D0822471

CROSS-TALK IN COMP THEORY

NCTE Editorial Board: Elizabeth Close, Willie Mae Crews, Colleen Fairbanks, Cora Lee Five, Ray Levi, Andrea Lunsford, Jaime Armin Mejía, Carolyn Phipps, Kyoko Sato, Zarina M. Hock, Chair, ex officio, Kent Williamson, ex officio, Kurt Austin, ex officio

CROSS-TALK IN COMP THEORY

A Reader

Second Edition
Revised and Updated

Edited by

Victor Villanueva
Washington State University

National Council of Teachers of English
1111 W. Kenyon Road, Urbana, Illinois 61801-1096

Staff Editor: Tom Tiller
Interior and Cover Design: Precision Graphics

NCTE Stock Number: 09764-3050

©2003 by the National Council of Teachers of English.

All rights reserved. No part of this publication may be reproduced or transmitted in any form or by any means, electronic or mechanical, including photocopy, or any information storage and retrieval system, without permission from the copyright holder. Printed in the United States of America.

It is the policy of NCTE in its journals and other publications to provide a forum for the open discussion of ideas concerning the content and the teaching of English and the language arts. Publicity accorded to any particular point of view does not imply endorsement by the Executive Committee, the Board of Directors, or the membership at large, except in announcements of policy, where such endorsement is clearly specified.

Although every attempt is made to ensure accuracy at the time of publication, NCTE cannot guarantee that all published addresses for electronic mail or Web sites are current.

Library of Congress Cataloging-in-Publication Data

Cross-talk in comp theory : a reader / edited by Victor Villanueva.–
2nd ed., rev. and updated.
    p. cm.
Includes bibliographical references and index.
    ISBN 0-8141-0976-4
    1. English language–Composition and exercises–Study and teaching.
2. English language–Rhetoric–Study and teaching. I. Villanueva,
Victor, 1948-
    PE1404.C755 2003
    808'.042'071–dc21

                                                            2002156573

Table of Contents

SECTION ONE

The Givens in Our Conversations: The Writing Process   1

v

SECTION TWO
Talking in Terms of Discourse:
What It Is; How It's Taught

SECTION THREE
Scientific Talk: Developmental Schemes

Acknowledgments

Joyce Middleton had picked up a copy of *Cross-Talk* from a table. "Good book," she says, kind of to herself, kind of to me. "But not much on women." Ritchie and Boardman had written the same.

Same meeting. John Scenters-Zapico: "Good book. How come nothing on technology?"

"Yep."

Samantha Andrus and Tom Henry liked the book too. And they too had suggestions. Sam and Tom are graduate students, tour guides on a campus visit some time back.

So—though I probably have not made John and Joyce or even Sam and Tom happy, I owe you thanks in rethinking *Cross-Talk*. I owe thanks to graduate students beyond Sam and Tom—thanks to the real users of *Cross-Talk*, for talking to me about the book as I travel to campuses and to conferences. You're the ones who tell me what works for you and what doesn't. You're the ones who tell me if and how the book has helped, causing me to rethink and recast. This second volume is yours, no less than the first. Thank you all for using the book and for talking to me about the book.

And thanks to NCTE. I mentioned a second edition to Zarina Hock. It was she who pursued "Son of Cross-Talk." Kurt Austin followed through, when too many commitments had me on the brink of saying "forget about it." Tom Tiller worked through the details. Thanks, Zarina, Kurt, and Tom (and Kent and Eileen and Jacqui, and all the NCTE folk I've worked with over the years).

Y Mami, mi corazón pa' casi un cuarto siglo, la madre de nos niñas, este libro no es para ti. Pero yo soy. Mi hijo y mis hijas—pienso de ti siempre.

Preface to the Second Edition

Second editions are like movie sequels. And I don't figure I've got a Part II to *The Godfather* or *Aliens*. But the profession has continued to move ahead, so the sequel to *Cross-Talk* seems like a good idea. One of the editors kept referring to it as "Son of Cross-Talk."

The acorn hasn't landed far from the tree, though. The book isn't all that different from the first edition. It's still divided into the same categories. My biases remain my biases, though as in the first edition, I try to remain true to the profession by giving preference to essays that are most frequently cited. And as in the first edition, there are a lot of interesting things going on in composition studies that don't get addressed, things like empirical research, assessment, or linguistics.

But some things have happened since I conducted the research for the first edition in 1992 to 1994. The most remarkable has been the technological explosion, with new software packages that affect our work coming out weekly, or so it seems, and with the pervasiveness of the Internet and its World Wide Web. The Net changed the way I conducted the research for this volume, a two-year process reduced to a few weeks on computerized databases and journal archives on the Web—often with whole texts available at the stroke of a few keys. Yet for all that, it doesn't appear as if technology has made its way into our theoretical discussions. Despite the great work of Cynthia Selfe and Gail Hawisher, not much has emerged in our journals that can stand the test of time—not because of any shortcoming in our scholars but because of the speed with which the things written about become archaic, this morning's innovation becoming this evening's anachronism. Technology has been included in this version, but not significantly, surely not as significantly as its presence in our lives would suggest.

In a very real sense, *Cross-Talk* is intended as a historical artifact, a way of tracking theoretical discussions in a field that continues to find itself forming its theoretical foundations. Even the givens of comp—writing as process—are contending with cross-talk, like post-process theory. It's hard to track the history we're in.

The other big change in composition studies—at least in our journals—has been the increased presence of writers of color and the greater acceptance of critical pedagogy. As I point out in the final essay to this volume, writers of color are still not present in this profession in the kinds of numbers that would affect our discussions on racism in truly meaningful ways, but something did happen in the second half of the 1990s: the beginnings of rich discussion on racism clearly centered on the concerns of this profession (a somewhat different set of discussions on racism from those which took place in journals like *College English* at the beginning of the second half of the twentieth century).

Readers of the first edition will likely miss the discussion between Peter Elbow and David Bartholomae. It was, I recognize, an interesting discussion centering on academic discourse versus other kinds of writing. It's gone because the discussion has taken a different turn—the personal versus the academic. That discussion has its representatives here, through Gesa Kirsch and Joy Ritchie, through Jacqueline Jones Royster, and in some sense through Richard Miller. Joy Ritchie and Kathleen Boardman broaden the discussion on feminism. And service learning is introduced, a relatively new entry into the conversation on composition.

Composition studies has moved on. New students are learning of our field, a field still in flux, still growing. It was time to account for the 1990s in the conversation, in the talk and cross-talk. Something gets lost with a sequel, I know, even a good sequel. Robert De Niro might have been great, but I missed Brando. Some of the Brandos will be missed in Son of Cross-Talk, but I trust this sequel will continue to serve, to initiate graduate students and more experienced teachers into the theories that inform composition studies.

Preface to the First Edition

I wanted to prepare a healthier pancake for the children. The whole-wheat recipe in the healthier cookbook hadn't quite gone over. But my adjustments made for pretty pancakes that came out, time and again, uncooked at the center. I figured I'd better add another egg to the batter next time around. And that worked. That egg added just the touch more leavening the batter needed, the touch more air to cook the batter through. If I had wanted to go just a bit healthier, I could have substituted that egg with two egg whites, beaten to a froth, since the fat of the yolk wouldn't have been necessary to the batter, as it would have been for, say, a custard. I made healthy pancakes that the kids would (and did and do) eat.

The point is this: I could adjust, take control of the process, because I had an understanding of how eggs work in cooking. I understood the theory.

But then, theories of leavening have been pretty well worked out. Theories of written composition have not. And operating from the gut, what feels right, what sounds right, what might be fun for the students, can too easily lead to theoretical contradictions. And students know. I don't know how they know, but they seem to sense or maybe outwardly recognize theoretical inconsistencies, reacting too often with passive compliance, never arriving at the full benefits possible in engaging—really engaging—in written discourse.

What those benefits of literacy might be aren't exactly clear, though. Plato tells of the god Thoth claiming that writing would be the key to remembrance. And writing was, we are told, used as a memory aid, a mnemonic device. In recent times, as we will find in the articles to follow, writing has been credited with learning, cognitive development, social cohesion, political power. What writing can provide has never been altogether clear.

So composition studies has divided itself, either to find out what writing is, or how to teach it better, or to discern the degree to which it either removes or bestows power. Composition studies finds its historicists (with some compositionists as revisionist historicists), current-traditionalists, cognitivists, expressionists, social-constructionists (who tend also to be epistemicists), empiricists, anti-foundationalists, and leftists, among others. Academic books on composition studies tend to historicize, theorize, polemicize, or synthesize, as well as proselytize. Composition is complex and diverse.

But with the greater diversity and sophistication has come greater confusion. I have seen teachers come to accept writing as a process, a common-enough notion nowadays, without recognizing the theoretical bases to different approaches to process. I have heard a new compositionist on the job market betray his confusion, claiming a Marxist bent, yet aligning himself with Kenneth Bruffee and Peter Elbow—highly respected compositionists, but hardly representatives of the political left. Another candidate clearly knew research on composition (for which there are several good collections) but seemed not to know of the philosophical objections to classical-empirical research. The overwhelming majority of candidates—even those fortunate enough to study with prestigious compositionists—seem unable to navigate their ways through composition's currents.

What follows, then, is an aid for you—the teacher of graduate composition theory, the graduate student of composition, the veteran teacher of composition back in the graduate comp course. What follows is a book of readings whose objective is to introduce you to some of the concepts and methods available to writing teachers today and to have you regard some of the controversy. This is a reader of previously published works, mainly by those who tend to be mentioned in the works of others. The book's further objective is to have you begin to consider your own predispositions toward language, discourse, writing, and writing instruction, predispositions which can then be considered critically and discussed knowledgeably. The list of suggested readings adds book-length considerations. With the books I have suggested, the books and articles cited in the essays that pique your interest, and the essays themselves, you should be able to come up with quite the pancake recipe, something you can swallow.

I mention the readings and the works the essays themselves cite because, though this book is comprehensive, it is not complete. It is not intended to establish a canon of comp. It's an overview, manageable within an academic quarter or semester. So the readings contained herein do not encompass all there is to composition studies. There are gaps. Writing across the curriculum is absent. Linguistics is minimally represented, which means there is little here on research on those who come into the classroom speaking a nonstandard dialect or those whose primary language is other than English (which includes sociolinguistic and applied linguistic studies of the hundreds of American Indian languages still spoken in the United States today). There is little on grammar, and the current discussions on multiculturalism and the comp classroom aren't explicitly represented. But all of these concerns really are here, in large terms, in the theoretical discussions concerning those who have been traditionally excluded or underrepresented in the academy.

Nor is evaluation explicitly represented. I know that the teacher is always concerned with evaluation and assessment. And how a teacher decides to respond, evaluate, and grade essays should be a reflection of the philosophy or theory of writing that the classroom curriculum embodies. But the subject of evaluation is large, almost another theoretical sphere, more concerned with what you do with writing in the classroom than with what writing is or even what writing instruction might be. I've relegated evaluation to the list of suggested readings. In other words, to learn more you'll still have to read those more complete academic books on composition contained in the list of readings or mentioned in the collection. But after going through this book, you will have a sense of who you might want to read. This book is intended as a primer, drops to activate the pump.

Selection suggests a selector, one with particular biases. But though my own biases in selecting the readings will no doubt come through, no single viewpoint is presented. The readings are presented in such a way as to establish a dialectic—a way for you to come to your own conclusions by considering opposing viewpoints. The process approach espoused in the first section receives a critical assessment in the "Mulligan Stew" article. Walter Ong provides a necessary reconsideration of product. The cognitive explanations of basic writers' problems advanced by Andrea Lunsford and by Frank D'Angelo are countered by Mike Rose's article on cognitive development. Cognitive explanations generally are countered by social-construction's explanations, with Patricia Bizzell explicitly drawing the comparison, offering the critique; both the cognitivist and the social-constructionist become subject to ideological critiques. Points find counterpoints throughout the book—talk and cross-talk.

Some articles will address matters of race or ethnicity, gender, the poor or working class. Considerations of race and the like have had a great deal to do with establishing the theoretical controversies. One compositionist of note, at least, Maxine Hairston, has argued that our changing theories of composition are in part the result of the introduction into our college classrooms of those we have come to call basic writers, those who come to college not quite prepared to undertake college writing, most often people of color and the poor. There are always a few in every composition classroom, at every level, from first-year college students to seniors. To ponder how composition might affect the more troublesome, those basic writers, would inform our approach to the less troublesome.

Although the book's layout is principally concerned with establishing a dialectic, presenting varying views, there is something of a chronology to the ordering, a near chronology of the profession's changes—process to cohesion to cognition to social construction to ideology. The first two sections present the views that seem to have lasted: writing-as-process, writing as a means of learning, James Kinneavy's aims of discourse, some basic research. Yet even these sections contain some controversial matters: the generalizability of case studies, Frank D'Angelo's ontogeny recapitulating phylogeny (terms you'll come to understand through the reading). The third section looks to the cognitive sciences and developmental psychology, pretty popular till recently. The fourth section addresses that which has compromised cognition's popularity: social construction. It introduces Kenneth Bruffee and something of a counter in John Trimbur; there is also Charles Schuster's reading of Mikhail Bakhtin as informing social construction. Section five looks to the debate over whether freshman composition courses should concern themselves with narration or with academic discourse, with the discourses about and by those traditionally excluded from the academy—women, people of color. Then an important set of postscripts. And so the profession stands, kind of, for the moment.

SECTION ONE

The Givens in Our Conversations
The Writing Process

That writing is a process sounds pretty obvious. We know that texts don't appear magically on pages as whole products. There is a process in getting from mind to page. As obvious as that might be, however, teachers of writing have until relatively recently been trained to behave as literary critics—looking at texts so as to analyze what happens within those texts. Students in composition classes were enjoined to look at texts, analyze and discuss what happens in those texts, and then produce something of their own that followed the patterns they found in those texts. Ideas were to be provided by the text, the form provided by the text, with evaluation based on how well the student paper emulated the ideal text. The process was rather like having students watch and discuss a videotape of a prima ballerina and having the students attempt the same dance, with the students then being evaluated based on how well they approximated the ballerina's performance—without knowing how the ballerina came to master those steps. No attention was given to the process of arriving at the product.

In 1959 the National Academy of Sciences sponsored the Woods Hole Conference. Its director was a cognitive psychologist with a keen interest in education and language—Jerome Bruner. The result of the conference was a shift in emphasis for all schooling to the process of cognitive development. "Process" became the new catchword. In 1966, about fifty teachers of English from England and from the United States met to discuss common problems. What the Americans discovered was that the British did not teach writing as discipline specific. The British, rather than teach writing to serve some external purpose or genre, taught writing as a process of individual development, a matter of self-discovery. This was the Dartmouth Conference. Its discoveries fit well with the Woods Hole discoveries.

Woods Hole and Dartmouth made for a new attention to the whole concept of process. Writers and teachers like Donald Murray, Ken Macrorie, and Peter Elbow turned to what they knew as writers and as teachers to shed light on what writers do when they write. At about the same time, researchers in composition were heeding the call provided by Richard Braddock, Richard Lloyd-Jones, and Lowell Schoer's *Research in Written Composition*, a collection of research on composing to 1963. Their call? More research on writing itself (as opposed to products or pedagogy). Janet Emig's *The Composing Processes of Twelfth Graders* was the first significant answer to the call. Others presented here looked to what professional writers do when they revise that students in writing classes don't do, and what Basic Writers—students not quite ready for the tasks of college literacy—do when they write.

So writing is a process. But that doesn't mean that at the end of the process there won't be a product. The idea is to place greater emphasis on the process than on the product. Rhetorician Walter Ong reminds us in a classic article that combines matters of literary criticism with rhetoric and the teaching of writing, that there are consequences to the writing produced, that what is written affects and is affected by audiences, by readers. Lisa Ede and Andrea Lunsford broaden the picture on audience. Then comes the question as to whether "process" has overshadowed other concerns with writing. This comes to be called "post-process theory," a reconsideration of the givens of our conversation. Lee-Ann M. Kastman Breuch tells us about post-process.

Teach Writing as a Process
Not Product

Donald M. Murray

Most of us are trained as English teachers by studying a product: writing. Our critical skills are honed by examining literature, which is finished writing; language as it has been used by authors. And then, fully trained in the autopsy, we go out and are assigned to teach our students to write, to make language live.

Naturally we try to use our training. It's an investment and so we teach writing as a product, focusing our critical attentions on what our students have done, as if they had passed literature in to us. It isn't literature, of course, and we use our skills, with which we can dissect and sometimes almost destroy Shakespeare or Robert Lowell to prove it.

Our students knew it wasn't literature when they passed it in, and our attack usually does little more than confirm their lack of self-respect for their work and for themselves; we are as frustrated as our students, for conscientious, doggedly responsible, repetitive autopsying doesn't give birth to live writing. The product doesn't improve, and so, blaming the student—who else?—we pass him along to the next teacher, who is trained, too often, the same way we were. Year after year the student shudders under a barrage of criticism, much of it brilliant, some of it stupid, and all of it irrelevant. No matter how careful our criticisms, they do not help the student since when we teach composition we are not teaching a product, we are teaching a process.

And once you can look at your composition program with the realization you are teaching a process, you may be able to design a curriculum which works. Not overnight, for writing is a demanding, intellectual process;

Pulitzer Prize–winning journalist Donald M. Murray presented this paper at the 1972 convention of the New England Association of Teachers of English; it appeared in their journal, *The Leaflet*, in November 1972. Reprinted with permission.

but sooner than you think, for the process can be put to work to produce a product which may be worth your reading.

What is the process we should teach? It is the process of discovery through language. It is the process of exploration of what we know and what we feel about what we know through language. It is the process of using language to learn about our world, to evaluate what we learn about our world, to communicate what we learn about our world.

Instead of teaching finished writing, we should teach unfinished writing, and glory in its unfinishedness. We work with language in action. We share with our students the continual excitement of choosing one word instead of another, of searching for the one true word.

This is not a question of correct or incorrect, of etiquette or custom. This is a matter of far higher importance. The writer, as he writes, is making ethical decisions. He doesn't test his words by a rule book, but by life. He uses language to reveal the truth to himself so that he can tell it to others. It is an exciting, eventful, evolving process.

This process of discovery through language we call writing can be introduced to your classroom as soon as you have a very simple understanding of that process, and as soon as you accept the full implications of teaching process, not product.

The writing process itself can be divided into three stages: *prewriting, writing,* and *rewriting.* The amount of time a writer spends in each stage depends on his personality, his work habits, his maturity as a craftsman, and the challenge of what he is trying to say. It is not a rigid lock-step process, but most writers most of the time pass through these three stages.

Prewriting is everything that takes place before the first draft. Prewriting usually takes about 85% of the writer's time. It includes the awareness of his world from which his subject is born. In prewriting, the writer focuses on that subject, spots an audience, chooses a form which may carry his subject to his audience. Prewriting may include research and daydreaming, note-making and outlining, title-writing and lead-writing.

Writing is the act of producing a first draft. It is the fastest part of the process, and the most frightening, for it is a commitment. When you complete a draft you know how much, and how little, you know. And the writing of this first draft—rough, searching, unfinished—may take as little as one percent of the writer's time.

Rewriting is reconsideration of subject, form, and audience. It is researching, rethinking, redesigning, rewriting—and finally, line-by-line editing, the demanding, satisfying process of making each word right. It may take many times the hours required for a first draft, perhaps the remaining fourteen percent of the time the writer spends on the project.

4

How do you motivate your student to pass through this process, perhaps even pass through it again and again on the same piece of writing?

First by shutting up. When you are talking he isn't writing. And you don't learn a process by talking about it, but by doing it. Next by placing the opportunity for discovery in your student's hands. When you give him an assignment you tell him what to say and how to say it, and thereby cheat your student of the opportunity to learn the process of discovery we call writing.

To be a teacher of a process such as this takes qualities too few of us have, but which most of us can develop. We have to be quiet, to listen, to respond. We are not the initiator or the motivator; we are the reader, the recipient.

We have to be patient and wait, and wait, and wait. The suspense in the beginning of a writing course is agonizing for the teacher, but if we break first, if we do the prewriting for our students they will not learn the largest part of the writing process.

We have to respect the student, not for his product, not for the paper we call literature by giving it a grade, but for the search for truth in which he is engaged. We must listen carefully for those words that may reveal a truth, that may reveal a voice. We must respect our student for his potential truth and for his potential voice. We are coaches, encouragers, developers, creators of environments in which our students can experience the writing process for themselves.

Let us see what some of the implications of teaching process, not product, are for the composition curriculum.

Implication No. 1. The text of the writing course is the student's own writing. Students examine their own evolving writing and that of their classmates, so that they study writing while it is still a matter of choice, word by word.

Implication No. 2. The student finds his own subject. It is not the job of the teacher to legislate the student's truth. It is the responsibility of the student to explore his own world with his own language, to discover his own meaning. The teacher supports but does not direct this expedition to the student's own truth.

cf. Bartholomae

Implication No. 3. The student uses his own language. Too often, as writer and teacher Thomas Williams points out, we teach English to our students as if it were a foreign language. Actually, most of our students have learned a great deal of language before they come to us, and they are quite willing to exploit that language if they are allowed to embark on a serious search for their own truth.

Implication No. 4. The student should have the opportunity to write all the drafts necessary for him to discover what he has to say on this particular

5

subject. Each new draft, of course, is counted as equal to a new paper. You are not teaching a product, you are teaching a process.

Implication No. 5. The student is encouraged to attempt any form of writing which may help him discover and communicate what he has to say. The process which produces "creative" and "functional" writing is the same. You are not teaching products such as business letters and poetry, narrative and exposition. You are teaching a product your students can use—now and in the future—to produce whatever product his subject and his audience demand.

Implication No. 6. Mechanics come last. It is important to the writer, once he has discovered what he has to say, that nothing get between him and his reader. He must break only those traditions of written communication which would obscure his meaning.

Implication No. 7. There must be time for the writing process to take place and time for it to end. The writer must work within the stimulating tension of unpressured time to think and dream and stare out windows, and pressured time—the deadline—to which the writer must deliver.

Implication No. 8. Papers are examined to see what other choices the writer might make. The primary responsibility for seeing the choices is the student. He is learning a process. His papers are always unfinished, evolving, until the end of the marking period. A grade finishes a paper, the way publication usually does. The student writer is not graded on drafts any more than a concert pianist is judged on his practice sessions rather than on his performance. The student writer is graded on what he has produced at the end of the writing process.

Implication No. 9. The students are individuals who must explore the writing process in their own way, some fast, some slow, whatever it takes for them, within the limits of the course deadlines, to find their own way to their own truth.

Implication No. 10. There are no rules, no absolutes, just alternatives. What works one time may not another. All writing is experimental.

None of these implications require a special schedule, exotic training, extensive new materials or gadgetry, new classrooms, or an increase in federal, state, or local funds. They do not even require a reduced teaching load. What they do require is a teacher who will respect and respond to his students, not for what they have done, but for what they may do; not for what they have produced, but for what they may produce, if they are given an opportunity to see writing as a process, not a product.

6

Writing as a Mode of Learning

JANET EMIG

Writing represents a unique mode of learning—not merely valuable, not merely special, but unique. That will be my contention in this paper. The thesis is straightforward. Writing serves learning uniquely because writing as process-and-product possesses a cluster of attributes that correspond uniquely to certain powerful learning strategies.

Although the notion is clearly debatable, it is scarcely a private belief. Some of the most distinguished contemporary psychologists have at least implied such a role for writing as heuristic. Lev Vygotsky, A. R. Luria, and Jerome Bruner, for example, have all pointed out that higher cognitive functions, such as analysis and synthesis, seem to develop most fully only with the support system of verbal language—particularly, it seems, of written language.[1] Some of their arguments and evidence will be incorporated here.

Here I have a prior purpose: to describe as tellingly as possible *how* writing uniquely corresponds to certain powerful learning strategies. Making such a case for the uniqueness of writing should logically and theoretically involve establishing many contrasts, distinctions between (1) writing and all other verbal languaging processes—listening, reading, and especially talking; (2) writing and all other forms of composing, such as composing a painting, a symphony, a dance, a film, a building; and (3) composing in words and composing in the two other major graphic symbol systems of mathematical equations and scientific formulae. For the purposes of this paper, the task is simpler, since most students are not permitted by most curricula to discover the values of composing, say, in dance, or even in film; and most students are not sophisticated enough to create, to originate formulations, using the highly abstruse symbol system of equations and formu-

Reprinted from *College Composition and Communication* 28.2 (May 1977): 122–28. Copyright © 1977 by Janet Emig. Used with permission.

lae. Verbal language represents the most *available* medium for composing; in fact, the significance of sheer availability in its selection as a mode for learning can probably not be overstressed. But the uniqueness of writing among the verbal languaging processes does need to be established and supported if only because so many curricula and courses in English still consist almost exclusively of reading and listening.

WRITING AS A UNIQUE LANGUAGING PROCESS

Traditionally, the four languaging processes of listening, talking, reading, and writing are paired in either of two ways. The more informative seems to be the division many linguists make between first-order and second-order processes, with talking and listening characterized as first-order processes; reading and writing, as second-order. First-order processes are acquired without formal or systematic instruction; the second-order processes of reading and writing tend to be learned initially only with the aid of formal and systematic instruction.

The less useful distinction is that between listening and reading as receptive functions and talking and writing as productive functions. Critics of these terms like Louise Rosenblatt rightfully point out that the connotation of passivity too often accompanies the notion of receptivity when reading, like listening, is a vital, construing act.

An additional distinction, so simple it may have been previously overlooked, resides in two criteria: the matters of origination and of graphic recording. Writing is originating and creating a unique verbal construct that is graphically recorded. Reading is creating or re-creating *but not* originating a verbal construct that is graphically recorded. Listening is creating or re-creating but not originating a verbal construct that is *not* graphically recorded. Talking is creating *and* originating a verbal construct that is *not* graphically recorded (except for the circuitous routing of a transcribed tape). Note that a distinction is being made between creating and originating separable processes.

For talking, the nearest languaging process, additional distinctions should probably be made. (What follows is not a denigration of talk as a valuable mode of learning.) A silent classroom or one filled only with the teacher's voice is anathema to learning. For evidence of the cognitive value of talk, one can look to some of the persuasive monographs coming from the London Schools Council project on writing: *From Information to Understanding* by Nancy Martin or *From Talking to Writing* by Peter Medway.[2] We also know that for some of us, talking is a valuable, even necessary, form of pre-writing. In his curriculum, James Moffett makes the value of such talk quite explicit.

8

But to say that talking is a valuable form of pre-writing is not to say that writing is talk recorded, an inaccuracy appearing in far too many composition texts. Rather, a number of contemporary trans-disciplinary sources suggest that talking and writing may emanate from different organic sources and represent quite different, possibly distinct, language functions. In *Thought and Language*, Vygotsky notes that "written speech is a separate linguistic function, differing from oral speech in both structure and mode of functioning."[3] The sociolinguist Dell Hymes, in a valuable issue of *Daedalus*, "Language as a Human Problem," makes a comparable point: "That speech and writing are not simply interchangeable, and have developed historically in ways at least partly autonomous, is obvious."[4] At the first session of the Buffalo Conference on Researching Composition (4-5 October 1975), the first point of unanimity among the participant-speakers with interests in developmental psychology, media, dreams and aphasia was that talking and writing were markedly different functions.[5] Some of us who work rather steadily with writing research agree. We also believe that there are hazards, conceptually and pedagogically, in creating too complete an analogy between talking and writing, in blurring the very real differences between the two.

What Are These Differences?

1. Writing is learned behavior; talking is natural, even irrepressible, behavior.

2. Writing then is an artificial process; talking is not.

3. Writing is a technological device—not the wheel, but early enough to qualify as primary technology; talking is organic, natural, earlier.

4. Most writing is slower than most talking.

5. Writing is stark, barren, even naked as a medium; talking is rich, luxuriant, inherently redundant.

6. Talk leans on the environment; writing must provide its own context.

7. With writing, the audience is usually absent; with talking, the listener is usually present.

8. Writing usually results in a visible graphic product; talking usually does not.

9. Perhaps because there is a product involved, writing tends to be a more responsible and committed act than talking.

10. It can even be said that throughout history, an aura, an ambience, a mystique has usually encircled the written word; the spoken word

9

has for the most part proved ephemeral and treated mundanely (ignore, please, our recent national history).

11. Because writing is often our representation of the world made visible, embodying both process and product, writing is more readily a form and source of learning than talking.

UNIQUE CORRESPONDENCES BETWEEN LEARNING AND WRITING

What then are some *unique* correspondences between learning and writing? To begin with some definitions: Learning can be defined in many ways, according to one's predilections and training, with all statements about learning of course hypothetical. Definitions range from the chemo-physiological ("Learning is changed patterns of protein synthesis in relevant portions of the cortex")[6] to transactive views drawn from both philosophy and psychology (John Dewey, Jean Piaget) that learning is the re-organization or confirmation of a cognitive scheme in light of an experience.[7] What the speculations seem to share is consensus about certain features and strategies that characterize successful learning. These include the importance of the classic attributes of re-inforcement and feedback. In most hypotheses, successful learning is also connective and selective. Additionally, it makes use of propositions, hypotheses, and other elegant summarizers. Finally, it is active, engaged, personal—more specifically, self-rhythmed—in nature.

Jerome Bruner, like Jean Piaget, through a comparable set of categories, posits three major ways in which we represent and deal with actuality: (1) enactive—we learn "by doing"; (2) iconic—we learn "by depiction in an image"; and (3) representational or symbolic—we learn "by restatement in words." To overstate the matter, in enactive learning, the hand predominates; in iconic, the eye; and in symbolic, the brain.

What is striking about writing as a process is that, by its very nature, all three ways of dealing with actuality are simultaneously or almost simultaneously deployed. That is, the symbolic transformation of experience through the specific symbol system of verbal language is shaped into an icon (the graphic product) by the enactive hand. If the most efficacious learning occurs when learning is re-inforced, then writing through its inherent re-inforcing cycle involving hand, eye, and brain marks a uniquely powerful multi-representational mode for learning.

Writing is also integrative in perhaps the most basic possible sense: the organic, the functional. Writing involves the fullest possible functioning of the brain, which entails the active participation in the process of both the left and the right hemispheres. Writing is markedly bispheral, although in some popular accounts, writing is inaccurately presented as a chiefly left-hemisphere activity, perhaps because the linear written product is somehow regarded as analogue for the process that created it; and the left hemisphere seems to process material linearly.

The right hemisphere, however, seems to make at least three, perhaps four, major contributions to the writing process—probably, to the creative process generically. First, several researchers, such as Geschwind and Snyder of Harvard and Zaidal of Cal Tech, through markedly different experiments, have very tentatively suggested that the right hemisphere is the sphere, even the *seat*, of emotions.[9] Second—or perhaps as an illustration of the first—Howard Gardner, in his important study of the brain-damaged, notes that our sense of emotional appropriateness in discourse may reside in the right sphere:

Emotional appropriateness, in sum—being related not only to *what* is said, but to how it is said and to what is *not* said, as well—is crucially dependent on right hemisphere intactness.[10]

Third, the right hemisphere seems to be the source of intuition, of sudden gestalts, of flashes of images, of abstractions occurring as visual or spatial wholes, as the initiating metaphors in the creative process. A familiar example: William Faulkner noted in his *Paris Review* interview that *The Sound and the Fury* began as the image of a little girl's muddy drawers as she sat in a tree watching her grandmother's funeral.[11]

Also, a unique form of feedback, as well as reinforcement, exists with writing, because information from the *process* is immediately and visibly available as that portion of the *product* already written. The importance for learning of a product in a familiar and available medium for immediate, literal (that is, visual) re-scanning and review cannot perhaps be overstated. In his remarkable study of purportedly blind sculptors, Géza Révész found that without sight, persons cannot move beyond a literal transcription of elements into any manner of symbolic transformation—by definition, the central requirement for reformulation and re-interpretation, i.e., revision, that most aptly named process.[12]

As noted in the second paragraph, Vygotsky and Luria, like Bruner, have written importantly about the connections between learning and writing. In his essay "The Psychobiology of Psychology," Bruner lists as one of six axioms regarding learning: "We are connective."[13] Another correspondence then between learning and writing: in *Thought and Language*, Vygotsky notes that writing makes a unique demand in that the writer must engage in "deliberate semantics"—in Vygotsky's elegant phrase, "deliberate structuring of the web of meaning."[14] Such structuring is required because, for Vygotsky, writing centrally represents an expansion of inner speech, that mode whereby we talk to ourselves, which is "maximally compact" and "almost entirely predicative"; written speech is a mode which is "maximally detailed" and which requires explicitly supplied subjects and topics. The medium then of written verbal language requires the establishment of systematic connections and relationships. Clear writing by definition is that writing which signals without ambiguity the nature of conceptual relationships, whether they be coordinate, subordinate, superordinate, causal, or something other.

Successful learning is also engaged, committed, personal learning. Indeed, impersonal learning may be an anomalous concept, like the very notion of objectivism itself. As Michael Polanyi states simply at the beginning of *Personal Knowledge*: "the ideal of strict objectivism is absurd." (How many courses and curricula in English, science, and all else does that one sentence reduce to rubble?) Indeed, the theme of *Personal Knowledge* is that

> into every act of knowing there enters a passionate contribution of the person knowing what is being known, . . . this coefficient is no mere imperfection but a vital component of his knowledge.[15]

In *Zen and the Art of Motorcycle Maintenance*, Robert Pirsig states a comparable theme:

> The Quality which creates the world emerges as *a relationship* between man and his experience. He is a *participant* in the creation of all things.[16]

Finally, the psychologist George Kelly has as the central notion in his subtle and compelling theory of personal constructs man as a scientist steadily and actively engaged in making and re-making his hypotheses about the nature of the universe.[17]

We are acquiring as well some empirical confirmation about the importance of engagement in, as well as self-selection of, a subject for the student learning to write and writing to learn. The recent Sanders and Littlefield study, reported in *Research in the Teaching of English*, is persuasive evidence on this point, as well as being a model for a certain type of research.[18]

As Luria implies in the quotation above, writing is self-rhythmed. One writes best as one learns best, at one's own pace. Or to connect the two processes, writing can sponsor learning because it can match its pace. Support for the importance of self-pacing to learning can be found in Benjamin Bloom's important study "Time and Learning."[19] Evidence for the significance of self-pacing to writing can be found in the reason Jean-Paul Sartre gave last summer for not using the tape-recorder when he announced that blindness in his second eye had forced him to give up writing:

> I think there is an enormous difference between speaking and writing. One rereads what one rewrites. But one can read slowly or quickly: in other words, you do not know how long you will have to take deliberating over a sentence. . . . If I listen to a tape recorder, the listening speed is determined by the speed at which the tape turns and not by my own needs. Therefore I will always be either lagging behind or running ahead of the machine.[20]

Writing is connective as a process in a more subtle and perhaps more significant way, as Luria points out in what may be the most powerful paragraph of rationale ever supplied for writing as heuristic:

> Written speech is bound up with the inhibition of immediate synpractical connections. It assumes a much slower, repeated mediating process of analysis and synthesis, which makes it possible not only to develop the required thought, but even to revert to its earlier stages, thus transforming the sequential chain of connections in a simultaneous, self-reviewing structure. Written speech thus represents a new and powerful instrument of thought.[21]

But first to explicate: writing inhibits "immediate synpractical connections." Luria defines *synpraxis* as "concrete-active" situations in which language does not exist independently but as a "fragment" of an ongoing action "outside of which it is incomprehensible."[22] In *Language and Learning*, James Britton defines it succinctly as "speech-cum-action."[23] Writing, unlike talking, restrains dependence upon the actual situation. Writing as a mode is inherently more self-reliant than speaking. Moreover, as Bruner states in explicating Vygotsky, "Writing virtually forces a remoteness of reference on the language user."[24]

Luria notes what has already been noted above: that writing, typically, is a "much slower" process than talking. But then he points out the relation of this slower pace to learning: this slower pace allows for—indeed, encourages—the shuttling among past, present, and future. Writing, in other words, connects the three major tenses of our experience to make meaning. And the two major modes by which these three aspects are united are the processes of analysis and synthesis: analysis, the breaking of entities into their constituent parts; and synthesis, combining or fusing these, often into fresh arrangements or amalgams.

Finally, writing is epigenetic, with the complex evolutionary development of thought steadily and graphically visible and available throughout as a record of the journey, from jottings and notes to full discursive formulations. For a summary of the correspondences stressed here between certain learning strategies and certain attributes of writing see Figure 1.

This essay represents a first effort to make a certain kind of case for writing—specifically, to show its unique value for learning. It is at once over-elaborate and under specific. Too much of the formulation is in the off-putting jargon of the learning theorist, when my own predilection would have been to emulate George Kelly and to avoid terms like *reinforcement* and *feedback* since their use implies that I live inside a certain paradigm about learning I don't truly inhabit. Yet I hope that the essay will start a crucial line of inquiry; for unless the losses to learners of not writing are compellingly described and substantiated by experimental and speculative research, writing itself as a central academic process may not long endure.

Figure 1 Unique cluster of correspondences between certain learning strategies and certain attributes of writing.

Selected Characteristics of Successful Learning Strategies	Selected Attributes of Writing Process and Product
1. Profits from multi-representational and integrative re-inforcement	1. Represents process uniquely multi-representational and integrative
2. Seeks self-provided feedback:	2. Represents powerful instance of self-provided feedback:
a. immediate	a. provides product uniquely available for *immediate* feedback (review and re-evaluation)
b. long-term	b. provides record of evolution of thought since writing is epigenetic as process-and-product
3. Is connective:	3. Provides connections:
a. makes generative conceptual groupings, synthetic and analytic	a. establishes explicit and systematic conceptual groupings through lexical, syntactic, and rhetorical devices
b. proceeds from propositions, hypotheses, and other elegant summarizers	b. represents most available means (verbal language) for economic recording of abstract formulations
4. Is active, engaged, personal— notably, self-rhythmed	4. Is active, engaged, personal— notably, self-rhythmed

NOTES

1. Lev S. Vygotsky, *Thought and Language*, trans. Eugenia Hanfmann and Gertrude Vakar (Cambridge: The M.I.T. Press, 1962); A. R. Luria and F. Ia. Yudovich, *Speech and the Development of Mental Processes in the Child*, ed. Joan Simon (Baltimore: Penguin, 1971); Jerome S. Bruner, *The Relevance of Education* (New York: W. W. Norton and Co., 1971).

2. Nancy Martin, *From Information to Understanding* (London: Schools Council Project Writing Across the Curriculum, 11-13, 1973); Peter Medway, *From Talking to Writing* (London: Schools Council Project Writing Across the Curriculum, 11-13, 1973).

3. Vygotsky, p. 98.

4. Dell Hymes, "On the Origins and Foundations of Inequality Among Speakers," *Daedalus*, 102 (Summer, 1973), 69.

5. Participant-speakers were Loren Barrett, University of Michigan; Gerald O'Grady, SUNY/Buffalo; Hollis Frampton, SUNY/Buffalo; and Janet Emig, Rutgers.

6. George Steiner, *After Babel: Aspects of Language and Translation* (New York: Oxford University Press, 1975), p. 287.

7. John Dewey, *Experience and Education* (New York: Macmillan, 1938); Jean Piaget, *Biology and Knowledge: An Essay on the Relations between Organic Regulations and Cognitive Processes* (Chicago: University of Chicago Press, 1971).

8. Bruner, pp. 7-8.

9. Boyce Rensberger, "Language Ability Found in Right Side of Brain," *New York Times*, 1 August 1975, p. 14.

10. Howard Gardner, *The Shattered Mind: The Person After Brain Damage* (New York: Alfred A. Knopf, 1975), p. 372.

11. William Faulkner, *Writers at Work: The Paris Review Interviews*, ed. Malcolm Cowley (New York: The Viking Press, 1959), p. 130.

12. Géza Révész, *Psychology and Art of the Blind*, trans. H. A. Wolff (London: Longmans-Green, 1950).

13. Bruner, p. 126.

14. Vygotsky, p. 100.

15. Michael Polanyi, *Personal Knowledge: Toward a Post-Critical Philosophy* (Chicago: University of Chicago Press, 1958), p. viii.

16. Robert Pirsig, *Zen and the Art of Motorcycle Maintenance* (New York: William Morrow and Co., Inc., 1974), p. 212.

17. George Kelly, *A Theory of Personality: The Psychology of Personal Constructs* (New York: W. W. Norton and Co., 1963).

18. Sara E. Sanders and John H. Littlefield, "Perhaps Test Essays Can Reflect Significant Improvement in Freshman Composition: Report on a Successful Attempt," *RTE*, 9 (Fall, 1975), 145-153.

19. Benjamin Bloom, "Time and Learning," *American Psychologist*, 29 (September 1974), 682-688.

20. Jean-Paul Sartre, "Sartre at Seventy: An Interview," with Michel Contat, *New York Review of Books*, 7 August 1975.

21. Luria, p. 118.

22. Luria, p. 50.

23. James Britton, *Language and Learning* (Baltimore: Penguin, 1971), pp. 10-11.

24. Bruner, p. 47.

The Composing Processes
of Unskilled College Writers

SONDRA PERL

This paper presents the pertinent findings from a study of the composing processes of five unskilled college writers (Perl, 1978). The first part summarizes the goals of the original study, the kinds of data collected, and the research methods employed. The second part is a synopsis of the study of Tony, one of the original five case studies. The third part presents a condensed version of the findings on the composing process and discusses these findings in light of current pedagogical practice and research design.

GOALS OF THE STUDY

This research addressed three major questions: (1) How do unskilled writers write? (2) Can their writing processes be analyzed in a systematic, replicable manner? and (3) What does an increased understanding of their processes suggest about the nature of composing in general and the manner in which writing is taught in the schools?

In recent years, interest in the composing process has grown (Britton, 1975; Burton, 1973; Cooper, 1974; Emig, 1967, 1971). In 1963, Braddock, Lloyd-Jones, and Schoer, writing on the state of research in written composition, included the need for "direct observation" and case study procedures in their suggestions for future research (pp. 24, 31-32). In a section entitled "Unexplored Territory," they listed basic unanswered questions such as, "What is involved in the act of writing?" and "Of what does skill in writing

Reprinted from *Research in the Teaching of English* 13.4 (December 1979): 317–36. Used with permission.

actually consist?" (p. 51). Fifteen years later, Cooper and Odell (1978) edited a volume similar in scope, only this one was devoted entirely to issues and questions related to research on composing. This volume in particular signals a shift in emphasis in writing research. Alongside the traditional, large scale experimental studies, there is now widespread recognition of the need for works of a more modest, probing nature, works that attempt to elucidate basic processes. The studies on composing that have been completed to date are precisely of this kind; they are small-scale studies, based on the systematic observation of writers engaged in the process of writing (Emig, 1971; Graves, 1973; Mischel, 1974; Pianko, 1977; Stallard, 1974).

For all of its promise, this body of research has yet to produce work that would insure wide recognition for the value of process studies of composing. One limitation of work done to date is methodological. Narrative descriptions of composing processes do not provide sufficiently graphic evidence for the perception of underlying regularities and patterns. Without such evidence, it is difficult to generate well-defined hypotheses and to move from exploratory research to more controlled experimental studies. A second limitation pertains to the subjects studied. To date no examination of composing processes has dealt primarily with unskilled writers. As long as "average" or skilled writers are the focus, it remains unclear as to how process research will provide teachers with a firmer understanding of the needs of students with serious writing problems.

The present study is intended to carry process research forward by addressing both of these limitations. One prominent feature of the research design involves the development and use of a meaningful and replicable method for rendering the composing process as a sequence of observable and scorable behaviors. A second aspect of the design is the focus on students whose writing problems baffle the teachers charged with their education.

DESIGN OF THE STUDY

This study took place during the 1975-76 fall semester at Eugenio Maria de Hostos Community College of the City University of New York. Students were selected for the study on the basis of two criteria: writing samples that qualified them as unskilled writers and willingness to participate. Each student met with the researcher for five 90-minute sessions (see Table 1). Four sessions were devoted to writing with the students directed to compose aloud, to externalize their thinking processes as much as possible, during each session. In one additional session, a writing profile on the students' perceptions and memories of writing was developed through the use of an open-ended interview. All of the sessions took place in a soundproof room in

Table 1 Design of the study.

	Session 1 (S1)	Session 2 (S2)	Session 3 (S3)	Session 4 (S4)	Session 5 (S5)
Mode	Extensive	Reflexive		Extensive	Reflexive
Topic	Society & Culture	Society & Culture	Interview: Writing Profile	Capitalism	Capitalism
Directions	Students told to compose aloud; no other directions given	Students told to compose aloud; no other directions given		Students told to compose aloud; also directed to talk out ideas before writing	Students told to compose aloud; also directed to talk out ideas before writing

the college library. Throughout each session, the researcher assumed a non-interfering role.

The topics for writing were developed in an introductory social science course in which the five students were enrolled. The "content" material they were studying was divided into two modes: extensive, in which the writer was directed to approach the material in an objective, impersonal fashion, and reflexive, in which the writer was directed to approach similar material in an affective, personalized fashion. Contrary to Emig's (1971) definitions, in this study it was assumed that the teacher was always the audience.

DATA ANALYSIS

Three kinds of data were collected in this study: the students' written products, their composing tapes, and their responses to the interview. Each of these was studied carefully and then discussed in detail in each of the five case study presentations. Due to limitations of space, this paper will review only two of the data sets generated in the study.

Coding the Composing Process

One of the goals of this research was to devise a tool for describing the movements that occur during composing. In the past such descriptions have taken the form of narratives which detail, with relative precision and insight, observable composing behaviors; however, these narratives provide no way of ascertaining the frequency, relative importance, and place of each behavior within an individual's composing process. As such, they are cumbersome and difficult to replicate. Furthermore, lengthy, idiosyncratic narratives run the risk of leaving underlying patterns and regularities obscure. In contrast, the method created in this research provides a means of viewing the composing process that is:

1. Standardized—it introduces a coding system for observing the composing process that can be replicated;

2. Categorical—it labels specific, observable behaviors so that types of composing movements are revealed;

3. Concise—it presents the entire sequence of composing movements on one or two pages;

4. Structural—it provides a way of determining how parts of the process relate to the whole; and

5. Diachronic—it presents the sequences of movements that occur during composing as they unfold in time.

In total, the method allows the researcher to apprehend a process as it unfolds. It lays out the movements or behavior sequences in such a way that if patterns within a student's process or among a group of students exist, they become apparent.

The Code

The method consists of coding each composing behavior exhibited by the student and charting each behavior on a continuum. During this study, the coding occurred after the student had finished composing and was done by working from the student's written product and the audiotape of the session. It was possible to do this since the tape captured both what the student was saying and the literal sound of the pen moving across the page. As a result, it was possible to determine when students were talking, when they were writing, when both occurred simultaneously, and when neither occurred.

The major categorical divisions in this coding system are talking, writing, and reading; however, it was clear that there are various kinds of talk and various kinds of writing and reading operations, and that a coding system would need to distinguish among these various types. In this study the following operations were distinguished:

1. General planning [PL]—organizing one's thoughts for writing, discussing how one will proceed.
2. Local planning [PLL]—talking out what idea will come next.
3. Global planning [PLG]—discussing changes in drafts.
4. Commenting [C]—sighing, making a comment or judgment about the topic.
5. Interpreting [I]—rephrasing the topic to get a "handle" on it.
6. Assessing [A(+); A(−)]—making a judgment about one's writing; may be positive or negative.
7. Questioning [Q]—asking a question.
8. Talking leading to writing [T→W]—voicing ideas on the topic, tentatively finding one's way, but not necessarily being committed to or using all one is saying.
9. Talking and writing at the same time [TW]—composing aloud in such a way that what one is saying is actually being written at the same time.
10. Repeating [re]—repeating written or unwritten phrases a number of times.
11. Reading related to the topic:
    a. Reading the directions [R_D]
    b. Reading the question [R_Q]
    c. Reading the statement [R_S]
12. Reading related to one's own written product:
    a. Reading one sentence or a few words [R^a]
    b. Reading a number of sentences together [R^{a-b}]
    c. Reading the entire draft through [R^{W1}]
13. Writing silently [W].
14. Writing aloud [TW].
15. Editing [E]:
    a. Adding syntactic markers, words, phrases, or clauses [Eadd]
    b. Deleting syntactic markers, words, phrases, or clauses [Edel]
    c. Indicating concern for a grammatical rule [Egr]
    d. Adding, deleting, or considering the use of punctuation [Epunc]

    e. Considering or changing spelling [Esp]

    f. Changing the sentence structure through embedding, coordination or subordination [Ess]

    g. Indicating concern for appropriate vocabulary (word choice) [Ewc]

    h. Considering or changing verb form [Evc]

16. Periods of silence [s].

By taking specific observable behaviors that occur during composing and supplying labels for them, this system thus far provides a way of analyzing the process that is categorical and capable of replication. In order to view the frequency and the duration of composing behaviors and the relation between one particular behavior and the whole process, these behaviors need to be depicted graphically to show their duration and sequence.

The Continuum

The second component of this system is the construction of a time line and a numbering system. In this study, blank charts with lines like the following were designed:

```
-------   -------   -------   -------   -------   -------   -------
   10        20        30        40        50        60        70
```

A ten-digit interval corresponds to one minute and is keyed to a counter on a tape recorder. By listening to the tape and watching the counter, it is possible to determine the nature and duration of each operation. As each behavior is heard on the tape, it is coded and then noted on the chart with the counter used as a time marker. For example, if a student during prewriting reads the directions and the question twice and then begins to plan exactly what she is going to say, all within the first minute, it would be coded like this:

If at this point the student spends two minutes writing the first sentence, during which time she pauses, rereads the question, continues writing, and then edits for spelling before continuing on, it would be coded like this:

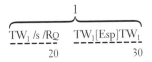

$$\overbrace{\underset{20}{\underline{\text{TW}_1\ /\text{s}\ /\text{R}\underline{\text{Q}}}}\qquad\underset{30}{\underline{\text{TW}_1[\text{Esp}]\text{TW}_1}}}^{1}$$

At this point two types of brackets and numbering systems have appeared. The initial sublevel number linked with the TW code indicates which draft the student is working on. TW_1 indicates the writing of the first draft; TW_2 and TW_3 indicate the writing of the second and third drafts. Brackets such as [Esp] separate these operations from writing and indicate the amount of time the operation takes. The upper-level number above the horizontal bracket indicates which sentence in the written product is being written and the length of the bracket indicates the amount of time spent on the writing of each sentence. All horizontal brackets refer to sentences, and from the charts it is possible to see when sentences are grouped together and written in a chunk (adjacent brackets) or when each sentence is produced in isolation (gaps between brackets). (See Appendix for sample chart.)

The charts can be read by moving along the time line, noting which behaviors occur and in what sequence. Three types of comments are also included in the charts. In bold-face type, the beginning and end of each draft are indicated; in lighter type-face, comments on the actual composing movements are provided; and in the lightest type-face, specific statements made by students or specific words they found particularly troublesome are noted.

From the charts, the following information can be determined:

1. the amount of time spent during prewriting;
2. the strategies used during prewriting;
3. the amount of time spent writing each sentence;
4. the behaviors that occur while each sentence is being written;
5. when sentences are written in groups or "chunks" (fluent writing);
6. when sentences are written in isolation (choppy or sporadic writing);
7. the amount of time spent between sentences;
8. the behaviors that occur between sentences;
9. when editing occurs (during the writing of sentences, between sentences, in the time between drafts);
10. the frequency of editing behavior;

11. the nature of the editing operations; and

12. where and in what frequency pauses or periods of silence occur in the process.

The charts, or *composing style sheets* as they are called, do not explain what students wrote but rather *how* they wrote. They indicate, on one page, the sequences of behavior that occur from the beginning of the process to the end. From them it is possible to determine where and how these behaviors fall into patterns and whether these patterns vary according to the mode of discourse.

It should be noted that although the coding system is presented before the analysis of the data, it was derived from the data and then used as the basis for generalizing about the patterns and behavioral sequences found within each student's process. These individual patterns were reported in each of the five case studies. Thus, initially, a style sheet was constructed for each writing session on each student. When there were four style sheets for each student, it was possible to determine if composing patterns existed among the group. The summary of results reported here is based on the patterns revealed by these charts.

Analyzing Miscues in the Writing Process

Miscue analysis is based on Goodman's model of the reading process. Created in 1962, it has become a widespread tool for studying what students do when they read and is based on the premise that reading is a psycholinguistic process which "uses language, in written form, to get to the meaning" (Goodman, 1973, p. 4). Miscue analysis "involves its user in examining the observed behavior of oral readers as an interaction between language and thought, as a process of constructing meaning from a graphic display" (Goodman, 1973, p. 4). Methodologically, the observer analyzes the mismatch that occurs when readers make responses during oral reading that differ from the text. This mismatch or miscueing is then analyzed from Goodman's "meaning-getting" model, based on the assumption that "the reader's preoccupation with meaning will show in his miscues, because they will tend to result in language that still makes sense" (Goodman, 1973, p. 9).

In the present study, miscue analysis was adapted from Goodman's model in order to provide insight into the writing process. Since students composed aloud, two types of oral behaviors were available for study: encoding processes or what students spoke while they were writing and decoding processes or what students "read"[1] after they had finished writing. When a discrepancy existed between encoding or decoding and what was on the paper, it was referred to as miscue.

24

For encoding, the miscue analysis was carried out in the following manner:

1. The students' written products were typed, preserving the original style and spelling.
2. What students said while composing aloud was checked against the written products; discrepancies were noted on the paper wherever they occurred.
3. The discrepancies were categorized and counted.

Three miscue categories were derived for encoding:

1. Speaking complete ideas but omitting certain words during writing.
2. Pronouncing words with plural markers or other suffixes completely but omitting these endings during writing.
3. Pronouncing the desired word but writing a homonym, an approximation of the word or a personal abbreviation of the word on paper.

For decoding, similar procedures were used, this time comparing the words of the written product with what the student "read" orally. When a discrepancy occurred, it was noted. The discrepancies were then categorized and counted.

Four miscue categories were derived for decoding:

1. "Reading in" missing words or word endings;
2. Deleting words or word endings;
3. "Reading" the desired word rather than the word on the page;
4. "Reading" abbreviations and misspellings as though they were written correctly.

A brief summary of the results of this analysis appears in the findings.

SYNOPSIS OF A CASE STUDY

Tony was a 20-year-old ex-Marine born and raised in the Bronx, New York. Like many Puerto Ricans born in the United States, he was able to speak Spanish, but he considered English his native tongue. In the eleventh grade, Tony left high school, returning three years later to take the New York State high school equivalency exam. As a freshman in college, he was also working part-time to support a child and a wife from whom he was separated.

Behaviors

The composing style sheets provide an overview of the observable behaviors exhibited by Tony during the composing process. (See Appendix for samples of Tony's writing and the accompanying composing style sheet.) The most salient feature of Tony's composing process was its recursiveness. Tony rarely produced a sentence without stopping to reread either a part or the whole. This repetition set up a particular kind of composing rhythm, one that was cumulative in nature and that set ideas in motion by its very repetitiveness. Thus, as can be seen from any of the style sheets, talking led to writing which led to reading which led to planning which again led to writing.

The style sheets indicated a difference in the composing rhythms exhibited in the extensive and reflexive modes. On the extensive topics there was not only more repetition within each sentence but also many more pauses and repetitions between sentences, with intervals often lasting as long as two minutes. On the reflexive topics, sentences were often written in groups, with fewer rereadings and only minimal time intervals separating the creation of one sentence from another.

Editing occurred consistently in all sessions. From the moment Tony began writing, he indicated a concern for correct form that actually inhibited the development of ideas. In none of the writing sessions did he ever write more than two sentences before he began to edit. While editing fit into his overall recursive pattern, it simultaneously interrupted the composing rhythm he had just initiated.

During the intervals between drafts, Tony read his written work, assessed his writing, planned new phrasings, transitions or endings, read the directions and the question over, and edited once again.

Tony performed these operations in both the extensive and reflexive modes and was remarkably consistent in all of his composing operations. The style sheets attest both to this consistency and to the densely packed, tight quality of Tony's composing process—indeed, if the notations on these sheets were any indication at all, it was clear that Tony's composing process was so full that there was little room left for invention or change.

Fluency

Table 2 provides a numerical analysis of Tony's writing performance. Here it is possible to compare not only the amount of time spent on the various

Table 2   Tony: Summary of four writing sessions (time in minutes).

		S1 TW$_1$			**S4 T→W**	
	Drafts	Words	Time	Drafts	Words	Time
Extensive Mode			Prewriting: 7.8			Prewriting: 8.0
	W1	132	18.8	W1	182	29.0
	W2	170	51.0	W2	174	33.9
	Total	302	Total composing: 91.2*	Total	356	Total composing: 82.0*
		S2 TW$_1$			**S5 T→W**	
	Drafts	Words	Time	Drafts	Words	Time
Reflexive Mode			Prewriting: 3.5			Prewriting: 5.7
	W1	165	14.5	W1	208	24.0
	W2	169	25.0	W2	190	38.3
	W3	178	24.2	W3	152	20.8
	Total	512	Total composing: 76.0*	Total	550	Total composing: 96.0*

* Total composing includes time spent on editing and rereading, as well as actual writing.

composing operations but also the relative fluency. For Sessions 1 and 2 the data indicate that while Tony spent more time prewriting and writing in the extensive mode, he actually produced fewer words. For Sessions 4 and 5, a similar pattern can be detected. In the extensive mode, Tony again spent more time prewriting and produced fewer words. Although writing time was increased in the reflexive mode, the additional 20 minutes spent writing did not sufficiently account for an increase of 194 words. Rather, the data indicate that Tony produced more words with less planning and generally in less time in the reflexive mode, suggesting that his greater fluency lay in this mode.

Strategies

Tony exhibited a number of strategies that served him as a writer whether the mode was extensive or reflexive. Given my topic, the first operation he performed was to focus in and narrow down the topic. He did this by rephrasing the topic until either a word or an idea in the topic linked up with something in his own experience (an attitude, an opinion, an event). In this way he established a connection between the field of discourse and himself and at this point he felt ready to write.

Level of Language Use

Once writing, Tony employed a pattern of classifying or dividing the topic into manageable pieces and then using one or both of the divisions as the basis for narration. In the four writing sessions, his classifications were made on the basis of economic, racial, and political differences. However, all of his writing reflected a low level of generality. No formal principles were used to organize the narratives nor were the implications of ideas present in the essay developed.

In his writing, Tony was able to maintain the extensive/reflexive distinction. He recognized when he was being asked directly for an opinion and when he was being asked to discuss concepts or ideas that were not directly linked to his experience. However, the more distance between the topic and himself, the more difficulty he experienced, and the more repetitive his process became. Conversely, when the topic was close to his own experience, the smoother and more fluent the process became. More writing was produced, pauses were fewer, and positive assessment occurred more often. However, Tony made more assumptions on the part of the audience in the reflexive mode. When writing about himself, Tony often did not stop to explain the context from which he was writing; rather, the reader's understanding of the context was taken for granted.

Editing

Tony spent a great deal of his composing time editing. However, most of this time was spent proofreading rather than changing, rephrasing, adding, or evaluating the substantive parts of the discourse. Of a total of 234 changes made in all of the sessions, only 24 were related to changes of content and included the following categories:

1. Elaborations of ideas through the use of specification and detail;
2. Additions of modals that shift the mood of a sentence;
3. Deletions that narrow the focus of a paper;
4. Clause reductions or embeddings that tighten the structure of a paper;
5. Vocabulary choices that reflect a sensitivity to language;

28

6. Reordering of elements in a narrative;

7. Strengthening transitions between paragraphs;

8. Pronoun changes that signal an increased sensitivity to audience.

The 210 changes in form included the following:

Additions	19	Verb changes	4
Deletions	44	Spelling	95
Word choice	13	Punctuation	35
Unresolved problems	89		

The area that Tony changed most often was spelling, although, even after completing three drafts of a paper, Tony still had many words misspelled.

Miscue Analysis

Despite continual proofreading, Tony's completed drafts often retained a look of incompleteness. Words remained misspelled, syntax was uncorrected or overcorrected, suffixes, plural markers, and verb endings were missing, and often words or complete phrases were omitted.

The composing aloud behavior and the miscue analysis derived from it provide one of the first demonstrable ways of understanding how such seemingly incomplete texts can be considered "finished" by the student. (See Table 3 for a summary of Tony's miscues.) Tony consistently voiced complete sentences when composing aloud but only transcribed partial sentences. The same behavior occurred in relation to words with plural or marked endings. However, during rereading and even during editing, Tony supplied the missing endings, words, or phrases and did not seem to "see" what was missing from the text. Thus, when reading his paper, Tony "read in" the meaning he expected to be there which turned him into a reader of content rather than form. However, a difference can be observed between the extensive and reflexive modes, and in the area of correctness Tony's greater strength lay in the reflexive mode. In this mode, not only were more words produced in less time (1,062 vs. 658), but fewer decoding miscues occurred (38 vs. 46), and fewer unresolved problems remained in the text (34 vs. 55).

When Tony did choose to read for form, he was handicapped in another way. Through his years of schooling, Tony learned that there were sets of rules to be applied to one's writing, and he attempted to apply these rules of form to his prose. Often, though, the structures he produced were far more

Table 3   Tony—Miscue analysis.

ENCODING

	Speaking complete ideas but omitting certain words during writing	Pronouncing words with plural markers or other suffixes completely but omitting these endings during writing	Pronouncing the desired word but writing a homonym, an approximation of the word or a personal abbreviation of the word on paper	Total
S1	1	4	11	16
S2	8	0	14	22
S4	4	0	16	20
S5	3	1	15	19
	16	5	56	77

DECODING

	Reading in missing words or word endings	Deleting words or word endings	Reading the desired word rather than the word on the page	Reading abbreviations and misspellings as though they were written correctly	Total
S1	10	1	1	15	27
S2	5	1	2	10	18
S4	3	3	0	13	19
S5	7	1	2	10	20
	25	6	5	48	84

complicated than the simple set of proofreading rules he had at his disposal. He was therefore faced with applying the rule partially, discarding it, or attempting corrections through sound. None of these systems was completely helpful to Tony, and as often as a correction was made that improved the discourse, another was made that obscured it.

Summary

Finally, when Tony completed the writing process, he refrained from commenting on or contemplating his total written product. When he initiated writing, he immediately established distance between himself as writer and his discourse. He knew his preliminary draft might have errors and might need revision. At the end of each session, the distance had decreased if not entirely disappeared. Tony "read in" missing or omitted features, rarely perceived syntactic errors, and did not untangle overly embedded sentences. It was as if the semantic model in his head predominated, and the distance with which he entered the writing process had dissolved. Thus, even with his concern for revision and for correctness, even with the enormous amount of time he invested in rereading and repetition, Tony concluded the composing process with unresolved stylistic and syntactic problems. The conclusion here is not that Tony can't write, or that Tony doesn't know how to write, or that Tony needs to learn more rules: Tony is a writer with a highly consistent and deeply embedded recursive process. What he needs are teachers who can interpret that process for him, who can see through the tangles in the process just as he sees meaning beneath the tangles in his prose, and who can intervene in such a way that untangling his composing process leads him to create better prose.

SUMMARY OF THE FINDINGS

A major finding of this study is that, like Tony, all of the students studied displayed consistent composing processes; that is, the behavioral subsequences prewriting, writing, and editing appeared in sequential patterns that were recognizable across writing sessions and across students.

This consistency suggests a much greater internalization of process than has ever before been suspected. Since the written products of basic writers often look arbitrary, observers commonly assume that the students' approach is also arbitrary. However, just as Shaughnessy (1977) points out that there is "very little that is random . . . in what they have written" (p. 5), so, on close observation, very little appears random in *how* they write. The students observed had stable composing processes which they used whenever they were presented with a writing task. While this consistency argues against seeing these students as beginning writers, it ought not necessarily imply that they are proficient writers. Indeed, their lack of proficiency may be attributable to the way in which premature and rigid attempts to correct and edit their work truncate the flow of composing without substantially improving the form of what they have written. More detailed findings will be reviewed in the following subsections which treat the three major aspects of composing: prewriting, writing, and editing.

Prewriting

When not given specific prewriting instructions, the students in this study began writing within the first few minutes. The average time they spent on prewriting in sessions 1 and 2 was four minutes (see Table 4), and the planning strategies they used fell into three principal types:

1. Rephrasing the topic until a particular word or idea connected with the student's experience. The student then had "an event" in mind before writing began.

2. Turning the large conceptual issue in the topic (e.g., equality) into two manageable pieces for writing (e.g., rich vs. poor; black vs. white).

3. Initiating a string of associations to a word in the topic and then developing one or more of the associations during writing.

When students planned in any of these ways, they began to write with an articulated sense of where they wanted their discourse to go. However, frequently students read the topic and directions a few times and indicated that they had "no idea" what to write. On these occasions, they began writing without any secure sense of where they were heading, acknowledging only that they would "figure it out" as they went along. Often their first sentence was a rephrasing of the question in the topic which, now that it was in their own handwriting and down on paper in front of them, seemed to enable them to plan what ought to come next. In these instances, writing led to planning which led to clarifying which led to more writing. This sequence of planning and writing, clarifying and discarding, was repeated frequently in all of the sessions, even when students began writing with a secure sense of direction.

Although one might be tempted to conclude that these students began writing prematurely and that planning precisely what they were going to write ought to have occurred before they put pen to paper, the data here suggest:

1. that certain strategies, such as creating an association to a key word, focusing in and narrowing down the topic, dichotomizing and classifying, can and do take place in a relatively brief span of time; and

2. that the developing and clarifying of ideas is facilitated once students translate some of those ideas into written form. In other words, seeing ideas on paper enables students to reflect upon, change and develop those ideas further.

Table 4 Overview of all writing sessions.

	Prewriting time*				Total words — Total composing time				Editing changes		Unresolved problems	Miscues during reading
	S1	S2	S4	S5	S1	S2	S4	S5	Content	Form		
Tony	7.8	3.5	8.0	5.7	302 / 91.2	512 / 76.0	356 / 82.0	550 / 96.0	24	210	89	84
Dee	2.5	2.9	5.0	5.0	409 / 55.5	559 / 65.0	91 / 24.5	212 / 29.0	7	24	40	32
Stan	3.5	4.3	14.8	14.7	419 / 62.0	553 / 73.1	365 / 73.0	303 / 68.0	13	49	45	55
Lueller	2.0	1.5	4.0	13.0	518 / 90.8	588 / 96.8	315 / 93.0	363 / 77.8	2	167	143	147
Beverly	5.5	7.0	32.0	20.0	519 / 79.0	536 / 80.3	348 / 97.4	776 / 120.0	21	100	55	30

* Due to a change in the prewriting directions, only Sessions 1 and 2 are used to calculate the average time spent in prewriting.

Writing

Careful study revealed that students wrote by shuttling from the sense of what they wanted to say forward to the words on the page and back from the words on the page to their intended meaning. This "back and forth" movement appeared to be a recursive feature: at one moment students were writing, moving their ideas and their discourse forward; at the next they were backtracking, rereading, and digesting what had been written.

Recursive movements appeared at many points during the writing process. Occasionally sentences were written in groups and then reread as a "piece" of discourse; at other times sentences and phrases were written alone, repeated until the writer was satisfied or worn down, or rehearsed until the act of rehearsal led to the creation of a new sentence. In the midst of writing, editing occurred as students considered the surface features of language. Often planning of a global nature took place: in the midst of producing a first draft, students stopped and began planning how the second draft would differ from the first. Often in the midst of writing, students stopped and referred to the topic in order to check if they had remained faithful to the original intent, and occasionally, though infrequently, they identified a sentence or a phrase that seemed, to them, to produce a satisfactory ending. In all these behaviors, they were shuttling back and forth, projecting what would come next and doubling back to be sure of the ground they had covered.

A number of conclusions can be drawn from the observations of these students composing and from the comments they made: although they produced inadequate or flawed products, they nevertheless seemed to understand and perform some of the crucial operations involved in composing with skill. While it cannot be stated with certainty that the patterns they displayed are shared by other writers, some of the operations they performed appear sufficiently sound to serve as prototypes for constructing two major hypotheses on the nature of their composing processes. Whether the following hypotheses are borne out in studies of different types of writers remains an open question:

1. Composing does not occur in a straightforward, linear fashion. The process is one of accumulating discrete bits down on the paper and then working from those bits to reflect upon, structure, and then further develop what one means to say. It can be thought of as a kind of "retrospective structuring"; movement forward occurs only after one has reached back, which in turn occurs only after one has some sense of where one wants to go. Both aspects, the reaching back and the sensing forward, have a clarifying effect.

2. Composing always involves some measure of both construction and discovery. Writers construct their discourse inasmuch as they begin with a sense of what they want to write. This sense, as long as it remains implicit, is not equivalent to the explicit form it gives rise to. Thus, a process of constructing meaning is required. Rereading or backward movements become a way of assessing whether or not the words on the page adequately capture the original sense intended. Constructing simultaneously affords discovery. Writers know more fully what they mean only after having written it. In this way the explicit written form serves as a window on the implicit sense with which one began.

Editing

Editing played a major role in the composing processes of the students in this study (see Table 5). Soon after students began writing their first drafts, they began to edit, and they continued to do so during the intervals between drafts, during the writing of their second drafts and during the final reading of papers.

While editing, the students were concerned with a variety of items: the lexicon (i.e., spelling, word choice, and the context of words); the syntax (i.e., grammar, punctuation, and sentence structure); and the discourse as a whole (i.e., organization, coherence, and audience). However, despite the students' considered attempts to proofread their work, serious syntactic and stylistic problems remained in their finished drafts. The persistence of these

Table 5 Editing changes.

	Tony	Dee	Stan	Lueller	Beverly	Totals
Total number of words produced	1720	1271	1640	1754	2179	8564
Total form	210	24	49	167	100	550
Additions	19	2	10	21	11	63
Deletions	44	9	18	41	38	150
Word choice	13	4	1	27	6	51
Verb changes	4	1	2	7	12	26
Spelling	95	4	13	60	19	191
Punctuation	35	4	5	11	14	69
Total content	24	7	13	2	21	67

errors may, in part, be understood by looking briefly at some of the problems that arose for these students during editing.

Rule Confusion

(1) All of the students observed asked themselves, "Is this sentence [or feature] correct?" but the simple set of editing rules at their disposal was often inappropriate for the types of complicated structures they produced. As a result, they misapplied what they knew and either created a hypercorrection or impaired the meaning they had originally intended to clarify; (2) The students observed attempted to write with terms they heard in lectures or class discussions, but since they were not yet familiar with the syntactic or semantic constraints one word placed upon another, their experiments with academic language resulted in what Shaughnessy (1977, p. 49) calls, "lexical transplants" or "syntactic dissonances"; (3) The students tried to rely on their intuitions about language, in particular the sound of words. Often, however, they had been taught to mistrust what "sounded" right to them, and they were unaware of the particular feature in their speech codes that might need to be changed in writing to match the standard code. As a result, when they attempted corrections by sound, they became confused, and they began to have difficulty differentiating between what sounded right in speech and what needed to be marked on the paper.

Selective Perception

These students habitually reread their papers from internal semantic or meaning models. They extracted the meaning they wanted from the minimal cues on the page, and they did not recognize that outside readers would find those cues insufficient for meaning.

A study of Table 6 indicates that the number of problems remaining in the students' written products approximates the number of miscues produced during reading. This proximity, itself, suggests that many of these errors persisted because the students were so certain of the words they wanted to have on the page that they "read in" these words even when they were absent; in other words, they reduced uncertainty by operating as though what was in their heads was already on the page. The problem of selective perception, then, cannot be reduced solely to mechanical decoding; the semantic model from which students read needs to be acknowledged and taken into account in any study that attempts to explain how students write and why their completed written products end up looking so incomplete.

Table 6 The talk-write paradigm.
Miscues—Decoding behaviors

	Tony	Dee	Stan	Lueller	Beverly	Totals
Unresolved problems	89	40	45	143	55	372
"Reading in" missing words or word endings	25	13	11	44	11	104
Deleting words or word endings	6	2	4	14	9	35
"Reading" the desired word rather than the word on the page	5	6	18	15	8	52
"Reading" abbreviations and misspellings as though they were written correctly	48	11	22	74	2	157
	84	32	55	147	30	348

Egocentricity

The students in this study wrote from an egocentric point of view. While they occasionally indicated a concern for their readers, they more often took the reader's understanding for granted. They did not see the necessity of making their referents explicit, of making the connections among their ideas apparent, of carefully and explicitly relating one phenomenon to another, or of placing narratives or generalizations within an orienting, conceptual framework.

On the basis of these observations one may be led to conclude that these writers did not know how to edit their work. Such a conclusion must, however, be drawn with care. Efforts to improve their editing need to be based on an informed view of the role that editing already plays in their composing processes. Two conclusions in this regard are appropriate here:

1. Editing intrudes so often and to such a degree that it breaks down the rhythms generated by thinking and writing. When this happens the students are forced to go back and recapture the strands of their thinking once the editing operation has been completed. Thus, editing occurs prematurely, before students have generated enough discourse to approximate the ideas they have, and it often results in their losing track of their ideas.

2. Editing is primarily an exercise in error-hunting. The students are prematurely concerned with the "look" of their writing; thus, as soon as a few words are written on the paper, detection and correction of errors replaces writing and revising. Even when they begin writing with a tentative, flexible frame of mind, they soon become locked into whatever is on the page. What they seem to lack as much as any rule is a conception of editing that includes flexibility, suspended judgment, the weighing of possibilities, and the reworking of ideas.

IMPLICATIONS FOR TEACHING AND RESEARCH

One major implication of this study pertains to teachers' conceptions of unskilled writers. Traditionally, these students have been labeled "remedial," which usually implies that teaching ought to remedy what is "wrong" in their written products. Since the surface features in the writing of unskilled writers seriously interfere with the extraction of meaning from the page, much class time is devoted to examining the rules of the standard code. The pedagogical soundness of this procedure has been questioned frequently,[2] but in spite of the debate, the practice continues, and it results in a further complication, namely that students begin to conceive of writing as a "cosmetic" process where concern for correct form supersedes development of ideas. As a result, the excitement of composing, of constructing and discovering meaning, is cut off almost before it has begun.

More recently, unskilled writers have been referred to as "beginners," implying that teachers can start anew. They need not "punish" students for making mistakes, and they need not assume that their students have already been taught how to write. Yet this view ignores the highly elaborated, deeply embedded processes the students bring with them. These unskilled college writers are not beginners in a *tabula rasa* sense, and teachers err in assuming they are. The results of this study suggest that teachers may first need to identify which characteristic components of each student's process facilitate writing and which inhibit it before further teaching takes place. If they do not, teachers of unskilled writers may continue to place themselves in a defeating position: imposing another method of writing instruction upon the students' already internalized processes without first helping students to extricate themselves from the knots and tangles in those processes.

A second implication of this study is that the composing process is now amenable to a replicable and graphic mode of representation as a sequence of codable behaviors. The composing style sheets provide researchers and teachers with the first demonstrable way of documenting how individual students write. Such a tool may have diagnostic as well as research benefits. It may be used to record writing behaviors in large groups, prior to and after instruction, as well as in individuals. Certainly it lends itself to the longitudinal study of the writing process and may help to elucidate what it is that changes in the process as writers become more skilled.

A third implication relates to case studies and to the theories derived from them. This study is an illustration of the way in which a theoretical model of the composing process can be grounded in observations of the individual's experience of composing. It is precisely the complexity of this experience that the case study brings to light. However, by viewing a series of cases, the researcher can discern patterns and themes that suggest regularities in composing behavior across individuals. These common features lead to hypotheses and theoretical formulations which have some basis in shared experience. How far this shared experience extends is, of course, a question that can only be answered through further research.

A final implication derives from the preponderance of recursive behaviors in the composing processes studied here, and from the theoretical notion derived from these observations: retrospective structuring, or the going back to the sense of one's meaning in order to go forward and discover more of what one has to say. Seen in this light, composing becomes the carrying forward of an implicit sense into explicit form. Teaching composing, then, means paying attention not only to the forms or products but also to the explicative process through which they arise.

APPENDIX

Composing Style Sheet

Name: **Tony**   Mode: **Extensive TW1**   Date: **October 31, 1975**

Session: **1**   Topic: **Society & Culture**   Time: **11:00 AM - 12:30 PM**

Prewriting

								1	
RDRQAPL	QWCRIQPLRQ	PLRQPLRQRI	PLRQPLRQPLRQ	TA(-)QRIP L	RIRI RQ T	QDQTPLRQPLG	RQ	TW1	AR^1[E$_{ap}$] R^1	PL RQPLG T
10	20 rephrasing question	30	40	50	60	70		80	90	100

				2			3		
RW1RQTQRW1	To	PL	RW1RW1RQRQ	RQ TPL	TW1[E(-)]	RW1→TW1	R^{2}T	RW1 RW1 E RW1	TW1	PLL R1-3	TW1 PLL TW1
10	developing ideas	20	30	40	50 not a good way to start a sentence	developing 60 narrative	70	80	90	200

4	5	6	7			8+9			
R$_5$T→TW1 TW1 TW1T→TW1	PLT TW1[re]	TW1 T RQ	PL R^2	TW1	[re]	TW1	PLG RQ RW1	[PL→E] RW1	TE	RW1 [Eadd] PL
10	20 ending 30	effects 40 of crisis	ending 50		60 End of W1 70		80 read for content first	90	300

						1		
RW1	A(-)	TPL	RW1	A(+) RW1	[E$_{as}$] T	RW1	PLW2	TW2	[E$_{gr}$	] TW2 [E$_{gr}$]TW2 PL
go into more depth 10	20	30	40	elaborating lay-offs—jobs 50		60	70 Begin W2 80	90	400

	2					3			
R2A (+) TW2	[R2]A(+) TW2	[E$_{ap}$]	R^2 R^3 PL	T[E$_{as}^{gr}$]PL	A(+)TW2 [PL→ E] TW2 [E$_{del}^{add}$	] TW2[E$_{gr}$] TW2 PLR^3 PL-R^3	Tadd
10	20	30	40 there is there are	50	60	70	80	90	500

4				5				
TW2−[EPL	]TW2	PL RW2 [E PL]RW2[EWC]RIQ	RW1 [EWC^{add}]	A(+) TW2 [re] TW2 T	TW2[re]RW1 T PL RW1 T [re] TW2 [re]
10	20	30	40	50	60	70 elaborating 80	90	600

	6				7			
[re][re]TW2 [re]	TW2 [re] TW2	PLRW1	RW2 [re] RW2	A(+) RW2 TE	PL RW1	RW2	PL
10	20	30	40	50	explaining changes 60	70	80	90	700

						10		
RW1 T PL	RW2 T R^4 T	R$^+$TW2	[re] TW2 [re] TW2	R$^{6-7}$ [Eadd] R$^{6-7}$ [re]	PL R$^{5-7}$ A(+)PlRW1
10	20 elaborating new sentence	30	40	50	60	70	80	90	800

		8	9			10		
Ts → PL	RQ	PL	T RW1 → TW2[re]	R^8 TW2	Tadd RQ	A(-)	RW1 A(+) R^9 TW2	PL	RQ RW2
should I add more? 10	20	30	40	50 elaborating	changes 60 mind	70 ending	End of W2 80	90	900

RW2	WS to 960							
10	Total 20 composing finished	30	40	50	60	70	80	90	1000

Writing Sample
TONY
Session 1
W1

All men can't be consider equal in a America base on financial situation.[1] Because their are men born in rich families that will never have to worry about any financial difficulties.[2]

           are

And then theyre / ~~the~~ another type of Americans that is born to a poor family and al-

    may

way / have some kind of fina—difficulty.[3] Espeicaly nowadays in New York city With

          and all   If he is able

the budgit Crisis /   .[4] ~~He may~~ be able To get a job.[5] But are now he lose the job just as easy as he got it.[6] So when he loses his job he'll have to try to get some fina—assistance.[7]

                                here

~~A~~ Then he'll probley have even more fin—diffuicuty.[8] So right / you can't see that In Ameri~~an~~, all men are not create equal in the fin—sense.[9]

Writing Sample
TONY
Session 1
W2

All men can not be consider equal in America base on financial situation.[1] Because their are men born in rich families that will never have to worry about any financial ~~diffuel~~

              the

diffuliculties.[2] And then they're are / another type of amer~~a~~icans that are born to a poor

            may

fami~~t~~ly.[3] And This is the type of Americans that ~~will~~ / alway have some kind of finanical diffuliculty.[4] Espeical today ~~today~~ ~~the~~in new york The way the city has fallen ~~has fallen~~

                      working

into fin—debt.[5] It has become such a big crisis for the ~~people~~people, in the [6] If the

            with the   the   ~~is~~

working man is able to find a job, espeicaly ~~for~~ / ~~city~~ a city The way ~~the way~~ city / fin— sitionu is set up now, ~~h~~He'll probley lose the job a whole lot faster than what he got it.[7] When he loses his job he'll ~~p~~ have even more fin—difficulty.[8] And then he'll be force to go~~t~~ to the city for some fini—assi—.[9] So right here you can see that all men in America are not create equal in the fin—sense.[10]

NOTES

1. The word "read" is used in a particular manner here. In the traditional sense, reading refers to accurate decoding of written symbols. Here it refers to students' verbalizing words or endings even when the symbols for those words are missing or only minimally present. Whenever the term "reading" is used in this way, it will be in quotation marks.

2. For discussions on the controversy over the effects of grammar instruction on writing ability, see the following: Richard Braddock, Richard Lloyd-Jones, and Lowell Schoer, *Research in Written Composition* (Urbana, Ill.: National Council of Teachers of English, 1963); Frank O'Hare, *Sentence Combining* (NCTE Research Report No. 15, Urbana, Ill.: National Council of Teachers of English, 1973); Elizabeth F. Haynes, "Using Research in Preparing to Teach Writing," *English Journal*, 1978, 67, 82-89.

REFERENCES

Braddock, R., Lloyd-Jones, R., & Schoer, L. *Research in written composition.* Urbana, Ill.: National Council of Teachers of English, 1963.

Britton, J., Burgess, T., Martin, N., McLeod, A., & Rosen, H. *The development of writing abilities (11-18).* London: Macmillan Education Ltd., 1975.

Burton, D. L. Research in the teaching of English: The troubled dream. *Research in the Teaching of English*, 1973, 1, 160-187.

Cooper, C. R. Doing research/reading research. *English Journal*, 1974, 63, 94-99.

Cooper, C. R., & Odell, L. (Eds.) *Research on composing: Points of departure.* Urbana, Ill.: National Council of Teachers of English, 1978.

Emig, J. A. On teaching composition: Some hypotheses as definitions. *Research in the Teaching of English*, 1967, 1, 127-135.

Emig, J. A. *The composing processes of twelfth graders.* Urbana, Ill.: National Council of Teachers of English, 1971. (Research Report No. 13) (Ed. D. Dissertation, Harvard University, 1969).

Goodman, K. S. (Ed.) *Miscue analysis: Applications to reading instruction.* Urbana, Ill.: NCTE and ERIC, 1973.

Graves, D. H. Children's writing: Research directions and hypotheses based upon an examination of the writing process of seven year old children (Doctoral dissertation, State University of New York at Buffalo, 1973). *Dissertation Abstracts International*, 1974, 34, 6255A.

Haynes, E. F. Using research in preparing to teach writing. *English Journal*, 1978, 67, 82-89.

Mischel, T. A case study of a twelfth-grade writer. *Research in the Teaching of English*, 1974, 8, 303-314.

O'Hare, F. *Sentence-combining: Improving student writing without formal grammar instruction.* Urbana, Ill.: National Council of Teachers of English, 1973. (Research Report No. 15)

Perl, S. *Five writers writing: Case studies of the composing processes of unskilled college writers.* Unpublished doctoral dissertation, New York University, 1978.

Pianko, S. *The composing acts of college freshmen writers.* Unpublished Ed.D. dissertation, Rutgers University, 1977.

Shaughnessy, M. P. *Errors and expectations: A guide for the teacher of basic writing.* New York: Oxford University Press, 1977.

Stallard, C. K. An analysis of the writing behavior of good student writers. *Research in the Teaching of English*, 1974, 8, 206-218.

Revision Strategies of Student Writers and Experienced Adult Writers

Nancy Sommers

Although various aspects of the writing process have been studied extensively of late, research on revision has been notably absent. The reason for this, I suspect, is that current models of the writing process have directed attention away from revision. With few exceptions, these models are linear; they separate the writing process into discrete stages. Two representative models are Gordon Rohman's suggestion that the composing process moves from prewriting to writing to rewriting and James Britton's model of the writing process as a series of stages described in metaphors of linear growth, conception—incubation—production. What is striking about these theories of writing is that they model themselves on speech: Rohman defines the writer in a way that cannot distinguish him from a speaker ("A writer is a man who . . . puts [his] experience into words in his own mind"—p. 15); and Britton bases his theory of writing on what he calls (following Jakobson) the "expressiveness" of speech. Moreover, Britton's study itself follows the "linear model" of the relation of thought and language in speech proposed by Vygotsky, a relationship embodied in the linear movement "from the motive which engenders a thought to the shaping of the thought, *first* in inner speech, *then* in meanings of words, and *finally* in words" (quoted in Britton, p. 40). What this movement fails to take into account in its linear structure—"first . . . then . . . finally"—is the recursive shaping of thought by language; what it fails to take into account is revision. In these linear

Reprinted from *College Composition and Communication* 31.4 (December 1980): 378–88. Used with permission.

conceptions of the writing process revision is understood as a separate stage at the end of the process—a stage that comes after the completion of a first or second draft and one that is temporally distinct from the prewriting and writing stages of the process.[3]

The linear model bases itself on speech in two specific ways. First of all, it is based on traditional rhetorical models, models that were created to serve the spoken art of oratory. In whatever ways the parts of classical rhetoric are described, they offer "stages" of composition that are repeated in contemporary models of the writing process. Edward Corbett, for instance, describes the "five parts of a discourse"—*inventio, dispositio, elocutio, memoria, pronuntiatio*—and, disregarding the last two parts since "after rhetoric came to be concerned mainly with written discourse, there was no further need to deal with them,"[4] he produces a model very close to Britton's conception [*inventio*], incubation [*dispositio*], production [*elocutio*]. Other rhetorics also follow this procedure, and they do so not simply because of historical accident. Rather, the process represented in the linear model is based on the irreversibility of speech. Speech, Roland Barthes says, "is irreversible":

> "A word cannot be retracted, except precisely by saying that one retracts it. To cross out here is to add: if I want to erase what I have just said, I cannot do it without showing the eraser itself (I must say: '*or rather. . .* ' '*I expressed myself badly. . .* '); paradoxically, it is ephemeral speech which is indelible, not monumental writing. All that one can do in the case of a spoken utterance is to tack on another utterance."[5]

What is impossible in speech is *revision:* like the example Barthes gives, revision in speech is an afterthought. In the same way, each stage of the linear model must be exclusive (distinct from the other stages) or else it becomes trivial and counterproductive to refer to these junctures as "stages."

By staging revision after enunciation, the linear models reduce revision in writing, as in speech, to no more than an afterthought. In this way such models make the study of revision impossible. Revision, in Rohman's model, is simply the repetition of writing; or to pursue Britton's organic metaphor, revision is simply the further growth of what is already there, the "preconceived" product. The absence of research on revision, then, is a function of a theory of writing which makes revision both superfluous and redundant, a theory which does not distinguish between writing and speech.

What the linear models do produce is a parody of writing. Isolating revision and then disregarding it plays havoc with the experiences composition teachers have of the actual writing and rewriting of experienced writers. Why should the linear model be preferred? Why should revision be forgotten, superfluous? Why do teachers offer the linear model and students accept it? One reason, Barthes suggests, is that "there is a fundamental tie between teaching and speech," while "writing begins at the point where speech becomes *impossible*."[6] The spoken word cannot be revised. The possibility of revision distinguishes the written text from speech. In fact, according to Barthes, this is the essential difference between writing and speaking. When we must revise, when the very idea is subject to recursive shaping by language, then speech becomes inadequate. This is a matter to which I will return, but first we should examine, theoretically, a detailed exploration of what student writers as distinguished from experienced adult writers *do* when they write and rewrite their work. Dissatisfied with both the linear model of writing and the lack of attention to the process of revision, I conducted a series of studies over the past three years which examined the revision processes of student writers and experienced writers to see what role revision played in their writing processes. In the course of my work the revision process was redefined as *a sequence of changes in a composition—changes which are initiated by cues and occur continually throughout the writing of a work.*

METHODOLOGY

I used a case study approach. The student writers were twenty freshmen at Boston University and the University of Oklahoma with SAT verbal scores ranging from 450–600 in their first semester of composition. The twenty experienced adult writers from Boston and Oklahoma City included journalists, editors, and academics. To refer to the two groups, I use the terms *student writers* and *experienced writers* because the principal difference between these two groups is the amount of experience they have had in writing.

Each writer wrote three essays, expressive, explanatory, and persuasive, and rewrote each essay twice, producing nine written products in draft and final form. Each writer was interviewed three times after the final revision of each essay. And each writer suggested revisions for a composition written by an anonymous author. Thus extensive written and spoken documents were obtained from each writer.

The essays were analyzed by counting and categorizing the changes made. Four revision operations were identified: deletion, substitution, addition, and reordering. And four levels of changes were identified: word, phrase, sentence, theme (the extended statement of one idea). A coding system was developed for identifying the frequency of revision by level and operation. In addition, transcripts of the interviews in which the writers

45

interpreted their revisions were used to develop what was called a *scale of concerns* for each writer. This scale enabled me to codify what were the writer's primary concerns, secondary concerns, tertiary concerns, and whether the writers used the same scale of concerns when revising the second or third drafts as they used in revising the first draft.

REVISION STRATEGIES OF STUDENT WRITERS

Most of the students I studied did not use the terms *revision* or *rewriting*. In fact, they did not seem comfortable using the word *revision* and explained that revision was not a word they used, but the word their teachers used. Instead, most of the students had developed various functional terms to describe the type of changes they made. The following are samples of these definitions:

> *Scratch Out and Do Over Again:* "I say scratch out and do over, and that means what it says. Scratching out and cutting out. I read what I have written and I cross out a word and put another word in; a more decent word or a better word. Then if there is somewhere to use a sentence that I have crossed out, I will put it there."
>
> *Reviewing:* "Reviewing means just using better words and eliminating words that are not needed. I go over and change words around."
>
> *Reviewing:* "I just review every word and make sure that everything is worded right. I see if I am rambling; I see if I can put a better word in or leave one out. Usually when I read what I have written, I say to myself, 'that word is so bland or so trite,' and then I go and get my thesaurus."
>
> *Redoing:* "Redoing means cleaning up the paper and crossing out. It is looking at something and saying, no that has to go, or no, that is not right."
>
> *Marking Out:* "I don't use the word rewriting because I only write one draft and the changes that I make are made on top of the draft. The changes that I make are usually just marking out words and putting different ones in."
>
> *Slashing and Throwing Out:* "I throw things out and say they are not good. I like to write like Fitzgerald did by inspiration, and if I feel inspired then I don't need to slash and throw much out."

The predominant concern in these definitions is vocabulary. The students understand the revision process as a rewording activity. They do so because they perceive words as the unit of written discourse. That is, they concentrate on particular words apart from their role in the text. Thus one student quoted above thinks in terms of dictionaries, and, following the eighteenth century theory of words parodied in *Gulliver's Travels*, he imagines a load of things carried about to be exchanged. Lexical changes are the major revision activities of the students because economy is their goal. They are governed, like the linear model itself, by the Law of Occam's razor that prohibits logically needless repetition: redundancy and superfluity. Nothing governs speech more than such superfluities; speech constantly repeats itself precisely because spoken words, as Barthes writes, are expendable in the cause of communication. The aim of revision according to the students' own description is therefore to clean up speech; the redundancy of speech is unnecessary in writing, their logic suggests, because writing, unlike speech, can be reread. Thus one student said, "Redoing means cleaning up the paper and crossing out." The remarkable contradiction of cleaning by marking might, indeed, stand for student revision as I have encountered it.

The students place a symbolic importance on their selection and rejection of words as the determiners of success or failure for their compositions. When revising, they primarily ask themselves: can I find a better word or phrase? A more impressive, not so cliched, or less hum-drum word? Am I repeating the same word or phrase too often? They approach the revision process with what could be labeled as a "thesaurus philosophy of writing"; the students consider the thesaurus a harvest of lexical substitutions and believe that most problems in their essays can be solved by rewording. What is revealed in the students' use of the thesaurus is a governing attitude toward their writing: that the meaning to be communicated is already there, already finished, already produced, ready to be communicated, and all that is necessary is a better word "rightly worded." One student defined revision as "redoing"; "redoing" meant "just using better words and eliminating words that are not needed." For the students, writing is translating: the thought to the page, the language of speech to the more formal language of prose, the word to its synonym. Whatever is translated, an original text already exists for students, one which need not be discovered or acted upon, but simply communicated.[7]

The students list repetition as one of the elements they most worry about. This cue signals to them that they need to eliminate the repetition either by substituting or deleting words or phrases. Repetition occurs, in large part, because student writing imitates—transcribes—speech: attention to repetitious words is a manner of cleaning speech. Without a sense of the developmental possibilities of revision (and writing in general) students seek, on the authority of many textbooks, simply to clean up their language and prepare to type. What is curious, however, is that students are aware of lexical repetition, but not conceptual repetition. They only notice the repetition if they can "hear" it; they do not diagnose lexical repetition as symptomatic of problems on a deeper level. By rewording their sentences to avoid the lexical repetition, the students solve the immediate problem, but blind themselves to problems on a textual level; although they are using different words, they are sometimes merely restating the same idea with different words. Such blindness, as I discovered with student writers, is the inability to "see" revision as a process: the inability to "re-view" their work again, as it were, with different eyes, and to start over.

The revision strategies described above are consistent with the students' understanding of the revision process as requiring lexical changes but not semantic changes. For the students, the extent to which they revise is a function of their level of inspiration. In fact, they use the word *inspiration* to describe the ease or difficulty with which their essay is written, and the extent to which the essay needs to be revised. If students feel inspired, if the writing comes easily, and if they don't get stuck on individual words or phrases, then they say that they cannot see any reason to revise. Because students do not see revision as an activity in which they modify and develop perspectives and ideas, they feel that if they know what they want to say, then there is little reason for making revisions.

The only modification of ideas in the students' essays occurred when they tried out two or three introductory paragraphs. This results, in part, because the students have been taught in another version of the linear model of composing to use a thesis statement as a controlling device in their introductory paragraphs. Since they write their introductions and their thesis statements even before they have really discovered what they want to say, their early close attention to the thesis statement, and more generally the linear model, function to restrict and circumscribe not only the development of their ideas, but also their ability to change the direction of these ideas.

Too often as composition teachers we conclude that students do not willingly revise. The evidence from my research suggests that it is not that students are unwilling to revise, but rather that they do what they have been taught to do in a consistently narrow and predictable way. On every occasion when I asked students why they hadn't made any more changes, they essentially replied, "I knew something larger was wrong, but I didn't think it would help to move words around." The students have strategies for handling words and phrases and their strategies helped them on a word or sentence level. What they lack, however, is a set of strategies to help them identify the "something larger" that they sensed was wrong and work from there. The students do not have strategies for handling the whole essay. They lack procedures or heuristics to help them reorder lines of reasoning or ask questions about their purposes and readers. The students view their compositions in a linear way as a series of parts. Even such potentially useful concepts as "unity" or "form" are reduced to the rule that a composition, if it is to have form, must have an introduction, a body, and a conclusion, or the sum total of the necessary parts.

The students decide to stop revising when they decide that they have not violated any of the rules for revising. These rules, such as "Never begin a sentence with a conjunction" or "Never end a sentence with a preposition," are lexically cued and rigidly applied. In general, students will subordinate the demands of the specific problems of their text to the demands of the rules. Changes are made in compliance with abstract rules about the product, rules that quite often do not apply to the specific problems in the text. These revision strategies are teacher-based, directed towards a teacher-reader who expects compliance with rules—with pre-existing "conceptions"—and who will only examine parts of the composition (writing comments about those parts in the margins of their essays) and will cite any violations of rules in those parts. At best the students see their writing altogether passively through the eyes of former teachers or their surrogates, the textbooks, and are bound to the rules which they have been taught.

REVISION STRATEGIES OF EXPERIENCED WRITERS

One aim of my research has been to contrast how student writers define revision with how a group of experienced writers define their revision processes. Here is a sampling of the definitions from the experienced writers:

> *Rewriting:* "It is a matter of looking at the kernel of what I have written, the content, and then thinking about it, responding to it, making decisions, and actually restructuring it."
>
> *Rewriting:* "I rewrite as I write. It is hard to tell what is a first draft because it is not determined by time. In one draft, I might cross out three pages, write two, cross out a fourth, rewrite it, and call it a draft. I am constantly writing and rewriting. I can only conceptualize so much in my first draft—only so much information can be held in my head at one time; my rewriting efforts are a reflection of how much information I can encompass at one time. There are levels and agenda which I have to attend to in each draft."
>
> *Rewriting:* "Rewriting means on one level, finding the argument, and on another level, language changes to make the argument more effective. Most of the time I feel as if I can go on rewriting forever. There is always one part of a piece that I could keep working on. It is always difficult to know at what point to abandon a piece of writing. I like this idea that a piece of writing is never finished, just abandoned."

Rewriting: "My first draft is usually very scattered. In rewriting, I find the line of argument. After the argument is resolved, I am much more interested in word choice and phrasing."

Revising: "My cardinal rule in revising is never to fall in love with what I have written in a first or second draft. An idea, sentence, or even a phrase that looks catchy, I don't trust. Part of this idea is to wait a while. I am much more in love with something after I have written it than I am a day or two later. It is much easier to change anything with time."

Revising: "It means taking apart what I have written and putting it back together again. I ask major theoretical questions of my ideas, respond to those questions, and think of proportion and structure, and try to find a controlling metaphor. I find out which ideas can be developed and which should be dropped. I am constantly chiseling and changing as I revise."

The experienced writers describe their primary objective when revising as finding the form or shape of their argument. Although the metaphors vary, the experienced writers often use structural expressions such as "finding a framework," "a pattern," or "a design" for their argument. When questioned about this emphasis, the experienced writers responded that since their first drafts are usually scattered attempts to define their territory, their objective in the second draft is to begin observing general patterns of development and deciding what should be included and what excluded. One writer explained, "I have learned from experience that I need to keep writing a first draft until I figure out what I want to say. Then in a second draft, I begin to see the structure of an argument and how all the various sub-arguments which are buried beneath the surface of all those sentences are related." What is described here is a process in which the writer is both agent and vehicle. "Writing," says Barthes, unlike speech, "develops like a seed, not a line," and like a seed it confuses beginning and end, conception and production. Thus, the experienced writers say their drafts are "not determined by time," that rewriting is a "constant process," that they feel as if (they) "can go on forever." Revising confuses the beginning and end, the agent and vehicle; it confuses, *in order to find*, the line of argument.

After a concern for form, the experienced writers have a second objective: a concern for their readership. In this way, "production" precedes "conception." The experienced writers imagine a reader (reading their product) whose existence and whose expectations influence their revision process. They have abstracted the standards of a reader and this reader seems to be partially a reflection of themselves and functions as a critical and productive collaborator—a collaborator who has yet to love their work. The anticipation of a reader's judgment causes a feeling of dissonance when the writer recognizes incongruities between intention and execution, and requires these writers to make revisions on all levels. Such a reader gives them just what the students lacked: new eyes to "re-view" their work. The experienced writers believe that they have learned the causes and conditions, the product, which will influence their reader, and their revision strategies are geared towards creating these causes and conditions. They demonstrate a complex understanding of which examples, sentences, or phrases should be included or excluded. For example, one experienced writer decided to delete public examples and add private examples when writing about the energy crisis because "private examples would be less controversial and thus more persuasive." Another writer revised his transitional sentences because "some kinds of transitions are more easily recognized as transitions than others." These examples represent the type of strategic attempts these experienced writers use to manipulate the conventions of discourse in order to communicate to their reader.

But these revision strategies are a process of more than communication; they are part of the process of *discovering meaning* altogether. Here we can see the importance of dissonance; at the heart of revision is the process by which writers recognize and resolve the dissonance they sense in their writing. Ferdinand de Saussure has argued that meaning is differential or "diacritical," based on differences between terms rather than "essential" or inherent qualities of terms. "Phonemes," he said, "are characterized not, as one might think, by their own positive quality but simply by the fact that they are distinct."[9] In fact, Saussure bases his entire *Course in General Linguistics* on these differences, and such differences are dissonant; like musical dissonances which gain their significance from their relationship to the "key" of the composition which itself is determined by the whole language, specific language (parole) gains its meaning from the system of language (langue) of which it is a manifestation and part. The musical composition— a "composition" of parts—creates its "key" as in an over-all structure which determines the value (meaning) of its parts. The analogy with music is readily seen in the compositions of experienced writers: both sorts of composition are based precisely on those structures experienced writers seek in their writing. It is this complicated relationship between the parts and the whole in the work of experienced writers which destroys the linear model; writing cannot develop "like a line" because each addition or deletion is a reordering of the whole. Explicating Saussure, Jonathan Culler asserts that "meaning depends on difference of meaning."[10] But student writers constantly struggle to bring their essays into congruence with a predefined meaning. The experienced writers do the opposite: they seek to discover (to create) meaning in the engagement with their writing, in revision. They seek to em-

phasize and exploit the lack of clarity, the differences of meaning, the dissonance, that writing as opposed to speech allows in the possibility of revision.
Writing has spatial and temporal features not apparent in speech—words
are recorded in space and fixed in time—which is why writing is susceptible
to reordering and later addition. Such features make possible the dissonance
that both provokes revision and promises, from itself, new meaning.

For the experienced writers the heaviest concentration of changes is on
the sentence level, and the changes are predominantly by addition and deletion. But, unlike the students, experienced writers make changes on all levels and use all revision operations. Moreover, the operations the students fail
to use—reordering and addition—seem to require a theory of the revision
process as a totality—a theory which, in fact, encompasses the *whole* of the
composition. Unlike the students, the experienced writers possess a nonlin-
ear theory in which a sense of the whole writing both precedes and grows
out of an examination of the parts. As we saw, one writer said he needed "a
first draft to figure out what to say," and "a second draft to see the structure of
an argument buried beneath the surface." Such a "theory" is both theoretical and strategical; once again, strategy and theory are conflated in ways that
are literally impossible for the linear model. Writing appears to be more like
a seed than a line.

Two elements of the experienced writers' theory of the revision process
are the adoption of a holistic perspective and the perception that revision is
a recursive process. The writers ask: what does my essay as a *whole* need for
form, balance, rhythm, or communication. Details are added, dropped, substituted, or reordered according to their sense of what the essay needs for
emphasis and proportion. This sense, however, is constantly in flux as ideas
are developed and modified; it is constantly "re-viewed" in relation to the
parts. As their ideas change, revision becomes an attempt to make their writing consonant with that changing vision.

The experienced writers see their revision process as a recursive
process—a process with significant recurring activities—with different levels
of attention and different agenda for each cycle. During the first revision
cycle their attention is primarily directed towards narrowing the topic and
delimiting their ideas. At this point, they are not as concerned as they are
later about vocabulary and style. The experienced writers explained that
they get closer to their meaning by not limiting themselves too early to lexical concerns. As one writer commented to explain her revision process, a
comment inspired by the summer 1977 New York power failure: "I feel like
Con Edison cutting off certain states to keep the generators going. In first
and second drafts, I try to cut off as much as I can of my editing generator,
and in a third draft, I try to cut off some of my idea generators, so I can make

52

sure that I will actually finish the essay." Although the experienced writers describe their revision process as a series of different levels or cycles, it is inaccurate to assume that they have only one objective for each cycle and that each cycle can be defined by a different objective. The same objectives and sub-processes are present in each cycle, but in different proportions. Even though these experienced writers place the predominant weight upon finding the form of their argument during the first cycle, other concerns exist as well. Conversely, during the later cycles, when the experienced writers' primary attention is focused upon stylistic concerns, they are still attuned, although in a reduced way, to the form of the argument. Since writers are limited in what they can attend to during each cycle (understandings are temporal), revision strategies help balance competing demands on attention. Thus, writers can concentrate on more than one objective at a time by developing strategies to sort out and organize their different concerns in successive cycles of revision.

It is a sense of writing as discovery—a repeated process of beginning over again, starting out new—that the students failed to have. I have used the notion of dissonance because such dissonance, the incongruities between intention and execution, governs both writing and meaning. Students do not see the incongruities. They need to rely on their own internalized sense of good writing and to see their writing with their "own" eyes. Seeing in revision—seeing beyond hearing—is at the root of the word *revision* and the process itself; current dicta on revising blind our students to what is actually involved in revision. In fact, they blind them to what constitutes good writing altogether. Good writing disturbs: it creates dissonance. Students need to seek the dissonance of discovery, utilizing in their writing, as the experienced writers do, the very difference between writing and speech—the possibility of revision.

NOTES

1. D. Gordon Rohman and Albert O. Wlecke, "Pre-writing: The Construction and Application of Models for Concept Formation in Writing," Cooperative Research Project No. 2174, U.S. Office of Education, Department of Health, Education, and Welfare; James Britton, Anthony Burgess, Nancy Martin, Alex McLeod, Harold Rosen, *The Development of Writing Abilities (11-18)* (London: Macmillan Education, 1975).

2. Britton is following Roman Jakobson, "Linguistics and Poetics," in T. A. Sebeok, *Style in Language* (Cambridge, Mass: MIT Press, 1960).

3. For an extended discussion of this issue see Nancy Sommers, "The Need for Theory in Composition Research," *College Composition and Communication*, 30 (February, 1979), 46-49.

4. *Classical Rhetoric for the Modern Student* (New York: Oxford University Press, 1965), p. 27.

5. Roland Barthes, "Writers, Intellectuals, Teachers," in *Image-Music-Text*, trans. Stephen Heath (New York: Hill and Wang, 1977), pp. 190-191.

6. "Writers, Intellectuals, Teachers," p. 190.

7. Nancy Sommers and Ronald Schleifer, "Means and Ends: Some Assumptions of Student Writers," *Composition and Teaching*, II (in press).

8. *Writing Degree Zero* in *Writing Degree Zero and Elements of Semiology*, trans. Annette Lavers and Colin Smith (New York: Hill and Wang, 1968), p. 20.

9. *Course in General Linguistics*, trans. Wade Baskin (New York, 1966), p. 119.

10. Jonathan Culler, *Saussure* (Penguin Modern Masters Series; London: Penguin Books, 1976), p. 70.

Acknowledgment: The author wishes to express her gratitude to Professor William Smith, University of Pittsburgh, for his vital assistance with the research reported in this article and to Patrick Hays, her husband, for extensive discussions and critical editorial help.

The Writer's Audience
Is Always a Fiction

Walter J. Ong, S.J.

Epistola . . . non erubescit.
    —*Cicero*, Epistolae ad familiares *v. 12.1.*

Ubi nihil erit quae scribas, id ipsum scribes.
    —*Cicero*, Epistolae ad Atticum *iv.8.4.*

I

Although there is a large and growing literature on the differences between oral and written verbalization, many aspects of the differences have not been looked into at all, and many others, although well known, have not been examined in their full implications. Among these latter is the relationship, of the so-called "audience" to writing as such, to the situation that inscribed communication establishes and to the roles that readers as readers are consequently called on to play. Some studies in literary history and criticism at times touch near this subject, but none, it appears, take it up in any detail.

The standard locus in Western intellectual tradition for study of audience responses has been rhetoric. But rhetoric originally concerned oral communication, as is indicated by its name, which comes from the Greek word for public speaking. Over two millennia, rhetoric has been gradually extended to include writing more and more, until today, in highly technological cultures, this is its principal concern. But the extension has come

Reprinted by permission of the Modern Language Association of America from *PMLA* 90.1 (January 1975): 9–21. Copyright © 1975 by the Modern Language Association of America.

gradually and has advanced pari passu with the slow and largely unnoticed emergence of markedly chirographic and typographic styles out of those originating in oral performance, with the result that the differentiation between speech and writing has never become a matter of urgent concern for the rhetoric of any given age: when orality was in the ascendancy, rhetoric was oral-focused; as orality yielded to writing, the focus of rhetoric was slowly shifted, unreflectively for the most part, and without notice.

Histories of the relationship between literature and culture have something to say about the status and behavior of readers, before and after reading given materials, as do mass media studies, readership surveys, liberation programs for minorities or various other classes of persons, books on reading skills, works of literary criticism, and works on linguistics, especially those addressing differences between hearing and reading. But most of these studies, except perhaps literary criticism and linguistic studies, treat only perfunctorily, if at all, the roles imposed on the reader by a written or printed text not imposed by spoken utterance. Formalist or structuralist critics, including French theorists such as Paul Ricoeur as well as Roland Barthes, Jacques Derrida, Michel Foucault, Philippe Sollers, and Tzvetan Todorov, variously advert to the immediacy of the oral as against writing and print and occasionally study differences between speech and writing, as Louis Lavelle did much earlier in *La Parole et l'écriture* (1942). In treating of masks and "shadows" in his *Sociologie du théâtre* (1965), Jean Duvignaud brilliantly discusses the projections of a kind of collective consciousness on the part of theater audiences. But none of these appear to broach directly the question of readers' roles called for by a written text, either synchronically as such roles stand at present or diachronically as they have developed through history. Linguistic theorists such as John R. Searle and John L. Austin treat "illocutionary acts" (denoted by "warn," "command," "state," etc.), but these regard the speaker's or writer's need in certain instances to secure a special hold on those he addresses,[1] not any special role imposed by writing.

Wayne Booth in *The Rhetoric of Fiction* and Walker Gibson, whom Booth quotes, come quite close to the concerns of the present study in their treatment of the "mock reader," as does Henry James, whom Booth also cites, in his discussion of the way an author makes "his reader very much as he makes his character."[2] But this hint of James is not developed—there is no reason why it should be—and neither Booth nor Gibson discusses in any detail the history of the ways in which readers have been called on to relate to texts before them. Neither do Robert Scholes and Robert Kellogg in their invaluable work, *The Nature of Narrative*: they skirt the subject in their chapter on "The Oral Heritage of Written Narrative,"[3] but remain chiefly concerned with the oral performer, the writer, and techniques, rather than with the recipient of the message. Yet a great many of the studies noted here as well as many others, among which might be mentioned Norman N. Holland's *The Dynamics of Literary Response* (1968), suggest the time is ripe for a study of the history of readers and their enforced roles, for they show that we have ample phenomenological and literary sophistication to manage many of the complications involved.

So long as verbal communication is reduced to a simplistic mechanistic model which supposedly moves corpuscular units of something labeled "information" back and forth along tracks between two termini, there is of course no special problem with those who assimilate the written or printed word. For the speaker, the audience is in front of him. For the writer, the audience is simply further away, in time or space or both. A surface inscribed with information can neutralize time by preserving the information and conquer space by moving the information to its recipient over distances that sound cannot traverse. If, however, we put aside this alluring but deceptively neat and mechanistic mock-up and look at verbal communication in its human actuality, noting that words consist not of corpuscular units but of evanescent sound and that, as Maurice Merleau-Ponty has pointed out,[4] words are never fully determined in their abstract signification but have meaning only with relation to man's body and to its interaction with its surroundings, problems with the writer's audience begin to show themselves. Writing calls for difficult, and often quite mysterious, skills. Except for a small corps of highly trained writers, most persons could get into written form few if any of the complicated and nuanced meanings they regularly convey orally. One reason is evident: the spoken word is part of present actuality and has its meaning established by the total situation in which it comes into being. Context for the spoken word is simply present, centered in the person speaking and the one or ones to whom he addresses himself and to whom he is related existentially in terms of the circumambient actuality.[5] But the meaning caught in writing comes provided with no such present circumambient actuality, at least normally. (One might except special cases of written exchanges between persons present to one another physically but with oral channels blocked: two deaf persons, for example, or two persons who use different variants of Chinese and are orally incomprehensible to one another but can communicate through the same written characters, which carry virtually the same meanings though they are sounded differently in the different varieties of Chinese.)

Such special cases apart, the person to whom the writer addresses himself normally is not present at all. Moreover, with certain special exceptions such as those just suggested, he must not be present. I am writing a book which will be read by thousands, or, I modestly hope, by tens of thousands. So, please, get out of the room. I want to be alone. Writing normally calls for some kind of withdrawal.

How does the writer give body to the audience for whom he writes? It would be fatuous to think that the writer addressing a so-called general audience tries to imagine his readers individually. A well-known novelist friend of mine only laughed when I asked him if, as he was writing a novel, he imagined his real readers—the woman on the subway deep in his book, the student in his room, the businessman on a vacation, the scholar in his study. There is no need for a novelist to feel his "audience" this way at all. It may be, of course, that at one time or another he imagines himself addressing one or another real person. But not all his readers in their particularities. Practically speaking, of course, and under the insistent urging of editors and publishers, he does have to take into consideration the real social, economic, and psychological state of possible readers. He has to write a book that real persons will buy and read. But I am speaking—or writing—here of the "audience" that fires the writer's imagination. If it consists of the real persons who he hopes will buy his book, they are not these persons in an untransmuted state.[6]

Although I have thus far followed the common practice in using the term "audience," it is really quite misleading to think of a writer as dealing with an "audience," even though certain considerations may at times oblige us to think this way. More properly, a writer addresses readers—only, he does not quite "address" them either: he writes to or for them. The orator has before him an audience which is a true audience, a collectivity. "Audience" is a collective noun. There is no such collective noun for readers, nor, so far as I am able to puzzle out, can there be. "Readers" is a plural. Readers do not form a collectivity, acting here and now on one another and on the speaker as members of an audience do. We can devise a singularized concept for them, it is true, such as "readership." We can say that the *Reader's Digest* has a readership of I don't know how many millions—more than it is comfortable to think about, at any rate. But "readership" is not a collective noun. It is an abstraction in a way that "audience" is not.

The contrast between hearing and reading (running the eye over signals that encode sound) can be caught if we imagine a speaker addressing an audience equipped with texts. At one point, the speaker asks the members of the audience all to read silently a paragraph out of the text. The audience immediately fragments. It is no longer a unit. Each individual retires into his own microcosm. When the readers look up again, the speaker has to gather them into a collectivity once more. This is true even if he is the author of the text they are reading.

58

To sense more fully the writer's problem with his so-called audience let us envision a class of students asked to write on the subject to which school-teachers, jaded by summer, return compulsively every autumn: "How I Spent My Summer Vacation." The teacher makes the easy assumption, inviting and plausible but false, that the chief problem of a boy and a girl in writing is finding a subject actually part of his or her real life. In-close subject matter is supposed to solve the problem of invention. Of course it does not. The problem is not simply what to say but also whom to say it to. Say? The student is not talking. He is writing. No one is listening. There is no feedback. Where does he find his "audience"? He has to make his readers up, fictionalize them.

If the student knew what he was up against better than the teacher giving the assignment seemingly does, he might ask, "Who wants to know?" The answer is not easy. Grandmother? He never tells grandmother. His father or mother? There's a lot he would not want to tell them, that's sure. His classmates? Imagine the reception if he suggested they sit down and listen quietly while he told them how he spent his summer vacation. The teacher? There is no conceivable setting in which he could imagine telling his teacher how he spent his summer vacation other than in writing this paper, so that writing for the teacher does not solve his problems but only restates them. In fact, most young people do not tell anybody how they spent their summer vacation, much less write down how they spent it. The subject may be in-close; the use it is to be put to remains unfamiliar, strained, bizarre.

How does the student solve the problem? In many cases, in a way somewhat like the following. He has read, let us say, *The Adventures of Tom Sawyer*. He knows what this book felt like, how the voice in it addressed its readers, how the narrator hinted to his readers that they were related to him and he to them, whoever they may actually have been or may be. Why not pick up that voice and, with it, its audience? Why not make like Samuel Clemens and write for whomever Samuel Clemens was writing for? This even makes it possible to write for his teacher—itself likely to be a productive ploy—whom he certainly has never been quite able to figure out. But he knows his teacher has read *Tom Sawyer*, has heard the voice in the book, and could therefore obviously make like a *Tom Sawyer* reader. His problem is solved, and he goes ahead. The subject matter now makes little difference, provided that it is something like Mark Twain's and that it interests him on some grounds or other. Material in-close to his real life is not essential, though, of course, it might be welcome now that he has a way to process it.

If the writer succeeds in writing, it is generally because he can fictionalize in his imagination an audience he has learned to know not from daily life but from earlier writers who were fictionalizing in their imagination audiences they had learned to know in still earlier writers, and so on back to the dawn of written narrative. If and when he becomes truly adept, an "original writer," he can do more than project the earlier audience, he can alter it. Thus it was that Samuel Clemens in *Life on the Mississippi* could not merely project the audience that the many journalistic writers about the Midwestern rivers had brought into being, but could also shape it to his own demands. If you had read Isaiah Sellers, you could read Mark Twain, but with a difference. You had to assume a part in a less owlish, more boisterous setting, in which Clemens' caustic humor masks the uncertainty of his seriousness. Mark Twain's reader is asked to take a special kind of hold on himself and on life.

II

These reflections suggest, or are meant to suggest, that there exists a tradition in fictionalizing audiences that is a component part of literary tradition in the sense in which literary tradition is discussed in T. S. Eliot's "Tradition and the Individual Talent." A history of the ways audiences have been called on to fictionalize themselves would be a correlative of the history of literary genres and literary works, and indeed of culture itself.

What do we mean by saying the audience is a fiction? Two things at least. First, that the writer must construct in his imagination, clearly or vaguely, an audience cast in some sort of role—entertainment seekers, reflective sharers of experience (as those who listen to Conrad's Marlow), inhabitants of a lost and remembered world of prepubertal latency (readers of Tolkien's hobbit stories), and so on. Second, we mean that the audience must correspondingly fictionalize itself. A reader has to play the role in which the author has cast him, which seldom coincides with his role in the rest of actual life. An office worker on a bus reading a novel of Thomas Hardy is listening to a voice which is not that of any real person in the real setting around him. He is playing the role demanded of him by this person speaking in a quite special way from the book, which is not the subway and is not quite "Wessex" either, though it speaks of Wessex. Readers over the ages have had to learn this game of literacy, how to conform themselves to the projections of the writers they read, or at least how to operate in terms of these projections. They have to know how to play the game of being a member of an audience that "really" does not exist. And they have to adjust when the rules change, even though no rules thus far have ever been published and even though the changes in the unpublished rules are themselves for the most part only implied.

A history of literature could be written in terms of the ways in which audiences have successively been fictionalized from the time when writing broke away from oral performance, for, just as each genre grows out of what went before it, so each new role that readers are made to assume is related to previous roles. Putting aside for the moment the question of what fictionalizing may be called for in the case of the audience for oral performance, we can note that when script first came on the scene, the fictionalizing of readers was relatively simple. Written narrative at first was merely a transcription of oral narrative, or what was imagined as oral narrative, and it assumed some kind of oral singer's audience, even when being read. The transcribers of the *Iliad* and the *Odyssey* presumably imagined an audience of real listeners in attendance on an oral singer, and readers of those works to this day do well if they can imagine themselves hearing a singer of tales.[7] How these texts and other oral performances were in fact originally set down in writing remains puzzling, but the transcribers certainly were not composing in writing, but rather recording with minimal alteration what a singer was singing or was imagined to be singing.

Even so, a scribe had to fictionalize in a way a singer did not, for a real audience was not really present before the scribe, so it would seem, although it is just possible that at times one may have been (Lord, pp. 125-28). But, as transcription of oral performance or imagined oral performance gave way gradually to composition in writing, the situation changed. No reader today imagines *Second Skin* as a work that John Hawkes is reciting extempore to a group of auditors, even though passages from it may be impressive when read aloud.

III

We have noted that the roles readers are called on to play evolve without any explicit rules or directives. How readers pick up the implicit signals and how writers change the rules can be illustrated by examining a passage from a specialist in unpublished directives for readers, Ernest Hemingway. The passage is the opening of *A Farewell to Arms*. At the start of my comment on the passage, it will be clear that I am borrowing a good deal from Walker Gibson's highly discerning book on modern American prose styles, *Tough, Sweet, and Stuffy*.[8] The Hemingway passage follows:

> In the late summer of that year we lived in a house in a village that looked across the river and the plain to the mountains. In the bed of the river there were pebbles and boulders, dry and white in the sun, and the water was clear and swiftly moving and blue in the channels.

Hemingway's style is often characterized as straightforward, unadorned, terse, lacking in qualifiers, close-lipped; and it is all these things. But none of them were peculiar to Hemingway when his writing began to command attention. A feature more distinctive of Hemingway here and elsewhere is the way he fictionalizes the reader, and this fictionalizing is often signaled largely by his use of the definite article as a special kind of qualifier or of the demonstrative pronoun "that," of which the definite article is simply an attenuation.

"The late summer of that year," the reader begins. What year? The reader gathers that there is no need to say. "Across the river." What river? The reader apparently is supposed to know. "And the plain." What plain? *The* plain"—remember? "To the mountains." What mountains? Do I have to tell you? Of course not. *The* mountains—*those* mountains we know. We have somehow been there together. Who? You, my reader, and I. The reader—every reader—is being cast in the role of a close companion of the writer. This is the game he must play here with Hemingway, not always exclusively or totally, but generally, to a greater or lesser extent. It is one reason why the writer is tight-lipped. Description as such would bore a boon companion. What description there is comes in the guise of pointing, in verbal gestures, recalling humdrum, familiar details. "In the bed of the river there were pebbles and boulders, dry and white in the sun." The known world, accepted and accepting. Not presentation, but recall. The writer needs only to point, for what he wants to tell you about is not the scene at all but his feelings. These, too, he treats as something you really had somehow shared, though you might not have been quite aware of it at the time. He can tell you what was going on inside him and count on sympathy, for you were there. You *know*. The reader here has a well-marked role assigned him. He is a companion-in-arms, somewhat later become a confidant. It is a flattering role. Hemingway readers are encouraged to cultivate high self-esteem.

The effect of the definite article in Hemingway here is quite standard and readily explicable. Normally, in English, we are likely to make an initial reference to an individual object by means of the indefinite article and to bring in the definite only subsequently. "Yesterday on the street *a* man came up to me, and when I stopped in my stride *the* man said. . . ." "A" is a modified form of the term "one," a kind of singular of "some." "A man" means "one man" (of many real or possible men). The indefinite article tacitly acknowledges the existence or possibility of a number of individuals beyond the immediate range of reference and indicates that from among them one is selected. Once we have indicated that we are concerned not with all but with one-out-of-many, we train the definite article or pointer article on the object of our attention.[9] The definite article thus commonly signals some previous, less definite acquaintanceship. Hemingway's exclusion of indefinite in favor of definite articles signals the reader that he is from the first on familiar ground. He shares the author's familiarity with the subject matter. The reader must pretend he has known much of it before.

Hemingway's concomitant use of the demonstrative distancing pronoun "that" parallels his use of "the." For "the" is only an attenuated "that." It is a modified form of the demonstrative pronoun that replaced the original Old English definite article "seo." Both hold their referents at a distance, "that" typically at a somewhat greater distance than "the." *That* mountain you see ten miles away is indicated there on *the* map on *the* wall. If we wish to think of the map as close, we would say, "*This* map on this wall." In distancing their objects, both "that" and "the" can tend to bring together the speaker and the one spoken to. "That" commonly means that-over-there at a distance from you-and-me here, and "the" commonly means much the same. These terms thus can easily implement the Hemingway relationship: you-and-me.

This you-and-me effect of the distancing demonstrative pronoun and the definite article can be seen perhaps more spectacularly in romance etymology. The words for "the" in the romance languages come from the Latin word *ille, illa, illud*, which yields in various romance tongues *il, le, la, el, lo*, and their cognates. *Ille* is a distancing demonstrative in Latin: it means "that-over-there-away-from-you-and-me" and stands in contrastive opposition to another Latin demonstrative which has no counterpart in English, *iste, ista, istud*, which means "that-over-there-by-you" (and thus can readily become pejorative—"that-little-no-account-thing-of-yours"). *Ille* brings together the speaker and the one spoken to by contrast with the distanced object; *iste* distances from the speaker the one spoken to as well as the object. *Ille* yields the romance definite articles, which correspond quite closely in function to the English "the," and thus advertises the close tie between "the" and "that."

Could readers of an earlier age have managed the Hemingway relationship, the you-and-me relationship, marked by tight-lipped empathy based on shared experience? Certainly from antiquity the reader or hearer of an epic was plunged in medias res. But this does not mean he was cast as the author's boon companion. It means rather that he was plunged into the middle of a narrative sequence and told about antecedent events only later. A feeling of camaraderie between companions-in-arms is conveyed in epics, but the companions-in-arms are fictional characters; they are not the reader or hearer and the narrator. *"Forsan et haec olim meminisse iuvabit"*—these words in the *Aeneid*, "perhaps some day it will help to recall these very things," are spoken by Aeneas to his companions when they are undergoing a period of hardships. They are one character's words to other characters, not Virgil's words to his hearer or reader. One might urge further that, like Hemingway's reader, the reader or hearer of an epic—most typically, of an oral folk epic—was hearing stories with which he was already acquainted, that he was thus on familiar ground. He was, but not in the sense that he was forced to pretend he had somehow lived as an alter ego of the narrator. His familiarity with the material was not a pretense at all, not a role, but a simple fact. Typically, the epic audience had heard the story, or something very much like it, before.

The role in which Hemingway casts the reader is somewhat different not only from anything these situations in early literature demand but also from anything in the time immediately before Hemingway. This is what makes Hemingway's writing interesting to literary historians. But Hemingway's demands on the reader are by no means entirely without antecedents. The existence of antecedents is indicated by the fact that Hemingway was assimilated by relatively unskilled readers with very little fuss. He does not recast the reader in a disturbingly novel role. By contrast, the role in which Faulkner casts the reader is a far greater departure from preceding roles than is Hemingway's. Faulkner demands more skilled and daring readers, and consequently had far fewer at first, and has relatively fewer even today when the Faulkner role for readers is actually taught in school. (Perhaps we should say the Faulkner roles.)

No one, so far as I know, has worked up a history of the readers' roles that prepared for that prescribed by Hemingway. But one can discern significantly similar demands on readers beginning as early as Addison and Steele, who assume a new fashionable intimacy among readers themselves and between all readers and the writer, achieved largely by casting readers as well as writer in the role of coffeehouse habitués. Defoe develops in his own way comparable author-reader intimacy. The roots of these eighteenth-century intimacies are journalistic, and from earlier journalism they push out later in Hemingway's own day into the world of sportswriters and war correspondents, of whom Hemingway himself was one. With the help of print and the near instantaneousness implemented by electronic media (the telegraph first, later radio teletype and electronic transmission of photography), the newspaper writer could bring his reader into his own on-the-spot experience, availing himself in both sports and war of the male's strong sense of camaraderie based on shared hardships. Virgil's *forsan et haec olim meminisse iuvabit* once more. But Virgil was telling a story of the days of old and, as has been seen, the camaraderie was among characters in the story, Aeneas and his men. Sports and war journalism are about the here and now, and, if the story can be got to the reader quickly, the camaraderie can be easily projected between the narrator and the reader. The reader is close enough temporally and photographically to the event for him to feel like a vicarious participant. In journalism Hemingway had an established foundation on which to build, if not one highly esteemed in snobbish literary circles. And he in turn has been built upon by those who have come later. Gibson has shown how much the style of *Time* magazine is an adaptation of Hemingway (pp. 48-54). To Hemingway's writer-reader camaraderie *Time* adds omniscience, solemnly "reporting," for example, in eyewitness style, the behavior and feelings of a chief of state in his own bedroom as he answers an emergency night telephone call and afterward returns to sleep. Hemingway encouraged his readers in high self-esteem. *Time* provides its readers, on a regular weekly basis, companionship with the all-knowing gods.

When we look the other way down the corridors of time to the period before the coffeehouses and the beginnings of intimate journalism, we find that readers have had to be trained gradually to play the game Hemingway engages them in. What if, *per impossibile*, a Hemingway story projecting the reader's role we have attended to here had turned up in Elizabethan England? It would probably have been laughed out of court by readers totally unable to adapt to its demands upon them. It would certainly have collided with representative literary theory, as propounded for example by Sir Philip Sidney in *The Defense of Poesie*. For Sidney and most of his age, poetry— that is to say, literature generally—had as its aim to please, but even more basically to teach, at least in the sense that it gave the reader to know what he did not know before. The Hemingway convention that the reader had somehow been through it all before with the writer would have been to Sidney's age at best confusing and at worst wrongheaded. One could argue that the Hemingway narrator would be telling the reader at least something he did not know before—that is, largely, the feelings of the narrator. But even this revelation, as we have seen, implies in Hemingway a covert awareness on the part of the reader, a deep sympathy or empathy of a basically romantic, nonpublic sort, grounded in intimacy. Sidney would have sent Hemingway back to his writing table to find something newer to write about, or to find a way of casting his material in a fresher-sounding form.

Another, and related, feature of the Hemingway style would have repelled sixteenth-century readers: the addiction to the "the" and "that" to the calculated exclusion of most descriptive qualifiers. There is a deep irony here. For in the rhetorical world that persisted from prehistoric times to the age of romanticism, descriptive qualifiers were commonly epithetic, expected qualifiers. The first chapter of Sidney's *Arcadia* (1590) presents the reader with "the hopeless shepheard," the "friendly rival," "the necessary food," "natural rest," "flowery fields," "the extreme heat of summer," and countless other souvenirs of a country every rhetorician had trod many times before. Is this not making the reader a recaller of shared experience much as Hemingway's use of "the" and "that" does? Not at all in the same way. The sixteenth-century reader recalls the familiar accouterments of literature, which are the familiar accouterments or commonplaces also of sculpture, painting, and all art. These are matters of shared public acquaintanceship, not of private experience. The sixteenth-century reader is walking through land all educated men know. He is not made to pretend he knows these familiar objects because he once shared their presence with this particular author, as a Hemingway reader is made to pretend. In Sidney, there is none of the you-and-I-know-even-if-others-don't ploy.

IV

To say that earlier readers would have been nonplussed at Hemingway's demands on them is not to say that earlier readers did not have special roles to play or that authors did not have their own problems in devising and signaling what the roles were. A few cases might be instanced here.

First of all, it is only honest to admit that even an oral narrator calls on his audience to fictionalize itself to some extent. The invocation to the Muse is a signal to the audience to put on the epic-listener's cap. No Greek, after all, ever talked the kind of language that Homer sang, although Homer's contemporaries could understand it well enough. Even today we do not talk in other contexts quite the kind of language in which we tell fairy stories to children. "Once upon a time," we begin. The phrase lifts you out of the real world. Homer's language is "once upon a time" language. It establishes a fictional world. But the fictionalizing in oral epic is directly limited by live interaction, as real conversation is. A real audience controls the narrator's behavior immediately. Students of mine from Ghana and from western Ireland have reported to me what I have read and heard from many other sources: a given story may take a skilled or "professional" storyteller anywhere from ten minutes to an hour and a half, depending on how he finds the audience relates to him on a given occasion. "You always knew ahead of time what he was going to say, but you never knew how long it would take him to say it," my Irish informant reported. The teller reacts directly to audience response. Oral storytelling is a two-way street.

Written or printed narrative is not two-way, at least in the short run. Readers' reactions are remote and initially conjectural, however great their ultimate effects on sales. We should think more about the problems that the need to fictionalize audiences creates for writers. Chaucer, for example, had a problem with the conjectural readers of the *Canterbury Tales*. There was no established tradition in English for many of the stories, and certainly none at all for a collection of such stories. What does Chaucer do? He sets the stories in what, from a literary-structural point of view, is styled a frame. A group of pilgrims going to Canterbury tell stories to one another: the pilgrimage frames the individual narratives. In terms of signals to his readers, we could put it another way: Chaucer simply tells his readers how they are to fictionalize themselves. He starts by telling them that there is a group of pilgrims doing what real people do, going to a real place, Canterbury. The reader is to imagine himself in their company and join the fun. Of course this means fictionalizing himself as a member of a nonexistent group. But the fictionalizing is facilitated by Chaucer's clear frame-story directives. And to minimize the fiction by maximizing real life, Chaucer installs himself, the narrator, as one of the pilgrims. His reader-role problem is effectively solved. Of course, he got the idea pretty much from antecedent writers faced with similar problems, notably Boccaccio. But he naturalizes the frame in the geography of southeast England.

The frame story was in fact quite common around Europe at this period. Audience readjustment was a major feature of mature medieval culture, a culture more focused on reading than any earlier culture had been. Would it not be helpful to discuss the frame device as a contrivance all but demanded by the literary economy of the time rather than to expatiate on it as a singular stroke of genius? For this it certainly was not, unless we define genius as the ability to make the most of an awkward situation. The frame is really a rather clumsy gambit, although a good narrator can bring it off pretty well when he has to. It hardly has widespread immediate appeal for ordinary readers today.

In the next period of major audience readjustment, John Lyly's *Euphues* and even more Thomas Nashe's *The Unfortunate Traveler* can be viewed as attempts to work out a credible role in which Elizabethan readers could cast themselves for the new medium of print. Script culture had preserved a heavy oral residue signaled by its continued fascination with rhetoric, which had always been orally grounded, a fascination that script culture passed on to early print culture. But the new medium was changing the noetic economy, and, while rhetoric remained strong in the curriculum, strain was developing. Lyly reacts by hyperrhetoricizing his text, tongue-in-cheek, drowning the audience and himself in the highly controlled gush being purveyed by the schools. The signals to the reader are unmistakable, if unconsciously conveyed: play the role of the rhetorician's listener for all you are worth (*Euphues* is mostly speeches), remembering that the response the rhetorician commands is a serious and difficult one—it takes hard work to assimilate the baroque complexity of Lyly's text—but also that there is something awry in all the isocola, apophonemata, and antisagogai, now that the reader is so very much more a reader than a listener. Such aural iconographic equipment had been functional in oral management of knowledge, implementing storage and recall, but with print it was becoming incidental—which is, paradoxically, why it could be so fantastically elaborated.

Nashe shows the same uneasiness, and more, regarding the reader's role. For in the phantasmagoria of styles in *The Unfortunate Traveler* he tries out his reader in every role he can think of: whoever takes on Nashe's story must become a listener bending his ear to political orations, a participant in scholastic disputations, a hanger-on at goliardic Woodstocks, a camp follower fascinated by merry tales, a simpering reader of Italian revenge stories and sixteenth-century true confessions, a fellow conspirator in a world of picaresque cheats, and much more.

Nashe gives a foretaste of other trial-and-error procedures by which recipes were to be developed for the reader of the narrative prose works we now call novels. Such recipes were being worked out in other languages, too: in French notably by Rabelais, whose calls for strenuous shifts in the reader's stance Nashe emulated, and in Spanish by Cervantes, who explores all sorts of ironic possibilities in the reader's relationship to the text, incorporating into the second part of *Don Quixote* the purported reactions of readers and of the tale's characters to the first part of the work. Picaresque travels, well known at least since Apuleius' *Golden Ass*, multiplied, with major audience adjustments, in English down through *Tom Jones:* the unsettled role of the reader was mirrored and made acceptable by keeping the hero himself on the move. Samuel Richardson has his readers pretend they have access to other persons' letters, out of which a story emerges. Journals and diaries also multiplied as narrative devices: the reader becoming a snooper or a collector of seeming trivia that turn out not to be trivia at all. Ultimately, Laurence Sterne is able to involve his reader not only in the procreation of his hero Tristram Shandy but also in the hero's writing of his autobiography, in which pages are left blank for the reader to put his "own fancy in." The audience-speaker interaction of oral narrative here shows the reader in a new ironic guise—somewhat destructive of the printed book, toward which, as an object obtruding in the person-to-person world of human communication, the eighteenth century was feeling some ambiguous hostilities, as Swift's work also shows.

The problem of reader adjustment in prose narrative was in great part due to the difficulty that narrators long had in feeling themselves as other than oral performers. It is significant that, although the drama had been tightly plotted from classical antiquity (the drama is the first genre controlled by writing, and by the same token, paradoxically, the first to make deliberate use of colloquial speech), until the late eighteenth century there is in the whole Western world (and I suspect in the East as well) no sizable prose narrative, so far as I know, with a tidy structure comparable to that known for two millennia in the drama, moving through closely controlled tensions to a climax, with reversal and denouement. This is not to say that until the modern novel emerged narrative was not organized, or that earlier narrators were trying to write modern novels but regularly fell short of their aims. (Scholes and Kellogg have warned in *The Nature of Narrative* against this retroactive analysis of literary history.) But it is to say that narrative had not fully accommodated itself to print or, for that matter, to writing, which drama had long before learned to exploit. *Tom Jones* is highly programed, but in plot it is still episodic, as all prose narrative had been all the way back through the Hellenic romances. With Jane Austen we are over the hurdle: but Jane Austen was a woman, and women were not normally trained in the Latin-based academic, rhetorical, oral tradition. They were not trained speechmakers who had turned belatedly to chirography and print.

Even by Jane Austen's time, however, the problem of the reader's role in prose narrative was by no means entirely solved. Nervousness regarding the role of the reader registers everywhere in the "dear reader" regularly invoked in fiction well through the nineteenth century. The reader had to be reminded (and the narrator, too) that the recipient of the story was indeed a reader—not a listener, not one of the crowd, but an individual isolated with a text. The relationship of audience-fictionalizing to modern narrative prose is very mysterious, and I do not pretend to explain it all here, but only to point to some of the strange problems often so largely overlooked in the relationship. Tightly plotted prose narrative is the correlative of the audiences fictionalized for the first time with the aid of print, and the demands of such narrative on readers were new.

V

The present reflections have focused on written fictional narrative as a kind of paradigm for the fictionalizing of writers' "audiences" or readers. But what has been said about fictional narrative applies ceteris paribus to all writing. With the possible[10] exception noted above of persons in the presence of one another communicating by writing because of inability to communicate orally, the writer's audience is always a fiction. The historian, the scholar or scientist, and the simple letter writer all fictionalize their audiences, casting them in a made-up role and calling on them to play the role assigned.

Because history is always a selection and interpretation of those incidents the individual historian believes will account better than other incidents for some explanation of a totality, history partakes quite evidently of the nature of poetry. It is a making. The historian does not make the elements out of which he constructs history, in the sense that he must build with events that have come about independently of him, but his selection of events and his way of verbalizing them so that they can be dealt with as "facts," and consequently the overall pattern he reports, are all his own creation, a making. No two historians say exactly the same thing about the same given events, even though they are both telling the truth. There is no *one* thing to say about anything; there are many things that can be said.

The oral "historian" captures events in terms of themes (the challenge, the duel, the arming of the hero, the battle, and so on), and formulas (the brave soldier, the faithful wife, the courageous people, the suffering people), which are provided to him by tradition and are the only ways he knows to talk about what is going on among men. Processed through these conventions, events become assimilable by his auditors and "interesting" to them. The writer of history is less reliant on formulas (or it may be he has such a variety of them that it is hard to tell that is what they are). But he comes to his material laden with themes in much vaster quantity than can be available to any oral culture. Without themes, there would be no way to deal with events. It is impossible to tell everything that went on in the Pentagon even in one day: how many stenographers dropped how many sheets of paper into how many wastebaskets when and where, what they all said to each other, and so on ad infinitum. These are not the themes historians normally use to write what really "happened." They write about material by exploiting it in terms of themes that are "significant" or "interesting." But what is "significant" depends on what kind of history you are writing—national political history, military history, social history, economic history, personal biography, global history. What is significant and, perhaps even more, what is "interesting" also depends on the readers and their interaction with the historian. This interaction in turn depends on the role in which the historian casts his readers. Although so far as I know we have no history of readers of history, we do know enough about historiography to be aware that one could well be worked out. The open-faced way the reader figures in Samuel Eliot Morison's writings is different from the more conspiratorial way he figures in Perry Miller's and both are quite different from the way the reader figures in Herodotus.

Scholarly works show comparable evolution in the roles they enforce on their readers. Aristotle's works, as has often been pointed out, are an agglomerate of texts whose relationship to his own holographs, to his students' notes, and to the work of later editors will remain always more or less a puzzle. Much of Aristotle consists of school logia or sayings, comparable to the logia or sayings of Jesus to his followers of which the Gospels chiefly consist. Aristotle's logia were addressed to specific individuals whom he knew, rather than simply to the wide world. Even his more patently written compositions retain a personal orientation: his work on ethics is the *Nicomachean Ethics*, named for his son. This means that the reader of Aristotle, if he wants to understand his text, will do well to cast himself in the role of one of Aristotle's actual listeners.

The practice of orienting a work, and thereby its readers, by writing it at least purportedly for a specific person or persons continues well through the Renaissance. The first edition of Peter Ramus' *Dialectic* was the French *Dialectique de Pierre de la Ramée à Charles de Lorraine Cardinal, son Mécène* (Paris, 1555), and the first edition of the far more widely used Latin version preserved the same personal address: *Dialectici Libri Duo . . . ad Carolum Lotharingum Cardinalem* (Paris, 1556). Sidney's famous romance or epic is *The Countess of Pembroke's Arcadia*. Often in Renaissance printed editions a galaxy of prefaces and dedicatory epistles and poems establishes a whole cosmos of discourse which, among other things, signals the reader what roles he is to assume. Sidney's, Spenser's, and Milton's works, for example, are heavily laden with introductory material—whole books have been devoted to the study of Sidney's introductory matter alone.

Until recent times the rhetorical tradition, which, with the allied dialectical or logical tradition, dominated most written as well as oral expression, helped in the fictionalizing of the audience of learned works in a generic but quite real way. Rhetoric fixed knowledge in agonistic structures.

For this reason, the roles of the reader of learned works until fairly recent times were regularly more polemic than those demanded of the reader today. Until the age of romanticism reconstituted psychological structures, academic teaching of all subjects had been more or less polemic, dominated by the ubiquitous rhetorical culture, and proceeding typically by proposing and attacking theses in highly partisan fashion. (The academic world today preserves much of the nomenclature, such as "thesis" and "defense" of theses, but less of the programed fighting spirit, which its members let loose on the social order more than on their subject matter or colleagues.) From Augustine through St. Thomas Aquinas and Christian Wolff, writers of treatises generally proceeded in adversary fashion, their readers being cast as participants in rhetorical contests or in dialectical scholastic disputations.

Today the academic reader's role is harder to describe. Some of its complexities can be hinted at by attending to certain fictions which writers of learned articles and books generally observe and which have to do with reader status. There are some things the writer must assume that every reader knows because virtually every reader does. It would be intolerable to write, "Shakespeare, a well-known Elizabethan playwright," not only in a study on Renaissance drama but even in one on marine ecology. Otherwise the reader's role would be confused. There are other things that established fiction holds all readers must know, even though everyone is sure all readers do not know them: these are handled by writing, "as everyone knows," and then inserting what it is that not quite everyone really does know. Other things the reader can safely be assumed not to know without threatening the role he is playing. These gradations of admissible ignorance vary from one level of scholarly writing to another, and since individual readers vary in knowledge and competence, the degree to which they must fictionalize themselves to match the level of this or that reading will vary. Knowledge of the degrees of admissible ignorance for readers is absolutely essential if one is to publish successfully. This knowledge is one of the things that separates the beginning graduate student or even the brilliant undergraduate from the mature scholar. It takes time to get a feel for the roles that readers can be expected comfortably to play in the modern academic world.

Other kinds of writing without end could be examined in our reflections here on the fictionalizing of readers' roles. For want of time and, frankly, for want of wider reflection, I shall mention only two others. These are genres that do not seem to fall under the rule that the writer's audience is always a fiction since the "audience" appears to be simply one clearly determined person, who hardly need fictionalize himself. The first of the genres is the familiar letter and the second the diary.

The case of the letter reader is really simple enough. Although by writing a letter you are somehow pretending the reader is present while you are writing, you cannot address him as you do in oral speech. You must fictionalize him, make him into a special construct. Whoever saluted a friend on the street with "Dear John"? And if you try the informal horrors, "Hi!" or "Greetings!" or whatever else, the effect is not less but more artificial. You are reminding him that you wish you were not writing him a letter, but, then, why are you? There is no way out. The writer has to set up another relationship to the reader and has to set the reader in a relationship to the writer different from that of nonchirographical personal contact.

The dimensions of fiction in a letter are many. First, you have no way of adjusting to the friend's real mood as you would be able to adjust in oral conversation. You have to conjecture or confect a mood that he is likely to be in or can assume when the letter comes. And, when it does come, he has to put on the mood that you have fictionalized for him. Some of this sort of adjustment goes on in oral communication, too, but it develops in a series of exchanges: a tentative guess at another's mood, a reaction from him, another from yourself, another from him, and you know about where you are. Letters do not have this normal give-and-take: they are one-way movements. Moreover, the precise relationships of writer to reader in letters vary tremendously from age to age even in intensively role-playing correspondence. No one today can capture exactly the fiction in Swift's *Journal to Stella*, though it is informative to try to reconstruct it as fully as possible, for the relationships of children to oldsters and even of man to woman have subtly altered, as have also a vast mesh of other social relationships which the *Journal to Stella* involves.

The epistolary situation is made tolerable by conventions, and learning to write letters is largely a matter of learning what the writer-reader conventions are. The paradoxes they involve were well caught some years ago in a Marx Brothers movie—if I recall correctly where the incident occurred. Letters start with "Dear Sir." An owlish, bemused businessman calls his secretary in. "Take this letter to Joseph Smithers," he directs. "You know his address. 'Dear Sir: You dirty rat. . . .'" The fiction of the exordium designed to create the *lector benevolens* is first honored and then immediately wiped out.

The audience of the diarist is even more encased in fictions. What is easier, one might argue, than addressing oneself? As those who first begin a diary often find out, a great many things are easier. The reasons why are not hard to unearth. First of all, we do not normally talk to ourselves—certainly not in long, involved sentences and paragraphs. Second, the diarist pretending to be talking to himself has also, since he is writing, to pretend he is somehow not there. And to what self is he talking? To the self he imagines he is? Or would like to be? Or really thinks he is? Or thinks other people think he is? To himself as he is now? Or as he will probably or ideally be twenty years hence? If he addresses not himself but "Dear Diary," who in the world is "Dear Diary"? What role does this imply? And why do more women than men keep diaries? Or if they don't (they really do—or did), why do people think they do? When did the diary start? The history of diaries, I believe, has yet to be written. Possibly more than the history of any other genre, it will have to be a history of the fictionalizing of readers.

The case of the diary, which at first blush would seem to fictionalize the reader least but in many ways probably fictionalizes him or her most, brings into full view the fundamental deep paradox of the activity we call writing, at least when writing moves from its initial account-keeping purposes to other more elaborate concerns more directly and complexly involving human persons in their manifold dealings with one another. We are familiar enough today with talk about masks—in literary criticism, psychology, phenomenology, and elsewhere. Personae, earlier generally thought of as applying to characters in a play or other fiction (dramatis personae), are imputed with full justification to narrators and, since all discourse has roots in narrative, to everyone who uses language. Often in the complexities of present-day fiction, with its "unreliable narrator" encased in layer after layer of persiflage and irony, the masks within masks defy complete identification. This is a game fiction writers play, harder now than ever.

But the masks of the narrator are matched, if not one-for-one, in equally complex fashion by the masks that readers must learn to wear. To whom is *Finnegans Wake* addressed? Who is the reader supposed to be? We hesitate to say—certainly I hesitate to say—because we have thought so little about the reader's role as such, about his masks, which are as manifold in their own way as those of the writer.

Masks are inevitable in all human communication, even oral. Role playing is both different from actuality and an entry into actuality: play and actuality (the world of "work") are dialectically related to one another. From the very beginning, an infant becomes an actual speaker by playing at being a speaker, much as a person who cannot swim, after developing some ancillary skills, one day plays at swimming and finds that he is swimming in truth. But oral communication, which is built into existential actuality more directly than written, has within it a momentum that works for the removal of masks. Lovers try to strip off all masks. And in all communication, insofar as it is related to actual experience, there must be a movement of love. Those who have loved over many years may reach a point where almost all masks are gone. But never all. The lover's plight is tied to the fact that every one of us puts on a mask to address himself, too. Such masks to relate ourselves to ourselves we also try to put aside, and with wisdom and grace we to some extent succeed in casting them off. When the last mask comes off, sainthood is achieved, and the vision of God. But this can only be with death.

No matter what pitch of frankness, directness, or authenticity he may strive for, the writer's mask and the reader's are less removable than those of the oral communicator and his hearer. For writing is itself an indirection. Direct communication by script is impossible. This makes writing not less but more interesting, although perhaps less noble than speech. For man lives largely by indirection, and only beneath the indirections that sustain him is his true nature to be found. Writing, alone, however, will never bring us truly beneath to the actuality. Present-day confessional writing—and it is characteristic of our present age that virtually all serious writing tends to the confessional, even drama—likes to make an issue of stripping off all masks. Observant literary critics and psychiatrists, however, do not need to be told that confessional literature is likely to wear the most masks of all. It is hard to bare your soul in any literary genre. And it is hard to write outside a genre. T. S. Eliot has made the point that so far as he knows, great love poetry is never written solely for the ear of the beloved (p. 97), although what a lover speaks with his lips is often indeed for the ear of the beloved and of no other. The point is well made, even though it was made in writing.

NOTES

1. See, e.g., J. R. Searle, *The Philosophy of Language* (London: Oxford Univ. Press, 1971), pp. 24–28, where Austin is cited, and Searle's bibliography, pp. 146–48.

2. *The Rhetoric of Fiction* (Chicago: Univ. of Chicago Press, 1961), pp. 49–52, 138, 363–64.

3. *The Nature of Narrative* (New York: Oxford Univ. Press, 1966), pp. 17–56. Among recent short studies exhibiting concerns tangent to but not the same as those of the present article might be mentioned three from *New Literary History*: Georges Poulet, "Phenomenology of Reading," 1 (1969–70), 53–68; Geoffrey H. Hartman, "History-Writing as Answerable Style," 2 (1970–71), 73–84; and J. Hillis Miller, "The Still Heart: Poetic Form in Wordsworth," 2 (1970–71), 297–310, esp. p. 310; as well as Gerald Prince, "Introduction à l'étude du narrataire," *Poétique*, No. 14 (1973), pp. 178–96, which is concerned with the "narrataire" only in novels ("narratee" in a related English-language study by the same author as noted by him here) and with literary taxonomy more than history. See also Paul Ricoeur, "What Is a Text? Explanation and Interpretation," Appendix, pp. 135–50, in David Rasmussen, *Mythic-Symbolic Language and Philosophical Anthropology: A Constructive Interpretation of the Thought of Paul Ricoeur* (The Hague: Martinus Nijhoff, 1971).

4. *Phenomenology of Perception*, trans. Colin Smith (London: Routledge, 1962), pp. 181–84.

5. See my *The Presence of the Word* (New Haven and London: Yale Univ. Press, 1967), pp. 116–17.

6. T. S. Eliot suggests some of the complexities of the writer-and-audience problem in his essay on "The Three Voices of Poetry," by which he means (1) "the voice of the poet talking to himself—or to nobody," (2) "the voice of the poet addressing an audience," and (3) "the voice of the poet when he attempts to create a dramatic character speaking" (*On Poetry and Poets*, New York: Noonday Press, 1961, p. 96). Eliot, in the same work, states that these voices often mingle and indeed, for him, "are most often found together" (p. 108). The approach I am here taking cuts across Eliot's way of enunciating the problem and, I believe, brings out some of the built-in relationships among the three voices which help account for their intermingling. The "audience" addressed by Eliot's second voice not only is elusively constituted but also, even in its elusiveness, can determine the voice of the poet talking to himself or to nobody (Eliot's first sense of "voice"), because in talking to oneself one has to objectify oneself, and one does so in ways learned from addressing others. A practiced writer talking "to himself" in a poem has a quite different feeling for "himself" than does a complete illiterate.

7. See Albert B. Lord, *The Singer of Tales*, Harvard Studies in Comparative Literature, No. 24 (Cambridge, Mass.: Harvard Univ. Press, 1964), pp. 124–38.

8. *Tough, Sweet, and Stuffy* (Bloomington and London: Indiana Univ. Press, 1966), pp. 28–54. In these pages, Gibson gets very close to the concern of the present article with readers' roles.

9. The present inclination to begin a story without the initial indefinite article, which tacitly acknowledges a range of existence beyond that of the immediate reference, and to substitute for the indefinite article a demonstrative pronoun of proximity, "this," is one of many indications of the tendency of present-day man to feel his lifeworld—which is now more than ever the whole world—as in-close to him, and to mute any references to distance. It is not uncommon to hear a conversation begin, "Yesterday on the street this man came up to me, and. . . ." A few decades ago, the equivalent would very likely have been, "Yesterday on the street a man came up to me, and. . . ." This widespread preference, which Hemingway probably influenced little if at all, does show that Hemingway's imposition of fellowship on the reader was an indication, perhaps moderately precocious, of a sweeping trend.

10. "Possible," because there is probably a trace of fictionalizing even when notes are being exchanged by persons in one another's presence. It appears unlikely that what is written in such script "conversations" is exactly the same as what it would be were voices used. The interlocutors are, after all, to some extent pretending to be talking, when in fact they are not talking but writing.

Audience Addressed/ Audience Invoked

The Role of Audience in Composition Theory and Pedagogy

Lisa Ede and Andrea Lunsford

One important controversy currently engaging scholars and teachers of writing involves the role of audience in composition theory and pedagogy. How can we best define the audience of a written discourse? What does it mean to address an audience? To what degree should teachers stress audience in their assignments and discussions? What *is* the best way to help students recognize the significance of this critical element in any rhetorical situation?

Teachers of writing may find recent efforts to answer these questions more confusing than illuminating. Should they agree with Ruth Mitchell and Mary Taylor, who so emphasize the significance of the audience that they argue for abandoning conventional composition courses and instituting a "cooperative effort by writing and subject instructors in adjunct courses. The cooperation and courses take two main forms. Either writing instructors can be attached to subject courses where writing is required, an organization which disperses the instructors throughout the departments participating; or the composition courses can teach students how to write the papers assigned in other concurrent courses, thus centralizing instruction but diversifying topics."[1] Or should teachers side with Russell Long, who asserts that those advocating greater attention to audience overemphasize the role of "observable physical or occupational characteristics" while

Reprinted from *College Composition and Communication* 35.2 (May 1984): 155–71. Used with permission.

ignoring the fact that most writers actually create their audiences. Long argues against the usefulness of such methods as developing hypothetical rhetorical situations as writing assignments, urging instead a more traditional emphasis on "the analysis of texts in the classroom with a very detailed examination given to the signals provided by the writer for his audience."[2]

To many teachers, the choice seems limited to a single option—to be for or against an emphasis on audience in composition courses. In the following essay, we wish to expand our understanding of the role audience plays in composition theory and pedagogy by demonstrating that the arguments advocated by each side of the current debate oversimplify the act of making meaning through written discourse. Each side, we will argue, has failed adequately to recognize (1) the fluid, dynamic character of rhetorical situations; and (2) the integrated, interdependent nature of reading and writing. After discussing the strengths and weaknesses of the two central perspectives on audience in composition—which we group under the rubrics of *audience addressed* and *audience invoked*[3]—we will propose an alternative formulation, one which we believe more accurately reflects the richness of "audience" as a concept.[*]

AUDIENCE ADDRESSED

Those who envision audience as addressed emphasize the concrete reality of the writer's audience; they also share the assumption that knowledge of this audience's attitudes, beliefs, and expectations is not only possible (via observation and analysis) but essential. Questions concerning the degree to which this audience is "real" or imagined, and the ways it differs from the speaker's audience, are generally either ignored or subordinated to a sense of the audience's powerfulness. In their discussion of "A Heuristic Model for Creating a Writer's Audience," for example, Fred Pfister and Joanne Petrik attempt to recognize the ontological complexity of the writer-audience relationship by noting that "students, like all writers, must fictionalize their audience."[4] Even so, by encouraging students to "construct in their imagina-

---

[*]A number of terms might be used to characterize the two approaches to audience which dominate current theory and practice. Such pairs as identified/envisaged, "real"/fictional, or analyzed/created all point to the same general distinction as do our terms. We chose "addressed/invoked" because these terms most precisely represent our intended meaning. Our discussion will, we hope, clarify their significance; for the present, the following definitions must serve. The "addressed" audience refers to those actual or real-life people who read a discourse, while the "invoked" audience refers to the audience called up or imagined by the writer.

tion an audience that is as nearly a replica as is possible of *those many readers who actually exist in the world of reality,*" Pfister and Petrik implicitly privilege the concept of audience as addressed.[5]

Many of those who envision audience as addressed have been influenced by the strong tradition of audience analysis in speech communication and by current research in cognitive psychology on the composing process.[6] They often see themselves as reacting against the current-traditional paradigm of composition, with its a-rhetorical, product-oriented emphasis.[7] And they also frequently encourage what is called "real-world" writing.[8]

Our purpose here is not to draw up a list of those who share this view of audience but to suggest the general outline of what most readers will recognize as a central tendency in the teaching of writing today. We would, however, like to focus on one particularly ambitious attempt to formulate a theory and pedagogy for composition based on the concept of audience as addressed: Ruth Mitchell and Mary Taylor's "The Integrating Perspective: An Audience-Response Model for Writing." We choose Mitchell and Taylor's work because of its theoretical richness and practical specificity. Despite these strengths, we wish to note several potentially significant limitations in their approach, limitations which obtain to varying degrees in much of the current work of those who envision audience as addressed.

In their article, Mitchell and Taylor analyze what they consider to be the two major existing composition models: one focusing on the writer and the other on the written product. Their evaluation of these two models seems essentially accurate. The "writer" model is limited because it defines writing as either self-expression or "fidelity to fact" (p. 255) — epistemologically naive assumptions which result in troubling pedagogical inconsistencies. And the "written product" model, which is characterized by an emphasis on "certain intrinsic features [such as a] lack of comma splices and fragments" (p. 258), is challenged by the continued inability of teachers of writing (not to mention those in other professions) to agree upon the precise intrinsic features which characterize "good" writing.

Most interesting, however, is what Mitchell and Taylor *omit* in their criticism of these models. Neither the writer model nor the written product model pays serious attention to invention, the term used to describe those methods designed to aid in retrieving information, forming concepts, analyzing complex events, and solving certain kinds of problems."[9] Mitchell and Taylor's lapse in not noting this omission is understandable, however, for the same can be said of their own model. When these authors discuss the writing process, they stress that "our first priority for writing instruction at every level ought to be certain major tactics for structuring material because these structures are the most important in guiding the reader's comprehension and memory" (p. 271). They do not concern themselves with where "the material" comes from—its sophistication, complexity, accuracy, or rigor.

Mitchell and Taylor also fail to note another omission, one which might be best described in reference to their own model (Figure 1). This model has four components. Mitchell and Taylor use two of these, "writer" and "written product," as labels for the models they condemn. The third and fourth components, "audience" and "response," provide the title for their own "audience-response model for writing" (p. 249).

Mitchell and Taylor stress that the components in their model interact. Yet, despite their emphasis on interaction, it never seems to occur to them to note that the two other models may fail in large part because they overemphasize and isolate one of the four elements—wrenching it too greatly from its context and thus inevitably distorting the composing process. Mitchell and Taylor do not consider this possibility, we suggest, because their own model has the same weakness.

Mitchell and Taylor argue that a major limitation of the "writer" model is its emphasis on the self, the person writing, as the only potential judge of effective discourse. Ironically, however, their own emphasis on audience leads to a similar distortion. In their model, the audience has the sole power of evaluating writing, the success of which "will be judged by the audience's reaction: 'good' translates into 'effective,' 'bad' into 'ineffective.'" Mitchell and Taylor go on to note that "the audience not only judges writing; it also motivates it" (p. 250),[10] thus suggesting that the writer has less control than the audience over both evaluation and motivation.

Despite the fact that Mitchell and Taylor describe writing as "an interaction, a dynamic relationship" (p. 250), their model puts far more emphasis on the role of the audience than on that of the writer. One way to pinpoint

Figure 1   Mitchell and Taylor's "general model of writing" (p. 250).

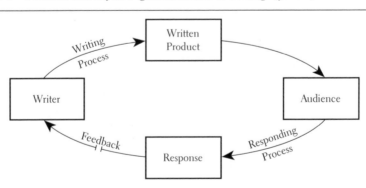

the source of imbalance in Mitchell and Taylor's formulation is to note that they are right in emphasizing the creative role of readers who, they observe, "actively contribute to the meaning of what they read and will respond according to a complex set of expectations, preconceptions, and provocations" (p. 251), but wrong in failing to recognize the equally essential role writers play throughout the composing process not only as creators but also as *readers* of their own writing.

As Susan Wall observes in "In the Writer's Eye: Learning to Teach the Rereading/Revising Process," when writers read their own writing, as they do continuously while they compose, "there are really not one but two contexts for rereading: there is the writer-as-reader's sense of what the established text is actually saying, as of this reading; and there is the reader-as-writer's judgment of what the text might say or should say. . . ."[11] What is missing from Mitchell and Taylor's model, and from much work done from the perspective of audience as addressed, is a recognition of the crucial importance of this internal dialogue, through which writers analyze inventional problems and conceptualize patterns of discourse. Also missing is an adequate awareness that, no matter how much feedback writers may receive after they have written something (or in breaks while they write), as they compose writers must rely in large part upon their own vision of the reader, which they create, as readers do their vision of writers, according to their own experiences and expectations.

Another major problem with Mitchell and Taylor's analysis is their apparent lack of concern for the ethics of language use. At one point, the authors ask the following important question: "Have we painted ourselves into a corner, so that the audience-response model must defend sociologese and its related styles?" (p. 265). Note first the ambiguity of their answer, which seems to us to say no and yes at the same time, and the way they try to deflect its impact:

> No. We defend only the right of audiences to set their own standards and we repudiate the ambitions of English departments to monopolize that standard-setting. If bureaucrats and scientists are happy with the way they write, then no one should interfere.
> But evidence is accumulating that they are not happy. (p. 265)

Here Mitchell and Taylor surely underestimate the relationship between style and substance. As those concerned with Doublespeak can attest, for example, the problem with sociologese is not simply its (to our ears) awkward, convoluted, highly nominalized style, but the way writers have in certain instances used this style to make statements otherwise unacceptable to lay persons, to "gloss over" potentially controversial facts about programs and their consequences, and thus violate the ethics of language use. Hence, although we support Mitchell and Taylor when they insist that we must better understand and respect the linguistic traditions of other disciplines and professions, we object to their assumption that style is somehow value free.

As we noted earlier, an analysis of Mitchell and Taylor's discussion clarifies weaknesses inherent in much of the theoretical and pedagogical research based on the concept of audience as addressed. One major weakness of this research lies in its narrow focus on helping students learn how to "continually modify their work with reference to their audience" (p. 251). Such a focus, which in its extreme form becomes pandering to the crowd, tends to undervalue the responsibility a writer has to a subject and to what Wayne Booth in *Modern Dogma and the Rhetoric of Assent* calls "the art of discovering good reasons."[12] The resulting imbalance has clear ethical consequences, for rhetoric has traditionally been concerned not only with the effectiveness of a discourse, but with truthfulness as well. Much of our difficulty with the language of advertising, for example, arises out of the ad writer's powerful concept of audience as addressed divorced from a corollary ethical concept. The toothpaste ad that promises improved personality, for instance, knows too well how to address the audience. But such ads ignore ethical questions completely.

Another weakness in research done by those who envision audience as addressed suggests an oversimplified view of language. As Paul Kameen observes in "Rewording the Rhetoric of Composition," "discourse is not grounded in forms or experience or audience; it engages all of these elements simultaneously."[13] Ann Berthoff has persistently criticized our obsession with one or another of the elements of discourse, insisting that meaning arises out of their synthesis. Writing is more, then, than "a means of acting upon a receiver" (Mitchell and Taylor, p. 250); it is a means of making meaning for writer *and* reader.[14] Without such a unifying, balanced understanding of language use, it is easy to overemphasize one aspect of discourse, such as audience. It is also easy to forget, as Anthony Petrosky cautions us, that "reading, responding, and composing are aspects of understanding, and theories that attempt to account for them outside of their interaction with each other run the serious risk of building reductive models of human understanding."[15]

AUDIENCE INVOKED

Those who envision audience as invoked stress that the audience of a written discourse is a construction of the writer, a "created fiction" (Long,

p. 225). They do not, of course, deny the physical reality of readers, but they argue that writers simply cannot know this reality in the way that speakers can. The central task of the writer, then, is not to analyze an audience and adapt discourse to meet its needs. Rather, the writer uses the semantic and syntactic resources of language to provide cues for the reader—cues which help to define the role or roles the writer wishes the reader to adopt in responding to the text. Little scholarship in composition takes this perspective; only Russell Long's article and Walter Ong's "The Writer's Audience Is Always a Fiction" focus centrally on this issue.[16] If recent conferences are any indication, however, a growing number of teachers and scholars are becoming concerned with what they see as the possible distortions and oversimplifications of the approach typified by Mitchell and Taylor's model.[17]

Russell Long's response to current efforts to teach students analysis of audience and adaptation of text to audience is typical: "I have become increasingly disturbed not only about the superficiality of the advice itself, but about the philosophy which seems to lie beneath it" (p. 221). Rather than detailing Long's argument, we wish to turn to Walter Ong's well-known study. Published in *PMLA* in 1975, "The Writer's Audience Is Always a Fiction" has had a significant impact on composition studies, despite the fact that its major emphasis is on fictional narrative rather than expository writing. An analysis of Ong's argument suggests that teachers of writing may err if they uncritically accept Ong's statement that "what has been said about fictional narrative applies ceteris paribus to all writing" (p. 17).

Ong's thesis includes two central assertions: "What do we mean by saying the audience is a fiction? Two things at least. First, that the writer must construct in his imagination, clearly or vaguely, an audience cast in some sort of role. . . . Second, we mean that the audience must correspondingly fictionalize itself" (p. 12). Ong emphasizes the creative power of the adept writer, who can both project and alter audiences, as well as the complexity of the reader's role. Readers, Ong observes, must learn or "know how to play the game of being a member of an audience that 'really' does not exist" (p. 12).

On the most abstract and general level, Ong is accurate. For a writer, the audience is not *there* in the sense that the speaker's audience, whether a single person or a large group, is present. But Ong's representative situations—the orator addressing a mass audience versus a writer alone in a room—oversimplify the potential range and diversity of both oral and written communication situations.

Ong's model of the paradigmatic act of speech communication derives from traditional rhetoric. In distinguishing the terms audience and reader, he notes that "the orator has before him an audience which is a true audience, a collectivity. . . . Readers do not form a collectivity, acting here and now on one another and on the speaker as members of an audience do" (p. 11). As this quotation indicates, Ong also stresses the potential for interaction among members of an audience, and between an audience and a speaker.

But how many audiences are actually collectives, with ample opportunity for interaction? In *Persuasion: Understanding, Practice, and Analysis,* Herbert Simons establishes a continuum of audiences based on opportunities for interaction.[18] Simons contrasts commercial mass media publics, which "have little or no contact with each other and certainly have no reciprocal awareness of each other as members of the same audience" with "face-to-face work groups that meet and interact continuously over an extended period of time." He goes on to note that: "Between these two extremes are such groups as the following: (1) the *pedestrian audience,* persons who happen to pass a soap box orator . . . ; (2) the *passive, occasional audience,* persons who come to hear a noted lecturer in a large auditorium . . . ; (3) the *active, occasional audience,* persons who meet only on specific occasions but actively interact when they do meet" (pp. 97-98).

Simons' discussion, in effect, questions the rigidity of Ong's distinctions between a speaker's and a writer's audience. Indeed, when one surveys a broad range of situations inviting oral communication, Ong's paradigmatic situation, in which the speaker's audience constitutes a "collectivity, acting here and now on one another and on the speaker" (p. 11), seems somewhat atypical. It is certainly possible, at any rate, to think of a number of instances where speakers confront a problem very similar to that of writers: lacking intimate knowledge of their audience, which comprises not a collectivity but a disparate, and possibly even divided, group of individuals, speakers, like writers, must construct in their imaginations "an audience cast in some sort of role."[19] When President Carter announced to Americans during a speech broadcast on television, for instance, that his program against inflation was "the moral equivalent of warfare," he was doing more than merely characterizing his economic policies. He was providing an important cue to his audience concerning the role he wished them to adopt as listeners—that of a people braced for a painful but necessary and justifiable battle. Were we to examine his speech in detail, we would find other more subtle, but equally important, semantic and syntactic signals to the audience.

We do not wish here to collapse all distinctions between oral and written communication, but rather to emphasize that speaking and writing are, after all, both rhetorical acts. There are important differences between speech and writing. And the broad distinction between speech and writing that Ong makes is both commonsensical and particularly relevant to his subject, fictional narrative. As our illustration demonstrates, however, when one turns to precise, concrete situations, the relationship between speech and writing can become far more complex than even Ong represents.

Just as Ong's distinction between speech and writing is accurate on a highly general level but breaks down (or at least becomes less clear-cut) when examined closely, so too does his dictum about writers and their audiences. Every writer must indeed create a role for the reader, but the constraints on the writer and the potential sources of and possibilities for the reader's role are both more complex and diverse than Ong suggests. Ong stresses the importance of literary tradition in the creation of audience: "If the writer succeeds in writing, it is generally because he can fictionalize in his imagination an audience he has learned to know not from daily life but from earlier writers who were fictionalizing in their imagination audiences they had learned to know in still earlier writers, and so on back to the dawn of written narrative" (p. 11). And he cites a particularly (for us) germane example, a student "asked to write on the subject to which schoolteachers, jaded by summer, return compulsively every autumn: 'How I Spent My Summer Vacation'" (p. 11). In order to negotiate such an assignment successfully, the student must turn his real audience, the teacher, into someone else. He or she must, for instance, "make like Samuel Clemens and write for whomever Samuel Clemens was writing for" (p. 11).

Ong's example is, for his purposes, well-chosen. For such an assignment does indeed require the successful student to "fictionalize" his or her audience. But why is the student's decision to turn to a literary model in this instance particularly appropriate? Could one reason be that the student knows (consciously or unconsciously) that his English teacher, who is still the literal audience of his essay, appreciates literature and hence would be entertained (and here the student may intuit the assignment's actual aim as well) by such a strategy? In Ong's example the audience—the "jaded" schoolteacher—is not only willing to accept another role but, perhaps, actually yearns for it. How else to escape the tedium of reading 25, 50, 75 student papers on the same topic? As Walter Minot notes, however, not all readers are so malleable:

> In reading a work of fiction or poetry, a reader is far more willing to suspend his beliefs and values than in a rhetorical work dealing with some current social, moral, or economic issue. The effectiveness of the created audience in a rhetorical situation is likely to depend on such constraints as the actual identity of the reader, the subject of the discourse, the identity and purpose of the writer, and many other factors in the real world.[20]

An example might help make Minot's point concrete.

Imagine another composition student faced, like Ong's, with an assignment. This student, who has been given considerably more latitude in her choice of a topic, has decided to write on an issue of concern to her at the moment, the possibility that a home for mentally-retarded adults will be built in her neighborhood. She is alarmed by the strongly negative, highly emotional reaction of most of her neighbors and wishes in her essay to persuade them that such a residence might not be the disaster they anticipate.

This student faces a different task from that described by Ong. If she is to succeed, she must think seriously about her actual readers, the neighbors to whom she wishes to send her letter. She knows the obvious demographic factors—age, race, class—so well that she probably hardly needs to consider them consciously. But other issues are more complex. How much do her neighbors know about mental retardation, intellectually or experientially? What is their image of a retarded adult? What fears does this project raise in them? What civic and religious values do they most respect? Based on this analysis—and the process may be much less sequential than we describe here—she must, of course, define a role for her audience, one congruent with her persona, arguments, the facts as she knows them, etc. She must, as Minot argues, *both* analyze and invent an audience.[21] In this instance, after detailed analysis of her audience and her arguments, the student decided to begin her essay by emphasizing what she felt to be the genuinely admirable qualities of her neighbors, particularly their kindness, understanding, and concern for others. In so doing, she invited her audience to see themselves as *she* saw them: as thoughtful, intelligent people who, if they were adequately informed, would certainly not act in a harsh manner to those less fortunate than they. In accepting this role, her readers did not have to "play the game of being a member of an audience that 'really' does not exist" (Ong, "The Writer's Audience," p. 12). But they did have to recognize in themselves the strengths the student described and to accept her implicit linking of these strengths to what she hoped would be their response to the proposed "home."

When this student enters her history class to write an examination she faces a different set of constraints. Unlike the historian who does indeed have a broad range of options in establishing the reader's role, our student has much less freedom. This is because her reader's role has already been established and formalized in a series of related academic conventions. If she is a successful student, she has so effectively internalized these conventions that she can subordinate a concern for her complex and multiple audiences to focus on the material on which she is being tested and on the single audience, the teacher, who will respond to her performance on the test.[22]

We could multiply examples. In each instance the student writing—to friend, employer, neighbor, teacher, fellow readers of her daily newspaper—

would need, as one of the many conscious and unconscious decisions required in composing, to envision and define a role for the reader. But *how* she defines that role—whether she relies mainly upon academic or technical writing conventions, literary models, intimate knowledge of friends or neighbors, analysis of a particular group, or some combination thereof—will vary tremendously. At times the reader may establish a role for the reader which indeed does not "coincide[s] with his role in the rest of actual life" (Ong, p. 12). At other times, however, one of the writer's primary tasks may be that of analyzing the "real life" audience and adapting the discourse to it. One of the factors that makes writing so difficult, as we know, is that we have no recipes: each rhetorical situation is unique and thus requires the writer, catalyzed and guided by a strong sense of purpose, to reanalyze and reinvent solutions.

Despite their helpful corrective approach, then, theories which assert that the audience of a written discourse is a construction of the writer present their own dangers.[23] One of these is the tendency to overemphasize the distinction between speech and writing while undervaluing the insights of discourse theorists, such as James Moffett and James Britton, who remind us of the importance of such additional factors as distance between speaker or writer and audience and levels of abstraction in the subject. In *Teaching the Universe of Discourse,* Moffett establishes the following spectrum of discourse: recording ("the drama of what is happening"), reporting ("the narrative of what happened"), generalizing ("the exposition of what happens") and theorizing ("the argumentation of what will, may happen").[24] In an extended example, Moffett demonstrates the important points of connection between communication acts at any one level of the spectrum, whether oral or written:

> Suppose next that I tell the cafeteria experience to a friend some time later in conversation. . . . Of course, instead of recounting the cafeteria scene to my friend in person I could write it in a letter to an audience more removed in time and space. Informal writing is usually still rather spontaneous, directed at an audience known to the writer, and reflects the transient mood and circumstances in which the writing occurs. Feedback and audience influence, however, are delayed and weakened. . . . *Compare in turn now the changes that must occur all down the line when I write about this cafeteria experience in a discourse destined for publication and distribution to a mass, anonymous audience of present and perhaps unborn people.* I cannot allude to things and ideas that only my friends know about. I must use a vocabulary, style, logic, and rhetoric that anybody in that mass audience can understand and respond to. I must name and organize what happened during those moments in the cafeteria that day in such a way that

this mythical average reader can relate what I say to some primary moments of experience of his own. (pp. 37-38; our emphasis)

Though Moffett does not say so, many of these same constraints would obtain if he decided to describe his experience in a speech to a mass audience—the viewers of a television show, for example, or the members of a graduating class. As Moffett's example illustrates, the distinction between speech and writing is important; it is, however, only one of several constraints influencing any particular discourse.

Another weakness of research based on the concept of audience as invoked is that it distorts the processes of writing and reading by overemphasizing the power of the writer and undervaluing that of the reader. Unlike Mitchell and Taylor, Ong recognizes the creative role the writer plays as reader of his or her own writing, the way the writer uses language to provide cues for the reader and tests the effectiveness of these cues during his or her own rereading of the text. But Ong fails adequately to recognize the constraints placed on the writer, in certain situations, by the audience. He fails, in other words, to acknowledge that readers' own experiences, expectations, and beliefs do play a central role in their reading of a text, and that the writer who does not consider the needs and interests of his audience risks losing that audience. To argue that the audience is a "created fiction" (Long, p. 225), to stress that the reader's role "seldom coincides with his role in the rest of actual life" (Ong, p. 12), is just as much an oversimplification, then, as to insist, as Mitchell and Taylor do, that "the audience not only judges writing, it also motivates it" (p. 250). The former view overemphasizes the writer's independence and power; the latter, that of the reader.

RHETORIC AND ITS SITUATIONS[25]

If the perspectives we have described as audience addressed and audience invoked represent incomplete conceptions of the role of audience in written discourse, do we have an alternative? How can we most accurately conceive of this essential rhetorical element? In what follows we will sketch a tentative model and present several defining or constraining statements about this apparently slippery concept, "audience." The result will, we hope, move us closer to a full understanding of the role audience plays in written discourse.

Figure 2 represents our attempt to indicate the complex series of obligations, resources, needs, and constraints embodied in the writer's concept of audience. (We emphasize that our goal here is *not* to depict the writing process as a whole—a much more complex task—but to focus on the

Figure 2   The concept of audience.

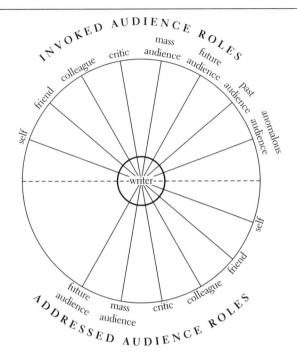

writer's relation to audience.) As our model indicates, we do not see the two perspectives on audience described earlier as necessarily dichotomous or contradictory. Except for past and anomalous audiences, special cases which we describe paragraphs hence, all of the audience roles we specify—self, friend, colleague, critic, mass audience, and future audience—may be invoked or addressed.[26] It is the writer who, as writer and reader of his or her own text, one guided by a sense of purpose and by the particularities of a specific rhetorical situation, establishes the range of potential roles an audience may play. (Readers may, of course, accept or reject the role or roles the writer wishes them to adopt in responding to a text.)

Writers who wish to be read must often adapt their discourse to meet the needs and expectations of an addressed audience. They may rely on past experience in addressing audiences to guide their writing, or they may engage a representative of that audience in the writing process. The latter occurs, for instance, when we ask a colleague to read an article intended for scholarly publication. Writers may also be required to respond to the intervention of others—a teacher's comments on an essay, a supervisor's suggestions for improving a report, or the insistent, catalyzing questions of an editor. Such intervention may in certain cases represent a powerful stimulus to the writer, but it is the writer who interprets the suggestions—or even commands—of others, choosing what to accept or reject. Even the conscious decision to accede to the expectations of a particular addressed audience may not always be carried out; unconscious psychological resistance, incomplete understanding, or inadequately developed ability may prevent the writer from following through with the decision—a reality confirmed by composition teachers with each new set of essays.

The addressed audience, the actual or intended readers of a discourse, exists outside of the text. Writers may analyze these readers' needs, anticipate their biases, even defer to their wishes. But it is only through the text, through language, that writers embody or give life to their conception of the reader. In so doing, they do not so much create a role for the reader—a phrase which implies that the writer somehow creates a mold to which the reader adapts—as invoke it. Rather than relying on incantations, however, writers conjure their vision—a vision which they hope readers will actively come to share as they read the text—by using all the resources of language available to them to establish a broad, and ideally coherent, range of cues for the reader. Technical writing conventions, for instance, quickly formalize any of several writer-reader relationships, such as colleague to colleague or expert to lay reader. But even comparatively local semantic decisions may play an equally essential role. In "The Writer's Audience Is Always a Fiction," Ong demonstrates how Hemingway's use of definite articles in *A Farewell to Arms* subtly cues readers that their role is to be that of a "companion in arms . . . a confidant" (p. 13).

Any of the roles of the addressed audience cited in our model may be invoked via the text. Writers may also invoke a past audience, as did, for instance, Ong's student writing to those Mark Twain would have been writing for. And writers can also invoke anomalous audiences, such as a fictional character—Hercule Poirot perhaps. Our model, then, confirms Douglas Park's observation that the meanings of audience, though multiple and complex, "tend to diverge in two general directions: one toward actual people external to a text, the audience whom the writer must accommodate; the other toward the text itself and the audience implied there: a set of suggested or evoked attitudes, interests, reactions, conditions of knowledge which may or may not fit with the qualities of actual readers or listeners."[27] The most complete understanding of audience thus involves a synthesis of the perspectives we have termed audience addressed, with its focus on the reader, and audience invoked, with its focus on the writer.

One illustration of this constantly shifting complex of meanings for "audience" lies in our own experiences writing this essay. One of us became interested in the concept of audience during an NEH Seminar, and her first audience was a small, close-knit seminar group to whom she addressed her work. The other came to contemplate a multiplicity of audiences while working on a textbook; the first audience in this case was herself, as she debated the ideas she was struggling to present to a group of invoked students. Following a lengthy series of conversations, our interests began to merge: we shared notes and discussed articles written by others on audience, and eventually one of us began a draft. Our long distance telephone bills and the miles we travelled up and down I-5 from Oregon to British Columbia attest most concretely to the power of a co-author's expectations and criticisms and also illustrate that one person can take on the role of several different audiences: friend, colleague, and critic.

As we began to write and re-write the essay, now for a particular scholarly journal, the change in purpose and medium (no longer a seminar paper or a textbook) led us to new audiences. For us, the major "invoked audience" during this period was Richard Larson, editor of this journal, whose questions and criticisms we imagined and tried to anticipate. (Once this essay was accepted by *CCC*, Richard Larson became for us an addressed audience: he responded in writing with questions, criticisms, and suggestions, some of which we had, of course, failed to anticipate.) We also thought of the readers of *CCC* and those who attend the annual CCCC, most often picturing you as members of our own departments, a diverse group of individuals with widely varying degrees of interest in and knowledge of composition. Because of the generic constraints of academic writing, which limit the range of roles we may define for our readers, the audience represented by the readers of *CCC* seemed most vivid to us in two situations: (1) when we were concerned about the degree to which we needed to explain concepts or terms; and (2) when we considered central organizational decisions, such as the most effective way to introduce a discussion. Another, and for us extremely potent, audience was the authors—Mitchell and Taylor, Long, Ong, Park, and others—with whom we have seen ourselves in silent dialogue. As we read and reread their analyses and developed our responses to them, we felt a responsibility to try to understand their formulations as fully as possible, to play fair with their ideas, to make our own efforts continue to meet their high standards.

Our experience provides just one example, and even it is far from complete. (Once we finished a rough draft, one particular colleague became a potent but demanding addressed audience, listening to revision upon revision and challenging us with harder and harder questions. And after this essay is published, we may revise our understanding of audiences we thought we knew or recognize the existence of an entirely new audience.

The latter would happen, for instance, if teachers of speech communication for some reason found our discussion useful.) But even this single case demonstrates that the term *audience* refers not just to the intended, actual, or eventual readers of a discourse, but to *all* those whose image, ideas, or actions influence a writer during the process of composition. One way to conceive of "audience," then, is as an overdetermined or unusually rich concept, one which may perhaps be best specified through the analysis of precise, concrete situations.

We hope that this partial example of our own experience will illustrate how the elements represented in Figure 2 will shift and merge, depending on the particular rhetorical situation, the writer's aim, and the genre chosen. Such an understanding is critical: because of the complex reality to which the term audience refers and because of its fluid, shifting role in the composing process, any discussion of audience which isolates it from the rest of the rhetorical situation or which radically overemphasizes or underemphasizes its function in relation to other rhetorical constraints is likely to oversimplify. Note the unilateral direction of Mitchell and Taylor's model (p. 5), which is unable to represent the diverse and complex role(s) audience(s) can play in the actual writing process—in the creation of meaning. In contrast, consider the model used by Edward P. J. Corbett in his *Little Rhetoric and Handbook*.[28] This representation, which allows for interaction among all the elements of rhetoric, may at first appear less elegant and predictive than Mitchell and Taylor's. But it is finally more useful since it accurately represents the diverse range of potential interrelationships in any written discourse.

We hope that our model also suggests the integrated, interdependent nature of reading and writing. Two assertions emerge from this relationship. One involves the writer as reader of his or her own work. As Donald Murray notes in "Teaching the Other Self: The Writer's First Reader," this role is

Figure 3   Corbett's model of "The Rhetorical Interrelationships" (p. 5).

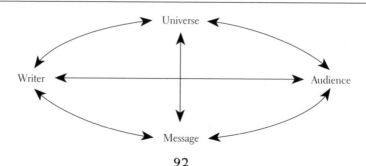

critical, for "the reading writer—the map-maker and map-reader—reads the word, the line, the sentence, the paragraph, the page, the entire text. This constant back-and-forth reading monitors the multiple complex relationships between all the elements in writing."[29] To ignore or devalue such a central function is to risk distorting the writing process as a whole. But unless the writer is composing a diary or journal entry, intended only for the writer's own eyes, the writing process is not complete unless another person, someone other than the writer, reads the text also. The second assertion thus emphasizes the creative, dynamic duality of the process of reading and writing, whereby writers create readers and readers create writers. In the meeting of these two lies meaning, lies communication.

A fully elaborated view of audience, then, must balance the creativity of the writer with the different, but equally important, creativity of the reader. It must account for a wide and shifting range of roles for both addressed and invoked audiences. And, finally, it must relate the matrix created by the intricate relationship of writer and audience to all elements in the rhetorical situation. Such an enriched conception of audience can help us better understand the complex act we call composing.

NOTES

1. Ruth Mitchell and Mary Taylor, "The Integrating Perspective: An Audience-Response Model for Writing," *CE*, 41 (November, 1979), 267. Subsequent references to this article will be cited in the text.

2. Russell C. Long, "Writer-Audience Relationships: Analysis or Invention," *CCC*, 31 (May, 1980), 223 and 225. Subsequent references to this article will be cited in the text.

3. For these terms we are indebted to Henry W. Johnstone, Jr., who refers to them in his analysis of Chaim Perelman's universal audience in *Validity and Rhetoric in Philosophical Argument: An Outlook in Transition* (University Park, PA: The Dialogue Press of Man & World, 1978), p. 105.

4. Fred R. Pfister and Joanne F. Petrik, "A Heuristic Model for Creating a Writer's Audience," *CCC*, 31 (May, 1980), 213.

5. Pfister and Petrik, 214; our emphasis.

6. See, for example, Lisa S. Ede, "On Audience and Composition," *CCC*, 30 (October, 1979), 291-295.

7. See, for example, David Tedlock, "The Case Approach to Composition," *CCC*, 32 (October, 1981), 253-261.

8. See, for example, Linda Flower's *Problem-Solving Strategies for Writers* (New York: Harcourt Brace Jovanovich, 1981) and John P. Field and Robert H. Weiss' *Cases for Composition* (Boston: Little Brown, 1979).

9. Richard E. Young, "Paradigms and Problems: Needed Research in Rhetorical Invention," in *Research on Composing: Points of Departure*, ed. Charles R. Cooper and Lee Odell (Urbana, IL: National Council of Teachers of English, 1978), p. 32 (footnote #3).

10. Mitchell and Taylor do recognize that internal psychological needs ("unconscious challenges") may play a role in the writing process, but they cite such instances as an "extreme

case (often that of the creative writer)" (p. 251). For a discussion of the importance of self-evaluation in the composing process see Susan Miller, "How Writers Evaluate Their Own Writing," *CCC*, 33 (May, 1982), 176-183.

11. Susan Wall, "In the Writer's Eye: Learning to Teach the Rereading/Revising Process," *English Education*, 14 (February, 1982), 12.

12. Wayne Booth, *Modern Dogma and the Rhetoric of Assent* (Chicago: The University of Chicago Press, 1974), p. xiv.

13. Paul Kameen, "Rewording the Rhetoric of Composition," *Pre/Text*, 1 (Spring-Fall, 1980), 82.

14. Mitchell and Taylor's arguments in favor of adjunct classes seem to indicate that they see writing instruction, wherever it occurs, as a skills course, one instructing students in the proper use of a tool.

15. Anthony R. Petrosky, "From Story to Essay: Reading and Writing," *CCC*, 33 (February, 1982), 20.

16. Walter J. Ong, S. J., "The Writer's Audience Is Always a Fiction," *PMLA*, 90 (January, 1975), 9-21. Subsequent references to this article will be cited in the text.

17. See, for example, William Irmscher, "Sense of Audience: An Intuitive Concept," unpublished paper delivered at the CCCC in 1981; Douglas B. Park, "The Meanings of Audience: Pedagogical Implications," unpublished paper delivered at the CCCC in 1981; and Luke M. Reinsma, "Writing to an Audience: Scheme or Strategy?" unpublished paper delivered at the CCCC in 1982.

18. Herbert W. Simons, *Persuasion: Understanding, Practice, and Analysis* (Reading, MA: Addison-Wesley, 1976).

19. Ong, p. 12. Ong recognizes that oral communication also involves role-playing, but he stresses that it "has within it a momentum that works for the removal of masks" (p. 20). This may be true in certain instances, such as dialogue, but does not, we believe, obtain broadly.

20. Walter S. Minot, "Response to Russell C. Long," *CCC*, 32 (October, 1981), 337.

21. We are aware that the student actually has two audiences, her neighbors and her teacher, and that this situation poses an extra constraint for the writer. Not all students can manage such a complex series of audience constraints, but it is important to note that writers in a variety of situations often write for more than a single audience.

22. In their paper on "Student and Professional Syntax in Four Disciplines" (unpublished paper delivered at the CCCC in 1981), Ian Pringle and Aviva Freedman provide a good example of what can happen when a student creates an aberrant role for an academic reader. They cite an excerpt from a third year history assignment, the tone of which "is essentially the tone of the opening of a television travelogue commentary" and which thus asks the reader, a history professor, to assume the role of the viewer of such a show. The result is as might be expected: "Although the content of the paper does not seem significantly more abysmal than other papers in the same set, this one was awarded a disproportionately low grade" (p. 2).

23. One danger which should be noted is a tendency to foster a questionable image of classical rhetoric. The agonistic speaker-audience relationship which Long cites as an essential characteristic of classical rhetoric is actually a central point of debate among those involved in historical and theoretical research in rhetoric. For further discussion, see: Lisa Ede and Andrea Lunsford, "On Distinctions Between Classical and Modern Rhetoric," in *Classical Rhetoric and Modern Discourse: Essays in Honor of Edward P. J. Corbett*, ed. Robert Connors, Lisa Ede, and Andrea Lunsford (Carbondale, IL: Southern Illinois University Press, 1984).

24. James Moffett, *Teaching the Universe of Discourse* (Boston: Houghton Mifflin, 1968), p. 47. Subsequent references will be mentioned in the text.

25. We have taken the title of this section from Scott Consigny's article of the same title, *Philosophy and Rhetoric*, 7 (Summer, 1974), 175-186. Consigny's effort to mediate between two opposing views of rhetoric provided a stimulating model for our own efforts.

26. Although we believe that the range of audience roles cited in our model covers the general spectrum of options, we do not claim to have specified all possibilities. This is particularly the case since, in certain instances, these roles may merge and blend—shifting subtly in character. We might also note that other terms for the same roles might be used. In a business setting, for instance, colleague might be better termed co-worker; critic, supervisor.

27. Douglas B. Park, "The Meanings of 'Audience,'" *CE*, 44 (March, 1982), 249.

28. Edward P. J. Corbett, *The Little Rhetoric & Handbook*, 2nd edition (Glenview, IL: Scott, Foresman, 1982), p. 5.

29. Donald M. Murray, "Teaching the Other Self: The Writer's First Reader," *CCC*, 33 (May, 1982), 142.

Post-Process "Pedagogy"

A Philosophical Exercise

Lee-Ann M. Kastman Breuch

Recently, "post-process" theories of composition instruction have suggested that process (prewriting, writing, rewriting) is no longer an adequate explanation of the writing act. Many post-process scholars, largely influenced by postmodernist and anti-foundationalist perspectives, suggest that the process paradigm has reduced the writing act to a series of codified phases that can be taught. These critics suggest that process pedagogy simply offers us another foundational explanation of writing.[1] Indeed, the dominant contention of post-process scholars is that process has come to represent Theory with a capital "T."[2] Gary Olson explains, for example, that the process approach is problematic because it attempts to generalize the writing act:

> The problem with process theory, then, is not so much that scholars are attempting to theorize various aspects of composing as it is that they are endeavoring (consciously or not) to construct a model of the composing process, thereby constructing a Theory of Writing, a series of generalizations about writing that supposedly hold true all or most of the time. (8)

This generalization can be especially problematic if teachers of writing present the writing process as one universal process rather than as plural processes (see Russell 80).

The suggestion that process is no longer a viable explanation for the writing act has spurred further discussion about the nature of the writing

First published in *JAC* 22.1 (Winter 2002): 119–50. Reprinted with permission.

process. For example, while some scholars suggest that the process approach may attempt to represent the act of writing universally, others find this characterization of process inaccurate. Bruce McComiskey notes his disagreement with this characterization: "Invention and revision strategies, as I understand and teach them, do not assume a stable and predictable linguistic system for generating universal meaning; their function is, instead, to harness the polyphonic character of language in communities, to develop rather than constrict a writer's sense of purpose" (39–40). David Russell also argues that the idea of a universal process—"*the* process," as he puts it—is less accurate than the idea of plural processes. He argues for a "progressively wider understanding of writing processes as they are played out in a range of activity systems in our culture(s)" (88). Joseph Petraglia suggests that we should not abandon or reject process, but simply move past it:

> Of course, the fundamental observation that an individual produces text by means of a writing process has not been discarded. Instead, it has dissolved and shifted from figure to ground. . . . We now have the theoretical and empirical sophistication to consider the mantra "writing is a process" as the right answer to a really boring question. We have better questions now, and the notion of process no longer counts as much of an insight. (53)

Because process is so often the topic of discussion in post-process scholarship, post-process has come to mean a critique of the process movement in composition studies. In response, I argue that post-process scholarship is shortchanged by the continued emphasis on process in that the broader implications of post-process theory have very little to do with process. Furthermore, I suggest that the only importance process has to post-process theory is in the form of an illustration—and a poor one at that. That is, "process" as it is cast by post-process scholarship is the scapegoat in an argument to forward postmodern and anti-foundationalist perspectives that are critical to post-process theory.

In this article, I attempt to clarify what I believe post-process theory can contribute to composition pedagogy. In accordance with Sidney Dobrin, who suggests that post-process theory should not fall into the "pedagogical imperative," I suggest that there is no identifiable post-process pedagogy that we can concretely apply to writing classrooms; however, I believe post-process theory offers many insights for the profession of teaching that we all should consider (*Constructing* 63). Specifically, I argue that post-process theory encourages us to reexamine our definition of writing as an activity rather than a body of knowledge, our methods of teaching as indeterminate activities rather than exercises of mastery, and our communicative interactions with students as dialogic rather than monologic. My mission to high-light these insights is driven by what I perceive to be a lack of clarity in post-process theory, fueled by a diversion into discussions of process and by arguments that seemingly resist pedagogical application. When we look past arguments that dominate current scholarship in post-process theory and in-stead uncover the assumptions that guide post-process theory, we may find helpful and even profound contributions that inform our pedagogical prac-tice—if not in specific pedagogical agendas, then in philosophical princi-ples that guide our practice.

In the next section, I explain how post-process theory may seemingly defy pedagogical application. I specifically review central arguments made by Thomas Kent, a prominent post-process scholar, and I offer a critique of current scholarship on post-process theory.

POST-PROCESS RESISTANCE

On the surface, post-process theory seems to resist pedagogical application because of post-process claims that writing cannot be taught, vague peda-gogical agendas, and divergent depictions of post-process pedagogy. If one were to casually explore post-process theory, these three characterizations might leave the impression that teaching writing is a hopeless endeavor. I argue that the wrong arguments are highlighted in this scholarship—argu-ments that focus on the negatives of process pedagogy rather than on the possibilities of post-process theory. In this section, I explore these argu-ments further to uncover central assumptions that inform the post-process perspective.

Pedagogical resistance is perhaps most apparent in the claim that writ-ing cannot be taught, which stems from the argument forwarded by Kent that writing is a situated, interpretive, and indeterminate act. In *Paralogic Rhetoric*, Kent suggests that accepting a post-process perspective (at least in a paralogic sense) means rejecting process as the ultimate explanation for the writing act and instead recognizing the role of interpretation and indetermi-nacy in the writing act. Consequently, if we consider writing as an indeter-minate and interpretive activity, he asserts, then "writing and reading—conceived broadly as processes or bodies of knowledge—cannot be taught, for nothing exists to teach" (161). This statement is critical to the post-process perspective for its rejection of process as both an explanation of the writing act and a method of teaching writing. Indeed, this claim seems to have spurred discussions about what Petraglia has called "life after process," so it is necessary to examine it more closely.

Certainly, the claim that writing cannot be taught—and that writing process is inadequate to explain the writing act—on the surface indicates resistance to pedagogical application. However, when investigating more closely, we see that Kent does not completely abandon writing pedagogy, as the following passage from *Paralogic Rhetoric* about his "externalist pedagogy" reveals:

> Stated baldly, an externalist pedagogy endorses the following claims: (1) writing and reading are kinds of communicative interaction; (2) communicative interaction requires triangulation; (3) triangulation requires us to make hermeneutic guesses about how others will interpret our utterances; (4) the process we employ to make our hermeneutic guesses cannot be codified; (5) consequently, no system or framework theory can predict in advance how our utterances will be interpreted; (6) therefore, neither writing nor reading can be reduced to a systemic process or to a codifiable set of conventions, although clearly some of the background knowledge useful for writing—like grammar, sentence structure, paragraph cohesion, and so forth—can be codified and reduced to a system. However, we should remember that knowing a framework or process is necessary but not sufficient for communicative interaction; knowing a grammar, for example, only prepares us to write or to read. (161)

I argue that this passage demonstrates not a total resistance to pedagogy, but rather a careful pedagogical position, for Kent's stance on teaching writing depends on the definition of *writing* that he has outlined in this passage. Kent distinguishes background knowledge—grammar systems and so forth—from the writing act, which he says is indeterminate and dynamic and defies systems. That is, while grammar and rules about cohesion or sentence structure can be easily codified and transmitted to students, these systems should not be confused with the writing act—an act that he describes as uncertain and indeterminate: "Certain background skills, such as an understanding of grammar, can be taught, but the acquisition of these skills never guarantees that a student will be able to communicate effectively; no framework theory of any kind can help a student predict in advance the interpretation that someone else may give to an utterance" (161).

It is important to note that Kent does not reject the instruction of system-based content such as grammar; rather, he suggests that these skills do not in themselves comprise the writing act and that we cannot reduce the writing act to a system that can then be taught. These statements help us to understand that in saying "nothing exists to teach," Kent is not rejecting pedagogical application altogether, but rather the specific pedagogical application of process pedagogy, which he claims attempts to reduce the writing act (not background knowledge) into content that can be taught to students:

> So, any composition or literature pedagogy that presupposes such a frame-
> work assumes that writing and reading consists of a well-defined process
> that, once mastered, allows us to engage unproblematically in commu-
> nicative interaction. These process-oriented pedagogies generally assume
> that discourse production and reception are cognitive activities that may be
> reduced either to frameworks that describe the mental processes writers
> and readers employ or to social activities that describe the conventions or
> conceptual schemes that hold together a discourse community. (161–62)

Let's take this claim for what it's worth. Kent suggests that writing is not a system or process and therefore cannot be taught as such. Consequently, he
does not suggest that teaching writing is impossible; he suggests that teaching writing *as a system* is impossible. Thus, while some may take the claim
that "nothing exists to teach" to mean that writing pedagogy is an impossible
project, I argue that the claim exists to attack process pedagogy specifically.

While Kent's project here seems to be to dismantle process pedagogy, he
does provide suggestions for reconceptualizing pedagogy based on the theoretical framework he has outlined. Yet these, too, demonstrate resistance to
pedagogical application. As some scholars have pointed out, Kent's discussions of pedagogy are "vague," "cautious," and "less developed" than his theoretical framework (Dobrin, *Constructing* 89; Ward 158). Nonetheless, in
order to illustrate the ways in which Kent moves away from process pedagogy, it is important to review the pedagogical insights he does offer. Kent's
reconceptualization of pedagogy begins with the suggestion that we use a
new vocabulary to discuss writing in relation to communicative interaction:

> As strong externalists, we would stop talking about writing and reading as
> processes and start talking about these activities as determinate social acts.
> This shift from an internalist conception of communicative interaction —
> the notion that communication is a product of the internal workings of the
> mind or the workings of the discourse communities in which we live — to
> an externalist conception that I have outlined here would challenge us to
> drop our current process-oriented vocabulary and to begin talking about
> our social and public uses of language. (169)

What results from this proposal is an increased emphasis on communicative
interaction between teachers and students. Kent discusses at length how this
emphasis would affect teacher-student roles in writing classrooms:

> Instead of dialecticians who initiate students into new knowledge, mentors
> who endorse a paralogic rhetoric become co-workers who actively collabo-
> rate with their students to help them through different communicative

situations both within and outside the university. As co-workers, these mentors—by relinquishing their roles as high priests—engender a new relationship with their students in that they actively collaborate with their students and become, in a sense, students themselves. (166)

Kent's (re)vision of writing pedagogy, then, pushes past process and toward a dialogic understanding of meaning-making. This dialogic pedagogy requires two-way rather than one-way communication, suggesting that teachers move away from a transmission model of education and toward a transformative model that includes active participation from both teachers and students as collaborators.

While Kent's comments about pedagogy do provide direction beyond process, some scholars have been quick to point out that his comments are not specific enough to outline any pedagogy that could be labeled "post-process," thus increasing the resistance to applying post-process theory to pedagogy. Indeed, the vagueness of Kent's proposed pedagogy has indicated to some that post-process theory should remain a theoretical enterprise. Dobrin in particular supports this viewpoint: "Perhaps Kent's own glossing of classroom application should serve as an indication that these theories, while informative about the nature of discourse, are not necessarily practice-oriented theories, a recognition which, of course, puts us at an awkward crossroads" (*Constructing* 86). Dobrin argues that post-process theory is not yet developed enough for pedagogical application: "Even those who see the classroom potential of post-process theory have too hastily fallen into the pedagogical imperative and seek to create pedagogies from theories we are just beginning to discuss" (64). Warning of the "pedagogical imperative," or the idea that a theory must have direct classroom application, Dobrin says that rushing to outline pedagogical application is "frivolous" (86).

Further resistance to pedagogical application of post-process theory exists in the inevitable trap of trying to specify a pedagogy that upholds anti-foundationalist and postmodern beliefs. That is, post-process theory as outlined by Kent upholds the anti-foundationalist view that knowledge is situated, indeterminate, and thoroughly hermeneutic. Thus, in advocating a pedagogy based on anti-foundationalism, one must wrestle with the paradox of any pedagogical agenda it forwards. David Wallace explains:

If we recognize that structural understandings of language and rhetoric are not *objective* and have no intrinsic basis in *reality*, then we must also recognize that any act of pedagogy that requires (or encourages) conformity to convention is ultimately a power move. . . . Thus *any* pedagogical act must be seen as socially and culturally implicated because asking students to move in any direction—whether that be toward mastery of the conventions of standard written English or toward a critical awareness of the social and political consequences of acts of literacy—is to ask them to change not just what they know but who they are. (110–11)

Wallace claims that any pedagogy—postmodern or anti-foundationalist— adopts a stance and therefore cannot be considered indeterminate or ambiguous. Note that Wallace suggests that *any* pedagogical act is an act of power, thus reinforcing the paradox of any anti-foundationalist pedagogy.

What results from this inherent paradox of pedagogical application is confusion about any pedagogical insights post-process theory might offer; in addition, the resistance to a single pedagogical agenda encourages pluralism. For example, in recent years, various "post-process pedagogies" have emerged that bear no resemblance to one another. One example of post-process pedagogy is offered by McComiskey, who openly rejects what he calls Kent's "anti-process" and builds a post-process pedagogy on the idea of "social-process rhetorical inquiry," which he defines as "a method of invention that usually manifests itself in composition classes as a set of heuristic questions based on the cycle of cultural production, contextual distribution, and critical consumption" (40, 42). Raúl Sánchez, who stays closer to Kent's arguments and advocates pedagogy as a one-to-one mentored relationship between teacher and student, articulates another pedagogy that claims to be post-process. In this proposed pedagogy, Sánchez suggests that writing courses no longer focus on process as content, but rather use class time to engage in discourse about writing (see Dobrin, *Constructing* 84). Irene Ward also builds on Kent's ideas to articulate a "functional dialogism" for writing pedagogy, which includes the following forms of dialogue in the writing classroom:

- internal dialogues between a self and an internalized audience
- dialogue between teacher and student
- dialogue between students and other larger social institutions, including but not limited to the educational institution or some other social institution within any one or more of the student's immediate communities
- dialogues among students about the formal matters of the composition or the ideas or subject of the discourse
- composing using dialogic forms in order to understand an issue or group of issues from various points of view and gain insight into one's relationship to those ideas and into multiple perspectives represented by many voices that have already entered into public dialogue. (171)

Still others articulate different visions for how post-process theory might apply to pedagogy. For example, Barbara Couture suggests that pedagogy must move beyond modeling a process and toward the development of agency in students:

> Our current scholarship on diverse ways of knowing, meaning, and com-
> municating strongly suggests that modeling specific conventions and pro-
> cedures will not ensure that writers learn all they need to know in order to
> communicate effectively to others. . . . Writers need to become subjective
> agents, making willful judgments effected in concrete actions that convey
> them successfully to others. (42)

Russell takes a different approach and does not advocate rejecting process outright but, rather, extending the notion of process—or, as he puts it, "to extend the activity system of the discipline of composition studies, to offer to teachers and students more and more refined tools for helping people in and entering various activity systems to write and learn to write and trans-form their activity through writing" (91).

Lest we become confused by these divergent attempts to apply post-process theory to pedagogy, Petraglia reminds us that given the increase in scholarship about writing in the past two decades, both qualitative and quantitative, it is "natural" for post-process theory to exhibit such complexity (53). Yet, this does not help us understand with any clarity just what post-process theory can offer. Kent admits to the hybrid nature of scholarship about post-process theory in the introduction to his edited collection about post-process theory: "Although the authors appearing in these pages may dis-agree about the nature of the 'post' in 'post-process' theory, all of them agree that change is in the air" (5). Further, he describes three assumptions that he claims most post-process scholars share: writing is public; writing is inter-pretive; and writing is situated (1). Perhaps these assumptions clarify to some degree how we might understand post-process theory, and I return to them later in this essay.

In sum, there are good reasons to believe that post-process theory resists pedagogical application: the declaration that writing cannot be taught, the lack of a clear pedagogical agenda, and the divergent applications thus far of post-process theory. With respect to Dobrin's insistence that we too easily fall into the "pedagogical imperative," I suggest that there are implications for pedagogy but that they are not highlighted in a productive way. The first implication is the recognition that writing is more than a body of knowledge to be mastered, which I address in the next section.

POST-PROCESS REJECTION OF MASTERY

While it is unclear what post-process theory offers in the way of concrete assignments or classroom environment, post-process theory does make an important pedagogical contribution through its rejection of mastery. Not coincidentally, many post-process scholars associate the process movement with mastery, suggesting (as Kent does) that process represents a system of writing that can be learned and perfected.[3] Couture explains: "We pay a price . . . by reducing those acts that make us uniquely human—speaking and writing—to a device or technology to be mastered, ignoring their more central role in shaping the way we are and live" (39). In this section, I explain in further detail the assumptions of mastery that post-process scholars have articulated (and rejected) about process pedagogy. I argue that whether or not we agree with the depiction of process as mastery, the post-process rejection of mastery is an important recognition for writing scholars and teachers.

One way post-process theorists depict process as mastery is by suggesting that writing process is a "thing"—a system, body of knowledge, or model—that can be skillfully practiced and conquered. When we reexamine Kent's claim about writing pedagogy, this language becomes apparent: "Writing and reading—conceived broadly as processes or bodies of knowledge—cannot be taught, for nothing exists to teach" (161). Helen Ewald observes that Kent's claim "seems based on the assumption that the ability to teach a subject rests on its having a codified body of knowledge that can be transmitted" (122). Of course, Kent ultimately rejects the idea that writing can be described as a body of knowledge, but in doing so process becomes the scapegoat, representing little more than a body of knowledge. Dobrin, also speaking from a post-process perspective, makes this point clear: "Certainly, process pedagogy is convenient; process pedagogy makes it easy to define texts and to write texts. We can unproblematically, clearly present a body of knowledge and evaluate students' abilities to absorb and rehash that body of knowledge, that process" ("Paralogic" 139). According to these and other post-process scholars, process means little more than content—a body of knowledge.

This depiction of process as a body of knowledge often leads to what Erika Lindemann calls "what-centered" teaching approaches, in which teachers emphasize subject matter above all else. It is helpful to examine process pedagogy in this light to better understand the post-process critique that process leads to mastery. According to Lindemann, a what-centered writing course might emphasize subject matter such as literature, films, linguistic systems (grammar and sentence structure), or even modes of writing. In contrast, "how-centered" approaches emphasize activities that occur in a writing class (Lindemann includes process pedagogy here) such as prewriting, writing, and rewriting, in addition to activities such as listening to and discussing the writing of students in class (251, 252). She suggests that "what-centered" courses emphasize nouns (content), while "how-centered" courses emphasize verbs (activities).

The distinction between what-centered and how-centered approaches is particularly important where process pedagogy is concerned. If process pedagogy is considered an approach that reduces writing to a thing—a body of knowledge that can be transmitted to students—then process pedagogy would certainly be considered a what-centered approach to teaching writing. However, Lindemann notes (and I agree) that process pedagogy as it was originally introduced in composition represents a *how-centered* approach because of its emphasis on the activities involved in process approaches to writing (prewriting, writing, rewriting). Indeed, process pedagogy and the research of Janet Emig, Ken Macrorie, and Peter Elbow in many ways encouraged a shift away from content-based approaches, such as current-traditional pedagogy, which emphasized grammatical structures. But viewed through post-process lenses, process seems to have lost its luster. Indeed, post-process scholarship has ignored process as how-centered and has curiously assumed that process is content-based.

Thinking about process or writing as "what-centered" facilitates mastery, as Lindemann explains: "We turn process-centered courses into what-centered courses every time we're tempted to interrupt students engaged in writing with an explanation of some subject matter. Or, if we 'explain' prewriting strategies during the first few weeks and never refer to them again, we've made prewriting a subject matter, a body of information to learn about rather than an activity to practice" (252). Lindemann argues that this turn is not productive and that teachers should be conscious of their efforts to uphold process as how-centered. However, post-process theory seems to be certain that this turn toward content has in fact occurred. Couture explains that instructors have emphasized process as content as a result of a historical habit of modeling writing in the classroom: "How did the emphasis upon process, like so many ideas about writing that are derived from scholarship and research, lose so much when applied en masse in our classrooms? At least one reason can be traced back to how we traditionally have approached composition instruction, teaching students to model technique rather than to emulate expression" (30). As Couture explains, our tendency to perceive process as mastery is historically consistent with past pedagogy, such as current-traditional approaches:

Teaching the writing process as the modeling of technique certainly is consistent with a tradition of composition pedagogy extending from the practice of imitating good writing by good writers; through the practice of perfecting the argumentative strategies of deduction, induction, comparing, contrasting, and defining; to following the basic pattern of the five-paragraph theme, mastered by most of us in high school English and freshman composition classes. And, too, emphasis on process as model has reflected an overt desire of many composition instructors to identify methods for improving writing instruction so as to "right" their students' writing. . . . (33)

Couture explains well how we—both students and teachers—might interpret process as mastery of writing techniques. From a student's perspective, process could be presented as a technique that could be mastered to improve student writing. From a teacher's perspective, process could be viewed as a pedagogical method that could be mastered in the classroom. Either way, the argument presented here suggests that process has been treated as a thing to master in writing pedagogy. Yet, this characterization of process as mastery seems too simple. Lisa Ede reminds us, for example, that research on writing process has displayed enormous complexity. To illustrate this complexity, she reviews the work of several process scholars such as Emig, Elbow, Donald Murray, Linda Flower, and John Hayes, and she reminds us of their divergent approaches to process. But, as Ede articulates, process became "co-opted and commodified—by textbooks that oversimplified and rigidified a complex phenomenon, by overzealous language arts coordinators and writing program administrators who assumed that the process approach to teaching could be 'taught' in one or two in-service sessions" (35–36; see also Russell 84).

I review these arguments to problematize the assumption that process is "what-centered," based solely on content or a body of knowledge. While it may be true that process has been "co-opted," as Ede suggests, I argue that this commodification of process should be considered as a slip and not as a fact. As Lindemann reminds us, the characterization of process as how-centered is more true to the origins of the process movement. Simply stated, before accepting post-process arguments about the failure of process, we need to examine the assumptions informing them. When we do, we can find value in the post-process insistence that we reexamine the way we think of process in the writing classroom, as well as our approaches to mastery. That is, post-process scholars seem most concerned about writing being characterized as a thing, whether that thing is process, grammatical systems, discourse conventions, and so on. When considering these arguments, the value in post-process scholarship appears not to be the rejection of process, but the rejection of mastery—the rejection of the belief that writing can be categorized as a thing to be mastered.

Post-process opposition to mastery is also apparent in arguments that characterize process as Theory—or process as having universal explanatory power. And, as in the "what-centered" characterization of process, process as a Theory is rejected by post-process scholars, as Olson reminds us:

> The problem with process theory, then, is not so much that scholars are attempting to theorize various aspects of composing as it is that they are endeavoring (consciously or not) to construct a model of the composing process, thereby constructing a Theory of Writing, a series of generalizations about writing that supposedly hold true all or most of the time. (8)

Couture's observation that process is a way to teach writing the "right" way also supports the argument that process presents a Theory. Like the rejection of mastery, these arguments illustrate the postmodern and anti-foundationalist influences on post-process theory. As Olson explains, "The postmodern critique of theory serves as a useful corrective in that it alerts us to the dangers of creating master narratives and then adhering to these explanations as if we have obtained truth" (8). Postmodern critique is especially helpful in deconstructing what Pullman describes as the "rhetorical narrative" of process pedagogy, a "motivated selection and sequencing of events that sacrifices one truth in order to more clearly represent another" (16; see also Foster 149). Indeed, the postmodern influences on post-process theory denounce the search for universal truth. Kent reminds us of the "master narrative of objectivity," the idea that truth resides outside of language and that knowledge is systematic rather than interpretive (*Paralogic* 63). At the root of the post-process critique of process pedagogy is the idea that process is a systematic method for learning writing—one that is objective rather than subjective.

Again, considering the post-process opposition to mastery, we must reexamine the claim that process represents a Theory or a grand narrative. I suggest that given the postmodern and anti-foundationalist influences on post-process theory, post-process scholars are more concerned with the rejection of universal theories in general than the rejection of process pedagogy in particular. Process appears to be merely a convenient illustration of the post-process perspective. For example, because process scholarship has been the dominant perspective in writing pedagogy, it is easy to paint it as an illustration of a master narrative, a Theory, or a model to be imitated. It is tempting to wonder if the purpose of post-process scholarship is to simply knock process off of its pedestal. Similar moves have been made in the past regarding the current-traditional movement in composition studies. Pull-man describes the rush to associate the term *current-traditional* with a movement, theory, or label about teaching writing effectively:

> We forget that [this] expression did not refer to a theory but was instead a shorthand and off-the-cuff way of alluding to the way the tradition of rhetoric was currently being purveyed in the Freshman Composition textbooks of [the] day. Because we forget this, we tend to think that current-traditional rhetoric was a bogus theory based on prejudice and misunderstanding, a kind of mindless application of traditional folklore or naive interpretations of Aristotle's *Rhetoric* when in fact it did not exist as a theory except to the extent one could extrapolate a theory from the textbooks current at the time. (22)

Pullman asserts that the rush to define current-traditional rhetoric forwarded the process movement: "The writing process was not, in other words, so much discovered as created . . ." (23). Further, he suggests that this "creation" of process gave scholars reason to reject current-traditional rhetoric: "In a sense, the reified expression *current-traditional rhetoric* does little more than create a daemon for the sake of expelling it" (23).

In describing the building and rejecting of current-traditional rhetoric, Pullman illustrates his perception of the rhetorical narrative of process. Ede makes a similar observation of this rhetorical move, suggesting that advocates of the process movement depicted current-traditional rhetoric negatively. She claims that the process movement "in effect constituted itself through a denial of origins that involves creating that which it wishes to oppose and then erasing the shared ground that made the original construction of the other possible. In an important sense current-traditional rhetoric did not exist until advocates of writing as a process created it" (37). Ede calls this strategy "a characteristic move of the western intellectual project," and the point I wish to make is that this same move may be apparent in post-process scholarship (37). Here, process is described as a master narrative, a Theory, a content- and what-centered approach. Process is first described as a thing and is then promptly rejected. Petraglia articulates this move: "As I understand it, 'post-process' signifies a rejection of the generally formulaic framework for understanding writing that process suggested" (53). It could easily be argued that post-process scholars have created their own rhetorical narrative of process as content-based, thus casting process as the scapegoat.

As I suggested previously, I disagree with the depiction of process as a formula, model, or "thing," but I do agree with Petraglia's assertion that post-process scholarship signifies a rejection of generally formulaic frameworks for explaining writing. This broader understanding of post-process scholarship—focused not on process, but on the rejection of formulaic explanations of writing—is a key contribution to the reconceptualization of writing. Petraglia explains this well: "This reconceptualization requires that the discipline let go of its current pedagogical shape (i.e., its focus on supplying students with productive rhetorical skills that can be exercised through writing) and instead deploy its efforts to inculcate *receptive* skills" (61–62). Thus, I argue that rather than the rejection of process, the post-process critique contributes to our discipline through the rejection of mastery—the description of writing as a "thing," and the description of a master narrative or theory of writing. In giving up the search for a way to teach writing, post-process theory advocates, in the words of Petraglia, the "letting go" of the discipline. As I explain in the next section, post-process theory can be more fully explained by reviewing key assumptions critical to the theory, assumptions that are informed by postmodern and anti-foundationalist perspectives.

POST-PROCESS ASSUMPTIONS ABOUT WRITING

In moving away from writing as a "thing," post-process theory encourages us to examine writing again as an activity—an indeterminate activity. By "indeterminate" I mean that the writing act cannot be predicted in terms of how students will write (through certain formulas or content) or how students will learn (through certain approaches). The shift from writing as content to writing as activity can be more fully explained by assumptions that are central to the post-process perspective. These are, according to Kent, the following: "(1) writing is public; (2) writing is interpretive; and (3) writing is situated" (Introduction 1). As I suggest in this section, because so much post-process scholarship has focused on the rejection of process, we need further explanation about assumptions that support a post-process view of writing. In my attempt to provide more background and explanation of these assumptions, I refer to the work of Donald Davidson, Richard Rorty, Thomas Kuhn, Stanley Fish, and scholars in composition who have discussed these assumptions.

Writing Is Public

The assumption that writing is public grows out of the post-process perspective that meaning making is a product of our communicative interaction with others rather than a product of an individual.[4] Acknowledging the public nature of writing means acknowledging a reading audience—people to whom the writing matters—whether that audience is oneself, another person, a group of people, or any other reader. Emphasizing the public nature of writing reminds us that beyond writing correctly, writers must work toward communicating their message to an audience. It is this goal—being understood—that Kent suggests cannot be "guaranteed"; therefore, we cannot know with certainty if students are successful, nor can we know how to teach students to be successful in communicative interaction. However, we *can* encourage students to become more aware of their interactions with others.

We can further understand the assumption that writing is public by examining the Davidsonian perspective of "language-in-use," a concept that has influenced some post-process scholars, particularly Kent. Davidson explains in "A Nice Derangement of Epitaphs" that language-in-use does not rely on some sort of foundational structure (like Noam Chomsky's deep structure) or even conventions of language. His description of language-in-use has radical implications for the idea that language is contextually or "convention" bound:

> There is no such thing as a language, not if a language is anything like what many philosophers and linguists have supposed. There is therefore no such thing to be learned, mastered, or born with. We must give up the idea of a clearly defined shared structure which language-users acquire and then apply to cases. And we should try again to say how convention in any important sense is involved in language; or, as I think, we should give up the attempt to illuminate how we communicate by appeal to conventions. (446)[5]

Davidson's version of communicative interaction suggests that meaning is not relative to a community or to discourse conventions but is a product of language-in-use, and language-in-use, as Reed Way Dasenbrock explains, is always public and accessible to other language users:

> Networks of meaning, thus, are both inner and outer, including ourselves and others in a web. It is not that we have something unique to say stemming from our personal experience before we negotiate the public structures of meaning, but what we have to say forms as a response to that public structure, to what has come before us and what is being said and done around us. (29)

Davidson terms this public interaction "triangulation," which he understands as the connection between language users and the world.[6] In explaining triangulation, Davidson writes that the "basic idea is that our concept of objectivity—our idea that our thoughts may or may not correspond to the truth—is an idea that we would not have if it weren't for interpersonal relations. In other words, the source of objectivity is intersubjectivity: the triangle consists of two people and the world" (Kent, "Language" 7–8). Triangulation is a key concept for explaining how meanings are located within our communicative interactions with others, and it suggests that we can't know things without knowing others.

The public aspect of writing, which incorporates Davidson's depiction of language-in-use, is already apparent in some writing pedagogies; however, these pedagogies are often described as "dialogic" instead of "post-process" because they emphasize communicative interaction in the teaching of writing. Sánchez outlines a writing pedagogy, for example, as a one-to-one mentored relationship between teacher and student that emphasizes communicative interaction. In this proposed pedagogy, writing instruction is no longer focused on process as content, but rather on class time used to engage students in discourse about writing (see Dobrin, *Constructing* 83–85). Similarly, Ewald suggests that a pedagogy emphasizing communicative interaction would "enjoy an intimate connection between instructional subjects and methods. Writing instruction could be organized around discourse moves" (128).

Other pedagogies that emphasize dialogue employ concepts from Bakhtin—particularly the concepts of heteroglossia and addressivity. Ward explains how these concepts relate to writing pedagogy: "The self in a dialogic pedagogy is not autonomous and solitary but multiple, composed of all the voices or texts one has ever heard or read and therefore capable of playing an infinite number of roles in service of the internal dialogic interaction" (172–73). Using Bakhtinian concepts of dialogue, Ward describes a "functional dialogism," a pedagogy that encourages students to interact with others, thus reinforcing the public aspect of writing:

> Because learning takes place best in communicative interaction, a functional dialogic pedagogy will have to employ a great deal of public writing—that is, writing directed to others capable of and interested in responding—if we are to produce students who are able to generate not only correct, readable prose, but also prose that can elicit a response from others, thereby enabling students to become active participants in communities beyond the classroom. (170)

Dialogue is even more prominent in Kay Halasek's *A Pedagogy of Possibility*, in which she argues that "dialogue has replaced writing as a process as a defining metaphor for the discipline" (3–4). Halasek's decidedly post-process pedagogy emphasizes Bakhtinian scholarship, which she conceptualizes as "a world that recognizes the viability and necessity of existing social, economic, and national languages. Through the concept of dialogism, Bakhtin establishes the critical need to sustain dialogue in the unending quest to maintain difference and diversity, hallmarks of intellectual growth and health . . ." (8). Emphasizing the importance of communicative interaction, Halasek suggests that heteroglossia—reflexivity and response—ought to characterize writing pedagogy.

The assumption that writing is public, therefore, incorporates the idea that meaning is made through our interactions. Terms used to describe this emphasis include language-in-use, communicative interaction, and dialogue, but they all point to the idea that writing is an activity—an interaction with others—rather than content to be mastered.

Writing Is Interpretive

A second assumption of the post-process perspective is that writing is interpretive. That is, the production—not just the reception—of discourse is thoroughly interpretive (or what Rorty calls "interpretation all the way down").[7] This assumption supports the belief that writing is indeterminate, for saying writing is interpretive suggests that meaning is not stable. We can better understand this assumption by reviewing what has been called the "interpretive turn" in philosophy, the claim that what we know is shaped by our interpretations. The interpretive turn, as described by James Bohman, David Hiley, and Richard Shusterman, follows previous philosophical movements such as the "epistemological turn" of the eighteenth century (where knowledge was equated with rational thought, especially the kind of rational thought exemplified by the scientific method) and the "linguistic turn" early in this century, where emphasis was placed on the structure of language and the meanings generated through language systems. According to Bohman, Hiley, and Shusterman, the interpretive turn breaks with these previous traditions by giving up the notion that the essence or the foundations of knowledge and meaning can be discovered: "The views about the foundations of knowledge and the knowing subject that were the basis for the epistemological turn have been called into question, and it has seemed to many philosophers that language and meaning cannot bear the kind of weight the linguistic turn required" (1). When we give up our search for the foundations of knowledge, and when we relinquish our attempts to reduce knowledge and meaning to foundational categories of linguistic or mental states, we encounter the interpretive turn—the acknowledgment that meaning is shaped by our interpretive acts.

Critical to the assumption that writing is interpretive is the degree to which interpretation penetrates. That is, are there some things, ideas, concepts, that are not subject to interpretation? The post-process assumption is that writing is thoroughly interpretive, or what Rorty calls "interpretation all the way down." Bohman, Hiley, and Shusterman explain that the move toward interpretation can take one of two forms: either "hermeneutic universalism" or "hermeneutic contextualism" (7). Hermeneutic universalism holds that interpretation never stops—that communication itself constitutes an interpretive act. Hermeneutic contextualism holds that interpretation takes place within some context, community, or background (7). In short, contextualism suggests that there are limits to interpretation, while universalism does not.

These competing conceptions of interpretation characterize a recurring debate within current hermeneutic theory, and clear examples of this debate are found in the writings of Kuhn and Rorty. For example, in "The Natural and the Human Sciences," Kuhn, a hermeneutic contextualist, notes that both the natural and the human sciences rely on interpretation, but the human sciences rely on interpretation more completely: "The natural sciences, therefore, though they may require what I have called a hermeneutic base, are not themselves hermeneutic enterprises. The human sciences, on the other hand, often are, and they may have no alternative." Kuhn endorses the idea that the natural sciences are more objective, and, finally, more "truthful" than the human sciences because the natural sciences "are not themselves hermeneutic enterprises" (23).

In contrast, Rorty, a hermeneutic universalist, argues that interpretation goes "all the way down": "My fantasy is of a culture so deeply anti-essentialist that it makes only a sociological distinction between sociologists and physicists, not a methodological or philosophical one" (71). In "Inquiry as Recontextualization," Rorty asserts that our minds are "webs of beliefs and desires, of sentential attitudes—webs that continually reweave themselves so as to accommodate new sentential attitudes" (59). For Rorty, both the human sciences and the natural sciences are thoroughly hermeneutic enterprises, and he argues that what we know or could ever know about the world derives from the webs of beliefs and desires that we continually reweave or "recontextualize":

> As one moves along the spectrum from habit to inquiry—from instinctive revision of intentions through routine calculation toward revolutionary science or politics—the number of beliefs added to or subtracted from the web increases. At a certain point in this process it becomes useful to speak of "recontextualization." The more widespread the changes, the more use

we have for the notion of "a new context." This new context can be a new explanatory theory, a new comparison class, a new descriptive vocabulary, a new private or political purpose, the latest book one has read, the last person one talked to; the possibilities are endless. (60–61)

According to Rorty, interpretation—what he calls "reinterpretation" and "recontextualization"—never ceases, for every interpretation is based on a previous interpretation. The different views about the power of interpretation held by Rorty and Kuhn exemplify the current debate concerning hermeneutic universalism and hermeneutic contextualization that we encounter in studies of both the reception and the production of discourse.

To understand writing as a thoroughly interpretive activity (in the spirit of hermeneutic universalism) means accepting that no foundational knowledge is the basis for writing as a discipline. Given this assumption, we can better understand the post-process rejection of mastery and its depiction and consequent rejection of process as a foundational body of knowledge. In addition, when we understand writing as thoroughly interpretive, we must also accept the indeterminate nature of the writing activity. Writing becomes an activity that requires an understanding of context, interaction with others, and our attempts to communicate a message. Understanding interpretation as universal helps illuminate the third post-process assumption: that writing is situated.

WRITING IS SITUATED

The assumption that writing is situated also illustrates the indeterminacy of the writing act, as writing must correspond to specific contexts that naturally vary. Of all three post-process assumptions, the assumption that writing is situated has been discussed most frequently by scholars interested in postmodern or anti-foundationalist perspectives. For example, James Sosnoski asserts that postmodern classrooms "do not have to follow a single blueprint and should change according to the situation" (210). Also endorsing situatedness, Thomas Barker and Fred Kemp explain that postmodernism is "a self-conscious acknowledgment of the immediate present and an attempt to respond to it in new ways" (1). James Berlin draws on postmodern thought and social-epistemic rhetoric to suggest that pedagogy becomes enforced through "dialectical interaction, working out a rhetoric more adequate to the historical moment and the actual conditions of teacher and students" (25). Situatedness, for these postmodern scholars, refers to the ability to respond to specific situations rather than rely on foundational principles or rules.

Situatedness has been discussed similarly in the anti-foundationalist perspective. For example, Patricia Bizzell asserts that "an anti-foundationalist understanding of discourse would see the student's way of thinking and interacting with the world, the student's very self, as fundamentally altered by participation in any new discourse" (43). She includes situatedness in her definition of rhetoric: "Rhetoric is the study of the personal, social and historical elements in human discourse—how to recognize them, interpret them, and act on them, in terms both of situational context and of verbal style" (52). Likewise, Susan Wells suggests that technical writing pedagogy should help students enter into communicative action and to help them understand their situatedness (264). Further, in "Teaching Professional Writing as Social Praxis," Thomas Miller suggests that we need to teach technical writing not as *techné* (or cognitive skills) but as *praxis*, which means that writers must understand the situations and contexts that surround them: "We can foster such 'practical wisdom' by developing a pedagogy that contributes to our students' ability to locate themselves and their professional communities in the larger public context" (68).

While situatedness has been addressed more explicitly in these passages, we can see traces of all three post-process assumptions in this scholarship. They are evident in assertions that writing should *change with the situation*, that students *interact with the world* through *dialectical interaction*, and that rhetoric involves *interpretation of social and historical elements of human discourse*. Given these similarities, we see that post-process scholarship is not advocating new directions, but rather endorsing anti-foundationalist and postmodern approaches that have already been articulated. To see writing in terms of post-process assumptions—as public, interpretive, and situated—encourages us to think of writing as an indeterminate activity rather than a body of knowledge to be mastered. These post-process assumptions (strongly influenced by postmodern and anti-foundationalist perspectives) finally shed light on how post-process theory might inform teaching.

POST-PROCESS PEDAGOGY?

My purpose thus far has been to reveal the post-process rejection of mastery and to outline the anti-foundationalist assumptions informing post-process theory. In doing so, I have suggested that post-process theory rejects system-based explanations of writing and embraces indeterminacy in the writing act. Given this understanding of post-process theory, in this final section I assert that post-process theory resists pedagogical agendas that are comprised of content, but that it offers valuable pedagogical principles about the activity of teaching. I discuss implications of these principles, which include mentoring and tutorial approaches to writing instruction.

Understanding the anti-foundationalist nature of post-process theory places us, as Dobrin suggests, "at an awkward crossroads" *(Constructing* 86). To articulate any kind of pedagogy based on anti-foundationalism would be to support the claim that knowledge can be rooted in a particular approach or system and, therefore, would no longer be anti-foundational. It is for this reason that I do not advocate a specific pedagogical agenda that espouses post-process theory, for I believe doing so presents an inherent paradox. Fish more clearly explains that we ought not to place too much pedagogical stock in anti-foundationalist assumptions such as situatedness:

> To put the matter in a nutshell, the knowledge that one is in a situation has no particular payoff for any situation you happen to be in, because the constraints of that situation will not be relaxed by that knowledge. It follows, then, that teaching our students the lesson of anti-foundationalism, while it will put them in possession of a new philosophical perspective, will not give them a tool for operating in the world they already inhabit. Being told that you are in a situation will help you neither to dwell in it more perfectly nor to *write* within it more successfully. (351)

Similarly, if we accept the post-process perspective that writing is indeterminate, public, interpretive, and situated, there is little we can do with this knowledge.

When it comes to pedagogy, however, the temptation is to turn our revelations into content to be delivered in the classroom, thereby falling prey to what Dobrin calls the "pedagogical imperative." While we may want to translate the post-process assumptions (writing is public, interpretive, and situated) into content to have our students learn, what good does this do? I completely agree with Dobrin that the force of the "pedagogical imperative" is alive and well and also that it is premature in relation to post-process theory. Dobrin suggests that post-process theory is too new to generate pedagogical insights—that its discussions should be theoretical at this point *(Constructing* 64). While I agree with Dobrin, I suggest that because of the anti-foundationalist influence on post-process theory, it is unlikely that we will *ever* see a "post-process pedagogy," complete with neat, bulleted points about applying a specific approach to the writing classroom. Fish is again insightful here, for he argues a similar point in declaring that the project to develop a postmodern or anti-foundationalist pedagogy should be abandoned—not simply because the project would be difficult, but because it is impossible. According to Fish, anti-foundationalism only helps us understand *that* we are situated. He argues that we can do nothing with this knowledge, and we certainly can't put it to use. In the conclusion of "Anti-Foundationalism, Theory Hope, and the Teaching of Composition," Fish offers a kind of apology for this view: "Perhaps I should apologize for taking up so much of your time in return for so small a yield; but the smallness of the yield has been my point. It is also the point of anti-foundationalism, which offers you nothing but the assurance that what it is unable to give you—knowledge, goals, purposes, strategies—is what you already have" (355). Similarly, I offer a kind of apology that I have no specific pedagogical agenda to offer that I could claim would be "post-process pedagogy," for I don't believe such an agenda is compatible with the theory.

More to the point, Fish's viewpoint actualizes, in my opinion, the "letting go" of the discipline that Petraglia spoke of in terms of post-process theory. Petraglia suggests that instructors of writing need to let go of the idea that writing is built on a foundational body of knowledge and accept the idea that we need to focus on situational response. Likewise, we must resist the temptation to turn our understanding of post-process assumptions into content to be delivered and mastered by students. Accepting post-process assumptions truly implies a "letting go" of the desire to find a right way to learn and teach writing.

While post-process theory does not offer concrete pedagogical agendas based on content, I believe that it offers valuable pedagogical principles that guide our practice as teachers. I see two main principles that post-process theory can offer pedagogy: the rejection of mastery and the engagement in dialogue rather than monologue with students. I have already illustrated these principles in my explanation of post-process assumptions (writing is public, interpretive, and situated), so I won't explain them again here. It is worth noting, however, that these principles have been present in previous scholarship about composition pedagogy, alternative pedagogies, and pragmatic theories dating back to John Dewey. We need to recognize that these post-process principles are not out in left field but, rather, that they support excellent scholarship in education. It is worth briefly reviewing these principles, most notably in the scholarship of Dewey and Paulo Freire.

We find traces of the rejection of mastery and engagement in dialogue in Dewey's declaration that education is a social process instead of subject matter (230). In "My Pedagogic Creed," Dewey suggests that "the only true education comes through the stimulation of the child's powers by the demands of the social situations in which he finds himself," that education is a lifelong process, and that school "must represent present life—life as real and vital to the child as that which he carries on in the home, in the neighborhood, or on the playground" (229, 230–31). In declaring these beliefs, he rejects the idea that education is a fixed body of knowledge to be transmitted passively to the student: "I believe, therefore, that the true centre of correlation of the school subjects is not science, nor literature, nor history, nor geography, but the child's own social activities" (232). The idea is that the rote learning of subject matter, without understanding its relevance to one's situation and the world, does not improve one's education. Dewey's ideas resonate with the post-process rejection of system-based writing approaches and its emphasis on language-in-use.

In some regards, an even more striking resemblance exists between post-process principles and the work of Freire, particularly his notion of the "banking concept." In *Pedagogy of the Oppressed*, Freire describes the banking concept as "an act of depositing, in which the students are the depositories and the teacher is the depositor. Instead of communicating, the teacher issues communiques and makes deposits which the students patiently receive, memorize, and repeat" (67). Freire considers the banking method of teaching to be a dehumanizing practice that ultimately reinforces teachers as oppressors, controlling knowledge, and students as the oppressed, incapable of response (68). In place of the banking concept of education, Freire advocates a "problem-posing" concept of education, which would require students to play active rather than passive roles:

> Those truly committed to liberation must reject the banking concept in its entirety, adopting instead a concept of women and men as conscious beings and consciousness intent upon the world. They must abandon the educational goal of deposit-making and replace it with the posing of the problems of human beings in their relationship with the world. (74)

By suggesting that critical consciousness requires that students must communicate with the world, not just be in the world, Freire illustrates the post-process emphasis on writing as public interaction with others and the world. And he emphasizes the social aspect of education when he asserts that human life can only have meaning through communication (72). He encourages the teacher-student relationship to be a "partnership" in which teacher and student engage in two-way dialogue. To do so requires a dialogic relationship between students and teacher in which roles of the traditional banking concept of education no longer exist and in which "the students—no longer docile listeners—are now critical co-investigators in dialogue with the teacher" (70,75). Although Freire's pedagogy is thoroughly ideological—a premise Dewey's pedagogy does not share to the same degree—both principles of rejection of mastery and engagement of dialogue can be seen in this scholarship.

In composition studies, we have also heard these principles before. As I outlined earlier in this essay, postmodern and anti-foundationalist "pedagogies" have advocated writing as situated, interpretive, and public rather than based on foundational knowledge, and several "dialogic" pedagogies have also been discussed in composition scholarship. Although the principles of rejection of mastery and engagement in dialogue have been discussed in previous scholarship, what is different about post-process theory is the combination of these principles in one theoretical perspective, as well as its sharp criticism of the dominant paradigm in composition studies. These features of post-process theory push the discipline forward in a most pronounced way, as its very name suggests.

Although I am unable to produce specific content-based pedagogical agendas that can be immediately transferred to the classroom, I do suggest that the rejection of mastery and engagement in dialogue lead to an important implication for how we teach writing: such a stance helps us reconsider teaching as an act of mentoring rather than a job in which we deliver content. To think of teaching as mentoring means spending time and energy on our interactions with students—listening to them, discussing ideas with them, letting them make mistakes, and pointing them in the right direction. This type of teacher-student relationship demonstrates instruction that is collaborative and dialogic, and it in fact reflects Kent's suggestions for pedagogy in *Paralogic Rhetoric*: "By working in partnership with their students, mentors would no longer stand outside their students' writing and reading experiences. Instead, they would become an integral part of their students' learning experiences . . ." (166). This type of mentoring suggests a release of the idea of mastery and the embrace of indeterminacy in teaching situations. Indeed, the connection could be made that like the post-process description of writing, the act of *teaching* is also public, interpretive, and situated—another type of indeterminate activity.

Given this emphasis on mentoring, I believe the strongest application of post-process theory is in the practice of one-to-one instruction that manifests itself in teacher-student interactions. Kent, Sánchez, Ward, and Halasek have come to similar conclusions, drawing attention to dialogue between teacher-student and to student-student interactions in the classroom. I support the kind of one-to-one, dialogic instruction these scholars have advocated; however, their descriptions of one-to-one interactions tend to be broad and abstract, leaving readers with little concrete sense of how post-process theory might apply to one-to-one instruction. For purposes of illustration, a more immediate and tangible application of post-process theory might exist in tutorial interactions between tutors and students in writing centers. Writing centers provide a concrete context for post-process theory because one-to-one interactions are the primary practice of writing center tutors, as well as the subject of writing center research. For example,

Christina Murphy and Steve Sherwood suggest that the essence of tutoring is *conversation,* or language-in-use (2). Similarly, Eric Hobson suggests that writing center scholarship often derives its credibility from practice, or "lore." In addition, illustrations of one-to-one teaching interactions abound in writing center literature; many scholars have addressed the dynamics of teaching interactions, teacher-student roles, and methods involved in one-to-one writing instruction.[8] Given that post-process theory emphasizes dialogue in writing instruction, as well as the importance of mentoring, and given that such dialogue in writing instruction is the core of writing center work, the connection between post-process theory and writing center pedagogy is easy to support.

Post-process theory, then, could find immediate application in writing center work and could benefit from writing center scholarship about one-to-one teaching. Alternatively, writing centers could benefit from post-process theory in exploring theoretical avenues to support writing center practice. There exists a wonderful irony in this connection because of the sometimes perceived gap in prestige between post-process theory and writing center practice. That is, post-process theory, at least in the terms Dobrin describes, appears on the surface to be an ivory-tower endeavor. Writing centers, on the other hand, because of their focus on practice, have historically been marginalized and have consequently struggled to legitimize scholarship based on tutorial practice. The connection between the two might result in a happy marriage. For instance, anti-foundationalist and postmodernist perspectives are appearing more frequently in writing center scholarship.[9] Traces of the public, situated, and interpretive aspects of post-process theory in writing centers exist in Joan Mullin's suggestion that writing centers "provide spaces where the personal and public, the individual and other, struggle to honor the singular voice, to recognize different language communities" (xiii). In addition, claims such as that expressed by Hobson ("no single theory can dictate writing center instruction") are reminiscent of the post-process rejection of a grand theory or narrative to describe communicative practice (8). The union of post-process theory and writing center practice could potentially demonstrate how theory and practice could live in harmony, providing both illustration and explanation of one-to-one writing instruction. Of course, while there are some interesting overlaps between post-process theory and writing center work, asserting a strong connection would require another lengthy and careful discussion, which I do not have time to develop here. But I do see this connection as a fruitful area for future research, and I see writing centers as an immediate illustration of the kind of instructional dialogue post-process theory endorses.

For the purposes of my discussion here, however, I wish to suggest that post-process theory is, at its very core, concerned with pedagogical practice.

In asserting this claim, I disagree with those scholars who suggest post-process theory should remain a theoretical enterprise, and I suggest that post-process theory is most decidedly connected to a *how-centered* approach to teaching. Critiques that deny any pedagogical relevance of post-process theory are, I believe, based on the expectation that pedagogy is what-centered and needs to produce a concrete pedagogical agenda based on content. The real pedagogical thrust of post-process theory has to do not with content or subject matter, but rather with *what we do with content*. As such, post-process theory has much to offer teachers in any discipline, whether they teach writing, math, physics, women's studies, history, or occupational therapy, for the pedagogical thrust of post-process theory is in its reminder that teaching does not equal mastery of content but rather how teachers and students can interact with one another *about* content. Thus, in addition to posing the question "what does it mean to write?" post-process theory also poses the question "what does it mean to teach?"

LETTING GO

As discerning scholars, we must not take post-process theory at face value, associating it only with a critique of process. If, as many post-process scholars articulate, post-process theory means accepting an anti-foundationalist perspective and adopting language-in-use, then its relevance to pedagogy is to encourage us to reexamine the "foundations" from which we may have been operating, as well as our communicative practices with students. Even if this examination does not make anti-foundationalists out of us, it reminds us to think carefully about our teaching practices, to avoid co-opting or reducing complex research in composition studies, and to become more aware of our interactions with students in the classroom.

"Letting go" in the case of post-process theory does not mean an avoidance of the teaching of writing; it does not mean becoming irresponsible teachers. It means, quite frankly, the opposite. It means becoming teachers who are more in tune to the pedagogical needs of students, more willing to discuss ideas, more willing to listen, more willing to be moved by moments of mutual understanding. It means, in sum, to be more conscientious in our attempts to meet the needs of students in their educational journeys. Post-process theory does not prescribe a pedagogy and ask us to adopt it blindly. Rather, it enhances our sensitivity as teachers, our knowledge and expertise, and the way we communicate with students to help them learn. In short, post-process theory asks us to take a close look at ourselves as teachers. Thinking through the principles of rejection of mastery and engagement in dialogue provides all teachers with a valuable philosophical exercise.[10]

NOTES

1. See, for example, Olson; Pullman; Kent, "Introduction."

2. See Petraglia; Dobrin, "Constructing"; Kent, "Introduction"; Pullman.

3. See, for example, Pullman, Olson, Couture.

4. In his *Paralogic Rhetoric*, Kent identifies this assumption with "externalism."

5. We can note similarities between Davidson's argument that "there is no such thing as language" and Kent's argument that "we cannot teach writing . . . for nothing exists to teach." Both arguments reject the idea that language and writing are comprised of foundational systems.

6. The term "triangulation" that Davidson uses is not to be confused with the term "triangulation" that denotes qualitative research methodology in which data are compiled from three or more perspectives to establish a more verifiable analysis.

7. While much has been discussed about interpretation in the reception of discourse—for example, Stanley Fish's concept of interpretive communities and how meaning is received—little has been discussed about the interpretive nature of writing or speaking.

8. See, for example, Murphy and Sherwood; Hobson; Harris; Black; Clark; Mullin and Wallace.

9. See Nancy Grimm's fine book, *Good Intentions: Writing Center Work for Postmodern Times*, as well as scholarship by Hobson and Abascal-Hildebrand.

10. I wish to thank colleagues who reviewed this article and provided comments that contributed to substantive improvements: Peter T. Breuch, Thomas Kent, Mary Lay, John Logie, David Beard, and James Thomas Zebroski.

WORKS CITED

Abascal-Hildebrand, Mary. "Tutor and Student Relations: Applying Gadamer's Notions of Translation." Mullin and Wallace 172–83.

Barker, Thomas T., and Fred O. Kemp. "Network Theory: A Postmodern Pedagogy for the Writing Classroom." *Computers and Community: Teaching Composition in the Twenty-First Century*. Ed. Carolyn Handa. Portsmouth: Boynton, 1990. 1–27.

Berlin, James A. "Poststructuralism, Cultural Studies, and the Composition Classroom: Postmodern Theory in Practice." *Rhetoric Review* 11 (1992): 16–33.

Bizzell, Patricia A. "Foundationalism and Anti-Foundationalism in Composition Studies." *Pre/Text* 7.1–2 (1986): 37–56.

Black, Laurel Johnson. *Between Talk and Teaching: Reconsidering the Writing Conference*. Logan: Utah State UP, 1998.

Bohman, James F., David R. Hiley, and Richard Shusterman. "Introduction: The Interpretive Turn." Hiley, Bohman, and Shusterman 1–14.

Clark, Gregory. *Dialogue, Dialectic, and Conversation: A Social Perspective on the Function of Writing*. Carbondale: Southern Illinois UP, 1990.

Couture, Barbara. "Modeling and Emulating: Rethinking Agency in the Writing Process." Kent, *Post-Process* 30–48.

Dasenbrock, Reed Way. "Do We Write the Text We Read?" *Literary Theory After Davidson*. Ed. Reed Way Dasenbrock. University Press: Pennsylvania State UP, 1993. 18–36.

———. "The Myths of the Subjective and of the Subject in Composition Studies." *Journal of Advanced Composition* 13 (1993): 21–32.

Davidson, Donald. "A Nice Derangement of Epitaphs." *Inquiries into Truth and Interpretation: Perspectives on the Philosophy of Donald Davidson.* Ed. Ernst LePore. New York: Oxford UP, 1984. 433–46.

Dewey, John. "My Pedagogic Creed." 1897. *The Essential Dewey: Pragmatism, Education, Democracy.* Ed. Larry A. Hickman and Thomas M. Alexander. Vol. 1. Bloomington: Indiana UP, 1998. 229–35.

Dobrin, Sidney I. *Constructing Knowledges: The Politics of Theory-Building and Pedagogy in Composition.* Albany: State U of New York P, 1997.

———. "Paralogic Hermeneutic Theories, Power, and the Possibility for Liberating Pedagogies." Kent, *Post-Process* 132–48.

Ede, Lisa. "Reading the Writing Process." *Taking Stock: The Writing Process Movement in the '90s.* Ed. Lad Tobin and Thomas Newkirk. Portsmouth: Boynton, 1994. 31–43.

Elbow, Peter. *Writing without Teachers.* New York: Oxford UP, 1973.

Emig, Janet. *The Composing Processes of Twelfth Graders.* Urbana, IL: NCTE, 1971.

Ewald, Helen Rothschild. "A Tangled Web of Discourses: On Post-Process Pedagogy and Communicative Interaction." Kent, *Post-Process* 116–31.

Fish, Stanley. "Anti-Foundationalism, Theory Hope, and the Teaching of Composition." *Doing What Comes Naturally: Change, Rhetoric, and the Practice of Theory in Literary and Legal Studies.* Durham: Duke UP, 1989. 315–41.

———. "Consequences." *Doing What Comes Naturally: Change, Rhetoric, and the Practice of Theory in Literary and Legal Studies.* Durham: Duke UP, 1989. 342–55.

Flower, Linda, and John Hayes. "Identifying the Organization of the Writing Processes." *Cognitive Processes in Writing.* Ed. Lee W. Gregg and Erwin R. Steinberg. Hillsdale: Erlbaum, 1980. 3–30.

Foster, David. "The Challenge of Contingency: Process and the Turn to the Social in Composition." Kent, *Post-Process* 149–62.

Freire, Paulo. *Pedagogy of the Oppressed.* Rpt. in *The Paulo Freire Reader.* Ed. Ana Maria Araujo Freire and Donaldo Macedo. New York: Continuum, 1998.

Grimm, Nancy Maloney. *Good Intentions: Writing Center Work for Postmodern Times.* Portsmouth: Boynton, 1999.

Halasek, Kay. *A Pedagogy of Possibility: Bakhtinian Perspectives on Composition Studies.* Carbondale: Southern Illinois UP, 1999.

Harris, Muriel. *Teaching One to One: The Writing Conference.* Urbana, IL: NCTE: 55–75,1986.

Hiley, David R., James F. Bohman, and Richard Shusterman, eds. *The Interpretive Turn: Philosophy, Science, Culture.* Ithaca: Cornell UP, 1991.

Hobson, Eric H. "Writing Center Practice Often Counters Its Theory. So What?" Mullin and Wallace 1–10.

Kent, Thomas. Introduction. Kent, *Post-Process* 1–6.

———. "Language Philosophy, Writing, and Reading: A Conversation with Donald Davidson." *Journal of Advanced Composition* 13 (1993): 1–20.

———. *Paralogic Rhetoric: A Theory of Communicative Interaction.* Lewisburg: Bucknell UP, 1993.

———, ed. *Post-Process Theory: Beyond the Writing-Process Paradigm.* Carbondale: Southern Illinois UP, 1999.

Kuhn, Thomas S. "The Natural and the Human Sciences." Hiley, Bohman, and Shusterman 17–24.

Lindemann, Erika. *A Rhetoric for Writing Teachers*. 3rd ed. New York: Oxford UP, 1995.

Macrorie, Ken. *Writing to Be Read*. Rochelle Park, NJ: Hayden, 1976.

McComiskey, Bruce. "The Post-Process Movement in Composition Studies." *Reforming College Composition: Writing the Wrongs*. Ed. Ray Wallace, Alan Jackson, and Susan Lewis Wallace. London: Greenwood, 2000. 37–53.

Miller, Thomas P. "Treating Professional Writing as Social *Praxis*." *Journal of Advanced Composition* 11 (1991): 57–72.

Mullin, Joan A. "Introduction: The Theory Behind the Centers." Mullin and Wallace vii–xiii.

Mullin, Joan A., and Ray Wallace, eds. *Intersections: Theory-Practice in the Writing Center*. Urbana, IL: NCTE, 1994.

Murphy, Christina, and Steve Sherwood. "The Tutoring Process: Exploring Paradigms and Practices." *The St. Martin's Sourcebook for Writing Tutors*. New York: St. Martin's, 1995. 1–18.

Murray, Donald M. *A Writer Teaches Writing*. Boston: Houghton, 1968.

Olson, Gary A. "Toward a Post-Process Composition: Abandoning the Rhetoric of Assertion." Kent, *Post-Process* 7–15.

Petraglia, Joseph. "Is There Life after Process? The Role of Social Scientism in a Changing Discipline." Kent, *Post-Process* 49–64.

Pullman, George. "Stepping Yet Again into the Same Current." Kent, *Post-Process* 16–29.

Rorty, Richard. "Inquiry as Recontextualization: An Anti-Dualist Account of Interpretation." Hiley, Bohman, and Shusterman 59–80.

Russell, David. "Activity Theory and Process Approaches: Writing in School and Society." Kent, *Post-Process* 80–95.

Sosnoski, James J. "Postmodern Teachers in Their Postmodern Classrooms: Socrates Begone!" *Contending with Words: Composition and Rhetoric in a Postmodern Age*. Ed. Patricia Harkin and John Schilb. New York: MLA, 1991. 198–219.

Wallace, David. "Reconsidering Behaviorist Composition Pedagogies: Positivism, Empiricism, and the Paradox of Postmodernism." *Journal of Advanced Composition* 6 (1996): 103–17.

Ward, Irene. *Literacy, Ideology, and Dialogue: Towards a Dialogic Pedagogy*. Albany: State U of New York P, 1994.

Wells, Susan. "Jürgen Habermas, Communicative Competence, and the Teaching of Technical Discourse." *Theory in the Classroom*. Ed. Cary Nelson. Urbana: U of Illinois P, 1986. 245–69.

Young, Richard E. "Paradigms and Problems: Needed Research in Rhetorical Invention." *Research on Composing: Points of Departure*. Ed. Charles R. Cooper and Lee Odell. Urbana: NCTE, 1978. 29–47.

Talking in Terms of Discourse
What It Is; How It's Taught

Research and introspection became the ways of discovering something about how one goes about writing. And part of that writing involves the writer's intentions in directing what is written to an audience: readers located in particular social contexts. In effect, then, the givens of our conversations include how our acts are rhetorical acts. That is, writing is a matter of someone saying something to someone within a given context using the tools of writing. The writer, the reader, and the text constitute the essential elements of the rhetorical triangle contained in classical rhetoric's *ethos*, *pathos*, and *logos*. James Kinneavy makes explicit the implicit fourth element in that triangle—the context. It is in this tradition of ancient rhetoric that James Kinneavy and Frank D'Angelo classify the various elements of written discourse, D'Angelo explicitly creating an ontology of discourse.

To some extent, each essay in this section is concerned with matters of mind: ontology, epistemology, psychology. The precedent is old. The second book to Aristotle's rhetoric, in many ways still the basis of academic rules of written discourse, provides a psychology of audiences. Eighteenth-century rhetorician George Campbell, and the nineteenth century's Alexander Bain, each turns to psychology to explain the processes involved in rhetorical acts. Kenneth Burke, perhaps the most noted rhetorician of the twentieth century, writes of a newly invigorated rhetoric that would turn to the insights of the "new sciences," including psychology. As we have seen, psychological matters influence the research that emerges as writing-as-process. Psychology also influences James Britton's looks to how early-childhood fluency in writing is accomplished. And there is a kind of psychology to Witte and Faigley's concerns with how coherence and cohesion are accomplished in writing.

James Berlin outlines the different epistemological assumptions that arise within the history of western rhetoric and their implications for composition theory by looking to the dynamic interplay among the various elements of the epistemological field. In other words, Berlin outlines what he sees as the underlying assumptions about the relations among words, thoughts, and the things represented in those words and thoughts that are implicit in various approaches to teaching composition. His categories (as presented both in his essay in this section and in another included later in this collection) become the terms with which we discuss ideological and epistemological assumptions about discourse and writing instruction. The other essays in this section look to the parts of a discourse in order to understand the whole more readily, asking how rigidly writers construct paragraphs or thesis sentences within paragraphs, and what it is that constitutes grammar and grammar instruction as part of teaching writing. All try to define what we're talking about when we talk about written discourse.

The Basic Aims of Discourse

JAMES L. KINNEAVY

INTRODUCTION

Most of us make implicit assumptions about the aims of discourse when we loosely distinguish expository writing from literature or creative writing, and, no doubt, there is some validity to the distinction. Many college composition textbooks often assume a similar distinction and address themselves to the province of expository writing. But it may be that this simple distinction is too simple and that other aims of discourse ought to be given some consideration. It is this question which I would like to investigate in this paper.

First, at least one working definition. I am concerned with complete discourse, not individual sentences or even paragraphs. It is often impossible to determine the aim of an individual sentence or paragraph without its full context. The same sentence or even paragraph in another context may have a very different aim. "Discourse" here means the full text, oral or written, delivered at a specific time and place or delivered at several instances. A discourse may be a single sentence, "Fire," screamed from a hotel window, or a joke, or a sonnet, or a three-hour talk, or a tragedy, or Toynbee's twelve volumes of *A Study of History*. Sometimes the determination of text is difficult: a conversation may trail off into another one; a novel like *Sanctuary* may pick up years later in *Requiem for a Nun*; there are trilogies in drama and novel, etc.; but usually the determination of text is a fairly simple matter.

By aim of discourse is meant the effect that the discourse is oriented to achieve in the average listener or reader for whom it is intended. It is the intent as embodied in the discourse, the intent of the work, as traditional

Reprinted from *College Composition and Communication* 20.4 (December 1969): 297–304. Used with permission.

philosophy called it. Is the work intended to delight or to persuade or to inform or to demonstrate the logical proof of a position? These would be typical aims.

The determination of the basic aims of discourse and some working agreement in this area among rhetoricians would be a landmark in the field of composition. For it is to the achievement of these aims that all our efforts as teachers of composition are directed.

Yet a classification of diverse aims of discourse must not be interpreted as the establishing of a set of iron-clad categories which do not overlap. Such an exercise must be looked upon as any scientific exercise—an abstraction from certain aspects of reality in order to focus attention on and carefully analyze the characteristics of some feature of reality in a scientific vacuum, as it were. The scientist who is attempting to formulate the law of gravity isolates the gravitational forces from air resistance, from surface variations, from electric attraction, etc., and hopefully postulates a principle of gravity. The re-insertion into real situations wherein wind, surface variations, electricity and other forces intervene comes later. Similarly, an attempt to formulate the nature of information, as such, must operate in a discourse vacuum which momentarily abstracts from the fact that information can be used in propaganda or be a component of a literary discourse. In actual practice such pure discourses as information devoid of persuasion, or persuasion devoid of information, or literature without some personal expression, and so forth, are almost non-existent or as rare as the laboratory concept of gravitation. But that does not destroy the validity of the classifications.

THE DETERMINATION OF THE AIMS OF DISCOURSE

Some Negative and Some External Norms

There are some useful cautions about determination of aims made in literary theory by W. K. Wimsatt and Monroe Beardsley which can be extended to discourse theory. It is dangerous in literature (and even more in persuasion) to assume that what the author says he is trying to do is actually what the work really accomplishes. To determine the aim by author intent is to run the risk of the "intentional fallacy." A parallel danger is to assume that the reaction of a given reader is an accurate indication of purpose. This fallacy has been termed the "affective fallacy" by Wimsatt and Beardsley.[1] The stated intentions of the author and the reactions of a given reader are useful markers that can point to significant evidence in the discourse itself, as the linguist Michael Riffaterre points out;[2] for this reason they should not be disregarded. Similarly, many authors advise us to take into account the cultural conventions of the genre employed; anthropologists like Malinowski warn of the importance of the immediate historical context; McLuhan emphasizes the significance of the medium used; Kenneth Burke writes a whole book on the influence of the semantic range, the grammar he calls it, of the motivational field; and even the grammatical choices offered by the language can restrict and modify the aim, as Sapir and Whorf caution us. All of these, external to the discourse, are nonetheless weighty determinants of aim and are so many arguments against the mythical autonomy of the text.

Internal Norms of Aim

Among the writers who have sought to establish the aims of discourse by norms internal to the discourse there is considerable variation in the kind of norm singled out. Yet there is a surprising measure of agreement among the analysts on so fundamental an issue. In Figure 1, I have attempted to show some of these various approaches, together with the principle of division and the resulting classifications of aims of discourse. The parallel classifications of the various systems are indicated in the horizontal rows. All of the authorities whom I have analyzed could not be presented on a single page, so I have only indicated typical representatives of various approaches.

The eldest and most persistent approach in western civilization is that beginning in Plato, codified by Aristotle, continued by the medieval Arab philosophers Averröes and Avicenna, Aquinas and Albertus Magnus, and passed on to modern times by the classical tradition and some comparative philologists, like Joshua Whatmough. Aristotle and Aquinas distinguish a *scientific* use of language achieving certainty, a *dialectical* use of language operating in the area of probability, a *rhetorical* or persuasive use of language based on seeming probability, and a *poetic* use of language incorporating a rigid but internal probability. The principle of division is obviously a scale of diminishing probability.[3]

Ernst Cassirer, examining the historical sequence of Greek views on the functions of language, sees first a *mythological* view of language as a medium for expressing the aspirations of early Greek society. This partially (though not at all totally) corresponds to Aristotle's poetic function. This was followed by a period in which it was felt by the philosophers that language was admirably suited to mirror or represent the universe. This *metaphysical* period, as he calls it, corresponds to Aristotle's scientific use of language. The practical or *pragmatic* use of language by the sophists and rhetoricians

Figure 1 A comparison of some systems of aims of discourse.

SCHOOL	Aristotle and Aquinas	Cassirer	Morris	Miller	Russell	Reichenbach	Richards	Bühler, Jakobson, Kinneavy
PRINCIPLE OF DIVISION	Level of Probability	Historical Sequence in Greece	Behavioral Reactions of Animals to Stimuli	Socio-Psych. Motives for Communications	Grammar (Kinds of Sentences)	Faculty Addresses to	Proportions of Reference and Emotion	Component of Communication Process Stressed
	Scientific —certain	Metaphysical —representative of the world	Informative	Informative —to increase uniformity of information	Informative —declarative	Communicative (thoughts to be believed)	Scientific (pure reference)	Reference Informative Scientific
	Dialectical —probable		Valuative	Opinion —to increase uniformity of opinions	Questioning —interrogative			Exploratory
	Rhetorical —seemingly probable	Pragmatic —practical use by Sophists	Incitive	Status change	Imperative —imperative	Promotive (actions to be accomplished)	Rhetorical (mixed reference and emotion)	Persuasive
	Poetic —internally probable						Poetic (pure emotion)	Literary
		Mythological —expressive of aspirations Interjectional	Systemic	Emotive	Expressive (of emotion) —exclamatory	Suggestive (emotions to be aroused)		Expressive

came next. Finally, Democritus pointed to a basic and initial *interjectional* or emotive use of language—to which Aristotle has no direct parallel.[4]

In the next column of Figure 1, C. W. Morris, the semiotician, bases his aims of discourse on a behavioral analysis of how animals react to stimuli. The animal first *informs* itself of the features of its environment, then *evaluates* the seemingly useful features, then responds to these as *incitive* "stimuli," and finally *systematizes* his signs in order to achieve the purpose for which he engaged in this expressive activity. There is a rough approximation here to Aristotle's scientific, dialectic, and rhetorical functions. Morris' systemic has some affinity with the expressive function of the others on the chart.[5]

George Miller, a communication theorist, establishes his distinctions on the socio-psychological motives for the communications which are revealed in the discourse. The *informative* use of language attempts to increase uniformity of fact and information in the community; the *opinion* use of language attempts to increase uniformity of the probable in the society; the *status change* use of language is oriented to improve one's societal position; and the *emotive* use is oriented to individual satisfaction in an expressive use of language. The similarities to the preceding systems are fairly obvious.[6]

In an interesting chapter on "The Uses of Language" in *Human Knowledge, Its Scope and Limits*, Bertrand Russell takes issue with the dominant logical positivist view of a simple dichotomy of referential and emotive uses of language and distinguishes the informative, the questioning, the promotive and the emotional uses of language. These correspond quite naturally to the kinds of rhetorical sentences in the language: declarative, interrogative, imperative, and exclamatory. These *image* quite closely Miller's, Morris' and Aristotle's categories, though the principle of division is different in each.[7]

Hans Reichenbach, a logical positivist, in a brief introduction to his book on symbolic logic, differentiates functions of language by the faculty appealed to in the discourse. He therefore distinguishes a communicative use emphasizing thoughts to be believed by the intellect, from a promotive use directed to actions to be accomplished, from a suggestive use oriented to emotions to be aroused.[8]

Both Reichenbach and Richards take the logical positivist position as their springboard. Richards emphasizes the kind of reference found in the discourse. In his various books, Richards suggests various categories of discourse. I have followed here the distinctions to be found in *How to Read a Page* and *Principles of Literary Criticism* rather than some of his other works. Discourses exist in a continuum with decreasing referential and increasing emotive affirmations. Pure reference discourse is scientific, pure emotive discourse is poetic. Any appreciable mixture of the two is rhetoric. Further subdivisions of the mixed area (rhetoric) are generally useless.[9]

The equating of poetry with emotive discourse in Richards is a common phenomenon among these classificatory systems—a fact the figure illustrates. Sometimes poetry is subsumed under emotive, sometimes poetry is equated to the emotive (as in Richards). Sometimes there is no provision for one or the other—thus Aristotle makes no room for expressive discourse as such, though emotion is important for his concept of catharsis in poetry and in the whole second book of his *Rhetoric*.

The last column of the figure distinguishes aims by the focus on the component of the communication process which is stressed in a given discourse. At one time I thought that this principle of classification was original with me, but I later found that Karl Bühler, a German psychologist, had used it in depth in the 1930's and that Roman Jakobson, acknowledging Bühler as his source, had also used it to classify aims of discourse in the early 1960's. The beginnings of this norm can be found in Aristotle who calls science language directed to things and rhetoric language directed to persons. Alan Gardiner, the linguist, had also suggested this principle of classification in the 1950's.[10]

This principle can be seen illustrated in Figure 2. If one represents the components of the communication process as a triangle composed of an encoder (writer or speaker), a decoder (reader or listener), a signal (the linguistic product), and a reality (that part of the universe to which the linguistic product refers), then a focus on one of these tends to produce a specific kind of discourse. Discourse dominated by subject matter (reality talked about) is called referential discourse. There are three kinds of referential discourse: exploratory, informative, and scientific. These correspond to elements in the first and second rows across Figure 1. Here, however, it seems important to distinguish the merely informative kind of writing (such as news stories in journalism, simple encyclopedia or textbook presentations) from the strictly scientific, though few authorities make the distinction. Aristotle, for example, has no theory of information, though he has one of science. And Miller has provision for informative, though he has no specific provision for the scientific. And it is equally important to distinguish a kind of discourse which asks a question (exploratory, dialectical, interrogative in some formulations) from discourse which answers it (informative) and proves the answer (scientific). Yet all three of these kinds of discourse are subject-matter or reference dominated. Examples of all three are given in Figure 2. These subdistinctions of reference discourse are my own and differ somewhat from Jakobson's.

Figure 2 The basic purposes of composition.

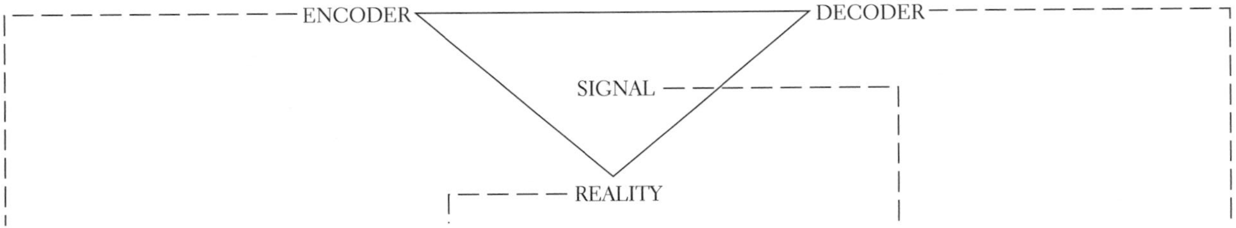

ENCODER — DECODER

SIGNAL

REALITY

EXPRESSIVE

Examples:

Of Individual
Conversation
Journals
Diaries
Gripe sessions
Prayer

Of Social
Minority protests
Manifestoes
Declarations of independence
Contracts
Constitutions of clubs
Myth
Utopia plans
Religious credos

REFERENTIAL

Examples:

Exploratory
Dialogues
Seminars
A tentative definition of . . .
Proposing a solution to problems
Diagnosis

Scientific
Proving a point by arguing from
  accepted premises
Proving a point by generalizing
  from particulars
A combination of both

Informative
News articles
Reports
Summaries
Non-technical encyclopedia
  articles
Textbooks

LITERARY

Examples:

Short story
Lyric
Short narrative
Limerick
Ballad, folk song
Drama
TV show
Movie
Joke

PERSUASIVE

Examples:

Advertising
Political speeches
Religious sermons
Legal oratory
Editorials

135

Secondly, as Bühler, Jakobson and Aristotle point out, discourse which focuses on eliciting a specific reaction from the decoder and is dominated by this request for reaction emerges as persuasion or rhetoric. In this use, the encoder may purposely disguise his own personality and purposely distort the picture of reality which language can paint in order to get the decoder to do something or believe something (as in dishonest advertising or some political propaganda). These distortions are not essential to persuasion, however. What is essential is that encoder, reality, and language itself all become instrumental to the achievement of some practical effect in the decoder. Obvious examples of such aims of discourse are given in the last column of Figure 2.

Thirdly, when the language product is dominated by the clear design of the writer or speaker to discharge his emotions or achieve his own individuality or embody his personal or group aspirations in a discourse, then the discourse tends to be expressive. The expressor or encoder here dominates the communication process. Sometimes in such uses the decoder and the referential components even become negligible—as with curse words uttered in private. But often such uses carry strong sub-components of information and persuasion, as in the *Declaration of Independence*. Some examples of such uses are given in the first column of the figure we have been analyzing.

Finally, the product or text or work itself may be the focus of the process as an object worthy of being appreciated in its own right. Such appreciation gives pleasure to the beholder. In this use of language, language calls attention to itself, to its own structures, not as references to reality or as expressions of personal aspirations or as instruments of persuasion, but as structures worthy of contemplation in their own right. Of course, reference, author personality, and persuasion may and usually are involved. But they are not rigidly relevant as primary foci. Indeed the reality may be fictional or very distorted; the author may be hidden under dramatic projections; and the persuasions involved may be quite trivial on occasion. This last use of language is called literature. It appears in such varied forms as the pun, the salacious joke, the sonnet, the novel, the TV drama, the epic, etc.

If a comparison may be drawn, it could be said that language is like a windowpane. I may throw bricks at it to vent my feelings about something; I may use a chunk of it to chase away an intruder; I may use it to mirror or explore reality; and I may use a stained-glass window to call attention to itself as an object of beauty. Windows, like language, can be used expressively, persuasively, referentially, and esthetically.

SOME CONCLUSIONS ABOUT
AIMS OF DISCOURSE

I have not included in Figure 1 many of the other approaches to aims of discourse, most of which are fairly symmetrical to those given here. These would include the several groups interested in the functions of language at its origin (was it imitative of reality, the bow-wow theory, was it a utilitarian rhetorical tool, the yo-he-ho theory, was it an expressive emotional theory, the ah-ah, pooh-pooh theory, or did language begin in play and poetry, the ding-dong theory). These theories, like the child function theories, do parallel the four functions arrived at. Some anthropologists, like Malinowski and Doob, have examined primitive societies and isolated the functions of language found there (they do not find a literary or play use, I might add, though Lévi-Strauss did). Nor have I mentioned the semanticists; Hayakawa's four uses of language also parallel the model sketched here. The uses of language, established by the Nebraska high school composition program and drawn heavily from the ordinary language philosophers, also closely parallel these distinctions.

The important lesson to be drawn from this almost fearful symmetry is that no composition program can afford to neglect any of these basic aims of discourse. There have been periods in the history of the teaching of composition, whether in the elementary or secondary or college level, when one or the other has been unduly prominent and others slighted or entirely neglected. The results have usually been educationally disastrous. In speech departments where persuasion was, for too long a time, too prominent, two cancerous effects have often followed: first, expository or reference discourse is assimilated into and made equivalent to persuasion and Aristotelian rhetorical proofs are extended to all discourse; secondly, even literature is reduced to persuasion, and some modern theories of oral interpretation now speak of the oral interpreter's function as one of coercing the audience into a desired emotional attitude. At the elementary and secondary school during the Deweyite progressive period, the reduction of all language to self-expression destroyed alike any objective scientific or literary norms. At the college level, in English departments during the period immediately preceding the present, the restriction of composition to expository writing and the reading of literary texts has had two equally dangerous consequences. First, the neglect of expressionism, as a reaction to progressive education, has stifled self-expression in the student and partially, at least, is a cause of the unorthodox and extreme forms of deviant self-expression now indulged in by college students on many campuses today.

Secondly, the neglect of persuasion has often caused persuasion to be as-similated and absorbed into literature in many cases. Expressionism has often been similarly absorbed so that literature has become prostituted to propaganda or the most weird forms of formless self-expression. In philosophy, with the logical positivists, interested solely in scientific statements, the ignoring of other uses of discourse has caused all of them to be lumped into the general category of nonsensical or meaningless. None of these situations is healthy. It is to the good of each of the aims of discourse to be studied in conjunction with the others.

The reason for this is to be seen in the various principles of classification used in the establishing of the aims by various writers. Scientific discourse is generally different in its logic, its level of probability, from the other aims of discourse. In fact, each aim of discourse has its own logic, its own kind of references, its own communication framework, its own patterns of organization, and its own stylistic norms. Sometimes these logics and stylistic principles even contradict each other. Overlaps certainly occur but the ultimate conflation and confusion of any of the aims of discourse with any other is pedagogically disastrous.

The study of these distinct aims of discourses is only a continuation of the basic liberal arts tradition. That tradition, coalesced into the trivium of grammar, rhetoric, and logic or dialectic, simply meant the study of literature, the study of persuasion, and the study of scientific and exploratory discourse. When the English departments presided over the dissolution of the liberal arts tradition in the early 1900's by exiling persuasion to speech departments and by exiling logic to philosophy departments, only literature (grammar) remained and literature, as such, had never been the only basis of the liberal arts. My plea is simply for a preservation of the liberal arts tradition with composition as the foundation stone.

NOTES

1. For the treatment of both fallacies, see W. K. Wimsatt and Monroe Beardsley, *The Verbal Icon* (Lexington, Kentucky, 1965), pp. 3-18, 21-39.

2. "Criteria for Style Analysis," in *Essays on the Language of Literature*, eds. Seymour Chatman and Samuel R. Levin (Boston, Massachusetts, 1967), pp. 419 ff.

3. For a historical survey of this school, see J. Craig LaDrière, "Rhetoric and 'Merely Verbal' Art," in *English Institute Essays, 1948*, ed. D. A. Robertson (New York, 1949), pp. 123-153.

4. See Ernst Cassirer, *An Essay on Man* (New Haven, 1944), pp. 109 ff.

5. See C. W. Morris, *Signs, Language and Behavior* (Englewood Cliffs, New Jersey, 1946), pp. 95 ff.

6. See George A. Miller, *Language and Communications* (New York, 1951), p. 253.

7. See Bertrand Russell, *Human Knowledge, Its Scope and Limits* (New York, 1948), pp. 58 ff.

8. See Hans Reichenbach, *Introduction to Symbolic Logic* (New York, 1947), pp. 17 ff.

9. See I. A. Richards, *How to Read a Page* (London, 1943), p. 100; and *Principles of Literary Criticism* (London, 1925), p. 261.

10. See Roman Jakobson, "Linguistics and Poetics," in *Essays on the Language of Literature*, eds. Seymour Chatman and Samuel R. Levin (Boston, 1967), pp. 299 ff.

An Ontological Basis
for a Modern Theory
of the Composing Process

FRANK J. D'ANGELO

In a recent article entitled "Tradition and Theory in Rhetoric," S. M. Hallo-ran comments that, in the past, the rhetorical tradition was built on the cultural ideal of the orator, the good man skilled in speaking who embodied the wisdom and knowledge of the culture. Because modern values are unstable and fragmented, Halloran continues, the orator no longer embodies the communal wisdom. Therefore, to base modern rhetorical theories on the cultural ideal of the orator would be difficult, if not impossible. Halloran concludes that "one cannot simply graft modern rhetorical or communication theory onto classical rhetoric."[1] Modern theorists, therefore, must base their rhetorical theories on different ontological assumptions.

I believe that a modern theory of the composing process can be based directly on evolutionary theory as it relates to the origins and history of consciousness. The composing process, being an aspect of consciousness, must necessarily develop along the same general lines as consciousness itself. What I have in mind, however, is not evolution conceived of in mechanistic terms, but evolution understood in teleological terms. In this view, the composing process is analogous to universal evolutionary processes, in which an original, amorphous, undifferentiated whole gradually evolves into a more complex, differentiated one. Like the processes of teleological evolution, the composing process is progress toward a goal that is directed by a conscious or

Reprinted from *Quarterly Journal of Speech* 64.1 (February 1978): 79–85. Used by permission of the National Communication Association.

unconscious intention or intelligence. My thesis is that *the process of composing is a movement from an undifferentiated to a differentiated whole*. It repeats in microcosm the history of the evolution of consciousness.[2]

THE COMPOSING PROCESS AND THE EVOLUTION OF CONSCIOUSNESS

The rhetorical topics themselves can be viewed as differentiations of basic mental processes that have evolved over thousands of years. So, also, can the figures of speech in Greek rhetoric. Paragraphing is the process of differentiating the parts from the whole. Invention, arrangement, and style are differentiations of a single, ongoing mental process.[3]

From the evolutionary point of view, composition is an organic development that begins with a kind of intuitive grasp of the end to be achieved and that concludes when that end is brought to fruition. The problem of composing is the problem of how an intention or purpose that is already partially realized in the mind gets what it needs to complete itself.[4]

It is not enough that in the process of composing the writer see the subject whole. One may know in general the end one wants to achieve without knowing all the details. The gestalt has to be brought to fulfillment, slowly, bit by bit, by linear methods. Thus the process of composing begins with a general idea, but the main process consists in filling in the details. Once the mind intuitively grasps the initial gestalt, then the rational mental processes can take over and the process of composition can be brought to completion in a logical, analytical manner.

Invention always seems to take place within a system. Some kind of structure always underlies the process. To invent is to extend a system which is already present in the mind.

There is purpose in the mind itself. The mind takes an active part in the composing process, supplying at one and the same time the ends and the means. Thus, a kind of necessity inheres in the process of invention. The mind, when faced with a problem, attempts to incorporate this problem within an existing structure. The mind of necessity must then invent because it is constantly active, always in process; it seeks to understand and to incorporate into its knowledge structure whatever is placed before it.

In the composing process, it seems that both conscious and subconscious processes take part. The subconscious mind provides the design, and the conscious mind provides its development. (A reverse process is also possible.) Actually, this is probably a simplification since there is a constant interplay between these two modes of consciousness. Since the subconscious part of the mind is not always accessible for invention, the writer must aid the subconscious as much as possible by a deliberate and conscious effort, by defining the problem, by filling in the details, by carefully working out the design—in brief, by preparing the mind so that the subconscious can take over.

STAGES OF EVOLUTION AND THE DEVELOPMENT OF CONSCIOUSNESS

I have said that the composing process is analogous to universal evolutionary processes, in which an original, amorphous, undifferentiated whole gradually evolves into a more complex, differentiated whole. The idea that evolution is taking us toward increasing complexity, differentiation, and unity has been admirably set forth by Pierre Teilhard de Chardin, who notes that historically the universe is becoming more and more concentrated into organized forms. In the beginning, the stuff of the universe was "virtually homogeneous," but with the passage of time, it segments, complicates, and differentiates itself into hierarchical units:

> . . . the ramifications of evolution reappear and go on close to us in a thousand social phenomena which we should never have imagined to be so closely linked with biology; in the formation and dissemination of languages, in the development and specialisation of new industries, in the formulation and propagation of philosophic and religious doctrines. In each of these groups of human activity a superficial glance would only detect a weak and haphazard answer to the procedure of life. It would accept without questioning the strange fact of parallelism—or it would account for it in terms of some abstract necessity.[5]

This differentiation is not merely fragmentation, though fragmentation there is, for the results of this differentiation are eventually being incorporated into a highly unified and organized pattern.

Differentiation manifests itself everywhere—on an inorganic level, on a biological level, and on a cultural level. Differentiation, together with its resulting and increasing complexity, is leading "to the evolution of progressively more conscious mind." As life advances, it transforms itself in depth, moving toward higher and higher levels of consciousness. It is gaining the "psychic zones of the world." As a result, humanity is achieving a more com-

143

plex mental activity to guide it along "the path of progress" to higher levels of consciousness.[6]

Teilhard believes that humanity is approaching a critical level of social organization. Evolution has reached a point where it is becoming conscious of itself, and in order to see where evolution is taking us, we must envision humankind as a single organism, growing, changing, and developing in a single direction. As a result of education, research, and the mass media, the human race has developed a collective memory and a generalized nervous system which is resulting in the super-organization of matter. Not only the individual, but the race as a whole is becoming *"totally reflexive upon itself."* Consequently, not only are we seeing a general heightening of consciousness in the individual, but also in the world:[7]

> What we see taking place in the world today is not merely the multiplication of *men* but the continued shaping of *Man*. Man . . . is not yet zoologically mature. Psychologically he has not spoken his last word. In one form or another something ultrahuman is being born which, through the direct or indirect effect of socialisation, cannot fail to make its appearance in the near future: a future that is not simply the unfolding of Time, but which is being constructed in advance of us.[8]

In his study of the origins and history of consciousness, Erich Neumann contends that the development of consciousness in the individual can be regarded as a repetition of the racial history of consciousness, that is, ontogeny repeats phylogeny. According to Neumann, "The individualized conscious man of our era is a late man, whose structure is built on early, pre-individual human stages from which individual consciousness has only detached itself step by step."[9] We can trace the stages in the evolution of consciousness, states Neumann, in mythological types, for ego consciousness in its evolution passes through a series of images or archetypes which are projections of the psyche and therefore must necessarily reveal themselves in dreams, fantasies, and myths. These images or archetypes are structural elements of the mind. To trace the stadial progression of archetypes in myths, therefore, is to trace the psychological stages in the development of the individual consciousness and the history of consciousness.[10]

To trace the mythological stages in the evolution of consciousness is not my main purpose, except insofar as it illuminates the study of the psychological stages in the development of consciousness. The three main stages of archetypal development are the creation myth, the hero myth, and the transformation myth. The creation myth symbolizes original unity, that stage of consciousness in which the ego is still submerged in the unconscious. The hero myth symbolizes separation from this original unity (the birth of the hero) and the growth of consciousness. The transformation myth symbolizes increasing differentiation of consciousness; it is the stage of the reflecting, self-conscious ego, the return to original unity in which the whole and its parts are synthesized into a unified system.[11]

What do these myths signify in terms of the ontogenetic and phylogenetic development of consciousness? We can imagine a time in prehistory when the person was not yet separated from nature, when the individual was a part of the group, the ego a part of the unconscious. All were parts of an undifferentiated whole. Just as the individual had, gradually, to escape the domination of the group, so also the ego had to emerge slowly from the sway of the unconscious. At this stage, states Neumann, consciousness was "still in abeyance, being not yet developed or only partially developed." This early stage in the development of consciousness corresponds to the dream state in which the individual consciousness breaks down easily and dissolves itself into images and symbols. This stage also corresponds to the state of consciousness of primitives, who are easily tired by any kind of self-conscious activity. Even in the modern individual the margin of conscious awareness is somewhat limited. Consciousness in prehistory, then, is characterized by non-differentiation and indeterminateness.[12] But slowly, over the course of thousands and thousands of years, the human mind becomes increasingly more complex and differentiated, and this differentiation is built into the structure of the brain. As the ego begins to gain its independence from the unconscious, it separates from it, yet still remains partially dependent on it. This splitting off of the ego from its origins in the unconscious leads to a kind of fragmentation in which the ego tries to become autonomous. As long as the ego attempts to cut off all of its ties with the unconscious, it is in danger of becoming sterile, emptied of all content. Like the hero in mythology, it must occasionally make a "descent" into the depths of the unconscious to recover its emotional components and images if it is to remain emotionally stable and creative.[13]

Neumann believes that Western civilization is in danger of upsetting the compensating balance of the unconscious forces of the psyche with the conscious forces. He claims that the human race is becoming increasingly more egocentric and that this egocentricity is responsible for the restlessness and meaninglessness of modern life. Not only are our traditional systems of values disintegrating, but also the very meaning of existence is being questioned.[14]

This increasing complexity and differentiation of consciousness is not necessarily bad in itself, argues Neumann. In fact, it is a necessary result of the process of evolution: "The development that has brought about the division of the two systems is in accord with a necessary process of psychic differentiation, but, like all differentiation, it runs the risk of becoming overdifferentiated and perverse."[15] Creative processes, then, must not exclude the unconscious. Although the ego is the directive force in the creative process, it must somehow assimilate aspects of the unconscious if it is to function properly. In so doing, it will be able to synthesize the differentiated parts previously broken down by the analytical mind into a new whole, into a new unity of the conscious and unconscious elements.

STAGES OF EVOLUTION AND THE ORGANIZATION OF KNOWLEDGE

In almost every field, the idea that evolution is moving from an undifferentiated to a differentiated whole manifests itself. For example, according to the Russian psychologist L. S. Vygotsky, in the acquisition of language the child begins with an undifferentiated whole. Vygotsky asserts that in terms of meaning, "the first word of the child is a whole sentence. Semantically, the child starts from the whole, from a meaningful complex, and only later begins to master the separate semantic units, the meanings of words, and to divide his formerly undifferentiated thought into those units."[16] Vygotsky continues: "A child's thought, precisely because it is born as a dim amorphous whole, must find expression in a single word. As his thought becomes more differentiated, the child is less apt to express it in single words but constructs a composite whole."[17]

The development of concept formation in the child seems to follow the same evolutionary stages as those enumerated by Neumann and Teilhard. In his study of *Thought and Language*, Vygotsky enumerates three basic stages of concept formation. The first stage is the placing of objects into unorganized heaps or congeries (that is, into undifferentiated wholes). In the first stage, in trying to solve a problem, the child brings together the most diffuse, seemingly unrelated objects into a highly unstable mental image. The concept, or rather perception, is vague and indefinite. The second stage consists of thinking in complexes. In this stage, the child no longer groups things together on the basis of subjective impressions alone, but brings them together by noting connections that actually exist between and among them. The final stage is that of abstracting, the process of isolating elements from a concrete experience and viewing them apart. At this time, the child is not only able to abstract and to analyze, but also to synthesize these abstracted elements into a coherent whole.[18]

A study of the history of the paragraph reveals that the paragraph as a differentiated unit is a relatively recent development. Edwin Lewis states that there has long been a unit of discourse in English prose larger than the sentence, but this unit was not really differentiated as our modern paragraph is: "In other words English writers have thought roughly in long stages before they have analyzed such stages into smaller steps."[19] Lewis then discusses the chief influences leading to the development of the modern paragraph: the scribal tradition which considers the paragraph as a unit of thought, the Latin tradition which regards the paragraph as a unit of emphasis, and the oral tradition which breaks up long stretches of discourse into easily understood smaller units for an uncultivated audience. In the eighteenth and nineteenth centuries, the tendency of writers was to reduce the length of the paragraph to a succession of smaller units of a more or less constant length.[20]

Supporting Lewis' point of view, Virginia Burke observes that "the paragraph was not sharply defined in the minds of many English prosaists, for it was often not distinguished from larger units (chapter and section) or from smaller units (sentences). Some writers frequently produced short paragraphs of fewer than three sentences. . . . Some writers. . . produced a high number of single sentence paragraphs, in which the single sentences were usually inordinately long. This practice seems to indicate that these writers frequently regarded sentences and paragraphs as identical or, more precisely, equivalent."[21] Burke concludes that "if the paragraph, as we know it, is possible only when internal arrangement is possible, and if internal arrangement is possible only when there are several sentences to organize, then the paragraph is a recent phenomenon."[22]

The foregoing examples suffice to demonstrate the extent to which scholars working in isolation in completely different fields have come to the realization of the importance of the stages of evolutionary development as a way of understanding and organizing knowledge. Yet, despite the significance of these ideas in other fields, little attempt has been made to apply them to the study of rhetoric.[23] I have already suggested that the composing process repeats in microcosm the history of the evolution of consciousness, in the mind's movement from an undifferentiated whole to a differentiated whole. Once the underlying pattern is grasped, almost anything can be assimilated to the overall design. Thus Alfred North Whitehead's three stages of education—the stage of romance, the stage of precision, and the stage of generalization—fit the pattern. So also do Piaget's psychological stages in the mental development of the child. For example, the first stage, the stage of egocentricity, is characterized by a high degree of subjectivity and little self-consciousness on the part of the child, who is hardly able to distinguish between the subjective and objective aspects of the world. The second stage is characterized by increasing differentiation of the subjective and objective. The third stage, the stage of abstract formal operations, is characterized by the child's ability to discern causal connections and general principles, and to relate the differentiated parts to the whole.

CONSIDERATION OF POSSIBLE OBJECTIONS

Let me at this point take up one or two possible objections. The first is that a part of my evidence seems to rest on outworn psychological knowledge. *Because our knowledge of the structure and functions of the human brain has increased, have not the ideas of psychoanalysts such as Jung or Freud grown increasingly irrelevant?* On the contrary, studies in psychoneurology suggest increasing specialization and differentiation in the two hemispheres of the cerebral cortex of the brain and that the psychoanalytical concepts of the ego and the id, the conscious and the subconscious, the rational and the intuitive, and the masculine and the feminine can easily be accommodated to the functions of the two hemispheres.[24]

A much more important objection, however, may be: *But doesn't the idea that the composing process must necessarily follow certain lines of development smack of a kind of evolutionary determinism? After all, rhetoric has traditionally been concerned with free choice.* The answer to this objection is that, as both Neumann and Teilhard point out, the evolutionary process that leads to greater complexity and differentiation can take a negative path. It can lead to egocentricity, fragmentation, and alienation. So free choice is still possible. That is why the task of rhetoric in the coming years is so important. Evolution has reached a point where it is partially self-controlled. According to Teilhard, it is up to us to further the progress of what he calls *hominisation*, that is, human beings rising from their animal natures toward higher things. This progress will take a very long time and will undoubtedly suffer setbacks along the way. Nevertheless, the ultimate goal is nothing less than universal convergence.

The function of rhetoric, therefore, is to guide individuals who are distinct and separate toward greater unity and identification of purpose and action. Of all the arts and sciences, rhetoric seems to be the discipline best able to induce cooperation among humankind. As Teilhard puts it: "Forced against one another by the increase in their numbers and the multiplication of their interrelations—compressed together by the activation of a common force and the awareness of a common distress—the men of the future will form, in some way, but one single consciousness."[25]

I realize, of course, that I have not necessarily shown a precise analogous relationship between the composing process and the evolution of consciousness. Yet the similarities between the two processes are so striking that we must either "accept without questioning the strange fact of parallelism" or "account verbally for it in terms of some abstract necessity."[26]

NOTES

1. S. M. Halloran, "Tradition and Theory in Rhetoric," *Quarterly Journal of Speech*, 62 (1976), 235-38, 241.

2. Dorothy C. Higginbotham, in some correspondence to me, has commented that what I "have defined as the composing process has relevance for the ontogeny of language in terms of spoken discourse long before the individual is capable of anything like written composition." This suggests that the composing process is "an example of the larger language organizing behavior that has evolved in man."

3. For one attempt at a theoretical application of these ideas to rhetoric, see Frank J. D'Angelo, *A Conceptual Theory of Rhetoric* (Cambridge, Ma.: Winthrop, 1975); for a pedagogical application, see Frank J. D'Angelo, *Process and Thought in Composition* (Cambridge, Ma.: Winthrop, 1977), especially Chapters 2, 3, and 8.

4. The generalized discussion of the composing process which follows is taken from D'Angelo, *A Conceptual Theory*, pp. 52-54.

5. Pierre Teilhard de Chardin, *The Phenomenon of Man*, intro. Sir Julian Huxley (New York: Harper Torchbooks, 1961), pp. 221-22.

6. Ibid., pp. 16, 17, 219.

7. Pierre Teilhard de Chardin, *The Future of Man*, trans. Norman Denny (New York: Harper Torchbooks, 1964), pp. 137-39.

8. Ibid., p. 275.

9. Erich Neumann, *The Origins and History of Consciousness*, foreword C. G. Jung, trans. R. F. C. Hull (Princeton: Princeton Univ. Press, 1954), p. xx.

10. Ibid., p. xvi.

11. Ibid., pp. 261-418, passim.

12. Ibid., pp. 266-70, 280-81, passim.

13. Ibid., p. 343.

14. Ibid., pp. 389-91.

15. Ibid., p. 383.

16. L. S. Vygotsky, *Thought and Language*, ed. and trans. Eugenia Hanfmann and Gertrude Vakar (Cambridge: The M.I.T. Press, 1962), p. 126.

17. Ibid.

18. Ibid., pp. 51, 60-61, 76.

19. Edwin H. Lewis, "The History of the Paragraph," in *Prose Style: A Historical Approach Through Studies*, ed. James R. Bennett (San Francisco: Chandler, 1971), p. 14.

20. Ibid., p. 14.

21. Virginia M. Burke, "The Continuity of the Paragraph," in *Prose Style: A Historical Approach Through Studies*, ed. James R. Bennett (San Francisco: Chandler, 1971), p. 19.

22. Ibid., p. 20.

23. Walter J. Ong's work, of course, is the most important attempt to study rhetoric in terms of evolving consciousness. See, especially, his *The Presence of the Word* (New Haven:

Yale Univ. Press, 1967) and *Rhetoric, Romance, and Technology* (Ithaca: Cornell Univ. Press, 1971).

24. See, for example, Stuart Dimond, *The Double Brain* (Edinburgh: Churchill Livingstone, 1972); Stuart J. Dimond and J. Graham Beaumont, eds., *Hemispheric Function in the Human Brain* (New York: Wiley, 1974); Michael S. Gazzaniga, *The Bisected Brain* (New York: Appleton-Century-Crofts, 1970); Julian Jaynes, *The Origin of Consciousness in the Breakdown of the Bicameral Mind* (Boston: Houghton Mifflin, 1977); Robert E. Ornstein, *The Psychology of Consciousness* (New York: Viking, 1972).

25. Teilhard, *Future of Man*, p. 321.

26. Teilhard, *Phenomenon of Man*, pp. 221-22.

Spectator Role
and the Beginnings of Writing

James Britton

*Only by understanding the entire history of sign development in the child
and the place of writing in it can we approach a correct solution of the psychology of writing.*
    —L. S. Vygotsky, Mind in Society, p. 106

IN SEARCH OF A THEORY

Literary and Nonliterary Discourse

Works of literature constitute a form of discourse: We have theories of
GENRE to distinguish among works of literature, but no satisfactory theory to
account for what is common to all such works and in what general ways
they differ from nonliterary discourse. The 1958 interdisciplinary symposium on "Style in Language" at Indiana University attempted to make
such a distinction, but the only consensus that seemed to emerge was the
low-level generalization that literary discourse is "noncasual discourse."
Moreover, in summing up that symposium, George Miller remarked, "I
gradually learned to understand a little of what the linguist has on his mind
when he begins to talk; his verbal behavior during these past days has not
puzzled me quite the way it once would have. But the critics have some
mystic entity called a 'poem' or 'literature,' whose existence I must take on
faith and whose defining properties still confuse me. (The fact that they

Reprinted from *What Writers Know: The Language, Process, and Structure of Written
Discourse*. Ed. Martin Nystrand. New York: Academic, 1982. 149–69. Used with permission
from Elsevier Science..

cannot agree amongst themselves on what a poem is adds to the mystery.) [Sebeok, 1960, p. 387]."

Since a great deal of (mostly unpublished) writing by nonprofessionals, by children in school and students in college, takes on forms that are clearly related to literary forms, it seems appropriate that any study of the psychology of writing should attempt to deal with this problem; and that the theory adumbrated should seek both to relate the artlike writings to literary works of art, and to distinguish between them.

One of the most important contributors to the Indiana symposium was Roman Jakobson who put forward his model of the 'constitutive factors' in a speech situation:

$$
\begin{array}{ccc}
 & \text{Context} & \\
 & \text{Message} & \\
\text{Addressor} & \text{Contact} & \text{Addressee} \\
 & \text{Code} &
\end{array}
$$

and the functions assignable to an utterance or part utterance in accordance with the factor on which it focuses:

$$
\begin{array}{ccc}
 & \text{Referential} & \\
\text{Emotive (or} & \text{Poetic} & \\
\text{Expressive)} & \text{Phatic} & \text{Conative} \\
 & \text{Metalingual} &
\end{array}
$$

He made it clear that a verbal message was very unlikely to be fulfilling one function only, but that in taking account of the various functions liable to be copresent we might expect to find them hierarchically ordered, one function being **dominant**. "The verbal structure," he added, "depends primarily on the dominant function [Sebeok, 1960, p. 353]."

I want to accept as starting point his view that the poetic function (in the broad sense of 'poetic,' equivalent to the verbal arts) may be defined as a "focus on the message for its own sake," and to agree in principle that the poetic function may be either dominant or merely accessory. But Jakobson goes on to say:

> Any attempt to reduce the sphere of poetic function to poetry or to confine poetry to poetic function would be a delusive oversimplification. Poetic function is not the sole function of verbal art but only its dominant, determining function, whereas in all other verbal activities it acts as a subsidiary, accessory constituent [Sebeok, 1960, p. 356].

Any linguistic choice made on the sole grounds that "it sounds better that way" would seem to exemplify Jakobson's conception of the poetic function in an accessory role. Yet it seems to me that the urgent necessity is to characterize the structure and status of verbal messages in which the poetic function is dominant, that is, to find ways of distinguishing poetic from nonpoetic discourse. Jakobson's model itself might even suggest a dichotomy of this kind, a dominant focus on the message itself for its own sake being in contrast with a message dominantly focused on something beyond or outside itself.

Susanne Langer (1953) recognizes such a dichotomy when she comments on the switch required when readers or listeners turn their attention from nonliterary to literary discourse. An "illusion of life," she says,

> is the primary illusion of all poetic art. It is at least tentatively established by the very first sentence, which has to switch the reader's or hearer's attitude from conversational interest to literary interest, i.e., from actuality to fiction. We make this shift with great ease, and much more often than we realize, even in the midst of conversation; one has only to say "You know about the two Scotchmen, who . . ." to make everybody in earshot suspend the actual conversation and attend to "the" two Scots and "their" absurdities. Jokes are a special literary form to which people will attend on the spur of the moment [1953 p. 213].

And, speaking of Blake's poem *Tyger*, she comments, "The vision of such a tiger is a virtual experience, built up from the first line of the poem to the last. But nothing can be built up unless the very first words of the poem EF-FECT THE BREAK WITH THE READER'S ACTUAL ENVIRONMENT [p. 214, emphasis added]."

In *The Reader, the Text, the Poem*, Louise Rosenblatt (1978) makes a broad distinction between two types of reading process, **efferent** and **aesthetic**. In efferent reading the reader's concern is with what he takes away from the reading (hence "efferent" from *effero* [I carry away]). In aesthetic reading, in contrast, "the reader's primary concern is with what happens during the actual reading event. . . . The reader's attention is centered directly on what he is living through during his relationship with that particular text [1978, pp. 24–25]." She is careful to point out that this is no hard and fast division but rather a continuum between two poles. Thus, "given the assumption that the text offers a potentially meaningful set of linguistic symbols, the reader is faced with the adoption of either a predominantly efferent or a predominantly aesthetic stance [1978, p. 78]." We shall return to this matter of the relation between a reader's and a writer's options.

Support for a general distinction between literary and nonliterary discourse comes also from a linguist's work in stylistics. Widdowson (1975) claims that what is crucial to the character of literature is that "the language of a literary work should be fashioned into patterns over and above those required by the actual language system [1975, p. 47]." I shall return to consider this claim in a later section.

Spectator and Participant Roles

As we have noted, many of the features we find in poetic discourse (the language of literature) we find also widely distributed in many other forms of discourse. A mere study of the distribution of such features will not, I believe, add up to an adequate description of the verbal structure of a message in which the poetic function is dominant. We have no difficulty in practice in recognizing the difference between a novel with a political purpose and a piece of political rhetoric or persuasive discourse. What are the factors that shape the literary work as a whole?

The theory I want to pursue is one that I first put forward many years ago (Britton, 1963), in what seems to me now a crude form. My purpose then was to find common ground between much of the writing children do in school and the literature they read. I was concerned that, unlike the arts of painting and music, literature, as far as schools and universities were concerned, was not something that students do, but always something that other people HAVE DONE. To bridge this gap, I looked for what seemed to be the informal spoken counterparts of written literature—not the anecdote as such, I decided (Langer's tale of the two Scotsmen)—but the kind of gossip about events that most of us take part in daily. To quote from that account, "The distinction that matters . . . is not whether the events recounted are true or fictional, but whether we recount them (or listen to them) as spectators or participants: and whenever we play the role of spectator of human affairs I suggest we are in the position of literature [Britton, 1963, p. 37]." The roles of spectator and participant were differentiated in this way:

> When we talk about our own affairs, clearly we can do so either as participant or as spectator. If I describe what has happened to me in order to get my hearer to do something for me, or even to change his opinion about me, then I remain a participant in my own affairs and invite him to become one. If, on the other hand, I merely want to interest him, so that he savours with me the joys and sorrows and surprises of my past experiences and appreciates with me the intricate patterns of events, then not only do I invite him to be a spectator, but I am myself a spectator of my own experience. . . . I don't think it is far-fetched to think of myself talking not about

my own past, but about my future, and, again, doing so in either of the two roles. As participant I should be planning, and asking my listener to participate by helping or advising or just 'giving me the necessary permission'. As spectator I should be day-dreaming, and inviting my listener to share in that kind of pleasure [Britton, 1963, p. 39].

To complete the account, I then made reference to taking up the role of spectator of imagined experiences in fantasy or fiction.

Three years later I prepared an advance paper for discussion at the Anglo-American Seminar at Dartmouth, a paper on "Response to Literature" (Britton, 1968), and as a brief postscript to that document, I referred to the "unorthodox view of literature" that characterized it as a written form of language in the role of spectator and so related it to the spoken form, gossip about events. The paper was discussed by a study group under the chairmanship of the British psychologist, D. W. Harding. It was not until the first meeting of the study group was over that he asked me whether I knew his own papers putting forward a similar view; and that evening, in Dartmouth College Library, I read for the first time "The Role of the Onlooker" (Harding, 1937) and "Psychological Processes in the Reading of Fiction" (Harding, 1962). There I found a fully and carefully argued case for distinguishing the role of an onlooker from that of a participant in events and for relating gossip to literature as activities in the former role.

The final report of that study group was prepared by Harding and included this comment:

> Though central attention should be given to literature in the ordinary sense, it is impossible to separate response to literature sharply from response to other stories, films, or television plays, or from children's own personal writing or spoken narrative. In all of these the student contemplates represented events in the role of a spectator, not for the sake of active intervention. But since his response includes in some degree accepting or rejecting the values and emotional attitudes which the narration implicitly offers, it will influence, perhaps greatly influence, his future appraisals of behavior and feeling [Harding, 1968, p. 11].

D. W. Harding

In the two articles I have referred to, Harding explored the relationship between three processes that seemed to him to have much in common: (*a*) watching events without taking part in them; (*b*) exchanging gossip — informal recounting or description of events; and (*c*) reading (or writing) fiction. An understanding of the first of these, that of being literally in the role of

155

spectator, is essential to an understanding of his view of the other two. An onlooker, he says, (*a*) ATTENDS (and this will range from "a passing glance" to a "fascinated absorption") and (*b*) EVALUATES (within a range from "an attitude of faint liking or disliking, hardly above indifference" to one of "strong, perhaps intensely emotional" response). What we attend to, he suggests, reflects our interests (if we take interest to mean "an enduring disposition to respond, in whatever way, to some class of objects or events"); how we evaluate reflects our sentiments, if we take a sentiment to be "an enduring disposition to evaluate some object or class of objects in a particular way [Harding, 1972, p. 134]."

A major aspect of a spectator's response to the events he witnesses will be a concern for the people involved and an interest in the way they react, but there is likely to be present also an interest in and evaluation of the pattern events take, with a sense that what is happening here might one day happen to him. Both aspects are, in a broad sense, learning experiences: As spectators we not only reflect our interests and sentiments but also modify and extend them. "In ways of this kind," Harding writes,

> the events at which we are "mere onlookers" come to have, cumulatively, a deep and extensive influence on our systems of value. They may in certain ways be even more formative than events in which we take part. Detached and distanced evaluation is sometimes sharper for avoiding the blurrings and bufferings that participant action brings, and the spectator often sees the event in a broader context than the participant can tolerate. To obliterate the effects on a man of the occasions on which he was only an onlooker would be profoundly to change his outlook and values [1962, p. 136].

To be one of a number of spectators is to take part in a mutual challenging and sanctioning of each other's evaluations. "Everything we look on at is tacitly and unintentionally treated as an object lesson by our fellow spectators; speech and gesture, smiles, nudges, clicks, tuts and glances are constantly at work to sanction or correct the feelings we have as spectators [Harding, 1937, p. 253]."

This aspect of a spectator's experience is sharply emphasized when we turn to the second of the three processes I have listed, that of deliberately taking up the role of spectator of represented or recounted experiences, as for example when we go home in the evening and chat about the day's events. We HAVE BEEN participants but are so no longer; taking up the role of spectator, we invite our listener to do the same. Harding goes so far as to imply that this familiar habit is something we indulge in for the purpose of testing out our modes of evaluating; having, in fact, our value systems sanctioned or modified by others whose values, in general, we reckon to share. We do not recount everything that happens to us: What we select constitutes a first level of evaluation. But it is as we recount the events in a manner designed to arouse in our listeners attitudes towards them that chime with our own that we more specifically invite corroboration of our ways of evaluating. On this basis, I think it is no distortion of Harding's account to suggest that as participants we APPLY our value systems, but as spectators we GENERATE AND REFINE the system itself. In applying our value systems we shall inevitably be constrained by self-interest, by concern for the outcome of the event we are participating in; as spectators we are freed of that constraint.

Harding goes on to suggest that what takes place informally in chat about events is in essence similar to what is achieved by a work of fiction or drama. "True or fictional, all these forms of narrative invite us to be onlookers joining in the evaluation of some possibility of experience [1962, p. 138]."

The London Writing Research Project

At the time of the Dartmouth Seminar my colleagues and I at the University of London Institute of Education were beginning to plan the Schools Council Project on the written language of 11- to 18-year-olds. Our first and major task was to devise modes of analysis of children's writings by means of which the development of writing abilities might be documented. We envisaged a multidimensional analysis and worked on what seemed to us two of the essential dimensions. The first resulted in a set of categories we called "sense of audience" (Who is the writing for?) and the second in a set of function categories (What is the writing for?). These are fully described in *The Development of Writing Abilities, 11–18* (Britton, Burgess, Martin, McLeod, & Rosen, 1975) and for my present purpose I need only indicate how the spectator-participant distinction was taken up and developed as the basis of the function category set.

To relate gossip to literature is not only to show a similarity in that they are both utterances in the spectator role, but also to indicate a difference. The formal and informal ends of the spectrum have very different potentials. One of the important ways in which we frame an evaluation and communicate it is by giving a particular shape to the events in narrating them; at the formal end of the scale all the resources of literary art, all the linguistic and conceptual forms that a literary artist molds into a unity, are at the service of that shaping and sharing.

Clearly, an account given of an experience in a letter to an intimate friend might also be placed at the informal end of the scale, in contrast perhaps to the same event narrated by the same writer as part of a short story or a published autobiography. (Dr. Johnson wrote a letter from the Hebrides to a friend in which he said, "When we were taken upstairs, a dirty fellow bounced out of the bed on which one of us was to lie"; this appears in his *Journal* as "Out of one of the couches on which we were to repose there started up at our entrance a man black as a Cyclops from the forge"—more of a parody of the point I am making than an illustration, I think!)

The informality of a chat or a personal letter is certainly in part a reflection of a relaxed relationship between the communicating parties—closeness rather than distance, warmth rather than coldness. Perhaps influenced also by Moffett's model of kinds of discourse in which he sees the **I–you** rhetorical relationship and the **I–it** referential relationship as intimately connected (Moffett, 1968, p. 33), we came to identify the informal end of this continuum with expressive language as Sapir (1961, p. 10) has defined it; further, to see that the "unshaped," loosely structured end of the spectator role continuum merged into the informal pole of language in the role of participant. This gave us three major categories of function: transactional, expressive, and poetic. **Transactional** is the form of discourse that most fully meets the demands of a participant in events (using language to get things done, to carry out a verbal transaction). **Expressive** is the form of discourse in which the distinction between participant and spectator is a shadowy one. And **poetic** discourse is the form that most fully meets the demands associated with the role of spectator—demands that are met, we suggested, by MAKING something with language rather than doing something with it.

Though our principal source for the term "expressive" was Edward Sapir, we found it was one widely used by other linguists. Jakobson labeled the function arising from a focus on the addressor either "emotive" or "expressive" and saw it as offering "a direct expression of the speakers attitude towards what he is speaking about [Sebeok, 1960, p. 354]"; a point that Dell Hymes later glossed: "A sender cannot help but express attitudes towards each of the other factors in a speech event, his audience, the style of the message, the code he is using, the channel he is using, his topic, the scene of the communication [1908, p. 106]." Labov (1966, p. 13) characterizes the expressive function as "the role of language as self-identification," and it is this aspect that Gusdorf elaborates: "The relation to others is only meaningful insofar as it reveals that personal identity within the person who is himself speaking. To communicate, man *expresses* himself, i.e. he actualizes himself, he creates from his own substance [1965, p. 69]." Thus the expressive function in our model is not simply the informal end of two scales, the neutral point between participant and spectator role language, but has its own positive function to perform—a function that profits from the indeterminacy between carrying out a verbal transaction and constructing a verbal object to be shared. The positive function of expressive speech is, in simple terms, to make the most of being with somebody, that is, to enjoy their company, to make their presence fruitful—a process that can profit from exploring with them both the inner and outer aspects of experience.

But in expressive writing the presence, the "togetherness" is simulated: The writer invokes the presence of the reader as he writes; the reader invokes the presence of the writer as he reads. Thus a working definition of expressive writing would be "writing that assumes an interest in the writer as well as in what he has to say about the world." We might add that it would be foolish to underestimate the importance of expressive speech or writing as means of influencing people and events. Advertisers and propagandists are only too ready to exploit its effectiveness.

Our description of expressive writing thus distinguished it from a verbal transaction on the one hand and a verbal object on the other. The verbal transaction and the verbal object are communicative rather than expressive, being in both cases language in the public domain; yet they communicate in very different ways. Expressive and referential strands, as Sapir explains, intermingle in all discourse, but the degree to which the former predominates is criterial in distinguishing expressive from transactional discourse. The change from expression to communication on the poetic side is brought about by an increasing degree of organization—organization into a single complex verbal symbol.

H. G. Widdowson

It is this last distinction that is illuminated by the work in stylistics of Widdowson (1975). He cites from literature examples of nongrammatical expressions that are nevertheless interpretable, finds such expressions in nonliterary texts, but concludes that they occur randomly in nonliterary writing, "whereas in literature they figure as part of a pattern which characterizes the literary work as a separate and self-contained whole [p. 36]." Interpretation of these expressions that violate the grammatical code relies on viewing them in the light of the context; and he goes on to show that this is also true of most metaphorical expressions (which again occur randomly in ordinary discourse but as part of a total pattern in a work of literature). Context, however, in ordinary language will include aspects of the social situation in which the utterance takes place and remarks that have gone before; whereas in literature context consists of the verbal fabric alone. Widdowson identifies patterns of three kinds to be found in literary works: phonological (metre and verse form are obvious examples), syntactical (parallel structures, for example, can invest an item with meaning which is, so to speak, by halo effect from other items in the series), and patterns formed by semantic links between individual lexical items. "At the heart of literary discourse," he concludes, "is the struggle to devise patterns of language which will bestow upon the linguistic items concerned just those values which convey the individual writer's personal vision [1975, p. 42]."

He goes on to suggest that the effect of the patterning over and above the patterns of the language code is "to create acts of communication which are self-contained units, independent of a social context and expressive of a reality other than that which is sanctioned by convention. In other words, I want to suggest that although literature need not be deviant as text it must of its nature be deviant as discourse [1975, p. 47]." This he achieves principally by pointing out that normal discourse features a sender of a message who is at the same time the addressor, and a receiver of a message who is also the addressee, whereas in literary discourse the author, as sender, is distinguished from the addressor, and the reader, as receiver, from the addressee. Striking examples of this disjunction illustrate his point ("I am the enemy you killed, my friend" from Owen; "With how sad steps, O moon" from Sidney), but he goes on to indicate that this modified relationship holds in general for works of literature. An addressor thus fuses meanings associated with a grammatical first person with those associated with a third, an addressee those of the second and third persons. This account of a systematic modification of the grammatical code he completes by showing how third person and first person are fused when in fiction a narrator describes the experiences of a third person sometimes in terms of what might have been observed, sometimes in terms of inner events that only the experiencer could know. On these grounds he concludes: "It would appear then that in literary discourse we do not have a sender addressing a message directly to a receiver, as is normally the case. Instead we have a communication situation within a communication situation and a message whose meaning is self-contained and not dependent on who sends it and who receives it [p. 50]."

In defending this view against likely objections, he makes two interesting points that are relevant to my theme. In many literary works, particularly perhaps in lyric poems, it is evident that the "I" of the work is the writer himself. In arguing that "it is not the writer as message sender, the craftsman, the 'maker' that the 'I' refers to but to the inner self that the writer is objectifying, and the very act of objectifying involves detaching this self and observing it as if it were a third person entity [1975, p. 53]," Widdowson sketches out, somewhat loosely, three forms of discourse in terms of the role of the "I": (*a*) In diaries and personal letters there is no distinction between sender and addressor: The writer may reveal his inner thoughts and feelings, and in doing so he takes responsibility—his readers may assume that he is "telling the truth." (*b*) In all other forms of nonliterary language, the writer, as sender and addressor, adopts a recognized social role and what he says and how he says it are determined by that role: "he is not at liberty to express his own individual sentiments at will. . . . [H]is addressee will be concerned with what he has to say in his role and not with his private and individual thoughts [p. 52]."; (*c*) literary discourse, where the sender and addressor are disjoined, is concerned with the private thoughts and feelings of the writer, but in "bringing them out of hiding" he objectifies them and may explore them through the creation of personae, so that "we cannot assume that when a literary writer uses the first person he is describing his own experiences or making a confession." The literary writer, in fact, aware of the convention that distinguishes sender from addressor, is "relieved from any social responsibility for what he says in the first person [p. 53]." (Love letters, he notes, count as evidence in a court of law, love poems don't!)

This analysis provides an interesting gloss on the three major function categories in our model: expressive, transactional, and poetic.

The second objection Widdowson anticipates relates to the familiar problem of "the novel with a message." Our claim that a literary work was a verbal object and not a verbal transaction was objected to on just these grounds, and we argued in reply that a poetic work achieved its effect indirectly, via the poetic construct taken as a whole. Widdowson's claim that a literary work is a self-contained unit independent of a social context risks the same kind of objection: His answer is

> that it may indeed be the purpose of a writer to stir the social conscience but he does not do so by addressing himself directly to those whose consciences he wishes to stir. He expresses a certain reality, a personal vision, and the reader, as an *observer* of this reality, might then feel constrained to act in a certain way. But he is not directed to act by the writer (1975, p. 53).

Widdowson then develops a point that will be familiar to readers of Jakobson (1971, e.g., p. 704); he explores the way paradigmatic relationships invade the area of syntagmatic relationships in poetic discourse, and illustrates this at the level of phonemes and the grammatical level of words and phrases. Phonological distinctions that by the normal language code exist as a range from which **selection** is made (the story for example is about a cat and not about a hat, a bat or a mat) invade the syntagmatic relationship, the process of **combination** in a literary work, as for example when a poet chooses "bright" in preference to "shining" because that word fits into the sound pattern, including perhaps both rhythm and rhyme, of his poem.

More germane to his principal argument is Widdowson's example of a series of verbal groups any one of which might have served to complete a sentence in a T. S. Eliot poem. Widdowson then shows how Eliot in fact does not SE-LECT, but COMBINES: "Words strain, Crack and sometimes break . . ." etc. This strategy, Widdowson notes, reflects the writer's struggle to resolve ambiguities and allows him to invite the reader to take part in that process. By such means works of literature communicate "an individual awareness of a reality other than that which is given general social sanction but nevertheless related to it [1971, p. 70]."

Contextualization

One of the important ways in which we may characterize the difference between transactional and poetic discourse is by reference to the way a reader grasps the message. If what a writer does when he draws from all he knows and selectively sets down what he wants to communicate is described as 'de-contextualization', then the complementary process on the part of a reader is to 'contextualize', interpreting the writer's meaning by building it into his existing knowledge and experience. We have suggested (Britton et al., 1975, pp. 85–86) that in reading a piece of transactional discourse we contextualize the material in piecemeal fashion; passing over what is familiar, rejecting what is incomprehensible to us or perceived as inconsistent with our own thinking, accepting in piecemeal fashion what seems to us interesting, building our own connections between these fragments and our existing knowledge (which is open to modification, of course, in the process). With poetic discourse, on the other hand (and much of what Widdowson has said will support this difference), we apply our own knowledge and experience to the reconstruction of the writer's verbal object, and until we have done this, until we have the sense of a completed whole, a single unique symbol, we are in no position to reexamine our own thoughts and feelings in the light of the author's work. This we have called **global contextualization.** I think our response to a novel with a message may sometimes be a deliberate reexamination of the kind this suggests, but I have come to believe that in most cases global contextualization is a process that goes on over time and one we may not even be conscious of. We are constantly learning from our own first-hand experiences and mostly, because of the wide-ranging and diffuse nature of the process, without being aware that we are doing so. I am inclined to think that our response to a work of literature is like that.

We do of course contextualize in piecemeal fashion while reading works of literature: We pick up clues as to what life is like in places we have never visited, what it was like at times before we were born. But this is quite subsidiary, for most of us, to the main effects of literature; and it has its risks, since the verbal object, as Widdowson shows, deals with a reality "other than that which is given social sanction." There may be pygmies in the Australian rain forests the novelist describes, but that is no guarantee that they exist in fact. Nevertheless, for historians or sociologists, say, to study literature for the information they can glean is of course a legitimate option; they will be employing a process of piecemeal contextualization where what the author offered was a work to be contextualized globally. Louise Rosenblatt (1978), as we have mentioned, has paid close attention to this matter of the reader's options and raised some important issues. In defining a literary work of art as "what happens when a reader and a text come together [p. 12]," she is I think loading the dice in the reader's favor, but the weight has for so long been on the author's side that this is understandable. There are of course anomalies, as when a text produced by an author as propaganda survives when its injunctions are no longer appropriate, and survives as a piece of literature; or when an informative text (Gibbon's *Decline and Fall* is the stock example) survives when much of its information has been superseded and even discredited, to be read now not as information but for the unique and individual qualities typical of a work of literature.

There are anomalies, but without wishing in any way to infringe on the reader's freedom to choose, I do suggest that in the vast majority of cases the general conventions chosen by the writer—whether to produce expressive, transactional, or poetic discourse—are in fact the conventions by which the reader chooses to interpret.

YOUNG FLUENT WRITERS

L. S. Vygotsky

I have known a number of children who by the age of 5 or 6 had taught themselves to write. In each case it was stories that they wrote, and usually the stories were made up into little books, with pictures as well as writing. I take it as some evidence of the extraordinary ability human beings have of succeeding in doing what they want to do. One of these young children, under the age of 4, began by producing a little book with "pretend writing" in it—and surely, just as we pretend to be someone we want to be, so we pretend to do something we want to do. Some 20 months later the scribbled lines had given place to a decipherable story. Evidence of this kind is too often ignored, and it takes a Vygotsky, speaking across the decades since his death, to observe that the attempt to teach writing as a motor skill is mistaken (Vygotsky, 1978, p. 117); that psychology has conceived of it as a motor skill and "paid remarkably little attention to the question of written language as such, that is, a particular system of symbols and signs whose mastery heralds a critical turning-point in the entire cultural development of the child [p. 106]." It was his view that make-believe play, drawing and writing should be seen as "different moments in an essentially unified process of development of written language [p. 116]." And this he contrasted with what he found in schools: "Instead of being founded on the needs of children as they naturally develop and on their own activity, writing is given to them from without, from the teacher's hands [p. 105]."

I suggest that the 4-year-old I have referred to made what Vygotsky calls "a basic discovery—namely that one can draw not only things but also speech [1978, p. 115]." Since pictorial representation is first-order symbolism and writing is second-order symbolism (designating words that are in turn signs for things and relationships), Vygotsky saw this discovery as a key point in the development of writing in a child; yet he recognized there was little understanding of how the shift takes place, since the necessary research had not been done (p. 115). We are not much wiser today, though the labors of Donald Graves and others give us good reason to hope.

Outline for a Case Study

My records of the development of Clare, the 4-year-old whose pretend writing I have referred to, may illustrate some of the points Vygotsky has made in his account of "the developmental history of written language."

(1) Her conversational speech was quite well developed by the time she was 2 years old. Much of her talk was playful (seeing me at the washbasin, *What have you got off, Daddy?*—at 2:3) and she used made-up forms freely (*I'm spoonfuling it in, I'm see-if-ing it will go through, smuttered in your eyes*—for uncombed hair—all at 2:7). Her curiosity about language was in evidence early (*When it's one girl you say "girl" and when it's two three four girls you say "girl s." Why when it's two three four childs you say "child ren?"*—at 2:10; *"Fairy girl with curly hair," that makes a rhyme, doesn't it?*— at 2:11; on hearing something described as 'delicious,' *Is delicious nicer than lovely?*—at 3:1).

(2) Extended make-believe play, involving her toy animals in family roles, was established by the time she was 3. Storytelling developed from it, the animals becoming the audience. The toy animals (she was given dolls from time to time but they were never adopted into the family) seem to have

sustained a key role. They were the *dramatis personae* of her make-believe play, the subject of the stories she told, of her drawings, and later of the stories she wrote. Vygotsky's point that in make-believe play the plaything is free to take on a meaning that does not rely on perceptual resemblance is amusingly illustrated by the fact that when Clare enacted a queen's wedding, the least suitable of the animals—a scraggy, loose-knit dog—was chosen for the role of queen!

(3) Her earliest recognizable drawings came just before she was 2 and though they are clearly attempts at human figures, the talk that always accompanied the drawing was often in anthropomorphic terms (*the mummy bird, the daddy bird*). A picture drawn in colored chalks at 3:5 shows a large figure of a girl on the left-hand side and a house on the right. Her commentary as she drew explained: *The girl is carrying a yellow handbag and she has a brown furry dog on a lead. Her feet are walking along. . . . I have put a car outside the house. I am putting blue sky, now I am putting in the sunshine.* (Here the diagonal blue strokes that had indicated the sky were interspersed with yellow ones.) *She's got a tricycle with blue wheels and a chain. Mrs. Jones across the road has yellow and brown on her windows. I shall put yellow and red on mine.*

It is an important part of Vygotsky's thesis that a young child's drawing is "graphic speech," dependent on verbal speech: The child draws, that is to say, from the memory of what he knows rather than from what he presently observes; and that what he knows has been processed in speech and is further processed in the speech that accompanies the drawing. The space in Clare's picture is well filled, but not in terms of topographical representation: The girl and the house are upright; the car is drawn vertically standing on its head; the dog vertically sitting on its tail; and the tricycle has its frame, wheels and chain spread out, looking more like an assembly kit.

(4) What circumstances could be supposed to facilitate the process that Vygotsky calls the move from drawing objects to drawing speech? Imitating the general pattern of writing behavior, Clare at the age of 3:6 produced parallel horizontal lines of cursive scribble, saying that she was *doing grownup's kind of writing.* At 3:11 she produced the little story book I have described with similar lines of scribble but interspersed with words she could actually write (*mummy, and, the*) and with a drawing on the cover. The stories she wrote from 5:6 onward were in cursive script with headings in capitals. She was by this time reading a good deal, mainly the little animal stories by Beatrix Potter and Alison Uttley.

Turning from the general pattern to the detail, Clare at the age of 3 played very often with a set of inch-high letters made of plastic in various colors. Among more random, playful uses, she learned to make her name in these letters and she was interested in what each letter was called. (One effect of this play was evident: When first she attempted to write words, an "E," for example, was an "E" for her whether it faced right or left or up or down.) One of her activities represented a link between letter recognition and writing behavior in general: At 3:5, in imitation of picture alphabets she knew, she was drawing a series of objects and writing the initial letter of each beside the drawing. Most of them she knew, but she came to one she did not: "rhubarb." When I told her, she said, *R—that's easy—just a girl's head and two up-and-downs!*

(5) The final stage in Vygotsky's "developmental history" is that by which the written language ceases to be second-order symbolism, mediated by speech, and becomes first-order symbolism. I can offer no evidence of this from the records of Clare, and indeed I seriously doubt whether that transition is ever entirely appropriate to the written language we have been concerned with, that of stories.

(6) I think the most important conclusion to be drawn from the case of Clare and other children who have taught themselves to write by writing stories is a point that is central to Vygotsky's argument, that of the effect of INTENTION on a child's performance. It would appear that the spoken language effectively meets young children's needs in general, and we must surmise that it is only as they come to value the written language as a vehicle for stories that they are likely to form an intention to write. Much of Clare's behavior indicated that she had done so. Slobin and Welsh (1973) have effectively demonstrated that mastery of the spoken language cannot be adequately assessed without account of "the intention to say so-and-so"—a lesson that as teachers or researchers we have been slow to learn.

Writing and Reading

Clare continued to read and write stories for many years. Animal fantasies predominated until the age of 7, pony stories and adventure stories (often featuring an animal) followed until, from the ages of 12 to 14 she gave herself up almost entirely to reading women's magazine stories and writing herself at great length in that vein. Here, to represent successive stages, are some opening lines:

> **At 6:** *I am a little Teddy Bear. I've got a pony called Snow and I live in a little house with a thatched roof.*
>
> **At 8½:** *Mrs. Hedgehog had just had three babies. Two of them were like ordinary hedgehog babies, covered with soft prickles. But the third had none. It was a dead calm as the Sand Martin and crew glided out of the small har-*

bour at Plymouth. Phillip and Jean were the eldest. They were twins of fourteen.

At 11: *Fiona Mackenzie lay in bed in her small attic bedroom. She turned sleepily over, but the morning sun streaming in at her small window dazzled her, and she turned back.* (A story about horses in the Highlands.)

At 12: *Derek looked into her face, and his green eyes burning fiercely with the white hot light of intense love gazed into the liquid depth of her melting, dark brown ones.*

At 14: *The dance was in full swing, and Giselle was the acknowledged belle of it. More radiant, more sparkling than ever before, she floated blissfully in the arms of James Wainforth.*

Her comments on her reading and writing were sometimes illuminating. At 3:8 she described the Cinderella story as *A bit sad book about two ugly sisters and a girl they were ugly to.* At 8:7 she was asked what sort of things she liked reading. *Well,* she said, *there's* Treasure Island—*that's a bloody one for when I'm feeling boyish. And* Little Men, *that's a sort of half-way one.* "And don't you ever feel girlish?" she was asked. *Yes. When I'm tired and then I read* The Smallest Dormouse. At 10:2 she wrote a story about children finding a treasure: *It's like Enid Blyton's story mostly,* she said, *except longer words.* A few months later she was struggling to get through Mrs. Craik's *John Halifax, Gentleman,* but gave up with the comment, *It's a bit Lorna Doonish, a lot of cissy boys in it. It's so sort of **genteel**—I can't stand it!*

That her writing was influenced by her reading shows up dramatically (though from a limited aspect) in the following figures relating to mean T-unit length and subordination at four age-points. The figures for a passage from a women's magazine story she had read are shown in parentheses.

Age:	6	9	13	(Magazine)	17
Number of words taken:	331	332	340	(330)	322
Mean T-Unit length:	4.1	8.0	6.9	(6.7)	11.5
Number of subordinate clauses:	7	17	6	(9)	19

Spectator Role and the Beginnings of Writing

In the light of current school practices, it is as important as ever today to stress Vygotsky's view that learning to read and learning to write must be seen as inseparable aspects of one process, that of mastering written language. We have come to recognize the way this process is grounded in speech but have not yet acknowledged the essential contribution of other forms of symbolic behavior, gesture, make-believe play, pictorial representation. In my account of Clare's development, I have added one other activity, that of manipulative play with the substance of written language. Bruner (1975) has pointed out that such play contributes to learning because it is a 'meta-process,' one that focuses on the nature itself of the activity. (Children learn to walk for the purpose of getting where they want to be; PLAY with walking—early forms of dancing—involves a concern with the nature of the walking process, an exploration of its manifold possibilities.)

It remains for me to point out that make-believe play (embracing the social environment children construct with their playthings), storytelling, listening to stories, pictorial representation and the talk that complements it, story reading and story writing—these are all activities in the role of spectator. As I have suggested, I believe it is this characteristic that develops a need for the written language in young children and the intention to master it. In such activities children are sorting themselves out, progressively distinguishing what is from what seems, strengthening their hold on reality by a consideration of alternatives. Clare, for example, at the age of 8:6, writes what at first sight appears to be a variant of the kind of animal fable she was familiar with from earlier reading of Beatrix Potter:

HEDGEHOG
Mrs. Hedgehog had just had three babies. Two of them were like ordinary hedgehog babies, covered with soft prickles.

But the third had none. He was like a hedgehog in any other way. He ate like a hedgehog and he lived like a hedgehog and he rolled up in a ball like a hedgehog, and he went to sleep in the winter like a hedgehog. But he had no prickles like a hedgehog.

When he was a year old a fairy came to him and said, "Go to China and get three hairs from the Emperor Ching Chang's seventh guinea-pig. Throw the hairs in the fire, and then put it out with six bucketfuls of water. Put some of the ash on your head, and leave it for the night. In the morning you will be covered with prickles." Then she faded away.

[The story tells how he carried out these instructions, and concludes:]

He went to sleep beside the stream. In the morning he woke up feeling rather strange. He looked at his back. It was covered in prickles. He spent four days in China, then he went home in the boat. His family were very surprised to see him!

For those who knew Clare, it was not difficult to recognize here an account of her own struggle to establish herself in the family in competition with a more confident and more relaxed younger sister. *His family were very surprised to see him!* Without knowing the writer, one might guess that a similar self-exploration was taking place, unconsciously, in the 6-year-old girl who wrote:

> *There was a child of a witch who was ugly. He had pointed ears thin legs and was born in a cave. he flew in the air holding on nothing just playing games.*
> *When he saw ordinary girls and boys he hit them with his broomstick. A cat came along. he arched his back at the girls and boys and made them run away. When they had gone far away the cat meeowed softly at the witch child. the cat loved the child. the child loved the cat the cat was the onlee thing the child loved in the world.*

It has often been pointed out that in one sense a tiny infant is lord of his universe, and that growing from infancy into childhood involves discovering one's own unimportance. But the world created in the stories children write is a world they control and this may be a source of deep satisfaction. As one of the children recorded by Donald Graves remarked, she liked writing stories because "you are the mother of the story."

Whether to read or to write, a story makes fewer demands than a piece of transactional writing since one essential element of the latter process is missing in the former. The reader of an informative or persuasive piece must construct himself the writer's meaning and inwardly debate it (an essential part of the piecemeal contextualization process); the reader of a story accepts, so to speak, an invitation to enter a world and see what happens to him there. The writer of a transactional piece must attempt to anticipate and make provision for the reader's inner debate; the writer of a story constructs a situation to his own satisfaction, though thereafter he may be willing, even eager, to share it.

Expressive Writing

Edward Sapir observed that "ordinary speech is directly expressive [1961, p. 10]." Because expressive writing, though it differs in substantial ways from speech, is the form of written discourse closest to speech, the London Writing Research team suggested that it provided a "natural" starting point for beginning writers, assisting them at a time when they have rich language resources recruited through speech, but few if any internalized forms of the written language. Progress from this point consists, we believe, in shuttling between those spoken resources and an increasing store of forms internalized from reading and being read to. (It may prove that vocal reading, whether their own or somebody else's, is in the early stages a more effective route to that internalization.)

We might describe this early form as an all-purpose expressive. As the writer employs it to perform different tasks, fulfill different purposes, and increasingly succeeds in meeting the different demands, his all-purpose expressive will evolve: He will acquire by dissociation a variety of modes. Expressive writing is thus a matrix from which will develop transactional and poetic writing, as well as the more mature forms of the expressive.

What the Young Writer Needs to Know

My argument has been that Vygotsky's account offers an explanation of the phenomenon I have noted, that of Clare and the other children who mastered written language by producing storybooks at an early age. Let me now go on to ask, "What does a writer acquiring mastery in this way need to know?"

First and foremost he must know from experience the SATISFACTION that can come from a story—perhaps first a story told to him, but then certainly a story read to him. Sartre (1967, p. 31) has commented on the difference: Accustomed to having his mother tell him stories, he describes his experience when first she reads to him: *The tale itself was in its Sunday best: the woodcutter, the woodcutter's wife and their daughter, the fairy, all those little people, our fellow-creatures, had acquired majesty; their rags were magnificently described, words left their mark on objects, transforming actions into rituals and events into ceremonies.*

Then he must know something of the structure of a story, a learning process that Applebee (1978) has very helpfully described in developmental terms for stories told by children between the ages of 2 and 5 (but with implications for later stages). He sees two principles at work, one of **centering,** a concern for the unity of a story, and one of **chaining,** a concern for sequence; and in terms of these two principles he outlines a series of plot structures that parallel the stages of concept development described by Vygotsky (1962). It should be noted, at the same time, that recall of events in narrative form is something that all children achieve a year or more before they are ready to tackle the written language.

Some forms of story writing will only be possible if the writer is familiar with the conventional associations that govern our expectations in listening to stories—the role expected of a wolf, a lion, a fox, a witch, a prince, and so on (Applebee, 1978, chap. 3). Such built-in associations are, of course, a resource that a young writer may in his own stories exploit, improvise on, invert, or ignore.

Knowledge of the linguistic conventions of stories—the *Once upon a time* and *happily ever after* conventions—are often familiar to children before they can read or write, as are more general features of the language of written stories. (I saw a story dictated by a 3-year-old which contained the sentence, *The king went sadly home for he had nowhere else to go*—a use of *for* which is certainly not a spoken form.)

But production of these and all other written forms relies, of course, on a knowledge of the written code itself, the formation of letters, words, sentences. How this is picked up from alphabet books and cornflake packets, picture books, TV advertisements, and street signs remains something of a mystery, though two governing conditions seem likely: a context of manipulative play and picture-making, and the association of this learning with the purpose of producing written stories. I am sure we underestimate the extent of such learning when a powerful interest is in focus. In my recent experience of reading stories to a 3-year-old, I have been amazed at her ability to fill the words into gaps I leave when the story I am reading is one she cannot have heard very often. Michael Polanyi's account of the relation of subsidiary to focal awareness certainly helps us to see this learning process as feasible (Polanyi, 1958, chap. 4).

Finally, the writer must know from experience the sound of a written text read aloud. How else can he come to hear an inner voice dictating to him the story he wants to produce? An apprenticeship of listening to others will enable him later to be aware of the rhythms of the written language in the course of his own silent reading.

A Final Speculation

I believe the successful writer learns all these things implicitly; that is to say, in Polanyi's terms, by maintaining a focal awareness of the desired performance that acts as a determining tendency guiding and controlling his subsidiary awareness of the means he employs. I believe, further, that any attempt to introduce explicit learning would be likely to hinder rather than help at this early stage. When we are dealing with poetic writing, there is much that could not in any case be made explicit: We simply do not know by what organizing principles experience is projected into a work of art.

It is this problem that Susanne Langer has been investigating over many years. Her distinction between discursive and presentational symbolism—between a message encoded in a symbol system and a message embodied in a single unique complex symbol; her recognition of the key role of the arts as offering an ordering of experience alternative to the cognitive, logical ordering achieved by discursive symbolism—these are foundation stones in our theory of language functions.

From her exploration of the laws governing a work of art she makes one very interesting suggestion: that in all works of art there is a building-up and resolution of tensions and that the intricate pattern of these movements, this rhythm, somehow reflects the "shape of every living act [Langer, 1967, chap. 7]."

To speculate on her speculations: We give and find shape in the very act of perception, we give and find further shape as we talk, write or otherwise represent our experiences. I say "give and find" because clearly there is order and pattern in the natural world irrespective of our perceiving and representing. At the biological level man shares that order, but at the level of behavior he appears to lose it: The pattern of his actions is more random than that of the instinctual behavior of animals. In learning to control his environment he has gained a freedom of choice in action that he may use constructively and harmoniously or to produce disharmony, shapelessness, chaos. When, however, he shapes his experience into a verbal object, an art form, in order to communicate it and to realize it more fully himself, he is seeking to recapture a natural order that his daily actions have forfeited. Understanding so little of the complexities of these processes, we can do no more than entertain that idea as a fascinating speculation.

REFERENCES

Applebee, A. N. *The child's concept of story.* Chicago: University of Chicago Press, 1978.

Britton, J. N. Literature. In J. N. Britton (Ed.), *The arts and current tendencies in education.* London: Evans, 1963. Pp. 34–61.

Britton, J. N. Response to literature. In J. R. Squire (Ed.), *Response to literature.* Champaign, Ill.: National Council of Teachers of English, 1968. Pp. 3–10.

Britton, J. N., Burgess, T., Martin, M., McLeod, A., and Rosen, H. *The development of writing abilities, 11–18.* London: Macmillan, 1975.

Bruner, J. S. The ontogenesis of speech acts. *Journal of Child Language,* 1975, 2, 1–19.

Gusdorf, G. *Speaking.* Evanston: Northwestern University Press, 1965.

Harding, D. W. The role of the onlooker. *Scrutiny,* 1937, 6, 247–258.

Harding, D. W. Psychological processes in the reading of fiction. *British Journal of Aesthetics,* 1962, 2, 133–147.

Harding, D. W. Response to literature: The report of the study group. In J. R. Squire (Ed.), *Response to literature.* Champaign, Ill.: National Council of Teachers of English, 1968. Pp. 11–27.

Hymes, D. The ethnography of speaking. In J. A. Fishman (Ed.), *Readings in the sociology of language.* The Hague: Mouton, 1968.

Jakobson, R. *Selected writings* (Vol. 2). *Word and language.* The Hague: Mouton, 1971.

Labov, W. *The social stratification of English in New York City.* Washington, D.C.: Center for Applied Linguistics, 1966.

Langer, S. K. *Feeling and form*. London: Routledge and Kegan Paul, 1953.

Langer, S. K. *Mind: An essay on human feeling*. Baltimore: Johns Hopkins Press, 1967.

Moffett, J. *Teaching the universe of discourse*. Boston: Houghton Mifflin, 1968.

Polanyi, M. *Personal knowledge*. London: Routledge and Kegan Paul, 1958.

Rosenblatt, L. *The reader, the text, the poem*. Carbondale, Ill.: Southern Illinois University Press, 1978.

Sapir, E. *Culture, language and personality*. Berkeley: University of California Press, 1961.

Sartre, J. P. *Words*. Harmondsworth: Penguin Books, 1967.

Sebeok, T. *Style in language*. Cambridge: M.I.T. Press, 1960.

Slobin, D. I., & Welsh, C. A. Elicited imitation as a research tool in developmental psycholinguistics. In C. A. Ferguson & D. I. Slobin (Eds.), *Studies of child language development*. New York: Holt, Rinehart and Winston, 1973.

Vygotsky, L. S. *Mind in society*. Cambridge: Harvard University Press, 1978.

Widdowson, H. G. *Stylistics and the teaching of literature*. London: Longman, 1975.

A Discourse-Centered Rhetoric of the Paragraph

PAUL C. RODGERS, JR.

Today's textbook paragraph, the paragraph taught by so many to so few—with its vision of triune organic integrity and its philosophy of mechanism—was unveiled almost precisely a century ago, in March 1866, by an unprepossessing Scottish logician and composition teacher named Alexander Bain. Bain laid no claim to infallibility as a rhetorician, and was more or less ignored in his own day, but the late nineteenth century chose to magnify his authority in retrospect: long after the man was forgotten, his dicta assumed something of the aura of revealed truth. In all the intervening years since 1866, though Bain's six "rules" have undergone considerable refinement and elaboration, virtually no one has ever challenged his basic concept of the paragraph or its underlying suppositions. In essence the paragraph today is just what it has been since the beginning, an "expanded sentence"—logically, structurally, semantically.[1]

Yet it has been obvious all along that Bain's analysis simply does not comprehend what goes on in many sound and effective paragraphs, and the language of its successive formulations never has given the student writer adequate guidance. As commonly defined (à la Bain), the paragraph is a group of sentences which develops the single idea conveyed in its topic sentence. Each of the key words in this definition offers pitfalls. What, for instance, is an "idea"? Does a noun or noun phrase express an idea, or must every idea be a proposition? Must the topic idea be carried as the major predication of the topic sentence? If not, then how does one distinguish topic material

---

Reprinted from *College Composition and Communication* 17.1 (February 1966): 2–11. Used with permission.

from its context? Can the topic be merely suggested, as by a question or exclamation or negative declaration or figure of speech, or must it be spelled out? If the paragraph is a group of sentences, how small can the group be? Do two sentences constitute a group? Does one? That is, can a paragraph properly be conterminous with its own topic sentence?

Bain and his immediate successors worked by deduction, first assuming a close organic parallel between sentence and paragraph and then applying traditional sentence-law to the paragraph. But questions like the ones suggested above provoked inductive study of actual paragraphs and eventually produced a mass of inductive qualifications grafted upon the original deductive formula:

Bain's Rules

♦ A proper paragraph always has a single central topic idea, except when it has two, three, or more.

♦ Development of the topic is always limited to the paragraph in which the topic is broached, except when the topic requires that exposition continue in the next.

♦ The topic sentence always expresses the topic idea, but the work of expression may be disposed of in a minor segment of the sentence; or, on the other hand, a complicated topic may take several sentences, and these sentences may be widely separated in the paragraph.

♦ There is always a topic sentence, yet it may not actually be stated. In this case, it is "implied," and serves as a sort of offstage influence directing the action in the paragraph.

♦ A paragraph by definition is a series of sentences, but now and then it turns out to be one sentence only. If the sentence-series seems too long for presentation as a unit, it can be subdivided into several paragraphs without loss of unity. Conversely, a series of short paragraphs can be combined into a single unit, sometimes with the original components identified by number or letter.

♦ Moreover there are certain very useful and common paragraph types that show little interest in amplifying topics: transitional, introductory, directive, summary, and concluding paragraphs.

In short, the paragraph is what the textbook says it is, except . . . it isn't. At least, not always; and if one happens to be working with the wrong handbook or the wrong anthology of prose models, it often isn't.

Faced with this congeries of paradoxes, recent commentators have tended to reject or simply ignore traditional theory:

> Since every paragraph of the essay is part of the general flow, it is difficult to find in many paragraphs anything so static that it can be isolated as the single idea, or topic, of that paragraph. The notion that every paragraph must have a topic sentence is hence a misleading one.[2]
>
> Obviously any piece of composition possessing even a minimum of unity may be summed up in some kind of sentence. The "implied" topic sentence, therefore, is an abstraction—a not very useful kind of ghost sentence.[3]
>
> [The paragraph] is simply a convenient grouping of sentences. In a progression of sentences a few places will be more suited to indentations than others, but you can justify an indentation before almost any sentence of sophisticated prose.[4]

However well grounded such pronouncements may be, they contribute little to prose criticism. If ideas flow, how shall we measure and define the current? If a sequence of ideas can be introduced without interpretive comment, how does the sequence relate to its context, the discourse? If indentations can occur almost anywhere, upon what basis shall we justify or challenge a given decision to indent?

The current situation may be summed up as follows: Deduction has failed to yield a fully satisfactory model of the paragraph, and interest in the putative organic parallel between paragraph and sentence has declined sharply. Reviewing Barrett Wendell's epochal commentary of 1890 in its reincarnation of 1963, one marvels at the man's poise and aplomb; and inevitably, and perhaps a bit sadly, one also notes the anachronism:

> A paragraph is to a sentence what a sentence is to a word. The principles which govern the arrangement of sentences in paragraphs, then, are identical with those that govern the arrangement of words in sentences.[5]

Piecemeal inductive observations over the years have so far undermined this notion of the paragraph that it scarcely seems worthwhile to state it. Yet we have not broken cleanly with the past: to the contrary, many teachers and textbook writers, possibly a majority, finding some value still in sentence-based tradition, seem to be fearful of pitching the baby out with the bath. As recently as October 1965, Francis Christensen prefaced his trail-breaking "Generative Rhetoric of the Paragraph" with these words:

> My purpose here is. . . to show that the paragraph has, or may have, a structure as definable and traceable as that of the sentence and that it can be analyzed in the same way. In fact . . . I have come to see that the parallel between sentence and paragraph is much closer than I suspected, so close, indeed, that as Josephine Miles put it (in a letter) the paragraph seems to be only a macro-sentence or meta-sentence.[6]

Christensen later went on to qualify his commentary with several of the usual exceptions.

My intention here is not to criticize Professor Christensen's approach, which strikes me as having great promise, but rather to argue for a concept of the paragraph that will comprehend *all* paragraphs.

Let me begin by pointing out again that the sentence-based notion of the paragraph was first introduced in words written, not in the skies, but at the University of Aberdeen, and by a man of strong logical predisposition. Secondly, when one explores its historical origin, one finds that the paragraph (from Gr. *para*, beside, + *graphos*, mark) began as a punctuation device, a symbol placed in the margin to indicate a noteworthy break in the flow of discourse; only later did the word come to signify the stretch of language between breaks. The original notion persists in our transitive verb *to paragraph*.

Thus paragraph structure precedes, in a certain very vital sense, the indentation that marks its physical limit; and rhetoric's proper task is to understand why indentations occur when they do, rather than to devise some Procrustean formula for governing the behavior of sentences between breaks, and to insist upon applying it over and over again throughout all written discourse. What we need is a philosophy of paragraph punctuation, a flexible, open-ended *discourse-centered* rhetoric of the paragraph.

What, then, may be the aspects or qualities of discourse that writers recognize when they indent? The late nineteenth century visualized discourse as a series of horizontal "leaps and pauses," a stream that "shoots toward some point of interest, eddies about it for a moment, then hurries on to another," with the paragraph indentations indicating successive conceptual leaps and lingerings.[7] As Edwin Lewis observed in 1894, the writer

> conceives his paragraph topic before he develops it, though of course in the process of development the associations of the symbols used may lead him afield. He thinks, so to speak, in successive nebulous masses, perceiving in each a luminous centre before he analyses the whole.[8]

This horizontal image still appears regularly in textbooks, but a second image now has been added. In 1946 the late Wendell Johnson pointed out that when the mind is "interested," attention fluctuates vertically, up and down the abstraction ladder:

> If you will observe carefully the speakers you find to be interesting, you are very likely to find that they play, as it were, up and down the levels of abstraction quite as a harpist plays up and down the strings of her harp.... the speaker who remains too long on the same general level of abstraction offends our evaluative processes—no matter what his subject may be.[9]

In 1964, John Lord applied Johnson's insight to prose analysis, visualizing good writing as "a constant weaving up and down between the concrete and the abstract, as well as a constant forward movement from a beginning through a middle to an end."[10]

The vertical image ties in nicely with traditional ideas of paragraph structure. Topic sentences coincide with certain emphasized peaks of abstraction. The most common methods of "amplification"—clarification of the topic by use of definition, analogy, comparison, or contrast; presentation of causes or logical proof; citation of examples, instances, and illustrations; accumulation of supporting details—all these methods tend strongly toward lower-level statement. The two main types of "movement"—variously spoken of as loose and periodic, deductive and inductive, regressive and progressive, and (perhaps most satisfactorily) as analytic and synthetic—refer simply to the upward or downward thrust of attention, toward or away from the abstract topic. Our thought-movement normally is synthetic, and moves upward from the particulars of experience to the high-level generalities of conceptual thought. The particulars "generate" the abstraction. When we write, however, we usually proceed by analysis, first stating the available generality, which stands first in consciousness, and then recovering or discovering ("generating") a sufficient bulk of particulars to support it. Extended synthetic movement accordingly is fairly uncommon in written discourse.

But neither horizontal leaps nor the vertical seesaw obligates a writer to indent. Both types of movement exist at all levels of discourse, in units smaller than the sentence and larger than the paragraph. Indentation frequently does mark major horizontal and vertical phases (which tend to coincide), but sometimes other considerations take precedence.

Like music, writing is a complex sequence of events in time. Subordinate patterns occur within the sequence, many of them interpenetrating and partly coinciding with others. The writer has at his disposal various punctuation devices with which he can tag and call attention to some of them. The paragraph break is only one such device, the most emphatic.

About all we can usefully say of *all* paragraphs at present is that their authors have marked them off for special consideration as *stadia of discourse,* in preference to other stadia, other patterns, in the same material. "At this point," the writer tells us with his indentation, "a major stadium of discourse has just been completed. Rest for a moment, recollect and consider, before the next begins." But his decision to indent may be taken for any one (or more) of at least half a dozen different reasons.

The great majority of stadia of course are logical, whatever else they may be, but thought-movement submits to very flexible partitioning; hence the size of a given logical paragraph frequently reflects secondary influences. Often the physical aspect of the paragraph must be controlled, especially in publications using narrow-column format. The reader must not be put off unnecessarily by paragraphs that seem overly bulky, and therefore indigestible, or by a long succession of thin, apparently anemic units. On the other hand, the need for rhetorical emphasis may dictate either bulk treatment or isolation of a short stadium in a paragraph of its own, and an impulse to vary paragraph length purely for variety's sake may have the same effect. To a lesser degree, patterns of prose rhythm may call for indentation;[11] so, too, may abrupt shifts in tone or strictly formal considerations, as when paragraphs are paired off for contrast or comparison or knit into some larger pattern involving paragraphs as units.

Thus the paragraph can be described very roughly as an autochthonous pattern in prose discourse, identified originally by application of logical, physical, rhythmical, tonal, formal, and other rhetorical criteria, set off from adjacent patterns by indentations, and commended thereby to the reader as a noteworthy stadium of discourse. Though all good paragraphs are distinct stadia, not all stadia are paragraphs. Many must always exist merely as emergent possibilities, potential paragraphs (as well as smaller units) dissolved in the flow of discourse. Paragraph structure is part and parcel of the structure of the discourse as a whole; a given stadium becomes a paragraph not by virtue of its structure but because the writer elects to indent, his indentation functioning, as does all punctuation, as a gloss upon the overall literary process under way at that point. Paragraphs are not composed; they are discovered. To compose is to create; to indent is to interpret. Accordingly, the qualities of the paragraph can no more be grasped through normative statement than can the qualities of discourse.

This conclusion is not wholly negative, of course. It denies only that the paragraph can be wrapped up conclusively in a tight deductive formula, and implies, positively, that inductive study of the art of paragraphing has an immense neglected potential. While intent upon determining what

The Paragraph is, <u>we have very</u> largely failed to appreciate what real paragraphs are.

To test this contention, let us contrast the traditional and discourse-centered views of a familiar paragraph sequence, Walter Pater's descant on "Style" (1888), an essay that recommends itself to our purpose for several special reasons. In it, Pater stresses what he calls "the necessity of *mind* in style," "that architectural conception of work, which foresees the end in the beginning and never loses sight of it," the underlying structural framework, which is "all-important, felt, or painfully missed, everywhere" (14.3).[12] One of the greatest pleasures in reading good prose, he tells us, lies in "the critical tracing out of that conscious artistic structure, and the pervading sense of it as we read" (15.16). Surely he must have foreseen that readers would judge his essay by its own forceful pronouncements; and he must therefore have paragraphed with unusual care.

But Pater always composed laboriously and deliberately. For thirty-five years, George Saintsbury admired his "wonderful perfection of craftsmanship,"[13] noting especially his sensitive control of prose rhythm and adroit management of the paragraph:

> Above all, no one, it must be repeated, has ever surpassed, and scarcely any one has ever equalled Mr. Pater in deliberate and successful architecture of the prose-paragraph—in what may, for the sake of a necessary difference, be called the scriptorial in opposition to the oratorical manner.[14]
>
> . . . it must always be remembered that the care of the paragraph was one of Mr. Pater's first and greatest anxieties; when I remarked on it [in 1876, apropos of Pater's *Renaissance*], . . . he wrote to me expressing special gratification, and acknowledging that it had been one of his principal objects.[15]

Such a conscious, calculated devotion to paragraph technique warrants close inspection.

But "Style" holds particular interest for us because of its structural subtlety and flexibility. As A. C. Benson observed, "<u>the bones do not show; not only does the rounded flesh conceal them, but they are still further disguised into a species of pontifical splendour by a rich and stiff embroidered robe of language.</u>"[16] The great variety in paragraph "shape" can be inferred from the following statistics. Though Pater's average paragraph in this essay is quite long (271 words), individual paragraphs range from 24 to 793 words, and the totals of sentences per paragraph range from one to 18. Two paragraphs have fewer than 100 words; 11 contain between 100 and 200 words;

9 contain between 200 and 300; and 9 run to more than 300. This break-down corresponds almost exactly to Edwin Lewis's conclusions regarding English prose in general.[17]

The traditional analysis of the first three paragraphs would view each block of writing individually, describing P1 and P2 as introductory paragraphs, informally assembled, lacking clear-cut central ideas and topic sentences, serving mainly to carry the reader in to P3, a single directive statement which lays out the ground to be covered in the sequel and initiates the essay proper. P3 reads as follows:

> Dismissing then, under sanction of Wordsworth, that harsher opposition of poetry to prose, as savouring in fact of the arbitrary psychology of the last century, and with it the prejudice that there can be but one only beauty of prose style, I propose here to point out certain qualities of all literature as a fine art, which, if they apply to the literature of fact, apply still more to the literature of the imaginative sense of fact, while they apply indifferently to verse and prose, so far as either is really imaginative—certain conditions of true art in both alike, which conditions may also contain in them the secret of the proper discrimination and guardianship of the peculiar excellences of either.

Despite its complexity, this paragraph plainly leans upon the previous discussion for its full implication. Wordsworth's "sanction" has just been examined at the close of P2; the prejudiced claim that there can be but "one only beauty" of prose style refers to earlier comments about Dryden's notions of prose (2.3) and overly narrow conceptions of literature in general (P1 *passim*, esp. 1.4); the distinction between verse and prose recalls a major motif recurring throughout both preceding paragraphs; the opposition of "fact" and "imaginative sense of fact" draws upon the climactic concluding clause of 2.5; and the unobtrusive reference to "discrimination and guardianship" reaches all the way back to 1.1, where Pater relates "the sense of achieved distinctions" to "progress of mind." Each of these references imparts vital meaning to the language of P3. In short, although P3 does direct the reader's attention forward, it simultaneously reminds him of ground already covered. Its gaze is at least as much retrospective as prospective. And it has to be, in view of the complexity of the idea it conveys.

Yet P3 does more than summarize: it selects, relates, disposes, and assigns varying degrees of emphasis to previously discrete ideas. Thus the task of P1-2 is not merely to introduce but to lay a necessary basis for P3; and the thought-movement throughout the sequence, despite occasional analytic eddies, can readily be identified as synthetic. Indeed, with only minor revisions, P1-3 could be combined into one huge synthetic paragraph, with the present P3 serving as its topic sentence.

Since an opening paragraph as bulky as this would obviously repel the reader, Pater divides his exposition into three manageable portions, arranging them in descending order of size as he moves toward his climax in P3. (The word count is 418-251-121; each succeeding unit contains roughly half as many words as its predecessor.) The pace is slow and even, transitions smooth. Although he regularly provides topic statements elsewhere, he omits them in P1 and P2—a further indication that he thinks of P1-3 as a single logical stadium. In a synthetic passage, the progression of ideas should unfold without interruption; otherwise it may not always be clear whether the writer is still approaching his as yet unstated conclusion, or making a new "leap." A topic sentence in either P1 or P2 would introduce just such an element of risk. Also, a terminal topic signals the close of a period of mental concentration. At this point, having surveyed the argument as a whole, and having judged it, the reader no longer feels obliged to bear in mind all the particulars from which the conclusion was drawn. He tends to relax his grip upon lesser elements as he pushes on toward the next major proposition. This is precisely what Pater has to prevent from happening: his reader must retain all the material of P1 and P2 till he arrives at P3.

To summarize, when we examine P1-3 closely, we discover a single synthetic logical stadium broken into three paragraphs, no doubt for physical or editorial reasons. Topic sentences are omitted, quite possibly deliberately, with the result that the thought-movement proceeds without that particular threat to continuity. Formal criteria may account for the length of the separate paragraphs, which descend in size to the relatively short and emphatic P3. *one line ¶*

None of these observations could be made by a strict traditional paragraph analysis.

The next passage of interest is P4-6. Pater opens P4 by commenting on the difficulty of discriminating "fact" from "sense of fact" in prose, and then develops this topic at length with illustrations, remarking at the close of 4.8 that historical writing enters the domain of "art proper" when it reflects the historian's sensibility and bias. Then (4.9) he digresses sharply, explaining that prose becomes "fine" art when it transcribes the writer's sense of fact and (second clause) "good" art when it renders the inner vision "truthfully." In 4.10 he drifts further from his topic, praising truth as a fundamental requirement of all good writing; and in 4.11 drifts yet again, defining beauty as a by-product of goodness (i.e., truthfulness), "the finer accommodation of speech to that vision within."

Here the paragraph ends, but the line of thought pushes on into P5 without interruption, and Pater seals the transition, oddly, by opening the new paragraph with a dash followed by what amounts to an appositive depending from the predicate of 4.11:

> —The transcript of his sense of fact rather than the fact, as being preferable, pleasanter, more beautiful to the writer himself.

Pater often opens a new phase of argument in a grammatically subordinate element emphasized by placement in terminal position; the present usage is unusual only because the appositive has been detached from the base construction and moved to the head of a new paragraph.

Logically complete and satisfying in itself, P5 nevertheless participates in the long disquisition upon fidelity-to-inner vision beginning at 4.9. And P6 extends the commentary even further. Not till the final phrase of 6.2 does Pater relinquish the theme he first introduced ostensibly to clarify the short prepositional phrase at the end of 4.8.

How shall we describe what happens in 4.9-6.2? The digression at the end of P4 is too long to be taken as a mildly irrelevant conclusion. Does it not then constitute a serious break in paragraph unity? Traditionalist critics doubtless would say it did. They might further object, on the same ground, to the weight of introductory material concentrated in 6.1-2, and probably would view the sequence 4.9-6.2 as a single unified paragraph which Pater has sadly misconceived.

Can Pater be defended? He can, I think, if we set aside our preconceptions and observe the general flow of discourse. A single logical stadium does of course exist, beginning at 4.9. It could easily be presented as a single analytic paragraph based on 4.9, conveying material which now requires 325 words. This would make a very substantial block of writing, but Pater's paragraphs frequently run to more than 300 words; so mere physical length cannot account for his decision to indent the way he has.

We can appreciate his strategy, once we note how deficient the whole passage is in "vertical" movement. His sole concern here is to clarify his notion of art, and this involves statement of four ideas: fact vs. sense of fact as the criterion for separating "fine" from "merely serviceable" art; adherence to inward truth as the criterion for recognizing "good" art; goodness in art as the foundation of beauty; and the inevitability of pleasure to be found in artistic self-expression. All these ideas are highly general and abstract, and he develops them mainly by repetition, a method which tends to maintain the same abstraction level as the topic. The passage consequently proceeds on a high abstraction plateau, and would surely risk boring the reader if it continued to its end without interruption.

Pater greatly reduces this hazard by dividing his material. Also, having worked out his four-point commentary in 4.9-5.1, he manages to repeat it in three separated contexts between 5.2 and 6.2, hammering his theses home not only by iteration but also by placement in terminal position, by isolation in a short paragraph, and by placement in initial position. He displays his argument much more forcefully in this way than he could have in a standard analytic paragraph. Further, if he had written such a paragraph, he probably would have felt obliged either to reduce the abstract exposition, thereby weakening its impact, or to introduce lower-level material—illustrations, causal statements, and the like—in order to generate interest.

Pater obviously found neither option appealing: to curtail treatment would have been to rob crucial ideas of emphasis they deserved—notably his doctrine of truth; to amplify them further, as by definition or illustration, would have been to raise problems he did not wish to handle, perhaps because of lack of space, perhaps because he sensed he could not handle them.[18]

Accordingly, rhetorical criteria in P4-6 take precedence over logical, the risk of dead-level dullness is reduced by partitioning, and a stadium of thought is allowed to straddle two paragraph breaks, exercising squatter's rights in paragraphs centered on other topics—to the dismay of traditionalist critics who perceive the massive breach of unity in P4, yet cannot honestly (I submit) find fault with it as they read.

Plainly, a stadium can be recognized as such without being punctuated as a paragraph. We have seen how Pater divides a stadium into separate paragraphs, and distributes portions of a divided stadium across paragraph breaks. He also does just the opposite, combines smaller stadia into a single paragraph. After a long series of routine analytic paragraphs dealing with diction and "contingent ornamentation" (P7-13), he broaches the general idea of structure in a synthetic transitional paragraph (P14), and then elaborates at great length in P15. The sequence 15.3-6 develops the topic by iteration; 15.7-8 concentrates on the structure of sentences; 15.9-10 deals with spontaneous structural elaborations, good and bad; 15.11-13 handles elaborations occurring after the main structure of a unit is complete; and 15.14-17 comments on the reader's pleasure in appreciating structure. Here, as elsewhere, Pater frequently advances in short, almost imperceptible steps taken in contexts otherwise devoted to illustration and repetition of previous points. His horizontal leaps, such as they are, often occur in minor subordinate structures within sentences, rather than across hiatuses between sentences, so that when a topic finally is granted full predication, it seems but an amplified echo. Heaping one "long-contending, victoriously intricate" sentence upon another, he pushes P15 to a length of 793 words and ends with the substance of a small essay, punctuated as a single paragraph.

Coherence, this passage undeniably possesses, but is it unified? Does it focus on one topic? Retracing the flow of ideas, we can argue with some difficulty that all this material is generated by 15.1-2. Or can we? Traditional criticism would point out that the paragraph moves in phases and could easily be broken at 15.7, 15.9, 15.10, 15.11, and 15.15, each resulting unit having its own topic sentence. As it is, we find several sub-topics, or possibly one "divided" topic, six identifiable stadia, all drawn into one union. The integrity of this union, assessed by the usual logical standards, is certainly open to question; to defend it on traditional grounds, we probably would have to abandon 15.1-2 as topic and invoke a ridiculously broad "implied" topic.

All the same, the paragraph reads well enough. And to mount a theoretical defense, we need only recognize that other legitimate criteria here have overridden the tug of logic. Obviously Pater wants to present his notion of structure as a single idea, regardless of its ramifications. Division of components would involve extensive expansion of this phase of the essay (cf. P4-6). By combining components, he avoids having to elaborate and at the same time stresses the whole by bulk treatment. However, I suspect that formal reasons also figured in the decision: P15 (793 words) and P16 (583 words) are by far the heaviest paragraphs in the essay,[19] and they deal with paired concepts, "mind" and "soul" in style. By cumulating the substance of P15 into one impressive mass, and juxtaposing it to the massive P16, he interprets the two concepts visually as a pair.

By contrast, the long stadium that follows, on Flaubert and the doctrine of the perfect word (P17-29), is far too heavy for block presentation. So he breaks it down into smaller stadia paragraphed in routine analytic fashion.

For the most part, of course, Pater's stadia follow the normal analytic pattern, whether or not they are set off as paragraphs. Synthesis is reserved for special situations. In P1-3 synthesis not only offers the advantages mentioned above but provides a gentle, gradual introit that accords well with his quiet tone and generally relaxed manner. In P14, where the movement sets up a definite contrast with the foregoing analytic sequence, it heralds an important phase of argument. At the conclusion of the essay (in P31), it allows him to end on a heavy note of emphasis.[20]

But the penultimate P30 is synthetic, too—the only synthetic paragraph in the essay that is not clearly an introduction or a conclusion. One wonders why, inevitably, for Pater rarely does anything without reason, yet the reason here is hard to find. I can offer only this suggestion: that P30 really is the

[margin handwritten note: it's not logical but works]

conclusion of the essay, and was conceived and written as such originally. It rounds out the argument beautifully, summing up the essay's central thesis in its final sentence, and has the characteristic force and rhythmic impact of a conclusion. Upon reviewing what he had written, however, if not before, Pater saw that his literary theory lay wide open to the same moralistic objections that had led him to withdraw the famous "Conclusion" to the *Renaissance* (1873) in its second edition (1877). Admittedly, he had recently restored a slightly modified version of the "Conclusion" in the third edition (1888), but he may very well have felt the present essay would revive old criticisms.

So in P31, having brought his commentary to a very satisfying close, he resumes exposition. He has shown how good art is achieved, he now informs us, but "great" art is something else. Here the criterion is matter, substance, not truth or form. To be great, a work of art must be more than good; it must also have "something of the soul of humanity in it," must increase the sum of human happiness, enlarge the sympathies, ennoble, fortify, redeem . . . and find "its logical architectural place in the great structure of human life" (31.4).

With these words, having barely introduced a major new idea which places the whole foregoing discussion in a new perspective, Pater abruptly ends. Even so sympathetic a reader as Saintsbury objects to the "appearance of 'hedging'" in P31, the sudden return to subject matter, which "as easily rememberable and with a virtuous high sound in it, appears to have greatly comforted some good but not great souls."[21] Pater's own judgment upon his paragraph perhaps can be inferred from his willingness to let its synthetic predecessor stand unrevised: P31 is distinct and supernumerary, both logically and structurally.

The foregoing observations in no way exhaust the possibilities of discourse-centered paragraph analysis. I have said nothing of tonal fluctuation, which does not strike me as being particularly significant in this essay, nor of rhythm, which is definitely significant but very hard to describe. Nor have I noted adequately the methods used to launch topic ideas, or the rise and fall of the abstraction level, or the use of ellipsis and the dash to tighten transitions between stadia, or Pater's unusual penchant for underplaying important ideas grammatically while stressing them rhetorically.

Inductive analysis of Pater's "Style" shows us something of what a paragraph *can* be, not what it must be; another writer, or another essay by the same writer, would reveal different possibilities, further precedents. I have been concerned mainly to demonstrate that the paragraph is just one of several kinds of stadia, and that the logical partitioning of complex discourse into paragraphs can occur at so many junctures that additional non-logical criteria often have to be invoked to account for a given decision to indent.

To insist that logic establish every indentation is to ignore several of the prime resources of good prose—which elevate and help transmute it from a merely serviceable "good round-hand" (1.3) into fine art.

NOTES

1. See my "Alexander Bain and the Rise of the Organic Paragraph," *Quarterly Journal of Speech*, LI (December 1965), 399-408.

2. James McConkey, *The Structure of Prose* (New York, 1963), p. 4.

3. Cleanth Brooks and Robert Penn Warren, *Modern Rhetoric* (2nd ed; New York, 1958), pp. 269-270.

4. Leo Rockas, *Modes of Rhetoric* (New York, 1964), p. 6.

5. Barrett Wendell, *English Composition* (New York, 1963), p. viii.

6. Francis Christensen, "A Generative Rhetoric of the Paragraph," *College Composition and Communication*, XVI (October 1965), 144.

7. Fred N. Scott and Joseph V. Denney, *Paragraph-Writing* (Ann Arbor, 1891), p. 71.

8. Edwin Herbert Lewis, *The History of the English Paragraph* (Chicago, 1894), p. 43.

9. Wendell Johnson, *People in Quandaries: The Semantics of Personal Adjustment* (New York, 1946), pp. 277-278. For a partial adumbration of this idea, see the "Introduction" to Lane Cooper's translation of *The Rhetoric of Aristotle* (New York, 1932), pp. xxxiv-xxxv.

10. John B. Lord, *The Paragraph: Structure and Style* (New York, 1964), p. 73.

11. Herbert Read, *English Prose Style* (Rev. ed; New York, 1952), pp. 58-65.

12. To facilitate reference to Pater, I shall use numbers to specify a given sentence (14.3 = fourteenth paragraph, third sentence) and a capital P to indicate "paragraph" (P4-6 = paragraphs four through six, inclusive).

13. George Saintsbury, *A History of Nineteenth Century Literature* (New York, 1896), p. 401.

14. *Ibid.*, p. 400.

15. George Saintsbury, *A History of English Prose Rhythm* (London, 1912), p. 421.

16. A. C. Benson, *Walter Pater* (New York, 1911), pp. 147-148.

17. Of 73 representative English prose writers studied by Lewis (p. 171), 27 average between 100 and 200 words per paragraph, 25 average between 200 and 300, and 21 average either below 100 or above 300, presumably the latter. In establishing the Pater word-counts, I have included quoted material.

18. See Edmund Chandler, "Pater on Style: An Examination of the Essay on 'Style' and the Textual History of 'Marius the Epicurean,'" *Anglistica*, XI (Copenhagen, 1958), pp. 95-99.

19. With the exception of P17 (573 words). P17 appears to be much lighter, however, since more than half of it consists of an inset block quotation.

20. It can easily be argued that P31 is analytic, comprising a definition (31.1) followed by illustrations and expanded repetitions of the same idea (31.2-4). I classify the paragraph as synthetic because 31.1-3 seems to me to build toward and to reach a climax in 31.4, which is by far the fullest and most emphatic of the four statements.

21. George Saintsbury, *A History of English Criticism* (New York, 1911), p. 501.

The Frequency and Placement
of Topic Sentences
in Expository Prose

Richard Braddock

Most textbooks on English composition have presented some concerted treatment of topic sentences, long hailed as means of organizing a writer's ideas and clarifying them for the reader. In the most popular composition textbook of the nineteenth century, for example, Alexander Bain recognized that topic sentences may come at the end of a descriptive or introductory paragraph, but he emphasized that expository paragraphs have topic sentences and that they usually come at the beginnings of paragraphs:

> 19. The opening sentence, unless obviously preparatory, is expected to indicate the scope of the paragraph. . . . This rule is most directly applicable to expository style, where, indeed, it is almost essential (Bain, 1890, p. 108).

In one of the more popular composition textbooks of the present, Gorrell and Laird present a similar statement about topic sentences—a statement which is paralleled in many other textbooks these days:

> Topic sentences may appear anywhere, or even be omitted. . . . but most modern, carefully constructed prose rests on standard paragraphs, most of which have topic sentences to open them.

And of 15 items on "Paragraph Patterns" in a commercial test of "writing," three involve the identification of topic sentences in brief paragraphs. In

Reprinted from *Research in the Teaching of English* 8.3 (Winter 1974): 287–302. Used with permission.

each of the three, the correct answer is the first sentence in the paragraph (*Basic Skills*, 1970).

How much basis is there for us to make such statements to students or to base testing on the truth of them? To clarify the matter, I studied the paragraphs in representative contemporary professional writing, seeking the answers to these two questions:

1. What proportion of the paragraphs contain topic sentences?
2. Where in the paragraphs do the topic sentences occur?

PROCEDURE

As a body of expository material representing contemporary professional writing, I used the corpus of 25 complete essays in American English selected by Margaret Ashida, using random procedures, from 420 articles published from January, 1964, through March, 1965, in *The Atlantic, Harper's, The New Yorker, The Reporter,* and *The Saturday Review.* Ashida indicated possible uses of the corpus:

> . . . this corpus could be used for a wealth of investigations by students, teachers, and research scholars—for anything from a relatively superficial examination of controversial matters of usage, to the exploration of the deep (and equally controversial) questions being raised by theoreticians of the new rhetorics. Because the sample has its own built-in validity, it represents a *common* corpus for use by many different scholars—something we desperately need in rhetorical research . . . (Ashida, 1968, pp. 14–23).

Paragraphs

Working one-by-one with zerographic copies of the 25 articles,[1] I numbered each paragraph from the first paragraph of the essay to the last. For this study, a paragraph was what we normally take to be one in printed material—a portion of discourse consisting of one or more sentences, the first line of type of which is preceded by more interlinear space than is otherwise found between lines in the text and the first sentence of which begins either with an indentation or with an unindented large initial capital.

Headnotes and footnotes were not counted as parts of the text for this study and hence were not numbered and analyzed. A problem appeared when one article included an insert, consisting of a diagram and some ten sentences of explanation, which was crucial to an understanding of the text

what he decided counts as a ¶

proper.[2] This insert arbitrarily was not counted as a paragraph in the article. In those few essays in which dialog was quoted, each separately indented paragraph was counted as a paragraph, even though it consisted in one case merely of one four-word sentence (Taper, p. 138).

T-units

After numbering the paragraphs in an essay, I proceeded to insert a pencilled slash mark after each T-unit in each paragraph and to write the total number of T-units at the end of each paragraph.

The T-unit, or "minimal terminable unit," is a term devised by Kellogg Hunt to describe the "shortest grammatically allowable sentences into which . . . [writing can] be segmented" (Hunt, 1965, pp. 20–21). In other words, consideration of the T-units of writing permits the researcher to use a rather standard conception of a sentence, setting aside the differences occurring between writers when they use different styles of punctuation. A T-unit, then, "includes one main clause plus all the subordinate clauses attached to or embedded within it. . . ." (Hunt, p. 141). Hunt wrote that an independent clause beginning with "and" or "but" is a T-unit, but I also included "or," "for," and "so" to complete what I take to be the coordinating conjunctions in modern usage.

Although in the vast majority of cases, there was no difficulty knowing where to indicate the end of a T-unit, several problems did arise. Take, for instance, the following sentence:

> The Depression destroyed the coalfield's prosperity, but the Second World War revived it, and for a few years the boom returned and the miner was again a useful and honored citizen (Caudill, p. 49). *3 T-units*

Obviously, one T-unit ends with "prosperity" and another with "revived it," but is what follows "revived it" one T-unit or two? I made the judgment that "for a few years" was an integral part of both clauses following it and that "and for a few years the boom returned and the miner was again a useful and honored citizen" was one T-unit. Similarly, I counted the following sentence as one T-unit, not two, judging the intent of the first clause in the speech of the Protocol man to be subordinate, as if he had said "If you put an ambassador in prison":

> For another, as a Protocol man said recently, "You put an ambassador in prison and you can't negotiate with him, which is what he's supposed to be here for" (Kahn, p. 75). *one T-unit*

In marking off T-units, a person must be prepared for occasional embedding. Sometimes a writer uses parentheses to help accomplish the embedding:

> Gibbs & Cox (Daniel H. Cox was a famous yacht designer who joined the firm in 1929, retired in 1943, and subsequently died) is the largest private ship-designing firm in the world (Sargeant, p. 49).

That sentence, of course, has one T-unit embedded within one other. In the following example, dashes enclose two T-units embedded within another, and the entire sentence consists of four T-units:

> "They're condescending, supercilious bastards, but when the 'United States' broke all the transatlantic records—it still holds them, and it went into service in 1952—they had to come down a peg" (Sargeant, p. 50).

But embedding does not prove to be a problem in determining what is and what is not a T-unit. With the exception of perhaps a dozen other problems in the thousands of sentences considered in the 25 essays, marking off and counting the T-units was a fairly mechanical operation.

Topic Sentences

The next problem was to decide which T-unit, if any, constituted a topic sentence in each paragraph. After several frustrating attempts merely to underline the appropriate T-unit where it occurred, I realized that the notion of what a topic sentence is, is not at all clear.

Consultation of composition textbooks provided no simple solution of the problem. Gorrell and Laird, for example, offered this definition of a topic sentence:

> Most paragraphs focus on a central idea or unifying device expressed in topical material. Occasionally this topical material is complex, involving more than one sentence and some subtopics; sometimes it carries over from a previous paragraph and is assumed to be understood or is referred to briefly; but usually it simply takes the form of a sentence, sometimes amplified or made more specific in a sentence or two following it. This topic sentence may appear at the end of the paragraph as a kind of summary or somewhere within the paragraph, but most frequently it opens the paragraph or follows an opening introduction or transition (Gorrell and Laird, p. 25).

The authors further clarify their definition (pp. 25–26) by stating that a topic sentence has three main functions: (1) to provide transition, (2) to suggest the organization of the paragraph, (3) to present a topic, either by naming or introducing a subject or by presenting a proposition or thesis for discussion. In the next several pages, the authors consider various types of "topic sentences as propositions" (or theses) and the problems in writing them with precision.

From my preliminary attempts to identify topic sentences in paragraphs, I could see the truth of a complex definition like Gorrell and Laird's. But such a comprehensive definition presents problems. Sometimes a paragraph opens with a sentence which we could all agree is transitional but which does not reveal much about the content of the paragraph. The second sentence may name the topic of the paragraph but not make a statement about it. The actual thesis of the paragraph may be stated explicitly in a succeeding sentence or in several sentences, or it may merely be inferred from what follows, even though it is never stated explicitly. In such a paragraph, which is the topic sentence—the first, second, a succeeding sentence, perhaps even all of them? Many of the sentences seem to fit the definition. An all-embracing definition does not seem helpful to me in deciding which sentence can be named the topic sentence.

Furthermore, as Paul Rodgers demonstrated (1966), paragraphing does not always correspond to a reader's perceived organization of ideas. Sometimes a paragraph presents an illustration of the thesis of the preceding paragraph. The second paragraph thus extends the previous paragraph, and the paragraph indentation seems quite arbitrary. Or sometimes a thesis is stated in a one-sentence paragraph and the following paragraph explains that thesis without restating it. In such situations, one cannot simply identify a topic sentence in each paragraph.

It seemed to me that the best test of topic sentences is the test a careful reader might make—the test offered when one constructs a sentence outline of the major points of an essay, drawing the sentences insofar as possible from the sentences the author has written. In constructing a sentence outline, one usually omits transitional and illustrative statements and concentrates on the theses themselves. Consequently, I decided to prepare a sentence outline of each of the 25 essays and *then* determine which paragraphs had topic sentences and where in the paragraphs they occurred.

Outlines

From the beginning of the first one, I was aware of the serious problems in constructing a sentence outline to study the organization of another person's

potential problems with his method

writing. To what degree would I tend to impose on an essay my own interpretation of what was written? Does it do violence to discursive writing to cast it into the form of a sentence outline, trying to make the outline understandable by itself when the essay includes details of thought and qualities of style omitted in the process? Would the paragraphing and other typographical features of the edited essay distract me from the ideas and structure of the written essay? Of course I would try to preserve the author's intent in all of these matters, but what I actually did would be so much a matter of judgment that I should expose my outlines for the criticism of others, permitting comparison to the original articles. Moreover, the outlines might be helpful to other investigators who would like to use them without going to the extensive effort of preparing their own. Although it is impractical to include the outlines here, I will make them available to others for the cost of the copying.

In outlining an article, I read it through in sections of a number of paragraphs which seemed to be related, underlining topic sentences where I could find them and constructing topic sentences where they were not explicit in the article. In constructing a topic sentence, I tried to include phrases from the original text as much as possible. Whatever sentences, phrases, or key words I did use from the original I was careful to enclose in quotation marks, indicating by ellipsis marks all omissions and by brackets all of my own insertions. Opposite each entry in the outline I indicated the number of the paragraph and T-unit of each quotation used. Thus the notation 20:2,3 and 4 indicates that quoted portions of the outline entry were taken from the second, third, and fourth T-units of the twentieth paragraph in the essay. On a few occasions where I took an idea from a paragraph but it did not seem possible to cast it in the author's original words at all, I put the paragraph number in parentheses to indicate that. But I tried to use the author's words as much as I could, even, in some cases, where it yielded a somewhat unwieldy entry in the outline.

To illustrate the approach, let me offer in Figure 1 the opening paragraphs from the first article in the corpus, indicating the corresponding entries in the outline.

Notice the different types of outline entries necessitated by the various kinds of paragraphs the author writes. Topic Sentence B is an example of what I would call a *simple topic sentence*, one which is quoted entirely or almost entirely from one T-unit in the passage, wherever that T-unit occurs. (Incidentally, the last sentence in Paragraph 2 is not reflected in Topic Sentence B because that last sentence is an early foreshadowing of the main idea of the entire article.)

Figure 1   Sample paragraphs and outline entries.

Opening Paragraphs from Drew, p. 33	Excerpt from Outline	
1. Among the news items given out to a shocked nation following the assassination of President Kennedy was the fact that Lee Harvey Oswald had purchased his weapon, a 6.5-mm Italian carbine, from a Chicago mail-order house under an assumed name. The rifle was sent, no questions asked, to one "A. Hidell," in care of a post-office box in Dallas. The transaction was routine in the mail-order trade; about one million guns are sold the same way each year.	I. "By the ordinary rules of the game, the events in Dallas should have ensured prompt enactment. . . ." of gun control legislation by Congress.	2:2
	A. "President Kennedy" had recently been shot with one of the "one million guns . . . sold . . . each year" through "the mail-order business in guns."	1:1,3,4
2. At the same time, a bill was pending in Congress to tighten regulation of the rapidly expanding mail-order business in guns. By the ordinary rules of the game, the events in Dallas should have ensured prompt enactment, just as the news of Thalidomide-deformed babies had provided the long-needed impetus for passage of stricter drug regulations in 1962. But Congress did not act—a testimonial to the deadly aim of the shotting lobby.	B. "At the same time, a bill was pending in Congress to tighten regulation of the rapidly expanding mail-order business in guns."	2:1
3. Two existing statutes presumably deal with the gun traffic. Both were passed in reaction to the gangsterism of the prohibition era. But, because of limited coverage, problems of proof, and various other quirks, they have had a negligible impact on the increasing gun traffic.	C. "Two existing statutes. . . . [had] a negligible impact on the increasing gun traffic."	3:1,3
4. The investigation of the mail-order traffic in guns began in 1961 under the auspices of the Juvenile Delinquency subcommittee. . . .		

Topic Sentence C is a fairly common type, one in which the topic sentence seems to begin in one T-unit but is completed in a later T-unit. In Paragraph 3, the first sentence does not make a specific enough statement about the two existing statutes to serve as a complete topic sentence, even though it reveals the subject of the paragraph. One must go to the third sentence to find the predicate for the topic sentence. Let us term this type a *delayed-completion topic sentence*. Not all delayed-completion topic sentences stem from separated subjects and predicates, though. Sometimes the two sentences present a question and then an answer (Fischer, 18: 1,2), a negative followed by a positive (Fischer, 38: 1,2), or metaphoric language subsequently explained by straight language (Drucker, 8: 1,2). The T-units from which a delayed-completion topic sentence is drawn are not always adjoining. In one instance, I discovered them separated by three T-units (Collado, 29: 1,2,6); in another, in adjoining paragraphs (Caudill, 17: 2 and 18: 1); in still another, nine paragraphs apart (Lear, 1: 1,2 and 10: 1).

Notice that Topic Sentence A is an example of a statement assembled by quotations from throughout the paragraph. The first sentence in Paragraph 1 cannot properly be considered the topic sentence: it includes such phrases as "the news item" and "a shocked nation" and such details as the name of the assassin, the size and make of the carbine, and the location of the mail order house—such matters as are not essential to the topic sentence; and it omits such a detail as the scope of the problem—"one million guns . . . sold . . . each year"—which helps convey the idea in Statement I. To ease later reference to this type of topic sentence, let us call it an *assembled topic sentence*.

Finally, there is what we might call an *inferred topic sentence*, one which the reader thinks the writer has implied even though the reader cannot construct it by quoting phrases from the original passage. Though the paragraph in Figure 2 comes out of context—from an article on cutting the costs of medical care—it may still be clear why the corresponding topic sentence had to be inferred.

As I was determining what were the topic sentences of an article, I was also keeping an eye out for what we might call the *major topic sentences* of the larger stadia of discourses. That is, a series of topic sentences all added up to a major topic sentence; a group of paragraphs all added up to what William Irmscher (1972) calls a "paragraph bloc" within the entire article. A major topic sentence (designated with a Roman numeral) might head as few as two topic sentences (designated with capital letters) in the outline or as many as 12 topic sentences (in the Kahn outline) or 15 (the most, in the Mumford outline). On the other hand, it was frequently apparent that the main idea of a paragraph was really a subpoint of the main idea of another

Figure 2 Sample of paragraph yielding inferred topic sentence.

Paragraph from Saunders, p. 24	Excerpt from Outline
Fortunately most ailments do not require such elaborate treatment. Pills cost a good deal less but even they are no small item in the medical bill. From 1929 to 1956 prescription sales climbed from $140 million to $1,466 million a year, and the average price per prescription rose from 85 cents to $2.62. Citing the findings of the Kefauver Committee, Professor Harris makes a strong case for more — and more stringent — regulation of the pharmaceutical industry by the government.	Prescription drug costs have risen.

can be assembled, inferred, or delayed completion

paragraph. Let us call these *subtopic sentences*. As few as two and as many as seven subtopic sentences (in the Taper outline) were headed by a topic sentence. Sometimes a major topic sentence or a subtopic sentence was simply stated in a single T-unit, but sometimes it had to be assembled, sometimes inferred. Some occurred as delayed-completion topic sentences.

After completing the rest of the outline, I arrived at the main idea (the thesis) or, in the case of the Kahn and Sargeant articles (both *New Yorker* "Profiles"), the purpose. And as with the various types of topic sentences, I drew quoted phrases from the article to construct the statement of the main idea whenever possible, but with one exception — if a term or phrase occurred frequently in the article, I would not enclose it in quotations and note its location unless it seemed to me to have been put by the author in a particular place or signalled in a particular way to suggest that he was at that time intentionally indicating to readers the nature of his main idea.

After all of the outlines were completed, I went back through each one, classifying each topic sentence as one of the four types and checking the outline against the text of the original essay.

FINDINGS

A tabulation of the frequency of each type of topic sentence for each of the 25 essays is presented in Table 1. It should not escape the reader that the number of topic sentences in an outline does not correspond directly to the number of paragraphs in its essay. Sometimes a major topic sentence and a topic sentence occurred in the same paragraph, and sometimes several para-

Table 1 Frequency of types of topic sentences in each of the 25 essays.

Essay No.	Author	Magazine	Main Idea	Simple			Del-comp.			Assembled			Inferred			Total TS's	Total Pars.
				MTS	TS	STS	MTS	TS	STS	MTS	TS	STS	MTS	TS	STS		
1	Drew	Reporter	Inf.	3	8	2	0	2	0	2	2	2	0	0	0	22	20
2	Tebbel	Sat. Rev.	D-C	1	5	2	1	2	0	0	5	2	1	2	1	23	25
3	Collado	Sat. Rev.	Sim.	3	8	3	1	1	2	0	4	9	0	1	0	33	50
4	Sargeant	New York.	Inf.	1	3	0	0	0	0	1	13	6	3	3	1	32	26
5	Chamberlain	Atlantic	Inf.	3	5	2	0	2	0	1	7	3	0	0	0	24	24
6	Daniels	Sat. Rev.	Sim.	3	8	0	0	2	0	0	6	0	0	0	0	18	27
7	E. Taylor	Reporter	Ass.	3	8	0	0	2	0	0	2	0	0	0	0	17	19
8	Kaufman	Atlantic	Ass.	2	13	5	1	2	7	1	0	2	0	1	0	35	41
9	Kahn	New York.	Inf.	0	7	0	0	1	0	1	25	0	4	5	0	44	45
10	Handlin	Atlantic	Sim.	4	11	0	0	7	0	1	4	0	0	0	0	28	35
11	Francois	Reporter	Ass.	2	5	0	0	1	0	0	3	0	0	1	0	13	13
12	Sanders	Harper's	Sim.	3	12	0	2	4	0	1	6	0	2	3	0	32	35
13	Lear	Sat. Rev.	Sim.	0	7	0	2	2	0	2	15	0	2	1	0	32	67
14	Lyons	Atlantic	Sim.	4	8	0	0	2	0	1	13	0	0	2	0	31	53
15	Ribman	Harper's	Inf.	5	20	1	0	4	0	1	12	0	1	0	0	44	56
16	Taper	New York.	Inf.	4	14	9	0	3	1	3	16	11	0	0	0	53	53
17	Fischer	Harper's	Inf.	4	11	9	0	1	1	1	9	3	0	1	0	41	42
18	Mumford	New York.	Inf.	2	17	0	0	2	0	3	27	0	2	0	0	54	49
19	Drucker	Harper's	Sim.	5	15	1	0	5	1	0	16	1	0	0	0	45	53
20	Caudill	Atlantic	Sim.	2	10	3	0	7	0	2	6	0	0	0	0	31	39
21	C. Taylor	Atlantic	Sim.	1	11	0	0	1	1	2	7	3	1	1	0	29	29
22	Cousins	Sat. Rev.	Sim.	1	2	0	1	2	0	1	3	0	0	0	0	11	13
23	Clark	Harper's	Sim.	4	8	0	1	1	1	0	4	1	0	0	0	21	26
24	Durrell	Atlantic	Sim.	1	5	0	1	0	0	1	6	0	0	0	0	15	13
25	Rule	Atlantic	Ass.	3	15	0	1	3	0	1	9	0	0	0	0	33	36
Totals			25	64	236	28	10	56	13	27	220	43	16	21	2	761	889

MTS = major topic sentence   TS = topic sentence   STS = subtopic sentence graphs seemed devoted to the presentation of one topic sentence. (The total number of topic sentences—including the main idea or purpose, major topic sentences, topic sentences, and subtopic sentences, if any—and the total number of paragraphs are given in the two columns at the right of the table.)

One conclusion from Table 1 is that the use made of the different types of topic sentences varies greatly from one writer to the next. Another is that the four articles taken from the *New Yorker* (each one a "Profile") tend to have yielded a higher proportion of assembled topic sentences than most of the other essays.

Frequency of Types of Topic Sentences

Table 2 combines the data for the 25 essays, indicating the distribution of topic sentences of each type. It is clear that less than half of all the topic sentences (45%) are simple topic sentences and almost as many (39%) are assembled. It is also apparent that—except for the statements of the main idea or purpose—the more of the text that the topic sentence covers, the more likely it is to be a simple topic sentence. That is, of the 117 major topic sentences, 55% were simple; of the 533 topic sentences, 44% were simple; of the 80 subtopic sentences, 33% were simple.

One might well maintain that simple and delayed-completion topic sentences are relatively explicit, that assembled and inferred topic sentences are relatively implicit. Pairing the types of topic sentences in that fashion, Table 2 reveals no great changes in the tendencies of the percentages. Slightly more than half of all the topic sentences (55%) are explicit, slightly less than half (45%) implicit. Again, with the exception of statements of

Table 2 Percentages of topic sentences of various types.

Types of Topic Sentences	No.	Percentages					
		Sim.	D-C	Explicit	Ass.	Inf.	Implicit
Main idea or purpose	25	48	4	52	16	32	48
Major topic sentences	117	55	9	63	23	14	37
Topic sentences	533	44	11	55	41	4	45
Subtopic sentences	86	33	15	48	50	2	52
All types together	761	45	11	55	39	6	45

main idea and purpose, <u>the more of the text which the topic sentence covers, the more likely it is to be explicit.</u>

If what the composition textbooks refer to as "the topic sentence" is the same thing as this study terms the simple topic sentence, it is apparent that <u>claims about its frequency</u> should be more cautious. <u>It just is not true that most expository paragraphs have topic sentences</u> in that sense. Even when simple and delayed-completion topic sentences are combined into the category "explicit topic sentences"—a broader conception than many textbook writers seem to have in mind—the frequency reaches only 55% of all the entries in a sentence outline. And when one remembers that only 761 outline topic sentences represent the 889 paragraphs in all 25 essays, he realizes that <u>considerably fewer than half of all the paragraphs in the essays have even explicit topic sentences</u>, to say nothing of simple topic sentences.

Placement of Simple Topic Sentences

How true is the claim that most expository paragraphs open with topic sentences? To find out, I studied the paragraph location of the 264 topic sentences and subtopic sentences in the outline. Gorrell and Laird, like others, had written that the "topic sentence may appear at the end of the paragraph as a kind of summary or somewhere within the paragraph, but most frequently it opens the paragraph or follows an opening introduction or transition (p. 25). Thus I decided to tabulate the occurrence of each simple topic sentence as it appeared in each of four positions: the first T-unit in the paragraph, the second T-unit, the last, or a T-unit between the second and last. To do that, of course, I could consider only paragraphs of four or more T-units. Consequently, I excluded from consideration paragraphs with three or fewer T-units. The results are presented in Table 3.

More than a fourth (28%) of all those paragraphs presenting simple topic sentences or simple subtopic sentences contained fewer than four T-units. Of the rest, 47% presented a simple topic sentence or simple subtopic sentence in the first T-unit, 15% in the second T-unit, 12% in the last T-unit, and 26% elsewhere. But these figures are based on the 190 paragraphs of four or more T-units which contain simple topic sentences or simple subtopic sentences. There were 355 paragraphs from which other topic sentences or subtopic sentences were drawn—delayed-completion, assembled, and inferred. One cannot say that they "have topic sentences to open them." <u>Consequently, it is obvious that much smaller percentages than the above pertain to expository paragraphs in general.</u> Furthermore, there were at least <u>128 paragraphs from which no topic</u> sentences at all

Table 3 Location of simple topic sentences and simple subtopic sentences.

Location	Essay Number																									Tot.	%
	1	2	3	4	5	6	7	8	9	10	11	12	13	14	15	16	17	18	19	20	21	22	23	24	25		
(Paragraph shorter than 4 T-units)	1	1	4	0	3	2	6	5	0	4	1	7	4	0	9	0	6	1	4	2	0	1	6	1	6	74	(28)
First T-unit	6	2	2	3	3	2	0	2	6	4	2	2	1	2	7	5	7	3	6	5	8	1	0	3	7	89	47
Second T-unit	1	4	2	0	0	1	1	2	0	1	0	1	0	1	1	0	4	5	0	2	2	0	1	0	0	29	15
Last T-unit	0	0	1	0	0	0	0	4	0	0	0	0	2	0	0	1	1	4	3	1	1	1	0	0	1	22	12
Elsewhere	2	0	2	0	1	2	1	5	1	2	2	2	0	5	3	9	2	4	3	2	0	0	1	1	1	50	26
Total no. of TS's and STS's in essay	10	7	11	3	7	8	8	18	7	11	5	12	7	8	20	15	20	17	16	13	11	2	8	5	15	264	
Total no. of paragraphs in essay	20	25	50	26	24	27	19	41	45	35	13	35	67	53	56	53	42	49	53	39	29	13	26	13	36	889	

were drawn. If one adds the 190, 355, and 128, he has a total of 673 from which percentages may be computed, if he wishes to estimate what percentage of *all* of the paragraphs in the 25 essays open with a topic sentence. Using those figures, I estimate that only 13% of the expository paragraphs of contemporary professional writers begin with a topic sentence, that only 3% end with a topic sentence.

IMPLICATIONS FOR TEACHING

Teachers and textbook writers should exercise caution in making statements about the frequency with which contemporary professional writers use simple or even explicit topic sentences in expository paragraphs. It is abundantly clear that students should not be told that professional writers usually begin their paragraphs with topic sentences. Certainly teachers of reading, devisers of reading tests, and authors of reading textbooks should assist students in identifying the kinds of delayed-completion and implicit topic statements which outnumber simple topic sentences in expository paragraphs.

This sample of contemporary professional writing did not support the claims of textbook writers about the frequency and location of topic sentences in professional writing. That does not, of course, necessarily mean the same findings would hold for scientific and technical writing or other types of exposition. Moreover, it does not all mean that composition teachers should stop showing their students how to develop paragraphs from clear topic sentences. Far from it. In my opinion, often the writing in the 25 essays would have been clearer and more comfortable to read if the paragraphs had presented more explicit topic sentences. But what this study does suggest is this: While helping students use clear topic sentences in their writing and identify variously presented topical ideas in their reading, the teacher should not pretend that professional writers largely follow the practices he is advocating.

NOTES

1. The copies were supplied through the generosity of the Department of English, University of Iowa.

2. Here and hereafter, reference to specific articles in the corpus will be made simply by using the author's last name—or, in the cases of the two articles by individuals of the same last name, by using the first initial and last name (see Table 1)—The paragraph referred to here is in Lear, p. 89.

REFERENCES

Ashida, M. E. Something for everyone: a standard corpus of contemporary American expository essays. *Research in the Teaching of English*, 1968, 2, 14–23.

Bain, A. *English Composition and Rhetoric*, enl. ed. London: Longmans, Green, 1890.

Basic skills system: writing test, Form A. New York: McGraw Hill, 1970.

Gorrell, R. M. and Laird, C. *Modern English handbook*, 4th ed. Englewood Cliffs, New Jersey: Prentice Hall, 1967.

Hunt, K. W. *Grammatical structures written at three grade levels*. Research Report No. 3. Urbana, Illinois: NCTE, 1965.

Irmscher, W.F. *The Holt guide to English*. New York: Holt, Rinehart and Winston, 1972.

Rodgers, P. Jr. A discourse-centered rhetoric of the paragraph. *College Composition and Communication*, 1966, 17, 2–11.

Grammar, Grammars,
and the Teaching of Grammar

Patrick Hartwell

For me the grammar issue was settled at least twenty years ago with the conclusion offered by Richard Braddock, Richard Lloyd-Jones, and Lowell Schoer in 1963.

> In view of the widespread agreement of research studies based upon many types of students and teachers, the conclusion can be stated in strong and unqualified terms: the teaching of formal grammar has a negligible or, because it usually displaces some instruction and practice in composition, even a harmful effect on improvement in writing.[1]

Indeed, I would agree with Janet Emig that the grammar issue is a prime example of "magical thinking": the assumption that students will learn only what we teach and only because we teach.[2]

But the grammar issue, as we will see, is a complicated one. And, perhaps surprisingly, it remains controversial, with the regular appearance of papers defending the teaching of formal grammar or attacking it.[3] Thus Janice Neuleib, writing on "The Relation of Formal Grammar to Composition" in *College Composition and Communication* (23 [1977], 247-50), is tempted "to sputter on paper" at reading the quotation above (p. 248), and Martha Kolln, writing in the same journal three years later ("Closing the Books on Alchemy," *CCC*, 32 [1981], 139-51), labels people like me "alchemists" for our perverse beliefs. Neuleib reviews five experimental studies, most of them concluding that formal grammar instruction has no effect

Reprinted from *College English* 47.2 (February 1985): 105–27. Used with permission.

on the quality of students' writing nor on their ability to avoid error. Yet she renders in effect a Scots verdict of "Not proven" and calls for more research on the issue. Similarly, Kolln reviews six experimental studies that arrive at similar conclusions, only one of them overlapping with the studies cited by Neuleib. She calls for more careful definition of the word *grammar*—her definition being "the internalized system that native speakers of a language share" (p. 140)—and she concludes with a stirring call to place grammar instruction at the center of the composition curriculum: "our goal should be to help students understand the system they know unconsciously as native speakers, to teach them the necessary categories and labels that will enable them to think about and talk about their language" (p. 150). Certainly our textbooks and our pedagogies—though they vary widely in what they see as "necessary categories and labels"—continue to emphasize mastery of formal grammar, and popular discussions of a presumed literacy crisis are almost unanimous in their call for a renewed emphasis on the teaching of formal grammar, seen as basic for success in writing.[4]

AN INSTRUCTIVE EXAMPLE

It is worth noting at the outset that both sides in this dispute—the grammarians and the anti-grammarians—articulate the issue in the same positivistic terms: what does experimental research tell us about the value of teaching formal grammar? But seventy-five years of experimental research has for all practical purposes told us nothing. The two sides are unable to agree on how to interpret such research. Studies are interpreted in terms of one's prior assumptions about the value of teaching grammar: their results seem not to change those assumptions. Thus the basis of the discussion, a basis shared by Kolln and Neuleib and by Braddock and his colleagues—"what does educational research tell us?"—seems designed to perpetuate, not to resolve, the issue. A single example will be instructive. In 1976 and then at greater length in 1979, W. B. Elley, I. H. Barham, H. Lamb, and M. Wyllie reported on a three-year experiment in New Zealand, comparing the relative effectiveness at the high school level of instruction in transformational grammar, instruction in traditional grammar, and no grammar instruction.[5] They concluded that the formal study of grammar, whether transformational or traditional, improved neither writing quality nor control over surface correctness.

> After two years, no differences were detected in writing performance or language competence; after three years small differences appeared in some

minor conventions favoring the TG [transformational grammar] group, but these were more than offset by the less positive attitudes they showed towards their English studies. (p. 18)

Anthony Petrosky, in a review of research ("Grammar Instruction: What We Know," *English Journal*, 66, No. 9 [1977], 86-88), agreed with this conclusion, finding the study to be carefully designed, "representative of the best kind of educational research" (p. 86), its validity "unquestionable" (p. 88). Yet Janice Neuleib in her essay found the same conclusions to be "startling" and questioned whether the findings could be generalized beyond the target population, New Zealand high school students. Martha Kolln, when her attention is drawn to the study ("Reply to Ron Shook," *CCC*, 32 [1981], 139-151), thinks the whole experiment "suspicious." And John Mellon has been willing to use the study to defend the teaching of grammar; the study of Elley and his colleagues, he has argued, shows that teaching grammar does no harm.[6]

It would seem unlikely, therefore, that further experimental research, in and of itself, will resolve the grammar issue. Any experimental design can be nitpicked, any experimental population can be criticized, and any experimental conclusion can be questioned or, more often, ignored. In fact, it may well be that the grammar question is not open to resolution by experimental research, that, as Noam Chomsky has argued in *Reflections on Language* (New York: Pantheon, 1975), criticizing the trivialization of human learning by behavioral psychologists, the issue is simply misdefined.

> There will be "good experiments" only in domains that lie outside the organism's cognitive capacity. For example, there will be no "good experiments" in the study of human learning.
>
> This discipline . . . will, of necessity, avoid those domains in which an organism is specially designed to acquire rich cognitive structures that enter into its life in an intimate fashion. The discipline will be of virtually no intellectual interest, it seems to me, since it is restricting itself in principle to those questions that are guaranteed to tell us little about the nature of organisms. (p. 36)

ASKING THE RIGHT QUESTIONS

As a result, though I will look briefly at the tradition of experimental research, my primary goal in this essay is to articulate the grammar issue in different and, I would hope, more productive terms. Specifically, I want to ask four questions:

1. Why is the grammar issue so important? Why has it been the dominant focus of composition research for the last seventy-five years?

2. What definitions of the word *grammar* are needed to articulate the grammar issue intelligibly?

3. What do findings in cognate disciplines suggest about the value of formal grammar instruction?

4. What is our theory of language, and what does it predict about the value of formal grammar instruction? (This question—"what does our theory of language predict?"—seems a much more powerful question than "what does educational research tell us?")

In exploring these questions I will attempt to be fully explicit about issues, terms, and assumptions. I hope that both proponents and opponents of formal grammar instruction would agree that these are useful as shared points of reference: care in definition, full examination of the evidence, reference to relevant work in cognate disciplines, and explicit analysis of the theoretical bases of the issue.

But even with that gesture of harmony it will be difficult to articulate the issue in a balanced way, one that will be acceptable to both sides. After all, we are dealing with a professional dispute in which one side accuses the other of "magical thinking," and in turn that side responds by charging the other as "alchemists." Thus we might suspect that the grammar issue is itself embedded in larger models of the transmission of literacy, part of quite different assumptions about the teaching of composition.

Those of us who dismiss the teaching of formal grammar have a model of composition instruction that makes the grammar issue "uninteresting" in a scientific sense. Our model predicts a rich and complex interaction of learner and environment in mastering literacy, an interaction that has little to do with sequences of skills instruction as such. Those who defend the teaching of grammar tend to have a model of composition instruction that is rigidly skills-centered and rigidly sequential: the formal teaching of grammar, as the first step in that sequence, is the cornerstone or linchpin. Grammar teaching is thus supremely interesting, naturally a dominant focus for educational research. The controversy over the value of grammar instruction, then, is inseparable from two other issues: the issues of sequence in the teaching of composition and of the role of the composition teacher. Consider, for example, the force of these two issues in Janice Neuleib's conclusion: after calling for yet more experimental research on the value of teaching grammar, she ends with an absolute (and unsupported) claim about sequences and teacher roles in composition.

> We do know, however, that some things must be taught at different levels. Insistence on adherence to usage norms by composition teachers does improve usage. Students can learn to organize their papers if teachers do not accept papers that are disorganized. Perhaps composition teachers can teach those two abilities before they begin the more difficult tasks of developing syntactic sophistication and a winning style. ("The Relation of Formal Grammar to Composition," p. 250)

(One might want to ask, in passing, whether "usage norms" exist in the monolithic fashion the phrase suggests and whether refusing to accept disorganized papers is our best available pedagogy for teaching arrangement.)[7]

But I want to focus on the notion of sequence that makes the grammar issue so important: first grammar, then usage, then some absolute model of organization, all controlled by the teacher at the center of the learning process, with other matters, those of rhetorical weight—"syntactic sophistication and a winning style"—pushed off to the future. It is not surprising that we call each other names: those of us who question the value of teaching grammar are in fact shaking the whole elaborate edifice of traditional composition instruction.

THE FIVE MEANINGS OF "GRAMMAR"

Given its centrality to a well-established way of teaching composition, I need to go about the business of defining grammar rather carefully, particularly in view of Kolln's criticism of the lack of care in earlier discussions. Therefore I will build upon a seminal discussion of the word *grammar* offered a generation ago, in 1954, by W. Nelson Francis, often excerpted as "The Three Meanings of Grammar."[8] It is worth reprinting at length, if only to re-establish it as a reference point for future discussions.

> The first thing we mean by "grammar" is "the set of formal patterns in which the words of a language are arranged in order to convey larger meanings." It is not necessary that we be able to discuss these patterns self-consciously in order to be able to use them. In fact, all speakers of a language above the age of five or six know how to use its complex forms of organization with considerable skill; in this sense of the word—call it "Grammar 1"—they are thoroughly familiar with its grammar.

The second meaning of "grammar"—call it "Grammar 2"—is "the branch of linguistic science which is concerned with the description, analysis, and formulization of formal language patterns." Just as gravity was in full operation before Newton's apple fell, so grammar in the first sense was in full operation before anyone formulated the first rule that began the history of grammar as a study.

The third sense in which people use the word "grammar" is "linguistic etiquette." This we may call "Grammar 3." The word in this sense is often coupled with a derogatory adjective: we say that the expression "he ain't here" is "bad grammar." . . .

As has already been suggested, much confusion arises from mixing these meanings. One hears a good deal of criticism of teachers of English couched in such terms as "they don't teach grammar any more." Criticism of this sort is based on the wholly unproven assumption that teaching Grammar 2 will improve the student's proficiency in Grammar 1 or improve his manners in Grammar 3. Actually, the form of Grammar 2 which is usually taught is a very inaccurate and misleading analysis of the facts of Grammar 1; and it therefore is of highly questionable value in improving a person's ability to handle the structural patterns of his language. (pp. 300-301)

Francis' Grammar 3 is, of course, not grammar at all, but usage. One would like to assume that Joseph Williams' recent discussion of usage ("The Phenomenology of Error," *CCC*, 32 [1981], 152-168), along with his references, has placed those shibboleths in a proper perspective. But I doubt it, and I suspect that popular discussions of the grammar issue will be as flawed by the intrusion of usage issues as past discussions have been. At any rate I will make only passing reference to Grammar 3—usage—naively assuming that this issue has been discussed elsewhere and that my readers are familiar with those discussions.

We need also to make further discriminations about Francis' Grammar 2, given that the purpose of his 1954 article was to substitute for one form of Grammar 2, that "inaccurate and misleading" form "which is usually taught," another form, that of American structuralist grammar. Here we can make use of a still earlier discussion, one going back to the days when *PMLA* was willing to publish articles on rhetoric and linguistics, to a 1927 article by Charles Carpenter Fries, "The Rules of the Common School Grammars" (42 [1927], 221-237). Fries there distinguished between the scientific tradition of language study (to which we will now delimit Francis' Grammar 2, scientific grammar) and the separate tradition of "the common school grammars," developed unscientifically, largely based on two inadequate principles—appeals to "logical principles," like "two negatives make a positive," and analogy to Latin grammar; thus, Charlton Laird's characterization, "the grammar of Latin, ingeniously warped to suggest English" (*Language in America* [New York: World, 1970], p. 294). There is, of course, a direct link between the "common school grammars" that Fries criticized in 1927 and the grammar-based texts of today, and thus it seems wise, as Karl W. Dykema suggests ("Where Our Grammar Came From," *CE*, 22 (1961), 455-465), to separate Grammar 2, "scientific grammar," from Grammar 4, "school grammar," the latter meaning, quite literally, "the grammars used in the schools."

Further, since Martha Kolln points to the adaptation of Christensen's sentence rhetoric in a recent sentence-combining text as an example of the proper emphasis on "grammar" ("Closing the Books on Alchemy," p. 140), it is worth separating out, as still another meaning of *grammar*, Grammar 5, "stylistic grammar," defined as "grammatical terms used in the interest of teaching prose style." And, since stylistic grammars abound, with widely variant terms and emphases, we might appropriately speak parenthetically of specific forms of Grammar 5—Grammar 5 (Lanham); Grammar 5 (Strunk and White); Grammar 5 (Williams, *Style*); even Grammar 5 (Christensen, as adapted by Daiker, Kerek, and Morenberg).[9]

THE GRAMMAR IN OUR HEADS

With these definitions in mind, let us return to Francis' Grammar 1, admirably defined by Kolln as "the internalized system of rules that speakers of a language share" ("Closing the Books on Alchemy," p. 140), or, to put it more simply, the grammar in our heads. Three features of Grammar 1 need to be stressed: first, its special status as an "internalized system of rules," as tacit and unconscious knowledge; second, the abstract, even counterintuitive, nature of these rules, insofar as we are able to approximate them indirectly as Grammar 2 statements; and third, the way in which the form of one's Grammar 1 seems profoundly affected by the acquisition of literacy. This sort of review is designed to firm up our theory of language, so that we can ask what it predicts about the value of teaching formal grammar.

A simple thought experiment will isolate the special status of Grammar 1 knowledge. I have asked members of a number of different groups—from sixth graders to college freshmen to high-school teachers—to give me the rule for ordering adjectives of nationality, age, and number in English. The response is always the same: "We don't know the rule." Yet when I ask these groups to perform an active language task, they show productive control over the rule they have denied knowing. I ask them to arrange the following words in a natural order:

French   the   young   girls   four

I have never seen a native speaker of English who did not immediately produce the natural order, "the four young French girls." The rule is that in English the order of adjectives is first, number, second, age, and third, nationality. Native speakers can create analogous phrases using the rule — "the seventy-three aged Scandinavian lechers"; and the drive for meaning is so great that they will create contexts to make sense out of violations of the rule, as in foregrounding for emphasis: "I want to talk to the French four young girls." (I immediately envision a large room, perhaps a banquet hall, filled with tables at which are seated groups of four young girls, each group of a different nationality.) So Grammar 1 is eminently usable knowledge — the way we make our life through language — but it is not accessible knowledge; in a profound sense, we do not know that we have it. Thus neurolinguist Z. N. Pylyshyn speaks of Grammar 1 as "autonomous," separate from common-sense reasoning, and as "cognitively impenetrable," not available for direct examination.[10] In philosophy and linguistics, the distinction is made between formal, conscious, "knowing about" knowledge (like Grammar 2 knowledge) and tacit, unconscious, "knowing how" knowledge (like Grammar 1 knowledge). The importance of this distinction for the teaching of composition — it provides a powerful theoretical justification for mistrusting the ability of Grammar 2 (or Grammar 4) knowledge to affect Grammar 1 performance — was pointed out in this journal by Martin Steinmann, Jr., in 1966 ("Rhetorical Research," CE, 27 [1966], 278-285).

Further, the more we learn about Grammar 1 — and most linguists would agree that we know surprisingly little about it — the more abstract and implicit it seems. This abstractness can be illustrated with an experiment, devised by Lise Menn and reported by Morris Halle,[11] about our rule for forming plurals in speech. It is obvious that we do indeed have a "rule" for forming plurals, for we do not memorize the plural of each noun separately. You will demonstrate productive control over that rule by forming the spoken plurals of the nonsense words below:

thole   flitch   plast

Halle offers two ways of formalizing a Grammar 2 equivalent of this Grammar 1 ability. One form of the rule is the following, stated in terms of speech sounds:

    a. If the noun ends in /s z š ž č ǰ/, add /ɨz/;

    b. otherwise, if the noun ends in /p t k f Ø/, add /s/;

    c. otherwise, add /z/.[11]

This rule comes close to what we literate adults consider to be an adequate rule for plurals in writing, like the rules, for example, taken from a recent "common school grammar," Eric Gould's *Reading into Writing: A Rhetoric, Reader, and Handbook* (Boston: Houghton Mifflin, 1983):

> *Plurals* can be tricky. If you are unsure of a plural, then check it in the dictionary. The general rules are
>   Add *s* to the singular: *girls, tables*
>   Add *es* to nouns ending in *ch, sh, x* or *s: churches, boxes, wishes*
>   Add *es* to nouns ending in *y* and preceded by a vowel once you have changed *y* to *i: monies, companies.* (p. 666)

(But note the persistent inadequacy of such Grammar 4 rules: here, as I read it, the rule is inadequate to explain the plurals of *ray* and *tray*, even to explain the collective noun *monies*, not a plural at all, formed from the mass noun *money* and offered as an example.) A second form of the rule would make use of much more abstract entities, sound features:

    a. If the noun ends with a sound that is [coronal, strident], add /ɨz/;

    b. otherwise, if the noun ends with a sound that is [non-voiced], add /s/;

    c. otherwise, add /z/.

(The notion of "sound features" is itself rather abstract, perhaps new to readers not trained in linguistics. But such readers should be able to recognize that the spoken plurals of *lip* and *duck*, the sound [s], differ from the spoken plurals of *sea* and *gnu*, the sound [z], only in that the sounds of the latter are "voiced"—one's vocal cords vibrate—while the sounds of the former are "non-voiced.")

    To test the psychologically operative rule, the Grammar 1 rule, native speakers of English were asked to form the plural of the last name of the composer Johann Sebastian *Bach*, a sound [x], unique in American (though not in Scottish) English. If speakers follow the first rule above, using word endings, they would reject a) and b), then apply c), producing the plural as /baxz/, with word-final /z/. (If writers were to follow the rule of the common school grammar, they would produce the written plural *Baches*, apparently, given the form of the rule, on analogy with *churches*.) If speakers follow the second rule, they would have to analyze the sound [x] as [non-labial, non-coronal, dorsal, non-voiced, and non-strident], producing the plural as /baxs/, with word-final /s/. Native speakers of American English overwhelmingly produce the plural as /baxs/. They use knowledge that Halle characterizes as "unlearned and untaught" (p. 140).

Now such a conclusion is counterintuitive—certainly it departs maximally from Grammar 4 rules for forming plurals. It seems that native speakers of English behave as if they have productive control, as Grammar 1 knowledge, of abstract sound features (± coronal, ± strident, and so on) which are available as conscious, Grammar 2 knowledge only to trained linguists—and, indeed, formally available only within the last hundred years or so. ("Behave as if," in that last sentence, is a necessary hedge, to underscore the difficulty of "knowing about" Grammar 1.)

Moreover, as the example of plural rules suggests, the form of the Grammar 1 in the heads of literate adults seems profoundly affected by the acquisition of literacy. Obviously, literate adults have access to different morphological codes: the abstract print -s underlying the predictable /s/ and /z/ plurals, the abstract print -ed underlying the spoken past tense markers /t/, as in "walked," /əd/, as in "surrounded," /d/, as in "scored," and the symbol /Ø/ for no surface realization, as in the relaxed standard pronunciation of "I walked to the store." Literate adults also have access to distinctions preserved only in the code of print (for example, the distinction between "a good sailer" and "a good sailor" that Mark Aranoff points out in "An English Spelling Convention," *Linguistic Inquiry*, 9 [1978], 299-303). More significantly, Irene Moscowitz speculates that the ability of third graders to form abstract nouns on analogy with pairs like *divine::divinity* and *serene::serenity*, where the spoken vowel changes but the spelling preserves meaning, is a factor of knowing how to read. Carol Chomsky finds a three-stage developmental sequence in the grammatical performance of seven-year-olds, related to measures of kind and variety of reading; and Rita S. Brause finds a nine-stage developmental sequence in the ability to understand semantic ambiguity, extending from fourth graders to graduate students.[12] John Mills and Gordon Hemsley find that level of education, and presumably level of literacy, influence judgments of grammaticality, concluding that literacy changes the deep structure of one's internal grammar; Jean Whyte finds that oral language functions develop differently in readers and non-readers; José Morais, Jésus Alegria, and Paul Bertelson find that illiterate adults are unable to add or delete sounds at the beginning of nonsense words, suggesting that awareness of speech as a series of phones is provided by learning to read an alphabetic code. Two experiments—one conducted by Charles A. Ferguson, the other by Mary E. Hamilton and David Barton—find that adults' ability to recognize segmentation in speech is related to degree of literacy, not to amount of schooling or general ability.[13]

It is worth noting that none of these investigators would suggest that the developmental sequences they have uncovered be isolated and taught as discrete skills. They are natural concomitants of literacy, and they seem best characterized not as isolated rules but as developing schemata, broad strategies for approaching written language.

GRAMMAR 2

We can, of course, attempt to approximate the rules or schemata of Grammar 1 by writing fully explicit descriptions that model the competence of a native speaker. Such rules, like the rules for pluralizing nouns or ordering adjectives discussed above, are the goal of the science of linguistics, that is, Grammar 2. There are a number of scientific grammars—an older structuralist model and several versions within a generative-transformational paradigm, not to mention isolated schools like tagmemic grammar, Montague grammar, and the like. In fact, we cannot think of Grammar 2 as a stable entity, for its form changes with each new issue of each linguistics journal, as new "rules of grammar" are proposed and debated. Thus Grammar 2, though of great theoretical interest to the composition teacher, is of little practical use in the classroom, as Constance Weaver has pointed out (*Grammar for Teachers* [Urbana, Ill.: NCTE, 1979], pp. 3-6). Indeed Grammar 2 is a scientific model of Grammar 1, not a description of it, so that questions of psychological reality, while important, are less important than other, more theoretical factors, such as the elegance of formulation or the global power of rules. We might, for example, wish to replace the rule for ordering adjectives of age, number, and nationality cited above with a more general rule— what linguists call a "fuzzy" rule—that adjectives in English are ordered by their abstract quality of "nouniness": adjectives that are very much like nouns, like *French* or *Scandinavian*, come physically closer to nouns than do adjectives that are less "nouny," like *four* or *aged*. But our motivation for accepting the broader rule would be its global power, not its psychological reality.[14]

I try to consider a hostile reader, one committed to the teaching of grammar, and I try to think of ways to hammer in the central point of this distinction, that the rules of Grammar 2 are simply unconnected to productive control over Grammar 1. I can argue from authority: Noam Chomsky has touched on this point whenever he has concerned himself with the implications of linguistics for language teaching, and years ago transformationalist Mark Lester stated unequivocally, "there simply appears to be no correlation between a writer's study of language and his ability to write."[15] I can cite analogies offered by others: Francis Christensen's analogy in an essay originally published in 1962 that formal grammar study would be "to invite a centipede to attend to the sequence of his legs in motion,"[16] or James Britton's analogy, offered informally after a conference presentation, that grammar study would be like forcing starving people to master the use of a knife and fork before allowing them to eat. I can offer analogies of my own, contemplating the wisdom of asking a pool player to master the physics of momentum before taking up a cue or of making a prospective driver get a degree in automotive engineering before engaging the clutch. I consider a hypothetical argument, that if Grammar 2 knowledge affected Grammar 1 performance, then linguists would be our best writers. (I can certify that they are, on the whole, not.) Such a position, after all, is only in accord with other domains of science: the formula for catching a fly ball in baseball ("Playing It by Ear," *Scientific American*, 248, No. 4 [1983], 76) is of such complexity that it is beyond my understanding—and, I would suspect, that of many workaday centerfielders. But perhaps I can best hammer in this claim—that Grammar 2 knowledge has no effect on Grammar 1 performance—by offering a demonstration.

The diagram below is an attempt by Thomas N. Huckin and Leslie A. Olsen (*English for Science and Technology* [New York: McGraw-Hill, 1983]) to offer, for students of English as a second language, a fully explicit formu-

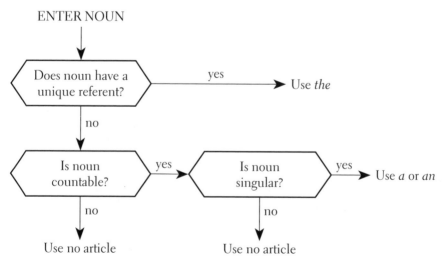

lation of what is, for native speakers, a trivial rule of the language—the choice of definite article, indefinite article, or no definite article. There are obvious limits to such a formulation, for article choice in English is less a matter of rule than of idiom ("I went to college" versus "I went to a university" versus British "I went to university"), real-world knowledge (using indefinite "I went into a house" instantiates definite "I looked at the ceiling," and indefinite "I visited a university" instantiates definite "I talked with the professors"), and stylistic choice (the last sentence above might alternatively end with "the choice of the definite article, the indefinite article, or no article"). Huckin and Olsen invite non-native speakers to use the rule consciously to justify article choice in technical prose, such as the passage below from P. F. Brandwein (*Matter: An Earth Science* [New York: Harcourt Brace Jovanovich, 1975]). I invite you to spend a couple of minutes doing the same thing, with the understanding that this exercise is a test case: you are using a very explicit rule to justify a fairly straightforward issue of grammatical choice.

> Imagine a cannon on top of _____ highest mountain on earth. It is firing _____ cannonballs horizontally. _____ first cannonball fired follows its path. As _____ cannonball moves, _____ gravity pulls it down, and it soon hits _____ ground. Now _____ velocity with which each succeeding cannonball is fired is increased. Thus, _____ cannonball goes farther each time. Cannonball 2 goes farther than _____ cannonball 1 although each is being pulled by _____ gravity toward the earth all _____ time. _____ last cannonball is fired with such tremendous velocity that it goes completely around _____ earth. It returns to _____ mountaintop and continues around the earth again and again. _____ cannonball's inertia causes it to continue in motion indefinitely in _____ orbit around earth. In such a situation, we could consider _____ cannonball to be _____ artificial satellite, just like _____ weather satellites launched by _____ U.S. Weather Service. (p. 209)

Most native speakers of English who have attempted this exercise report a great deal of frustration, a curious sense of working against, rather than with, the rule. The rule, however valuable it may be for non-native speakers, is, for the most part, simply unusable for native speakers of the language.

COGNATE AREAS OF RESEARCH

We can corroborate this demonstration by turning to research in two cognate areas, studies of the induction of rules of artificial languages and studies of the role of formal rules in second language acquisition. Psychologists have studied the ability of subjects to learn artificial languages, usually constructed of nonsense syllables or letter strings. Such languages can be described by phrase structure rules:

$S \Rightarrow VX$

$X \Rightarrow MX$

More clearly, they can be presented as flow diagrams, as below:

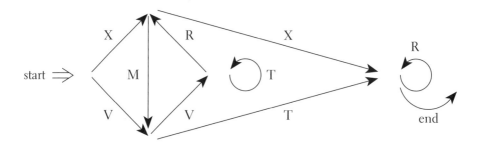

This diagram produces "sentences" like the following:

VVTRXRR.	XMVTTRX.	XXRR.
XMVRMT.	VVTTRMT.	XMTRRR.

The following "sentences" would be "ungrammatical" in this language:

*VMXTT.	*RTXVVT.	*TRVXXVVM.

Arthur S. Reber, in a classic 1967 experiment, demonstrated that mere exposure to grammatical sentences produced tacit learning: subjects who copied several grammatical sentences performed far above chance in judging the grammaticality of other letter strings. Further experiments have shown that providing subjects with formal rules—giving them the flow diagram above, for example—remarkably degrades performance: subjects given the "rules of the language" do much less well in acquiring the rules than do subjects not given the rules. Indeed, even telling subjects that they are to induce the rules of an artificial language degrades performance. Such laboratory experiments are admittedly contrived, but they confirm predictions that our theory of language would make about the value of formal rules in language learning.[17]

The thrust of recent research in second language learning similarly works to constrain the value of formal grammar rules. The most explicit statement of the value of formal rules is that of Stephen D. Krashen's monitor model.[18] Krashen divides second language mastery into *acquisition*—tacit, informal mastery, akin to first language acquisition—and formal learning—conscious application of Grammar 2 rules, which he calls "monitoring" output. In another essay Krashen uses his model to predict a highly individual use of the monitor and a highly constrained role for formal rules:

> Some adults (and very few children) are able to use conscious rules to increase the grammatical accuracy of their output, and even for these people, very strict conditions need to be met before the conscious grammar can be applied.[19]

In *Principles and Practice in Second Language Acquisition* (New York: Pergamon, 1982) Krashen outlines these conditions by means of a series of concentric circles, beginning with a large circle denoting the rules of English and a smaller circle denoting the subset of those rules described by formal linguists (adding that most linguists would protest that the size of this circle is much too large):

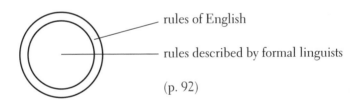

rules of English

rules described by formal linguists

(p. 92)

Krashen then adds smaller circles, as shown below—a subset of the rules described by formal linguists that would be known to applied linguists, a subset of those rules that would be available to the best teachers, and then a subset of those rules that teachers might choose to present to second language learners:

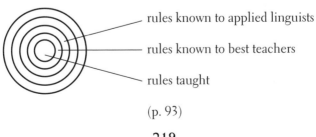

rules known to applied linguists

rules known to best teachers

rules taught

(p. 93)

219

Of course, as Krashen notes, not all the rules taught will be learned, and not all those learned will be available, as what he calls "mental baggage" (p. 94), for conscious use.

An experiment by Ellen Bialystock, asking English speakers learning French to judge the grammaticality of taped sentences, complicates this issue, for reaction time data suggest that learners first make an intuitive judgment of grammaticality, using implicit or Grammar 1 knowledge, and only then search for formal explanations, using explicit or Grammar 2 knowledge.[20] This distinction would suggest that Grammar 2 knowledge is of use to second language learners only after the principle has already been mastered as tacit Grammar 1 knowledge. In the terms of Krashen's model, learning never becomes acquisition (*Principles*, p. 86).

An ingenious experiment by Herbert W. Seliger complicates the issue yet further ("On the Nature and Function of Language Rules in Language Learning," *TESOL Quarterly*, 13 [1979], 359-369). Seliger asked native and non-native speakers of English to orally identify pictures of objects (e.g., "an apple," "a pear," "a book," "an umbrella"), noting whether they used the correct form of the indefinite articles *a* and *an*. He then asked each speaker to state the rule for choosing between *a* and *an*. He found no correlation between the ability to state the rule and the ability to apply it correctly, either with native or non-native speakers. Indeed, three of four adult non-native speakers in his sample produced a correct form of the rule, but they did not apply it in speaking. A strong conclusion from this experiment would be that formal rules of grammar seem to have no value whatsoever. Seliger, however, suggests a more paradoxical interpretation. Rules are of no use, he agrees, but some people think they are, and for these people, assuming that they have internalized the rules, even inadequate rules are of heuristic value, for they allow them to access the internal rules they actually use.

THE INCANTATIONS OF THE "COMMON SCHOOL GRAMMARS"

Such a paradox may explain the fascination we have as teachers with "rules of grammar" of the Grammar 4 variety, the "rules" of the "common school grammars." Again and again such rules are inadequate to the facts of written language; you will recall that we have known this since Francis' 1927 study. R. Scott Baldwin and James M. Coady, studying how readers respond to punctuation signals ("Psycholinguistic Approaches to a Theory of Punctuation," *Journal of Reading Behavior*, 10 [1978], 363-83), conclude that conventional rules of punctuation are "a complete sham" (p. 375). My own favorite is the Grammar 4 rule for showing possession, always expressed in terms of adding -'s or -s' to nouns, while our internal grammar, if you think about it, adds possession to noun phrases, albeit under severe stylistic constraints: "the horses of the Queen of England" are "the Queen of England's horses" and "the feathers of the duck over there" are "the duck over there's feathers." Suzette Haden Elgin refers to the "rules" of Grammar 4 as "incantations" (*Never Mind the Trees*, p. 9: see footnote 3).

It may simply be that as hyperliterate adults we are conscious of "using rules" when we are in fact doing something else, something far more complex, accessing tacit heuristics honed by print literacy itself. We can clarify this notion by reaching for an acronym coined by technical writers to explain the readability of complex prose—COIK: "clear only if known." The rules of Grammar 4—no, we can at this point be more honest—the incantations of Grammar 4 are COIK. If you know how to signal possession in the code of print, then the advice to add -'s to nouns makes perfect sense, just as the collective noun *monies* is a fine example of changing -*y* to -*i* and adding -*es* to form the plural. But if you have not grasped, tacitly, the abstract representation of possession in print, such incantations can only be opaque.

Worse yet, the advice given in "the common school grammars" is unconnected with anything remotely resembling literate adult behavior. Consider, as an example, the rule for not writing a sentence fragment as the rule is described in the best-selling college grammar text, John C. Hodges and Mary S. Whitten's *Harbrace College Handbook*, 9th ed. (New York: Harcourt Brace Jovanovich, 1982). In order to get to the advice, "as a rule, do not write a sentence fragment" (p. 25), the student must master the following learning tasks:

Recognizing verbs.

Recognizing subjects and verbs.

Recognizing all parts of speech. (*Harbrace* lists eight.)

Recognizing phrases and subordinate clauses. (*Harbrace* lists six types of phrases, and it offers incomplete lists of eight relative pronouns and eighteen subordinating conjunctions.)

Recognizing main clauses and types of sentences.

These learning tasks completed, the student is given the rule above, offered a page of exceptions, and then given the following advice (or is it an incantation?):

> Before handing in a composition, . . . proofread each word group written as
> a sentence. Test each one for completeness. First, be sure that it has at least
> one subject and one predicate. Next, be sure that the word group is not a
> dependent clause beginning with a subordinating conjunction or a relative
> clause. (p. 27)

The school grammar approach defines a sentence fragment as a conceptual error—as not having conscious knowledge of the school grammar definition of *sentence*. It demands heavy emphasis on rote memory, and it asks students to behave in ways patently removed from the behaviors of mature writers. (I have never in my life tested a sentence for completeness, and I am a better writer—and probably a better person—as a consequence.) It may be, of course, that some developing writers, at some points in their development, may benefit from such advice—or, more to the point, may think that they benefit—but, as Thomas Friedman points out in "Teaching Error, Nurturing Confusion" (*CE*, 45 [1983], 390-399), our theory of language tells us that such advice is, at the best, COIK. As the Maine joke has it, about a tourist asking directions from a farmer, "you can't get there from here."

REDEFINING ERROR

In the specific case of sentence fragments, Mina P. Shaughnessy (*Errors and Expectations* [New York: Oxford University Press, 1977]) argues that such errors are not conceptual failures at all, but performance errors—mistakes in punctuation. Muriel Harris' error counts support this view ("Mending the Fragmented Free Modifier," *CCC*, 32 [1981], 175-182). Case studies show example after example of errors that occur *because of* instruction—one thinks, for example, of David Bartholmae's student explaining that he added an -s to *children* "because it's a plural" ("The Study of Error," *CCC*, 31 [1980], 262). Surveys, such as that by Muriel Harris ("Contradictory Perceptions of the Rules of Writing," *CCC*, 30 [1979], 218-220), and our own observations suggest that students consistently misunderstand such Grammar 4 explanations (COIK, you will recall). For example, from Patrick Hartwell and Robert H. Bentley and from Mike Rose, we have two separate anecdotal accounts of students, cited for punctuating a *because*-clause as a sentence, who have decided to avoid using *because*. More generally, Collette A. Daiute's analysis of errors made by college students shows that errors tend to appear at clause boundaries, suggesting short-term memory load and not conceptual deficiency as a cause of error.[21]

Thus, if we think seriously about error and its relationship to the worship of formal grammar study, we need to attempt some massive dislocation of our traditional thinking, to shuck off our hyperliterate perception of the value of formal rules, and to regain the confidence in the tacit power of unconscious knowledge that our theory of language gives us. Most students, reading their writing aloud, will correct in essence all errors of spelling, grammar, and, by intonation, punctuation, but usually without noticing that what they read departs from what they wrote.[22] And Richard H. Haswell ("Minimal Marking," *CE*, 45 [1983], 600-604) notes that his students correct 61.1% of their errors when they are identified with a simple mark in the margin rather than by error type. Such findings suggest that we need to redefine error, to see it not as a cognitive or linguistic problem, a problem of not knowing a "rule of grammar" (whatever that may mean), but rather, following the insight of Robert J. Bracewell ("Writing as a Cognitive Activity," *Visible Language*, 14 [1980], 400-422), as a problem of metacognition and metalinguistic awareness, a matter of accessing knowledges that, to be of any use, learners must have already internalized by means of exposure to the code. (Usage issues—Grammar 3—probably represent a different order of problem. Both Joseph Emonds and Jeffrey Jochnowitz establish that the usage issues we worry most about are linguistically unnatural, departures from the grammar in our heads.)[23]

The notion of metalinguistic awareness seems crucial. The sentence below, created by Douglas R. Hofstadter ("Metamagical Themas," *Scientific American*, 235, No. 1 [1981], 22-32), is offered to clarify that notion; you are invited to examine it for a moment or two before continuing.

Their is four errors in this sentence. Can you find them?

Three errors announce themselves plainly enough, the misspellings of *there* and *sentence* and the use of *is* instead of *are*. (And, just to illustrate the perils of hyperliteracy, let it be noted that, through three years of drafts, I referred to the choice of *is* and *are* as a matter of "subject-verb agreement.") The fourth error resists detection, until one assesses the truth value of the sentence itself—the fourth error is that there are not four errors, only three. Such a sentence (Hofstadter calls it a "self-referencing sentence") asks you to look at it in two ways, simultaneously as statement and as linguistic artifact—in other words, to exercise metalinguistic awareness.

A broad range of cross-cultural studies suggest that metalinguistic awareness is a defining feature of print literacy. Thus Sylvia Scribner and Michael Cole, working with the triliterate Vai of Liberia (variously literate in English, through schooling; in Arabic, for religious purposes; and in an indigenous Vai script, used for personal affairs), find that metalinguistic awareness, broadly conceived, is the only cognitive skill underlying each of the three literacies. The one statistically significant skill shared by literate Vai was the recognition of word boundaries. Moreover, literate Vai tended to answer "yes" when asked (in Vai), "Can you call the sun the moon and the moon the sun?" while illiterate Vai tended to have grave doubts about such metalinguistic play. And in the United States Henry and Lila R. Gleitman report quite different responses by clerical workers and PhD candidates asked to interpret nonsense compounds like "house-bird glass": clerical workers focused on meaning and plausibility (for example, "a house-bird made of glass"), while PhD candidates focused on syntax (for example, "a very small drinking cup for canaries" or "a glass that protects house-birds").[24] More general research findings suggest a clear relationship between measures of metalinguistic awareness and measures of literacy level.[25] William Labov, speculating on literacy acquisition in inner-city ghettoes, contrasts "stimulus-bound" and "language-bound" individuals, suggesting that the latter seem to master literacy more easily.[26] The analysis here suggests that the causal relationship works the other way, that it is the mastery of written language that increases one's awareness of language as language.

This analysis has two implications. First, it makes the question of socially nonstandard dialects, always implicit in discussions of teaching formal grammar, into a non-issue.[27] Native speakers of English, regardless of dialect, show tacit mastery of the conventions of Standard English, and that mastery seems to transfer into abstract orthographic knowledge through interaction with print.[28] Developing writers show the same patterning of errors, regardless of dialect.[29] Studies of reading and of writing suggest that surface features of spoken dialect are simply irrelevant to mastering print literacy.[30] Print is a complex cultural code—or better yet, a system of codes—and my bet is that, regardless of instruction, one masters those codes from the top down, from pragmatic questions of voice, tone, audience, register, and rhetorical strategy, not from the bottom up, from grammar to usage to fixed forms of organization.

Second, this analysis forces us to posit multiple literacies, used for multiple purposes, rather than a single static literacy, engraved in "rules of grammar." These multiple literacies are evident in cross-cultural studies.[31] They are equally evident when we inquire into the uses of literacy in American communities.[32] Further, given that students, at all levels, show widely variant interactions with print literacy, there would seem to be little to do with grammar—with Grammar 2 or with Grammar 4—that we could isolate as a basis for formal instruction.[33]

GRAMMAR 5: STYLISTIC GRAMMAR

Similarly, when we turn to Grammar 5, "grammatical terms used in the interest of teaching prose style," so central to Martha Kolln's argument for teaching formal grammar, we find that the grammar issue is simply beside the point. There are two fully-articulated positions about "stylistic grammar," which I will label "romantic" and "classic," following Richard Lloyd-Jones and Richard E. Young.[34] The romantic position is that stylistic grammars, though perhaps useful for teachers, have little place in the teaching of composition, for students must struggle with and through language toward meaning. This position rests on a theory of language ultimately philosophical rather than linguistic (witness, for example, the contempt for linguists in Ann Berthoff's *The Making of Meaning: Metaphors, Models, and Maxims for Writing Teachers* [Montclair, N.J.: Boynton/Cook, 1981]); it is articulated as a theory of style by Donald A. Murray and, on somewhat different grounds (that stylistic grammars encourage overuse of the monitor), by Ian Pringle. The classic position, on the other hand, is that we can find ways to offer developing writers helpful suggestions about prose style, suggestions such as Francis Christensen's emphasis on the cumulative sentence, developed by observing the practice of skilled writers, and Joseph Williams' advice about predication, developed by psycholinguistic studies of comprehension.[35] James A. Berlin's recent survey of composition theory (*CE*, 45 [1982], 765-777) probably understates the gulf between these two positions and the radically different conceptions of language that underlie them, but it does establish that they share an overriding assumption in common: that one learns to control the language of print by manipulating language in meaningful contexts, not by learning about language in isolation, as by the study of formal grammar. Thus even classic theorists, who choose to present a vocabulary of style to students, do so only as a vehicle for encouraging productive control of communicative structures.

We might put the matter in the following terms. Writers need to develop skills at two levels. One, broadly rhetorical, involves communication in meaningful contexts (the strategies, registers, and procedures of discourse across a range of modes, audiences, contexts, and purposes). The other, broadly metalinguistic rather than linguistic, involves active manipulation of language with conscious attention to surface form. This second level may be developed tacitly, as a natural adjunct to developing rhetorical competencies—I take this to be the position of romantic theorists. It may be developed formally, by manipulating language for stylistic effect, and such manipulation may involve, for pedagogical continuity, a vocabulary of style. But it is primarily developed by any kind of language activity that enhances the awareness of language as language.[36] David T. Hakes, summarizing the research on metalinguistic awareness, notes how far we are from understanding this process:

> the optimal conditions for becoming metalinguistically competent involve growing up in a literate environment with adult models who are themselves metalinguistically competent and who foster the growth of that competence in a variety of ways as yet little understood. ("The Development of Metalinguistic Abilities," p. 205: see footnote 25)

Such a model places language, at all levels, at the center of the curriculum, but not as "necessary categories and labels" (Kolln, "Closing the Books on Alchemy," p. 150), but as literal stuff, verbal clay, to be molded and probed, shaped and reshaped, and, above all, enjoyed.

THE TRADITION OF EXPERIMENTAL RESEARCH

Thus, when we turn back to experimental research on the value of formal grammar instruction, we do so with firm predictions given us by our theory of language. Our theory would predict that formal grammar instruction, whether instruction in scientific grammar or instruction in "the common school grammar," would have little to do with control over surface correctness nor with quality of writing. It would predict that any form of active involvement with language would be preferable to instruction in rules or definitions (or incantations). In essence, this is what the research tells us. In 1893, the Committee of Ten (*Report of the Committee of Ten on Secondary School Studies* [Washington, D.C.: U.S. Government Printing Office, 1893]) put grammar at the center of the English curriculum, and its report established the rigidly sequential mode of instruction common for the last century. But the committee explicitly noted that grammar instruction did not aid correctness, arguing instead that it improved the ability to think logically (an argument developed from the role of the "grammarian" in the classical rhetorical tradition, essentially a teacher of literature—see, for example, the etymology of *grammar* in the *Oxford English Dictionary*).

But Franklin S. Hoyt, in a 1906 experiment, found no relationship between the study of grammar and the ability to think logically; his research led him to conclude what I am constrained to argue more than seventy-five years later, that there is no "relationship between a knowledge of technical grammar and the ability to use English and to interpret language" ("The Place of Grammar in the Elementary Curriculum," *Teachers Col-*

lege Record, 7 [1906], 483-484). Later studies, through the 1920s, focused on the relationship of knowledge of grammar and ability to recognize error; experiments reported by James Boraas in 1917 and by William Asker in 1923 are typical of those that reported no correlation. In the 1930s, with the development of the functional grammar movement, it was common to compare the study of formal grammar with one form or another of active manipulation of language; experiments by I. O. Ash in 1935 and Ellen Frogner in 1939 are typical of studies showing the superiority of active involvement with language.[37] In a 1959 article, "Grammar in Language Teaching" (*Elementary English*, 36 [1959], 412-421), John J. DeBoer noted the consistency of these findings.

> The impressive fact is . . . that in all these studies, carried out in places and at times far removed from each other, often by highly experienced and disinterested investigators, the results have been consistently negative so far as the value of grammar in the improvement of language expression is concerned. (p. 417)

In 1960 Ingrid M. Strom, reviewing more than fifty experimental studies, came to a similarly strong and unqualified conclusion:

> direct methods of instruction, focusing on writing activities and the structuring of ideas, are more efficient in teaching sentence structure, usage, punctuation, and other related factors than are such methods as nomenclature drill, diagramming, and rote memorization of grammatical rules.[38]

In 1963 two research reviews appeared, one by Braddock, Lloyd-Jones, and Schorer, cited at the beginning of this paper, and one by Henry C. Meckel, whose conclusions, though more guarded, are in essential agreement.[39] In 1969 J. Stephen Sherwin devoted one-fourth of his *Four Problems in Teaching English: A Critique of Research* (Scranton, Penn.: International Textbook, 1969) to the grammar issue, concluding that "instruction in formal grammar is an ineffective way to help students achieve proficiency in writing" (p. 135). Some early experiments in sentence combining, such as those by Donald R. Bateman and Frank J. Zidonnis and by John C. Mellon, showed improvement in measures of syntactic complexity with instruction in transformational grammar keyed to sentence combining practice. But a later study by Frank O'Hare achieved the same gains with no grammar instruction, suggesting to Sandra L. Stotsky and to Richard Van de Veghe that active manipulation of language, not the grammar unit, explained the earlier results.[40] More recent summaries of research—by Elizabeth I. Haynes,

Hillary Taylor Holbrook, and Marcia Farr Whiteman—support similar conclusions. Indirect evidence for this position is provided by surveys reported by Betty Bamberg in 1978 and 1981, showing that time spent in grammar instruction in high school is the least important factor, of eight factors examined, in separating regular from remedial writers at the college level.[41]

More generally, Patrick Scott and Bruce Castner, in "Reference Sources for Composition Research: A Practical Survey" (*CE*, 45 [1983], 756-768), note that much current research is not informed by an awareness of the past. Put simply, we are constrained to reinvent the wheel. My concern here has been with a far more serious problem: that too often the wheel we reinvent is square.

It is, after all, a question of power. Janet Emig, developing a consensus from composition research, and Aaron S. Carton and Lawrence V. Castiglione, developing the implications of language theory for education, come to the same conclusion: that the thrust of current research and theory is to take power from the teacher and to give that power to the learner.[42] At no point in the English curriculum is the question of power more blatantly posed than in the issue of formal grammar instruction. It is time that we, as teachers, formulate theories of language and literacy and let those theories guide our teaching, and it is time that we, as researchers, move on to more interesting areas of inquiry.

NOTES

1. *Research in Written Composition* (Urbana, Ill.: National Council of Teachers of English, 1963), pp. 37-38.

2. "Non-magical Thinking: Presenting Writing Developmentally in Schools," in *Writing Process, Development and Communication*, Vol. II of *Writing: The Nature, Development and Teaching of Written Communication*, ed. Charles H. Frederiksen and Joseph F. Dominic (Hillsdale, N.J.: Lawrence Erlbaum, 1980), pp. 21-30.

3. For arguments in favor of formal grammar teaching, see Patrick F. Basset, "Grammar—Can We Afford Not to Teach It?" *NASSP Bulletin*, 64, No. 10 (1980), 55-63; Mary Epes, et al., "The COMP-LAB Project: Assessing the Effectiveness of a Laboratory-Centered Basic Writing Course on the College Level" (Jamaica, N.Y.: York College, CUNY, 1979) ERIC 194 908; June B. Evans, "The Analogous Ounce: The Analgesic for Relief," *English Journal*, 70, No. 2 (1981), 38-39; Sydney Greenbaum, "What Is Grammar and Why Teach It?" (a paper presented at the meeting of the National Council of Teachers of English, Boston, Nov. 1982) ERIC 222 917; Marjorie Smelstor, *A Guide to the Role of Grammar in Teaching Writing* (Madison: University of Wisconsin School of Education, 1978) ERIC 176 323; and A. M. Tibbetts, *Working Papers: A Teacher's Observations on Composition* (Glenview, Ill.: Scott, Foresman, 1982).

For attacks on formal grammar teaching, see Harvey A. Daniels, *Famous Last Words: The American Language Crisis Reconsidered* (Carbondale: Southern Illinois University Press, 1983); Suzette Haden Elgin, *Never Mind the Trees: What the English Teacher Really Needs to*

Know about Linguistics (Berkeley: University of California College of Education, Bay Area Writing Project Occasional Paper No. 2, 1980) ERIC 198 536; Mike Rose, "Remedial Writing Courses: A Critique and a Proposal." *College English*, 45 (1983), 109-128; and Ron Shook, "Response to Martha Kolln," *College Composition and Communication*, 34 (1983), 491-495.

4. See, for example, Clifton Fadiman and James Howard, *Empty Pages: A Search for Writing Competence in School and Society* (Belmont, Cal.: Fearon Pitman, 1979); Edwin Newman, *A Civil Tongue* (Indianapolis, Ind.: Bobbs-Merrill, 1976); and *Strictly Speaking* (New York: Warner Books, 1974); John Simons, *Paradigms Lost* (New York: Clarkson N. Potter, 1980); A. M. Tibbetts and Charlene Tibbetts, *What's Happening to American English?* (New York: Scribner's, 1978); and "Why Johnny Can't Write," *Newsweek*, 8 Dec. 1975, pp. 58-63.

5. "The Role of Grammar in a Secondary School English Curriculum." *Research in the Teaching of English*, 10 (1976), 5-21; *The Role of Grammar in a Secondary School Curriculum* (Wellington: New Zealand Council of Teachers of English, 1979).

6. "A Taxonomy of Compositional Competencies," in *Perspectives on Literacy*, ed. Richard Beach and P. David Pearson (Minneapolis: University of Minnesota College of Education, 1979), pp. 247-272.

7. On usage norms, see Edward Finegan, *Attitudes toward English Usage: The History of a War of Words* (New York: Teachers College Press, 1980), and Jim Quinn, *American Tongue in Cheek: A Populist Guide to Language* (New York: Pantheon, 1980); on arrangement, see Patrick Hartwell, "Teaching Arrangement: A Pedagogy," *CE*, 40 (1979), 548-554.

8. "Revolution in Grammar," *Quarterly Journal of Speech*, 40 (1954), 299-312.

9. Richard A. Lanham, *Revising Prose* (New York: Scribner's, 1979); William Strunk and E. B. White, *The Elements of Style*, 3rd ed. (New York: Macmillan, 1979); Joseph Williams, *Style: Ten Lessons in Clarity and Grace* (Glenview, Ill.: Scott, Foresman, 1981); Christensen, "A Generative Rhetoric of the Sentence," *CCC*, 14 (1963), 155-161; Donald A. Daiker, Andrew Kerek, and Max Morenberg, *The Writer's Options: Combining to Composing*, 2nd ed. (New York: Harper & Row, 1982).

10. "A Psychological Approach," in *Psychobiology of Language*, ed. M. Studdert-Kennedy (Cambridge, Mass.: MIT Press, 1983), pp. 16-19. See also Noam Chomsky, "Language and Unconscious Knowledge," in *Psychoanalysis and Language: Psychiatry and the Humanities*, Vol. III, ed. Joseph H. Smith (New Haven, Conn.: Yale University Press, 1978), pp. 3-44.

11. Morris Halle, "Knowledge Unlearned and Untaught: What Speakers Know about the Sounds of Their Language," in *Linguistic Theory and Psychological Reality*, ed. Halle, Joan Bresnan, and George A. Miller (Cambridge, Mass.: MIT Press, 1978), pp. 135-140.

12. Moscowitz, "On the Status of Vowel Shift in English," in *Cognitive Development and the Acquisition of Language*, ed. T. E. Moore (New York: Academic Press, 1973), pp. 223-60; Chomsky, "Stages in Language Development and Reading Exposure," *Harvard Educational Review*, 42 (1972), 1-33; and Brause, "Developmental Aspects of the Ability to Understand Semantic Ambiguity, with Implications for Teachers," *RTE*, 11 (1977), 39-48.

13. Mills and Hemsley, "The Effect of Levels of Education on Judgments of Grammatical Acceptability," *Language and Speech*, 19 (1976), 324-342; Whyte, "Levels of Language Competence and Reading Ability: An Exploratory Investigation," *Journal of Research in Reading*, 5 (1982, 123-132; Morais, et al., "Does Awareness of Speech as a Series of Phones Arise Spontaneously," *Cognition*, 7 (1979), 323-331; Ferguson, *Cognitive Effects of Literacy: Linguistic Awareness in Adult Non-readers* (Washington, D.C.: National Institute of Educa-

tion Final Report, 1981) ERIC 222 85; Hamilton and Barton, "A Word Is a Word: Metalinguistic Skills in Adults of Varying Literacy Levels" (Stanford, Cal.: Stanford University Department of Linguistics, 1980) ERIC 222 859.

14. On the question of the psychological reality of Grammar 2 descriptions, see Maria Black and Shulamith Chiat, "Psycholinguistics without 'Psychological Reality'," *Linguistics*, 19 (1981), 37-61; Joan Bresnan, ed., *The Mental Representation of Grammatical Relations* (Cambridge, Mass.: MIT Press, 1982); and Michael H. Long, "Inside the 'Black Box': Methodological Issues in Classroom Research on Language Learning," *Language Learning*, 30 (1980), 1-42.

15. Chomsky, "The Current Scene in Linguistics," *College English*, 27 (1966), 587-595; and "Linguistic Theory," in *Language Teaching: Broader Contexts*, ed. Robert C. Meade, Jr. (New York: Modern Language Association, 1966), pp. 43-49; Mark Lester, "The Value of Transformational Grammar in Teaching Composition," *CCC*, 16 (1967), 228.

16. Christensen, "Between Two Worlds," in *Notes toward a New Rhetoric: Nine Essays for Teachers*, rev. ed., ed. Bonniejean Christensen (New York: Harper & Row, 1978), pp. 1-22.

17. Reber, "Implicit Learning of Artificial Grammars," *Journal of Verbal Learning and Verbal Behavior*, 6 (1967), 855-863; "Implicit Learning of Synthetic Languages: The Role of Instructional Set," *Journal of Experimental Psychology: Human Learning and Memory*, 2 (1976), 889-894; and Reber, Saul M. Kassin, Selma Lewis, and Gary Cantor, "On the Relationship Between Implicit and Explicit Modes in the Learning of a Complex Rule Structure," *Journal of Experimental Psychology: Human Learning and Memory*, 6 (1980), 492-502.

18. "Individual Variation in the Use of the Monitor," in *Principles of Second Language Learning*, ed. W. Richie (New York: Academic Press, 1978), pp. 175-185.

19. "Applications of Psycholinguistic Research to the Classroom," in *Practical Applications of Research in Foreign Language Teaching*, ed. D. J. James (Lincolnwood, Ill.: National Textbook, 1983), p. 61.

20. "Some Evidence for the Integrity and Interaction of Two Knowledge Sources," in *New Dimensions in Second Language Acquisition Research*, ed. Roger W. Anderson (Rowley, Mass.: Newbury House, 1981), pp. 62-74.

21. Hartwell and Bentley, *Some Suggestions for Using Open to Language* (New York: Oxford University Press, 1982), p. 73; Rose, *Writer's Block: The Cognitive Dimension* (Carbondale: Southern Illinois University Press, 1983), p. 99; Daiute, "Psycholinguistic Foundations of the Writing Process," *RTE*, 15 (1981), 5-22.

22. See Bartholomae, "The Study of Error"; Patrick Hartwell, "The Writing Center and the Paradoxes of Written-Down Speech," in *Writing Centers: Theory and Administration*, ed. Gary Olson (Urbana, Ill.: NCTE, 1984), pp. 48-61; and Sondra Perl, "A Look at Basic Writers in the Process of Composing," in *Basic Writing: A Collection of Essays for Teachers, Researchers, and Administrators* (Urbana, Ill.: NCTE, 1980), pp. 13-32.

23. Emonds, *Adjacency in Grammar: The Theory of Language-Particular Rules* (New York: Academic, 1983); and Jochnowitz, "Everybody Likes Pizza, Doesn't He or She?" *American Speech*, 57 (1982), 198-203.

24. Scribner and Cole, *Psychology of Literacy* (Cambridge, Mass.: Harvard University Press, 1981); Gleitman and Gleitman, "Language Use and Language Judgment," in *Individual Differences in Language Ability and Language Behavior*, ed. Charles J. Fillmore, Daniel Kempler, and William S.-Y. Wang (New York: Academic Press, 1979), pp. 103-126.

25. There are several recent reviews of this developing body of research in psychology and child development: Irene Athey, "Language Development Factors Related to Reading Development," *Journal of Educational Research*, 76 (1983), 197-203; James Flood and Paula

Menyuk, "Metalinguistic Development and Reading/Writing Achievement," *Claremont Reading Conference Yearbook,* 46 (1982), 122-132; and the following four essays: David T. Hakes, "The Development of Metalinguistic Abilities: What Develops?," pp. 162-210; Stan A. Kuczaj, II, and Brooke Harbaugh, "What Children Think about the Speaking Capabilities of Other Persons and Things," pp. 211-227; Karen Saywitz and Louise Cherry Wilkinson, "Age-Related Differences in Metalinguistic Awareness," pp. 229-250; and Harriet Salatas Waters and Virginia S. Tinsley, "The Development of Verbal Self-Regulation: Relationships between Language, Cognition, and Behavior," pp. 251-277; all in *Language, Thought, and Culture,* Vol. II of *Language Development,* ed. Stan Kuczaj, Jr. (Hillsdale, N.J.: Lawrence Erlbaum, 1982). See also Joanne R. Nurss, "Research in Review: Linguistic Awareness and Learning to Read," *Young Children,* 35, No. 3 [1980], 57-66.

26. "Competing Value Systems in Inner City Schools," in *Children In and Out of School: Ethnography and Education,* ed. Perry Gilmore and Allan A. Glatthorn (Washington, D.C.: Center for Applied Linguistics, 1982), pp. 148-171; and "Locating the Frontier between Social and Psychological Factors in Linguistic Structure," in *Individual Differences in Language Ability and Language Behavior,* ed. Fillmore, Kempler, and Wang, pp. 327-340.

27. See, for example, Thomas Farrell, "IQ and Standard English," *CCC,* 34 (1983), 470–84; and the responses by Karen L. Greenberg and Patrick Hartwell, *CCC,* in press.

28. Jane W. Torrey, "Teaching Standard English to Speakers of Other Dialects," in *Applications of Linguistics: Selected Papers of the Second International Conference of Applied Linguistics,* ed. G. E. Perren and J. L. M. Trim (Cambridge, Mass.: Cambridge University Press, 1971), pp. 423-428; James W. Beers and Edmund H. Henderson, "A Study of the Developing Orthographic Concepts among First Graders," *RTE,* 11 (1977), 133-148.

29. See the error counts of Samuel A. Kirschner and G. Howard Poteet, "Non-Standard English Usage in the Writing of Black, White, and Hispanic Remedial English Students in an Urban Community College," *RTE,* 7 (1973), 351-355; and Marilyn Sternglass, "Close Similarities in Dialect Features of Black and White College Students in Remedial Composition Classes," *TESOL Quarterly,* 8 (1974), 271-283.

30. For reading, see the massive study by Kenneth S. Goodman and Yetta M. Goodman, *Reading of American Children whose Language Is a Stable Rural Dialect of English or a Language other than English* (Washington, D.C.: National Institute of Education Final Report, 1978) ERIC 175 754; and the overview by Rudine Sims, "Dialect and Reading: Toward Redefining the Issues," in *Reader Meets Author/Bridging the Gap: A Psycholinguistic and Sociolinguistic Approach,* ed. Judith A. Langer and M. Tricia Smith-Burke (Newark, Del.: International Reading Association, 1982), pp. 222-232. For writing, see Patrick Hartwell, "Dialect Interference in Writing: A Critical View," *RTE,* 14 (1980), 101-118; and the anthology edited by Barry M. Kroll and Roberta J. Vann, *Exploring Speaking-Writing Relationships: Connections and Contrasts* (Urbana, Ill.: NCTE, 1981).

31. See, for example, Eric A. Havelock, *The Literary Revolution in Greece and its Cultural Consequences* (Princeton, N.J.: Princeton University Press, 1982); Lesley Milroy on literacy in Dublin, *Language and Social Networks* (Oxford: Basil Blackwell, 1980); Ron Scollon and Suzanne B. K. Scollon on literacy in central Alaska, *Interethnic Communication: An Athabascan Case* (Austin, Tex.: Southwest Educational Development Laboratory Working Papers in Sociolinguistics, No. 59, 1979) ERIC 175 276; and Scribner and Cole on literacy in Liberia, *Psychology of Literacy* (see footnote 24).

32. See, for example, the anthology edited by Deborah Tannen, *Spoken and Written Language: Exploring Orality and Literacy* (Norwood, N.J.: Ablex, 1982); and Shirley Brice Heath's continuing work: "Protean Shapes in Literacy Events: Ever-Shifting Oral and Liter-

ate Traditions," in *Spoken and Written Language*, pp. 91-117; *Ways with Words: Language, Life and Work in Communities and Classrooms* (New York: Cambridge University Press, 1983); and "What No Bedtime Story Means," *Language in Society*, 11 (1982), 49-76.

33. For studies at the elementary level, see Dell H. Hymes, et al., eds., *Ethnographic Monitoring of Children's Acquisition of Reading/Language Arts Skills In and Out of the Classroom* (Washington, D.C.: National Institute of Education Final Report, 1981) ERIC 208 096. For studies at the secondary level, see James L. Collins and Michael M. Williamson, "Spoken Language and Semantic Abbreviation in Writing," *RTE*, 15 (1981), 23-36. And for studies at the college level, see Patrick Hartwell and Gene LoPresti, "Sentence Combining as Kid-Watching," in *Sentence Combining: Toward a Rhetorical Perspective*, ed. Donald A. Daiker, Andrew Kerek, and Max Morenberg (Carbondale: Southern Illinois University Press, in press).

34. Lloyd-Jones, "Romantic Revels—I Am Not You," *CCC*, 23 (1972), 251-271; and Young, "Concepts of Art and the Teaching of Writing," in *The Rhetorical Tradition and Modern Writing*, ed. James J. Murphy (New York: Modern Language Association, 1982), pp. 130-141.

35. For the romantic position, see Ann E. Berthoff, "Tolstoy, Vygotsky, and the Making of Meaning," *CCC*, 29 (1978), 249-255; Kenneth Dowst, "The Epistemic Approach," in *Eight Approaches to Teaching Composition*, ed. Timothy Donovan and Ben G. McClellan (Urbana, Ill.: NCTE, 1980), pp. 65-85; Peter Elbow, "The Challenge for Sentence Combining"; and Donald Murray, "Following Language toward Meaning," both in *Sentence Combining: Toward a Rhetorical Perspective* (in press; see footnote 33); and Ian Pringle, "Why Teach Style? A Review-Essay," *CCC*, 34 (1983), 91-98.

For the classic position, see Christensen's "A Generative Rhetoric of the Sentence"; and Joseph Williams' "Defining Complexity," *CE*, 41 (1979), 595-609; and his *Style: Ten Lessons in Clarity and Grace* (see footnote 9).

36. Courtney B. Cazden and David K. Dickinson, "Language and Education: Standardization versus Cultural Pluralism," in *Language in the USA*, ed. Charles A. Ferguson and Shirley Brice Heath (New York: Cambridge University Press, 1981), pp. 446-468; and Carol Chomsky, "Developing Facility with Language Structure," in *Discovering Language with Children*, ed. Gay Su Pinnell (Urbana, Ill.: NCTE, 1980), pp. 56-59.

37. Boraas, "Formal English Grammar and the Practical Mastery of English." Diss. University of Illinois, 1917; Asker, "Does Knowledge of Grammar Function?" *School and Society*, 17 (27 January 1923), 109-111; Ash, "An Experimental Evaluation of the Stylistic Approach in Teaching Composition in the Junior High School," *Journal of Experimental Education*, 4 (1935), 54-62; and Frogner, "A Study of the Relative Efficacy of a Grammatical and a Thought Approach to the Improvement of Sentence Structure in Grades Nine and Eleven," *School Review*, 47 (1939), 663-675.

38. "Research on Grammar and Usage and Its Implications for Teaching Writing," *Bulletin of the School of Education*, Indiana University, 36 (1960), pp. 13-14.

39. Meckel, "Research on Teaching Composition and Literature," in *Handbook of Research on Teaching*, ed. N. L. Gage (Chicago: Rand McNally, 1963), pp. 966-1006.

40. Bateman and Zidonis, *The Effect of a Study of Transformational Grammar on the Writing of Ninth and Tenth Graders* (Urbana, Ill.: NCTE, 1966); Mellon, *Transformational Sentence Combining: A Method for Enhancing the Development of Fluency in English Composition* (Urbana, Ill.: NCTE, 1969); O'Hare, *Sentence-Combining: Improving Student Writing without Formal Grammar Instruction* (Urbana, Ill.: NCTE, 1971); Stotsky, "Sentence-Combining as a Curricular Activity: Its Effect on Written Language Development," *RTE*, 9

(1975), 30-72; and Van de Veghe, "Research in Written Composition: Fifteen Years of Investigation," ERIC 157 095.

41. Haynes, "Using Research in Preparing to Teach Writing," *English Journal*, 69, No. 1 (1978), 82-88; Holbrook, "ERIC/RCS Report: Whither (Wither) Grammar," *Language Arts*, 60 (1983), 259-263; Whiteman, "What We Can Learn from Writing Research," *Theory into Practice*, 19 (1980), 150-156; Bamberg, "Composition in the Secondary English Curriculum: Some Current Trends and Directions for the Eighties," *RTE*, 15 (1981), 257-266; and "Composition Instruction Does Make a Difference: A Comparison of the High School Preparation of College Freshmen in Regular and Remedial English Classes," *RTE*, 12 (1978), 47-59.

42. Emig, "Inquiry Paradigms and Writing," *CCC*, 33 (1982), 64-75; Carton and Castiglione, "Educational Linguistics: Defining the Domain," in *Psycholinguistic Research: Implications and Applications*, ed. Doris Aaronson and Robert W. Rieber (Hillsdale, N.J.: Lawrence Erlbaum, 1979), pp. 497-520.

Coherence, Cohesion, and Writing Quality

Stephen P. Witte and Lester Faigley

A question of continuing interest to researchers in writing is what internal characteristics distinguish essays ranked high and low in overall quality. Empirical research at the college level has for the most part taken two approaches to this question, examining errors[1] and syntactic features[2] while generally ignoring the features of texts that extend across sentence boundaries.[3] Neither the error approach nor the syntactic approach has been entirely satisfactory. For example, Elaine Maimon and Barbara Nodine's sentence-combining experiment suggests that, as is true when other skills and processes are learned, certain kinds of errors accompany certain stages in learning to write.[4] Because the sources of error in written discourse are often complex and difficult to trace, researchers can conclude little more than what is obvious: low-rated papers usually contain far more errors than high-rated papers. With regard to syntax, Ann Gebhard found that with few exceptions the syntactic features of high- and low-rated essays written by college students are not clearly differentiated. Indeed, research in writing quality based on conventions of written English and on theories of syntax, particularly transformational grammar, has not provided specific directions for the teaching of writing.

Such results come as no surprise in light of much current research in written discourse. This research—published in such fields as linguistics, cybernetics, anthropology, psychology, and artificial intelligence—addresses questions, concerned with extended discourse rather than with individual sentences, questions about how humans produce and understand discourse

Reprinted from *College Composition and Communication* 32.2 (May 1981): 189–204. Used with permission.

units often referred to as *texts*.[5] One such effort that has attracted the attention of researchers in writing is M. A. K. Halliday and Ruqaiya Hasan's *Cohesion in English*.[6] Although Halliday and Hasan do not propose a theory of text structure or examine how humans produce texts, they do attempt to define the concept of *text*. To them a text is a semantic unit, the parts of which are linked together by explicit cohesive ties. Cohesion, therefore, defines a text as text. A *cohesive tie* "is a semantic relation between an element in a text and some other element that is crucial to the interpretation of it" (p. 8). The two semantically connected elements can lie within the text or one element can lie outside the text. Halliday and Hasan call within-text cohesive ties *endophoric* and references to items outside the text *exophoric*. An example of an exophoric reference is the editorial "we" in a newspaper. Such references are exophoric because no antecedent is recoverable within the text. Exophoric references often help link a text to its situational context; but, as far as Halliday and Hasan are concerned, exophoric references do not contribute to the cohesion of a text. For Halliday and Hasan, cohesion depends upon lexical and grammatical relationships that allow sentence sequences to be understood as connected discourse rather than as autonomous sentences. Even though within-sentence cohesive ties do occur, the cohesive ties across "sentence boundaries" are those which allow sequences of sentences to be understood as a text.

Halliday and Hasan's concept of textuality, defined with reference to relationships that obtain across "sentence boundaries," suggests a number of possibilities for extending composition research beyond its frequent moorings in sentence-level operations and features. The major purpose of the present study is to apply two taxonomies of cohesive ties developed by Halliday and Hasan to an analysis of essays of college freshmen rated high and low in quality. Because *Cohesion in English* is a pioneering effort to describe relationships between and among sentences in text, we anticipate that cohesion will be studied in future research addressing the linguistic features of written texts. We are particularly interested in identifying what purposes Halliday and Hasan's taxonomies can serve in composition research and what purposes they cannot serve.

HALLIDAY AND HASAN'S SYSTEM FOR ANALYZING AND CLASSIFYING COHESIVE TIES

Cohesion in English specifies five major classes of cohesive ties, nineteen subclasses, and numerous sub-subclasses. In the analysis of cohesion which follows, we will be concerned with only the five major classes—*reference*, *substitution, ellipsis, conjunction,* and *lexical reiteration and collocation* — and their respective subclasses. Two of the major classes — *substitution* and *ellipsis* — are more frequent in conversation than in written discourse. *Substitution* replaces one element with another which is not a personal pronoun, and *ellipsis* involves a deletion of a word, phrase, or clause. The effect of both substitution and ellipsis is to extend the textual or semantic domain of one sentence to a subsequent sentence. The word *one* in sentence (2) illustrates cohesion based on substitution and the word *do* in sentence (4) illustrates cohesion based on ellipsis.

Substitution

1. Did you ever find a lawnmower?
2. Yes, I borrowed *one* from my neighbor.

Ellipsis

3. Do you want to go with me to the store?
4. Yes, I *do.*

The remaining three categories include the bulk of explicit cohesive ties in written English. The categories of *reference* and *conjunction* contain ties that are both grammatical and lexical. *Lexical reiteration and collocation* is restricted to ties which are presumably only lexical.

Reference cohesion occurs when one item in a text points to another element for its interpretation. Reference ties are of three types: *pronominals, demonstratives and definite articles,* and *comparatives.* Each of the sentence pairs below illustrates a different type of reference cohesion.

Reference Cohesion (Pronominal)

5. At home, my father is himself.
6. *He* relaxes and acts in *his* normal manner.

Reference Cohesion (Demonstratives)

7. We question why they tell us to do things.
8. *This* is part of growing up.

Reference Cohesion (Definite Article)

9. Humans have many needs, both physical and intangible.
10. It is easy to see *the* physical needs such as food and shelter.

Reference Cohesion (Comparatives)

11. The older generation is often quick to condemn college students for being carefree and irresponsible.

12. But those who remember their own youth do so *less* quickly.

The interpretation of the underlined elements in sentences (6), (8), (10), and (12) depends in each case upon presupposed information contained in the sentences immediately above it.

A fourth major class of cohesive ties frequent in writing is *conjunction.* Conjunctive elements are not in themselves cohesive, but they do "express certain meanings which presuppose the presence of other components in the discourse" (p. 226). Halliday and Hasan distinguish five types of conjunctive cohesion—*additive, adversative, causal, temporal,* and *continuative.* Examples of these subclasses of conjunctive cohesion appear below and illustrate how conjunctive cohesion extends the meaning of one sentence to a subsequent one.

Conjunctive Cohesion (Additive)

13. No one wants to be rejected.

14. *And* to prevent rejection we change our behavior often.

Conjunctive Cohesion (Adversative)

15. Small children usually change their behavior because they want something they don't have.

16. Carol, *however,* changed her behavior because she wanted to become part of a new group.

Conjunctive Cohesion (Causal)

17. Today's society sets the standards.

18. The people more or less follow it [sic].

19. *Consequently,* there exists the right behavior for the specific situation at hand.

Conjunctive Cohesion (Temporal)

20. A friend of mine went to an out-of-state college.

21. *Before* she left, she expressed her feelings about playing roles to win new friends.

Conjunctive Cohesion (Continuative)

22. Different social situations call for different behaviors.

23. This is something we all learn as children and we, *of course*, also learn which behaviors are right for which situations.

Coordinating conjunctions (such as *and, but,* and *so*), conjunctive adverbs (such as *however, consequently,* and *moreover*), and certain temporal adverbs and subordinating conjunctions (such as *before, after,* and *now*) supply cohesive ties across sentence boundaries.

The last major class of cohesive ties includes those based on *lexical* relationships. *Lexical* cohesion differs from *reference* cohesion and *conjunctive* cohesion because every lexical item is potentially cohesive and because nothing in the occurrence of a given lexical item necessarily makes it cohesive. If we were to encounter the word *this* in a text, we would either supply a referent from our working memory of the text or reread the text to find a referent. Similarly, when we encounter a conjunctive adverb such as *however*, we attempt to establish an adversative relationship between two text elements. In contrast, lexical cohesion depends on some "patterned occurrence of lexical items" (p. 288). Consider the following sentences adapted from a mountaineering guidebook:

24. The ascent up the Emmons Glacier on Mt. Rainier is long but relatively easy.

25. The only usual problem in the climb is finding a route through the numerous crevasses above Steamboat Prow.

26. In late season a *bergschrund* may develop at the 13,000-foot level, which is customarily bypassed to the right.

Three cohesive chains bind together this short text. The first chain (*ascent, climb, finding a route, bypassed to the right*) carries the topic—the way up the mountain. The second and third chains give the setting (*Glacier, crevasses, bergschrund*) (*Mt. Rainier, Steamboat Prow, 13,000-foot level*). These chains give clues to the interpretation of unfamiliar items. For most readers, *Steamboat Prow* is unknown, but one can infer that it is a feature on Mt. Rainier. Similarly, *bergschrund* is a technical term referring to a crevasse at the head of a glacier where the moving ice breaks apart from the stationary ice clinging to the mountain. In this text, a reader can infer that *bergschrunds* are associated with glaciers and that they present some type of obstacle to climbers, even without the final clause in (26).

Lexical cohesion is the predominant means of connecting sentences in discourse. Halliday and Hasan identify two major subclasses of lexical cohesion: *reiteration* and *collocation. Reiteration* is in turn divided into four subclasses, ranging from repetition of the *same item* to repetition through the use of a *synonym or near-synonym*, a *superordinate item*, or a *general item*.

Lexical reiteration is usually easy to identify. An example of synonymy occurs in (25) and (26) with the pairing of ascent *and* climb. The three other subclasses are illustrated in the following student example:

Lexical Reiteration (Same Item), (Superordinate), and (General Item)

27. Some professional tennis players, for example, grandstand, using obscene gestures and language to call attention to themselves.

28. Other *professional athletes* do similar *things*, such as spiking a football in the end zone, to attract *attention*.

In (28), *professional athletes* is, in this case, a superordinate term for *professional tennis players*. Professional athletes in other sports are encompassed by the term. *Things*, in contrast, is a general term. Here *things* is used to refer anaphorically to two behaviors, "using obscene gestures and language." While superordinates are names of specific classes of objects, general terms are even more inclusive, not restricted to a specific set of objects. The other type of lexical reiteration, illustrated by sentences (27) and (28), is same-item repetition: *attention* is simply repeated.

All the lexical cohesive relationships which cannot be properly subsumed under lexical reiteration are included in a "miscellaneous" class called *collocation*. Collocation refers to lexical cohesion "that is achieved through the association of lexical items that regularly co-occur" (p. 284). Lexical cohesion through collocation is the most difficult type of cohesion to analyze because items said to collocate involve neither repetition, synonymy, superordination, nor mention of general items. What is important is that the items said to collocate "share the same lexical environment" (p. 286). The following student example illustrates this principle:

Lexical Cohesion (Collocation)

29. On a camping trip with their parents, teenagers willingly do the household chores that they resist at home.

30. They gather *wood for a fire*, help put up the *tent*, and carry *water from a creek or lake*.

Although the underlined items in (30) are presented as the "camping trip" equivalents of *household chores,* the cohesion between sentences (29) and (30) results more directly from the associations of the underlined items with *camping trip.* The underlined items in sentence (30) collocate with *camping trip* in sentence (29). The mountaineering guidebook passage, however, is much more difficult to analyze. For one of the authors of the present article, antecedent knowledge of mountaineering allows *Steamboat Prow* to collocate with *Mt. Rainier* and *bergschrund* to collocate with *glacier.* For the other author, neither pair is lexically related by collocation apart from the text where they are connected by inference. We will return to this problem later in this essay.

In addition to the taxonomy that allows cohesive ties to be classified according to function, Halliday and Hasan introduce a second taxonomy. This second taxonomy allows cohesive ties to be classified according to the amount of text spanned by the *presupposed* and *presupposing* elements of a given tie. Halliday and Hasan posit four such "text-span" classes. Membership in a class is determined by the number of T-units a given cohesive tie spans.[7] Taken together, the two taxonomies Halliday and Hasan present allow any given cohesive tie to be classified in two different ways, one according to function and one according to distance. The four "text-span" classes contained in Halliday and Hasan's second taxonomy are illustrated in the following paragraph from a student paper:

Text-Span Classes (Immediate, Mediated, Remote, Mediated-Remote)

31. *Respect* is one reason people change their behavior.

32. For example, one does not speak with his *boss* as he would talk to a friend or co-worker.

33. One might use four-letter words in talking to a co-worker, but probably not in talking to his *boss.*

34. In talking to teachers or *doctors,* people also use bigger words than normal.

35. Although the situation is different than when one speaks with a *boss* or a *doctor,* one often talks with a minister or priest different [sic] than he talks with friends or *family.*

36. With the *family,* most people use a different language when they talk to parents or grandparents than when they talk to younger brothers and sisters.

37. People's ability to use language in different ways allows them to show the *respect* they should toward different people, whether they are professionals, *family* members, clergy, friends and co-workers, or *bosses*.

Immediate cohesive ties semantically linked adjacent T-units. The repetition of *doctor* in sentences (34) and (35) creates an *immediate* tie, forcing the reader to assimilate the content of (34) into the content of (35). In contrast, the repetition of *family* in sentences (35), (36), and (37) forms a *mediated* tie. The semantic bridge established by the occurrence of *family* in (35) and (37) is channelled through or mediated by the repetition of *family* in (36). The cohesive tie involving the repetition of *family* is not simply a series of immediate ties, because once a lexical item appears in a text all subsequent uses of that item presuppose the first appearance. *Immediate* and *mediated* ties join items in adjacent T-units. Such ties enable writers to introduce a concept in one T-unit and to extend, modify, or clarify that concept in subsequent and successive T-units.

Remote ties, on the other hand, result when the two elements of a tie are separated by one or more intervening T-units. The tie between *respect* in (31) and (37) is *remote*; here the repetition of the word signals to the reader that the semantic unit represented by the paragraph is now complete. Finally, ties which are both mediated and remote are called *mediated-remote*. An example of this type of cohesive tie appears in the repetition of *bosses* in sentences (32), (33), (35), and (37). Here the presupposing *bosses* in (37) is separated from the presupposed *boss* in (32) by intervening T-units (34) and (36) which contain no element relevant to the particular cohesive tie. Thus the tie is *remote*. However, the presupposing *bosses* is also *mediated* through repetitions of *boss* in (33) and (35). Hence the term *mediated-remote*. Skilled writers use mediated-remote ties to interweave key "themes" within the text.

ANALYSIS OF STUDENT ESSAYS

To explore the usefulness of Halliday and Hasan's theory of cohesion in writing research, we used their two taxonomies in an analysis of ten student essays. These essays were written by beginning University of Texas freshmen on the "changes in behavior" topic used in the Miami University sentence-combining experiment.[8] From 90 essays which had been rated holistically by two readers on a four-point scale, we selected five essays given the lowest score by both raters and five essays given the highest score. We analyzed these ten essays according to categories of error and according to syntactic features, as well as according to the number and types of cohesive ties. Our analyses of error and content variables yielded results similar to those other researchers have reported—that high-rated essays are longer and contain larger T-units and clauses, more nonrestrictive modifiers, and fewer errors.[9]

We anticipated that an analysis of cohesive ties in the high- and low-rated essays would reveal similar gross differences. The results of our analysis confirmed this expectation. At the most general level of analysis, the high rated essays are much more dense in cohesion than the low-rated essays. In the low-rated essays, a cohesive tie of some type occurs once every 4.9 words; in the high-rated essays, a tie occurs once every 3.2 words, a difference in mean frequency of 1.7 words. Likewise, a large difference in the mean number of cohesive ties per T-unit appears, with 2.4 ties per T-unit in the low-rated essays and 5.2 ties per T-unit in the high-rated essays. The figures for this and the preceding index, however, are not precisely comparable because the T-units in the high-rated essays are, on the average, 1.64 words longer than those in the low-rated essays. By dividing the number of cohesive ties in an essay set by the number of words in that set, we arrived at another general index of cohesive density. In the high-rated essays, 31.7% of all words contribute to explicit cohesive ties while only 20.4% of the words in the low-rated essays contribute to such ties.

The ways in which writers of the high- and low-rated essays form cohesive ties also distinguish the two groups of five essays from each other. Writers of the high-rated essays use a substantially higher relative percentage of *immediate* (High: 41.6%/Low: 32.8%) and *mediated* (High: 7.6%/Low: 0.8%) cohesive ties than do the writers of the low-rated essays. On the other hand, writers of the low-rated essays use more *mediated-remote* (High: 25.9%/Low: 36.7%) and *remote* ties (High: 26.9%/Low: 29.7%). These percentages allow us to focus on some crucial differences between the two essay sets. The larger relative percentage of *immediate* cohesive ties in the high-rated essays suggests, among other things, that the better writers tend to establish stronger cohesive bonds between individual T-units than do the writers of the low-rated essays. Analyses of *reference* and *conjunctive cohesion* support this observation. Writers of high-rated essays employ reference cohesion about twice as often, 84.1 times to 47.8 times per 100 T-units, as the writers of low-rated papers. The largest difference in the occurrence of referential cohesion is reflected in the higher frequency of third-person pronouns in the high-rated essays (High: 25.1 per 100 T-units/Low: 5.1 per 100 T-units). This lower frequency of third-person pronouns in the low-rated essays may be a direct result of the less skilled writers' attempts to avoid errors such as ambiguous pronoun reference. Because third-person pronouns usually refer back to the T-unit immediately preceding, we can infer that the writers of high-rated essays more often elaborate, in subsequent and adjacent T-units, topics introduced in a given T-unit.

Also contributing importantly to the greater use of *immediate* cohesive ties is the frequency with which the more skillful writers use *conjunction* to link individual T-units. Conjunctive ties most often result in *immediate* cohesive ties between T-units. It is not surprising, then, to find that the writers of high-rated essays employ over three times as many conjunctive ties (High: 65.4 per 100 T-units/Low: 20.4 per 100 T-units) as the writers of low-rated essays. Neither is it surprising to discover that the more skillful writers employ all five types of conjunction while the less skillful writers use only three. As is the case with pronominal references that cross T-unit boundaries, conjunctives are most often used to extend concepts introduced in one T-unit to other T-units which follow immediately in the text. Thus the more skillful writers appear to extend the concept introduced in a given T-unit considerably more often than do the less skillful writers. One major effect of such semantic extensions is, of course, essay length; and this finding helps to explain why the high-rated essays are, on the average, 375 words longer than the low-rated essays.

The relative frequency of *lexical cohesion* gives another indication that the writers of high-rated essays are better able to expand and connect their ideas than the writers of the low-rated essays. By far the largest number of cohesive ties, about two-thirds of the total ties for both the high and low samples, fall into the general category of *lexical cohesion*. Writers of the high-rated essays create some type of lexical tie 340 times per 100 T-units or every 4.8 words. Writers of the low-rated essays, however, manage a lexical tie just 161 times per 100 T-units or every 7.4 words. The majority of lexical ties (65%) in the low essays are repetitions of the same item. This distribution is reflected to a smaller degree in the high essays, where 52% of the total lexical ties fall into the *same item* subcategory. Writers of high-rated essays, however, form many more lexical collocations. Lexical collocations appear 94 times per 100 T-units in the high-rated essays in contrast to 28.8 times per 100 T-units in the low-rated essays.

COHESION AND INVENTION

These cohesion profiles suggest to us an important difference between the invention skills of the two groups of writers. The better writers seem to have a better command of invention skills that allow them to elaborate and extend the concepts they introduce. The poorer writers, in contrast, appear deficient in these skills. Their essays display a much higher degree of lexical and conceptual redundancy. The high percentage of lexical redundancy and the low frequency of lexical collocation in the low-rated essays are indications of this difference. The text-span categories also point to this difference. In the low-rated essays two-thirds of the cohesive ties are interrupted ties—*mediated-remote* or *remote* ties—which reach back across one or more T-units, indicating that the writers of the low-rated essays generally fail to elaborate and extend concepts through successive T-units.

The larger proportion of interrupted ties in the low-rated papers strongly suggests that substantially less new information or semantic content is introduced during the course of a low-rated essay than during the course of a high-rated essay. If more new information had been introduced in the low-rated essays, the writers would have had to rely more heavily than they did on *immediate* and *mediated* cohesive ties in order to integrate, to weave, the new information into the text. The writers of the low-rated papers tend more toward reiteration of previously introduced information than do the writers of the high-rated papers. Indeed, in reading the low-rated essays one can not help noting a good deal of what might be called conceptual and lexical redundancy. The following example illustrates this characteristic:

> Some people have to change their behavior around different acquaintances. One reason is that they want to make a good impression on others. You have to act different in front of a person who is giving you a job interview because you want to make a good impression. You, most of the time, act differently to fit in a crowd. You will change your behavior to get people to like you. You change your behavior to agree with peoples [sic] in the crowd.

This paragraph from a low-rated paper has a fairly strong beginning: it states a topic in the first sentence, modifies that topic in the second sentence, illustrates the topic in the third sentence, and gives another example in the fourth sentence. The next two sentences, however, simply reiterate what is said in the fourth sentence. The principal lexical items in the last two sentences—*change, behavior, people*, and *crowd*—are repetitions of items introduced earlier in the paragraph and offer little new information. Although for purposes of attaining cohesion in a text some redundancy is a virtue, the redundancy in the low-rated essays seems to be a flaw because these writers failed to supply additional information at the point where it would be expected to appear. Had this additional information been supplied, the writers would have had to use *immediate* and *mediated* ties in order to connect it to the rest of the text.

Compare the previous example paragraph from a low-rated paper with the following paragraph from a high-rated paper.

> It is a job that really changes our behavior. Among other changes, we change the way we dress. In many jobs college graduates want to look responsible and mature, projecting an image of competence. The college student who wore faded blue jeans is now in three-piece suits. He feels the need to be approved of and accepted by his boss and associates. While he talked of socialism in college, he now reaps the profits of capitalism. While in college he demanded honesty in the words and actions of others, on the job he is willing to "kiss ass" to make friends or get a promotion. Indeed, working can change behavior.

Notice that in the paragraph from the high-rated paper, *behavior* is repeated only one time. Yet the reader never questions that the paragraph is about changes in behavior. The writer repeatedly supplies examples of types of behavior, which are linked to the topic by a series of lexical collocations (e.g., *behavior, dress, look responsible, blue jeans, three-piece suits*). Clearly, the paragraph from the high-rated paper extends the semantic domain of the concept *behavior* to include a number of differentiated lexical items. Low-rated papers rarely show such extended series of collocations.

Analyses of cohesion thus measure some aspects of invention skills. The low-rated essays stall frequently, repeating ideas instead of elaborating them. Our analyses also suggest that the writers of the low-rated papers do not have working vocabularies capable of extending, in ways prerequisite for good writing, the concepts and ideas they introduce in their essays. Indeed, skill in invention, in discovering what to say about a particular topic, may depend in ways yet unexplored on the prior development of adequate working vocabularies. If students do not have in their working vocabularies the lexical items required to extend, explore, or elaborate the concepts they introduce, practice in invention can have only a limited effect on overall writing quality.

Our analyses further point to the underdevelopment of certain cognitive skills among the writers of the low-rated papers. The low-rated papers not only exhibit a great deal of redundancy, but (as noted earlier) also include relatively fewer *conjunctive* and *reference* ties and *immediate* and *mediated* ties. Besides lacking adequate vocabularies, writers of the low-rated essays seem to lack in part the ability to perceive and articulate abstract concepts with reference to particular instances, to perceive relationships among ideas, and to reach beyond the worlds of their immediate experience.

All this is to suggest that analyses of cohesion may be potentially useful in distinguishing between stages of writing development. Clearly, cohesion analyses measure more sophisticated aspects of language development than do error analyses and syntactic analyses. Cohesion analyses also give us some concrete ways of addressing some of the differences between good and poor writing, differences which heretofore could not be explained either to ourselves or to our students in any but the most abstract ways. We thus anticipate that Halliday and Hasan's taxonomies can be usefully applied in developmental studies as well as in studies such as the present one.

COHESION, COHERENCE, AND WRITING QUALITY

However promising cohesion analysis appears as a research tool and however encouraging the results of the present study seem, we feel that a number of important questions cannot be answered by analyzing cohesion. The first of these questions concerns writing quality. The quality or "success" of a text, we would argue, depends a great deal on factors outside the text itself, factors which lie beyond the scope of cohesion analyses. Recall that Halliday and Hasan exclude *exophoric*, or outside-text, references from their taxonomy of explicit cohesive ties. We think that writing quality is in part defined as the "fit" of a particular text to its context, which includes such factors as the writer's purpose, the discourse medium, and the audience's knowledge of an interest in the subject—the factors which are the cornerstones of discourse theory and, *mutatis mutandis*, should be the cornerstones of research in written composition.[10] We are not alone in this view. Several students of written discourse—among them Joseph Grimes,[11] Teun van Dijk,[12] Nils Enkvist,[13] and Robert de Beaugrande[14]—distinguish *cohesion* and *coherence*. They limit cohesion to explicit mechanisms in the text, both the types of cohesive ties that Halliday and Hasan describe and other elements that bind texts such as parallelism, consistency of verb tense, and what literary scholars have called "point of view."[15] Coherence conditions, on the other hand, allow a text to be understood in a real-world setting. Halliday and Hasan's theory does not accommodate real-world settings for written discourse or, consequently, the conditions through which texts become coherent. We agree with Charles Fillmore's contention that

> the scenes . . . [audiences] construct for texts are partly justified by the lexical and grammatical materials in the text and partly by the interpreter's own contributions, the latter being based on what he knows about the

current context, what he knows about the world in general, and what he assumes the speaker's intentions might be.[16]

Hence lexical collocations within a text are understood through cues which the writer provides and through the reader's knowledge of general discourse characteristics and of the world to which the discourse refers.

Thus lexical collocation is in all likelihood the subcategory of cohesion that best indicates overall writing ability, as well as disclosing distinctions among written texts that represent different discourse modes and purposes. An examination of lexical cohesive ties shows how writers build ideas, how they are able to take advantage of associations to weave together a text. But a fundamental problem lies in the analysis of a writer's text. Whose collocations do we analyze—the reader's or the writer's? One simple proof that the two do not always coincide can be found in the unintentional sexual references that students occasionally produce—the kind that get passed around the faculty coffee room.

Consider again the mountaineering guidebook passage in sentences (24), (25), and (26). We have already established that for mountaineers and glaciologists, *bergschrund* probably collocates with *glacier*, but for many other persons the two items do not collocate. Yet a naive reader presented this text probably would not stop to consult a dictionary for the lexical item, *bergschrund*, but would infer from its context that it is some type of obstacle to climbers and continue reading. Herbert Clark theorizes that we comprehend unknown items like *bergschrund* by drawing inferences.[17] We make inferences on the basis of what we can gather from the explicit content and the circumstances surrounding a text, through a tacit contract between the writer and reader that the writer will provide only information relevant to the current topic. In the case of the mountaineering passage, the circumstances of the text greatly affect our understanding of it. The type of text—a guidebook—follows a predictable organization, what has been called a *script* in research on artificial intelligence.[18] The guidebook contains a series of topics with a clear, yet implicit, goal: to inform the reader how to get to the top of a mountain. We expect the author to give us only information relevant to the particular route. Accordingly, readers understand *bergschrund* as an obstacle through a combination of cues—overt signals in the text such as the parallelism of the *bergschrund* sentence with the sentence about crevasses above it and, for those readers familiar with the type of text, implicit signals such as the following of the guidebook "script." Although Halliday and Hasan do not include parallelism in their taxonomy, parallelism often creates a cohesive tie.

Cohesion and coherence interact to a great degree, but a cohesive text may be only minimally coherent. Thus cohesion-based distinctions between texts rated high and low in quality can be misleading. Besides explicit links within a text, a text must conform to a reader's expectations for particular types of texts and the reader's knowledge of the world. A simple example will illustrate this point:

38. The quarterback threw the ball toward the tight end.

39. Balls are used in many sports.

40. Most balls are spheres, but a football is an ellipsoid.

41. The tight end leaped to catch the ball.

Sentences (39) and (40), while cohesive, violate a coherence condition that the writer provide only information relevant to the topic. The major problem with this short text is that a reader cannot construct what Fillmore calls a real-world scene for it; that is, the text neither seems to have a clear purpose nor appears to meet the needs of any given audience. Because it has no clear purpose, it lacks coherence, in spite of the cohesive ties which bind it together. In addition to a cohesive unity, written texts must have a pragmatic unity, a unity of a text and the world of the reader. A description of the fit of a text to its context, as well as descriptions of what composition teachers call writing quality, must specify a variety of coherence conditions, many of them outside the text itself.

IMPLICATIONS FOR THE TEACHING OF COMPOSITION

One implication of the present study is that if cohesion is better understood, it can be better taught. At present, in most college writing classes, cohesion is taught, explicitly or implicitly, either through exercises, classroom instruction, or comments on student papers. Many exercises not explicitly designed to teach cohesion do in fact demand that students form cohesive ties. Open sentence-combining exercises, for example, offer as much practice in forming cohesive ties as they do in manipulating syntactic structures, a fact which may explain the success of certain sentence-combining experiments as well as the failure of research to link syntactic measures such as T-unit and clause length to writing quality.[19] An open sentence-combining exercise about Charlie Chaplin might contain a series of sentences beginning with the name *Charlie Chaplin*. Such an exercise would, at the very least, demand that students change most of the occurrences of *Charlie Chaplin* to *he* in order to produce an acceptable text. Students working either from contextual cues or from their knowledge of Chaplin might also use phrases like *the comic genius* or *the little tramp* to substitute for the proper name *Chaplin*.

If cohesion is often implicitly incorporated in writing curricula, coherence is often ignored. A great portion of the advice in composition textbooks stops at sentence boundaries. Numerous exercises teach clause and sentence structure in isolation, ignoring the textual, and the situational, considerations for using that structure. The passive is a classic example:

42. The police apprehended the suspect as he left the bank.

43. He is being held in the county jail.

43a. The police are holding the suspect in the county jail.

A student following her teacher's advice to avoid the passive construction might revise sentence (43) to (43a). If she did so, she would violate the usual sequence of information in English, where the topic or "old" information is presented first.[20] In active sentences, such as (43a), where the object expresses the topic, a revision to the passive is often preferable. Avoiding the passive with (43a) would also require the unnecessary and uneconomical repetition of *police* and *suspect*. Consequently, maxims such as "Avoid passives" ignore the coherence conditions that govern the information structure of a text.

Other discourse considerations are similarly ignored in traditional advice on how to achieve coherence. As E. K. Lybert and D. W. Cummings have observed, the handbook injunction "Repeat key words and phrases" often *reduces* coherence.[21] Our analysis of cohesive ties in high- and low-rated essays substantiates Lybert and Cummings' point. While the low-rated papers we examined contain fewer cohesive ties than the high-rated papers in equivalent spans of text, the low-rated papers rely more heavily on lexical repetition. Also contrary to a popular notion, frequent repetition of lexical items does not necessarily increase readability. Roger Shuy and Donald Larkin's recent study shows lexical redundancy to be a principal reason why insurance policy language is difficult to read.[22]

Our analysis of cohesion suggests that cohesion is an important property of writing quality. To some extent the types and frequencies of cohesive ties seem to reflect the invention skills of student writers and to influence the stylistic and organizational properties of the texts they write. However, our analysis also suggests that while cohesive relationships may ultimately affect writing quality in some ways, there is no evidence to suggest that a large number (or a small number) of cohesive ties of a particular type will positively affect writing quality. All discourse is context bound—to the demands of the subject matter, occasion, medium, and audience of the text. Cohesion defines those mechanisms that hold a text together, while coherence defines those underlying semantic relations that allow a text to be understood and used. Consequently, coherence conditions—conditions governed by the writer's purpose, the audience's knowledge and expectations, and the information to be conveyed—militate against prescriptive approaches to the teaching of writing. Indeed, our exploration of what cohesion analyses can and cannot measure in student writing points to the necessity of placing writing exercises in the context of complete written texts. Just as exclusive focus on syntax and other formal surface features in writing instruction probably will not better the overall quality of college students' writing, neither will a narrow emphasis on cohesion probably produce significantly improved writing.[23]

NOTES

1. Most notably, Mina Shaughnessy, *Errors and Expectations,* (New York: Oxford University Press, 1977).

2. See Ann O. Gebhard, "Writing Quality and Syntax: A Transformational Analysis of Three Prose Samples," *Research in the Teaching of English,* 12 (October, 1978), 211-231.

3. Composition theorists, however, have not stopped at sentence boundaries. Several of the early efforts to describe relationships across sentences are summarized in Richard L. Larson, "Structure and Form in Non-Fiction Prose," in *Teaching Composition: Ten Bibliographical Essays,* ed. Gary Tate (Fort Worth, Texas: Texas Christian University Press, 1976), pp. 45-71. The reader will note certain similarities between Halliday and Hasan's taxonomy of cohesive ties set out later in the present essay and the work of previous composition theorists.

4. "Measuring Syntactic Growth: Errors and Expectations in Sentence-Combining Practice with College Freshmen," *Research in the Teaching of English,* 12 (October, 1978), 233-244.

5. No comprehensive overview of work in discourse in all of these fields exists at present. Extensive bibliographies, however, can be found in *Current Trends in Textlinguistics,* ed. Wolfgang U. Dressler (Berlin: de Gruyter, 1978) and Robert de Beaugrande, *Text, Discourse, and Process* (Norwood, N.J.: Ablex, 1980).

6. (London: Longman, 1976).

7. The term *T-unit,* of course, comes from Kellogg Hunt's *Grammatical Structures Written at Three Grade Levels,* NCTE Research Report No. 3 (Champaign, Ill.: National Council of Teachers of English, 1965). Hunt defined a *T-unit* as an independent clause and all subordinate elements attached to it, whether clausal or phrasal. Halliday and Hasan do not use the term *T-unit,* but they do define their four "text-span" classes according to the number of simple and complex sentences that the presupposing element of a cohesive tie must reach across

for the presupposed element (see pp. 340-355). There is good reason to define the four "text-span" classes in terms of T-units. To examine only cohesive ties that span the boundaries of orthographic sentences would ignore the large number of conjunctive relationships, such as addition and causality, between independent clauses.

8. Max Morenberg, Donald Daiker, and Andrew Kerek, "Sentence Combining at the College Level: An Experimental Study," *Research in the Teaching of English*, 12 (October, 1978), 245-256. This topic asks students to write about why we act differently in different situations, using specific illustrations from personal experience.

9. Detailed analyses for data summarized in this section are reported in Stephen P. Witte and Lester Faigley, *A Comparison of Analytic and Synthetic Approaches to the Teaching of College Writing*. Unpublished manuscript. The high-rated essays are, on the average, more than twice as long as the low-rated essays (647 words/270 words). Errors in three major categories were counted—punctuation, spelling, and grammar. Grammatical errors include errors in verb tenses, subject-verb agreement, pronoun reference, pronoun number agreement, and dangling or misplaced modifiers. The low-rated essays exhibit an error of some type nearly three times as often as the high-rated essays—one every 29 words as opposed to one every 87 words. For example, errors in end-stop punctuation, resulting in either a comma splice or a fragment, occur nearly eight times as often in the low-rated essays as in the high-rated essays. Misspelled words are over four times as frequent in the low-rated essays, and grammatical errors appear over twice as often.

Syntactic comparisons were made according to the number of words per T-unit and clause, and according to the frequency and placement of nonrestrictive or "free" modifiers. The low-rated essays contain T-units and clauses considerably shorter than the high-rated essays (High: 15.3 words per T-unit, 9.3 words per clause/Low: 13.7 words per T-unit, 7.5 words per clause). Nonrestrictive modifiers in all positions—initial, medial, and final—appear in the T-units of the high-rated essays nearly three times as frequently as in the low-rated essays (High: 28.5% of all T-units contain nonrestrictive modifiers/Low: 10.1% contain nonrestrictive modifiers). The high-rated essays also have twice the percentage of total words in nonrestrictive modifiers that the low-rated essays have.

10. Stephen P. Witte, "Toward a Model for Research in Written Composition," *Research in the Teaching of English*, 14 (February, 1980), 73-81.

11. *The Thread of Discourse* (The Hague: Mouton, 1975).

12. *Text and Context* (London: Longman, 1977).

13. "Coherence, Pseudo-Coherence, and Non-Coherence," in *Reports on Text Linguistics: Semantics and Cohesion*, ed. Jan-Ola Ostman (Abo, Finland: Research Institute of the Abo Akademi Foundation, 1978), pp. 109-128.

14. "The Pragmatics of Discourse Planning," *Journal of Pragmatics*, 4 (February, 1980), 15-42.

15. Susumo Kuno describes some linguistic features controlled by point of view, which he calls "empathy." See "Subject, Theme and the Speaker's Empathy—A Reexamination of Relativization Phenomena," in *Subject and Topic*, ed. Charles N. Li (New York: Academic Press, 1976), pp. 417-444.

16. "Topics in Lexical Semantics," in *Current Issues in Linguistic Theory*, ed. Roger W. Cole (Bloomington: Indiana University Press, 1977), p. 92.

17. "Inferences in Comprehension," in *Basic Processes in Reading: Perception and Comprehension*, ed. David LaBerge and S. Jay Samuels (Hillsdale, N.J.: Erlbaum, 1977), pp. 243-263.

18. R. C. Schank and R. P. Abelson, *Scripts, Plans, Goals, and Understanding: An Inquiry into Human Knowledge Structures* (Hillsdale, N.J.: Erlbaum, 1977).

19. See Lester Faigley, "Names in Search of a Concept: Maturity, Fluency, Complexity, and Growth in Written Syntax," *College Composition and Communication*, 31 (October, 1980), 291-300.

20. The theme-rheme distinction is the product of the Prague school of linguistics. Other researchers use the terms "topic-comment" or "given-new" information to refer to essentially the same concept. See Vilem Mathesius, *A Functional Analysis of Present Day English on a General Linguistic Basis*, ed Josef Vachek (Prague: Academia, 1975). Also relevant are Wallace L. Chafe, *Meaning and the Structure of Language* (Chicago: University of Chicago Press, 1970); M. A. K. Halliday, "Notes on Transitivity and Theme in English: II," *Journal of Linguistics*, 3 (October, 1967), 199-244; Herbert Clark and Susan Haviland, "Comprehension and the Given-New Contract," in *Discourse Production and Comprehension*, ed. Roy Freedle (Norwood, N.J.: Ablex, 1977), pp. 1-40; and Liisa Lautamatti, "Observations on the Development of Topic in Simplified Discourse," in *Text Linguistics, Cognitive Learning, and Language Teaching*, ed. Viljo Kohonen and Nils Erik Enkvist (Turku, Finland: University of Turku, 1978), pp. 71-104.

21. "On Repetition and Coherence," *College Composition and Communication*, 20 (February, 1969), 35-38.

22. "Linguistic Consideration in the Simplification/Clarification of Insurance Policy Language," *Discourse Processes*, 1 (October-December, 1978), 305-321.

23. John Mellon and James Kinneavy both make the point that while the Miami University sentence-combining students improved significantly in writing quality, they may not have done so because they learned to manipulate syntactic structures better, but because they were taught to put together complete texts. See "Issues in the Theory and Practice of Sentence Combining A Twenty-Year Perspective," in *Sentence Combining and the Teaching of Writing*, ed. Donald Daiker, Andrew Kerek, and Max Morenberg (Akron, Oh.: University of Akron, 1979), p. 10; and "Sentence Combining in a Comprehensive Language Framework" in the same volume, p. 66.

Contemporary Composition

The Major Pedagogical Theories

JAMES A. BERLIN

A number of articles attempting to make sense of the various approaches to teaching composition have recently appeared. While all are worth considering, some promote a common assumption that I am convinced is erroneous.[1] Since all pedagogical approaches, it is argued, share a concern for the elements of the composing process—that is, for writer, reality, reader, and language—their only area of disagreement must involve the element or elements that ought to be given the most attention. From this point of view, the composing process is always and everywhere the same because writer, reality, reader, and language are always and everywhere the same. Differences in teaching theories, then, are mere cavils about which of these features to emphasize in the classroom.

I would like to say at the start that I have no quarrel with the elements that these investigators isolate as forming the composing process, and I plan to use them myself. While it is established practice today to speak of the composing process as a recursive activity involving prewriting, writing, and rewriting, it is not difficult to see the writer-reality-audience-language relationship as underlying, at a deeper structural level, each of these three stages. In fact, as I will later show, this deeper structure determines the shape that instruction in prewriting, writing, and rewriting assumes—or does not assume, as is sometimes the case.

I do, however, strongly disagree with the contention that the differences in approaches to teaching writing can be explained by attending to the degree of emphasis given to universally defined elements of a universally

Reprinted from *College English* 44.8 (December 1982): 765–77. Used with permission.

defined composing process. The differences in these teaching approaches should instead be located in diverging definitions of the composing process itself—that is, in the way the elements that make up the process—writer, reality, audience, and language—are envisioned. Pedagogical theories in writing courses are grounded in rhetorical theories, and rhetorical theories do not differ in the simple undue emphasis of writer or audience or reality or language or some combination of these. Rhetorical theories differ from each other in the way writer, reality, audience, and language are conceived—both as separate units and in the way the units relate to each other. In the case of distinct pedagogical approaches, these four elements are likewise defined and related so as to describe a different composing process, which is to say a different world with different rules about what can be known, how it can be known, and how it can be communicated. To teach writing is to argue for a version of reality, and the best way of knowing and communicating it—to deal, as Paul Kameen has pointed out, in the metarhetorical realm of epistemology and linguistics.[2] And all composition teachers are ineluctably operating in this realm, whether or not they consciously choose to do so.

Considering pedagogical theories along these lines has led me to see groupings sometimes similar, sometimes at variance, with the schemes of others. The terms chosen for these categories are intended to prevent confusion and to be self-explanatory. The four dominant groups I will discuss are the Neo-Aristotelians or Classicists, the Positivists or Current-Traditionalists, the Neo-Platonists or Expressionists, and the New Rhetoricians. As I have said, I will be concerned in each case with the way that writer, reality, audience, and language have been defined and related so as to form a distinct world construct with distinct rules for discovering and communicating knowledge. I will then show how this epistemic complex makes for specific directives about invention, arrangement, and style (or prewriting, writing, and rewriting). Finally, as the names for the groups suggest, I will briefly trace the historical precedents of each, pointing to their roots in order to better understand their modern manifestations.

My reasons for presenting this analysis are not altogether disinterested. I am convinced that the pedagogical approach of the New Rhetoricians is the most intelligent and most practical alternative available, serving in every way the best interests of our students. I am also concerned, however, that writing teachers become more aware of the full significance of their pedagogical strategies. Not doing so can have disastrous consequences, ranging from momentarily confusing students to sending them away with faulty and even harmful information. The dismay students display about writing is, I am convinced, at least occasionally the result of teachers unconsciously offering contradictory advice about composing—guidance grounded in assumptions that simply do not square with each other. More important, as I have already indicated and as I plan to explain in detail later on, in teaching writing we are tacitly teaching a version of reality and the student's place and mode of operation in it. Yet many teachers (and I suspect most) look upon their vocations as the imparting of a largely mechanical skill, important only because it serves students in getting them through school and in advancing them in their professions. This essay will argue that writing teachers are perforce given a responsibility that far exceeds this merely instrumental task.[3]

I begin with revivals of Aristotelian rhetoric not because they are a dominant force today—far from it. My main purpose in starting with them is to show that many who say that they are followers of Aristotle are in truth opposed to his system in every sense. There is also the consideration that Aristotle has provided the technical language most often used in discussing rhetoric—so much so that it is all but impossible to talk intelligently about the subject without knowing him.

In the Aristotelian scheme of things, the material world exists independently of the observer and is knowable through sense impressions. Since sense impressions in themselves reveal nothing, however, to arrive at true knowledge it is necessary for the mind to perform an operation upon sense data. This operation is a function of reason and amounts to the appropriate use of syllogistic reasoning, the system of logic that Aristotle himself developed and refined. Providing the method for analyzing the material of any discipline, this logic offers, as Marjorie Grene explains, "a set of general rules for scientists (as Aristotle understood science) working each in his appropriate material. The rules are rules of validity, not psychological rules" (*A Portrait of Aristotle* [London: Faber and Faber, 1963], p. 69). Truth exists in conformance with the rules of logic, and logic is so thoroughly deductive that even induction is regarded as an imperfect form of the syllogism. The strictures imposed by logic, moreover, naturally arise out of the very structure of the mind and of the universe. In other words, there is a happy correspondence between the mind and the universe, so that, to cite Grene once again, "As the world is, finally, so is the mind that knows it" (p. 234).

Reality for Aristotle can thus be known and communicated, with language serving as the unproblematic medium of discourse. There is an uncomplicated correspondence between the sign and the thing, and—once again emphasizing the rational—the process whereby sign and thing are united is considered a mental act: words are not a part of the external world, but both word and thing are a part of thought.[4]

Rhetoric is of course central to Aristotle's system. Like dialectic—the method of discovering and communicating truth in learned discourse—

rhetoric deals with the realm of the probable, with truth as discovered in the areas of law, politics, and what might be called public virtue. Unlike scientific discoveries, truth in these realms can never be stated with absolute certainty. Still, approximations to truth are possible. The business of rhetoric then is to enable the speaker—Aristotle's rhetoric is preeminently oral—to find the means necessary to persuade the audience of the truth. Thus rhetoric is primarily concerned with the provision of inventional devices whereby the speaker may discover his or her argument, with these devices naturally falling into three categories: the rational, the emotional, and the ethical. Since truth is rational, the first is paramount and is derived from the rules of logic, albeit applied in the relaxed form of the enthymeme and example. Realizing that individuals are not always ruled by reason, however, Aristotle provides advice on appealing to the emotions of the audience and on presenting one's own character in the most favorable light, each considered with special regard for the audience and the occasion of the speech.

Aristotle's emphasis on invention leads to the neglect of commentary on arrangement and style. The treatment of arrangement is at best sketchy, but it does display Aristotle's reliance on the logical in its commitment to rational development. The section on style is more extensive and deserves special mention because it highlights Aristotle's rationalistic view of language, a view no longer considered defensible. As R. H. Robins explains:

> The word for Aristotle is thus the minimal meaningful unit. He further distinguishes the meaning of a word as an isolate from the meaning of a sentence; a word by itself "stands for" or "indicates" . . . something, but a sentence affirms or denies a predicate of its subject, or says that its subject exists or does not exist. One cannot now defend this doctrine of meaning. It is based on the formal logic that Aristotle codified and, we might say, sterilized for generations. The notion that words have meaning just by standing for or indicating something, whether in the world at large or in the human mind (both views are stated or suggested by Aristotle), leads to difficulties that have worried philosophers in many ages, and seriously distorts linguistic and grammatical studies.[5]

It should be noted, however, that despite this unfavorable estimate, Robins goes on to praise Aristotle as in some ways anticipating later developments in linguistics.

Examples of Aristotelian rhetoric in the textbooks of today are few indeed. Edward P. J. Corbett's *Classical Rhetoric for the Modern Student* (1971) and Richard Hughes and Albert Duhamel's *Principles of Rhetoric* (1967) revive the tradition. Most textbooks that claim to be Aristotelian are operating within the paradigm of what has come to be known as Current-Traditional Rhetoric, a category that might also be called the Positivist.

The Positivist or Current-Traditional group clearly dominates thinking about writing instruction today. The evidence is the staggering number of textbooks that yearly espouse its principles. The origins of Current-Traditional Rhetoric, as Albert Kitzhaber showed in his dissertation (University of Washington, 1953) on "Rhetoric in American Colleges," can be found in the late nineteenth-century rhetoric texts of A. S. Hill, Barett Wendell, and John F. Genung. But its epistemological stance can be found in eighteenth-century Scottish Common Sense Realism as expressed in the philosophy of Thomas Reid and James Beattie, and in the rhetorical treatises of George Campbell, Hugh Blair, and to a lesser extent, Richard Whately.

For Common Sense Realism, the certain existence of the material world is indisputable. All knowledge is founded on the simple correspondence between sense impressions and the faculties of the mind. This so far sounds like the Aristotelian world view, but is in fact a conscious departure from it. Common Sense Realism denies the value of the deductive method—syllogistic reasoning—in arriving at knowledge. Truth is instead discovered through induction alone. It is the individual sense impression that provides the basis on which all knowledge can be built. Thus the new scientific logic of Locke replaces the old deductive logic of Aristotle as the method for understanding experience. The world is still rational, but its system is to be discovered through the experimental method, not through logical categories grounded in a mental faculty. The state of affairs characterizing the emergence of the new epistemology is succinctly summarized by Wilbur Samuel Howell:

> The old science, as the disciples of Aristotle conceived of it at the end of the seventeenth century, had considered its function to be that of subjecting traditional truths to syllogistic examination, and of accepting as new truth only what could be proved to be consistent with the old. Under that kind of arrangement, traditional logic had taught the methods of deductive analysis, had perfected itself in the machinery of testing propositions for consistency, and had served at the same time as the instrument by which truths could be arranged so as to become intelligible and convincing to other learned men. . . . The new science, as envisioned by its founder, Francis Bacon, considered its function to be that of subjecting physical and human facts to observation and experiment, and of accepting as new truth only what could be shown to conform to the realities behind it.[6]

The rhetoric based on the new logic can be seen most clearly in George Campbell's *Philosophy of Rhetoric* (1776) and Hugh Blair's *Lectures on*

Rhetoric and Belles Lettres (1783). The old distinction between dialectic as the discipline of learned discourse and rhetoric as the discipline of popular discourse is destroyed. Rhetoric becomes the study of all forms of communication: scientific, philosophical, historical, political, legal, and even poetic. An equally significant departure in this new rhetoric is that it contains no inventional system. Truth is to be discovered outside the rhetorical enterprise—through the method, usually the scientific method, of the appropriate discipline, or, as in poetry and oratory, through genius.

The aim of rhetoric is to teach how to adapt the discourse to its hearers—and here the uncomplicated correspondence of the faculties and the world is emphasized. When the individual is freed from the biases of language, society, or history, the senses provide the mental faculties with a clear and distinct image of the world. The world readily surrenders its meaning to anyone who observes it properly, and no operation of the mind—logical or otherwise—is needed to arrive at truth. To communicate, the speaker or writer—both now included—need only provide the language which corresponds either to the objects in the external world or to the ideas in his or her own mind—both are essentially the same—in such a way that it reproduces the objects and the experience of them in the minds of the hearers (Cohen, pp. 38-42). As Campbell explains, "Thus language and thought, like body and soul, are made to correspond, and the qualities of the one exactly to co-operate with those of the other."[7] The emphasis in this rhetoric is on adapting what has been discovered outside the rhetorical enterprise to the minds of the hearers. The study of rhetoric thus focuses on developing skill in arrangement and style.

Given this epistemological field in a rhetoric that takes all communication as its province, discourse tends to be organized according to the faculties to which it appeals. A scheme that is at once relevant to current composition theory and typical in its emulation of Campbell, Blair, and Whately can be found in John Francis Genung's *The Practical Elements of Rhetoric* (1886).[8] For Genung the branches of discourse fall into four categories. The most "fundamental" mode appeals to understanding and is concerned with transmitting truth, examples of which are "history, biography, fiction, essays, treatises, criticism." The second and third groups are description and narration, appealing again to the understanding, but leading the reader to "feel the thought as well as think it." For Genung "the purest outcome" of this kind of writing is poetry. The fourth kind of discourse, "the most complex literary type," is oratory. This kind is concerned with persuasion and makes its special appeal to the will, but in so doing involves all the faculties. Genung goes on to create a further distinction that contributed to the departmentalization of English and Speech and the division of English into literature and composition. Persuasion is restricted to considerations of experts in the spoken language and poetry to discussions of literature teachers, now first appearing. College writing courses, on the other hand, are to focus on discourse that appeals to the understanding—exposition, narration, description, and argumentation (distinct now from persuasion). It is significant, moreover, that college rhetoric is to be concerned solely with the communication of truth that is certain and empirically verifiable—in other words, not probabilistic.

Genung, along with his contemporaries A. S. Hill and Barrett Wendell, sets the pattern for most modern composition textbooks, and their works show striking similarities to the vast majority of texts published today.[9] It is discouraging that generations after Freud and Einstein, college students are encouraged to embrace a view of reality based on a mechanistic physics and a naive faculty psychology—and all in the name of a convenient pedagogy.

The next theory of composition instruction to be considered arose as a reaction to current-traditional rhetoric. Its clearest statements are located in the work of Ken Macrorie, William Coles, Jr., James E. Miller and Stephen Judy, and the so-called "Pre-Writing School" of D. Gordon Rohman, Albert O. Wlecke, Clinton S. Burhans, and Donald Stewart (see Harrington, et al., pp. 645-647). Frequent assertions of this view, however, have appeared in American public schools in the twentieth century under the veil of including "creative expression" in the English curriculum.[10] The roots of this view of rhetoric in America can be traced to Emerson and the Transcendentalists, and its ultimate source is to be found in Plato.

In the Platonic scheme, truth is not based on sensory experience since the material world is always in flux and thus unreliable. Truth is instead discovered through an internal apprehension, a private vision of a world that transcends the physical. As Robert Cushman explains in *Therepeia* (Chapel Hill: University of North Carolina Press, 1958), "The central theme of Platonism regarding knowledge is that truth is not brought to man, but man to the truth" (p. 213). A striking corollary of this view is that ultimate truth can be discovered by the individual, but cannot be communicated. Truth can be learned but not taught. The purpose of rhetoric then becomes not the transmission of truth, but the correction of error, the removal of that which obstructs the personal apprehension of the truth. And the method is dialectic, the interaction of two interlocutors of good will intent on arriving at knowledge. Because the respondents are encouraged to break out of their ordinary perceptual set, to become free of the material world and of past error, the dialectic is often disruptive, requiring the abandonment of long held conventions and opinions. Preparing the soul to discover truth is often painful.

Plato's epistemology leads to a unique view of language. Because ultimate truths cannot be communicated, language can only deal with the realm of error, the world of flux, and act, as Gerald L. Bruns explains, as "a preliminary exercise which must engage the soul before the encounter with 'the knowable and truly real being' is possible" (p. 16). Truth is finally inexpressible, is beyond the resources of language. Yet Plato allows for the possibility that language may be used to communicate essential realities. In the *Republic* he speaks of using analogy to express ultimate truth, and in the *Phaedrus,* even as rhetoric is called into question, he employs an analogical method in his discussion of the soul and love. Language, it would appear, can be of some use in trying to communicate the absolute, or at least to approximate the experience of it.

The major tenets of this Platonic rhetoric form the center of what are commonly called "Expressionist" textbooks. Truth is conceived as the result of a private vision that must be constantly consulted in writing. These textbooks thus emphasize writing as a "personal" activity, as an expression of one's unique voice. In *Writing and Reality* (New York: Harper and Row, 1978), James Miller and Stephen Judy argue that "all good writing is *personal,* whether it be an abstract essay or a private letter," and that an important justification for writing is "to sound the depths, to explore, and to discover." The reason is simple: "Form in language grows from content—something the writer has to say—and that something, in turn, comes directly from the self" (pp. 12, 15). Ken Macrorie constantly emphasizes "Telling Truths," by which he means a writer must be "true to the feeling of his experience." His thrust throughout is on speaking in "an authentic voice" (also in Donald Stewart's *The Authentic Voice: A Pre-Writing Approach to Student Writing,* based on the work of Rohman and Wlecke), indicating by this the writer's private sense of things.[11] This placement of the self at the center of communication is also, of course, everywhere present in Coles' *The Plural I* (New York: Holt, Rinehart, and Winston, 1978).

One obvious objection to my reading of these expressionist theories is that their conception of truth can in no way be seen as comparable to Plato's transcendent world of ideas. While this cannot be questioned, it should also be noted that no member of this school is a relativist intent on denying the possibility of any certain truth whatever. All believe in the existence of verifiable truths and find them, as does Plato, in private experience, divorced from the impersonal data of sense experience. All also urge the interaction between writer and reader, a feature that leads to another point of similarity with Platonic rhetoric—the dialectic.

Most expressionist theories rely on classroom procedures that encourage the writer to interact in dialogue with the members of the class. The purpose is to get rid of what is untrue to the private vision of the writer, what is, in a word, inauthentic. Coles, for example, conceives of writing as an unteachable act, a kind of behavior that can be learned but not taught. (See especially the preface to *The Plural I.*) His response to this denial of his pedagogical role is to provide a classroom environment in which the student learns to write—although he or she is not taught to write—through dialectic. *The Plural I*, in fact, reveals Coles and his students engaging in a dialogue designed to lead both teacher and class—Coles admits that he always learns in his courses—to the discovery of what can be known but not communicated. This view of truth as it applies to writing is the basis of Coles' classroom activity. Dialogue can remove error, but it is up to the individual to discover ultimate knowledge. The same emphasis on dialectic can also be found in the texts of Macrorie and of Miller and Judy. Despite their insistence on the self as the source of all content, for example, Miller and Judy include "making connections with others in dialogue and discussion" (p. 5), and Macrorie makes the discussion of student papers the central activity of his classroom.

This emphasis on dialectic, it should be noted, is not an attempt to adjust the message to the audience, since doing so would clearly constitute a violation of the self. Instead the writer is trying to use others to get rid of what is false to the self, what is insincere and untrue to the individual's own sense of things, as evidenced by the use of language—the theory of which constitutes the final point of concurrence between modern Expressionist and Platonic rhetorics.

Most Expressionist textbooks emphasize the use of metaphor either directly or by implication. Coles, for example, sees the major task of the writer to be avoiding the imitation of conventional expressions because they limit what the writer can say. The fresh, personal vision demands an original use of language. Rohman and Wlecke, as well as the textbook by Donald Stewart based on their research, are more explicit. They specifically recommend the cultivation of the ability to make analogies (along with meditation and journal writing) as an inventional device. Macrorie makes metaphor one of the prime features of "good writing" (p. 21) and in one form or another takes it up again and again in *Telling Writing*. The reason for this emphasis is not hard to discover. In communicating, language does not have as its referent the object in the external world or an idea of this object in the mind. Instead, to present truth language must rely on original metaphors in order to capture what is unique in each personal vision. The private apprehension of the real relies on the metaphoric appeal from the known to the unknown, from the public and accessible world of the senses to the inner and privileged immaterial realm, in order to be made available to others. As in Plato, the analogical method offers the only avenue to expressing the true.

The clearest pedagogical expression of the New Rhetoric—or what might be called Epistemic Rhetoric—is found in Ann E. Berthoff's *Forming/Thinking/Writing: The Composing Imagination* (Rochelle Park, N.J.: Hayden, 1978) and Richard E. Young, Alton L. Becker, and Kenneth L. Pike's *Rhetoric: Discovery and Change* (New York: Harcourt Brace Jovanovich, 1970). These books have behind them the rhetorics of such figures as I. A. Richards and Kenneth Burke and the philosophical statements of Susan Langer, Ernst Cassirer, and John Dewey. Closely related to the work of Berthoff and Young, Becker, and Pike are the cognitive-developmental approaches of such figures as James Moffett, Linda Flower, Andrea Lunsford, and Barry Kroll. While their roots are different—located in the realm of cognitive psychology and empirical linguistics—their methods are strikingly similar. In this discussion, however, I intend to call exclusively upon the textbooks of Berthoff and of Young, Becker, and Pike to make my case, acknowledging at the start that there are others that could serve as well. Despite differences, their approaches most comprehensively display a view of rhetoric as epistemic, as a means of arriving at truth.

Classical Rhetoric considers truth to be located in the rational operation of the mind, Positivist Rhetoric in the correct perception of sense impressions, and Neo-Platonic Rhetoric within the individual, attainable only through an internal apprehension. In each case knowledge is a commodity situated in a permanent location, a repository to which the individual goes to be enlightened.

For the New Rhetoric, knowledge is not simply a static entity available for retrieval. Truth is dynamic and dialectical, the result of a process involving the interaction of opposing elements. It is a relation that is created, not pre-existent and waiting to be discovered. The basic elements of the dialectic are the elements that make up the communication process—writer (speaker), audience, reality, language. Communication is always basic to the epistemology underlying the New Rhetoric because truth is always truth for someone standing in relation to others in a linguistically circumscribed situation. The elements of the communication process thus do not simply provide a convenient way of talking about rhetoric. They form the elements that go into the very shaping of knowledge.

It is this dialectical notion of rhetoric—and of rhetoric as the determiner of reality—that underlies the textbooks of Berthoff and of Young, Becker, and Pike. In demonstrating this thesis I will consider the elements of the dialectic alone or in pairs, simply because they are more easily handled this way in discussion. It should not be forgotten, however, that in operation they are always simultaneously in a relationship of one to all, constantly modifying their values in response to each other.

The New Rhetoric denies that truth is discoverable in sense impression since this data must always be interpreted—structured and organized—in order to have meaning. The perceiver is of course the interpreter, but she is likewise unable by herself to provide truth since meaning cannot be made apart from the data of experience. Thus Berthoff cites Kant's "Percepts without concepts are empty; concepts without percepts are blind" (p. 13). Later she explains: "The brain puts things together, composing the percepts by which we can make sense of the world. We don't just 'have' a visual experience and then by thinking 'have' a mental experience; the mutual dependence of seeing and knowing is what a modern psychologist has in mind when he speaks of 'the intelligent eye'" (p. 44). Young, Becker, and Pike state the same notion:

> Constantly changing, bafflingly complex, the external world is not a neat, well-ordered place replete with meaning, but an enigma requiring interpretation. This interpretation is the result of a transaction between events in the external world and the mind of the individual—between the world "out there" and the individual's previous experience, knowledge, values, attitudes, and desires. Thus the mirrored world is not just the sum total of eardrum rattles, retinal excitations, and so on; it is a creation that reflects the peculiarities of the perceiver as well as the peculiarities of what is perceived. (p. 25)

Language is at the center of this dialectical interplay between the individual and the world. For Neo-Aristotelians, Positivists, and Neo-Platonists, truth exists prior to language so that the difficulty of the writer or speaker is to find the appropriate words to communicate knowledge. For the New Rhetoric truth is impossible without language since it is language that embodies and generates truth. Young, Becker, and Pike explain:

> Language provides a way of unitizing experience: a set of symbols that label recurring chunks of experience.. . . Language depends on our seeing certain experiences as constant or repeatable. And seeing the world as repeatable depends, in part at least, on language. A language is, in a sense, a theory of the universe, a way of selecting and grouping experience in a fairly consistent and predictable way. (p. 27)

Berthoff agrees: "The relationship between thought and language is dialectical: ideas are conceived by language; language is generated by thought" (p. 47). Rather than truth being prior to language, language is prior to truth and determines what shapes truth can take. Language does not correspond to the "real world." It creates the "real world" by organizing it, by determining what will be perceived and not perceived, by indicating what has meaning and what is meaningless.

The audience of course enters into this play of language. Current-Traditional Rhetoric demands that the audience be as "objective" as the writer; both shed personal and social concerns in the interests of the unobstructed perception of empirical reality. For Neo-Platonic Rhetoric the audience is a check to the false note of the inauthentic and helps to detect error, but it is not involved in the actual discovery of truth—a purely personal matter. Neo-Aristotelians take the audience seriously as a force to be considered in shaping the message. Still, for all its discussion of the emotional and ethical appeals, Classical Rhetoric emphasizes rational structures, and the concern for the audience is only a concession to the imperfection of human nature. In the New Rhetoric the message arises out of the interaction of the writer, language, reality, and the audience. Truths are operative only within a given universe of discourse, and this universe is shaped by all of these elements, including the audience. As Young, Becker, and Pike explain:

> The writer must first understand the nature of his own interpretation and how it differs from the interpretations of others. Since each man segments experience into discrete, repeatable units, the writer can begin by asking how his way of segmenting and ordering experience differs from his reader's. How do units of time, space, the visible world, social organization, and so on differ? . . .
>
> Human differences are the raw material of writing—differences in experiences and ways of segmenting them, differences in values, purposes, and goals. They are our reason for wishing to communicate. Through communication we create community, the basic value underlying rhetoric. To do so, we must overcome the barriers to communication that are, paradoxically, the motive for communication. (p. 30)

Ann E. Berthoff also includes this idea in her emphasis on meaning as a function of relationship.

> *Meanings are relationships.* Seeing means "seeing relationships," whether we're talking about seeing as *perception* or seeing as *understanding.* "I see what you mean" means "I understand how you put that together so that it makes sense." The way we make sense of the world is to see something *with respect to, in terms of, in relation to* something else. We can't make sense of one thing by itself; it must be seen as being *like* another thing; or *next to, across from, coming after* another thing; or as a repetition of another thing. *Something* makes sense—is meaningful—only if it is taken with *something else.* (p. 44)

The dialectical view of reality, language, and the audience redefines the writer. In Current-Traditional Rhetoric the writer must efface himself; stated differently, the writer must focus on experience in a way that makes possible the discovery of certain kinds of information—the empirical and rational—and the neglect of others—psychological and social concerns. In Neo-Platonic Rhetoric the writer is at the center of the rhetorical act, but is finally isolated, cut off from community, and left to the lonely business of discovering truth alone. Neo-Aristotelian Rhetoric exalts the writer, but circumscribes her effort by its emphasis on the rational—the enthymeme and example. The New Rhetoric sees the writer as a creator of meaning, a shaper of reality, rather than a passive receptor of the immutably given. "When you write," explains Berthoff, "you don't follow somebody else's scheme; you design your own. As a writer, you learn to make words behave the way you want them to. . . . Learning to write is not a matter of learning the rules that govern the use of the semicolon or the names of sentence structures, nor is it a matter of manipulating words; it is a matter of making meanings, and that is the work of the active mind" (p. 11). Young, Becker, and Pike concur: "We have sought to develop a rhetoric that implies that we are all citizens of an extraordinarily diverse and disturbed world, that the 'truths' we live by are tentative and subject to change, that we must be discoverers of new truths as well as preservers and transmitter of old, and that enlightened cooperation is the preeminent ethical goal of communication" (p. 9).

This version of the composing process leads to a view of what can be taught in the writing class that rivals Aristotelian rhetoric in its comprehensiveness. Current-Traditional and Neo-Platonic Rhetoric deny the place of invention in rhetoric because for both truth is considered external and self-evident, accessible to anyone who seeks it in the proper spirit. Like Neo-Aristotelian Rhetoric, the New Rhetoric sees truth as probabilistic, and it provides students with techniques—heuristics—for discovering it, or what might more accurately be called creating it. This does not mean, however, that arrangement and style are regarded as unimportant, as in Neo-Platonic Rhetoric. In fact, the attention paid to these matters in the New Rhetoric rivals that paid in Current-Traditional Rhetoric, but not because they are the only teachable part of the process. Structure and language are a part of the formation of meaning, are at the center of the discovery of truth, not simply the dress of thought. From the point of view of pedagogy, New Rhetoric thus treats in depth all the offices of classical rhetoric that apply to written language—invention, arrangement, and style—and does so by calling upon the best that has been thought and said about them by contemporary observers.

In talking and writing about the matters that form the substance of this essay, at my back I always hear the nagging (albeit legitimate) query of the overworked writing teacher: But what does all this have to do with the teaching of freshman composition? My answer is that it is more relevant than most of us are prepared to admit. In teaching writing, we are not simply offering training in a useful technical skill that is meant as a simple complement to the more important studies of other areas. We are teaching a way of experiencing the world, a way of ordering and making sense of it. As I have shown, subtly informing our statements about invention, arrangement, and even style are assumptions about the nature of reality. If the textbooks that sell the most copies tell us anything, they make abundantly clear that most writing teachers accept the assumptions of Current-Traditional Rhetoric, the view that arose contemporaneously with the positivistic position of modern science. Yet most of those who use these texts would readily admit that the scientific world view has demonstrated its inability to solve the problems that most concern us, problems that are often themselves the result of scientific "breakthroughs." And even many scientists concur with them in this view—Oppenheimer and Einstein, for example. In our writing classrooms, however, we continue to offer a view of composing that insists on a version of reality that is sure to place students at a disadvantage in addressing the problems that will confront them in both their professional and private experience.

Neo-Platonic, Neo-Aristotelian, and what I have called New Rhetoric are reactions to the inadequacy of Current-Traditional Rhetoric to teach students a notion of the composing process that will enable them to become effective persons as they become effective writers. While my sympathies are obviously with the last of these reactions, the three can be considered as one in their efforts to establish new directions for a modern rhetoric. Viewed in this way, the difference between them and Current-Traditional Rhetoric is analogous to the difference Richard Rorty has found in what he calls, in *Philosophy and the Mirror of Nature* (Princeton, N.J.: Princeton University Press, 1979), hermeneutic and epistemological philosophy. The hermeneutic approach to rhetoric bases the discipline on establishing an open dialogue in the hopes of reaching agreement about the truth of the matter at hand. Current-Traditional Rhetoric views the rhetorical situation as an arena where the truth is incontrovertibly established by a speaker or writer more enlightened than her audience. For the hermeneuticist truth is never fixed finally on unshakable grounds. Instead it emerges only after false starts and failures, and it can only represent a tentative point of rest in a continuing conversation. Whatever truth is arrived at, moreover, is always the product of individuals calling on the full range of their humanity, with esthetic and moral considerations given at least as much importance as any others. For Current-Traditional Rhetoric truth is empirically based and can only be achieved through subverting a part of the human response to experience. Truth then stands forever, a tribute to its method, triumphant over what most of us consider important in life, successful through subserving writer, audience, and language to the myth of an objective reality.

One conclusion should now be incontestable. The numerous recommendations of the "process"-centered approaches to writing instruction as superior to the "product"-centered approaches are not very useful. Everyone teaches the process of writing, but everyone does not teach the *same* process. The test of one's competence as a composition instructor, it seems to me, resides in being able to recognize and justify the version of the process being taught, complete with all of its significance for the student.

NOTES

1. I have in mind Richard Fulkerson, "Four Philosophies of Composition," *College Composition and Communication*, 30 (1979), 343-48; David V. Harrington, et al., "A Critical Survey of Resources for Teaching Rhetorical Invention," *College English*, 40 (1979), 641-61; William F. Woods, "Composition Textbooks and Pedagogical Theory 1960-80," *CE*, 43 (1981), 393-409.

2. "Rewording the Rhetoric of Composition," *PRE/TEXT*, 1 (1980), 39. I am indebted to Professor Kameen's classification of pedagogical theories for the suggestiveness of his method; my conclusions, however, are substantially different.

3. There is still another reason for pursuing the method I recommend, one that explains why rhetorical principles are now at the center of discussions in so many different disciplines. When taken together, writer, reality, audience, and language identify an epistemic field—the basic conditions that determine what knowledge will be knowable, what not knowable, and how the knowable will be communicated. This epistemic field is the point of departure for numerous studies, although the language used to describe it varies from thinker to thinker. Examples are readily available. In *Science and the Modern World* (New York: Macmillan, 1926), A. N. Whitehead sees this field as a product of the "fundamental assumptions which adherents of all variant systems within the epoch unconsciously presuppose" (p. 71). Susanne Langer, in *Philosophy in a New Key* (Cambridge, Mass.: Harvard University Press, 1979), calls it the "tacit, fundamental way of seeing things" (p. 6). Michael Polanyi uses the terms "tacit knowledge" in *Personal Knowledge* (Chicago: University of Chicago Press, 1962). Michel Foucault, in *The Order of Things* (1971; rpt. New York: Vintage Books, 1973), speaks of the "episteme," and Thomas Kuhn, in *Structure of Scientific Revolutions* (Chicago: University of Chicago Press, 1970), discusses at length the "paradigm" that underlies a scientific discipline. The historian Hayden White, in *Metahistory: The Historical Imagination in Nineteenth-Century Europe* (Baltimore: Johns Hopkins University Press, 1973), has translated the elements of the composing process into terms appropriate to the writing of history, seeing the historical field as being made up of the historian, the historical record, the historical accounts, and an audience. One compelling reason for studying composition theory is that it so readily reveals its epistemic field, thus indicating, for example, a great deal about the way a particular historical period defines itself—a fact convincingly demonstrated in Murray Cohen's *Sensible Words: Linguistic Practice in England 1640-1785* (Baltimore: Johns Hopkins University Press, 1977), a detailed study of English grammars.

4. See Gerald L. Bruns, *Modern Poetry and the Idea of Language* (New Haven, Ct.: Yale University Press, 1974), p. 34.

5. *Ancient and Mediaeval Grammatical Theory in Europe* (London: G. Bell and Sons, 1951), pp. 20-21.

6. *Eighteenth-Century British Logic and Rhetoric* (Princeton, N.J.: Princeton University Press, 1971), pp. 5-6.

7. *The Philosophy of Rhetoric*, ed. Lloyd F. Bitzer (Carbondale: Southern Illinois University Press, 1963), p. 215.

8. For a more detailed discussion of Genung see my "John Genung and Contemporary Composition Theory: The Triumph of the Eighteenth Century," *Rhetoric Society Quarterly*, 11 (1981), 74-84.

9. For an analysis of modern composition textbooks, see James A. Berlin and Robert P. Inkster, "Current-Traditional Rhetoric: Paradigm and Practice," *Freshman English News*, 8 (1980), 1-4, 13-14.

10. Kenneth J. Kantor, "Creative Expression in the English Curriculum: A Historical Perspective," *Research in the Teaching of English*, 9 (1975), 5-29.

11. *Telling Writing* (Rochelle Park, N.J.: Hayden Book Company, 1978), p. 13.

Scientific Talk

Developmental Schemes

Among James Berlin's epistemological categories in "Contemporary Composition" there is positivism. The assumptions that are carried by positivism remain the most pervasive for our society and for composition studies (though not without some sharp criticism). Implicit in the term (and the concept) is that knowledge is scaffolded, building upon itself, always ascending. So given rhetoric's and thereby composition's concern with mind, and given the cognitive emphasis of Woods Hole, the positivistic schemes that composition found most attractive were those concerning cognitive development.

The stages of development were determined by Jean Piaget's developmental scheme, and the approach to tapping into the "natural" process of cognitive development was inductive reasoning, a process of discovery. In 1968, James Moffett published *Teaching the Universe of Discourse*, a developmental scheme for teaching discourse that spanned from the elementary grades to the secondary. The curricular stages he developed—from the egocentric to the public: interior dialogue to conversation to correspondence to public narrative—follow the cognitive stages of development offered by Piaget. Piaget's interpretation of the mind as structuring knowledge systematically, his genetic epistemology, continues to hold sway with the education community. And since language plays a crucial role in his developmental scheme, it holds a particular attraction for compositionists. This attraction becomes magnified in the work of Lev Vygotsky, a contemporary of Piaget's. For Vygotsky, language doesn't just play a role; language is central, that which provides for our conceptions of reality. Vygotsky's concept of "inner speech," in which Piaget's egocentric speech doesn't disappear but becomes internalized and removed from the sounds of discourse, causes Piaget to revise his theories.

So intriguing and suggestive are the language and thought connections provided by Piaget and Vygotsky that composition becomes obsessed with recognizing those stages, fostering their development, believing in their lack when expectations for student writing are not met. Other developmental schemes, like William Perry's scheme of ethical and intellectual development in college, gain new attention. Mina Shaughnessy—who first coins the term "Basic Writer" to describe college writers otherwise termed "developmental" or "remedial"—creates a parody of developmental schemes to discuss how teachers come to consider basic writers when first confronted with them. And although not developmental, Linda Flower and John R. Hayes turn to the cognitive sciences, the research method of protocol analysis developed by Carl Jung, to build a model of the composing process. Mike Rose, Ann Berthoff, and Patricia Bizzell provide the cross-talk: Rose using his own understanding of cognitive psychology to question some of the assertions arising within composition studies' cognitivists, Berthoff looking to other schemes, and Bizzell calling the whole turn to cognition into question.

A Cognitive Process Theory of Writing

Linda Flower and John R. Hayes

There is a venerable tradition in rhetoric and composition which sees the composing process as a series of decisions and choices.[1] However, it is no longer easy simply to assert this position, unless you are prepared to answer a number of questions, the most pressing of which probably is: "What then are the criteria which govern that choice?" Or we could put it another way: "What guides the decisions writers make as they write?" In a recent survey of composition research, Odell, Cooper, and Courts noticed that some of the most thoughtful people in the field are giving us two reasonable but somewhat different answers:

> How do writers actually go about choosing diction, syntactic and organizational patterns, and context? Kinneavy claims that one's purpose — informing, persuading, expressing, or manipulating language for its own sake — guides these choices. Moffett and Gibson contend that these choices are determined by one's sense of the relation of speaker, subject, and audience. Is either of these two claims borne out by the actual practice of writers engaged in drafting or revising? Does either premise account adequately for the choices writers make?[2]

Rhetoricians such as Lloyd Bitzer and Richard Vatz have energetically debated this question in still other terms. Lloyd Bitzer argues that speech always occurs as a response to a rhetorical situation, which he succinctly defines as containing an exigency (which demands a response), an audience,

Reprinted from *College Composition and Communication* 32.4 (December 1981): 365–87. Used with permission.

and a set of constraints.[3] In response to this "situation-driven" view, Vatz claims that the speaker's response, and even the rhetorical situation itself, are determined by the imagination and art of the speaker.[4]

Finally, James Britton has asked the same question and offered a linguist's answer, namely, that syntactic and lexical choices guide the process.

> It is tempting to think of writing as a process of making linguistic choices from one's repertoire of syntactic structures and lexical items. This would suggest that there is a meaning, or something to be expressed, in the writer's mind, and that he proceeds to choose, from the words and structures he has at his disposal, the ones that best match his meaning. But is that really how it happens?[5]

To most of us it may seem reasonable to suppose that all of these forces — "purposes," "relationships," "exigencies," "language" — have a hand in guiding the writer's process, but it is not at all clear how they do so or how they interact. Do they, for example, work in elegant and graceful coordination, or as competitive forces constantly vying for control? We think that the best way to answer these questions — to really understand the nature of rhetorical choices in good and poor writers — is to follow James Britton's lead and turn our attention to the writing process itself: to ask, "but is that really how it happens?"

This paper will introduce a theory of the cognitive processes involved in composing in an effort to lay groundwork for more detailed study of thinking processes in writing. This theory is based on our work with protocol analysis over the past five years and has, we feel, a good deal of evidence to support it. Nevertheless, it is for us a working hypothesis and springboard for further research, and we hope that insofar as it suggests testable hypotheses it will be the same for others. Our cognitive process theory rests on four key points, which this paper will develop:

1. The process of writing is best understood as a set of distinctive thinking processes which writers orchestrate or organize during the act of composing.

2. These processes have a hierarchical, highly embedded organization in which any given process can be embedded within any other.

3. The act of composing itself is a goal-directed thinking process, guided by the writer's own growing network of goals.

4. Writers create their own goals in two key ways: by generating both high-level goals and supporting sub-goals which embody the writer's · developing sense of purpose, and then, at times, by changing major

goals or even establishing entirely new ones based on what has been learned in the act of writing.

1. Writing is best understood as a set of distinctive thinking processes which writers orchestrate or organize during the act of composing.

To many this point may seem self-evident, and yet it is in marked contrast to our current paradigm for composing—the stage process model. This familiar metaphor or model describes the composing process as a linear series of stages, separated in time, and characterized by the gradual development of the written product. The best examples of stage models are the Pre-Write/Write/Re-Write model of Gordon Rohman[6] and The Conception/Incubation/Production model of Britton et al.[7]

STAGE MODELS OF WRITING

Without doubt, the wide acceptance of Pre-Writing has helped improve the teaching of composition by calling attention to planning and discovery as legitimate parts of the writing process. Yet many question whether this linear stage model is really an accurate or useful description of the composing process itself. The problem with stage descriptions of writing is that they model the growth of the written product, not the inner process of the person producing it. "Pre-Writing" is the stage before words emerge on paper; "Writing" is the stage in which a product is being produced; and "Re-Writing" is a final reworking of that product. Yet both common sense and research tell us that writers are constantly planning (pre-writing) and revising (re-writing) as they compose (write), not in clean-cut stages.[8] Furthermore, the sharp distinctions stage models make between the operations of planning, writing, and revising may seriously distort how these activities work. For example, Nancy Sommers has shown that revision, as it is carried out by skilled writers, is not an end-of-the-line repair process, but is a constant process of "re-vision" or re-seeing that goes on while they are composing.[9] A more accurate model of the composing process would need to recognize those basic thinking processes which unite planning and revision. Because stage models take the final product as their reference point, they offer an inadequate account of the more intimate, moment-by-moment intellectual process of composing. How, for example, is the output of one stage, such as pre-writing or incubation, transferred to the next? As every writer knows, having good ideas doesn't automatically produce good prose. Such models are typically silent on the inner processes of decision and choice.

A COGNITIVE PROCESS MODEL

A cognitive process theory of writing, such as the one presented here, represents a major departure from the traditional paradigm of stages in this way: in a stage model the major units of analysis are *stages* of completion which reflect the growth of a written product, and these stages are organized in a *linear* sequence or structure. In a process model, the major units of analysis are elementary mental *processes,* such as the process of generating ideas. And these processes have a *hierarchical* structure (see p. 288, below) such that idea generation, for example, is a sub-process of Planning. Furthermore, each of these mental acts may occur at any time in the composing process. One major advantage of identifying these basic cognitive processes or thinking skills writers use is that we can then compare the composing strategies of good and poor writers. And we can look at writing in a much more detailed way.

In psychology and linguistics, one traditional way of looking carefully at a process is to build a model of what you see. A model is a metaphor for a process: a way to describe something, such as the composing process, which refuses to sit still for a portrait. As a hypothesis about a dynamic system, it attempts to describe the parts of the system and how they work together. Modeling a process starts as a problem in design. For example, imagine that you have been asked to start from scratch and design an imaginary, working "Writer." In order to build a "Writer" or a theoretical system that would reflect the process of a real writer, you would want to do at least three things:

1. First, you would need to define the major elements or sub-processes that make up the larger process of writing. Such sub-processes would include planning, retrieving information from long-term memory, reviewing, and so on.

2. Second, you would want to show how these various elements of the process interact in the total process of writing. For example, how is "knowledge" about the audience actually integrated into the moment-to-moment act of composing?

3. And finally, since a model is primarily a tool for thinking with, you would want your model to speak to critical questions in the discipline. It should help you see things you didn't see before.

Obviously, the best way to model the writing process is to study a writer in action, and there are many ways to do this. However, people's after-the-fact, *introspective analysis* of what they did while writing is noto-riously inaccurate and likely to be influenced by their notions of what they should have done. Therefore we turned to *protocol analysis*, which has been successfully used to study other cognitive processes.[10] Unlike in-trospective reports, thinking aloud protocols capture a detailed record of what is going on in the writer's mind during the act of composing itself. To collect a protocol, we give writers a problem, such as "Write an article on your job for the readers of *Seventeen* magazine," and then ask them to compose out loud near an unobtrusive tape recorder. We ask them to work on the task as they normally would—thinking, jotting notes, and writing—except that they must think out loud. They are asked to verbal-ize everything that goes through their minds as they write, including stray notions, false starts, and incomplete or fragmentary thought. The writers are *not* asked to engage in any kind of introspection or self-analysis while writing, but simply to think out loud while working like a person talking to herself.

The transcript of this session, which may amount to 20 pages for an hour session, is called a protocol. As a research tool, a protocol is extraordi-narily rich in data and, together with the writer's notes and manuscript, it gives us a very detailed picture of the writer's composing process. It lets us see not only the development of the written product but many of the intel-lectual processes which produced it. The model of the writing process pre-sented in Figure 1 attempts to account for the major thinking processes and constraints we saw at work in these protocols. But note that it does *not* spec-ify the order in which they are invoked.

The act of writing involves three major elements which are reflected in the three units of the model: **the task environment, the writer's long-term memory, and the writing processes.** The task environment includes all of those things outside the writer's skin, starting with the rhetorical problem or assignment and eventually including the growing text itself. The second ele-ment is the writer's long-term memory in which the writer has stored knowl-edge, not only of the topic, but of the audience and of various writing plans. The third element in our model contains writing processes themselves, specifically the basic processes of **Planning, Translating, and Reviewing,** which are under the control of a Monitor.

This model attempts to account for the processes we saw in the compos-ing protocols. It is also a guide to research, which asks us to explore each of these elements and their interaction more fully. Since this model is de-scribed in detail elsewhere,[11] let us focus here on some ways each element contributes to the overall process.

Figure 1 Structure of the writing model. (For an explanation of how to read a process model, please see endnote 11.)

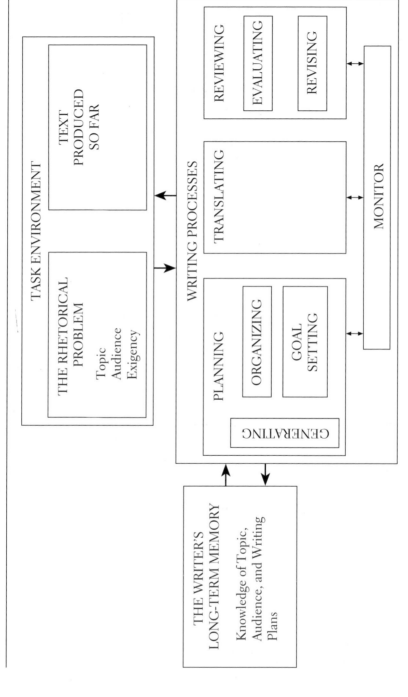

OVERVIEW OF THE MODEL

The Rhetorical Problem

At the beginning of composing, the most important element is obviously the **rhetorical problem** itself. A school assignment is a simplified version of such a problem, describing the writer's topic, audience, and (implicitly) her role as student to teacher. Insofar as writing is a rhetorical act, not a mere artifact, writers attempt to "solve" or respond to this rhetorical problem by writing something.

In theory this problem is a very complex thing: it includes not only the rhetorical situation and audience which prompts one to write, it also includes the writer's own goals in writing.[12] A good writer is a person who can juggle all of these demands. But in practice we have observed, as did Britton,[13] that writers frequently reduce this large set of constraints to a radically simplified problem, such as "write another theme for English class." Redefining the problem in this way is obviously an economical strategy as long as the new representation fits reality. But when it doesn't, there is a catch: people only solve the problems they define for themselves. If a writer's representation of her rhetorical problem is inaccurate or simply underdeveloped, then she is unlikely to "solve" or attend to the missing aspects of the problem. To sum up, defining the rhetorical problem is a major, immutable part of the writing process. But the way in which people choose to define a rhetorical problem to themselves can vary greatly from writer to writer. An important goal for research then will be to discover how this process of representing the problem works and how it affects the writer's performance.

The Written Text

As composing proceeds, a new element enters the task environment which places even more constraints upon what the writer can say. Just as a title constrains the content of a paper and a topic sentence shapes the options of a paragraph, each word in the growing text determines and limits the choices of what can come next. However, the influence that the growing text exerts on the composing process can vary greatly. When writing is incoherent, the text may have exerted too little influence; the writer may have failed to consolidate new ideas with earlier statements. On the other hand, one of the earmarks of a basic writer is a dogged concern with extending the previous sentence[14] and a reluctance to jump from local, text-bound planning to more global decisions, such as "what do I want to cover here?"

279

As we will see, the growing text makes large demands on the writer's time and attention during composing. But in doing so, it is competing with two other forces which could and also should direct the composing process; namely, the writer's knowledge stored in long-term memory and the writer's plans for dealing with the rhetorical problem. It is easy, for example, to imagine a conflict between what you know about a topic and what you might actually want to say to a given reader, or between a graceful phrase that completes a sentence and the more awkward point you actually wanted to make. Part of the drama of writing is seeing how writers juggle and integrate the multiple constraints of their knowledge, their plans, and their text into the production of each new sentence.[15]

The Long-Term Memory

The writer's long-term memory, which can exist in the mind as well as in outside resources such as books, is a storehouse of knowledge about the topic and audience, as well as knowledge of writing plans and problem representations. Sometimes a single cue in an assignment, such as "write a persuasive . . . ," can let a writer tap a stored representation of a problem and bring a whole raft of writing plans into play.

Unlike short-term memory, which is our active processing capacity or conscious attention, long-term memory is a relatively stable entity and has its own internal organization of information. The problem with long-term memory is, first of all, getting things out of it—that is, finding the cue that will let you retrieve a network of useful knowledge. The second problem for a writer is usually reorganizing or adapting that information to fit the demands of the rhetorical problem. The phenomena of "writer-based" prose nicely demonstrates the results of writing strategy based solely on retrieval. The organization of a piece of writer-based prose faithfully reflects the writer's own discovery process and the structure of the remembered information itself, but it often fails to transform or reorganize the knowledge to meet the different needs of a reader.[16]

Planning

People often think of planning as the act of figuring out how to get from here to there, i.e., making a detailed plan. But our model uses the term in its much broader sense. In the **planning** process writers form an internal representation of the knowledge that will be used in writing. This internal representation is likely to be more abstract than the writer's prose representation will eventually be. For example, a whole network of ideas might be represented by a single key word. Furthermore, this representation of one's knowledge will not necessarily be made in language, but could be held as a visual or perceptual code, e.g., as a fleeting image the writer must then capture in words.

Planning, or the act of building this internal representation, involves a number of sub-processes. The most obvious is the act of generating ideas, which includes retrieving relevant information from long-term memory. Sometimes this information is so well developed and organized *in memory* that the writer is essentially generating standard written English. At other times one may generate only fragmentary, unconnected, even contradictory thoughts, like the pieces of a poem that hasn't yet taken shape.

When the structure of ideas already in the writer's memory is not adequately adapted to the current rhetorical task, the sub-process of organizing takes on the job of helping the writer make meaning, that is, give a meaningful structure to his or her ideas. The process of organizing appears to play an important part in creative thinking and discovery since it is capable of grouping ideas and forming new concepts. More specifically, the organizing process allows the writer to identify categories, to search for subordinate ideas which develop a current topic, and to search for superordinate ideas which include or subsume the current topic. At another level the process of organizing also attends to more strictly textual decisions about the presentation and ordering of the text. That is, writers identify first or last topics, important ideas, and presentation patterns. However, organizing is much more than merely ordering points. And it seems clear that all rhetorical decisions and plans for reaching the audience affect the process of organizing ideas at all levels, because it is often guided by major goals established during the powerful process of goal-setting.

Goal-setting is indeed a third, little-studied but major, aspect of the planning process. The goals writers give themselves are both procedural (e.g., "Now let's see—a—I want to start out with 'energy'") and substantive, often both at the same time (e.g., "I have to relate this [engineering project] to the economics [of energy] to show why I'm improving it and why the steam turbine needs to be more efficient" or "I want to suggest that—that—um—the reader should sort of—what—what should one say—the reader should look at what she is interested in and look at the things that give her pleasure . . . ").

The most important thing about writing goals is the fact that they are *created* by the writer. Although some well-learned plans and goals may be drawn intact from long-term memory, most of the writer's goals are generated, developed, and revised by the same processes that generate and organize new ideas. And this process goes on throughout composing. Just as goals lead a writer to generate ideas, those ideas lead to new, more complex goals which can then integrate content and purpose.

Our own studies on goal setting to date suggest that the act of defining one's own rhetorical problem and setting goals is an important part of "being creative" and can account for some important differences between good and poor writers.[17] As we will argue in the final section of this paper, the act of developing and refining one's own goals is not limited to a "pre-writing stage" in the composing process, but is intimately bound up with the ongoing, moment-to-moment process of composing.

Translating

This is essentially the process of putting ideas into visible language. We have chosen the term **translate** for this process over other terms such as "transcribe" or "write" in order to emphasize the peculiar qualities of the task. The information generated in **planning** may be represented in a variety of symbol systems other than language, such as imagery or kinetic sensations. Trying to capture the movement of a deer on ice in language is clearly a kind of translation. Even when the **planning** process represents one's thought in words, that representation is unlikely to be in the elaborate syntax of written English. So the writer's task is to translate a meaning, which may be embodied in key words (what Vygotsky calls words "saturated with sense") and organized in a complex network of relationships, into a linear piece of written English.

The process of **translating** requires the writer to juggle all the special demands of written English, which Ellen Nold has described as lying on a spectrum from generic and formal demands through syntactic and lexical ones down to the motor tasks of forming letters. For children and inexperienced writers, this extra burden may overwhelm the limited capacity of short-term memory.[18] If the writer must devote conscious attention to demands such as spelling and grammar, the task of translating can interfere with the more global process of planning what one wants to say. Or one can simply ignore some of the constraints of written English. One path produces poor or local planning, the other produces errors, and both, as Mina Shaughnessy showed, lead to frustration for the writer.[19]

In some of the most exciting and extensive research in this area, Marlene Scardamalia and Carl Bereiter have looked at the ways children cope with the cognitive demands of writing. Well-learned skills, such as sentence construction, tend to become automatic and lost to consciousness. Because so little of the writing process is automatic for children, they must devote conscious attention to a variety of individual thinking tasks which adults perform quickly and automatically. Such studies, which trace the development of a given skill over several age groups, can show us the hidden components of an adult process as well as show us how children learn. For example, these studies have been able to distinguish children's ability to handle idea complexity from their ability to handle syntactic complexity; that is, they demonstrate the difference between seeing complex relationships and translating them into appropriate language. In another series of studies Bereiter and Scardamalia showed how children learn to handle the translation process by adapting, then eventually abandoning, the discourse conventions of conversation.[20]

Reviewing

As you can see in Figure 1, **reviewing** depends on two sub-processes: **evaluating** and **revising**. Reviewing, itself, may be a conscious process in which writers choose to read what they have written either as a springboard to further translating or with an eye to systematically evaluating and/or revising the text. These periods of planned reviewing frequently lead to new cycles of planning and translating. However, the reviewing process can also occur as an unplanned action triggered by an evaluation of either the text or one's own planning (that is, people revise written as well as unwritten thoughts or statements). The sub-processes of revising and evaluating, along with generating, share the special distinction of being able to interrupt any other process and occur at any time in the act of writing.

The Monitor

As writers compose, they also monitor their current process and progress. The **monitor** functions as a writing strategist which determines when the writer moves from one process to the next. For example, it determines how long a writer will continue generating ideas before attempting to write prose. Our observations suggest that this choice is determined both by the writer's goals and by individual writing habits or styles. As an example of varied composing styles, writers appear to range from people who try to move to polished prose as quickly as possible to people who choose to plan the entire discourse in detail before writing a word. Bereiter and Scardamalia have shown that much of a child's difficulty and lack of fluency lies in their lack of an "executive routine" which would promote switching between processes or encourage the sustained generation of ideas.[21] Children for example, possess the skills necessary to generate ideas, but lack the kind of monitor which tells them to "keep using" that skill and generate a little more.

IMPLICATIONS OF A COGNITIVE PROCESS MODEL

A model such as the one presented here is first and foremost a tool for researchers to think with. By giving a testable shape and definition to our observations, we have tried to pose new questions to be answered. For example, the model identifies three major processes (**plan, translate, and review**) and a number of sub-processes available to the writer. And yet the first assertion of this cognitive process theory is that people do not march through these processes in a simple 1, 2, 3 order. Although writers may spend more time in planning at the beginning of a composing session, planning is not a unitary stage, but a distinctive thinking process which writers use over and over during composing. Furthermore, it is used at all levels, whether the writer is making a global plan for the whole text or a local representation of the meaning of the next sentence. This then raises a question: if the process of writing is not a sequence of stages but a set of optional actions, how are these thinking processes in our repertory actually orchestrated or organized as we write? The second point of our cognitive process theory offers one answer to this question.

2. The processes of writing are hierarchically organized, with component processes embedded within other components.

A hierarchical system is one in which a large working system such as composing can subsume other less inclusive systems, such as generating ideas, which in turn contain still other systems, and so on. Unlike those in a linear organization, the events in a hierarchical process are not fixed in a rigid order. A given process may be called upon at any time and embedded within another process or even within another instance of itself, in much the same way we embed a subject clause within a larger clause or a picture within a picture.

For instance, a writer trying to construct a sentence (that is, a writer in the act of **translating**) may run into a problem and call in a condensed version of the entire writing process to help her out (e.g., she might generate and organize a new set of ideas, express them in standard written English, and review this new alternative, all in order to further her current goal of translating). This particular kind of embedding, in which an entire process is embedded within a larger instance of itself, is known technically in linguistics as recursion. However, it is much more common for writers to simply embed individual processes as needed—to call upon them as sub-routines to help carry out the task at hand.

284

Writing processes may be viewed as the writer's tool kit. In using the tools, the writer is not constrained to use them in a fixed order or in stages. And using any tool may create the need to use another. Generating ideas may require evaluation, as may writing sentences. And evaluation may force the writer to think up new ideas.

Figure 2 demonstrates the embedded processes of a writer trying to compose (translate) the first sentence of a paper. After producing and reviewing two trial versions of the sentence, he invokes a brief sequence of planning, translating, and reviewing—all in the service of that vexing sentence. In our example the writer is trying to translate some sketchily represented meaning about "the first day of class" into prose, and a hierarchical process allows him to embed a variety of processes as sub-routines within his overall attempt to translate.

A process that is hierarchical and admits many embedded sub-processes is powerful because it is flexible: it lets a writer do a great deal with only a few relatively simple processes—the basic ones being **plan**, **translate**, and **review**. This means, for instance, that we do not need to define "revision" as a unique stage in composing, but as a thinking process that can occur at any time a writer chooses to evaluate or revise his text or his plans. As an important part of writing, it constantly leads to new planning or a "re-vision" of what one wanted to say.

Embedding is a basic, omni-present feature of the writing process even though we may not be fully conscious of doing it. However, a theory of composing that only recognized embedding wouldn't describe the real complexity of writing. It wouldn't explain *why* writers choose to invoke the processes

Figure 2   An example of embedding.

(Plan)   Ok, first day of class. . . . . just jot down a possibility.

(Translate)   *Can you imagine what your first day of a college English class will be like?*

(Review)   I don't like that sentence, it's lousy—sounds like theme talk.

(Review)   Oh Lord—I get closer to it and I get closer—

(Plan)   Could play up the sex thing a little bit

(Translate)   *When you walk into an English class the first day you'll be interested, you'll be thinking about boys, tasks, and professor—*

(Review)   That's banal—that's awful.

285

they do or how they know when they've done enough. To return to Lee Odell's question, what guides the writers' decisions and choices and gives an overall purposeful structure to composing? The third point of the theory is an attempt to answer this question.

3. Writing is a goal-directed process. In the act of composing, writers create a hierarchical network of goals and these in turn guide the writing process.

This proposition is the keystone of the cognitive process theory we are proposing—and yet it may also seem somewhat counter-intuitive. According to many writers, including our subjects, writing often seems a serendipitous experience, as act of discovery. People start out writing without knowing exactly where they will end up; yet they agree that writing is a purposeful act. For example, our subjects often report that their writing process seemed quite disorganized, even chaotic, as they worked, and yet their protocols reveal a coherent underlying structure. How, then, does the writing process manage to seem so unstructured, open-minded, and exploratory ("I don't know what I mean until I see what I say") and at the same time possess its own underlying coherence, direction, or purpose?

One answer to this question lies in the fact that people rapidly forget many of their own local working goals once those goals have been satisfied. This is why thinking aloud protocols tell us things retrospection doesn't.[22] A second answer lies in the nature of the goals themselves, which fall into two distinctive categories: process goals and content goals. Process goals are essentially the instructions people give themselves about how to carry out the process of writing (e.g., "Let's doodle a little bit." "So . . . , write an introduction." "I'll go back to that later."). Good writers often give themselves many such instructions and seem to have greater conscious control over their own process than the poorer writers we have studied. Content goals and plans, on the other hand, specify all things the writer wants to say or to do to an audience. Some goals, usually ones having to do with organization, can specify both content and process, as in, "I want to open with a statement about political views." In this discussion we will focus primarily on the writer's content goals.

The most striking thing about a writer's content goals is that they grow into an increasingly elaborate network of goals and sub-goals as the writer composes. Figure 3 shows the network one writer had created during four minutes of composing. Notice how the writer moves from a very abstract goal of "appealing to a broad range in intellect" to a more operational definition of that goal, i.e., "explain things simply." The eventual plan to "write

Figure 3   Beginning of a network of goals.

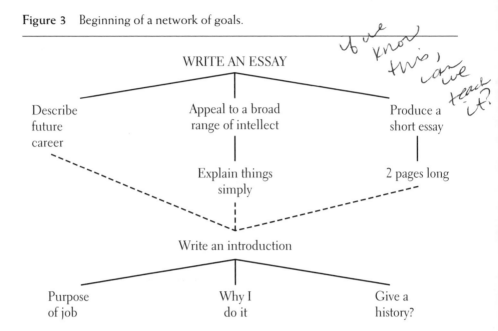

an introduction" is a reasonable, if conventional, response to all three top-level goals. And it too is developed with a set of alternative sub-goals. Notice also how this network is hierarchical in the sense that new goals operate as a functional part of the more inclusive goals above them.

These networks have three important features:

1. They are created as people compose, throughout the entire process. This means that they do not emerge full-blown as the result of "pre-writing." Rather, as we will show, they are created in close interaction with ongoing exploration and the growing text.

2. The goal-directed thinking that produces these networks takes many forms. That is, goal-setting is not simply the act of stating a well-defined end point such as "I want to write a two-page essay." Goal-directed thinking often involves describing one's starting point ("They're not going to be disposed to hear what I'm saying"), or laying out a plan for reaching a goal ("I'd better explain things simply"), or evaluating one's success ("That's banal—that's awful"). Such statements are often setting implicit goals, e.g., "Don't be banal." In order to understand a writer's goals, then, we must be sensitive to the broad range of plans, goals, and criteria that grow out of goal-directed thinking.

Goal-directed thinking is intimately connected with discovery. Consider for example, the discovery process of two famous explorers—Cortez, silent on his peak in Darien, and that bear who went over the mountain. Both, indeed, discovered the unexpected. However, we should note that both chose to climb a long hill to do so. And it is this sort of goal-directed search for the unexpected that we often see in writers as they attempt to explore and consolidate their knowledge. Furthermore, this search for insight leads to new, more adequate goals, which in turn guide further writing.

The beginning of an answer to Odell's question, "What guides composing?" lies here. The writer's own set of self-made goals guide composing, but these goals can be inclusive and exploratory or narrow, sensitive to the audience or chained to the topic, based on rhetorical savvy or focused on producing correct prose. All those forces which might "guide" composing, such as the rhetorical situation, one's knowledge, the genre, etc., are mediated through the goals, plans, and criteria for evaluation of discourse actually set up by the writer.

This does not mean that a writer's goals are necessarily elaborate, logical, or conscious. For example, a simple-minded goal such as "Write down what I can remember" may be perfectly adequate for writing a list. And experienced writers, such as journalists, can often draw on elaborate networks of goals which are so well learned as to be automatic. Or the rules of a genre, such as those of the limerick, may be so specific as to leave little room or necessity for elaborate rhetorical planning. Nevertheless, whether one's goals are abstract or detailed, simple or sophisticated, they provide the "logic" that moves the composing process forward.

3. Finally writers not only create a hierarchical network of guiding goals, but, as they compose, they continually return or "pop" back up to their higher-level goals. And these higher-level goals give direction and coherence to their next move. Our understanding of this network and how writers use it is still quite limited, but we can make a prediction about an important difference one might find between good and poor writers. Poor writers will frequently depend on very abstract, undeveloped top-level goals, such as "appeal to a broad range of intellect," even though such goals are much harder to work with than a more operational goal such as "give a brief history of my job." Sondra Perl has seen this phenomenon in the basic writers who kept returning to reread the assignment, searching, it would seem, for ready-made goals, instead of forming their own. Alternatively, poor writers will depend on only very low-level goals, such as finishing a sentence or correctly spelling a word. They will be, as Nancy Sommers' student revisers were, locked in by the myopia in their own goals and criteria.

Therefore, one might predict that an important difference between good and poor writers will be in both the quantity and quality of the middle range of goals they create. These middle-range goals, which lie between intention and actual prose (cf., "give a brief history" in Figure 3), give substance and direction to more abstract goals (such as "appealing to the audience") and they give breadth and coherence to local decisions about what to say next.

GOALS, TOPIC, AND TEXT

We have been suggesting that the logic which moves composing forward grows out of the goals which writers create as they compose. However, common sense and the folklore of writing offer an alternative explanation which we should consider, namely, that one's own knowledge of the topic (memories, associations, etc.) or the text itself can take control of this process as frequently as one's goals do. One could easily imagine these three forces constituting a sort of eternal triangle in which the writer's goals, knowledge, and current text struggle for influence. For example, the writer's initial planning for a given paragraph might have set up a goal or abstract representation of a paragraph that would discuss three equally important, parallel points on the topic of climate. However, in trying to write, the writer finds that some of his knowledge about climate is really organized around a strong cause-and-effect relationship between points 1 and 2, while he has almost nothing to say about point 3. Or perhaps the text itself attempts to take control, e.g., for the sake of a dramatic opening, the writer's first sentence sets up a vivid example of an effect produced by climate. The syntactic and semantic structure of that sentence now demand that a cause be stated in the next, although this would violate the writer's initial (and still appropriate) plan for a three-point paragraph.

Viewed this way, the writer's abstract plan (representation) of his goals, his knowledge of the topic, and his current text are all actively competing for the writer's attention. Each wants to govern the choices and decisions made next. This competitive model certainly captures that experience of seeing the text run away with you, or the feeling of being led by the nose by an idea. How then do these experiences occur within a "goal-driven process"? First, as our model of the writing process describes, the processes of **generate** and **evaluate** appear to have the power to interrupt the writer's process at any point—and they frequently do. This means that new knowledge and/or some feature of the current text can interrupt the process at any time through the processes of **generate** and **evaluate**. This allows a flexible collaboration among goals, knowledge, and text. Yet this collaboration often culminates in a revision of previous goals. The persistence and functional importance of initially established goals is reflected by a number of signs:

the frequency with which writers refer back to their goals; the fact that writers behave consistently with goals they have already stated; and the fact that they evaluate text in response to the criteria specified in their goals.

Second, some kinds of goals steer the writing process in yet another basic way. In the writers we have studied, the overall composing process is clearly under the direction of global and local *process* goals. Behind the most free-wheeling act of "discovery" is a writer who has recognized the heuristic value of free exploration or "just writing it out" and has chosen to do so. Process goals such as these, or "I'll edit it later," are the earmarks of sophisticated writers with a repertory of flexible process goals which let them use writing for discovery. But what about poorer writers who seem simply to free associate on paper or to be obsessed with perfecting the current text? We would argue that often they too are working under a set of implicit process goals which say "write it as it comes," or "make everything perfect and correct as you go." The problem then is not that knowledge or the text have taken over, so much as that the writer's own goals and/or images of the composing process put these strategies in control.[23]

To sum up, the third point of our theory—focused on the role of the writer's own goals—helps us account for purposefulness in writing. But can we account for the dynamics of discovery? Richard Young, Janet Emig, and others argue that writing is uniquely adapted to the task of fostering insight and developing new knowledge.[24] But how does this happen in a goal-directed process?

We think that the remarkable combination of purposefulness and openness which writing offers is based in part on a beautifully simple, but extremely powerful principle, which is this: *In the act of writing, people regenerate or recreate their own goals in the light of what they learn.* This principle then creates the fourth point of our cognitive process theory.

4. Writers create their own goals in two key ways: by generating goals and supporting sub-goals which embody a purpose; and, at times, by changing or regenerating their own top-level goals in light of what they have learned by writing.

We are used, of course, to thinking of writing as a process in which our *knowledge* develops as we write. The structure of knowledge for some topic becomes more conscious and assertive as we keep tapping memory for related ideas. That structure, or "schema," may even grow and change as a result of library research or the addition of our own fresh inferences. However, writers must also generate (i.e., create or retrieve) the unique goals which guide their process.

290

In this paper we focus on the goals writers create for a particular paper, but we should not forget that many writing goals are well-learned, standard ones stored in memory. For example, we would expect many writers to draw automatically on those goals associated with writing in general, such as, "interest the reader," or "start with an introduction," or on goals associated with a given genre, such as making a jingle rhyme. These goals will often be so basic that they won't even be consciously considered or expressed. And the more experienced the writer the greater this repertory of semi-automatic plans and goals will be.

Writers also develop an elaborate network of working "sub-goals" as they compose. As we have seen, these sub-goals give concrete meaning and direction to their more abstract top-level goals, such as "interest the reader," or "describe my job." And then on occasion writers show a remarkable ability to regenerate or change the very goals which had been directing their writing and planning: that is, they replace or revise major goals in light of what they learned through writing. It is these two creative processes we wish to consider now.

We can see these two basic processes—creating sub-goals and regenerating goals—at work in the following protocol, which has been broken down into episodes. As you will see, writers organize these two basic processes in different ways. We will look here at three typical patterns of goals which we have labeled **"Explore and Consolidate," "State and Develop," "Write and Regenerate."**

EXPLORE AND CONSOLIDATE

This pattern often occurs at the beginning of a composing session, but it could appear anywhere. The writers frequently appear to be working under a high-level goal or plan to explore: that is, to think the topic over, to jot ideas down, or just start writing to see what they have to say. At other times the plan to explore is subordinate to a very specific goal, such as to find out "what on earth can I say that would make a 15-year-old girl interested in my job?" Under such a plan, the writer might explore her own knowledge, following out associations or using more structured discovery procedures such as tagmemics or the classical topics. But however the writer chooses to explore, the next step is the critical one. The writer pops back up to her top-level goal and from that vantage point reviews the information she has generated. She then consolidates it, producing a more complex idea than she began with by drawing inferences and creating new concepts.

Even the poor writers we have studied often seem adept at the exploration part of this process, even to the point of generating long narrative trains of association—sometimes on paper as a final draft. The distinctive thing about good writers is their tendency to return to that higher-level goal and to review and consolidate what has just been learned through exploring. In the act of consolidating, the writer sets up a *new goal* which replaces the goal of explore and directs the subsequent episode in composing. If the writer's topic is unfamiliar or the task demands creative thinking, the writer's ability to explore, to consolidate the results, and to regenerate his or her goals will be a critical skill.

The following protocol excerpt, which is divided into episodes and sub-episodes, illustrates this pattern of **explore and consolidate**.

Episode 1 a, b

In the first episode, the writer merely reviews the assignment and plays with some associations as he attempts to define his rhetorical situation. It ends with a simple process goal—"On to the task at hand"—and a reiteration of the assignment.

(1a) Okay - Um . . . Open the envelope - just like a quiz show on TV - My job for a young thirteen to fourteen teenage female audience - Magazine - *Seventeen*. My job for a young teenage female audience - Magazine - *Seventeen*. I never have read *Seventeen*, but I've referred to it in class and other students have. (1b) This is like being thrown the topic in a situation - you know - in an expository writing class and asked to write on it on the board and I've done that and had a lot of fun with it - so on to the task at hand. My job for a young teenage female audience - Magazine - *Seventeen*.

Episode 2 a, b, c, d

The writer starts with a plan to explore his own "job," which he initially defines as being a teacher and not a professor. In the process of exploring he develops a variety of sub-goals which include plans to: make new meaning by exploring a contrast; present himself or his persona as a teacher; and affect his audience by making them reconsider one of their previous notions. The extended audience analysis of teen-age girls (sub-episode 2c) is in response to his goal of affecting them.

At the end of episode 2c, the writer reaches tentative closure with the statement, "By God, I can change that notion for them." There are significantly long pauses on both sides of this statement, which appears to consolidate much of the writer's previous exploration. In doing this, he dramatically extends his earlier, rather vague plan to merely "compare teachers and professors"—he has regenerated and elaborated his top-level goals. This consolidation leaves the writer with a new, relatively complex, rhetorically sophisticated working goal, one which encompasses plans for a topic, a persona, and the audience. In essence the writer is learning through planning and his goals are the creative bridge between his exploration and the prose he will write.

Perhaps the writer thought his early closure at this point was too good to be true, so he returns at 2d to his initial top-level or most inclusive goal (write about my job) and explores alternative definitions of his job. The episode ends with the reaffirmation of his topic, his persona, and, by implication, the consolidated goal established in Episode 2c.

(2a) Okay lets see - lets doodle a little bit - Job - English teacher rather than professor - I'm doodling this on a scratch sheet as I say it. -ah- (2b) In fact that might be a useful thing to focus on - how a professor differs from - how a teacher differs from a professor and I see myself as a teacher - that might help them - my audience to reconsider their notion of what an English teacher does. (2c) -ah- English teacher - young teen-age female audience - they will all have had English - audience - they're in school - they're taking English - for many of them English may be a favorite subject - doodling still - under audience, but for the wrong reasons - some of them will have wrong reasons in that English is good because its tidy - can be a neat tidy little girl - others turned off of it because it seems too prim. By God I can change that notion for them. (2d) My job for a young teenage female audience - Magazine - *Seventeen*. -ah- Job - English teacher - guess that's what I'll have to go - yeah - hell - go with that - that's a challenge - rather than - riding a bicycle across England that's too easy and not on the topic - right, or would work in a garden or something like that - none of those are really my jobs - as a profession - My job for a young teenage female audience - Magazine - *Seventeen*. All right - I'm an English teacher.

STATE AND DEVELOP

This second pattern accounts for much of the straightforward work of composing, and is well illustrated in our protocol. In it the writer begins with a relatively general high-level goal which he then proceeds to develop or flesh out with sub-goals. As his goals become more fully specified, they form a bridge from his initial rather fuzzy intentions to actual text. Figure 4 is a

Figure 4   Writer developing a set of sub-goals.

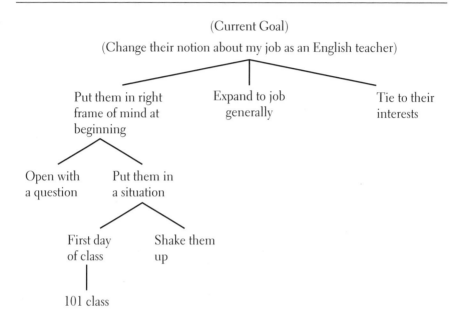

schematic representation of the goals and sub-goals which the writer eventually creates.

Episode 3 a, b, c

The episode starts with a sub-goal directly subordinate to the goal established in Episode 2 (change their notion of English teachers). It takes the pattern of a search in which the writer tries to find ways to carry out his current goal of "get [the audience?] at the beginning." In the process he generates yet another level of sub-goals (i.e., open with a question and draw them into a familiar situation). (A note on our terminology: in order to focus on the overall structure of goals and sub-goals in a writer's thinking, we have treated the writer's plans and strategies all as sub-goals or operational definitions of the larger goal.)

Notice how the content or ideas of the essay are still relatively unspecified. The relationship between creating goals and finding ideas is clearly reciprocal: it was an initial exploration of the writer's ideas which produced these goals. But the writing process was then moved forward by his attempt to flesh out a network of goals and sub-goals, not just by a mere "pre-writing" survey of what he knew about the topic. Episode 3c ends in an effort to test one of his new goals against his own experience with students.

(3a) All right - I'm an English teacher. I want to get at the beginning - I know that they're not going to be disposed - to hear what I'm saying - partly for that reason and partly to put them in the right, the kind of frame of mind I want - I want to open with an implied question or a direct one and put them in the middle of some situation - then expand from there to talk about my job more generally . . . and try to tie it in with their interest. (3b) So one question is where to begin - what kind of situation to start in the middle of - probably the first day of class. . . . They'd be interested - they'd probably clue into that easily because they would identify with first days of school and my first days are raucous affairs - it would immediately shake-em up and get them to thinking a different context. (3c) Okay - so - First day of class - lets see. - Maybe the first 101 class with that crazy skit I put on - that's probably better than 305 because 101 is freshmen and that's nearer their level and that skit really was crazy and it worked beautifully.

WRITE AND REGENERATE

This pattern is clearly analogous to the explore and consolidate pattern, except that instead of planning, the writer is producing prose. A miniature example of it can be seen in Figure 2, in which the writer, whose planning we have just seen, attempts to compose the first sentence of his article for *Seventeen*. Although he had done a good deal of explicit planning before this point, the prose itself worked as another, more detailed representation of what he wanted to say. In writing the sentence, he not only saw that it was inadequate, but that his goals themselves could be expanded. The reciprocity between writing and planning enabled him to learn even from a failure and to produce a new goal, "play up sex." Yet it is instructive to note that once this new plan was represented in language—subjected to the acid test of prose—it too failed to pass, because it violated some of his tacit goals or criteria for an acceptable prose style.

The examples we cite here are, for the purposes of illustration, small and rather local ones. Yet this process of setting and developing sub-goals, and—at times—regenerating those goals is a powerful creative process. Writers and teachers of writing have long argued that one learns through the act of writing itself, but it has been difficult to support the claim in other ways. However, if one studies the process by which a writer uses a goal to generate ideas, then consolidates those ideas and uses them to revise or regenerate new, more complex goals, one can see this learning process in action. Furthermore, one sees why the process of revising and clarifying goals has such a broad effect, since it is through setting these new goals that the fruits of discovery come back to inform the continuing process of writing. In this instance, some of our most complex and imaginative acts can depend on the elegant simplicity of a few powerful thinking processes. We feel that a cognitive process explanation of discovery, toward which this theory is only a start, will have another special strength. By placing emphasis on the inventive power of the writer, who is able to explore ideas, to develop, act on, test, and regenerate his or her own goals, we are putting an important part of creativity where it belongs—in the hands of the working, thinking writer.

NOTES

1. Aristotle, *The Rhetoric,* trans. Lane Cooper (New York: Appleton-Century-Crofts, 1932); Richard Lloyd-Jones, "A Perspective on Rhetoric," in *Writing: The Nature, Development and Teaching of Written Communication,* ed. C. Frederiksen, M. Whiteman, and J. Dominic (Hillsdale, NJ: Lawrence Erlbaum Associates, in press.)

2. Lee Odell, Charles R. Cooper, and Cynthia Courts, "Discourse Theory: Implications for Research in Composing," in *Research on Composing: Points of Departure,* ed. Charles Cooper and Lee Odell (Urbana, IL: National Council of Teachers of English, 1978), p. 6.

3. Lloyd Bitzer, "The Rhetorical Situation," *Philosophy and Rhetoric,* 1 (January, 1968), 1-14.

4. Richard E. Vatz, "The Myth of the Rhetorical Situation," in *Philosophy and Rhetoric,* 6 (Summer, 1973), 154-161.

5. James Britton et al., *The Development of Writing Abilities, 11-18* (London: Macmillan, 1975), p. 39.

6. Gordon Rohman, "Pre-Writing: The Stage of Discovery in the Writing Process," *CCC,* 16 (May, 1965), 106-112.

7. See Britton et al., *The Development of Writing Abilities,* pp. 19-49.

8. Nancy Sommers, "Response to Sharon Crowley, 'Components of the Process,'" *CCC,* 29 (May, 1978), 209-211.

9. Nancy Sommers, "Revision Strategies of Student Writers and Experienced Writers," *CCC,* 31 (December, 1980), 378-388.

10. John R. Hayes, *Cognitive Psychology: Thinking and Creating* (Homewood, IL: Dorsey Press, 1978); Herbert A. Simon and John R. Hayes, "Understanding Complex Task Instruction," in *Cognition and Instruction,* ed. D. Klahr (Hillsdale, NJ: Lawrence Erlbaum Associates, 1976), pp. 269-285.

11. John R. Hayes and Linda S. Flower, "Identifying the Organization of Writing Processes," in *Cognitive Processes in Writing: An Interdisciplinary Approach,* ed. Lee Gregg and Erwin Steinberg (Hillsdale, NJ: Lawrence Erlbaum Associates, 1980), pp. 3-30. Although diagrams of the sort in Figure 1 help distinguish the various processes we wish our model to describe, these schematic representations of processes and elements are often misleading. The arrows indicate that *information* flows from one box or process to another; that is, knowledge about the writing assignment or knowledge from memory can be transferred or

used in the **planning** process, and information from **planning** can flow back the other way. What the arrows *do not mean* is that such information flows in a predictable left to right circuit, from one box to another as if the diagram were a one-way flow chart. This distinction is crucial because such a flow chart implies the very kind of stage model against which we wish to argue. One of the central premises of the cognitive process theory presented here is that writers are constantly, instant by instant, orchestrating a battery of cognitive processes as they integrate planning, remembering, writing, and rereading. The multiple arrows, which are conventions in diagramming this sort of model, are unfortunately only weak indications of the complex and active organization of thinking processes which our work attempts to model.

12. Linda S. Flower and John R. Hayes, "The Cognition of Discovery: Defining a Rhetorical Problem," CCC, 31 (February, 1980), 21-32.

13. Britton et al., *The Development of Writing Abilities*, pp. 61-65.

14. Sondra Perl, "Five Writers Writing: Case Studies of the Composing Process of Unskilled College Writers," Diss. New York University, 1978.

15. Linda S. Flower and John R. Hayes, "The Dynamics of Composing: Making Plans and Juggling Constraints," in *Cognitive Processes in Writing: An Interdisciplinary Approach*, ed. Lee Gregg and Erwin Steinberg (Hillsdale, NJ: Lawrence Erlbaum Associates, 1980), pp. 31-50.

16. Linda S. Flower, "Writer-Based Prose: A Cognitive Basis for Problems in Writing," *College English*, 41 (September, 1979), 19-37.

17. Flower, "The Cognition of Discovery," pp. 21-32.

18. Ellen Nold, "Revising," in *Writing: The Nature, Development, and Teaching of Written Communication*, ed. C. Frederiksen et al. (Hillsdale, NJ: Lawrence Erlbaum Associates, in press).

19. Mina Shaughnessy, *Errors and Expectations* (New York: Oxford University Press, 1977).

20. Marlene Scardamalia, "How Children Cope with the Cognitive Demands of Writing," in *Writing: The Nature, Development and Teaching of Written Communication*, ed. C. Frederiksen et al. (Hillsdale, NJ: Lawrence Erlbaum Associates, in press). Carl Bereiter and Marlene Scardamalia, "From Conversation to Composition: The Role of Instruction in a Developmental Process," in *Advances in Instructional Psychology*, Volume 2, ed. R. Glaser (Hillsdale, NJ: Lawrence Erlbaum Associates, in press).

21. Bereiter and Scardamalia, "From Conversation to Composition."

22. John R. Hayes and Linda Flower, "Uncovering Cognitive Processes in Writing: An Introduction to Protocol Analysis," in *Methodological Approaches to Writing Research*, ed. P. Mosenthal, L. Tamor, and S. Walmsley (in press).

23. Cf. a recent study by Mike Rose on the power of ineffective process plans, "Rigid Rules, Inflexible Plans, and the Stifling of Language: A Cognitivist's Analysis of Writer's Block," CCC, 31 (December, 1980), 389-400.

24. Janet Emig, "Writing as a Mode of Learning," CCC, 28 (May, 1977), 122-128; Richard E. Young, "Why Write? A Reconsideration," unpublished paper delivered at the convention of the Modern Language Association, San Francisco, California, 28 December 1979.

Cognitive Development and the Basic Writer

Andrea A. Lunsford

In her article, "Writing as a Mode of Learning," Janet Emig argues that

> Writing . . . connects the three major tenses of our experience to make meaning. And the two major modes by which these three aspects are united are the processes of analysis and synthesis: analysis, the breaking of entities into their constituent parts; and synthesis, combining or fusing these, often into fresh arrangements or amalgams.[1]

I agree with Professor Emig, and her work as well as that of Mina Shaughnessy has led me to ponder the relationship of writing and the processes of analysis and synthesis to the teaching of basic writers. In general, my study of basic writers—their strategies, processes, and products[2]—leads me to believe that they have not attained that level of cognitive development which would allow them to form abstractions or conceptions. That is, they are most often unable to practice analysis and synthesis and to apply successfully the principles thus derived to college tasks. In short, our students might well perform a given task in a specific situation, but they have great difficulty abstracting from it or replicating it in another context.

Let me offer one concrete example to illustrate this point. Asked to read ten consecutive issues of a comic strip, choose one of the major characters, and infer the basic values of that character from the information provided in the ten issues, typical basic writing students find it almost impossible to articulate anything about the values of characters unlike themselves. In short, they have problems drawing inferences or forming concepts based on what they have read. Instead, they tend either to describe the characters or, more

Reprinted from *College English* 41.1 (September 1979): 449–59. Used with permission.

typically, to drop the comic strip character after a few sentences and shift to what they see as their own values. When I first began teaching basic writers, their response to this type of assignment gave me the first hint of how their difficulties were related to cognitive development.

In *Thought and Language,* the Russian psychologist Lev Vygotsky identifies three basic phases in the ascent to concept formation: the initial syncretic stage, in which "word meaning denotes nothing more to the child than a vague syncretic conglomeration of individual objects that have . . . coalesced into an image"; the "thinking in complexes" stage during which "thought . . . is already coherent and objective . . . , although it does not reflect objective relationships in the same way as conceptual thinking"; and, finally, the true-concept formation stage.[3] Vygotsky cautions, however, that

> even after the adolescent has learned to produce concepts, . . . he does not abandon elementary forms; they continue for a long time to operate, indeed to predominate, in many areas of his thinking. . . . The transitional character of adolescent thinking becomes especially evident when we observe the actual functioning of the newly acquired concepts. Experiments specially devised to study the adolescent's operations bring out. . . a striking discrepancy between his ability to form concepts and his ability to define them. (p. 79)

Vygotsky goes on to distinguish between "spontaneous" concepts, those which are formed as a result of ordinary, day-to-day experiences, and "scientific" concepts, which are formed largely in conjunction with instruction. The student described above by Vygotsky is like my basic writing students confronted with the comic strips in that they all are able to formulate spontaneous concepts, but not able to remove themselves from such concepts, to abstract from them, or to define them into the scientific concepts necessary for successful college work. In my experience, basic writing students most often work at what Vygotsky calls the "thinking in complexes" stage and the spontaneous-concept stage rather than at the true-concept formation stage. While these writers may have little difficulty in dealing with familiar everyday problems requiring abstract thought based on concepts, they are *not aware of the processes they are using.* Thus they often lack the ability to infer principles from their own experience. They are not forming the "scientific concepts" which are basic to mastery of almost all college material.

Jean Piaget categorizes mental development basically into four stages: the sensori-motor stage; the pre-operational stage; the concrete-operations stage; and the formal-operations stage characterized by the ability to abstract, synthesize, and form coherent logical relationships.[4] At the stage of concrete operations, the child's thought is still closely linked to concrete data; completely representational, hypothetical, or verbal thought still eludes him. As the child moves through the stages of cognitive development, he goes through what Piaget calls the process of "de-centering," a process further defined by Lee Odell as "getting outside one's own frame of reference, understanding the thoughts, values, feelings of another person; . . . projecting oneself into unfamiliar circumstances, whether factual or hypothetical; . . . learning to understand why one reacts as he does to experience."[5] Although children first begin to "de-center" as early as the pre-operational stage, egocentricity is still strong in the concrete stage, and, indeed, we apparently continue the process of "de-centering" throughout our lives.

The relationship of Piaget's concrete stage to Vygotsky's "thinking in complexes" stage and "spontaneous-concept formation" stage is, I believe, clear. Furthermore, the work of both Piaget and Vygotsky strongly indicates that cognitive development moves first from doing, to doing consciously, and only then to formal conceptualization. As Eleanor Duckworth says in an essay in *Piaget in the Classroom*, "thoughts are our way of connecting things up for ourselves. If somebody else tells us about the connections he has made, we can only understand him to the extent that we do the work of making those connections ourselves."[6] This notion is directly related to the highly influential work of Gilbert Ryle. In *The Concept of Mind* (New York: Barnes and Noble, 1949), Ryle makes his crucial distinction between knowing *how* and knowing *that*.

> Learning *how* or improving in ability is not like learning *that* or acquiring information. Truths can be imparted, procedures can only be inculcated, and while inculcation is a gradual process, imparting is relatively sudden. It makes sense to ask at what moment someone became apprised of a truth, but not to ask at what moment someone acquired a skill. "Part-trained" is a significant phrase, "part-informed" is not. Training is the art of setting tasks which the pupils have not yet accomplished but are not any longer quite incapable of accomplishing. . . . Misunderstanding is a by-product of knowing how. Only a person who is at least a partial master of the Russian tongue can make the wrong sense of a Russian expression. Mistakes are exercises of competences. (pp. 59-60)

Chomsky's distinction between "competence" and "performance" has similar implications. Chomsky's views as expressed in *Aspects of the Theory of Syntax* (Cambridge, Mass.: MIT Press, 1965) can be used to argue against the notion that "language is essentially an adventitious construct, taught by 'conditioning' . . . or by a drill and explicit explanation" (p. 51). In other words, students learn by doing and *then* by extrapolating principles from their activities. This theory informs an educational model proposed by James Britton in a recent lecture at Ohio State University (and based on his 1970 *Language and Learning*). Essentially, this paradigm incorporates learning by doing as opposed to learning solely by the study of abstract principles or precepts.

Britton's model is closely related to that articulated in Michael Polanyi's discussion of skills in *Personal Knowledge* (New York: Harper and Row, 1964). Polanyi begins his discussion by citing "the well-known fact that the *aim of a skillful performance is achieved by the observance of a set of rules which are not known as such to the person following them*" (p. 49). Polanyi uses examples of the person who rides a bicycle, keeps afloat in the water, or plays a musical instrument without at all comprehending the underlying rules. "Rules of art can be useful," Polanyi says, "but they do not determine the practice of an art; they are maxims, which can serve as a guide to an art only if they can be integrated into the practical knowledge" (p. 50). Polanyi goes on to discuss the importance of apprenticeship in acquiring a skill or an art, by which he means that we learn by doing *with* a recognized "master" or "connoisseur" better than by studying or reading about abstract principles. Vygotsky puts it quite succinctly: "What a child can do in cooperation today he can do alone tomorrow. Therefore the only good kind of instruction is that which marches ahead of development and leads it; it must be aimed not so much at the ripe as at the ripening functions" (*Thought and Language*, p. 104).

I have attempted this very cursory theoretical review partially in support of the premise asserted at the beginning of my essay: that most of our basic writing students are operating well below the formal-operations or true-concept formation stage of cognitive development, and hence they have great difficulty in "de-centering" and performing tasks which require analysis and synthesis. But once we are convinced that our basic writing students are most often characterized by the inability to analyze and synthesize, what then? How can we, as classroom teachers, use what we know about theory and about our students' levels of cognitive development to guide the ways in which we organize our basic writing classes and create effective assignments?

The theory reviewed above offers, I believe, a number of implications which will help us answer these questions. First, basic writing classes should never be teacher-centered; set lectures should always be avoided. Instead, the classes should comprise small workshop groups in which all members are active participants, apprentice-writers who are "exercising their competence" as they learn *how* to write well. Class time should be spent writing, reading what has been written aloud to the group/audience, and talking about that writing.

Such sessions require an atmosphere of trust, and they demand careful diagnosis and preparation by the teacher. But these suggestions offer only a very general guide. Exactly *what* preparation should the basic writing teacher do?

The best way to move students into conceptualization and analytic and synthetic modes of thought is to create assignments and activities which allow students to practice or exercise themselves in these modes continuously. While an entire course plan would take more space than is available here, I can offer a series of examples, from activities focusing on grammatical categories and sentence-building to essay assignments, each of which is designed to foster conceptualization and analytic thinking.

One reason drill exercises have so often failed to transfer a skill into a student's own writing is that the student is operating below the cognitive level at which he or she could abstract and generalize a principle from the drill and then apply that principle to enormously varied writing situations. Memorizing precepts has been equally ineffective. Instead of either one, why not present students with a set of data, from their own writing or from that of someone else, and help them approach it inductively? Following is an exercise on verb recognition which attempts to engage students in inferential reasoning.

RECOGNIZING VERBS

Read the following sentences, filling in the missing word(s) in each one:

a. The cow _____ over the moon.

b. The farmer _____ a wife.

c. Jack Sprat _____ _____ no fat; his
wife _____ _____ no lean.

d. Jack Horner _____ in a corner.

e. Jack _____ over the candlestick.

f. Don't _____ on my blue suede shoes.

g. The cat _____ away with the spoon.

h. Sunshine on my shoulder _____ me happy.

i. Little Miss Muffett _____ on a tuffet.

j. He _____ for his pipe, and he _____ for
his fiddlers three.

k. The three little kittens _____ their mittens.

l. Little Boy Blue, come _____ your horn.

m. They all _____ in a yellow submarine.

n. The three little pigs _____ to market.

o. Jack and Jill _____ up the hill.

p. One _____ over the cuckoo's nest.

q. Everywhere that Mary _____ the lamb was sure to _____

Whether or not you recognize the songs and rhymes these sentences come from, you will have filled in the blanks with VERBS. Look back over the verbs you have used, and then list five other lines from songs or rhymes and underline the verbs in them.

1.
2.
3.
4.
5.

Now try your hand at formulating the rest of the following definition: Verbs are words which _____

_____

You may have noted in your definition that verbs *do something;* or you may have remembered learning a traditional definition of verbs. No matter what definition we come up with, though, verbs are essential to our communication: they complete or comment on the subjects of our sentences. Now revise your definition so that it includes the major *function* which verbs have in sentences:

_____

_____

CHARACTERISTICS OF VERBS

In this assignment, your job is to discover some major characteristics of verbs. To find the first one, begin studying the following lists of verbs. Then try to determine what characterizes each group. How do the groups differ?

Group One	*Group Two*	*Group Three*
break	prayed	will go
sweep	climbed	will run
strikes	altered	will fall
say	passed	will listen
heeds	dug	will look
catch	failed	will move
engages	wrote	will organize
operates	chose	will win
arrests	swore	will answer
play	questioned	will ride
reads	promised	will act
study	gave	will sing

Can you state what characterizes each group? _____

_____

_____

If you are having difficulty answering this question, try answering the next three questions first.

The action named by the verbs in Group One takes place at what time?

_____

The action named by the verbs in Group Two takes place at what time?

_____

The action named by the verbs in Group Three takes place at what time?

_____

Now go back and fill in an answer to the first question about what characterizes each group.

By now, you will have been able to identify the TENSE of the verbs in the three groups. Tense, or relation to time, is one of the major characteristics of verbs; it distinguishes them from other kinds of words such as nouns. Do you know the names of the three tenses represented in Group One, Group Two, and Group Three?

This same inductive or analytic approach can be applied to any grammatical concept or convention we wish our students to become familiar with. Rather than asking students to memorize the functions of the semi-colon, for instance, workshop groups can be presented with a passage or short essay which uses semi-colons frequently. The students' task is to isolate those sentences which use semi-colons and then draw some conclusions based on their data: they might be asked to group sentences which use semi-colons in the same way, to define the semi-colon, etc. Whatever the task, the group will be engaged in inferential problem-solving rather than in isolated drill or memorization. In Vygotsky's terms, analytic thinking is the "ripening function" we are attempting to foster.

In spite of their general effectiveness, sentence-combining drills will often fail to transfer new patterns into the basic writer's own writing—unless the sentence-combining work helps build inferential bridges. The sequential sentence-combining exercise below is designed to give students practice in inferring and analyzing. It is based primarily on the ancient practice of *imitatio*, which we would do well to introduce in all of our basic writing classes.

Pattern Sentence: The General Motors assembly line grinds out cars
        swiftly, smoothly, and almost effortlessly.

A. After studying the sentence pattern, combine each of the following sets
of sentences into a sentence which imitates the pattern.

1. The cat eyed its prey.
2. The cat was scruffy.
3. The cat was yellow.
4. The prey was imaginary.
5. The cat eyed it craftily.
6. It eyed it tauntingly.
7. It even eyed it murderously.

---

1. Oil massages you.
2. The oil is bath oil.
3. It is Beauty's oil.
4. The massaging is gentle.
5. The massaging is soothing.
6. The massaging is almost loving.

---

1. We tend to use technologies.
2. The technologies are new.
3. Our use of them is profuse.
4. Our use is unwise.
5. Our use is even harmful.

---

1. H. L. Mencken criticized foibles.
2. The foibles belonged to society.
3. The society was American.
4. The criticism was witty.
5. It was sarcastic.
6. It was often unmerciful.

---

1. The lecturer droned.
2. The lecturer was nondescript.
3. The lecturer was balding.
4. The droning went on and on.
5. The droning was mechanical.
6. It was monotonous.
7. It was interminable.

B. Now fill in appropriate words to complete the following sentence, again being careful to imitate the pattern sentence.

The _____ _____ wins _____
_____ly, _____ly, and almost _____ly.

C. Now write a series of seven sentences and then combine them into one sentence which imitates the pattern sentence. Then write at least one more sentence which imitates the pattern.

Such exercises are not difficult to create; they can easily be adapted to specialized interests of any particular group or class. And they can lead to the kind of paragraph- and theme-length sentence-combining exercises recommended recently by Donald Daiker, Andrew Kerek, and Max Morenberg of Miami of Ohio.[7] Furthermore, such exercises can be supplemented by visual stimuli, pictures or video tapes, which can be used as raw material from which to generate new sentences in imitation of the pattern. But to be maximally effective, sentence-combining exercises must be designed to lead basic writing students to bridge the cognitive gap between imitating and generating.

I have yet to offer any sample essay assignments, but I do not thereby mean to imply that writing whole essays should only occur at or toward the end of a basic writing course. On the contrary, basic writers should begin composing whole paragraphs and essays, practicing the entire process of writing, from the very onset of the course. A pitcher does not practice by articulating one mini-movement at a time but by engaging in an entire, continuous process, from warm-up and mental preparation, to the wind-up, the release, and the follow-through: an analogy, to be sure, but one which I hope is not overly-strained. In addition to having students write paragraphs and essays early in the course, I would like especially to emphasize the importance of working with analytic modes in basic writing classes. Basic writers often fall back on narrative and descriptive modes because these modes are more adaptable to their own experience, or to what Linda Flower has described as "writer-based prose."[8] Yet the work of Ed White in California and of James Britton and his colleagues in England has shown us that little correlation exists in student performance between the spatial and temporal modes of narration and description and the logical and analytic modes of exposition and argumentation. Therefore, the basic writing course that works exclusively on narration and description will probably fail to build the cognitive skills its students will need to perform well in other college courses.

The comic-strip assignment I described earlier in this essay helped me learn that my students needed practice in using and assimilating analytic modes; it also helped me see that I had made several crucial mistakes in giving that assignment. First, I assigned it when the students had had little or no formal practice in inferential reasoning; second, I asked students to do the assignment at home rather than in workshop groups. In short, I ignored one of the lessons both Polanyi and Vygotsky have taught us: that often we learn best by working at a task in cooperation with a "master" or "connoisseur." I have since profited from these mistakes, and that same assignment, properly prepared for by workshop discussion and practice, has proven considerably more effective. Following are two other assignments, one calling for a brief response, the other for a longer essay, which are designed to help students gain control of analytic modes.

WRITING ASSIGNMENT A

Study the following set of data:

1. New York City lost 600,000 jobs between 1969-76.
2. In 1975, twenty buildings in prime Manhattan areas were empty.
3. Between 1970-75, ten major corporations moved their headquarters from New York City to the Sunbelt.
4. In 1976, New York City was on the brink of bankruptcy.
5. Between February, 1977 and February, 1978, New York City gained 9,000 jobs.
6. Since January, 1978, one million square feet of Manhattan floor space has been newly rented.
7. AT&T has just built a $110 million headquarters in New York.
8. IBM has just built an $80 million building at 55th and Madison in New York.
9. Co-op prices and rents have increased since 1977.
10. Even $1 million luxury penthouses are sold out.
11. There is currently an apartment shortage in Manhattan.
12. The President recently signed a bill authorizing $1.65 billion in federal loan guarantees for New York City.

After reading and thinking about the information listed above, how would you describe the current economic trend in New York City? Using your answer to that question as an opening sentence, write a paragraph in which you explain and offer support for your conclusion by using the information provided in the original set of data.

An assignment like the one above, which gives students practice in analyzing, generalizing, and abstracting, can be readily adapted to workshop groups in which discussion, criticism, and revision can take place.

WRITING ASSIGNMENT B

Preparing: Choose a person (but NOT someone you know well) whom you can observe on at least 5-7 occasions. You might choose someone who rides the same bus as you do, or one of your instructors, or someone who is in one of your classes. Be sure that you are on no closer than "how are you today?" terms with the person you choose.

Gathering Data: Arrange the times you can observe your person so that you can make notes during or immediately after the observation. Note down anything that seems important to you. For a start, answer these questions after each observation.

1. What is X wearing? (Be detailed; include colors, types of fabric, etc.)
2. How is X's hair fixed? (What kind of hair-cut, length of hair, style, etc.)
3. What, if anything, does X have with him or her? (Bag, knapsack, purse, books, etc.)
4. What is X doing? (Be as detailed as possible.)
5. What does X say? (Get exact wording whenever you can.)
6. Who does X associate with?
7. What seems to be X's mood?

Grouping Data: Study all your notes. Then group them under the following headings: APPEARANCE, ACTIONS, WORDS.

Analyzing Data: Now study all the information you have categorized. Based on that information, what would you say is X's lifestyle? What does your observation suggest about X's top priorities? What is most important to X?

Writing About your Data: Write a short essay which begins by answering the questions asked under "Analyzing Data." Use the data you have grouped in your notes to explain and support your analysis of the lifestyle and priorities of X.

This assignment begins with workshop discussion; the results of each stage are discussed by the group. Revision, sorting, and excluding are thus continuous, with the teacher helping students move more and more surely from *describing* their subjects to *analyzing* them. To save space, I have omitted the revising stages, which involve group response to and criticism of the essays and which vary, of course, with the particular difficulties encountered by each group.

Writing projects based on inference-drawing and conceptualization are easily adapted to almost any topic. I have used excerpts from the *Foxfire* books as the basis for essays in which students draw conclusions and generalize about the people interviewed. David Bartholomae, of the University of Pittsburgh, recommends Studs Terkel's *Working* as the basis for similar assignments building conceptual skills. Role-playing exercises and persona paraphrases offer other effective means of helping students "de-center" and hence gain the distance necessary to effective analysis and synthesis. In fact, it is possible and, I would urge, highly profitable, to build an entire basic writing course on exercises like the ones described above, assignments which "march ahead of development and lead it." If we can do so successfully, and if we can find valid ways to substantiate our success, certainly we will have put all our theory to the best practical use. And as a bonus, we will help to establish what Janet Emig argues is the unique value of writing to the entire learning process.

NOTES

1. "Writing as a Mode of Learning," CCC, 28 (1977), 127.

2. "The Ohio State University Remedial English Pilot Project: Final Report and Follow-Up Study," Ohio State University, 1977, and "An Historical, Descriptive, and Evaluative Study of Remedial English in American Colleges and Universities," Diss. Ohio State University, 1977.

3. Lev Semenovich Vygotsky, *Thought and Language*, trans. Eugenia Hanfmann and Gertrude Vakar (Cambridge, Mass.: MIT Press, 1962), pp. 59-61.

4. *Six Psychological Studies* (New York: Random House, 1967).

5. "Teaching Reading: An Alternative Approach," *English Journal*, 22 (1973), 455.

6. "Language and Thought," in *Piaget in the Classroom*, ed. Milton Schwebel and Jane Raph (New York: Basic Books, 1973), p. 148.

7. *The Writer's Options: College Sentence Combining* (New York: Harper and Row, 1979).

8. Linda Flower and John R. Hayes, "Problem Solving Strategies and the Writing Process," *College English*, 39 (1977), 449-461.

Diving In

An Introduction to Basic Writing

Mina P. Shaughnessy

Basic writing, alias remedial, developmental, pre-baccalaureate, or even handicapped English, is commonly thought of as a writing course for young men and women who have many things wrong with them. Not only do medical metaphors dominate the pedagogy (*remedial, clinic, lab, diagnosis,* and so on), but teachers and administrators tend to discuss basic-writing students much as doctors tend to discuss their patients, without being tinged by mortality themselves and with certainly no expectations that questions will be raised about the state of *their* health.

Yet such is the nature of instruction in writing that teachers and students cannot easily escape one another's maladies. Unlike other courses, where exchanges between teacher and student can be reduced to as little as one or two objective tests a semester, the writing course requires students to write things down regularly, usually once a week, and requires teachers to read what is written and then write things back and every so often even talk directly with individual students about the way they write.

This system of exchange between teacher and student has so far yielded much more information about what is wrong with students than about what is wrong with teachers, reinforcing the notion that students, not teachers, are the people in education who must do the changing. The phrase "catching up," so often used to describe the progress of BW students, is illuminating here, suggesting as it does that the only person who must move in the teaching situation is the student. As a result of this view, we are much more likely

Reprinted from *College Composition and Communication* 27.3 (October 1976): 234–39.
Used with permission.

in talking about teaching to talk about students, to theorize about *their* needs and attitudes or to chart *their* development and ignore the possibility that teachers also change in response to students, that there may in fact be important connections between the changes teachers undergo and the progress of their students.

I would like, at any rate, to suggest that this is so, and since it is common these days to "place" students on developmental scales, saying they are eighth-graders or fifth-graders when they read and even younger when they write or that they are stalled some place on Piaget's scale without formal propositions, I would further like to propose a developmental scale for teachers, admittedly an impressionistic one, but one that fits the observations I have made over the years as I have watched traditionally prepared English teachers, including myself, learning to teach in the open-admissions classroom.

My scale has four stages, each of which I will name with a familiar metaphor intended to suggest what lies at the center of the teacher's emotional energy during that stage. Thus I have chosen to name the first stage of my developmental scale GUARDING THE TOWER, because during this stage the teacher is in one way or another concentrating on protecting the academy (including himself) from the outsiders, those who do not seem to belong in the community of learners. The grounds for exclusion are various. The mores of the times inhibit anyone's openly ascribing the exclusion to genetic inferiority, but a few teachers doubtless still hold to this view.

More often, however, the teacher comes to the basic-writing class with every intention of preparing his students to write for college courses, only to discover, with the first batch of essays, that the students are so alarmingly and incredibly behind any students he has taught before that the idea of their ever learning to write acceptably for college, let alone learning to do so in one or two semesters, seems utterly pretentious. Whatever the sources of their incompetence—whether rooted in the limits they were born with or those that were imposed upon them by the world they grew up in—the fact seems stunningly, depressingly obvious: they will never "make it" in college unless someone radically lowers the standards.

The first pedagogical question the teacher asks at this stage is therefore not "How do I teach these students?" but "What are the consequences of flunking an entire class?" It is a question that threatens to turn the class into a contest, a peculiar and demoralizing contest for both student and teacher, since neither expects to win. The student, already conditioned to the idea that there is something wrong with his English and that writing is a device for magnifying and exposing this deficiency, risks as little as possible on the page, often straining with what he does write to approximate the academic style and producing in the process what might better be called "written Anguish" rather than English—sentences whose subjects are crowded out by such phrases as "it is my conviction that" or "on the contrary to my opinion," inflections that belong to no variety of English, standard or non-standard, but grow out of the writer's attempt to be correct, or words whose idiosyncratic spellings reveal not simply an increase in the number of conventional misspellings but new orders of difficulty with the correspondences between spoken and written English. Meanwhile, the teacher assumes that he must not only hold out for the same product he held out for in the past but teach unflinchingly in the same way as before, as if any pedagogical adjustment to the needs of students were a kind of cheating. Obliged because of the exigencies brought on by open admissions to serve his time in the defense of the academy, he does if not his best, at least his duty, setting forth the material to be mastered, as if he expected students to learn it, but feeling grateful when a national holiday happens to fall on a basic-writing day and looking always for ways of evading conscription next semester.

But gradually, student and teacher are drawn into closer range. They are obliged, like emissaries from opposing camps, to send messages back and forth. They meet to consider each other's words and separate to study them in private. Slowly, the teacher's preconceptions of his students begin to give way here and there. It now appears that, in some instances at least, their writing, with its rudimentary errors and labored style has belied their intelligence and individuality. Examined at a closer range, the class now appears to have at least some members in it who might, with hard work, eventually "catch up." And it is the intent of reaching these students that moves the teacher into the second stage of development—which I will name CONVERTING THE NATIVES.

As the image suggests, the teacher has now admitted at least some to the community of the educable. These learners are perceived, however, as empty vessels, ready to be filled with new knowledge. Learning is thought of not so much as a constant and often troubling reformulation of the world so as to encompass new knowledge but as a steady flow of truth into a void. Whether the truth is delivered in lectures or modules, cassettes or computers, circles or squares, the teacher's purpose is the same: to carry the technology of advanced literacy to the inhabitants of an underdeveloped country. And so confident is he of the reasonableness and allure of what he is presenting, it does not occur to him to consider the competing logics and values and habits that may be influencing his students, often in ways that they themselves are unaware of.

Sensing no need to relate what he is teaching to what his students know, to stop to explore the contexts within which the conventions of academic discourse have developed, and to view these conventions in patterns large enough to encompass what students do know about language already, the teacher becomes a mechanic of the sentence, the paragraph, and the essay. Drawing usually upon the rules and formulas that were part of his training in composition, he conscientiously presents to his students flawless schemes for achieving order and grammaticality and anatomizes model passages of English prose to uncover, beneath brilliant, unique surfaces, the skeletons of ordinary paragraphs.

Yet too often the schemes, however well meant, do not seem to work. Like other simplistic prescriptions, they illuminate for the moment and then disappear in the melee of real situations, where paradigms frequently break down and thoughts will not be regimented. S's keep reappearing or disappearing in the wrong places; regular verbs shed their inflections and irregular verbs acquire them; tenses collide; sentences derail; and whole essays idle at one level of generalization.

Baffled, the teacher asks, "How is it that these young men and women whom I have personally admitted to the community of learners cannot learn these simple things?" Until one day, it occurs to him that perhaps these simple things—so transparent and compelling to him—are not in fact simple at all, that they only appear simple to those who already know them, that the grammar and rhetoric of formal written English have been shaped by the irrationalities of history and habit and by the peculiar restrictions and rituals that come from putting words on paper instead of into the air, that the sense and nonsense of written English must often collide with the spoken English that has been serving students in their negotiations with the world for many years. The insight leads our teacher to the third stage of his development, which I will name SOUNDING THE DEPTHS, for he turns now to the careful observation not only of his students and their writing but of himself as writer and teacher, seeking a deeper understanding of the behavior called writing and of the special difficulties his students have in mastering the skill. Let us imagine, for the sake of illustration, that the teacher now begins to look more carefully at two common problems among basic writers—the problem of grammatical errors and the problem of undeveloped paragraphs.

Should he begin in his exploration of error not only to count and name errors but to search for patterns and pose hypotheses that might explain them, he will begin to see that while his lessons in the past may have been "simple," the sources of the error he was trying to correct were often complex. The insight leads not inevitably or finally to a rejection of all rules and standards, but to a more careful look at error, to the formulation of what might be called a "logic" of errors that serves to mark a pedagogical path for teacher and student to follow.

Let us consider in this connection the "simple" *s* inflection on the verb, the source of a variety of grammatical errors in BW papers. It is, first, an alien form to many students whose mother tongues inflect the verb differently or not at all. Uniformly called for, however, in all verbs in the third person singular present indicative of standard English, it would seem to be a highly predictable or stable form and therefore one easily remembered. But note the grammatical concepts the student must grasp before he can apply the rule: the concepts of person, tense, number, and mood. Note that the *s* inflection is an atypical inflection within the modern English verb system. Note too how often it must seem to the student that he hears the stem form of the verb after third person singular subjects in what sounds like the present, as he does for example whenever he hears questions like "Does *she want* to go?" or "Can the *subway stop?*" In such sentences, the standard language itself reinforces the student's own resistance to the inflection.

And then, beyond these apparent unpredictabilities within the standard system, there is the influence of the student's own language or dialect, which urges him to ignore a troublesome form that brings no commensurate increase in meaning. Indeed, the very *s* he struggles with here may shift in a moment to signify plurality simply by being attached to a noun instead of a verb. No wonder then that students of formal English throughout the world find this inflection difficult, not because they lack intelligence or care but because they think analogically and are linguistically efficient. The issue is not the capacity of students finally to master this and the many other forms of written English that go against the grain of their instincts and experience but the priority this kind of problem ought to have in the larger scheme of learning to write and the willingness of students to mobilize themselves to master such forms at the initial stages of instruction.

Somewhere between the folly of pretending that errors don't matter and the rigidity of insisting that they matter more than anything, the teacher must find his answer, searching always under pressure for short cuts that will not ultimately restrict the intellectual power of his students. But as yet, we lack models for the maturation of the writing skill among young, native-born adults and can only theorize about the adaptability of other models for these students. We cannot say with certainty just what progress in writing ought to look like for basic-writing students, and more particularly how the elimination of error is related to their over-all improvement.

Should the teacher then turn from problems of error to his students' difficulties with the paragraphs of academic essays, new complexities emerge. Why, he wonders, do they reach such instant closure on their ideas, seldom moving into even one subordinate level of qualification but either moving on to a new topic sentence or drifting off into reverie and anecdote until the point of the essay has been dissolved? Where is that attitude of "suspended conclusion" that Dewey called thinking, and what can one infer about their intellectual competence from such behavior?

Before consigning his students to some earlier stage of mental development, the teacher at this stage begins to look more closely at the task he is asking students to perform. Are they aware, for example, after years of right/wrong testing, after the ACT's and the GED's and the OAT's, after straining to memorize what they read but never learning to doubt it, after "psyching out" answers rather than discovering them, are they aware that the rules have changed and that the rewards now go to those who can sustain a play of mind upon ideas—teasing out the contradictions and ambiguities and frailties of statements?

Or again, are the students sensitive to the ways in which the conventions of talk differ from those of academic discourse? Committed to extending the boundaries of what is known, the scholar proposes generalizations that cover the greatest possible number of instances and then sets about supporting his case according to the rules of evidence and sound reasoning that govern his subject. The spoken language, looping back and forth between speakers, offering chances for groping and backing up and even hiding, leaving room for the language of hands and faces, of pitch and pauses, is by comparison generous and inviting. The speaker is not responsible for the advancement of formal learning. He is free to assert opinions without a display of evidence or recount experiences without explaining what they "mean." His movements from one level of generality to another are more often brought on by shifts in the winds of conversation rather than by some decision of his to be more specific or to sum things up. For him the injunction to "be more specific" is difficult to carry out because the conditions that lead to specificity are usually missing. He may not have acquired the habit of questioning his propositions, as a listener might, in order to locate the points that require amplification or evidence. Or he may be marooned with a proposition he cannot defend for lack of information or for want of practice in retrieving the history of an idea as it developed in his own mind.

Similarly, the query "What is your point?" may be difficult to answer because the conditions under which the student is writing have not allowed for the slow generation of an orienting conviction, that underlying sense of the direction he wants his thinking to take. Yet without this conviction, he cannot judge the relevance of what comes to his mind, as one sentence branches out into another or one idea engenders another, gradually crowding from his memory the direction he initially set for himself.

Or finally, the writer may lack the vocabulary that would enable him to move more easily up the ladder of abstraction and must instead forge out of a nonanalytical vocabulary a way of discussing thoughts about thoughts, a task so formidable as to discourage him, as travelers in a foreign land are discouraged, from venturing far beyond bread-and-butter matters.

From such soundings, our teacher begins to see that teaching at the remedial level is not a matter of being simpler but of being more profound, of not only starting from "scratch" but also determining where "scratch" is. The experience of studenthood is the experience of being just so far over one's head that it is both realistic and essential to work at surviving. But by underestimating the sophistication of our students and by ignoring the complexity of the tasks we set before them, we have failed to locate in precise ways where to begin and what follows what.

But I have created a fourth stage in my developmental scheme, which I am calling DIVING IN in order to suggest that the teacher who has come this far must now make a decision that demands professional courage—the decision to remediate himself, to become a student of new disciplines and of his students themselves in order to perceive both their difficulties and their incipient excellence. "Always assume," wrote Leo Strauss, to the teacher, "that there is one silent student in your class who is by far superior to you in head and in heart." This assumption, as I have been trying to suggest, does not come easily or naturally when the teacher is a college teacher and the young men and women in his class are labeled remedial. But as we come to know these students better, we begin to see that the greatest barrier to our work with them is our ignorance of them and of the very subject we have contracted to teach. We see that we must grope our ways into the turbulent disciplines of semantics and linguistics for fuller, more accurate data about words and sentences; we must pursue more rigorously the design of developmental models, basing our schemes less upon loose comparisons with children and more upon case studies and developmental research of the sort that produced William Perry's impressive study of the intellectual development of Harvard students; we need finally to examine more closely the nature of speaking and writing and divine the subtle ways in which these forms of language both support and undo each other.

The work is waiting for us. And so irrevocable now is the tide that brings the new students into the nation's college classrooms that it is no longer within our power, as perhaps it once was, to refuse to accept them into the community of the educable. They are here. DIVING IN is simply deciding that teaching them to write well is not only suitable but challenging work for those who would be teachers and scholars in a democracy.

William Perry
and Liberal Education

Patricia Bizzell

The work of psychologist William G. Perry, Jr. has attracted much attention recently from college writing teachers who seek a developmental model to inform composition courses and writing-across-the-curriculum programs. To assess Perry's usefulness to writing instruction, I would like first to summarize his work, giving his own interpretation of its significance, and then to say how I think we should, and should not, use it.

After taking a BA in psychology at Harvard College, Perry began his academic career teaching English literature at Williams College. In 1947 he returned to Harvard to head the Bureau of Study Counsel, and there he performed the research that led to the publication of his influential book, *Forms of Intellectual and Ethical Development in the College Years: A Scheme* (New York: Holt, Rinehart, and Winston, 1968). Perry describes how college students pass from childhood to adulthood by moving through nine developmental positions. The shape of this process and the nature of the positions were defined through a series of interviews with Harvard undergraduate men in each of their four years in college.

Perry's nine-position scheme chronicles movement through three world views, "Dualism," "Relativism," and "Commitment in Relativism." The young person typically passes through them in this order, sometimes pausing or backtracking. Each world view shapes value judgments on religion, politics, family relations, and so on. Drawing on the student interviews, Perry depicts each world view primarily in terms of the young person's attitude toward schoolwork.

Reprinted from *College English* 46.5 (September 1984): 447–54. Used with permission.

The first world view, "Dualism," is characterized by the belief that everything in the world can be ordered in one of two categories—right or wrong. These categories are defined by axiomatic statements or "Absolutes," which are possessed by "Authority," adults who have perfect knowledge of the Absolutes. The proper task of Authority is to convey the Absolutes to the ignorant. For the dualist, knowing the world means memorizing the Absolutes and applying them to individual instances. For the student Dualist, education is a process of finding right answers (correct applications of Absolutes), with the help of the teacher (Authority). The student Dualist resists exploring academic problems that have no one right solution, and prefers teachers who supply answers and disciplines in which answers can be securely quantified.

In the second world view, "Relativism," Absolutes either are unknowable or no longer exist. Without them Authority can no longer empower one to categorize the world as right or wrong. In place of these generally applicable standards, selfish interest becomes the basis for each individual's decisions. For the Relativist, knowing the world means devising an individual strategy for survival. For the student Relativist, education is a process of devising persuasive answers, since right answers no longer exist. The teacher judges persuasiveness according to idiosyncratic criteria, not Absolute standards. As the student Relativist learns how to satisfy teachers' demands, he or she enjoys exploring problematic questions and prefers disciplines in which they abound. This student also prefers teachers who do not stand on the (now unfounded) authority of their office but relate personally to the student.

In the third world view, "Commitment in Relativism," the world is still without Absolutes and Authority. Nevertheless, it is not without order, and decisions need not be based on solitary self-interest. For the Committed Relativist, knowing the world means understanding what has been rendered important by one's family, friends, religious and ethnic traditions, and intellectual interests. These priorities derived from social surroundings guide choices about the values that will order one's life, choices that Perry calls "Commitments." As one's Commitments develop, one can make confident judgments of what is better or worse relative to them, while still realizing that other people who have sufficiently examined their values may employ different but valid standards of judgment. For the student Committed Relativist, education is a process of achieving the knowledge necessary for making Commitments. Once Committed to a field of study, this student does not seek right or glib answers; rather he or she tries to start working productively in the chosen field. The teacher is neither Authority nor personal friend during this process, but rather a more experienced fellow worker, or mentor.

Perry does not clearly explain what his developmental scheme describes. Is it a process through which all normal 18- to 21-year-olds can be expected to pass, a process that is automatic, genetically determined? If so, Perry's scheme would extend the developmental scheme put forward for younger children by Jean Piaget. Piaget sees children moving through a series of stages of cognitive activity, from sensori-motor on to formal-operational; this process unfolds independent of a child's particular cultural context. Most researchers in the development of adolescents seek to complete Piaget's scheme, that is, to describe the stages children pass through after puberty; and Perry, too, nods in the direction of Piaget. He suggests that he follows Piaget in the notion that developmental processes repeat themselves on different levels—in other words, that we can expect to find some process in the adolescent analogous to the movement through cognitive stages in the young child.

Perry differentiates his study from Piaget's, however, when he says that *Forms of Intellectual and Ethical Development* focuses on "the level at which a person undertakes the development of his 'philosophical assumptions' about his world" (p. 29). I see two distinctions from Piaget here. First, Perry describes this development as something a person "undertakes"; in other words, it is a process of which the person is conscious and which he or she can guide to some extent. In contrast, Piaget describes cognitive development as unfolding naturally, with only occasional awareness on the child's part that changes are occurring, and without much possibility of anyone, child or observing adult, altering the course of the development. The second distinction follows from this self-conscious aspect of the development Perry describes: what are developed are "philosophical assumptions," not cognitive stages. Philosophical assumptions, I take it, can be examined, revised, and consciously affirmed by their possessor, unlike cognitive stages. Perry puts the phrase in quotation marks to indicate that he does not see the typical undergraduate as a systematic thinker; nevertheless, he wants to use such language because it suggests that the scheme focuses on beliefs consciously held in the mind. The process of developing philosophical assumptions may be analogous to that of developing mature cognitive abilities, but it is not the same kind of process.

But if Perry derives from Piaget only the concept of a developmental process, then what kind of process does Perry's scheme describe? Perry's answer to this question is not clear. I think, however, that in spite of Perry's nod to Piaget, his developmental scheme describes something that does not necessarily happen to all cognitively normal 18- to 21-year-olds. Perry drops many hints that what he is describing is what happens to young people when they receive an education. Furthermore, he suggests that an education-induced developmental process should not be regarded as value-neutral, as we would presumably have to regard a process that unfolded according to some genetic necessity, such as that described by Piaget. Education initiates one into the traditions, habits, and values of a community. Perry's scheme focuses particularly on liberal arts education and the world view it inculcates. Obviously, then, it is possible to pass through the ages of 18 to 21 quite "normally" from the psychological point of view without undergoing this kind of development.

Perry aims in his book to convince us that undergraduates in a liberal arts college do pass through the developmental process he describes, but he also does something more. He tries, I think, to persuade us that this development, although not necessary for normal cognition, is desirable. There is, of course, an implicit argument for the desirability of a developmental process in any work that claims simply to describe such a process. If the process is developmental, then by definition, movement through it must be good and arrest at an early stage bad. The researcher is not supposed to assign such values to the stages being described and therefore is not expected to defend the implicit values. Perry, however, has openly assigned values to his developmental stages: successful completion of a liberal arts education requires moving eventually into the world view of Committed Relativism. Perry must either defend the values or be charged with bias in his research.

Consequently Perry openly states: "The values built into our scheme are those we assume to be commonly held in significant areas of our culture, finding their most concentrated expression in such institutions as colleges of liberal arts, mental health movements, and the like" (p. 45). He understands that these values are "statements of opinion," with which others may differ (p. 45), and that framing these values in a developmental scheme implicitly argues for them by implying that the closer one adheres to them, the more one "grows" (p. 44). But he is unembarrassed at arguing for these values because he believes that they lead ultimately to the truest world view, or as he puts it, "an optimally congruent and responsible address to the present state of man's predicament" (p. 45). Ultimately Perry sees the achievement of this world view as having spiritual significance; he refers several times to his scheme's being a sort of modern-day *Pilgrim's Progress*, and he stresses the courage it takes for young people to win through to the end (see pp. 37, 44).

Perry's scheme, then, charts the creation of, not just any intellectually and ethically mature adult, but precisely "the liberally educated man," a man (or woman) "who has learned to think about even his own thoughts, to examine the way he orders his data and the assumptions he is making, and to compare these with other thoughts that other men might have" (p. 39). Perry characterizes the adult who cannot be self-reflective in this way as "anti-intellectual," even if he or she is otherwise intelligent (p. 39). To develop this kind of self-reflective intellectual maturity, Perry explicitly recommends a pedagogy of pluralism, which forces students to confront opposing views on an issue, forcing them out of the Dualist world view on into Relativism and beyond. Persuasively arguing for this pedagogy, Perry cites Socrates as its first practitioner and finds an American supporter for it in Henry Adams (p. 35). Pluralism is also the pedagogy of Harvard College. Perry recognizes that its pervasiveness at Harvard has conditioned his research results, but he does not seek to claim universality for his results. Rather, he argues for this particular education-induced development. Let other colleges, Perry implies, follow Harvard, as they have done in the past, in defining "the very heart of liberal education" (pp. 35-36).

Perry does not discuss the place of writing in the development for which he argues. He does not say, for example, that a Dualist student will write a particular kind of essay. Indeed, to determine a student's position in the scheme, Perry looks at nothing other than what the student tells the interviewer about his experiences. From the transcript of the interview Perry derives the student's attitudes toward schoolwork, which serve to characterize the positions in the scheme, as I explain above.

These general attitudes toward schoolwork presumably do inform particular kinds of academic performance, however. In a much anthologized essay Perry has distinguished between the attitudes that produce "cow" writing, or data unorganized by theory, and "bull" writing, or theory unsupported by data.[1] He does not use the descriptive terms from his scheme to characterize "cow" and "bull" writers, but he does connect students' papers with their understanding of academic ways of thinking.

With this indirect encouragement from Perry, many writing teachers have found it easy to match typical kinds of student essays with positions in the scheme. For example, a familiar sort of undergraduate essay is the one without an organizing thesis, the essay that is simply a collocation of facts strung together like beads with connectives such as "another" or "next." Typically, too, this kind of essay is either hypercorrect or fraught with errors that seem to have kept the student's attention fixed on the sentence level, so underdeveloped are the ideas in the whole paper. In place of generalizations from data this paper relies on maxims used so uncritically as to strike us as dreadful clicheés. Mina Shaughnessy has found these characteristics in the writing of students at the most "basic" level of approximation to academic discourse (*Errors and Expectations* [New York: Oxford University Press, 1977], pp. 198-202). Building on Shaughnessy's work, Andrea Lunsford finds similar characteristics in the essays of some of her Basic Writers.[2] It seems easy to identify such writing as the work of what Perry calls Dualist students, with their belief in unquestionable Absolutes and their view of education as the collecting of right answers.

Much more research is needed, however, before we can use Perry's scheme to classify kinds of student writing. No doubt there are common kinds of undergraduate essays other than that described above, which seems to fit the scheme so neatly; we do not know whether Perry's scheme can provide an exhaustive explanation of variation in student writing. We should remember that Perry's scheme was based on the experiences of students who were highly successful academically and who were attending one of the most selective liberal arts colleges in the country. Although Shaughnessy and Lunsford, working with students somewhat different from Perry's, found signs in student writing of a development similar to the one he describes (neither of them refers to Perry), we do not know to what extent Perry's scheme can extend its explanatory power across a variety of student abilities, academic preparation, and college experiences. We should also note that Perry provides no timetable for progress through his scheme; nowhere does he suggest that all freshmen can be expected to be Dualists, who then as sophomores and juniors traverse Relativism and achieve Committed Relativism as seniors. The existence of these gaps in our knowledge of the scheme's application to student writing argues against using the scheme to classify student writing in any detailed way.

Furthermore, I would argue that we should not use Perry's scheme as a blueprint for writing curricula. Mechanical applications of Perry's scheme will tend to trivialize it while producing curricula that really tell us nothing new. For example, one freshman composition curriculum based on Perry uses his analysis of Relativism to justify the already familiar recommendation to ask students to read several essays that take opposing views on a controversial issue and then to develop their own argumentative positions.[3] The method is so familiar as already to have been embodied in numberless freshman composition anthologies. Furthermore, because students require prolonged exposure to pluralistic methods in many disciplines, and time to reduce the domain of Dualism, this curriculum does not do justice to the rather elaborate process whereby a student achieves the Relativist world view, according to Perry. Some research has suggested that Dualists make more progress if teachers initially take a nurturing, rather than a challenging, stance with them.[4] Moreover, students who have already achieved Relativism may not be greatly benefited by lessons in recognizing and arguing from opposing views on a controversial issue. Such practice may only entrench them in intransigently held personal views, a mind-set which, according to Perry, often retards students' progress through Relativism to Commitment.

If we agree with Perry that students pass through certain positions on their way to the kind of intellectual maturity valued in liberal arts colleges, it does not necessarily follow that we can get them to progress faster by forcing them to imitate more advanced positions until their brains kick on and hold these positions on their own. We should not, in other words, commit a version of what has come to be known as the "American heresy" with respect to the work of Piaget, that is, the attempt to find ways of moving children faster through the Piagetian levels. Perry's scheme describes the effects of a certain liberal arts curriculum, to be sure—Harvard's—but this does not mean that we can turn the effects into a model of causes for a new curriculum that will perform the same changes more efficiently. To try would be to neglect the emphasis Perry himself places on the function of education as acculturation, not training; inculcation of values, not practice in techniques.

Of what use, then, is Perry's work to college writing teachers? I think his scheme can help us to understand why the differences occur in student writing, even if we cannot apply his classification scheme rigidly. Shaughnessy and Lunsford do not agree on why such differences occur. Shaughnessy suggests that they arise from students' unequal ability to meet the expectations of the academic discourse community. Lunsford argues that the students are at different levels of cognitive development in the Piagetian sense—Basic Writers are "egocentric" (p. 284). Perry's scheme forges a link between these social and cognitive explanations because, as I argued above, he is describing a developmental process that is only analogous to but not identical with Piaget's. Perry's analysis describes the changes in student thinking that result from their socialization into the academic community. The great strength of his scheme is its focus on one important constant in the struggles of all college writers: the intellectual demands of liberal education.

Perry's work should make us realize that as we bring our students through the process of liberal education, we are not simply teaching them to think or to grow up, as we sometimes like to say that we are. Rather, we are teaching them to think in a certain way, to become adults with a certain set of intellectual habits and ethical predilections. We are asking them to accept a certain kind of relation to their culture, from among the range of relations that are possible.

Thus Perry's greatest use to writing teachers is to provide us with a sort of philosophical map of the changes liberal education seeks to induce in our students. Such a map can help us understand that certain typical problems students have with writing in college should be regarded as problems with accepting the academic community's preferred world view, and not necessarily as problems with achieving "normal" cognition. This is supported by the rough match between Perry's scheme and the characteristics Shaughnessy and Lunsford note in the writing of students who are different from those in Perry's research sample.

In short, Perry provides us with a useful picture of the kind of "cultural literacy" required in a liberal arts college. The term "cultural literacy" refers to the objects of knowledge and the ways of thinking that one must master in order to participate in a particular community.[5] Following Perry we come to realize that the academic community requires students to know, for example, not only what Genesis says about the creation of the earth but also what geologists, biologists, and other scientists say about it. A community of religious fundamentalists might require only knowledge of Genesis. Furthermore, the academic community requires students to know how to evaluate competing ideas according to criteria of logical structure, adequate evidence, and so on; this academic way of thinking might not be valued, for instance, in a fundamentalist community in which tradition or the judgment of a revered authority is sufficient to validate arguments.

Literacy in the more usual sense of the ability to read and write is also highly valued in the academic community. Clearly, literacy is not required for participation in every sort of community. Some communities, too, value reading over writing—when there is a sacred text to be chanted, for example. But the academic community places a high value on writing, and Perry can help us see why. The whole thrust of his developmental scheme is toward an increasing distance on the beliefs of one's childhood. These beliefs can no longer be accepted uncritically as Absolutes, once we realize that well-intentioned people may hold beliefs different from our own. As the pedagogical pluralism which Perry recommends widens the students' perspectives, it also fosters relativism by casting their beliefs into comparative relations with those of others.

Many theorists in composition studies have argued that writing is a unique mode of learning precisely because it fosters this kind of distancing.[6] One's ideas can be more easily examined, critiqued in comparison with other views, and reformulated as they are worked out in written form. Learning to write, then, can be seen as a process of learning to think about one's own thinking, a process which may well be unfamiliar to students in their home communities.

Furthermore, Perry's quasi-spiritual tone should remind us that we tend to invest teaching with moral fervor. I submit that most teachers will recognize in themselves a sort of moral repugnance about bad writing, a feeling that students "ought" to be able to organize and develop their ideas better, even while recognizing that this feeling partakes of the irrational blaming of the victim. Given that we do have this moral investment in the objects of knowledge and the ways of thinking that we teach, it seems hypocritical to pretend that academic activity is value-neutral, that we are merely teaching "thinking," not thinking in a certain way. And it seems more respectful to our students to see what we are doing when we teach as attempting to persuade them to accept our values, not simply inculcating our values.

Is this development desirable? The nature of Perry's scheme makes this question inevitable, fortunately. As in all discussions of cultural literacy the issue is, whose culture will be empowered to set the terms of literacy? Writing teachers are already acquainted with one such discussion in the debate over students' right to their own language. Personally, I believe that the kind of cultural literacy whose development is both chronicled and advocated in Perry's scheme is desirable for all students. But I do not want to begin here the lengthy argument that would be needed to defend that view.

Here I would simply like to make the point that our assumptions about the ends of education are strongly culture-bound, as Perry helps us see. Furthermore, Perry gives us a perspective on all college teachers as, in effect, rhetors. To a high degree we persuade students to our values through our use of language, in lectures, textbooks, informal discussions, and writing assignments. Writing-across-the-curriculum programs do not so much create important roles for writing in all disciplines as they render us self-conscious about the role writing already plays. Some college teachers may not be comfortable with the view of themselves as rhetors, preferring to see themselves as investigators, reporters, value-neutral conveyors of truth. Perry's most important contribution to writing instruction may well be the critique he implies of this positivistic view of the teacher's role.

NOTES

1. "Examsmanship and the Liberal Arts," in *Examining at Harvard College*, ed. L. Bramson (Cambridge, Mass.: Faculty of the Arts and Sciences, Harvard University, 1963).

2. "The Content of Basic Writers' Essays," *College Composition and Communication*, 31 (1980), 279-283, 285.

3. This new, experimental composition program was described in a paper presented by Professor Gene Krupa of the University of Iowa at the 1983 Conference on College Composition and Communication. Professor Krupa did not want to draw any conclusions yet about its worth.

4. See, for example, Kiyo Morimoto, "Notes on the Context for Learning," *Harvard Educational Review*, 43 (1973), 245-257.

5. For a definition of the term, and an argument in favor of a cultural literacy similar to that in Perry's scheme, see Richard Hoggart, "The Importance of Literacy," *Journal of Basic Writing*, 3 (1980), 74-87.

6. See, for example, Janet Emig, "Writing as a Mode of Learning," *College Composition and Communication*, 28 (1977), 122-128; and Linda Flower, "Writer-Based Prose: A Cognitive Basis for Problems in Writing," *College English*, 41 (1979), 19-37.

Is Teaching Still Possible?

Writing, Meaning, and Higher Order Reasoning

ANN E. BERTHOFF

In the memorable disquisition with which he begins *Permanence and Change* (Indianapolis, Ind.: Bobbs Merrill, 1954), Kenneth Burke explains how thinking which does not include thinking about thinking is merely problem-solving, an activity carried out very well by trouts.

> Though all organisms are critics in the sense that they interpret the signs about them, the experimental speculative technique made available by speech would seem to single out the human species as the only one possessing an equipment for going beyond the criticism of experience to a criticism of criticism. We not only interpret the characters of events. . . . We may also interpret our interpretations. (pp. 5-6)

That species-specific capacity for thinking about thinking, for interpreting interpretations, for knowing our knowledge, is, I think, the chief resource for any teacher and the ground of hope in the enterprise of teaching reading and writing.

I plan to be cheerful but there is a certain amount of setting aside which needs to be done before I can confidently claim that teaching is still possible. About half my time will go to nay-saying: I want first to assess the hazards of developmental models and the positivist views of language which underwrite them. I will turn then to a consideration of how alternative views of language and learning can help us invent a pedagogy that views reading and writing as interpretation and the making of meaning.

Reprinted from *College English* 46.8 (December 1984): 743–55. Used with permission.

What we have these days is properly described, I think, as a pedagogy of exhortation: "Feel comfortable. . . . Wake up! . . . Find something you're interested in. . . . Get your thesis statement. . . . Say what you really think. . . . Go over your paper and take out all unnecessary words." But exhortation, whether left-wing or right-wing, is not instructive. (No writer ever puts in words which he or she thinks are unnecessary; learning to discover that some *are* is one of the chief challenges in learning to write.) What must supplant the pedagogy of exhortation is a "pedagogy of knowing." The phrase is Paulo Freire's, and he means by it what Socrates, Montessori, Jane Addams, I. A. Richards, Roger Ascham, or other great teachers would have meant, namely, that unless and until the mind of the learner is engaged, no meaning will be made, no knowledge can be won.

What chiefly forestalls our moving from a pedagogy of exhortation to a pedagogy of knowing is a dependence on a view of language which cannot account *for* meaning nor give an account *of* meanings. A positivist conception of language as a "communication medium," as a set of muffin tins into which the batter of thought is poured, leads to question-begging representations and models of the composing process. Understanding what a pedagogy of knowing would involve is prevented by an unhealthy confusion about what development means and a damaging dependence on the stage models which cognitive psychologists have elaborated, supposedly for the benefit of rhetoricians as well as for guidance counsellors, therapists, curriculum designers, and the publishers of values clarification kits.

Let me begin with a passage from an article by a rhetorician who is discussing cross-disciplinary programs.

> Since the early 1970s evidence has been accumulating which suggests that up to fifty percent of the adolescent population in this country fail to make the transition from the concrete operational stage to formal operations by the time they have reached late high school or college age. Judging from this empirical research, it would appear that as many as half of our students from junior high on into adulthood are unable to think abstractly, to process and produce logical propositions.[1]

Three points are notable: First, the Piagetian model, which is of course intended to represent the stages of development of the language and thought of the child, is here applied to the reasoning of young adults; second, "empirical research" is taken as providing evidence in support of certain claims about learning; third, the failure to reach the stage of formal operations is made equivalent to an inability to "think abstractly," which, in turn, is identified as processing and producing logical propositions. These are all misconceptions. The attempt to apply the Piagetian stage model to non-children is futile; the claim that empirical research supports the efficacy of doing so is false; the identification of abstract thought with processing propositions begs the question of what constitutes that process.

What the child does or does not do may look like what the incompetent or deficient or uneducated adult does or does not do, but it does not follow that the two instances are alike so far as motivation or function are concerned. Just so, the savage is not a child; the lunatic is not a poet; the chimp who has been taught sign language cannot be said to be using it as either the hearing or deaf human being does. To see the similarities without noting the differences is to settle for pseudo-concepts, in Vygotsky's phrase.

If we do form a concept of language as not just a medium of communication but a means of making meaning, we preclude a dependence on empirical research to find out what is happening in our classrooms, to see what writers do when they compose. If you start with a working concept of language as a means of making meaning, you are recognizing that language can only be studied by means of language. Understood in such terms as *context, purpose, intention, import, reference, significance, ambiguity, representation,* and so on, linguistic structures or texts or speech acts can only be studied by interpreting the interdependencies of meanings—and by interpreting our interpretations. But if these conceptions are central, what is there for empirical researchers to investigate? Empiricists do not generally recognize that all method, including scientific method, entails interpretation; they do not generally recognize that there are no raw data; there are no self-sufficient facts; there is no context-free evaluation. Their method is not to recognize the fact that all knowledge is mediated and that facts must be formulated, but to proceed as if interpretation were supererogatory. Empirical researchers leave out of account meaning because they have no means of accounting for it. I. A. Richards observed of this kind of investigator that he "does not know how to respect the language."

> He does not yet have a conception of the language which would make it respectable. He thinks of it as a code and has not yet learned that it is an organ—the supreme organ of the mind's self-ordering growth. Despite all his claims to be expert in collecting, reporting, comparing, and systematizing linguistic facts, he has not yet apprehended the greatest of them all: that language is an instrument for controlling our becoming.[2]

Some of the human sciences have seen the folly of denying the very subject which should be at the heart of the study of the language animal, the *animal symbolicum*. The anthropologist Clifford Geertz, in a wonderful essay called "Thick Description," shows just what it means to ask questions about what human beings are doing.[3] He undertakes to explain how context and perspective function in interpretation by subjecting an example of Gilbert Ryle's to analysis: A boy is seen to wink; another boy has a tic which involves his eyelid; a third boy is seen practicing an imitation of the boy with the tic. Try describing these "behaviors," as the empirical researcher would call them, and watch two of them become human acts, motivated and meaningful—and subject to interpretation.

If meaning is set aside in the search for "data," the findings will not then be applicable to the making of meaning. But composition specialists who follow psycholinguistic principles of analysis want to have it both ways: their empirical research requires that meaning be left out of account, but they also want to claim that their findings are relevant to pedagogy. What writers do is thus confused with what psycholinguists want to study. This methodological pitfall is impossible to avoid when the investigator is guided by a conception of language as a code.[4]

The empiricist needs something to measure, and cohesive devices can be counted, once there is a taxonomy. They are a feature of discourse analysis, which is not, as one might have thought, a matter of studying the dialectic of what-is-said and what-is-meant; it is not the analysis of intention and recalcitrant linguistic structures in dialectic, the relationship that makes the representation of meaning possible; it is by no means simply a fancy name for "critical reading": discourse analysis is the study of "information management," "thematic structure," "sentence rules," and, preeminently, of "cohesion." Now the "cohesiveness" of a text is not the same thing as "coherence." Coherence is mentalistic; it isn't there on the page; it cannot be measured and graphed; it can only be interpreted in terms of the emergent meanings of the writer. But for the psycholinguistic investigator, it is not writers who produce texts; texts are created by cohesive devices.

At a recent conference I heard a psycholinguist explain how, in order to foreground the cohesive devices, he had to reduce the role of meaning. The first problem in the design of his experiment was to find a passage or a stretch of discourse in which meaning was not important so that it would be easier to measure the responsiveness of college students to cohesive devices. He spent some time in preparing the text, but I wondered why he didn't simply excise something from any textbook in any discipline published in any year, since they are generally written so that readers will not be irritated or distracted by the need to interpret what is being said in an attempt to understand what was intended.

This kind of empirical research institutionalizes the pedagogy of exhortation: "Does your paper flow? If not, check your transitions. Can your reader follow you? Be sure to give him clues." Thus we get papers full of roadsigns pointing in the wrong direction—*however*, when there is no *however* relationship; *on the other hand*, introducing a faulty parallel; redundancy (the uninstructed writer's only means of emphasis); end linkages—which I call Nixonian Syntactic Ligature—with the beginning of each sentence picking up the exact wording of the end of the preceding sentence. Research on cohesive devices easily seeps into composition theory because it sounds scientific and because anything that lets us count will seem helpful in evaluating what we think we are teaching. But the fact that cohesive ties may be identified and classified can easily distract us from the problem of learning how to help writers discover, in the very act of realizing their intentions, the discursive power of language itself, what Edward Sapir meant by calling language heuristic. Empirical research into "discourse acquisition" is likely, I think, to mislead us—to lead us away from thinking about thinking, to keep us from studying the process whereby writers discover the resources of language and learn to control them in the making of meaning.[5]

The challenge to experimental design should be not to reduce meaning or to try to eliminate it; this is a primitive conception of what disembedding involves. The challenge to experimental design is not to dispense with meaning but to control language so that there are not too many meanings at a time; so that the learners can discern, in I. A. Richards' words, "the partially parallel task" (*Speculative Instruments*, p. 96) when they confront it; so that the teacher, by means of a careful sequence of lessons or assignments, can assure that the students are conscious of their minds in action, can develop their language by means of exercising deliberate choice. Positivists see no virtue whatsoever in consciousness of consciousness since they model conceptualization on motor skills—and everybody knows that there consciousness becomes self-consciousness: you'll fall off the bicycle if you think hard about what you're doing. What is forgotten is that wherever language is concerned we are dealing with symbolic acts. Consciousness there is not that "self" consciousness which is so destructive but Freire's "conscientization" or Burke's "interpretation of our interpretations" or Richards' "comprehending our comprehensions more comprehensively" or Coleridge's "knowing our knowledge" or Cassirer's "confrontation of an act of awareness" and so on. Consciousness of consciousness is entailed in our activity as language animals.

If psychologists would read Susanne K. Langer's *Mind: An Essay on Human Feeling*, they would have a clearer idea of what they are about. Or they could read a little phenomenology, but psychology is usually about a generation behind. Thus psychologists have recently taken up structuralism, just as it's being laid to rest elsewhere. And before that it was operationalism, which fed itself on hard data. Robert Oppenheimer, in a brilliant talk to the American Psychological Association in 1955, urged the members not to mimic a determinist physics "which is not there any more" ("Analogy in Science," reprinted in *Reclaiming the Imagination*, pp. 189-202). He suggested, rather, that they listen to a man named Jean Piaget. Nowadays, when psychology is awash in Piagetian concepts, it is hard to imagine that this warning was necessary, but Oppenheimer realized that those in charge were the successors to those whom William James had called "brass instrument psychologists." Oppenheimer said: "I make this plea not to treat too harshly those who tell you a story, having observed carefully without having established that they are sure that the story is the whole story and the general story" (p. 201).

The story Piaget had to tell was certainly interesting, but it isn't the whole story or the general story, and some psychologists, by examining Piaget's experimental designs very carefully, have shown how and where he went wrong. I call your attention to an excellent little book, *Children's Minds*, by Margaret Donaldson (New York: Norton, 1979). (She is neither polemical about Piaget nor worshipful of some anti-Piaget.) Dozens of experiments are described which offer alternative explanations of children's responses to certain questions and situations designed to test their cognitive skills. They clearly establish that Piaget's findings, in instance after instance, are the artifacts of his procedures. The alleged incapacity to "decenter" is seen to be a matter of difficulty in locomotion and movement and not in a lack of "object concept" or an incapacity to entertain other points of view. It seems clear that children who made "egocentric" responses in various experiments of Piaget did not fully understand what they were supposed to do.

Margaret Donaldson writes in one of the summaries:

> Children are not at any stage as egocentric as Piaget has claimed . . . [they] are not so limited in ability to reason deductively as Piaget—and others— have claimed. . . . There is no reason to suppose that [the child] is born with an 'acquisitive device' which enables him to structure and make sense of the language he hears while failing to structure and make sense of the other features of his environment. (pp. 55-56)

The recent corrective experiments she discusses are fascinating, but there are precedents. What Margaret Donaldson's psychologists have done for the semantics and syntax of Piagetian questions, Rudolf Arnheim did for visual representation in Piagetian problems. Ever alert to the powers of visual thinking, Arnheim illustrates what he calls "visual illiteracy" with a pair of drawings in cross section of a water tap in open and closed position, schematic representations used in one of Piaget's perceptual problems. In a series of devastating questions in *Visual Thinking* (Berkeley: University of California Press, 1969) he points out the ambiguities and concludes as follows:

> I am not denying that a person, immunized and warned by years of exposure to mediocre textbook illustrations, mail order catalogues, and similar products of visual ineptness, can figure out the meaning of these drawings, especially if helped by verbal explanation. But surely, if a child passes the test he does so in spite of the drawing, not with the help of it; and if he fails, he has not shown that he does not understand the working of a tap. He may simply be unable to extricate himself from a visual pitfall. (p. 312)

But of course the centrally important critique of Piaget's work came from Lev Vygotsky as early as 1932. Vygotsky's strictures concern not only the relationship of language and thought but also that of learning and instruction.[6] All study of language and thought, Vygotsky argued, must begin with the "unit of meaning," since neither language as element nor thought as element can be apprehended in its real character without the context provided by the other. Speech is not articulated sound plus intention; it is not speech until and unless it is meaningful. Neither language nor thought is meaningful outside a social context—which is to say that purpose and intention are from the first constrained not by a need for "communication" but by a need for representation, which of course invites and demands interpretation. Language is symbolic activity and from the first establishes itself in a social setting. The crucial difference between Vygotsky's procedures and Piaget's is that language is built into Vygotsky's test design and the tester is actively involved in exchanges with the subject. Piaget, Vygotsky thought, did not appreciate the complex dialectic of the learning curve and the role of instruction. The explanation for the misleading questions and the ambiguous directions is to be sought in the fact that Piaget thought that the only way to test cognitive skills was to isolate them as far as possible from language-dependent settings. The failure to understand the interdependence of language and thought is consonant with the misconception of the role of instruction which, like test design, is considered by Piaget in mechanistic terms.

Why should we care about Piaget and his critics? Don't we have enough to do, taking care of course design and teacher training and writing across the curriculum and trying to assure the survival of departments of English and to assuage deans who are counting FTE's—don't we have enough to do without worrying over arguments which may or may not be intelligible or important? The answer is that if we don't understand the grounds for a critical appraisal of theories of cognitive development, if we let our practice be guided by whatever we are told has been validated by empirical research, we will get what we have got: a conception of learning as contingent on development in a straightforward, linear fashion; of development as a pre-set program which is autonomous and does not require instruction; of language as words used as labels; of meaning as a one-directional, one-dimensional attribute; of the human mind as an adaptive mechanism. Thus are we wrecked on the rocks of teaching seen as intervention; of the so-called student-centered classroom; of single-skill correction; of discourse analysis, in which the chief function of discourse is disregarded; of reading instruction in which language is considered solely as a graphic code; of writing seen as the assignment of topics sequenced according to the commonplaces of classical rhetoric, as interpreted by associationist psychology: narrative before description, compare-contrast separate from definition, expression way before exposition; an affective English 101 (Turn off your mind and float downstream) and a cognitive English 102 (Get your thesis statement! Generalize! Be brief! Don't generalize!).

Developmental models uncritically deployed lead to the kind of judgment exemplified in the final sentence of the text I took as my point of departure, the one stating that students can't think abstractly, that they can't "produce or process logical propositions." We should not be surprised that this writer goes on to say that "It is fairly obvious from work done in psychology that we cannot accelerate the transition from concrete to formal operations." What is surprising is the rest of the sentence: "but we may be able to promote its natural development by creating a more natural classroom environment" (Freisinger, p. 163). Why would we aim to promote its "natural development" if we don't think we can "accelerate the transition" to a stage now long overdue? Yet I am cheered by this absurd contradiction, cheered according to the same logic by which Gide was led to praise hypocrisy as a step in the right direction. I think the writer is a better teacher than the theory he explicitly depends on lets him be; so he discards it! He finds another which allows him to speak of promoting natural development in a natural environment. That sounds like somebody who believes that teaching is still possible!

I am now ready to be cheerful. The first piece of good news is that what college students find difficult—what everybody finds difficult, what diplomats and doctors, of medicine and of philosophy, find difficult, is not *abstraction* but *generalization*. These acts of mind are conflated by positivists, but they are not the same. Abstraction is not generalization. This is not a quibble; if it were, our enterprise would be futile and the very idea of education fatuous.

Abstraction is natural, normal: it is the way we make sense of the world in perception, in dreaming, in all expressive acts, in works of art, in all imagining. Abstraction is the work of the active mind; it is what the mind does as it forms. The name for this power of mind used to be imagination. We do not have to teach it: it is the work of our Creator. It is a God-given power or, if you prefer, it is a specific power the *animal symbolicum* has in lieu of a repertory of instincts which obviate the necessity of interpreting interpretations. We do not have to teach abstraction. What we do have to do is to show students how to reclaim their imaginations so that "the prime agent of all human perception" can be for them a living model of what they do when they write. What we must learn to do, if we are to move from the pedagogy of exhortation to a pedagogy of knowing, is to show our students how to use what they already do so cleverly in order to learn how to generalize—how to move from abstraction in the non-discursive mode to discursive abstraction, to generalization. We must strive to "raise implicit recognitions to explicit differentiations": that phrase comes from a book called *The Philosophy of Rhetoric*, published nearly fifty years ago by I. A. Richards. We do not yet have a philosophy of rhetoric, for the very good reason that we, teachers of reading and writing and those responsible for literacy at all levels, have not "taken charge of the criticism of our own assumptions," as Richards urged. The second piece of good news is that there is a semiotics which can guide that enterprise.

It starts from a triadic rather than a dyadic conception of the sign and you can represent it rather easily by drawing two triangles. Draw first an equilateral triangle, pointing upward. At the southwest corner write "Writer or encoder"; at the southeast, write "Audience or decoder" and at the top, write "Message." This constitutes what positivist rhetoricians call the triangle of discourse: It is worthless. As you can easily see, it leaves out purpose, meaning, and intention; it confuses message with signal. Now draw another equilateral triangle and make the base a dotted line. Label the southwest angle "representamen or symbol"; the southeast angle, "object or referent"; at the apex, write "interpretant or reference." You can get from the symbol to what it represents only by means of a meaning, a mediating idea. This curious triangle represents the triadicity central to C. S. Peirce's *semeiotics* and it appears in *The Meaning of Meaning* (New York: Harcourt, Brace, 1944) by Ogden and Richards, a work first published in 1922. I know of no evidence that Vygotsky had read either Peirce or Ogden and Richards, but the triangle with the dotted line appears in an excellent paper of his on symbolization as mediated activity, first published in 1930 ("Mind in Society," reprinted in *Reclaiming the Imagination*, pp. 61-72).

Triadicity is an idea whose time has surely come. It can help us take charge of the criticism of our assumptions about teaching because in the triadic conception of the sign, the symbol-user, the knower, the learner is integral to the process of making meaning. The curious triangle, by thus representing the mediating function of interpretation, can serve as an emblem for a pedagogy of knowing. Indeed, my third piece of good news is that triadicity can help us reclaim imagination and the idea of language as "the supreme organ of the mind's self-ordering growth." I will conclude now with a sketch of this view of language and how it can lead us towards an authentic pedagogy of knowing.

Language seen as a means of making meaning has two aspects, the hypostatic and the discursive. By naming the world, we hold images in mind; we remember; we can return to our experience and reflect on it. In reflecting, we can change, we can transform, we can envisage. Language thus becomes the very type of social activity by which we might move towards changing our lives. The hypostatic power of language to fix and stabilize frees us from the prison of the moment. Language recreates us as historical beings. In its discursive aspect language runs along and brings thought with it, as Cassirer puts it. Discourse grows from inner dialogue (and the differing accounts by Piaget and Vygotsky of that development make a fascinating study). From this earliest activity of the mind, language gradually takes on the discursive forms which serve the communicative function. Because of this tendency to syntax, we can articulate our thoughts; we can think about thinking and thus interpret our interpretations.

Seeing language in this perspective encourages the recognition that meaning comes first; that it is complex from the start; that its articulation is contingent on the mind's activity in a human world. The chief hazard of the developmental model is that it sanctions the genetic fallacy—that what comes first is simple, not complex, and that what comes after is a bigger version of a little beginning. Thus we have the idea that there is first one word and then another, another, another, until there is enough to fill out the awaiting syntactic structures. But this isn't the way it happens. The hypostatic word, the single uttered syllable, is a protosentence; syntax is deeply implicated, we might say, in every human cry. Children let a single word do the work of the sentence until the discursive power of language can draw out and articulate the meaning. The conception of a semantic component added to a syntactic structure is a mechanistic conception which must be supplanted. I suggest as an image of the growth and development of language one of those little wooden flowers which the Japanese used to make—before they turned to silicon chips—a tiny compacted form which, placed in a dish of water, opens and expands, blossoming in the shape of a fully articulated flower. Please note the dialectic: it is the water which acts to release the form. In my extended metaphor, the water is our social life, the essential context for the making of meaning. Cognitive psychologists who deliberately ignore it have not advanced over those early kings whose hobby it was to try to discover which language is oldest. They sequestered newborn twins in castle keep or cottage, in the care of a mute nurse, and breathlessly awaited news of what language it would be, when the babies came to speak. And you can safely bet that the court astrologer—that proto-psycholinguist—saw to it that the first reported syllables were construed as Swedish or Hebrew or whatever language it was that the monarch—that proto-funding agency—expected.

In my opinion the ambiguities of the determinism suggested by any account of natural, normal development can serve as the hinges of our thinking about thinking in the interest of discovering the laws of growth, the interdependency of nature and nurture, seed and soil. Language and learning, like syntax and semantics, are in a dialectical relationship which we must learn to construe and represent so that it is accessible to our students. Just so, we must guide their consciousness of consciousness so that it can become the means of freeing the self from itself: as a pleasant way of resolving that paradox, I recommend Walker Percy's new book, *Lost in the Cosmos: The Last Self-Help Book*. After a startling and instructive analysis of twenty versions of the lost self, we have a chapter on triadicity, the means of reclaiming the self. Dr. Percy is an artist, a scientist, and a philosopher for whom triadicity provides the means of conceiving that symbolic activity which defines the mind.

Because they make interpretation central, triadic models of the composing process are the trustworthy ones we need in developing a pedagogy of knowing. The two I consider most useful are perception and dialogue. Every course I teach begins with observation—with looking and looking again. It is my strong conviction that what is looked at should include organic objects, themselves compositions. But of course we must also "problematize the existential situation," as Freire rather infelicitously puts it. I bring seaweed and crab legs to class, the seed pods of sedges and five kinds of pine cones, but I also ask students to problematize the soda cans and milk cartons left from the last class.[7] (I haven't dared to undertake the archeology of the waste basket: God knows what we might find!) We use my version of the journalist's heuristic, *HDWDWW?*—deliberately constructed to resist becoming an acronym: *How does who do what and why?* How does that come to be on your desk? Who left it there? Why do you leave this junk around? What are these things in evidence of? What is the meaning of this litter? Looking and looking again helps students learn to transform things into questions; they learn to see names as "titles for situations," as Kenneth Burke puts it. In looking and naming, looking again and re-naming, they develop perspectives and contexts, discovering how each controls the other. They are composing; they are forming; they are abstracting.

Perception is non-discursive abstraction; the questioning of perceptions is the beginning of generalization, of discursive abstraction. Perception as a model of the composing process lets us capitalize on the hypostatic function of language. Students can discover that they are already thinking; by raising implicit recognitions to explicit differentiations, they can, as it were, *feel* the activity of their minds. By beginning with meaning, with complexity, we assure that minds will, indeed, be active. As I've been arguing, that complexity must be controlled by the way we use language or it will overwhelm, but the complexity entailed in making meaning should never be put off: *elements of what we want to end with must be present in some form from the first or we will never get to them.* That, I take it, is the chief law of growth.

Dialogue is the other triadic model. The "natural environment" necessary to the growth and development of the discursive power of language requires dialogue. Looking again starts that questioning which is the beginning of dialectic and it should be practiced in dialogue in class, of course, but also in what I call a "dialectical notebook," the facing pages offering a structure which enables the student to talk to herself. Dialogue is essential not only because it provides practice in those other uses of language—speaking and listening—but because it can model that constant movement from the particular to the general and back again which for Vygotsky is the defining characteristic of concept formation. But let me be explicit about this natural environment: it is a *prepared* environment, in the sense in which Montessori spoke of her classroom as a prepared environment. This dialectic of particularizing and generalizing, this conceptualizing, this thinking, though it is a power natural by reason of language itself, though it is natural to the human mind, must be put into practice. Like speech itself, it requires a social context in which purposes can be arrived at, intentions discovered and formulated and represented in different modes of discourse.

If college students find generalizing difficult, it's because nobody has ever taught them how to go about it, and abstraction which proceeds by means of generalizing—*concept formation*, as it is often called—must be deliberately learned and should therefore be deliberately taught. But few methods for doing so have been developed and those which have are, generally speaking, of the type Freire calls the banking model: the teacher deposits valuable information. Developmental models are most dangerous when they distract teachers from recognizing the deficiencies of their pedagogy. When we are told, as we are by almost everybody reporting research, that students are good at narrative but fall apart when faced with exposition, it is not necessary to hypothesize that students have come bang up against a developmental fence. The first step of the analysis should be to look at the character of the assignments, at the sequence of "tasks." In an interesting variation on this theme of "narrative good, exposition terrible," one researcher contrasts how well students do with persuasion and how poorly they do with argument.[8] She reports how intelligently students have jumped through the hoops of compare-contrast, "explain a process," "describe an incident," etc., etc.—all in the interest of composing in the persuasive mode—only to fall flat on their faces with the argumentation paper. And guess where it came from? Not from exploration or dialogue or observation or a close reading of texts. No: it came from an assigned topic on euthanasia. Why is anybody surprised when they get terrible writing from a terrible assignment? "Who is to get the kidney machine?" is no advance at all over "Which is greater, fire or water?" "Provocative" topics stimulate cant and cliché; they breed Engfish; they lead to debate, which is by no means dialectic. Nobody learns from debate because, as Richards often observed, the disputant is commonly too busy making a point to trouble to see what it is.

Assigning topics—the essential strategy of the pedagogy of exhortation—is no substitute for instruction. But the deeper reason for the failure in the argumentation paper is the same as for the proclaimed success in the persuasion paper. Persuasion is the air we breathe; it is the mode of advertisement. But where do our students hear argument? Mine do not have the faintest idea of the conventions of an editorial—and when have they ever heard an authentic, dialectical exchange on television information shows? The discourse we find familiar to the point of being able to reproduce it has nothing to do with developmental stages, once childhood is passed—or maybe even before. You may be sure that prepubescent Presbyterians in the eighteenth century were capable of composing arguments on natural depravity, while pre-pubescent Baptists were writing on grace abounding unto the chief of sinners, and little Methodists were writing on topics like "Must the drunkard be an unhappy man?" My advanced composition students find almost intolerably difficult Huxley's "On a Piece of Chalk," a public lecture which a century ago famously enthralled workers with no secondary education—but Huxley's audience had heard two or three sermons every week of their lives! Argument was the air you breathed, a hundred years ago. I am not, of course, claiming authenticity or moral superiority for those who can argue. I mean only that the capacity to manage disputation is a culture-bound skill and that its dependence on neurobiological development is a necessary but not a sufficient condition.

Ironically, it is sometimes students themselves who misconceive the developmental model. Especially older students fear that they must return to Square One. They have to make it all up, they think. When we ask them, like everybody else, to look and look again, we must, by a careful choice of reading—on the model of malt whiskey, not diet soda—lead them to discover that scientists and lawyers and poets look and look again. Of course we must begin with where they are—as meaning makers. We must, in I. A. Richards' phrase, offer them "assisted invitations" to look carefully at what they are doing—observing a weed or drawing up a shopping list—in order to discover *how* to do it.[9] Our job is to devise sequences of assignments which encourage conscientization, the discovery of the mind in action. That will not be accomplished by setting topics, no matter how nicely matched to the "appropriate" developmental stage they might be.

Rather, in our pedagogy of knowing, we will encourage the discovery of mind by assuring that language is seen not as a set of slots, not as an inert code to be mastered by drill, but as a means of *naming* the world; of holding the images by whose means we human beings recognize the forms of our experience; of reflecting on those images, as we do on other words. We teachers will assure that language is continually exercised to name and establish likes and differents so that by sorting and gathering, students will learn to define: they will learn to abstract in the discursive mode; they will learn to generalize. They will thus be able to "think abstractly" because they will be learning how meanings make further meanings possible, how form finds further form. And we will, in our pedagogy of knowing, be giving our students back their language so that they can reclaim it as an instrument for controlling their becoming.

NOTES

1. Randall Freisinger, "Cross-Disciplinary Writing Workshops: Theory and Practice," *College English*, 42 (1980), 163.

2. *Speculative Instruments* (New York: Harcourt Brace, 1955), p. 9. It is the lack of a philosophy of language that could properly account for meaning which invalidates the procedures so frequently recommended for students of the composing process. George Hillocks, for instance, suggests that inquiry procedures are well-modelled by ethology. (See his article "Inquiry and the Composing Process: Theory and Research," *College English*, 44 [1982], 659-673.) But as Susanne K. Langer has shown in the second volume of *Mind: An Essay on Human Feeling* (Baltimore, Md.: Johns Hopkins University Press, 1972), Frisch, Tinbergen, et al. are unaware of the role metaphor plays in their descriptions; of presuppositions which remain entirely unexamined; of distortions resulting from a failure to differentiate animal and human acts. Ethological interpretations are shown to be pseudoconcepts, generalizations about particular cases, not authentic concepts.

3. *The Interpretation of Cultures* (New York: Basic Books, 1973), pp. 3-30. Reprinted in my *Reclaiming the Imagination*, (Upper Montclair, N.J.: Boynton/Cook, 1984), pp. 226-248.

4. Max Black in an essay on Whorf entitled "Linguistic Relativity" notes "the linguist's fallacy of imputing his own sophisticated attitudes to the speakers he is studying" (*Models and Metaphors* [Ithaca, N.Y.: Cornell University Press, 1962], p. 247).

5. I do not deny the value of analyzing cohesive devices in the context of discourse; this, I take it, is precisely what Richards had in mind when he called rhetoric "the study of how words work." But "discourse analysis," as presently practiced, does not always take into account the interdependence of linguistic and rhetorical functions. It begs the question of the relationship of language and thought, because the positivist conception of language by which it is guided does not provide the means for accounting for meaning. Discourse analysts separate thinking from writing, which they conceive of as the manipulation of *devices*. When Charles R. Cooper tells us in "Procedures for Describing Written Texts" (in *Research on Writing*, ed. Peter Mosenthal and Shaun Walmsley [New York: Longman, 1983]) that the "thinking process leads the writer to choose appropriate strategies and forms for presenting the outcomes of thought *as written text*" (p. 291), he has not been alert to those hazards Vygotsky urges us to avoid by beginning with the unit of meaning. For Professor Cooper it is clearly not part of the procedure for describing, much less for producing, "texts" to take into account the heuristic powers of language or the interplay of feedback and what Richards calls "feedforward." Yet "shaping at the point of utterance" is not exclusively an oral phenomenon.

It should be noted that for Halliday and Hasan, whose taxonomy is widely used, the working concept of a text is as a semantic unit. For an excellent discussion of the interdependence of meaning and grammatical, logical, and rhetorical forms, see Jeanne Fahnestock, "Semantic and Lexical Coherence," *College Composition and Communication*, 34 (1983), 400-416. And see anything Josephine Miles has ever written.

6. See especially "Development of Scientifc Concepts in Childhood" in *Thought and Language*, trans. and ed. Eugenia Hanfman and Gertrude Vakar (Cambridge, Mass.: MIT Press, 1962). Vygotsky analyzes the theories of the relationship of learning and development held by Piaget, William James, and the Gestaltists and then goes on to outline his own theory, the central feature of which is "the zone of proximal development." The interdependence of "scientific" and "spontaneous" concepts is exactly analogous to that of discursive and mythic forms of thought in Cassirer's philosophy of symbolic forms and Susanne K. Langer's philosophy of mind. The idea of development "upward" in spontaneous conceptualization and "downward" in the formation of scientific concepts is fundamental to Vygotsky's dialectical conception of learning and development as set forth in *Mind in Society: The Development of Higher Psychological Processes*, ed. Michael Cole, Vera John-Steiner, Sylvia Scribner, and Ellen Souberman (Cambridge, Mass.: Harvard University Press, 1978). See especially pp. 78-91.

7. For excellent examples and interesting procedures, see Ira Shor, *Critical Teaching and Everyday Life* (Boston: South End Press, 1980), pp. 155-194.

8. Susan Miller, "Rhetorical Maturity: Definition and Development," in *Reinventing the Rhetorical Tradition*, ed. Aviva Freedman and Ian Pringle (Conway, Ark.: L & S Books, 1980), pp. 119-127.

9. I have borrowed the phrase "assisted invitations" for the exercises in *Forming/Thinking/Writing: The Composing Imagination* (Upper Montclair, N.J.: Boynton/Cook, 1982). Richards returns continually to the importance of the conscious and deliberate auditing of meaning as a means of making further meaning. See Ann E. Berthoff, "I. A. Richards and the Audit of Meaning," *New Literary History*, 14 (1982), 64-79.

Narrowing the Mind and Page
Remedial Writers and Cognitive Reductionism

MIKE ROSE

There has been a strong tendency in American education—one that took modern shape with the I.Q. movement—to seek singular, unitary cognitive explanations for broad ranges of poor school performance. And though this trend—I'll call it cognitive reductionism—has been challenged on many fronts (social and political as well as psychological and psychometric), it is surprisingly resilient. It re-emerges. We see it in our field in those discussions of basic and remedial writers that suggest that unsuccessful writers think in fundamentally different ways from successful writers. Writing that is limited to the concrete, that doesn't evidence abstraction or analysis, that seems illogical is seen, in this framework, as revealing basic differences in perception, reasoning, or language.[1] This speculation has been generated, shaped, and supported by one or more theories from psychology, neurology, and literary studies.

Studies of cognitive style suggest that people who can be characterized as "field-dependent" (vs. those who are "field-independent") might have trouble with analytical tasks. *Popular articles on brain research* claim a neurophysiological base for some humans to be verbal, logical, analytical thinkers and for others to be spatial, holistic, non-verbal thinkers. *Jean Piaget's work on the development of logical thought* seems pertinent as well: some students might not have completed their developmental ascent from concrete to abstract reasoning. And *orality-literacy theorists* make connections between literacy and logic and suggest that the thinking of some minority groups might

Reprinted from *College Composition and Communication* 39.3 (October 1988): 267–98.
Used with permission.

be affected by the degree to which their culture has moved from oral to literate modes of behavior.

The applications of these theories to poor writers appear in composition journals and papers at English, composition, and remedial education conferences. This is by no means the only way people interested in college-age remedial writers talk about thinking-writing connections, but the posing of generalized differences in cognition and the invoking of Piaget, field dependence and the rest has developed into a way of talking about remediation. And though this approach has occasionally been challenged in journals, it maintains a popular currency and encourages a series of bold assertions: poor writers can't form abstractions; they are incapable of analysis; they perceive the world as an undifferentiated whole; the speech patterns they've acquired in their communities seriously limit their critical capacity.

I think we need to look closely at these claims and at the theories used to support them, for both the theories and the claims lead to social distinctions that have important consequences, political as well as educational. This is not to deny that the theories themselves have contributed in significant ways to our understanding of mental processes (and Piaget, of course, shaped an entire field of research), but their richness should not keep us from careful consideration of their limits, internal contradictions, and attendant critical discussions and counterstatements. Consideration of the theories leads us naturally to consideration of their applicability to areas beyond their original domain. Such application often overgeneralizes the theory: Ong's brilliant work on orality and literacy, for example, moves beyond its history-of-consciousness domain and becomes a diagnostic framework. A further problem—sometimes inherent in the theories themselves, sometimes a result of reductive application—is the tendency to diminish cognitive complexity and rely on simplified cognitive oppositions: independent vs. dependent, literate vs. oral, verbal vs. spatial, concrete vs. logical. These oppositions are textbook-neat, but, as much recent cognitive research demonstrates, they are narrow and misleading. Yet another problem is this: these distinctions are usually used in a way meant to be value-free (that is, they highlight differences rather than deficits in thinking), but, given our culture, they are anything but neutral. Social and political hierarchies end up encoded in sweeping cognitive dichotomies.

In this article I would like to reflect on the problems with and limitations of this particular discourse about remediation. To do this, I'll need to provide a summary of the critical discussion surrounding each of the theories in its own field, for that complexity is too often lost in discussions of thought and writing. As we move through the essay, I'll point out the problems in applying these theories to the thought processes of poor writers.

And, finally, I'll conclude with some thoughts on studying cognition and writing in less reductive ways.

COGNITIVE STYLE:
FIELD DEPENDENCE-INDEPENDENCE

Cognitive style, broadly defined, is an "individual's characteristic and consistent manner of processing and organizing what he [or she] sees and thinks about" (Harré and Lamb 98). In theory, cognitive style is separate from verbal, quantitative, or visual intelligence; it is not a measure of how much people know or how well they mentally perform a task, but the manner in which they perform, their way of going about solving a problem, their style. Cognitive style research emerges out of the study of individual differences, and there have been a number of theories of cognitive style proposed in American and British psychology since the late 40's. Varied though they are, all the theories discuss style in terms of a continuum existing between two polar opposites: for example, reflectivity vs. impulsivity, analytic vs. global, complexity vs. simplicity, levelling vs. sharpening, risk-taking vs. cautiousness, field-dependence vs. field-independence. Field dependence-independence, first described by Herman A. Witkin in 1949, is, by far, the most researched of the cognitive styles, and it is the style that seems to be most discussed in composition circles.

The origins of the construct are, as Witkin, Moore, Goodenough, and Cox note, central to its understanding. Witkin's first curiosity concerned the degree to which people use their surrounding visual environment to make judgments about the vertical position of objects in a field. Witkin devised several devices to study this issue, the best known being the Rod and Frame Test. A square frame on a dark background provides the surrounding visual field, and a rod that rotates within it is the (potentially) vertical object. Both the frame and the rod can separately be rotated clockwise or counterclockwise, and "[t]he subject's task is to adjust the rod to a position where he perceives it as upright, while the frame around it remains in its initial position of tilt" ("Field-Dependent" 3). Witkin, et al.'s early findings revealed some interesting individual differences:

> For some, in order for the rod to be apprehended as properly upright, it must be fully aligned with the surrounding frame, whatever the position of the frame. If the frame is tilted 30 [degrees] to the right, for example, they will tilt the rod 30 [degrees] to the right, and say the rod is perfectly straight in that position. At the opposite extreme of the continuous performance

range are people who adjust the rod more or less close to the upright in making it straight, regardless of the position of the surrounding frame. They evidently apprehend the rod as an entity discrete from the prevailing visual frame of reference and determine the uprightness of the rod according to the felt position of the body rather than according to the visual frame immediately surrounding it. ("Field-Dependent" 3-4)

A subject's score is simply the number of degrees of actual tilt of the rod when the subject claims it is straight.

Witkin and his associates later developed another measure—one that was much less cumbersome and could be given to many people at once—The Embedded Figures Test.[2] Witkin, et al. considered the Embedded Figures Test to be similar to the Rod and Frame Test in its "essential perceptual structure." The subject must locate a simple geometric design in a complex figure, and "once more what is at issue is the extent to which the surrounding visual framework dominates perception of the item within it" (6). A subject's score on the test is the number of such items he or she can disembed in a set time.

The "common denominator" between the two tests is "the extent to which the person perceives part of the field as discrete from the surrounding field as a whole, rather than embedded in the field; or the extent to which the organization of the prevailing field determines perception of its components" (7). Put simply, how strong is our cognitive predisposition to let surrounding context influence what we see? Witkin soon began to talk of the differences between field dependence vs. independence as differences between articulated (or analytic) vs. global perception:

> At one extreme there is a consistent tendency for experience to be global and diffuse; the organization of the field as a whole dictates the manner in which its parts are experienced. At the other extreme there is a tendency for experience to be delineated and structured; parts of a field are experienced as discrete and the field as a whole organized. To these opposite poles of the cognitive styles we may apply the labels "global and articulated." ("Psychological Differentiation" 319)

Witkin's tests were tapping interesting individual differences in perception and cognition, but the really tantalizing findings emerged as Witkin and his colleagues began pursuing a wide-ranging research agenda that, essentially, sought correlations between performance on field dependence-independence tests and performance on a variety of other cognitive, behavioral, and personality tests, measures, and activities. Hundreds of these studies followed, ranging from the insightful (correlating cognitive style with the way teachers structure social science concepts) to the curious (correlating cognitive style with the shortness of women's skirts). Some of the studies yielded low correlations, and some were inconclusive or were contradictory—but, in general, the results, as summarized by educational psychologist Merlin Wittrock, resulted in the following two profiles:

♦ To the degree that people score high on field independence they tend to be: "relatively impersonal, individualistic, insensitive to others and their reinforcements, interested in abstract subject matter, and intrinsically motivated. They have internalized frames of reference, and experience themselves as separate or differentiated from others and the environment. They tend to use previously learned principles and rules to guide their behavior" (93).

♦ To the degree that people score low on field independence they are, by default, field-dependent, and they tend to be: "more socially oriented, more aware of social cues, better able to discern feelings of others from their facial expressions, more responsive to a myriad of information, more dependent on others for reinforcement and for defining their own beliefs and sentiments, and more in need of extrinsic motivation and externally defined objectives" (93).

The tendency of the field-independent person to perceive particular shapes and orientations despite context, and the tendency of the field-dependent person to let "the organization of the field as a whole dictate the manner in which its parts are experienced" seemed to be manifesting themselves in motivation, cognition, and personality. A few relatively simple tests were revealing wide-ranging differences in the way people think and interact.

The psychometric neatness of this work seems a little too good to be true, and, in fact, problems have been emerging for some time. My discussion of them will be oriented toward writing.

You'll recall that it is central to the theory that cognitive style is not a measure of ability, of how well people perform a task, but a measure of their manner of performance, their style. If we applied this notion to writing, then, we would theoretically expect to find interesting differences in the way discourse is produced, in the way a rhetorical act is conceived and executed: maybe the discourse of field independents would be more analytical and impersonal while field-dependent discourse would be richer in social detail. But these differences should not, theoretically, lead to gross differences in quality. By some general measure, papers written by field-dependent and field-independent students should have equal possibility of being acceptable discourse. They would just be different. However, the most detailed and comprehensive cognitive style study of college-level writers I've yet seen yields this: papers written by field-dependent students are simply poor papers, and along most dimensions—spelling, grammar, development (Williams). This doesn't fit. Conclusions emerge, but they don't jibe with what the theory predicts.

Such conceptual and testing perplexities are rooted, I believe, in the field dependence-independence work itself. My review of the psychological literature revealed seven problems with the construct, and they range from the technical to the conceptual level.

For cognitive style to be a legitimate construct, it has to be distinct from general intelligence or verbal ability or visual acuity, because cognitive style is not intended to be a measure of how "smart" someone is, but of the manner in which she or he engages in an intellectual task. Unfortunately, there are a number of studies which suggest that field dependence-independence significantly overlaps with measures of intelligence, which are, themselves, complex and controversial. As early as 1960, Lee J. Cronbach wrote in his authoritative *Essentials of Psychological Testing*: "General reasoning or spatial ability accounts for much of Embedded Figures performance as does difficulty in handling perceptual interference" (549). In 1972, Philip Vernon, also a prominent researcher of individual differences, reviewed studies that investigated relations between scores on field dependence-independence and various measures of "visual intelligence." He concluded that "the strong positive correlation with such a wide range of spatial tests is almost embarrassing" (368). And after conducting his own study, Vernon declaimed that Embedded Figures Tests "do not define a factor distinct from general intelligence . . . and spatial ability or visualization" (386). Things become more complicated. Vernon, and other researchers (see, for example, Linn and Kyllonen), present factor-analytic data that suggest that determining the position of the rod within the frame and disembedding the hidden figures tap *different* mental constructs, not the unitary construct Witkin had initially postulated.[3] It is possible, of course, that different aspects of field dependence-independence are being tapped by the different tests and that two of them should be administered together—as Witkin, in fact, recommended. But even if researchers used multiple measures (as few have—most use only the Embedded Figures Test because of its utility), the problem of overlap with measures of intelligence would remain. In short, it's not certain just what the field dependence-independence tests are measuring, and it's very possible that they are primarily tapping general or spatial intelligence.

There is a further testing problem. In theory, each pole of a cognitive style continuum "has adaptive value in certain circumstances . . . neither end of [a] cognitive style dimension is uniformly more adaptive . . . adaptiveness depends upon the nature of the situation and upon the cognitive requirements of the task at hand" (Messick 9). Now, there have been studies which show that field-dependent people seem to attend more readily than field-independent people to social cues (though the effects of these studies tend to be small or inconsistent—see McKenna), but it is important to note that Witkin and his colleagues have never been able to develop a test that *positively* demonstrates field dependence. The Rod and Frame Test, the Embedded Figures Test—and all the other tests of field dependence-independence—assess how well a person displays field *in*dependence. Field dependence is essentially determined by default—the more a person fails at determining the true position of the rod or the slower he is at disembedding the figure, the more field dependent he is. This assessment-by-default would not be a problem if one were testing some level of skill or intellectual ability, say, mechanical aptitude. But where a bipolar and "value-free" continuum is being assessed—where one is not "deficient" or "maladaptive" regardless of score, but only different, where both field-independent and field-dependent people allegedly manifest cognitive strengths as well as limitations—then it becomes a problem if you can't devise a test on which field-dependent subjects would score well. Witkin, et al. admit that the development of such a test is "an urgent task" (16). It has not yet been developed.

But even if a successful test of field dependence could be created, problems with assessment would not be over. All existing tests of field dependence-independence are, as Paul L. Wachtel points out:

> in certain respects poorly suited for exploration of the very problem [they were] designed to deal with—that of style. It is difficult to organize ideas about different directions of development upon a framework which includes only one dimension, and only the possibility of "more" or "less." (186)

Consider the notion of style. It would seem that style is best assessed by the observation and recording of a range of behaviors over time. Yet the Rod and Frame and Embedded Figures Tests don't allow for the revelation of the cognitive processes in play as the person tries to figure them out. That is, there is no provision made for the subject to speak aloud her mental processes or offer a retrospective account of them or explain—as in Piagetian method—

why she's doing what she's doing. We have here what Michael Cole and Barbara Means refer to as the problem of drawing process inferences from differences in task performance (65). It would be unfair to lay this criticism on Witkin's doorstep alone, for it is a general limitation with psychometric approaches to cognition. (See, for example, Hunt.) But Witkin's work, since it purports to measure style, is especially vulnerable to it.

Let us now rethink those composite profiles of field-independent vs. field-dependent people. You'll recall that the correlations of all sorts of measures suggest that field-dependent people are more socially oriented, more responsive to a myriad of information, etc., while field-independent people tend to be individualistic, interested in abstract subject matter, and so on. These profiles can be pretty daunting; they're built on hundreds of studies, and they complement our folk wisdom about certain kinds of personalities. But we must keep in mind that the correlations between tests of field independence and personality or cognitive measures are commonly .25 to .3 or .4; occasionally, correlations as high as .5 or .6 are recorded, but they are unusual. That means that, typically, 84% to 94% of the variance between one measure and the other remains to be accounted for by factors other than those posited by the cognitive style theorist. Such studies accrue, and eventually the theorist lays them all side by side, notes the seeming commonalities, and profiles emerge. You could consider these profiles telling and veridical, but you could also consider them webs of thin connection.

We in the West are drawn to the idea of consistency in personality (from Renaissance humors to Jungian types), and that attraction, I think, compels us to seek out similar, interrelated consistencies in cognition. Certainly there are regularities in the way human beings approach problems; we don't go at our cognitive tasks willy-nilly. But when cognitive researchers try to chart those consistencies by studying individual people solving multiple problems they uncover a good deal of variation, variation that is potentially efficient and adaptive. William F. Battig, for example, found in his studies of adult verbal learning that most subjects employed different strategies at different times, even when working on a single problem. At least in the cognitive dimension, then, it has proven difficult to demonstrate that people approach different problems, in different settings, over time in consistent ways. This difficulty, it seems to me, presents a challenge to the profiles provided by cognitive style theorists.

There are, finally, troubling conceptual-linguistic problems with field dependence-independence theory, and they emerge most dramatically for me when I try to rephrase some of Witkin's discussions of the two styles. Here is one example:

> Persons with a global style are more likely to go along with the field "as is," without using such mediational processes as analyzing and structuring. In many situations field-independent people tend to behave as if governed by general principles which they have actively abstracted from their experiences. . . . In contrast, for field-dependent people information processing systems seem to make less use of such mediators. (Witkin, et al. 21)

Statements like this are common in Witkin, and they flow along and make sense in the discussion he offers us—but you stop cold if you consider for a minute what it might mean for people to have a tendency to operate in the world "without using such mediational processes as analyzing and structuring" or, by implication, to not "behave as if governed by general principles which they have actively abstracted from their experiences." These seem like pretty extreme claims, given the nature and limitations of tests of cognitive style. All current theories of cognition that I'm familiar with posit that human beings bring coherence to behavior by abstracting general principles from experiences, by interpreting and structuring what they see and do. When people can't do this sort of thing, or can only do it minimally, we assume that something is seriously wrong with them.

Witkin and his colleagues faced the dilemma that all theory builders face: how to find a language with which to express complex, abstract ideas. (For a Wittgensteinian analysis of Witkin's language, see Kurtz.) And given the nature of language, such expression is always slippery. I think, though, that Witkin and company get themselves into more than their fair share of trouble. The language they finally choose is often broad and general: it is hard to operationalize, and, at times, it seems applicable post hoc to explain almost any result (see Wachtel 184-85). It is metaphoric in troubling ways. And it implies things about cognition that, upon scrutiny, seem problematic. I would suggest that if we're going to apply Witkin's notions to the assessment of writing and cognition we'll need more focussed, less problematic definitions. Now, Witkin does, in fact, occasionally provide such definitions, but they raise problems of a different order. And here again we see the complications involved in connecting Witkin's theory to composing.

In an admirably precise statement, Witkin, et al. note:

> The individual who, in perception, cannot keep an item separate from the surrounding field—in other words, who is relatively field-dependent—is likely to have difficulty with that class of problems, and, we must emphasize, *only* with that class of problems, where the solution depends on

taking some critical element out of the context in which it is presented and restructuring the problem material so that the item is now used in a different context. (9)

Consider rhetoric and the production of written language. For Witkin's formulation to apply, we would have to define rhetorical activity and written language production as *essentially* involving the disembedding of elements from contexts and concomitant restructuring of those contexts. It seems to me that such application doesn't hold. Even if there were a rhetorical-linguistic test of cognitive style—and there isn't; the tests are visual, perceptual-orientational—I think most of us would say that while we could think of linguistic-rhetorical problems that might fit Witkin's description, it would be hard to claim that it characterizes rhetorical activity and linguistic production in any broad and inclusive way.

Second of all, it's important to remember that Witkin is talking about a *general* disembedding skill, a skill that would be effective in a wide range of contexts: engineering, literature, social relations. A number of contemporary students of cognition, however, question the existence of such general cognitive skills and argue for more domain-specific strategies, skills, and abilities (see, for example, Carey; Fodor; Gardner, *Frames*; Glaser; Perkins). Given our experience in particular domains, we may be more or less proficient at disembedding and restructuring problem areas in literature but not in engineering. Our ability to disembed the hidden geometric figures in Witkin's test may be more related to our experience with such visual puzzles than to some broad cognitive skill at disembedding. If a student can't structure an essay or take a story apart in the way we've been trained to do, current trends in cognitive research would suggest that her difficulties have more to do with limited opportunity to build up a rich network of discourse knowledge and strategy than with some general difference or deficit in her ability to structure or analyze experience.

HEMISPHERICITY

The French physician Paul Broca announced in 1865 that "we speak with the left hemisphere"; neurologists have had clinical evidence for some time that damage to certain areas of the left side of the brain could result in disruptions in production or comprehension of speech-aphasia—and that damage to certain areas of the right could result in space and body orientation problems; laboratory experiments with healthy people over the last 25 or so years have demonstrated that particular linguistic or spatial capacities seem to require the function of regions in the left or right brain respectively (though it is also becoming clear that there is some degree of right hemisphere involvement in language production and comprehension and left hemispheric involvement in spatial tasks); and radical neurosurgery on a dozen or so patients with intractable epilepsy—a severing of the complex band of neural fibers (the commissures) that connect the left and right cerebral hemispheres—has provided dramatic, if highly unusual, illustration of the anatomical specialization of the hemispheres. It is pretty much beyond question, then, that different areas of the brain contribute to different aspects of human cognition. As with any biological structure there is variation, but in 98% of right handers and 70% of "non-right" handers, certain areas of the left hemisphere are critical for the processing of phonology and syntax and for the execution of fine motor control, and certain areas of the right hemisphere are involved in various kinds of visual and spatial cognition.

These conclusions evolve from either clinical observation or experimental studies. Most studies fit the following paradigm: a set of tasks is presented to a subject, and the tasks are either isomorphic with the process under investigation (e.g., distinguishing nonsense syllables like "pa," "ta," "ka," "ba" as a test of phonetic discrimination) or can be assumed, in a common sense way, to tap the activity under investigation (e.g., mentally adding a list of numbers as a test of serial processing). The subject's speed or accuracy is recorded and, in some studies, other measures are taken that are hypothesized to be related to the mental processes being studied (e.g., recording the brain wave patterns or blood flow or glucose metabolism of the cerebral hemispheres while the subject performs the experimental task).

Studies of this type have enabled researchers to gain some remarkable insight into the fine neuropsychological processes involved in understanding language and, to a lesser degree, in making spatial-orientational discriminations. But it is also true that, ingenious as the work has been, the field is still at a relatively primitive state: many studies are difficult to duplicate (a disturbing number of them yield conflicting results), and the literature is filled with methodological quarrels, competing theories, and conceptual tangles. (For a recent, and very sympathetic, overview see Benson and Zaidel.)

In spite of the conflicts, there are various points of convergence in the data, and, in the yearning for parsimony that characterizes science, the areas of agreement have led some neuroscientists to seek simple and wide-ranging characterizations of brain function. They suggest that beneath all the particular findings about syntax and phonetics and spatial discrimination lie *fundamental* functional differences in the left and right cerebral hemispheres: each is best suited to process certain kinds of stimuli and/or each processes stimuli in distinct ways. A smaller number of neuroscientists—and many popularizers—go a step further and suggest that people tend toward reliance on one hemisphere or the other when they process information. This theory is commonly referred to as "hemisphericity" (Bogen, DeZure, TenHouton, and Marsh). And a few sociologically oriented theorists take another, truly giant, step and suggest that entire dominant and subdominant groups of people can be characterized by a reliance on left or right hemispheric processing (TenHouten). We have, then, the emergence of a number of cognitive dichotomies: the left hemisphere is characterized as being analytic while the right is holistic (or global or synthetic); the left is verbal, the right non-verbal (or spatial); the left a serial processor, the right a parallel processor—and the list continues: focal vs. diffuse, logical vs. intuitive, propositional vs. appositional, and so on.

The positing of hemispheric dichotomies is understandable. Human beings are theory-makers, and parsimony is a fundamental criterion by which we judge the value of a theory: can it account for diverse data with a simple explanation? But, given the current state of brain research, such generalizations, to borrow Howard Gardner's phrase, leapfrog from the facts ("What We Know" 114). Gardner is by no means alone in his criticism. My reading of the neuroscientific literature reveals that the notion of dichotomous hemispheric function is very controversial, and the further notion of hemisphericity is downright dismissed by a broad range of neuroscientists, psychologists, psycholinguists, and research psychiatrists:

> [T]he concepts [analytic/synthetic, temporal/spatial, etc.] are currently so slippery that it sometimes proves impossible to maintain consistency throughout one paper. (John C. Marshall in Bradshaw and Nettleton 72)

> [M]uch of perception (certainly of visual perception) is very difficult to split up this way. The alleged dichotomy [between temporal-analytic and spatial-holistic] is, if it exists at all, more a feature of laboratory experiments than of the real world. (M.J. Morgan in Bradshaw and Nettleton 74)

> [T]he idea of hemisphericity lacks adequate foundation and. . . because of the assumptions implicit in the idea of hemisphericity, it will never be possible to provide such a foundation. The idea is a misleading one which should be abandoned. (Beaumont, Young, and McManus 191)

The above objections rise from concerns about method, subjects, and conceptualization. Let me survey each of these concerns.

A significant amount of the data used to support hemisphericity—and certainly the most dramatic—is obtained from people in whom accident or pathology has highlighted what particular sections of the brain can or can't do. The most unusual group among these (and they are much-studied) is the handful of people who have had severe and life-threatening epilepsy alleviated through a radical severing of the neural fibers that connect the right and left hemispheres. Such populations, however, present a range of problems: tumors and wounds can cause disruptions in other areas of the brain; stroke victims could have had previous "silent strokes" and could, as well, be arteriosclerotic; long disease histories (certainly a characteristic of the severe epileptics who underwent split-brain surgery) can lead to compensatory change in brain function (Bogen, "The Dual Brain"; Whitaker and Ojemann). Furthermore, extrapathological factors, such as education and motivation, can, as Bradshaw and Nettleton put it, also "mask or accentuate the apparent consequences of brain injury" (51). And, as a final caution, there is this: the whole enterprise of localizing linguistic function through pathological performance is not without its critics (see Caplan).

Studies with healthy subjects—and there are increasing numbers of these—remove one major difficulty with hemisphericity research, though here methodological problems of a different sort arise. Concern not with subjects but with instruments and measures now comes into focus. Space as well as my own technological shortcomings prohibit a full review of tools and methods, but it might prove valuable to briefly survey the problems with a representative research approach: electroencephalographic methods. (Readers interested in critical reviews of procedures other than the one I cover can consult the following: Regional Cerebral Blood Flow: Beaumont; Lateral Eye Movements: Ehrlichman and Weinberger; Tachistoscopic Methods: Young; Dichotic-Listening Tests: Efron.)

If you hypothesize that certain kinds of tasks (like discriminating between syllables or adding a list of numbers) are primarily left-brain tasks and that others (like mentally rotating blocks or recognizing faces) are primarily right-brain tasks, then neuroelectric activity in the target hemisphere should vary in predictable ways when the subject performs the respective tasks. And, in fact, such variation in brain wave activity has been empirically demonstrated for some time. Originally, such studies relied on the electroencephalogram (EEG)—the ongoing record of brain wave activity—but now it is possible to gain a more sophisticated record of what are called event-related potentials (ERP). ERP methods use the electroencephalographic machinery, but rely on computer averaging and formalization to more precisely relate brain wave activity to repeated presentations of specific stimuli (thus the waves are "event-related"). The advantage of EEG and ERP methods is that they offer a direct electrophysiological measurement of brain activity and, especially in the case of ERP, "can track rapid fluctuation in brain electrical fields related to cognitive processing . . ." (Brown, Marsh, and Ponsford 166). Such tracking is important to hemisphericity theorists, for it can lend precision to their claims.

There are problems, however. EEG/ERP methods are among the most technically demanding procedures in psychology, and that technical complexity gives rise to a number of difficulties involving variation in cortical anatomy, electrode placement, and data analysis (Beaumont; Gevins, Zeitlin, Doyle, Schaffer, and Callaway). And, when it comes to the study of language processing—certainly an area of concern to writing researchers— ERP procedures give rise to problems other than the technical. Most ERP studies must, for purposes of computer averaging, present each stimulus as many as 50 times, and such repetition creates highly artificial linguistic processing conditions. Even relatively natural language processing studies have trouble determining which perceptual, linguistic, or cognitive factors are responsible for results (see, e.g., Hillyard and Woods). So, though hemispheric differences in brain wave patterns can be demonstrated, the exceptional technical and procedural difficulties inherent in the EEG/ERP studies of language processing make it hard to interpret data with much precision. Cognitive psychophysiologists Emanuel Donchin, Gregory McCarthy and Marta Kutas summarize this state of affairs:

> [A]lthough a substantial amount of clinical data support the theory of left hemisphere superiority in language reception and production, the ERP data regarding this functional asymmetry are far from consistent. The methodological and statistical shortcomings which exist in some of the studies cited [in their review article] along with inconsistencies in the others render any decision about the efficacy of ERP's as indices of linguistic processing inconclusive. (239. For similar, more recent, assessments, see Rugg; Beaumont, Young, and McManus.)

In considering the claims of the hemisphericity theorists, we have reviewed problems with subjects, techniques, and procedures. There is yet a further challenge to the notion of hemisphericity. Some hemisphericity theorists believe that since people can be characterized by a tendency to rely on one hemisphere or the other, then such reliance should manifest itself in the way people lead their lives: in the way they solve problems, in the jobs they choose, and so on. Yet the few studies that have investigated this dimension of the theory yielded negative results. Hemisphericity advocates Robert Ornstein and David Galin failed to find overall systematic EEG differences between lawyers (assumed to be left hemispheric) and sculptors and ceramicists (assumed to be right hemispheric). In a similar study, Dumas and Morgan failed to find EEG differences between engineers and artists, leading the researchers to conclude that "the conjecture that there are 'left hemispheric' people and 'right hemispheric' people seems to be an oversimplification" (227). In a more ambitious study, Arndt and Berger gave graduate students in law, psychology, and sculpture batteries of tests to assess verbal analytic ability (for example, a vocabulary test) and spatial ability (for example, a figure recognition test), and, as well, tests to assess hemisphericity (letter and facial recognition tachistoscopic tasks). While they found—as one would expect—a significant correlation between verbal or spatial ability and occupation (e.g., sculptors scored better than lawyers on the spatial tests), they *did not* find significant correlations between the verbal or spatial tests and the hemisphericity task; nor did they find significant correlation between the hemisphericity task and occupation.

A postscript on the above. Failures to find hemispheric differences between individuals of various occupational groups—along with the methodological difficulties mentioned earlier—throw into serious doubt the neurosociological claim that entire *groups* of people can be characterized as being left or right hemispheric. The neurosociological literature makes some remarkable speculative leaps from the existence of left-right dualities in cultural myth and symbol to asymmetries in left-right brain function, and relies, for empirical support, on the results of individual verbal and spatial tests (like the sub-tests in I.Q. assessments)—precisely the kinds of tests that a number of psychologists and neurologists have shown to be limited in assessing left or right hemispheric performance (see, e.g., DeRenzi).

Let me try to draw a few conclusions for rhetoric and composition studies.

It is important to keep in mind that the experimental studies that do support hemispheric specialization suggest small differences in performance capacities, and the differences tend to be of degree more than kind: in the range of 6-12%. Researchers have to expose subjects to many trials to achieve these differences. (One hundred and fifty to two hundred is common; one facial recognition study ran subjects through 700 trials.) And the experiments deal with extremely specific—even atomistic—functions. (Researchers consider the distinguishing of homonyms in a sentence—"bear" vs. "bare"—to be a "complex verbal task.") It is difficult to generalize from results of this type and magnitude to broad statements about one hemisphere being the seat of logic and the other of metaphor. What happens, it seems, is that theorists bring to very particular (though, admittedly, very important) findings about phonology or syntax or pattern recognition a whole array of cultural beliefs about analytic vs. synthetic thinking and logic vs. creativity and apply them in blanket fashion. There is a related problem here, and it concerns the hemisphericity theorists' assumption that, say, distinguishing phonemes is an analytical or serial or propositional task while, say, facial recognition is synthetic or holistic or appositional. These assumptions are sensible, but they are not proven. In fact, *one could argue the other way around*: e.g., that recognizing faces, for example, is not a holistic but a features analysis task. Unfortunately, neuroscientists don't know enough to resolve this very important issue. They work with indirect measures of information processing: differences in reaction time or variations in electrophysiological measures. They would need more direct access than they now have to the way information is being represented and problems are being solved.

Because the accounts of cerebral asymmetry can be so dramatic—particularly those from split-brain studies—it is easy to dwell on differences. But, in fact, there is wide-ranging similarity, overlap, and cooperation in the function of the right and left hemispheres:

> Complex psychological processes are not 'localized' in any one hemisphere but are the result of integration between hemispheres. (Alexander Luria cited in LeDoux 210)

If Luria's dictum applied anywhere, it would certainly be to the "complex psychological processes" involved in reading and writing. Under highly controlled laboratory conditions researchers can show that phoneme discrimination or word recognition can be relatively localizable to one hemisphere or the other. But attempts to comprehend or generate writing—what is perceived or produced as logical or metaphoric or coherent or textured—involve a stunning range of competencies: from letter recognition to syntactic fluency to an understanding of discourse structure and genre (see, e.g., Gardner and Winner 376-80). And such a range, according to everything we know, involves the whole brain in ways that defy the broad claims of the hemisphericity theorists. When students have trouble structuring an argument or providing imagistic detail, there is little neurophysiological evidence to support contentions that their difficulties originate in organic predisposition or social conditioning to rely on one hemisphere or the other.

JEAN PIAGET AND STAGES OF COGNITIVE DEVELOPMENT

Piaget's theory of cognitive development is generally held to be, even by its revisors and detractors, the modern West's most wide-ranging and significant

account of the way children think. The theory, which Piaget began to articulate over 50 years ago, covers infancy to adolescence and addresses the development of scientific and mathematical reasoning, language, drawing,
morality, and social perception; it has shaped the direction of inquiry into
childhood cognition; and it has led to an incredible number of studies, a
good many of which have been cross-cultural. In holding to the focus of this
article, then, there's a lot I'll have to ignore — I'll be limiting myself to those
aspects of Piaget's theory that have been most widely discussed in reference
to college-age writers.

Though Piaget and his colleagues adjusted their theory to account for
the wealth of data being generated by researchers around the world, there
are several critical features that remain central to the theory. Piaget's theory
is a stage theory. He posits four general stages (some with substages), and all
children pass through them in the same order. A child's reasoning at each
stage is *qualitatively* different from that at earlier or later stages, though the
knowledge and strategies of earlier stages are incorporated into later ones.
During any given stage, the child reasons in *similar* ways regardless of the
kinds of problems she or he faces, and Piaget tended to rule out the possibility that, during a given stage, a child could be trained to reason in much
more sophisticated ways. Passage, evolution really, from one stage to the
next occurs over time, an interaction of genetic processes and engagement
with the world. The child continually assimilates new information which
both reshapes and is reshaped by the knowledge structures the child currently has — and, as the child continues to interact with the world, she or he
experiences discontinuities between the known and the new, and these discontinuities lead to further development of knowledge of how things work.
Thinking, then, gradually evolves to ever more complex levels, represented
by each of the stages.

It is important to keep in mind that Piaget's perspective on cognition is
fundamentally logical and mathematical. Late in his life he observed that
he did not wish "to appear only as a child psychologist":

> My efforts, directed toward the psychogenesis of thought, were for me only
> a link between two dominant preoccupations: the search for the mecha-
> nisms of biological adaptation and the analysis of that higher form of adap-
> tation which is scientific thought, the epistemological interpretation of
> which has always been my central aim. (in Gruber and Vonèche xi)

With this perspective in mind, let us very briefly consider the stages of
Piaget's theory that are appropriated to discussions of college-age remedial
writers.

♦ *Concrete Operational* (6-7 to 11-12 years). The cognitive milestone here is that children are freed from immediate perception and enter the realm of logical—if concrete—operations. They can use logic to solve everyday problems, can take other points of view, can simultaneously take into account more than one perspective. In many ways, though, the child's reasoning is still linked to the environment, to tasks that are concrete and well-specified: "Tasks that demand very abstract reasoning, long chains of deduction, or the recognition that the available evidence is insufficient to reach any conclusion are thought to be beyond the reach" of children at the concrete operational stage (Siegler 89). Children have trouble separating out and recombining variables, performing sophisticated conservation tasks, and solving proportionality problems. They also have trouble planning systematic experiments and understanding "purely hypothetical questions that are completely divorced from anything in their experience" (Siegler 90).

♦ *Formal Operational* (11-15 years). During this stage, children develop into sophisticated logical thinkers—Piaget compared them to scientists—and can solve problems that throw concrete-operational children: like the pendulum task described below. Flavell summarizes the ability of the formal-operational child this way: "His thinking is *hypothetico-deductive* rather than *empirico-inductive*, because he creates hypotheses and then deduces the empirical states of affairs that should occur if his hypotheses are correct . . . The older individual's thinking can . . . be totally abstract, totally formal-logical in nature." (145. For a critical discussion of the notion of stages, see Brainerd.)

Piaget and his colleagues developed a number of tasks to distinguish concrete from formal operational thinking. The pendulum task is representative:

Children observed strings with metal balls at their ends swinging from a metal frame. The strings varied in length and the metal balls varied in how much they weighed; the task was to identify the factor or combination of factors that determined the pendulum's period. Plausible hypotheses included the weight of the metal balls, the length of the strings, the height from which the strings were dropped, and the force with which they were pushed. Although the length of the string is in fact the only relevant factor . . . 10- and 11-year olds almost always concluded that the metal ball's weight played a key role, either as the sole determining factor or in combination with the string's length. Thus the children failed to disentangle the influence of the different variables to determine which one caused the effect. (Siegler 89-90)

In the 1970's a number of studies appeared reporting that up to 50% of American college freshmen could not solve formal-operational problems like the pendulum task. The conclusion was that an alarming number of our 18-year-olds were locked at the level of concrete operations, a stage Piaget contends they should have begun evolving beyond by early and certainly by mid-adolescence. These data quickly found their way to a more general readership, and some people in composition understandably saw relevance in them and began to use them to explain the problems with the writing of remedial students. With support of the data, they wrote that up to 50% of college freshmen were locked into the level of the concrete, couldn't think abstractly, couldn't produce logical propositions, couldn't conceptualize—and, borrowing further from Piagetian terminology, they speculated that these students couldn't decenter, couldn't take another's point of view, were cognitively egocentric. The last two stages of the Piagetian framework became in application a kind of cognitive dichotomy unto themselves. If students couldn't produce coherent abstractions in writing, if they wrote about what was in front of them and couldn't express themselves on the conceptual level, if they described something in writing as though their reader shared their knowledge of it—then those limits in written expression suggested something broad and general about the state of their thinking: they might be unable to form abstractions . . . any abstractions; they couldn't decenter . . . at all. There are problems with this line of reasoning, however, and they have to do with the application of the framework as well as with the framework itself.

As any developmental psychologist will point out, there are major conceptual problems involved in applying a *developmental* model to adults. Piaget's theory was derived from the close observation of infants, children, and early- to mid-adolescents; it was intended as a description of the way thinking evolves in the growing human being. Applying it to college-age students and, particularly, to adult learners is to generalize it to a population other than the one that yielded it. There are more specific problems to consider as well, and they have to do with testing.

It is important to underscore the fact that Piaget implies broad limitations in cognition from specific inadequacies on a circumscribed set of tasks. This is not an unreasonable induction—all sorts of general theories are built on the performance of specific tasks—but it must be pointed out that we are dealing with an inference of major consequence. As developmental psychologist Rochelle Gelman put it: "The child is said to lack cognitive principles of broad significance simply because he fails a particular task involving those principles" (326). It is, then, an inferential leap of some magnitude to say that because college students fail to separate out variables and formally test hypotheses in a few tasks typical of the physics lab, they cannot conceptualize or abstract or tease out variables in any other sphere of their lives. Piaget himself said as much in one of his late articles:

> In our investigation of formal structures we used rather specific types of experimental situations which were of a physical and logical-mathematical nature because these seemed to be understood by the school children we sampled. However, it is possible to question whether these situations are, fundamentally, very general and therefore applicable to any school or professional environment. . . . It is highly likely that [people like apprentice carpenters, locksmiths, or mechanics] will know how to reason in a hypothetical manner in their speciality, that is to say, dissociating the variables involved, relating terms in a combinatorial manner and reasoning with propositions involving negations and reciprocities. (10)

Piaget's tests are clever and complex. To assist in replication, Piaget and his colleagues provided explicit instructions on how to set up the tests, what to say, and how to assess performance. This clarity contributed to the welter of Piagetian studies conducted over the years, many of which supported the theory. A significant body of recent research, however, has raised serious questions about the social conditions created when these tests are given. Most of this research has been done with younger children, and probably the best summary of it is Donaldson's. The thrust of this work is contained in one of Donaldson's chapter titles; when a child performs poorly on a Piagetian task, is it because of a "failure to reason or a failure to understand"? The tasks might be unfamiliar; the child might misunderstand the instructions; because psychological experiments are new to her, she might confuse the experimenter's intentions and "not see the experiment as the experimenter hopes [she] will" (Gelman 324). (See also philosopher Jonathan Adler's Grician critique of Piagetian testing.) What psychologists like Donaldson have done is keep the formal requirements of Piagetian tasks but change the particular elements to make them more familiar (e.g., substituting a toy policeman and a wall for a doll and a mountain), provide a chance for children to get familiar with the tasks, and rephrase instructions to make sure children understand what is being asked. Children in these conditions end up performing remarkably better on the tasks; significantly higher percentages of them can, for example, adopt other points of view, conserve quantity and number, and so on. What limited some children on Piaget's tasks, then, seems to be more related to experimental conditions rather than some absolute restriction in their ability to reason.

A somewhat related set of findings has do with training—one of the more controversial issues in Piagetian theory. This is not the place to recap the controversy; suffice it to say that a large number of studies has demonstrated that brief training sessions can have dramatic results on performance. One such study has direct bearing on our discussion. Kuhn, Ho, and Adams provided training to college freshman who failed at formal-operational tasks. After training, the students were once again presented with the tests, and "most of the college subjects showed immediate and substantial formal reasoning." The authors go on to speculate that the absence of formal-operational performance "may to a large extent reflect cognitive processing difficulties in dealing with the problem formats, rather than absence of underlying reasoning competencies" (1128).

I will conclude this brief critique by considering, once again, the mathematico-logical base of Piaget's theory. There is a tradition in the 20th century West—shaped by Russell, Whitehead, Carnap, and others—to study human reasoning within the framework of formal, mathematical logic, to see logic not only as a powerful tool, but as a representation of how people actually reason—at least when they're reasoning effectively. This tradition had a strong influence on Piaget's theory. In Toulmin's words, Piaget's "overall intellectual goal" was to:

> discover how growing children "come to *recognize the necessity* of" conforming to the intellectual structures of logic, Euclidean geometry, and the other basic Kantian forms. (256)

And as Inhelder and Piaget themselves said: "[R]easoning is nothing more than the propositional calculus itself" (305).

Mathematical logic is so privileged that we tend to forget that this assumption about logic being isomorphic with reasoning is highly controversial; it lies at the center of a number of current debates in cognitive psychology, artificial intelligence, and philosophy. Here is one of many counterstatements:

> Considerations of pure logic . . . may be useful for certain kinds of information under certain circumstances by certain individuals. But logic cannot serve as a valid model of how most individuals solve most problems most of the time. (Gardner, *Mind's New Science* 370)

Formal logic essentially strips away all specific connections to human affairs and things of the world; it allows us to represent relations and interactions within a wholly abstract system. Our elevation of this procedure blinds us to the overwhelming degree to which powerful and effective reasoning can be practical, non-formal, and concrete. As psychologist Barbara Rogoff puts it, "thinking is intricately interwoven with the context of the problem to be solved" (2). She continues:

> Evidence suggests that our ability to control and orchestrate cognitive skills is not an abstract context-free competence which may be easily transferred across widely diverse problem domains but consists rather of cognitive activity tied specifically to context. (3)

Much problem-solving and, I suspect, the reasoning involved in the production of most kinds of writing rely not only on abstract logical operations, but, as well, on the rich interplay of visual, auditory, and kinesthetic associations, feeling, metaphor, social perception, the matching of mental representations of past experience with new experience, and so on. And writing, as the whole span of rhetorical theory makes clear, is deeply embedded in the particulars of the human situation. It is a context-dependent activity that calls on many abilities. We may well need to engage in formal-logical reasoning when writing certain kinds of scientific or philosophical papers or when analyzing certain kinds of hypotheses and arguments, but we cannot assume that the ability or inability to demonstrate formal-operational thought on one or two Piagetian tasks has a necessary connection to our students' ability or inability to produce coherent, effective discourse.

ORALITY-LITERACY

Orality-literacy theory draws on the studies of epic poetry by Milman Parry and Albert Lord, the classical-philological investigations of Eric Havelock, the wide-ranging theoretical work of Walter Ong, and, to a lesser degree, on the compelling, though dated, cross-cultural investigations of thought in primitive, non-literate cultures. The work is broad, rich, and diverse—ranging from studies of the structure of the epic line to the classification schemes of unlettered rural farmers—but as it comes to those of us in composition, its focus is on the interrelation of language and cognition. Various scholars say it in various ways, but the essential notion is that the introduction of literacy into a society affects the way the members of the society think. There seem to be strong and weak versions of this theory.

The strong version states that the acquisition of literacy brings with it not only changes in linguistic possibilities—e.g., subordinative and discursive rather than additive and repetitive styles, less reliance on epithets and maxims and other easily remembered expressions—but *necessarily* results in a wide variety of changes in thinking: only after the advent of literacy do humans possess the ability to engage in abstraction, generalization, systematic thinking, defining, logos rather than mythos, puzzlement over words as words, speculation on the features of language. And these abilities, depending on who you read, lead to even wider changes in culture, summarized, not without exasperation, by social historian Harvey Graff:

> These characteristics include, in typical formulations or listings, attitudes ranging *from* empathy, innovativeness, achievement orientation, "cosmopoliteness," information and media awareness, national identification, technological acceptance, rationality, and commitment to democracy, *to* opportunism, linearity of thought and behavior, or urban residence. ("Reflections" 307)

The operative verb here is "transformed." Writing *transforms* human cognition.

The weak version of the oral-literate construct acknowledges the role literacy plays in developing modes of inquiry, building knowledge, etc., but tends to rely on verbs like "facilitate," "favor," "enable," "extend"—the potential of human cognition is extended more than transformed. Here's Jack Goody, an anthropologist who is often lumped in with those holding to the "strong version," but who, at least in his late work, takes issue with the oral-literate dichotomy. In discussing various differences between literate and oral expression, for example, he warns that such differences "do not relate primarily to differences of 'thought' or 'mind' (though there are consequences for these) but to differences in the nature of communicative acts" (26). So though Goody grants that writing "made it possible to scrutinize discourse in a different kind of way" and "increased the potentiality for cumulative knowledge" and freed participants from "the problem of memory storage" dominating "intellectual life," (37), he also insists that:

> Even in non-literate societies there is no evidence that individuals were prisoners of pre-ordained schemes, of primitive classifications, of the structures of myth. Constrained, yes; imprisoned, no. Certain, at least, among them could and did use language in a generative way, elaborating metaphor, inventing songs and "myths", creating gods, looking for new solutions to recurring puzzles and problems, changing the conceptual universe. (33)

The theory is a sensible one: literacy must bring with it tremendous repercussions for the intellect. The problem is that when the theory, particularly the strong version, is applied to composition studies, it yields some troubling consequences. Late twentieth-century American inner-city adolescents and adults are thought to bear cognitive resemblance to (ethnocentric notions of) primitive tribesmen in remote third-world cultures (or these adolescents and adults think like children, and children think like primitives): they don't practice analytic thinking; they are embedded in the context of their lives and cannot analyze it; they see things only as wholes; they think that printed words are concrete things; they cannot think abstractly.

A little reflection on this application of orality-literacy theory—given its origins—reveals a serious problem of method. The theory emerges from anthropological work with primitive populations, from historical-philological study of Homeric texts, from folkloric investigations of non-literate tale-tellers, and from brilliant, though speculative, literary-theoretical reflection on what might have happened to the human mind as it appropriated the alphabet. It is, then, a tremendous conceptual leap to apply this theory to urban-industrial Americans entering school in the penultimate decade of the twentieth century. We have here a problem of generalizability.

Now one could admit these problems yet still see some analogic value in applying the oral-literate construct with a hedge—for it at least, as opposed to the other theories we've been exploring, is directly concerned with written language. Fair enough. Yet my reading has led me to doubt the strength and utility of the theory on its own terms. (My concern rests primarily with the strong version. The weak version makes less dramatic claims about cognition, though some of what I found would qualify weak versions as well.) There are problems with what the theory implies about the way written language emerges in society and the role it plays in determining how people lead their linguistic lives and conduct their cognitive affairs. This is not to deny the profound effects literacy can have on society; it is to question the strength of the orality-literacy construct in characterizing those effects. Let me briefly survey some of the difficulties.

Literacy and Society

The historical record suggests that the technology and conventions of literacy work their way slowly through a society and have gradual—and not necessarily linearly progressive—influence on commerce, politics, bureaucracy, law, religion, education, the arts. (See, e.g., Marrou; Clanchy; Cressy.) Furthermore, it is hard to maintain, as the strong version does, that literacy is the primum mobile in social-cultural change. What emerges, instead, is a complex interaction of economic, political, and religious forces of which literacy is a part—and not necessarily the strongest element. Though there is no doubt that literacy shapes the way commerce, government, and religion are conducted, it, as John Oxenham puts it: "would have followed, not preceded, the formation of certain kinds of society" (59). And Harvey Graff, pointing out all the "discontinuities" and "contradictions" in linear, evolutionary assumptions about the spread of literacy, emphasizes that "[n]either writing [n]or printing alone is an 'agent of change'; their impacts are determined by the manner in which human agency exploits them in a specific setting" (Reflections" 307).[4]

Another way to view the problems with the transformational claims about literacy is to consider the fact that a number of societies have appropriated literacy to traditional, conservative purposes. In such societies literacy did not trigger various cultural-cognitive changes—changes in mores, attitudes, etc.—but reinforced patterns already in place. Again, John Oxenham:

> We have always to bear in mind that there have been literate social groups, who so far from being inventive and trusting, have been content merely to copy their ancient scriptures and pass them on virtually unaltered. It may be, then, that literate people can respond more readily to leadership for change in culture, technology, social mores, but that literacy by itself does not induce appetites for change, improvement or exploration. (52)

There are a number of illustrations of this; one specific case-study is provided by Kenneth Lockridge, whose inquiry into the social context of literacy in Colonial New England leads him to conclude:

> [T]here is no evidence that literacy ever entailed new attitudes among men, even in the decades when male literacy was spreading rapidly toward universality, and there is positive evidence that the world view of literate New Englanders remained as traditional as that of their illiterate neighbors. (4)

It is even difficult to demonstrate causal links between reading and writing and changes in the economic sphere—an area that "modernization theorists" generally thought to be particularly sensitive to gains in literacy. Harvey Graff's study of social mobility in three mid-19th century towns revealed that "systematic patterns of inequality and stratification . . . were deep and pervasive and relatively unaltered by the influence of literacy." He continues:

> Class, ethnicity, and sex were the major barriers of social inequality. The majority of Irish Catholic adults, for example, were literate . . . but they

stood lowest in wealth and occupation, as did laborers and servants. Women and blacks faired little better, regardless of literacy . . . social realities contradicted the promoted promises of literacy. (*The Literacy Myth* 320-21)

Similar assertions are made closer to home by Carman St. John Hunter and David Harmon, whose overview of the research on contemporary adult illiteracy leads to this conclusion:

For most persons who lack literacy skills, illiteracy is simply one factor interacting with many others—class, race and sex discrimination, welfare dependency, unemployment, poor housing, and a general sense of powerlessness. The acquisition of reading and writing skills would eliminate conventional illiteracy among many but would have no appreciable effect on the other factors that perpetuate the poverty of their lives. (9-12. See also Ogbu.)

The oral-literate distinction can help us see differences in the communicative technologies available to the members of a society, to get a sense of formats, means, and forums through which communication occurs (Enos and Ackerman). But it appears to be historically, culturally, and economically reductive—and politically naive—to view literacy as embodying an automatic transformational power. What is called for is a contextual view of literacy: the ability to read or to write is a technology or a method or a behavior, a set of conventions that interact in complex ways with a variety of social forces to shape society and culture. It is, to use Harvey Graff's phrasing, a "myth" to assume that literacy necessarily sparks social change.

Literacy and Cognition

Let us move now from the social-cultural realm to some of the claims made about cognition. These come from two highly diverse sources: classical philological studies of epic poetry and anthropological studies of thought and language. There are problems with both.

The key work in the classicist vein is Eric Havelock's investigation of Greek culture before and after the advent of the alphabet. In books ranging from *Preface to Plato* (published in 1963) to *The Muse Learns to Write* (1986) Havelock has made the strong claim that pre-alphabetic Greeks, ingenious as they were, were barred from philosophical thought because oral discourse could not generate abstract, propositional language or self-conscious reflection on language as language. To be sure, there are times when Havelock's claims are less extreme, but even in *The Muse Learns to*

Write, a tempered book, one finds questions and statements like these: "May not all logical thinking as commonly understood be a product of Greek alphabetic literacy?" (39) and "it is only as language is written down that it becomes possible to think about it" (112). And such theorizing quickly leads to a troublesome alphabetic determinism.

Havelock's work is compelling, but we must remember that when it comes to cognition, he is operating very much in the realm of speculation. That is, he infers things about cognitive processes and the limits of reasoning ability from the study of ancient texts, some of which represent genres that one would not expect to give rise to philosophic inquiry. Furthermore, even if we accepted his method, we could find powerful counterstatements to his thesis—and some of these are contained in a festschrift issued by the Monist Press. Examining the same texts from which Havelock built his case, University of Chicago classicist Arthur W. H. Adkins provides evidence of abstraction, verbal self-consciousness, and the linguistic resources to engage in systematic thinking. He concludes that:

> Havelock has not as yet demonstrated any *necessary* link between literacy and abstract thought . . . he has not as yet demonstrated that *in fact* the stimulus to abstract thought in early Greece was the invention of writing; [and] some features denied by Havelock to be available in oral speech are found in the Homeric poems. (220. See also Margolis.)

The other line of argument about literacy and cognition comes from twentieth-century anthropological studies of the reasoning of rural farmers and primitive tribesmen. These studies tend not to be of literacy-orality per se, but are appropriated by some orality-literacy theorists. A good deal of this cross-cultural research has involved classification tasks: a set of objects (or a set of pictures of the objects) is given to a tribesman, and the investigator asks the tribesman to group the objects/pictures. The key issue is the scheme by which the tribesman completes the grouping: does he, for example, place a hoe with a potato and offer the *concrete* reason that they go together because you need one to get the other, or does he place the hoe with a knife because he reasons *abstractly* that they are both tools? The Western anthropologist considers concrete reasoning to be less advanced than abstract reasoning, and orality-literacy theorists like to pose literacy as the crucial variable fostering abstract reasoning. It is because the tribesman lacks letters that he is locked into the concrete. This is an appealing conjecture, but, as I hope the previous discussion suggests, literacy is too intertwined with schooling and urbanization, with economics, politics, and religion to be able to isolate it and make such a claim. There are other problems too, not just with the causal linking of literacy and abstraction, but with traditional comparative research itself. Cole and Means put it this way:

> [D]epartures from the typical performance patterns of American adults are not necessarily deficits, but may indeed be excellent adaptations to the life circumstances of the people involved. . . . Which type of classification is preferable will depend upon the context, that is, the number of different types of objects to be grouped and the way in which the materials are going to be used . . . preference for one type of grouping over another is really no more than that—just a matter of preference. (161-62)

In line with the above, it must be kept in mind that because "primitive" subjects tend to classify objects in ways we label concrete does not necessarily mean that they can think in no other way. Consider, as we close this section, a wonderful anecdote from anthropologist Joseph Glick, as retold by Jacqueline Goodenow:

> The investigators had gathered a set of 20 objects, 5 each from 4 categories: food, clothing, tools, and cooking utensils. . . . [W]hen asked to put together the objects that belonged together, [many of the tribesmen produced] not 4 groups of 5 but 10 groups of 2. Moreover, the type of grouping and the type of reason given were frequently of the type we regard as extremely concrete, e.g., "the knife goes with the orange because it cuts it." Glick . . . notes, however, that subjects at times volunteered "'that a wise man would do things in the way this was done.' When an exasperated experimenter asked finally, 'How would a fool do it?' he was given back groupings of the type . . . initially expected—four neat piles with foods in one, tools in another." (170-71. For fuller cross-cultural discussions of concrete vs. abstract reasoning see Ginsburg; Lave; and Tulkin and Konner.)

Literacy and Language

It is problematic, then, to claim that literacy necessarily causes a transformation of culture, society, or mind or that societies without high levels of literacy are barred from the mental activities that some theorists have come to associate with literacy: verbal self-consciousness, abstraction, etc. Perhaps, though, the orality-literacy construct does have value if one strips away the cultural-cognitive baggage; its real benefit might be its ability to help us understand the nature of the language experiences students received in their homes and communities and further help to distinguish between the oral and literate features in their writing. But even here there are problems, for the reality of speaking-writing relationships seems to be more complex than the oral-literate distinction suggests.

Certainly, there are bioanatomical and perceptual differences between speech and writing—differences in the way each is acquired, produced, and comprehended. And if you examine very different types of language (e.g., dinner-table conversation vs. academic prose), you will find significant grammatical and stylistic differences as well. (See, for example, Chafe.) But the oral-literate construct leads us to focus attention too narrowly on the channel, the mode of communication, in a way that can (a) imply a distinctive uniformity to oral modes vs. written modes and (b) downplay the complex interaction among human motive, language production, and social setting. Linguists currently working with oral narratives and written texts suggest that the notion of an oral narrative itself is problematic, for oral traditions can differ in major ways (Scollon and Scollon); that the narrative variations we see may have less to do with literateness than with cultural predispositions (Tannen, "A Comparative Analysis"); that features often defined as literate are frequently found in oral discourse and vice versa (Polanyi; Tannen, "Relative Focus"); that characteristics identified by some as a mark of preliterate discourse—e.g., formulaic expressions—are woven throughout the language of literate people (Fillmore); that while spoken sentences can be shown to differ from written sentences, they are not necessarily less complex grammatically (Halliday); and so on. Finally, it seems that many of the differences we can find between stretches of speech and writing might, as Karen Beamon suggests, depend on factors such as genre, context, register, topic, level of formality, and purpose as much as whether the passage is spoken or written.

These closer examinations of a wide variety of texts and utterances should make us wary of neat, bipolar characterizations—whether dichotomies or simple continua—of oral vs. written language. And it seems to me that this caution about the linguistic reality of the oral-literate distinction could lead to reservations about its contemporary social reality—that is, can we accurately and sensitively define, in late twentieth-century America, entire communities and subcultures as being oral and others as being literate? By what criteria, finally, will we be able to make such a distinction? In asking these questions, I am not trying to downplay the obvious: children enter school with widely different degrees of exposure to literacy activities and with significantly different experiences as to how those activities are woven into their lives. And these differences clearly have consequences for schooling.

What I do want to raise, though, is the possibility that the oral-literate continuum does not adequately characterize these differences. The continuum, because it moves primarily along the single dimension of speech-print, slights history and politics—remember, it weights literacy as *the* primary force in cognitive development and social change—and it encourages, because of its bipolarity, a dichotomizing of modes where complex interweaving seems to exist. Finally, the orality-literacy construct tends to reduce the very social-linguistic richness it is meant to describe. Here is Shirley Brice Heath on the language behaviors of two working-class communities in the Carolinas:

> The residents of each community are able to read printed and written materials in their daily lives and, on occasion, they produce written messages as part of the total pattern of communication in the community. In both communities, the residents turn from spoken to written uses of language and vice versa as the occasion demands, and the two modes of expression serve to supplement and reinforce each other. Yet, in terms of the usual distinctions made between oral and literate traditions, neither community may be simply classified as either "oral" or "literate." (*Ways with Words* 203)

Work like Heath's challenges the sociological and linguistic utility of the orality-literacy construct; in fact, elsewhere Heath directly criticizes "current tendencies to classify communities as being at one or another point along a hypothetical [oral-literate] continuum which has no societal reality" ("Protean Shapes" 116).

What is most troubling on this score is the way the orality-literacy construct is sometimes used to represent language use in the urban ghetto. What emerges is a stereotypic characterization of linguistic homogeneity— all the residents learn from the sermon but not the newspaper; they run the dozens but are ignorant of print. The literacy backgrounds of people who end up in remedial, developmental, or adult education classes are more complex than that: they represent varying degrees of distance from or involvement with printed material, various attitudes toward it and skill with it, various degrees of embracement of or complicated rejection of traditions connected with their speech. Important here is what Mina Shaughnessy and Glynda Hull so carefully demonstrate: some of the most vexing problems writing teachers face are rooted in the past attempts of educationally marginalized people *to make sense of the uses of print.* Print is splattered across the inner city, and, in effective and ineffective ways, people incorporate it into their lives.

There is a related problem. Some theorists link Piagetian notions of cognitive egocentrism with generalizations about orality and conclude that without the language of high literacy, people will be limited in their ability to "decenter," to recognize the need to "decontextualize" what they are communicating, to perceive and respond to the social and informational needs of the other. Certainly, people with poor educations will have a great deal of trouble doing such things in writing, but one must be very cautious about leaping from stunted and limited texts to inferences about deficits in social cognition or linguistic flexibility. Developmentally and sociologically oriented linguists have demonstrated for some time that human beings are not locked into one way of speaking, one register, and develop, at quite a young age, the recognition that different settings call for different kinds of speech (Hudson). Poor writers are not as a population cognitively egocentric; they are aware of the other, of "audience"—some disenfranchised people acutely so. What they lack are the opportunities to develop both oral and written communicative facility in a range of settings. Or they may resist developing that facility out of anger or fear or as an act of identity. They may prefer one way of speaking, most of us do, and thus haven't developed a fluency of voices. But rather than being cognitively locked out of other registers, other linguistic roles, other points of view, they are more likely emotionally and politically barred from them.

It is obvious that literacy enables us to do a great deal. It provides a powerful solution to what Walter Ong calls "the problem of retaining and retrieving carefully articulated thought" (34). It enables us to record discourse, scan and scrutinize it, store it—and this has an effect on the way we educate, do business, and run the courts. And as we further pursue intellectual work, reading and writing become integral parts of inquiry, enable us to push certain kinds of analysis to very sophisticated levels. In fact, as investigations of academic and research settings like Latour and Woolgar's *Laboratory Life* suggest, it becomes virtually impossible to tease writing and reading out of the conduct and progress of Western humanistic *or* scientific inquiry. One of the values of the orality-literacy construct is that it makes us aware of how central literacy is to such inquiry. But, finally, the bipolarity of the construct (as with the others we've examined) urges a way of thinking about language, social change, and cognition that easily becomes dichotomous and reductive. "The tyranny of conceptual dichotomies," Graff calls it ("Reflections" 313). If writing is thought to possess a given characteristic—say, decontextualization or abstraction—then the dichotomy requires you to place the opposite characteristic—contextualization, concreteness—in the non-writing category (cf. Elbow). We end up splitting cognition along linguistic separations that exist more in theory than in social practice.

CONCLUSION

Witkin uncovered interesting perceptual differences and led us toward a deeper consideration of the interrelations of personality, problem solving, and social cognition. Hemisphericity theorists call our attention to the neurological substrate of information processing and language production. Piaget developed an insightful, non-behaviorist method to study cognitive growth and, more comprehensively than anyone in our time, attempted to articulate the changes in reasoning we see as children develop. And the orality-literacy theorists give us compelling reflection on spoken and written language and encourage us to consider the potential relations between modes of communication and modes of thought. My intention in this essay is not to dismiss these thinkers and theories but to present the difficulties in applying to remedial writers these models of mind. For there is a tendency to accept as fact condensed deductions from them—statements stripped away from the questions, contradictions, and complexities that are central to them. Let me summarize the problems I see with the theories we've been considering.

First, the theories end up levelling rather than elaborating individual differences in cognition. At best, people are placed along slots on a single continuum; at worst they are split into mutually exclusive camps—with one camp clearly having cognitive and social privilege over the other. The complexity of cognition—its astounding glides and its blunderous missteps as well—is narrowed, and the rich variability that exists in any social setting is ignored or reduced. This reductive labelling is going on in composition studies at a time when cognitive researchers in developmental and educational psychology, artificial intelligence, and philosophy are posing more elaborate and domain-specific models of cognition.

Second, and in line with the above, the four theories encourage a drift away from careful, rigorous focus on student writing and on the cognitive processes that seem directly related to it, that reveal themselves as students compose. That is, field dependence-independence, hemisphericity, etc., lead us from a close investigation of the production of written discourse and toward general, wide-ranging processes whose link to writing has, for the most part, been *assumed rather than demonstrated*. Even orality-literacy theory, which certainly concerns language, urges an antagonism between speech and writing that carries with it sweeping judgments about cognition.

The theories also avert or narrow our gaze from the immediate social and linguistic conditions in which the student composes: the rich interplay of purpose, genre, register, textual convention, and institutional expectation (Bartholomae; Bizzell; McCormick). When this textual-institutional context is addressed, it is usually in simplified terms: the faculty—and their discourse—are literate, left-hemispheric, field-independent, etc., and underprepared students are oral, right-hemispheric, and field dependent. I hope my critical surveys have demonstrated the conceptual limits of such labelling.

Third, the theories inadvertently reflect cultural stereotypes that should, themselves, be the subject of our investigation. At least since Plato, we in the West have separated heart from head, and in one powerful manifestation of that split we contrast rational thought with emotional sensibility, intellectual acuity with social awareness—and we often link the analytical vs. holistic opposition to these polarities. (I tried to reveal the confusion inherent in such talk when discussing cognitive style and hemisphericity.) These notions are further influenced by and play into other societal notions about independence and individuality vs. communal and tribal orientations and they domino quickly toward stereotypes about race, class, and gender.

Let me say now that I am not claiming that the research in cognitive style or hemisphericity or any of the other work we surveyed is of necessity racist, sexist, or elitist. The conclusions that can be drawn from the work, however, mesh with—and could have been subtly influenced by—cultural biases that are troubling. This is an important and, I realize, sensitive point. Some assert that student writers coming from particular communities can't reason logically or analytically, that the perceptual processes of these students are more dependent on context than the processes of white, middle-class students, that particular racial or social groups are right-hemispheric, that the student writers we teach from these groups are cognitively egocentric.

A number of recent books have amply demonstrated the way 19th and early 20th century scientific, social scientific, and humanistic assessments of mental capacity and orientation were shaped by that era's racial, gender, and class biases (see, for example, Gilman; Gould; Kamin; and Valenstein). We now find these assessments repellent, but it's important to remember that while some were made by reactionary social propagandists, a number were made as well by thinkers operating with what they saw as rigorous method—and some of those thinkers espoused a liberal social philosophy. This is a powerful illustration of the hidden influences of culture on allegedly objective investigations of mind. We all try to make sense of problematic performance—that's part of a teacher's or a researcher's job—but we must ask ourselves if speculation about cognitive egocentrism and concrete thinking and holistic perception embodies unexamined cultural biases about difference—biases that would be revealed to us if we could adopt other historical and social perspectives.

These summary statements have a number of implications for research.

The leap to theory is a privileged move—it is revered in the academy and allows parsimonious interpretations of the baffling variability of behavior. But a theory, any theory, is no more than a best guess at a given time, simultaneously evocative and flawed. Especially when it comes to judging cognition, we need to be particularly aware of these flaws and limitations, for in our culture judgments about mind carry great weight. A good deal of careful, basic descriptive and definitional work must be done before we embrace a theory, regardless of how compelling it is.

A series of fundamental questions should precede the application of theory: Is the theory formulated in a way that allows application to writing; that is, can it be defined in terms of discourse? Given what we know about writing, how would the theory be expected to manifest itself—i.e., what would it mean textually and dynamically for someone to be a field-dependent writer? What will the theory allow us to explain about writing that we haven't explained before? What will it allow us to do pedagogically that we weren't able to do as well before? Will the theory strip and narrow experience and cognition, or does it promise to open up the histories of students' involvement with writing, their rules, strategies, and assumptions, the invitations and denials that characterized their encounters with print?

Beyond such general questions are more specific guidelines for those of us doing psychological research. Once we undertake an investigation of cognition we must be careful to discuss our findings in terms of the kinds of writing we investigate. Generalizing to other tasks, and particularly to broad cognitive processes, is not warranted without evidence from those other domains. If theories like the four we discussed, but others too (e.g., theories of moral development, social cognition, metacognition, etc.), are appropriated that are built on particular tests, then researchers must thoroughly familiarize themselves with the tests beneath the theories and consult with psychologists who use them. People who are going to administer such tests should take the tests themselves—see what they're like from the inside. My mentor Richard Shavelson also urges researchers to administer the tests to individual students and have them talk about what they're doing, get some sense of how students might interpret or misinterpret the instructions, the various ways they represent the task to themselves, what cognitive processes seem to come into play as the students work with the tests. Furthermore, it must be remembered that the results of testing will be influenced by the degree of familiarity the students have with the tests and by the social situation created in the administration of them. How will these conditions be adjusted for and acknowledged? Finally, the resulting data must be discussed as being specific to the students tested. Generalizing to others must be done with caution.

A special word needs to be said here about comparative studies. If we employ hi-lo designs, expert-novice studies, and the like—which can be powerfully revealing designs—we need to consider our design and our results from historical and sociopolitical perspectives as well as cognitive ones. That is, if class, gender, or race differences emerge—and they certainly could—they should not automatically be assumed to reflect "pure" cognitive differences, but rather effects that might well be conditioned by and interpreted in light of historical, socio-political realities. There is currently a lot of talk about the prospect of forging a social-cognitive orientation to composition research (see, for example, Freedman, Dyson, Flower, and Chafe; Bizzell and Herzberg). One of the exciting results of such an endeavor could be an increased sensitivity to the social forces that shape cognitive activity. I've argued elsewhere for a research framework that intersects the cognitive, affective, and situational dimensions of composing and that involves the systematic combination of multiple methods, particularly ones traditionally thought to be antagonistic. My assumption is that the careful integration of, say, cognitive process-tracing and naturalistic observation methods can both contribute to fresh and generative insight and provide a guard against reductive interpretation (Rose, "Complexity").

Much of this essay has concerned researchers and theoreticians, but at the heart of the discussion is a basic question for any of us working with poor writers: How do we go about judging the thought processes involved with reading and writing when performance is problematic, ineffective, or stunted? If I could compress this essay's investigation down to a single conceptual touchstone, it would be this: Human cognition—even at its most stymied, bungled moments—is rich and varied. It is against this assumption that we should test our theories and research methods and classroom assessments. Do our practices work against classification that encourages single, monolithic explanations of cognitive activity? Do they honor the complexity of interpretive efforts even when those efforts fall short of some desired goal? Do they foster investigation of interaction and protean manifestation rather than investigation of absence: abstraction is absent, consciousness of print is absent, logic is absent? Do they urge reflection on the cultural biases that might be shaping them? We must be vigilant that the systems of intellect we develop or adapt do not ground our students' difficulties in sweeping, essentially one-dimensional perceptual, neurophysiological, psychological, or linguistic processes, systems that drive broad cognitive wedges between those who do well in our schools and those who don't.[5]

NOTES

1. For presentation, qualification, or rebuttal of this orientation see, for example: Ann E. Berthoff, "Is Teaching Still Possible?" *College English* 46 (1984): 743-55; Thomas J. Farrell, "I.Q. and Standard English," *CCC* 34 (1983): 470-85 and the replies to Farrell by

Greenberg, Hartwell, Himley, and Stratton in *CCC* 35 (1984): 455-78; George H. Jensen, "The Reification of the Basic Writer," *Journal of Basic Writing* 5 (1986): 52-64; Andrea Lunsford, "Cognitive Development and the Basic Writer," *College English* 41 (1979): 38-46 and Lunsford, "Cognitive Studies and Teaching Writing," *Perspectives on Research and Scholarship in Composition*, Ed. Ben W. McClelland and Timothy R. Donovan, New York: MLA, (1986): 145-61; Walter J. Ong, "Literacy and Orality in Our Times," *Profession 79*, Ed. Jasper P. Neel, New York: MLA, 1979: 1-7; Lynn Quitman Troyka, "Perspectives on Legacies and Literacy in the 1980s," *CCC* 33 (1982): 252-62 and Troyka, "Defining Basic Writers in Context," *A Sourcebook for Basic Writing Teachers*, Ed. Theresa Enos, New York: Random House, 1987: 2-15; James D. Williams, "Coherence and Cognitive Style," *Written Communication* 2 (1985): 473-91. For illustration of the transfer of this issue to the broader media, see Ellen K. Coughlin, "Literacy: 'Excitement' of New Field Attracts Scholars of Literature," *The Chronicle of Higher Education* 29 (9 Jan. 1985): 1, 10.

2. For a description of the other tests—the Body Adjustment Test and the rarely used auditory and tactile embedded figures tests—see Witkin, et al.

3. Witkin later revised his theory, suggesting that the rod and frame test and the embedded figures test were tapping different dimensions of the field dependence-independence construct. This revision, however, gives rise to further problems—see Linn and Kyllonen.

4. Educators and evaluators often seem locked into a 19th century linear progress conception of the way both societies and individuals appropriate literacy. Graff presents a provocative historical challenge to such notions; here's Vygotsky on individual development: "together with processes of development, forward motion, and appearance of new forms, we can discern processes of curtailment, disappearance, and reverse development of old forms at each step . . . only a naive view of development as a purely evolutionary process. . . can conceal from us the true nature of these processes" (106).

5. Particular sections of this paper were discussed with or reviewed by specialists who provided a great deal of expert help: Susan Curtiss (neurolinguistics), Richard Leo Enos (classical studies), Sari Gilman (research psychiatry), John R. Hayes, Richard Shavelson, and Catherine Stasz (cognitive and educational psychology), Thomas Huckin (linguistics), Robert Siegler (developmental psychology). David Bartholomae, Linda Flower, Glynda Hull, David Kaufer, and Stephen Witte commented generously on the entire manuscript. The project benefited as well from rich conversation with Mariolina Salvatori and Kathryn Flannery. Versions of the paper were read at Carnegie Mellon, Pitt, Indiana University of Pennsylvania, UCLA, Berkeley, CCCC (Atlanta), Penn State, and UCSD. My thanks for all the ideas generated at those conferences and colloquia. Finally, appreciation is due to Sally Magargee for her research assistance and the Carnegie Mellon Department of English and the Spencer Foundation for their support.

WORKS CITED

Adkins, Arthur W.H. "Orality and Philosophy." Robb 207-27.

Adler, Jonathan. "Abstraction is Uncooperative." *Journal for the Theory of Social Behavior* 14 (1984): 165-81.

Arndt, Stephen, and Dale E. Berger. "Cognitive Mode and Asymmetry in Cerebral Functioning." *Cortex* 14 (1978): 78-86.

Bartholomae, David. "Inventing the University." Rose, *When a Writer Can't Write* 134-65.

Battig, William F. "Within-Individual Differences in 'Cognitive' Processes." *Information Processing and Cognition*. Ed. Robert L. Solso. Hillsdale, NJ: Erlbaum, 1975. 195-228.

Beamon, Karen. "Coordination and Subordination Revisited: Syntactic Complexity in Spoken and Written Narrative Discourse." Tannen, *Coherence in Spoken and Written Discourse* 45-80.

Beaumont, J. Graham. "Methods for Studying Cerebral Hemispheric Function." *Functions of the Right Cerebral Hemisphere*. Ed. A.W. Young. London: Academic Press, 1983. 113-46.

Beaumont, J. Graham, A.W. Young, and I.C. McManus. "Hemisphericity: A Critical Review." *Cognitive Neuropsychology* 2 (1984): 191-212.

Benson, D. Frank, and Eran Zaidel, eds. *The Dual Brain: Hemispheric Specialization in Humans*. New York: Guilford, 1985.

Berthoff, Ann E. "Is Teaching Still Possible?" *College English* 46 (1984): 743-55.

Bizzell, Patricia. "Cognition, Convention, and Certainty: What We Need to Know about Writing." *Pre/Text* 3 (1982): 213-44.

Bizzell, Patricia, and Bruce Herzberg. *The Bedford Bibliography for Teachers of Writing*. Boston: Bedford Books, 1987.

Bogen, Joseph. "The Dual Brain: Some Historical and Methodological Aspects." Benson and Zaidel 27-43.

Bogen, Joseph, et al. "The Other Side of the Brain: The A/P Ratio." *Bulletin of Los Angeles Neurological Society* 37 (1972): 49-61.

Bradshaw, J.L., and N.C. Nettleton. "The Nature of Hemispheric Specialization in Man." *Behavioral and Brain Sciences* 4 (1981): 51-91.

Brainerd, Charles J. "The Stage Question in Cognitive-Developmental Theory." *The Behavioral and Brain Sciences* 2 (1978): 173-81.

Brown, Warren S., James T. Marsh, and Ronald E. Ponsford. "Hemispheric Differences in Event-Related Brain Potentials." Benson and Zaidel 163-79.

Caplan, David. "On the Cerebral Localization of Linguistic Functions: Logical and Empirical Issues Surrounding Deficit Analysis and Functional Localization." *Brain and Language* 14 (1981): 120-37.

Carey, Susan. *Conceptual Change in Childhood*. Cambridge: MIT P, 1985.

Chafe, Wallace L. "Linguistic Differences Produced by Differences in Speaking and Writing." Olson, Torrance, and Hildyard 105-23.

Clanchy, M.T. *From Memory to Written Record: England 1066-1307*. Cambridge: Harvard UP, 1979.

Cole, Michael, and Barbara Means. *Comparative Studies of How People Think*. Cambridge: Harvard UP, 1981.

Cressy, David. "The Environment for Literacy: Accomplishment and Context in Seventeenth-Century England and New England." *Literacy in Historical Perspective*. Ed. Daniel P. Resnick. Washington: Library of Congress, 1983. 23-42.

Cronbach, Lee J. *Essentials of Psychological Testing*. New York: Harper and Row, 1960.

DeRenzi, Ennio. *Disorders of Space Exploration and Cognition*. London: Wiley, 1982.

Donaldson, Margaret. *Children's Minds*. New York: Norton, 1979.

Donchin, Emanuel, Gregory McCarthy, and Marta Kutas. "Electroencephalographic Investigations of Hemispheric Specialization." *Language and Hemispheric Specialization in Man: Cerebral Event-Related Potentials*. Ed. John E. Desmedt. Basel, NY: Karger, 1977. 212-42.

Dumas, Roland, and Arlene Morgan. "EEG Asymmetry as a Function of Occupation, Task and Task Difficulty." *Neuropsychologia* 13 (1975): 214-28.

Efron, Robert. "The Central Auditory System and Issues Related to Hemispheric Specialization." *Assessment of Central Auditory Dysfunction: Foundations and Clinical Correlates.* Ed. Marilyn L. Pinheiro and Frank E. Musiek. Baltimore: Williams and Wilkins, 1985. 143-54.

Ehrlichman, Howard, and Arthur Weinberger. "Lateral Eye Movements and Hemispheric Asymmetry: A Critical Review." *Psychological Bulletin* 85 (1978): 1080-1101.

Elbow, Peter. "The Shifting Relationships Between Speech and Writing." *CCC* 34 (1985): 283-303.

Enos, Richard Leo, and John Ackerman. "*Letteraturizzazione* and Hellenic Rhetoric: An Analysis for Research with Extensions." *Proceedings of 1984 Rhetoric Society of America Conference.* Ed. Charles Kneupper, forthcoming.

Fillmore, Charles J. "On Fluency." *Individual Differences in Language Ability and Language Behavior.* Ed. Charles J. Fillmore, Daniel Kempler, and William S.Y. Wang. New York: Academic Press, 1979. 85-101.

Flavell, John H. *Cognitive Development.* Englewood Cliffs: Prentice-Hall, 1977.

Fodor, Jerry A. *The Modularity of Mind.* Cambridge: MIT P, 1983.

Freedman, Sarah, et al. *Research in Writing: Past, Present, and Future.* Berkeley: Center for the Study of Writing, 1987.

Gardner, Howard. *Frames of Mind.* New York: Basic Books, 1983.

———. *The Mind's New Science.* New York: Basic Books, 1985.

———. "What We Know (and Don't Know) About the Two Halves of the Brain." *Journal of Aesthetic Education* 12 (1978): 113-19.

Gardner, Howard, and Ellen Winner. "Artistry and Aphasia." *Acquired Aphasia.* Ed. Martha Taylor Sarno. New York: Academic Press, 1981. 361-84.

Gelman, Rochelle. "Cognitive Development." *Ann. Rev. Psychol.* (1978): 297-332.

Gevins, A.S., et al. "EEG Patterns During 'Cognitive' Tasks." *Electroencephalography and Clinical Neurophysiology* 47 (1979): 704-10.

Gilman, Sander. *Difference and Pathology.* Ithaca, NY: Cornell UP, 1985.

Ginsburg, Herbert. "Poor Children, African Mathematics, and the Problem of Schooling." *Educational Research Quarterly* 2 (1978): 26-44.

Glaser, Robert. "Education and Thinking: The Role of Knowledge." *American Psychologist* 39 (1984): 93-104.

Goodenow, Jacqueline. "The Nature of Intelligent Behavior: Questions Raised by Cross-Cultural Studies." *The Nature of Intelligence.* Ed. Lauren B. Resnick. Hillsdale, NJ: Erlbaum, 1976. 168-88.

Goody, Jack. *The Domestication of the Savage Mind.* London: Cambridge UP, 1977.

Gould, Stephen Jay. *The Mismeasure of Man.* New York: Norton, 1981.

Graff, Harvey. *The Literacy Myth.* New York: Academic Press, 1979.

———. "Reflections on the History of Literacy: Overview, Critique, and Proposals." *Humanities and Society* 4 (1981): 303-33.

Gruber, Howard E., and J. Jacques Vonèche, eds. *The Essential Piaget.* New York: Basic Books, 1977.

Halliday, M.A.K. "Differences Between Spoken and Written Language." *Communication through Reading.* Vol. 2. Ed. Glenda Page, John Elkins, and Barrie O'Connor. Adelaide, SA: Australian Reading Association, 1979. 37-52.

Havelock, Eric. *The Muse Learns to Write.* Cambridge: Harvard UP, 1986.

———. *Preface to Plato.* Cambridge: Harvard UP, 1963.

Harré, Rom, and Roger Lamb. *The Encyclopedic Dictionary of Psychology.* Cambridge: MIT P, 1983.

Heath, Shirley Brice. "Protean Shapes in Literacy Events: Ever-Shifting Oral and Literate Traditions." *Spoken and Written Language.* Ed. Deborah Tannen. Norwood, NJ: Ablex, 1982. 91-117.

———. *Ways With Words.* London: Cambridge UP, 1983.

Hillyard, Steve A., and David L. Woods. "Electrophysiological Analysis of Human Brain Function." *Handbook of Behavioral Neurobiology.* Vol. 2. Ed. Michael S. Gazzaniga. New York: Plenum, 1979. 343-78.

Hudson, R.A. *Sociolinguistics.* Cambridge: Cambridge UP, 1986.

Hull, Glynda. "The Editing Process in Writing: A Performance Study of Experts and Novices." Diss. U of Pittsburgh, 1983.

Hunt, Earl. "On the Nature of Intelligence." *Science* 219 (1983): 141-46.

Hunter, Carman St. John, and David Harmon. *Adult Illiteracy in the United States.* New York: McGraw-Hill, 1985.

Inhelder, Barbel, and Jean Piaget. *The Growth of Logical Thinking from Childhood to Adolescence.* Trans. Anne Parsons and Stanley Milgram. New York: Basic Books, 1958.

Jensen, George H. "The Reification of the Basic Writer." *Journal of Basic Writing* 5 (1986): 52-64.

Kamin, Leon J. *The Science and Politics of I.Q.* Hillsdale, NJ: Erlbaum, 1974.

Kuhn, Deanna, Victoria Ho, and Catherine Adams. "Formal Reasoning Among Pre- and Late Adolescents." *Child Development* 50 (1979): 1128-35.

Kurtz, Richard M. "A Conceptual Investigation of Witkin's Notion of Perceptual Style." *Mind* 78 (1969): 522-33.

Latour, Bruno, and Steve Woolgar. *Laboratory Life.* Beverly Hills, CA: Sage, 1979.

Lave, Jean. "Cognitive Consequences of Traditional Apprenticeship Training in West Africa." *Anthropology and Education Quarterly* 8 (1977): 177-80.

LeDoux, Joseph E. "Cerebral Asymmetry and the Integrated Function of the Brain." *Functions of the Right Cerebral Hemisphere.* Ed. Andrew W. Young. London: Academic Press, 1983. 203-16.

Linn, Marcia C., and Patrick Kyllonen. "The Field Dependence-Independence Construct: Some, One, or None." *Journal of Educational Psychology* 73 (1981): 261-73.

Lockridge, Kenneth. *Literacy in Colonial New England.* New York: Norton, 1974.

Margolis, Joseph. "The Emergence of Philosophy." Robb 229-43.

Marrou, H.I. *A History of Education in Antiquity.* Madison, WI: U of Wisconsin P, 1982.

McCormick, Kathleen. *The Cultural Imperatives Underlying Cognitive Acts.* Berkeley: Center for The Study of Writing, 1986.

McKenna, Frank P. "Field Dependence and Personality: A Re-examination." *Social Behavior and Personality* 11 (1983): 51-55.

Messick, Samuel. "Personality Consistencies in Cognition and Creativity." *Individuality in Learning.* Ed. Samuel Messick and Associates. San Francisco: Jossey-Bass, 1976. 4-22.

Ogbu, John U. *Minority Education and Caste.* New York: Academic Press, 1978.

Olson, David R., Nancy Torrance, and Angela Hildyard, eds. *Literacy, Language, and Learning.* New York: Cambridge UP, 1981.

Ong, Walter J. *Orality and Literacy: The Technologizing of the Word.* New York: Methuen, 1982.

Ornstein, Robert E., and David Galin. "Psychological Studies of Consciousness." *Symposium on Consciousness.* Ed. Philip R. Lee et al. New York: Viking, 1976. 53-66.

Oxenham, John. *Literacy: Writing, Reading, and Social Organisation.* London: Routledge and Kegan Paul, 1980.

Perkins, D.N. "General Cognitive Skills: Why Not?" *Thinking and Learning Skills.* Ed. Susan F. Chipman, Judith W. Segal, and Robert Glaser. Hillsdale, NJ: Erlbaum, 1985. 339-63.

Piaget, Jean. "Intellectual Evolution from Adolescence to Adulthood." *Human Development* 15 (1972): 1-12.

Polanyi, Livia. *Telling the American Story: A Structural and Cultural Analysis of Conversational Storytelling.* Norwood, NJ: Ablex, 1985.

Robb, Kevin, ed. *Language and Thought in Early Greek Philosophy.* LaSalle, IL: Monist Library of Philosophy, 1983.

Rogoff, Barbara. *Everyday Cognition.* Cambridge: Harvard UP, 1984.

Rose, Mike. "Complexity, Rigor, Evolving Method, and the Puzzle of Writer's Block: Thoughts on Composing Process Research." Rose, *When a Writer Can't Write* 227-60.

——, ed. *When a Writer Can't Write: Studies in Writer's Block and Other Composing Process Problems.* New York: Guilford, 1985.

Rugg, Michael D. "Electrophysiological Studies." *Divided Visual Field Studies of Cerebral Organization.* Ed. J. Graham Beaumont. New York: Academic Press, 1982. 129-46.

Scollon, Ron, and Suzanne B.K. Scollon. "Cooking It Up and Boiling It Down: Abstracts in Athabascan Children's Story Retellings." Tannen, *Coherence in Spoken and Written Discourse* 173-97.

Shaughnessy, Mina. *Errors and Expectations.* New York: Oxford UP, 1977.

Siegler, Robert S. "Children's Thinking: The Search For Limits." *The Function of Language and Cognition.* Ed. G.J. Whitehurst and Barry J. Zimmerman. New York: Academic Press, 1979. 83-113.

Sperry, Roger W. "Consciousness, Personal Identity, and the Divided Brain." Benson and Zaidel 11-26.

Tannen, Deborah, ed. *Coherence in Spoken and Written Discourse.* Norwood, NJ: Ablex, 1984.

——. "A Comparative Analysis of Oral Narrative Strategies: Athenian Greek and American English." *The Pear Stories.* Ed. Wallace Chafe. Norwood, NJ: Ablex, 1980. 51-87.

——. "Relative Focus on Involvement in Oral and Written Discourse." Olson, Torrance, and Hildyard 124-47.

TenHouten, Warren D. "Social Dominance and Cerebral Hemisphericity: Discriminating Race, Socioeconomic Status, and Sex Groups by Performance on Two Lateralized Tests." *Intern J. Neuroscience* 10 (1980): 223-32.

Toulmin, Stephen. "Epistemology and Developmental Psychology." *Developmental Plasticity.* Ed. Eugene S. Gollin. New York: Academic Press, 1981. 253-67.

Tulkin, S.R., and M.J. Konner. "Alternative Conceptions of Intellectual Functioning." *Human Development* 16 (1973): 33-52.

Valenstein, Elliot S. *Great and Desperate Cures.* New York: Basic Books, 1986.

Vernon, Philip. "The Distinctiveness of Field Independence." *Journal of Personality* 40 (1972): 366-91.

Vygotsky, L.S. *Mind in Society.* Cambridge: Harvard UP, 1978.

Wachtel, Paul L. "Field Dependence and Psychological Differentiation: Reexamination." *Perceptual and Motor Skills* 35 (1972): 174-89.

Whitaker, Harry A., and George A. Ojemann. "Lateralization of Higher Cortical Functions: A Critique." *Evolution and Lateralization of the Brain.* Ed. Stuart Dimond and David Blizard. New York: New York Academy of Science, 1977. 459-73.

Williams, James Dale. "Coherence and Cognitive Style." Diss. U of Southern California, 1983.

Witkin, Herman A. "Psychological Differentiation and Forms of Pathology." *Journal of Abnormal Psychology* 70 (1965): 317-36.

Witkin, Herman A., et al. "Field-Dependent and Field-Independent Cognitive Styles and Their Educational Implications." *Review of Educational Research* 47 (1977): 1-64.

Wittrock, Merlin. "Education and the Cognitive Processes of the Brain." *Education and The Brain.* Ed. Jeanne S. Chall and Allen S. Mirsky. Chicago: U of Chicago P, 1978. 61-102.

Young, Andrew W. "Methodological and Theoretical Bases of Visual Hemifield Studies." *Divided Visual Field Studies of Cerebral Organisation.* Ed. J. Graham Beaumont. New York: Academic Press, 1982. 11-27.

Cognition, Convention, and Certainty

What We Need to Know about Writing

PATRICIA BIZZELL

What do we need to know about writing? Only recently have we needed to ask this question, and the asking has created composition studies. We have needed to ask it because of changing circumstances in the classroom, and our answers will be put to the test there with a speed uncommon in other academic disciplines. The current theoretical debate over how to go about finding these answers, therefore, is not merely an empty exercise. Students' lives will be affected in profound ways.

This profound effect on students is the more to be expected because of the terms in which the "writing problem" has appeared to us—terms that suggest that students' thinking needs remediation as much as their writing. Seeing the problem this way makes it very clear that our teaching task is not only to convey information but also to transform students' whole world view. But if this indeed is our project, we must be aware that it has such scope. Otherwise, we risk burying ethical and political questions under supposedly neutral pedagogical technique. Some of our answers to the question of what we need to know about writing are riskier in this regard than others.

We now see the "writing problem" as a thinking problem primarily because we used to take our students' thinking for granted. We used to assume that students came to us with ideas and we helped them put those ideas into words. We taught style, explaining the formal properties of model essays and evaluating students' products in the light of these models. Some students

Previously published in the journal *PRE/TEXT* 3.3 (1982): 213–243. Used by permission of Patricia Bizzell.

came to us with better ideas than others, but these were simply the brighter or more mature students. All we could do for the duller, more immature students was to hope that exposure to good models might push them along the developmental path.[1]

Over the last twenty years, however, we have encountered in our classrooms more and more students whose ideas seem so ill-considered, by academic standards, that we can no longer see the problem as primarily one of expression. Rather, we feel, "Now I have to teach them to think, too!" And at the same time, students have so much trouble writing Standard English that we are driven away from stylistic considerations back to the basics of grammar and mechanics. Teaching style from model essays has not prepared us to explain or repair these students' deficiencies. The new demands on us as teachers can only be met, it seems, by a reconsideration of the relationship between thought and language. We are pretty much agreed, in other words, that what we need to know about writing has to do with the thinking processes involved in it.

Composition specialists generally agree about some fundamental elements in the development of language and thought. We agree that the normal human individual possesses innate mental capacities to learn a language and to assemble complex conceptual structures. As the individual develops, these capacities are realized in her learning a native tongue and forming thought patterns that organize and interpret experience. The mature exercise of these thought and language capacities takes place in society, in interaction with other individuals, and this interaction modifies the individual's reasoning, speaking, and writing within society. Groups of society members can become accustomed to modifying each other's reasoning and language use in certain ways. Eventually, these familiar ways achieve the status of conventions that bind the group in a discourse community, at work together on some project of interaction with the material world. An individual can belong to more than one discourse community, but her access to the various communities will be unequally conditioned by her social situation.

If composition specialists generally agree about this description, however, we disagree about what part of it is relevant to composition studies. One theoretical camp sees writing as primarily inner-directed, and so is more interested in the structure of language-learning and thinking processes in their earliest state, prior to social influence. The other main theoretical camp sees writing as primarily outer-directed, and so is more interested in the social processes whereby language-learning and thinking capacities are shaped and used in particular communities. In the current debate, each camp seeks to define what we *most* need to know about writing.

Inner-directed theorists seek to discover writing processes that are so fundamental as to be universal. Later elaborations of thinking and language-using should be understood as outgrowths of individual capacities (see Figure 1). Hence, inner-directed theorists are most interested in individual capacities and their earliest interactions with experience (locations #1 and 2, Figure 1). The inner-directed theorists tend to see the kinds of reasoning occurring at all four locations as isomorphic—all the same basic logical structures.[2] They also tend to see differences in language use at different locations as superficial matters of lexical choice; the basic structure of the language cannot change from location to location because this structure is isomorphic with the innate mental structures that enabled one to learn a language, and hence presumably universal and independent of lexical choice. Nevertheless, looking for an argument to justify teaching one form of a language, some inner-directed theorists treat one set of lexical choices as better able than others to make language embody the innate structures.

Figure 1   An inner-directed model of the development of language and thought writing. Arrows indicate direction of individual's development, beginning with innate capacities and issuing finally in particular instances of use.

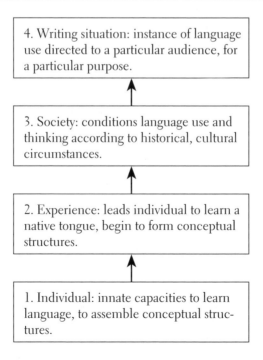

4. Writing situation: instance of language use directed to a particular audience, for a particular purpose.

3. Society: conditions language use and thinking according to historical, cultural circumstances.

2. Experience: leads individual to learn a native tongue, begin to form conceptual structures.

1. Individual: innate capacities to learn language, to assemble conceptual structures.

Insofar as these better choices fall into the patterns of, for example, a "standard" form of a native tongue, they make the standard intellectually superior to other forms.[3]

Inner-directed theorists further claim, in a similar paradox, that the universal, fundamental structures of thought and language can be taught. If our students are unable to have ideas, we should look around locations # 1 and 2 for structural models of the mental processes that are not happening in these students' minds. Once we find these models, we can guide students through the processes until the students' own thought-forming mechanisms "kick on" and they can make concepts on their own. An heuristic procedure is often presented as such a process model.[4] Similarly, if our students are unable to write English, we should look in the same locations for patterns of correct syntax, which we can then ask the students to practice until they internalize the patterns. Sentence-combining exercises offer such pattern practice.[5]

Once students are capable of cognitively sophisticated thinking and writing, they are ready to tackle the problems of a particular writing situation. These problems are usually treated by inner-directed theory as problems of audience analysis. Audience analysis seeks to identify the personal idiosyncracies of readers so that the writer can communicate her message to them in the most persuasive form. The changes made to accommodate an audience, however, are not seen as substantially altering the meaning of the piece of writing because that is based in the underlying structure of thought and language.[6]

In contrast, outer-directed theorists believe that universal, fundamental structures can't be taught; thinking and language use can never occur free of a social context that conditions them (see Figure 2). The outer-directed theorists believe that teaching style from model essays failed not because we were doing the wrong thing but because we weren't aware of what we were doing. Teaching style from model essays, in this view, is teaching the discourse conventions of a particular community—in this case, a community of intellectuals including, but not limited to, academics. But because we were unaware that we were in a discourse community, we taught the conventions as formal structures, as if they were universal patterns of thought and language. What we should do is to teach students that there are such things as discourse conventions.

The outer-directed theorists are sceptical about how we can obtain knowledge of what thinking and language-learning processes are innate. Moreover, they would argue that the individual is already inside a discourse community when she learns a native tongue, since the infant does not learn

Figure 2   An outer-directed model of the development of language and thought. Note that innate capacities have no expression outside discourse communities and that society is made up entirely of discourse communities. Individual has unequal access to different communities. Direction of development is outward from native community.

2. Society: aggregate of discourse communities that all share certain patterns of language-using, thinking conditioned by historical, cultural circumstances.

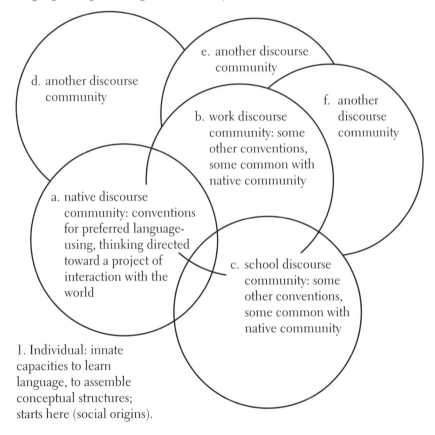

some generalized form of language but rather the habits of language use in the neighborhood, or the discourse community into which she is born.[7] Since this discourse community already possesses traditional, shared ways of understanding experience, the infant doesn't learn to conceptualize in a social vacuum, either, but is constantly being advised by more mature community members whether her inferences are correct, whether her groupings of experiential data into evidence are significant, and so on.[8] Some outer-directed theorists would go so far as to say that the lines of develop-ment of thought and language merge when the native tongue is learned, since one learns to think only by learning a language and one can't have an idea one doesn't have a word for.[9]

Outer-directed theorists would argue that we have no reason to believe, and no convincing way to determine, that our students can't think or use language in complex ways. It's just that they can't think or use language in the ways we want them to. To help them, then, we should be looking for ways to explain discourse conventions. We might find patterns of language use and reasoning that are common to all members of a society, patterns that are part of the set of conventions of every discourse community within the society. Conventions that are common in the society could be used as bridges between different discourse communities—for example, to ease the transition into the academic discourse community for students who come from discourse communities far removed from it.[10]

The staple activity of outer-directed writing instruction will be analysis of the conventions of particular discourse communities (see Figure 2). For example, a major focus of writing-across-the-curriculum programs is to demystify the conventions of the academic discourse community.[11] Dis-course analysis goes beyond audience analysis because what is most signifi-cant about members of a discourse community is not their personal preferences, prejudices, and so on, but rather the expectations they share by virtue of belonging to that particular community. These expectations are embodied in the discourse conventions, which are in turn conditioned by the community's work. Audience analysis aims to persuade readers that you're right; it is to dress your argument in flattering apparel. Discourse analysis aims to enable you to make that argument, to do intellectual work of significance to the community, and hence, to persuade readers that you are a worthy co-worker.[12]

Answers to what we need to know about writing will have to come from both the inner-directed and the outer-directed theoretical schools if we wish to have a complete picture of the composing process. We need to explain the cognitive and the social factors in writing development, and even more important, the relationship between them. Therefore, we should think of the current debate between the two schools as the kind of fruitful exchange that enlarges knowledge, not as a process that will lead to its own termina-tion, to a theory that silences debate. I would like to show here how one inner-directed theoretical model of writing can be enlarged by an outer-directed critique.

The inner-directed school has been distinguished by its fostering of research on writing that follows scientific methodology, and two of the most important researchers are Linda Flower, a professor of English at Carnegie-Mellon University, and John R. Hayes, a professor of psychology at the same school. They have been conducting research for about six years on what people do when they compose. The goal of this research is to formulate "A Cognitive Process Theory of Writing," according to the title of their recent *College Composition and Communication* essay, under review here.[13] Their work's roots in cognitive psychology can be seen in *Cognitive Processes in Writing*, also reviewed here, the proceedings of a 1978 symposium at Carnegie-Mellon.[14] Flower and Hayes see composing as a kind of problem-solving activity; what interests them are the "invariant" thought processes called into play whenever one is confronted with a writing task. In other words, they assume that although each writing task will have its own environment of purposes and constraints, the mental activity involved in juggling these constraints while moving to accomplish one's purposes does not change from task to task. This problem-solving thought process is the "cognitive process of writing."

In Figure 1, location 2 is approximately where Flower and Hayes would place what they are studying. The cognitive process is triggered by what goes on at location 4 (imposition of a particular writing task); the process may also be shaped by attitudes absorbed at location 3 and modified in the light of success or failure in problem-solving at location 4. Not everyone uses the same cognitive process in writing, some processes are more successful than others, and one's process can be consciously or unconsciously modified. Flower and Hayes seek to describe a model of the most complete and successful composing process they can find through their research.

Protocol analysis is their principle research tool. First, the researcher asks a person (the test subject) to say aloud whatever she is thinking while solving a problem posed by the researcher. For example, Flower and Hayes have asked English teachers to describe what goes through their minds while composing an article describing their jobs for the readers of *Seventeen* magazine. The transcription of what the subject says is the protocol. Next, the researcher scans the protocol looking in the subject's self-description for features predicted by the theory of cognitive activity guiding the research. Flower and Hayes have looked for descriptions of behavior common to current accounts of the writing process, such as "organizing" and "revising." In analyzing the protocol, the researcher must bridge gaps in the protocol caused by the subject's forgetting to mention some of her problem-solving steps. The theory is tested by its ability to bridge these gaps as well as by the appearance in the protocol of features it predicts (Flower and Hayes explain their procedure in "Identifying the Organization of Writing Processes," *Cognitive Processes*, pp. 3-30).

Through their research, Flower and Hayes have been gradually refining a process model of composing (see "Process Theory," p. 370). Its most current version divides the writing situation into three main parts: one, the "task environment," subdivided into "rhetorical problem" and "text produced so far"; two, the "writing process," subdivided into "reviewing" (further subdivided into "revising" and "evaluating"), "translating," and "planning" (further subdivided into "generating," "goal-setting," and "organizing"); and three, the "writer's long-term memory." The task environment is outside the writer, the writing process is inside the writer, and long-term memory can be both inside and outside—that is, in the writer's mind or in books. Task environment and memory are seen as information sources upon which the writer draws while performing the composing activities grouped under "writing process."

This model is hierarchical and recursive rather than sequential in structure; that is, Flower and Hayes do not see the writing process as an invariant order of steps. What is invariant, in their view, is the structural relation of the steps. A writer can "access" memory or task environment, and switch from one composing subprocess to another, at any time while the writing task is being completed; an entity in the model called "monitor" executes these switches. This model does not tell us how to proceed through the composing process, but only that in proceeding, there are certain subprocesses we must include if we want to compose successfully.

Flower and Hayes see this model as resolving current theoretical disagreements about what guides composing. Beginning their "Process Theory" essay with summaries of different but compatible views on composing, Flower and Hayes seem to suggest that while other theorists are like blind men describing an elephant, in the Flower-Hayes model we see the whole beast—or at least we can infer its shape when the porpoise occasionally breaks water, to switch to the animal metaphor Flower and Hayes use (*Cognitive Processes*, pp. 9-10). It is the hierarchical and recursive structure of this model, in Flower and Hayes's view, that makes it superior to other theorists' work and able to control and reconcile other theorists' work.

The Flower-Hayes model may, however, strike many readers as a surprising mix of daunting complexity and disappointing familiarity. When we finally get the new terminology straight in our minds, we find in the model's elaborate cognitive processes just the same writing activities we have been debating about. Consider, for example, the Flower-Hayes model's "monitor," the entity that executes switches between composing subprocesses. On the one hand, the term, borrowed from computer programming, is rather intimidating, especially if we imagine that it names something we didn't know was there before. On the other hand, we find out eventually that "monitor" means simply "the writer's mind making decisions." Borrowing a term from programming masks the question of *why* the writer makes certain decisions. The Flower-Hayes model consistently presents a description of *how* the writing process goes on as if it were capable of answering questions about *why* the writer makes certain choices in certain situations. While it is useful for us to have an overview of the "how," such as the Flower-Hayes model offers, we should not suppose that this will enable us to advise students on difficult questions of practice. To put it another way, if we are going to see students as problem-solvers, we must also see them as problem-solvers situated in discourse communities that guide problem definition and the range of alternative solutions. Outer-directed theory can thus shore up the Flower-Hayes model in two critical areas, planning and translating.

"Translating," according to Flower and Hayes, is "the process of putting ideas into visible language" ("Process Theory," p. 373). They treat written English as a set of containers into which we pour meaning, regardless of how meaning exists before the pouring. The containers may not seem to be in convenient sizes at first—we have to struggle with their "constraints" or "special demands"—but once we internalize these, written language as a factor in the composing process essentially disappears. Writing does not so much contribute to thinking as provide an occasion for thinking—or, more precisely, a substrate upon which thinking can grow. Beyond minor matters of spelling, diction, and so on, we do not have to worry about how students are going to find out about the features of written language because these are already innate.

"Translating," then, remains the emptiest box in the Flower-Hayes model, while "planning" becomes the fullest. During planning, the writer generates and organizes ideas before struggling to put them into words. Language itself is not seen as having a generative force in the planning process, except insofar as it stands as a record of the current progress of the writer's thinking in "text produced so far." Planning processes, therefore, have to be elaborated because they are all the writer has to guide her toward a solution to the particular writing problem. What's missing here is the connection to social context afforded by recognition of the dialectical relationship between thought and language. We can have thoughts for which we have no words, I think, but learning language, though it doesn't exactly teach us to think, teaches us what thoughts matter. To put it another way, we can *know* nothing but what we have words for, if knowledge is what language makes of experience.

Vygotsky has characterized this dialectical relationship of thought and language as the development of "verbal thought." At first, language use and thinking develop separately in the child. But eventually the child comes to understand that language not only names ideas but develops and evaluates them, and then, *"the nature of the* [child's] *development itself changes,* from biological to historical."[15] The child's linguistic and cognitive development culminates in "verbal thought," which "is not a natural, innate form of behavior but is determined by a historical-cultural process and has specific properties and laws that cannot be found in the natural forms of thought and speech" (Vygotsky, p. 51). To illustrate the mature relationship between thought and language, Vygotsky uses situations that are strongly context-bound, such as conversations between lovers or among actors in a play.

Vygotsky's analysis suggests that a model that separates planning and translating will not be fruitful for describing adult language-using because these activities are never separate in adult language-using. There is, to be sure, a basis in the human organism for language-using behavior; Vygotsky calls it "biological," Flower and Hayes call it "cognitive." But while this basis is a legitimate object of study in its own right, even the most complete anatomy of it will not explain adult language-using because, as Vygotsky emphasizes, with the advent of verbal thought the very nature of language-using processes changes. The writing process can only take place after this change occurred. Vygotsky's analysis would suggest, then, not only that we should not separate planning and translating but also that we should understand them as conditioned by social context.

If we accept Vygotsky's analysis as indicating the need to fill in Flower and Hayes's empty "translating" box, then to look for knowledge to fill it, we can turn to sociolinguistics. This discipline seeks to analyze the ways thinking and language-using are conditioned by social context. In studying writing, sociolinguists look for the verbal ties with context. They argue that certain genres, implying certain relations between people, are typical of certain situations. Furthermore, readers do not perceive a text as hanging together logically unless its connections with the social context are as clear as the markers of internal coherence.[16] Therefore, for example, students who struggle to write Standard English need knowledge beyond the rules of grammar, spelling, and so on. They need to know: the habitual attitudes of Standard English users toward this preferred form; the linguistic features that most strongly mark group identity; the conventions that can sometimes be ignored; and so on. Students who do know the rules of Standard English may still seem to academics to be writing "incorrectly" if the students are insensitive to all these other features of language use in the community—then the students are using academic language in unacademic ways.[17]

Composition specialists can learn from sociolinguists to avoid what George Dillon has called the "bottom-to-top" fallacy: the notion that a writer first finds meaning, then puts it into words, then organizes the words into sentences, sentences into paragraphs, etc.[18] Dillon argues, rather, that it is the sense of her whole project that most stimulates a writer's thinking and guides her language use. The discourse gives meaning to the words and not vice versa. For example, such phrases as "it seems to me" and "these results suggest . . ." do not themselves tell us how to interpret such a pattern of qualifying statements. When we encounter these words in a student paper, we are likely to chide the writer for covering up poor research or for being unduly humble. When we encounter the very same words in a scholarly paper, we simply take them to mean that the writer is establishing a properly inquiring persona (see Dillon, p. 91).

Even something as cognitively fundamental as sentence structure takes on meaning from the discourse in which it is deployed. For this reason, for example, revising rules are notoriously unhelpful: they always require further knowledge in order to be applied. We can't "omit needless words" unless we have some additional criteria for "needlessness." We can't even "avoid passive voice" all the time. Passive voice might be preferred by a writer who wants to head her sentence with words that tie it closely to the previous sentence, especially if the kind of discourse she is producing places a high value on markers of internal coherence.[19]

"Putting meaning into words," then, cannot be seen as a mechanical process of finding the right size containers. Instead, with a form of discourse we take on a whole range of possibilities for making meaning. Language-using in social contexts is connected not only to the immediate situation but to the larger society, too, in the form of conventions for construing reality. This relationship between language and world view has prompted M.A.K. Halliday to argue that "the problem of educational failure is not a linguistic problem, if by linguistic we mean a problem of different urban dialects"; at bottom, "it is a semiotic problem, concerned with the different ways in which we have constructed our social reality, and the styles of meaning: we have learned to associate with the various aspects of it."[20] In short, educational problems associated with language use should be understood as difficulties with joining an unfamiliar discourse community.

To look at writing as situated in a discourse community is to blur over the lines between translating and planning in the Flower-Hayes model. Finding words is not a separate process from setting goals. It *is* setting goals, because finding words is always a matter of aligning oneself with a particular discourse community. The community's conventions will include instructions on a preferred form of the native tongue, a specialized vocabulary, a polite technique for establishing persona, and so on. To some extent, the community's conventions can be inferred from analyzing the community's texts. But because the conventions also shape world view, the texts can never be an adequate index of community practice.

Therefore, we should not think of what I am calling a discourse community simply as a group who have decided to abide by certain language-using rules. Rather, we should see the group as an "interpretive community," to use Stanley Fish's term, whose language-using habits are part of a larger pattern of regular interaction with the material world.[21] Because this interaction is always an historical process, changing over time, the community's conventions also change over time. This is not to say that the community's interpretive conventions are arbitrary or that they totally determine individual behavior. They are not arbitrary because they are always conditioned by the on-going work in the community and sanctioned by consensus. At any given time, community members should have no trouble specifying that some kinds of thinking and language-using are obviously appropriate to the community and some are not. Changes in conventions can only define themselves in terms of what is already acceptable (even if such definition means negation of the currently acceptable).

At the same time, some kinds of thinking and language-using are not obviously either appropriate or inappropriate; they are open to debate. An individual who abides by the community's conventions, therefore, can still find areas for initiative—adherence is slavish adherence only for the least productive community members. These "open" areas may be the unsolved problems of the community, experiences that remain anomalous in the community's interpretive scheme, or they may be areas the community has never even considered dealing with. An individual may, however, bring one of these open areas into the range of the community's discourse if her argument for an interpretation of it is sufficiently persuasive in terms the community already understands. As an example of this activity, Mina Shaughnessy has cited Freud's introductory lectures on psychoanalysis.[22]

Producing text within a discourse community, then, cannot take place unless the writer can define her goals in terms of the community's interpretive conventions. Writing is always already writing for some purpose that can only be understood in its community context. Fish has argued not only that the community of literary critics proceeds in this way but furthermore, that the main business of English studies should be to investigate the nature of discourse communities (see Fish, pp. 338-55). It is exactly this sort of analysis that the Flower-Hayes model lacks when trying to explain planning. For Flower and Hayes, "generating" (a subdivision of planning) means finding ideas by using heuristics, not by responding with individual initiative to the community's needs. "Organizing" (another subdivision) means fitting ideas into the range of logical structures available from human thought processes, not finding out what's reasonable in terms of a community's interpretive conventions. In other words, all that's needed for generating and organizing is access to the invariant, universal structures of human cognition (for a critique of this assumption, see Dillon, pp. 50-82).

The weakness of this approach is most apparent in Flower and Hayes's treatment of "goal-setting." They correctly identify goal-setting as the motor of the composing process, its most important element, but in their model they close it off in the most subordinate position (a subdivision of a subdivision of the writing process). In the "Process Theory" essay, Flower and Hayes elaborate their description into "process goals" (directions for the writing process) and "content goals" (directions for affecting the audience), and they also classify goals in terms of levels of abstraction (see "Process Theory," p. 377). Their model's structure cannot order this multifarious account.

Flower and Hayes end the "Process Theory" essay with analysis of a "good" writer's protocol, aimed to explicate the process of goal-setting. The writer is having trouble deciding how to tell *Seventeen* readers about his job as a college English teacher until he decides that many girls think of English as a "tidy" and "prim" subject and that "By God I can change that notion for them." He goes on to frame an introduction that recounts a "crazy skit" his 101 class liked on the first day of school ("Process Theory," pp. 383, 385). Of his "By God" moment of decision, Flower and Hayes say that "he has regenerated and elaborated his top-level goals," and "this consolidation leaves the writer with a new, relatively complex, rhetorically sophisticated working goal, one which encompasses plans for a topic, a persona, and an audience" (p. 383).

Notice the verbs in this explanation: "regenerating" and "elaborating" goals "leave" the writer with regenerated ("new") and elaborated ("complex") goals—which "encompass" what he needs to know to go on writing. The action described here has no force as an explanation not only because it is circular (regeneration causes regeneration), but also because we still don't know where the new goals come from. Flower and Hayes suggest that going through a process simply "leaves" one with the goals, as if the process itself brought them into being. Upon arrival, the goals are found to contain ("encompass") the necessary knowledge—but we still don't know how that knowledge got there.

The *Seventeen* article writer's process of goal-setting, I think, can be better understood if we see it in terms of writing for a discourse community. His initial problem (which seems to be typical of most subjects confronted with this writing task) is to find a way to include these readers in a discourse community for which he is comfortable writing. He places them in the academic discourse community by imagining the girls as students ("they will all have had English," p. 383). Once he has included them in a familiar discourse community, he can find a way to address them that is common in the community: he will argue with them, putting a new interpretation on information they possess in order to correct misconceptions (his "By God" decision). In arguing, he can draw on all the familiar habits of persuasion he has built up in his experience as a teacher (his "crazy skit" decision). He could not have found a way to write this article if he did not have knowledge of a discourse community to draw on.

The Flower-Hayes model does, of course, include a "long-term memory" where such knowledge could be stored, and Flower and Hayes even acknowledge its importance:

> Sometimes a single cue in an assignment, such as "write a persuasive. . . ,"
> can let a writer tap a stored representation of a problem and bring a whole
> raft of writing plans into play. (p. 371)

A "stored representation of a problem" must be a set of directions for producing a certain kind of text—what I have been calling discourse conventions. I would argue that the writer doesn't just tap this representation sometimes but every time a writing task is successfully accomplished. Flower and Hayes give this crucial determinant of text production very offhand treatment, however. They seem to see writing in response to discourse conventions as response to "semiautomatic plans and goals" that contrast with "goals writers create for a particular paper" (p. 381). Evidently they are seeing discourse conventions simply as rules to be internalized, similar to their treatment of the "constraints" of written English. This reduction of conventions to sets of rules is also suggested by their choice of the limerick as a good example of a "genre" (p. 379).

Hence, although Flower and Hayes acknowledge the existence of discourse conventions, they fail to see conventions' generative power, which is to say that their notion of conventions does not include the interpretive function for which I have been arguing. This neglect of the role of knowledge in composing makes the Flower-Hayes theory particularly insensitive to the problems of poor writers.

> Poor writers will frequently depend on very abstract, undeveloped top-level goals, such as "appeal to a broad range of intellect," even though such goals are much harder to work with than a more operational goal such as "give a brief history of my job." Sondra Perl has seen this phenomenon in the basic writers who kept returning to reread the assignment, searching, it would seem, for ready-made goals, instead of forming their own. Alternatively, poor writers will depend on only very low-level goals, such as finishing a sentence or correctly spelling a word. They will be, as Nancy Sommers's student revisers were, locked in by the myopia in their own goals and criteria. (p. 379)

The implication here seems to be that cognitive deficiency keeps poor writers from forming their own goals, keeps them locked in the myopia of goals appropriate to a much earlier stage of cognitive development. The physical image of poor eyesight is revealing of Flower and Hayes's assumptions about the innate sources of writing problems.

I think these students' difficulties with goal-setting are better understood in terms of their unfamiliarity with the academic discourse community, combined, perhaps, with such limited experience outside their native discourse communities that they are unaware that there is such a thing as a discourse community with conventions to be mastered. What is underdeveloped is their knowledge of the ways experience is constituted and interpreted in the academic discourse community and of the fact that all discourse communities constitute and interpret experience. Basil Bernstein has shown that British working-class students are not cognitively deficient but that, first, their native discourse community's conventions are very different from school conventions, and, second, their lack of a variety of speech partners makes it hard for them to see their problems in school as problems of learning to relate to new speech partners (or an unfamiliar discourse community).[23]

Such students may be unable to set a more operational goal because they do not know the conventions of language-using that define such goals as, for example, a "history." Without such knowledge, they may fall back on goals that worked in the past—perhaps in grammar school where close attention to spelling and grammar was rewarded. Or they may sensibly try to enlarge their knowledge by rereading the assignment, seeking clues to the conventions of this new discourse community or those "ready-made goals" without which no writing gets accomplished. Of course, their search of the assignment may be fruitless if the teacher has not been sufficiently explicit about her expectations. Academics are, perhaps, too ready to assume that such operations as "describe" or "analyze" are self-evident, when in fact they have meanings specific to the academic discourse community and specific to disciplines within that community.

To help poor writers, then, we need to explain that their writing takes place within a community, and to explain what the community's conventions are. Another way of putting this would be to borrow Thomas Kuhn's terminology and explain that "puzzle-solving" writing can go on only under the direction of an established "paradigm" for community activity.[24] As Charles Bazerman's work has shown, the writer within the academic community knows how to relate her text to "the object under study, the literature of the field, the anticipated audience, and the author's own self" via discipline-specific conventions governing "lexicon," "explicit citation and implicit knowledge," "knowledge and attitudes the text assumes that the readers will have," and the "features" of a "public face" (Bazerman, pp. 362-63).

The Flower-Hayes model of writing, then, cannot alone give us a complete picture of the process. We might say that if this model describes the *form* of the composing process, the process cannot go on without the *content* which is knowledge of the conventions of discourse communities. In practice, however, form and content cannot be separated in this way, since discourse conventions shape the goals that drive the writing process. To let the model stand alone as an account of composing is to mask the necessity for the socially situated knowledge without which no writing project gets under way. The problems of letting this model stand alone can be seen in the pedagogy emerging from Flower and Hayes's work. They are inclined to treat the model itself as an heuristic:

> Our model is a model of competent writers. Some writers, though, perhaps to their disadvantage, may fail to use some of the processes. (*Cognitive Processes*, p. 29)

Flower has recently published a textbook that aims to guide students through a complete repertoire of composing strategies.[25]

The difficulty with the textbook's view of writing as problem-solving is that it treats problem-solving as an unfiltered encounter with the underlying structure of reality—"the act of discovering key issues in a problem that often lie hidden under the noisy details of the situation" (p. 21). Having defined a problem, one should: first, "fit it into a category of similar problems"; next, decide on a possible course of action against the problem ("make the problem definition more operational"); "tree" the problem or

analyze its parts into a hierarchical structure; "generate alternative solutions"; present a conclusion, which weighs alternatives and acknowledges
assumptions and implications of the conclusion (see pp. 21-26). But *first*,
how does one define a problem? Although Flower says that "problems are
only problems for someone," she doesn't talk about this necessary link between problem definition and interpretive communities (p. 21). Rather, it
seems that we will *find* (not make) the problem if we strip away the "noisy
details of the situation." I would argue, in contrast, that only the noisy details of the situation can define a problem. To "define" a problem is to interact with the material world according to the conventions of a particular
discourse community; these conventions are the only source for categories
of similar problems, operational definitions, and alternative solutions, and a
conclusion can only be evaluated as "well supported" in terms of a particular community's standards.

 I certainly do not mean to suggest that students should not be encouraged to look at reality when they compose—far from it, since I have emphasized the function of writing in doing (intellectual) work in the world. But I
do mean to point out that we cannot look at reality in an unfiltered way—
"reality" only makes sense when organized by the interpretive conventions
of a discourse community. Students often complain that they have nothing
to say, whereas "real-world" writers almost never do, precisely because real-
world writers are writing for discourse communities in which they know
their work can matter, whereas students can see little purpose for their own
attempts ("essais") other than to get a grade. For example, Erwin Steinberg
has suggested that the superior organization of an electrical engineer's report, as compared to a freshman composition, stems from the engineer's superior knowledge of and experience in a field; what looks like a cognitive
difference turns out to have a large social component (see "A Garden of Opportunities and a Thicket of Dangers," *Cognitive Processes*, pp. 163-165).
Hence, although Steinberg is sympathetic to the project of finding writing
models and heuristics, he cautions, "We must always be careful not to think
in terms of a single model, because if we do we'll find one and force everyone to use it—the way English teachers used to require students to make formal outlines before they wrote" (p. 163).
 The cognitive psychology approach cuts off writing-as-problem-solving
from the context of a discourse community precisely because *one* model is
sought (Steinberg's caveat notwithstanding). Discourse communities are
tied to historical and cultural circumstances, and hence can only be seen as
unenlightening instances of the general theory the cognitive approach
seeks: the one model is the universal one. All of the theoretical essays in

Cognitive Processes in Writing seek to find this model. Carl Bereiter offers an account of the stages of development in children's writing processes. Like the Flower-Hayes model, his is recursive—that is, he suggests that children's development includes a certain set of stages but that the order of these stages can be changed. There is, however, a "preferred or 'natural' order of writing development," an order in which the constraints on composing imposed by the necessity of putting thoughts into words are gradually reduced by being "automatized." Bereiter suggests that this order should be adopted in the schools (see "Development in Writing," p. 89).

Collins and Gentner seek to go even further in schematizing their theory as a rule-governed model because they hope to end with a program enabling a computer to compose (see "A Framework for a Cognitive Theory of Writing," pp. 51-52). This would permit the creation of "Writing Land," where computers would guide students through the patterns of the writing process and enhance the students' cognitive activities (see "Framework," pp. 67-70). Computer-assisted composition will help students reduce the constraints imposed by the struggle to put thoughts into words by separating "idea production" and "text production" ("Framework," p. 53). Once the ideas are under control, "the next stage is to impose text structure on the ideas" ("Framework," p. 59).

During text production, Collins and Gentner confidently state, the writer can call on "structural devices, stylistic devices, and content devices"—the term "devices" suggesting rule-governed mechanisms. Yet "unfortunately for the writer, there is no one-to-one correspondence between means and end here"—in other words, no consistency in situation that would permit reliance on rule-governed mechanisms ("Framework," p. 60). Collins and Gentner's analysis frequently bumps up against language's opacity, the contribution to thinking of densely situation-bound meanings embodied in habits of language-using. Because they cannot account for this situational aspect of writing, Collins and Gentner can only define "good writing" as writing that conforms to a set of rules set by some authority (see "Framework," pp. 52-53). This approach leaves them no way to justify the authority's decisions as other than arbitrary, and hence their "rules" turn out to be situation-bound: "Delete extraneous material," "Shorten long paragraphs," and so on ("Framework," p. 65). Such advice is unhelpful to students without other knowledge that enables them to identify the extraneous and over-lengthy, as I noted earlier in my discussion of revising rules.

The fundamental problem with this approach is that it assumes that the rules we can formulate to describe behavior are the same rules that produce the behavior. As attempts to program language-using computers have shown, such structures reveal their lack of explanatory power when applied to an actual situation in which discourse conventions come into play. Programming a computer to use language comes up against a problem of infinite regress of context—or, how do we tell the computer how to tell what's important when things are important only in terms of purposive activity? How can we define, for example, what is "extraneous material," when the quality of being extraneous resides not in the material itself but in its relation to discourse? Or, to use a simpler example, how can we tell the computer when a paragraph is too long except by specifying a range of lines that constitute acceptable lengths? Is there any form of discourse in which 20-line paragraphs are acceptable and 21-line paragraphs are not? As the competence/performance debate in linguistics has suggested, it may be that we cannot have a completely descriptive theory of behavior in widely varying specific situations—that is, we cannot formulate universal rules for context-bound activities. If language-using isn't rule-governed in this sense, however, it still may be regular—that is, we may be able to group situations as likely to share a number of language-using features. But to do this is to describe the conventions of discourse communities.[26]

As I have been arguing, then, both the inner-directed and the outer-directed theoretical schools will have to contribute to a synthesis capable of providing a comprehensive new agenda for composition studies. My critique of Flower and Hayes's work is intended to contribute to such a synthesis, not to delegitimate what they are doing. I do want to raise a serious question, however, about another feature of the inner-directed school, a feature that works against fruitful discussion and synthesis: the quest for certainty. In seeking one universal model of the composing process, inner-directed theorists seek a new set of principles for our discipline that will raise their arguments, as one has put it, "above mere ideology" (Hirsch, p. 4). They seek a kind of certainty they believe is accessible only to science, and their talk of paradigm-shifting invokes Kuhn to announce that our discipline will soon have a scientific basis.[27]

This kind of certainty is presumably analogous to the commonplace elevation of fact over opinion, since it is supposed to end all debate. The inner-directed school therefore has redefined composition research to mean a search for the facts in the real world that prove a theory beyond debate. The Flower-Hayes model claims much prestige from being derived from such supposedly unimpeachable evidence. But its reliance on empirical evidence can be questioned on several grounds. For one thing, protocol analysis is a controversial method even within cognitive psychology because it tends to affect what is being observed (see Gould's remarks, *Cognitive Processes*, p. 125). Flower and Hayes's work is particularly vulnerable because most of their adult subjects have been English teachers who are familiar with the specialized vocabulary of the theory Flower and Hayes have used to analyze the protocols. Under any circumstances, protocol analysis can lead to "self-fulfilling" prophecy because its assumption that the subject's words mirror her thinking allows the researcher to claim that certain thought processes have occurred if certain words appear in the protocol. Self-fulfilling prophecy is even more likely when test subjects share expert knowledge of these words with the researchers.

The larger point to be made here, however, is that no scientific research, no matter how rigorously it is conducted, possesses the kind of authoritative certainty inner-directed theorists are seeking.[28] It is always desirable, of course, to know more about composing, but it is also necessary to treat this knowledge as provisional, the way scientists treat their findings, if inquiry is not to end. We may wonder, then, why inner-directed theorists are so ready to invest their results with final authority and rush to pedagogical applications. I think it is that certainty appeals to composition specialists these days for various reasons. For one, until recently composition studies was a low-status enclave it was hard to escape; a powerful theory would help us retaliate against the literary critics who dominate English studies. Moreover, such a theory might help us survive what appears to be the long slide of all humanistic disciplines into a low-status enclave. A scientific-sounding theory promises an "accountability" hedge against hard times.

The strongest appeal of certainty, however, is its offer of a solution to our new students' problems that will enable us to undertake their socialization into the academic discourse community without having to consider the ethical and political dimensions of this act. We are reluctant to take up ethical and political questions about what we do because writing teachers have been under a terrific strain. Pressured with increasing asperity by our colleges to prepare students for their other courses, we have also felt anxious in the classroom both when our teaching worked—because we sensed that we were wiping out the students' own culture—and when it didn't—because we were cheating them of a chance to better their situations. Inner-directed pedagogy meets teachers' emotional needs because it can be defended on grounds that are likely to satisfy complaining faculty and administrators, and because its claim to a basis in universals assures us that when we inculcate it, we aren't touching the students' own culture but merely giving them a way around it and up the ladder of success. The corollary is that students for whom the pedagogy doesn't work need no longer be seen as victims of our incompetence but simply as innately inferior.

Invocation of certainty, then, performs the rhetorical function of invocation of the Deity. It guarantees the transcendent authority of values for which we do not need to argue but which we can now apply with the confidence of a "good cause." I would argue, however, that we must understand such a move as the assigning of superhuman authority to a human construction. All knowledge, that is, is of human origin, even scientific knowledge. Indeed, modern philosophy has centered around a critique of scientific knowledge precisely because such knowledge is most likely now to be treated as certain. As Richard Rorty has recently shown, the history of Western philosophy since the Renaissance can be seen as a series of unsuccessful attempts to fight off the admission that such claims for certainty are no longer tenable.[29] There is no way out of confrontation, except among fellow believers, with the necessity of arguing for one's ethical choices.

This confrontation is especially necessary in a pluralistic society such as the United States, in which a heterogeneous school population ensures that pedagogical choices will affect students unequally. Under such circumstances, as Rorty cautions, claims to certainty often express simply a desire for agreement which masks the question of whose interests are being served (see Rorty, p. 335). Teachers' individual ethical choices add up to political consequences, responsibility for which we cannot avoid. We are better off, then, with a disciplinary theory that encourages examination of consequences. For example, inner-directed research might come up with an heuristic that is useful in Basic Writing classes. But if we use it there, we should not imagine that the heuristic allows us to forget who the students are in Basic Writing classes, where they come from, what their prospects are — in short, why these particular students are having educational difficulties.

Ultimately, I am calling for the inspection of what some curriculum theorists have called the "hidden curriculum": the project of initiating students into a particular world view that gives rise to the daily classroom tasks without being consciously examined by teacher or students.[30] If we call what we are teaching "universal" structures or processes, we bury the hidden curriculum even deeper by claiming that our choice of material owes nothing to historical circumstances. To do this is to deny the school's function as an agent of cultural hegemony, or the selective valuation and transmission of world views. The result for students who don't share the school's preferred world views is either failure or deracination. I think we must acknowledge cultural differences in the classroom, even though this means increasing our emotional strain as members of one group trying to mediate contacts among various others.

The kind of pedagogy that would foster responsible inspection of the politically loaded hidden curriculum in composition class is discourse analysis. The exercise of cultural hegemony can be seen as the treatment of one community's discourse conventions as if they simply mirrored reality. To point out that discourse conventions exist would be to politicize the classroom—or rather, to make everyone aware that it is already politicized. World views would become more clearly a matter of conscious commitment, instead of unconscious conformity, if the ways in which they are constituted in discourse communities were analyzed.

This is not to say that we can make the school an ideologically neutral place. The whole force of my argument is that there is no way to *escape* all discourse communities, stand outside them and pronounce judgment. Furthermore, I assent to most of the conventions of the academic discourse community and believe that students from other communities can benefit from learning about them, and learning them. But perhaps we can break up the failure/deracination dilemma for students from communities at a distance from academe. Through discourse analysis we might offer them an understanding of their school difficulties as the problems of a traveler to an unfamiliar country—yet a country in which it is possible to learn the language and the manners and even "go native" while still remembering the land from which one has come.

In his discussion of literary criticism and interpretive communities, Stanley Fish has offered us one set of suggestions for how such ethically and politically conscious education might proceed. Richard Rorty offers another in his vision of philosophy becoming not the arbiter of disciplines but the mediator among them. This "edifying" philosophy will have as its task making us realize that agreement that looks like certainty can occur only "because when a practice has continued long enough the conventions which make it possible—and which permit a consensus on how to divide it into parts—are relatively easy to isolate" (p. 321). Rorty's is not a positivist notion of arbitrary conventions; he sees conventions as the product of communities, situation-bound but also subject to change. Rorty generalizes Kuhn's notions of "normal" and "revolutionary" science to argue that the edifying philosopher's task is to keep reminding us that "normal" discourse is evidently clear and above debate only because we agree about its conventions. Education must begin with normal discourse but should not be limited to it, with its unhelpful distinction between facts and values (see p. 363). For the goal of discovering Truth, Rorty substitutes the goal of continuing conversation, but this will not be a dangerously relativistic goal because always conditioned by and having to answer to an historical framework. Rorty's philosophical community thus resembles Fish's interpretive community.

Finally, then, we should see our answers to the question of what we need to know about writing in the light of a new humanistic synthesis. Philosophy has moved to the position that discourse communities are all we have to rely upon in our quest for certainty. Literary criticism is analyzing how discourse communities function as historically situated interpretive communities. Composition studies should focus upon practice within interpretive communities—exactly how conventions work in the world and how they are transmitted. If the work of these disciplines continues to converge, a new synthesis will emerge that revivifies rhetoric as the central discipline of human intellectual endeavor. In view of such a synthesis, the project to make composition studies merely scientific looks obsolete.

I hope that this rhetorical synthesis, because it turns our attention to questions of value and persuasion, will also reawaken us to the collective nature of the whole educational endeavor. There should be no disgrace in discovering that one's work and the understanding that guides it cannot be achieved autonomously. Then the main casualty of our theoretical debate can be the debilitating individualism that adds so much to classroom strain. In other words, let us emphasize not only discourse but also community. I do not mean that we should seek to eliminate the conflicts that arise from our coming from different historical and cultural situations. We should recognize that being so situated is the most important thing we have in common.[31]

NOTES

1. The attitude I'm describing here has been called current-traditionalism, and it still dominates textbooks in the field; see Donald C. Stewart, "Composition Textbooks and the Assault on Tradition," *College Composition and Communication,* 29 (May 1978), pp. 171-76.

2. I am taking this sense of "isomorphic" from Frank D'Angelo, *A Conceptual Theory of Rhetoric* (Cambridge, Mass.: Winthrop, 1975), pp. 16, 26-36.

3. I have in mind here the justification for teaching Standard English advanced in E.D. Hirsch, Jr., *The Philosophy of Composition* (Chicago: Univ. of Chicago Press, 1977).

4. For example, Richard Young has recently characterized his particle-wave-field heuristic as based on "universal invariants that underlie all human experience as characteristic of rationality itself"; in "Arts, Crafts, Gifts, and Knacks: Some Disharmonies in the New Rhetoric," *Visible Language,* 14, no. 4 (1980), 347.

5. For an overview of research on sentence-combining and the arguments for teaching it, see Frank O'Hare, *Sentence Combining: Improving Student Writing without Formal Grammar Instruction* (Urbana, Illinois: NCTE, 1973).

6. A new textbook that operates from these principles of audience analysis (and other inner-directed pedagogy) is Janice M. Lauer, Gene Montague, Andrea Lunsford, and Janet Emig, *Four Worlds of Writing* (New York: Harper and Row, 1981).

7. Typically, a discourse community prefers one form of the native tongue, which may be characterized simply by level of formality and specialized vocabulary, or which may be a

dialect, or a fully constituted language (in the native tongue's family) with its own grammar rules. The outer-directed theorists thus emphasize "parole" over "langue," to use de Saussure's terms, "performance" over "competence," to use Chomsky's terms. For a good account of such language differences in an American setting, see William Labov, *The Study of Nonstandard English* (1969; revised and enlarged; Urbana, Illinois: NCTE, 1975).

8. See, for example, M.A.K. Halliday, "Language as Social Semiotic," *Language as Social Semiotic* (Baltimore: University Park Press, 1978), pp. 108-26.

9. This attitude has been called the Sapir-Whorf hypothesis, because arguments are advanced for it by linguists Edward Sapir and his pupil, Benjamin Lee Whorf; for a good summary and critique of the Sapir-Whorf hypothesis, see Adam Schaff, *Language and Cognition* (1964; trans. Olgierd Wojtasiewicz, ed. Robert S. Cohen; New York: McGraw-Hill, 1973).

10. This, I think, is the gist of the analysis offered by Mina Shaughnessy, "Beyond the Sentence," *Errors and Expectations* (New York: Oxford Univ. Press, 1977), pp. 226-72.

11. A new textbook that operates from some principles of outer-directed pedagogy is Elaine Maimon, Gerald L. Belcher, Gail W. Hearn, Barbara F. Nodine, and Finbarr W. O'Connor, *Writing in the Arts and Sciences* (Cambridge, Massachusetts: Winthrop, 1981).

12. For an exemplary analysis of academic discourse conventions and how they lead to the accomplishment of the community's work, see Charles Bazerman, "What Written Knowledge Does: Three Examples of Academic Discourse," *Philosophy of the Social Sciences*, 11 (September 1981), pp. 361-87; further references in text.

13. Linda Flower and John R. Hayes, "A Cognitive Process Theory of Writing," *College Composition and Communication*, 32 (December 1981), pp. 365-87; further references in text.

14. Lee W. Gregg and Erwin R. Steinberg, editors, *Cognitive Processes in Writing* (Hillsdale, New Jersey: Lawrence Erlbaum, 1980); further references in text.

15. Lev Vygotsky, *Thought and Language* (1934; rpt. ed. & trans. Eugenia Hanfmann and Gertrude Vakar; Cambridge, Mass.: MIT Press, 1962), p. 51, author's emphasis; further references in text. Vygotsky's pupil A.R. Luria did research among Uzbek peasants which suggests that thought and language interpenetrate to such a degree that perception of optical illusions, for example, changes with cultural experience and level of education; see A.R. Luria, *Cognitive Development* (1974; rpt. trans. Martin Lopez-Morillas and Lynn Solotaroff, ed. Michael Cole; Cambridge, Mass.: Harvard Univ. Press, 1976).

16. See M.A.K. Halliday and Ruqaiya Hasan, *Cohesion in English* (London: Longman, 1976), pp. 19-26.

17. My line of argument here is based on Dell Hymes, "Bilingual Education: Linguistic vs. Sociolinguistic Bases," *Foundations in Sociolinguistics* (Philadelphia: Univ. of Pennsylvania Press, 1974), pp. 119-24; in the same volume, Hymes argues that to uncover the extralinguistic attitudes lending significance to language use, linguists need more contributions from folklorists.

18. George L. Dillon, *Constructing Texts* (Bloomington, Indiana: Indiana Univ. Press, 1981), pp. 1-20; further references in text.

19. A critique of the notion of simplicity-as-clarity has been offered by Richard Lanham, *Style: An Anti-Textbook* (New Haven, Conn.: Yale Univ. Press, 1974). Lanham's later work in composition pedagogy suggests, however, that he is cynical about the position taken in *Style* and not really ready to defend "ornate" language choices outside of special literary circumstances; see Richard Lanham, *Revising Prose* (New York: Scribner, 1979). Dillon, pp. 21-49, is more helpful on understanding the problems with revising rules.

20. Halliday, "Language in Urban Society," p. 163; Halliday suggests that our current difficulties in the composition class may be at least in part a function of the increasing number of students who come from urban areas.

21. See Stanley Fish, *Is There a Text in this Class?* (Cambridge, Mass.: Harvard Univ. Press, 1980), further references in text; the following argument is heavily indebted to Fish's work.

22. Mina Shaughnessy, "Some Needed Research on Writing," *College Composition and Communication*, 27 (December 1977), p. 319.

23. See Basil Bernstein, *Class, Codes and Control* (1971; rpt. New York: Schocken, 1975); and to correct the vulgar error that Bernstein is diagnosing a cognitive deficiency in working-class language, see "The Significance of Bernstein's Work for Sociolinguistic Theory" in Halliday, pp. 101-107. Many dangerous misinterpretations of Bernstein could perhaps have been avoided if he had not chosen to call working-class language-using habits a "restricted code" and middle-class (school-oriented) habits an "elaborated code."

24. The seminal text here is Thomas Kuhn, *The Structure of Scientific Revolutions*, 2d. edition, enlarged (Chicago: Univ. of Chicago Press, 1970). Kuhn is now going so far as to say that "proponents of different theories (or different paradigms, in the broader sense of the term) speak different languages—languages expressing different cognitive commitments, suitable for different worlds"; he announces the study of language's function in theory-making as his current project. See Thomas Kuhn, *The Essential Tension* (Chicago: Univ. of Chicago Press, 1977), pp. 22-23.

25. Linda Flower, *Problem-Solving Strategies for Writing* (New York: Harcourt Brace Jovanovich, 1981); further references in text.

26. In my discussion of Collins and Gentner, I am following the line of argument offered by Hubert L. Dreyfus, *What Computers Can't Do* (New York: Harper and Row, 1972); rpt. 2d. edition, San Francisco: Freeman, 1979). Flower and Hayes's sympathy with the Collins-Gentner approach is suggested not only by the large amount of agreement between the two accounts of composing, but also by the numerous borrowings in the Flower-Hayes model from computer terminology and by Flower and Hayes's suggestion that their model will contribute toward "building a Writer" ("Process Theory," p. 368).

27. For an example of this use of Kuhn, see Maxine Hairston, "The Winds of Change: Thomas Kuhn and the Revolution in the Teaching of Writing," *College Composition and Communication*, 33 (February 1982), pp. 76-88.

28. This argument follows the account of rhetoric's function in the scientific discourse community given by Kuhn in *Structure* and (in a more radical version) by Paul Feyerabend, *Against Method* (1975; rpt. London: Verso, 1978).

29. Richard Rorty, *Philosophy and the Mirror of Nature* (Princeton, NJ: Princeton Univ. Press, 1979); further references in text.

30. On the hidden curriculum and its reproduction of oppressive social power relations, see Michael Apple, *Ideology and Curriculum* (London: Routledge and Kegan Paul, 1979).

31. I would like to thank Bruce Herzberg for the many ideas and the editorial guidance that he has, as usual, contributed to my work.

Talking about Writing in Society

Positivism has been the dominant paradigm for Western society for nearly four centuries, its premises and assumptions rarely questioned for most of that time. It is no wonder, then, that contemporary composition studies would look to the sciences for explanations about what happens in writing. But anthropological study and various elements of critical theory, beginning in the later 1960s, put serious questions to positivism, to positivism's search for universal answers, to the very idea that we can think in terms of universal.

Composition studies turned to three lines of inquiry in its search for alternatives to positivism. Comp turned to anthropology's social construction theory and its ethnographic research methodologies. Composition also turned to continental philosophical, psychological, and critical theories of poststructuralism. And composition turned to Stanley Fish's term "anti-foundationalism," contained in his 1989 *Doing What Comes Naturally: Change, Rhetoric, and the Practice of Theory in Literary and Legal Studies* (Durham, NC: Duke UP). Anti-foundationalism, poststructuralism, social construction theory say in common that there can be no universal truths, no truths free from contextual particularities. Everything contains reflections, to some degree or other, of the cultural, historical, and political contexts in which inquiry takes place. And to the extent that they are political, they also include points of contact, places where cultures collide and eventually intermingle. These spaces where cultures meet (usually in unequal terms, as matters of conquest and conquered) are what linguist Mary Louise Pratt terms "contact zones," a term which has captured the imagination of those who would turn to the social in composition studies, since it captures the cultural, the historical, the political, and the rhetorical. Scientism or positivism, on the other hand, appears inherently flawed, in its claiming to transcend the social and political, thereby failing to make explicit (or even to recognize) the effects of the social and the political in its inquiries.

Collaborative Learning and the "Conversation of Mankind"

KENNETH A. BRUFFEE

There are some signs these days that collaborative learning is of increasing interest to English teachers.[1] Composition teachers seem to be exploring the concept actively. Two years ago the term appeared for the first time in the list of topics suggested by the Executive Committee of the Conference on College Composition and Communication for discussion at the CCCC annual convention. It was eighth or ninth on a list of ten items. Last year it appeared again, first on the list.

Teachers of literature have also begun to talk about collaborative learning, although not always by that name. It is viewed as a way of engaging students more deeply with the text and also as an aspect of professors' engagement with the professional community. At its 1978 convention the Modern Language Association scheduled a multi-session forum entitled "Presence, Knowledge, and Authority in the Teaching of Literature." One of the associated sessions, called "Negotiations of Literary Knowledge," included a discussion of the authority and structure (including the collaborative classroom structure) of "interpretive communities." At the 1983 MLA convention collaborative practices in reestablishing authority and value in literary studies were examined under such rubrics as "Talking to the Academic Community: Conferences as Institutions" and "How Books 11 and 12 of *Paradise Lost* Got to be Valuable" (changes in interpretive attitudes in the community of Miltonists).

Reprinted from *College English* 46.7 (November 1984): 635–52. Used with permission. Readers may find more recent explorations of issues discussed in this article in Kenneth A. Bruffee, *Collaborative Learning: Higher Education, Interdependence, and the Authority of Knowledge* (Baltimore: Johns Hopkins University Press, 2nd edition, 1999).

In both these contexts collaborative learning is discussed sometimes as a process that constitutes fields or disciplines of study and sometimes as a pedagogical tool that "works" in teaching composition and literature. The former discussion, often highly theoretical, usually manages to keep at bay the more troublesome and problematic aspects of collaborative learning. The discussion of classroom practice is less fortunate. What emerges there is that many teachers are unsure about how to use collaborative learning and about when and where, appropriately, it should be used. Many are concerned also that when they try to use collaborative learning in what seem to be effective and appropriate ways, it sometimes quite simply fails.

I sympathize with these experiences. Much the same thing has happened to me. Sometimes collaborative learning works beyond my highest expectations. Sometimes it doesn't work at all. Recently, though, I think I have been more successful. The reason for that increased success seems to be that I know a little more now than I did in the past about the complex ideas that lie behind collaborative learning. This essay is frankly an attempt to encourage other teachers to try collaborative learning and to help them use collaborative learning appropriately and effectively. But it offers no recipes. It is written instead on the assumption that understanding both the history and the complex ideas that underlie collaborative learning can improve its practice and demonstrate its educational value.

The history of collaborative learning as I know it can be briefly sketched. Collaborative learning began to interest American college teachers widely only in the 1980s, but the term was coined and the basic idea first developed in the 1950s and 1960s by a group of British secondary school teachers and by a biologist studying British post-graduate education— specifically, medical education. I myself first encountered the term and some of the ideas implicit in it in Edwin Mason's still interesting but now somewhat dated polemic entitled *Collaborative Learning* (London: Ward Lock Educational Co., 1970), and in Charity James' *Young Lives at Stake: A Reappraisal of Secondary Schools* (London: Collins, 1968). Mason, James, and Leslie Smith, colleagues at Goldsmith's College, University of London, were committed during the Vietnam era to democratizing education and to eliminating from education what were perceived then as socially destructive authoritarian social forms. Collaborative learning as they thought of it emerged from this largely political, topical effort.

The collaborative forms that Mason and his colleagues proposed to establish in education had already been explored and their educational value affirmed, however, by the earlier findings of M. L. J. Abercrombie. Abercrombie's *Anatomy of Judgment* (Harmondsworth: Penguin, 1964) culminated ten years of research on the selection and training of medical students at University College, University of London. The result of her research was to suggest that diagnosis, the art of medical judgment and the key element in successful medical practice, is better learned in small groups of students arriving at diagnoses collaboratively than it is learned by students working individually. Abercrombie began her study by observing the scene that lay people think is most typical of medical education: the group of medical students with a teaching physician gathered around a ward bed to diagnose a patient. She then made a seemingly slight but in outcome enormously important change in the way that scene is usually played out. Instead of asking each individual member of the group of students to diagnose the patient on his or her own, Abercrombie asked the whole group to examine the patient together, discuss the case as a group, and arrive at a consensus, a single diagnosis that they could all agree to. What she found was that students learning diagnosis this way acquired good medical judgment faster than individuals working alone (p. 19).

For American college teachers the roots of collaborative learning lie neither in radical politics nor in research. They lie in the nearly desperate response of harried colleges during the early 1970s to a pressing educational need. A decade ago, faculty and administrators in institutions throughout the country became aware that, increasingly, students entering college had difficulty doing as well in academic studies as their native ability suggested they should be able to do. Of course, some of these students were poorly prepared academically. Many more of them, however, had on paper excellent secondary preparation. The common denominator among both the poorly prepared and the seemingly well-prepared was that, for cultural reasons we may not yet fully understand, all these students seemed to have difficulty adapting to the traditional or "normal" conventions of the college classroom.

One symptom of the difficulty these students had adapting to college life and work was that many refused help when it was offered. The help colleges offered, in the main, were tutoring and counseling programs staffed by graduate students and other professionals. These programs failed because undergraduates refused to use them. Many solutions to this problem were suggested and tried, from mandated programs that forced students to accept help they evidently did not want, to sink-or-swim programs that assumed that students who needed help but didn't seek it out didn't belong in college anyway. One idea that seemed at the time among the most exotic and unlikely (that is, in the jargon of the 60s, among the most "radical") turned out in the event to work rather well. Taking hints about the social organization of learning given by John Bremer, Michael von Moschzisker, and others writing at that time about changes in primary and secondary education, some college faculty members guessed that students were refusing help because the kind of help provided seemed merely an extension of the work, the expectations, and above all the social structure of traditional classroom learning (*The School Without Walls* [New York: Holt, 1971], p. 7). It was traditional classroom learning that seemed to have left these students unprepared in the first place. What they needed, it seemed, was help that was not an extension of but an alternative to traditional classroom teaching.

To provide that alternative some colleges turned to peer tutoring. Through peer tutoring teachers could reach students by organizing them to teach each other. And peer tutoring, it turned out, was just one way of doing that, although perhaps the most readily institutionalized way. Collectively, peer tutoring and similar modes such as peer criticism and classroom group work could be sensibly classified under the convenient term provided by our colleagues in Britain: collaborative learning. What the term meant in practice was a form of indirect teaching in which the teacher sets the problem and organizes students to work it out collaboratively. For example, in one type of collaborative learning, peer criticism (also called peer evaluation), students learn to describe the organizational structure of a peer's paper, paraphrase it, and comment both on what seems well done and what the author might do to improve the work. The teacher then evaluates both the essay and the critical response. In another type of collaborative learning, classroom group work, students in small groups work toward a consensus in response to a task set by the teacher, for example, a question about a play, a poem, or another student's paper. What distinguished collaborative learning in each of its several types from traditional classroom practice was that it did not seem to change what people learned (a supposition that now seems questionable) so much as it changed the social context in which they learned it. Students' work tended to improve when they got help from peers; peers offering help, furthermore, learned from the students they helped and from the activity of helping itself. Collaborative learning, it seemed, harnessed the powerful educative force of peer influence that had been—and largely still is—ignored and hence wasted by traditional forms of education.[2]

More recently, those of us actively interested in collaborative learning have begun to think further about this practical experience. Recent developments in philosophy seem to suggest a conceptual rationale for collaborative learning that yields some unexpected insights into pedagogical practice. A new conception of the nature of knowledge provides direction that we lacked earlier as we muddled through, trying to solve practical problems in practical ways. The better we understand this conceptional rationale, it seems, the more effective our practice of collaborative learning becomes.

418

In the hope that this experience will prove true for others, the following three sections outline the rationale of collaborative learning as I currently understand it and the relation of that rationale to classroom practice. The final section outlines some as yet not fully worked out implications both of collaborative learning as a practice and of some aspects of its conceptual rationale. Practice and rationale together, I will argue there, have the potential to challenge fairly deeply the theory and practice of traditional classroom teaching.

CONVERSATION AND THE NATURE OF THOUGHT AND KNOWLEDGE

In an important essay on the place of literature in education published some twenty years ago, "The Voice of Poetry in the Conversation of Mankind," Michael Oakeshott argues that what distinguishes human beings from other animals is our ability to participate in unending conversation. "As civilized human beings," Oakeshott writes,

> we are the inheritors, neither of an inquiry about ourselves and the world, nor of an accumulating body of information, but of a conversation, begun in the primeval forests and extended and made more articulate in the course of centuries. It is a conversation which goes on both in public and within each of ourselves. . . . Education, properly speaking, is an initiation into the skill and partnership of this conversation in which we learn to recognize the voices, to distinguish the proper occasions of utterance, and in which we acquire the intellectual and moral habits appropriate to conversation. And it is this conversation which, in the end, gives place and character to every human activity and utterance. (*Rationalism in Politics* [New York: Basic Books, 1962], p. 199)

Oakeshott argues that the human conversation takes place within us as well as among us, and that conversation as it takes place within us is what we call reflective thought. In making this argument he assumes that conversation and reflective thought are related in two ways: causally and functionally. That is, Oakeshott assumes what the work of Lev Vygotsky and others has shown, that reflective thought is public or social conversation internalized (see, for example, Vygotsky, *Mind and Society* [Cambridge, Mass.: Harvard University Press, 1978]). We first experience and learn "the skill and partnership of conversation" in the external arena of direct social exchange with other people. Only then do we learn to displace that "skill and

419

partnership" by playing silently ourselves, in imagination, the parts of all the participants in the conversation. As Clifford Geertz has put it,

> thinking as an overt, public act, involving the purposeful manipulation of objective materials, is probably fundamental to human beings; and thinking as a covert, private act, and without recourse to such materials [is] a derived, though not unuseful, capability. . . . Human thought is consumately social: social in its origins, social in its functions, social in its form, social in its applications.[3]

Since what we experience as reflective thought is related causally to social conversation (we learn one from the other), the two are also related functionally. That is, because thought is internalized conversation, thought and conversation tend to work largely in the same way. Of course, in thought some of the limitations of conversation are absent. Logistics, for example, are no problem at all. I don't have to take the A train or Eastern Airlines flight #221 to get together with myself for a chat. And in thought there are no differences among the participants in preparation, interest, native ability, or spoken vernacular. Each one is just as clever as I can be, or just as dull. On the other hand, in thought some of the less fortunate limitations of conversation may persist. Limitations that may be imposed, for example, by ethnocentrism, inexperience, personal anxiety, economic interests, and paradigmatic inflexibility can constrain my thinking just as they can constrain conversation. If my talk is narrow, superficial, biased, and confined to cliches, my thinking is likely to be so too.

Still, it remains the case that according to this concept of mental activity many of the social forms and conventions of conversation, most of the grammatical, syntactical and rhetorical structures of conversation, and the range, flexibility, impetus, and goals of conversation are the sources of the forms and conventions, structures, impetus, range and flexibility, and the issues of reflective thought.

The relationship I have been drawing here between conversation and thought illuminates the source of the quality, depth, terms, character, and issues of thought. The assumptions underlying my argument differ considerably, however, from the assumptions we ordinarily make about the nature of thought. We ordinarily assume that thought is some sort of given, an "essential attribute" of the human mind. The view that conversation and thought are causally related assumes not that thought is an essential attribute of the human mind but that it is instead an artifact created by social interaction. We can think because we can talk, and we think in ways we have learned to talk. As Stanley Fish has put it, the thoughts we "can think and the mental

[handwritten marginalia:] What about people who can't talk? or could talk or never talk

operations [we] can perform have their source in some or other interpretive community."[4] The range, complexity, and subtlety of our thought, its power, the practical and conceptual uses we can put it to, and the very issues we can address result in large measure directly from the degree to which we have been initiated into what Oakeshott calls the potential "skill and partnership" of human conversation in its public and social form.

To the extent that thought is internalized conversation, then, any effort to understand how we think requires us to understand the nature of conversation; and any effort to understand conversation requires us to understand the nature of community life that generates and maintains conversation. *talking in class* Furthermore, any effort to understand and cultivate in ourselves the kind of thought we value most requires us to understand and cultivate the kinds of community life that establish and maintain conversation that is the origin of that kind of thought. To think well as individuals we must learn to think well collectively—that is, we must learn to converse well. The first steps to learning to think better, therefore, are learning to converse better and learning to establish and maintain the sorts of social context, the sorts of community life, that foster the sorts of conversation members of the community value.

This principle has broad applicability and has implications far beyond those that may be immediately apparent. For example, Thomas Kuhn has argued in *The Structure of Scientific Revolutions*, (2nd ed.: Chicago: University of Chicago Press, 1970) that to understand scientific thought and knowledge we must understand the nature of scientific communities. Scientific knowledge changes not as our "understanding of the world" changes. It changes as scientists organize and reorganize relations among themselves (pp. 209-10). Carrying Kuhn's view and terminology further, Richard Rorty argues in *Philosophy and the Mirror of Nature* (Princeton: Princeton University Press, 1979) that to understand any kind of knowledge we must understand what he calls the social justification of belief. That is, we must understand how knowledge is established and maintained in the "normal discourse" of communities of knowledgeable peers.[5] Stanley Fish completes the argument by saying that these "interpretive communities" are the source of our thought and of the "meanings" we produce through the use and manipulation of symbolic structures, chiefly language. Fish suggests further, reflecting Erving Goffman's conclusion to *The Presentation of Self in Everyday Life* ([New York: Doubleday Anchor, 1959], pp. 252-53), that interpretative communities may also be in large measure the source of what we regard as our very selves (Fish, p. 14). Our feelings and intuitions are as much the product of social relations as our knowledge.

EDUCATIONAL IMPLICATIONS:
CONVERSATION, COLLABORATIVE LEARNING
AND "NORMAL DISCOURSE"

The line of argument I have been pursuing has important implications for educators, and especially for those of us who teach English—both literature and composition. If thought is internalized public and social talk, then writing of all kinds is internalized social talk made public and social again. If thought is internalized conversation, then writing is internalized conversation re-externalized.[6]

[margin handwriting: Takes it a step further]

Like thought, writing is related to conversation in both time and function. Writing is a technologically displaced form of conversation. When we write, having already internalized the "skill and partnership" of conversation, we displace it once more onto the written page. But because thought is already one step away from conversation, the position of writing relative to conversation is more complex than the position of thought relative to conversation. Writing is at once two steps away from conversation and a return to conversation. We converse; we internalize conversation as thought; and then by writing, we re-immerse conversation in its external, social medium.

My ability to write this essay, for example, depends on my ability to talk through with myself the issues I address here. And my ability to talk through an issue with myself derives largely from my ability to converse directly with other people in an immediate social situation. The point is not that the particular thing I write every time must necessarily be something I have talked over with other people first, although I may well often do just that. What I have to say can, of course, originate in thought, and it often does. But my thought itself is conversation as I have learned to internalize it. The point, therefore, is that writing always has its roots deep in the acquired ability to carry on the social symbolic exchange we call conversation.

The inference writing teachers should make from this line of reasoning is that our task must involve engaging students in conversation among themselves at as many points in both the writing and the reading process as possible, and that we should contrive to ensure that students' conversation about what they read and write is similar in as many ways as possible to the way we would like them eventually to read and write. The way they talk with each other determines the way they will think and the way they will write.

To organize students for these purposes is, in as general a way as I can put it, to organize collaborative learning. Collaborative learning provides a social context in which students can experience and practice the kinds of conversation valued by college teachers. The kind of conversation peer tutors engage in with their tutees, for example, can be emotionally involved,

[margin handwriting: Not just silently listening (that's easy!)]

422

intellectually and substantively focused, and personally disinterested. There could be no better source than this of the sort of displaced conversation—writing—valued by college teachers. Similarly, collaborative classroom group work guided by a carefully designed task makes students aware that writing is a social artifact, like the thought that produces it. Writing may seem to be displaced in time and space from the rest of a writer's community of readers and other writers, but in every instance writing is an act, however much displaced, of conversational exchange.

Besides providing a particular kind of conversation, collaborative learning also provides a particular kind of social context for conversation, a particular kind of community—a community of status equals: peers. Students learn the "skill and partnership" of re-externalized conversation, writing, not only in a community that fosters the kind of conversation college teachers value most, but also in a community that approximates the one most students must eventually write for in everyday life, in business, government, and the professions.

It is worthwhile to disgress a moment here to establish this last point. In most cases people write in business, government, and the professions mainly to inform and convince other people within the writer's own community, people whose status and assumptions approximate the writer's own.[7] That is, the sort of writing most people do most in their everyday working lives is what Richard Rorty calls "normal discourse." Normal discourse (a term of Rorty's coinage based on Thomas Kuhn's term "normal science") applies to conversation within a community of knowledgeable peers. A community of knowledgeable peers is a group of people who accept, and whose work is guided by, the same paradigms and the same code of values and assumptions. In normal discourse, as Rorty puts it, everyone agrees on the "set of conventions about what counts as a relevant contribution, what counts as a question, what counts as having a good argument for that answer or a good criticism of it." The product of normal discourse is "the sort of statement that can be agreed to be true by all participants whom the other participants count as 'rational'" (p. 320).

The essay I am writing here is an example of normal discourse in this sense. I am writing to members of my own community of knowledgeable peers. My readers and I (I presume) are guided in our work by the same set of conventions about what counts as a relevant contribution, what counts as a question, what counts as having a good argument for that answer or a good criticism of it. I judge my essay finished when I think it conforms to that set of conventions and values. It is within that set of conventions and values that my readers will evaluate the essay, both in terms of its quality and in terms of whether or not it makes sense. Normal discourse is pointed; it is explanatory and argumentative. Its purpose is to justify belief to the satisfaction of other people within the author's community of knowledgeable peers. Much of what we teach today—or should be teaching—in composition courses is the normal discourse of most academic, professional, and business communities. The rhetoric taught in our composition textbooks comprises—or should comprise—the conventions of normal discourse of those communities.[8]

Teaching normal discourse in its written form is central to a college curriculum, therefore, because the one thing college teachers in most fields commonly want students to acquire, and what teachers in most fields consistently reward students for, is the ability to carry on in speech and writing the normal discourse of the field in question. Normal discourse is what William Perry describes as discourse in the established contexts of knowledge in a field, discourse that makes effective reference to facts as defined within those contexts. In a student who can integrate fact and context together in this way, Perry says, "we recognize a colleague."[9] This is so because to be conversant with the normal discourse in a field of study or endeavor is exactly what we mean by being knowledgeable—that is, knowledge-able—in that field. Not to have mastered the normal discourse of a discipline, no matter how many "facts" or data one may know, is not to be knowledgeable in that discipline. Mastery of a knowledge community's normal discourse is the basic qualification for acceptance into that community.

The kind of writing students find most useful to learn in college, therefore, is not only the kind of writing most appropriate to work in fields of business, government, and the professions. It is also the writing most appropriate to gaining competence in most academic fields that students study in college. What these two kinds of writing have in common is that they are both written within and addressed to a community of status equals: peers. They are both normal discourse.

This point having, I hope, been established, the nature of the particular kind of community that collaborative learning forms becomes clearer. Collaborative learning provides the kind of social context, the kind of community, in which normal discourse occurs: a community of knowledgeable peers. This is one of its main goals: to provide a context in which students can practice and master the normal discourse exercised in established knowledge communities in the academic world and in business, government, and the professions.

But to say this only raises a host of questions. One question is, how can student peers, who are not members of the knowledge communities they hope to enter, who lack the knowledge that constitutes those communities, help other students enter them? The first, more concrete answer to this question is that no student is wholly ignorant and inexperienced. Every student is already a member of several knowledge communities, from canoeing to computers, baseball to ballet. Membership in any one of these communities may not be a resource that will by itself help much directly in learning to organize an essay or explicate a poem. But pooling the resources that a group of peers brings with them to the task may make accessible the normal discourse of the new community they together hope to enter. Students are especially likely to be able to master that discourse collaboratively if their conversation is structured indirectly by the task or problem that a member of that new community (the teacher) has judiciously designed.[10] To the conversation between peer tutors and their tutees in writing, for example, the tutee brings knowledge of the subject to be written about and knowledge of the assignment. The tutor brings sensitivity to the needs and feelings of peers and knowledge of the conventions of discourse and of standard written English. And the conversation is structured in part by the demands of the teacher's assignment and in part by the formal conventions of the communities the teacher represents, the conventions of academic discourse and standard English.

Such conversation among students can break down, of course, if any one of these elements is not present. It can proceed again if the person responsible for providing the missing element, usually but not always the teacher, is flexible enough to adjust his or her contribution accordingly. If, for example, tutees do not bring to the conversation knowledge of the subject and the assignment, then the teacher helps peer tutors see that their most important contribution may be to help tutees begin at the very beginning: how to go about making sufficient acquaintance with the subject matter and how to set out to clarify the assignment. If tutors lack sensitivity to language and to the feelings and needs of their peers, tutees must contribute by making those feelings and needs more clearly evident. If the task or assignment that the teacher has given is unclear or too difficult or too simple-minded to engage students effectively, then the teacher has to revise it. Throughout this process the teacher has to try to help students negotiate the rocks and shoals of social relations that may interfere with their getting on with their work together.

What students do when working collaboratively on their writing is not write or edit or, least of all, read proof. What they do is converse. They talk about the subject and about the assignment. They talk through the writer's understanding of the subject. They converse about their own relationship and, in general, about relationships in an academic or intellectual context between students and teachers. Most of all they converse about and as a part of writing. Similarly, what students do when working collaboratively in small groups in order to read a text with understanding—a poem, a story, or another student's paper—is also to converse. They converse in order to reach consensus in answer to questions the teacher has raised about the text. They converse about and as a part of understanding. In short, they learn, by practicing it in this orderly way, the normal discourse of the academic community.

COLLABORATIVE LEARNING
AND THE AUTHORITY OF KNOWLEDGE

The place of conversation in learning, especially in the humanities, is the largest context in which we must see collaborative learning. To say that conversation has a place in learning should not of course seem peculiar to those of us who count ourselves humanists, a category that includes all of us who teach literature and most of us who teach writing. Furthermore, most of us believe that "class discussion" is one of the most effective ways of teaching. The truth, however, is that despite this belief the person who does most of the discussing in most of our discussion classes is the teacher.

This tends to happen because behind our enthusiasm for discussion lies a fundamental distrust of it. The graduate training most of us have enjoyed—or endured—has taught us, in fact, that collaboration and community activity is inappropriate and foreign to work in humanistic disciplines such as English. Humanistic study, we have been led to believe, is a solitary life, and the vitality of the humanities lies in the talents and endeavors of each of us as individuals. What we call discussion is more often than not an adversarial activity pitting individual against individual in an effort to assert what one literary critic has called "will to power over the text," if not over each other. If we look at what we do instead of what we say, we discover that we think of knowledge as something we acquire and wield as individuals relative to each other, not something we generate and maintain in company with and in dependency upon each other.[11]

Only recently have humanists of note, such as Stanley Fish in literary criticism and Richard Rorty in philosophy, begun to take effective steps toward exploring the force and implications of knowledge communities in the humanistic disciplines, and toward redefining the nature of our knowledge as a social artifact. Much of this recent work follows a trail blazed two decades ago by Thomas Kuhn. The historical irony of this course of events lies in the fact that Kuhn developed his notion about the nature of scientific knowledge after first examining the way knowledge is generated, established, and maintained in the humanities and social sciences. For us as humanists to discover in Kuhn and his followers the conceptual rationale of collaborative learning is to see our own chickens come home to roost.

Kuhn's position that even in the "hard" sciences knowledge is a social artifact emerged from his attempt to understand the implications of the increasing indeterminacy of knowledge of all kinds in the twentieth century.[12] To say that knowledge is indeterminate is to say that there is no fixed and certain point of reference, no Arnoldian "touchstone" against which we can measure truth. If there is no such absolute referent, then knowledge must be a thing people make and remake. Knowledge must be a social artifact. But to call knowledge a social artifact, Kuhn argues, is not to say that knowledge is merely relative, that knowledge is what any one of us says it is. Knowledge is maintained and established by communities of knowledgeable peers. It is what together we agree it is, for the time being. Rorty, following Kuhn, argues that communities of knowledgeable peers make knowledge by a process of socially justifying belief. Collaborative learning models this process.

This then is a second and more general answer to the question raised in the preceding section. How can student peers, who are not themselves members of the knowledge communities they hope to enter, help other students to enter those communities? Isn't collaborative learning the blind leading the blind?

It is of course exactly the blind leading the blind if we insist on the Cartesian model of knowledge: that to know is to "see," and that knowledge is information impressed upon the individual mind by some outside source. But if we accept the premise that knowledge is an artifact created by a community of knowledgeable peers constituted by the language of that community, and that learning is a social and not an individual process, then to learn is not to assimilate information and improve our mental eyesight. To learn is to work collaboratively to establish and maintain knowledge among a community of knowledgeable peers through the process that Richard Rorty calls "socially justifying belief." We socially justify belief when we explain to others why one way of understanding how the world hangs together seems to us preferable to other ways of understanding it. We establish knowledge or justify belief collaboratively by challenging each other's biases and presuppositions; by negotiating collectively toward new paradigms of perception, thought, feeling, and expression; and by joining larger, more experienced communities of knowledgeable peers through assenting to those communities' interests, values, language, and paradigms of perception and thought.

If we accept this concept of knowledge and learning even partially and tentatively, it is possible to see collaborative learning as a model of the way that even the most sophisticated scientific knowledge is established and maintained. Knowledge is the product of human beings in a state of continual negotiation or conversation. Education is not a process of assimilating "the truth" but, as Rorty has put it, a process of learning to "take a hand in what is going on" by joining "the conversation of mankind." Collaborative learning is an arena in which students can negotiate their way into that conversation.

COLLABORATIVE LEARNING AND NEW KNOWLEDGE

Seen this way, collaborative learning seems unexceptionable. It is not hard to see it as comfortable, not very surprising, not even very new. In discovering and applying collaborative learning we seem to be, if not exactly reinventing the wheel, certainly rediscovering some of the more obvious implications of that familiar and useful device. Collaborative learning, it seems, is no new thing under the sun. However much we may explore its conceptual ramifications, we must acknowledge the fact that people have always learned from their peers and doggedly persist in doing so whether we professional teachers and educators take a hand in it or not. In Thomas Wolfe's *Look Homeward, Angel* Eugene Gant records how in grammar school he learned to write (in this case, form the words on a page) from his "comrade," learning from a peer what "all instruction failed" to teach him. In business and industry, furthermore, and in professions such as medicine, law, engineering, and architecture—where to work is to learn or fail—collaboration is the norm. All that is new in collaborative learning, it seems, is the systematic application of collaborative principles to that last bastion of hierarchy and individualism, the American college classroom.

This comfortable view, while appropriate, may yet be deceptive. If we follow just a bit further the implications of the rationale for collaborative learning that I have been outlining here, we catch a glimpse of a somewhat startling educational scene. Take, for example, the principle that entering an existing knowledge community involves a process of negotiation. Followed to its logical conclusion this principle implies that education is not a rite of passage in which students passively become initiated into an institution that is monolithic and unchanging. It implies that the means by which students learn to negotiate this entry, collaborative learning, is not merely a better pedagogy, a better way of initiating new members into existing knowledge communities. And it implies that collaborative learning as a classroom practice models more than how knowledge is established and maintained.

The argument pursued here implies, in short, that in the long run collaborative learning models how knowledge is generated, how it changes and grows.

This way of thinking about collaborative learning is somewhat speculative, but it is nevertheless of considerable interest and importance to teachers of English. If, as Rorty suggests, knowledge is a social artifact, if knowledge is belief justified through normal discourse, then the generation of knowledge, what we call "creativity," must also be a social process. It too must involve discourse. But the discourse involved in generating knowledge cannot be normal discourse, since normal discourse maintains knowledge. It is inadequate for generating new knowledge. Knowledge-generating discourse is discourse of quite another kind. It is, to use Rorty's phrase, abnormal discourse.

In contrast to normal discourse, abnormal discourse occurs between coherent communities or within communities when consensus no longer exists with regard to rules, assumptions, goals, values, or mores. Abnormal discourse, Rorty says, "is what happens when someone joins in the discourse who is ignorant of the conventions governing that discourse "or who sets them aside." Whereas normal discourse produces "the sort of statement which can be agreed to be true by all participants whom the other participants count as 'rational,'" "the product of abnormal discourse can be anything from nonsense to intellectual revolution." Unlike the participants in normal discourse who sound "rational" to the others in the community, a person speaking abnormal discourse sounds "either 'kooky' (if he loses his point) or 'revolutionary' (if he gains it)" (pp. 320, 339).

The importance of abnormal discourse to the discussion of collaborative learning is that abnormal discourse serves the function of helping us—immersed as we inevitably are in the everyday normal discourse of our disciplines and professions—to see the provincial nature of normal discourse and of the communities defined by normal discourse. Abnormal discourse sniffs out stale, unproductive knowledge and challenges its authority, that is, the authority of the community which that knowledge constitutes. Its purpose, Rorty says, is to undermine "our reliance upon the knowledge we have gained" through normal discourse. We must occasionally undermine this reliance because normal discourse tends to "block the flow of conversation by presenting [itself] as offering the canonical vocabulary for discussion of a given topic" (pp. 386-387).

Abnormal discourse is therefore necessary to learning. But, ironically, abnormal discourse cannot be directly taught. "There is no discipline that describes" abnormal discourse, Rorty tells us, "any more than there is a discipline devoted to the study of the unpredictable or of 'creativity'" (p. 320).

What we can teach are the tools of normal discourse; that is, both practical rhetoric and rhetorically based modes of literary criticism such as the taxonomy of figures, new-critical analysis, and deconstructive criticism.[13] To leave openings for change, however, we must not teach these tools as universals. We must teach practical rhetoric and critical analysis in such a way that, when necessary, students can turn to abnormal discourse in order to undermine their own and other people's reliance on the canonical conventions and vocabulary of normal discourse. We must teach the use of these tools in such a way that students *can* set them aside, if only momentarily, for the purpose of generating new knowledge, for the purpose, that is, of reconstituting knowledge communities in more satisfactory ways.

It is just here that, as I mentioned at the beginning of this essay, we begin to move beyond our earlier suppositions about what people learn through collaborative learning. Defining knowledge as a social artifact established and maintained through normal discourse challenges the authority of knowledge as we traditionally understand it. But by changing what we usually call the process of learning—the work, the expectations, and the social structure of the traditional classroom—collaborative learning also changes what we usually call the substance of learning. It challenges the authority of knowledge by revealing, as John Trimbur has observed, that authority itself is a social artifact. This revelation and the new awareness that results from it makes authority comprehensible both to us as teachers and to our students. It involves a process of reacculturation. Thus collaborative learning can help students join the established knowledge communities of academic studies, business, and the professions. But it should also help students learn something else. They should learn, Trimbur says, "something about how this social transition takes place, how it involves crises of identity and authority, how students can begin to generate a transitional language to bridge the gap between communities" (private correspondence).

Challenging the traditional authority of knowledge in this way, collaborative learning naturally challenges the traditional basis of the authority of those who teach. Our authority as teachers always derives directly or indirectly from the prevailing conception of the authority of knowledge. In the pre-Cartesian world people tended to believe that the authority of knowledge lodged in one place, the mind of God. In that world teachers derived their authority from their godliness, their nearness to the mind of God. In Cartesian, Mirror-of-Nature epistemology, the authority of knowledge has had three alternative lodgings, each a secular version of the mind of God. We could believe if we chose that the authority of knowledge lodged in some touchstone of value and truth above and beyond ourselves, such as mathematics, creative genius, or the universals of sound reasoning. We

430

could believe that the authority of knowledge lodged in the mind of a person of genius: a Wordsworth, an Einstein, or a Freud. Or we could believe that the authority of knowledge lodged in the nature of the object objectively known: the universe, the human mind, the text of a poem.

Our authority as teachers, accordingly, has had its source in our nearness to one of these secular versions of the mind of God. In the first case we derive our authority from our identification with the "touchstone" of value and truth. Thus, for some of us, mathematicians and poets have, generally speaking, greater authority than, say, sociologists or literary critics. According to the second alternative we derive our authority from intimacy with the greatest minds. Many of us feel that those who have had the good fortune to study with Freud, Faraday, or Faulkner, for example, have greater authority than those who studied with their disciples; or, those who have studied the manuscripts of Joyce's fiction have greater authority than those who merely studied the edited texts. According to the third alternative, we derive our authority as teachers from being in direct touch with the objective world. Most of us feel that those whose knowledge is confirmed by hands-on laboratory experimentation have greater authority than those whose knowledge is based on a synthesis of secondary sources.

Because the concept that knowledge is socially justified belief denies that the authority of knowledge lodges in any of these places, our authority as teachers according to that concept has quite another source as well. Insofar as collaborative learning inducts students into established knowledge communities and teaches them the normal discourse of those communities, we derive our authority as teachers from being certified representatives of the communities of knowledgeable peers that students aspire to join, and that we, as members of our chosen disciplines and also members of the community of the liberally educated public at large, invite and encourage them to join. Teachers are defined in this instance as those members of a knowledge community who accept the responsibility for inducting new members into the community. Without successful teachers the community will die when its current members die, and knowledge as assented to by that community will cease to exist.

Insofar as collaborative learning helps students understand how knowledge is generated through abnormal discourse, however, our authority as teachers derives from another source. It derives from the values of a larger—indeed, the largest possible—community of knowledgeable peers, the community that encompasses all others. The interests of this largest community contradict one of the central interests of local communities such as professional disciplines and fields of study: to maintain established knowledge. The interest of the larger community is to resist this conservative tendency.

Its interest is to bridge gaps among knowledge communities and to open them to change.

The continued vitality of the knowledge communities we value—in particular the community of liberally educated people and its sub-communities, the scholarly and professional disciplines—depends on both these needs being met: to maintain established knowledge and to challenge and change it. As representatives and delegates of a local, disciplinary community, and of the larger community as well, teachers are responsible for the continued vitality of both of the knowledge communities we value. Responsible to both sets of values, therefore, we must perform as conservators *and* agents of change, as custodians of prevailing community values *and* as agents of social transition and reacculturation.

Because by giving students access to the "conversation of mankind," to return to Oakeshott's phrase, collaborative learning can serve both of these seemingly conflicting educational aims at once, it has an especially important role to play in studying and teaching English. It is one way of introducing students to the process by which communities of knowledgeable peers create referential connections between symbolic structures and "reality," that is, by which they establish knowledge and by doing so maintain community growth and coherence. To study adequately any text—student theme or play by Shakespeare—is to study an entire social symbolic process, not just part of it. To study and teach English is to study and teach the social origin, nature, reference, and function of symbolic structures.

The view that knowledge is a social artifact, furthermore, requires a re-examination of our premises as students of English and as teachers. To date, very little work of this sort has been done. One can only guess what might come of a concerted effort on the part of the profession as a whole. The effort might ultimately involve "demystifying" much that we now do as humanists and teachers of the humanities. If we bring to mind, for example, a sampling of important areas of current theoretical thought in and allied to literary criticism, we are likely to find mostly bipolar forms: text and reader, text and writer, symbol and referent, signifier and signified. On the one hand, a critique along the lines I have been following here might involve examining how these theories would differ if they included the third term missing from most of them. How would a psychoanalytically oriented study of metaphor differ, for example, if it acknowledged that psychotherapy is fundamentally a kind of social relationship based on the mutual creation or recreation of symbolic structures by therapist and patient? How would semiotics differ if it acknowledged that all "codes" are symbolic structures constituting language communities and that to understand these codes requires us to examine and understand the complex social symbolic relations among the people who make up language communities? How would practical rhetoric look if we assumed that writer and reader were not adversaries but partners in a common, community-based enterprise? How would it look if we no longer assumed that people write to persuade or to distinguish themselves and their points of view and to enhance their own individuality by gaining the acquiescence of other individuals? How would it look if we assumed instead that people write for the very opposite reason: that people write in order to be accepted, to join, to be regarded as another member of the culture or community that constitutes the writer's audience?

Once we had reexamined in this way how English is studied professionally, we could on the other hand also undertake to reexamine how English is taught as well. If we did that, we might find ourselves taking issue with Stanley Fish's conclusion that to define knowledge as a social artifact generated by interpretive communities has no effect whatsoever on the way we read and teach literature and composition. My argument in this essay suggests, on the contrary, that some changes in our pedagogical attitudes and classroom practices are almost inevitable. These changes would result from integrating our understanding of social symbolic relationships into our teaching—not just into what we teach but also into how we teach it. For example, so long as we think of knowledge as a reflection and synthesis of information about the objective world, then to teach *King Lear* seems to involve providing a "correct" text and rehearsing students in "correct" interpretations of it. "Correct" here means the text and the interpretations that, as Fish puts it, seem "obvious and inescapable" within the knowledge community, within the "institutional or conventional structure," of which we happen to be members (p. 370).

But if we think of knowledge as socially justified belief, then to teach *King Lear* seems to involve creating contexts where students undergo a sort of cultural change. This change would be one in which they loosen ties to the knowledge communities they currently belong to and join another. These two communities would be seen as having quite different sets of values, mores, and goals, and above all quite different languages. To speak in one community of a person asking another to "pray you undo this button" (V, iii) might be merely to tell a mercantile tale, or a prurient one, while in another community such a request could be both a gesture of profound human dignity and a metaphor of the dissolution of a world.

Similarly, so long as we think of learning as reflecting and synthesizing information about the objective world, to teach expository writing is to provide examples, analysis, and exercises in the traditional modes of practical rhetoric—description, narration, comparison-contrast—or examples, analysis, and exercises in the "basic skills" of writing, and to rehearse students in their proper use. But if we think of learning as a social process, the process of socially justifying belief, then to teach expository writing seems to involve something else entirely. It involves demonstrating to students that they know something only when they can explain it in writing to the satisfaction of the community of their knowledgeable peers. To teach this way, in turn, seems to require us to engage students in collaborative work that does not just reinforce the values and skills they begin with, but that promotes a sort of reacculturation.[14]

The argument I have been making here implies, in short, that students and teachers of literature and writing must begin to develop awareness and skill that may seem foreign and irrelevant to our profession at the present time. Organizing collaborative learning effectively requires doing more than throwing students together with their peers with little or no guidance or preparation. To do that is merely to perpetuate, perhaps even aggravate, the many possible negative efforts of peer group influence: conformity, anti-intellectualism, intimidation, and leveling-down of quality. To avoid these pitfalls and to marshal the powerful educational resource of peer group influence requires us to create and maintain a demanding academic environment that makes collaboration—social engagement in intellectual pursuits—a genuine part of students' educational development. And that in turn requires quite new and perhaps more thorough analyses of the elements of our field than we have yet attempted.

NOTES

1. I am indebted for conversation regarding substantive issues raised in this essay to Fellows of the Brooklyn College Institute for Training Peer Tutors and of the Asnuntuck Community College Institute in Collaborative Learning and Peer-Tutor Training, and to Peter Elbow. Both Institutes were supported by grants from the Fund for the Improvement of Postsecondary Education. I am particularly grateful to Peter Hawkes, Harvey Kail, Ronald Maxwell, and John Trimbur for reading the essay in early drafts and for offering suggestions for improvement. The essay is in many ways and at many levels a product of collaborative learning.

2. The educative value of peer group influence is discussed in Theodore M. Newcomb and Everett K. Wilson, eds., *College Peer Groups* (Chicago: Aldine, 1966).

3. *The Interpretation of Cultures* (New York: Basic Books, 1971), pp. 76-77, 360. In addition to "The Growth of Culture and the Evolution of Mind," also relevant in the same volume are "The Impact of the Concept of Man" and "Ideology as a Cultural System," parts four and five.

4. *Is There a Text in This Class?: The Authority of Interpretive Communities* (Cambridge, Mass.: Harvard University Press, 1980), p. 14. Fish develops his argument fully in part 2, pp. 303-371. On the distinction between "interiority" or "inwardness" and "internalization," see Stephen Toulmin, "The Inwardness of Mental Life," *Critical Inquiry*, 6 (1979), 1-16.

5. I have explored some of the larger educational implications of Rorty's argument in "Liberal Education and the Social Justification of Belief," *Liberal Education*, 68 (1982), 95-114.

6. I make a case for this position in "Writing and Reading as Collaborative or Social Acts," in Janice N. Hays, et al, eds., *The Writer's Mind: Writing as a Mode of Thinking* (Urbana, Ill.: National Council of Teachers of English, 1983), pp. 159-169. In the current critical climate the distinction between conversation and speech as sources of writing and thought is important to maintain. Deconstructionist critics such as Paul de Man argue (e.g., in his *Blindness and Insight* [Minneapolis: University of Minnesota Press, 1983]), following Derrida, that writing is not displaced speech but a primary act. This argument defines "writing" in a much broader sense than we are used to, to mean something like "making public" in any manner, including speech. Hence deconstructionist "writing" can be construed as a somewhat static conception of what I am here calling "conversation": a social act. So long as the conversational, hence social, nature of "writing" in the deconstructionist sense remains unrecognized, the aversion of deconstructionist criticism to the primacy of speech as embodying the phenomenological "metaphysics of presence" remains circular. The deconstructionist argument holds that privileging speech "centers" language in persons. But "persons" are fictions. The alternative proposal by deconstruction, however, that writing is "free play," invites centering once again, since the figure of play personifies language. The deconstructionist critique has thus yet to acknowledge sufficiently that language, and its products such as thought and the self, are social artifacts constituted by "interpretive communities."

7. Some writing in business, government, and the professions may of course be like the writing students do in school for teachers, that is, for the sake of practice and evaluation. Certainly some writing in everyday working life is done purely as performance to please superiors in the corporate or department hierarchy, tell them what they already know, and demonstrate to them the writer's proficiency *as* a writer. It may be true, therefore, that learning to write to a person who is not a member of one's own status and knowledge community, that is, to a teacher, has some practical everyday value. But the value of writing of this type is hardly proportionate to the amount of time students normally spend on it.

8. A textbook that acknowledges the normal discourse of academic disciplines and offers ways of learning it in a context of collaborative learning is Elaine Maimon, et al., *Writing in the Arts and Sciences* (Boston: Little Brown, 1981).

9. "Examsmanship and the Liberal Arts," in *Examining in Harvard College: A Collection of Essays by Members of the Harvard Faculty* (Cambridge, Mass.: Harvard University Press, 1963). Quoted from Kenneth A. Bruffee, *A Short Course in Writing* (Boston: Little, Brown, 1980), p. 221.

10. For examples and an explanation of this technique, see my *A Short Course in Writing*, cited above, and "CLTV: Collaborative Learning Television," *Educational Communication and Technology Journal*, 30 (1982), 26-40. Also see Clark Bouton and Russell Y. Garth, eds., *Learning in Groups* (San Francisco: Jossey-Bass, 1983).

11. I discuss the individualistic bias of our current interpretation of the humanistic tradition in "The Structure of Knowledge and the Future of Liberal Education," *Liberal Education*, 67 (1981), 181-185.

12. I trace briefly the history of the growing indeterminacy of knowledge and its relevance to the humanities in "The Structure of Knowledge," cited above.

13. Christopher Norris defines deconstruction somewhat simplistically but usefully for most purposes as "rhetorical questioning" (*Deconstruction: Theory and Practice* [London: Methuen, 1982], p. 21).

14. I suggest some possible curricular implications of the concept of knowledge as socially justified belief in "Liberal Education and the Social Justification of Belief," cited above. See also Clifford Geertz, *Local Knowledge* (New York: Basic Books, 1983), pp. 14-15, 161; Richard M. Rorty, "Hermeneutics, General Studies, and Teaching," *Synergos: Selected Papers from the Synergos Seminars*, George Mason University, 2 (Fall 1982), 1-15; and my "Learning to Live in a World out of Joint: Thomas Kuhn's Message to Humanists Revisited," *Liberal Education*, 70 (1984), 77-81.

Reality, Consensus, and Reform in the Rhetoric of Composition Teaching

GREG MYERS

I would like to raise some political questions about two methods of teaching I use in my writing classes: having small groups of students collaborate on and critique each others' writing, and having case assignments based on some actual writing situation, whether a technical proposal or an anthropology exam. My thinking about these methods is based largely on the detailed and practical suggestions of Peter Elbow and Kenneth Bruffee, and on discussion of their works with other teachers. My means of raising questions will be to compare the writings of Elbow and Bruffee to the work of an earlier writer, Sterling Andrus Leonard (1888-1931), whose Dewey-inspired English education textbook, *English Composition as a Social Problem*, suggested these two teaching methods, which I had considered new, back in 1917. I revive this now-forgotten writer and make these comparisons for two reasons: 1) the distance in time makes it easier for us to see his social context than it is to see the context of Elbow or Bruffee, and 2) the recurrence of these ideas as new ideas suggests that those of us who want to change the way writing is taught tend to overlook the efforts and the lessons of earlier reformers. As Lawrence Cremin says in his history of the progressive movement in education, of which Leonard was a part, "Reform movements are notoriously ahistorical in outlook" (8). Until recently, this ahistoricism has

Reprinted from *College English* 48.2 (February 1986): 154–71. Used with permission.

been characteristic of composition theory, with its reformist attacks on a monolithic tradition.[1]

Leonard's writings are interesting in themselves, even considered apart from their historical importance, and deserve to be rescued from the storage rooms of teachers' college libraries. Besides the comments on collaborative learning and "real" writing that I will be considering, he made a number of other criticisms and suggestions between 1914 and 1930 that could be taken from this year's issues of *College Composition and Communication* or *College English*:

> *On the composing process:* "The ideal of the finished product is absolutely vicious, except as it functions to determine the remote goal." (*English Composition* 190)
>
> *On the development of writing abilities:* "Indeed, growth in the art of writing or speaking may be defined simply as a process of becoming increasingly reader-minded." (*English Composition* 14)
>
> *On freewriting:* "Some may really do best to write first in mad and scrabble haste, for themselves only, and thus clear their thoughts before they attempt to talk or write for anyone else." (*English Composition* 111)
>
> *On the modes:* "Useful as this [classification of the forms of discourse] doubtless is for sorting completed pieces of writing, it does not view the process of writing from the side of the thoughts or ideas the writer has to express and particularly of his purpose in expressing those." ("As to the Forms of Discourse" 202)

He also makes suggestions on invention, on sentence combining, on Piaget's theories, and on the need to avoid petty criticisms of errors and unrealistic, "schoolmastering" standards of usage.[2] But what most interests me is his answer to what he calls "the central problem" of his English education work:

> How, stirred by. . . interesting problems requiring expressing, can the school class be knit into a social group organized for mutual help, and aided to move steadily forward in the arduous way of attaining effective expression? (35).

His emphases on the class as a social group, and on the real basis of writing in "interesting problems" of the students' communities inside and outside the school, anticipate the current interest in what Patricia Bizzell calls "social processes whereby language learning and thinking capacities are shaped and used in particular communities" (215). I will try to show that he also anticipates some of the political dilemmas of present-day reformers.

SOME TERMS: IDEOLOGY, CONSENSUS, AND REALITY

I will be criticizing two sorts of rhetorical appeals that Leonard, and later Elbow and Bruffee, use in arguing for the teaching of writing through groups: an appeal to the authority of consensus, and an appeal to the authority of reality. It may seem perverse to object to appeals that are so common in our field and that are apparently progressive: surely we all see the need to come to reasoned agreement within a community, and to relate our teaching to the real world. To explain why I find these appeals problematic, I need to draw on an indispensible piece of Marxist jargon, the concept of *ideology*. I am not using the word the way it is commonly used to criticize any systematic political belief, as, say, an unsympathetic reader of this article might say my views were distorted by Left wing ideology. I am using it in the sense established by Marx, and modified by twentieth-century Marxists, to describe the whole system of thought and belief that goes with a social and economic system, the thoughts that structure our thinking so deeply that we take them for granted, as the nature of the real world. The concept has been much discussed by Marxists because it helps explain the apparent stability of the capitalist system, despite all its contradictions. It helps explain why people who are oppressed seem to go along with their oppression; the ideology of the oppressive system gives them the structures through which they make sense of their world.[3]

The concept of ideology has been of particular interest to Marxist sociologists of education, who see the school as, at least in part, an institution that adapts ideology to changing economic and social conditions, and produces a new version of ideology for each generation. Schools not only teach academic knowledge; they teach work according to schedule, acceptance of authority, and competition among individuals and between groups. They also help provide a justification for the hierarchies of society, so that, for instance, people accept that manual labor should pay less than mental labor. This process of adapting and carrying on the assumptions of our society is called *reproducing ideology*, by analogy with Marx's description of the reproduction of capital. Recently, radical teachers have asked if school can also be a place where people can resist the reproduction of ideology; they have put less emphasis on the all-embracing power of ideology as a structure, and have focused on the ways students and teachers can break this unthinking acceptance of ideas that support the way things are.[4] Of course, many teachers who are not Marxists agree that the vast differences in our society between rich and poor, black and white, men and women, are bad, and many teachers agree that critical thinking is a good thing. Where Marxist teachers differ from other critics of these injustices is in arguing that the social and economic system that perpetuates the injustices builds a protective structure of ideology that prevents us from thinking critically about it. Thus, what we might think is free and progressive thought may be another way of perpetuating a system we want to change.

I will argue that ideas of *consensus* and *reality*, as they are used by Leonard, though they seem so progressive, are part of the structure of ideology. The construction of a sense of general agreement is as important to the rhetoric of composition teaching as it is to the rhetoric of national politics; look, for instance, at all the articles in this journal asserting a new paradigm in the profession. But if conflict is part of the system, and is necessary to change the system, then consensus, within the system as it is, must mean that some interests have been suppressed or excluded. Similarly, it is common in our profession to show oneself as escaping tired academic forms to enter the real world. But if what we take as reality is always a social construction, then to accept the reality we see now is to accept the structure of illusion our system gives us. Worse, it is to see reality as something natural, outside our control, rather than to see it as something we make in our actions in society.

Since many readers who see the same economic, racial, and sexist injustices I do may not share my conviction that the problems are fundamental and systematic, it may help to use a familiar example from a society all readers will believe is fundamentally and systematically unjust. Huckleberry Finn's thinking is structured by the ideology of a slave-holding society. Though Huck himself does not own any slaves or benefit from this society (recall that he has invested some capital that he found), he hates abolitionists, and he can only think about blacks and whites in the terms he has learned. (Every reader must recall the exchange he has when he tells Aunt Sally the steamboat had blown a cylinder head: "Good gracious! Anybody hurt?—No'm. Killed a nigger.—Well, it's lucky; because sometimes people do get hurt.") But for reasons Huck doesn't entirely understand, and which he would not consider as being in any way political, he is capable of some remarkable acts of resistance to this system: for instance, he makes up elaborate lies on the spur of the moment to keep slave hunters away. There is some chance for change as long as he and others are capable of such resistance. But still he consciously believes in the institution of slavery enough so that he thinks worse of Tom Sawyer, a good boy, for apparently helping free

Jim. Huck himself is an agreeable sort who prefers to avoid trouble. Whenever he tries to approach the *consensus* view, to do what he believes is right, he thinks of returning his friend Jim to slavery. Towards the end of the book, he believes he is finally facing *reality* when he admits to himself that in helping Jim escape, he is guilty of stealing property from Jim's owner. Now I am not saying that the social system of present day New York or Texas or Lancashire, where I have been teaching, is like that of ante-bellum Missouri where Huck grows up; what I am saying is that our social system constructs our view of the world as slavery does Huck's, and that the appeals to consensus and to reality may support that ideological view, as they did for Huck.

STERLING LEONARD AND CONSENSUS

I have commented on how current Sterling Leonard's ideas sound today. I would argue that this is because the historical conditions of high school English education in his period, 1900-1930, have some similarities to those in college, and particularly community college, English education in our own time. The high schools then were adapting to a massive influx of immigrants, and to the enrollment of working class students who had previously left school early, if they had attended at all.[5] In a similar way, writing programs like those at the City University of New York have faced the institutional challenge of coping with a group of students who would not previously have attended a university. In both periods, the new students changed the institutions, as well as being changed by them. In both periods, the institutions were responding to the demands of business for a large workforce with a different kind of skills. And in both periods, the teachers of writing were trying to establish their own professional status. A sense of historical conditions can help us see Leonard's progressivism in a social context.

Leonard was a typical reformer of this period, and one could find ideas similar to his in the work of John Dewey, E. L. Thorndike, George Philip Krapp, Fred Newton Scott, C. C. Fries, and I. A. Richards.[6] Leonard worked with all these teachers, in his own schooling at Michigan and Columbia Teachers' College or in his later work as a professor at Wisconsin and a leader of the then new NCTE. But the most important influence on him, and an important influence still on composition theory, was the work of John Dewey. It was from Dewey that Leonard took his central theme—and the theme of most importance to us in trying to criticize his work—the idea of the school as an image of society. For instance, in *The School and Society* (1898), Dewey says, "The great thing to keep in mind, then, regarding the introduction into the school of various forms of active occupation, is that through them the entire spirit of the school is renewed. . . . It gets a chance to become a miniature community, an embryonic society" (15). This quotation refers to both the elements I want to discuss in Leonard's work, the use of the social group of the class, and the emphasis on "real projects," with their reality defined by the analogy to the world outside the school.

Leonard's emphasis on the class as a social group is not just dogmatic Deweyism; he has clearly taught and learned from classes taught this way. In *English Composition as a Social Problem*, for example, he anticipates current ideas in using group work as the basis for "prevision of ideas" (invention), for revision suggestions, and for setting standards of usage. He has practical suggestions to make on teachers' direction of class experimentation (22), on responding (or not responding) to spoken errors (42), on introducing the class to criticism of students' writing (47), on letting the class make up terminology (77), on withholding one's criticisms (97), and on restraining students' carping criticisms of each other: "We must encourage prompt condemnation of guerilla pettifogging whenever we discover signs of it" (164). These passages remind the reader today of the practical advice in Bruffee's *A Short Course in Writing* or Elbow's *Writing Without Teachers.*

But there are passages in which Leonard describes the authority of the classroom group that should make us aware of the dangers of a consensus-based method. Leonard sees his method as furthering the sort of democracy in education promised by Dewey, a democracy he does not see in the traditional classroom. "Our present classrooms are designed chiefly for securing a maximum of order and dispatch. Parliamentary practice is demanded in the custom of addressing the teacher always, and is parodied in the raising of right hands for recognition" (40). Leonard's students have much more to do with each other than this; they are "an interested group of cooperative workers" (65). The danger is that the teacher has merely embodied his or her authority in the more effective guise of class consensus. This guided consensus has a power over individual students that a teacher can not have alone. "What the class may be able, with the help and suggestion of their leader, truly to realize as quite undesirable—cheap or smart or the like—may be quietly branded by the common judgment as unacceptable, and really eliminated" (130). Any teacher who uses group discussions or projects has seen that they can, on occasion, be fierce enforcers of conformity. And Leonard welcomes this enforcement with less worry than we might have. "The erring will be helped sufficiently by a sensation of lowered class temperature, so sharp that even the least sensitive cannot escape it" (149). Leonard does not himself use, but refers to, another teacher's "device . . . of having all children look for such violations [of rules of usage] by any member of the group anywhere and report complete statements and names, and then of deputing committees to write out all such reports on the blackboard each week" (150). Such elaborate machinery might occur to a teacher only during a period of war-time red-baiting hysteria (this was written in 1917), but the tendency to unthinking conformity is always there when consensus is used to set and enforce standards.

The emphasis on the authority of the group that we see in Leonard's textbook is apparent also in his most influential research, his usage studies that attempt to show the differences between formal textbook prescriptions and the language actually used in social transactions. For him the choice is not between correct and incorrect forms, but between the real world of actual usage and the unreal world of school English: "The question appears to turn on whether we wish in these grade and high school years to cultivate excellent homely expressions to fit the daily, informal occasions that we all have to meet most often, or rather a bookish and formal type exclusively" (132). Here he attacks something like what Ken Macrorie calls "Engfish." Leonard does believe that there are some arbitrary rules that must be taught as arbitrary rules. But he believes these rules are very few; thus he is interested in the definition of what the NCTE then called "Minimum Essentials," making a short list of items to be taught by all teachers and consigning the rest of the handbook items to oblivion.

Leonard's authority for the selection of these "essential" items would be actual usage; he has nothing but scorn for the John Simons and Edwin Newmans of his day who would try to impose puristic usage by fiat. "It is easy," he wrote in an early article, "to compile and propagate handbooks of baseless prescriptions; and people will buy them, just as they will buy manuals of etiquette, simply because these announce so many things which 'aren't done' that everyone is convicted of a sin and hastens to remedy the evil. But neither language nor other phases of good manners are settled by these means" ("What About Correct English?" 255). In his Columbia dissertation, *The Doctrine of Correctness in English Usage, 1700-1800,* he traces the origins of many of the handbook rules, and shows they have no basis in the actual usage of any period. This study led to *Current English Usage,* a massive survey to show how little "cultivated usage" supports the handbooks on most disputed items.[7] His views, progressive for the time, had a strong influence on the NCTE's position on usage. But we should note that Leonard's constant appeal to consensus usage assumes the inherent superiority of certain language groups. When he compares grammar books to etiquette books, he assumes, correctly I think, that issues of grammar are debated with such heat because they conceal issues of class, and especially the uneasiness of the middle class about its status. But there is little sense in his usage studies that there might not be just one answer for each item, that different classes or regions or races might have different usages, and that conflicts between these usages reflect other social conflicts. Instead, he carefully chooses certain kinds of respondents, and carefully figures the percentages of respondents approving of each item, and takes the majority vote as the right answer. His authority, he says, is "what various judges have observed about actual use or non-use by cultivated persons" ("Current Definition of Levels in English Usage" 345). But note it is cultivated persons who are to be considered, and experts who are to be the judges. The notion of consensus in usage, while it seems democratic, ignores the conflicts that characterize language change, and leaves the authority of certain types of language unquestioned.

It may seem odd to insist that large social conflicts are behind the use of groups to critique students' papers or the decision on when to use the subjunctive. But Leonard's exercises in democracy can be seen as part of a larger effort to create consensus by eliminating or at least concealing diversity and conflict. This diversity is so well concealed that anyone reading Leonard's articles now, or reading any sampling of articles from the NCTE's *English Journal* of his period, could remain unaware that teachers in many cities would be teaching classes in which most students were foreign born.[8] The only indication of potential conflict would be the way that progressive and traditional educators alike made every class into a civics lesson. If one believes that the society of that time was basically just, and that the treatment of the immigrants and workers, and their children, was just, then the attempt to integrate these newcomers into a consensus view, into the melting pot, was a generous project. But if one reads the history of that period as a history of challenges to a system that promoted great extremes of poverty and wealth, and terrible conditions of living and work, challenges by labor unions, immigrant communities, and new black urban communities, then the attempt by educators to deny the existence of these challenges can be seen as part of a repressive response by the government and corporations. Leonard's Deweyan individualism, though it still sounds progressive to us, strips the student of any identification with class, religion, family, or origins. And these identifications, as we are now coming to see in the controversies over bi-cultural education, can be the beginnings of political action. Deweyan education reassembles these students as units in a classroom group, in which they are conscious only of the demands of a monolithic "society" as enforced by the school and by other students.

Leonard and Reality

It may seem paradoxical, or even perverse, for a radical who keeps referring to the social and economic basis of education to criticize the emphasis on *re-*

ality in the work of Leonard and other progressive educators. Aren't they trying to do, in a practical way, just what I insist on doing in theory? The difference in our views is in how we define reality. For Leonard, what is real is
given; we gain knowledge of it through our senses, if we are not deceived by
non-empirical assumptions, and we adapt to it as best we can. For a Marxist,
reality is not a monolithic thing out there, but a process in society, an ongoing conflict between various groups, which in turn structures that society.
People have no simple unmediated perception of reality; the facts we are
likely to take as reality are most likely parts of another ideological structure.
Think, for example, of the very limited sense "the real world" has had in recent discussion of writing courses—it becomes synonymous with the demands of employers as shown in surveys. By treating the "real world" as the
bedrock of our teaching, we perpetuate the idea that reality is something
outside us and beyond our efforts to change it.

We have seen that Leonard's rhetorical strategy in his attacks on what he
calls "Old Purist Junk" about usage is to compare the formalism of textbooks
with the way people use language in the "real world." He makes a similar appeal in replacing the teaching of the modes of discourse with a developmental classification based on the stages a child is supposed to go through in
learning the presentation and interpretation of facts. In the earliest assignments a student receives, the student simply reports observations: "All these
matters are to be presented as objectively as possible; they are to set forth all
the writer's senses have apprehended" ("As to the Forms of Discourse" 202).
The purpose of this exercise is to root out merely conventional beliefs, by
making the students stick to the facts: "Nothing is of more doubtful value, as
an exercise in composition or anything else, than the restatement of fact or
interpretation the writer has absorbed but not lived or thought through himself" ("As to the Forms of Discourse" 204). Now I have been attacking just
this handing on of uncriticized assumptions. But I disagree with Leonard's
belief that the *facts* lie outside these assumptions. If what we think of as facts
are determined by our ideological framework, the facts cannot themselves
get us beyond that framework.[9] Leonard's textbook says, as do many textbooks today, "The whole art of helping children in writing or speaking, as
this study urges it, is based on the idea of showing them how to search out
and give not general but specific details" (*English Composition* 105). I too
am always asking students for more details. But I am interested in what such
details reveal about our assumptions, not in getting beyond assumptions to
some external reality.

To take an example, Leonard asks his students to describe a place, and
to cut out any statements unsupported by facts. That may lead to a more
readable and more academic sounding paper, but it will not tell us what the

place is really like. When, for instance, the various students in a basic writing course at Queens College write comparisons of the places they live to the places their parents lived as children, what these places are "really like" is determined by conventional frameworks of progress or nostalgia. What the place is really like might be better understood by comparing all those unsupported generalizations that various people would bring to such a description, comparing, say, the Lower East Side described as oppressive ghetto with the Lower East Side described as warm community, Forest Hills described as success and security with Forest Hills described as silent streets and alienating apartment blocks. No careful attention to the description of stoops or wide lawns will reconcile these descriptions in one objective reality. Both express deeper tensions that go beyond the rhetorical problems set by the assignment.

There is at times an alarming sound to Leonard's enthusiasm for the real world, as there is to his enthusiasm for consensus, that should make us examine our own enthusiasms today. His demand that development in school lead to the world of work and community responsibility, while it frees the school from the empty formalism of lectures, drills, and theme topics, ironically makes it more subservient to ideology. The real world is indistinguishable from the world defined by business publicists: "Meat packers, electric companies, millers, dog breeders, and others have free advertising matter and exhibits which are of the greatest value. Whatever your children want to know is likely to be covered by government or advertising material" ("Composition and Grammar in the Junior High School" 410). Despite the apparent naiveté of this view, Leonard is not by any means a promoter of a narrowly vocational education. Dewey had described the relation between business and education in broad terms.

> Though there should be an organic connection between the school and business life, it is not meant that the school is to prepare the student for any particular business, but that there should be a natural connection of the everyday life of a child with the business environment around him, and that it is the affair of the school to clarify and liberalize this connection, to bring it to consciousness, not by introducing special studies, like commercial geography and arithmetic, but by keeping alive the ordinary bonds of relation. (68)

It is not the connection of business that is in itself disturbing, but the sense of the naturalness and inevitability of this connection as the one way of reaching out to the world outside the school. For Leonard, as for Dewey, to criticize the subordination of education to the needs of business and government is to fail to face reality.

Teachers today are likely to be more skeptical about the uses of advertising. But we still assume the value of making the classroom represent "reality," and we still define this reality in very limited terms which we take uncritically from our economic system. For instance, many of the research studies that seek to define a body of good writing compare the writing of students to that of published writers. Now this makes for some valuable comparisons, but we should note how we just assume, lacking an agreed standard of writing quality, that good writing is writing that can be sold for money. Some editors of composition readers argue, using rhetoric very similar to Leonard's, that this sort of contemporary professional writing is more real than, say, readings taken from the canon of English and American literature. Or other editors of readers argue that the writing of students who have won a national essay contest is more real than the writing of professional magazine writers. All these assertions, whatever the pedagogical value of the materials they propose, beg the question of just how we come to define a real world, and accept that world as something given.

LEONARD AND REFORM

Anyone who has sat through a dull writing class (or has oneself taught a dull class with growing frustration) would recognize Leonard's descriptions of traditional methods of teaching English. He attacks these classes using a rhetoric similar to that of composition reformers today, who present themselves as fighting for more realistic views against the tradition that prevailed before the mid-1960s.[10] Much as I sympathize with the critique given by both periods of reform, I have questions about the way these reformers define themselves against the dubious practices of traditional teachers, who are often at a lower level of the hierarchy of educational prestige. The attack on tradition shifts our focus from the conflicting goals of the school in society to the simpler issue of the competence of individual teachers and the practicality of specific methods.

These questions may be raised most clearly by considering one of Leonard's articles from 1923. "How English Teachers Correct Papers" reports a study in which various groups of student-teachers and teachers were given a list of sentences from both students and famous authors and asked to mark any errors they would require a student to correct (517). Leonard's whole study is something of a trap for the unsuspecting teachers, practically all of whom "fatigued themselves to a point close to insensibility by meticulous correction of a great number of idioms in sentences by De Quincey, Lamb, Pater, Symonds, and authors of similar standing" (517), so that they were too tired to see what Leonard considered actual errors. To complete his attack, Leonard lists "constructive comments" the teachers gave on whole papers they were asked to mark, including "corrections" that made the correct incorrect, "puristic or wholly captious excisions, restatements, arrangements, and additions," and foolish or irrelevant criticisms. Leonard's suggestion that "the wisest teacher proceeds always by way of queries and suggestion, not by dogmatic rules and requirements," is a good one, and has been reiterated recently in articles in the composition journals reporting studies similar to Leonard's.[11] But Leonard's article, like some recent critiques, presents a polemic against dogmatism without either an understanding of its origins, or a model for a new method based on queries and suggestion.

The study shows how much Leonard needs bad teachers to make his argument. I would not deny that there was, and is, a plentiful supply of such teachers to provide examples of arbitrary traditionalism. But I am uneasy with the way the university expert makes them the enemy. He shows how their habits fly in the face of the "reality" revealed by current research, and he judges their judgment against an absolute level of cultivation represented by the writing of "De Quincey, Lamb, Pater, Symonds, and authors of similar standing." I would argue that this kind of top-down reform leads nowhere, because it just reinforces the hierarchy of the teaching profession, reminding teachers that the expertise is somewhere else. Thus in each generation it is the reformers who chair committees, write articles, and edit the journals; by these standards it is the reformers who are the establishment, and the opponents they label traditionalists are the outsiders. And in the 1980s we use the same sort of rhetoric, on the same sort of issues, to the same sort of teachers, to distinguish ourselves from tradition, that the members of that "tradition" used against a previous generation. What is needed to break this circle is more understanding of the conditions under which people teach, and the ideological frameworks within which they think. We should be opposing, not traditional teachers, but a system in which such repressive teaching is, in fact, perfectly appropriate.

I am annoyed with Leonard's rhetoric as a reformer because he assumes authority over other teachers and over students while denying he has it. He assumes authority as trained expert, university professor, empirical researcher, voice of the downtrodden students, bringing enlightenment to normal-school-trained teachers. But he denies his personal authority by saying the students are controlling the classroom, and his curriculum just follows the real world, and his reforms are based on the latest research. If we see that schools can be both places of liberation and places of oppression, then we have to ask how we are using what limited power over people's lives we do have.

CONSENSUS AND REALITY IN ELBOW AND BRUFFEE

If Leonard were just a forgotten hero of composition theory, like Alexander Bain or Fred Newton Scott, to revive him and then criticize him would be unnecessary and rather unfair. But the example of Leonard can help us criticize the presentation of consensus, reality, and reform in two theorists who carry on the tradition of progressive education, Peter Elbow and Ken Bruffee.

Elbow's *Writing Without Teachers* first introduced many of us to the usefulness of groups in the teaching of writing, and gave us some insights into their dynamics. But his more recent book, *Writing With Power*, shifts the emphasis away from the social context, returning to some essential internal power as a way of control of self and others. For Elbow, language may get work done in the social world, and the individual learner may use that social world as a tool to help him or her learn writing, but the system of language is produced by individuals, not by society. It is true that he seems to emphasize the social context of writing and the uses of consensus in his chapters on "Audience" and "Feedback." And he emphasizes the need to make the classroom reflect the world, using terms very much like those of Leonard: "any 'back to basics' movement in the teaching of writing needs to start by ensuring each child the most basic thing of all: a real audience for his written words—an audience that really listens and takes the interchange seriously" (184). This might seem to be a difficult need to satisfy in the composition class, but even in the artificial world of the classroom, "there is always a useful real audience available to whom writing can easily be delivered: other members of the class" (230).

For Elbow, as for Leonard, power over real audiences comes from an immediate connection with reality gained through a breaking down of stifling conventions. Writing with power requires authenticity of expression ("voice") and unmediated realism of perception in which the writer and reader must "see" the object written about (316). The problem with this call for direct experience of reality is that, as with Leonard, one must ask to which reality is one admitted. Elbow, unlike Leonard, acknowledges the existence of fundamentally different views of the world. But he still sees these views as free and individual, not acknowledging the way they are structured by ideology. So in his book, reality is divided between a cold, clear outside and a warm, messy inside. Writing consists of the negotiation between these two sides of the individual. In Elbow's model, the audience is essential to help in revision, but the best words come from deep down inside, from one's voice. Problems are solved in this model by changing the inside; change in the outside, that is, power over others, follows from this success in dealing with oneself. No wonder Elbow ends with a chapter on "Writing and Magic"; magic is the only possible source for such ineffable energies. This relentlessly internal approach to writing is both the book's strength and its weakness. *Writing With Power* consists almost entirely of vivid, often visceral, usually organic metaphors for creation.[12] These metaphors may help us see our processes of writing in new ways, but they also prevent any analysis of the social conditions of our writing. There is no real place in this model for a discourse group that gives one the structures of words one takes for granted.

Elbow has been a powerful writer for reform. Does his insistence that personal authenticity is the source of power apply to his own writing? He refers often to his own internal struggles in writing the book. I would argue, though, that its rhetorical power comes not from these struggles, but from its place in a group of texts. It gives a new metaphorical guise to familiar progressive education concepts, and makes an appeal to individualism that is a commonplace of American rhetoric. It has some affinities with a long line of straight-talking guides to self-improvement. Take, for example, the tone of hip moralism that combines with the traditional moralism of delayed reward in this passage: "If you slip into free-writing for the sake of producing good pieces of writing, then you put a kind of short-run utilitarian pressure on the process, and hinder yourself from getting all the other benefits" (*Writing With Power* 17). Now there is nothing wrong with using the jargon of self-improvement, any more than there is with using Marxist jargon as I do. My point is that both Elbow and I write within discourses developed in social processes, and that his account ignores these processes.

The work of Kenneth Bruffee can help us critique the appeal to reality that Leonard and Elbow make, especially in the recent essays in which Bruffee attempts to establish the theoretical grounds of collaborative learning. But his appeal to consensus is similar to theirs, and I think a lack of analysis of this consensus is the weak point of his theory. We might not see, at first, how different he is from Leonard and Elbow; he says in his textbook *A Short Course in Writing* that he starts with a search for a method of writing that will be *real*. "Peer criticism," he says, "is the most *real* writing students will ever do as students," because the writer has an immediate and actual audience and purpose (115). Similarly, an exercise on reminiscence tells the student, "Just begin at the beginning and tell the whole truth" (3). Where Bruffee differs from Leonard and Elbow begins to be apparent in the next exercise, when he asks the student to retell a "family story" that has become formalized with retelling over time. This exercise suggests, as the personal reminiscence assignment in most textbooks cannot, the degree to which language is given by the social group, in this case the family. The student must try to translate the private language of the family into the language of the classroom, noticing the difference.

For Bruffee, "writing is a communal activity," not just an essence of meaning given by the individual to the community. Instead of tracing language to an original voice inside, Bruffee asks questions to make the reader "see an essay as a 'thing' someone has made, like a table or a chair—something artificially designed, shaped, and put together to serve a purpose" (122). He says his system of peer criticism will enable students to "gain a stronger sense of the degree to which knowledge, like writing itself, is a social phenomenon, and the degree to which the social context in which we learn permeates what we know and how we know it" (116). In his view of knowledge, the group is there from the beginning, defining the terms of thought, and does not simply come in at the end, as an audience.

But while Bruffee shows that reality can be seen as a social construct, he does not give us any way to criticize this construct. Having discovered the role of consensus in the production of knowledge, he takes this consensus as something that just is, rather than a something that might be good or bad. For instance, in his recent essays, he argues for collaborative learning because it is the norm in business, industry, and the professions. This is true enough, but I question whether analogy to these institutions is, in itself, an argument for a teaching method. We need to look at the consensus within these institutions as the result of conflicts, not as a monolith. To decide whether the groups in our classes are introducing students to new communities of discourse, or are confining them in ideological structures, we need a clearer definition than he gives of what these interpretive communities are, and a sense of the historical processes shaping them.

Bruffee defines discourse communities in terms of certain kinds of academic or non-academic knowledge. For instance, he says, "Every student is already a member of several knowledge communities, from canoeing to computers, baseball to ballet" ("Collaborative Learning" 644). Bruffee suggests in another article that social differences are incidental to the process of education and should drop away if the students share an educational goal. "Outside the learning group . . . people may have widely different positions in the management hierarchy of a union or corporation, in the professional or student hierarchy of an educational institution, or in a system of economic or social class. But as collaborative learners all these people are peers. With regard to a course in ethnography or elementary Chinese, the vice-president of a corporation, the janitor, the English professor, the freshman, the society matron, and the shoe salesman must leave their social differences behind" ("CLTV" 38).[13]

This is an attractive and idealistic vision, but it assumes that knowledge is outside the realm of these people's social differences. Look over the list and ask who is most likely to be in a course on ethnography or elementary Chinese? Who, on the other hand, is likely to be in a course on English as a second language or on basic office skills? Who is likely to be in a basic writing course at the City University? To ask such questions is to realize that knowledge is not uniformly distributed in our society, and that it is not all of a piece. If we turn a blind eye to social factors we are likely merely to perpetuate the provision of different kinds of knowledge for the rich and the poor.

Bruffee sometimes includes non-academic knowledge in examples of discourse communities. For instance, he talks in one article about the contribution to the writing group of knowledge gained in office work, or in organizing a household. But what if one considers the knowledge of communities whose interests might be opposed, say the knowledge of social workers and the knowledge of welfare clients, or the knowledge of an accountant and the knowledge of employees in a factory to be closed? Such bodies of knowledge cannot be resolved into a consensus without one side losing something.

How are discourse communities made? Bruffee sees how society furthers thought or hinders it, but he does not see social and economic factors as providing his structures. For him, these factors are unfortunate limitations to our thought and conversation that must be eliminated as much as possible.

> Limitations that may be imposed for example, by ethnocentrism, inexperience, personal anxiety, economic interests, and paradigmatic inflexibility can constrain my thinking just as they can constrain conversation. If my talk is narrow, superficial, biased, and confined to clichés, my thinking is likely to be so too. ("Collaborative Learning" 639)

I would see such limitations as giving the structure to our thought. Ethnocentrism and economic interests are not just unfortunate habits, they are whole systems of ideas that people take for granted and use to make sense of the world. One cannot escape from one's economic interests and ethnic background, but one can try to understand how they shape one's thinking and social actions.

452

The model Bruffee gives for change in knowledge, adapted from Thomas Kuhn and Richard Rorty, leads us away from such analysis. It attributes the growth of knowledge and change of paradigms to factors internal to the discipline, such as the multiplication of anomalies and the shift of paradigms. The only conflict is between normal science and extraordinary science, or normal discourse and abnormal discourse. An alternative model would be in the work of historians and sociologists of science who see change in terms of social and economic factors.[14] For instance, Bruffee might call his own composition theory a new paradigm, resulting from the new models of Kuhn and Rorty. I might call it an attempt to rationalize theoretically the methods he earlier developed, and I would trace these methods to the institutional need, which he describes in his article, to deal with new kinds of university students. Similarly, I might trace my interest in these questions to my teaching of basic writing at Queens College. Ultimately, I would trace both his thinking and mine to the challenges of Open Admissions at CUNY. And Open Admissions was not the result of a paradigm shift in the philosophy of education; it emerged from the political conflicts of New York City in the 1960s.

Bruffee's recent essay points out that "The view that knowledge is a social artifact . . . requires a reexamination of our premises as students of English and as teachers" ("Collaborative Learning" 650). His suggestions for reform are excellent: he would "demystify" the humanities and the relation of teacher to student by putting them in a social context. But I think he underestimates the difficulty of the reforms he proposes, because he sees the resistance to them as a matter of habit, not of ideology. In A *Short Course*, he describes the problem he is addressing in terms of what he sees as "a conflict between two forces: the docility and dependence created in young people by American schooling and the increasing demand of modern life that human beings be autonomous, flexible, and self-possessed" (vii). But these two forces are not in conflict if we see the interests of employers, rather than "modern life" as the force that makes demands here. Students can be both docile and convinced of their autonomy, freedom of choice, and control of their lives. A school that reproduced this ideological construct would be a successful school.

In his recent article, Bruffee sees some of these dangers clearly enough. He points out the "provincial" nature of what he and Rorty call normal discourse. He also seems to recognize the kinds of possible dangers in the use of collaborative learning that I pointed out in some of Leonard's examples. He refers to the need to avoid "the many possible negative effects of peer group influence: conformity, anti-intellectualism, intimidation, and leveling-down of quality." He would do this by making "collaboration . . . a genuine part of students' educational development" (652). I would do it by emphasizing conflict as well as collaboration. I think he is referring to the same sense of a divided role I have described when he says "we must perform as conservators *and* agents of change, as custodians of prevailing community values *and* as agents of social transition and reacculturation" (650).

LESSONS FOR REFORMERS

I find I have no suggestions for assignments that are as innovative as those of the authors I am criticizing. But that is partly because what I have to suggest is not a method but a stance toward one's teaching. This stance requires a sort of doubleness: an awareness that one's course is part of an ideological structure that keeps people from thinking about their situation, but also a belief that one can resist this structure and help students to criticize it.

The sense of conflict in these three writers is clear enough when they describe their work as teachers. In each case they have a problem with existing institutions; in each case they offer an escape that I don't think works. Leonard, for instance, offers professionalism as an escape from the sense of pointlessness many teachers have: "It becomes clear how different a subject it is coming to be from the sodden, idealless drudgery of themes swoopingly red-inked and at the nearest possible moment thrown into the wastebasket" (193). Escape for him is through attention to the new research in composition in the 1920s ("Research on the Teaching of English"). But research will not change the basic antagonism of student and teacher he describes here.

Elbow, in his advice to students about writing in school, presents powerfully the role and limitations of the teacher:

> Teachers are good for giving criticism because they read papers in piles of 25 or 50. Take that criticism and use it. They are good at making you write when you don't feel like it, simply because they have authority. Instead of resenting this, try appreciating it and internalizing from it what may be the most important skill of all: the ability to write when you are in the wrong mood. They are *not* good at telling you what your writing feels like to a real human being, at taking your words seriously as messages directed to them, at praising you, or perhaps even at noticing you. Get these things elsewhere. (*Writing With Power* 234)

This is excellent advice, but Elbow's solution, that of using the tension between teacher and student, is based on his assumption that there is a world elsewhere of "real human beings." There is, of course, a world outside of school, and he is right to remind us of these other readers and writers. But the kinds of authority embodied in the school are present in the rest of the culture as well. The writer of an engineering proposal, a magazine article, or even a poem, is constrained by structures as powerful as those determining the freshman composition theme. The classroom alienation he takes for granted, in which the teacher processes batches of student raw material, is characteristic, not only of school, but of other institutions in our society. Bruffee traces his own interest in collaborative learning to a similar realization of how alienating his work had become:

> When I began teaching composition, I was still in graduate school. I had large classes, and I did not really know what I was doing. Every class hour seemed to stretch on to eternity. Grading papers took hours and was a dreadful grind. I kept hoping my classes would get smaller and the hour shorter. Instead, my classes got larger and the hour longer. I kept hoping I would learn to grade papers more easily and quickly. That did not happen either. Worst of all, I was not really sure that I was teaching anybody anything. (*Short Course* 184)

All three writers start by considering the drudgery of the work, the enormous numbers of papers, and the opposition of teachers and students. They want a change in the conditions of work, and a system that allows them to teach as well as just evaluate. They make a good case in these passages, whether they realize it or not, that our problems will not be solved just by new methods, or new theories, or new knowledge. We should begin by realizing that our interests are not the same as those of the institutions that employ us, and that the improvement of our work will involve social changes. No amount of merely educational reform will end the alienation described in these passages.

But this is not to say that all attempts at change are foiled by an all-powerful system, and that real change must wait until a revolution. Paul Willis warns other Marxist theorists against such an attitude at the end of *Learning to Labour*, his fine book on ideological reproduction in a British secondary school. He suggests the sort of double role for teachers that I have been arguing for here.

> If we have nothing to say about what to do on Monday morning then everything is yielded to a purist structuralist Marxist tautology: nothing can be done until the basic structures of society are changed but the structures prevent us from making any changes. There is no contradiction in asking practitioners to work on two levels simultaneously—to face immediate

problems in doing 'the best' (so far as they can see it) for their clients whilst appreciating all the time that these very actions may help to produce the structures within which the problems arise. (186)

What this approach means for, say, a basic writing teacher is that one teaches the forms of academic writing, so that students who might not finish four years of college have a better chance of finishing, without assuming that there is anything liberating about these forms or about academic discourse. One teaches job letters to the business communications students who need to get jobs downtown, without teaching that a job downtown is the answer to their problems. I have no specific new ideas for what we should do Monday morning, but I follow with interest those of other radical teachers. In this article, I am asking, not for a new kind of assignment, but for more skepticism about what assignments do to reproduce the structures of our society.

We should keep a similar skepticism about the appeals to reality and consensus in composition theory and research. There have been a number of recent articles calling for a view of writing as a social process.[15] This is a welcome corrective to the individualism of the cognitive psychology models of the 1970s. But we should not let our enthusiasm for this social view lead us to accepting social construction of knowledge as something good in itself. The kind of critique begun in *College English* by Richard Ohmann, Stanley Aronowitz, and others is even more appropriate now that we are seeing writing in a social context. I think these theories will be developed with more sophistication if we draw on critiques developed by such sociologists of education as Apple and Giroux, and on materials provided by historians of education.[16]

Leonard in the 1920s, and Elbow and Bruffee today, have made teachers aware of the need for changes in the way we teach. The work of sociologists and historians of education would help us to remain aware that the changes we propose may finally support an existing consensus and a conception of reality that supports those now in power. Our sense that something is wrong should lead us to criticize our own function in society, as well as our pedagogy. Otherwise, to use a comment of Leonard's from another, entirely different context, "It has less effect than a spoonful of water poured over a flock of ducks" ("Composition and Grammar" 448).

NOTES

1. Some recent historical studies that discuss reform in composition include those by James Berlin (whose book has an extensive bibliography), Michael Halloran, Robert Conners, Wallace Douglas, (whose article appears in a special issue of the *English Journal* devoted to the history of the profession), and Evelyn Wright.

2. See *English Composition as a Social Problem* for references to invention (81), sentence-combining (158), "schoolmastering" (183 and many other references). On Piaget, see "Relating the Teaching of English to Reality" (45).

3. For a discussion of the term, see Raymond Williams, *Keywords*. For a series of reviews of various studies of ideology, see Centre for Contemporary Cultural Studies, *On Ideology*.

4. Several detailed historical and sociological studies along these lines are collected in Michael Apple, ed., *Cultural and Economic Reproduction in Education*. Important earlier articles on ideology in education are collected in the Open University reader, Roger Dale et al., eds., *Schooling and Capitalism: A Sociological Reader*. A recent analysis of educational theories, in clear but rather abstract terms, is Henry Giroux, *Theory and Resistance in Education: A Pedagogy for the Opposition*. Current critical articles on the sociology of education often appear in the journal *Curriculum Inquiry*.

5. See Cremin; David Hogan, "Education and Class Formation: The Peculiarities of Americans," in Apple's collection; and Diane Ravitch's quite readable book on the case of New York City.

6. Biographical information on Leonard is from W. E. Leonard's *DAB* entry. Background to the period is from the books by J. N. Hook and Arthur Applebee, and from Merle Curti's contemporary study. Curti, like me, looks at these ideas from the left, but he considers Dewey's influence entirely progressive. A reviewer of my article recommended the chapter on Leonard by John Brereton in *Traditions of Inquiry* (New York: Oxford UP, 1985). The whole book should be relevant to my topic here, but it was unavailable in Britain as I revised this article.

7. Leonard's study, which he left incomplete at his death, is included in Albert Marckwardt's *Facts About Current English Usage*.

8. On Americanization, see Cremin; Hook; Ravitch; and *English Journal in the 1920s*.

9. See Richard Ohmann, "Use Specific, Definite, Concrete Language."

10. For an example of the rhetoric of composition reform, see Donald Stewart, "Composition Textbooks and the Assault on Tradition," and some of the other articles collected in Gary Tate and Edward P. J. Corbett, eds., *The Writing Teacher's Sourcebook*.

11. Leonard's study is similar to that in Nancy Sommer's recent article, "Responding to Student Writing." Like Leonard, Sommers only gives examples of comments that are badly done. Dan Moshenberg pointed out to me the similarity of Leonard's study to the experiment in poetry criticism I. A. Richards reports in *Practical Criticism*.

12. Those who favor such visceral metaphors should see Lester Faigley's paper, "Peristalsis as Paradigm: From Process to Product."

13. See also two other essays by Bruffee, "The Structure of Knowledge and the Future of Liberal Education," and "Liberal Education and the Social Justification of Belief."

14. A good introduction to the sociology of scientific knowledge is another Open University reader, edited by Barry Barnes and David Edge.

15. See, for example, the very different approaches of Patricia Bizzell, of Bruffee ("Writing and Reading as Collaborative Social Acts"), and of Charles Bazerman ("Scientific Writing as a Social Act"). Bazerman, like Bruffee, has a textbook based on his approach (*The Informed Writer*).

16. For example, one way of seeing how deeply ingrained and uncritical are the psychological categories we use to define basic writers is to read the historical treatment of these categories in Steven Shapin and Barry Barnes, "Head and Hand: Rhetorical Resources in British Pedagogical Writing 1770-1850."

WORKS CITED

Apple, Michael, ed. *Cultural and Economic Reproduction in Education.* London: Routledge, 1982.

Applebee, Arthur. *Tradition and Reform in the Teaching of English.* Urbana: NCTE, 1974.

Aronowitz, Stanley. "Mass Culture and the Eclipse of Reason: The Pedagogical Implications." *College English* 38 (1977): 768-72.

Barnes, Barry, and David Edge, eds. *Science in Context.* Milton Keynes: Open UP, 1982.

Bazerman, Charles. *The Informed Writer.* 2nd ed. Boston: Houghton, 1985.

———. "Scientific Writing as a Social Act." *New Essays in Scientific and Technical Communication.* Ed. Carolyn Miller, et al. Farmingdale, New York: Baywood, 1983. 157-84.

Berlin, James. *Writing Instruction in Nineteenth-Century American Colleges.* Carbondale: Southern Illinois UP Press, 1984.

Bizzell, Patricia. "Cognition, Convention, and Certainty: What We Need to Know About Writing." *Pre/Text* 3 (1982): 213-43.

Bruffee, Kenneth. "CLTV: Collaborative Learning Television." *Educational Communication and Technology Journal* 30 (1982): 26-40.

———. "Collaborative Learning and the 'Conversation of Mankind.'" *College English* 46 (1984): 635-52.

———. "Liberal Education and the Social Justification of Belief." *Liberal Education* 68 (1982): 95-114.

———. *A Short Course in Writing.* 2nd ed. Boston: Winthrop, 1980.

———. "The Structure of Knowledge and the Future of Liberal Education." *Liberal Education* 67 (1981): 177-86.

———. "Writing and Reading as Collaborative Social Acts." *The Writer's Mind.* Ed. Janice Hays. Urbana: NCTE, 1983.

Centre for Contemporary Cultural Studies. *On Ideology.* London: Hutchinson University Library, 1978.

Connors, Robert. "The Rise and Fall of the Modes of Discourse." *College Composition and Communication* 32 (1981): 444-55.

Cremin, Lawrence. *The Transformation of the School.* New York: Vintage, 1961.

Curti, Merle. *The Social Ideas of American Educators.* New York: Scribner's, 1935.

Dale, Roger, et al., eds. *Schooling and Capitalism: A Sociological Reader.* London: Routledge, 1976.

Dewey, John. *The School and Society.* Chicago: U of Chicago P, 1898.

Douglas, Wallace. "Why Know Our History." *English Journal* 68 (1979): 16-21.

Elbow, Peter. *Writing With Power.* New York: Oxford UP, 1982.

———. *Writing Without Teachers.* New York: Oxford UP, 1973.

Faigley, Lester. "Peristalsis as Paradigm: From Process to Product." Paper presented at the panel on "Nutrastylistics" at the Conference on College Composition and Communication, Minneapolis, March 1985.

Giroux, Henry. *Theory and Resistance in Education: A Pedagogy for the Opposition.* London: Heinemann Educational Books, 1983.

Halloran, Michael. "Rhetoric in the American College Curriculum: The Decline of Public Discourse." *Pre/Text* 3 (1982): 245-269.

Hook, J. N. *A Long Way Together.* Urbana: NCTE, 1979.

Kantor, Kevin. "Creative Expression in the English Curriculum: An Historical Perspective." *Research in the Teaching of English* 9 (1975): 5-29.

Leonard, Sterling. "As to the Forms of Discourse." *English Journal* 3 (1914): 201-211.

———. "Composition and Grammar in the Junior High School." *The Classroom Teacher* 10 (1927): 309-449.

———. "Current Definition of Levels in English Usage." *English Journal* 16 (1926): 345-59.

———. *The Doctrine of Correctness in English Usage, 1700-1800.* Madison: U of Wisconsin P, 1929.

———. *English Composition as a Social Problem.* Boston: Houghton, 1917.

———. "How English Teachers Correct Papers." *English Journal* 20 (1923): 517-31.

———. "Relating the Teaching of English to Reality." *Nation's Schools* 4 (1929): 45-48.

———. "Research on the Teaching of English." *Journal of Educational Research* 19 (1929): 317-21.

———. "What About Correct English?" *The Teachers Journal and Abstract* 6 (1931): 252-56.

Leonard, W. E. "Sterling Andrus Leonard." *Dictionary of American Biography.* 9: 168-9.

Marckwardt, Albert. *Facts About Current English Usage.* New York: Appleton-Century, 1938.

Ohmann, Richard. *English in America: A Radical View of the Profession.* New York: Oxford UP, 1976.

———. "Use Specific, Definite, Concrete Language." *College English* 41 (1979): 379-89.

Ravitch, Diane. *The Great School Wars: New York City, 1805-1973.* New York: Basic, 1974.

Richards, I. A. *Practical Criticism.* New York: Harcourt, 1929.

Shapin, Steven, and Barry Barnes. "Head and Hand: Rhetorical Resources in British Pedagogical Writing 1770-1850." *Oxford Review of Education* 2 (1976): 235-50.

Sommers, Nancy. "Responding to Student Writing." *College Composition and Communication* 32 (1982): 148-56.

Tate, Gary, and Edward P. J. Corbett, eds. *The Writing Teacher's Sourcebook.* New York: Oxford, 1981.

Williams, Raymond. *Keywords.* London: Oxford UP, 1976.

Willis, Paul. *Learning to Labour: How Working Class Kids Get Working Class Jobs.* Farnborough, England: Saxon, 1977.

Wright, Evelyn. "School English and Public Policy." *College English* 42 (1980): 327-42.

Consensus and Difference in Collaborative Learning

JOHN TRIMBUR

Kenneth A. Bruffee, Harvey S. Wiener, and others have argued that collaborative learning may be distinguished from other forms of group work on the grounds that it organizes students not just to work together on common projects but more important to engage in a process of intellectual negotiation and collective decision-making. The aim of collaborative learning, its advocates hold, is to reach consensus through an expanding conversation. This conversation takes place at a number of levels—first in small discussion groups, next among the groups in a class, then between the class and the teacher, and finally among the class, the teacher, and the wider community of knowledge. In Bruffee's social constructionist pedagogy, the language used to reach consensus acquires greater authority as it acquires greater social weight: the knowledge students put into words counts for more as they test it out, revising and relocating it by taking into account what their peers, the teacher, and voices outside the classroom have to say.

The purpose of this essay is to examine two important criticisms of the politics of collaborative learning in order to explore one of the key terms in collaborative learning, consensus. This seems worth doing because the notion of consensus is one of the most controversial and misunderstood aspects of collaborative learning.

One line of criticism argues that the use of consensus in collaborative learning is an inherently dangerous and potentially totalitarian practice that stifles individual voice and creativity, suppresses differences, and enforces conformity. Thomas S. Johnson, for example, believes that consensus is just

Reprinted from *College English* 51.6 (October 1989): 602–16. Used with permission.

another name for "group think" and conjures images of 1984. Pedro Beade worries that consensus might be used to justify the practices of "a crazy, totalitarian state" (708). These critics of collaborative learning want to rescue the sovereignty and autonomy of the individual from what Johnson calls collaborative learning's "peer indoctrination classes." Underlying these political objections is the sense, as David Foster puts it, that the human mind is "far too mysterious and fascinating" to take the social constructionist route and "ground its utterances" in a "normative social community." According to Foster, collaborative learning is based on an epistemological mistake: Bruffee's "overeager application of the social constructionist label" causes him to overvalue social practices and thus to deny the primacy of individual consciousness in creating knowledge.

A second line of criticism, on the other hand, agrees with Bruffee that things like selves, knowledge, discourse, readers, and writers are indeed socially constructed. What left-wing critics such as Greg Myers do worry about, however, is that Bruffee's social constructionist pedagogy runs the risk of limiting its focus to the internal workings of discourse communities and of overlooking the wider social forces that structure the production of knowledge. To understand the production and validation of knowledge, Myers argues, we need to know not just how knowledge communities operate consensually but how knowledge and its means of production are distributed in an unequal, exclusionary social order and embedded in hierarchical relations of power. Without a critique of the dominant power relations that organize the production of knowledge, left-wing critics hold, the social constructionist rationale for collaborative learning may, unwittingly or not, accommodate its practices to the authority of knowledge it believes it is demystifying.

In this essay I propose to extend the left critique, not to abandon the notion of consensus but to revise it, as a step toward developing a critical practice of collaborative learning. I want to concede that consensus in some of its pedagogical uses may indeed be an accommodation to the workings of normal discourse and function thereby as a component to promote conformity and improve the performance of the system. My point will be, however, that consensus need not inevitably result in accommodation. The politics of consensus depends on the teacher's practice. Consensus, I will argue, can be a powerful instrument for students to generate differences, to identify the systems of authority that organize these differences, and to transform the relations of power that determine who may speak and what counts as a meaningful statement.

Before I outline the critical and transformative projects I believe are implied in collaborative learning, I want to address the fear of conformity in the first line of criticism—the fear that collaborative learning denies differences and threatens individuality. It is important to acknowledge that this fear points to some real problems that arise when students work together in groups—problems such as parochialism, demagoguery, narrow appeals to common sense, an urge to reach noncontroversial consensus without considering alternatives. After all, we cannot realistically expect that collaborative learning will lead students spontaneously to transcend the limits of American culture, its homogenizing force, its engrained suspicion of social and cultural differences, its tendency to reify the other and blame the victim. But if the fear of conformity is a legitimate one, it is not for the reasons the first group of Bruffee's critics gives. Their effort to save the individual from the group is based on an unhelpful and unnecessary polarization of the individual and society.

The limits of these critics' fear of conformity can best be seen, I think, by emphasizing the influence of John Dewey's educational pragmatism on collaborative learning. What Bruffee takes from Dewey is a strong appreciation of the generativity of group life and its promise for classroom teaching. Consensus represents the potentiality of social agency inherent in group life— the capacity for self-organization, cooperation, shared decision-making, and common action. From a pragmatist perspective, the goal of reaching consensus gives the members of a group a stake in collective projects. It does not inhibit individuality, as it does for those who fear consensus will lead to conformity. Rather it enables individuals to participate actively and meaningfully in group life. If anything, it is through the social interaction of shared activity that individuals realize their own power to take control of their situation by collaborating with others.

For Deweyans, the effort to save the individual from the group is at best misguided and at worst reactionary. On one hand, pragmatists see no reason to rescue the individual from "normative communities" because in effect there is nowhere else the individual can be: consciousness is the extension of social experience inward. On the other hand, the desire to escape from "normative communities" and break out of the "prison house of language" by grounding utterances in the generative force of individual consciousness springs from an ideological complex of belief and practice.

Dewey's educational pragmatism recasts the fear that consensus will inevitably lead to conformity as a fear of group life itself. Pedagogies that take the individual as the irreducible, inviolate starting point of education— whether through individualized instruction, cultivation of personal voice, or an emphasis on creativity and self-actualization—inscribe a deeply contradictory ideology of individualism in classroom practice. If these pedagogies seek to liberate the individual, they also simultaneously constitute the student as a social atom, an accounting unit under the teacher's gaze, a record kept by the teacher. The fear of consensus often betrays a fear of peer group influence—a fear that students will keep their own records, work out collective norms, and take action. Rather than the liberation of the individual it claims to be, the fear of "group-think" is implicitly teacher-centered and authoritarian. It prevents a class of students from transforming themselves from an aggregate of individuals into a participatory learning community. The mode of teaching and learning remains what Bruffee calls "authoritarian-individualist": the atomization of students locks them into a one-to-one relation to the teacher, the repository of effective authority in the classroom, and cuts them off from the possibilities of jointly empowering activities carried out in the society of peers. In short, the critique of consensus in the name of individualism is baseless. Consensus does not necessarily violate the individual but instead can enable individuals to empower each other through social activity.

We may now take up the left-wing critique. Here the issue is not the status of the individual but the status of exchange among individuals. We should note, first of all, that Bruffee and his left-wing critics occupy a good deal of common ground concerning the social relationships of intellectual exchange as they are played out in the classroom. For teachers and theorists looking for a critical pedagogy, Bruffee's work has been important because it teaches us to read the classroom and the culture of teaching and learning as a social text.

How we teach, Bruffee suggests, is what we teach. For Bruffee, pedagogy is not a neutral practice of transmitting knowledge from one place to another, from the teacher's head to the students'. The pedagogical project that Bruffee initiated in the early seventies calls into question the dynamics of cultural reproduction in the classroom, a process that normally operates, as it were, behind our backs. What before had seemed commonsensical became in Bruffee's reading of the classroom as a social text a set of historically derived practices—an atomized and authoritarian culture that mystifies the production of knowledge and reproduces hierarchical relations of power and domination. Bruffee's formulation of collaborative learning in the early seventies offers an implicit critique of the culture of the classroom, the sovereignty of the teacher, the reification of knowledge, the atomized authority-dependence of students, and the competitiveness and intellectual hoarding encouraged by the traditional reward system and the wider meritocratic order in higher education.

In his early work, Bruffee sees collaborative learning as part of a wider movement for participatory democracy, shared decision-making, and non-authoritarian styles of leadership and group life. "In the world which surrounds the classroom," Bruffee says in 1973, "people today are challenging and revising many social and political traditions which have heretofore gone unquestioned"; if education has been resistant to collaboration, "[e]lsewhere, everywhere, collaborative action increasingly pervades our society" ("Collaborative Learning" 634). In Bruffee's account, collaborative learning occurs—along with free universities, grass-roots organizing, the consciousness-raising groups of women's liberation, the anti-war movement, and so on—as a moment in the cultural history of the sixties, the name we now give to signify delegitimation of power and the search for alternative forms of social and political life. I think it is not accidental that collaborative learning emerged initially within open admissions programs, as part of a wider response to political pressures from below to extend literacy and access to higher education to black, Hispanic, and working-class people who had formerly been excluded.

From the late seventies to the present, Bruffee has asked what it means to reorganize the social relations in the classroom and how the decentering of authority that takes place in collaborative learning might change the way we talk about the nature of liberal education and the authority of knowledge and its institutions. Bruffee's ongoing efforts to find a language adequate to this task—to theorize collaborative learning as a social constructionist pedagogy—have turned, in the ensuing discussion, into the source of recent left-wing challenges to his work. One of the central issues of contention concerns Bruffee's appropriation of Richard Rorty's notion of conversation.

The term conversation has become a social constructionist code word to talk about knowledge and teaching and learning as social—not cognitive—acts. Knowledge, in this account, is not the result of the confrontation of the individual mind with reality but of the conversation that organizes the available means we have at any given time to talk about reality. Learning, therefore, cannot be understood strictly on cognitive grounds; it means rather joining new communities and taking part in new conversations. Learning, as Rorty puts it, "is a shift in a person's relations with others, not a shift inside the person that now *suits* him to enter new relationships" (*Philosophy* 187). By organizing students to participate in conversation, Bruffee argues, collaborative learning forms transitional communities to help students undergo the stressful and anxiety-inducing process of moving out of their indigenous communities and acquiring fluency in the conversation of liberally educated men and women. For Bruffee, Rorty's notion of conversation provides a rationale for collaborative learning as a process of re-acculturation, of learning to participate in the ongoing discussions of new communities.

This is a powerful rationale because it translates a wider reinterpretation of knowledge taking place in contemporary critical theory to the classroom—and gives us a way to incorporate what Bruffee calls the "social turn" in twentieth-century thought into the theory and practice of teaching. Still, for left-wing teachers and theorists, there is something troubling about Rorty's notion of conversation, something in the metaphor worth unpacking.

For Rorty, the term conversation offers a useful way to talk about the production of knowledge as a social process without reference to metaphysical foundations. Rorty's notion of conversation describes a discourse that has no beginning or end, but no crisis or contradiction, either. Cut loose from metaphysical moorings and transcendental backups, the conversation keeps rolling of its own accord, reproducing itself effortlessly, responsible only to itself, sanctioned by what Rorty sees as the only sanction credible: our loyalty to the conversation and our solidarity with its practices. All we can do is to continue the conversation initiated before we appeared on the scene. "We do not know," Rorty says, "what 'success' would mean except simply 'continuance'" (*Consequences* 172).

In political terms, what Rorty calls "postmodernist bourgeois liberalism" hangs onto the "ideals of the Enlightenment" but gives up the belief in Enlightenment reason. In Rorty's hands, the metaphor of conversation invokes an eighteenth-century vision of freely constituted, discoursing subjects taking part in polite speech, in Enlightenment salons and coffee houses, in the "republic of letters" emerging in the interstices of the absolutist state. To historicize Rorty's metaphor is to disclose what Terry Eagleton calls the "bourgeoisie's dream of freedom": "a society of petty producers whose endlessly available, utterly inexhaustible commodity is discourse itself" (16-17). As Eagleton argues, the "bourgeoisie . . . discovers in discourse an idealized image of its own social relations" (16). Conversation becomes the only truly free market, an ideal discursive space where exchange without domination is possible, where social differences are converted into abstract equalities at the level of speech acts.

Only now, Rorty says, the discourse must operate without the consensus of universal reason that eighteenth-century speakers took to be the normative grounding of their utterances. Given the postmodernist's disbelief in metanarratives of reason and freedom, Rebecca Comay argues, the conversation loses its emancipatory edge and "adapts to the episodic rhythms of commercial culture" (122). If we've traded in the old metaphysical comforts for a cheerful, if ungrounded affirmation of conversation, we do so, Rorty says, so we can "read more, talk more, write more" (*Philosophy* 375). The logic of planned obsolescence drives the conversation as we look for the "new, better, more interesting, more fruitful ways of speaking" (*Philosophy* 360). In a world without foundations, "nobody is so passe as the intellectual czar of the previous generation. . . the man who redescribed all those old descriptions, which, thanks in part to his redescriptions of them, nobody now wants to know anything about" (*Consequences* xl–xli). According to the idealized exchange of a free and open market, conversation keeps circulating in a spectacle of production and consumption. The new becomes old, the fashionable out-of-date, but the conversation itself is inexhaustible. "Evanescent moments in a continuing conversation . . . we keep the conversation going" (*Philosophy* 378).

Stripped of its universalist principles, the conversation turns into an act of assimilation. Unpacked, Rorty's metaphor of conversation offers a version of nonfoundationalism without tears. The consensus that keeps things rolling is no longer based on higher purposes but instead on the recognition that if we cannot discover the truth in any final sense, what we can do is to keep on talking to each other: we can tell stories, give accounts, state reasons, negotiate differences, and so on. The conversation, that is, gives up teleological ends to reaffirm the sociability of intellectual exchange. And if, as Rorty says, the conversation is simply the way we justify our beliefs socially, then we might as well relax, get good at it, and enjoy it.

Of course there are considerable attractions to this view. But there are some problems too. Rorty acknowledges, for example, the tendency of discourse to normalize itself and to block the flow of conversation by posing as a "canonical vocabulary." The conversation, as Rorty starts to acknowledge here, is perpetually materializing itself in institutional forms, alloting the opportunity to speak and arbitrating the terms of discussion. But Rorty, finally, backs away from the full consequences of conversation's normative force. At just the point where we could name the conversation and its underlying consensus as a technology of power and ask how its practices enable and constrain the production of knowledge, privilege and exclude forms of discourse, set its agenda by ignoring or suppressing others. Rorty builds a self-correcting mechanism into the conversation, an invisible hand to keep the discourse circulating and things from going stale. This is abnormal discourse or, as Rorty says, "what happens when someone joins in the discourse who is ignorant of . . . conventions or who sets them aside" (*Philosophy* 320).

Rorty's view of abnormal discourse is, I think, a problematical one. On one hand, it identifies abnormal discourse with a romantic realm of thinking the unthinkable, of solitary voices calling out, of the imagination cutting against the grain. In keeping with this romantic figure of thought, Rorty makes abnormal discourse the activity par excellence not of the group but of the individual—the genius, the rebel, the fool, "some*one* . . . who is ignorant of . . . conventions or sets them aside." This side of abnormal discourse, moreover, resists formulation. There is, Rorty says, "no discipline which describes it, any more than there is a discipline devoted to a study of the unpredictable, or of 'creativity'" (*Philosophy* 320). It is simply "generated by free and leisured conversation . . . as the sparks fly up" (321).

At the same time, though we can't know abnormal discourse on its own terms, we can identify how it functions, but now from a pragmatist perspective, to keep the conversation going. In other words, at just the moment Rorty seems to introduce difference and destabilize the conversation, he turns crisis, conflict, and contradiction into homeostatic gestures whose very expression restabilizes the conversation. What remains, once we've removed universal reason, narratives of emancipation, or "permanent neutral frameworks" as the grounds for adjudicating knowledge claims, is civility, the agreement to keep on talking. The "power of strangeness" in abnormal discourse "to take us out of our old selves" and "to make us into new beings" (*Philosophy* 360) simply reaffirms our solidarity with the conversation.

Left-wing critics are uncomfortable with this position. They want to interrupt the conversation, to denaturalize its workings, and to talk about the way conversation legitimizes itself by its very performance. Left-wing critics worry that Rortyian conversation downplays its own social force and the conflict it generates, the discourses silenced or unheard in the conversation and its representation of itself. They suspect there are other voices to take into account—voices constituted as otherness outside the conversation. For this reason, left-wing critics want to redefine consensus by locating it in the prevailing balance of power, as a marker that sets the boundaries between discourses. As Myers suggests, we need to see consensus in terms of differences and not just of agreements, "as the result of conflicts, not as a monolith" (166). Redefining consensus as a matter of conflict suggests, moreover, that consensus does not so much reconcile differences through rational negotiation. Instead, such a redefinition represents consensus as a strategy that structures differences by organizing them in relation to each other. In this sense, consensus cannot be known without its opposite—without the other voices at the periphery of the conversation.

By looking at consensus in terms of conflict rather than agreement, we get a somewhat different picture of the relationship between normal and abnormal discourse than the one Rorty and Bruffee have offered. Redefining consensus leads us, I think, to abandon the view that abnormal discourse functions as a complement to normal discourse, something which, as Bruffee says, students can turn to from time to time to question business as usual and to keep the conversation going. Instead, abnormal discourse represents the result at any given time of the set of power relations that organizes normal discourse: the acts of permission and prohibition, of incorporation and exclusion that institute the structure and practices of discourse communities. Abnormal discourse is not so much a homeostatic mechanism that keeps the conversation and thereby the community renewed and refreshed. Instead, it refers to dissensus, to marginalized voices, the resistance and contestation both within and outside the conversation, what Roland Barthes calls acratic discourse—the discourses out of power. Abnormal discourse, that is, refers not only to surprises and accidents that emerge when normal discourse reaches a dead end, when, as Wittgenstein puts it, "language goes on holiday." In the account I'm suggesting, it also refers to the relations of power that determine what falls within the current consensus and what is assigned the status of dissent. Abnormal discourse, from this perspective, is neither as romantic nor as pragmatic as Rorty makes it out to be. Rather it offers a way to analyze the strategic moves by which discourse communities legitimize their own conversation by marginalizing others. It becomes a critical term to describe the conflict among discourses and collective wills in the heterogeneous conversation in contemporary public life.

Bruffee argues that such an emphasis on conflict has led his left-wing critics to want to "turn to 'struggle' to force change in 'people's interests'" (Response 714). I would reply that struggle is not something people, left-wing or otherwise, can "turn to" or choose to do. "Struggle," at least the way I understand it, is something we're born into: it's a standard feature of contemporary social existence. We experience "struggle" all the time in everyday life precisely because, as Bruffee points out, we "all belong to many overlapping, mutually inclusive communities." We "experience belonging to each of these communities as both limiting and liberating" (715) in part because we experience the discourses, or what Bruffee calls the "vernacular languages of the communities one belongs to," as a polyphony of voices, an internal conversation traversed by social, cultural, and linguistic differences.

Bruffee uses the term vernacular to call attention to the plurality of voices that constitute our verbal thought. The intersecting vernaculars that we experience contending for our attention and social allegiance, however, are not just plural. They are also organized in hierarchical relations of power. The term vernacular, after all, as Houston Baker reminds us, "signals" on etymological and ideological grounds "'a slave born on his master's estate'" (2). The term vernacular, that is, cannot be understood apart from the relations of domination and subordination it implies. The conversation, in Bakhtin's word, is "heteroglot," a mosaic of vernaculars, the multi-accented idiomatic expression of race, class, and gender differences. The conversation gives voice to the conflicts inherent in an unequal social order and in the asymmetrical relations of power in everyday life.

Bruffee worries that "struggle" means interrupting the conversation to "force change in people's interests." Bruffee's worries here betray what seems to me a persistent anxiety in non-foundationalist versions of social constructionist thought about its own radical disclosure: that once we give up extra-historical and universal criteria and reduce the authority of knowledge to a self-legitimizing account of its own practices, we won't have a way to separate persuasion from force, validity claims from plays of power. As Rorty puts it, to "suggest that there is *no* . . . common ground seems to endanger rationality. . . . To question the need for commensuration seems the first step toward a return to a war of 'all against all'" (*Philosophy* 317). In the account I'm suggesting, "struggle" is not a matter of interrupting the conversation to replace consensual validation with force. It refers rather to the relations between the two terms—intellectual negotiation and power—in what we think of as rational argument and public discourse. The term "struggle" is simply a way of shifting rhetorical analysis, as Victor Vitanza has suggested, from Aristotelean persuasion or Burkean identification to an agonistic framework of conflict and difference—to a rhetoric of dissensus.

The choice, as I see it, does not consist of solidarity with a self-explaining conversation or violence. I want to preserve, along with Bruffee and Rorty, the value of civility and consensus. But to do this we will need to rehabilitate the notion of consensus by redefining it in relation to a rhetoric of dissensus. We will need, that is, to look at collaborative learning not merely as a process of consensus-making but more important as a process of identifying differences and locating these differences in relation to each other. The consensus that we ask students to reach in the collaborative classroom will be based not so much on collective agreements as on collective explanations of how people differ, where their differences come from, and whether they can live and work together with these differences.

To think of consensus in terms of dissensus is to challenge a central rationale Bruffee has offered for collaborative learning. Bruffee currently holds that one of the benefits of collaborative learning is that its consensual practices model the normal workings of discourse communities in business, government, the professions, and academia. Myers argues, correctly I think, that Bruffee's use of consensus risks accepting the current production and distribution of knowledge and discourse as unproblematical and given. The limit of Myers' critique, however, is that it concedes Bruffee's claim that consensus is in fact the norm in business, industry, and the professions. In this regard, both Bruffee and Myers seriously underestimate the extent to which the conversations of these discourse communities are regulated not so much by consensual negotiation and shared decision-making as by what

Jürgen Habermas calls a "success orientation" of instrumental control and rational efficiency.

It can be misleading, therefore, to tell students, as social constructionists do, that learning to write means learning to participate in the conversation and consensual practices of various discourse communities. Instead, we need to ask students to explore the rhetoric of dissensus that pervades writing situations. As Susan Wells argues, even such apparently prosaic and "unheroic" tasks as writing manuals for the computer-assisted redesign of an auto body section take place within a complicated network of competing and contradictory interests. In the case of the design manual that Wells cites, the technical writer faces three different audiences. Concerned with the overall operation of a computer system, the first audience of systems programmers may be just as likely to guard their professional knowledge of the system as to collaborate with others. They may, in fact, see the second audience, application programmers responsible for writing programs for specific design tasks, as "enemies" looking for ways to "tweak" or "jiggle" the system to get their work done—and who thereby threaten the overall performance of the system. The third audience of users, on the other hand, needs to know how to operate the system on narrow job-related grounds. But from both the programmers' perspective, this group is an unknown variable, men and women who may be "demonically curious" and want to play with the system, to see how it really works.

By exploring the differential access to knowledge and the relations of power and status that structure this writing situation, Wells says, students can learn not only how technical writers "write for success" by adjusting to multiple audiences. (As it turned out, the technical writer produced a separate manual containing quite different information for each of the audiences.) Students can also learn to articulate a rhetoric of dissensus that will lead them to see that the goal of discourse in this case, as Wells puts it, "is systematic misunderstanding and concealment. . . the total fragmentation and dispersal of knowledge" (256). They can learn, that is, not how consensus is achieved through collaborative negotiation but rather how differences in interest produce conflicts that may in fact block communication and prohibit the development of consensus.

Of course, it is true, as Wells notes, that not all organizations rely upon such a rigid division of labor. Collaboration and consensual decision-making, after all, have become buzz words for "new age" managers and technocrats. Part of the current conventional wisdom about the new information society is that cooperation and collaboration will replace the competitive and individualistic ethos of the entrepreneurial age of industrial capitalism. But finally what collaboration and consensus amount to are not so much new paradigms for a high-tech post-industrial order as new versions of an older industrial psychology adopted to late capitalism—human relations techniques to bolster morale, promote identification with the corporation, legitimize differential access to knowledge and status, and increase productivity. Even in the ostensibly disinterested realm of academics, the production of knowledge is motivated as much by career moves as by consensus, by the efforts of individuals to enhance their credentials and relative position in a field, to build up their fund of cultural capital.

At issue here is not whether collaborative learning reflects more accurately than traditional pedagogies the actual social relations that produce knowledge and make organizations run. Surely it does. But by modeling collaborative learning on the normal workings of discourse communities, Bruffee identifies the authority of knowledge with the prevailing productive apparatus. For social constructionists, this is an uncontroversial point. In one sense, it is the point—that the present configuration of knowledge and its institutions is a social artifact. But in another sense, this line of thought also concedes the authority of knowledge to the professional judgment of experts, to academic specialties and professional training, to the wider meritocratic order of a credentialed society.

If one of the goals of collaborative learning is to replace the traditional hierarchical relations of teaching and learning with the practices of participatory democracy, we must acknowledge that one of the functions of the professions and the modern university has been to specialize and to remove knowledge from public discourse and decision-making, to reduce it to a matter of expertise and technique. By the same token, we must acknowledge that it devalues the notion of consensus to identify it with the current professional monopolies of knowledge. If anything, the prevailing configuration of knowledge and its institutions *prevents* the formation of consensus by shrinking the public sphere and excluding the majority of the population from the conversation.

The effect of Bruffee's use of consensus is to invest a kind of "real world" authority in the discursive practices and tacit understandings that bind the discourse communities of specialists and experts together. It makes the conversation a self-explaining mechanism that legitimizes itself through its performances. "This," we tell students, "is the way we [English teachers, biologists, lawyers, chemical engineers, social workers, whatever] do things around here. There's nothing magical about it. It's just the way we talk to each other." The problem is that invoking the "real world" authority of such consensual practices neutralizes the critical and transformative project of collaborative learning, depoliticizes it, and reduces it to an acculturative technique.

To develop a critical version of collaborative learning, we will need to distinguish between consensus as an acculturative practice that reproduces business as usual and consensus as an oppositional one that challenges the prevailing conditions of production. The point of collaborative learning is not simply to demystify the authority of knowledge by revealing its social character but to transform the productive apparatus, to change the social character of production. In this regard, it will help to cast consensus not as a "real world" practice but as a utopian one.

To draw out the utopian possibilities I believe are implied in collaborative learning, we will need to distinguish between "spurious" and "genuine" consensus, as grounded and problematical as these terms may appear to be. In his theory of "communicative action," Habermas defines "genuine" consensus not as something that actually happens but instead as the counterfactual anticipation that agreement can be reached without coercion or systematic distortion. Consensus, for Habermas, is not, as it is for social constructionists like Bruffee, an empirical account of how discourse communities operate but a critical and normative representation of the conditions necessary for fully realized communication to occur. In Habermas' view, we should represent consensus not as the result at any given time of the prevailing conversation but rather as an aspiration to organize the conversation according to relations of non-domination. The anticipation of consensus, that is, projects what Habermas calls an "ideal speech situation," a utopian discursive space that distributes symmetrically the opportunity to speak, to initiate discourse, to question, to give reasons, to do all those other things necessary to justify knowledge socially. From this perspective, consensus becomes a necessary fiction of reciprocity and mutual recognition, the dream of conversation as perfect dialogue. Understood as a utopian desire, assembled from the partial and fragmentary forms of the current conversation, consensus does not appear as the end or the explanation of the conversation but instead as a means of transforming it.

To cast consensus as a utopian instead of a "real world" practice has a number of implications for the collaborative classroom. For one thing, a utopian representation of consensus offers students a powerful critical instrument to interrogate the conversation—to interrupt it in order to investigate the forces which determine who may speak and what may be said, what inhibits communication and what makes it possible. The normal workings of collaborative learning, as Bruffee describes them, ask students to generate an interpretive response to a literary work or a rhetorical analysis of a piece of writing and then to compare the results to the responses or analyses of their teacher and the community of scholars the teacher represents. The pedagogical goal is to negotiate a common language in the classroom, to draw students into a wider consensus, and to initiate them into the conversation as it is currently organized in the academy. The utopian view of consensus, on the other hand, would abandon this expert-novice model of teaching and learning. Instead consensus would provide students with a critical measure to identify the relations of power in the formation of expert judgment.

Let me give an example here. Collaborative learning in literature classes is often based on the idea that students need to avoid, on the one hand, the objectivism that assumes the meaning is in the text and, on the other, the radical pluralism that assumes we cannot distinguish the merits of one reading from another. Collaborative learning, that is, seeks to locate authority in neither the text nor the reader but in what Stanley Fish calls interpretive communities. From the perspective I am suggesting, however, the identification of collaborative learning with interpretive communities takes for granted the enterprise of interpretation as an end in itself.

In contrast, I think we need to begin collaborative classes by asking why interpretation has become the unquestioned goal of literary studies and what other kinds of readings thereby have been excluded and devalued. We would be interested in the forces which have produced dissensus about how to go about reading a literary text and about what constitutes a literary text in the first place. Students, of course, already know a good deal about all this: they are used to naming Shakespeare and Dickens and Hemingway as literature and disqualifying Stephen King, thrillers, and science fiction. What students have had less opportunity to do is to investigate collectively these implicit hierarchies in terms of the relations of power that organize them. Their literature classes have taught them to segregate kinds of reading but without asking them where these differences come from.

For this reason, we might begin the conversation in literature classes by talking not about how to read a literary text but rather about how the students in the course have been trained to read literature and how their schooled reading differs from the way they read outside of school. By examining these differences, freshmen and sophomores in introductory literature courses, I have found, can begin to examine critically the prevailing representation of literature and the institutional base on which it rests. Students rather quickly will distinguish between literature—which is assigned by teachers and is "good for you"—and the other reading they do—which is "for fun." They explain to each other and to me that literature is filled with "hidden meanings" and that the point of schooled reading is to dig them out, while the reading they do for "fun" produces strong identification with characters and teaches them about "life" or gives them the opportunity to escape from it.

The point of such discussion is not to reach agreement about what properly belongs in the realm of literature and what lies outside of it. Nor is it to abandon the usefulness of schooled reading. Rather what students begin to see is that literature exists as a social category that depends on its relation to non-literature. Students, that is, can begin to sketch the rhetoric of dissensus that structures the dominant representation of what literature is and is not and that produces marked differences in the way they read and experience texts.

Such discussions, moreover, give students permission to elaborate what they already know—namely, that schooled reading for "hidden meanings" reinforces the authority of expert readers and creates professional monopolies of knowledge. By drawing on their own experience as readers in and out of school, students regularly and spontaneously make the same telling point William E. Cain makes in *The Crisis in Criticism* that the institution of literature depends upon the "close reading" of specialist critics. In this regard, one of the most valuable things students bring to a literature class is what we as professional readers have largely forgotten—the imprecise, unanalytical act of non-close reading, the experience of ordinary readers at home, on the subway, or at the beach in the summer, the kind of reading that schooled reading marks as different.

One of the benefits of emphasizing the dissensus that surrounds the act of reading is that it poses consensus not as the goal of the conversation but rather as a critical measure to help students identify the structures of power that inhibit communication among readers (and between teachers and students) by authorizing certain styles of reading while excluding others. What students in introductory literature classes learn, I think, is to overcome the feeling that they don't get the point of literature or that they just like to read "trash." Instead, they learn why readers disagree about what counts as a reading, where the differences they experience as readers come from, and how we might usefully bring these differences into relation to each other. They learn to probe not only the ideology of the institution of literature but also the ideologies of popular reading. Just as they learn how schooled reading constitutes them as students in a complicated relationship to the authority of teachers and the institution of literature, students also learn that the reading they do outside of school is not simply a pastime but more important represents an act of self-formation that organizes their experience and desire in imaginary relations to the popular culture of late capitalism and its construction of race, class, and gender differences.

The revised notion of consensus I am proposing here depends paradoxically on its deferral, not its realization. I am less interested in students achieving consensus (although of course this happens at times) as in their using consensus as a critical instrument to open gaps in the conversation through which differences may emerge. In this regard, the Habermasian representation of consensus as a counterfactual anticipation of fully realized communication offers students a critical tool to identify the structures of power which determine who may speak and what may be said. But more important, this notion of consensus also offers students utopian aspirations to transform the conversation by freeing it from the prevailing constraints on its participants, the manipulations, deceptions, and plays of power. Through a collective investigation of differences, students can begin to imagine ways to change the relations of production and to base the conversation not on consensus but on reciprocity and the mutual recognition of the participants and their differences.

Unlike Habermas, however, I do not believe removing relations of domination and systematic distortion, whether ideological or neurotic, from the conversation is likely to establish the conditions in which consensus will express a "rational will" and "permit what *all* can want" (108). Instead, I want to displace consensus to a horizon which may never be reached. We need to see consensus, I think, not as an agreement that reconciles differences through an ideal conversation but rather as the desire of humans to live and work together with differences. The goal of consensus, it seems to me, ought to be not the unity of generalizable interests but rather what Iris Marion Young calls "an openness to unassimilated otherness" (22). Under the utopian aegis of consensus, students can learn to agree to disagree, not because "everyone has their own opinion," but because justice demands that we recognize the inexhaustibility of difference and that we organize the conditions in which we live and work accordingly.

By organizing students non-hierarchically so that all discursive roles are available to all the participants in a group, collaborative learning can do more than model or represent the normal workings of discourse communities. Students' experience of non-domination in the collaborative classroom can offer them a critical measure to understand the distortions of communication and the plays of power in normal discourse. Replacing the "real world" authority of consensus with a rhetoric of dissensus can lead students to demystify the normal workings of discourse communities. But just as important, a rhetoric of dissensus can lead them to redefine consensus as a utopian project, a dream of difference without domination. The participatory and democratic practices of collaborative learning offer an important instance of what Walter Benjamin, in "The Author as Producer," calls the "exemplary character of production"—the collective effort to "induce other producers to produce" and to "put an improved apparatus at their disposal" (233). In this regard, the exemplary character of production in collaborative learning can release collective energies to turn the means of criticism into a means of transformation, to tap fundamental impulses toward emancipation and justice in the utopian practices of Habermas' "ideal speech situation."

It would be fatuous, of course, to presume that collaborative learning can constitute more than momentarily an alternative to the present asymmetrical relations of power and distribution of knowledge and its means of production. But it can incite desire through common work to resolve, if only symbolically, the contradictions students face because of the prevailing conditions of production—the monopoly of expertise and the impulse to know, the separation of work and play, allegiance to peers and dependence on faculty esteem, the experience of cooperation and the competitiveness of a ranking reward system, the empowering sense of collectivity and the isolating personalization of an individual's fate. A rehabilitated notion of consensus in collaborative learning can provide students with exemplary motives to imagine alternative worlds and transformations of social life and labor. In its deferred and utopian form, consensus offers a way to orchestrate dissensus and to turn the conversation in the collaborative classroom into a heterotopia of voices—a heterogeneity without hierarchy.

WORKS CITED

Baker, Houston A., Jr. *Blues, Ideology, and Afro-American Literature.* Chicago: U of Chicago P, 1984.

Beade, Pedro. Comment. *College English* 49 (1987): 708.

Benjamin, Walter. "The Author as Producer." *Reflections.* Ed. Peter Demetz. New York: Schocken, 1986. 220-38.

Bruffee, Kenneth A. "Collaborative Learning: Some Practical Models." *College English* 34 (1973): 634-43.

———. Response. *College English* 49 (1987): 711-16.

Cain, William E. *The Crisis in Criticism: Theory, Literature, and Reform in English Studies.* Baltimore: John Hopkins UP, 1984.

Comay, Rebecca. "Interrupting the Conversation: Notes on Rorty." *Telos* 69 (1986): 119-30.

Eagleton, Terry. *The Function of Criticism.* London: Verso, 1984.

Foster, David. Comment. *College English* 49 (1987): 709-11.

Habermas, Jürgen. *Legitimation Crisis.* Trans. Thomas McCarthy. Boston: Beacon, 1975.

Johnson, Thomas S. Comment. *College English* 48 (1986): 76.

Myers, Greg. "Reality, Consensus, and Reform in the Rhetoric of Composition Teaching." *College English* 48 (1986): 154-74.

Rorty, Richard. *The Consequences of Pragmatism.* Minneapolis: U of Minnesota P, 1982.
_____. *Philosophy and the Mirror of Nature.* Princeton: Princeton UP, 1979.
Vitanza, Victor. "Critical Sub/Versions of the History of Philosophical Rhetoric." *Rhetoric Review* 6.1 (1987): 41-66.
Wells, Susan. "Habermas, Communicative Competence, and the Teaching of Technical Discourse." *Theory in the Classroom.* Ed. Cary Nelson. Urbana: U of Illinois P, 1986. 245-69.
Young, Iris Marion. "The Ideal of Community and the Politics of Difference." *Social Theory and Practice* 12.1 (1986): 1-26.

"Contact Zones"
and English Studies

PATRICIA BIZZELL

Our Ptolemaic system of literary categories goes creaking and groaning onward, in spite of the widely acknowledged need to overhaul it in response to multiculturalism. This is not to say that there have not been attempts to revise course design in light of new materials and methods. For example, G. Douglas Atkins and Michael L. Johnson's *Writing and Reading Differently* (1985), Susan L. Gabriel and Isaiah Smithson's *Gender in the Classroom* (1990), and James A. Berlin and Michael J. Vivion's *Cultural Studies in the English Classroom* (1992) address the pedagogical consequences of deconstruction, feminist literary theory, and cultural studies, respectively, and also incorporate more diverse literatures. But these attempts to foster innovation in the individual classroom still leave the basic structure of English studies intact.

In Kristin Ross's description of the multicultural world literature and cultural studies program at the University of California at Santa Cruz, she comments indirectly on this problem when she identifies as one stumbling block to the Santa Cruz program the faculty's unwillingness "to depart from their specialized fields" (668). They fended off demands to diversify their course material with plaints like "But I don't have a PhD in South African literature" (668). Ross gives good reasons for forging ahead in spite of such protests, but she doesn't say much about the underlying structure of English studies that still makes us think our scholarship must be organized along national or chronological lines, even though these are inimical to the process of integrating new materials and methods because devised to serve and protect the old ones.

Reprinted from *College English* 56.2 (February 1994): 163–69. Used with permission.

The persistence of the old basic structure can be seen even in an impressive new collection published by the Modern Language Association with the avowed intention of fostering innovation: Stephen Greenblatt and Giles Gunn's *Redrawing the Boundaries: The Transformation of English and American Literary Studies* (1992). Even here, boundaries are not redrawn in fundamentally new ways. Rather, the old, familiar structure of English studies is visible, for instance in chapter divisions that carve literary studies into chronological periods, such as "Seventeenth-Century Studies" (British literature) and "American Literary Studies to the Civil War." Ten such chapters are followed by eleven more, most with the word "Criticism" in the title, implying that here we turn from primary to secondary texts. Yet it is here that we find the most attention to literature by women, gay people, and people of color: separate chapters are devoted, for example, to "Feminist Criticism" and "African American Criticism." Thus other traditional boundaries appear to be reasserted rather than redrawn. Moreover, the field of composition studies appears to remain behind even more impenetrable traditional boundaries. Not only is "Composition Studies" given a separate chapter (in the second set of eleven), but there must be an additional, separate chapter just to explain why composition studies is included in this book at all ("Composition and Literature").

I think we need a radically new system to organize English studies, and I propose that we develop it in response to the materials with which we are now working. Instead of finagling the new literatures and the new pedagogical and critical approaches into our old categories, we should try to find comprehensive new forms that seem to spring from and respond to the new materials. Instead of asking ourselves, for example, "How can I fit Frederick Douglass into my American Renaissance course?" we need to ask, "How should I reconceive my study of literature and composition now that I regard Douglass as an important writer?"

It could be argued that we don't need any new system of categories, that what we should do is simply to knock down the old system and then let everyone do what he or she pleases. This appears to be the approach taken by another recent attempt to chart new courses, the MLA's 1987 English Coalition Conference. Peter Elbow, in his account of this conference, *What Is English?* (1990), tells us there was a "remarkable consensus" at the conference on "the central business of English studies" (17), and it was as follows:

> *Using language* actively in a diversity of ways and settings—that is, not only in the classroom as exercises for teachers but in a range of social settings with various audiences where the language makes a difference.

Reflecting on language use. Turning back and self-consciously reflecting on how one has been using language—examining these processes of talking, listening, writing, and reading.

Trying to ensure that this using and reflecting go on in *conditions of both nourishment and challenge,* that is, conditions where teachers care about students themselves and what they actively learn—not just about skills or scores or grades. (18; emphasis in original)

The tone here, of course, is quite different from that of *Redrawing the Boundaries*—the focus is clearly on pedagogy rather than on the body of scholarly knowledge. I applaud this focus on pedagogy, and I admire the principles laid down above. But I can't help noticing that they appear to have very little to do specifically with the discipline of English studies. To me, they sound like the kind of principles I urge on faculty from all disciplines in my school's writing-across-the-curriculum program. There isn't a course at my school where these principles couldn't be put advantageously into practice. How, then, do they define "the central business of English studies"?

What these principles leave out, as Elbow himself notes, is what people read and write *about* in literary studies. He acknowledges that "you can't make meaning unless you are writing or reading about *something*; . . . practices are always practices *of* a content" (19; emphasis in original). Yet the topic of literary content appeared to be taboo at the conference. As Elbow tells it:

The question of literature was left strikingly moot. Not only was there no consensus, there was a striking avoidance of the issue. It's not that it didn't come up; the question of literature arose recurrently. . . . Yet every time we somehow slid away from the issue into something else. (96, 97)

This sounds to me like repression, not freedom, but I sympathize with the conference members. Small wonder they could not find a way to talk about literature, with the old system of organizing it discredited for lack of inclusiveness and no new system yet accepted. But I am concerned that this kind of avoidance leaves graduate and undergraduate curricula dangerously lacking in guidance—dangerously vulnerable to "cultural literacy" pundits who would shove into the breach the only system still known, namely the old, bad traditional one. Indeed, this threat appeared at the conference itself, and Elbow, although an advocate of composition pedagogies in which each writer is to do pretty much as he or she pleases, was sufficiently troubled by it that he proposes his own list of literary contents for English studies in an appendix.

But exactly how are we to develop a new system of organization from the new materials of study, supposing we agree that this is needed? To do so would seem to require that we make generalizations about the new material—about what, say, might be required to study Asian-American literature adequately—that would be extremely difficult, if not downright presumptuous, to make. I think we need an approach to the diverse world literatures written in English we are now studying that focuses not on their essential nature, whatever that may be, but rather on how they might, not "fit" together exactly, but come into productive dialogue with one another.

I suggest that we address this problem by employing Mary Louise Pratt's concept of the "contact zone":

> I use this term to refer to social spaces where cultures meet, clash, and grapple with each other, often in contexts of highly asymmetrical relations of power, such as colonialism, slavery, or their aftermaths as they are lived out in many parts of the world today. (34)

This concept can aid us both because it emphasizes the conditions of difficulty and struggle under which literatures from different cultures come together (thus forestalling the disrespectful glossing over of differences), and because it gives us a conceptual base for bringing these literatures together, namely, when they occur in or are brought to the same site of struggle or "contact zone."

A "contact zone" is defined primarily in terms of historical circumstances. It is circumscribed in time and space, but with elastic boundaries. Focusing on a contact zone as a way of organizing literary study would mean attempting to include *all* material relevant to the struggles going on there. Pratt's main example of a "contact zone" here is Peru in the late sixteenth and early seventeenth centuries, where she wants to study the interaction among texts by Native Americans (newly discovered by twentieth-century scholars) and the canonical Spanish accounts. I submit that the United States is another such contact zone, or more precisely, a congeries of overlapping contact zones, considered from the first massive immigration of Europeans in the seventeenth century up to the present day. "Multiculturalism" in English studies is a name for our recognition of this condition of living on contested cultural ground, and our desire to represent something of this complexity in our study of literature and literacy.

If we understand that we are teaching in, and about, contact zones, Pratt suggests that we must stop imagining our job to be transmitting a unitary literature and literacy. Under this old model,

The prototypical manifestation of language is generally taken to be the speech of individual adult native speakers face-to-face (as in Saussure's famous diagram) in monolingual, even monodialectal situations—in short, the most homogeneous case, linguistically and socially. The same goes for written communication. (38)

Now, Pratt suggests that we need a new model:

a theory that assumed different things—that argued, for instance, that the most revealing speech situation for understanding language was one involving a gathering of people each of whom spoke two languages and understood a third and held only one language in common with any of the others. (38)

This model treats difference as an asset, not a liability.

Given American diversity, our classrooms are getting to be more like Pratt's new model than the old one. If we respond by "teaching the contact zone," we can foster classrooms where, as in Pratt's experience,

All the students in the class . . . [heard] their culture discussed and objectified in ways that horrified them; all the students saw their roots traced back to legacies of both glory and shame; . . . [but] kinds of marginalization once taken for granted were gone. Virtually every student was having the experience of seeing the world described with him or her in it. (39)

Acknowledging its difficulties, I am suggesting that we need a new system of organization in English studies to make this kind of teaching—and scholarship—not only possible, but normative.

In short, I am suggesting that we organize English studies not in terms of literary or chronological periods, nor essentialized racial or gender categories, but rather in terms of historically defined contact zones, moments when different groups within the society contend for the power to interpret what is going on. As suggested above, the chronological, geographical, and generic parameters of any contact zone are defined on the basis of including as much material as possible that is relevant to the issue being contested. Time periods can be short or long, literatures of different groups, languages, or continents can be considered together, all genres are admitted, and so on.

For example, the New England region from about 1600 to about 1800 might be defined as a contact zone in which different groups of Europeans and Native Americans were struggling for the power to say what had happened in their relations with each other. Thus canonical Puritan histories, autobiographies, and captivity narratives would be studied in connection with historical commentaries and memoirs by non-Puritan Europeans (traditionally treated as "minor"), European transcriptions of Native American speeches (problematic but invaluable), and letters, histories, and spiritual autobiographies written by Native Americans in English (unknown in the academy until very recently). The object would not be to represent what the lives of the diverse European immigrant and Native American groups were really like. Rather, the attempt would be to show how each group represented itself imaginatively in relation to the others. We would, in effect, be reading all the texts as brought to the contact zone, for the purpose of communicating across cultural boundaries.

There are several advantages to this approach. First, it provides a rationale for integrating English studies multiculturally. No longer would we be trying to squeeze new material into inappropriate old categories, where its importance could not be adequately appreciated. We would be working with categories that treated multiculturalism as a defining feature, that assumed the richest literary treasures could be found in situations in which different histories, lifeways, and languages are trying to communicate and to deal with the unequal power distribution among them. We would no longer need to ask prejudicial questions, such as whether Frederick Douglass was as "good" on some putative absolute scale of expository value as Henry Thoreau. Rather, we would look at the rhetorical effectiveness of each writer in dealing with the matter in hand, for example, the need to promote civil disobedience in the contact zone created by white and black efforts to define and motivate action in response to slavery in the antebellum U.S.

Second, this approach fully integrates composition and rhetoric into literary studies. Studying texts as they respond to contact zone conditions is studying them rhetorically, studying them as efforts of rhetoric. The historical context provides a way to focus the rhetorical analysis. Moreover, professional and student writing can also be seen as contending in contact zones and experimenting with the textual arts of the contact zone that rhetorical analysis emphasizes. Thus boundaries between "content" (literature) and its traditional inferior, pedagogy (composition), are usefully blurred, as are the distinctions between "high" literature and other kinds of writing, including student writing. Donald McQuade makes a persuasive argument for blurring these boundaries in "Composition and Literature."

At the end of her essay, Pratt calls for the development of what she calls "the pedagogical arts of the contact zone":

> exercises in storytelling and in identifying with the ideas, interests, histories, and attitudes of others; experiments in transculturation and collaborative work and in the arts of critique, parody, and comparison (including

unseemly comparisons between elite and vernacular cultural forms); the redemption of the oral; ways for people to engage with suppressed aspects of history (including their own histories); ways to move *into and out of* rhetorics of authenticity; ground rules for communication across lines of difference and hierarchy that go beyond politeness but maintain mutual respect; a systematic approach to the all-important concept of *cultural mediation.* (40; emphasis in original)

David Bartholomae has recently suggested that we imagine these "arts" translated into exercises in an English class. Imagine, for example, a class in which literature is analyzed for the ways it moves among rhetorics of authenticity, students experiment with attending to suppressed aspects of their own history as part of establishing their writerly personae, and scholarly writing is both shared and opened for parody. Pratt calls this work "cultural mediation"; my phrase for it is "negotiating difference"—studying how various writers in various genres have grappled with the pervasive presence of difference in American life and developed virtues out of necessity. I would include analysis of student writing, for its employment of contact zone rhetorical strategies, and I would include "texts" of all kinds, as required by the contact zones under study—posters, songs, films, videos, and so forth.

Reorganizing literary studies along these lines would mean redesigning courses. For example, at Holy Cross we offer first-year students a choice of either a composition course (a course in the personal essay) or a course that introduces them to literary study by teaching the close reading of works grouped according to genre. Under the new paradigm, there would be no need for two separate courses. The abilities needed both to enter literary studies and to refine one's own writing would be the skills of analyzing and imitating rhetorical arts of the contact zone. Students would learn to critique strategies of negotiating difference in the writing of others and to practice them in their own. So we could offer just one course, writing-intensive but including some reading and analysis of literature (broadly defined).

It would also mean reorganizing graduate study and professional scholarly work in ways I hardly dare to suggest. I suppose that one would no longer become a specialist in American literature, a "Shakespeare man," or a "compositionist." Rather, people's areas of focus would be determined by the kinds of rhetorical problems in which they were interested.

My main object is to get people to work on the project. I have no coherent alternative program to present. But I believe that if we reorganize literary studies in this way, we will be giving a dynamic new direction to our profession. We will be creating disciplinary parameters within which boundaries really can be redrawn to come to terms with the demands of multiculturalism.

This new paradigm will stimulate scholarship and give vitally needed guidance to graduate and undergraduate curricula. It might also lead us, in the multicultural literary archives, to stories of hope that can lend us all spiritual sustenance as we renew efforts to make the United States a multicultural democracy. If we are not given to complete the task, neither are we allowed to desist from it.

WORKS CITED

Atkins, G. Douglas, and Michael L. Johnson, eds. *Writing and Reading Differently: Deconstruction and the Teaching of Composition and Literature.* Lawrence: U of Kansas P, 1985.

Bartholomae, David. "The Tidy House: Basic Writing in the American Curriculum." *Journal of Basic Writing* 12 (Spring 1993): 4-21.

Berlin, James A., and Michael J. Vivion, eds. *Cultural Studies in the English Classroom.* Portsmouth, NH: Heinemann-Boynton/Cook, 1992.

Elbow, Peter. *What is English?* New York: MLA, 1990.

Gabriel, Susan L., and Isaiah Smithson, eds. *Gender in the Classroom: Power and Pedagogy.* Urbana: U of Illinois P, 1990.

Greenblatt, Stephen, and Giles Gunn, eds. *Redrawing the Boundaries: The Transformation of English and American Literary Studies.* New York: MLA, 1992.

McQuade, Donald. "Composition and Literature." Greenblatt and Gunn 482-519.

Pratt, Mary Louise. "Arts of the Contact Zone." *Profession 91.* New York: MLA, 1991. 33-40.

Ross, Kristin. "The World Literature and Cultural Studies Program." *Critical Inquiry* 19 (Summer 1993): 666-676.

Professing Multiculturalism

The Politics of Style in the Contact Zone

MIN-ZHAN LU

In her 1991 "Arts of the Contact Zone," Mary Louise Pratt points out that while colleges and universities have increasingly deployed a rhetoric of diversity in response to the insistence of non-mainstream groups for fuller participation, the "import" of "multiculturalism" remains "up for grabs across the ideological spectrum" (39). I begin with Pratt's reminder because I want to call attention to the images of "grabbing" and "import." These depict "multiculturalism" as a construct whose "import"—meanings, implications, and consequences—is available only to those willing to expend the energy to "grab" it: to search, envision, grasp, articulate, and enact it. And these images conjure up the act of importing—of bringing in—perspectives and methods formerly excluded by dominant institutions. I want to articulate one "import" of multiculturalism here by exploring the question of how to conceive and practice teaching methods which invite a multicultural approach to style, particularly those styles of student writing which appear to be ridden with "errors." And I situate this question in the context of English Studies, a discipline which, on the one hand, has often proclaimed its concern to profess multiculturalism but, on the other hand, has done little to combat the ghettoization of two of its own cultures, namely composition teaching and student writing.

My inquiry is motivated by two concerns which I believe I share with a significant number of composition teachers. The first results from a sense of division between the ways in which many of us approach style in theory and in our teaching practices. I have in mind teachers who are aligned in theory

Reprinted from *College Composition and Communication* 45.4 (December 1994): 442–58. Used with permission.

with a view of composition which contests the separation of form and meaning and which also argues against a conception of "academic discourse" as discrete, fixed, and unified. This alignment, while generating a critical perspective towards traditional methods of teaching style through drills in "correct usage," does not always result in any immediate revision of such methods in classroom practice. Some of us tend to resolve this gap between theory and practice in one of two ways: (1) We set aside a few weeks to teach "usage" or "copyediting" in the traditional way while spending the rest of the term helping students to revise their work on a more conceptual level; or (2) we send students who have "problems" with "usage" to the writing center. Such "resolutions" often leave the teacher frustrated. Because she recognizes the burden on those at the fringe of having to "prove" themselves to those at the center by meeting the standards set by the latter, she cannot but take seriously students' anxiety to master "correct" usage. Nevertheless, she is aware that instead of helping them to overcome such an anxiety, her teaching strategies risk increasing it, as they may reinforce students' sense of the discrepancy between their inability to produce "error-free" prose and their ability to come up with "good ideas," and they may confirm these students' impression that only those who make "errors" need to worry about issues of usage and editing. My second concern has to do with a division many of us feel between our role as composition teachers and the role we play as students, teachers, or scholars in other, supposedly more central areas of English Studies. As our interest in composition teaching, theory, and research evolves, we are increasingly interested in contesting the second-class status of work in composition. At the same time, we are often all too aware that we ourselves are guilty of perpetuating the divisions between composition and other areas of English Studies by approaching the writings of "beginners" or "outsiders" in a manner different from the approach we take to the writings of "experts."

Two stories, both of which took place around the turn of this century, illustrate part of the historical power of that kind of division. The first story comes from Gertrude Stein's *The Autobiography of Alice B. Toklas.* According to Stein, right after she had made arrangements to have her book *Three Lives* printed by Grafton Press of New York, "a very nice American young man" was sent by the press to Paris to check on her:

> You see, [the young man] said slightly hesitant, the director of the Grafton Press is under the impression that perhaps your knowledge of english. But I am an american, said Gertrude Stein indignantly. Yes yes I understand that perfectly now, he said, but perhaps you have not had much experience in writing. I suppose, said [Stein] laughing, you were under the impression

that I was imperfectly educated. He blushed, why no, he said, but you might not have had much experience in writing. Oh yes, she said, oh yes. . . . and you might as well tell [the director] . . . that everything that is written in the manuscript is written with the intention of its being so written and all he has to do is to print it and I will take the responsibility. The young man bowed himself out. (68)

This exchange between an indignant Stein and an embarrassed "young man" reveals some of the criteria used by "educated america" when dealing with an idiosyncratic style. These criteria are (a) the writer's "knowledge of english," which is seen as somehow dependent on whether she is a native speaker, and (b) the writer's "experience in writing," which is seen as related to whether she has been "[im]perfectly educated." Stein, an "American" bearing certification of a "perfect" education from Radcliffe and Johns Hopkins Medical School, knew she had the authority to maintain that everything in her manuscript was "written with the intention of its being so written." Stein's indignation and the embarrassment she elicited from the "young man" suggest that in the early 1900s, ethnic and educational backgrounds were two common denominators for determining whether style represented self-conscious and innovative experimentation or blundering "errors."

The second story took place a few years prior to the Stein event, when the style of another writer, Theodore Dreiser, was also questioned by a publisher to whom he had submitted his first novel, *Sister Carrie*. The rejection letter from Harper faults Dreiser for his "uneven" style which, according to the editors, was "disfigured by . . . colloquialisms" (*Sister Carrie* 519). Existing manuscripts of the book's revision indicate that Dreiser did not defend his style with the kind of authority Stein exhibited. Instead he sought editorial help from his wife Jug and friend Henry because he deemed both to have been better educated than himself. There is evidence in the revised manuscript that Dreiser adopted nearly all of Jug's corrections of grammar and Henry's rewording of his Germanic rhythms and cumulative sentence structures (*Sister Carrie* 580–81). Read in the context of Stein's story, Dreiser's willingness to have all aspects of his style "corrected" might be attributed in part to his acute awareness of the criteria used by "educated america" when dealing with the writing of the son of an impoverished German immigrant with extremely sporadic formal education. The early reception of *Sister Carrie* proves the validity of Dreiser's concern, as even its defenders attributed its "crude" style to his ethnic background and lack of formal education.[1]

Almost a century after these events, more and more English courses are now informed by a view of language as a site of struggle among conflicting discourses with unequal socio-political power. Students in these courses are beginning to approach the style of what they call "real" writers like Stein and Dreiser very differently. Interest in multiculturalism has also shifted the attention of some teachers to writers' success at what Bakhtin calls "dialogically coordinating" a varied and profound "heteroglossia" (295–96). Analysis of style in these classrooms often centers on the politics of the writer's stylistic decisions: (a) mapping the "heteroglossia" on the internal and external scenes of writing, (b) attending to the writer's effort to look at one discourse through the eyes of another, and (c) considering the writer's willingness to resist the centripetal forces of "official" discourses. Viewed from this multicultural perspective on style, the writings of both Dreiser and Stein could be considered in terms of the efforts of each to dialogically coordinate the profound heteroglossia within and outside official "educated" discourses. For readers adopting this perspective, neither Dreiser's ethnic background nor his "imperfect" educational background would be used to dismiss his "uneven" style solely as evidence of "error"—that is, to conclude that his style merely reflects his lack of knowledge or experience in writing. In fact, given the frequency with which writings from what Gloria Anzaldua has called the "borderlands" are being currently assigned in some English courses and the praise this type of writing receives for its hybridization of "official" discourses, Dreiser's readiness to yield to the authority of the "better educated" now appears conservative—indicating a passive stance towards the hegemony of ethnocentrism and linguistic imperialism. In fact, the publication of the Pennsylvania edition of *Sister Carrie* in 1987 indicates that such a critical view privileging resistance was in operation when the editors decided to delete many of the changes made by the "better educated" Jug and Henry in the hope of preserving the "power and forcefulness" of Dreiser's original prose (*Sister Carrie* 581).

However, Dreiser's reaction still haunts me, especially when I move from teaching students to analyze the idiosyncratic style of "real" writers to helping them to work on their own styles. In my "literature" courses for junior- or senior-level college students or "writing" courses for first-year students, students learn to talk with considerable eloquence about the politics of stylistic decisions made by "real" writers, especially those writing from the borderlands by choice or necessity. Most of the readings I assign for these classes call attention to writers' need and right to contest the unifying force of hegemonic discourses, and thus make Dreiser's submission to the authority of the "better educated" appear dated and passive. Yet the meaning of Dreiser's submissiveness changes for me and most of my students as soon as we move to work on the style of a student writer, especially when we tinker with what we call the writer's "discursive voice"—that is, when dealing with deviations in diction, tone, voice, structure, and so on (which we loosely call the "rhetorical register"), or with punctuation, syntax, sentence structure, and so on (which we refer to as the "grammatical register"). On those occasions, how to sound "right" suddenly becomes a "real" concern for my students: pervasive, immediate, and difficult for me to dismiss. My students' apparent anxiety to reproduce the conventions of "educated" English poses a challenge for my teaching and research. Why is it that in spite of our developing ability to acknowledge the political need and right of "real" writers to experiment with "style," we continue to cling to the belief that such a need and right does not belong to "student writers"? Another way of putting the question would be, why do we assume—as Dreiser did—that until one can prove one's ability to produce "error-free" prose, one has not earned the right to innovative "style"?

[handwritten margin note: Do you need to know the rules to break them?]

Again, I believe Dreiser's account of his own educational experience might shed some light on the question. In *Dawn*, Dreiser writes about his opportunity to attend the University of Indiana, Bloomington for two short terms. A former teacher made arrangements to exempt Dreiser from the preliminary examinations because, Dreiser points out, these exams would have quickly "debarred" him (342). Life as what we might today call an open admissions student at Indiana made Dreiser feel "reduced." He "grieved" at his "inability to grasp . . . such a commonplace as grammar" (378). Even though he knew he was able to apprehend many things and to demonstrate his apprehensions "quite satisfactorily" to himself, he found the curriculum "oppressive," leaving him "mute" with "a feeling of inadequacy" (425). The events surrounding the efforts of Dreiser and Stein to publish their first books indicate that the common approach of the editors, publishers, and critics to their idiosyncratic styles was not coincidental. Dreiser's experience at Indiana, his willingness to have his "uneven" style "corrected," and Stein's quick rebuttal to the "young man" all point to the institutional source of this approach. A common view of "style" as belonging only to those who are beyond "error," and a certain type of college curriculum treating matters of grammar or usage as the prerequisites to higher education, seem mutually reinforcing. It is this belief that pushes students identified as having "problems" to meet such "prerequisites" and assigns teachers trained to deal with such "problems" to the periphery or borderlands of higher education.

Dreiser's memories of Indiana seem symptomatic of the feelings of a significant number of college students I encounter. I have in mind particularly students who seem quick to admit that they are "not good" at writing because they have been identified at some point in their education as needing special—remedial, laboratory, or intensive—instruction in the "basics." Like Dreiser, they are frustrated at their inability to grasp "grammar" because they have been encouraged to view it as "such a commonplace"—something everyone who aspires to become anyone ought to be able to master. And they feel muted and reduced by the curriculum because it does not seem to recognize that they are quite able to grasp subjects other than "grammar" and demonstrate their understanding of such subjects satisfactorily to themselves, if perhaps not in writing to others. It seems to me that one way of helping students to deal with this frustration would be to connect their "difficulties" with the refusal of "real" writers to reproduce the hegemonic conventions of written English. And it seems to me that this will not take place until teachers like myself contest the distinction between "real" and "student" writers and stop treating the idiosyncratic style of the not yet "perfectly educated" solely in terms of "error." One form of contestation could be to apply to student writing the same multicultural approach we have been promoting when analyzing the work of "real" writers. Susan Miller has argued in *Textual Carnivals* that the tendency to treat student writers as "emerging, or as failed, but never as actually responsible 'authors'" has served to maintain the low status of composition studies in its relations to those "outside it, and its self-images and ways of working out its new professionalization" (195–96). An approach to student writing that treats students as real writers would undo such binaries and thus assert the right and ability of writing teachers and students to fully participate in a truly multicultural curriculum.

My aim here is to discuss a teaching method formulated out of my attempt to apply a multicultural approach to student writing: an approach which views the classroom as a potential "contact zone"—which Pratt describes as a space where various cultures "clash, and grapple with each other, often in contexts of highly asymmetrical relations of power" (34). In arguing for a multicultural approach to styles traditionally displaced to the realm of "error," I align my teaching with a tradition in "error" analysis which views even "error-ridden" student writings as texts relevant to critical approaches available to English Studies. I am particularly interested in explicitly foregrounding the category of "resistance" and "change" when helping students to conceptualize the processes of producing and interpreting an idiosyncratic style in students' own writings. In the classroom I envision, the notion of "intention" is presented as the decision of a writer who understands not only the "central role of human agency" but also that such agency is often "enacted under circumstances not of one's choosing" (West 31). I define the writer's attempt to "reproduce" the norms of academic discourses as necessarily involving the re-production—approximating, negotiating, and revising—of these norms. And I do so by asking students to explore the full range of choices and options, including those excluded by the conventions of academic discourses.

These aspects in the classroom I envision inevitably distance it from classrooms influenced by one belief prevalent in ESL courses or courses in "Basic Writing": namely, that a monolingual environment is the most conducive to the learning of "beginners" or "outsiders." This belief overlooks the dialogical nature of students' "inner voices" as well as the multicultural context of students' lives. The classroom I envision also differs from approaches to students' ambivalence towards the effects of education exemplified by Mina Shaughnessy's *Errors and Expectations.* Shaughnessy convincingly shows the relevance to error analysis of a range of feelings common to students likely to be identified as basic writers: their anxiety to "sound academic" and to self-consciously emulate the formal style (194), their low self-esteem as learners and writers, and their sense of ambivalence towards academic discourse. But as I have argued in "Conflict and Struggle," Shaughnessy's goal in acknowledging students' ambivalence is only to help them dissolve it (904–06). Because this ambivalence arises from sources well beyond the classroom—coming from the unequal power relationships pervading the history, culture, and society my students live in—not all students can or even want to get rid of all types of ambivalence. On the contrary, the experiences of writers like Gloria Anzaldúa, bell hooks, and Mike Rose suggest that, appropriately mobilized, a sense of ambivalence might be put to constructive uses in writing.

To foreground the concepts of "resistance" and "change" when analyzing the styles of a student or "real" writer, I ask students to read deviations from the official codes of academic discourses not only in relation to the writer's knowledge of these codes but also in terms of her efforts to negotiate and modify them. Aside from increasing the student's knowledge of and experience in reproducing these official forms, I am most interested in doing three things: (1) enabling students to hear discursive voices which conflict with and struggle against the voices of academic authority; (2) urging them to negotiate a position in response to these colliding voices; and (3) asking them to consider their choice of position in the context of the socio-political power relationships within and among diverse discourses and in the context of their personal life, history, culture, and society.

Because of the tendency in English Studies to ghettoize the culture of composition, I will use some student writing produced in writing courses for first-year students to illustrate how I would actually go about teaching a multicultural approach to style. And I am going to focus on features of writing styles which are commonly displaced to the realm of "error" and thus viewed as peripheral to college English teaching. In using these rather than other types of examples, I hope to illustrate as well the need to view composition as a site which might inform as well as be informed by our effort to profess multiculturalism in other, supposedly more "advanced" and "central" areas of English Studies. David Bartholomae has recently reminded us that there is no need "to import 'multiple cultures' [into the classroom, via anthologies]. They are there, in the classroom, once the institution becomes willing to pay that kind of attention to student writing" (14–15). Such attention, he explains, could produce composition courses in multiculturalism "that worked with the various cultures represented in the practice of its students" (14). My second reason for using these examples is related to the ways in which conflict and struggle have been perceived by teachers specializing in error analysis. These teachers tend to hear arguments foregrounding conflict and struggle in the classroom as sloganeering "the students' right to their own language" in order to eliminate attention to error, or as evidence of a "PC" attack on the "back to basics" movement (see, for example, Traub). The examples I use here, I hope, will demonstrate a way of teaching which neither overlooks the students' potential lack of knowledge and experience in reproducing the dominant codes of academic discourses *nor* dismisses the writer's potential social, political, and linguistic interest in modifying these codes, with emphasis on the word "potential."

When teaching first-year writing classes, I usually introduce the multicultural approach to student writing style around the mid-point of the term, when I feel that students are beginning to apply to their actual practices a view of writing as a process of re-seeing. To present the writer's experimentation with style (including what is generally called "copyediting" or the "correction of error") as an integral part of the revision process, I look for sample student writings with two characteristics. First, I am interested in writings with the kinds of "error" a majority of the class would feel they can easily "spot" and "fix." This type of writing allows me to acknowledge some potential causes of non-conventional styles and effective methods of revising them which are more widely disseminated in traditional writing classrooms and familiar to most students. Second, I look for styles which are also more conducive to my attempt to help the writer to negotiate a new position in relation to the colliding voices active in the scenes of writing.[2]

Following is a handout I have used when teaching first-year composition classes. The two segments on the handout are from the papers one student wrote in response to two assignments, one asking her to discuss an essay, "From a Native Daughter," by Haunani-Kay Trask, and another asking her to comment on the kind of "critical thinking" defined in the "Introduction" to an anthology called *Rereading America*. For the convenience of discussion in this essay, I have added emphasis to the handout:

Segment One:

As a Hawaiian native historian, Trask *can able to* argue for her people. As a Hawaiian native, she was exposed to two totally different viewpoints about her people. She was brought up in Hawaii. During this time, she heard the stories about her people from her parents. Later on she was send to America mainland to pursue higher education, in which she learnt a different stories about her people. Therefore, she understood that the interpretation of land was different between the "haole" and the native. To prove that the "haole" were wrong, she went back to Hawaii and work on the land with other native, so she *can* feel the strong bond with land her people have which the "haole" *could* not feel. The "haole" historians never bother to do so as they were more interested in looking for written evidence. That was why Trask, as a native Hawaiian historian, argued that these "haole" historians were being ignorant and ethnocentric. That is also why Trask suggested the "haole" historians learn the native tongue.

———

Segment Two:

Elements like perceiving things from different perspective, finding and validating each alternative solutions, questioning the unknown and breaking the nutshell of cultural norms are important for developing the ability of "critical thinking." . . . Most of the new universities' students are facing new challenges like staying away from family, peer pressure, culture shock, heavy college work etc. I *can* say that these are the "obstacles" to success. If a student *can able to* approach each situation with different perspectives than the one he brought from high school, I *may* conclude that this particular student has climbed his first step to become a "critical thinker." . . . However, there is one particular obstacle that is really difficult for almost everyone to overcome, that is the cultural rules. From the textbook, I found that cultural rules are deep rooted in our mind and cause us to view things from our respective cultural viewpoint. Even though cultural values lead the way of life of a particular group of people, they blind us as well. I relate to this because I truly believe that the cultural rules of my country, Malaysia, make my life here difficult. In order to achieve a "critical mind," one should try to break from his own cultural rules.

———

"can," verb:

1. to be able to; have the ability, power, or skill to. 2. to know how to. 3. to have the power or means to. 4. to have the right or qualifications to. 5. *may*; *have permission to. (The Random House Dictionary)*

"able," adjective:

1. having necessary power, skill, resources, or qualifications; qualified; able to lift a trunk; . . . able to vote. *(The Random House Dictionary)*

When using this handout, I usually begin by asking students what particularly about the two segments might be said to make the voice of the writer idiosyncratic. My students in both writing and literature classes have been fairly quick in tracing it to the "can able to" structure in the two segments. Then I ask the class to speculate on potential causes of that idiosyncrasy. Students' responses to this question usually go something like this: Here is a "foreign" speaker, a student from Malaysia, trying to use the English idiom "to be able to" and ending up with an "error." So we usually talk a little bit about the difference in grammatical function between the verb "can" and the verb "to be" in relation to the adjective "able." And I describe the writer's own initial interpretation of the cause of this "error": her native language is Chinese. With the help of a tutor, she had realized that the Chinese translation for both "can" and "be able to" is the same. When using the expression "be able to," she would be thinking in Chinese. As a result, she often ended up writing "can able to." I would refer to her own initial reading because I am interested in complicating but not denying the relationship between style and the writer's knowledge of and experience with the conventions of written English. So I try to acknowledge first that exposure to and practice in reproducing the "be able to" structure could be one of the ways to revise these segments.

I then go on to complicate this approach by also calling attention to the relationship between form and meaning. What might be the difference in meaning between "can," "be able to," and "can able to"? Most of the students I have encountered tend to see "can" as interchangeable with "be able to." To them, "can able to" appears redundant, like a double negative. To problematize this reading, I usually call attention to the two dictionary entries included in the handout, especially to definition 5 under "can." Definition 5 opens up a new reading by presenting the word "can" as having one more meaning than "to be able to." Rather than approaching the issue of ability from the perspective of what an individual possesses, definition 5 approaches it from the perspective of the external forces *permitting* something, as in the verb "may."

Most native English speakers among my students tend to argue that in actual usage, only grandmas and schoolteachers make the distinction between "can" and "may." *Everyone* uses "can" and "be able to" interchangeably nowadays. In response, I tell them the writer's position on the issue. She was aware of the distinction—she was the one who first called my attention to definition 5. At this point, a "contact zone" would begin to take shape with three conflicting positions on the meanings of "can" and "able to": the position of a speaker of idiomatic English, the position of the dictionary, and the position of a "foreign" student writer. Since the "foreign" student writer position is here being cast as that of someone lacking knowledge and expertise in formal and idiomatic English and thus the least powerful of the three, I am most interested in furthering the students' existing construction of that position so it is not so easily silenced.

To that end, I pose the question of whether, read in the context of the two segments in the handout, one might argue that the "can" in the two "can able to" structures does not take on the same meaning as the other uses of "can" in the rest of the segments. This line of inquiry usually leads us to compare the meaning of the "can" in the first sentence in Segment One to the two "can's" in the seventh sentence and to the meaning of the "can" in the "can able to" in Segment Two as well as the "can" in the previous sentence or the "may" in the second half of the same sentence. My aim here is to get students to re-construct the voice of the writer by focusing on the various uses of the word "can" in the two segments. When exploring the question, I also try to direct attention to the passive voice (Trask was "brought up in Hawaii" and "send to America mainland to pursue higher education") in the sentences following the statement "Trask can able to argue for her people." I explore with the class how and why this passive voice might be read as indicating that the student writer is approaching Trask's ability from the perspective of the external circumstances of Trask's life—using "can" in the sense of her having the "permission to" become a native Hawaiian historian—as well as from the perspective of her having the qualifications to argue as a historian. The two uses of "can" in sentence seven, however, present Trask's and the "haole" historians' (in)ability to "feel" the Hawaiian's bond with the land as more related to a person's will and attitude rather than to whether each "may"—has the permission to—learn the Hawaiian language or work with the people. ("The 'haole' historians never bother to do so.") Similarly, in the second segment, the "can" in "a student can able to adopt different perspectives," when read in the context of the writer's discussion of the difficulties for "everyone to overcome" the "obstacle" of cultural rules and of her own experience of that difficulty, again foregrounds the role of external conditions and their effect on one's ability to do something. In that sense, this "can" is closer in meaning to the "may" in "I may conclude," a conclusion presented as depending more on the action of someone else than on the ability of the "I" drawing the conclusion. At the same time, this "can" is different from the "can" in the "I can say . . ." since the latter seems to depend on the ability of the speaker to name the situations as "obstacles" rather than on whether or not the speaker has permission to so name them.

In getting the class to enact a "close reading" of the two segments, I aim to shift attention to the relationship between a discursive form, "can able to," and the particular meanings it might be said to create in particular contexts.

As a result, a new question often surfaces: What kind of approach to "ability" is enacted by a speaker of idiomatic English who sees "can" and "be able to" as completely interchangeable in meaning? In exploring this question, students have mentioned popular sayings such as "if there is a will, there is a way"; TV shows such as *Mr. Rogers' Neighborhood* which teach viewers to believe "everyone is special," possessing unique qualities; and various discourses promoting the power of positive thinking. Students begin to perceive the way in which a common treatment of "can" and "to be able to" as interchangeable in meaning might be seen as contributing to a popular American attitude towards the transcendental power of the individual. Once we locate these conflicting approaches to the notion of ability, it becomes clear that the revision or "correction" of the "can able to" in these two segments can no longer take place simply at the level of linguistic form. It must also involve a writer's negotiating a position in relation to value systems with unequal social power in the U.S.: one "popular" and the others "alien," "dated," or "formal" but critical. Once this structural "error" is contextualized in conflicting attitudes towards a belief in the transcendental power of the individual, the issue can no longer be merely one's knowledge of or respect for the authorities of a dictionary English versus colloquial English, or one's competency in a particular language, but also one's alignment with competing discursive positions.

At this point, we will have mapped a contact zone with a range of choices and options both among linguistic forms and among discursive alignments. As we move on to the question of how each of us might revise these two segments, I would make sure that each student further enlarges this contact zone by taking into consideration the specific conditions of her or his life. I would have already introduced my definition of the "conditions of life" in previous assignments and class discussions, a definition that includes a whole range of discursive sites, including those of race, ethnicity, gender, sex, economic class, education, religion, region, recreation, and work. I also encourage each student to think about "life" in terms of the life she has lived in the past, is living in the present, and envisions for the future. Furthermore, I stress that decisions on how to revise should also be related to each student's interpretation(s) of the two texts discussed in the segments. To summarize, the contact zone in which the revision takes place would encompass the collision of at least the following voices: the voice of a "foreign" student writer (as constructed by the class at the beginning of the discussion), the voice(s) of the writer of the two segments (as constructed by the class discussion resulting from a "close reading" of the various uses of "can"), the voice of a dictionary, the voice of a speaker of idiomatic English, the voices important to the specific conditions of each student's life, the voice of a teacher, and the voice emerging from each student's interpretation of the two texts discussed in the two segments.

Since decisions on how to revise the "can able to" structure depend on who is present, the particular ways in which the discussion unfolds, and who is doing the revision, such decisions vary from class to class and student to student. To illustrate the unpredictability of the outcome, let me use two decisions made in two different courses, one by the original writer of the two segments and one by another student whose native language is also Chinese. Like all other students in my class, during the process of a "close reading" of the uses of "can" in these two segments, the original writer encountered a construction of her "voices" which she may not have fully considered before the discussion. Therefore, when revising the two segments, she too had to negotiate with these forms of reading and constructions of voices. Upon reflecting on the conditions of her life, she reviewed the attitude towards "ability" promoted in the particular neighborhood in Malaysia where she grew up. In view of that as well as of her own experience as a daughter (especially her difficulties persuading her parents to let her rather than only their sons go abroad for college), her current difficulty in adjusting to the kind of "critical thinking" promoted in my classroom (which she felt was the direct opposite of what she was told to do in her schooling back home), and her admiration of Trask's courage to "argue for her people," the writer decided to foreground the relationship between individual ability and the conditions in which that ability "may" be realized. With the help of her classmates, she came up with several options. One was to add an "if" clause to a sentence using "be able to." Another was to change "can able to" to "may be able to." One student suggested that she use "can able to" and then tag a sentence to explain her reasoning—her view of "ability." Among the suggestions, the writer picked "may be able to" because, as she put it, it was clearly "grammatically correct" and "says what I want to say." As the term progressed, one of the students in the class used "can able to" playfully in a class discussion, and others caught on. It became a newly coined phrase we shared throughout the term.

However, a Vietnamese American student whose home language is also Chinese took a very different stance towards the hegemonic attitude toward "ability" and for a quite different reason from what led some of my American-born students to identify with the voice of an idiomatic speaker. Using examples from his immigrant community, he argued for the importance of believing in the capacity of the individual. He pointed out that the emphasis on external conditions had made some people in his community fatalistic and afraid to take up the responsibility to make changes. According to him, there is a saying in classic Chinese similar to "if there is a will, there is a way." His parents used it repeatedly when lecturing him. So he was all for using "can" and "be able to" interchangeably to foreground the power of the individual. He hoped more people in his community would adopt this outlook. Accordingly, his revision changed "can able to" to "be able to." At the same time, he also changed the passive voice in the sentences referring to Trask's childhood and education in the first segment to the active voice, arguing that there is enough basis in the essays to sustain that reading.

Given the frequency with which students opt for the voices of academic authority, I used to wonder if this kind of teaching is driven more by my view of language as a site of struggle than by the needs of students eager to internalize and reproduce the conventions of academic discourse. My conclusion is: No, this process of negotiation is particularly meaningful for students anxious to master the codes of academic discourse, especially because their discursive practices are most likely to have to take place in the kind of postmodern capitalist world critics such as Fredric Jameson have characterized. Although the product, their decision to reproduce the code, might remain the same whether it is made with or without a process of negotiation, the activities leading to that decision, and thus its significance, are completely different. Without the negotiation, their choice would be resulting from an attempt to passively absorb and automatically reproduce a predetermined form. In such cases, the student would perceive different discourses, to borrow from Bakhtin, as belonging to different, fixed, and indisputable "chambers" in her consciousness and in society. And she would evaluate her progress by the automatism with which she was able to move in and out of these "chambers." If and when this student experienced some difficulty mastering a particular code, she would view it as a sign of her failure as a learner and writer.

On the other hand, if the student's decision to reproduce a code results from a process of negotiation, then she would have examined the conflict between the codes of Standard English and other discourses. And she would have deliberated not only on the social power of these colliding discourses but also on who she was, is, and aspires to be when making this decision. If the occasion arises in the future when she experiences difficulty in reproducing a particular code, as it very likely will, her reaction may be much more positive and constructive. Learning to work on style in the contact zone is also useful for those students interested in exploring ways of resisting the unifying force of "official" discourse. First, it can help students hear a range of choices and options beyond the confines of their immediate life. Second, negotiating as a group gives them the distance they need but might not have when dealing with their own writing in isolation. Therefore, devoting a few class periods to familiarizing students with this approach to style can be fruitful, especially if students are asked to theorize their action afterwards by reflecting on its strengths and limitations.

Obviously, one of the challenges for such a teaching method is that one can only project but not predict a class discussion on the basis of the chosen sample. In fact, life in the contact zone is by definition dynamic, heterogeneous, and volatile. Bewilderment and suffering as well as revelation and exhilaration are experienced by everyone, teacher and students, at different moments. No one is excluded, no one is safe (Pratt 39). Therefore, learning to become comfortable in making blunders is central to this type of teaching. In fact, there is no better way to teach students the importance of negotiation than by allowing them the opportunity to watch a teacher work her way through a chancy and volatile dialogue. Seemingly simple markers such as skin color, native tongue, ethnic heritage or nationality can neither prescribe nor pre-script the range of voices likely to surface. How to voice and talk to rather than speaking for or about the voices of the "other" within and among cultures is thus not a question which can be resolved prior to or outside of the process of negotiation. Rather, it must remain a concern guiding our action as we take part in it.

Needless to say, this type of teaching would work better when students are also asked to try the same method when analyzing the style of "real" writers so they understand that the "problems" they have with style are shared by all writers. For example, when students in a first-year writing course were reading Trask's essay "From a Native Daughter," I asked them to discuss or write about aspects of her style which seemed to deviate from the style of other historians they had encountered. Several students observed that the paragraphs in Trask's essay are shorter, including a series of one-sentence paragraphs with parallel structures of "And when they wrote . . . they meant . . ." (123–24). Others were struck by the opening of Trask's essay, where she addresses her audience directly and asks that they "greet each other in friendship and love." She tells many more personal stories and uses fewer references for support, and she uses the imagery of a lover to depict the role of language. I urged them to examine these stylistic features in relation to the particular stance Trask seems to have taken towards the conflict between "haole" (white) culture and the native Hawaiian culture. Having approached the writing of a "real" writer from the perspective of the relationship between meaning, form, and social identifications, students are likely to be more motivated in applying this perspective to their own style and its revision.

At the same time, using a student paper to enact a negotiation in the contact zone can create a sense of immediacy and a new level of meaningfulness about abstract concepts discussed or enacted in the assigned readings for students in "literature" and "critical theory" classes. For example, I have used the handout with the "can able to" construction in senior-level critical theory courses when discussing Bahktin's notion of "internal dialogism," Raymond Williams's concept of "structures of feeling," Cornel West's "prophetic critics and artists of color," and "dense" critiques of colonial discourse by such writers as Edward Said or Homi K. Bhabha. In the process of revising the "can able to" structure in the handout, in actively negotiating conflict in a contact zone, students in literature and cultural critical theory courses can gain a concrete opportunity to test the theories of various critics against their own practice. This type of activity reduces the "alienation" students often experience when asked to "do" theory. Testing theories against their own writing practices can also enable students to become more aware of the specific challenges such theories pose as well as the possibilities they open up for the individual writers committed to practicing these viewpoints. And I have used this method in upper-level literature courses when teaching such "borderland" literature as Sandra Cisneros's short story "Little Miracle, Kept Promises" or *Breaking Bread* by Cornel West and bell hooks. Reading and revising a student text, students can become more sensitive to the ways in which a "real" writer negotiates her way through contending discourses. At the same time, such reading and revision of their own writing allows students to enter into dialogue with "real" writers as "fellow travelers," active learners eager to compare and contrast one another's trials and triumphs.

One reaction to teaching style in the contact zone is fear that it will keep students from wanting to learn the conventions of academic discourse. My experience so far suggests that the unequal sociopolitical power of diverse discourses exerts real pressures on students' stylistic choices. After all, students choose to come to college, the choice of which speaks volumes on that power. The need to write for professors who grade with red pens circling all "errors" is also real for a majority of our students in most classrooms outside English departments. Therefore, although the process of negotiation encourages students to struggle with such unifying forces, it does not and cannot lead them to ignore and forget them. It acknowledges the writer's right and ability to experiment with innovative ways of deploying the codes taught in the classroom. It broadens students' sense of the range of options and choices facing a writer. But it does not choose for the students. Rather, it leaves them to choose in the context of the history, culture, and society in which they live.

NOTES

1. See Anderson, "An Apology for Crudity"; Kazin, *On Native Grounds*; and Mencken, "The Dreiser Bugaboo."

2. For an extended discussion of teaching editing that informs my own, see Horner, "Rethinking," especially pages 188–96.

WORKS CITED

Anderson, Sherwood. "An Apology for Crudity." *The Stature of Theodore Dreiser: A Critical Survey of the Man and His Work.* Ed. Alfred Kazin and Charles Shapiro. Bloomington: Indiana UP, 1965. 81–84.

Anzaldúa, Gloria. *Borderlands/La Frontera: The New Mestiza.* San Francisco: aunt lute, 1987.

Bakhtin, Mikhail. *The Dialogic Imagination.* Ed. Michael Holquist. Trans Caryl Emerson and Michael Holquist. Austin: U of Texas P, 1981.

Bartholomae, David. "The Tidy House: Basic Writing in the American Curriculum." *Journal of Basic Writing* 12 (1993): 4–21.

Dreiser, Theodore. *Dawn.* New York: Fawcett, 1931.

———. *Sister Carrie: The Pennsylvania Edition.* Philadelphia: U of Pennsylvania P. 1981.

Horner, Bruce. "Mapping Errors and Expectations for Basic Writing: From the 'Frontier Field' to 'Border Country.'" *English Education* 26 (1994): 29–51.

———. "Rethinking the 'Sociality' of Error: Teaching Editing as Negotiation." *Rhetoric Review* 11 (1992): 172–99.

Kazin, Alfred. *On Native Grounds: An Interpretation of Modern American Prose Literature.* New York: Harcourt, 1942.

Lu, Min-Zhan. "Conflict and Struggle: The Enemies or Preconditions of Basic Writing?" *College English* 54 (1992): 887–913.

Mencken, H. L. "The Dreiser Bugaboo." *Seven Arts* 2 (1917): 507–17.

Miller, Susan. *Textual Carnivals: The Politics of Composition.* Carbondale: Southern Illinois UP, 1991.

Pratt, Mary Louise. "Arts of the Contact Zone." *Profession* 91 (1991): 33–40.

Shaughnessy, Mina. *Errors and Expectations: A Guide for the Teacher of Basic Writing.* New York: Oxford UP, 1977.

Stein, Gertrude. *The Autobiography of Alice B. Toklas.* New York: Vintage, 1933.

Trask, Haunani-Kay. "From a Native Daughter." *Rereading America: Cultural Contexts for Critical Thinking and Writing.* 2nd ed. Ed. Gary Colombo, Robert Cullen, and Bonnie Lisle. Boston: Bedford, 1989. 118–27.

Traub, James. "P.C. vs. English: Back to Basic." *The New Republic* 8 Feb. 1993: 18–19.

West, Cornel. "The New Cultural Politics of Difference." *Out There: Marginalization and Contemporary Cultures.* Ed. Russel Ferguson, Martha Gever, Trinh T. Minh-Ha, and Cornel West. Cambridge, MA: MIT P, 1990. 19–36.

Acknowledgments: Earlier versions of this paper were delivered at the 1993 CCCC and at the University of Washington. My thanks go to the respondents in the audiences at both occasions. I am also grateful for comments on drafts of this piece from Elizabeth Robertson, Ira Shor, Anne Herrington, and James Seitz. Work on this essay was supported by a grant from the Drake University Center for the Humanities. And I offer special thanks to Bruce Horner for his contributions to the conception and revisions of this essay.

SECTION FIVE

Talking about Selves and Schools

On Voice, Voices, and Other Voices

Once we claim that all knowledge is socially constructed, imbricated in times and places and cultures, we are compelled to articulate those times and places and cultures. What is the academic discourse community? Is it as homogeneous as it appears? And if it is, what does that suggest—that there are cultures (which includes the cultures as defined by gender and sexual preferences) which are not part of, or at least not recognized by, the academic community? Who comprises the academic community? Who are its students? Each question generates another.

The first answer says, "Let's hear from the members of the community, its teachers and its students." The essay form returns to a central place in the curriculum, narrative discourse, the autobiographical. There was precedent. In the 1930s Fred Newton Scott of the University of Michigan advocated a writing instruction consisting of the relation between personal experience and the external world, an individual within society, a matter of civic responsibility. Scott's theory would regain popularity in the 1980s, though the curriculum would be associated with the Brazilian pedagogical theorist Paulo Freire rather than Scott, insofar as Freire adds an overtly political impetus to literacy and to writing from what one knows experientially.

When in the early 1970s the City University of New York opens its doors to any high school graduate wanting admission, the social and the political join the discussion on the value of narrative and the value of more conventional forms of academic discourse. With open admissions the colleges of the CUNY system were besieged by scores of students who would not have been able to attend college under older admissions policies. These were students—mainly from among the poor and mainly people of color—who believed themselves college material. And their college teachers agreed that these students were otherwise bright—except that the students' reading and writing abilities were so significantly lower than what would be necessary for success in college that, as we have seen, many came to believe that the students were victims of some sort of cognitive shortcoming.

The colleges were baffled. A new range of research was developed to confront and assist these "new" students, nontraditional students, remedial, developmental students. Finally, Mina Shaughnessy coins the term "basic writers," and in the first truly empathetic research work on basic writers, she looks to patterns of error in these students' writing, not cognitive dysfunction. This takes shape as *Errors and Expectations* (New York: Oxford UP, 1977).

But for all its sympathy, there are those who would go a step further, would try to understand the social processes that could relegate such a large number to the trouble-heap, a large number with two essential qualities in common—being poor and not being from the racial or ethnic majority. And in trying to understand, this newer line of scholarship tries to circumvent the reproduction of a school system that has traditionally failed to educate the woman, the poor, or the person of color at the same grade of efficiency as others. This gets complicated as rhetorical theory looks to how language is not just the conveyor of knowledge; language is the way knowledge becomes known.

Women show a way. They assert their role within the society at large and within the academy. The central role of women in composition studies makes feminist issues unignorable, with women making up the greater portion of the teaching force, with women playing key roles in developing contemporary composition, figures like Janet Emig, Mina Shaughnessy, Andrea Lunsford, to name too few. And given American feminism's turn to the autobiographical in its popular and its academic writing, composition's turn to narrative receives further reinforcement.

Others follow suit. In some sense, Richard Rodriguez's *Hunger of Memory* (New York: Bantam, 1983) opens the door, as he writes of his experiences in acquiring abilities in English literacy, the child of Mexican immigrants who becomes a doctoral candidate in British literature. Gloria Anzaldúa publishes *Borderlands/La Frontera* in 1987 (San Francisco: Aunt Lute), crossing ancient native languages, Spanish, English, and exploring matters of sexuality. Mike Rose, already a known figure in composition studies, writes in *Lives on the Boundary* (New York: Penguin, 1990) of his experiences as a working-class remedial student who eventually succeeds, thanks to some wonderful teachers. A year after Mike Rose's book, Keith Gilyard's *Voices of the Self* (Detroit: Wayne State UP, 1991) is released, the story of an African American growing up in New York. His is a story in multiple genres—autobiography and linguistic analysis of code switching in alternating chapters. Two years later, Victor Villanueva publishes *Bootstraps* (Urbana: NCTE, 1993), a mix of several genres including autobiography, now firmly located within rhetoric and composition studies. In 1994 bell hooks comes out with *Teaching to Transgress* (New York: Routledge). The concerns with "voice" that had arisen in the 1960s and 1970s thanks to pioneers like Ken Macrorie, Walker Gibson, Donald Murray, and especially Peter Elbow emerge in the writings of women and people of color. But what James Berlin had seen as a too-strong concern with individualism in these "expressionists" is responded to by the women and people of color writing critical autobiographies. The turn to autobiography becomes autobiography *as* social and political, with some asking if the political has any place in the composition classroom.

Democracy, Pedagogy, and the Personal Essay

Joel Haefner

Is the personal essay "democratic"?

Over the last several years, several writers have, overtly or covertly, made the assertion that it is. Chris Anderson, for example, claims that "The essay is fundamentally democratic. It enfranchises both the reader and the writer" ("Hearsay" 303). Anderson, along with writers like Graham Good, Dennis Rygiel, William Zeiger, and Kurt Spellmeyer, is attempting to claim a special epistemological role for the essay in American higher education because it is highly accessible as a model or as a vehicle for student writing. But these calls for reviving the personal essay in higher education carry a hidden agenda: to justify the personal essay as one of the privileged forms of discourse for American democracy and for the future of American society.

This pedagogical and critical project rests on several premises: that the essay is inherently formless, that it is accessible to a universal audience, that it uses common, referential language, and ultimately that it is grounded in the personal experience of the essayist. Behind these premises lies the shibboleth of individualism, and, concomitantly, the ideology of American democracy. But this distorts the adaptability of the essay for different writers and different audiences at different moments. As we interrogate our assumptions about the essay genre and its role in a "democratic" and "individualistic" pedagogy, we will find, I think, that it makes more sense to see the essay as a cultural product, as a special kind of collective discourse. Hence there is still a place for the "personal" essay in a collaborative pedagogy.

Reprinted from *College English* 54.2 (February 1992): 127–37. Used with permission.

I want to address first the question of whether the essay is truly formless and anti-systematic. One of Good's primary points in *The Observing Self: Rediscovering the Essay* is that the essay is not anti-empirical but anti-structural. Even Bacon's essays, Good claims, resist structure and logical method, and he claims that the "birth" of the genre with Montaigne was a reaction to the growing emphasis on method. Spellmeyer also argues, using Montaigne as his quintessential example, that "the form of the essay nonetheless demands a self-conscious formlessness, a con-vention through contravention" (263).

Not only does this strategy rely on dichotomies, it replaces one kind of structure—empiricism or interpretive method or rhetorical *dispositio*—with other structures, specifically structures of voice, audience, and space. R. Lane Kauffmann argues that the essay is methodical in its opposition to dogma, ideology, and method—"unmethodical method" is the oxymoron Kauffmann assigns to the essay genre. And just as importantly, this initial premise about the essay genre clearly links its "formlessness" with "freedom"—explicitly epistemological freedom, but implicitly political freedom, especially freedom of expression.

Both Good and Spellmeyer use what I call the "originative fallacy." Many speculations about the essay are based on the notion that the genre began with Montaigne, and that Montaigne's *Essais* imprinted the essential qualities of the genre. To base a theory of the genre on the conviction that the essay began with the Great Father, Montaigne, both commits the genre (and critical approaches to it) to radical individualism and to patriarchal myths of fathering and genesis (see, e.g., Haefner).

But the context in which essays are written *and* published affects the form and nature of the genre, and since those contexts change it is impossible to talk about an "essential" or "original" form of the essay. "Even 'informal' essays," cautions Douglas Hesse, "are historically situated and generically contextualized" (328). Montaigne and Bacon, for example, had no set limits on the length of their pieces, and so could vary that length at will. But since the essay genre was adopted by the periodical press, the length of essays has been circumscribed by economic and editorial factors. The organization of Hazlitt and De Quincey's essays was often a matter of pecuniary necessity, with quotations growing longer as they struggled to fill out their quota of pages before the printer's deadline. Essays, like periodicals, amalgamate a variety of forms (see Williams 214; Starobinski; Regosin; Cottrell). Several critics have pointed out that the essay has close affinities with earlier literary genres (see Auer). The essay is not anti-form, but synthesizes a diversity of forms.

Good, Spellmeyer, and others also argue, implicitly or explicitly, that the essay is accessible to any intelligent reader. If the essay is available to anyone who can read intelligently, then it is a kind of classless genre, an "egalitarian" mode. "The informal essay," Zeiger writes, "is well known and much beloved for its egalitarian spirit—the congeniality and deference of the writer toward both the topic and the reader" (236). This "egalitarian" approach to the essay parallels a supposed tenet of American democracy: equal access and opportunity for all, at least equal access based on liberal, humanistic knowledge.

The variety of forms operating in the essay may have something to do with the variety of published forums the essay has found. And these varied forums—from books to revised editions to general interest magazines to specialized magazines to newspapers—imply a spectrum of discourse groups, not a universal audience. It is difficult, then, to claim that the personal essay is "accessible" to almost any audience. In fact, the audiences involved in the writing of personal essays were restricted by a number of factors, chiefly economic means, educational level, occupation, interest, and available leisure time. Certainly, all writers construct fictive audiences, as Walter Ong has suggested, but essayists also work with given audiences, the readers of the periodical, even the "readers" who evaluate manuscripts at publishing houses.

In fact, the "universal" audiences claimed by many essayists and essay theorists are careful fictions that counterbalance the restrictive discourse communities that inform different essays. "The reader indeed—that great idea!—is very often a more important person towards the fortune of an essay than the writer," De Quincey wrote in 1839; he goes on to make it clear that "the reader" is a verbal construct, a "great noun-substantive" (250-52). Look, in addition, at the way in which Virginia Woolf fictionalizes her audience, the space of the essay, and the narrator's relationship with her readers in this passage from "The Modern Essay":

> It [the essay] should lay us under a spell with its first word, and we should only wake, refreshed with its last. In the interval we may pass through the most various experiences of amusement, surprise, interest, indignation; we may soar to the heights of fantasy with Lamb or plunge to the depths of wisdom with Bacon, but we must never be roused. The essay must lap us about and draw its curtain across the world. (216–17)

Even in terms of syntax and lexicon, Woolf presumes her readers possess performative linguistic skills, a presumption that undermines the idea of a "common" reader. Audience is constructed; narrator is constructed; even the space of the essay is carefully constructed to promote the fictions of intimacy, of confession, and of the writing closet. The scene of the essay is as much a myth of individualism as the myth of the writer's garret, as Linda Brodkey observes (396–98).

These issues of audience and the "scene" of the personal essay are intertwined with the premise that the personal essay uses "common" language. Good employs a strategy of discriminating between the subjective skepticism presented in the personal essay and the "objective" skepticism represented by poststructuralism and textuality (180–81). Good, Anderson, and others are confronted with a paradox: how can we claim universal knowledge and common language for the essay when we presume the essay is personal and limited to the vision of a specific writer?

We can also argue that language is deeply embedded in discourse communities, is often non-referential, and is communal, not individualistic, at base, an argument that Susan Miller makes in response to Spellmeyer. As David Bleich observes:

> In psychology, biology, and chemistry/physics, respectively, the idea of the origin of knowledge in individuals has been gradually replaced by the belief in its origins in groups, in history, and in social purposes. The role of language is fundamental in all. But this sense of "language" is no longer familiar: it is not a code or a self-enclosed system of rules and words, or any other entity that is separable from the social interests and collective experiences that emerge in public as language initiatives. (39)

If the self is not unitary, if language is not based on individual knowledge but on collective experience, then the referentiality of personal, expressive prose is called into question, and the accessibility of the personal essay to a universal readership that shares "human experience" is also in doubt.

The linchpin for all these recent arguments for the revival of the essay remains the idea that the essay presents individualistic, "personal" knowledge. According to Good, "The essayist's personality is offered as a 'universal particular,' an example not of a particular virtue or vice, but of an 'actually existing' individual and the unorganized 'wholeness' of his experience" (8). The problem raised here reflects what Terry Eagleton calls the "humanistic fallacy," "the naive notion that a literary text is just a kind of transcript of the living voice of a real man or woman addressing us" (120).

Few of these recent theorists of the essay take the argument to its logical conclusion: that the personal essay, individualistic and democratic *in radix*, is opposed to the discourse of Marxism. But Good does make the point explicit: the resistance of the essay to system and dogma means that it resists, not only existentialism and poststructuralism, but Marxism and religion as well. "The essay," he writes, "must obviously be at odds to some extent with Marxism and religion in that both the latter approach phenomena in the light of accepted principles or articles of faith, where the essay works from particular phenomenon outwards (and not very far outwards)" (25). If we allow Good's dichotomy between deduction and induction to stand, then the conclusion is inescapable: the essay is an essential tool for Western democracy. Indeed, that is the note with which he ends his book:

> The essay is neither an elite form nor a mass form, and when it treats those forms it is generally critical of both. It is a democratic form, open to any-one who can see clearly and think independently. As such it is vital to our educational, cultural, and political health. (186)

The linking of Good's adjectives—educational, cultural, and political—and his medical metaphor make my point clear. The essay, as interpreted by these writers, is not simply a form of expressive discourse, but an essential element in the perpetuation of epistemological, cultural, and above all, political traditions. To admit this interpretation of the essay genre is to confirm the "health" and well-being of our educational system, Western culture, and democracy; to affirm other interpretations introduces the question of disease. But how well does this pathology of the essay match the realities of the genre, and what does it mean for American pedagogy?

Questioning the assumptions that the personal essay is individualistic, accessible, and ultimately democratic must lead us to scrutinize the pedagogy that valorizes this kind of discourse. As both James Berlin and Robert J. Connors have noted, the development of textbooks that used personal essays as models was an outgrowth of what Berlin calls "expressionistic rhetoric" (Berlin 62; Connors 177). By the 1920s, exploring students' experiences and cultivating their personalities were the explicit goals of most composition readers and remain the premise underlying many contemporary anthologies. Under the influence of John Dewey the coupling of expressive rhetoric, the imprinting of democratic progressivism, and the personal essay became universal. "The very idea of education," Dewey wrote, is "a freeing of individual capacity in a progressive growth directed to social aims" (98). As Karen Burke LeFevre points out, "radical individualism" has permeated our pedagogy, rhetoric, and politics, and we need to be aware of that pervasiveness. One symptom of that pervasiveness is the use of the personal essay—interpreted as subjective, "personal" discourse—in writing textbooks, composition curricula, and in the recent theoretical statements I have been scrutinizing here.

Hence even as composition pedagogy disposed of the notion of writing as product and embraced the paradigm of writing as process, the personal essay was still a useful tool in propagating the myth of writing as individualistic expression. It is in the last six or seven years, when Cooper, Brodkey, Burke, LeFevre, and others anatomized the unicentric basis of composition theory that writers like Spellmeyer, Anderson, and Good have felt the need to defend the subjective, individualistic, democratic qualities of the personal essay.

Frederic Jameson has pointed out that genre and form function as "ideograms," encoded systems of ideology (6). Most significantly for our purposes here, in analyzing Adorno's essays, Jameson sees the fragmentation and indirection of the essay genre *not* as the mimesis of an individual writer's associative mental process, but as the linguistic representation of the dialectical process (52–53). Even if we grant that the essay genre has been imprinted with the ideology of bourgeois capitalism, that does not imply that our pedagogy needs to reaffirm that ideology, or that our interpretive strategies toward the genre are also constricted by the same ideology. I would challenge the notion that the essay genre is necessarily middle-class at base. After all, essayists and their audiences can range from Bacon's aristocracy to Alice Walker's rural African-American culture. Thanks to the diversity of the genre, essays are continually being "remade" by different communities at different points of time, with new textual elements and traditions added, deleted, modified.

The point is that the essay is not inherently individualistic and subjective, and hence that its only place in composition pedagogy is as a model of "writer-based prose." In fact, there is no evidence that using personal essays as expressive discourse does promote a spirit of democracy or egalitarianism in the writing or literature classroom. Students may find some topics that speak directly to them, but the personal essay often remains alien, a species of discourse imposed by the institution. What matters is what uses we make of the essay in our courses, the nature of our pedagogical assumptions.

If our pedagogy asserts that the personal essay is intrinsically "democratic," then we had better define just what we mean by "democracy." The unstated assumption is that we mean American, capitalistic, individualistic democracy. In light of the evolution of political systems around the world, that easy assumption becomes increasingly problematic, especially when we are talking about pedagogy and the social utility of education. So one of our first steps must be to either free ourselves of the ideological burden of calling personal essays "democratic," or at the very least define what that adjective means.

A second pedagogical step in dealing with the issues I raise here is to question the whole notion of the social performance of higher education.

And traditionally in the United States the notions of social performance and democracy have been inextricably linked. Almost every college mission statement implies this connection: the duty of a university is to promote rationality which promotes intellectual freedom which promotes democracy. Look, for example, at a draft of a "Philosophy of University Studies" proposed at my institution:

> Historically, education has always been charged with civic obligations. Freedom without enlightenment could not and will not long endure. The best safeguard of democracy, the key to its life, lies in the people themselves, specifically in their rational, intellectual empowerment. (10)

I am not claiming that we should not be making these connections and assertions. What I am suggesting is that we need to be aware that such premises affect everyday decisions we make in the classroom and the texts and methods we select for our classes, and that those premises need to be articulated and continually questioned.

My critique of the common critical approach to the essay and the pedagogy that has accommodated that approach may seem to imply that I see no role for the personal essay in the composition or literature classroom. Actually, I enjoy personal essays too much, and find them too useful in teaching, to banish them, and I would also argue that the greater variety of discourse forms our students explore the better. I also realize that personal essays are too deeply embedded in educational institutions and the publishing industry to be easily extricated. If, as Robert Scholes suggests, "the whole naive epistemology" that "a complete self confronts a solid world, perceiving it directly and accurately, always capable of capturing it perfectly" is now "lying in ruins around us" (655), then we need to find a new pedagogy that can still make use of the personal essay. Ultimately what my critique suggests is a pedagogy that attempts to balance the individualistic, expressive view of knowledge with a social, collective perspective.

The best answer at the moment, it seems to me, is to bring the personal essay into the collaborative writing project. At first glance this seems like an impossible task: how could one reconcile a form that typically uses the first-person singular pronoun with group production? This problem confronts any advocate of collaborative writing, most recently Lisa Ede and Andrea Lunsford, who write that their research "has led us not to assent to the 'death of the author' but to try to conceive new and more expansive ways of experiencing and representing authorship" (131).

Ede and Lunsford identify two major pitfalls for collaborative writing pedagogy: that collaborative writing remains largely based on a notion of individualistic authorship, and that texts written in groups will be hierarchical, authoritative, consensual, masculine, and product-oriented (112–36). They find the former problem in the work of Peter Elbow and the early writings of Kenneth Bruffee, and indeed this is common practice. We have students write and read personal essays within the framework of a cognitive composition process, and collaborative work is limited to the invention and revising, but not the drafting, stages. When collaborative work is practiced at all stages of the composing process, students typically generate—and are asked to generate—what Ede and Lunsford call "hierarchical" texts, texts which are "rigidly structured, driven by highly specified goals, and carried out by people playing clearly defined and delimited roles" (133). The usual model for these texts are committee reports drawn from business or academic administration, and most of us would not call these "personal essays" at all. In fact, they are articles, reports, arguments that have been traditionally contrasted to the personal essay.

I want to suggest three ways in which the personal essay can be integrated into a collaborative writing pedagogy. First, by asking students to reconstruct the cultural context in which personal essays are written. Second, by urging students to test the *ethos* of the rhetorical situation, by challenging the unity of the first-person narrator that is a hallmark of the personal essay. Third, by asking students to examine for themselves the place of the personal essay in the university curriculum. Like Ede and Lunsford, I am not going to lay down rules and laws for such a pedagogy; to do so would be to lapse back into a sense of *author*ity which my preceding critique has questioned. And I am not arguing the personal essay as a panacea for our pedagogical conundrums. But I do think there are ways to continue to use the genre in the classroom, and I hope these ideas begin a dialogue that will lead to more possibilities.

To return to my first point: I hardly need to recapitulate the demands for the re-contextualization of the literary text in our classes that have been voiced by feminists, New Historicists, cultural critics, structuralists, reader-response theorists, and others. But it seems clear that the paradigm of the isolated text is as limiting as the myth of the isolated writer, and in fact the two are linked through an aesthetics of expressive referentiality. The first step in re-constructing the personal essay as something other than "one man's meat" (to borrow E. B. White's title) must be teaching the "cultural text," as Gerald Graff calls it. "If there is any point of agreement" among literary theorists today, Graff claims, "it is on the principle that texts are not, after all, autonomous and self-contained, that the meaning of any text . . . depends . . . on other texts and textualized frames of reference" (256). Pursuing a dialogic pedagogy, Graff writes that "the unit of study should cease to be the isolated text (or author) and become the virtual space or cultural conversation that the text presupposes" (257).

One of our first aims, then, is to present the "cultural text" of a personal essay to our students. This means, in practice, drawing together earlier essays, other works by the essayist, the essayist's biography, newspaper accounts, movies, music, art, politics—whatever illuminated and broadened the context of the essay. For example, an examination of Lamb's "The Old South-Sea House" might involve not only other Elian essays but the works, letters, and recorded conversations of his circle, the political climate of the Regency, the economic fortunes of the British Empire, Lamb's personal life, ballads, pictures, and so forth. Another example: a class reading an essay from Joan Didion's *Slouching Towards Bethlehem* might explore Didion's life, pop music, war and protest, television—in short, the culture of California—in trying to grasp the full context of a particular essay.

My second point in a new pedagogical approach is more profoundly tied to the personal essay genre and to the critique I have advanced. We can perhaps most effectively challenge the whole idea of singular authorship by stretching the limits of the first-person pronoun, the "I" narrative strategy composition classes have followed in expressive, writer-based instruction. The sanctity of the "I" and the assumption that the persona of the personal essay *is* the writer herself could be challenged in a number of ways: by having writing groups create a personal essay that purports to be the work of a single author; by encouraging individual students to write a personal essay using "we"; by having teams re-write personal essays from other singular viewpoints—say, Didion's "Some Dreamers of the Golden Dream" rewritten from the persona of a Latina woman. A critique or review of the process of composing as a group behind the fiction of a singular author would be an essential part of any such project.

Both in terms of composition theory and the nature of the personal essay that I have advanced here, this is not a radical departure. Rhetoricians have long focused on the nature of the speaker's *ethos*, and there have been practical applications for the composition classroom, as in Walker Gibson's valuable *Persona: A Style Study for Readers and Writers*. But the assumption is almost always that a single author will don a variety of masks, not that a group of writers will be speaking from a single persona or many singular personae. The *Tatler* and *Spectator* papers, after all, featured several writers composing behind a singular persona.

The personal persona could be destabilized further by encouraging students not to create a unified, coherent first-persona singular voice, but rather a mix of "I" speakers. Annie Dillard achieves something like this in many of her essays. Ede and Lunsford might call this kind of collaborative writing dialogic, and given the variety of forms and audiences that the essay genre has accommodated, I think the personal essay is particularly well suited to this pedagogy.

We need to be very careful, however, about how we use the notion of dialogism in our pedagogies. Spellmeyer, for example, stresses the dialogic nature and potentials of the essay in interaction with student writers/readers. I feel he misreads Bakhtin, limiting dialogism to exchanges between individuals, not social groups. Bakhtin claimed that the novel "and those artistic-prose genres that gravitate towards it" (implicitly including the essay) organize "a diversity of social speech types" on "socio-ideological languages" that comprise "heteroglossia"; individual voices are bearers of those social speech types, not vice versa. Thomas E. Recchio explores the application of Bakhtinian dialogism to the essay genre thoroughly and suggests (like Spellmeyer, in my opinion) that the essay is essentially subjective but ameliorated by the concept of social dialogue. In her address to the 1989 CCCC Meeting, Andrea Lunsford cited Bakhtin as a model for composition pedagogy and research. Despite the fact that Lunsford extols collaborative writing as a vital new direction for composition, she nevertheless asserts that "writing was necessary for the invention of the self . . . [and] the reification of that self in the Romantic 'author,' and its crossing to America as rugged individualism, self-reliance, and intellectual property . . ." (73). And that premise leads her to the conclusion that composition teachers are "radically democratic" (76).

That brings me to my last point in a pedagogy that attempts to re-situate the personal essay: let the students—collaboratively or individually—address the issue of the personal essay and its place in the curriculum. Let them explore and debate the issues of individualism and collectivism which have informed our recent re-evaluations of the personal essay. At the end of *Professing Literature*, Graff quotes James Kincaid's vision of an ideal literature course, one where we "teach not the texts themselves but how we situate ourselves in reference to those texts" (262). We can use personal essays to raise important questions with our students about the nature of knowledge and education. We can ask them: What is a personal essay? What makes it "personal"? Does it have any role in a writing class? Why are personal essays so widely used in writing classes?

We would probably not get a clear consensus from our students on these questions, and that is all to the good. As several writers have pointed out, much work in collaborative writing relies on the idea of consensus—that the group writing or the group being written to is a unit, a community without difference or dissent. Bruffee asks us to quit assuming that people write "to enhance their own individuality" and instead assume "that people write in order to be accepted, to join, to be regarded as another member of the culture or community that constitutes the writer's audience" (651). It would not be difficult, if one valorized the idea of consensus within the collaborative project, as Bruffee does here, to argue that this pedagogy is indeed "democratic." And it would not be difficult to fit the personal essay into this kind of pedagogy. But we may not want to privilege consensus in our pedagogy, nor will our students' best writing necessarily grow out of consensus.

The issue of consensus brings us back to our starting point: is the essay intrinsically democratic? Only if we confirm that the essay conveys personal, subjective knowledge, that it inscribes the self and that it is accessible to all. Is the personal essay even at base personal and subjective, as Good and others claim? Not necessarily. We can construe the essay as intrinsically collaborative; even when essays are written by what Cooper calls "the solitary author" those essays were often a collaborative effort. We could explore the ways in which readership shaped particular essays and was constructed by essayists. And we could use those insights to help student groups generate essays that are collaborative and "dialogic," that take into account actual and fictionalized audiences, that construct a kind of knowledge that is not limited to individual experience and that is not simply an adjunct to the proselytization of American democracy. If we do not, we may, as Hesse writes, "insulate students from vital questions about relationships among language, individualism, and discursive formation" (324).

What I have been trying to highlight here is that the conventional wisdom for both literary critics and composition pedagogues affirms the ideologies of individualism and "democracy," and that we need to be aware of and examine those premises. I am not arguing that "democracy" should be replaced with some other political ideology, or that we should try to generate a pedagogy that is apolitical. Indeed, the latter is impossible, the former probably impractical. Ohmann and Cooper, among others, have pointed out that a pedagogy that is not "inner-directed" (Patricia Bizzell's term) or individualistic usually collides with vast institutional conventions, like grading. But teachers of composition and literature should, I think, know and discuss the kinds of ideology genre bears, and our appropriations of the personal essay are a good case in point.

WORKS CITED

Anderson, Chris. "Hearsay Evidence and Second-Class Citizenship." *College English* 50 (1988): 300–08.

———, ed. *Literary Nonfiction: Theory, Criticism, Pedagogy.* Carbondale: Southern Illinois UP, 1989.

Auer, Annemarie. *Ein Essay ueber den Essay.* Halle: Mitteldeutscher Verlag, 1974.

Bakhtin, M. M. *The Dialogic Imagination: Four Essays.* Trans. Caryl Emerson and Michael Holquist. Austin: U of Texas P, 1981.

Berlin, James A. *Rhetoric and Reality: Writing Instruction in American Colleges, 1900–1985.* Carbondale: Southern Illinois UP, 1987.

Bleich, David. *The Double Perspective: Language, Literacy, and Social Relations.* New York: Oxford UP, 1988.

Brodkey, Linda. "Modernism and the Scene(s) of Writing." *College English* 49 (1987): 396–418.

Bruffee, Kenneth. "Collaborative Writing and the 'Conversation of Mankind.'" *College English* 46 (1984): 635–52.

Butrym, Alexander J., ed. *Essays on the Essay: Redefining the Genre.* Athens: U of Georgia P, 1989.

Connors, Robert J. "Personal Writing Assignments." *College Composition and Communication* 39 (1987): 166–83.

Cooper, Marilyn M., and Michael Holzman. *Writing as Social Action.* Portsmouth, NH: Boynton/Cook, 1989.

Core, George. "Stretching the Limits of the Essay." Butrym 207–20.

Cottrell, Robert D. *Sexuality/Textuality: A Study of the Fabric of Montaigne's Essais.* Columbus: Ohio State UP, 1981.

De Quincey, Thomas. *De Quincey as Critic.* Ed. John E. Jordan. London: Routledge, 1973.

Dewey, John. *Democracy and Education.* New York: Free Press, 1944.

Eagleton, Terry. *Literary Theory: An Introduction.* Minneapolis: U of Minnesota P, 1983.

Ede, Lisa, and Andrea Lunsford. *Singular Texts/Plural Authors: Perspectives on Collaborative Writing.* Carbondale: Southern Illinois UP, 1990.

Gibson, Walker. *Persona: A Style Study for Readers and Writers.* New York: Random, 1969.

Good, Graham. *The Observing Self: Rediscovering the Essay.* London: Routledge, 1988.

Graff, Gerald. *Professing Literature: An Institutional History.* Chicago: U of Chicago P, 1987.

Haefner, Joel. "Unfathering the Essay: Resistance and Intergenerality in the Essay Genre." *Prose Studies* 12 (1989): 259–73.

Hesse, Douglas. "The Recent Rise of Literary Nonfiction: A Cautionary Assay." *Journal of Advanced Composition* 11 (1991): 323–33.

Jameson, Frederic. *Marxism and Form: Twentieth-Century Dialectical Theories of Literature.* Princeton: Princeton UP, 1971.

Kauffmann, R. Lane. "The Skewed Path: Essaying as Unmethodical Method." Butrym 221–40.

LeFevre, Karen Burke. *Invention as a Social Act.* Carbondale: Southern Illinois UP, 1987.

Lunsford, Andrea A. "Composing Ourselves: Politics, Commitment, and the Teaching of Writing." *College Composition and Communication* 41 (1990): 71–82.

Miller, Susan. "Comment on 'A Common Ground: The Essay in Academe.'" *College English* 52 (1990): 330–34.

Ong, Walter J. "The Writer's Audience Is Always a Fiction." *PMLA* 90 (1975): 9–21.

"Philosophy of University Studies at Illinois State University." Draft. University Studies Review Committee. Normal, IL. October, 1990.

Recchio, Thomas E. "A Dialogic Approach to the Essay." Butrym 271–88.

Regosin, Richard L. *"The Matter of My Book": Montaigne's Essais as the Book of the Self.* Berkeley: U of California P, 1977.

Reither, James A., and Douglas Vipond. "Writing as Collaboration." *College English* 51 (1989): 855–67.

Rygiel, Dennis. "On the Neglect of Twentieth-Century Nonfiction: A Writing Teacher's View." *College English* 46 (1984): 392–400.

Scholes, Robert. "Is There a Fish in this Text?" *College English* 46 (1984): 653–64.

Spellmeyer, Kurt. "A Common Ground: The Essay in the Academy." *College English* 51 (1989): 262–76. (Rpt. in Butrym 253–70.)

Starobinski, Jean. "'This Mask Torn Away.'" *Michel de Montaigne's Essays.* Ed. Harold Bloom. New York: Chelsea, 1987. 97–118.

Williams, Raymond. *The Long Revolution.* New York: Penguin, 1961.

Woolf, Virginia. *The Common Reader.* New York: Harcourt, 1925.

Zeiger, William. "The Personal Essay and Egalitarian Rhetoric." Anderson, *Literary Nonfiction* 235–44.

Beyond the Personal

Theorizing a Politics of Location in Composition Research

GESA E. KIRSCH AND JOY S. RITCHIE

In recent years, feminist scholarship has begun to inform much research in composition studies. One particular emphasis has been on admitting the "personal" into our public discourse, on locating ourselves and research participants in our research studies. In what Adrienne Rich calls "a politics of location," theorizing begins with the material, not transcending the personal, but claiming it. The goal is, Rich says in an echo of Hélène Cixous, "to reconnect our thinking and speaking with the body of this particular living human individual, a woman" (213).[1] This new emphasis on the personal, on validating experience as a source of knowledge, raises a number of recurring questions: How does a politics of location inform—and change—research practices? How do we both affirm the importance of "location," and yet understand the limitations of our ability to locate ourselves and others? How do issues of power, gender, race, and class shape a politics of location? What ethical principles are consistent with feminist scholarship and can guide researchers? Although these questions are clearly important in feminist scholarship, they are not merely feminist issues. They mark an important point where feminist theories can inform composition studies. And although we believe women's experiences are an important starting point for research because they have been ignored and omitted in studies of many kinds, we also believe that what can be learned from women's experiences

Reprinted from *College Composition and Communication* 46.1 (February 1995): 7–29. Used with permission.

and from feminist theory has wider implications for composition research; it can become a location for reconsidering what counts as knowledge and for revitalizing research in composition.

In this article, we begin by examining what it means to bring a politics of location to composition research and by foregrounding some of the difficulties of assuming that perspective. We argue that it is not enough to claim the personal and locate ourselves in our scholarship and research. In doing so, we risk creating another set of "master narratives," risk speaking for and essentializing others, and risk being blinded by our own culturally determined world views. Instead, we propose that composition researchers theorize their locations by examining their experiences as reflections of ideology and culture, by reinterpreting their own experiences through the eyes of others, and by recognizing their own split selves, their multiple and often unknowable identities. Further, we propose changes in research practices, such as collaborating with participants in the development of research questions, the interpretation of data at both the descriptive and interpretive levels, and the writing of research reports. Finally, we raise ethical questions that arise from these new research practices. We illustrate our argument with examples drawn from composition, including our own research, but also from scholarship in anthropology, oral history, and sociology. Scholars in those fields have a long history of using ethnomethodological research, have reflected on the role of the personal in research, and have encountered a range of ethical dilemmas.

A POLITICS OF LOCATION
IN FEMINIST RESEARCH

We begin this essay by locating ourselves in this writing, although we recognize that any location is fluid, multiple, and illusive. The impulse to write this article came from a day-long conversation among several women during a workshop on feminism and composition at the 1992 CCCC.[2] These women, though mostly tenured and tenure-tracked and with successful teaching and publication records, were nevertheless frustrated because of the conflicts they experience as feminists in composition living in English departments. The issues we talked about that day suggested that we have been taught to devalue our own experiences as researchers and writers, our relationships with students and other teachers, and our own histories as sources for research and scholarship. As a result, we have often stripped the personal from our writing and research.

As we continued to think about the conflicts women expressed in that group, we began to realize that in part, these conflicts arise from our varied and shifting locations in our discipline, particularly from attempts to hold feminist values and to focus on issues of gender in research, while we still accept the existing epistemologies and methodologies in the field—methodologies that often presuppose objectivity and gender-neutrality. We recognize this tension in our own research. Instead of working to question, resist, and transform traditional research practices, we often find ourselves attempting to live within the contradictions between our feminist beliefs and those traditionally valued in our discipline, even as we write this essay. As we explored these contradictions, we found that many feminists in other disciplines have already begun this work.

We believe researchers in composition must engage in the same kinds of discussions that feminist researchers are having in other disciplines concerning the "politics of location" in research. We hope to advance that discussion by presenting some of the feminist critiques of philosophical, methodological, and ethical assumptions underlying traditional research. In doing so we assert the importance of interrogating the motives for our research and the unspoken power relationships with the "subjects" of our research, considerations we hope will assist us in developing a more ethical approach to research.[3]

If we are to move beyond what Sandra Harding calls an "add women and stir" approach to research (*Feminism* 3), we need to examine just what a politics of location means for research, what are its implications and its limitations. How might we achieve a more problematized politics of location? Rich says that we can no longer utter phrases like "women always. . . ." Instead, she argues: "If we have learned anything in these years of late twentieth-century feminism, it's that that 'always' blots out what we really need to know: When, where, and under what conditions has the statement been true" (214)? But Rich does not suggest that research simply needs to provide the ethnographer's "thick descriptions" of context or to engage in superficial reflexivity. It is not enough to make the facile statements that often occur at the beginning of research articles, to say, "I am a white, middle-class woman from a Midwestern university doing research." She urges women to investigate what has shaped their own perspectives and acknowledge what is contradictory, and perhaps unknowable, in that experience.

In addition to acknowledging our multiple positions, a politics of location must engage us in a rigorous ongoing exploration of *how* we do our research: What assumptions underlie our approaches to research and methodologies? And a politics of location must challenge our conception of *who* we are in our work: How are our conflicting positions, histories, and desires for power implicated in our research questions, methodologies, and conclusions? A politics of location allows us to claim the legitimacy of our experience, but it must be accompanied by a rigorously reflexive examination of ourselves as researchers that is as careful as our observation of the object of our inquiry (Harding, *Whose Science?* 149–50, 161–63). Thus, for example, researchers need to acknowledge the way race (and for most composition scholars this means examining their whiteness), social class, and other circumstances have structured their own thinking and how that, in turn, has shaped their own questions and interpretations. Rich observes: "Marginalized though we have been as women, as white and Western makers of theory, we also marginalize others because our lived experience is thoughtlessly white, because even our 'women's cultures' are rooted in some Western tradition" (219).

Finally, a postmodern feminist perspective leads us to continually question our ability to locate ourselves as researchers and to locate the participants in our research. We need to take into account what psychoanalytic, hermeneutic, and postmodern critics have already shown us about the limitations of our ability to fully understand our own motivations and perspectives. These scholars remind us that we can never fully step outside our culture in order to examine our assumptions, values, and goals. Pretending to do so amounts to what Stanley Fish calls the "theory hope of antifoundationalism" (qtd. in Bizzell 40), the belief that although we reject foundational truth as the basis of knowledge, we can nevertheless use critical analysis to interrogate the historical, political, and social contexts of our knowledge. But, as Fish reminds us, no attempt at analyzing our assumptions is neutral or value-free; it is always a culturally and politically charged activity.

This problematized "politics of location" may seem to make our task impossible; it may make us wonder if we can claim anything for our research. But instead of falling into inaction and despair, we move forward with the awareness that we can only approximate an understanding, noticing the multiple and contradictory positions researchers and participants occupy, complicating and politicizing our investigation, valuing the individual and the local, although we can never hope to understand them fully. We move forward with a willingness to pursue the difficulties inherent in a politics of location accompanied by an equal willingness to be unrelentingly self-reflective.

THE RISK OF ESSENTIALISM

While locating research questions in ourselves and our own experience is vital, it also creates unsettling problems and possibilities for the way we think about knowledge, authority, and power. Feminists have rightly challenged the claims to objectivity in traditional research, arguing that inattention to the researcher's location and subjectivity has led to what Donna Haraway calls the "god trick," researchers' false claims to an ahistorical and universal perspective that has caused gross omissions and erasures in claims of knowledge (qtd. in Harding, *Whose Science?* 153). But feminist theorists have also argued against the uncritical celebration of female experience situated in a fixed or "natural" female identity (Ritchie 255). In fact, it would be dangerous for women, as Teresa Ebert argues, to invest so much in the "local," the individual, the unique, that we forget the global power structures that oppress women (902).

It is not enough, then, to begin locating ourselves and our experiences. In doing so naively, we risk ignoring hierarchies and creating the same unifying and totalizing master narratives that feminist scholars have sought to revise and oppose. More specifically, we risk defining gender biologically rather than recognizing it as a varied set of social relationships. We risk limiting our definitions to a binary of male and female as opposite, inherently different human beings, without seeing the multiple permutations of gendered experience. Jane Flax argues that this will prevent us from adequately asking and answering the questions we need to articulate in order to understand how both men and women are affected by cultural contexts (*Thinking Fragments* 182).

In composition studies we risk making essentializing distinctions about writers: If they are male they must write or think *this* way; if they are female, they must write or think another. New research on gender and writing has made important contributions to composition studies and moved the field from being "gender-blind to [being] gender-sensitive" (Peaden 260), but there remains the tendency to polarize—to essentialize—accounts of gender differences.[4] Don Kraemer suggests that in considering gender and language we look at the "range of social relations they imply" rather than read gender as "one monolithic language" (328). We argue that composition researchers need to resist the drive to generalize about men and women, that we can learn much from studying the multiple ways in which both men and women can express themselves, and that composition teachers need to develop pedagogical practices that encourage students to write in a wide variety of discourse forms, a task that Lillian Bridwell-Bowles has begun to map out successfully in "Discourse and Diversity."

Claiming our experience, then, may be as inadequate for making claims to knowledge as traditional claims from objectivity are. Harding points out that "our experience may lie to us" just as it has lied to male researchers who believed their positions were value-free or universal (*Whose Science?* 286). A number of African American, lesbian, and third world feminists, including bell hooks, have argued that simply privileging our experience may lead us to posit rigid and exclusionary definitions of experience that erase the interlocking structures of race, social class, and heterosexist oppression for men and women ("Feminist Politicization" 107–08). The result is that we create definitions of experience that produce dominant group "common-sense" norms so exclusive that the experience of nonwhite, nondominant people is eliminated, while dominant gender, class, race, and sexuality produce more airtight, fastened down, comprehensive theories. Sidonie Smith observes that feminist researchers "from the dominant culture" can easily appropriate the experiences of others if they are "unselfconscious about the possibility of such cultural appropriation" (401). Consider, for example, the experience that taught one of us (Ritchie) about the problems of cultural appropriation and representation.

Joy Ritchie: As I observed the writing of two women students in an advanced composition class—Manjit Kaur, a Punjabi from Malaysia and BeeTin Choo, a Chinese woman from Singapore—I was struck by the rich and contradictory construction of selfhood in their writing. When I decided to report on their writing, I quickly recognized the political and ethical problems involved in writing *about* them, speaking *for* them, or attempting to represent their experiences. Instead, I invited them to co-author an article, thinking that allowing them to speak for themselves would help me avoid appropriating their writing for my purposes. But I discovered that we still faced many difficult decisions because of the complexity and multiplicity of each of our identities and motivations, most obviously because of our cultural differences, because of the complex power relations between students and professor, and because of the constraints of academic writing. For example, during the time we were writing our essay, after our proposal had been accepted by the editors, BeeTin became increasingly committed to a Christian perspective and was, therefore, uncomfortable with the feminist theoretical framework the other two of us favored. Both women were concerned particularly that their representations of their cultures, written in the relative safety of a classroom, would be misinterpreted by readers and used to solidify existing negative stereotypes of their culture. Whose theory, whose language, whose interpretation, and whose narrative voice would prevail? We had to negotiate these and other questions. I drafted the introduction and conclusion for the essay because I felt some responsibility for ensuring coherence among our three distinct voices, but I struggled, without complete success, to minimize the dominance of my narrative voice.

In a continuing dialogue as we wrote together, I learned more about the way my own cultural context constrained my perspective and often caused me to objectify "others." First, I had to recognize that my assumptions about international students and "Asian women students" led to limited and essentialized understanding of their lives as students, as women, and as writers. BeeTin's silence was not Asian acquiescence to authority; it was a form of resistance. Manjit's exploration of the roles of women in Malaysia and in the United States did not necessarily fit within my western feminist assumptions about women's oppression. I realized that I set apart Manjit and BeeTin as essentialized "others" as I sought to define their voices and to analyze the style, form, and rhetorical features of their writing according to my own training in rhetoric. Although we finished the article, we considered abandoning it at several points because each of us felt at least slightly compromised in the essay that resulted (Ritchie, Kaur, Choo Meyer).

If researchers are to preserve the value of experience as a source of knowledge, they need to locate the experience of others, especially those previously excluded or devalued. But they also need to recognize the impossibility of ever fully understanding another's experiences and to question their motives in gathering, selecting, and presenting those stories. It is important to step back from our own experience, to understand it as a reflection of ideology and culture. But this may not be enough. As Ritchie's work with her students suggests, the tendency to essentialize is only one symptom of what Michelle Fine calls the "knotty entanglement" of self and other (72). As researchers examine more carefully the relationship between themselves and participants, they will need to consider the provocative advice of Trinh Minh-ha: "In writing close to the other of the other, I can only choose to maintain a self-reflexively critical relationship toward the material, a relationship that defines both the subject written and the writing subject undoing the I while asking 'what do I want, wanting to *know* you—or me?'" (76).

Since researchers cannot assume that they understand what is relevant in the lives of others or even what are the important questions to ask, research participants must be invited to articulate research questions, to speak for themselves, to choose the occasions for and forms of representing their experiences. Inevitably, as in Ritchie's work with her students, participants' perspectives will reshape the assumptions and methodologies on which research is based, leading to more collaborative, complex, and "knottily entangled" research practices.

RELATIONSHIP OF THE KNOWER TO THE KNOWN

We have been focusing on the "knower" and her perspective on research. But feminist researchers have another significant and related concern—the "known" and its relationship to the "knower." One of the methodological changes proposed by feminist scholars is to establish more interactive, collaborative, and reciprocal relations between researchers and participants. These changes have come to us from pioneering work of scientists like Barbara McClintock and Evelyn Fox Keller, whose ideas about "objectivity" and the relationship between subject and object of study have complicated feminist research. McClintock's discoveries (documented by Keller) about genetic transposition in maize arose from her unconventional view of the role of the scientist and the relationship of observer and the observed. She no longer thought of the scientist as combative, manipulative, or dominant but rather in a relationship of intimacy and empathy with nature (Keller 117).

As scholars in composition we are uniquely positioned to interact closely with participants since much of our work involves us directly in the lives of students, teachers, and writers as we study their written and oral language. Our research strategies often bring us into lived daily relationships with research participants in ways not possible for biologists or even sociologists. Shirley Brice Heath's *Ways with Words* provides examples of daily lived interactions among research participants and researcher, although she mentions them only occasionally in her narrative: Heath's children played with the children in her study; she transported them in her car; she socialized with them in homes and churches. In the context of her work, Heath's participants became partners in research. Black and white teachers, mill workers, businessmen, and parents whose communities Heath was studying, began themselves to observe and analyze the patterns of language use around them and could therefore begin to formulate questions and initiate change.

One of the assumptions underlying collaboration between researchers and participants is that it will benefit all parties involved in the interaction: Researchers can gather additional insights by getting to know participants in the context of their daily lives, and participants can gain new knowledge about themselves and their lives through the research project. Collaborative research practices often bring about methodological changes as well. One frequently quoted example of methodological innovation resulting from collaborative research is Ann Oakley's interview study of working-class pregnant women. When Oakley encountered women who asked her about prenatal care or other medical information, for example, she found that she could not follow traditional interview procedures: to deflect questions, withhold information, and maintain the role of distanced interviewer. Instead, Oakley decided that she had a moral obligation to assist these women in their quest for information. Consequently, she changed her research methodology in response to research participants: she engaged in dialogue with the women, provided them with information available to her, and helped them get access to prenatal care. Thus, she launched one of the early feminist critiques of social science research methodology. In composition studies, we need to be similarly sensitive to research procedures. Whether we study basic or professional writers, we need to ask participants to collaborate with us, to help us design our research questions, to ask for their feedback, to answer their questions, and to share our knowledge with them.

This formulation of collaborative research still does not go far enough. A feminist politics of location would require the learning about self to be as *reciprocal* as possible—with the researcher also gaining knowledge about her own life or at least reexamining her cultural and gender biases. Sherry Gorelick suggests that "the researcher is transformed in the process of research—influenced and taught by her respondent-participants as she influences them. Theory and practice emerge from their interaction" (469). In composition there are few published accounts in which researchers reflect on the knowledge they gained about themselves and their relations with others due to the research they conducted, and in the few places where such accounts appear, they are often relegated to a preface or epilogue. We suspect this has to do with the format of traditional research reports which do not invite researchers' self-reflections and introspections. But we have anecdotal evidence from colleagues and friends who have discovered that interactive, collaborative research leaves them with a changed understanding of themselves. We have already mentioned one such example: the collaborative writing project Ritchie undertook with two students and the profound questions it raised for her and her position as a white female university professor. Another example emerged in an interview study Kirsch conducted with academic women (*Women Writing the Academy*).

Gesa Kirsch: In my effort to learn more about the concerns of academic women in different disciplines and at different stages of their careers, I invited participants to collaborate with me during various stages of the research: I developed interview questions with the help of women who participated in the study, adding and revising questions in response to initial conversations. I also collaborated with women in the interpretation of interviews. As I began to record and transcribe interviews, I consulted with women about the themes I identified as important in their lives. Thus, I entered into a cycle of conversation whereby both researcher and participants shaped, to some extent, the interpretation of interviews. In many cases, the collaboration between myself and participants was mutually beneficial: the stories women told me transformed my sense of self as writer, as scholar, and as participant in the academic community; women themselves also reported gaining insights into their writing and research processes through the interviews. In some cases, the interviews led to friendships that extended well beyond the duration of my research.

But the cycle of collaboration also had limitations. For example, it was cut short by time constraints I faced as researcher and by participants' interest, availability, and willingness to collaborate with me. I also have to assume that some participants may have felt disappointed, misunderstood, or even manipulated. Although no woman directly expressed this sentiment to me, lack of interest in follow-up conversations and resistance to collaboration suggest that possibility.

Relations between researcher and participants will always retain the potential for misunderstandings, even exploitation—much like other human relationships do. This potential risk, however, should not lead to inaction; rather, researchers can learn to explore sites of conflict for the shifting, multiple, and contradictory positions researchers and participants inevitably occupy and for the ethical questions raised by collaborative research.

ETHICAL QUESTIONS:
ISSUES OF POWER AND COLONIZATION

So far we have argued that a politics of location must begin with researchers who recognize their own subjectivity, who draw on their experiences to formulate research questions even as they recognize the limitations of their perspective, experiences, and understanding. Researchers' reflective and critical stance, however, is only the beginning. They must also investigate the relation between the knower and the known and explore the possibilities of collaboration with participants as they develop research questions, collect data, interpret findings, and write research reports. Finally, they must be open to change themselves, reexamining their own perspective continually as they collaborate with participants and come to recognize how their cultural, ethnic, gendered, and personal histories influence the shape of their research. Ideally, a politics of location enables reciprocal, dialogic, collaborative, and mutually beneficial relations between researchers and participants. However, this "ideal" research scenario often remains just that—an ideal. More often, researchers encounter epistemological, methodological, and—perhaps most troubling—ethical dilemmas. We now turn to ethical issues, such as questions of power and colonization, that scholars are likely to face in the research process.

The work of Michel Foucault and others has allowed us to see how observation, classification, and codification in the discourse of the academy are always exercises of power, sometimes more coercive than others. Issues of power and colonization can become particularly prominent in studies of oppressed or disenfranchised groups, as the example of Daphne Patai's work illustrates. She reflects on her experience of interviewing working-class women in Brazil, many of whom lived in poverty and lacked access to adequate health care and education.

> The dilemma of feminist researchers working on groups less privileged than themselves can be succinctly stated as follows: is it possible—not in theory, but in the actual conditions of the real world today—to write about the oppressed without becoming one of the oppressors? (139)

Patai ultimately answers this question in the negative, arguing that the material, economic, and political conditions that separate privileged feminist researchers from disenfranchised or oppressed women cannot easily be overcome, no matter how emancipatory the research methods are or how much good will the researcher brings to the project. She does not, however, suggest that scholars abandon all research that involves oppressed or disenfranchised people; instead, she suggests that scholars abandon their naiveté and learn to make professional judgments about the context, consequences, and potential benefits and drawbacks of their work.

Other ethical dilemmas can emerge when researchers solicit highly personal information from participants. Judith Stacey, a sociologist, faced an ethical dilemma when she interviewed a fundamentalist Christian woman. This woman revealed that she had been involved in a lesbian relationship before her marriage, but asked Stacey not to disclose that information. Thus, the researcher faced a dilemma:

> What feminist ethical principles could I invoke to guide me here? Principles of respect for research subjects and for a collaborative, egalitarian research relationship demand compliance, but this forced me to collude with the homophobic silencing of lesbian experience, as well as consciously to distort what I considered to be a crucial component of the ethnographic "truth" in my study. Whatever we [the interviewer and interviewee] decided, my ethnography was forced to betray a feminist principle. (114)

At times researchers will find that feminist principles are at odds with ethnographic ones. Feminist principles urge researchers to listen to women's voices, to cooperate with women in the telling of their stories, and to honor their trust. Ethnographic principles, on the other hand, urge researchers to be as accurate, exhaustive, and frank as possible in the process of gathering and presenting information about other people and cultures.

The kinds of ethical dilemmas Patai and Stacey describe also concern composition researchers. While composition research does not necessarily involve "disenfranchised groups," it often concerns groups who have less power and fewer resources than the researchers, such as students, basic writers, K–12 teachers, minorities, and women. Furthermore, composition scholars frequently solicit highly personal information from research participants, much in the same way that writing teachers who assign autobiographical essays can find themselves confronted with details about their students' lives that they never anticipated.[5] Researchers need to consider, for example, the dynamics of the interview situation. Although it may be dishonest to assume the stance of objective, detached interviewer, Sheila Riddell points out that it is equally problematic to position oneself as "just another woman" whose concerns in life are similar to those of the research participant (83–84). Because it creates a false atmosphere of equality and mutuality in which women are often eager to talk, this stance may seem to break down barriers between the researcher and participants, but it may also be manipulative or even coercive, while giving participants a false sense of control. Riddell's interviews with teenaged girls led her to speculate that women may talk more openly in some situations because of their social powerlessness and are thus easily exploited. In a long-term study of English teachers Ritchie faced similar issues.

Joy Ritchie: As my colleague David Wilson and I conducted a study of teachers' developing knowledge of their discipline and its pedagogy, I interviewed Carol Gulyas, one of our participants, several times over a period of four years while she completed her course work and began teaching. Because of the many hours I spent in interviews with her and because of her position as a student in some of our classes and as a research and teaching assistant in our project, we developed a closer relationship with Carol than with other participants, a relationship she described as one of "love and caring." My position of authority, but also our frequent and extended contacts, as well as my position as a woman with similar concerns about children and parents, for example, no doubt caused Carol to be less reserved in revealing connections between her personal life and the development of her voice as a writer, as a teacher, and as a woman. According to Carol, our frequent prompts to reflect on and articulate her learning over several semesters encouraged and deepened her learning. Because Carol was so articulate, self-reflective, and astute in her analyses of herself and her peers, the data she provided, and especially the connection between her personal history and her theoretical learning, were crucial in shaping our conclusions. David and I recognized that our representation of her personal experience in our writing might be a distortion or an appropriation. But because we had been so intrusive in Carol's life, we could not withdraw—nor would we have wanted to—from Carol after the study was over.

We felt more than the usual obligation to become an advocate for Carol in her emerging career, to encourage her to write her own account of her learning, even in counterpoint to our representation of it, and to continue to learn from her as a colleague (Gulyas; Wilson and Ritchie).

A final ethical dilemma we want to discuss concerns anthropologists, oral historians, and composition scholars alike: How can or should researchers respond to participants who do not share the researcher's values, who oppose feminist research goals, or who do not identify with feminist causes? We draw on another example from oral history to illustrate this ethical issue. Sondra Hale, an anthropologist who studies African and Middle Eastern women, reports on the dissonance she experienced in interviews with women who either did not identify themselves as feminists or did not share the researcher's notion of what it means to be a feminist. Hale describes her disappointment with an interview of a Sudanese women's movement leader who ignored Hale's invitation to reflect on her role and position in the movement. Instead, the woman chose to use the interview as an occasion to promote the "party line," to enhance the image of the Sudanese women's movement, even when it meant providing inaccurate information or exaggerating accomplishments. In composition studies, we can face similar dissonances in our interactions with research participants. In the interview study of academic women mentioned above, Kirsch also faced questions of how to interpret women's lives.

Gesa Kirsch: I interviewed a history professor who chose to distance herself from the feminist movement and repeatedly disavowed any interest in, sympathy with, or connections to feminist ideas. Yet she had been a "pioneer" in a field dominated by men and made many comments that were feminist in nature, such as pointing to the discrepancy between her values and those of her male colleagues, describing herself as a woman living in a "foreign" male culture, and expressing an interest in experimenting with forms of writing that went "against the academic grain." How was I to represent her views and comments? Should I use her comments that emphasized dissonance from feminist ideas, or should I offer my feminist reading of her interview? Taking my cues from feminist scholars, I addressed these questions by doing both; I juxtaposed her comments (in extended interview quotes) with my analysis and commentary, thereby giving readers evidence that allowed both perspectives to emerge. Of course, as the writer of the research report, I still retain authority by selecting interview quotes, arranging the text, and drawing on supporting theories.

To some degree, researchers cannot escape a position of power and the potential for appropriating or manipulating information. The point here, however, is not to suggest that scholars ignore or omit data that seem to con-

tradict their views. Rather, the point is to encourage researchers to view dissonances as opportunities to examine deeply held assumptions and to allow
multiple voices to emerge in their research studies, an act that will require innovation in writing research reports. (We discuss possibilities for new forms of
writing below.) Only in that manner will researchers be able to allow readers
to see the conflicting pieces of information they often gather in their work
and the potential contradictions inherent in their interpretations.

We are not advocating a relativist approach to research here, however.
Instead, we argue that feminist research goals should guide researchers' decisions. Feminist research can be distinguished from other research traditions by its emancipatory goals.[6] Feminist researchers not only set out to
study and describe women's lives and experiences, but actively seek to understand and change the conditions of women's social and political realities.
Thus, feminist researchers advocate using guiding questions like these for
responding to ethical dilemmas: Who benefits from the research/theories?
What are the possible outcomes of the research and the possible consequences for research participants? Whose interests are at stake? How and to
what extent will the research change social realities for research participants? There are no easy solutions to the range of ethical dilemmas researchers can face. Like Patai, we do not think

> that generic solutions can be found to the dilemmas feminists [and other
> researchers] face in conducting research, nor do [we] for an instant hold
> out the hope of devising exact "rules" that will resolve these issues for us. In
> [our] view, this is impossible because ethical problems do not arise as ab-
> solutes requiring "blind justice." (145)

Researchers will face difficult decisions in the research process, but a politics of location requires that researchers interrogate their relations with the
people they study and the power they hold over them. Linda Alcoff suggests
that "in order to evaluate attempts to speak for others in particular instances,
we need to analyze the probable or actual effects of the words on the discursive and material context" (26). At times, researchers will have to refocus
their research questions, find additional or different participants, assume
roles other than that of participant-observer, leave some data unpublished,
or even abandon a research project.

TOWARDS AN ETHICS OF RESEARCH

In the previous section we have raised some of the ethical questions inherent in a feminist politics of location. Although we do not claim to have all

the answers, we want to suggest how composition researchers can begin to address these questions. As we have shown, these questions are intertwined with—and highlight the necessity for articulating—ethical concerns. However, as we have attempted earlier in this essay to problematize our understanding of a politics of location, we also need to problematize ethics, informing our view with the vigorous discussion of ethics in which feminists from various disciplines have recently engaged.[7] First we will consider how we might revise our definition of ethics based on caring, collaborative relationships with participants. Next, we suggest changes in research methods and forms of writing to meet these ethical demands, changes that allow multi-vocal, dialogic representations in our research narratives. Finally, we propose a reexamination of the goals and implications of research in a further attempt to examine an ethical stance in our work.

Feminist discussions of ethics call for a fundamental change in the way ethics is conceived. Traditional ethics are based on a fixed set of principles determined through rational means to guide one's approach to all problems. That approach assumes a universal applicability and fails to question beliefs in objectivity and neutrality. It also homogenizes differences in contexts and perspectives and fails to take into account the connection between political and moral questions. In general, feminist philosophers disavow traditional rule-governed ethics based on "universal" principles and on unbending rules, because acting from principle entails acting without experience and context, without a politics of location (e.g., Noddings; Schweickart; Young). An ethic of care often comes to different conclusions than an ethic of principle. Ethical behavior must be guided by natural sentiment or what Noddings calls "caring" within the context of human relationships. Unlike rule-bound ethics, "caring" requires one to place herself in an empathetic relationship in order to understand the other's point of view. For this reason an ethic of care is dependent on the engagement of "the personal"—a particular person of ethical character engaged in the examination of context, motivations, relationships, and responsibility (Tronto, "Beyond Gender" 657–58).

But empathy is not an unproblematic concept. Gregory Clark, paraphrasing Wyschogrod, notes that "an act of empathy is inherently an interpretation that eclipses, at least partially, the full reality of another's difference: it directs me to 'understand' another in my own terms" (66). Feminist critics, while acknowledging the importance of an ethic of care, point out the inherent hierarchies, paternalism, and inequalities even in this "caring" ethical model. Patrocinio Schweickart observes that "an ethic of care is no guarantee against self-deception—a discourse of care can be used to mask exploitative and uncaring conditions" (187). Further, Sarah

Hoagland suggests that Noddings's ethic still posits a one-way relationship rather than a truly reciprocal relationship between the caring and cared-for. Such unidirectional relationships of care, she argues, reinforce oppressive institutions (250–53).

Hoagland's concern seems especially relevant for composition researchers because of the problems inherent in seemingly benevolent but unequal relationships. It suggests that researchers continually interrogate their relations with participants, working toward dialogic, mutually educative, caring relations while at the same time recognizing that the complex power dynamics between researcher and participants can undermine, threaten, or manipulate those relations. Engaging in more collaborative approaches to research can help reduce the distance between researchers and participants. Participants can be brought in as co-researchers; those who have been marginalized can be encouraged to join in posing research questions that matter to them. Not only should participants co-author the questions, they can also work with researchers to negotiate the interpretations of data at both the descriptive and interpretive level. bell hooks is most insistent that white, privileged researchers and writers stop asking disempowered women to tell their stories so that these women can rewrite them in their own language, making their stories their own ("Choosing the Margin" 152). Madeleine Grumet provides further suggestions for reciprocal relationships between researchers and participants.

> So if telling a story requires giving oneself away, then we are obligated to devise a method of receiving stories that mediates the space between the self that tells, the self that told, and the self that listens: a method that returns a story to the teller that is both hers and not hers, that contains her self in good company. (70)

Inevitably caring, reciprocal, collaborative research will lead to complications, but it may also lead to richer, more rigorously examined results. Despite the potential problems of an ethic of care, we prefer, along with Tronto, "a moral theory that can recognize and identify these issues [problems of otherness, privilege, and paternalism] . . . to a moral theory that, because it presumes that all people are equal, is unable even to recognize them" (*Moral Boundaries* 147).

Reciprocal relations also imply that researchers attempt to open themselves to change and learning, to reinterpreting their own lives, and to reinventing their own "otherness" (Harding, *Whose Science?* 217). This means doing more than listening to and becoming more sensitive to the experiences of those who are disenfranchised. It requires researchers to attempt to identify what may be repressed and unconscious in their own experiences, and to claim their own contradictory social and gendered identities. Women can explore their marginality, for example, by considering that a woman scholar is at some level a contradiction in terms, that women in the academy still continue to occupy marginal positions because of their gender (Harding, "Who Knows?" 103). Marginality is not merely determined by sex or skin color; we sometimes make choices that place us in such positions. Men in composition studies, for example, can explore how their work as teachers and scholars often positions them as "other" in English departments that tend to privilege the study of literature and critical theory.[8] African American scholars have theorized the importance of using this perspective to generate new understandings of our discipline (Collins 40–41; hooks, "Choosing the Margin" 149). Collins argues that our own devalued identities can be powerful resources for knowing because the tension that arises from assuming the perspective of "outsiders within" allows us to see what privileged insiders cannot (59). Patricia J. Williams in *The Alchemy of Race and Rights* combines her privileged perspective as a legal scholar and her marginalized personal history as an African American woman to analyze the social and political contexts of such seemingly arcane matters as contract law.[9]

Working from a marginal position also offers the potential for research that moves beyond analyzing gender or race as though they are someone else's problem—not ours. It can lead the more privileged to consider themselves as potential "subjects" of study, and, therefore, reveal more clearly their privileged positions as well as their unacknowledged marginality. In her analysis of self-other relations, Michelle Fine describes the study of one of her students, Nancy Porter. Porter interviewed white "Main Line" women in Philadelphia and revealed how white people's lives are protected from surveillance and how scholars have "sanitized" evidence of the dysfunctional in such privileged lives (73).[10] Historian Minnie Bruce Pratt provides another example of this process. She uses her identity as a white Southerner at the center, but also her identity as a lesbian on the margin, to analyze her understanding of Southern history, to see how her white perspective is challenged by the perspective of African American lives, and by her own "outsider" position as a lesbian. We are not suggesting that scholars engage in self-indulgent privileging of their own stories or that they superimpose their stories on those of others; instead, we suggest that they can place their stories and those of their research participants in dialogue with each other to gain new insights into their own and others' lives. As the women in our discussion group at CCCC acknowledged, because our gender and our position in composition still locates us in a marginal position in many English departments, it gives us one important site from which to see with the perspective of outsiders.

We have already asserted the importance of rigorous self-reflection on the part of the researcher in order to avoid essentializing others and to clarify her own motives, desires, and interests. We also understand that to some extent these will always remain unconscious and unknowable. However, neutrality and objectivity are also myths that mask the power-relations always present in research endeavors. That does not mean that relativism is the only alternative, however. Harding's notion of "strong objectivity" may help us understand how to negotiate this apparent dichotomy between a humanist belief in our ability to represent experience and a paralyzed postmodernist stance that denies the possibility of making any claims or taking action. "Strong objectivity" recognizes the historical, social, culturally situated nature of our motives and values, continually theorizes the impact of those values on our work, and searches for what is being eliminated, distorted, or masked in the process (*Whose Science?* 145–47).[11] As part of this activity we can look at the relationship between our theories and our conclusions. The questions that guide our data collection, the stories we decide to tell or eliminate from our research narratives, the range of conclusions we suppress or include—all are guided by our own positionality and must be acknowledged. This process is difficult because "working from a perspective in which we are trained to want to give a reasoned and connected account, we face live material [such as interviews and ethnographic observations] that is constantly in the process of transformation, that is not organized in the way of academic theories" (Acker, Barry, and Esseveld 149).

In addition to acting from an ethic of care and from the perspective offered by rigorous ongoing scrutiny of our motivations and methods, an ethical stance also suggests that we encode in our research narratives the provisional nature of knowledge that our work generates and the moral dilemmas inherent in research. We need to reconsider our privileging of certain, coherent, and univocal writing and include multiple voices and diverse interpretations in our research narratives, highlighting the ideologies that govern our thinking as well as those that may contradict our own. These "rupturing narratives," as Michelle Fine describes them, "allow us to hear the uppity voices of informants and researchers" (78). Finally, of course, we must be prepared to make the case for new forms of research and writing in our discipline as McCarthy and Fishman and others have begun to do. Traditional research reports, for example, urge writers to come to conclusions and announce their findings. That process demands that researchers make coherent what might be fragmented, and thus that they might sometimes reduce complex phenomena or erase differences for the sake of developing coherent theories.[12]

To avoid such erasing of differences, we need to continue experimenting with new ways of reporting research. In composition, a number of scholars have begun to invent writing that highlights multiple narratives and diverse perspectives. Several examples come to mind: Beverly Clark and Sonja Wiedenhaupt published an article on writers' block that took the form of a dialogue between the researcher and the writer, thereby allowing two distinct voices to tell the story from two different vantage points; Jill Eichhorn, Sara Farris, Karen Hayes, Adriana Hernandez, Susan Jarratt, Karen Powers-Stubbs, and Marian Sciachitano used a symposium to reflect on and theorize their experiences as feminist teachers, writing "both as a collective and in [their] seven different voices" (297); and Susan Miller collaborated and co-authored a study of "academic underlife" with several of her undergraduate students, Worth Anderson, Cynthia Best, Alycia Black, John Hurst, and Brandt Miller.[13] Such innovative writing challenges scholars to find new ways of presenting research, challenges journal editors to develop a greater tolerance for ambiguity and unconventional forms of discourse, and challenges readers to learn new ways of reading and interpreting texts. Fine observes, "When we construct texts collaboratively, self-consciously examining our relations with/for/despite those who have been contained as Others, we move against, we enable resistance to, "Othering" (74). Multivocal reports also disrupt the smooth research narratives we have come to know and expect, highlight rather than suppress the problems of representation in our writing, and expose the multiple, shifting, and contradictory subject positions of researchers and participants.[14]

Finally, a problematized politics of location leads us to research centered in the local and the individual while at the same time acknowledging that research has social consequences in the world. If we work from an ethic of care, we cannot ignore the political and cultural conditions that place us in unequal power relationships with the participants of our research (Hoagland 260). We have seen in the studies of Patai and Oakley and in our own research how deeply implicated issues of power are, in our work. Patti Lather is one of many feminist thinkers who argues strongly that we cannot be satisfied with more research and better data concerning women (or other groups we choose to study). If our research is centered on a politics of location it demands an extra measure of responsibility and accountability on our part. It requires using research as "praxis" to help those who participate with us in research to understand and change their situation, to help those who have been marginalized to speak for themselves. Under these circumstances, it will not be possible to walk away from the research site or those who live in it. Our research instead will need to extend to theory-generating in a self-reflexive and mutually dialogic context to help researchers and participants challenge and change the conditions that keep oppressive structures in place. Only in this extra measure of "care" can our research truly be ethical.

Pursuing the difficulties inherent in a politics of location may lead us beyond some of the frustrations we experience in our work in English departments, because these discussions will inevitably lead us to question our accommodation with the status quo in our discipline, to more seriously question the discipline's traditional ways of asking and answering research questions, to examine the internalized structures, the standard conventions for generating and communicating knowledge in the discipline, and to reshape our agendas for research and action in the field. It will engage us in a rigorous process of analyzing the meaning of the "personal" in our work.

NOTES

1. We frame our article with Adrienne Rich's words realizing that she has been criticized for some of her earlier writing in which she seems to advocate an essentialist position that reinscribes bourgeois individualism and an unproblematic universal feminism. We think her position is an important starting point for discussions of a politics of location, however, because Rich was one of the early theorists attempting to reintroduce the personal in order to challenge the impersonal authority and false universality of interpretive practices that exclude women's writing and women's lives altogether from the academy and other public sites. In the essay we quote, she does acknowledge the social and psychological construction of women's lives and defines "location" as a space in which we move, not as a fixed site. She also foregrounds the tension we want to explore between the degendered, depoliticized subject of post-modernist aesthetics and the universalizing, unified, humanist subject—both positions which can erase the specificity and lived experience of particular women.

2. We realize that our attempt to locate the origins of this article in a single event misrepresents the many origins our work inevitably has. In the first place we had to be motivated to attend the workshop, a motivation we could trace to our reading of feminist literature, to conversations with colleagues and friends, and to our lived everyday experiences as women in the academy and in the culture at large. If we continue this search for origins, we quickly come to realize that questions of location are complex and call for an analysis of the many conflicting layers of reality we experience in our multiple and shifting subject positions.

3. People participating in research studies are traditionally called "subjects." This term, however, is problematic, implying a division if not hierarchy between researchers and subjects, thereby positioning participants as objects of study, not as the complex and contradictory human beings they are. Since we are questioning precisely this division between researchers and subjects, we have chosen to use the terms "research participants" or simply "participants" throughout this article when we are referring to human beings involved in research studies.

4. Heather Brodie Graves, for example, argues that traditional "feminine" and "masculine" traits can be found in writers of both genders; she analyzes the writing of Kenneth Burke for "feminine" traits and that of Julia Kristeva for "masculine" traits to illustrate her point.

5. For discussions of writing teachers faced with highly personal and at times disturbing information in their students' writing, see Carole Deletiner; Cheryl Johnson; Richard E. Miller.

6. For discussions of feminist research goals and methods, see *Beyond Methodology* (Fonow and Cook), *Feminism and Methodology* (Harding), *Feminist Research Methods* (Nielsen), *Feminist Methods in Social Research* (Reinharz).

7. Space does not permit a full discussion of feminist approaches to ethics, particularly an ethic of care. We refer interested readers to discussions in political science (Tronto; Young), in feminist theory and philosophy (Card; Friedman; Hoagland; Houston; Lather; Schweickart), in education and psychology (Fine; Gilligan; Grumet; Noddings; Punch), and in composition studies (Clark; Mortensen and Kirsch).

8. We do not mean to suggest that only scholars who are marginalized can engage in feminist or care-based approaches to research. Rather, we argue for a sense of location that one can actively learn to choose. But we believe that attending to the experiences of marginalized people as well as examining aspects of one's identity that are suppressed are important points of departure for a critical perspective on research.

9. We do not wish to minimize differences among women of different backgrounds, generations, race, class, ethnicity, or other identity-shaping factors. In fact, the position of African American women in the academy is distinctly different from those of white, middle class women and has caused much debate and tension among feminist theorists. We use this example only to suggest that a marginal position can be a source of strength and insight, allowing researchers to formulate new research questions and gain knowledge not readily available to those who occupy more privileged positions.

10. For another revealing study of "whiteness," see *White Women, Race Matters: The Social Construction of Whiteness* by Ruth Frankenberg.

11. Harding's concept of "strong objectivity" is not unproblematic. Flax, for example, argues that it is still based on a notion of "transcendental truth" because it suggests that once we eliminate or reduce gender biases we will have come closer to 'the truth' (Disputed Subjects 141–47). We concur with Flax's critique but find Harding's notion useful as a working concept for researchers trying to assess the ethical dimensions of their work.

12. We recognize the irony of the text we have produced: a relatively univocal, coherent text that argues for experimental, multivocal writing. We have attempted to present multivocality by writing in our individual voices when describing our own research projects and in our collective voice in other sections of this text, but we can imagine more experimental and innovative ways of writing.

13. We list names of all collaborators/authors here to give full credit to the nature of collaborative work; all too often multiple authors disappear in the "et al." convention, a practice that reinforces the dominant single-author model of scholarship.

14. The multivocal texts we advocate are not without risk; besides making new demands on readers, writers, and editors, these texts pose special risks for untenured faculty and graduate students who still have to "prove"—or feel that they still have to prove—their disciplinary membership by using conventional research methods and forms.

WORKS CITED

Acker, Joan, Kate Barry, and Johanna Esseveld. "Objectivity and Truth: Problems in Doing Feminist Research." *Beyond Methodology: Feminist Scholarship as Lived Research.* Ed. Mary Fonow and Judith Cook. Bloomington: Indiana UP, 1991. 133–53.

Alcoff, Linda. "The Problem of Speaking for Others." *Cultural Critique* 20 (1991–92): 5–32.

Anderson, Worth, Cynthia Best, Alycia Black, John Hurst, Brandt Miller, and Susan Miller. "Cross-Curricular Ablex: A Collaborative Report on Ways with Academic Words." *College Composition and Communication* 41 (1990): 11–36.

Bizzell, Patricia. "Foundationalism and AntiFoundationalism in Composition Studies." *Pre/Text* 7 (1986): 37–56.

Bridwell-Bowles, Lillian. "Discourse and Diversity: Experimental Writing Within the Academy." *College Composition and Communication* 43 (1992): 349–68.

Card, Claudia, ed. *Feminist Ethics.* Lawrence: UP of Kansas. 1991.

Clark, Beverly Lyon, and Sonja Wiedenhaupt. "On Blocking and Unblocking Sonja: A Case Study in Two Voices." *College Composition and Communication* 43 (1992): 55–74.

Clark, Gregory. "Rescuing the Discourse of Community." *College Composition and Communication* 45 (1994): 61–74.

Collins, Patricia Hill. "Learning from the Outsider Within: The Sociological Significance of Black Feminist Thought." *(En)Gendering Knowledge: Feminists in Academe.* Ed. Joan Hartman and Ellen Messer-Davidow. Knoxville: U of Tennessee P, 1991. 40–65.

Deletiner, Carole. "Crossing Lines." *College English* 54 (1992): 809–17.

Ebert, Teresa. "The 'Difference' of Postmodern Feminism." *College English* 53 (1991): 886–904.

Eichhorn, Jill, Sara Farris, Karen Hayes, Adriana Hernandez, Susan Jarratt, Karen Powers-Stubbs, and Marian Sciachitano. "A Symposium on Feminist Experiences in the Composition Classroom." *College Composition and Communication* 43 (1992): 297–322.

Fine, Michelle. "Working the Hyphens: Reinventing Self and Other in Qualitative Research." *Handbook of Qualitative Research.* Ed. Norman Denzin and Yvonna Lincoln. Thousand Oaks, CA: Sage, 1994. 70–82.

Flax, Jane. *Thinking Fragments: Psychoanalysis, Feminism, and Postmodernism in the Contemporary West.* Berkeley: U of California P, 1990.

———. *Disputed Subjects: Essays on Psychoanalysis, Politics, and Philosophy.* New York: Routledge, 1993.

Fonow, Mary Margaret, and Judith A. Cook, eds. *Beyond Methodology: Feminist Scholarship as Lived Research.* Bloomington: Indiana UP, 1991.

Friedman, Marilyn. "Beyond Caring: The De-Moralization of Gender." *Science, Morality, and Feminist Theory.* Ed. Marsha Hanen and Kai Nielsen. Calgary: U of Calgary P, 1987. 87–110.

Frankenberg, Ruth. *White Women, Race Matters: The Social Construction of Whiteness.* Minneapolis: U of Minnesota P. 1993.

Gilligan, Carol. *In a Different Voice: Psychological Theory and Women's Development.* Cambridge, MA: Harvard UP, 1982.

Gorelick, Sherry. "Contradictions of Feminist Methodology." *Gender and Society* 4 (1991):459–77.

Graves, Heather Brodie. "Regrinding the Lens of Gender: Problematizing 'Writing as a Woman.'" *Written Communication* 10 (1993):139–63.

Grumet, Madeleine R. "The Politics of Personal Knowledge." *Stories Lives Tell: Narrative and Dialogue in Education.* Ed. Carol Witherell and Nel Noddings. New York: Teachers College P, 1991. 67–77.

Gulyas, Carol. "Reflections on Telling Stories." *English Education* 18 (1994): 189–94.

Hale, Sondra. "Feminist Methods, Process, and Self-Criticism: Interviewing Sudanese Women." *Women's Words: The Feminist Practice of Oral History.* Ed. Sherna Gluck and Daphne Patai. New York: Routledge, 1991. 121–36.

Haraway, Donna. "Situated Knowledges: The Science Question in Feminism and the Privilege of Partial Perspective. *Feminist Studies* 14 (1988): 575–99.

Harding, Sandra, ed. *Feminism and Methodology: Social Science Issues.* Bloomington: Indiana UP, 1987.

———. "Who Knows? Identities and Feminist Epistemology." *(En)Gendering Knowledge: Feminists in Academe.* Ed. Joan Hartman and Ellen Messer-Davidow. Knoxville, TN: U of Tennessee P, 1991. 100–15.

———. *Whose Science? Whose Knowledge? Thinking from Women's Lives.* Ithaca: Cornell UP, 1991.

Heath, Shirley Brice. *Ways With Words: Language, Life, and Work in Communities and Classrooms.* New York: Cambridge UP, 1983.

Hoagland, Sarah Lucia. "Some Thoughts about 'Caring'." *Feminist Ethics.* Ed. Claudia Card. Lawrence: UP of Kansas, 1991. 246–63.

hooks, bell. "Feminist Politicization: A Comment." *Talking Back: Thinking Feminist, Thinking Black.* Boston: South End P, 1985. 105–11.

———. "Choosing the Margin as a Space of Radical Openness." *Yearning: Race, Gender, and Cultural Politics.* Boston: South End P, 1990. 145–54.

Houston, Barbara. "Rescuing Womanly Virtues: Some Dangers of Moral Reclamation." *Science, Morality, and Feminist Theory.* Ed. Marsha Hanen and Kai Nielsen. Calgary: U of Calgary P, 1987. 237–62.

Johnson, Cheryl L. "Participatory Rhetoric and the Teacher as Racial/Gendered Subject." *College English* 56 (1994): 409–19.

Keller, Evelyn Fox. "Dynamic Objectivity: Love, Power, and Knowledge." *Reflections on Gender and Science.* New Haven: Yale UP, 1985. 115–26.

Kirsch, Gesa, E. *Women Writing the Academy: Audience, Authority, and Transformation.* Carbondale: Southern Illinois UP, 1993.

Kraemer, Don J. "Gender and the Autobiographical Essay: A Critical Extension of the Research." *College Composition and Communication* 43 (1992): 323–39.

Lather, Patti. *Getting Smart: Feminist Research and Pedagogy With/In the Postmodern.* New York: Routledge, 1991.

McCarthy, Lucille Parkinson, and Stephen M. Fishman. "A Text for Many Voices: Representing Diversity in Reports of Naturalistic Research." *Ethics and Representation in Qualitative Studies of Literacy.* Ed. Peter Mortensen and Gesa E. Kirsch. Urbana, IL: National Council of Teachers of English, 1996. 155–76.

Miller, Richard E. "Fault Lines in the Contact Zone." *College English* 56 (1994): 389–408.

Minh-ha, Trinh T. *Women, Native, Other: Writing Postcoloniality and Feminism.* Bloomington: Indiana UP, 1989.

Mortensen, Peter, and Gesa Kirsch. "On Authority in the Study of Writing." *College Composition and Communication* 44 (1993): 556–72.

Nielsen, Joyce McCarl, ed. *Feminist Research Methods: Exemplary Readings in the Social Sciences.* San Francisco: Westview, 1990.

Noddings, Nel. *Caring: A Feminine Approach to Ethics and Moral Education.* Berkeley: U of California P, 1984.

Oakley, Ann. "Interviewing Women: A Contradiction in Terms?" *Doing Feminist Research.* Ed. Helen Roberts. New York: Routledge, 1981. 30–61.

Patai, Daphne. "U.S. Academics and Third World Women: Is Ethical Research Possible?" *Women's Words: The Feminist Practice of Oral History.* Ed. Sherna Gluck and Daphne Patai. New York: Routledge, 1991. 137–53.

Peaden, Catherine Hobbs. Rev. of *Gender Issues in the Teaching of English.* Ed. Nancy McCracken and Bruce Appleby. *Journal of Advanced Composition* 13 (1993): 260–63.

Pratt, Minnie Bruce. "Identity: Skin Blood Heart." *Yours in Struggle: Three Feminist Perspectives on Anti-Semitism and Racism.* Ed. Elly Bulkin, Minnie Bruce Pratt, and Barbara Smith. Ithaca, NY: Long Haul P, 1984. 11–63.

Punch, Maurice. "Politics and Ethics in Qualitative Research." *Handbook of Qualitative Research.* Ed. Norman Denzin and Yvonna Lincoln. Thousand Oaks, CA: Sage, 1994. 83–97.

Reinharz, Shulamit. *Feminist Methods in Social Research.* New York: Oxford UP, 1992.

Rich, Adrienne. "Notes on a Politics of Location." *Blood, Bread, and Poetry.* New York: Norton, 1989. 210–31.

Riddell, Sheila. "Exploiting the Exploited? The Ethics of Feminist Educational Research." *The Ethics of Educational Research.* Ed. Robert Burgess. New York: Falmer, 1989. 77–99.

Ritchie, Joy S. "Confronting the Essential Problem: Reconnecting Feminist Theory and Pedagogy." *Journal of Advanced Composition* 10 (1990): 249–71.

Ritchie, Joy S., Manjit Kaur, and Bee Tin Choo Meyer. "Women Students' Autobiographical Writing: The Rhetoric of Discovery and Defiance." *Situated Stories: Valuing Diversity in Composition Research.* Ed. Emily Decker and Kathleen Mary Geissler. Portsmouth, NH: Boynton/Cook Heinemann, 1998. 173–89.

Schweickart, Patrocinio. "In Defense of Femininity: Commentary on Sandra Bartky's Femininity and Domination." *Hypatia* 8 (1993): 178–91.

Smith, Sidonie. "Who's Talking/Who's Talking Back? The Subject of Personal Narrative." *Signs: Journal of Women in Culture and Society* 18 (1993): 392–407.

Stacey, Judith. "Can There Be a Feminist Ethnography?" *Women's Words: The Feminist Practice of Oral History.* Ed. Sherna Gluck and Daphne Patai. New York: Routledge, 1991. 111–19.

Tronto, Joan. "Beyond Gender Difference to a Theory of Care." *Signs: Journal of Women in Culture and Society* 12 (1987): 644–63.

_____. *Moral Boundaries: A Political Argument for an Ethic of Care.* New York: Routledge, 1993.

Williams, Patricia J. *The Alchemy of Race and Rights.* Boston: Harvard UP, 1991.

Wilson, David E., and Joy S. Ritchie. "Resistance, Revision, and Representation: Narrative in Teacher Education." *English Education* 18 (1994): 177–88.

Young, Iris Marion. *Justice and the Politics of Difference.* Princeton: Princeton UP, 1990.

Acknowledgments: We wish to thank colleagues, friends, and CCC reviewers for their comments and encouragement as we developed this essay: Lil Brannon, Robert Brooke, Gregory Clark, Lisa Ede, Elizabeth Flynn, Min-Zhan Lu, and Kate Ronald.

The Language of Exclusion

Writing Instruction at the University

MIKE ROSE

"How many '*minor* errors' are acceptable?"

"We must try to isolate and define those *further* skills in composition . . ."

". . . we should provide a short remedial course to patch up any deficiencies."

"Perhaps the most striking feature of this campus' siege against illiteracy . . ."

"One might hope that, after a number of years, standards might be set in the high schools which would allow us to abandon our own defensive program."

These snippets come from University of California and California state legislative memos, reports, and position papers and from documents produced during a recent debate in UCLA's Academic Senate over whether a course in our freshman writing sequence was remedial. Though these quotations— and a half dozen others I will use in this essay—are local, they represent a kind of institutional language about writing instruction in American higher education. There are five ideas about writing implicit in these comments: Writing ability is judged in terms of the presence of error and can thus be quantified. Writing is a skill or a tool rather than a discipline. A number of our students lack this skill and must be remediated. In fact, some percentage of our students are, for all intents and purposes, illiterate. Our remedial efforts, while currently necessary, can be phased out once the literacy crisis is solved in other segments of the educational system.

Reprinted from *College English* 47.4 (April 1985): 341–59. Used with permission.

This kind of thinking and talking is so common that we often fail to notice that it reveals a reductive, fundamentally behaviorist model of the development and use of written language, a problematic definition of writing, and an inaccurate assessment of student ability and need. This way of talking about writing abilities and instruction is woven throughout discussions of program and curriculum development, course credit, instructional evaluation, and resource allocation. And, in various ways, it keeps writing instruction at the periphery of the curriculum.

It is certainly true that many faculty and administrators would take issue with one or more of the above notions. And those of us in writing would bring current thinking in rhetoric and composition studies into the conversation. (Though we often—perhaps uncomfortably—rely on terms like "skill" and "remediation.") Sometimes we successfully challenge this language or set up sensible programs in spite of it. But all too often we can do neither. The language represented in the headnotes of this essay reveals deeply held beliefs. It has a tradition and a style, and it plays off the fundamental tension between the general education and the research missions of the American university. The more I think about this language and recall the contexts in which I've heard it used, the more I realize how caught up we all are in a political-semantic web that restricts the way we think about the place of writing in the academy. The opinions I have been describing are certainly not the only ones to be heard. But they are strong. Influential. Rhetorically effective. And profoundly exclusionary. Until we seriously rethink it, we will misrepresent the nature of writing, misjudge our students' problems, and miss any chance to effect a true curricular change that will situate writing firmly in the undergraduate curriculum.

Let us consider the college writing course for a moment. Freshman composition originated in 1874 as a Harvard response to the poor writing of *upper*classmen, spread rapidly, and became and remained the most consistently required course in the American curriculum. Upper division writing courses have a briefer and much less expansive history, but they are currently receiving a good deal of institutional energy and support. It would be hard to think of an ability more desired than the ability to write. Yet, though writing courses are highly valued, even enjoying a boom, they are also viewed with curious eyes. Administrators fund them—often generously—but academic senates worry that the boundaries between high school and college are eroding, and worry as well that the considerable investment of resources in such courses will drain money from the research enterprise. They deny some of the courses curricular status by tagging them remedial, and their members secretly or not-so-secretly wish the courses could be moved to community colleges. Scientists and social scientists underscore the importance of effective writing, yet find it difficult—if not impossible—to restructure their own courses of study to encourage and support writing. More than a few humanists express such difficulty as well. English departments hold onto writing courses but consider the work intellectually second-class. The people who teach writing are more often than not temporary hires; their courses are robbed of curricular continuity and of the status that comes with tenured faculty involvement. And the instructors? Well, they're just robbed.

The writing course holds a very strange position in the American curriculum. It is within this setting that composition specialists must debate and defend and interminably evaluate what they do. And how untenable such activity becomes if the very terms of the defense undercut both the nature of writing and the teaching of writing, and exclude it in various metaphorical ways from the curriculum. We end up arguing with words that sabotage our argument. The first step in resolving such a mess is to consider the language institutions use when they discuss writing. What I want to do in this essay is to look at each of the five notions presented earlier, examine briefly the conditions that shaped their use, and speculate on how it is that they misrepresent and exclude. I will conclude by entertaining a less reductive and exclusionary way to think—and talk—about writing in the academy.

BEHAVIORISM, QUANTIFICATION, AND WRITING

A great deal of current work in fields as diverse as rhetoric, composition studies, psycholinguistics, and cognitive development has underscored the importance of engaging young writers in rich, natural language use. And the movements of the last four decades that have most influenced the teaching of writing—life adjustment, liberal studies, and writing as process—have each, in their very different ways, placed writing pedagogy in the context of broad concerns: personal development and adjustment, a rhetorical-literary tradition, the psychology of composing. It is somewhat curious, then, that a behaviorist approach to writing, one that took its fullest shape in the 1930s and has been variously and severely challenged by the movements that followed it, remains with us as vigorously as it does. It is atomistic, focusing on isolated bits of discourse, error centered, and linguistically reductive. It has a style and a series of techniques that influence pedagogy, assessment, and evaluation. We currently see its influence in workbooks, programmed instruction, and many formulations of behavioral objectives, and it gets most of its airplay in remedial courses. It has staying power. Perhaps we can better understand its resilience if we briefly survey the history that gives it its current shape.

When turn-of-the-century educational psychologists like E. L. Thorndike began to study the teaching of writing, they found a Latin and Greek-influenced school grammar that was primarily a set of prescriptions for conducting socially acceptable discourse, a list of the arcane do's and don'ts of usage for the ever-increasing numbers of children—many from lower classes and immigrant groups—entering the educational system. Thorndike and his colleagues also found reports like those issuing from the Harvard faculty in the 1890s which called attention to the presence of errors in handwriting, spelling, and grammar in the writing of the university's entering freshmen. The twentieth-century writing curriculum, then, was focused on the particulars of usage, grammar, and mechanics. Correctness became, in James Berlin's words, the era's "most significant measure of accomplished prose" (*Writing Instruction in Nineteenth-Century American Colleges* [Carbondale: Southern Illinois University Press, 1984], p. 73).

Such particulars suited educational psychology's model of language quite well: a mechanistic paradigm that studied language by reducing it to discrete behaviors and that defined language growth as the accretion of these particulars. The stress, of course, was on quantification and measurement. ("Whatever exists at all exists in some amount," proclaimed Thorndike.[1]) The focus on error—which is eminently measurable—found justification in a model of mind that was ascending in American academic psychology. Educators embraced the late Victorian faith in science.

Thorndike and company would champion individualized instruction and insist on language practice rather than the rote memorization of rules of grammar that characterized nineteenth-century pedagogy. But they conducted their work within a model of language that was tremendously limited, and this model was further supported and advanced by what Raymond Callahan has called "the cult of efficiency," a strong push to apply to education the principles of industrial scientific management (*Education and the Cult of Efficiency* [Chicago: University of Chicago Press, 1962]). Educational gains were defined as products, and the output of products could be measured. Pedagogical effectiveness—which meant cost-effectiveness—could be determined with "scientific" accuracy. This was the era of the educational efficiency expert. (NCTE even had a Committee on Economy of Time in English.) The combination of positivism, efficiency, and skittishness about correct grammar would have a profound influence on pedagogy and research.

This was the time when workbooks and "practice pads" first became big business. Their success could at least partly be attributed to the fact that they were supported by scientific reasoning. Educational psychologists had demonstrated that simply memorizing rules of grammar and usage had no discernible effect on the quality of student writing. What was needed was application of those rules through practice provided by drills and exercises. The theoretical underpinning was expressed in terms of "habit formation" and "habit strength," the behaviorist equivalent of learning—the resilience of an "acquired response" being dependent on the power and number of reinforcements. The logic was neat: specify a desired linguistic behavior as precisely as possible (e.g., the proper use of the pronouns "he" and "him") and construct opportunities to practice it. The more practice, the more the linguistic habit will take hold. Textbooks as well as workbooks shared this penchant for precision. One textbook for teachers presented a unit on the colon.[2] A text for students devoted seven pages to the use of a capital letter to indicate a proper noun.[3] This was also the time when objective tests—which had been around since 1890—enjoyed a sudden rebirth as "new type" tests. And they, of course, were precision incarnate. The tests generated great enthusiasm among educators who saw in them a scientific means accurately and fairly to assess student achievement in language arts as well as in social studies and mathematics. Ellwood Cubberley, the dean of the School of Education at Stanford, called the development of these "new type" tests "one of the most significant movements in all our educational history."[4] Cubberley and his colleagues felt they were on the threshold of a new era.

Research too focused on the particulars of language, especially on listing and tabulating error. One rarely finds consideration of the social context of error, or of its cognitive-developmental meaning—that is, no interpretation of its significance in the growth of the writer. Instead one finds W. S. Guiler tallying the percentages of 350 students who, in misspelling "mortgage," erred by omitting the "t" vs. those who dropped the initial "g."[5] And one reads Grace Ransom's study of students' "vocabularies of errors"—a popular notion that any given student has a more or less stable set of errors he or she commits. Ransom showed that with drill and practice, students ceased making many of the errors that appeared on pretests (though, unfortunately for the theory, a large number of new errors appeared in their posttests).[6] One also reads Luella Cole Pressey's assertion that "everything needed for about 90 per cent of the writing students do . . . appears to involve only some 44 different rules of English composition." And therefore, if mastery of the rules is divided up and allocated to grades 2 through 12, "there is an average of 4.4 rules to be mastered per year."[7]

Such research and pedagogy was enacted to good purpose, a purpose stated well by H. J. Arnold, Director of Special Schools at Wittenberg College:

> [Students'] disabilities are specific. The more exactly they can be located, the more promptly they can be removed. . . . It seems reasonably safe to predict that the elimination of the above mentioned disabilities through adequate remedial drill will do much to remove students' handicaps in certain college courses. ("Diagnostic and Remedial Techniques for College Freshmen," *Association of American Colleges Bulletin*, 16 [1930], pp. 271–272).

The trouble, of course, is that such work is built on a set of highly questionable assumptions: that a writer has a relatively fixed repository of linguistic blunders that can be pinpointed and then corrected through drill, that repetitive drill on specific linguistic features represented in isolated sentences will result in mastery of linguistic (or stylistic or rhetorical) principles, that bits of discourse bereft of rhetorical or conceptual context can form the basis of curriculum and assessment, that good writing is correct writing, and that correctness has to do with pronoun choice, verb forms, and the like.

Despite the fact that such assumptions began to be challenged by the late 30s,[8] the paraphernalia and the approach of the scientific era were destined to remain with us. I think this trend has the staying power it does for a number of reasons, the ones we saw illustrated in our brief historical overview. It gives a method—a putatively objective one—to the strong desire of our society to maintain correct language use. It is very American in its seeming efficiency. And it offers a simple, understandable view of complex linguistic problems. The trend seems to reemerge with most potency in times of crisis: when budgets crunch and accountability looms or, particularly, when "nontraditional" students flood our institutions.[9] A reduction of complexity has great appeal in institutional decision making, especially in difficult times: a scientific-atomistic approach to language, with its attendant tallies and charts, nicely fits an economic/political decision-making model. When in doubt or when scared or when pressed, count.

And something else happens. When student writing is viewed in this particularistic, pseudo-scientific way, it gets defined in very limited terms as a narrow band of inadequate behavior separate from the vastly complex composing that faculty members engage in for a living and delve into for work and for play. And such perception yields what it intends: a behavior that is stripped of its rich cognitive and rhetorical complexity. A behavior

552

that, in fact, looks and feels basic, fundamental, atomistic. A behavior that certainly does not belong in the university.

ENGLISH AS A SKILL

As English, a relatively new course of study, moved into the second and third decades of this century, it was challenged by efficiency-obsessed administrators and legislators. Since the teaching of writing required tremendous resources, English teachers had to defend their work in utilitarian terms. One very successful defense was their characterization of English as a "skill" or "tool subject" that all students had to master in order to achieve in almost any subject and to function as productive citizens. The defense worked, and the utility of English in schooling and in adult life was confirmed for the era.

The way this defense played itself out, however, had interesting ramifications. Though a utilitarian defense of English included for many the rhetorical/conceptual as well as the mechanical/grammatical dimensions of language, the overwhelming focus of discussion in the committee reports and the journals of the 1920s and 1930s was on grammatical and mechanical error. The narrow focus was made even more narrow by a fetish for "scientific" tabulation. One could measure the degree to which students mastered their writing skill by tallying their mistakes.

We no longer use the phrase "tool subject," and we have gone a long way in the last three decades from error tabulation toward revitalizing the rhetorical dimension of writing. But the notion of writing as a skill is still central to our discussions and our defenses: we have writing skills hierarchies, writing skills assessments, and writing skills centers. And necessary as such a notion may seem to be, I think it carries with it a tremendous liability. Perhaps the problem is nowhere more clearly illustrated than in this excerpt from the UCLA academic senate's definition of a university course:

> A university course should set forth an integrated body of knowledge with primary emphasis on presenting principles and theories rather than on developing skills and techniques.

If "skills and techniques" are included, they must be taught "primarily as a means to learning, analyzing, and criticizing theories and principles." There is a lot to question in this definition, but for now let us limit ourselves to the distinction it establishes between a skill and a body of knowledge. The distinction highlights a fundamental tension in the American university: between what Laurence Veysey labels the practical-utilitarian dimension (applied, vocational, educationalist) and both the liberal culture and the research dimensions—the latter two, each in different ways, elevating appreciation and pure inquiry over application (*The Emergence of the American University* [Chicago: University of Chicago Press, 1965]). To discuss writing as a skill, then, is to place it in the realm of the technical, and in the current, research-ascendant American university, that is a kiss of death.

Now it is true that we commonly use the word *skill* in ways that suggest a complex interweaving of sophisticated activity and rich knowledge. We praise the interpretive skills of the literary critic, the diagnostic skills of the physician, the interpersonal skills of the clinical psychologist. Applied, yes, but implying a kind of competence that is more in line with obsolete definitions that equate skill with reason and understanding than with this more common definition (that of the *American Heritage Dictionary*): "An art, trade, or technique, particularly one requiring use of the hands or body." A skill, particularly in the university setting, is, well, a tool, something one develops and refines and completes in order to take on the higher-order demands of purer thought. Everyone may acknowledge the value of the skill (our senate praised our course to the skies as it removed its credit), but it is valuable as the ability to multiply or titrate a solution or use an index or draw a map is valuable. It is absolutely necessary but remains second-class. It is not "an integrated body of knowledge" but a technique, something acquired differently from the way one acquires knowledge—from drill, from practice, from procedures that conjure up the hand and the eye but not the mind. Skills are discussed as separable, distinct, circumscribable activities; thus we talk of subskills, levels of skills, sets of skills. Again writing is defined by abilities one can quantify and connect as opposed to the dynamism and organic vitality one associates with thought.

Because skills are fundamental tools, basic procedures, there is the strong expectation that they be mastered at various preparatory junctures in one's educational career and in the places where such tools are properly crafted. In the case of writing, the skills should be mastered before one enters college and takes on higher-order endeavors. And the place for such instruction—before or after entering college—is the English class. Yes, the skill can be refined, but its fundamental development is over, completed via a series of elementary and secondary school courses and perhaps one or two college courses, often designated remedial. Thus it is that so many faculty consider upper-division and especially graduate-level writing courses as de jure remedial. To view writing as a skill in the university context reduces the possibility of perceiving it as a complex ability that is continually developing as one engages in new tasks with new materials for new audiences.

If the foregoing seems a bit extreme, consider this passage from our Academic Senate's review of UCLA Writing Programs:

> . . . it seems difficult to see how *composition*—whose distinctive aspect seems to be the transformation of language from thought or speech to hard copy—represents a distinct further step in shaping cogitation. There don't seem to be persuasive grounds for abandoning the view that composition is still a *skill* attendant to the attainment of overall linguistic competence.

The author of the report, a chemist, was reacting to some of our faculty's assertions about the interweaving of thinking and writing; writing for him is more or less a transcription skill.

So to reduce writing to second-class intellectual status is to influence the way faculty, students, and society view the teaching of writing. This is a bitter pill, but we in writing may have little choice but to swallow it. For, after all, is not writing simply different from "integrated bodies of knowledge" like sociology or biology? Is it? Well, yes and no. There are aspects of writing that would fit a skills model (the graphemic aspects especially). But much current theory and research are moving us to see that writing is not simply a transcribing skill mastered in early development. Writing seems central to the shaping and directing of certain modes of cognition, is integrally involved in learning, is a means of defining the self and defining reality, is a means of representing and contextualizing information (which has enormous political as well as conceptual and archival importance), and is an activity that develops over one's lifetime. Indeed it is worth pondering whether many of the "integrated bodies of knowledge" we study, the disciplines we practice, would have ever developed in the way they did and reveal the knowledge they do if writing did not exist. Would history or philosophy or economics exist as we know them? It is not simply that the work of such disciplines is recorded in writing, but that writing is intimately involved in the nature of their inquiry. Writing is not just a skill with which one can present or analyze knowledge. It is essential to the very existence of certain kinds of knowledge.

REMEDIATION

Since the middle of the last century, American colleges have been establishing various kinds of preparatory programs and classes within their halls to maintain enrollments while bringing their entering students up to curricular par.[10] One fairly modern incarnation of this activity is the "remedial class," a designation that appears frequently in the education and language arts journals of the 1920s.[11] Since that time remedial courses have remained very much with us: we have remedial programs, remedial sections, remedial textbooks, and, of course, remedial students. Other terms with different twists (like "developmental" and "compensatory") come and go, but "remedial" has staying power. Exactly what the adjective "remedial" means, however, has never quite been clear. To remediate seems to mean to correct errors or fill in gaps in a person's knowledge. The implication is that the material being studied should have been learned during prior education but was not. Now the reasons why it was not could vary tremendously: they could rest with the student (physical impairment, motivational problems, intelligence), the family (socio-economic status, stability, the support of reading-writing activities), the school (location, sophistication of the curriculum, adequacy of elementary or secondary instruction), the culture or subculture (priority of schooling, competing expectations and demands), or some combination of such factors. What "remedial" means in terms of curriculum and pedagogy is not clear either. What is remedial for a school like UCLA might well be standard for other state or community colleges, and what is considered standard during one era might well be tagged remedial in the next.

It is hard to define such a term. The best definition of remedial I can arrive at is a highly dynamic, contextual one: The function of labelling certain material remedial in higher education is to keep in place the hard fought for, if historically and conceptually problematic and highly fluid, distinction between college and secondary work. "Remedial" gains its meaning, then, in a political more than a pedagogical universe.

And the political dimension is powerful—to be remedial is to be substandard, inadequate, and, because of the origins of the term, the inadequacy is metaphorically connected to disease and mental defect. It has been difficult to trace the educational etymology of the word "remedial," but what I have uncovered suggests this: Its origins are in law and medicine, and by the late nineteenth century the term fell pretty much in the medical domain and was soon applied to education. "Remedial" quickly generalized beyond the description of students who might have had neurological problems to those with broader, though special, educational problems and then to those normal learners who are not up to a particular set of standards in a particular era at particular institutions. Here is some history.

Most of the enlightened work in the nineteenth century with the training of special populations (the deaf, the blind, the mentally retarded) was conducted by medical people, often in medical settings. And when young people who could hear and see and were of normal intelligence but had unusual—though perhaps not devastating—difficulties began to seek help, they too were examined within a medical framework. Their difficulties had to do with reading and writing—though mostly reading—and would today be classified as learning disabilities. One of the first such difficulties to be studied was dyslexia, then labelled "congenital word blindness."

In 1896 a physician named Morgan reported in the pages of *The British Medical Journal* the case of a "bright and intelligent boy" who was having great difficulty learning to read. Though he knew the alphabet, he would spell some words in pretty unusual ways. He would reverse letters or drop them or write odd combinations of consonants and vowels. Dr. Morgan examined the boy and had him read and write. The only diagnosis that made sense was one he had to borrow and analogize from the cases of stroke victims, "word blindness," but since the child had no history of cerebral trauma, Morgan labelled his condition "*congenital* word blindness" (W. Pringle Morgan, "A Case of Congenital Word Blindness," *The British Medical Journal*, 6, Part 2 [1896], 1378). Within the next two decades a number of such cases surfaced; in fact another English physician, James Hinshelwood, published several books on congenital word blindness.[12] The explanations were for the most part strictly medical, and, it should be noted, were analogized from detectable cerebral pathology in adults to conditions with no detectable pathology in children.

In the 1920s other medical men began to advance explanations a bit different from Morgan's and Hinshelwood's. Dr. Samuel Orton, an American physician, posed what he called a "cerebral physiological" theory that directed thinking away from trauma analogues and toward functional explanations. Certain areas of the brain were not defective but underdeveloped and could be corrected through "remedial effort." But though he posed a basically educational model for dyslexia, Dr. Orton's language should not be overlooked. He spoke of "brain habit" and the "handicap" of his "physiological deviates."[13] Though his theory was different from that of his forerunners, his language, significantly, was still medical.

As increasing access to education brought more and more children into the schools, they were met by progressive teachers and testing experts interested in assessing and responding to individual differences. Other sorts of reading and writing problems, not just dyslexia, were surfacing, and increasing numbers of teachers, not just medical people, were working with the special students. But the medical vocabulary—with its implied medical model—remained dominant. People tried to *diagnose* various *disabilities, defects, deficits, deficiencies,* and *handicaps,* and then tried to *remedy* them.[14] So one starts to see all sorts of reading/writing problems clustered together and addressed with this language. For example, William S. Gray's important monograph, *Remedial Cases in Reading: Their Diagnosis and Treatment* (Chicago: University of Chicago Press, 1922), listed as "specific causes of failure in reading" inferior learning capacity, congenital word blindness, poor auditory memory, defective vision, a narrow span of recognition, ineffective eye movements, inadequate training in phonetics, inadequate attention to the content, an inadequate speaking vocabulary, a small meaning vocabulary, speech defects, lack of interest, and timidity. The remedial paradigm was beginning to include those who had troubles as varied as bad eyes, second language interference, and shyness.[15]

It is likely that the appeal of medical-remedial language had much to do with its associations with scientific objectivity and accuracy—powerful currency in the efficiency-minded 1920s and 30s. A nice illustration of this interaction of influences appeared in Albert Lang's 1930 textbook, *Modern Methods in Written Examinations* (Boston: Houghton Mifflin, 1930). The medical model is quite explicit:

> teaching bears a resemblance to the practice of medicine. Like a successful physician, the good teacher must be something of a diagnostician. The physician by means of a general examination singles out the individuals whose physical defects require a more thorough testing. He critically scrutinizes the special cases until he recognizes the specific troubles. After a careful diagnosis he is able to prescribe intelligently the best remedial or corrective measures. (p. 38)

By the 1930s the language of remediation could be found throughout the pages of publications like *English Journal*, applied now to writing (as well as reading and mathematics) and to high school and college students who had in fact learned to write but were doing so with a degree of error thought unacceptable. These were students—large numbers of them—who were not unlike the students who currently populate our "remedial" courses: students from backgrounds that did not provide optimal environmental and educational opportunities, students who erred as they tried to write the prose they thought the academy required, second-language students. The semantic net of "remedial" was expanding and expanding.

There was much to applaud in this focus on writing. It came from a progressive era desire to help *all* students progress through the educational system. But the theoretical and pedagogical model that was available for "corrective teaching" led educators to view writing problems within a medical-remedial paradigm. Thus they set out to diagnose as precisely as possible the errors (defects) in a student's paper—which they saw as symptomatic of equally isolable defects in the student's linguistic capacity—and devise drills and exercises to remedy them. (One of the 1930s nicknames for remedial sections was "sick sections." During the next decade they would be tagged "hospital sections.") Such corrective teaching was, in the words of H. J. Arnold, "the most logical as well as the most scientific method" ("Diagnostic and Remedial Techniques for College Freshmen," p. 276).

These then are the origins of the term, remediation. And though we have, over the last fifty years, moved very far away from the conditions of its origins and have developed a richer understanding of reading and writing difficulties, the term is still with us. A recent letter from the senate of a local liberal arts college is sitting on my desk. It discusses a "program in remedial writing for . . . [those] entering freshmen suffering from severe writing handicaps." We seem entrapped by this language, this view of students and learning. Dr. Morgan has long since left his office, but we still talk of writers as suffering from specifiable, locatable defects, deficits, and handicaps that can be localized, circumscribed, and remedied. Such talk reveals an atomistic, mechanistic-medical model of language that few contemporary students of the use of language, from educators to literary theorists, would support. Furthermore, the notion of remediation, carrying with it as it does the etymological wisps and traces of disease, serves to exclude from the academic community those who are so labelled. They sit in scholastic quarantine until their disease can be diagnosed and remedied.

ILLITERACY

In a recent meeting on graduation requirements, a UCLA dean referred to students in remedial English as "the truly illiterate among us." Another administrator, in a memorandum on the potential benefits of increasing the number of composition offerings, concluded sadly that the increase "would not provide any assurance of universal literacy at UCLA." This sort of talk about illiteracy is common. We hear it from college presidents, educational foundations, pop grammarians, and scores of college professors like the one who cried to me after a recent senate meeting, "All I want is a student who can write a simple declarative sentence!" We in the academy like to talk this way.[16] It is dramatic and urgent, and, given the current concerns about illiteracy in the United States, it is topical. The trouble is, it is wrong. Perhaps we can better understand the problems with such labelling if we leave our colleagues momentarily and consider what it is that literacy means.

To be literate means to be acquainted with letters or writings. But exactly how such acquaintance translates into behavior varies a good deal over time and place. During the last century this country's Census Bureau defined as literate anyone who could write his or her name. These days the government requires that one be able to read and write at a sixth-grade level to be *functionally* literate: that is, to be able to meet—to a minimal degree—society's reading and writing demands. Things get a bit more complex if we consider the other meanings "literacy" has acquired. There are some specialized uses of the term, all fairly new: computer literacy, mathematical literacy, visual literacy, and so on. Literacy here refers to an acquaintance with the "letters" or elements of a particular field or domain. And there are also some very general uses of the term. Cultural literacy, another new construction, is hard to define because it is so broad and so variously used, but it most often refers to an acquaintance with the humanistic, scientific, and social scientific achievements of one's dominant culture. Another general use of the term, a more traditional one, refers to the attainment of a liberal education, particularly in belles-lettres. Such literacy, of course, is quite advanced and involves not only an acquaintance with a literary tradition but interpretive sophistication as well.

Going back over these definitions, we can begin by dismissing the newer, specialized uses of "literacy." Computer literacy and other such literacies are usually not the focus of the general outcries we have been considering. How about the fundamental definition as it is currently established? This does not seem applicable either, for though many of the students entering American universities write prose that is grammatically and organizationally flawed, with very few exceptions they can read and write at a sixth-grade level. A sixth-grade proficiency is, of course, absurdly inadequate to do the work of higher education, but the definition still stands. By the most common measure the vast majority of students in college are literate. When academics talk about illiteracy they are saying that our students are "without letters" and cannot "write a simple declarative sentence." And such talk, for most students in most segments of higher education, is inaccurate and misleading.

One could argue that though our students are literate by common definition, a significant percentage of them might not be if we shift to the cultural and belletristic definitions of literacy or to a truly functional-contextual definition: that is, given the sophisticated, specialized reading and writing demands of the university—and the general knowledge they require—then it might be appropriate to talk of a kind of cultural illiteracy among some percentage of the student body. These students lack knowledge of the achievements of a tradition and are not at home with the ways we academics write about them. Perhaps this use of illiteracy is more warranted than the earlier talk about simple declarative sentences, but I would still advise caution. It is my experience that American college students tend to have learned more about western culture through their twelve years of schooling than their papers or pressured classroom responses demonstrate. (And, of course, our immigrant students bring with them a different cultural knowledge that we might not tap at all.) The problem is that the knowledge these students possess is often incomplete and fragmented and is not organized in ways that they can readily use in academic writing situations. But to say this is not to say that their minds are cultural blank slates.

There is another reason to be concerned about inappropriate claims of illiteracy. The term illiteracy comes to us with a good deal of semantic baggage, so that while an appropriately modified use of the term may accurately denote, it can still misrepresent by what it suggests, by the traces it carries from earlier eras. The social historian and anthropologist Shirley Brice Heath points out that from the mid-nineteenth century on, American school-based literacy was identified with "character, intellect, morality, and good taste . . . literacy skills co-occurred with moral patriotic character."[17] To be literate is to be honorable and intelligent. Tag some group illiterate, and you've gone beyond letters; you've judged their morals and their minds.

Please understand, it is not my purpose here to whitewash the very real limitations a disheartening number of our students bring with them. I dearly wish that more of them were more at home with composing and could write critically better than they do. I wish they enjoyed struggling for graceful written language more than many seem to. I wish they possessed more knowledge about humanities and the sciences so they could write with more authority than they usually do. And I wish to God that more of them read novels and poems for pleasure. But it is simply wrong to leap from these unrequited desires to claims of illiteracy. Reading and writing, as any ethnographic study would show, are woven throughout our students' lives. They write letters; some keep diaries. They read about what interests them, and those interests range from rock and roll to computer graphics to black holes. Reading, for many, is part of religious observation. They carry out a number of reading and writing acts in their jobs and in their interactions with various segments of society. Their college preparatory curriculum in high school, admittedly to widely varying degrees, is built on reading, and even the most beleaguered schools require some kind of writing. And many of these students read and even write in languages other than English. No, these students are not illiterate, by common definition, and if the more sophisticated definitions apply, they sacrifice their accuracy by all they imply.

Illiteracy is a problematic term. I suppose that academics use it because it is rhetorically effective (evoking the specter of illiteracy to an audience of peers, legislators, or taxpayers can be awfully persuasive) or because it is emotionally satisfying. It gives expression to the frustration and disappointment in teaching students who do not share one's passions. As well, it affirms the faculty's membership in the society of the literate. One reader of this essay suggested to me that academics realize the hyperbole in their illiteracy talk, do not really mean it to be taken, well, literally. Were this invariably true, I would still voice concern over such exaggeration, for, as with any emotionally propelled utterance, it might well be revealing deeply held attitudes and beliefs, perhaps not unlike those discussed by Heath. And, deeply felt or not, such talk in certain political and decision-making settings can dramatically influence the outcomes of deliberation.

The fact remains that cries of illiteracy substitute a fast quip for careful analysis. Definitional accuracy here is important, for if our students are in fact adult illiterates, then a particular, very special curriculum is needed. If they are literate but do not read much for pleasure, or lack general knowledge that is central to academic inquiry, or need to write more than they do and pay more attention to it than they are inclined to, well, then these are very different problems. They bring with them quite different institutional commitments and pedagogies, and they locate the student in a very different place in the social-political makeup of the academy. Determining that place is crucial, for where but in the academy would being "without letters" be so stigmatizing?

THE MYTH OF TRANSIENCE

I have before me a report from the California Postsecondary Education Commission called *Promises to Keep*. It is a comprehensive and fair-minded assessment of remedial instruction in the three segments of California's public college and university system. As all such reports do, *Promises to Keep* presents data on instruction and expenses, discusses the implications of the data, and calls for reform. What makes the report unusual is its inclusion of an historical overview of preparatory instruction in the United States. It acknowledges the fact that such instruction in some guise has always been with us. In spite of its acknowledgement, the report ends on a note of optimism characteristic of similar documents with less historical wisdom. It calls for all three segments of the higher education system to "implement . . . plans to reduce remediation" within five years and voices the hope that if secondary education can be improved, "within a very few years, the state and its institutions should be rewarded by . . . lower costs for remediation as the need for remediation declines." This optimism in the face of a disconfirming historical survey attests to the power of what I will call the myth of transience. Despite the accretion of crisis reports, the belief persists in the American university that if we can just do *x* or *y*, the problem will be solved—in five years, ten years, or a generation—and higher education will be able to return to its real work. But entertain with me the possibility that such peaceful reform is a chimera.

Each generation of academicians facing the characteristic American shifts in demographics and accessibility sees the problem anew, laments it in the terms of the era, and optimistically notes its impermanence. No one seems to say that this scenario has gone on for so long that it might not be temporary. That, in fact, there will probably *always* be a significant percentage of students who do not meet some standard. (It was in 1841, not 1985 that the president of Brown complained, "Students frequently enter college almost wholly unacquainted with English grammar . . ." [Frederick Rudolph, *Curriculum: A History of the American Undergraduate Course of Study* (San Francisco: Jossey-Bass, 1978), p. 88].) The American higher educational system is constantly under pressure to expand, to redefine its boundaries, admitting, in turn, the sons of the middle class, and later the daughters, and then the American poor, the immigrant poor, veterans, the racially segregated, the disenfranchised. Because of the social and educational conditions these groups experienced, their preparation for college will, of course, be varied. Add to this the fact that disciplines change and society's needs change, and the ways society determines what it means to be educated change.

All this works itself rather slowly into the pre-collegiate curriculum. Thus there will always be a percentage of students who will be tagged substandard. And though many insist that this continued opening of doors will sacrifice excellence in the name of democracy, there are too many economic, political, and ethical drives in American culture to restrict higher education to a select minority. (And, make no mistake, the history of the American college and university from the early nineteenth century on could also be read as a history of changes in admissions, curriculum, and public image in order to keep enrollments high and institutions solvent.[18] The research institution as we know it is made possible by robust undergraduate enrollments.) Like it or not, the story of American education has been and will in all likelihood continue to be a story of increasing access. University of Nashville President Philip Lindsley's 1825 call echoes back and forth across our history: "The farmer, the mechanic, the manufacturer, the merchant, the sailor, the soldier . . . must be educated" (Frederick Rudolph, *The American College and University: A History* [New York: Vintage, 1962], p. 117).

Why begrudge academics their transience myth? After all, each generation's problems are new to those who face them, and people faced with a problem need some sense that they can solve it. Fair enough. But it seems to me that this myth brings with it a powerful liability. It blinds faculty members to historical reality and to the dynamic and fluid nature of the educational system that employs them. Like any golden age or utopian myth, the myth of transience assures its believers that the past was better or that the future will be.[19] The turmoil they are currently in will pass. The source of the problem is elsewhere; thus it can be ignored or temporarily dealt with until the tutors or academies or grammar schools or high schools or families make the changes they must make. The myth, then, serves to keep certain fundamental recognitions and thus certain fundamental changes at bay. It is ultimately a conservative gesture, a way of preserving administrative and curricular status quo.

And the myth plays itself out against complex social-political dynamics. One force in these dynamics is the ongoing struggle to establish admissions requirements that would protect the college curriculum, that would, in fact, define its difference from the high school course of study. Another is the related struggle to influence, even determine, the nature of the high school curriculum, "academize" it, shape it to the needs of the college (and the converse struggle of the high school to declare its multiplicity of purposes, college preparation being only one of its mandates). Yet another is the tension between the undergraduate, general education function of the university vs. its graduate, research function. To challenge the myth is to vibrate these complex dynamics; thus it is that it is so hard to dispel. But I would suggest that it must be challenged, for though some temporary "remedial" measures are excellent and generously funded, the presence of the myth does not allow them to be thought through in terms of the whole curriculum and does not allow the information they reveal to reciprocally influence the curriculum. Basic modifications in educational philosophy, institutional purpose, and professional training are rarely considered. They do not need to be if the problem is temporary. The myth allows the final exclusionary gesture: The problem is not ours in any fundamental way; we can embrace it if we must, but with surgical gloves on our hands.

There may be little anyone can do to change the fundamental tension in the American university between the general educational mission and the research mission, or to remove the stigma attached to application. But there is something those of us involved in writing can do about the language that has formed the field on which institutional discussions of writing and its teaching take place.

We can begin by affirming a rich model of written language development and production. The model we advance must honor the cognitive and emotional and situational dimensions of language, be psycholinguistic as well as literary and rhetorical in its focus, and aid us in understanding what we can observe as well as what we can only infer. When discussions and debates reveal a more reductive model of language, we must call time out and reestablish the terms of the argument. But we must also rigorously examine our own teaching and see what model of language lies beneath it. What linguistic assumptions are cued when we face freshman writers? Are they compatible with the assumptions that are cued when we think about our own writing or the writing of those we read for pleasure? Do we too operate with the bifurcated mind that for too long characterized the teaching of "remedial" students and that is still reflected in the language of our institutions?

Remediation. It is time to abandon this troublesome metaphor. To do so will not blind us to the fact that many entering students are not adequately prepared to take on the demands of university work. In fact, it will help us perceive these young people and the work they do in ways that foster appropriate notions about language development and use, that establish a framework for more rigorous and comprehensive analysis of their difficulties, and that do not perpetuate the raree show of allowing them entrance to the academy while, in various symbolic ways, denying them full participation.

Mina Shaughnessy got us to see that even the most error-ridden prose arises from the confrontation of inexperienced student writers with the complex linguistic and rhetorical expectations of the academy. She reminded us that to properly teach writing to such students is to understand "the intelligence of their mistakes."[20] She told us to interpret errors rather than circle them, and to guide these students, gradually and with wisdom, to be more capable participants within the world of these conventions. If we fully appreciate her message, we see how inadequate and limiting the remedial model is. Instead we need to define our work as transitional or as initiatory, orienting, or socializing to what David Bartholomae and Patricia Bizzell call the academic discourse community.[21] This redefinition is not just semantic sleight-of-hand. If truly adopted, it would require us to reject a medical-deficit model of language, to acknowledge the rightful place of all freshmen in the academy, and once and for all to replace loose talk about illiteracy with more precise and pedagogically fruitful analysis. We would move from a mechanistic focus on error toward a demanding curriculum that encourages the full play of language activity and that opens out onto the academic community rather than sequestering students from it.

A much harder issue to address is the common designation of writing as a skill. We might begin by considering more fitting terms. Jerome Bruner's "enabling discipline" comes to mind. It does not separate skill from discipline and implies something more than a "tool subject" in that to enable means to make possible. But such changes in diction might be little more than cosmetic.

If the skills designation proves to be resistant to change, then we must insist that writing is a very unique skill, not really a tool but an ability fundamental to academic inquiry, an ability whose development is not fixed but ongoing. If it is possible to go beyond the skills model, we could see a contesting of the fundamental academic distinction between integrated bodies of knowledge and skills and techniques. While that distinction makes sense in many cases, it may blur where writing is concerned. Do students really *know* history when they learn a "body" of facts, even theories, or when they act like historians, thinking in certain ways with those facts and theories? Most historians would say the latter. And the academic historian (vs. the chronicler or the balladeer) conducts inquiry through writing; it is not just an implement but is part of the very way of doing history.

It is in this context that we should ponder the myth of transience. The myth's liability is that it limits the faculty's ability to consider the writing problems of their students in dynamic and historical terms. Each academic generation considers standards and assesses the preparation of its students but seems to do this in ways that do not call the nature of the curriculum of the time into question. The problem ultimately lies outside the academy. But might not these difficulties with writing suggest the need for possible far-ranging changes within the curriculum as well, changes that *are* the proper concern of the university? One of the things I think the myth of transience currently does is to keep faculty from seeing the multiple possibilities that exist for incorporating writing throughout their courses of study. Profound reform could occur in the much-criticized lower-division curriculum if writing were not seen as only a technique and the teaching of it as by and large a remedial enterprise.

The transmission of a discipline, especially on the lower-division level, has become very much a matter of comprehending information, committing it to memory, recalling it, and displaying it in various kinds of "objective" or short-answer tests. When essay exams are required, the prose all too often becomes nothing more than a net in which the catch of individual bits of knowledge lie. Graders pick through the essay and tally up the presence of key phrases. Such activity trivializes a discipline; it reduces its methodology, grounds it in a limited theory of knowledge, and encourages students to operate with a restricted range of their cognitive abilities. Writing, on the other hand, assumes a richer epistemology and demands fuller participation. It requires a complete, active, struggling engagement with the facts and principles of a discipline, an encounter with the discipline's texts and the incorporation of them into one's own work, the framing of one's knowledge within the myriad conventions that help define a discipline, the persuading of other investigators that one's knowledge is legitimate. So to consider the relationship between writing and disciplinary inquiry may help us decide what is central to a discipline and how best to teach it. The university's research and educational missions would intersect.

Such reform will be difficult. True, there is growing interest in writing adjuncts and discipline-specific writing courses, and those involved in writing-across-the-curriculum are continually encouraging faculty members to evaluate the place of writing in their individual curricula. But wide-ranging change will occur only if the academy redefines writing for itself, changes the terms of the argument, sees instruction in writing as one of its central concerns.

Academic senates often defend the labelling of a writing course as remedial by saying that they are defending the integrity of the baccalaureate, and they are sending a message to the high schools. The schools, of course, are so beleaguered that they can barely hear those few units ping into the bucket. Consider, though, the message that would be sent to the schools and to the society at large if the university embraced—not just financially but conceptually—the teaching of writing: if we gave it full status, championed its rich relationship with inquiry, insisted on the importance of craft and grace, incorporated it into the heart of our curriculum. What an extraordinary message that would be. It would affect the teaching of writing as no other message could.

Author's note: I wish to thank Arthur Applebee, Robert Connors, Carol Hartzog, and William Schaefer for reading and generously commenting on an earlier version of this essay. Connors and Hartzog also helped me revise that version. Bill Richey provided research assistance of remarkably high caliber, and Tom Bean, Kenyon Chan, Patricia Donahue, Jack Kolb, and Bob Schwegler offered advice and encouragement. Finally, a word of thanks to Richard Lanham for urging me to think of our current problem in broader contexts.

NOTES

1. Quoted in Lawrence A. Cremin, *The Transformation of the School: Progressivism in American Education* (New York: Alfred A. Knopf, 1961), p. 185.

2. Arthur N. Applebee, *Tradition and Reform in the Teaching of English: A History* (Urbana, Ill.: National Council of Teachers of English, 1974), pp. 93–94.

3. P. G. Perrin, "The Remedial Racket," *English Journal*, 22 (1993), 383.

4. From Cubberley's introduction to Albert R. Lang, *Modern Methods in Written Examinations* (Boston: Houghton Mifflin, 1930), p. vii.

5. "Background Deficiencies," *Journal of Higher Education,* 3 (1932), 371.

6. "Remedial Methods in English Composition," *English Journal,* 22 (1933), 749–754.

7. "Freshmen Needs in Written English," *English Journal,* 19 (1930), 706.

8. I would mislead if I did not point out that there were cautionary voices being raised all along, though until the late 1930s they were very much in the minority. For two early appraisals, see R. L. Lyman, *Summary of Investigations Relating to Grammar, Language, and Composition* (Chicago: University of Chicago Press, 1924), and especially P. G. Perrin, "The Remedial Racket," *English Journal,* 22 (1933), 382–388.

9. Two quotations. The first offers the sort of humanist battle cry that often accompanies reductive drill, and the second documents the results of such an approach. Both are from NCTE publications.

"I think . . . that the chief objective of freshman English (at least for the first semester and low or middle—but not high—sections) should be ceaseless, brutal drill on mechanics, with exercises and themes. Never mind imagination, the soul, literature, for at least one semester, but pray for literacy and fight for it" (A University of Nebraska professor quoted with approval in Oscar James Campbell, *The Teaching of College English* [New York: Appleton-Century, 1934], pp. 36–37).

"Members of the Task Force saw in many classes extensive work in traditional school-room grammar and traditional formal English usage. They commonly found students with poor reading skills being taught the difference between *shall* and *will* or pupils with serious difficulties in speech diagraming sentences. Interestingly, observations by the Task Force reveal far more extensive teaching of traditional grammar in this study of language programs for the disadvantaged than observers saw in the National Study of High School English Programs, a survey of comprehensive high schools known to be achieving important results in English with college-bound students able to comprehend the abstractions of such grammar" (Richard Corbin and Muriel Crosby, *Language Programs for the Disadvantaged* [Urbana, Ill.: NCTE, 1965], pp. 121–122).

10. In 1894, for example, over 40% of entering freshmen came from the preparatory divisions of the institutions that enrolled them. And as late as 1915—a time when the quantity and quality of secondary schools had risen sufficiently to make preparatory divisions less necessary—350 American colleges still maintained their programs. See John S. Brubacher and Willis Rudy, *Higher Education in Transition: A History of American Colleges and Universities, 1636–1976,* 3rd ed. (New York: Harper and Row, 1976), pp. 241 ff., and Arthur Levine, *Handbook on Undergraduate Curriculum* (San Francisco: Jossey-Bass, 1981), pp. 54 ff.

11. Several writers point to a study habits course initiated at Wellesley in 1894 as the first modern remedial course in higher education (K. Patricia Cross, *Accent on Learning* [San Francisco: Jossey-Bass, 1979], and Arthur Levine, *Handbook on Undergraduate Curriculum*). In fact, the word "remedial" did not appear in the course's title and the course was different in kind from the courses actually designated "remedial" that would emerge in the 1920s and 30s. (See Cross, pp. 24–25, for a brief discussion of early study skills courses.) The first use of the term "remedial" in the context I am discussing was most likely in a 1916 article on the use of reading tests to plan "remedial work" (Nila Banton Smith, *American Reading Instruction* [Newark, Delaware: International Reading Association, 1965], p. 191). The first elementary and secondary level remedial courses in reading were offered in the early 1920s; remedial courses in college would not appear until the late 20s.

12. *Letter-, Word-, and Mind-Blindness* (London: Lewis, 1902); *Congenital Word-Blindness* (London: Lewis, 1917).

13. "The 'Sight Reading' Method of Teaching Reading, as a Source of Reading Disability," *Journal of Educational Psychology*, 20 (1929), 135–143.

14. There were, of course, some theorists and practitioners who questioned medical-physiological models, Arthur Gates of Columbia Teacher's College foremost among them. But even those who questioned such models—with the exception of Gates—tended to retain medical language.

15. There is another layer to this terminological and conceptual confusion. At the same time that remediation language was being used ever more broadly by some educators, it maintained its strictly medical usage in other educational fields. For example, Annie Dolman Inskeep has only one discussion of "remedial work" in her book *Teaching Dull and Retarded Children* (New York: Macmillan, 1926), and that discussion has to do with treatment for children needing health care: "Children who have poor teeth, who do not hear well, or who hold a book when reading nearer than eight inches to the eyes or further away than sixteen. . . . Nervous children, those showing continuous fatigue symptoms, those under weight, and those who are making no apparent bodily growth" (p. 271).

16. For a sometimes humorous but more often distressing catalogue of such outcries, see Harvey A. Daniels, *Famous Last Words* (Carbondale: Southern Illinois University Press, 1983), especially pp. 31–58.

17. "Toward an Ethnohistory of Writing in American Education," in Marcia Farr Whiteman, ed., *Writing: The Nature, Development, and Teaching of Written Communication*, Vol. 1 (Hillsdale, N.J.: Erlbaum, 1981), 35–36.

18. Of turn-of-the-century institutions, Laurence Veysey writes: "Everywhere the size of enrollments was closely tied to admission standards. In order to assure themselves of enough students to make a notable "splash," new institutions often opened with a welcome to nearly all comers, no matter how ill prepared; this occurred at Cornell, Stanford, and (to a lesser degree) at Chicago" (*The Emergence of the American University*, p. 357).

19. An appropriate observation here comes from Daniel P. and Lauren B. Resnick's critical survey of reading instruction and standards of literacy: "there is little to go back to in terms of pedagogical method, curriculum, or school organization. The old tried and true approaches, which nostalgia prompts us to believe might solve current problems, were designed neither to achieve the literacy standard sought today nor to assure successful literacy for everyone . . . there is no simple past to which we can return" ("The Nature of Literacy: An Historical Exploration," *Harvard Educational Review*, 47 [1977], 385).

20. *Errors and Expectations* (New York: Oxford University Press, 1977), p. 11.

21. David Bartholomae, "Inventing the University," in Mike Rose, ed., *When a Writer Can't Write: Studies in Writer's Block and Other Composing Process Problems* (New York: Guilford, 1985); Patricia Bizzell, "College Composition: Initiation into the Academic Discourse Community," *Curriculum Inquiry*, 12 (1982), 191–207.

Composing as a Woman

Elizabeth A. Flynn

It is not easy to think like a woman in a man's world, in the world of the professions; yet the capacity to do that is a strength which we can try to help our students develop. To think like a woman in a man's world means thinking critically, refusing to accept the givens, making connections between facts and ideas which men have left unconnected. It means remembering that every mind resides in a body; remaining accountable to the female bodies in which we live; constantly retesting given hypotheses against lived experience. It means a constant critique of language, for as Wittgenstein (no feminist) observed, "The limits of my language are the limits of my world." And it means that most difficult thing of all: listening and watching in art and literature, in the social sciences, in all the descriptions we are given of the world, for silences, the absences, the nameless, the unspoken, the encoded—for there we will find the true knowledge of women. And in breaking those silences, naming ourselves, uncovering the hidden, making ourselves present, we begin to define a reality which resonates to us, which affirms our being, which allows the woman teacher and the woman student alike to take ourselves, and each other, seriously: meaning, to begin taking charge of our lives.

—Adrienne Rich, "Taking Women Students Seriously"

The emerging field of composition studies could be described as a feminization of our previous conceptions of how writers write and how writing should be taught.[1] In exploring the nature of the writing process, composition specialists expose the limitations of previous product-oriented approaches by

---

Reprinted from *College Composition and Communication* 39.4 (December 1988): 423–35. Used with permission.

demystifying the product and in so doing empowering developing writers and readers. Rather than enshrining the text in its final form, they demonstrate that the works produced by established authors are often the result of an extended, frequently enormously frustrating process and that creativity is an activity that results from experience and hard work rather than a mysterious gift reserved for a select few. In a sense, composition specialists replace the figure of the authoritative father with an image of a nurturing mother. Powerfully present in the work of composition researchers and theorists is the ideal of a committed teacher concerned about the growth and maturity of her students who provides feedback on ungraded drafts, reads journals, and attempts to tease out meaning from the seeming incoherence of student language. The field's foremothers come to mind—Janet Emig, Mina Shaughnessy, Ann Berthoff, Win Horner, Maxine Hairston, Shirley Heath, Nancy Martin, Linda Flower, Andrea Lunsford, Sondra Perl, Nancy Sommers, Marion Crowhurst, Lisa Ede. I'll admit the term foremother seems inappropriate as some of these women are still in their thirties and forties—we are speaking here of a very young field. Still, invoking their names suggests that we are also dealing with a field that, from the beginning, has welcomed contributions from women—indeed, has been shaped by women.

The work of male composition researchers and theorists has also contributed significantly to the process of feminization described above. James Britton, for instance, reverses traditional hierarchies by privileging private expression over public transaction, process over product. In arguing that writing for the self is the matrix out of which all forms of writing develop, he valorizes an activity and a mode of expression that have previously been undervalued or invisible, much as feminist literary critics have argued that women's letters and diaries are legitimate literary forms and should be studied and taught alongside more traditional genres. His work has had an enormous impact on the way writing is taught on the elementary and high school levels and in the university, not only in English courses but throughout the curriculum. Writing-Across-the-Curriculum Programs aim to transform pedagogical practices in all disciplines, even those where patriarchal attitudes toward authority are most deeply rooted.

FEMINIST STUDIES
AND COMPOSITION STUDIES

Feminist inquiry and composition studies have much in common. After all, feminist researchers and scholars and composition specialists are usually in the same department and sometimes teach the same courses. Not surprisingly, there have been wonderful moments when feminists have expressed their commitment to the teaching of writing. Florence Howe's essay, "Identity and Expression: A Writing Course for Women," for example, published in *College English* in 1971, describes her use of journals in a writing course designed to empower women. Adrienne Rich's essay, "'When We Dead Awaken': Writing as Re-Vision," politicizes and expands our conception of revision, emphasizing that taking another look at the texts we have generated necessitates revising our cultural assumptions as well.

There have also been wonderful moments when composition specialists have recognized that the marginality of the field of composition studies is linked in important ways to the political marginality of its constituents, many of whom are women who teach part-time. Maxine Hairston, in "Breaking Our Bonds and Reaffirming Our Connections," a slightly revised version of her Chair's address at the 1985 convention of the Conference on College Composition and Communication, draws an analogy between the plight of composition specialists and the plight of many women. For both, their worst problems begin at home and hence are immediate and daily. Both, too, often have complex psychological bonds to the people who frequently are their adversaries (273).

For the most part, though, the fields of feminist studies and composition studies have not engaged each other in a serious or systematic way. The major journals in the field of composition studies do not often include articles addressing feminist issues, and panels on feminism are infrequent at the Conference on College Composition and Communication.[2] As a result, the parallels between feminist studies and composition studies have not been delineated, and the feminist critique that has enriched such diverse fields as linguistics, reading, literary criticism, psychology, sociology, anthropology, religion, and science has had little impact on our models of the composing process or on our understanding of how written language abilities are acquired. We have not examined our research methods or research samples to see if they are androcentric. Nor have we attempted to determine just what it means to compose as a woman.

Feminist research and theory emphasize that males and females differ in their developmental processes and in their interactions with others. They emphasize, as well, that these differences are a result of an imbalance in the social order, of the dominance of men over women. They argue that men have chronicled our historical narratives and defined our fields of inquiry. Women's perspectives have been suppressed, silenced, marginalized, written out of what counts as authoritative knowledge. Difference is erased in a desire to universalize. Men become the standard against which women are judged.

A feminist approach to composition studies would focus on questions of difference and dominance in written language. Do males and females compose differently? Do they acquire language in different ways? Do research methods and research samples in composition studies reflect a male bias? I do not intend to tackle all of these issues. My approach here is a relatively modest one. I will survey recent feminist research on gender differences in social and psychological development, and I will show how this research and theory may be used in examining student writing, thus suggesting directions that a feminist investigation of composition might take.

GENDER DIFFERENCES IN SOCIAL AND PSYCHOLOGICAL DEVELOPMENT

Especially relevant to a feminist consideration of student writing are Nancy Chodorow's *The Reproduction of Mothering*, Carol Gilligan's *In a Different Voice*, and Mary Belenky, Blythe Clinchy, Nancy Goldberger, and Jill Tarule's *Women's Ways of Knowing*. All three books suggest that women and men have different conceptions of self and different modes of interaction with others as a result of their different experiences, especially their early relationship with their primary parent, their mother.

Chodorow's book, published in 1978, is an important examination of what she calls the "psychoanalysis and the sociology of gender," which in turn influenced Gilligan's *In a Different Voice* and Belenky et al.'s *Women's Ways of Knowing*. Chodorow tells us in her preface that her book originated when a feminist group she was affiliated with "wondered what it meant that women parented women." She argues that girls and boys develop different relational capacities and senses of self as a result of growing up in a family in which women mother. Because all children identify first with their mother, a girl's gender and gender role identification processes are continuous with her earliest identifications whereas a boy's are not. The boy gives up, in addition to his oedipal and preoedipal attachment to his mother, his primary identification with her. The more general identification processes for both males and females also follow this pattern. Chodorow says,

> Girls' identification processes, then, are more continuously embedded in and mediated by their ongoing relationship with their mother. They develop through and stress particularistic and affective relationships to others. A boy's identification processes are not likely to be so embedded in or mediated by a real affective relation to his father. At the same time, he tends to deny identification with and relationship to his mother and reject

what he takes to be the feminine world; masculinity is defined as much negatively as positively. Masculine identification processes stress differentiation from others, the denial of affective relation, and categorical universalistic components of the masculine role. Feminine identification processes are relational, whereas masculine identification processes tend to deny relationship. (176)

Carol Gilligan's *In a Different Voice,* published in 1982, builds on Chodorow's findings, focusing especially, though, on differences in the ways in which males and females speak about moral problems. According to Gilligan, women tend to define morality in terms of conflicting responsibilities rather than competing rights, requiring for their resolution a mode of thinking that is contextual and narrative rather than formal and abstract (19). Men, in contrast, equate morality and fairness and tie moral development to the understanding of rights and rules (19). Gilligan uses the metaphors of the web and the ladder to illustrate these distinctions. The web suggests interconnectedness as well as entrapment; the ladder suggests an achievement-orientation as well as individualistic and hierarchical thinking. Gilligan's study aims to correct the inadequacies of Lawrence Kohlberg's delineation of the stages of moral development. Kohlberg's study included only male subjects, and his categories reflect his decidedly male orientation. For him, the highest stages of moral development derive from a reflective understanding of human rights (19).

Belenky, Clinchy, Goldberger, and Tarule, in *Women's Ways of Knowing,* acknowledge their debt to Gilligan, though their main concern is intellectual rather than moral development. Like Gilligan, they recognize that male experience has served as the model in defining processes of intellectual maturation. The mental processes that are involved in considering the abstract and the impersonal have been labeled "thinking" and are attributed primarily to men, while those that deal with the personal and interpersonal fall under the rubric of "emotions" and are largely relegated to women. The particular study they chose to examine and revise is William Perry's *Forms of Intellectual and Ethical Development in the College Years* (1970). While Perry did include some women subjects in his study, only the interviews with men were used in illustrating and validating his scheme of intellectual and ethical development. When Perry assessed women's development on the basis of the categories he developed, the women were found to conform to the patterns he had observed in the male data. Thus, his work reveals what women have in common with men but was poorly designed to uncover those themes that might be more prominent among women. *Women's Ways of Knowing* focuses on "what else women might have to say about the development of their minds and on alternative routes that are sketchy or missing in Perry's version" (9).

Belenky et al. examined the transcripts of interviews with 135 women from a variety of backgrounds and of different ages and generated categories that are suited for describing the stages of women's intellectual development. They found that the quest for self and voice plays a central role in transformations of women's ways of knowing. Silent women have little awareness of their intellectual capacities. They live—selfless and voiceless— at the behest of those around them. External authorities know the truth and are all-powerful. At the positions of received knowledge and procedural knowledge, other voices and external truths prevail. Sense of self is embedded either in external definitions and roles or in identifications with institutions, disciplines, and methods. A sense of authority arises primarily through identification with the power of a group and its agreed-upon ways for knowing. Women at this stage of development have no sense of an authentic or unique voice, little awareness of a centered self. At the position of subjective knowledge, women turn away from others and any external authority. They have not yet acquired a public voice or public authority, though. Finally, women at the phase of constructed knowledge begin an effort to reclaim the self by attempting to integrate knowledge they feel intuitively with knowledge they have learned from others.

STUDENT WRITING

If women and men differ in their relational capacities and in their moral and intellectual development, we would expect to find manifestations of these differences in the student papers we encounter in our first-year composition courses. The student essays I will describe here are narrative descriptions of learning experiences produced in the first of a two-course sequence required of first-year students at Michigan Tech. I've selected the four because they invite commentary from the perspective of the material discussed above. The narratives of the female students are stories of interaction, of connection, or of frustrated connection. The narratives of the male students are stories of achievement, of separation, or of frustrated achievement.

Kim's essay describes a dreamlike experience in which she and her high school girlfriends connected with each other and with nature as a result of a balloon ride they decided to take one summer Sunday afternoon as a way of relieving boredom. From the start, Kim emphasizes communion and tranquility: "It was one of those Sunday afternoons when the sun shines brightly and a soft warm breeze blows gently. A perfect day for a long drive on a country road with my favorite friends." This mood is intensified as they ascend in the balloon: "Higher and higher we went, until the view was overpowering. What once was a warm breeze turned quickly into a cool crisp wind. A feeling of freedom and serenity overtook us as we drifted along slowly." The group felt as if they were "just suspended there on a string, with time non-existent." The experience made them contemplative, and as they drove quietly home, "each one of us collected our thoughts, and to this day we still reminisce about that Sunday afternoon." The experience solidified relationships and led to the formation of a close bond that was renewed every time the day was recollected.

The essay suggests what Chodorow calls relational identification processes. The members of the group are described as being in harmony with themselves and with the environment. There is no reference to competition or discord. The narrative also suggests a variation on what Belenky et al. call "connected knowing," a form of procedural knowledge that makes possible the most desirable form of knowing, constructed knowledge. Connected knowing is rooted in empathy for others and is intensely personal. Women who are connected knowers are able to detach themselves from the relationships and institutions to which they have been subordinated and begin to trust their own intuitions. The women in the narrative were connected doers rather than connected knowers. They went off on their own, left their families and teachers behind (it was summer vacation, after all), and gave themselves over to a powerful shared experience. The adventure was, for the most part, a silent one but did lead to satisfying talk.

Kathy also describes an adventure away from home, but hers was far less satisfying, no doubt because it involved considerably more risk. In her narrative she makes the point that "foreign countries can be frightening" by focusing on a situation in which she and three classmates, two females and a male, found themselves at a train station in Germany separated from the others because they had gotten off to get some refreshments and the train had left without them. She says,

> This left the four of us stranded in an unfamiliar station. Ed was the only person in our group that could speak German fluently, but he still didn't know what to do. Sue got hysterical and Laura tried to calm her down. I stood there stunned. We didn't know what to do.

What they did was turn to Ed, whom Kathy describes as "the smartest one in our group." He told them to get on a train that was on the same track as the original. Kathy realized, though, after talking to some passengers, that they were on the wrong train and urged her classmates to get off. She says,

> I almost panicked. When I convinced the other three we were on the wrong train we opened the doors. As we were getting off, one of the conductors started yelling at us in German. It didn't bother me too much because I couldn't understand what he was saying. One thing about trains in Europe is that they are always on schedule. I think we delayed that train about a minute or two.

In deciding which train to board after getting off the wrong one, they deferred to Ed's judgment once again, but this time they got on the right train. Kathy concludes, "When we got off the train everyone was waiting. It turned out we arrived thirty minutes later than our original train. I was very relieved to see everyone. It was a very frightening experience and I will never forget it."

In focusing on her fears of separation, Kathy reveals her strong need for connection, for affiliation. Her story, like Kim's, emphasizes the importance of relationships, though in a different way. She reveals that she had a strong need to feel part of a group and no desire to rebel, to prove her independence, to differentiate herself from others. This conception of self was a liability as well as a strength in the sense that she became overly dependent on the male authority figure in the group, whom she saw as smarter and more competent than herself. In Belenky et al.'s terms, Kathy acted as if other voices and external truths were more powerful than her own. She did finally speak and act, though, taking it on herself to find out if they were on the right train and ushering the others off when she discovered they were not. She was clearly moving toward the development of an authentic voice and a way of knowing that integrates intuition with authoritative knowledge. After all, she was the real hero of the incident.

The men's narratives stress individuation rather than connection. They are stories of individual achievement or frustrated achievement and conclude by emphasizing separation rather than integration or reintegration into a community. Jim wrote about his "Final Flight," the last cross-country flight required for his pilot's license. That day, everything seemed to go wrong. First, his flight plan had a mistake in it that took $1\frac{1}{2}$ hours to correct. As a result, he left his hometown 2 hours behind schedule. Then the weather deteriorated, forcing him to fly as low as a person can safely fly, with the result that visibility was very poor. He landed safely at his first destination but flew past the second because he was enjoying the view too much. He says,

Then I was off again south bound for Benton Harbor. On the way south along the coast of Lake Michigan the scenery was a beautiful sight. This relieved some of the pressures and made me look forward to the rest of the flight. It was really nice to see the ice flows break away from the shore. While enjoying the view of a power plant on the shore of Lake Michigan I discovered I had flown past the airport.

He finally landed and took off again, but shortly thereafter had to confront darkness, a result of his being behind schedule. He says,

The sky turned totally black by the time I was half-way home. This meant flying in the dark which I had only done once before. Flying in the dark was also illegal for me to do at this time. One thing that made flying at night nice was that you could see lights that were over ninety miles away.

Jim does not emphasize his fear, despite the fact that his situation was more threatening than the one Kathy described, and his reference to his enjoyment of the scenery suggests that his anxiety was not paralyzing or debilitating. At times, his solitary flight was clearly as satisfying as Kim's communal one. When he focuses on the difficulties he encountered, he speaks only of his "problems" and "worries" and concludes that the day turned out to be "long and trying." He sums up his experience as follows: "That day I will long remember for both its significance in my goal in getting my pilot's license and all the problems or worries that it caused me during the long and problem-ridden flight." He emerges the somewhat shaken hero of his adventure; he has achieved his goal in the face of adversity. Significantly, he celebrates his return home by having a bite to eat at McDonald's by himself. His adventure does not end with a union or reunion with others.

Jim's story invites interpretation in the context of Chodorow's claims about male interactional patterns. Chodorow says that the male, in order to feel himself adequately masculine, must distinguish and differentiate himself from others. Jim's adventure was an entirely solitary one. It was also goal-directed—he wanted to obtain his pilot's license and, presumably, prove his competence to himself and others. His narrative calls into question, though, easy equations of abstract reasoning and impersonality with male modes of learning since Jim was clearly as capable as Kim of experiencing moments of exultation, of communion with nature.

Joe's narrative of achievement is actually a story of frustrated achievement, of conflicting attitudes toward an ethic of hard work and sacrifice to achieve a goal. When he was in high school, his father drove him twenty miles to swim practice and twenty miles home every Tuesday through

Friday night between October and March so he could practice for the swim team. He hated this routine and hated the Saturday morning swim meets even more but continued because he thought his parents, especially his father, wanted him to. He says, "I guess it was all for them, the cold workouts, the evening practices, the weekend meets. I had to keep going for them even though I hated it." Once he realized he was going through his agony for his parents rather than for himself, though, he decided to quit and was surprised to find that his parents supported him. Ultimately, though, he regretted his decision. He says,

> As it turns out now, I wish I had stuck with it. I really had a chance to go somewhere with my talent. I see kids my age who stuck with something for a long time and I envy them for their determination. I wish I had met up to the challenge of sticking with my swimming, because I could have been very good if I would have had their determination.

Joe is motivated to pursue swimming because he thinks his father will be disappointed if he gives it up. His father's presumed hold on him is clearly tenuous, however, because once Joe realizes that he is doing it for him rather than for himself, he quits. Finally, though, it is his gender role identification, his socialization into a male role and a male value system, that allows him to look back on his decision with regret. In college, he has become a competitor, an achiever. He now sees value in the long and painful practices, in a single-minded determination to succeed. The narrative reminds us of Chodorow's point that masculine identification is predominantly a gender role identification rather than identification with a particular parent.

I am hardly claiming that the four narratives are neat illustrations of the feminist positions discussed above. For one thing, those positions are rich in contradiction and complexity and defy easy illustration. For another, the narratives themselves are as often characterized by inconsistency and contradiction as by a univocality of theme and tone. Kathy is at once dependent and assertive; Joe can't quite decide if he should have been rebellious or disciplined. Nor am I claiming that what I have found here are characteristic patterns of male and female student writing. I would need a considerably larger and more representative sample to make such a claim hold. I might note, though, that I had little difficulty identifying essays that revealed patterns of difference among the twenty-four papers I had to choose from, and I could easily have selected others. Sharon, for instance, described her class trip to Chicago, focusing especially on the relationship she and her classmates were able to establish with her advisor. Diane described "An Unwanted Job" that she seemed unable to quit despite unpleasant working conditions. Mike, like Diane, was dissatisfied with his job, but he expressed his dissatisfaction and was fired. The frightening experience Russ described resulted from his failed attempt to give his car a tune-up; the radiator hose burst, and he found himself in the hospital recovering from third-degree burns. These are stories of relatedness or entanglement; of separation or frustrated achievement.

The description of the student essays is not meant to demonstrate the validity of feminist scholarship but to suggest, instead, that questions raised by feminist researchers and theorists do have a bearing on composition studies and should be pursued. We ought not assume that males and females use language in identical ways or represent the world in a similar fashion. And if their writing strategies and patterns of representation do differ, then ignoring those differences almost certainly means a suppression of women's separate ways of thinking and writing. Our models of the composing process are quite possibly better suited to describing men's ways of composing than to describing women's.[5]

PEDAGOGICAL STRATEGIES

The classroom provides an opportunity for exploring questions about gender differences in language use. Students, I have found, are avid inquirers into their own language processes. An approach I have had success with is to make the question of gender difference in behavior and language use the subject to be investigated in class. In one honors section of first-year English, for instance, course reading included selections from Mary Anne Ferguson's *Images of Women in Literature*, Gilligan's *In a Different Voice*, Alice Walker's *Meridian*, and James Joyce's *A Portrait of the Artist as a Young Man*. Students were also required to keep a reading journal and to submit two formal papers. The first was a description of people they know in order to arrive at generalizations about gender differences in behavior, the second a comparison of some aspect of the Walker and Joyce novels in the light of our class discussions.

During class meetings we shared journal entries, discussed the assigned literature, and self-consciously explored our own reading, writing, and speaking behaviors. In one session, for instance, we shared retellings of Irwin Shaw's "The Girls in Their Summer Dresses," an especially appropriate story since it describes the interaction of a husband and wife as they attempt to deal with the husband's apparently chronic habit of girl-watching. Most of the women were sympathetic to the female protagonist, and several males clearly identified strongly with the male protagonist.

The students reacted favorably to the course. They found Gilligan's book to be challenging, and they enjoyed the heated class discussions. The final journal entry of one of the strongest students in the class, Dorothy, suggests the nature of her development over the ten-week period:

> As this is sort of the wrap-up of what I've learned or how I feel about the class, I'll try to relate this entry to my first one on gender differences.
>
> I'm not so sure that men and women are so similar anymore, as I said in the first entry. The reactions in class especially make me think this. The men were so hostile toward Gilligan's book! I took no offense at it, but then again I'm not a man. I must've even overlooked the parts where she offended the men!
>
> Another thing really bothered me. One day after class, I heard two of the men talking in the hall about how you just have to be really careful about what you say in HU 101H about women, etc. *Why* do they have to be careful?! What did these two *really* want to say? That was pretty disturbing.
>
> However, I do still believe that MTU (or most any college actually) does bring out more similarities than differences. But the differences are still there—I know that.

Dorothy has begun to suspect that males and females read differently, and she has begun to suspect that they talk among themselves differently than they do in mixed company. The reading, writing, and discussing in the course have clearly alerted her to the possibility that gender affects the way in which readers, writers, and speakers use language.

This approach works especially well with honors students. I use somewhat different reading and writing assignments with non-honors students. In one class, for instance, I replaced the Gilligan book with an essay by Dale Spender on conversational patterns in high school classrooms. Students wrote a paper defending or refuting the Spender piece on the basis of their experiences in their own high schools. I have also devised ways of addressing feminist issues in composition courses in which the focus is not explicitly on gender differences. In a course designed to introduce students to fundamentals of research, for instance, students read Marge Piercy's *Woman on the Edge of Time* and did research on questions stimulated by it. They then shared their findings with the entire class in oral presentations. The approach led to wonderful papers on and discussions of the treatment of women in mental institutions, discrimination against minority women, and the ways in which technology can liberate women from oppressive roles.

I return now to my title and to the epigraph that introduces my essay. First, what does it mean to "compose as a woman"? Although the title invokes Jonathan Culler's "Reading as a Woman," a chapter in *On Deconstruction*, I do not mean to suggest by it that I am committed fully to Culler's deconstructive position. Culler maintains that "to read as a woman is to avoid reading as a man, to identify the specific defenses and distortions of male readings and provide correctives" (54). He concludes,

> For a woman to read as a woman is not to repeat an identity or an experience that is given but to play a role she constructs with reference to her identity as a woman, which is also a construct, so that the series can continue: a woman reading as a woman reading as a woman. The noncoincidence reveals an interval, a division within woman or within any reading subject and the "experience" of that subject. (64)

Culler is certainly correct that women often read as men and that they have to be encouraged to defend against this form of alienation. The strategy he suggests is almost entirely reactive, though. To read as a woman is to avoid reading as a man, to be alerted to the pitfalls of men's ways of reading.[4] Rich, too, warns of the dangers of immasculation, of identifying against oneself and learning to think like a man, and she, too, emphasizes the importance of critical activity on the part of the woman student—refusing to accept the givens of our culture, making connections between facts and ideas which men have left unconnected. She is well aware that thinking as a woman involves active construction, the recreation of one's identity. But she also sees value in recovering women's lived experience. In fact, she suggests that women maintain a critical posture in order to get in touch with that experience—to name it, to uncover that which is hidden, to make present that which has been absent. Her approach is active rather than reactive. Women's experience is not entirely a distorted version of male reality, it is not entirely elusive, and it is worthy of recuperation. We must alert our women students to the dangers of immasculation and provide them with a critical perspective. But we must also encourage them to become self-consciously aware of what their experience in the world has been and how this experience is related to the politics of gender. Then we must encourage our women students to write from the power of that experience.

NOTES

1. I received invaluable feedback on drafts of this essay from Carol Berkenkotter, Art Young, Marilyn Cooper, John Willinsky, Diane Shoos, John Flynn, Richard Gebhardt, and three anonymous *CCC* reviewers.

2. The 1988 Conference on College Composition and Communication was a notable exception. It had a record number of panels on feminist or gender-related issues and a number of sessions devoted to political concerns. I should add, too, that an exception to the generalization that feminist studies and composition studies have not confronted each other is Cynthia Caywood and Gillian Overing's very useful anthology, *Teaching Writing: Pedagogy, Gender, and Equity.* In their introduction to the book, Caywood and Overing note the striking parallels between writing theory and feminist theory. They conclude, "[T]he process model, insofar as it facilitates and legitimizes the fullest expression of the individual voice, is compatible with the feminist re-visioning of hierarchy, if not essential to it" (xiv). Pamela Annas, in her essay, "Silences: Feminist Language Research and the Teaching of Writing," describes a course she teaches at the University of Massachusetts at Boston, entitled "Writing as Women." In the course, she focuses on the question of silence — "what kinds of silence there are; the voices inside you that tell you to be quiet, the voices outside you that drown you out or politely dismiss what you say or do not understand you, the silence inside you that avoids saying anything important even to yourself, internal and external forms of censorship, and the stress that it produces" (3-4). Carol A. Stanger in "The Sexual Politics of the One-to-One Tutorial Approach and Collaborative Learning" argues that the one-to-one tutorial is essentially hierarchical and hence a male mode of teaching whereas collaborative learning is female and relational rather than hierarchical. She uses Gilligan's images of the ladder and the web to illustrate her point. Elisabeth Daeumer and Sandra Runzo suggest that the teaching of writing is comparable to the activity of mothering in that it is a form of "women's work." Mothers socialize young children to insure that they become acceptable citizens, and teachers' work, like the work of mothers, is usually devalued (45-46).

3. It should be clear by now that my optimistic claim at the outset of the essay that the field of composition studies has feminized our conception of written communication needs qualification. I have already mentioned that the field has developed, for the most part, independent of feminist studies and as a result has not explored written communication in the context of women's special needs and problems. Also, feminist inquiry is beginning to reveal that work in cognate fields that have influenced the development of composition studies is androcentric. For an exploration of the androcentrism of theories of the reading process see Patrocinio P. Schweickart, "Reading Ourselves: Toward a Feminist Theory of Reading."

4. Elaine Showalter, in "Reading as a Woman: Jonathan Culler and the Deconstruction of Feminist Criticism," argues that "Culler's deconstructionist priorities lead him to overstate the essentialist dilemma of defining the *woman* reader, when in most cases what is intended and implied is a *feminist* reader" (126).

WORKS CITED

Annas, Pamela J. "Silences: Feminist Language Research and the Teaching of Writing." *Teaching Writing: Pedagogy, Gender, and Equity.* Ed. Cynthia L. Caywood and Gillian R. Overing. Albany: State U of New York P, 1987. 3-17.

Belenky, Mary Field, et al. *Women's Ways of Knowing: The Development of Self, Voice, and Mind.* New York: Basic Books, 1986.

Britton, James, et al. *The Development of Writing Abilities (11-18).* London: Macmillan Education, 1975.

Caywood, Cynthia L., and Gillian R. Overing. Introduction. *Teaching Writing: Pedagogy, Gender, and Equity.* Ed. Cynthia L. Caywood and Gillian R. Overing. Albany: State U of New York P, 1987. xi-xvi.

Chodorow, Nancy. *The Reproduction of Mothering: Psychoanalysis and the Sociology of Gender*. Berkeley: U of California P, 1978.

Culler, Jonathan. *On Deconstruction: Theory and Criticism after Structuralism*. Ithaca: Cornell UP, 1982.

Daeumer, Elisabeth, and Sandra Runzo. "Transforming the Composition Classroom." *Teaching Writing: Pedagogy, Gender, and Equity*. Ed. Cynthia L. Caywood and Gillian R. Overing. Albany: State U of New York P, 1987. 45-62.

Gilligan, Carol. *In a Different Voice: Psychological Theory and Women's Development*. Cambridge: Harvard UP, 1982.

Hairston, Maxine. "Breaking Our Bonds and Reaffirming Our Connections." *College Composition and Communication* 36 (October 1985): 272-82.

Howe, Florence. "Identity and Expression: A Writing Course for Women." *College English* 32 (May 1971): 863-71. Rpt. in Howe, *Myths of Coeducation: Selected Essays, 1964-1983*. Bloomington: Indiana UP, 1984. 28-37.

Kohlberg, Lawrence. "Moral Stages and Moralization: The Cognitive-Development Approach." *Moral Development and Behavior*. Ed. T. Lickona. New York: Holt, 1976. 31-53.

Perry, William G. *Forms of Intellectual and Ethical Development in the College Years*. New York: Holt, Rinehart & Winston, 1970.

Rich, Adrienne. "Taking Women Students Seriously." *On Lies, Secrets, and Silence: Selected Prose, 1966-1978*. New York: W.W. Norton, 1979. 237-45.

_____. "'When We Dead Awaken': Writing as Re-Vision." *On Lies, Secrets, and Silence: Selected Prose, 1966-1978*. New York: W.W. Norton, 1979. 33-49.

Schweickart, Patrocinio P. "Reading Ourselves: Toward a Feminist Theory of Reading." *Gender and Reading: Essays on Readers, Texts and Contexts*. Ed. Elizabeth A. Flynn and Patrocinio P. Schweickart. Baltimore: Johns Hopkins UP, 1986. 31-62.

Showalter, Elaine. "Reading as a Woman: Jonathan Culler and the Deconstruction of Feminist Criticism." *Men and Feminism*. Ed. Alice Jardine and Paul Smith. New York: Methuen, 1987. 123-27.

Stanger, Carol A. "The Sexual Politics of the One-to-One Tutorial Approach and Collaborative Learning." *Teaching Writing: Pedagogy, Gender, and Equity*. Ed. Cynthia L. Caywood and Gillian R. Overing. Albany: State U of New York P, 1987. 31-44.

Feminism in Composition

Inclusion, Metonymy, and Disruption

Joy Ritchie and Kathleen Boardman

At a time when composition is engaged in clarifying its theoretical, political, and pedagogical histories, it is appropriate to construct a story of feminism's involvement in the disciplinary conversations. Despite the recent burgeoning of feminist perspectives in our discipline, it is not easy to delineate how feminism has functioned over the past three decades to shape and critique our understandings of the gendered nature of writing, teaching, and institutions. Although some accounts suggest that feminism, until recently, has been absent or at least late-blooming in the field, we find a more complex relationship in our rereading of essays and books in composition written from a feminist perspective—in particular, the many accounts of personal experience in the field written by feminists and by women since the 1970s. In this essay we look, and look again, at the few articles and notes that appeared in *CCC*, *College English*, and *English Journal* in the early 1970s. We also focus on feminist retrospective accounts—re-visions of composition written since the mid-1980s.

In writing this brief critical historical survey, we have found ourselves working from various impulses. First, we want to document and celebrate the vitality of feminism in composition, from its early manifestations in the small scattering of essays published in the 1970s (some of them frequently cited, others forgotten) to the explosion of feminist theory and well-documented feminist practice of the last decade. We wish to point out that much early feminist work in composition is not documented in our official publications,

Reprinted from *College Composition and Communication* 50.4 (June 1999): 585–606. Used with permission.

having occurred in informal conversations, in classrooms, and in committee meetings. At the same time, we want to suggest ways to examine and theorize experiential accounts—both published and unpublished—of feminism in composition. We must also consider seriously the causes and consequences of the delay in feminism's emergence in the published forums of our discipline and the extent to which feminism, despite its recent vitality, has remained contained or marginalized in composition. Finally, we hope to speculate on the positive and negative potential of inclusive, metonymic, and disruptive strategies for feminism's contribution to composition's narratives.

In the past decade, feminists have been visibly active in our discipline. They have examined the subjectivity of the gendered student and the position of women writers in the profession. Questioning assumptions about genre, form, and style, they have provided an impetus to seek alternative writing practices. Feminist perspectives have produced analyses of the gendered nature of the classroom, the feminization of English teaching, the working conditions for female teachers, and the implications of feminist theory for scholarship. Feminist scholars like Andrea Lunsford and Cheryl Glenn have begun rewriting the rhetorical tradition by reclaiming, refiguring, and regendering "Rhetorica." They are also critiquing earlier constructions of history and scholarship in composition. And from a different direction, scholars are drawing upon feminist, African American, lesbian, Native American, and class-based examinations of difference in order to complicate definitions of diversity within composition. Two recent essay collections, Susan Jarratt and Lynn Worsham's *Feminism and Composition Studies: In Other Words,* and Louise Phelps and Janet Emig's *Feminine Principles and Women's Experience in American Composition and Rhetoric,* especially highlight the strength of feminism(s) in composition and show how important feminism has been in shaping women's definitions of themselves, their work, and their commitment to pursuing questions of equity in the field.

Yet in the 1970s, while the work of composition as an emerging discipline was occurring right next door to, down the hall from, or in the basement under the work of feminist linguists and literary scholars, composition's official published discussions were largely silent on issues of gender. There is little explicit evidence of systematic theorizing about gender from the 1950s to the late 1980s. As late as 1988, Elizabeth Flynn could write, "For the most part . . . the fields of feminist studies and composition studies have not engaged each other in a serious or systematic way" (425). Indeed, when we began this study, we framed it as a paradox: prior to the mid-1980s, feminism seemed absent from composition but present among compositionists. From those early investigations we pulled one useful reminder: that the connections of composition and feminism have not been an inevitable result of the presence of so many women in the field. But subsequent conversations with a number of longtime teachers and scholars, who spoke to us about their own feminist beliefs and activities in composition dating back to the 1960s, reminded us that the near-absence of feminism from our publications does not constitute absence from the field.

The absence-presence binary also did not help us explain our own history as feminists in composition. As secondary English teachers, teaching women's literature and applying our feminist perspectives to high school courses in the 1970s, we moved into graduate courses and tenure track jobs in composition in the late 1980s and 1990s. Reflecting on our own experience, we recognized that much of the creative feminist energy in composition's history is not visible in the publications we searched: it appeared in informal conversations, in basement classrooms, and in committees on which women served. This energy might be viewed as ephemeral, yet we can testify, along with others, that it created solidarity among women, influenced students and colleagues, and helped form an epistemology on which later feminist work could grow. Sharon Crowley reminds us further that composition allowed and acknowledged women's participation in teaching and scholarship before many other disciplines began to do so—as we see from the important work of Josephine Miles, Winifred Horner, Ann Berthoff, Janet Emig and others. Still, Theresa Enos' collection of anecdotes from women in the field over the last several decades cautions us that the job conditions and security for many of these practitioners were terrible.

Crowley's and Enos' different perspectives point again to a history of women and feminism in composition that cannot be constructed in a tidy narrative. In the documents and accounts we have read and heard, we find three overlapping tropes that shed light on the roles feminism has played in composition and in the strategies women have used to gain a place in its conversations: (1) Following the pattern of developing feminist thought in the 1970s and 1980s, many early feminist accounts in composition sought *inclusion* and equality for women. (2) More recent accounts like those of Louise Phelps and Janet Emig posit feminism as a "subterranean" unspoken presence (xv), and Susan Jarratt and Laura Brady suggest the *metonymy* or contiguity of feminism and composition. (3) Also developing during this time has been what feminist postmodernists define as *disruption* and critique of hegemonic narratives—resistance, interruption, and finally redirection of composition's business as usual.

While it's tempting to posit this as a linear, evolutionary set of tropes— that women have grown out of and into as we've matured theoretically—we find it too restrictive to do so. These narratives coexist and have multiple functions, often depending on the historical or theoretical context in which they are read. For example, some early attempts at inclusion, based on experiential accounts, function also as disruptive narratives, and a number of very recent accounts might be characterized as primarily metonymic narratives. Furthermore, each of these tropes has both advantages and disadvantages for feminism in composition: for example, a narrative aimed at *including* women may also function to *contain* feminism within narrow boundaries. We also emphasize that we are not interested in categorizing narratives (and narrators) as "inclusionist," "disruptionist," and so on. Rather we hope to tease out the tropes, show how these narratives can be reread in multiple ways, and suggest how each one enacts one or more epistemological positions with respect to women's experience, identity, and difference.

As we reread for these rhetorical strategies, we find that the conceptions of experience in each of these sets of narratives also require examination. Most of the feminist writing in composition is grounded in accounts of personal experience. For example, many women have told powerful stories of their first recognition of their marginality in a field they had previously thought of as theirs. We must beware of reading these moving accounts too transparently and untheoretically. In her essay "Experience," Joan W. Scott offers a useful caution:

> When experience is taken as the origin of knowledge, the vision of the individual subject (the person who had the experience or the historian who recounts it) becomes the bedrock of evidence upon which explanation is built. Questions about the constructed nature of experience, about how subjects are constituted as different in the first place, about how one's vision is structured—about language (or discourse) and history—are left aside. (25)

Scott reminds us that narratives of experience should be encountered not as uncontested truth but as catalysts for further analysis of the conditions that shape experience.

We want to be clear about our view of experience: we are not dismissing such accounts but only suggesting ways to read and listen to them. The problem is not that these narratives are personal or that they are experiential, but that they are often untheorized. In understanding both the value and the limitations of feminist uses of experience in our field, we have found the work of Scott and of Rosemary Hennessy particularly useful. Both address "experience" as a construct and show ways to continue to value women's experiences as sources of knowledge; but they also suggest ways to theorize experience to make it a more critical rhetorical tool. Scott advises us to keep in mind that "experience is at once always already an interpretation and is in need of interpretation. What counts as experience is neither self-evident nor straightforward; it is always contested, always therefore political" (37). Hennessy views experience as a critical tool for examining the values and ideologies used to construct women's experiences, but she adds an important qualification for ensuring that women's experience is not narrowly read. Any critical theorizing of women's experience must be undertaken in the context of a continual "re-contextualization of the relationship between personal and group history and political priorities" (Minnie Bruce Pratt, qtd in Hennessy 99) and in relation to the "counterhegemonic discourses" of others (99). We have found that by attending to certain feminist tropes in our discipline, we can not only begin to tease out the relationships between composition and feminism, but also gain a better sense of the important dialectical relationships between experience and theory.

ADDING WOMEN: NARRATIVES AIMED AT INCLUSION

Correcting the long absence of women from intellectual and political landscapes, inserting women's perspectives into contexts dominated by patriarchy, and giving women equal status with men have constituted one of the central feminist projects—that of *inclusion*. This effort to add women has been criticized retrospectively as ineffective because it arises from Enlightenment conceptions of individual autonomy and the unquestioned "truth" of individual experience. Discussions of inclusion of women *as* women may reinforce essentialist or biological definitions of gender, and they often neglect to theorize the discourses that keep women and minorities marginalized. Most critically, many attempts to include women in the conversations of the field have in fact added only white, middle-class, heterosexual women. Despite these criticisms, we need to reread these attempts from their cultural context and for their first steps toward gender awareness. As Suzanne Clark reminds us, "feminists challenging a certain kind of feminism in composition represent a luxury: women now have a sufficient number to play out [their] anxieties of influence" (94). Our analyses need to take into account cultural and historical contexts out of which women were working that made these assumptions viable at the time.

Some of the first published evidence of the initiative to add women to the conversation came in NCTE publications aimed primarily at secondary teachers. The March 1972 *English Journal* printed "The Undiscovered," Robert A. Bennett's NCTE presidential address of the previous November.

591

In highlighting "the undiscovered human resources of our professional organization" (352), Bennett includes girls and women among "those peoples of American society who have not yet been allowed to make their fullest contribution":

> The talents of the great number of women teachers who are today still non-members of the Council or who are inactive in Council affairs, provide another undiscovered resource. As a professional organization, we must reach out to these women and encourage them . . . to become full partners in our common effort. (353)

After urging the organization to examine wage and promotion policies, document discriminatory practices, and work for recognition of women in curriculum and pedagogy, Bennett declares, "NCTE must take a stand for recognition of the contribution of women to society and to our profession. We have not done it. Let's get at it" (353).

Two months later, *English Journal* carried a short "Open Letter from Janet Emig, Chairwoman, NCTE Committee on the Role and Image of Women," asking the membership to nominate committee members and to send information about any "instances of discrimination against women in the profession, either in the form of a brief narrative or, if you are the woman involved, as a signed or as an anonymous case history" (710). A direct result of NCTE's new commitment to include women, Emig's committee was soliciting stories that would potentially disrupt business-as-usual in the profession, (a practice that Theresa Enos repeated more than 20 years later for *Gender Roles and Faculty Lives in Rhetoric and Composition*). The CCCC Committee on the Status of Women also continues to solicit narratives, in various forums, in order to ascertain more clearly the status of women in the field.

While a review of *CCC* from the late 1960s through the late 1980s uncovers few essays or other documents that would indicate a gendered feminist consciousness in composition, two landmark special issues of *College English*, in 1971 and 1972, report on the newly formed MLA Commission on the Status of Women in the Profession and document courses designed by feminists in English to reshape the curriculum from the standpoint of women students. The narratives in these special issues set the pattern for the impulse a decade or more later in composition to add women to its perspectives. Arising from the writers' own consciousness-raising experiences, the narratives articulate the potential for student and teacher subjectivities that are not neutral or universal but uniquely influenced by the textual, social, and political context of gender. Florence Howe's impassioned 1971 essay, in which she inserts her own personal account of discrimination, reports the inequities in women's status she uncovered as chair of the MLA commission. In addition to these first attempts to address women's low status in the profession, Howe and Elaine Showalter both illustrate their efforts to rectify the lack of women's texts and perspectives in English courses. Showalter describes her newly organized course, "The Educated Woman in Literature," in practical terms, and Howe presents a writing course she designed to help women alter their self-image "from centuries of *belief* in their inferiority, as well as from male-dominated and controlled institutions" (863). A second special issue of *College English* (October 1972) contains important essays concerning women's inclusion in the discipline of English, among them Tillie Olsen's "Women Who Are Writers in Our Century: One Out of Twelve" and Adrienne Rich's "When We Dead Awaken: Writing as Re-vision." Each of these essays seeks to insert women—their perspectives, their writing, their lived experiences—into a discipline from which they had been excluded.

In "Taking Women Students Seriously," her important 1978 essay emphasizing the necessity of including women's perspectives in education, Adrienne Rich described how the experience of changing from one teaching context to another allowed her to translate the critical questions she asked as a writing instructor of minority students into parallel questions she needed to ask about women students:

> How does a woman gain a sense of her *self* in a system . . . which devalues work done by women, denies the importance of female experience, and is physically violent toward women? . . . How do we, as women, teach women students a canon of literature which has consistently excluded or depreciated female experience? (239)

These early essays set a pattern for subsequent inclusive questions that women in composition began asking. Beginning by describing their own consciousness-raising experiences in their essays, the writers moved on to document the concrete changes in teaching and critical perspectives they advocated. What are women's experiences in classrooms, in institutions? How do women use language? How are women writers different from male writers? Questions like these included women in ways that had not been possible in a "gender-blind" field of composition; they set the stage for writers in the 1980s like Pamela Annas and Elizabeth Flynn to engage them further in work that again sought women's inclusion in the field and sparked feminist discussions for a newer generation of women.[1]

In the late 70s, the trope of inclusion appeared in essays applying feminist language research to composition by investigating claims made by

Robin Lakoff in her 1975 *Language and Woman's Place*—that women, by using a ladylike middle-class language, contributed to their own oppression. Lakoff's argument reflected the "dominance" approach to women's language use that was prominent among feminists of the 70s: attributing gender differences in language mainly to social oppression of women. Joan Bolker's 1979 *College English* article, "Teaching Griselda to Write," is a practitioner's account of her experience struggling with the absence of voice and authority in the work of "good-girl" student writers. The many citations of this short article in the past 19 years suggest that it has resonated with feminists in composition. In 1978, two articles examining women's "different" style appeared in *CCC*. In "The Feminine Style: Theory and Fact," Mary P. Hiatt discusses her study of the stylistic features of women's and men's writing. She reports "clear evidence of a feminine style . . . [that] is in fact rather different from the common assumptions about it" (226). Contrary to Lakoff's generalizations about women's oral language, women's written style, according to Hiatt, has "no excesses of length or complexity or emotion" (226). In "Women in a Double-Bind: Hazards of the Argumentative Edge," Sheila Ortiz Taylor draws composition instructors' attention to the "invisible, though real, disadvantage" that women students face in writing courses because "both the methods and the goals of such classes are alien to them" (385). She argues that the competitive, impersonal style of traditional argument alienates women; she urges instructors to validate "conversational tone, dramatic technique, and intimate reader involvement" (389).

Among the first composition articles to train the spotlight on women's language experiences, these essays highlight deficiency. (Ironically, as in Lakoff's book, an essentialized "woman" is both *included* and *found lacking*.) Bolker, Taylor, and Hiatt respond differently to the idea that women students must have special problems because a feminine style represents deficiency. Taylor uses the language of victimization to describe the woman student: "She must feel that something is wrong with her, a self-destructive disapproval common enough in women. . . . of course, much of the damage has been done by the time our students reach us. They have been taught a special language" (385). But Taylor adds that a feminine style of argument is only "deficient" because society has refused to validate it. Bolker believes that with more self-esteem and voice, the good girl can be a contender in the arena of the dominant discourse. Hiatt implies that readers need to be more discerning about the gender differences they *think* they see. None of these articles is heavily theorized; with the possible exception of Hiatt's, they arise from and return directly to classroom experience. Because they do not attend closely to larger systemic issues of power and discourse, these studies also make it possible for feminist concerns to be contained, encapsulated, or dismissed as "women's issues." Yet essays like these deserve credit for challenging the field's gender-blindness by insisting that women be included in narratives of classroom writing practices. They have contributed to a sense of intuitive connection between composition and those who ask, at least implicitly, "What difference might it make if the student (or teacher) is female?"

MAKING INTUITIVE CONNECTIONS: NARRATIVES OF METONYMIC RELATIONSHIP

In their introduction to *Teaching Writing: Pedagogy, Gender, and Equity*, one of the first books to connect writing and feminism in composition, Cynthia Caywood and Gillian Overing say that despite the absence of explicit discussion, they had experienced as practitioners an "intuitive understanding" of a "fundamental connection" between feminism and revisionist writing theory. While highlighting an absence of attention to gender, they also posit a more complicated reading of this absence by pointing to the nearly parallel lives of composition and feminist theory. According to this story, the two have run for years in the same direction, along close trajectories; to bring the fields together it is necessary only to notice the shared goals and common directions, and to make connections more visible and explicit. Caywood and Overing ask, "At what point did our parallel interests in feminism and revisionist writing theory converge?" (xi). More recently Susan Jarratt, Laura Brady, Janet Emig, and Louise Phelps have suggested that the boundaries have been permeable between feminist work in literary studies, the social sciences, and composition. This resonates with our own sense, as practitioners in the 70s, that boundaries between feminism and composition were often marked by unarticulated overlaps and crossovers. This permeability may have been partly the result of the interdisciplinary nature of composition, which drew for its theoretical substance from linguistics, cognitive and developmental psychology, and literary criticism. But while this intuitive connection may have created alliances among women in composition and feminists in other fields, it may also have delayed the emergence of feminist theory and continued its marginalization in the field.

Various factors account for the intuitive sense of connection that many of us have experienced and narrated. First, emerging pedagogical theories spoke a language that resonated with feminism's concerns of the time: coming to voice and consciousness, illuminating experience and its relationship to individual identity, playing the believing game rather than the doubting game, collaborating rather than competing, subverting hierarchy in the

classroom. These watchwords characterized composition's link to liberal political and social agendas shared by feminist scholars in other disciplines and
aimed at challenging established traditions, epistemologies, and practices of
the academy.[2] Sharon Crowley explicitly connects Dewey's progressivism
with Janet Emig's development of "process pedagogies," arguing that this
link between progressivism and process pedagogies was vitally important in
reconceptualizing composition "as an art rather than a course," and
"because its theorists discovered a way to talk about student writing that authorized teachers to think of themselves as researchers" (17). This reconceptualization resonated for feminists theoretically and politically.

Secondly, at that time many women in the profession were doing dou-
ble-duty as composition and literature teachers. Among the *College English*
authors represented in the special issues we have pointed out, Florence
Howe taught composition and wrote about how her course focused on
women, and Adrienne Rich taught writing with Mina Shaughnessy in the
SEEK program at CCNY. Many feminist composition instructors, coming
from literary critical backgrounds, continued reading in their fields and appropriating whatever feminist approaches seemed useful—much as compositionists of the 80s and 90s have appropriated the work of Belenky, Clinchy,
Goldberger, and Tarule and poststructuralist feminists.

The material conditions surrounding women in composition have also
contributed to a felt sense of the feminist connections to our work. Composition was and still is constructed as women's work, and the majority of workers were women; many of us teaching writing or working on composition
degrees during the 70s and 80s were newly arrived from secondary teaching.
Surrounded by colleagues with similar career patterns, we entered conversations that enacted an interplay between our lives and our professional work.
The drawbacks of the "feminization" of the field were not theorized until
several years later.

Finally, as the field developed in the 1970s, although journal editors
and the professional hierarchy were primarily male, the names of women
were also moving into prominent places: Mina Shaughnessy, Janet Emig,
Ann Berthoff, Sondra Perl, Anne Gere, Lillian Bridwell-Bowles, and others
were writing many of the important articles and books we studied. Many
feminists refer with appreciation to the "foremothers," first for their presence
as models, and secondly for their ideas which, though not articulated in
terms of gender, are often read, in retrospect, as consistent with feminist
practice. In many cases, these ideas have to do with nurturing, collaboration, revisioning, and decentering.

Some retrospective accounts use theory to make the composition-
feminism connections less intuitive, more explicit. Turning from fore-

mothers to "midwives," Carolyn Ericksen Hill uses feminist theory to read composition history through the gendering of practices, of theories, and of the field itself.[3] She reads the label "midwives" back onto male composition theorists active in the 60s and early 70s: Peter Elbow, Ken Macrorie, John Schultz, and William Coles, Jr. Without necessarily claiming them as feminists, she can, with the aid of postmodern theory, gender their approach as feminine and place their work in a certain feminist context: they helped "birth" the experiential self. The expressivist/nurturing feminist connection has often been made in passing, but Hill's label "midwives" claims these key composition figures for feminist theorizing—and also marginalizes them. In the 1990s, Hill argues, these four "expressivist" figures have been pushed to the edge of a newly theorized and professionalized field; their gender-blindness and humanistic model of the autonomous self have had to make way for gender difference and shifting subject positions, powerful constructs for feminist analysis. Hill sees in the compartmentalization—rather than dynamic rereading—of the four men's so-called expressivism a parallel with the "othering" of "woman," and of feminism, that continues to occur.

The rereading of "foremothers"—or even "midwives"—as feminist precursors may also be problematic if it ignores context and complexity, as we see from a few examples of foremothers who resist labeling. In the late 1970s, Ann Berthoff roundly rejected the gendering of logic and the either/ or-ism of all discussions of women's ways of knowing; she reaffirmed this rejection at the 1998 CCCC convention. Still, the foremother figures can both exemplify and disrupt the notion of the feminization of the field. As fore*mothers* they are both marginalized and typically characterized as nurturers. But insofar as they are envisioned as *fore*mothers, as founders, they are not feminized but rather constructed in a traditionally masculine position.

Evidence that stories of connection continue to resonate with us may be found in Jan Zlotnik Schmidt's introduction to *Women/Writing/Teaching*, a 1998 collection of essays by women writers and teachers. Schmidt emphasizes the importance of women's experience in making writing-teaching connections and expresses her hope that readers will also "explore their own life stories, their development of selfhood, their multiple identities as writers, teachers, and writing teachers" (xii). Retrospective narratives that create foremothers, midwives, connections, and nurturing community in composition's history foreground the double potential of the metonymic relationship between feminism and composition. This intuitive connection helps to create a sense of solidarity and vitality. But it may also reinforce the very structures that keep feminist perspectives contained in a separate, benign category rather than giving feminist analysis a central place, or at least keeping it insistently, vocally disruptive of the discipline's metanarratives. For example, some feminist practitioners have told powerful stories about replacing hierarchical, agonistic classroom environments with decentered, nurturing classrooms based on an ethic of care. But, as Eileen Schell argues, "femin*in*ist pedagogy, although compelling, may reinforce rather than critique or transform patriarchal structures by reinscribing what Magda Lewis calls the 'woman as caretaker ideology'" ("The Cost" 74, our italics).

Granting feminism's intuitive connections with a discipline that challenged current-traditional conceptions of language and introduced new decentered writing pedagogies, it is also important to recognize that some feminist agendas were more likely to disrupt than to aid composition's early progress toward full disciplinary status. Composition needed to build institutional legitimacy in the traditional academy; a fundamental feminist goal was to disrupt rather than extend patriarchal discourses and their assumptions about knowledge. Composition sought a single theory of the writing process and the writing subject; feminist theorists challenged notions of a singular universal concept of truth. The trope of metonymy may have difficulty expanding to cover some of these adversarial relationships.

FEMINIST DISRUPTIONS

Composition has many narratives of feminist disruption which emphasize neither inclusion nor intuitive connection but rather represent some form of feminism (newly experienced or theorized) reaching back to reread and even reconfigure past experience and practice. We see increasing numbers of current feminists drawing on postmodern theories to analyze and critique the basic "process" narratives of composition's first 20 years, to raise questions about difference(s), and to critique disciplinary practices and structures that have shaped composition. Disruption is often linked to postmodern theories of power, discourse, and ideology rather than to consciousness-raising sessions, discussions of pedagogy, or attempts to create equitable and inclusive conditions for women. In order to intervene significantly in power structures that keep women subordinate, feminists investigate and uncover the contradictions in those dominant structures. The feminist narratives we have reread remind us, however, that efforts at inclusion, connection, and disruption often work synthetically rather than as adversaries or as unequal partners. As Theresa Enos says, her book's "most powerful use of 'data' is the narrative, in the stories that help us define our places in academia so that we can better trace our future" (1).

The explicit recognition of composition's lack of attention to women's material lives has led women in anger, frustration, and recognition to tell the stories of their coming to awareness. A classic feminist narrative of the early 70s is the story of a "good girl," silenced by her compulsion to please, whose recognition of her oppression releases an anger strong enough to overcome politeness and fear; thus she finds both her voice and an agenda for change. The consciousness-raising sessions of the late 60s and early 70s provided a model for this narrative, as did the two special women's issues of *College English,* 1971–72, that we have mentioned. In "When We Dead Awaken," Rich told her own story of frustration at the demands that she be good at all the roles women were supposed to play, while Howe, after narrating how she had acquiesced in years of inequitable treatment, wrote, "Eighteen months as commission Chairwoman [of the MLA Commission on the Status of Women] has eroded that wry smile. I feel now a growing anger as I come to realize that . . . I am not alone in my state" (849).

Many of today's feminist accounts of the 60s and 70s follow a similar pattern. Lynn Z. Bloom's essay, "Teaching College English as a Woman" (1992), is a scathing look at the bad old days in college English, when a woman in the field—whether student or teacher—would be exploited if she did not get angry and speak up. Bloom recalls a conversion experience when, as a part-time composition instructor, she finally was able to obtain office space: in a basement room full of desks, on the floor under the stairs, next to the kitty litter. Surveying these wretched conditions, she told herself, "If I ever agree to do this again, I deserve what I get" (821). Separated by more than 20 years, Bloom's and Howe's angry accounts illustrate what we might call individual, liberal disruption: the idea that once a woman sees clearly, her life is changed, and she is thus empowered to become effectively active for change and reform. These accounts show the "revisioning" that feminist thinking has enabled individual women to do. We read these accounts as disruptive because in addition to realizing that the liberal Enlightenment agenda hasn't included *her,* each of these women also recognizes that she must take action to disrupt and change the structures that have kept her subordinate.

Other women who are currently doing feminist work in composition studies have provided similar testimonies of naive compliance, oppressed silence, eventual recognition, and new outspokenness.[4] That we now have so many such narratives may mean that women in composition today are finally in a position to claim the authority of the autobiographical; it may also mean that, largely due to feminist efforts, the conventions of scholarly discourse have expanded to include the personal narrative as a way of situating oneself in one's scholarship. But perhaps the personal testimony remains an effective—and still necessary—tool of disruption. Many of these stories are disruptive because they expose "the pattern of well-rewarded, male supervision of under-rewarded, female workers" that has existed in composition and "is entrenched in our whole culture" (Enos vii). The disruption that is so central to the consciousness-raising narrative itself also highlights gaps in our reading of our past and of business as usual. Rereading the consciousness-raising essays that have recurred in composition over the past 25 years can show us more sites where women have been silent but where feminists want to rupture that silence.

Many narratives deal with experiences in teaching and department politics, but a 1993 retrospective account by Nancy McCracken, Lois Green, and Claudia Greenwood tells how they acquiesced as researchers to a field characterized by "a persistent silence on the subject of gender" in its "landmark research studies on writing development and writing processes" (352). Now writing collaboratively, they return to studies of teacher responses to student writing that they had published earlier (and separately), reinterpreting those studies in terms of gender differences. These authors emphasize that until the late 80s the climate in composition studies had made it difficult to notice or report gender differences in empirical studies: "None of us went looking for gender differences. When the data began to speak of gender, we dared not listen" (356). They recount their worries about being accused of biological determinism, about seeming to exclude men, about appearing unprofessional, and about calling attention to themselves as women. Now, they say, they feel empowered not only to note gender difference but to insist on it. Theirs is not a story of breaking silence by themselves. Instead, the current "research environment in which it is both important and safe to study the interplay between students' gender and their development as writers" (354) has made it possible to revise their findings. Their story is not about singular heroism but about collaboration, in a network of mutual support, in a research/scholarly environment that has made discursive structures more visible. Their story is not about going solo against a hostile discipline but about rereading the field and their own complicity. Their reading disrupts, among other things, their *own* research, by requiring that they return to it and revise it.

Some of the early disruptive narratives we have mentioned are reformist, and they may even be read as attempts at inclusion as well as disruption. Another form of disruptive narrative is less grounded in the impulse for individual disruption and change, but seeks wider consideration of difference. Such critiques often create conflict and may evoke more resistance because they demand changes in institutional and epistemological structures that

600

conflict with composition's continuing need to establish legitimacy. They support the emergence of different perspectives rather than suppressing them. In these accounts difference is expanded from the single male/female binary to differences, taking into account multiple inflections of social class, sexual orientation, and race. For example, Harriet Malinowitz's study of lesbian and gay students in writing classes and Shirley Wilson Logan's writing on the confluence of race and gender in composition both attempt to expand our understanding of what differences can mean in composition classrooms. They articulate the connections among differences as well as show the privileging or erasure of some categories by others. Writing out of her own experience as a Chinese student speaking several languages, Min-Zhan Lu has drawn upon third-world and minority feminisms as well as other cultural theorists to disrupt composition teachers' view of the conflicts students face in negotiating the political, linguistic, and rhetorical "borderlands" between home and school. She reopens a debate about the processes of acculturation and accommodation at work in writing classrooms, particularly those that serve minority and immigrant students. In doing so, she rereads the work of Mina Shaughnessy, Thomas Farrell, Kenneth Bruffee, and others in light of current contexts in order to critique the wider public debates about literacy and to highlight the cultural conflicts and necessary resistances of today's students on the margins.

At times these disruptions can create tension and anger even among feminists, highlighting the way feminism itself is shaped by and embedded in existing hierarchical discourses. This conflict may seem to undermine any sense of solidarity that existed when feminism appeared in a more intuitive rather than carefully articulated and scrutinized form. But in fact, such conflict may produce one of feminism's most important benefits—the proliferation of differences. Nedra Reynolds argues: "Feminists daring to criticize other feminists have opened up spaces for analyzing difference; they interrupted the discourses of feminism in the singular to make possible feminism in the plural" (66). Other disruptive narratives of difference are only now emerging and await further exploration. Constructs like Gloria Anzaldúa's *mestiza*, Trinh T. Minh-ha's subject-in-the-making, Donna Haraway's cyborg, and Judith Butler's performer of gender extend postmodern notions of difference in disruptive directions with their advocacy of multiplicity, fluidity, hybridity, and indeterminacy.

Feminists in composition in the past decade have used postmodern theories to reread the feminization and the femin*in*ization of composition as problematic and to seek to revise institutional frameworks. The preponderance of women in composition has not led inevitably to the triumph of feminist interests and values in the field. For example, Susan Miller tells the story of the "sad women in the basement" and describes feminization as the "female coding" of the "ideologically constructed identity for the teacher of composition" (123); it involves constructing composition as "women's work." Feminization refers to the gendering of the entire field of composition and of various activities that have taken place within it (nonhierarchical pedagogy, the writing process movement, "romantic" philosophies, nurturing of writers). For Miller, feminization points to the devaluation of the composition instructor, and the subordination of composition to literature, throughout the history of the field. For Rhonda Grego and Nancy Thompson, compositionists "still reside within our gendered roles," but we are not limited to a traditional "wifely" role because the field has lately been "developing terms and methods through which to name our work at least to ourselves, if not yet fully to the ruling apparatus of the academic system" (68). In *Gypsy Academics and Mother Teachers*, Eileen Schell combines materialist feminist and postmodern perspectives, labor and institutional history, and the personal narratives of women nontenure-track teachers to analyze the gendered division of labor in composition and to critique femin*in*ization — the coopting of the "ethic of care." She also provides strategies for coalition-building and tangible plans of action for reconceptualizing women's positions and reshaping institutional structures. Feminization narratives like these work disruptively in two directions: their analysis foregrounds the political position of composition within institutional structures, but it also highlights tensions within women's roles and interests in composition.

Finally, disruptive narratives in composition have begun to analyze the established narratives of the discipline and the agency of students and teachers constructed by those narratives. They explore the ideologies underlying the discourses where composition has been situated, including those espoused by feminists, to underscore the contradictions and dangers that those create for women as well as for the field in general. An early example is Susan Jarratt's rereading of Peter Elbow's work and of the tendency in feminism and expressivism to suppress conflict and promote consensus.[5] She argues that such a stance fails to arm women students and teachers with the tools to confront the power relations inherent in their positions. An important recent example of disruption is Nedra Reynolds' rereading of several major narratives in the field. Reynolds emphasizes that interruption — talking back, forcibly breaking into the prevailing discourse of a field — is a way to create agency: "Agency is not simply about finding one's own voice but also about intervening in discourses of the everyday [this would include personal experience narratives] and cultivating rhetorical tactics that make interruption and resistance an important part of any conversation" (59). She points out the tendency of "some of the most important voices in composition today . . . to ignore work in feminism that might complement or complicate their ideas" (66). She not only "interrupts" some of the major cultural studies theorists but also analyzes the conceptions of subjectivity and agency in the work of James Berlin, John Trimbur, and Lester Faigley. She criticizes the dominant narrative's tendency to compartmentalize interrupters and disrupters as "rude women," thereby denying them agency. As part of the evidence for her argument, she tells stories about a cultural studies conference where bell hooks and other women participants analyzed the "terror" of the typical "white supremacist hierarchy" (65). Reynolds urges women to develop strategies for interrupting dominant discourses in composition and challenges them to offer their students the means to resist rigid forms of discourse.

CONCLUSION: IN EXCESS

These three different but also converging narratives of feminism suggest a rich tradition of feminist thought and activity in composition: pushing for admission, working intuitively alongside, and interrupting the conversation. We believe these three tropes may help us read and revise feminism's evolving place in the narratives of composition; they provide useful insight for feminists about existing tensions in the relationship of theory to experience and practice; and they point to strategies feminists may seek to promote or avoid in the future.

In composition's last three decades, the impulse has been toward legitimation, theory-building, and consolidation. The disruption and the assertion of difference that feminists and others represent have come slowly and with struggle; they have been delayed and even suppressed by the need to build a more unified disciplinary discourse. In several recent metanarratives that assess where composition has come from and where it is going, we find traces of these three lines of feminist thought that may help us see where feminism might most usefully lead composition and where they might go together. These recent commentaries demonstrate that tropes of inclusion and metonymic connection still define feminism's relationship to the field.

In *Fragments of Rationality*, Lester Faigley practices inclusion as he credits feminism for its efforts to theorize a postmodern subject with agency; he also cites the contributions of feminists in foregrounding important pedagogical and political questions. James Berlin's *Rhetorics, Poetics, Cultures* does not mention feminism, but this book, like Faigley's, does cite several postmodern feminists' efforts to theorize subjectivity and difference. In Joseph Harris' *A Teaching Subject: Composition Since 1966*, the connections between women practitioners, feminism, and "the teaching subject" are neither articulated nor connected; they remain an unspoken presence. Like Berlin, Sharon Crowley argues in *Composition in the University* that despite its progress over the past 30 years, composition has remained a conservative discipline, still trapped in current-traditionalism, still shackled to the service role of Freshman English, and still bound to the limitations of humanism in English departments. Unlike Berlin, she looks to feminist thought for its disruptive power, as one of several theoretical perspectives that might help dislodge composition from narrow disciplinary confines.

The representation of feminist perspectives in these recent commentaries suggests that in the future these relationships will persist—with unspoken alliances between feminist thought and composition, and inclusive reliance on postmodern feminism(s) where they advance the general argument. But it is to the disruptive strategy, framed in dialogue with inclusivity and metonymy, that we return. It is tempting to see disruption as the newest and best hope for feminism and to privilege theorizing as the most worthwhile activity for feminism and composition. But it's also clear that different emphases may be more effective as rhetorical contexts shift and historical moments change. While efforts at inclusion suffer from the limitations we've outlined, and untheorized or unarticulated practices also create risks of marginalization and erasure, disruptive strategies, by themselves, also have limitations. The history of feminism suggests that it is necessary to do more than interrupt a disciplinary conversation. Disruption may be only temporary, and as Reynolds and others point out, it's easy to push disrupters to the sidelines, to stop listening to them and to marginalize them once again. In addition, the task of disruption requires rhetorical skill. Those who interrupt may gain momentary attention, but those who can't sustain the conversation, hold up the argument, or tell an absorbing story will soon drop—or be dropped—from the discussion.

Certainly feminists in composition have provided the field with models for persuasive and beautiful writing that tells and disrupts stories of experience. (Lynn Worsham's "After Words: A Choice of Words Remains" is a recent example.) If theorizing and disruption are detached from lived experience and material history, they may remain irrelevant. And if disruption only fractures and doesn't again create connection, a sense of an even tentatively inclusive agenda, it will lack the vital energy and supportive alliances to sustain its own taxing work. Over the last 30 years, feminists have demonstrated that critique and disruption are never finished and that coalition-building and collaboration are vital for change.

Our rereading of 30 years of feminist writing suggests that in both early and more recent work, feminism has been most challenging and disruptive and also provided a sense of alliance and inclusion when it has maintained a dialogical relationship between theory and experience. Despite its short history, feminist work in composition can certainly provide many revitalizing demonstrations of this dialogical relationship as one of its contributions to academic feminism. Virtually all the feminist work we've reviewed and see emerging has, at least in part, claimed, interpreted, and revised accounts of experience and history: the personal history of one's life as a woman, the practice of the teacher, or the experience of the scholar. As Suzanne Clark points out, narratives of experience theorized become possible sites of agency: "At the same time that stories of personal experience invoke and re-cite determinant categories of identity . . . such stories also produce an excess not easily retrofitted as the norm" (98). Rather than dismissing stories of experience, Clark suggests that we look at them for what is "excessive," that is, for parts of the narrative that do not fit our current explanations: "What refuses, despite the sometimes daunting applications of straitjacket pseudo-sciences, to be contained?" (98). One of feminism's most potentially powerful tools is the deployment of what is excessive, what is other. Difference, "otherness," disrupts, as Rosemary Hennessy argues, because the "gaps, contradictions, *aporias*" that otherness creates force dominant perspectives into crisis management to "seal over or manage the contradictions. . . . But they also serve as the inaugural space for critique" (92).

Many gaps remain for feminists to explore in composition and in its relationship to English and the broader culture. Although researchers have now examined from a feminist perspective the status of women in composition and the feminized status of composition within English studies, many women still teach composition in the "basement," and the wider institutional, economic, and cultural conditions continue to create barriers against improving their status. Although women and men in our field have considered how class, gender, and race may shape their pedagogy, we have not thoroughly come to terms with students' or teachers' gendered, classed, or raced position in the academy—or the continuing failure to provide a viable education for many minority students or encouragement for minority colleagues in our field. Although various critics have highlighted the gender blindness of liberatory and critical pedagogies, we have not thoroughly considered how such theories and pedagogies stop short of realizing their goals where women students, minorities, and gay and lesbian students are concerned. Although we have a body of metacommentary on research methodologies and ethical representation of research subjects, we have only begun to explore effective ways to connect our research to wider public concerns and debates about literacy.

Our own interest in diversity and multiplicity makes us curious about the possible uses of "excess" as a trope for feminists in composition of the present and future. Already we are exploring feminist or "diverse discourses," which are in excess of what a singular linear argument requires. We are pushing for notions and accounts of agency that exceed limited ideas of the determined subject. Might the re-visionary stories of the next generation refer to greedy visions of *more* as well as angry recognitions of *lack*? Can we envision narratives of a disruptive practice that overflows as well as challenges? Excess might be proposed as inclusion with a difference: uncontained and without limits.

At this time when composition is reviewing its past and seeking to chart new directions, a glance beyond the academy suggests that political and economic conditions will create continuing intellectual and practical "straitjackets" in composition's next 50 years. The energy of feminists will be vital to the disruption of restrictive theory and practice. This energy will be important for sustaining coalitions for change; it is our best hope for inclusion and proliferation of difference, multiplicity, and uncontainable excess.

NOTES

1. In two recent collections of essays on composition, Villanueva's *Cross-Talk in Comp Theory*, and Bloom, Daiker, and White's *Composition in the Twenty-First Century*, the only essay specifically from a feminist perspective is Flynn's 1988 "Composing as a Woman." The frequent inclusion of this essay suggests the impact it has had; the fact that it is the only one included suggests that, in some venues at least, it has been used to contain feminism at the same time.

2. For example, the February 1970 issue of *CCC* contains articles by Donald Murray and by William Coles articulating many of the crucial progressive assumptions emerging in composition: the value of individual students' writing as an articulation of agency and selfhood rather than merely as an object of diagnosis and correction. The CCC journals of that year also contain several proposals for alternative freshman English courses for minority students, and the October 1972 issue contains the CCCC Executive Committee's Resolution, "The Student's Right to His Own Language." Although they remain steadfastly gender-blind, essays like these attest to the profession's increasing attempts in the late 60s and 70s to redefine writing and writing instruction. These disciplinary calls for cultural diversity in the curriculum and for the students' rights to their own language caused a great deal of ferment in the profession and foregrounded issues of difference, yet they still did not open a discursive space for women to speak as women writers and teachers or to consider the gendered implications of Coles' goal for writing: "to allow the student to put himself together" (28).

3. Belenky, Clinchy, Goldberger, and Tarule are noted for their use of "midwife" in their discussion of educators who promote constructed knowledge. But the term was applied to writing instructors much earlier. In 1970, Stephen Judy wrote in *English Journal* (which he was later to edit): "We need to discard the structure of the composition teacher as one who passes on knowledge about writing, makes assignments, and corrects errors on themes. A more appropriate role can be described as that of coach or catalyst, or one that I prefer, that of midwife: one who assists in the process of bringing something forth but does not participate in the process himself" (217). This passage suggests possibilities for metonymy; the mascu-

line pronoun may simply illustrate composition's gender-blindness, but it may also be a trace of the gender-shifting that Hill does twenty years later. Judy adds, "It would be difficult for a midwife to do *her* job adequately if the expectant mother knew she were going to be graded on the results" (217, italics ours).

4. Wendy Bishop, Lillian Bridwell-Bowles, Louise Phelps, and Nancy Sommers are just a few of the women who have written personal narratives that practice and reflect on disruption of a status quo. Jacqueline Jones Royster writes, "I have been compelled on too many occasions to count to sit as a well-mannered Other" (30). Theresa Enos' *Gender Roles and Faculty Lives in Rhetoric and Composition* contains a number of anonymous stories from women in composition, along with her narrative of her own experience as an "academically battered woman" (ix). Gesa Kirsch's interviews with women in various academic disciplines explore their interpretations of their experiences as writers and raise "questions of gender and language, women's participation in public discourse, and women's 'ways of writing'" (xvii). A new collection, *Women/Writing/Teaching*, edited by Jan Zlotnik Schmidt presents ten previously published and ten new essays by women that examine their personal experiences as writers and teachers.

5. We could cite numerous other examples: Patricia Sullivan's rereading of Stephen North's *The Making of Knowledge in Composition*; Nancy Welch's use of feminist theory and her own experience to reread Lacan and other theorists and to disrupt composition's conceptualization of revision; and the important work of increasing numbers of feminists rereading and regendering the rhetorical tradition from Aspasia to Ida B. Wells, from Gertrude Buck to Toni Morrison.

WORKS CITED

Annas, Pamela J. "Style as Politics: A Feminist Approach to the Teaching of Writing." *College English* 47 (1985): 360–71.

Belenky, Mary Field, Blythe McVicker Clinchy, Nancy Rule Goldberger, and Jill Mattuck Tarule. *Women's Ways of Knowing: The Development of Self, Voice, and Mind.* New York: Basic, 1986.

Bennett, Robert A. "NCTE Presidential Address: The Undiscovered." *English Journal* 61 (1972): 351–57.

Berlin, James. *Rhetorics, Poetics and Cultures: Refiguring College English Studies.* Urbana: NCTE, 1996.

Berthoff, Ann E. "Rhetoric as Hermeneutic." *CCC* 42 (1991): 279–87.

Bishop, Wendy. "Learning Our Own Ways to Situate Composition and Feminist Studies in the English Department." *Journal of Advanced Composition* 10 (1990): 339–55.

Bloom, Lynn Z. "Teaching College English as a Woman." *College English* 54 (1992): 818–25.

Bloom, Lynn Z., Donald A. Daiker, and Edward M. White, eds. *Composition in the Twenty-First Century: Crisis and Change.* Carbondale: Southern Illinois UP, 1996.

Bolker, Joan. "Teaching Griselda to Write." *College English* 40 (1979): 906–08.

Brady, Laura. "The Reproduction of Othering." Jarratt and Worsham 21–44.

Bridwell-Bowles, Lillian. "Freedom, Form, Function: Varieties of Academic Discourse." *CCC* 46 (1995): 46–61.

Caywood, Cynthia, and Gillian Overing, eds. *Teaching Writing: Pedagogy, Gender, and Equity.* Albany: State U of New York P, 1987.

Clark, Suzanne. "Argument and Composition." Jarratt and Worsham 94–99.

Coles, William, Jr. "The Sense of Nonsense as a Design for Sequential Writing Assignments." *CCC* 21 (1970): 27–34.

Crowley, Sharon. *Composition in the University: Historical and Polemical Essays.* Pittsburgh Series in Composition, Literacy, and Culture. Pittsburgh: U of Pittsburgh P, 1998.

Enos, Theresa. *Gender Roles and Faculty Lives in Rhetoric and Composition.* Carbondale: Southern Illinois UP, 1996.

Faigley, Lester. *Fragments of Rationality: Postmodernity and the Subject of Composition.* Pittsburgh Series in Composition, Literacy, and Culture. Pittsburgh, U of Pittsburgh P, 1992.

Flynn, Elizabeth A. "Composing as a Woman." *CCC* 39 (1988) : 423–35.

Fontaine, Sheryl I., and Susan Hunter, eds. *Writing Ourselves into the Story: Unheard Voices from Composition Studies.* Carbondale: Southern Illinois UP, 1993. 1–17.

Grego, Rhonda, and Nancy Thompson. "Repositioning Remediation: Renegotiating Composition's Work in the Academy." *CCC* 47 (1996): 62–84.

Harris, Joseph. *A Teaching Subject: Composition Since 1966.* Upper Saddle River: Prentice, 1997.

Hennessy, Rosemary. *Materialist Feminism and the Politics of Discourse.* Thinking Gender Series. New York: Routledge, 1992.

Hiatt, Mary P. "The Feminine Style: Theory and Fact." *CCC* 29 (1978): 222–26.

Hill, Carolyn Ericksen. *Writing from the Margins: Power and Pedagogy for Teachers of Composition.* New York: Oxford UP, 1990.

Howe, Florence. "A Report on Women and the Profession." *College English* 32 (1971): 847–54.

———. "Identity and Expression: A Writing Course for Women." *College English* 32 (1971): 863–71.

Jarratt, Susan C. "Feminism and Composition: The Case for Conflict." *Contending with Words: Composition and Rhetoric in a Postmodern Age.* Ed. Patricia Harkin and John Schilb. New York: MLA, 1991. 105–23.

Jarratt, Susan C.,and Lynn Worsham, eds. *Feminism and Composition Studies: In Other Words.* New York: MLA, 1998.

Judy, Stephen. "The Search for Structures in the Teaching of Composition." *English Journal* 59 (1970): 213–18.

Kirsch, Gesa E. *Women Writing the Academy: Audience, Authority, and Transformation.* Studies in Writing and Rhetoric. Carbondale: Southern Illinois UP, 1992.

Kirsch, Gesa E., and Patricia A. Sullivan, eds. *Methods and Methodology in Composition Research.* Carbondale: Southern Illinois UP, 1992.

Lakoff, Robin. *Language and Woman's Place.* New York: Harper, 1975.

Logan, Shirley W., ed. *With Pen and Voice: The Rhetoric of Nineteenth Century African-American Women.* Carbondale: Southern Illinois UP, 1995.

Lu, Min-Zhan. "Conflict and Struggle: The Enemies or Preconditions of Basic Writing?" *College English* 54 (1992): 887–913.

———. "From Silence to Words: Writing as Struggle." Perl 165–76.

Malinowitz, Harriet. *Textual Orientations: Lesbian and Gay Students and the Making of Discourse Communities.* Portsmouth: Boynton, Heinemann, 1995.

McCracken, Nancy, Lois Green, and Claudia Greenwood. "Gender in Composition Research: A Strange Silence." Fontaine and Hunter 352–73.

Miller, Susan. *Textual Carnivals: The Politics of Composition.* Carbondale: Southern Illinois UP, 1991.

Murray, Donald M. "The Interior View: One Writer's Philosophy of Composition." *CCC* 21 (1970): 21–26.

Olsen, Tillie. "Women Who Are Writers in Our Century: One Out of Twelve." *College English* 34 (1972): 6–17.

"Open Letter from Janet Emig, Chairwoman, NCTE Committee on the Role and Image of Women." *English Journal* 61 (1972): 710.

Perl, Sondra, ed. *Landmark Essays on Writing Process.* Landmark Essays Series 7. Davis: Hermagoras, 1994.

Phelps, Louise W. "Becoming a Warrior: Lessons of the Feminist Workplace." Phelps and Emig 289–339.

Phelps, Louise W., and Janet Emig, eds. *Feminine Principles and Women's Experience in American Composition and Rhetoric.* Pittsburgh Series in Composition, Literacy, and Culture. Pittsburgh: U of Pittsburgh P, 1995.

Reynolds, Nedra. "Interrupting Our Way to Agency: Feminist Cultural Studies and Composition." Jarratt and Worsham 58–73.

Rich, Adrienne. "When We Dead Awaken: Writing as Re-vision." *College English* 34 (1972): 18–25.

——. "Taking Women Students Seriously." *On Lies, Secrets, and Silence: Selected Prose 1966–1978.* New York: Norton, 1979. 237–45.

Royster, Jacqueline Jones. "When the First Voice You Hear Is Not Your Own." *CCC* 47 (1996): 29–40.

Schell, Eileen. *Gypsy Academics and Mother-Teachers: Gender, Contingent Labor, and Writing Instruction.* Portsmouth: Boynton, 1998.

——. "The Costs of Caring: 'Feminism' and Contingent Women Workers in Composition Studies." Jarratt and Worsham 74–93.

Schmidt, Jan Zlotnik, ed. *Women/Writing/Teaching.* Albany: State U of New York P, 1998.

Scott, Joan. "Experience." *Feminists Theorize the Political.* Ed. Judith Butler and Joan W. Scott. New York: Routledge, 1992. 22–40.

Showalter, Elaine. "Women and the Literary Curriculum." *College English* 32 (1971): 855–62.

Sommers, Nancy. "Between the Drafts." Perl 217–24.

Sullivan, Patricia A. "Feminism and Methodology." Kirsch and Sullivan 37–61.

Taylor, Sheila Ortiz. "Women in a Double-Bind: Hazards of the Argumentative Edge." *CCC* 29 (1978): 385–89.

"The Students' Right to Their Own Language." *CCC* 25 Special Issue (1974): 1–32.

The Secretary's Report of Executive Committee. "The Student's Right to His Own Language." *CCC* 21 (1970): 319–28.

Villanueva Jr., Victor, ed. *Cross-Talk in Comp Theory.* Urbana: NCTE, 1997.

Welch, Nancy. *Getting Restless: Rethinking Revision in Writing Instruction.* Portsmouth: Boynton, 1997.

Worsham, Lynn. "After Words: A Choice of Words Remains." Jarratt and Worsham 329–56.

When the First Voice You Hear
Is Not Your Own

Jacqueline Jones Royster

[handwritten marginalia: Subjectivity as defining a value]

This essay emerged from my desire to examine closely moments of personal challenge that seem to have import for cross-boundary discourse. These types of moments have constituted an ongoing source of curiosity for me in terms of my own need to understand human difference as a complex reality, a reality that I have found most intriguing within the context of the academic world. From a collectivity of such moments over the years, I have concluded that the most salient point to acknowledge is that "subject" position really is everything.

Using subject position as a terministic screen in cross-boundary discourse permits analysis to operate kaleidoscopically, thereby permitting interpretation to be richly informed by the converging of dialectical perspectives. Subjectivity as a defining value pays attention dynamically to context, ways of knowing, language abilities, and experience, and by doing so it has a consequent potential to deepen, broaden, and enrich our interpretive views in dynamic ways as well. Analytical lenses include the process, results, and impact of negotiating identity, establishing authority, developing strategies for action, carrying forth intent with a particular type of agency, and being compelled by external factors and internal sensibilities to adjust belief and action (or not). In a fundamental way, this enterprise supports the sense of rhetoric, composition, and literacy studies as a field of study that embraces the imperative to understand truths and consequences of language use more fully. This enterprise supports also the imperative to reconsider the beliefs and values which inevitably permit our attitudes and

Reprinted from *College Composition and Communication* 47.1 (February 1996): 29–40. Used with permission.

actions in discourse communities (including colleges, universities, and classrooms) to be systematic, even systemic.

Adopting subjectivity as a defining value, therefore, is instructive. However, the multidimensionality of the instruction also reveals the need for a shift in paradigms, a need that I find especially evident with regard to the notion of "voice," as a central manifestation of subjectivity. My task in this essay, therefore, is threefold. First, I present three scenes which serve as my personal testimony as "subject." These scenes are singular in terms of their being my own stories, but I believe that they are also plural, constituting experiential data that I share with many. My sense of things is that individual stories placed one against another build credibility and offer, as in this case, a litany of evidence from which a call for transformation in theory and practice might rightfully begin. My intent is to suggest that my stories in the company of others demand thoughtful response.

Second, I draw from these scenes a specific direction for transformation, suggesting dimensions of the nature of voicing that remain problematic. My intent is to demonstrate that our critical approaches to voice, again as a central manifestation of subjectivity, are currently skewed toward voice as a spoken or written phenomenon. This intent merges the second task with the third in that I proceed to suggest that theories and practices should be transformed. The call for action in cross-boundary exchange is to refine theory and practice so that they include voicing as a phenomenon that is constructed and expressed visually and orally, *and* as a phenomenon that has import also in being a *thing* heard, perceived, and reconstructed.

SCENE ONE

I have been compelled on too many occasions to count to sit as a well-mannered Other, silently, in a state of tolerance that requires me to be as expressionless as I can manage, while colleagues who occupy a place of entitlement different from my own talk about the history and achievements of people from my ethnic group, or even about their perceptions of our struggles. I have been compelled to listen as they have comfortably claimed the authority to engage in the construction of knowledge and meaning about me and mine, without paying even a passing nod to the fact that sometimes a substantive version of that knowledge might already exist, or to how it might have already been constructed, or to the meanings that might have already been assigned that might make me quite impatient with gaps in their understanding of my community, or to the fact that I, or somebody within my ethnic group, might have an opinion about what they are doing. I have been compelled to listen to speakers, well-meaning though they may think they are, who signal to me rather clearly that subject position is everything. I have come to recognize, however, that when the subject matter is me and the voice is not mine, my sense of order and rightness is disrupted. In metaphoric fashion, these "authorities" let me know, once again, that Columbus has discovered America and claims it now, claims it still for a European crown.

Such scenes bring me to the very edge of a principle that I value deeply as a teacher and a scholar, the principle of the right to inquiry and discovery. When the discovering hits so close to home, however, my response is visceral, not just intellectual, and I am made to look over a precipice. I have found it extremely difficult to allow the voices and experiences of people that I care about deeply to be taken and handled so carelessly and without accountability by strangers.

At the extreme, the African American community, as my personal example, has seen and continues to see its contributions and achievements called into question in grossly negative ways, as in the case of *The Bell Curve*. Such interpretations of who we are as a people open to general interrogation, once again, the innate capacities of "the race" as a whole. As has been the case throughout our history in this country, we are put in jeopardy and on trial in a way that should not exist but does. We are compelled to respond to a rendering of our potential that demands, not that we account for attitudes, actions, and conditions, but that we defend ourselves as human beings. Such interpretations of human potential create a type of discourse that serves as a distraction, as noise that drains off energy and sabotages the work of identifying substantive problems within and across cultural boundaries and the work also of finding solutions that have import, not simply for "a race," but for human beings whose living conditions, values, and preferences vary.

All such close encounters, the extraordinarily insidious ones and the ordinary ones, are definable through the lens of subjectivity, particularly in terms of the power and authority to speak and to make meaning. An analysis of subject position reveals that these interpretations by those outside of the community are not random acts of unkindness. Instead, they embody ways of seeing, knowing, being, and acting that probably suggest as much about the speaker and the context as they do about the targeted subject matter. The advantage with this type of analysis, of course, is that we see the obvious need to contextualize the stranger's perspective among other interpretations and to recognize that an interpretive view is just that—interpretive. A second advantage is that we also see that in our nation's practices these types of interpretations, regardless of how superficial or libelous they may actually be within the context of a more comprehensive view, tend to have considerable consequence in the lives of the targeted group, people in this case whose own voices and perspectives remain still largely under considered and uncredited.

Essentially, though, having a mechanism to see the under considered helps us see the extent to which we add continually to the pile of evidence in this country of cross-cultural misconduct. These types of close encounters that disregard dialectical views are a type of free touching of the powerless by the power-full. This analytical perspective encourages us to acknowledge that marginalized communities are not in a good position to ward off the intrusion of those authorized in mainstream communities to engage in willful action. Historically, such actions have included everything from the displacement of native people from their homelands, to the use of unknowing human subjects in dangerous experiments, to the appropriation and misappropriation of cultural artifacts—art, literature, music, and so on. An insight using the lens of subjectivity, however, is a recognition of the ways in which these moments are indeed moments of violation, perhaps even ultimate violation.

This record of misconduct means that for people like me, on an instinctive level, all outsiders are rightly perceived as suspect. I suspect the genuineness of their interest, the altruism of their actions, and the probability that whatever is being said or done is not to the ultimate benefit and understanding of the people who are subject matter but not subjects. People in the neighborhood where I grew up would say, "Where is their home training?" Imbedded in the question is the idea that when you visit other people's "home places," especially when you have not been invited, you simply can not go tramping around the house like you own the place, no matter how smart you are, or how much imagination you can muster, or how much authority and entitlement outside that home you may be privileged to hold. And you certainly can not go around name calling, saying things like, "You people are intellectually inferior and have a limited capacity to achieve," without taking into account who the family is, what its living has been like, and what its history and achievement have been about.

The concept of "home training" underscores the reality that point of view matters and that we must be trained to respect points of view other than our own. It acknowledges that when we are away from home, we need to know that what we think we see in places that we do not really know very well may not actually be what is there at all. So often, it really is a matter of time, place, resources, and our ability to perceive. Coming to judgment too quickly, drawing on information too narrowly, and saying hurtful, discrediting, dehumanizing things without undisputed proof are not appropriate. Such behavior is not good manners. What comes to mind for me is another saying that I heard constantly when I was growing up, "Do unto others as you would have them do unto you." In this case, we would be implored to draw conclusions about others with care and, when we do draw conclusions, to use the same type of sense and sensibility that we would ideally like for others to use in drawing conclusions about us.

This scene convinces me that what we need in a pressing way in this country and in our very own field is to articulate codes of behavior that can sustain more concretely notions of honor, respect, and good manners across boundaries, with cultural boundaries embodying the need most vividly. Turning the light back onto myself, though, at the same time that my sense of violation may indeed be real, there is the compelling reality that many communities in our nation need to be taken seriously. We all deserve to be taken seriously, which means that critical inquiry and discovery are absolutely necessary. Those of us who love our own communities, we think, most deeply, most uncompromisingly, without reservation for what they are and also are not, must set aside our misgivings about strangers in the interest of the possibility of deeper understanding (and for the more idealistic among us, the possibility of global peace). Those of us who hold these communities close to our hearts, protect them, and embrace them; those who want to preserve the goodness of the minds and souls in them; those who want to preserve consciously, critically, and also lovingly the record of good work within them must take high risk and give over the exclusivity of our rights to know.

It seems to me that the agreement for inquiry and discovery needs to be deliberately reciprocal. All of us, strangers and community members, need to find ways to sustain productivity in what Pratt calls contact zones (199), areas of engagement that in all likelihood will remain contentious. We need to get over our tendencies to be too possessive and to resist locking ourselves into the tunnels of our own visions and direct experience. As community members, we must learn to have new faith in the advantage of sharing. As strangers, we must learn to treat the loved people and places of Others with care and to understand that, when we do not act respectfully and responsibly, we leave ourselves rightly open to wrath. The challenge is not to work with a fear of abuse or a fear of retaliation, however. The challenge is to teach, to engage in research, to write, and to speak with Others with the determination to operate not only with professional and personal integrity, but also with the specific knowledge that communities and their ancestors are watching. If we can set aside our rights to exclusivity in our own home cultures, if we can set aside the tendencies that we all have to think too narrowly, we actually leave open an important possibility. In our nation, we have little idea of the potential that a variety of subjectivities—operating with honor, respect, and reasonable codes of conduct—can bring to critical inquiry or critical problems. What might happen if we treated differences in subject position as critical pieces of the whole, vital to thorough understanding, and central to both problem-finding and problem-solving? This society has not, as yet, really allowed that privilege in a substantial way.

SCENE TWO

As indicated in Scene One, I tend to be enraged at what Tillie Olsen has called the "trespass vision," a vision that comes from intellect and imagination (62), but typically not from lived experience, and sometimes not from the serious study of the subject matter. However, like W. E. B. Du Bois, I've chosen not to be distracted or consumed by my rage at voyeurs, tourists, and trespassers, but to look at what I can do. I see the critical importance of the role of negotiator, someone who can cross boundaries and serve as guide and translator for Others.

In 1903, Du Bois demonstrated this role in *The Souls of Black Folk*. In the "Forethought" of that book, he says: "Leaving, then, the world of the white man, I have stepped within the Veil, raising it that you may view faintly its deeper recesses—the meaning of its religion, the passion of its human sorrow, and the struggle of its greater souls" (1). He sets his rhetorical purpose to be to cross, or at least to straddle, boundaries with the intent of shedding light, a light that has the potential of being useful to people on both sides of the veil. Like Du Bois, I've accepted the idea that what I call my "home place" is a cultural community that exists still quite significantly beyond the confines of a well-insulated community that we call the "mainstream," and that between this world and the one that I call home, systems of insulation impede the vision and narrow the ability to recognize human potential and to understand human history both microscopically and telescopically.

Like Du Bois, I've dedicated myself to raising this veil, to overriding these systems of insulation by raising another voice, my voice in the interest of clarity and accuracy. What I have found too often, however, is that, unlike those who have been entitled to talk about me and mine, when I talk about my own, I face what I call the power and function of deep disbelief, and what Du Bois described as "the sense of always looking at one's self through the eyes of others, of measuring one's soul by the tape of a world that looks on in amused contempt and pity" (5).

An example comes to mind. When I talk about African American women, especially those who were writing non-fiction prose in the nineteenth century, I can expect, even today after so much contemporary scholarship on such writers, to see people who are quite flabbergasted by anything that I share. Reflected on their faces and in their questions and comments, if anyone can manage to speak back to me, is a depth of surprise that is always discomforting. I sense that the surprise, or the silence, if there is little response, does not come from the simple ignorance of unfortunate souls who just happen not to know what I have spent years coming to know. What I suspect is that this type of surprise rather "naturally" emerges in a society that so obviously has the habit of expecting nothing of value, nothing of consequence, nothing of importance, nothing at all positive from its others, so that anything is a surprise; everything is an exception; and nothing of substance can really be claimed as a result.

In identifying this phenomenon, Chandra Talpade Mohanty speaks powerfully about the ways in which this culture co-opts, dissipates, and displaces voices. As demonstrated by my example, one method of absorption that has worked quite well has been essentially rhetorical. In discussing nineteenth century African American women's work, I bring tales of difference and adventure. I bring cultural proofs and instructive examples, all of which invariably must serve as rites of passage to credibility. I also bring the power of storytelling. These tales of adventure in odd places are the transitions by which to historicize and theorize anew with these writers re-inscribed in a rightful place. Such a process respects long-standing practices in African-based cultures of theorizing in narrative form. As Barbara Christian says, we theorize "in the stories we create, in riddles and proverbs, in the play with language, since dynamic rather than fixed ideas seem more to our liking" (336).

The problem is that in order to construct new histories and theories such stories must be perceived not just as "simple stories" to delight and entertain, but as vital layers of a transformative process. A reference point is Langston Hughes and his Simple stories, stories that are a model example of how apparent simplicity has the capacity to unmask truths in ways that are remarkably accessible—through metaphor, analogy, parable, and symbol. However, the problem of articulating new paradigms through stories becomes intractable, if those who are empowered to define impact and consequence decide that the stories are simply stories and if the record of achievement is perceived, as Audre Lorde has said, as "the random droppings of birds" (Foreword xi).

If I take my cue from the life of Ida Wells, and I am bold enough and defiant enough to go beyond the presentation of my stories as juicy tidbits for the delectation of audiences, to actually shift or even subvert a paradigm, I'm much more likely to receive a wide-eyed stare and to have the value and validity of my conceptual position held at a distance, in doubt, and wonderfully absorbed in the silence of appreciation. Through the systems of deep disbelief I become a storyteller, a performer. With such absorptive ability in the systems of interpretation, I have greater difficulty being perceived as a person who theorizes without the mediating voices of those from the inner sanctum, or as a person who might name myself a philosopher, a theorist, a historian who creates paradigms that allow the experiences and the insights of people like me to belong.

What I am compelled to ask when veils seem more like walls is who has the privilege of speaking first? How do we negotiate the privilege of interpretation? When I have tried to fulfill my role as negotiator, I have often walked away knowing that I have spoken, but also knowing, as Anna Julia Cooper knew in 1892, that my voice, like her voice, is still a muted one. I speak, but I can not be heard. Worse, I am heard but I am not believed. Worse yet, I speak but I am not deemed believable. These moments of deep disbelief have helped me to understand much more clearly the wisdom of Audre Lorde when she said: "I have come to believe over and over again that what is most important to me must be spoken, made verbal and shared, even at the risk of having it bruised or misunderstood" (*Sister* 40). Lorde teaches me that, despite whatever frustration and vulnerability I might feel, despite my fear that no one is listening to me or is curious enough to try to understand my voice, it is still better to speak (*Black* 31). I set aside the distractions and permeating noise outside of myself, and I listen, as Howard Thurman recommended, to the sound of the genuine within. I go to a place inside myself and, as Opal Palmer Adisa explains, I listen and learn to "speak without clenching my teeth" (56).

SCENE THREE

There have been occasions when I have indeed been heard and positively received. Even at these times, however, I sometimes can not escape responses that make me most weary. One case in point occurred after a presentation in which I had glossed a scene in a novel that required cultural understanding. When the characters spoke in the scene, I rendered their voices, speaking and explaining, speaking and explaining, trying to translate the experience, to share the sounds of my historical place and to connect those sounds with systems of belief so that deeper understanding of the scene might emerge, and so that those outside of the immediacy of my home culture, the one represented in the novel, might see and understand more and be able to make more useful connections to their own worlds and experiences.

One very well-intentioned response to what I did that day was, "How wonderful it was that you were willing to share with us your 'authentic' voice!" I said, "My 'authentic' voice?" She said, "Oh yes! I've never heard you talk like that, you know, so relaxed. I mean, you're usually great, but, this was really great! You weren't so formal. You didn't have to speak in appropriated academic language. You sounded 'natural.' It was nice to hear you be yourself." I said, "Oh, I see. Yes, I do have a range of voices, and I take quite a bit of pleasure actually in being able to use any of them at will." Not understanding the point that I was trying to make gently, she said, "But this time, it was really you. Thank you."

The conversation continued, but I stopped paying attention. What I didn't feel like saying in a more direct way, a response that my friend surely would have perceived as angry, was that all my voices are authentic, and like bell hooks, I find it "a necessary aspect of self-affirmation not to feel compelled to choose one voice over another, not to claim one as more authentic, but rather to construct social realities that celebrate, acknowledge, and affirm differences, variety" (12). Like hooks, I claim all my voices as my own very much authentic voices, even when it's difficult for others to imagine a person like me having the capacity to do that.

From moments of challenge like this one, I realize that we do not have a paradigm that really allows for what scholars in cultural and postcolonial studies (Anzaldúa, Spivak, Mohanty, Bhabha) have called hybrid people—people who either have the capacity by right of history and development, or who might have created the capacity by right of history and development, to move with dexterity across cultural boundaries, to make themselves comfortable, and to make sense amid the chaos of difference.

As Cornel West points out, most African Americans, for example, dream in English, not in Yoruba, or Hausa, or Wolof. Hybrid people, as demonstrated by the history of Africans in the Western hemisphere, manage a fusion process that allows for survival, certainly. However, it also allows for the development of a peculiar expertise that extends one's range of abilities well beyond ordinary limits, and it supports the opportunity for the development of new and remarkable creative expression, like spirituals, jazz, blues, and what I suspect is happening also with the essay as genre in the hands of African American women. West notes that somebody gave Charlie Parker a saxophone, Miles Davis a trumpet, Hubert Laws a flute, and Les McCann a piano. I suggest that somebody also gave Maria Stewart, Gertrude Mossell, Frances Harper, Alice Walker, Audre Lorde, Toni Morrison, Patricia Williams, June Jordan, bell hooks, Angela Davis and a cadre of other African American women a pencil, a pen, a computer keyboard. In both instances, genius emerges from hybridity, from Africans who, over the course of time and circumstance, have come to dream in English, and I venture to say that all of their voices are authentic.

In sharing these three scenes, I emphasize that there is a pressing need to construct paradigms that permit us to engage in better practices in cross-boundary discourse, whether we are teaching, researching, writing, or talking with Others, whoever those Others happen to be. I would like to emphasize, again, that we look again at "voice" and situate it within a world of symbols, sound, and sense, recognizing that this world operates symphonically. Although the systems of voice production are indeed highly integrated and appear to have singularity in the ways that we come to sound, voicing actually sets in motion multiple systems; prominent among them are systems for speaking but present also are the systems for hearing. We speak within systems that we know significantly through our abilities to negotiate noise and to construct within that noise sense and sensibility.

Several questions come to mind. How can we teach, engage in research, write about, and talk across boundaries *with* others, instead of for, about, and around them? My experiences tell me that we need to do more than just talk and talk back. I believe that in this model we miss a critical moment. We need to talk, yes, and to talk back, yes, but when do we listen? How do we listen? How do we demonstrate that we honor and respect the person talking and what that person is saying, or what the person might say if we valued someone other than ourselves having a turn to speak? How do we translate listening into language and action, into the creation of an appropriate response? How do we really "talk back" rather than talk also? The goal is not, "You talk, I talk." The goal is better practices so that we can exchange perspectives, negotiate meaning, and create understanding with the intent of being in a good position to cooperate, when, like now, cooperation is absolutely necessary.

When I think about this goal, what stands out most is that these questions apply in so much of academic life right now. They certainly apply as we go into classrooms and insist that our students trust us and what we contend is in their best interest. In light of a record in classrooms that seriously questions the range of our abilities to recognize potential, or to appreciate students as non-generic human beings, or to appreciate that they bring with them, always, knowledge, we ask a lot when we ask them to trust. Too often, still, institutionalized equations for placement, positive matriculation, progress, and achievement name, categorize, rank, and file, while our true-to-life students fall between the cracks. I look again to Opal Palmer Adisa for an instructive example. She says:

> Presently, many academics advocate theories which, rather than illuminating the works under scrutiny, obfuscate and problematize these works so that students are rendered speechless. Consequently, the students constantly question what they know, and often, unfortunately, they conclude that they know nothing. (54)

Students may find what we do to be alienating and disheartening. Even when our intentions are quite honorable, silence can descend. Their experiences are not seen, and their voices are not heard. We can find ourselves participating, sometimes consciously, sometimes not, in what Patricia Williams calls "spirit murder" (55). I am reminded in a disconcerting way of a troubling scene from Alex Haley's *Roots*. We engage in practices that say quite insistently to a variety of students in a variety of ways, "Your name is Toby." Why wouldn't students wonder: Who can I trust here? Under what kinds of conditions? When? Why?

In addition to better practices in our classrooms, however, we can also question our ability to talk convincingly with deans, presidents, legislators, and the general public about what we do, how we do it, and why. We have not been conscientious about keeping lines of communication open, and we are now experiencing the consequences of talking primarily to ourselves as we watch funds being cut, programs being eliminated, and national agencies that are vital to our interests being bandied about as if they are post-it notes, randomly stuck on by some ill-informed spendthrift. We must learn to raise a politically active voice with a socially responsible mandate to make a rightful place for education in a country that seems always ready to place the needs of quality education on a sideboard instead of on the table. Seemingly, we have been forever content to let voices other than our own speak authoritatively about our areas of expertise and about us. It is time to speak for ourselves, in our own interests, in the interest of our work, and in the interest of our students.

Better practices are not limited, though, even to these concerns. Of more immediate concern to me this year, given my role as Chair of CCCC, is how to talk across boundaries within our own organization as teachers of English among other teachers of English and language arts from kindergarten through university with interests as varied as those implied by the sections, conferences, and committees of our parent organization, the National Council of Teachers of English (NCTE). Each of the groups within NCTE has its own set of needs, expectations, and concerns, multiplied across the amazing variety of institutional sites across which we work. In times of limited resources and a full slate of critical problems, we must find reasonable ways to negotiate so that we can all thrive reasonably well in the same place.

In our own case, for years now, CCCC has recognized changes in our relationships with NCTE. Since the mid-1980s we have grown exponentially. The field of rhetoric and composition has blossomed and diversified. The climate for higher education has increasingly degenerated, and we have struggled in the midst of change to forge a more satisfying identity and a more positive and productive working relationship with others in NCTE who are facing crises of their own. After 50 years in NCTE, we have grown up, and we have to figure out a new way of being and doing in making sure that we can face our challenges well. We are now in the second year of a concerted effort to engage in a multi-leveled conversation that we hope will leave CCCC well-positioned to face a new century and ongoing challenges. Much, however, depends on the ways in which we talk and listen and talk again in crossing boundaries and creating, or not, the common ground of engagement.

As I look at the lay of this land, I endorse Henry David Thoreau's statement when he said, "Only that day dawns to which we are awake" (267). So my appeal is to urge us all to be awake, awake and listening, awake and operating deliberately on codes of better conduct in the interest of keeping our boundaries fluid, our discourse invigorated with multiple perspectives, and our policies and practices well-tuned toward a clearer respect for human potential and achievement from whatever their source and a clearer understanding that voicing at its best is not just well-spoken but also well-heard.

WORKS CITED

Adisa, Opal Palmer. "I Must Write What I Know So I'll Know That I've Known It All Along." *Sage: A Scholarly Journal on Black Women* 9.2 (1995): 54–57.

Anzaldúa, Gloria. *Borderlands/La Frontera.* San Francisco: Aunt Lute, 1987.

Bhabha, Homi K. *The Location of Culture.* London: Routledge, 1994.

Christian, Barbara. "The Race for Theory." *Cultural Critique* 6 (1987): 335–45.

Cooper, Anna Julia. *A Voice from the South.* New York: Oxford UP, 1988.

Du Bois, W. E. B. *The Souls of Black Folk.* New York: Grammercy, 1994.

Haley, Alex. *Roots.* Garden City: Doubleday, 1976.

Hernstein, Richard J., and Charles Murray. *The Bell Curve: Intelligence and Class Structure in American Life.* New York: Free, 1994.

hooks, bell. *Talking Back: Thinking Feminist, Thinking Black.* Boston: South End, 1989.

Lorde, Audre. *The Black Unicorn.* New York: Norton, 1978.

———. Foreword. *Wild Women in the Whirlwind.* Ed. Joanne M. Braxton and Andree Nicola McLaughlin. New Brunswick: Rutgers UP, 1990. xi–xiii.

———. *Sister Outsider.* Freedom: The Crossing Press, 1984.

Mohanty, Chandra Talpade. "On Race and Voice: Challenges for Liberal Education in the 1990s." *Cultural Critique* 14 (Winter 1989–90): 179–208.

———. "Decolonizing Education: Feminisms and the Politics of Multiculturalism in the 'New' World Order." Ohio State University, Columbus, April 1994.

Olsen, Tillie. *Silences.* New York: Delta, 1978.

Pratt, Mary Louise. "Arts of the Contact Zone." *Profession* 91 (1991): 33–40.

Spivak, Gayatri Chakravorty. *In Other Worlds: Essays in Cultural Politics.* New York: Routledge, 1988.

Thoreau, Henry David. *Walden.* New York: Vintage, 1991.

Thurman, Howard. "The Sound of the Genuine." Spelman College, Atlanta, April 1981.

West, Cornel. "Race Matters." Ohio State U, Columbus, OH, February 1995.

Williams, Patricia. *The Alchemy of Race and Rights.* Cambridge: Harvard UP, 1991.

Inventing the University

DAVID BARTHOLOMAE

(*Education may well be, as of right, the instrument whereby every individual,
in a society like our own, can gain access to any kind of discourse. But we
well know that in its distribution, in what it permits and in what it prevents,
it follows the well-trodden battle-lines of social conflict. Every educational
system is a political means of maintaining or of modifying the appropriation
of discourse, with the knowledge and the powers it carries with it.*
    —Michel Foucault, The Discourse on Language)

*. . . the text is the form of the social relationships made visible, palpable,
material.*
    —*Basil B. Bernstein,* Codes, Modalities and the Process of Cultural
    Reproduction: A Model

I

Every time a student sits down to write for us, he has to invent the university
for the occasion—invent the university, that is, or a branch of it, like history
or anthropology or economics or English. The student has to learn to speak
our language, to speak as we do, to try on the peculiar ways of knowing, selecting, evaluating, reporting, concluding, and arguing that define the discourse of our community. Or perhaps I should say the *various* discourses of
our community, since it is in the nature of a liberal arts education that a

Reprinted from *When a Writer Can't Write: Studies in Writer's Block and Other Composing-
Process Problems.* Ed. Mike Rose. New York: Guilford, 1985. 134–65. Copyright © 1985 by
the Guilford Press. All rights reserved.

student, after the first year or two, must learn to try on a variety of voices and interpretive schemes—to write, for example, as a literary critic one day and as an experimental psychologist the next; to work within fields where the rules governing the presentation of examples or the development of an argument are both distinct and, even to a professional, mysterious.

The student has to appropriate (or be appropriated by) a specialized discourse, and he has to do this as though he were easily and comfortably one with his audience, as though he were a member of the academy or an historian or an anthropologist or an economist; he has to invent the university by assembling and mimicking its language while finding some compromise between idiosyncrasy, a personal history, on the one hand, and the requirements of convention, the history of a discipline, on the other hand. He must learn to speak our language. Or he must dare to speak it or to carry off the bluff, since speaking and writing will most certainly be required long before the skill is "learned." And this, understandably, causes problems.

Let me look quickly at an example. Here is an essay written by a college freshman.

> In the past time I thought that an incident was creative was when I had to make a clay model of the earth, but not of the classical or your everyday model of the earth which consists of the two cores, the mantle and the crust. I thought of these things in a dimension of which it would be unique, but easy to comprehend. Of course, your materials to work with were basic and limited at the same time, but thought help to put this limit into a right attitude or frame of mind to work with the clay.
>
> In the beginning of the clay model, I had to research and learn the different dimensions of the earth (in magnitude, quantity, state of matter, etc.) After this, I learned how to put this into the clay and come up with something different than any other person in my class at the time. In my opinion, color coordination and shape was the key to my creativity of the clay model of the earth.
>
> Creativity is the venture of the mind at work with the mechanics relay to the limbs from the cranium, which stores and triggers this action. It can be a burst of energy released at a precise time a thought is being transmitted. This can cause a frenzy of the human body, but it depends on the characteristics of the individual and how they can relay the message clearly enough through mechanics of the body to us as an observer. Then we must determine if it is creative or a learned process varied by the individuals thought process. Creativity is indeed a tool which has to exist, or our world will not succeed into the future and progress like it should.

I am continually impressed by the patience and goodwill of our students. This student was writing a placement essay during freshman orientation. (The problem set to him was: "Describe a time when you did something you felt to be creative. Then, on the basis of the incident you have described, go on to draw some general conclusions about 'creativity.'") He knew that university faculty would be reading and evaluating his essay, and so he wrote for them.

In some ways it is a remarkable performance. He is trying on the discourse even though he doesn't have the knowledge that would make the discourse more than a routine, a set of conventional rituals and gestures. And he is doing this, I think, even though he *knows* he doesn't have the knowledge that would make the discourse more than a routine. He defines himself as a researcher working systematically, and not as a kid in a high school class: "I thought of these things in a dimension of . . ."; "I had to research and learn the different dimensions of the earth (in magnitude, quantity, state of matter, etc.)." He moves quickly into a specialized language (his approximation of our jargon) and draws both a general, textbook-like conclusion— "Creativity is the venture of the mind at work . . ."—and a resounding peroration—"Creativity is indeed a tool which has to exist, or our world will not succeed into the future and progress like it should." The writer has even picked up the rhythm of our prose with that last "indeed" and with the qualifications and the parenthetical expressions of the opening paragraphs. And through it all he speaks with an impressive air of authority.

There is an elaborate but, I will argue, a necessary and enabling fiction at work here as the student dramatizes his experience in a "setting"—the setting required by the discourse—where he can speak to us as a companion, a fellow researcher. As I read the essay, there is only one moment when the fiction is broken, when we are addressed differently. The student says, "Of course, your materials to work with were basic and limited at the same time, but thought help to put this limit into a right attitude or frame of mind to work with the clay." At this point, I think, we become students and he the teacher giving us a lesson (as in, "You take your pencil in your right hand and put your paper in front of you"). This is however, one of the most characteristic slips of basic writers. (I use the term "basic writers" to refer to university students traditionally placed in remedial composition courses.) It is very hard for them to take on the role—the voice, the persona—of an authority whose authority is rooted in scholarship, analysis, or research. They slip, then, into a more immediately available and realizable voice of authority, the voice of a teacher giving a lesson or the voice of a parent lecturing at the dinner table. They offer advice or homilies rather than "academic" conclusions. There is a similar break in the final paragraph, where the conclusion that pushes for a definition ("Creativity is the venture of the mind at work with the mechanics relay to the limbs from the cranium") is replaced by a conclusion that speaks in the voice of an elder ("Creativity is indeed a tool which has to exist, or our world will not succeed into the future and progress like it should").

It is not uncommon, then, to find such breaks in the concluding sections of essays written by basic writers. Here is the concluding section of an essay written by a student about his work as a mechanic. He had been asked to generalize about work after reviewing an on-the-job experience or incident that "stuck in his mind" as somehow significant.

> How could two repairmen miss a leak? Lack of pride? No incentive? Lazy? I don't know.

At this point the writer is in a perfect position to speculate, to move from the problem to an analysis of the problem. Here is how the paragraph continues, however (and notice the change in pronoun reference).

> From this point on, I take *my* time, do it right, and don't let customers get under *your* skin. If they have a complaint, tell them to call your boss and he'll be more than glad to handle it. Most important, worry about yourself, and keep a clear eye on everyone, for there's always someone trying to take advantage of you, anytime and anyplace. (Emphasis added)

We get neither a technical discussion nor an "academic" discussion but a Lesson on Life.[1] This is the language he uses to address the general question, "How could two repairmen miss a leak?" The other brand of conclusion, the more academic one, would have required him to speak of his experience in our terms; it would, that is, have required a special vocabulary, a special system of presentation, and an interpretive scheme (or a set of commonplaces) he could have used to identify and talk about the mystery of human error. The writer certainly had access to the range of acceptable commonplaces for such an explanation: "lack of pride," "no incentive," "lazy." Each commonplace would dictate its own set of phrases, examples, and conclusions; and we, his teachers, would know how to write out each argument, just as we know how to write out more specialized arguments of our own. A "commonplace," then, is a culturally or institutionally authorized concept or statement that carries with it its own necessary elaboration. We all use commonplaces to orient ourselves in the world; they provide points of reference and a set of "prearticulated" explanations that are readily available to organize and interpret experience. The phrase, "lack of pride" carries with it its own account of the repairman's error, just as at another point in time a reference to "original sin" would have provided an explanation, or

626

just as in certain university classrooms a reference to "alienation" would enable writers to continue and complete the discussion. While there is a way in which these terms are interchangeable, they are not all permissible: A student in a composition class would most likely be turned away from a discussion of original sin. Commonplaces are the "controlling ideas" of our composition textbooks, textbooks that not only insist on a set form for expository writing but a set view of public life.[2]

When the writer says, "I don't know," then, he is not saying that he has nothing to say. He is saying that he is not in a position to carry on this discussion. And so we are addressed as apprentices rather than as teachers or scholars. In order to speak as a person of status or privilege, the writer can either speak to us in our terms—in the privileged language of university discourse—or, in default (or in defiance) of that, he can speak to us as though we were children, offering us the wisdom of experience.

I think it is possible to say that the language of the "Clay Model" paper has come *through* the writer and not from the writer. The writer has located himself (more precisely, he has located the self that is represented by the "I" on the page) in a context that is finally beyond him, not his own and not available to his immediate procedures for inventing and arranging text. I would not, that is, call this essay an example of "writer-based" prose. I would not say that it is egocentric or that it represents the "interior monologue or a writer thinking and talking to himself" (Flower, 1981, p. 63). It is, rather, the record of a writer who has lost himself in the discourse of his readers. There is a context beyond the intended reader that is not the world but a way of talking about the world, a way of talking that determines the use of examples, the possible conclusions, acceptable commonplaces, and key words for an essay on the construction of a clay model of the earth. This writer has entered the discourse without successfully approximating it.

Linda Flower (1981) has argued that the difficulty inexperienced writers have with writing can be understood as a difficulty in negotiating the transition between "writer-based" and "reader-based" prose. Expert writers, in other words, can better imagine how a reader will respond to a text and can transform or restructure what they have to say around a goal shared with a reader. Teaching students to revise for readers, then, will better prepare them to write initially with a reader in mind. The success of this pedagogy depends on the degree to which a writer can imagine and conform to a reader's goals. The difficulty of this act of imagination and the burden of such conformity are so much at the heart of the problem that a teacher must pause and take stock before offering revision as a solution. A student like the one who wrote the "Clay Model" paper is not so much trapped in a private language as he is shut out from one of the privileged languages of public life, a language he is aware of but cannot control.

II

Our students, I've said, have to appropriate (or be appropriated by) a specialized discourse, and they have to do this as though they were easily or comfortably one with their audience. If you look at the situation this way, suddenly the problem of audience awareness becomes enormously complicated. One of the common assumptions of both composition research and composition teaching is that at some "stage" in the process of composing an essay a writer's ideas or his motives must be tailored to the needs and expectations of his audience. Writers have to "build bridges" between their point of view and the reader's. They have to anticipate and acknowledge the reader's assumptions and biases. They must begin with "common points of departure" before introducing new or controversial arguments. Here is what one of the most popular college textbooks says to students.

> Once you have your purpose clearly in mind, your next task is to define and analyze your audience. A sure sense of your audience—knowing who it is and what assumptions you can reasonably make about it—is crucial to the success of your rhetoric. (Hairston, 1978, p. 107)

It is difficult to imagine, however, how writers can have a purpose before they are located in a discourse, since it is the discourse with its projects and agendas that determines what writers can and will do. The writer who can successfully manipulate an audience (or, to use a less pointed language, the writer who can accommodate her motives to her reader's expectations) is a writer who can both imagine and write from a position of privilege. She must, that is, see herself within a privileged discourse, one that already includes and excludes groups of readers. She must be either equal to or more powerful than those she would address. The writing, then, must somehow transform the political and social relationships between students and teachers.

If my students are going to write for me by knowing who I am—and if this means more than knowing my prejudices, psyching me out—it means knowing what I know; it means having the knowledge of a professor of English. They have, then, to know what I know and how I know what I know (the interpretive schemes that define the way I would work out the problems I set for them); they have to learn to write what I would write or to offer up some approximation of that discourse. The problem of audience awareness, then, is a problem of power and finesse. It cannot be addressed, as it is in most classroom exercises, by giving students privilege and denying the situation of the classroom—usually, that is, by having students write to an outsider, someone excluded from their privileged circle: "Write about 'To His Coy Mistress,' not for your teacher but for the students in your class"; "Describe Pittsburgh to someone who has never been there"; "Explain to a high school senior how best to prepare for college"; "Describe baseball to an Eskimo." Exercises such as these allow students to imagine the needs and goals of a reader, and they bring those needs and goals forward as a dominant constraint in the construction of an essay. And they argue, implicitly, what is generally true about writing—that it is an act of aggression disguised as an act of charity. What these assignments fail to address is the central problem of academic writing, where a student must assume the right of speaking to someone who knows more about baseball or "To His Coy Mistress" than the student does, a reader for whom the general commonplaces and the readily available utterances about a subject are inadequate.

Linda Flower and John Hayes, in an often quoted article (1981), reported on a study of a protocol of an expert writer (an English teacher) writing about his job for readers of *Seventeen* magazine. The key moment for this writer, who seems to have been having trouble getting started, came when he decided that teenage girls read *Seventeen*; that some teenage girls like English because it is tidy ("some of them will have wrong reasons in that English is good because it's tidy—can be a neat tidy little girl"); that some don't like it because it is "prim" and that, "By God, I can change that notion for them." Flower and Hayes's conclusion is that this effort of "exploration and consolidation" gave the writer "a new, relatively complex, rhetorically sophisticated working goal, one which encompasses plans for topic, a persona, and the audience" (p. 383).[3]

Flower and Hayes give us a picture of a writer solving a problem, and the problem as they present it is a cognitive one. It is rooted in the way the writer's knowledge is represented in the writer's mind. The problem resides there, not in the nature of knowledge or in the nature of discourse but in a mental state prior to writing. It is possible, however, to see the problem as (perhaps simultaneously) a problem in the way subjects are located in a field of discourse.

Flower and Hayes divide up the composing process into three distinct activities: "planning or goal-setting," "translating," and "reviewing." The last of these, reviewing (which is further divided into two subprocesses, "evaluating" and "revising"), is particularly powerful, for as a writer continually generates new goals, plans, and text, he is engaging in a process of learning and discovery. Let me quote Flower and Hayes's conclusion at length.

> If one studies the process by which a writer uses a goal to generate ideas, then consolidates those ideas and uses them to revise or regenerate new, more complex goals, one can see this learning process in action. Furthermore, one sees why the process of revising and clarifying goals has such a broad effect, since it is through setting these new goals that the fruits of discovery come back to inform the continuing process of writing. In this instance, some of our most complex and imaginative acts can depend on the elegant simplicity of a few powerful thinking processes. We feel that a cognitive process explanation of discovery, toward which this theory is only a start, will have another special strength. By placing emphasis on the inventive power of the writer, who is able to explore ideas, to develop, act on, test, and regenerate his or her own goals, we are putting an important part of creativity where it belongs—in the hands of the working, thinking writer. (1981, p. 386)

While this conclusion is inspiring, the references to invention and creativity seem to refer to something other than an act of writing—if writing is, finally, words on a page. Flower and Hayes locate the act of writing solely within the mind of the writer. The act of writing, here, has a personal, cognitive history but not a history as a text, as a text that is made possible by prior texts. When located in the perspective afforded by prior texts, writing is seen to exist separate from the writer and his intentions; it is seen in the context of other articles in *Seventeen*, of all articles written for or about women, of all articles written about English teaching, and so on. Reading research has make it possible to say that these prior texts, or a reader's experience with these prior texts, have bearing on how the text is read. Intentions, then, are part of the history of the language itself. I am arguing that these prior texts determine not only how a text like the *Seventeen* article will be read but also how it will be written. Flower and Hayes show us what happens in the writer's mind but not what happens to the writer as his motives are located within our language, a language with its own requirements and agendas, a language that limits what we might say and that makes us write and sound, finally, also like someone else. If you think of other accounts of the composing process—and I'm thinking of accounts as diverse as Richard Rodriguez's *Hunger of Memory* (1983) and Edward Said's *Beginnings* (1975)—you get a very different account of what happens when private motive enters into public discourse, when a personal history becomes a public account. These accounts place the writer in a history that is not of the writer's own invention; and they are chronicles of loss, violence, and compromise.

It is one thing to see the *Seventeen* writer making and revising his plans for a topic, a persona, and an audience; it is another thing to talk about discovery, invention, and creativity. Whatever plans the writer had must finally have been located in language and, it is possible to argue, in a language that is persistently conventional and formulaic. We do not, after all, get to see the *Seventeen* article. We see only the elaborate mental procedures that accompanied the writing of the essay. We see a writer's plans for a persona; we don't see that persona in action. If writing is a process, it is also a product; and it is the product, and not the plan for writing, that locates a writer on the page, that locates him in a text and a style and the codes or conventions that make both of them readable.

Contemporary rhetorical theory has been concerned with the "codes" that constitute discourse (or specialized forms of discourse). These codes determine not only what might be said but also who might be speaking or reading. Barthes (1974), for example, has argued that the moment of writing, where private goals and plans become subject to a public language, is the moment when the writer becomes subject to a language he can neither command nor control. A text, he says, in being written passes through the codes that govern writing and becomes "de-originated," becomes a fragment of something that has always been *already* read, seen, done, experienced" (p. 21). Alongside a text we have always the presence of "off-stage voices," the oversound of all that has been said (e.g., about girls, about English). These voices, the presence of the "already written," stand in defiance of a writer's desire for originality and determine what might be said. A writer does not write (and this is Barthes's famous paradox) but is, himself, written by the languages available to him.

It is possible to see the writer of the *Seventeen* article solving his problem of where to begin by appropriating an available discourse. Perhaps what enabled that writer to write was the moment he located himself as a writer in a familiar field of stereotypes: Readers of *Seventeen* are teenage girls; teenage girls think of English (and English teachers) as "tidy" and "prim," and, "By God, I can change that notion for them." The moment of eureka was not simply a moment of breaking through a cognitive jumble in that individual writer's mind but a moment of breaking into a familiar and established territory—one with insiders and outsiders; one with set phrases, examples, and conclusions.

I'm not offering a criticism of the morals or manners of the teacher who wrote the *Seventeen* article. I think that all writers, in order to write, must imagine for themselves the privilege of being "insiders"—that is, the privilege both of being inside an established and powerful discourse and of being granted a special right to speak. But I think that right to speak is seldom conferred on us—on any of us, teachers or students—by virtue of the fact that we have invented or discovered an original idea. Leading students to believe that they are responsible for something new or original, unless they understand what those words mean with regard to writing, is a dangerous and counterproductive practice. We do have the right to expect students to be active and engaged, but that is a matter of continually and stylistically working against the inevitable presence of conventional language; it is not a matter of inventing a language that is new.

When a student is writing for a teacher, writing becomes more problematic than it was for the *Seventeen* writer (who was writing a version of the "Describe baseball to an Eskimo" exercise). The student, in effect, has to assume privilege without having any. And since students assume privilege by locating themselves within the discourse of a particular community—within a set of specifically acceptable gestures and commonplaces—learning, at least as it is defined in the liberal arts curriculum, becomes more a matter of imitation or parody than a matter of invention and discovery.

To argue that writing problems are also social and political problems is not to break faith with the enterprise of cognitive science. In a recent paper reviewing the tremendous range of research directed at identifying general cognitive skills, David Perkins (in press) has argued that "the higher the level of competence concerned," as in the case of adult learning, "the fewer *general* cognitive control strategies there are." There comes a point, that is, where "field-specific" or "domain-specific" schemata (what I have called "interpretive strategies") become more important than general problem-solving processes. Thinking, learning, writing—all these become bound to the context of a particular discourse. And Perkins concludes:

> Instruction in cognitive control strategies tends to be organized around problem-solving tasks. However, the isolated problem is a creature largely of the classroom. The nonstudent, whether operating in scholarly or more everyday contexts, is likely to find himself or herself involved in what might be called "projects"—which might be anything from writing a novel to designing a shoe to starting a business.

It is interesting to note that Perkins defines the classroom as the place of artificial tasks and, as a consequence, has to place scholarly projects outside the classroom, where they are carried out by the "nonstudent." It is true, I think, that education has failed to involve students in scholarly projects, projects that allow students to act as though they were colleagues in an academic enterprise. Much of the written work that students do is test-taking, report or summary—work that places them outside the official discourse of the academic community, where they are expected to admire and report on what we do, rather than inside that discourse, where they can do its work and participate in a common enterprise.[4] This, however, is a failure of teachers and curriculum designers, who speak of writing as a mode of learning but all too often represent writing as a "tool" to be used by an (hopefully) educated mind.

It could be said, then, that there is a bastard discourse peculiar to the writing most often required of students. Carl Bereiter and Marlene Scardamalia (in press) have written about this discourse (they call it "knowledge-telling"; students who are good at it have learned to cope with academic tasks by developing a "knowledge-telling strategy"), and they have argued that insistence on knowledge-telling discourse undermines educational efforts to extend the variety of discourse schemata available to students.[5] What they actually say is this:

> When we think of knowledge stored in memory we tend these days to think of it as situated in three-dimensional space, with vertical and horizontal connections between sites. Learning is thought to add not only new elements to memory but also new connections, and it is the richness and structure of these connections that would seem . . . to spell the difference between inert and usable knowledge. On this account, the knowledge-telling strategy is educationally faulty because it specifically avoids the forming of connections between previously separated knowledge sites.

It should be clear by now that when I think of "knowledge" I think of it as situated in the discourse that constitutes "knowledge" in a particular discourse community, rather than as situated in mental "knowledge sites." One can remember a discourse, just as one can remember an essay or the movement of a professor's lecture; but this discourse, in effect, also has a memory of its own, its own rich network of structures and connections beyond the deliberate control of any individual imagination.

There is, to be sure, an important distinction to be made between learning history, say, and learning to write as an historian. A student can learn to command and reproduce a set of names, dates, places, and canonical interpretations (to "tell" somebody else's knowledge); but this is not the same thing as learning to "think" (by learning to write) as an historian. The former requires efforts of memory; the latter requires a student to compose a text out of the texts that represent the primary materials of history and in accordance with the texts that define history as an act of report and interpretation.

Let me draw on an example from my own teaching. I don't expect my students to *be* literary critics when they write about *Bleak House*. If a literary critic is a person who wins publication in a professional journal (or if he or she is one who could), the students aren't critics. I do, however, expect my students to be, themselves, invented as literary critics by approximating the language of a literary critic writing about *Bleak House*. My students, then, don't invent the language of literary criticism (they don't, that is, act on their own) but they are, themselves, invented by it. Their papers don't begin with a moment of insight, a "by God" moment that is outside of language. They begin with a moment of appropriation, a moment when they can offer up a sentence that is not theirs as though it were their own. (I can remember when, as a graduate student, I would begin papers by sitting down to write literally in the voice—with the syntax and the key words—of the strongest teacher I had met.)

What I am saying about my students' essays is that they are approximate, not that they are wrong or invalid. They are evidence of a discourse that lies between what I might call the students' primary discourse (what the students might write about *Bleak House* were they not in my class or in any class, and were they not imagining that they were in my class or in any class—if you can imagine any student doing any such thing) and standard, official literary criticism (which is imaginable but impossible to find). The students' essays are evidence of a discourse that lies between these two hypothetical poles. The writing is limited as much by a student's ability to imagine "what might be said" as it is by cognitive control strategies.[6] The act of writing takes the student away from where he is and what he knows and allows him to imagine something else. The approximate discourse, therefore, is evidence of a change, a change that, because we are teachers, we call "development." What our beginning students need to learn is to extend themselves, by successive approximations, into the commonplaces, set phrases, rituals and gestures, habits of mind, tricks of persuasion, obligatory conclusions and necessary connections that determine the "what might be said" and constitute knowledge within the various branches of our academic community.[7]

Pat Bizzell is, I think, one of the most important scholars writing now on "basic writers" (and this is the common name we use for students who are refused unrestrained access to the academic community) and on the special characteristics of academic discourse. In a recent essay, "Cognition, Convention, and Certainty: What We Need to Know about Writing" (1982a), she looks at two schools of composition research and the way they represent the problems that writing poses for writers.[8] For one group, the "inner-directed theorists," the problems are internal, cognitive, rooted in the way the mind represents knowledge to itself. These researchers are concerned with discovering the "universal, fundamental structures of thought and language" and with developing pedagogies to teach or facilitate both basic, general cognitive skills and specific cognitive strategies, or heuristics, directed to serve more specialized needs. Of the second group, the "outer-directed theorists," she says that they are "more interested in the social processes whereby language-learning and thinking capacities are shaped and used in particular communities."

> The staple activity of outer-directed writing instruction will be analysis of the conventions of particular discourse communities. For example, a main focus of writing-across-the-curriculum programs is to demystify the conventions of the academic discourse community. (1982a, p. 218)

The essay offers a detailed analysis of the way the two theoretical camps can best serve the general enterprise of composition research and composition teaching. Its agenda, however, seems to be to counter the influence of the cognitivists and to provide bibliography and encouragement to those interested in the social dimension of language learning.

As far as basic writers are concerned, Bizzell argues that the cognitivists' failure to acknowledge the primary, shaping role of convention in the act of composing makes them "particularly insensitive to the problems of poor writers." She argues that some of those problems, like the problem of establishing and monitoring overall goals for a piece of writing, can be

> better understood in terms of the unfamiliarity with the academic discourse community, combined, perhaps, with such limited experience outside their native discourse communities that they are unaware that there is such a thing as a discourse community with conventions to be mastered. What is underdeveloped is their knowledge both of the ways experience is constituted and interpreted in the academic discourse community and of the fact that all discourse communities constitute and interpret experience. (1982a, p. 230)

One response to the problems of basic writers, then, would be to determine just what the community's conventions are, so that those conventions could be written out, "demystified" and taught in our classrooms. Teachers, as a result, could be more precise and helpful when they ask students to "think," "argue," "describe," or "define." Another response would be to examine the essays written by basic writers—their approximations of academic discourse—to determine more clearly where the problems lie. If we look at their writing, and if we look at it in the context of other student writing, we can better see the points of discord that arise when students try to write their way into the university.

The purpose of the remainder of this chapter will be to examine some of the most striking and characteristic of these problems as they are presented in the expository essays of first-year college students. I will be concerned, then, with university discourse in its most generalized form—as it is represented by introductory courses—and not with the special conventions required by advanced work in the various disciplines. And I will be concerned with the difficult, and often violent accommodations that occur when students locate themselves in a discourse that is not "naturally" or immediately theirs.

III

I have reviewed 500 essays written, as the "Clay Model" essay was, in response to a question used during one of our placement exams at the University of Pittsburgh: "Describe a time when you did something you felt to be creative. Then, on the basis of the incident you have described, go on to draw some general conclusions about "creativity." Some of the essays were written by basic writers (or, more properly, those essays led readers to identify the writers as basic writers); some were written by students who "passed" (who were granted immediate access to the community of writers at the university). As I read these essays, I was looking to determine the stylistic resources that enabled writers to locate themselves within an "academic" discourse. My bias as a reader should be clear by now. I was not looking to see how a writer might represent the skills demanded by a neutral language (a language whose key features were paragraphs, topic sentences, transitions, and the like—features of a clear and orderly mind). I was looking to see what happened when a writer entered into a language to locate himself (a textual self) and his subject; and I was looking to see how, once entered, that language made or unmade the writer.

Here is one essay. Its writer was classified as a basic writer and, since the essay is relatively free of sentence level errors, that decision must have been rooted in some perceived failure of the discourse itself.

> I am very interested in music, and I try to be creative in my interpretation of music. While in highschool, I was a member of a jazz ensemble. The members of the ensemble were given chances to improvise and be creative in various songs. I feel that this was a great experience for me, as well as the other members. I was proud to know that I could use my imagination and feelings to create music other than what was written.
>
> Creativity to me, means being free to express yourself in a way that is unique to you, not having to conform to certain rules and guidelines.

Music is only one of the many areas in which people are given opportunities to show their creativity. Sculpting, carving, building, art, and acting are just a few more areas where people can show their creativity.

Through my music I conveyed feelings and thoughts which were important to me. Music was my means of showing creativity. In whatever form creativity takes, whether it be music, art, or science, it is an important aspect of our lives because it enables us to be individuals.

Notice the key gesture in this essay, one that appears in all but a few of the essays I read. The student defines as his own that which is a commonplace. "Creativity, *to me,* means being free to express yourself in a way that is unique to you, not having to conform to certain rules and guidelines." This act of appropriation constitutes his authority; it constitutes his authority as a writer and not just as a musician (that is, as someone with a story to tell). There were many essays in the set that told only a story—where the writer established his presence as a musician or a skier or someone who painted designs on a van, but not as a person at a remove from that experience interpreting it, treating it as a metaphor for something else (creativity). Unless those stories were long, detailed, and very well told—unless the writer was doing more than saying, "I am a skier" or a musician or a van-painter—those writers were all given low ratings.

Notice also that the writer of the "Jazz" paper locates himself and his experience in relation to the commonplace (creativity is unique expression; it is not having to conform to rules or guidelines) regardless of whether the commonplace is true or not. Anyone who improvises "knows" that improvisation follows rules and guidelines. It is the power of the commonplace—its truth as a recognizable and, the writer believes, as a final statement—that justifies the example and completes the essay. The example, in other words, has value because it stands within the field of the commonplace.[9] It is not the occasion for what one might call an "objective" analysis or a "close" reading. It could also be said that the essay stops with the articulation of the commonplace. The following sections speak only to the power of that statement. The reference to "sculpting, carving, building, art, and acting" attest to the universality of the commonplace (and it attests the writer's nervousness with the status he has appropriated for himself—he is saying, "Now, I'm not the only one here who has done something unique"). The commonplace stands by itself. For this writer, it does not need to be elaborated. By virtue of having written it, he has completed the essay and established the contract by which we may be spoken to as equals: "In whatever form creativity takes, whether it be music, art, or science, it is an important aspect of *our* lives because it enables *us* to be individuals." (For me to break that contract, to argue that *my* life is not represented in that essay, is one way for me to begin as a teacher with that student in that essay.)

All of the papers I read were built around one of three commonplaces: (1) creativity is self-expression, (2) creativity is doing something new or unique, and (3) creativity is using old things in new ways. These are clearly, then, key phrases from the storehouse of things to say about creativity. I've listed them in the order of the students' ratings: A student with the highest rating was more likely to use number three than number one, although each commonplace ran across the range of possible ratings. One could argue that some standard assertions are more powerful than others, but I think the ranking simply represents the power of assertions within our community of readers. Every student was able to offer up an experience that was meant as an example of "creativity"; the lowest range of writers, then, was not represented by students who could not imagine themselves as creative people.[10]

I said that the writer of the "Jazz" paper offered up a commonplace regardless of whether it was true or not; and this, I said, was an instance of the power of a commonplace to determine the meaning of an example. A commonplace determines a system of interpretation that can be used to "place" an example within a standard system of belief. You can see a similar process at work in this essay.

> During the football season, the team was supposed to wear the same type of cleats and the same type socks, I figured that I would change this a little by wearing my white shoes instead of black and to cover up the team socks with a pair of my own white ones. I thought that this looked better than what we were wearing, and I told a few of the other people on the team to change too. They agreed that it did look better and they changed there combination to go along with mine. After the game people came up to us and said that it looked very good the way we wore our socks, and they wanted to know why we changed from the rest of the team.
>
> I feel that creativity comes from when a person lets his imagination come up with ideas and he is not afraid to express them. Once you create something to do it will be original and unique because it came about from your own imagination and if any one else tries to copy it, it won't be the same because you thought of it first from your own ideas.

This is not an elegant paper, but it seems seamless, tidy. If the paper on the clay model of the earth showed an ill fit between the writer and his project, here the discourse seems natural, smooth. You could reproduce this paper and hand it out to a class, and it would take a lot of prompting before the students sensed something fishy and one of the more aggressive ones said something like, "Sure he came up with the idea of wearing white shoes

638

and white socks. Him and Billy 'White-Shoes' Johnson. Come on. He copied the very thing he said was his own idea, 'original and unique.' "

The "I" of this text—the "I" who "figured," "thought," and "felt"—is located in a conventional rhetoric of the self that turns imagination into origination (I made it), that argues an ethic of production (I made it and it is mine), and that argues a tight scheme of intention (I made it because I decided to make it). The rhetoric seems invisible because it is so common. This "I" (the maker) is also located in a version of history that dominates classrooms, the "great man" theory: History is rolling along (the English novel is dominated by a central, intrusive narrative presence; America is in the throes of a Great Depression; during football season the team was supposed to wear the same kind of cleats and socks) until a figure appears, one who can shape history (Henry James, FDR, the writer of the "White Shoes" paper), and everything is changed. In the argument of the "White Shoes" paper, the history goes "I figured . . . I thought . . . I told . . . They agreed . . ." and, as a consequence, "I feel that creativity *comes from when* a person lets his imagination come up with ideas and he is not afraid to express them." The act of appropriation becomes a narrative of courage and conquest. The writer was able to write that story when he was able to imagine himself in that discourse. Getting him out of it will be a difficult matter indeed.

There are ways, I think, that a writer can shape history in the very act of writing it. Some students are able to enter into a discourse but, by stylistic maneuvers, to take possession of it at the same time. They don't originate a discourse, but they locate themselves within it aggressively, self-consciously. Here is another essay on jazz, which for sake of convenience I've shortened. It received a higher rating than the first essay on jazz.

> Jazz has always been thought of as a very original creative field in music. Improvisation, the spontaneous creation of original melodies in a piece of music, makes up a large part of jazz as a musical style. I had the opportunity to be a member of my high school's jazz ensemble for three years, and became an improvisation soloist this year. Throughout the years, I have seen and heard many jazz players, both professional and amateur. The solos performed by these artists were each flavored with that particular individual's style and ideas, along with some of the conventional premises behind improvisation. This particular type of solo work is creative because it is, done on the spur of the moment and blends the performer's ideas with basic guidelines.
>
> I realized my own creative potential when I began soloing. . . .
>
> My solos, just as all the solos generated by others, were original because I combined and shaped other's ideas with mine to create something completely new. Creativity is combining the practical knowledge and

guidelines of a discipline with one's original ideas to bring about a new, original end result, one that is different from everyone else's. Creativity is based on the individual. Two artists can interpret the same scene differently. Each person who creates something does so by bringing out something individual in himself.

The essay is different in some important ways from the first essay on jazz. The writer of the second is more easily able to place himself in the context of an "academic" discussion. The second essay contains an "I" who realized his "creative potential" by soloing; the first contained an "I" who had "a great experience." In the second essay, before the phrase, "I had the opportunity to be a member of my high school's jazz ensemble," there is an introduction that offers a general definition of improvisation and an acknowledgment that other people have thought about jazz and creativity. In fact, throughout the essay the writer offers definitions and counterdefinitions. He is placing himself in the context of what has been said and what might be said. In the first paper, before a similar statement about being a member of a jazz ensemble, there was an introduction that locates jazz solely in the context of this individual's experience: "I am very interested in music." The writer of this first paper was authorized by who he is, a musician, rather than by what he can say about music in the context of what is generally said. The writer of the second essay uses a more specialized vocabulary; he talks about "conventional premises," "creative potential," "musical style," and "practical knowledge." And this is not just a matter of using bigger words, since these terms locate the experience in the context of a recognizable interpretive scheme—on the one hand there is tradition and, on the other, individual talent.

It could be said, then, that this essay is also framed and completed by a commonplace: "Creativity is combining the practical knowledge and guidelines of a discipline with one's original ideas to bring about a new, original end result, one that is different from everyone else's." Here, however, the argument is a more powerful one; and I mean "powerful" in the political sense, since it is an argument that complicates a "naive" assumption (it makes scholarly work possible, in other words), and it does so in terms that come close to those used in current academic debates (over the relation between convention and idiosyncrasy or between rules and creativity). The assertion is almost consumed by the pleas for originality at the end of the sentence; but the point remains that the terms "original" and "different," as they are used at the end of the essay, are problematic, since they must be thought of in the context of "practical knowledge and guidelines of a discipline."

The key distinguishing gesture of this essay, that which makes it "better" than the other, is the way the writer works against a conventional point of view, one that is represented within the essay by conventional phrases that the writer must then work against. In his practice he demonstrates that a writer, and not just a musician, works within "conventional premises." The "I" who comments in this paper (not the "I" of the narrative about a time when he soloed) places himself self-consciously within the context of a conventional discourse about the subject, even as he struggles against the language of that conventional discourse. The opening definition of improvisation, where improvisation is defined as spontaneous creation, is rejected when the writer begins talking about "the conventional premises behind improvisation." The earlier definition is part of the conventional language of those who "have always thought" of jazz as a "very original creative field in music." The paper begins with what "has been said" and then works itself out against the force and logic of what has been said, of what is not only an argument but also a collection of phrases, examples, and definitions.

I had a teacher who once told us that whenever we were stuck for something to say, we should use the following as a "machine" for producing a paper: "While most readers of _____ have said _____, a close and careful reading shows that _____." The writer of the second paper on jazz is using a standard opening gambit, even if it is not announced with flourish. The essay becomes possible when he sets himself against what must become a "naive" assumption—what "most people think." He has defined a closed circle for himself. In fact, you could say that he has laid the ground work for a discipline with its own key terms ("practical knowledge," "disciplinary guidelines," and "original ideas"), with its own agenda and with its own investigative procedures (looking for common features in the work of individual soloists).

The history represented by this student's essay, then, is not the history of a musician and it is not the history of a thought being worked out within an individual mind; it is the history of work being done within and against conventional systems.

In general, as I reviewed essays for this study, I found that the more successful writers set themselves in their essays against what they defined as some more naive way of talking about their subject—against "those who think that . . ."—or against earlier, more naive versions of themselves—"once I thought that. . . ." By trading in one set of commonplaces at the expense of another, they could win themselves status as members of what is taken to be some more privileged group. The ability to imagine privilege enabled writing. Here is one particularly successful essay. Notice the specialized vocabulary, but notice also the way in which the text continually refers to its own language and to the language of others.

> Throughout my life, I have been interested and intrigued by music. My mother has often told me of the times, before I went to school, when I would "conduct" the orchestra on her records. I continued to listen to music and eventually started to play the guitar and the clarinet. Finally, at about the age of twelve, I started to sit down and to try to write songs. Even though my instrumental skills were far from my own high standards, I would spend much of my spare time during the day with a guitar around my neck, trying to produce a piece of music.
>
> Each of these sessions, as I remember them, had a rather set format. I would sit in my bedroom, strumming different combinations of the five or six chords I could play, until I heard a series of which sounded particularly good to me. After this, I set the music to a suitable rhythm, (usually dependent on my mood at the time), and ran through the tune until I could play it fairly easily. Only after this section was complete did I go on to writing lyrics, which generally followed along the lines of the current popular songs on the radio.
>
> At the time of the writing, I felt that my songs were, in themselves, an original creation of my own; that is, I, alone, made them. However, I now see that, in this sense of the word, I was not creative. The songs themselves seem to be an oversimplified form of the music I listened to at the time.
>
> In a more fitting sense, however, I *was* being creative. Since I did not purposely copy my favorite songs, I was, effectively, originating my songs from my own "process of creativity." To achieve my goal, I needed what a composer would call "inspiration" for my piece. In this case the inspiration was the current hit on the radio. Perhaps, with my present point of view, I feel that I used too much "inspiration" in my songs, but, at that time, I did not.
>
> Creativity, therefore, is a process which, in my case, involved a certain series of "small creations" if you like. As well, it is something, the appreciation of which varies with one's point of view, that point of view being set by the person's experience, tastes, and his own personal view of creativity. The less experienced tend to allow for less originality, while the more experienced demand real originality to classify something a "creation." Either way, a term as abstract as this is perfectly correct, and open to interpretation.

This writer is consistently and dramatically conscious of herself forming something to say out of what has been said *and* out of what she has been saying in the act of writing this paper. "Creativity" begins in this paper as "original creation." What she thought was "creativity," however, she now says was imitation; and, as she says, "in a sense of the word" she was not "creative." In another sense, however, she says that she *was* creative, since she didn't purposefully copy the songs but used them as "inspiration."

While the elaborate stylistic display—the pauses, qualifications, and the use of quotation marks—is in part a performance for our benefit, at a more obvious level we as readers are directly addressed in the first sentence of the last paragraph: "Creativity, therefore, is a process which, in my case, involved a certain series of 'small creations' if you like." We are addressed here as adults who can share her perspective on what she has said and who can be expected to understand her terms. If she gets into trouble after this sentence, and I think she does, it is because she doesn't have the courage to generalize from her assertion. Since she has rhetorically separated herself from her younger "self," and since she argues that she has gotten smarter, she assumes that there is some developmental sequence at work here and that, in the world of adults (which must be more complete than the world of children) there must be something like "real creativity." If her world is imperfect (if she can only talk about creation by putting the word in quotation marks), it must be because she is young. When she looks beyond herself to us, she cannot see our work as an extension of her project. She cannot assume that we too will be concerned with the problem of creativity and originality. At least she is not willing to challenge us on those grounds, to generalize her argument, and to argue that even for adults creations are really only "small creations." The sense of privilege that has allowed her to expose her own language cannot be extended to expose ours.

The writing in this piece—that is, the work of the writer within the essay—goes on in spite of, or against, the language that keeps pressing to give another name to her experience as a songwriter and to bring the discussion to closure. (In comparison, think of the quick closure of the "White Shoes" paper.) Its style is difficult, highly qualified. It relies on quotation marks and parody to set off the language and attitudes that belong to the discourse (or the discourses) that it would reject, that it would not take as its own proper location.

David Olson (1981) has argued that the key difference between oral language and written language is that written language separates both the producer and the receiver from the text. For my student writers, this means that they had to learn that what they said (the code) was more important than what they meant (the intention). A writer, in other words, loses his primacy at the moment of writing and must begin to attend to his and his words' conventional, even physical presence on the page. And, Olson says, the writer must learn that his authority is not established through his presence but through his absence—through his ability, that is, to speak as a god-like source beyond the limitations of any particular social or historical moment;

to speak by means of the wisdom of convention, through the oversounds of official or authoritative utterance, as the voice of logic or the voice of the community. He concludes:

> The child's growing competence with this distinctive register of language in which both the meaning and the authority are displaced from the intentions of the speaker and lodged "in the text" may contribute to the similarly specialized and distinctive mode of thought we have come to associate with literacy and formal education. (1918, p. 110)

Olson is writing about children. His generalizations, I think I've shown, can be extended to students writing their way into the academic community. These are educated and literate individuals, to be sure, but they are individuals still outside the peculiar boundaries of the academic community. In the papers I've examined in this chapter, the writers have shown an increasing awareness of the codes (or the competing codes) that operate within a discourse. To speak with authority they have to speak not only in another's voice but through another's code; and they not only have to do this, they have to speak in the voice and through the codes of those of us with power and wisdom; and they not only have to do this, they have to do it before they know what they are doing, before they have a project to participate in, and before, at least in terms of our disciplines, they have anything to say. Our students may be able to enter into a conventional discourse and speak, not as themselves, but through the voice of the community; the university, however, is the place where "common" wisdom is only of negative values—it is something to work against. The movement toward a more specialized discourse begins (or, perhaps, best begins) both when a student can define a position of privilege, a position that sets him against a "common" discourse, and when he or she can work self-consciously, critically, against not only the "common" code but his or her own.

IV

Pat Bizzell, you will recall, argues that the problems of poor writers can be attributed both to their unfamiliarity with the conventions of academic discourse and to their ignorance that there are such things as discourse communities with conventions to be mastered. If the latter is true, I think it is true only in rare cases. All the student writers I've discussed (and, in fact, most of the student writers whose work I've seen) have shown an awareness that something special or something different is required when one writes for an academic classroom. The essays that I have presented in this chapter all, I think, give evidence of writers trying to write their way into a new community. To some degree, however, all of them can be said to be unfamiliar with the conventions of academic discourse.

Problems of convention are both problems of finish and problems of substance. The most substantial academic tasks for students, learning history or sociology or literary criticism, are matters of many courses, much reading and writing, and several years of education. Our students, however, must have a place to begin. They cannot sit through lectures and read textbooks and, as a consequence, write as sociologists or write literary criticism. There must be steps along the way. Some of these steps will be marked by drafts and revisions. Some will be marked by courses, and in an ideal curriculum the preliminary courses would be writing courses, whether housed in an English department or not. For some students, students we call "basic writers," these courses will be in a sense the most basic introduction to the language and methods of academic writing.

Our students, as I've said, must have a place to begin. If the problem of a beginning is the problem of establishing authority, of defining rhetorically or stylistically a position from which one may speak, then the papers I have examined show characteristic student responses to that problem and show levels of approximation or stages in the development of writers who are writing their way into a position of privilege.

As I look over the papers I've discussed, I would arrange them in the following order: the "White Shoes" paper; the first "Jazz" essay; the "Clay Model" paper; the second "Jazz" essay; and, as the most successful paper, the essay on "Composing Songs." The more advanced essays for me, then, are those that are set against the "naive" codes of "everyday" life. (I put the terms "naive" and "everyday" in quotation marks because they are, of course, arbitrary terms.) In the advanced essays one can see a writer claiming an "inside" position of privilege by rejecting the language and commonplaces of a "naive" discourse, the language of "outsiders." The "I" of those essays locates itself against the specialized language of what is presumed to be a more powerful and more privileged community. There are two gestures present then—one imitative and one critical. The writer continually audits and pushes against a language that would render him "like everyone else" and mimics the language and interpretive systems of the privileged community.

At a first level, then, a student might establish his authority by simply stating his own presence within the field of a subject. A student, for example, writes about creativity by telling a story about a time he went skiing. Nothing more. The "I" on the page is a skier, and skiing stands as a representation of a creative act. Neither the skier nor skiing are available for interpretation; they cannot be located in an essay that is not a narrative essay (where skiing might serve metaphorically as an example of, say, a sport where set movements also allow for a personal style). Or a student, as did the one who wrote the "White Shoes" paper, locates a narrative in an unconnected rehearsal of commonplaces about creativity. In both cases, the writers have finessed the requirement to set themselves against the available utterances of the world outside the closed world of the academy. And, again, in the first "Jazz" paper, we have the example of a writer who locates himself within an available commonplace and carries out only rudimentary procedures for elaboration, procedures driven by the commonplace itself and not set against it. Elaboration, in this latter case, is not the opening up of a system but a justification of it.

At a next level I would place student writers who establish their authority by mimicking the rhythm and texture, the "sound," of academic prose, without there being any recognizable interpretive or academic project under way. I'm thinking, here, of the "Clay Model" essay. At an advanced stage, I would place students who establish their authority as *writers*; they claim their authority, not by simply claiming that they are skiers or that they have done something creative, but by placing themselves both within and against a discourse, or within and against competing discourses, and working self-consciously to claim an interpretive project of their own, one that grants them their privilege to speak. This is true, I think, in the case of the second "Jazz" paper and, to a greater degree, in the case of the "Composing Songs" paper.

The levels of development that I've suggested are not marked by corresponding levels in the type or frequency of error, at least not by the type or frequency of sentence-level error. I am arguing, then, that a basic writer is not necessarily a writer who makes a lot of mistakes. In fact, one of the problems with curricula designed to aid basic writers is that they too often begin with the assumption that the key distinguishing feature of a basic writer is the presence of sentence-level error. Students are placed in courses because their placement essays show a high frequency of such errors, and those courses are designed with the goal of making those errors go away. This approach to the problems of the basic writer ignores the degree to which error is less often a constant feature than a marker in the development of a writer. A student who can write a reasonably correct narrative may fall to pieces when faced with a more unfamiliar assignment. More important, however, such courses fail to serve the rest of the curriculum. On every campus there is a significant number of college freshmen who require a course to introduce them to the kinds of writing that are required for a university education. Some of these students can write correct sentences and some cannot; but, as a group, they lack the facility other freshmen possess when they are faced with an academic writing task.

The "White Shoes" essay, for example, shows fewer sentence-level errors than the "Clay Model" paper. This may well be due to the fact that the writer of the "White Shoes" paper stayed well within safe, familiar territory. He kept himself out of trouble by doing what he could easily do. The tortuous syntax of the more advanced papers on my list is a syntax that represents a writer's struggle with a difficult and unfamiliar language, and it is a syntax that can quickly lead an inexperienced writer into trouble. The syntax and punctuation of the "Composing Songs" essay, for example, shows the effort that is required when a writer works against the pressure of conventional discourse. If the prose is inelegant (although I confess I admire those dense sentences) it is still correct. This writer has a command of the linguistic and stylistic resources—the highly embedded sentences, the use of parentheses and quotation marks—required to complete the act of writing. It is easy to imagine the possible pitfalls for a writer working without this facility.

There was no camera trained on the "Clay Model" writer while he was writing, and I have no protocol of what was going through his mind, but it is possible to speculate on the syntactic difficulties of sentences like these: "In the past time I thought that an incident was creative was when I had to make a clay model of the earth, but not of the classical or your everyday model of the earth which consists of the two cores, the mantle and the crust. I thought of these things in a dimension of which it would be unique, but easy to comprehend." The syntactic difficulties appear to be the result of the writer's attempt to use an unusual vocabulary and to extend his sentences beyond the boundaries of what would have been "normal" in his speech or writing. There is reason to believe, that is, that the problem was with *this* kind of sentence, in this context. If the problem of the last sentence is that of holding together the units "I thought," "dimension," "unique" and "easy to comprehend," then the linguistic problem was not a simple matter of sentence construction. I am arguing, then, that such sentences fall apart not because the writer lacked the necessary syntax to glue the pieces together but because he lacked the full statement within which these key words were already operating. While writing, and in the thrust of his need to complete the sentence, he had the key words but not the utterance. (And to recover the utterance, I suspect, he would need to do more than revise the sentence.) The invisible conventions, the prepared phrases remained too distant for the statement to be completed. The writer would have needed to get inside of a discourse that he could in fact only partially imagine. The act of constructing a sentence, then, became something like an act of transcription in which the voice on the tape unexpectedly faded away and became inaudible.

Shaughnessy (1977) speaks of the advanced writer as one who often has a more facile but still incomplete possession of this prior discourse. In the case of the advanced writer, the evidence of a problem is the presence of dissonant, redundant, or imprecise language, as in a sentence such as this: "No education can be *total*, it must be *continuous*."

Such a student, Shaughnessy says, could be said to hear the "melody of formal English" while still unable to make precise or exact distinctions. And, she says,

> the pre-packaging feature of language, the possibility of taking over phrases and whole sentences without much thought about them, threatens the writer now as before. The writer, as we have said, inherits the language out of which he must fabricate his own messages. He is therefore in a constant tangle with the language, obliged to recognize its public, communal nature and yet driven to invent out of this language his own statements. (1977, pp. 207–208)

For the unskilled writer, the problem is different in degree and not in kind. The inexperienced writer is left with a more fragmentary record of the comings and goings of academic discourse. Or, as I said above, he or she often has the key words without the complete statements within which they are already operating.

Let me provide one final example of this kind of syntactic difficulty in another piece of student writing. The writer of this paper seems to be able to sustain a discussion only by continually repeating his first step, producing a litany of strong, general, authoritative assertions that trail quickly into confusion. Notice how the writer seems to stabilize his movement through the paper by returning again and again to recognizable and available commonplace utterances. When he has to move away from them, however, away from the familiar to statements that would extend those utterances, where he, too, must speak, the writing—that is, both the syntax and the structure of the discourse—falls to pieces.

> Many times the times drives a person's life depends on how he uses it. I would like to think about if time is twenty-five hours a day rather than twenty-four hours. Some people think it's the boaring or some people might say it's the pleasure to take one more hour for their life. But I think the time is passing and coming, still we are standing on same position. We should use time as best as we can use about the good way in our life. Everything we do, such as sleep, eat, study, play and doing something for our-

selves. These take the time to do and we could find the individual ability and may process own. It is the important for us and our society. As time going on the world changes therefor we are changing, too. When these situation changes we should follow the suitable case of own. But many times we should decide what's the better way to do so by using time. Sometimes like this kind of situation can cause the success of our lives or ruin. I think every individual of his own thought drive how to use time. These affect are done from environmental causes. So we should work on the better way of our life recognizing the importance of time.

There is a general pattern of disintegration when the writer moves off from standard phrases. This sentence, for example, starts out coherently and then falls apart: "*We should use time as best as we can* use about the good way in our life." The difficulty seems to be one of extending those standard phrases or of connecting them to the main subject reference, "time" (or "the time," a construction that causes many of the problems in the paper). Here is an example of a sentence that shows, in miniature, this problem of connection: "*I think every individual* of his own thought drive how to use *time*.

One of the remarkable things about this paper is that, in spite of all the syntactic confusion, there is the hint of an academic project here. The writer sets out to discuss how to creatively use one's time. The text seems to allude to examples and to stages in an argument, even if in the end it is all pretty incoherent. The gestures of academic authority, however, are clearly present, and present in a form that echoes the procedures in other, more successful papers. The writer sets himself against what "some people think"; he speaks with the air of authority: "But I think. . . . Everything we do. . . . When these situation changes. . . ." And he speaks as though there were a project underway, one where he proposes what he thinks, turns to evidence, and offers a conclusion: "These affect are done from environmental causes. So we should work. . . ." This is the case of a student with the ability to imagine the general outline and rhythm of academic prose but without the ability to carry it out, to complete the sentences. And when he gets lost in the new, in the unknown, in the responsibility of his own commitment to speak, he returns again to the familiar ground of the commonplace.

The challenge to researchers, it seems to me, is to turn their attention again to products, to student writing, since the drama in a student's essay, as he or she struggles with and against the languages of our contemporary life, is as intense and telling as the drama of an essay's mental preparation or physical production. A written text, too, can be a compelling model of the "composing process" once we conceive of a writer as at work within a text and simultaneously, then, within a society, a history, and a culture.

It may very well be that some students will need to learn to crudely mimic the "distinctive register" of academic discourse before they are prepared to actually and legitimately do the work of the discourse, and before they are sophisticated enough with the refinements of tone and gesture to do it with grace or elegance. To say this, however, is to say that our students must be our students. Their initial progress will be marked by their abilities to take on the role of privilege, by their abilities to establish authority. From this point of view, the student who wrote about constructing the clay model of the earth is better prepared for his education than the student who wrote about playing football in white shoes, even though the "White Shoes" paper is relatively error-free and the "Clay Model" paper is not. It will be hard to pry loose the writer of the "White Shoes" paper from the tidy, pat discourse that allows him to dispose of the question of creativity in such a quick and efficient manner. He will have to be convinced that it is better to write sentences he might not so easily control, and he will have to be convinced that it is better to write muddier and more confusing prose (in order that it may sound like ours), and this will be harder than convincing the "Clay Model" writer to continue what he has already begun.

ACKNOWLEDGMENTS

Preparation of this chapter was supported by the Learning Research and Development Center of the University of Pittsburgh, which is supported in part by the National Institute of Education.

NOTES

1. David Olson (1981) has made a similar observation about school-related problems of language learning in younger children. Here is his conclusion: "Hence, depending upon whether children assumed language was primarily suitable for making assertions and conjectures or primarily for making direct or indirect commands, they will either find school texts easy or difficult" (p. 107).

2. For Aristotle, there were both general and specific commonplaces. A speaker, says Aristotle, has a "stock of arguments to which he may turn for a particular need."

> If he knows the *topoi* (regions, places, lines of argument)—and a skilled speaker will know them—he will know where to find what he wants for a special case. The general topics, or *common*places, are regions containing arguments that are common to all branches of knowledge. . . . But there are also special topics (regions, places, *loci*) in which one looks for arguments appertaining to particular branches of knowledge, special sciences, such as ethics or politics. (1932, pp. 154–155)

And, he says, "the topics or places, then, may be indifferently thought of as in the science that is concerned, or in the mind of the speaker." But the question of location is "indifferent" *only* if the mind of the speaker is in line with set opinion, general assumption. For the speaker (or writer) who is not situated so comfortably in the privileged public realm, this is indeed not an indifferent matter at all. If he does not have the commonplace at hand, he will not, in Aristotle's terms, know where to go at all.

3. Pat Bizzell has argued that the *Seventeen* writer's process of goal-setting

> can be better understood if we see it in terms of writing for a discourse community. His initial problem . . . is to find a way to include these readers in a discourse community for which he is comfortable writing. He places them in the academic discourse community by imagining the girls as students. . . . Once he has included them in a familiar discourse community, he can find a way to address them that is common in the community: he will argue with them, putting a new interpretation on information they possess in order to correct misconceptions. (1982a, p. 228)

4. See Bartholomae (1979, 1983) and Rose (1983) for articles on curricula designed to move students into university discourse. The movement to extend writing "across the curriculum" is evidence of a general concern for locating students within the work of the university; see Bizzell (1982a) and Maimon *et al.* (1981). For longer works directed specifically at basic writing, see Ponsot and Deen (1982) and Shaughnessy (1977). For a book describing a course for more advanced students, see Coles (1978).

5. In spite of my misgivings about Bereiter and Scardamalia's interpretation of the cognitive nature of the problem of "inert knowledge," this is an essay I regularly recommend to teachers. It has much to say about the dangers of what seem to be "neutral" forms of classroom discourse and provides, in its final section, a set of recommendations on how a teacher might undo discourse conventions that have become part of the institution of teaching.

6. Stanley Fish (1980) argues that the basis for distinguishing novice from expert readings is the persuasiveness of the discourse used to present and defend a given reading. In particular, see the chapter, "Demonstration vs. Persuasion: Two Models of Critical Activity" (pp. 356–373).

7. Some students, when they come to the university, can do this better than others. When Jonathan Culler says, "the possibility of bringing someone to see that a particular interpretation is a good one assumes shared points of departure and common notions of how to read," he is acknowledging that teaching, at least in English classes, has had to assume that students, to be students, were already to some degree participating in the structures of reading and writing that constitute English studies (quoted in Fish, 1980, p. 366).

Stanley Fish tells us "not to worry" that students will violate our enterprise by offering idiosyncratic readings of standard texts:

> The fear of solipsism, of the imposition by the unconstrained self of its own prejudices, is unfounded because the self does not exist apart from the communal or conventional categories of thought that enable its operations (of thinking, seeing, reading). Once we realize that the conceptions that fill consciousness, including any conception of its own status, are culturally derived, the very notion of an unconstrained self, of a consciousness wholly and dangerously free, becomes incomprehensible. (1980, p. 335)

He, too, is assuming that students, to be students (and not "dangerously free"), must be members in good standing of the community whose immediate head is the English teacher. It is interesting that his parenthetical catalogue of the "operations" of thought, "thinking, seeing, reading," excludes writing, since it is only through written records that we have any real indication of how a student thinks, sees, and reads. (Perhaps "real" is an inappropriate word to use here, since there is certainly a "real" intellectual life that goes on, independent of writing. Let me say that thinking, seeing, and reading are valued in the academic community *only* as they are represented by extended, elaborated written records.) Writing, I presume, is a given for Fish. It is the card of entry into this closed community that constrains and excludes dangerous characters. Students who are excluded from this community are students who do poorly on written placement exams or in freshman composition. They do not, that is, move easily into the privileged discourse of the community, represented by the English literature class.

8. My debt to Bizzell's work should be evident everywhere in this essay. See also Bizzell (1978, 1982b) and Bizzell and Herzberg (1980).

9. Fish says the following about the relationship between student and an object under study:

> we are not to imagine a moment when my students "simply see" a physical configuration of atoms and *then* assign that configuration a significance, according to the situation they happen to be in. To be in the situation (this or any other) is to "see" with the eyes of its interests, its goals, its understood practices, values, and norms, and so to be conferring significance *by* seeing, not after it. The categories of my students' vision are the categories by which they understand themselves to be functioning as students . . . and objects will appear to them in forms related to that way of functioning rather than in some objective or preinterpretive form. (1980, p. 334)

10. I am aware that the papers given the highest rankings offer arguments about creativity and originality similar to my own. If there is a conspiracy here, that is one of the points of my chapter. I should add that my reading of the "content" of basic writers' essays is quite different from Lunsford's (1980).

REFERENCES

Aristotle. (1932). *The Rhetoric of Aristotle* (L. Cooper, Trans.) Englewood Cliffs, NJ: Prentice-Hall.

Barthes, R. (1974). *S/Z* (R. Howard, Trans.). New York: Hill & Wang.

Bartholomae, D. (1979). Teaching basic writing: An alternative to basic skills. *Journal of Basic Writing, 2,* 85–109.

Bartholomae, D. (1983). Writing assignments: Where writing begins. In P. Stock (Ed.), *Forum* (pp. 300–312). Montclair, NJ: Boynton/Cook.

Bereiter, C., & Scardamalia, M. (in press). Cognitive coping strategies and the problem of "inert knowledge." In S. S. Chipman, J. W. Segal, & R. Glaser (Eds.), *Thinking and learning skills: Research and open questions* (Vol. 2). Hillsdale, NJ: Erlbaum.

Bizzell, P. (1978). The ethos of academic discourse. *College Composition and Communication, 29,* 351–355.

Bizzell, P. (1982a). Cognition, convention, and certainty: What we need to know about writing. *Pre/text, 3,* 213–244.

Bizzell, P. (1982b). College composition: Initiation into the academic discourse community. *Curriculum Inquiry, 12,* 191–207.

Bizzell, P., & Herzberg, B. (1980). "Inherent" ideology, "universal" history, "empirical" evidence, and "context-free" writing: Some problems with E. D. Hirsch's *The Philosophy of Composition. Modern Language Notes, 95,* 1181–1202.

Coles, W. E., Jr. (1978). *The plural I.* New York: Holt, Rinehart & Winston.

Fish, S. (1980). *Is there a text in this class? The authority of interpretive communities.* Cambridge, MA: Harvard University Press.

Flower, L. S. (1981). Revising writer-based prose. *Journal of Basic Writing, 3,* 62–74.

Flower, L., & Hayes, J. (1981). A cognitive process theory of writing. *College Composition and Communication, 32,* 365–387.

Hairston, M. (1978). *A contemporary rhetoric.* Boston: Houghton Mifflin.

Lunsford, A. A. (1980). The content of basic writers' essays. *College Composition and Communication, 31,* 278–290.

Maimon, E. P., Belcher, G. L., Hearn, G. W., Nodine, B. F., & O'Conner, F. X. (1981). *Writing in the arts and sciences.* Cambridge, MA: Winthrop.

Olson, D. R. (1981). Writing: The divorce of the author from the text. In B. M. Kroll & R. J. Vann (Eds.), *Exploring speaking–writing relationships: Connections and contrasts.* Urbana, IL: National Council of Teachers of English.

Perkins, D. N. (in press). General cognitive skills: Why not? In S. S. Chipman, J. W. Segal, & R. Glaser (Eds.), *Thinking and learning skills: Research and open questions* (Vol. 2). Hillsdale, NJ: Earlbaum.

Ponsot, M., & Deen, R. (1982). *Beat not the poor desk.* Montclair, NJ: Boynton/Cook.

Rodriguez, R. (1983). *Hunger of memory.* New York: Bantam.

Rose, M. (1983). Remedial writing courses: A critique and a proposal. *College English, 45,* 109–128.

Said, E. W. (1975). *Beginnings: Intention and method.* Baltimore: The Johns Hopkins University Press.

Shaughnessy, M. (1977). *Errors and expectations.* New York: Oxford University Press.

The Arts of Complicity

Pragmatism and the Culture of Schooling

RICHARD E. MILLER

> *Those truly committed to liberation must reject the banking concept in its*
> *entirety, adopting instead a concept of men as conscious beings, and con-*
> *sciousness as consciousness intent upon the world. They must abandon the*
> *educational goal of deposit-making and replace it with the posing of the*
> *problems of men in their relations with the world.*
>
> —*Paulo Freire*, Pedagogy of the Oppressed, 66

For nearly thirty years, Paulo Freire's name and his writings have signified our brightest hopes about the importance of what we do: to invoke Freire is to declare one's allegiance to education as a practice of freedom and one's commitment to "revolution," "liberation," "conscientization," "problem-posing." And so, when scholars outside of composition wish to join in our discussions, they turn, more often than not, to Freire's work to establish the sincerity of their interest in pedagogical practice and their belief that teaching others to read and write has political consequences. Citing Freire is, thus, a way of establishing one's credentials in the field, of showing one's true colors. We see this, for example, in Jane Tompkins's much-discussed, "Pedagogy of the Distressed," where Tompkins links her discovery of "a way to make teaching more enjoyable and less anxiety-producing" to a set of reflections prompted by Freire's insistence that "you cannot have a revolution unless education becomes a practice of freedom" (656, 653). And we see this, as well, in bell hooks's *Teaching to Transgress*, where hooks identifies Freire as one of two teachers who has deeply influenced her efforts to enact a liberatory practice

Reprinted from *College English* 61.1 (September 1998): 10–28. Used with permission.

that "enables transgressions—a movement against and beyond boundaries" (12). And, as news of Freire's death spreads throughout the profession, such public testaments to his influence on our ways of thinking are bound to proliferate exponentially. Indeed, at the 1998 4Cs, Freire was posthumously commemorated for his contributions to the field and those presentations which reflected his work were specially marked in the program.

What are we to make of Freire's place in our profession's history? Why does his representation of the power of teaching hold such an appeal for so many of us? From a certain perspective, the answer to these questions is obvious. Freire has given teachers a way to see themselves as something other than the mindless functionaries of the state apparatus responsible for tidying the prose of the next generation of bureaucrats. His liberatory pedagogy has long provided an attractive alternative to the grinding and effacing processes of professional training that are so popular among those who equate education with vocationalism. Freirian pedagogy foregrounds the politics of teaching; it recognizes the interrelationship of word and world, language and power; it requires teachers to construct a teaching practice that is responsive to the students' needs and abilities; it offers a powerful critique of dominant educational practice. And, of course, Freire's well-known critique of "the banking concept" of education has succinctly captured all that is wrong with a teaching practice that has teachers deposit the oppressor's knowledge in the students in such a way that the students are sure to remain docile, unthreatening servants of the state. Freire's work has, in short, given weapons of resistance to those dissatisfied with instrumentalist approaches to education: it has offered a critical vocabulary, a philosophically grounded and politically defensible pedagogy, a vision of a better world.

When I entered graduate school more than a decade ago, I was among those swept away by Freire's vision and the possibilities opened up by renaming the goal of our work in the classroom as "conscientization." Having spent three years employed as a "learning skills specialist" on the margins of a major research university, I was only too well acquainted with institutional indifference and its consequences. I longed to work in the learning environment Freire advocated, where institutionally enforced passivity would be eliminated and the teacher, as problem-poser, would create, "together with the students, the conditions under which knowledge at the level of the *doxa* is superseded by true knowledge, at the level of the *logos*" (68). In such a place, where students were moved from *doxa* to *logos*, from belief to "true knowledge," the groundwork for radical social change would be put into place.

Of course, when I actually set out to do this kind of work I ran into a set of difficulties that, in retrospect, seem all too predictable: many of my students resisted the "politicization" of the classroom; those who didn't seemed overly eager to ventriloquize sentiments they didn't believe or understand; and, at the end of the semester, no matter how spirited and engaging the discussions had been, the quality of writing I received seemed, if I was honest with myself, to vary little from work elicited in other, more traditional classrooms. That there are problems involved in adopting Freire's pedagogy— originally developed to address the needs of the illiterate and dispossessed peoples of Brazil—to teach undergraduates in the United States is now commonly recognized (Elbow; North; Berlin; McCormick); and for those committed to getting Freire's project to work with students in the United States, there are considerable resources to turn to for support (Berthoff; Shor; Kutz and Roskelly; Bizzell). What I wish to consider here is a rather different matter, though: why is it that this image of the teacher as liberator of the oppressed, upon which Freire's pedagogy relies so heavily, has had such a perduring appeal? Or, to put this another way, working in the spirit of Freire's own pedagogical practice, what can we learn by problematizing our community's most cherished self-representation? If we aren't in the business of liberation, uplift, and movement, however slow, towards a better social world, what is it we're doing in our classrooms?

EVERYBODY GET IN LINE: LIBERATION AND THE OBEDIENT RESPONSE

Given the choice between the "mechanistic," "necrophilic" banking model of instruction and the life-affirming, consciousness-raising, history-transforming pedagogy of the problem-poser, it's not hard to see why so many of us have embraced the rhetoric of Freire's emancipatory practice and have continued to deploy it long after our own experiences have demonstrated its inutility. Of course, Freire long ago anticipated the possibility that his "problem-posing" approach would be accused of being nothing more than the "banking concept" in disguise, one that extolled the virtues of freedom while imposing a uniform vision. To counter such charges, Freire insisted from the beginning that the problem-posing approach had to "be forged *with*, not *for*, the oppressed (whether individuals or peoples) in the incessant struggle to regain their humanity" (33). Freire's commitment to the principle that a liberatory pedagogy should at every stage enact its participatory politics distinguishes him from those who think that social change requires giving the oppressed a healthy dose of revolutionary indoctrination before allowing them to participate in their own education. And, for this very reason, Freire's commitment to refiguring the teacher-student relationship creates a significant problem at the level of practice: as Freire himself posed the question, "how can the oppressed, as divided, unauthentic beings, participate in developing the pedagogy of their libera-tion?" (33). That is, if one begins, as Freire does, with a Marxist theory of the so-cial sphere, where the oppressed are cast as the faceless masses who have been deluded into accepting their own powerlessness, then "collaborating" with the oppressed seems positively counterproductive. After all, given *their* false con-sciousness, *their* "divided, unauthentic beings," *their* lust for individual rewards over communal gains, what could *they* possibly have to contribute to the revo-lutionary project?

Freire's resolution of this problem is straightforward enough, though not without its own complications. In order for the oppressed to participate ac-tively in the creation of their own pedagogical apparatus, they must first come to see that they have become host bodies for the oppressor's ideology and that they have molded their lives to conform to this ideology's image. To assist the oppressed in acquiring this insight, Freire sends teams of investiga-tors to the community that has been targeted for his educational project. These investigators approach the area "as if it were for them an enormous, unique, living 'code' to be deciphered" (103). Working in concert with local representatives, over time the investigators detect "generative words" and "generative thematics," revealing the contradictions that lie at the core of the target community's world of concerns. These words and themes are cod-ified in familiar images from the community that are then "re-presented" to the learners for them to reflect on: the learners look at a picture of a well, say, and women carrying water bottles; they decode the images; they begin to speak of their frustrations over access to clean water in their neighbor-hoods; when the co-ordinator "poses as problems both the codified existen-tial situation and their own answers," the learners begin to make connections between the themes evoked by the images and their own posi-tions of powerlessness (110). And, presumably, as the learners come to this realization, by having their "false consciousness of reality" posed to them as a problem or "through revolutionary action, developing a consciousness which is less and less false" (125), they begin to liberate themselves from the oppressor's dehumanizing ideology.

One might think that turning to Freire's own examples of what his peda-gogy looks like in practice would help to further clarify the differences be-tween the banking and problem-posing methods. As it turns out, though, *Pedagogy of the Oppressed* provides few glimpses of what it means to be a student under the problem-posing system, devoting its attention, instead, to presenting the theory and the methodology that gives rise to liberatory prac-tice. Curiously, when the scene of instruction does surface in *Pedagogy of the Oppressed*, it seamlessly illustrates the smooth functioning of Freire's lib-eratory machine and the ease with which those in his system come to see the error of their former ways. Thus, for example, after Freire has argued that the oppressed internalize a logic of self-depreciation, he turns to one of his educational meetings to show how this logic can be exposed and dismantled. Here, we are treated to the following quotation from an unidentified Chilean peasant: "They used to say we were unproductive because we were lazy and drunkards. All lies. Now that we are respected as men, we're going to show everyone that we were never drunkards or lazy. We were exploited!" (50). And, in another example, where workers in Santiago were asked to discuss two pictures — one of a drunken man walking on the street and another of three young men talking on a street corner — Freire records the workers' open identification with and defense of the drunken man. For Freire, this response proves the value of the problem-posing method, which in this instance allowed the workers to say "what they really felt" (111). Although it may not be pleasing to learn, in this case, that the workers defend drunkenness, conscientization begins with the subjective perception of the world of lived experience and then "through action prepares men for the struggle against the obstacles to their humanization" (112). Thus, in the first example, the Chilean peasants come to see that they never were drunkards, but rather were oppressed; in the second, the workers from Santiago have taken their first steps toward changing their lives by objectifying and naming their own way of being in the world. In both cases, it seems, the drunken consciousness is on its way to sobering up.

Freire offers up these examples of spontaneous assent as illustrations of the positive effects of his practice; we just have to take his word for it that the workers in these learning situations were saying "what they really felt" — on the assumption, perhaps, that the illiterate and downtrodden can only speak without guile or nuance or that Freire, in some way, knows how to divine when such authentic speech has occurred. Of course, in order to maintain the essential distinction between the two pedagogical approaches, Freire must insist that those on the receiving end of his problem-posing pedagogy are free to come to whatever conclusions they like because his teaching method leeches the power dynamic out of the teacher-student relationship. Acknowledging that all teachers have "values which influence their perceptions," Freire adamantly insists that the only value his teachers seek to share with the oppressed "is a critical perception of the world, which implies a correct method of approaching reality in order to unveil it" (103). Given Freire's examples of the ever-pliable peasantry and the force of his own argument, however, it is hard to believe that the "critical perception of the world" he seeks to impart through the problem-posing method is meant to produce anything other than a new citizenry with a shared set of values. What else could be the outcome of teaching others the ways to "unveil" reality, to shed their "false consciousness," to "cut the umbilical cord of magic and myth which binds them to the world of oppression" (176)?

One reason that Freire's pedagogy has so much appeal is that it comes armed with a rhetoric that overwhelms and neutralizes any effort to point out this tension between the Freirian insistence on a collaborative methodology, where people are taught not what to think but how, and a practice that, almost magically, produces people who know exactly what to think about injustice and how it should be redressed. Freire explains that those who resist his pedagogy with the complaint that they are being led by the hand to certain foregone conclusions respond in this way because they have begun "to realize that if their analysis of the situation goes any deeper they will either have to divest themselves of their myths, or reaffirm them" (155). Since divestment involves the painful process of renouncing whatever privilege it is that one has acquired, Freire continues, some choose instead to "reaffirm" their myths by accusing his pedagogy of "their own usual practices: *steering, conquering, and invading*" (155). In other words, with this brilliant reversal, Freire argues that those who feel that they are not, in fact, free or equal collaborators in his venture are the ones most lost to "false consciousness"—they are, in effect, the bankers among us.

As Freire would have it, "well-intentioned professionals" are the ones most likely to fall prey to this way of thinking: they understand that following out his method of analysis would require that they "cease being *over* or *inside* (as foreigners) in order to be *with* (as comrades)" and they are afraid (154). Borrowing a phrase from Althusser, Freire then goes on to say that, although these professionals are "men who have been 'determined from above' by a culture of domination which has constituted them as dual beings," and despite the fact that they "are in truth more misguided than anything else, they not only could be, but ought to be, reclaimed by the revolution" (156). In effect, then, Freire, the educator, is saying that it is those who have been most successful in school who are the ones most likely to be deeply wedded to the ideology that stands in the way of communal action. And, were it not for Freire's reassurance that even these professionals can and should be "reclaimed by the revolution," it might appear that he feels professionally trained educators are unsalvageable since they have been so successfully confused by the dominant logic.

Again, what puzzles me is why this vision of teaching and the rhetoric that surrounds it should appeal to teachers, particularly teachers of reading and writing. Why, as a profession, would we be drawn to an approach that depicts professionals in such a negative light? Is it the institutionally marginalized position of composition instruction that allows us to see ourselves as beyond the reach of Freire's critique? Do we imagine ourselves as somehow outside the very system that employs us to instruct entering students in the language arts? Is there something about literacy work that makes its practitioners immune to the desires for advancement upon which hierarchical systems depend? Or is this just a story teachers like to tell themselves about themselves—a way to make it from semester to semester that preserves the teacher's sense of self-esteem? And, thus, is the appeal of the image of teacher as liberator itself proof that liberatory teachers are, in fact, filled with the very false consciousness that they're determined to eradicate in others?

BENEATH THE RHETORIC OF RELEASE: STUDENTS SILENTLY MAKING THE GRADE

In *Domination and the Arts of Resistance*, James Scott sets out to disrupt the discussion about false consciousness by arguing that all social action involves the performance of a "public transcript" and a "hidden transcript." As Scott defines these two modes of discourse, the public transcript serves "as a shorthand way of describing the open interaction between subordinates and those who dominate" (2); it is a text that rarely fails to "provide convincing evidence for the hegemony of dominant values, for the hegemony of dominant discourse" (4). If the public transcript is, by definition, always available for inspection, the hidden transcript describes the discourse "that takes place 'offstage,' beyond direct observation by powerholders," and for this reason, Scott insists, "whatever form it assumes—offstage parody, dreams of violent revenge, millennial visions of a world turned upside down—this collective hidden transcript is essential to any dynamic view of power relations" (4, 9).

It is Scott's provocative contention that, because the analysis of power has focused almost exclusively on the public transcript, it has, to this point, ceaselessly produced evidence that the disempowered willingly and thoughtlessly participate in the system that insures their own subordination. Proof of this domination is always everywhere ready to hand in the public transcript: it's on the news, it's in the libraries, it's in the critique of mass culture; it's there to be ferreted out of the sales figures for televisions, VCRs, minivans, cellular phones, home security systems; it's in our students' papers, which never seem to tire of mindlessly reproducing "original" arguments about the virtues of individuality, hard work, self-determination. Focusing exclusively on the public transcript, in short, supports the view that subordinates are, in fact, mired in false consciousness; it supports as well the corollary belief that it is the job of the media and their analysts, including the functionaries in the academy, to make sense of the world for those less well able, translating the chaos of experience into a digestible and entertaining form that ultimately serves to reinforce the status quo. Scott disrupts this familiar depiction of the world gone wrong by observing that it rests on the assumption that there are those who misperceive reality and those who perceive it clearly, those with false consciousness and those with a scientific or true understanding of social reality. Drawing on his notion of a hidden transcript, though, Scott rejects what he calls the "thick version" of false consciousness, which casts subordinates as actively believing "in the values that explain and justify their own subordination," and the "thin version" of false consciousness, which argues that subordinates comply with the social order because they have come to accept that it "is natural and inevitable" (72). Although subordinates neither consent nor resign themselves to their fate, Scott argues, they do reliably collaborate in the production of a public transcript which creates the impression that they have accepted the tenets of the dominant ideology. They do this, he says, to avoid any "*explicit* display of insubordination" (86). Thus, so long as we are without access to the subordinates' "hidden transcript," so long as we are ignorant of what they say or think when they are outside the reach of those in power, we are left only with the image of the subordinates "on their best behavior," doing what is called for in order not to put themselves in harm's way (87). Off-stage, though, subordinates rehearse "the anger and reciprocal aggression denied by the presence of domination" (37–38), jointly creating "a discourse of dignity, of negation, of justice" (114). Away from the boss, away from the classroom, away from the oppressor's gaze, we all fantasize about alternative world orders.

Obviously, Scott is no easier to argue with than Freire. Where Freire argues that proof of one's false consciousness may be found in one's rejection of his ideas, Scott's sleight of hand is to maintain that proof of his theory's validity is to be found in the fact that the archives, home to the public transcript, house almost no evidence of the private transcript! Absence equals presence. As Scott puts it, "the logic of infrapolitics is to leave few traces in the wake of its passage. By covering its tracks it not only minimizes the risks its practitioners run but it also eliminates much of the documentary evidence that might convince social scientists and historians that real politics was taking place" (200). Regardless of whether one finds this line of reasoning suggestive or solipsistic, it is important to recognize that the circularity of Scott's argument (proof of the hidden transcript's existence is to be found in its absence from the public transcript) leads to an understanding of what constitutes a "real politics" that differs markedly from the understanding produced by the circularities in Freire's argument. For, unlike Freire, Scott insists that, in comparing the subordinate and dominant classes, it is

> more accurate to consider subordinate classes *less* constrained at the level of thought and ideology [than the dominant classes], since they can in se-cluded settings speak with comparative safety, and *more* constrained at the level of political action and struggle, where the daily exercise of power sharply limits the options available to them. (91)

With this startling reversal, Scott relocates his version of false conscious-ness—that is, being more constrained at the level of thought and ideology—among the dominant classes; indeed, as he sees it, there is an inverse proportion between one's freedom to think and one's ability to function visi-bly as a political agent. The higher one climbs the social ladder, the more one must, in all phases of one's life, ascribe to the dominant ideology, the more confined are those spaces for voicing one's doubts about that ideology, the more one must see oneself as always on stage. And the lower one goes on that ladder, the less one must ascribe to party lines and ideological pieties, the freer one is to imagine other viable social arrangements, the less likely one is to be in a position to bring those utopian visions to pass.

Scott finds proof for this part of his theory in the fact that, historically, subordinates have repeatedly given voice to imaginative renderings that de-pict the collapse of the current dominant system and its replacement by a more just system; if one looks hard enough, one is sure to find in every cul-tural milieu a version of the idea that, someday, the last shall be first and the first shall be last. This is because, as Scott sees it, subordinates have no diffi-culty *imagining* a "counterfactual social order," one that involves either "a total reversal of the existing distribution of status and rewards" or the nega-tion of "the existing social order" (80–81)—this capability is "part and parcel of the religiopolitical equipment of historically disadvantaged groups" (91). Thus, it is a mistake to think that subordinates have been so thoroughly colo-nized that they cannot conceive of or desire a better world. It is more accu-rate to say that they have no access to the channels of social power that might bring this better world into being. And, following this logic, we might say that it is not that students have been so mystified by the Ideological State Apparatus of higher education that they can't see or understand how the sys-tem has been designed to deprive them of a sense of individual autonomy. It is, rather, that they are powerless to change the system and know only too well its ability to punish them for not complying with its demands. So they do what is required of them, slipping in enough of the hidden transcript to preserve their sense of self-respect: they write papers that lifelessly respond to the assignment; they contradict themselves, saying what they want to say and what they think the teacher wants them to say at the same time; they publicly announce their interest in the work at hand while manifesting no visible sign that their interest requires anything from them. They hunker down and try to get by.

Of course, in making this analogy between subordinates and students, the oppressed and those paying individuals seated in our classes trying to earn their degrees in business, say, I have opened myself to the criticism that I am trivializing the manifest differences between the two groups. Freire, as previously noted, wasn't concerned with teaching first-year college students the nuances of academic prose or the virtues of the expository essay. His work was with illiterate peasants who were struggling to combat their government's oppressive policies. And Scott, too, is generally more interested in forms of domination which carry the threat of physical violence, such as "slavery, serfdom, and the caste system [which] routinely generate practices and rituals of denigration, insult, and assaults on the body" (23). It would be foolish to equate the challenges Freire has confronted in the field or the oppressive situations that interest Scott with the challenges we face teaching composition in the academy: we teach those who have already found their way into the system, those who wish, at some level, to gain access to the material benefits that higher education is understood to promise. But, in making this analogy, I do not mean to imply the general commensurability of systems of oppression; rather, by noting that students occupy a subordinate position in the educational system, I mean only to suggest that they, too, have their "hidden transcripts" where they store their reservations about what is happening to them in the classroom.

I also mean to suggest that, however tempting it may be to describe our work as teachers as being pursued in the interests of "liberation" or "consciousness-raising" or "resistance," the truth is that this rhetoric's appeal is so attractive because it covers over our more primary role as functionaries of the administration's educational arm. In the right setting, we can forget that we are the individuals vested with the responsibility for soliciting and assessing student work; we can imagine that power has left the room at the moment the student announces the insight, "we're going to show everyone that we were never drunkards or lazy. We were exploited!"; we can convince ourselves to accept whatever gets said at face value. The students, however, never forget where they are, no matter how carefully we arrange the desks in the classroom, how casually we dress, how open we are to disagreement, how politely we respond to their journal entries, their papers, their portfolios. They don't forget; we often do.

This is not to imply that no "authentic" interactions can occur within the space of the classroom or, conversely, that all interactions in that space are necessarily duplicitous, cynical, self-serving, or self-protective. I think it more accurate to say that we will never know, in any absolute sense, if the work our students do is "authentic" or if that work reflects their achieved level of "consciousness." Indeed, I would argue that the prevailing desire to re-construct the scene of instruction as a site where authenticity is forged and layers of false consciousness are peeled away indicates a general commitment in our profession to imagining that the power dynamic in the teacher-student relationship can, under ideal conditions, be erased. Thus, Freire presents the recipients of his pedagogy as coming to their own conclusions, as learning to think for themselves. He doesn't linger over the fact that all this self-motivated thinking leads his students to think exactly what he would like them to think; he doesn't imagine that, possibly, his students are mouthing his pieties, silently collaborating in the production of the desired public transcript and then sneaking back home where they are free to question his lessons or force others to accept them or forget them altogether. And Althusser invokes those few teachers who work against ideology ("They are a kind of hero," he tells us), while lamenting the fact that the majority of instructors little suspect that their labor "contributes to the maintenance and nourishment of this ideological representation of the School, which makes the School today as 'natural,' indispensable—useful and even beneficial for our contemporaries"—as the Church was in the days of old (157). Althusser doesn't think it possible that these benighted teachers might have reservations about the educational system, but know the professional consequences of giving voice to those reservations. Nor does he suspect that he too might have been captured by the ideology that draws people to the teaching profession, where the ideal pedagogue is in fact typically cast as the one who works against the system, critical of its movements, free of its impurities, allied with science and reason rather than myth and folklore.

While Freire and Althusser thus struggle, in different ways, to establish the possibility that the classroom can indeed function as the site of authentic engagement, Scott argues that, historically, the classroom has promoted "radicalism" precisely because it has served so well as a scene of betrayal. That is, because the classroom is the place that promotes "the implicit promise of the dominant ideology (If you work hard, obey authority, do well in school, and keep your nose clean you will advance by merit and have satisfying work)," it functions to encourage students to conform, to make sacrifices, and to develop often highly unrealistic expectations about what the future holds for them (107). And, when those expectations are not realized—when a good job isn't waiting at the end of all those years of smiling subservience—a general, almost palpable sense of betrayal spreads among those who formerly believed in the dominant ideology. (Think, for instance, of the prevailing mood among those about to enter the academic job market.) And for this reason Scott sees the gravest threat to hegemony as resting not with the oppressed masses, but rather with those individuals who have worked their way up through the system, believing all the rhetoric about equality, liberty, opportunity, and merit, only to have those beliefs betrayed by a system dominated by glass ceilings, old-boy networks, off-stage agreements, and double-dealing administrators.

Scott momentarily entertains the idea that the potential for radical institutional change resides in this untapped reservoir of betrayed individuals: "the system may have most to fear from those subordinates among whom the institutions of hegemony have been most successful" (107). Perhaps this is an instant when Scott's own "hidden transcript" surfaces in his argument, a place where he can revel in the subordinate's familiar fantasy that raging against the machine constitutes a viable politics. For whatever reason, Scott quickly drops this detour into the roots of radicalism and returns to his original concern—how one cultivates the arts of resistance when revolutionary transformation is out of the question. His value to us here lies precisely in this refusal to lead us down the path to revolution: that is, his refusal to repeat the pieties of those committed to the liberatory project allows him to focus on the actual actions and experiences of those who labor under conditions of constraint. The classroom is, of course, one such place where the labor of others—both teachers and students—is constrained to meet the demands of outside forces. It is to that compromised space that we must now turn our attention.

RUPTURING THE PUBLIC TRANSCRIPT: "ALL MY MOST BRILLIANT PROFESSORS ARE TRULY MEDIOCRE TEACHERS"

Although Scott is, as I've already noted, generally concerned with more repressive forms of domination than those found in the classroom, he does invoke the teacher's mastery as an example of a particular kind of authority, one that "can tolerate a remarkably high level of practical nonconformity so long as it does not actually tear the public fabric of hegemony" (204). Thus, the teacher can lecture about the beauty of literature or the politics of literacy or the liberatory powers of the cultural studies paradigm, say, knowing all the while that the students aren't paying attention, aren't taking notes, aren't even listening. As long as no one actually stops the class to say it's all nonsense or to perform some other public gesture of contempt, the teacher's role as the ultimate arbiter of meaning is never really in danger. Any student who has made it to college knows these rules of behavior and knows, as well, the boundaries of permissible signs of disengagement (or learns them soon enough): eyes may close, pencils may doodle or be laid to rest, in some classes newspapers may be allowed to open, heads even may go down. Snoring, listening to headsets, audibly parroting the teacher's remarks are all ill-advised, as is — in most cases — openly contesting the teacher's point of view. The classroom can tolerate all manner of nonconformity, but every classroom has its limit, whether it be the expression of doubt about the virtue of the academic enterprise, open speculation about the teacher's qualifications for running the class, or insistent disrespect for the methods of assigning and assessing the work the students produce. At some point, every teacher must enforce the boundary between the concerns of the hidden transcript, where students regularly rehearse their misgivings about the education they're receiving, and the public transcript, where the virtues of the educational system are taken for granted.

The violation of this boundary can be quite shocking, but it is important to recognize that the shock arises not because the public revelation of the hidden transcript discloses unknown information but rather because, in the act itself, the revelation threatens to "tear the public fabric of hegemony." Thus, if we take, for example, the frustrated student who suddenly "goes off" in class — announcing he's only taking the expository writing course because it's required, that he was graded more fairly in high school, that all this writing about culture has nothing to do with what he plans to do with his life — it is safe to say that nothing in the content of what the student has said can be construed as surprising; rather, what grabs everyone's attention is the fact that the student has chosen to make this statement within his teacher's hearing. Or, to refer to a recent example from my own experience, when I summoned a graduate student to my office to discuss the open disrespect he had shown his peers in our Teaching Seminar by reading through the course catalogue during their presentations, the content of the graduate student's response was not shocking, but the fact that he shared that content with me was. He said he really had no interest in pedagogy, but had come to the university to study literature. He told me he was taking the course because it was what was required of him to be eligible for funding. And then he said, "all my most brilliant professors are truly mediocre teachers." In the silence that followed, we were both embarrassed, I think, by the fact that he made this final statement in my presence. To quell such "revolts" we teachers often do what we do best: we start talking. Perhaps we are solicitous, perhaps

667

not. Perhaps we invite the student to reflect on the assumptions that inform the stated critique, perhaps we tell the student exactly what those assumptions are and why they are so pernicious. But the goal, more often than we care to admit, I'd say, is to restore order, return to the lesson plan, get the hidden transcript back offstage and out of sight.

One essay that seems to go out of its way to transgress the boundary that separates what can and what cannot be said about the culture of schooling is Richard Rodriguez's frequently anthologized "The Achievement of Desire." In this piece, Rodriguez recounts how disorienting his academic success has been for him: the son of Mexican immigrants, Rodriguez describes his increasing alienation from his parents as he began to excel at school, his growing embarrassment at their broken English, their apparent ignorance, their impoverished state. Mechanically devoting himself to his studies, Rodriguez rises through the ranks, goes to graduate school to study Renaissance literature, wins a scholarship to pursue research at the British Museum. To all outward appearances, he would seem to have realized the American Dream; inwardly, though, Rodriguez is consumed with doubt about what he has done and where it has taken him. He feels that he has betrayed his parents and that he has been betrayed by a system that has left him incapable of producing anything but "pedantic, lifeless, unassailable prose" (499). He is, in short, the very kind of person that Scott would be willing to describe as having "false consciousness," one of those trusting people who "made sacrifices of self-discipline and control and developed expectations that were usually betrayed" (Scott 107).

When I first assigned Rodriguez in my composition courses, I was surprised at the amount of hostility that students unleashed in response to his essay. Far from seeing Rodriguez's reflection on the long-term effects of schooling and the consequences of committing oneself to always pleasing the teacher as an invitation to air their own critiques of institutionalized education, the students responded, as a rule, by accusing Rodriguez of being a traitor to his parents, his heritage, even his teachers. One didn't have to sacrifice anything to do well in school, the students would say; indeed, many went out of their way to demonstrate that as far as they were concerned doing well in school was all but irrelevant to how they thought about the world, related to others, moved through the social sphere. And thus, in their own rush to rehearse again the lines about the virtues of education drawn from the public transcript, they transformed Rodriguez into a two-time loser: first, for betraying his parents and his heritage; and second, for allowing his education to play such a large role in his life that it shaped who he was and how he thought about himself and the world. As one of Rodriguez's more vocal critics put it: "The way in which he treats his parents angers me, he is so obsessed with his studies that he neglects his parents and his child-hood. In the second grade all I remember was having fun with friends, feel-ing love from my parents and always respecting my parents. This punk shows no love to his parents, and that is what I can't understand. . . . I see his parents in my mind. They are just like my parents, and I feel like hugging them and telling them that they are great parents. At the same time I feel like taking Rodriguez and wringing his neck."

It's hard to know what to make of such responses. For my purposes, though, they are of interest because, on the surface at least, they appear to articulate a desire about how schooling should function—that is, that schools should restrict themselves to providing "know-how" and that they should not disturb one's place in the world. And such responses suggest a fear that schools do not actually function in this isolated way, but rather pro-duce (or reinforce) an estrangement from one's past, an uncertainty about one's place in the world, a resigned sense that what one must give up during the educational process can never be recovered. While this fear of educa-tion's disruptive powers is something that Freire and Scott would both agree is well warranted, Rodriguez concludes his essay by declaring that it is his education that has allowed him to see the consequences of his own acade-mic success: "If, because of my schooling, I had grown culturally separated from my parents, my education finally had given me ways of speaking and caring about that fact" (585). What many students and teachers can't forgive Rodriguez for is his public insistence that education inevitably alienates one in these ways and that this is one of the appeals of scholarly work.

So, when confronted with this argument, the students put on a good show of being shocked that Rodriguez was attracted to something that cre-ated a barrier between himself and his family. They are less sure, though, about how to respond to Rodriguez's critical description of schooling; for good reason, they are wary, knowing that to speak openly in class of what one loses through academic advancement (or of what one gains in the way that Rodriguez does) is to risk rupturing the public transcript about educa-tion's unquestioned virtues. And so, rather than have this piece of the hid-den transcript of schooling make its way onto the public stage, the students collaborate in repairing the rupture and rise, in unison, to the defense of self-determination, freedom, individuality. They argue that being good at school need not change one in any substantial way; they insist that this son of immigrants could have had the best of both worlds; they declare that the rewards of a loving family far outweigh whatever benefits one might receive from mastering the scholarly apparatus. They lay it on thick. And, in the right context, everyone can sigh with relief that a catastrophe has been averted.

TO TEACH AND TO LIVE IN A
BUREAUCRATIC WORLD: ON THE USES
OF INSTITUTIONAL AUTOBIOGRAPHY

Between the poles of these two representations of schooling as either radically liberating and empowering or ceaselessly oppressive and instrumentalist, one finds a vast, unexplored territory—the fraught, compromised world where all of our classes are actually convened. I have detailed the attractions and the perils of the rhetorics of liberation and violation most frequently deployed in analyses of the political consequences of teaching; in closing I would like to suggest that, in order for students to begin to imagine other ways of framing their experience of schooling, they must first be given an opportunity to formulate a more nuanced understanding of how power gets exercised in the social sphere. And for this to happen, we must provide them with opportunities to discover the virtues of discursive versatility, by which I mean the ability to speak, read, and write persuasively across a wide range of social contexts. Lest this sound like a refurbished but thinly disguised call to renew our commitment to rhetorical instruction, let me make clear that I am interested in promoting a fluency in the languages of the bureaucratic systems that regulate all our lives; a familiarity with the logics, styles of argumentation, repositories of evidence deployed by these organizational bodies; a fuller understanding of what can and cannot be gained through discursive exchanges, with a concomitant recalibration of the horizon of expectations. Were I a polemicist, I might say what I was after is a pragmatic pedagogy, one grounded in "the arts of complicity, duplicity, and compromise," the very same arts that are deployed, with such enervating effect, by the host of social, bureaucratic, and corporate institutions that govern all our lives.

But, if Scott is right in positing the existence of a hidden transcript that runs alongside the public transcript, it would seem that there is little need for inaugurating this pragmatic pedagogy: that is, according to Scott's theory, everyone already has a sensitivity to context and learns, through the process of familiarization, where and with whom it is safe to speak openly and when discretion is the better part of valor. The goal of a pragmatic pedagogy, though, is not to create discursive versatility where none existed before; it is, rather, to build on the discursive versatility that our very humanity has bestowed upon us. Thus, with regard to the classroom, the goal is not to teach the students that there is a difference between the literate practices valued in the academic and domestic spheres: undergraduates are already well aware of this differential valuation and its consequences. (Rodriguez is hardly exceptional in being able to detect this difference the moment he entered *primary* school.) The problem, thus, is not that students are unaware of the conflicts between these competing spheres, but that, within the space of the classroom, their very sensitivity to the differing contexts manifests itself, more often than not, either as silence or as open assent to the teacher's position. And, as every teacher who has heard the exasperated plea, "just tell me what you want and I'll do it," knows, when the students set out to conform to what they believe are the teacher's expectations, more often than not they simultaneously convey the impression that what a teacher finds most pleasing is the fully compliant, obedient, perhaps even unthinking student. As Scott explains, all students have been taught the consequences of not assuming this pose: "One deserter shot, one assertive slave whipped, one unruly student rebuked; these acts are meant as public events for an audience of subordinates. They are intended as a kind of preemptive strike to nip in the bud any further challenges of the existing frontier" (197).

And, of course, as teachers we too are subject to the demands of the classroom drama, which requires that we meet the ambient expectations about what it means to teach and to be an authority on one's subject. Thus, we are quick to cover our own ignorance, talk over our own confusion, hide our own doubts about the rewards of learning because, if we act otherwise, we would risk rending education's public transcript by exposing the highly credentialed person at the front of the room as nothing more than a fraud. Under such learning conditions, it is hard to know what lasting lesson anyone is getting from the experience, beyond sustained instruction in the ways educated people are meant to carry themselves in public. This is, to be sure, an important lesson, but it's one that's all about the deadening effects of formal compliance—a lesson that leaves no room for thinking about the range of permissible forms of action that can occur within the flexibly bounded, inevitably permeable space of enforced compliance.

By providing a forum for teachers to discuss what actually occurs in their classrooms, composition studies has helped to show that there are other roles for the teacher to occupy besides unquestioned master and final arbiter of meaning. The discipline's abiding interest in reconsidering how power and authority are distributed and conferred in the classroom reflects a genuine desire on the part of the majority of its members to be seen as working to undermine an overarching system that is hierarchically organized ("We'll sit in a circle," I say), status-conscious ("Please, just call me Richard"), exclusive ("Everyone's opinion is valued here"). Similarly, the waxings and wanings of the discipline's debate about whether composition instruction should introduce students to academic discourse or help them articulate and generate insights about their personal experiences reveal a constitutive ambivalence in the workforce about what it means to write in the academy: when you teach composition, are you working for the system or against it?

This ambivalence about the status of our work is easy enough to understand. After all, since composition is situated on the margins of the academy, in the borderland of remedial and basic instruction, it is regularly staffed by people who know firsthand how casually and quietly the bureaucratic system of higher education parcels out economic injustice. Why prepare students to produce work that is valued by such a system? Why not teach them to resist, to intervene, to dismantle?

I don't believe that these two activities are mutually exclusive—that preparing a student to succeed in business, say, is incompatible with the project of teaching a student to think about the effects of discriminatory hiring practices. In the current fraught environment, though, I've stopped trying to convince teachers and teachers-in-training about the "merits of complicity" through argument: with the seductive rhetorics of liberation and resistance in the air, I've learned that it isn't long before the conversation produces charges that I'm selling out, cashing in my ideals, kissing up to the man. To circumvent this thoroughly familiar exchange, where the principled work of education in this corner squares off against the mercenary interests of the business world in the other, I've designed an assignment that asks teachers-in-training to write in the entirely unfamiliar (perhaps nonexistent) genre of the institutional autobiography, a genre which unites the seemingly opposed worlds of the personal—where one is free, unique, and outside of history— and the institutional—where one is constrained, anonymous, and imprisoned by the accretion of past practices. In this genre, the conventional questions that reside at the heart of the autobiographical enterprise about how one has become the person one has, overcome the obstacles one has, achieved what one has, get inflected in such a way that the concern becomes locating one's narrative within a specific institutional context. So inflected, the questions become: What experiences have led you to teach, study, read, and write in the ways you do? What institutional policies have promoted or inhibited your success?

When I assigned this project in a graduate seminar this past summer, I didn't know what I'd get in return and the students weren't sure what to produce. We had watched the film *Dangerous Minds* and critiqued Hollywood's fascination with producing classroom narratives of conversion and redemption; we had noted the prevalence of this narrative at our own conferences and in our journals where, as one student put it, after some initial difficulties, the teacher-hero gets down to the business of "liberating right, left, and center." Critiquing the master narrative was easy enough; the challenge lay in figuring out how to work within and against its constraints simultaneously, acknowledging but not overstating the influence of past teachers and one's own work in the classroom. Although the students had no models for how to do this at their immediate disposal, they were not working in a vacuum; I encouraged them to return to the archives—their own personal archive, including the papers, notes, and other pedagogical paraphernalia they'd saved, and the public record, including transcripts, graduation requirements, professional correspondence, and so forth—to unearth material evidence of past practices. I also had the students read a set of texts that focus on the institutional constraints that shape the business of higher education: Ian Hunter's *Rethinking the School*, Robin Varnum's *Fencing with Words*, Howard Tinberg's *Border Talk*, and David Tyack and Larry Cuban's *Tinkering Toward Utopia*. Then I stood back and waited to see what would happen.

One of the teachers responded to the assignment by recounting how she moved from being a part-time instructor on the fringes of her home institution to being a full-time member of her department as a result of the governor's decision to commit the state's educational system to technological innovation. Surrounded by others who were understandably reluctant, in the early eighties, to learn about computers and computerized instruction, this teacher volunteered to give it a try and slowly made her way to seemingly permanent employment, only to learn that, in the competitive market of the late nineties, she needed to show progress toward the doctorate to maintain her position. Neither wholly the victor nor the victim in this process, this teacher concluded her institutional autobiography with this observation:

> I know I am a better teacher than I would have been if technology hadn't interfered. That technology, forced into my teaching career by the bureaucracy, pushed me to "see" writing courses and writing itself in a new framework. That new framework emphasized my lack of knowledge in a subject I was struggling to teach and forced me to read, research, and realize how much more I needed to know.

Though this teacher had begun the course by describing herself as working in a state educational system that was ruled by bankers and businessmen, by the end of the semester she had revised her story so that it could account for the relative freedom she had experienced while working within a system governed by shifting and arbitrary requirements.

This is not to say, though, that this is an ideal story or that it is one with a happy ending. The state educational system that employs this teacher continues to be dependent on the whims of corporate culture; she finds her classes filled with students who are driven by an interest in financial success that she does not share; and her own ongoing employment is contingent upon her upgrading her credentials—a requirement that means she must move away from her family while she does her coursework. Pointing out the manifest injustices of this situation may be personally cathartic; it does not, however, alter the fact that the most pressing problem this teacher confronts is how to construct an inhabitable and hospitable life within these constraining conditions. There are those who would use this situation to raise once more the call to overthrow the system; others would say that the teacher has no choice but to roll over and take it. I would suggest, however, that none of us knows for certain what lies ahead for this teacher, her institution, or the state she works in. We don't know what will happen. All we know for sure is that the future will be like the past in that it will ceaselessly demand of us all that we improvise solutions to problems we never imagined possible.

Far from being powerless, as teachers who have years of experience in this frequently capricious and indifferent system for distributing social privilege, we are actually very well positioned to assist our students in acquiring the skills necessary for persisting in the ongoing project of navigating life in a bureaucracy. Specifically, we can teach them how to work within and against discursive constraints simultaneously, thereby helping them to experience the mediated access to "authenticity" that social action allows. Having our students develop this kind of discursive versatility won't serve to knock down or permanently remove the barrier that will always separate the public and the hidden transcripts, nor will it necessarily produce supporters of the kind of social justice Freire envisions. Rather, the more modest goal of the pragmatic pedagogy I've outlined here is to provide our students with the opportunity to speak, read, and write in a wider range of discursive contexts than is available to them when they labor under the codes of silence and manufactured consent that serve to define the lived experience of subordinates in the culture of schooling. If, through this process, the students learn how to register their reservations about academic practice in ways that can be heard as reasoned arguments rather than dismissed as the plaintive bleating of sheep, if they learn to pose their questions about the work before them in ways that invite response, and if, finally, they learn how to listen to and learn from the responses they receive, they may well be in a better position to negotiate the complex social and intellectual experiences that await them just beyond the classroom's walls. There is no knowing if the students will, in fact, be in this better position at some future moment, but this is the goal. It is only the polemical rhetoric that surrounds the discussion of pedagogical practice that would lead us to expect that any more definite outcome could be guaranteed.

WORKS CITED

Althusser, Louis. "Ideology and Ideological State Apparatuses (Notes Towards an Investigation)." *For Marx.* Trans. Ben Brewster. London: Allen Lane, 1969. 127–86.

Berlin, James. "Not a Conclusion: A Conversation." *Into the Field: Sites of Composition Studies.* Ed. Anne Ruggles Gere. New York: MLA, 1993. 193–206.

Berthoff, Ann. E. *Reclaiming the Imagination.* Upper Montclair, NJ: Boynton/Cook, 1984.

Bizzell, Patricia. *Academic Discourse and Critical Consciousness.* Pittsburgh, U of Pittsburgh P, 1992.

Elbow, Peter. "Pedagogy of the Bamboozled." *Embracing Contraries.* New York: Oxford UP, 1986. 85–98.

Freire, Paulo. *Pedagogy of the Oppressed.* 1968. Trans. Myra Bergman Ramos. New York: Continuum, 1989.

hooks, bell. *Teaching to Transgress.* New York: Routledge, 1994.

Kutz, Eleanor, and Hephzibah Roskelly. *An Unquiet Pedagogy: Transforming Practice in the English Classroom.* Portsmouth, NH: Boynton/Cook-Heinemann, 1991.

McCormick, Kathleen. "Always Already Theorists: Literary Theory and Theorizing in the Undergraduate Curriculum." *Pedagogy is Politics: Literary Theory and Critical Teaching.* Ed. Maria-Regina Kecht. Urbana: U of Illinois P, 1992. 111–31.

North, Stephen M. "Rhetoric, Responsibility, and the 'Language of the Left.'" *Composition & Resistance.* Ed. C. Mark Hurlbert and Michael Blitz. Portsmouth, NH: Boynton/Cook, 1991. 127–36.

Rodriguez, Richard. "The Achievement of Desire." Rpt. in *Ways of Reading.* Ed. David Bartholomae and Anthony Petrosky. 3d ed. Boston: Bedford, 1993. 481–504.

Scott, James C. *Domination and the Arts of Resistance: Hidden Transcripts.* New Haven: Yale UP, 1990.

Shor, Ira, ed. *Freire for the Classroom: A Sourcebook for Liberatory Teaching.* Portsmouth, NH: Boynton/Cook, 1987.

Tompkins, Jane. "Pedagogy of the Distressed." *College English* 52.6 (October 1990): 653–60.

On the Subjects of Class and Gender in "The Literacy Letters"

LINDA BRODKEY

In "The Discourse on Language," Michel Foucault dramatizes the desire to be "on the other side of discourse, without having to stand outside it, pondering its particular, fearsome, and even devilish features" (215) in this whimsical colloquy between the individual and the institution.

> Inclination speaks out: "I don't want to have to enter this risky world of discourse; I want nothing to do with it insofar as it is decisive and final; I would like to feel it all around me, calm and transparent, profound, infinitely open, with others responding to my expectations, and truth emerging, one by one. All I want is to allow myself to be borne along, within it, and by it, a happy wreck." Institutions reply: "But you have nothing to fear from launching out; we're here to show you discourse is within the established order of things, that we've waited a long time for its arrival, that a place has been set aside for it—a place that both honours and disarms it; and if it should have a certain power, then it is we, and we alone, who give it that power." (215-16)

What Foucault and other poststructuralists have been arguing the last fifteen or twenty years is considerably easier to state than act on: we are at once constituted and unified as subjects in language and discourse. The discursive subject is of particular interest to those of us who teach writing because language and discourse are understood to be complicit in the representation of

Reprinted from *College English* 51.2 (February 1989): 125–41. Used with permission.

self and others, rather than the neutral or arbitrary tools of thought and expression that they are in other modern theories, not to mention handbooks and rhetorics. Among other things, this means that since writers cannot avoid constructing a social and political reality in their texts, as teachers we need to learn how to "read" the various relationships between writer, reader, and reality that language and discourse supposedly produce.

New theories of textuality are inevitably new theories of reading. And in the field of writing, those who teach basic writers and welcome new ways to read their texts are perhaps the most likely to recognize the possibilities of discursive subjectivity. The poststructural David Bartholomae of "Inventing the University," for example, writes less confidently but more astutely of what student errors may signify than the Bartholomae of "The Study of Error," published some years earlier at the height of the field's enthusiasm for empirical research and error analysis. For the startling power of a discourse to confer authority, name errors, and rank order student texts speaks more readily to the experience of reading basic writing than promises of improved reliability or validity in the empirical study of errors. While empiricality is far from moot, it makes little difference if one is right if one is not talking about that which most concerns writing and the teaching of writing. Or, as Sharon Crowley has put it, "the quality of the power that is associated with writing varies with the degree of author-ity granted by a culture to its texts" (96). In this society the authority that teachers are empowered to grant to or withhold from student texts derives from the theory of textuality governing their reading.

The question then is how to read what students write. And at issue is the unquestioned power of a pedagogical authority that insists that teachers concentrate on form at the expense of content.

> I'm siting at home now when I have more time to write to you I enjoyed rending your letters. I under stand reading them one word I had a little trouble with the word virginia but know about me well that is hard but I will try.

The errors in spelling and punctuation in this passage are serious, but not nearly as egregious, I suspect, as the tradition that warrants reducing a text to its errors. Remember the anger you feel when someone corrects your pronunciation or grammar while you are in the throes of an argument, and you can recover the traces of the betrayal students must experience when a writing assignment promises them seemingly unlimited possibilities for expression, and the response or evaluation notes only their limitations. The errors are there, and the passage is hard to read. Yet to see only the errors strikes me as an unwarranted refusal to cede even the possibility of discursive subjectivity and authority to the woman who wrote this passage, barring of course that of basic writer which an error analysis would without question grant her.

CHANGING THE SUBJECT

This is an essay about the ways discourses construct our teaching. In postmodern theories of subjectivity:

1. all subjects are the joint creations of language and discourse;
2. all subjects produced are ideological;
3. all subject positions are vulnerable to the extent that individuals do not or will not identify themselves as the subjects (i.e., the effects) of a discourse.

Those who occupy the best subject positions a discourse has to offer would have a vested interest in maintaining the illusion of speaking rather than being spoken by discourse. Postmodern rhetoric would begin by assuming that all discourses warrant variable subject positions ranging from mostly satisfying to mostly unsatisfying for those individuals named by them. Each institutionalized discourse privileges some people and not others by generating uneven and unequal subject positions as various as stereotypes and agents. Hence, it is at least plausible to expect most, though not all, of those individuals whose subjectivity is the most positively produced by a discourse to defend its discursive practices against change. And it is equally plausible to expect some, though again not all, of those individuals whose subjectivity is the most negatively produced to resist its discursive practices. Feminists, for example, regularly resist discursive practices that represent female subjectivity solely in terms of reproductive biology. Of course, neither verbal resistance nor other material forms of protest to such reduced subject positions are universal among women.

Discursive resistance requires opportunities for resistance. Altering an institutionalized discourse probably requires an unremitting negative critique of its ideology, a critique that is most often carried out in the academy by attempting to replace a particular theory (e.g., of science or art or education or law) with another. Recently, theoretical battles have proliferated to such an extent that a cover term, *critical theory*, has come to refer to a variety of ideological critiques of theory, research, and practice across the academy: critical legal studies, critical practice, critical anthropology, critical pedagogy, and so on.

Discursive resistance, however, need not be conducted in such abstract terms as we have recently witnessed in the academy. The more usual practice would be for those individuals who are ambivalent or threatened by their subject positions in a given discourse to interrupt the very notion of the unified self—the traditional Cartesian notion that the self is a transcendent and absolute entity rather than a creation of language and ideology—in their spoken and written texts. Such interruptions are likely to take one of two forms: reversing the negative and positive subject positions in a given discourse—as Carol Gilligan does in her feminist revision of the research on the development of moral reasoning among adolescent girls; or representing a stereotype as an agent in a discourse the least committed to the preservation of the stereotype—as Toni Morrison does when representing Afro-American women and men as the agents rather than the victims of events in her novels.

Studies of these and other interruptive practices, rhetorics of resistance in which individuals shift subject positions from one discourse to another or within a discourse in their speaking and writing, would constitute empirical inquiry into the postmodern speculation that language and discourse are material to the construction of reality, not simply by-products reflecting or reproducing a set of non-discursive, material social structures and political formations. Knowledge of multiple subject positions makes possible both the practical and the theoretical critiques that interrupt the assumption of unchanging, irreversible, and asymmetrical social and political relations between the privileged and unprivileged subjects represented in a particular discourse (see Williams, esp. 75-141).

What is needed is research that addresses what Stuart Hall has recently called "a theory of articulation," which he describes as "a way of understanding how ideological elements come, under certain conditions, to cohere together within a discourse, and a way of asking how they do or do not become articulated, at specific junctures, to certain political subjects" (53). Since articulation separates intentions from effects, or production from reception, Hall has reinserted the possibility of human agency into poststructural theory. More specifically, articulation distinguishes between the desire to be unified in a discourse and what happens in practice, namely, what individuals do in and with the unified subject positions offered them by such recognizable institutional discourses as, say, science, art, education, law, and religion or ethics.

"THE LITERACY LETTERS"

What I mean by research on the rhetorics of discursive practice and attendant practices of resistance is amply illustrated in a curriculum project I have referred to elsewhere as "the Literacy Letters" (see Brodkey). The letters were generated in the discourse of education, since they were initiated by six white middle-class teachers (four women and two men) taking my graduate course on teaching basic writing and sustained by six white working-class women enrolled in an Adult Basic Education (ABE) class. The woman who was teaching the ABE class and taking my course hoped that corresponding would provide the students in her class with what she called an <u>authentic reason to write</u>—on the order of a pen-pal experience for adults. The experienced English teachers from my class, most of whom had not taught basic writing, set out to learn more about the reading and writing concerns of their adult correspondents. As for me, I welcomed the chance to study correspondence itself, which seemed to me a remarkable opportunity to examine both the production and reception of self and other in the writing and reading of personal letters.

Permission to photocopy the letters as data for research was granted by all correspondents before the first exchange. For the two months that they wrote, the correspondents agreed not to meet or talk on the phone. The data, then, are the letters written by the six pairs who wrote regularly: one pair exchanged letters eight times; one pair seven times; two pairs six times; and two pairs five times.

When the teachers first reported that they found writing the letters stressful, I attributed their anxiety to the fact that I would be reading and evaluating their letters as well as those written by the students in the ABE class. But their uneasiness persisted despite repeated assurances that I couldn't look at or read the letters until the semester's end, a standard procedure meant to protect the educational rights of those who agree to participate in classroom research. After reading and thinking about the letters, however, I am no longer so inclined to assume that my presence as such was as threatening or intrusive as I first thought, though doubtless it contributed some to their anxiety.

Learning to Read "The Literacy Letters"

Research on basic writers as well as my own experience teaching amply prepared me for the ungainly prose produced by the women in the ABE class (e.g., Bartholomae, Perl, Shaughnessy). But nothing I had read or remembered from my own teaching prepared me for occasional moments of linguistic as well as discursive awkwardness from the teachers. I am not referring to the necessary clumsiness with which the teachers sought their footing before they knew anything about their correspondents, but to intermittent improprieties that occurred once several letters had been exchanged. In fact, I found these occasional lapses so perplexing that it's fair to say that the teachers' unexpected errors, rather than the students' expected ones, led me to think about the literacy letters in terms of the poststructural discursive practices of reproduction and resistance. Only discourse, more specifically the power of a discourse over even its fluent writers, I decided, could begin to explain the errors of these otherwise literate individuals.

That educational discourse grants teachers authority over the organization of language in the classroom, which includes such commonplace privileges as allocating turns, setting topics, and asking questions, is clear from sociolinguistic studies of classroom language interaction (e.g., Stubbs). Many teachers, including those in this study, attempt to relinquish their control by staging opportunities for students to take the privileged subject position of teacher in, say, group discussions or collaborative assignments that grant them, at least temporarily, a measure of control over educational discursive practice. Attempts to transform classroom discussions into conversations between peers are thwarted to the extent that teachers fail to realize that their interpersonal relationships with students, as well as their institutional ones, are constituted by educational discourse. While the power of a discourse is not absolute, neither is it vulnerable to change by individuals who ignore its power, only by those who interrupt or resist or challenge the seemingly immutable reality of unified subjectivity. In much the same way that you don't resist racism by denying that racism exists, but by confronting it in yourself and others, teachers cannot divest themselves of those vestiges of authority that strike them as unproductive by ignoring the institutional arrangements that unequally empower teachers and students.

At the outset, the teachers in this study attempted to mitigate the power of educational discourse over themselves and their correspondents by "playing" student. Their letters are replete with the desire to represent themselves as students of writing pedagogy and their correspondents as their teachers. The longest running correspondence, for instance, was initiated by a teacher who wrote: "I think that some of the things you could tell me might help me to understand what I can do better when I try to help my students learn to improve thier (sic) writing." Since none of the students made suggestions about either curriculum or instruction, roles were not reversed. But making the requests seems to have mooted the possibility of the teachers practicing the most authoritarian "dialect" of educational discourse in their correspondence. To wit, no teacher reduced personal correspondence to spelling or grammar lessons; nor, for that matter, did any of the students from the ABE class ask to be taught or corrected.

Bear in mind that the writers of the literacy letters are not held by the usual arrangements between teachers and students. To be sure, the teachers are teachers and the students are students. But theirs is what might be called an extracurricular relationship, arranged by the authorized teacher. While the teachers assiduously avoided lessons and hence avoided even the possibility of displacing the classroom teacher's authority, there are nevertheless times in the letters when it certainly looks as if by ignoring rather than contesting the authority of educational discourse, they retained control over such discursive privileges as determining what is and what is not an appropriate topic. The teachers exercise their authority infrequently, but decisively, whenever one of their correspondents interrupts, however incidentally, the educational discursive practice that treats class as irrelevant to the subjectivity of teachers and students. Telegraphed by linguistic and/or discursive lapses, the refusal that signals the teachers' unspoken commitment to a classless discourse provokes additional and more pronounced discursive resistance from the ABE writers.

Personal Narratives in "The Literacy Letters"

Discursive hegemony on the part of the teachers is most obvious and discursive resistance on the part of the students is most dramatic during storytelling episodes. Personal correspondence evokes personal narratives. The teachers tell a variety of stories in which they represent themselves as busy professionals trying to resolve conflicts among work, family, and school. Social research on storytelling suggests that in exchange for being granted the time it takes to tell a story, the teller is expected to make it worth the listener's while by raising for evaluation or contemplation that which is problematic or unusual about the narrative conflict and its resolution (see Labov, Pratt). That the teachers tell stories representing themselves as guilty about their inability to find enough time is not surprising, since their busy lives have been made all the more complicated by recently adding course work to schedules already overburdened by responsibilities at work and home. Nor are the responses to their stress stories unexpected, for the women from the Adult Basic Education class console and commiserate with the teachers in much the way that research suggests interlocutors ordinarily do. The teachers, however, occasionally respond in extraordinary ways when their correspondents reciprocate with stories about their lives.

The ABE students do not tell narratives about not having the time to fulfill their obligations to the three spheres of work, school, and family. Nor are their stories about internal conflicts like guilt. Instead, they write most frequently about external threats to the well-being of themselves and their families or their neighbors. While work and education often figure in their stories, they are important only insofar as they materially affect their lives: a family is besieged by the threat of layoffs; lack of educational credentials means the low paychecks and the moonlighting that robs families of time with the overworked wage earner.

Clearly teachers and students alike told class-based narratives. Yet the teachers' markedly inept responses to their correspondents' narratives suggest that the hegemony of educational discourse warrants teachers not only to represent themselves as subjects unified by the internal conflicts like guilt that preoccupy professionals, but to disclaim narratives that represent a subject alternatively unified in its conflicts with an external material reality. This refusal to acknowledge the content of their correspondents' narratives, most explicable as a professional class narcissism that sees itself everywhere it looks, alienates the ABE writers from educational discourse and, more importantly, from the teachers it ostensibly authorizes.

Don and Dora

The seven-letter exchange between the teacher and student I'll call Don and Dora is disarming. Frequency alone suggests that both teacher and student found corresponding satisfying. For some weeks they wrote about movies, food, and their families, all topics introduced by Don who represented himself in his initial letter as a complex subject, specifically, as a young man beset by personal failings his correspondent would find amusing:

> I won't tell you how long I like to stay in bed in the morning—though I do stay up very late at night (watching old movies)—but let's just say that it's past 11 AM. Oh well, we all have to have at least one vice. Unfortunately, I have more than one. One of my others is Chinese food. There's a Chinese food cart parked right outside the window of the library where I work, so every afternoon I dash out when the line slacks off . . . I usually try to get some vegetable dishes, even though I most always end up getting the most highly caloric item on the menu.

His comedic self-presentation is amplified by this final request: "Please let me know what you're doing: do you like Chinese food (and if so, what kind?), do you like old movies (and if so, which ones?), do you think I'm too weird to write back to? I'll look forward to your responses, comments, complaints, etc." In her response letter, Dora picks up the topics of movies and food. "I to enjoy the old movies and (love Chinese food)," she writes, but then goes on to conclude about them both, "so [I] guess that make two of us that are (weird)." Notice that while she responds to his question, "do you think I'm too weird to write back to?", writing back is itself material evidence that Dora doesn't find Don's tastes *too* weird. Dora is, as she puts it, "looking forward to writing back this is my first letter I ever wrote."

Over the next few weeks, their letters follow this pattern. Don writes extended and humorous anecdotes that portray him as a man at odds with himself at work, school, and home, and Dora offers consolation by letting him know how amusing she and the other women in her class find his stories: "Rachel [her teacher] ask me to read your letter to the class we all though that your grandmother and father was funning about the candy." After dutifully playing audience for some weeks, however, Dora dramatically reverses the pattern when she not only asserts herself as a narrator, but as the narrator of tragic rather than comedic events, in this letter which in its entirety reads as follows:

> I don't have must to siad this week a good frineds husband was kill satday at 3:15 the man who kill-him is a good man he would give you the shirt off of his back it is really self-defense but anyway I see police academy three it was funny but not is good as the first two

Dora's narrative limns as stark a reality as any represented in the literacy letters. However, the abrupt shift from herself as a narrator who reflects on the aftermath of violence to herself as the student who answers a teacher's questions—"but anyway I see police academy three it was funny but not is good as the first two"—is, for me, one of those moments when the power of discourse seems the most absolute.

It's not implausible to imagine that in telling a narrative Dora is trying out the more positive subject position afforded narrators by the discourse of art, and that Don has held throughout their correspondence. But art is only a respite, it seems, for Dora shifts quickly from narrator back to student. Yet in that brief moment when she inserts herself as the narrator, Dora takes on the more complex subjectivity afforded by the discourse of art to narrators. Though short, the story she tells is one in which the narrator's sympathies are clearly divided between the survivors—the friend and the murderer—a narrative position that Dora grounds in the extenuating circumstances of moral character (a good man "would give you the shirt off of his back") and law ("it is really self-defense"). Her narrative point of view considers not the grisly fact of murder and not even what motivated the murder, but the notion that murder is a consequence of circumstances rather than character.

Narrative strikes me as a potentially effective mode of resistance, for the rules governing storytelling more or less require Don to respond to the content of Dora's narrative. Since Dora attentuated the full interruptive force of the discourse of art on educational discourse, however, by interjecting the comment about the movie, she effectively lost her hold on the rhetorical practice in which the narrative critiques a teacher's exclusive right to initiate topics. The abrupt shift from narrator back to audience returns, or offers to return, teacher and student alike to the already established subject positions of teacher/narrator and student/audience.

Even if Dora's interjection is understood as hesitation, Don might have assisted her by simply responding to the content of her story. He might have asked about motive or even asked why she says nothing about the victim. But Don's response suggests only that he is nonplussed:

> I'm sorry to hear about the problem that you wrote about last week. It's always hard to know what to say when the situation is as unusual as that one. I hope that everything is getting a little better, at least for you trying to know what to say and do in that situation.

Several issues about the fragility of the unity that even the most privileged subjects are able to achieve in language and discourse come immediately to mind. Most obvious, perhaps, is the syntactic lapse in the final sentence ("I hope that everything is getting a little better, at least for *you* trying to know what to say and do in that situation"). Less obvious, though equally to the point, is the way that Don's linguistic facility, under the circumstances, only amplifies the discursive inadequacy of this passage as a response to the content of her narrative.

Bearing in mind that she has just told a story in which the "problem" is the aftermath of murder—her friend's husband is dead and the good man who killed him presumably faces prison—the assertion that this is a matter of manners—"It's always hard to know what to say when the situation is as unusual as that one"—is not simply inappropriate. It constitutes a discursive retreat that threatens to reconstitute Don and Dora in the most profoundly alienated subject relationship of all—self and other—and to give over their more or less satisfying discursive relationship as narrator and audience. Even the demonstrative adjective, *that*, underscores the distance Don places between himself and the world in which he resides and the other and the world in which she resides. The contrast between this awkward first paragraph and the plans to visit his grandmother on Mother's Day that complete his letter effectively reiterates the terms of their continued correspondence.

In her next letter, Dora again responds to the content of Don's letter, "I am glad to hear that you are going to see your grandmother." And though she makes no further mention in this or any letter of the murder, she writes "I hope you get more energy about work," which remark is followed by:

> I wouldn't want to see you living in Kensington with the rest of us bums, ha ha

It certainly looks as if she has acknowledged the threat of othering by noting that his self-proclaimed and amply documented laziness throughout their correspondence would, in the eyes of many, make him one of the others— "the rest of us bums"—whose subjectivity he's denying. That her class antagonism increases after the next letter, in which he narrates in the usual humorous detail his visit with his grandmother, is evident in the fact that for the first time she makes no reference to his anecdote and ends a brief account of her own Mother's Day with, "I got call back to work today. I am very nervous about it. it like started a new job." In his next letter, in which he makes no mention of her job, Don follows yet another extended narrative about a day at the beach with "Keep cool and write soon!" But this time Dora ignores both the narrative and the imperatives and does not write again.

Don's response is characteristic of the kind of discursive uneasiness that arises whenever one of the students interrupts the educational practice that deems such working-class concerns as neighborhood violence irrelevant. And while this is admittedly one of the more dramatic examples, it suggests the extent to which unacknowledged tension over the control of subject positions contributes to rather than alleviates class antagonism, for we see that the teacher's desire to be preserved as the unified subject of an educational discursive practice that transcends class overrides the student's desire to narrate herself as a subject unified in relation to the violence that visited her working-class neighborhood.

Rita and Esther

The second example comes from the six-letter exchange between an experienced secondary English teacher I'll call Rita and the most fluent and prolific writer from the ABE class, a student I'll call Esther. The set itself is unusual, since these are the only correspondents whose letters are often of similar length. From the outset, it's easy to see that Esther is not only actively resisting playing "student" but sometimes even tries to play "teacher." In response to Rita's initial letter, for instance, Esther first compliments her— "My classmates and I read your wonderful letter"—but then faults her for what she neglected to mention: "you never stated your age or your country in the letter. And also where your Grandmother's home was." And unlike the other ABE writers, in her first and subsequent letters, Esther asks for information that Rita has neither offered nor alluded to:

> What is it like where you live and what are the shopping areas like. How is the transportation and the Climate there. What kind of food do you like to eat. You didn't say if you were married, or if you have children. Please write back and let me know.

Though this is admittedly an insight considerably improved by hindsight, the class antagonism that erupts later can probably be traced to Rita's ambivalance about their relationship, for she seems unable either to accept Esther's assumption that they are peers or to assert herself as a teacher. Rita's reluctance to declare herself as either a teacher or a peer may explain her refusal to do more than name the suburb she lives in or the nearby mall in answer to questions like "What is it like where you live and what are the shopping areas like." In short, Rita replies but does not answer Esther's questions.

In a letter near the end of their correspondence, following yet one more futile effort to establish what Rita's life is like — "Do you live near a beach or the shore? Are you going anywhere special this Summer?" — Esther writes this explanation in response to Rita's comment that she sounded "a little discouraged" in her last letter:

> I'm going to have to look for another house because, the Restate is Selling the house unless somebody invests in it and wants me to stay his or her tennant. That is why I was a little discourage because I didn't have a chance to save any money. I'll still answer your letters. Thank you for writing back.

This is a remarkable passage if only because it is one of the few times in the literacy letters when anyone mentions money by name. There are plenty of coded references to money: vacations taken or not taken, the buying of gifts, the cost of public transportation and food. But this particular statement is about money, about the simple economic fact that changing housing requires capital. And given what Esther has written, Rita's response strikes me as a perverse misreading:

> It is difficult to save money. Do you have any idea where you will move? What kind of home are you planning to buy? Interest rates are low now.

The peculiarity arises in the increasing unconnectedness of Rita's sentences to Esther's assertions. The first sentence is a response to Esther's assertion that she hasn't "had a chance to save any money." And the second sentence relates to Esther's claim that she will probably have to move. But in light of what Esther wrote, the assumption that Esther is planning to buy a house or that interest rates are of any consequence to her is, to say the least, surprising. That the question confounds Esther is evident in her next letter, which begins with a passing reference to Rita's sister, whose illness Rita mentioned in her last letter, followed by a brief but pointed attempt to correct the misunderstanding:

> I'm very sorry to hear about your sister. I hope she gets better. About the house. The only way I could buy a house is by hitting a number in the Lotto.

As lessons in elementary economics go this is about as clear as any I know. Yet Rita's response to this assertion is, on the face of it, even more bizarre than her statement that "Interest rates are low now." To wit, she ignores Esther's topic, which is housing, and reintroduces gambling, Lotto, as a topic they might discuss:

> Do you play Lotto frequently? I never think that I can ever win one of those lotteries. Did you ever know anyone who won? Some people play faithfully.

This is a near perfect example of cross-talk, for two conversations are now in play—one about housing and another about gambling. And were this a conversation between peers, Rita would be charged with illicitly changing the topic, since it is she who played the conversational gambit in which Esther's instructive hyperbole—"the only way I could buy a house is if I win the Lotto"—is taken at its face value, and Lotto, which is not the topic but the comment, is transformed into the topic, now in the form of questions about gambling. It's a familiar teacher's gambit for controlling what does and does not count as knowledge, a remnant, perhaps, of the institutionalized silencing that Michelle Fine suggests "more intimately informs low-income, public schooling than relatively privileged situations" (158).

The salient fact here is that educational discourse empowers teachers to determine what is worthwhile in a student's contributions, presumably even if that judgment has little or no linguistic basis and even if a teacher-student relationship is not entirely warranted. Remember that Esther has been representing herself as an adult whose financial status is precarious and that she has gone to some pains not to occupy the student position that Rita has finally assigned her. It is in Esther's final letter, in which she makes one last attempt to establish subjective parity between herself and Rita, that we see the devastating pedagogical consequences of preserving this particular privilege of educational discursive practice.

> I don't play the Lotto everyday except on my birthday when it July 11 (7/11). I'm really messing up this letter. I'm going to an award dinner on May 30th at 7 p.m. And when I get a lucky number. I don't know anyone that ever won. Thank you for your nice letter. Bye for now.

Esther wrote better letters at the beginning than at the end of the semester. The disintegration of syntax in this her last letter ("when it" for "which is") augurs the disappearance of the working-class adult subject she has been representing and the articulation of the Adult Basic Writer, a subject unified by its errors, its sentence fragments ("And when I get a lucky number") and its rhetorical disjunctures (the sentences and phrases whose meanings are recoverable only by association). That Esther sees the failure as her own, "I'm really messing up this letter," echoes Foucault's assertion that it is the power of discourse to create the illusion that "it is we, and we alone, who give it that power." Finally overwhelmed by educational discourse, the adult subject retreats into silence.

Ellen and Pat

The eight-letter exchange between the student and teacher I'll call Pat and Ellen is by many standards, including my own, the most successful not simply because they wrote the most often, but because Pat's letters grew longer and her errors fewer over the two months she corresponded with Ellen. While she shares the other teachers' aversion to class, Ellen differs considerably from them in her initial and repeated representation of herself as unified in relation to family: "I have been married for 21 years," "[I am] the mother of two teenagers," "I'm a very family-centered person." Ellen's representation of her familial self is often completed or articulated by Pat, when, for example, she writes "I'm all so marry for 22½ year. I have 4 kids." The self unified in relation to family is reminiscent of that represented in many of the working-class narratives, except that the self articulated in their letters is decidedly female.

That gender is a crucial dimension of their subjectivity first becomes apparent when Ellen responds to Pat's physical description of herself with this measured assertion of identification: "It sounds as though you and I look somewhat alike." In this instance, it is Ellen who articulates or completes a representation of self initiated by Pat and hence Ellen who identifies herself as the embodied female subject represented in Pat's physical description. This particular articulation stands out because it is the only corporeal representation of self in the letters and because it is also the only self-representation offered by one of the students with which a teacher identifies or articulates. To be sure, Ellen's articulation is tenuous, qualified immediately by "somewhat," and later by assertions such as "I'm trying to lose some weight before the summer season comes so I won't be so embarrassed in my bathing suit" that suggest the middle-class woman's all too familiar and uneasy relationship to her body.

In the course of their reciprocal articulation, and the co-construction of themselves as gendered subjects, Pat and Ellen tell and respond to stories that narrate their shared concerns as mothers. And it is as mother-women that they ignore the class differences that overwhelm the correspondents in the other two examples. Their mutual concern for their children's education, for instance, overrides material differences between their children's actual access to education. Ellen writes that she and her husband will be traveling to Williamsburg to bring their daughter home from college for the summer: "So far, each year that we've gone we've had to move her in the rain. It would be nice to be able to keep dry for once during all of the trips back and forth to the car." Pat advises Ellen to "think positive," attending not to the fact that Ellen's daughter attends a private college while her son goes to a local community college, but to the prediction that it will probably rain. In what appears to be yet another attempt to lift Ellen's spirits, Pat then recalls that she, her husband, and three children took a trip to Williamsburg eight years earlier, about which she has only this to say: "Williamsburg is a beautiful place."

Toward the end of their correspondence, Ellen and Pat recount their Mother's Days. Ellen's story is short:

> I hope you had an enjoyable Mother's Day. Did your family treat you to dinner? B [Ellen's daughter] cooked the meal and we had a combination Mother's Day and birthday celebration. My husband was one of those Mother's Day presents when he was born so every eighth year his birthday and Mother's Day fall on the same weekend so it was quite a festive time with lots going on.

Pat responds with an elaborate narrative, at least four times longer than any letter she has written, in the course of which she introduces class concerns that unify her identity as the mother and hence differentiate her experience as a mother from Ellen's. In other words, Pat's narrative interrupts their mutually constructed gender identity with a representation of herself as a subject unified in relation to Mother's Day that differs considerably from the self represented in Ellen's narrative.

In the first of five episodes, Pat establishes mood, explaining that on the Thursday evening before Mother's Day, after finally succeeding in bathing and putting the younger children to bed, she found herself "down hartit" and worrying about how hard her husband works at his two jobs and how his not being at home much means that she feels "like a mom and a dad." She follows this orientation to her state of mind with a second episode in which her two older children ask what she wants for Mother's Day. She reports telling her son that "a card will do" but confiding to her daughter that "what I want you can't affordit." Pressed by the daughter to tell, she admits to wanting "a ciling fane for my dinning room." Pat indicates that a ceiling fan is out of the question by writing "she laugh and so did I laugh." The third episode, which opens with an account of the complicated childcare arrangements made in order for her son to take her window shopping for ceiling fans that Friday evening, includes: a brief description of the shopping spree ("there are lots of fanes to look at but I like this one fane a lots"); a scene in which the son surprises her by giving her the money to buy the fan; and an account of what happens when they return home where the children are waiting ("They all where happy for mom but not as thrill as I was inside of me"). On Saturday, the fourth episode begins with a gift of flowers from her son and his "girl friend" and concludes with dinner with the younger children at McDonald's, where a young woman at the counter tells Pat that her son "is an inspiration to the young people here" who "miss he but there is hope for the future." (In a previous letter Pat has explained that her son worked at McDonald's for a year and a half while attending a local community college, but had since taken a job at a hospital where, after three promotions, he was making 10% more than he had as manager of the night shift at McDonald's.) She concludes the fourth episode with "I was so proud of him. Went I was told this." The fifth and final episode begins on Mother's Day morning with her husband making breakfast, after which she receives a box of candy from the smaller children, a card containing ten dollars from all the children, two "short sets" from her grandson, and yet another box of candy from the son's "girl friend." Reflecting on events in the conclusion of her letter, Pat writes: "I was surprize it was a beautiful motherday weekend. I feel like I writing a book so I am lifeing now."

The demonstrations of familial affection in Pat's narrative apparently resolve her internal conflict (discouragement). In a family where money is scarce—the husband works two jobs, the son holds a full-time job while attending community college, and the daughter is employed—the members shower the mother with cash and commodities. Rather than confine their celebration of the mother to service—cooking for her or dining out—the family extends it to include both the material tokens—the flowers, the fan, the clothes, and the candy—and the thrill of consumption—the material event of shopping and paying for the fan. The ritual acts of consumption and service that dramatize the mother's value in this working-class family temporarily align all its members with the economy. In other words, the economic realities that are continually threatening its unity are replaced by a four-day fantasy in which the family compensates the mother for her emotional and physical labor.

Middle-class families do not ordinarily celebrate motherhood with consumption rituals. What Ellen has described is the familiar middle-class service ritual in which the mother is released from the specific task of cooking, a symbol of the domestic responsibilities that threaten to alienate those mothers who also work outside the home from their families. In response to Pat's narrative, Ellen writes, "I enjoyed hearing about all your very nice Mother's Day surprises. It sounds as though you have a very loving and considerate family. They must really appreciate how hard you work and all of the many things you do for them." Ellen's is a gracious comment that fully acknowledges their shared understanding of mothers' work and once again articulates their mutual identity as gendered subjects. But Ellen's response fails to articulate Pat's representation of her own and, by extension, Ellen's subjectivity as contingent on class. It's not just that their families understand the mother differently. I suspect that the working-class celebration of the mother would strike Ellen as too much and that the middle-class celebration would strike Pat as too little. Differences in their material circumstances separate them as mothers (neither Ellen nor her middle-class family need ritual relief from economic hardships), and Ellen's comment fails to acknowledge that Pat's class-based narrative places them in distinct rather than the same subject positions as women.

Ellen concludes her letter with a suggestion that draws Pat's attention to what is not said. "Since this is the last week of your classes you can wrtie (sic) me at my home address if you think that you will have the time and would like to continue writing. I know that I would enjoy hearing from you." Pat understands the absence of any expressed desire to write as well as read her letters to mean that Ellen has lost the enthusiasm for writing she expressed in earlier correspondence: "At first I was nervous about writing to someone I didn't know, but now I enjoy writing them and look forward to your letter each week." By invoking the institutional auspices under which they have been corresponding—"this is the last week of your classes"—Ellen effectively shifts from the discourse of art in which they have both been representing and articulating their subjectivity as mothers in personal narratives to the educational discourse in which Pat would presumably be a student writing for a teacher.

Pat interrupts the shift in discourse and subject positions that Ellen has suggested when she writes: "I would like to know, if you would still writing me, or not if not it has been nice writing to you. I don't know if it help you are not, I know it has help me a lot. Thank you very must." Pat offers yet another version of their educational relationship in which she and Ellen would continue to learn from one another by corresponding, but she makes it clear, I think, that the decision to write as well as read is Ellen's. And Ellen chooses not to write back.

CONCLUSION

Since the late 1970s, that is, since the publication of Pierre Bourdieu and Jean-Claude Passeron's *Reproduction in Education, Society and Culture*, many teachers and parents, and some administrators and social theorists and social scientists, have been concerned about the extent to which schools not only tolerate but legitimate the very forms of classism, racism, and sexism that American education is publicly charged with eliminating. I mention this by way of pointing out that law provides educational opportunity for those it designates as the subjects of social and economic discrimination. Indeed, it is the state that provides a good deal of the funding for the Adult Basic Education program that the working-class students in the study were attending. Yet the data remind us that law does not protect these students from the dialect of educational discourse in which a teacher's control over discursive practice is contingent on the ideology that classroom language transcends class, race, and gender.

The teachers in this study are not ogres—far from it. They are energetic and inventive practitioners committed to universal education. In their writing, however, that commitment manifests itself in an approach to teaching and learning that many educators share in this country, a view that insists that the classroom is a separate world of its own, in which teachers and students relate to one another undistracted by the classism, racism, and sexism that rage outside the classroom. Discursive hegemony of teachers over students is usually posed and justified in developmental terms—as cognitive deficits, emotional or intellectual immaturity, ignorance, and most recently, cultural literacy—any one of which would legitimate asymmetrical relationships between its knowing subjects, teachers, and its unknowing subjects, students. To the credit of the teachers who participated in this study, none took the usual recourse of justifying their discursive control by focusing on errors in spelling, grammar, and mechanics that are indubitably there and that make reading the literacy letters as difficult as reading Lacan, Derrida, Foucault, or Althusser. Yet the teachers frenetically protected educational discourse from class, and in their respective refusals to admit class concerns into the letters, they first distanced and then alienated themselves from their correspondents.

While educational discourse defends its privileged subjects against resistance, against the violence that Dora narrates, against Esther's lesson in economics, and even against Pat's much celebrated mother, the linguistic and rhetorical uneasiness with which these attempts to articulate working-class subjectivity were met suggests that the class-free discourse that seems immutable in theory is, in practice, a source of some ambivalence for the teachers in this study. What is immediately challenged by the narratives is the rhetorical practice in which the privileges of one subject—to tell stories or decide what the topic is—materially diminish the rights of other subjects. What is ultimately challenged is the ideology that class, and by extension race and gender differences, are present in American society but absent from American classrooms. If that's true, it is only true because the representation by students of those concerns inside educational discourse goes unarticulated by teachers.

To teach is to authorize the subjects of educational discourse. We have all been faced with the choice that Pat gave Ellen. To say no to writing is to say no to differences that matter to those students who live on the margins of an educational discourse that insists that they articulate themselves as the subjects teachers represent, or not at all. To say yes to writing is to say yes to those alternative subjectivities that Dora, Esther, and Pat represent in their writing and that are left unchallenged when unarticulated by Don, Rita, and Ellen. In this instance, teachers and students alike lose the opportunity to question the extent to which class figures in any individual's rendering of a unified self. Resistance inside educational discourse is then a practice in cooperative articulation on the part of students and teachers who actively seek to construct and understand the differences as well as similarities between their respective subject positions.

WORKS CITED

Bartholomae, David. "Inventing the University." *When a Writer Can't Write.* Ed. Mike Rose. New York: Guilford P, 1985. 134-65.

_____. "The Study of Error." *College Composition and Communication* 31 (1980): 253-69.

Bourdieu, Pierre, and Jean-Claude Passeron. *Reproduction in Education, Society and Culture*. Beverly Hills: Sage, 1977.

Brodkey, Linda. "Tropics of Literacy." *Journal of Education* 168 (1986): 47-54.

Crowley, Sharon. "writing and Writing." *Writing and Reading Differently: Deconstruction and the Teaching of Composition and Literature*. Ed. Douglas Atkins and Michael L. Johnson. Lawrence: UP of Kansas, 1985. 93-100.

Fine, Michelle. "Silencing in the Public Schools." *Language Arts* 64 (1987): 157-74.

Foucault, Michel. "The Discourse on Language." *The Archeology of Knowledge*. New York: Harper & Row, 1976. 215-37.

Hall, Stuart. "On Postmodernism and Articulation: An Interview with Stuart Hall." Ed. Larry Grossberg. *Journal of Communication Inquiry* 10 (1986): 45-60.

Labov, William. *Language in the Inner City: Studies in the Black English Vernacular*. Philadelphia: U of Pennsylvania P, 1972.

Perl, Sandra. "The Composing Processes of Unskilled College Writers." *Research in the Teaching of English* 13 (1979): 317-36.

Pratt, Mary Louise. *Toward a Speech Act Theory of Literary Discourse*. Bloomington: Indiana UP, 1977.

Shaughnessy, Mina. *Errors and Expectations: A Guide for the Teacher of Basic Writing*. New York: Oxford UP, 1977.

Stubbs, Michael. *Language, Schools and Classrooms*. London: Methuen, 1976.

Williams, Raymond. *Marxism and Literature*. New York: Oxford UP, 1977.

Diversity, Ideology, and Teaching Writing

Maxine Hairston

WHERE WE HAVE COME FROM

In 1985, when I was chair of CCCC, as my chair's address I gave what might be called my own State of the Profession Report. On the whole it was a positive report. I rejoiced in the progress we had made in the previous fifteen years in establishing our work as a discipline and I pointed out that we were creating a new paradigm for the teaching of writing, one that focused on process and on writing as a way of learning. I asserted that we teach writing for its own sake, as a primary intellectual activity that is at the heart of a college education. I insisted that writing courses must not be viewed as service courses. Writing courses, especially required freshman courses, should not be *for* anything or *about* anything other than writing itself, and how one uses it to learn and think and communicate.

I also warned in my Chair's address that if we hoped to flourish as a profession, we would have to establish our psychological and intellectual independence from the literary critics who are at the center of power in most English departments; that we could not develop our potential and become fully autonomous scholars and teachers as long as we allowed our sense of self worth to depend on the approval of those who define English departments as departments of literary criticism.

We've continued to make important strides since 1985. We have more graduate programs in rhetoric and composition, more tenure track positions

Reprinted from *College Composition and Communication* 43.2 (May 1992): 179–95. Used with permission.

in composition created each year, more and larger conferences, and so many new journals that one can scarcely keep up with them. In those years, I've stayed optimistic about the profession and gratified by the role I've played in its growth.

WHERE WE SEEM TO BE HEADING

Now, however, I see a new model emerging for freshman writing programs, a model that disturbs me greatly. It's a model that puts dogma before diversity, politics before craft, ideology before critical thinking, and the social goals of the teacher before the educational needs of the student. It's a regressive model that undermines the progress we've made in teaching writing, one that threatens to silence student voices and jeopardize the process-oriented, low-risk, student-centered classroom we've worked so hard to establish as the norm. It's a model that doesn't take freshman English seriously in its own right but conceives of it as a tool, something to be used. The new model envisions required writing courses as vehicles for social reform rather than as student-centered workshops designed to build students' confidence and competence as writers. It is a vision that echoes that old patronizing rationalization we've heard so many times before: students don't have anything to write about so we have to give them topics. Those topics used to be literary; now they're political.

I don't suggest that all or even most freshman writing courses are turning this way. I have to believe that most writing teachers have too much common sense and are too concerned with their students' growth as writers to buy into this new philosophy. Nevertheless, everywhere I turn I find composition faculty, both leaders in the profession and new voices, asserting that they have not only the right, but the duty, to put ideology and radical politics at the center of their teaching.

Here are four revealing quotations from recent publications. For instance, here is James Laditka in the *Journal of Advanced Composition*:

> All teaching supposes ideology; there simply is no value free pedagogy. For these reasons, my paradigm of composition is changing to one of critical literacy, a literacy of political consciousness and social action. (361)

Here is Charles Paine in a lead article in *College English*:

> Teachers need to recognize that methodology alone will not ensure radical visions of the world. An appropriate course content is necessary as well. . . .

698

[E]quality and democracy are not transcendent values that inevitably emerge when one learns to seek the truth through critical thinking. Rather, if those are the desired values, the teacher must recognize that he or she must influence (perhaps manipulate is the more accurate word) students' values through charisma or power—he or she must accept the role as manipulator. Therefore it is of course reasonable to try to inculcate into our students the conviction that the dominant order is repressive. (563-64)

Here is Patricia Bizzell:

We must help our students . . . to engage in a rhetorical process that can collectively generate . . . knowledge and beliefs to displace the repressive ideologies an unjust social order would prescribe. . . . I suggest that we must be forthright in avowing the ideologies that motivate our teaching and research. For instance, [in an experimental composition course he teaches at Purdue] James Berlin might stop trying to be value-neutral and anti-authoritarian in the classroom. Berlin tells his students he is a Marxist but disavows any intention of persuading them to his point of view. Instead, he might openly state that this course aims to promote values of sexual equality and left-oriented labor relations and that this course will challenge students' values insofar as they conflict with these aims. Berlin and his colleagues might openly exert their authority as teachers to try to persuade students to agree with their values instead of pretending that they are merely investigating the nature of sexism and capitalism and leaving students to draw their own conclusions. (670)

Here is C. H. Knoblauch:

We are, ultimately, compelled to choose, to make, express, and act upon our commitments, to denounce the world, as Freire says, and above all oppression and whatever arguments have been called upon to validate it. Moreover our speech may well have to be boldly denunciative at times if it is to affect its hearers in the midst of their intellectual and political comfort. . . . We are obliged to announce ourselves so that, through the very process of self-assertion, we grow more conscious of our axioms. . . . The quality of our lives as teachers depends on our willingness to discover through struggle ever more fruitful means of doing our work. The quality of our students' lives depends on [it]. ("Rhetorical" 139)

These quotations do not represent just a few instances that I ferreted out to suit my thesis; you will find similar sentiments if you leaf through only a few of the recent issues of *College English, Rhetoric Review, College Composition and Communication, Journal of Advanced Composition, Focuses,* and others. Some names that you might look for in addition to the ones I've quoted are James Berlin, John Trimbur, Lester Faigley, Richard Ohmann, and Linda Brodkey. At least forty percent of the essays in *The Right to Literacy*, the proceedings of a 1988 conference sponsored by the Modern Language Association in Columbus, Ohio, echo such sentiments, and a glance at the program for the 1991 CCCC convention would confirm how popular such ideas were among the speakers. For that same convention, the publisher HarperCollins sponsored a contest to award grants to graduate students to attend; the topic they were asked to write on was "Describe the kind of freshman writing course you would design." Nearly all of the contestants described a politically-focused course. All ten essays in the 1991 MLA publication *Contending with Words* recommend turning writing courses in this direction.

Distressingly often, those who advocate such courses show open contempt for their students' values, preferences, or interests. For example, in an article in *College English*, Ronald Strickland says, "The teacher can best facilitate the production of knowledge by adapting a confrontational stance toward the student. . . . Above all, the teacher should avoid the pretense of detachment, objectivity, and autonomy." He admits that his position "conflicts with the expectations of some students [and] these students make it difficult for me to pursue my political/intellectual agenda" (293).

David Bleich dismisses his students' resistance with equal ease:

> There is reason to think that students want to write about what they say they don't want to write about. They want a chance to write about racism, classism, and homophobia even though it makes them uncomfortable. But what I think makes them most uncomfortable is to surrender the paradigm of individualism and to see that paradigm in its sexist dimensions.

He cites his students' religion as one of the chief obstacles to their enlightenment:

> Religious views collaborate with the ideology of individualism and with sexism to censor the full capability of what people can say and write. . . . By "religious values" I mean belief in the savability of the individual human soul. The ideal of the nuclear family, as opposed to the extended or communal family, permits the overvaluation of the individual child and the individual soul. (167)

And here is Dale Bauer in an article from *College English*:

> I would argue that political commitment—especially feminist commitment—is a legitimate classroom strategy and rhetorical imperative. The

feminist agenda offers a goal toward our students' conversions to emancipatory critical action. . . . In teaching identification and teaching feminism, I overcome a vehement insistence on pluralistic relativism or on individualism.

Bauer acknowledges that her students resist her political agenda. She says,

There is an often overwhelming insistence on individualism and isolation . . . [They] labor at developing a critical distance to avoid participating in "the dialectic of resistance and identification."

Bauer quotes one of her students as saying in an evaluation,

"The teacher consistently channels class discussions around feminism and does not spend time discussing the comments that oppose her beliefs. In fact, she usually twists them around to support her beliefs."

Bauer dismisses such objections, however, claiming she has to accept her authority as rhetor because "anything less ends up being an expressivist model, one which reinforces . . . the dominant patriarchal culture" (389). Often these advocates are contemptuous of other teachers' approaches to teaching or the goals those teachers set for their students. For example, Lester Faigley assails the advice given about writing a job application letter in a standard business writing text:

In the terms of [the Marxist philosopher] Althusser, [the applicant who writes such a letter] has voluntarily assented his subjectivity within the dominant ideology and thus has reaffirmed relations of power. By presenting himself as a commodity rather than as a person, he has not only made an initial gesture of subservience like a dog presenting its neck, but he has also signaled his willingness to continue to be subservient. (251)

In discussing Linda Flower's cognitive, problem-solving approach to teaching writing, James Berlin calls it, "the rationalization of economic activity. The pursuit of self-evident and unquestioned goals in the composing process parallels the pursuit of self-evident and unquestioned profit-making goals in the corporate market place." (What a facile non-logical leap!) He continues in the same article to deride Donald Murray's and Peter Elbow's approaches to writing because of their focus on the individual, saying

Expressionist rhetoric is inherently and debilitatingly divisive of political protest. . . . Beyond that, expressionist rhetoric is easily co-opted by the very capitalist forces it opposes. After all, this rhetoric can be used to reinforce the entrepreneurial virtues capitalism values most: individualism, private initiative, the confidence for risk taking, the right to be contentious with authority (especially the state). (491)

HOW WE GOT HERE

But how did all this happen? Why has the cultural left suddenly claimed writing courses as their political territory?

There's no simple answer, of course. Major issues about social change and national priorities are involved, and I cannot digress into those concerns in this essay. But my first response is, "You see what happens when we allow writing programs to be run by English departments?" I'm convinced that the push to change freshman composition into a political platform for the teacher has come about primarily because the course is housed in English departments.

As the linguistics scholar John Searle pointed out in a detailed and informative article in *The New York Review of Books*, the recent surge of the cultural left on major American campuses has centered almost entirely in English departments. He says,

> The most congenial home left for Marxism, now that it has been largely discredited as a theory of economics and politics, is in departments of literary criticism. And [because] many professors of literature no longer care about literature in ways that seemed satisfactory to earlier generations . . . they teach it as a means of achieving left-wing political goals or as an occasion for exercises in deconstruction, etc. (38)

I theorize that the critical literary theories of deconstruction, poststructuralism (both declining by now), and Marxist critical theory have trickled down to the lower floors of English departments where freshman English dwells. Just as they have been losing their impact with faculty above stairs, they have taken fresh root with those dwelling below.

Deconstructionists claim that the privileged texts of the canon are only reflections of power relations and the dominant class structures of their eras. Thus the job of the literary critic is to dissect Shakespeare or Milton or Eliot or Joyce to show how language reflects and supports the "cultural hegemony" of the time. They also claim that all meaning is indeterminate and socially constructed; there is no objective reality nor truth that can be agreed on.

Marxist criticism echoes these sentiments. For example, Ronald Strickland writes in *College English*:

> Marxist critics have demonstrated that conventional literary studies have been more complicitous . . . than any other academic discipline in the reproduction of the dominant ideology. . . . Traditional English studies helps to maintain liberal humanism through its emphasis on authorial genius. . . . [Thus] there is a political imperative to resist the privileging of individualism in this practice, for, as Terry Eagleton has demonstrated, it amounts to a form of coercion in the interests of conservative, elitist politics. (293)

All these claims strike me as silly, simplistic, and quite undemonstrable. Nevertheless, if one endorses these intellectual positions—and sympathizes with the politics behind them—it's easy to go to the next step and equate conventional writing instruction with conventional literary studies. Then one can say that because standard English is the dialect of the dominant class, writing instruction that tries to help students master that dialect merely reinforces the status quo and serves the interest of the dominant class. An instructor who wants to teach students to write clearly becomes part of a capitalistic plot to control the workforce. What nonsense! It seems to me that one could argue with more force that the instructor who fails to help students master the standard dialect conspires against the working class.

How easy for theorists who, by the nature of the discipline they have chosen, already have a facile command of the prestige dialect to denigrate teaching that dialect to students. Have they asked those students what *they* want to learn? And how easy for these same theorists to set up straw men arguments that attack a mechanistic, structuralist, literature-based model of composition and call it "conservative, regressive, deterministic, and elitist" (Knoblauch, "Literacy" 76) when they know such models have long been discredited in the professional literature.

But I think this is what happens when composition theorists remain psychologically tied to the English departments that are their base. Partly out of genuine interest, I'm sure, but also out of a need to belong to and be approved by the power structure, they immerse themselves in currently fashionable critical theories, read the authors that are chic—Foucault, Bahktin, Giroux, Eagleton, and Cixous, for example—then look for ways those theories can be incorporated into their own specialty, teaching writing.

This, according to Searle's article, means that they subscribe to a view of the role of the humanities in universities that is

> . . . based on two primary assumptions. 1. They believe that Western civilization in general, and the United States in particular, are in large part oppressive, patriarchal, hegemonic, and in need of replacement or at least transformation. 2. The primary function of teaching the humanities is

political; they [the cultural left] do not really believe the humanities are valuable in their own right except as a means of achieving social transformation. (38)

Searle goes on to point out that this debate about what is "hegemonic," "patriarchal," or "exclusionary" has been focused almost entirely in English departments.

I find it hard to believe that most English professors seriously hold these opinions or that they are ready to jettison their lifelong commitment to the humanities, but evidently significant numbers do. News releases and many professional articles suggest that these attitudes have permeated the Modern Language Association, and the associate chair of the English Department at the University of Texas recently said in a colloquium of the College of Liberal Arts that the "mission of English departments is always to oppose the dominant culture."

For those who agree, how natural to turn to the freshman writing courses. With a huge captive enrollment of largely unsophisticated students, what a fertile field to cultivate to bring about political and social change. Rhetoric scholars who go along will also get new respect now that they have joined the ideological fray and formed alliances with literature faculty who have been transforming their own courses.

Composition faculty who support such change can bring fresh respectability and attention to those often despised introductory English courses now that they can be used for "higher purposes." They may even find some regular faculty who will volunteer to teach freshman writing when they can use it for a political forum. Five years ago the regular faculty in our department at Texas tried to get rid of freshman English altogether by having it taught entirely in extension or at the local community college; this past year, many of those who had previously advocated abandoning the course were in the forefront of the battle to turn it into a course about racism and sexism. Now the course was suddenly worth their time.

The opportunity to make freshman English a vehicle for such social crusades is particularly rich: in many universities, graduate students in English teach virtually all of the sections, graduate students who are already steeped in post-structuralism and deconstruction theory, in the works of Foucault, Raymond Williams, Terry Eagleton, and Stanley Fish, and in feminist theory. Too often they haven't been well trained in how to teach writing and are at a loss about what they should be doing with their students. How easy then to focus the course on their own interests, which are often highly political. Unfortunately, when they try to teach an introductory composition course by concentrating on issues rather than on craft and critical thinking, large numbers of their students end up feeling confused, angry—and cheated.

I also believe that two major social forces outside the liberal arts are contributing to creating the environment that has given rise to this new model. The first is the tremendous increase in diversity of our student population, especially in states like California and Texas and in all our major cities. With changing demographics, we face an ethnic and social mix of students in our classes that previews for us what our institutions are going to be like in the year 2000. These students bring with them a kaleidoscope of experiences, values, dialects, and cultural backgrounds that we want to respond to positively and productively, using every resource we can to help them adapt to the academic world and become active participants in it. The code words for our attempts to build the kind of inclusive curriculum that we need have become "multiculturalism" and "cultural diversity." They're good terms, of course. Any informed and concerned educator endorses them in the abstract. The crucial question, however, is how one finds concrete ways to put them into practice, and also how one guards against their becoming what Richard Weaver called "god terms" that can be twisted to mean anything an ideologue wants them to mean.

As writing teachers, I think all of us are looking for ways to promote genuine diversity in our classes and yet keep two elements that are essential for any state-of-the-art composition course.

First, students' own writing must be the center of the course. Students need to write to find out how much they know and to gain confidence in their ability to express themselves effectively. They do not need to be assigned essays to read so they will have something to write about—they bring their subjects with them. The writing of others, except for that of their fellow students, should be supplementary, used to illustrate or reinforce.

Second, as writing teachers we should stay within our area of professional expertise: helping students to learn to write in order to learn, to explore, to communicate, to gain control over their lives. That's a large responsibility, and all that most of us can manage. We have no business getting into areas where we may have passion and conviction but no scholarly base from which to operate. When classes focus on complex issues such as racial discrimination, economic injustices, and inequities of class and gender, they should be taught by qualified faculty who have the depth of information and historical competence that such critical social issues warrant. Our society's deep and tangled cultural conflicts can neither be explained nor resolved by simplistic ideological formulas.

But one can run a culturally diverse writing course without sacrificing any of its integrity as a writing course. Any writing course, required or not, can be wonderfully diverse, an exciting experience in which people of different cultures and experience learn about difference first-hand. More about that shortly.

FORCES FROM OUTSIDE

The second major force I see at work is directly political. There's no question in my mind that this new radical stance of many composition faculty is in some ways a corollary of the angry response many intellectuals have to the excesses of right-wing, conservative forces that have dominated American politics for the past decade. Faculty in the liberal arts tend to be liberals who are concerned about social problems and dislike the trends we've seen in cutting funds for human services and for education. We're sick over the condition of our country: one child in five living in poverty; one person in eight hungry; 33 million people with no health insurance; a scandalous infant mortality rate; hundreds of thousands homeless. Yet we see our government spend billions on a dubious war. No need to go on—we all know the terrible inequities and contradictions of our society.

As educators of good will, we shouldn't even have to mention our anger about racism and sexism in our society—that's a given, as is our commitment to work to overcome it. I, for one, refuse to be put on the defensive on such matters of personal conscience or to be silenced by the fear that someone will pin a label on me if I don't share his or her vision of the world or agree on how to improve it. Ad hominem arguments don't impress me.

But it's entirely understandable that academics who are traditional liberals sympathize at first with those who preach reform, even when they sound more radical than we'd like. On the surface we share common ground: we'd all like to bring about a fairer, more compassionate society. But I fear that we are in real danger of being co-opted by the radical left, coerced into acquiescing to methods that we abhor because, in the abstract, we have some mutual goals. Some faculty may also fear being labeled "right-wing" if they oppose programs that are represented as being "liberating." But we shouldn't be duped. Authoritarian methods are still authoritarian methods, no matter in what cause they're invoked. And the current battle is *not* one between liberals and conservatives. Those who attempt to make it so—columnists like George Will—either do not understand the agenda of the cultural left, or they make the association in order to discredit liberal goals. Make no mistake—those on the cultural left are not in the least liberal; in fact, they despise liberals as compromising humanists. They're happy, however, to stir up traditional liberal guilt and use it for their purposes.

706

WHAT'S WRONG WITH THEIR GOALS?

Why do I object so strongly to the agenda that these self-styled radical teachers want to establish for composition courses and freshman English in particular?

First, I vigorously object to the contention that they have a right—even a *duty*—to use their classrooms as platforms for their own political views. Such claims violate all academic traditions about the university being a forum for the free exchange of ideas, a place where students can examine different points of view in an atmosphere of honest and open discussion, and, in the process, learn to think critically. It is a teacher's obligation to encourage diversity and exploration, but diversity and ideology will not flourish together. By definition, they're incompatible.

By the logic of the cultural left, any teacher should be free to use his or her classroom to promote any ideology. Why not facism? Racial superiority? Religious fundamentalism? Anti-abortion beliefs? Can't any professor claim the right to indoctrinate students simply because he or she is right? The argument is no different from that of any true believers who are convinced that they own the truth and thus have the right to force it on others. My colleague John Ruszkiewicz compares them to Milton's "the new forcers of conscience." We don't have to look far to see how frightening such arguments really are. They represent precisely the kind of thinking that leads to "reeducation camps" in totalitarian governments, to putting art in the service of propaganda, and to making education always the instrument of the state.

Those who want to bring their ideology into the classroom argue that since any classroom is necessarily political, the teacher might as well make it openly political and ideological. He or she should be direct and honest about his or her political beliefs; then the students will know where they stand and everyone can talk freely. Is any experienced teacher really so naive as to believe that? Such claims are no more than self-serving rationalizations that allow a professor total freedom to indulge personal prejudices and avoid any responsibility to be fair. By the same reasoning, couldn't one claim that since we know it is impossible to find absolute, objective truths, we might just as well abandon the search for truth and settle for opinion, superstition and conjecture? Would that advance our students' education? Couldn't one also say that since one can never be completely fair with one's children, one might as well quit trying and freely indulge one's biases and favoritism? It's astonishing that people who purport to be scholars can make such specious arguments.

The real political truth about classrooms is that the teacher has all the power; she sets the agenda, she controls the discussion, and she gives the grades. She also knows more and can argue more skillfully. Such a situation is ripe for intellectual intimidation, especially in required freshman composition classes, and although I think it is unprofessional for teachers to bring their ideology into any classroom, it is those freshman courses that I am especially concerned about.

THE THREAT TO FRESHMAN COURSES

I believe that the movement to make freshman English into courses in which students must write about specific social issues threatens all the gains we have made in teaching writing in the last fifteen years. I also think that rather than promoting diversity and a genuine multicultural environment, such courses actually work against those goals. Here are my reasons.

First, we know that students develop best as writers when they can write about something they care about and want to know more about. Only then will they be motivated to invest real effort in their work; only then can we hope they will avoid the canned, clichéd prose that neither they nor we take seriously. Few students, however, will do their best when they are compelled to write on a topic they perceive as politically charged and about which they feel uninformed, no matter how thought-provoking and important the instructor assumes that topic to be. If freshmen choose to write about issues involving race, class, and gender, that's fine. They should have every encouragement. I believe all topics in a writing class should be serious ones that push students to think and to say something substantial. But the topic should be their choice, a careful and thoughtful choice, to be sure, but not what someone else thinks is good for them.

Second, we know that young writers develop best as writers when teachers are able to create a low-risk environment that encourages students to take chances. We also know that novice writers can virtually freeze in the writing classroom when they see it as an extremely high-risk situation. Apprehensive about their grades in this new college situation, they nervously test their teachers to see what is expected of them, and they venture opinions only timidly. It is always hard to get students to write seriously and honestly, but when they find themselves in a classroom where they suspect there is a correct way to think, they are likely to take refuge in generalities and responses that please the teacher. Such fake discourse is a kind of silence, the silence we have so often deplored when it is forced on the disadvantaged. But when we stifle creative impulse and make students opt for survival over honesty, we have done the same thing. In too many instances, the first lesson they will learn as college students is that hypocrisy pays—so don't try to think for yourself.

My third objection to injecting prescribed political content into a required freshman course is that such action severely limits freedom of expression for both students and instructors. In my view, the freshman course on racism and sexism proposed at the University of Texas at Austin in the spring of 1990 would have enforced conformity in both directions. Students would have had no choice of what to write about, and the instructors who were graduate students would have had no choice about what to teach. Even if they felt unqualified to teach the material—and many did—or believed that the prescribed curriculum would work against their students' learning to write—and many did—they had to conform to a syllabus that contradicted their professional judgment and, often, their personal feelings. That course has since been revised and the freshman course in place since the fall of 1991 offers choices to both students and teachers.

NEW POSSIBILITIES FOR FRESHMAN COURSES

I believe we can make freshman English—or any other writing course—a truly multicultural course that gives students the opportunity to develop their critical and creative abilities and do it in an intellectually and ethically responsible context that preserves the heart of what we have learned about teaching writing in the past two decades.

First, I resist the effort to put any specific multicultural content at the center of a writing course, particularly a freshman course, and particularly a required course. Multicultural issues are too complex and diverse to be dealt with fully and responsibly in an English course, much less a course in which the focus should be on writing, not reading. Too often attempts to focus on such issues encourage stereotyping and superficial thinking. For instance, what English teacher wouldn't feel presumptuous and foolish trying to introduce Asian culture into a course when he or she can quickly think of at least ten different Asian cultures, all of which differ from each other drastically in important ways? What about Hispanic culture? Can the teacher who knows something of Mexico generalize about traditions of other Hispanic cultures? Can anyone teach the "black experience"? Do black men and women whose forebears come from Haiti and Nigeria and Jamaica share the experiences and heritage of African-Americans? Is Southern culture a valid topic for study? Many people think so. What about Jewish culture? But I don't need to labor the point. I only want to highlight the

709

concerns any of us should have when the push for so-called multicultural courses threatens the integrity of our discipline and the quality of our teaching.

I believe, however, that we can create a culturally inclusive curriculum in our writing classes by focusing on the experiences of our students. They are our greatest multicultural resource, one that is authentic, rich, and truly diverse. Every student brings to class a picture of the world in his or her mind that is constructed out of his or her cultural background and unique and complex experience. As writing teachers, we can help students articulate and understand that experience, but we also have the important job of helping every writer to understand that each of us sees the world through our own particular lens, one shaped by unique experiences. In order to communicate with others, we must learn to see through their lenses as well as try to explain to them what we see through ours. In an interactive classroom where students collaborate with other writers, this process of decentering so one can understand the "other" can foster genuine multicultural growth.

Imagine, for example, the breadth of experience and range of difference students would be exposed to in a class made up of students I have had in recent years.

One student would be from Malawi. The ivory bracelet he wears was put on his arm at birth and cannot be removed; he writes about his tribal legends. Another student is a young Vietnamese man who came to America when he was eight; he writes about the fear he felt his first day in an American school because there were no walls to keep out bullets. Another is a young Greek woman whose parents brought her to America to escape poverty; she writes about her first conscious brush with sexism in the Greek orthodox church. One student is the son of illegal aliens who followed the harvests in Texas; he writes with passion about the need for young Hispanics to get their education. A young black man writes about college basketball, a culture about which he is highly knowledgeable. A young man from the Texas panhandle writes about the traditions of cowboy boots and the ethical dimensions of barbed wire fences. Another young black man writes about the conflicts he feels between what he is learning in astronomy, a subject that fascinates him, and the teachings of his church.

It's worth noting here that religion plays an important role in the lives of many of our students—and many of us, I'm sure—but it's a dimension almost never mentioned by those who talk about cultural diversity and difference. In most classrooms in which there is an obvious political agenda, students—even graduate students—are very reluctant to reveal their religious beliefs, sensing they may get a hostile reception. And with reason—remember the quotation from David Bleich. But a teacher who believes in diversity must pay attention to and respect students with deep religious convictions, not force them too into silence.

Real diversity emerges from the students themselves and flourishes in a collaborative classroom in which they work together to develop their ideas and test them out on each other. They can discuss and examine their experiences, their assumptions, their values, and their questions. They can tell their stories to each other in a nurturant writing community. As they are increasingly exposed to the unique views and experiences of others, they will begin to appreciate differences and understand the rich tapestry of cultures that their individual stories make up. But they will also see unified motifs and common human concerns in that tapestry.

In this kind of classroom not all writing should be personal, expressive writing. Students need a broader range of discourse as their introduction to writing in college. The teacher can easily design the kinds of writing assignments that involve argument and exposition and suggest options that encourage cross-cultural awareness. For instance, some suggested themes for development might be these: family or community rituals; power relationships at all levels; the student's role in his or her family or group; their roles as men and women; the myths they live by; cultural tensions within groups. There are dozens more rich possibilities that could be worked out with the cooperation of colleagues in other departments and within the class itself.

The strength of all the themes I've mentioned is that they're both individual and communal, giving students the opportunity to write something unique to them as individuals yet something that will resonate with others in their writing community. The beauty of such an approach is that it's *organic*. It grows out of resources available in each classroom, and it allows students to make choices, then discover more about others and themselves through those choices. This approach makes the teacher a midwife, an agent for change rather than a transmitter of fixed knowledge. It promotes a student-centered classroom in which the teacher doesn't assume, as our would-be forcers of conscience do, that he or she owns the truth. Rather the students bring their own truths, and the teacher's role is to nurture change and growth as students encounter individual differences. Gradually their truths will change, but so will ours because in such a classroom one continually learns from one's students.

This is the kind of freshman English class from which students can emerge with confidence in their ability to think, to generate ideas, and to present themselves effectively to the university and the community. It is a class built on the scholarship, research, and experience that has enabled us to achieve so much growth in our profession in the last fifteen years. It is the kind of classroom we can be proud of as a discipline. I don't think we necessarily have to take freshman English out of English departments in order to establish this model, but we do have to assert our authority as writing professionals within our departments and fiercely resist letting freshman English be used for anyone else's goals. We must hold on to the gains we have made and teach writing in the ways we know best. Above all, we must teach it for the *students*' benefit, not in the service of politics or anything else.

Freshman English is a course particularly vulnerable to takeover because English departments in so many universities and colleges refuse to take it seriously and thus don't pay much attention to what happens in it. They can wake up, however, to find that some political zealots take the course very seriously indeed and will gladly put it to their own uses. The scores of us who have been studying, writing, speaking, and publishing for two decades to make freshman English the solid intellectual enterprise that it now is must speak out to protect it from this kind of exploitation. It is time to resist, time to speak up, time to reclaim freshman composition from those who want to politicize it.

What is at stake is control of a vital element in our students' education by a radical few. We can't afford to let that control stand.

WORKS CITED

Bauer, Dale. "The Other 'F' Word: Feminist in the Classroom." *College English* 52 (Apr. 1990): 385-96.

Berlin, James A. "Rhetoric and Ideology in the Writing Class." *College English* 50 (Sep. 1988): 477-94.

Bizzell, Patricia. "Beyond Anti-Foundationalism to Rhetorical Authority: Problems in Defining 'Cultural Literacy.' " *College English* 52 (Oct. 1990): 661-75.

Bleich, David. "Literacy and Citizenship: Resisting Social Issues." Lunsford, Moglen, and Slevin 163-69.

Faigley, Lester. "The Study of Writing and the Study of Language." *Rhetoric Review* 7 (Spring 1989): 240-56.

Harkin, Patricia, and John Schilb. *Contending with Words: Composition and Rhetoric in a Postmodern Age.* New York: MLA, 1991.

Knoblauch, C. H. "Literacy and the Politics of Education." Lunsford, Moglen, and Slevin 74-80.

———. "Rhetorical Constructions: Dialogue and Commitment." *College English* 50 (Feb. 1988): 125-40.

Laditka, James N. "Semiology, Ideology, Praxis: Responsible Authority in the Composition Classroom." *Journal of Advanced Composition* 10.2 (Fall 1990): 357-73.

Lunsford, Andrea A., Helen Moglen, and James Slevin, eds. *The Right to Literacy.* New York: MLA and NCTE, 1990.

Paine, Charles. "Relativism, Radical Pedagogy, and the Ideology of Paralysis." *College English* 51 (Oct. 1989): 557-70.

Searle, John. "The Storm Over the University." Rev. of *Tenured Radicals*, by Roger Kimball; *The Politics of Liberal Education*, ed. by Darryl L. Gless and Barbara Hernstein Smith; and *The Voice of Liberal Learning: Michael Oakeshott on Education*, ed. by Timothy Fuller. *The New York Review of Books* 6 Dec. 1990: 34-42.

Strickland, Ronald. "Confrontational Pedagogy and Traditional Literary Studies." *College English* 52 (Mar. 1990): 291-300.

Weaver, Richard M. *The Ethics of Rhetoric.* Chicago: Henry Regnery, 1953.

SECTION SIX

Continuing the Conversation

The 1990s find composition studies again reevaluating itself—asking important questions with which to continue the conversation. Linda Flower asks if the turn to the social necessarily has to mean a turn away from cognitive studies. Paul Matsuda asks if we've ignored those students in our classrooms for whom English is not their primary language. Ellen Cushman asks how we can claim a turn to the social without going out into society by way of service learning. Chris Anson asks about the impact of technology on composition studies. Berlin recasts his essay on epistemological fields, asking for a consideration of the possible ideological foundations to our pedagogy. Villanueva's keynote address at the 1999 meeting of the Conference on College Composition and Communication is a call to continue the conversation, to broaden the parameters of the conversation. The conversation must continue.

Rhetoric and Ideology
in the Writing Class

JAMES BERLIN

The question of ideology has never been far from discussions of writing instruction in the modern American college. It is true that some rhetorics have denied their imbrication in ideology, doing so in the name of a disinterested scientism—as seen, for example, in various manifestations of current-traditional rhetoric. Most, however, have acknowledged the role of rhetoric in addressing competing discursive claims of value in the social, political, and cultural. This was particularly evident during the sixties and seventies, for example, as the writing classroom became one of the public arenas for considering such strongly contested issues as Vietnam, civil rights, and economic equality. More recently the discussion of the relation between ideology and rhetoric has taken a new turn. Ideology is here foregrounded and problematized in a way that situates rhetoric within ideology, rather than ideology within rhetoric. In other words, instead of rhetoric acting as the transcendental recorder or arbiter of competing ideological claims, rhetoric is regarded as always already ideological. This position means that any examination of a rhetoric must first consider the ways its very discursive structure can be read so as to favor one version of economic, social, and political arrangements over other versions. A rhetoric then considers competing claims in these three realms from an ideological perspective made possible both by its constitution and by its application—the dialectical interaction between the rhetoric as text and the interpretive practices brought to it. A rhetoric can never be innocent, can never be a disinterested arbiter of the ideological claims of others because it is always already serving

Reprinted from *College English* 50.5 (September 1988): 477–94. Used with permission.

certain ideological claims. This perspective on ideology and rhetoric will be discussed in greater detail later. Here I merely wish to note that it has been forwarded most recently by such figures as Patricia Bizzell, David Bartholomae, Greg Myers, Victor Vitanza, and John Schilb and John Clifford. I have also called upon it in my monograph on writing instruction in twentieth-century American colleges. I would like to bring the discussion I began there up to date, focusing on ideology in the three rhetorics that have emerged as most conspicuous in classroom practices today: the rhetorics of cognitive psychology, of expressionism, and of a category I will call social-epistemic.

Each of these rhetorics occupies a distinct position in its relation to ideology. From the perspective offered here, the rhetoric of cognitive psychology refuses the ideological question altogether, claiming for itself the transcendent neutrality of science. This rhetoric is nonetheless easily preempted by a particular ideological position now in ascendancy because it encourages discursive practices that are compatible with dominant economic, social, and political formations. Expressionistic rhetoric, on the other hand, has always openly admitted its ideological predilections, opposing itself in no uncertain terms to the scientism of current-traditional rhetoric and the ideology it encourages. This rhetoric is, however, open to appropriation by the very forces it opposes in contradiction to its best intentions. Social-epistemic rhetoric is an alternative that is self-consciously aware of its ideological stand, making the very question of ideology the center of classroom activities, and in so doing providing itself a defense against preemption and a strategy for self-criticism and self-correction. This third rhetoric is the one I am forwarding here, and it provides the ground of my critique of its alternatives. In other words, I am arguing from ideology, contending that no other kind of argument is possible—a position that must first be explained.

Ideology is a term of great instability. This is true whether it is taken up by the Left or Right—as demonstrated, for example, by Raymond Williams in *Keywords* and *Marxism and Literature* and by Jorge Larrain in *The Concept of Ideology*. It is thus necessary to indicate at the outset the formulation that will be followed in a given discussion. Here I will rely on Göran Therborn's usage in *The Ideology of Power and the Power of Ideology*. Therborn, a Marxist sociologist at the University of Lund, Sweden, calls on the discussion of ideology found in Louis Althusser and on the discussion of power in Michel Foucault. I have chosen Therborn's adaptation of Althusser rather than Althusser himself because Therborn so effectively counters the ideology-science distinction of his source, a stance in which ideology is always false consciousness while a particular version of Marxism is defined as its scientific alternative in possession of objective truth. For Therborn, no position can lay claim to absolute, timeless truth, because finally all formulations are historically specific, arising out of the material conditions of a particular time and place. Choices in the economic, social, political, and cultural are thus always based on discursive practices that are interpretations, not mere transcriptions of some external, verifiable certainty. The choice for Therborn then is never between scientific truth and ideology, but between competing ideologies, competing discursive interpretations. Finally, Therborn calls upon Foucault's "micropolitics of power" (7) without placing subjects within a seamless web of inescapable, wholly determinative power relations. For Therborn, power can be identified and resisted in a meaningful way.

Therborn offers an especially valuable discussion for rhetoricians because of his emphasis on the discursive and dialogic nature of ideology. In other words, Therborn insists that ideology is transmitted through language practices that are always the center of conflict and contest:

> The operation of ideology in human life basically involves the constitution and patterning of how human beings live their lives as conscious, reflecting initiators of acts in a structured, meaningful world. Ideology operates as discourse, addressing or, as Althusser puts it, interpellating human beings as subjects. (15)

Conceived from the perspective of rhetoric, ideology provides the language to define the subject (the self), other subjects, the material world, and the relation of all of these to each other. Ideology is thus inscribed in language practices, entering all features of our experience.

Ideology for Therborn addresses three questions: "What exists? What is good? What is possible?" The first deals with epistemology, as Therborn explains: "what exists, and its corollary, what does not exist: that is, who we are, what the world is, what nature, society, men and women are like. In this way we acquire a sense of identity, becoming conscious of what is real and true; the visibility of the world is thereby structured by the distribution of spotlights, shadows, and darkness." Ideology thus interpellates the subject in a manner that determines what is real and what is illusory, and, most important, what is experienced and what remains outside the field of phenomenological experience, regardless of its actual material existence. Ideology also provides the subject with standards for making ethical and aesthetic decisions: "*what is good*, right, just, beautiful, attractive, enjoyable, and its opposites. In this way our desires become structured and normalized." Ideology provides the structure of desire, indicating what we will long for and pursue.

Finally, ideology defines the limits of expectation: *"what is possible* and impossible; our sense of the mutability of our being-in-the-world and the consequences of change are hereby patterned, and our hopes, ambitions, and fears given shape" (18). This last is especially important since recognition of the existence of a condition (poverty, for example) and the desire for its change will go for nothing if ideology indicates that a change is simply not possible (the poor we have always with us). In other words, this last mode of interpellation is especially implicated in power relationships in a group or society, in deciding who has power and in determining what power can be expected to achieve.

Ideology always carries with it strong social endorsement, so that what we take to exist, to have value, and to be possible seems necessary, normal and inevitable—in the nature of things. Ideology also, as we have seen, always includes conceptions of how power should—again, in the nature of things—be distributed in a society. Power here means political force but covers as well social forces in everyday contacts. Power is an intrinsic part of ideology, defined and reinforced by it, determining, once again, who can act and what can be accomplished. These power relationships, furthermore, are inscribed in the discursive practices of daily experience—in the ways we use language and are used (interpellated) by it in ordinary parlance. Finally, it should be noted that ideology is always pluralistic, a given historical moment displaying a variety of competing ideologies and a given individual reflecting one or another permutation of these conflicts, although the overall effect of these permutations tends to support the hegemony of the dominant class.

COGNITIVE RHETORIC

Cognitive rhetoric might be considered the heir apparent of current-traditional rhetoric, the rhetoric that appeared in conjunction with the new American university system during the final quarter of the last century. As Richard Ohmann has recently reminded us, this university was a response to the vagaries of competitive capitalism, the recurrent cycles of boom and bust that characterized the nineteenth-century economy. The university was an important part of the strategy to control this economic instability. Its role was to provide a center for experts engaging in "scientific" research designed to establish a body of knowledge that would rationalize all features of production, making it more efficient, more manageable, and, of course, more profitable. These experts were also charged with preparing the managers who were to take this new body of practical knowledge into the marketplace.

The old nineteenth-century college had prepared an elite to assume its rightful place of leadership in church and state. The economic ideal outside the college was entirely separate, finding its fulfillment in the self-made, upwardly mobile entrepreneur who strikes it rich. The academic and the economic remained divided and discrete. In the new university, the two were joined as the path to success became a university degree in one of the new scientific specialties proven to be profitable in the world of industry and commerce. The new middle class of certified meritocrats had arrived. As I have indicated in my monograph on the nineteenth century, current-traditional rhetoric with its positivistic epistemology, its pretensions to scientific precision, and its managerial orientation was thoroughly compatible with the mission of this university.

Cognitive rhetoric has made similar claims to being scientific, although the method called upon is usually grounded in cognitive psychology. Janet Emig's *The Composing Processes of Twelfth Graders* (1971), for example, attempted an empirical examination of the way students compose, calling on the developmental psychology of Jean Piaget in guiding her observations. In studying the cognitive skills observed in the composing behavior of twelve high school students, Emig was convinced that she could arrive at an understanding of the entire rhetorical context—the role of reality, audience, purpose, and even language in the composing act. Richard Larson was equally ambitious as throughout the seventies he called upon the developmental scheme of Jerome Bruner (as well as other psychologists) in proposing a problem-solving approach to writing, once again focusing on cognitive structures in arriving at an understanding of how college students compose. James Moffett and James Britton used a similar approach in dealing with the writing of students in grade school. For cognitive rhetoric, the structures of the mind correspond in perfect harmony with the structures of the material world, the minds of the audience, and the units of language (see my *Rhetoric and Reality* for a fuller discussion of this history). This school has been the strongest proponent of addressing the "process" rather than the "product" of writing in the classroom—although other theories have also supported this position even as they put forward a different process. Today the cognitivists continue to be a strong force in composition studies. The leading experimental research in this area is found in the work of Linda Flower and John Hayes, and I would like to focus the discussion of the relation of ideology and cognitive rhetoric on their contribution.

There is no question that Flower considers her work to fall within the domain of science, admitting her debt to cognitive psychology (Hayes' area of specialization), which she describes as "a young field—a reaction, in part, against assumptions of behaviorism" (*Problem-Solving* vii). Her statements

about the composing process of writing, furthermore, are based on empirical findings, on "data-based" study, specifically the analysis of protocols
recording the writing choices of both experienced and inexperienced writers. This empirical study has revealed to Flower and Hayes—as reported in
"A Cognitive Process Theory of Writing"—that there are three elements involved in composing: the task environment, including such external constraints as the rhetorical problem and the text so far produced; the writer's
long-term memory, that is, the knowledge of the subject considered and the
knowledge of how to write; and the writing processes that go on in the
writer's mind. This last is, of course, of central importance to them, based as
it is on the invariable structures of the mind that operate in a rational, although not totally predictable, way.

The mental processes of writing fall into three stages: the planning
stage, further divided into generating, organizing, and goal setting; the translating stage, the point at which thoughts are put into words; and the reviewing stage, made up of evaluating and revising. This process is hierarchical,
meaning that "components of the process [are] imbedded within other components" ("A Cognitive Process" 375), and it is recursive, the stages repeating themselves, although in no predetermined order. In other words, the
elements of the process can be identified and their functions described, but
the order of their operation will vary from task to task and from individual to
individual, even though the practices of good writers will be very similar to
each other (for a rich critique, see Bizzell). The "keystone" of the cognitive
process theory, Flower and Hayes explain, is the discovery that writing is a
goal-directed process: "In the act of composing, writers create a hierarchical
network of goals and these in turn guide the writing process." Because of this
goal directedness, the protocols of good writers examined consistently "reveal a coherent underlying structure" ("A Cognitive Process" 377).

It is clear from this brief description that Flower and Hayes focus on the
individual mind, finding in the protocol reports evidence of cognitive structures in operation. Writing becomes, as Flower's textbook indicates, just another instance of "problem-solving processes people use every day," most
importantly the processes of experts, such as "master chess players, inven-
tors, successful scientists, business managers, and artists" (*Problem-Solving*
2-3). Flower's textbook says little about artists, however, focusing instead on
"real-world" writing. She has accordingly called upon the help of a colleague from the School of Industrial Management (vi), and she includes a
concern for consulting reports and proposals as well as ordinary academic
research reports—"the real world of college and work" (4). This focus on the
professional activity of experts is always conceived in personal and managerial terms: "In brief, the goal of this book is to help you gain more control of

722

your own composing process: to become more efficient as a writer and more effective with your readers" (2). And the emphasis is on self-made goals, "on your own goals as a writer, on what you want to do and say" (3).

As I said at the outset, the rhetoric of cognitive psychology refuses the ideological question, resting secure instead in its scientific examination of the composing process. It is possible, however, to see this rhetoric as being eminently suited to appropriation by the proponents of a particular ideological stance, a stance consistent with the modern college's commitment to preparing students for the world of corporate capitalism. And as we have seen above, the professional orientation of *Problem-Solving Strategies for Writing*—its preoccupation with "analytical writing" (4) in the "real world" of experts—renders it especially open to this appropriation.

For cognitive rhetoric, the real is the rational. As we observed above, for Flower and Hayes the most important features of composing are those which can be analyzed into discrete units and expressed in linear, hierarchical terms, however unpredictably recursive these terms may be. The mind is regarded as a set of structures that performs in a rational manner, adjusting and reordering functions in the service of the goals of the individual. The goals themselves are considered unexceptionally apparent in the very nature of things, immediately identifiable as worthy of pursuit. Nowhere, for example, do Flower and Hayes question the worth of the goals pursued by the manager, scientist, or writer. The business of cognitive psychology is to enable us to learn to think in a way that will realize goals, not deliberate about their value: "I have assumed that, whatever your goals, you are interested in discovering better ways to achieve them" (*Problem-Solving* 1). The world is correspondingly structured to foreground goals inherently worth pursuing—whether these are private or professional, in writing or in work. And the mind is happily structured to perceive these goals and, thanks to the proper cognitive development of the observer—usually an expert—to attain them. Obstacles to achieving these goals are labelled "problems," disruptions in the natural order, impediments that must be removed. The strategies to resolve these problems are called "heuristics," discovery procedures that "are the heart of problem solving" (36). Significantly, these heuristics are not themselves rational, are not linear and predictable—"they do not come with a guarantee" (37). They appear normally as unconscious, intuitive processes that problem solvers use without realizing it, but even when formulated for conscious application they are never foolproof. Heuristics are only as good or bad as the person using them, so that problem solving is finally the act of an individual performing in isolation, solitary and alone (see Brodkey). As Flower explains: "Good writers not only have a large repertory of powerful strategies, but they have sufficient self-awareness of their own process to draw on these alternative techniques as they need them. In other words, they guide their own creative process" (37). The community addressed enters the process only after problems are analyzed and solved, at which time the concern is "adapting your writing to the needs of the reader" (1). Furthermore, although the heuristics used in problem solving are not themselves rational, the discoveries made through them always conform to the mensurable nature of reality, displaying "an underlying hierarchical organization" (10) that reflects the rationality of the world. Finally, language is regarded as a system of rational signs that is compatible with the mind and the external world, enabling the "translating" or "transforming" of the non-verbal intellectual operations into the verbal. There is thus a beneficent correspondence between the structures of the mind, the structures of the world, the structures of the minds of the audience, and the structures of language.

This entire scheme can be seen as analogous to the instrumental method of the modern corporation, the place where members of the meritocratic middle class, the twenty percent or so of the work force of certified college graduates, make a handsome living managing a capitalist economy (see Braverman, ch. 18). Their work life is designed to turn goal-seeking and problem-solving behavior into profits. As we have seen in Flower, the rationalization of the writing process is specifically designated an extension of the rationalization of economic activity. The pursuit of self-evident and unquestioned goals in the composing process parallels the pursuit of self-evident and unquestioned profit-making goals in the corporate marketplace: "whatever your goals are, you are interested in achieving better ways to achieve them" (*Problem-Solving* 12). The purpose of writing is to create a commodified text (see Clines) that belongs to the individual and has exchange value—"problem solving turns composing into a goal-directed journey—writing my way to where I want to be" (4)—just as the end of corporate activity is to create a privately-owned profit. Furthermore, while all problem solvers use heuristic procedures—whether in solving hierarchically conceived writing problems or hierarchically conceived management problems—some are better at using them than are others. These individuals inevitably distinguish themselves, rise up the corporate ladder, and leave the less competent and less competitive behind. The class system is thus validated since it is clear that the rationality of the universe is more readily detected by a certain group of individuals. Cognitive psychologists specializing in childhood development can even isolate the environmental features of the children who will become excellent problem solvers, those destined to earn the highest grades in school, the highest college entrance scores, and, finally, the highest salaries. Middle class parents are thus led to begin the cultivation of their children's cognitive skills as soon as possible—even in utero—and of course there are no shortage of expert-designed commodities that can be purchased to aid in the activity. That the cognitive skills leading to success may be the product of the experiences of a particular social class rather than the perfecting of inherent mental structures, skills encouraged because they serve the interests of a ruling economic elite, is never considered in the "scientific" investigation of the mind.

Cognitive rhetoric can be seen from this perspective as compatible with the ideology of the meritocratic university described in Bowles and Gintis' *Schooling in Capitalist America.* Power in this system is relegated to university-certified experts, those individuals who have the cognitive skills and the training for problem solving. Since social, political, and cultural problems are, like the economic, the result of failures in rational goal-seeking behavior, these same experts are the best prepared to address these matters as well. Furthermore, the agreement of experts in addressing commonly-shared problems in the economic and political arenas is additional confirmation of their claim to power: all trained observers, after all, come to the same conclusions. Once again, the possibility that this consensus about what is good and possible is a product of class interest and class experience is never seriously entertained. Cognitive rhetoric, then, in its refusal of the ideological question leaves itself open to association with the reification of technocratic science characteristic of late capitalism, as discussed, for example, by Georg Lukács, Herbert Marcuse, and Jürgen Habermas (see Larrain, ch. 6). Certain structures of the material world, the mind, and language, and their correspondence with certain goals, problem-solving heuristics, and solutions in the economic, social, and political are regarded as inherent features of the universe, existing apart from human social intervention. The existent, the good, and the possible are inscribed in the very nature of things as indisputable scientific facts, rather than being seen as humanly devised social constructions always remaining open to discussion.

EXPRESSIONISTIC RHETORIC

Expressionistic rhetoric developed during the first two decades of the twentieth century and was especially prominent after World War I. Its earliest predecessor was the elitist rhetoric of liberal culture, a scheme arguing for writing as a gift of genius, an art accessible only to a few, and then requiring years of literary study. In expressionistic rhetoric, this gift is democratized, writing becoming an art of which all are capable. This rhetoric has usually been closely allied with theories of psychology that argued for the inherent goodness of the individual, a goodness distorted by excessive contact with others in groups and institutions. In this it is the descendant of Rousseau on the one hand and of the romantic recoil from the urban horrors created by nineteenth-century capitalism on the other. Left to our own devices, this position maintains, each of us would grow and mature in harmony. Unfortunately, hardly anyone is allowed this uninhibited development, and so the fallen state of society is both the cause and the effect of its own distortion, as well as the corrupter of its individual members. In the twenties, a bowdlerized version of Freud was called upon in support of this conception of human nature. More recently—during the sixties and after—the theories of such figures as Carl Rogers, Abraham Maslow, Eric Fromm, and even Carl Jung have been invoked in its support. (For a fuller discussion of the history and character of expressionistic rhetoric offered here, see my "Contemporary Composition," and *Rhetoric and Reality* 43-46, 73-81, 159-65).

For this rhetoric, the existent is located within the individual subject. While the reality of the material, the social, and the linguistic are never denied, they are considered significant only insofar as they serve the needs of the individual. All fulfill their true function only when being exploited in the interests of locating the individual's authentic nature. Writing can be seen as a paradigmatic instance of this activity. It is an art, a creative act in which the process—the discovery of the true self—is as important as the product—the self discovered and expressed. The individual's use of the not-self in discovering the self takes place in a specific way. The material world provides sensory images that can be used in order to explore the self, the sensations leading to the apprehending-source of all experience. More important, these sense impressions can be coupled with language to provide metaphors to express the experience of the self, an experience which transcends ordinary non-metaphoric language but can be suggested through original figures and tropes. This original language in turn can be studied by others to understand the self and can even awaken in readers the experience of their selves. Authentic self-expression can thus lead to authentic self-experience for both the writer and the reader. The most important measure of authenticity, of genuine self-discovery and self-revelation, furthermore, is the presence of originality in expression; and this is the case whether the writer is creating poetry or writing a business report. Discovering the true self in writing will simultaneously enable the individual to discover the truth of the situation which evoked the writing, a situation that, needless to say, must always be compatible with the development of the self, and this leads to the ideological dimension of the scheme.

Most proponents of expressionistic rhetoric during the sixties and seventies were unsparingly critical of the dominant social, political, and cultural practices of the time. The most extreme of these critics demanded that the writing classroom work explicitly toward liberating students from the shackles of a corrupt society. This is seen most vividly in the effort known as "composition as happening." From this perspective, the alienating and fragmenting experience of the authoritarian institutional setting can be resisted by providing students with concrete experiences that alter political consciousness through challenging official versions of reality. Writing in response to such activities as making collages and sculptures, listening to the same piece of music in different settings, and engaging in random and irrational acts in the classroom was to enable students to experience "structure in unstructure; a random series of ordered events; order in chaos; the logical illogicality of dreams" (Lutz 35). The aim was to encourage students to resist the "interpretations of experience embodied in the language of others [so as] to order their own experience" (Paull and Kligerman 150). This more extreme form of political activism in the classroom was harshly criticized by the moderate wing of the expressionist camp, and it is this group that eventually became dominant. The names of Ken Macrorie, Walker Gibson, William Coles, Jr., Donald Murray, and Peter Elbow were the most visible in this counter effort. Significantly, these figures continued the ideological critique of the dominant culture while avoiding the overt politicizing of the classroom. In discussing the ideological position they encouraged, a position that continues to characterize them today, I will focus on the work of Murray and Elbow, both of whom explicitly address the political in their work.

From this perspective, power within society ought always to be vested in the individual. In Elbow, for example, power is an abiding concern—apparent in the title to his recent textbook (*Writing With Power*), as well as in the opening pledge of his first to help students become "less helpless, both personally and politically" by enabling them to get "control over words" (*Writing Without Teachers* vii). This power is consistently defined in personal terms: "power comes from the words somehow fitting the *writer* (not necessarily the reader) . . . power comes from the words somehow fitting *what they are about*" (*Writing With Power* 280). Power is a product of a configuration involving the individual and her encounter with the world, and for both Murray and Elbow this is a function of realizing one's unique voice. Murray's discussion of the place of politics in the classroom is appropriately titled "Finding Your Own Voice: Teaching Composition in an Age of Dissent," and Elbow emphasizes, "If I want power, I've got to use *my* voice" (*Embracing Contraries* 202). This focus on the individual does not mean that no community is to be encouraged, as expressionists repeatedly acknowledge that communal arrangements must be made, that, in Elbow's words, "the less acceptable hunger for participation and merging is met" (98). The community's right to exist, however, stands only insofar as it serves all of its members as individuals. It is, after all, only the individual, acting alone and apart from others, who can determine the existent, the good, and the possible. For Murray, the student "must hear the contradictory counsel of his readers, so that he learns when to ignore his teachers and his peers, listening to himself after evaluating what has been said about his writing and considering what he can do to make it work" ("Finding Your Own Voice" 144-45). For Elbow, the audience can be used to help improve our writing, but "the goal should be to move toward the condition where we don't necessarily need it in order to speak or write well." Since audiences can also inhibit us, Elbow continues, "we need to learn to write what is true and what needs saying even if the whole world is scandalized. We need to learn eventually to find in *ourselves* the support which—perhaps for a long time—we must seek openly from others" (*Writing With Power* 190).

Thus, political change can only be considered by individuals and in individual terms. Elbow, for example, praises Freire's focus on the individual in seeking the contradictions of experience in the classroom but refuses to take into account the social dimension of this pedagogy, finally using Freire's thought as an occasion for arriving at a personal realization of a "psychological contradiction, not an economic one or political one," at the core of our culture (*Embracing Contraries* 98). The underlying conviction of expressionists is that when individuals are spared the distorting effects of a repressive social order, their privately determined truths will correspond to the privately determined truths of all others: my best and deepest vision supports the same universal and external laws as everyone else's best and deepest vision. Thus, in *Writing Without Teachers* Elbow admits that his knowledge about writing was gathered primarily from personal experience, and that he has no reservations about "making universal generalizations upon a sample of one" (16). Murray is even more explicit in his first edition of *A Writer Teaches Writing:* "the writer is on a search for himself. If he finds himself he will find an audience, because all of us have the same common core. And when he digs deeply into himself and is able to define himself, he will find others who will read with a shock of recognition what he has written" (4).

This rhetoric thus includes a denunciation of economic, political, and social pressures to conform—to engage in various forms of corporate-sponsored thought, feeling, and behavior. In indirectly but unmistakably decrying the dehumanizing effects of industrial capitalism, expressionistic rhetoric insists on defamiliarizing experience, on getting beyond the corruptions of the individual authorized by the language of commodified culture in order to re-experience the self and through it the external world, finding in this activity possibilities for a new order. For expressionistic rhetoric, the correct response to the imposition of current economic, political, and social arrangements is thus resistance, but a resistance that is always construed in individual terms. Collective retaliation poses as much of a threat to individual integrity as do the collective forces being resisted, and so is itself suspect. The only hope in a society working to destroy the uniqueness of the individual is for each of us to assert our individuality against the tyranny of the authoritarian corporation, state, and society. Strategies for doing so must of course be left to the individual, each lighting one small candle in order to create a brighter world.

Expressionistic rhetoric continues to thrive in high schools and at a number of colleges and universities. At first glance, this is surprising, unexpected of a rhetoric that is openly opposed to establishment practices. This subversiveness, however, is more apparent than real. In the first place, expressionistic rhetoric is inherently and debilitatingly divisive of political protest, suggesting that effective resistance can only be offered by individuals, each acting alone. Given the isolation and incoherence of such protest, gestures genuinely threatening to the establishment are difficult to accomplish. Beyond this, expressionistic rhetoric is easily co-opted by the very capitalist forces it opposes. After all, this rhetoric can be used to reinforce the entrepreneurial virtues capitalism most values: individualism, private initiative, the confidence for risk taking, the right to be contentious with authority (especially the state). It is indeed not too much to say that the ruling elites in business, industry, and government are those most likely to nod in assent to the ideology inscribed in expressionistic rhetoric. The members of this class see their lives as embodying the creative realization of the self, exploiting the material, social, and political conditions of the world in order to assert a private vision, a vision which, despite its uniqueness, finally represents humankind's best nature. (That this vision in fact represents the interests of a particular class, not all classes, is of course not acknowledged.) Those who have not attained the positions which enable them to exert this freedom have been prevented from doing so, this ideology argues, not by economic and class constraints, but by their own unwillingness to pursue a private vision, and this interpretation is often embraced by those excluded from the ruling elite as well as by the ruling elite itself. In other words, even those most constrained by their positions in the class structure may support the ideology found in expressionistic rhetoric in some form. This is most commonly done by divorcing the self from the alienation of work, separating work experience from other experience so that self discovery and fulfillment take place away from the job. For some this may lead to the pursuit of self expression in intellectual or aesthetic pursuits. For most this quest results in a variety of forms of consumer behavior, identifying individual self expression with the consumption of some commodity. This separation of work from authentic human activity is likewise reinforced in expressionistic rhetoric, as a glance at any of the textbooks it has inspired will reveal.

SOCIAL-EPISTEMIC RHETORIC

The last rhetoric to be considered I will call social-epistemic rhetoric, in so doing distinguishing it from the psychological-epistemic rhetoric that I am convinced is a form of expressionism. (The latter is found in Kenneth Dowst and in Cyril Knoblauch and Lil Brannon, although Knoblauch's recent *College English* essay displays him moving into the social camp. I have discussed the notion of epistemic rhetoric and these two varieties of it in *Rhetoric and Reality* 145-55, 165-77, and 184-85.) There have been a number of spokespersons for social-epistemic rhetoric over the last twenty years: Kenneth Burke, Richard Ohmann, the team of Richard Young, Alton Becker and Kenneth Pike, Kenneth Bruffee, W. Ross Winterowd, Ann Berthoff, Janice Lauer, and, more recently, Karen Burke Lefever, Lester Faigley, David Bartholomae, Greg Myers, Patricia Bizzell, and others. In grouping these figures together I do not intend to deny their obvious disagreements with each other. For example, Myers, a Leftist, has offered a lengthy critique of Bruffee, who—along with Winterowd and Young, Becker and Pike—is certainly of the Center politically. There are indeed as many conflicts among the members of this group as there are harmonies. They are brought together here, however, because they share a notion of rhetoric as a political act involving a dialectical interaction engaging the material, the social, and the individual writer, with language as the agency of mediation. Their positions, furthermore, include an historicist orientation, the realization that a rhetoric is an historically specific social formation that must perforce change over time; and this feature in turn makes possible reflexiveness and revision as the inherently ideological nature of rhetoric is continually acknowledged. The most complete realization of this rhetoric for the classroom is to be found in Ira Shor's *Critical Teaching and Everyday Life*. Before considering it, I would like to discuss the distinguishing features of a fully articulated social-epistemic rhetoric.

For social-epistemic rhetoric, the real is located in a relationship that involves the dialectical interaction of the observer, the discourse community (social group) in which the observer is functioning, and the material conditions of existence. Knowledge is never found in any one of these but can only be posited as a product of the dialectic in which all three come together. (More of this in a moment.) Most important, this dialectic is grounded in language: the observer, the discourse community, and the material conditions of existence are all verbal constructs. This does not mean that the three do not exist apart from language: they do. This does mean that we cannot talk and write about them—indeed, we cannot know them— apart from language. Furthermore, since language is a social phenomenon that is a product of a particular historical moment, our notions of the observing self, the communities in which the self functions, and the very structures of the material world are social constructions—all specific to a particular time and culture. These social constructions are thus inscribed in the very language we are given to inhabit in responding to our experience. Language, as Raymond Williams explains in an application of Bakhtin (*Marxism and Literature* 21-44), is one of the material and social conditions involved in producing a culture. This means that in studying rhetoric—the ways discourse is generated—we are studying the ways in which knowledge comes into existence. Knowledge, after all, is an historically bound social fabrication rather than an eternal and invariable phenomenon located in some uncomplicated repository—in the material object or in the subject or in the social realm. This brings us back to the matter of the dialectic.

Understanding this dialectical notion of knowledge is the most difficult feature of social-epistemic rhetoric. Psychological-epistemic rhetoric grants that rhetoric arrives at knowledge, but this meaning-generating activity is always located in a transcendent self, a subject who directs the discovery and arrives through it finally only at a better understanding of the self and its operation—this self comprehension being the end of all knowledge. For social-epistemic rhetoric, the subject is itself a social construct that emerges through the linguistically-circumscribed interaction of the individual, the community, and the material world. There is no universal, eternal, and authentic self that beneath all appearances is at one with all other selves. The self is always a creation of a particular historical and cultural moment. This is not to say that individuals do not ever act as individuals. It is to assert, however, that they never act with complete freedom. As Marx indicated, we make our own histories, but we do not make them just as we wish. Our consciousness is in large part a product of our material conditions. But our material conditions are also in part the products of our consciousness. Both consciousness and the material conditions influence each other, and they are both imbricated in social relations defined and worked out through language. In other words, the ways in which the subject understands and is affected by material conditions is circumscribed by socially-devised definitions, by the community in which the subject lives. The community in turn is influenced by the subject and the material conditions of the moment.

Thus, the perceiving subject, the discourse communities of which the subject is a part, and the material world itself are all the constructions of an historical discourse, of the ideological formulations inscribed in the language-mediated practical activity of a particular time and place. We are lodged within a hermeneutic circle, although not one that is impervious to change.

This scheme does not lead to an anarchistic relativism. It does, however, indicate that arguments based on the permanent rational structures of the universe or on the evidence of the deepest and most profound personal intuition should not be accepted without question. The material, the social, and the subjective are at once the producers and the products of ideology, and ideology must continually be challenged so as to reveal its economic and political consequences for individuals. In other words, what are the effects of our knowledge? Who benefits from a given version of truth? How are the material benefits of society distributed? What is the relation of this distribution to social relations? Do these relations encourage conflict? To whom does our knowledge designate power? In short, social-epistemic rhetoric views knowledge as an arena of ideological conflict: there are no arguments from transcendent truth since all arguments arise in ideology. It thus inevitably supports economic, social, political, and cultural democracy. Because there are no "natural laws" or "universal truths" that indicate what exists, what is good, what is possible, and how power is to be distributed, no class or group or individual has privileged access to decisions on these matters. They must be continually decided by all and for all in a way appropriate to our own historical moment. Finally, because of this historicist orientation, social-epistemic rhetoric contains within it the means for self-criticism and self-revision. Human responses to the material conditions of existence, the social relations they encourage, and the interpellations of subjects within them are always already ideological, are always already interpretations that must be constantly revised in the interests of the greater participation of all, for the greater good of all. And this of course implies an awareness of the ways in which rhetorics can privilege some at the expense of others, according the chosen few an unequal share of power, perquisites, and material benefits.

Social-epistemic rhetoric thus offers an explicit critique of economic, political, and social arrangements, the counterpart of the implicit critique found in expressionistic rhetoric. However, here the source and the solution of these arrangements are described quite differently. As Ira Shor explains, students must be taught to identify the ways in which control over their own lives has been denied them, and denied in such a way that they have blamed themselves for their powerlessness. Shor thus situates the individual within social processes, examining in detail the interferences to critical thought that would enable "students to be their own agents for social change, their own creators of democratic culture" (48). Among the most important forces preventing work toward a social order supporting the student's "full humanity" are forms of false consciousness—reification, pre-scientific thought, acceleration, mystification—and the absence of democratic practices in all areas of experience. Although Shor discusses these forms of false consciousness in their relation to working class students, their application to all students is not hard to see, and I have selected for emphasis those features which clearly so apply.

In falling victim to reification, students begin to see the economic and social system that renders them powerless as an innate and unchangeable feature of the natural order. They become convinced that change is impossible, and they support the very practices that victimize them—complying in their alienation from their work, their peers, and their very selves. The most common form of reification has to do with the preoccupation with consumerism, playing the game of material acquisition and using it as a substitute for more self-fulfilling behavior. In pre-scientific thinking, the student is led to believe in a fixed human nature, always and everywhere the same. Behavior that is socially and self destructive is then seen as inevitable, in the nature of things, or can be resisted only at the individual level, apart from communal activity. Another form of pre-scientific thinking is the belief in luck, in pure chance, as the source of social arrangements, such as the inequitable distribution of wealth. The loyalty to brand names, the faith in a "common sense" that supports the existing order, and the worship of heroes, such as actors and athletes, are other forms of this kind of thought, all of which prevent "the search for rational explanations to authentic problems" (66). Acceleration refers to the pace of everyday experience—the sensory bombardment of urban life and of popular forms of entertainment—which prevents critical reflection. Mystifications are responses to the problems of a capitalist society which obscure their real sources and solutions, responses based on racism, sexism, nationalism, and other forms of bigotry. Finally, students are constantly told they live in the most free, most democratic society in the world, yet they are at the same time systematically denied opportunities for "self-discipline, self-organization, collective work styles, or group deliberation" (70), instead being subjected at every turn to arbitrary authority in conducting everyday affairs.

Shor's recommendations for the classroom grow out of an awareness of these forces and are intended to counter them. The object of this pedagogy is to enable students to *"extraordinarily reexperience the ordinary"* (93), as they critically examine their quotidian experience in order to externalize false consciousness. (Shor's use of the term "critical" is meant to recall Freire as well as the practice of the Hegelian Marxists of the Frankfurt School.) The point is to "address self-in-society and social-relations-in-self" (95). The self then is regarded as the product of a dialectical relationship between the individual and the social, each given significance by the other. Self-autonomy and self-fulfillment are thus possible not through becoming detached from the social, but through resisting those social influences that alienate and disempower, doing so, moreover, in and through social activity. The liberatory classroom begins this resistance process with a dialogue that inspires "a democratic model of social relations, used to problematize the undemocratic quality of social life" (95). This dialogue—a model inspired by Paulo Freire—makes teacher and learner equals engaged in a joint practice that is "[l]oving, humble, hopeful, trusting, critical" (95). This is contrasted with the unequal power relations in the authoritarian classroom, a place where the teacher holds all power and knowledge and the student is the receptacle into which information is poured, a classroom that is "[l]oveless, arrogant, hopeless, mistrustful, acritical" (95). Teacher and student work together to shape the content of the liberatory classroom, and this includes creating the materials of study in the class—such as textbooks and media. Most important, the students are to undergo a conversion from "manipulated objects into active, critical subjects" (97), thereby empowering them to become agents of social change rather than victims. Shor sums up these elements: "social practice is studied in the name of freedom for critical consciousness; democracy and awareness develop through the form of dialogue; dialogue externalizes false consciousness, changing students from reactive objects into society-making subjects; the object-subject switch is a social psychology for empowerment; power through study creates the conditions for reconstructing social practice" (98).

This approach in the classroom requires interdisciplinary methods, and Shor gives an example from the study of the fast-food hamburger: "Concretely my class' study of hamburgers not only involved English and philosophy in our use of writing, reading, and conceptual analysis, but it also included economics in the study of the commodity relations which bring hamburgers to market, history and sociology in an assessment of what the everyday diet was like prior to the rise of the hamburger, and health science in terms of the nutritional value of the ruling burger" (114). This interdisciplinary approach to the study of the reproduction of social life can also lead to "the unveiling of hidden social history" (115), the discovery of past attempts to resist self-destructive experience. This in turn can lead to an examination of the roots of sexism and racism in our culture. Finally, Shor calls upon comedy to reunite pleasure and work, thought and feeling, and upon a

He wants them to be aware of inherent power structures

resourceful use of the space of the classroom to encourage dialogue that provides students with information withheld elsewhere on campus—"informational, conceptual, personal, academic, financial" (120)—ranging from the location of free or inexpensive services to the location of political rallies.

This survey of the theory and practice of Ira Shor's classroom is necessarily brief and reductive. Still, it suggests the complexity of the behavior recommended in the classroom, behavior that is always open-ended, receptive to the unexpected, and subversive of the planned. Most important, success in this classroom can never be guaranteed. This is a place based on dialectical collaboration—the interaction of student, teacher, and shared experience within a social, interdisciplinary framework—and the outcome is always unpredictable. Yet, as Shor makes clear, the point of this classroom is that the liberated consciousness of students is the only educational objective worth considering, the only objective worth the risk of failure. To succeed at anything else is no success at all.

It should now be apparent that a way of teaching is never innocent. Every pedagogy is imbricated in ideology, in a set of tacit assumptions about what is real, what is good, what is possible, and how power ought to be distributed. The method of cognitive psychology is the most likely to ignore this contention, claiming that the rhetoric it recommends is based on an objective understanding of the unchanging structures of mind, matter, and language. Still, despite its commitment to the empirical and scientific, as we have seen, this rhetoric can easily be made to serve specific kinds of economic, social, and political behavior that works to the advantage of the members of one social class while disempowering others—doing so, moreover, in the name of objective truth. Expressionistic rhetoric is intended to serve as a critique of the ideology of corporate capitalism, proposing in its place an ideology based on a radical individualism. In the name of empowering the individual, however, its naivety about economic, social, and political arrangements can lead to the marginalizing of the individuals who would resist a dehumanizing society, rendering them ineffective through their isolation. This rhetoric also is easily co-opted by the agencies of corporate capitalism, appropriated and distorted in the service of the mystifications of bourgeois individualism. Social-epistemic rhetoric attempts to place the question of ideology at the center of the teaching of writing. It offers both a detailed analysis of dehumanizing social experience and a self-critical and overtly historicized alternative based on democratic practices in the economic, social, political, and cultural spheres. It is obvious that I find this alternative the most worthy of emulation in the classroom, all the while admitting that it is the least formulaic and the most difficult to carry out. I would also add that even those who are skeptical of the Marxian influence found in my description of this rhetoric have much to learn from it. As Kenneth Burke has shown, one does not have to accept the Marxian promise in order to realize the value of the Marxian diagnosis (*Rhetoric of Motives* 109). It is likewise not necessary to accept the conclusions of Ira Shor about writing pedagogy in order to learn from his analysis of the ideological practices at work in the lives of our students and ourselves. A rhetoric cannot escape the ideological question, and to ignore this is to fail our responsibilities as teachers and as citizens.

WORKS CITED

Bartholomae, David. "Inventing the University." *When a Writer Can't Write: Studies in Writer's Block and other Composing-Process Problems.* Ed. Mike Rose. New York: Guilford, 1986.

Berlin, James A. "Contemporary Composition: The Major Pedagogical Theories." *College English* 44 (1982): 765-77.

_____. *Rhetoric and Reality: Writing Instruction in American Colleges, 1900-1985.* Carbondale: Southern Illinois UP, 1987.

_____. *Writing Instruction in Nineteenth-Century American Colleges.* Carbondale: Southern Illinois UP, 1984.

Bizzell, Patricia. "Cognition, Convention, and Certainty: What We Need to Know about Writing." *PRE/TEXT* 3 (1982): 213-43.

Bowles, Samuel, and Herbert Gintis. *Schooling in Capitalist America.* New York: Basic, 1976.

Braverman, Harry. *Labor and Monopoly Capital: The Degradation of Work in the Twentieth Century.* New York: Monthly Review Press, 1974.

Brodkey, Linda. "Modernism and the Scene of Writing." *College English* 49 (1987): 396-418.

Bruner, Jerome S. *The Process of Education.* Cambridge: Harvard UP, 1960.

Burke, Kenneth. *A Rhetoric of Motives.* Berkeley: U of California P, 1969.

Clifford, John, and John Schilb. "A Perspective on Eagleton's Revival of Rhetoric." *Rhetoric Review* 6 (1987): 22-31.

Clines, Ray. "Composition and Capitalism." *Progressive Composition* 14 (March 1987): 4-5.

Dowst, Kenneth. "The Epistemic Approach: Writing, Knowing, and Learning." *Eight Approaches to Teaching Composition.* Ed. Timothy Donovan and Ben W. McClelland. Urbana: NCTE, 1980.

_____. "An Epistemic View of Sentence Combining: A Rhetorical Perspective." *Sentence Combining: A Rhetorical Perspective.* Ed. Donald A. Daiker, Andrew Kerek, and Max Morenberg. Carbondale: Southern Illinois UP, 1986. 321-33.

Elbow, Peter. *Embracing Contraries: Explorations in Learning and Teaching.* New York: Oxford, 1981.

_____. *Writing Without Teachers.* New York: Oxford UP, 1973.

_____. *Writing with Power: Techniques for Mastering the Writing Process.* New York: Oxford UP, 1981.

Emig, Janet. *The Composing Processes of Twelfth Graders.* Research Report No. 13. Urbana: NCTE, 1971.

Flower, Linda. *Problem-Solving Strategies for Writing.* 2nd ed. San Diego: Harcourt, 1985.

Flower, Linda, and John R. Hayes. "A Cognitive Process Theory of Writing." *College Composition and Communication* 32 (1981): 365-87.

Knoblauch, C. H. "Rhetorical Constructions: Dialogue and Commitment." *College English* 50 (1988): 125-40.

_____, and Lil Brannon. *Rhetorical Traditions and the Teaching of Writing.* Upper Montclair: Boynton/Cook, 1984.

Larrain, Jorge. *The Concept of Ideology.* Athens: U of Georgia P, 1979.

Larson, Richard. "Discovery Through Questioning: A Plan for Teaching Rhetorical Invention." *College English* 30 (1968): 126-34.

_____. "Invention Once More: A Role for Rhetorical Analysis." *College English* 32 (1971): 665-72.

_____. "Problem-Solving, Composing, and Liberal Education." *College Composition and Communication* 23 (1972): 208-10.

Lutz, William D. "Making Freshman English a Happening." *College Composition and Communication* 22 (1971): 35-38.

Murray, Donald. *A Writer Teaches Writing.* Boston: Houghton, 1968.

_____. "Finding Your Own Voice in an Age of Dissent." *College Composition and Communication* 20 (1969): 118-23.

Myers, Greg. "Reality, Consensus, and Reform in the Rhetoric of Composition Teaching." *College English* 48 (1986): 154-74.

Ohmann, Richard. "Literacy, Technology, and Monopoly Capital." *College English* 47 (1985): 675-89.

Paull, Michael, and Jack Kligerman. "Invention, Composition, and the Urban College." *College English* 33 (1972): 651-59.

Shor, Ira. *Critical Teaching and Everyday Life.* 1980. Chicago: U of Chicago, 1987.

Therborn, Göran. *The Ideology of Power and the Power of Ideology.* London: Verso, 1980.

Vitanza, Victor. "'Notes' Towards Historiographies of Rhetorics; or, Rhetorics of the Histories of Rhetorics: Traditional, Revisionary, and Sub/Versive." *PRE/TEXT* 8 (1987): 63-125.

Williams, Raymond. *Keywords: A Vocabulary of Culture and Society.* Revised Edition. New York: Oxford UP, 1977.

_____. *Marxism and Literature.* Oxford UP, 1977.

Cognition, Context, and Theory Building

LINDA FLOWER

English studies are caught up in a debate over whether we should see individual cognition or social and cultural context as the motive force in literate acts. This conflict between cognition and context (Bartholomae, Berlin, Bizzell, Knoblauch) has special force in rhetoric and composition because it touches some deeply-rooted assumptions and practices. Can we, for instance, reconcile a commitment to nurturing a personal voice, individual purpose, or an inner, self-directed process of meaning making, with rhetoric's traditional assumption that both inquiry and purpose are a response to rhetorical situations, or with the more recent assertions that inquiry in writing must start with social, cultural, or political awareness? These values and assertions run deep in the discipline. One response to these differences is to build theoretical positions that try to polarize (or moralize) cognitive and contextual perspectives. We know that critiques based on dichotomies can fan lively academic debates. They can also lead, Mike Rose has argued, to reductive, simplified theories that "narrow the mind and page" of student writers. In the end, these attempts to dichotomize may leave us with an impoverished account of the writing process as people experience it and a reductive vision of what we might teach.

We need, I believe, a far more integrated theoretical vision which can explain how context cues cognition, which in its turn mediates and interprets the particular world that context provides. This paper is about ways we might build such a vision by using what we have learned from arguments which problematize or reify this conflict but by also taking a step beyond

Reprinted from *College Composition and Communication* 40.3 (October 1989): 282–311. Used with permission.

them. Currently, our competing images of the composing process reflect a cognitive/contextual polarization that seems to shrink understanding and threatens to break up our vision of writing into floating islands of theory. What we don't know is how cognition and context do in fact interact, in specific but significant situations. We have little precise understanding of how these "different processes" feed on one another. My intention here is not to propose a specific theory, but to explore some ways we might use research— observational research, specifically—to create a well-supported, theoretical understanding of this interaction.

PART ONE: TOWARD INTERACTIVE THEORY

Constructing an interactive theory would make some significant demands upon us. First we would have to go beyond current partial positions. Early work in cognition, like most other work at the time, focused on the individual (Emig, Flower and Hayes). The Hayes/Flower cognitive process model is a case in point. Although this model suggests key *places where* social and contextual knowledge operate within a cognitive framework, that early research did little more than specify that the "task environment" was an important element in the process; it failed to account for *how* the situation in which the writer operates might shape composing, and it had little to say about the specific conventions, schemata, or commonplaces that might inform the writer's "long term memory." Other elements of the cognitive theory presented in 1981, such as the role of recursion, the shifting shape of writing plans, and the way a writer's own goals and vision of the task shape composing, may stand as strong claims, but claims focused nonetheless on describing basic processes and the individual writer. Early work that focused on the social context, wanting to see people as a social/political aggregate or as members of a discourse community, is likewise limited by a failure to account for the experience of individual students or writers within a group and to accommodate a vision of human agency, original contributions, and personal or intellectual development (Bizzell, "College Composition"; Bruffee). An interactive theory can build on what we already know and find valuable, but must go beyond.

To do so will demand both an openness to discovery and rigor. If we would understand how cognition and context interact, we cannot remain satisfied with speculative theories based only on abstract social or political imperatives. Even as we champion our values, we must distinguish prescription and assertion from description and evidence. Nor can we rely on contributions that offer us only a deconstruction or critique without offering in turn a substantive—and in some way substantiated—alternative. We need what ethnographers describe as "grounded theory" (Spradley)—a vision that is grounded in specific knowledge about real people writing in significant personal, social, or political situations. This grounding can come from many sources: from the comparative analysis of student texts (Bartholomae, Shaughnessy) or of talk at home and in school (Heath), from detailed discourse studies of the reading process, plans, and drafts of writers within specific communities (Bazerman, Myers), or from historical reconstructions of early rhetors in action (Enos). This grounding may emerge from the thick descriptions of field notes, plans, drafts, and process logs (Herrington, Nelson and Hayes), or from tracking how students represent writing tasks to themselves in their protocols, texts, and self-reflections (Flower, "Role"). It may come from the long-term observation of an educational experiment (Freire). Although these examples of observation operate out of different paradigms, with different immediate goals and values, they all offer the basis for learning something we didn't already "know" and for grounding and testing a developing theory within its own framework.

The interactive vision I am proposing would do one more thing. It would help us teach. Though we embrace multiple conceptual frameworks, we share the goal of helping writers understand themselves as constructors of meaning within a social and cultural context—a context that can both nurture and consume an individual writer. Educators do not work with abstractions; they work with students. As a teacher, I need an interactive vision of the writing process that can address the hurdles student writers often face, that can account for the cognitive and social sources of both success and failure, and that can talk about the experience of writing by being adequately fine-grained and situated in that experience. I want a framework that acknowledges the pressure and the potential the social context can provide, at the same time it explains how writers negotiate that context, create their own goals, and develop a sense of themselves as problem-solvers, speakers, or subjects who create meaning and affect other people through their writing. Although journal articles have the luxury of assuming a cognitive/contextual dichotomy, teachers cannot afford to present only half the picture. We need a grounded vision that can place cognition in its context, while celebrating the power of cognition to change that context, in a theory so richly specified that it can describe how individual writers develop those powers for themselves.

Peer response is a case in point where critical examination of how cognition and context affect one another seems called for. In theory, using peer response can be seen as invoking either a cognitive or a social experience. However, the "writing process" envisioned in each case is described quite differently. When one's image of writing is derived from social theory that foregrounds the role of "context," composing can be seen as a move within a discourse community, as a contribution to a larger conversation, as an interpersonal gesture, or as an act (acknowledged or not) of collaboration. If one emphasizes a cultural over a social context, the process of writing might be described as the enactment of the writer's assumptions and prior knowledge, or as the expression of (or resistance to) the political, economic, and historical forces that could be said to write the writer. As a classroom activity, peer response seems a "natural" extension of this social/cultural vision of writing. On the other hand, when one's image of writing foregrounds the experience and cognition of the individual writer, composing is at once a goal-directed rhetorical act and a cognitive and personal act of constructing meaning. Tracking the writer's tumbling stream of consciousness, we see a recursive thinking process guided (with or without conscious awareness) by the goals and knowledge the writer invokes and by the rhetorical situation—as the writer interprets it. In learning to write, writers not only increase their knowledge of discourse conventions and specific literate practices, they build a repertory of thinking strategies, and—at times—achieve a reflective awareness of their own constructive and interpretive processes.

Peer response places writing in a teacher-designed community of response. If we see writing as a social, context-driven event, this instructional move makes sense because it seems to enact our image of writing as a social, cultural process, happening within a classroom community. But what is happening to the cognition of individual students in this instructional context? Can we, for instance, predict that certain kinds of thinking will occur as a result of our social engineering? Many of the arguments for using peer response presume that the group will affect the cognition of the individual student: groups intervene within and can affect the writing process itself; they prompt students to work collectively to discover ideas; they create a live audience to which students can respond, which, it is argued, leads the individual to an internalized sense of how readers respond; and finally, they shift the emphasis in a classroom from product to process and from teacherly evaluation to writers' goals and readers' response (Freedman). But what actually happens in the minds of students? There is little question that at times peer response—as a teacher-generated social activity—*can* achieve these particular cognitive goals. However, Freedman's close analysis of response groups at work in two exemplary middle school classrooms reveals a mismatch between an instructional process or activity in the classroom and the cognitive process it was presumed to stimulate. Although both classes used dittoed response sheets specifically designed to prompt evaluation, students went to great lengths to avoid evaluating each other and to maintain smooth social relations with their peers. One response prompt asked: "What words or sentences seem out of place?" Students refused to answer in various ways:

> *Mike:* I'm not going to say anything's out of place. Okay?
>
> *Donald:* Yeah. Everything's great. Perfect!
>   [both laugh] (15)

Although the sheets kept students on task and did prompt problem solving, much of their thinking, it seems, was directed to solving the puzzle of how to fill out the teachers' sheets while avoiding an evaluative response. When students in one class were allowed to function in a more natural manner without sheets, the mismatch between the cognitive process promised in the literature and the very lively social classroom process that actually went on appeared even greater. Students spent an average of only 52% of their time on the task, with the rest of their attention devoted to "telling one another jokes or talking about weekend plans, friends, or hair-coloring" (22). Freedman's study is not a critique of peer response, but it exemplifies how these different processes—the instructional one we design, the cognitive one we presume it will support, and the social one that goes on anyway—can be strikingly out of synch. The critical, self-monitoring cognitive process we want students to develop may be in unstated conflict with far more pressing interpersonal needs for social affiliation, where acts of evaluation and criticism threaten solidarity.

As this small example suggests, it seems naive to assume that the cognitive processes we desire will naturally follow from the social situations we engineer. If we ignore the dialectic between cognition and context or if we try to enact one image of a "good" writing process but ignore the other, we may be building instructional delusions. We can't afford to speculate about students' thinking from the armchair of social theory. Nor can we place the mind in a bell jar and divorce the writing process from the social and emotional tide of talk on which it flows. The problem for peer response is that even if we acknowledge the significance of this dialectic, there are few studies that have, like Freedman's, carefully tracked the path it actually takes.

Elements of a More Interactive Theory

In asking us to examine how cognition and context interact, I do not want to suggest that we need a single image of the writing process or a single "integrated theory"—writing is too complex a phenomenon, and history tells us that single visions rarely satisfy many people for very long. What I would argue for is, first, the need for more balanced, multi-perspective descriptions and more rigorously grounded theoretical explanations of various aspects of the writing process: of the process of meaning making, of constructing knowledge, of working collaboratively, of planning and revising, of reading-to-write, of entering academic discourse, and so on (cf. Rose, "Complexity"). We already hold implicit theories about these acts. Even if we disavow the practice of theorizing, our images of the process and our priorities in teaching constitute a tacit theory. However, the wedding of composition with rhetoric, psychology, and now reading has called on us to theorize our understanding of composing in more reflective and testable ways. The sudden growth of research, scholarship, and new ideas, as well as the sometimes precipitous rush to polemical stands based on various moral, teacherly, or political imperatives, makes this a good time to reach for more analytical and balanced visions, for a greater sense of the conditional nature of our various perspectives. It is time for the systematic and self-questioning stance that goes with theoretical explanations—whether we are explaining a historical event, an experimental or observational study, or an approach to teaching.

Second, these attempts to build integrated, theory-conscious accounts of writing need, I believe, to address the apparent dichotomy of cognition and context in a direct way and in a spirit of open inquiry. It would be simple to frame this question in terms of a conflict—as much of the current discussion tends to. To ask, for instance, which element dominates or determines writing; what constitutes the balance of power; which is most important? But defining that relation as conflict might lead us to a simplistic conceptualization if these forces are, in fact, strongly interactive.

Let me propose three principles that inform this more complicated interaction and suggest that both cognition and context may in a sense *construct* one another. One principle is that cultural and social context can provide direct *cues* to cognition. The second is that that context is also and always *mediated* by the cognition of the individual writer. And the third is that the bounded purposes that emerge from this process are highly constrained but at the same time *meaningful, rhetorical acts.*

Principle One: Context Cues Cognition

One does need at least one writer to produce writing. But as we shed the romantic mythology of the isolated creator, we see the ways other people, the past, and the social present contribute to the production of a text, through cultural norms, available language, intertextuality, and through the more directly social acts of assignment giving, collaboration, and so on. The context in many ways determines, directs, or prompts the kind of thinking the individual writer will do—even if the writer's response to that context is resistance. It operates as a sign and a cue to cognitive action.

Rhetoric has traditionally affirmed this principle by treating the rhetor/writer as a social actor within a public forum. The art of persuasion is described as creating identity or a shared image with others, and the available "means" of persuasion rely on using those patterns and conventions of thought the audience will find convincing. The rhetor of classical theory literally stands within a public circle of peers, speaking to and within an exigency which has prompted the discourse. Although the rhetor of modern theory sits at a keyboard, invention is still described as a response to stasis and the shared problem that motivates discourse.

When we try to account for the influence of context in cognitive terms, we notice that the language of "problem-solving" itself places the writer in a responsive stance. Cognitive action is often initiated in response to a cue from the environment—in response to an "ill-defined problem" that the "solver" may have to define from limited and ambiguous cues in the world around. Research in cognition tends to concentrate on the response of the individual rather than on the situational cues, for obvious reasons: one can observe a writer's actions with some clarity; however, the cues which stimulated a given action may often need to be inferred or may even remain a mystery (e.g., Was the shift in the writer's argument a response to her own text, to possibilities inherent in her own language? Or did a quick glance at the assignment trigger a private association or an intuition about the unstated intentions of the instructor?) We may be unable to trace these multiple signs and causal links in many, even most cases, but we can describe some ways this cuing process works.

Context guides cognition in multiple ways. In its least visible role, context affects us in the form of past experience that supplies a wealth of prior knowledge, assumptions, and expectations, many of which can operate without our conscious awareness. These conceptual frameworks may even passively determine what it is possible to think or see. However—and I think this "however" is a strong rebuttal to linguistic determinism—adults possess an enormous repertoire of conceptual frameworks and, in any given situation, we can not predict which will be activated, which quiescent, or how any given framework will be used. In situated cognition it is not what is known, but the knowledge one uses that matters.

Context can also interact with the mind of the writer in a more direct and forceful way as a *cue to action*. Context selectively taps knowledge and triggers specific processes. For good or for ill, these cues to mental action may activate only a portion of what a given writer knows or could do, but they influence three key areas of cognition in writing: goals, criteria, and strategies. When context guides the process of setting goals, it can in essence dictate the problem the writer tries to solve, even when that cue is in conflict with other goals and values. For example, many students leave high school seeing school writing as an occasion for recitation or a tool teachers use to evaluate their comprehension of the textbook. When a college assignment asks, instead, for interpretation, critical analysis, or argument, they may continue to see their writing task as knowledge telling, a goal which leads them to suppress their own ideas and to avoid critical engagement with the texts they read—all in good faith that they are doing what is expected in school writing (Ackerman, Stein).

Context also guides action by setting the criteria by which a text or even one's own thinking process is monitored and evaluated. In Freedman's peer response study, for example, the dittoed assignment sheets and the demands of social maintenance set the standards for students' response to writing. These sheets were so good at doggedly focusing the attention of the group that students rarely interrupted with a personal or readerly response to the content. Finally, context cues action by suggesting appropriate strategies. Teachers, for instance, hope the holy words of college assignments (e.g., "analyze," "interpret") will cue the bundle of intellectual maneuvers every student should have learned. But "transfer" is a perennial problem in education in part because the context of a new class may fail to cue a student to use strategies which are appropriate, but were learned elsewhere in a different context. Because the new situation fails to contain meaningful cues to action (i.e., signs or signals that the student recognizes as such "cues"), the cognition in which he or she could engage is never invoked.

The principle that context cues cognition is important to an interactive theory because it helps explain both the nurturing and oppressive power of context within the mind of the writer and without. It suggests some ways context can operate within a writer's thinking and the problem of transfer these context-specific cues pose for education. It also leads us to ask: could metaknowledge and awareness of one's own process play a role in expanding the cues students perceive and the options they entertain?

Principle Two: Cognition Mediates Context

Context is a powerful force. However, it does not produce a text through immaculate conception. It is a semiotic source of signs, not a program for action. Context in its many forms is mediated—at all levels of awareness—by the cognition of the individual writer. A case in point: in a study of the reading-to-write process, my colleagues and I tried to track the ways in which a group of 72 first-semester freshmen interpreted an open-ended college writing assignment, in the act of reading and writing (Flower et al., *Reading*). At one level of analysis, the broad outlines of a shared culture emerged as a dominant force in this situation; one could see how the process of task representation was shaped by the legacy of school and the habits of recitation these successful students quickly invoked. But at another level of analysis, the striking fact was the constructive process of the individual student. The tasks students built for themselves differed from one another in the goals students set, the strategies they invoked, the knowledge they chose to use (which included or rigorously excluded the writer's own ideas), and the different organizing plans they thought appropriate for the assignment (which ranged from simple summaries, to free response, to careful synthesis, to interpretations of the reading for a purpose of the writer's own). These individual differences in task representation, which emerge from this more fine-grained analysis, are very meaningful differences: they affect the likelihood that a student will actually transform information; they dictate the role of the writer's own ideas and affect the usefulness of the text for readers; and in many cases they could determine the grade the paper would receive and the instructor's evaluation of the student. However, as this study showed, students may fail to perform an expected writing and thinking task which they could do because, through their own constructive process of task representation, they gave themselves a different task to do.

This study graphically illustrates how students from similar backgrounds, doing a shared assignment in a common freshman writing class, interpreted that situation in different ways in terms of the goals they set for themselves, the criteria they invoked, and the strategies they called upon. The shared context was mediated by individual cognition. However, this mediation did not occur as a single, self-conscious decision. In fact, most students did not appear to be aware that such diversity of interpretation regularly happened, that so many live options existed for them, or that their own interpretive process played such a large role in creating the task they actually did. Nor was this interpretive, mediating process limited to occasional instances of pondering over the terms of the assignment; it went on as a part of the sustained cognitive process of planning, problem-solving, and making trial-and-error stabs at doing the task. It is important to see that, as with any interpretive process, cognition takes action through interaction.

At times, the mediating work of cognition is tacit, immediate, and swift; at others it is explicit, alive to alternatives, and maybe even self-conscious or reflective. When the process of interpretation is tacit—fast and automatic— it may seem as though the cues of the context are simply governing the process. For example, a student "reads" an extended paper comment as simple criticism and a signal to delete the contested idea; a journalist "reads" a situation as a news story. In both cases the response to context was immediate and uncontested, but neither response was merely "natural" or "determined" by the context. Automated processes often reflect the rewards of learning; actions which were once the slow product of effortful concentration by the novice journalist give way to sophisticated cognition that transforms a situation into its own image. The downside of such practiced cognition is that it runs unexamined and remains closed to critical thinking. A student who "reads" the context of assigned school writing as a cue to knowledge-telling and who mediates that context in limited and tacit ways, may never notice the other cues that could prompt her to interpret or adapt her ideas for an original purpose.

At other times the process of mediation is sustained and complex. Writers read a rhetorical situation, mulling over its implications and their goals; they may evaluate their own plans; they may imagine how readers could respond. In this intuitive strategic and interpretive process, we can see the rhetorical context being constructed. Out of the writer's storehouse of frames, scripts, and schemata and the plethora of potential cues the situation affords, a rhetorical situation is created by the writer's own inferences and selective attention. I do not want to suggest that writers are necessarily aware of this process or the role of their own mediation, even when they wrestle with, think through, and worry over "what I should do here." As thinking-aloud protocols show, it is easy to be immersed in a tense, absorbing cognitive drama and not spare attention to monitoring that process itself.

Here is an example of a student actively mediating various aspects of the writing situation as she works on a reading-to-write assignment which asked her to use a brief set of readings to write her own statement on the topic of "revision." We see a writer caught up in conflicting cues to action, looking at the draft text and text plan she wants to save, on the one hand, and, on the other, at the assignment demands for an integrated statement. To complicate the situation, she has just realized that her source text is asserting a structure that is at odds with her own focus on the topic of revision. [Underlined words indicate notes and sentences written as the writer was thinking aloud; dots indicate brief pauses.]

And then, the third part will be <u>how poor writers</u>, um, <u>rewrite</u>.
No, how poor writers <u>revise.</u>
Hmm. Right now I'm thinking I don't really like the way this is structured.
It doesn't seem to integrate ideas.
It's hard to write this

because I'm being basically asked to write what I've just read
and I don't want to copy exactly.
So I keep thinking there must be more in the assignment than what I'm
seeing.
And I'm looking at the task and reading it again [page turned]
I guess I'll just go ahead and do it this way and see what happens,
because I'm not sure what more I should be doing in this.
OK Let's see. I'm going to . . . write this part.
Skimming through the paper, I'm picking out what I think are the main
points . . .
I know this differs earlier from the goals that I set up previously,
but I'm going to go ahead and do it this way.
OK . . . um, the first paragraph, generally the main ideas of that is that
<u>stronger writers do more planning than did the weaker writers.</u>
Hey, that doesn't really fit into my structure though, where I would have
the goals of revision written first.
So I'm going to read on further and see if I can find anything that
pertains to it.

Although the contextual cues here are relatively local ones, they illustrate the problem of mediating conflicting cues that can come from an assignment, from one's own draft text, and from the implicit expectations set by a course (e.g., "there must be more" than I'm seeing). We can see some of this writer's interpretive moves (and some of her unquestioned assumptions) as she tries to deal with (1) the conflict between her goals to "not copy" but still to use the source text's "main ideas" and (2) the related dilemma that one of the "main ideas" from the source (on the subject of planning) is at odds with her own structure focused on how writers revise. The writer mediates these conflicting cues to action by first recognizing the conflict itself and locating its sources, and then by choosing a tentative solution. At one point she rises to awareness of this strategic process itself (i.e., "It's hard to write this because . . .") which becomes the object of her own reflective thought.

Principle Three: A Bounded Purpose Is a Meaningful Rhetorical Act

An interactive theory, I believe, will have to recognize both the mediating power of cognition and the directive cues of context. And in doing so, it must face the troubled issue of intentionality. Are writers "determined" by their situation, do they "control" the meanings they make, or is "originality" only an illusion and "purpose" a fiction of rhetoric texts? Once again, dichotomies and uncontextualized, unconditionalized claims may obscure the issue. Social theorists who attack the illusion of control, who would locate purpose in the unconscious and dismiss the ephemera of cognition, have a special agenda—to understand *why* context and culture controls us as much as it does. Writing researchers and educators may be quite happy to acknowledge such forces, but their agenda is not to explicate or reify them. Rather it is to ask *where*, within this looming landscape of internalized forces we do not control, does human agency and intention insert itself? And when it does, *how* does it do so? From an educator's point of view, it may be better to praise a small doughnut than bemoan a large hole.

Purpose in writing is always a bounded purpose. Whether one is constrained by the assumptions of one's culture, the material realities of the publishing industry, the demands of one's job, or the terms of an assignment, purpose takes shape in a context that both demands and entices the writer to walk into the embrace of purposes that are in some sense not her own. And yet, within this ring of constraints, writers make critical choices at two levels. On one, they may choose to make some of these "given" purposes their own (to embrace the goals of a course or an assignment as a statement of shared intentions) or to resist "given" purposes or ignore chosen constraints. Though we may be more inclined to attribute purpose and independence to visible resistance, both acts make choices *among* constraints. The construction of purpose also goes on at another level: within these global givens, one must still construct an individual, if bounded, purpose that not only meets but mediates all of one's goals. Forming a rhetorical purpose is a complex and creative act of negotiation. Although the writer we saw above was constrained by the assigned goal to "integrate ideas," she was facing the writers' task of instantiating that goal with an individual rhetorical plan, with ideas, and with sentences on a page. In turning that abstract intention into a specific rhetorical action she is indeed creating a conditioned or *bounded* purpose, but it is the construction of meaning at just this level that often consumes the energy and attention of writers, that can distinguish expert from novice, and that constitutes some of the bold and integrative moves we call original.

When we look closely at how writers construct these bounded purposes we do not see a single statement of purpose, but a web of purpose—a complex network of goals, plans, intentions, and ideas (Flower, "Construction"). The creation of this web is a richly interactive social and cognitive event; however, the way in which people manage or mediate the constraints upon them may depend on whether they recognize the significance of their own choices within this web. The following comments come from another segment of the Reading-to-Write project in which we talked with students about the differences in task representation we had seen in the initial data. Ron, the student quoted below, did not have much to say about his strategies for writing *per se*—monitoring his own thinking process seemed new to him. On the other hand, he was quite articulate, even savvy about the social strategies and behavior that support his highly intentional effort to mediate and interpret the context of assigned writing. Talking about classes in general he said:

> *Ron:* I try to write [an assignment] as soon as I can and let them look at it. Even take it right to the teacher, and say, look at this. Am I going in the right direction or not?
>
> *Interviewer:* That's a kind of expensive way to do it, isn't it?
>
> *Ron:* You pick up things. You pick up good things. It's expensive in terms of that paper, but it's not expensive in terms of putting that away for future reference for the rest of the course. Really, its pretty practical if you think about it. Rather than going about it and getting two, three "C"s on a paper.

Ron, it seems, is not talking just about getting help on this paper, but about using audience to figure out the ways to think, goals to set—especially when he must face the problem of using his own knowledge.

> It's not really a conscious process that I go through. You just got to listen. I don't know if it sounds weird or what. But I sit there and I watch them during the lecture, I listen to key words that they use. They register.

Ron then goes on to articulate what is essentially a theory of negotiated meaning:

> And to be honest with you, I think it has a lot to do with my being . . . I've been out for 10 years, and I came back. And this is more related to real-world experiences. How it goes. I mean, you can go out and you can tell your boss—"Well, I think we could do it this way." And you have a real good idea. And he just says—"Get outa here." Meanwhile, if you really think it's a good idea you can twist it around and maintain the gist of the whole thing and maybe get it pushed through. Mutually beneficial: it's gonna help him and help you.

Ron came to college seeing meaning as something you negotiate with your reader. Using your own knowledge, he says in the interview, is "a risky decision." It is obvious Ron would prefer direct feedback and negotiation on a given text—he would prefer the audience to act as a direct cue to immediate action. But when Ron talks about listening, finding old tests, and investing time in the first paper, that context is being translated into a unique mental representation of an audience and expectations that will guide his thinking on the next paper.

As a writer, Ron seems most aware of his process in terms of feedback and social maneuvers. At the same time, his own comments raise questions about that less visible interpretive process he describes elsewhere as "filtering." One wants to know what happens when Ron decides to "sit there and watch," when he "listens to key words," and when they "register." How does his interpretive process and his way of mediating that context differ from that of other students who are also "listening" in class, but who hear it differently? What effect does the very fact of Ron's strategic decision to make meaning, to seek cues and actively filter his context, have on his writing? To me, these questions call for a new kind of research that could reveal the social and cognitive process by which Ron mediated the situation he found himself in and in doing so translated that context into action.

As an educator one can also feel uneasy about the way this writer depends on feedback for self-direction (a concern also voiced by his teacher in this study). Talking about a history paper, Ron told us:

> You get an answer in your mind as to what your interpretation of the task is and what the answer is. But then, you filter that through the realities of your environment and what's going on. . . . But that doesn't mean that you have to abandon your original thought on that. It's just a matter of practicality really.

Are these assumptions about meaning making, forged over ten years of rising from stock boy to assistant manager of a large store, going to be a sensitive guide to the academic discourse valued in college and to independent thinking? Ron, in his own way, seems to be facing one of the problems of integrating cognition and context. In his context-dominated image of the process there seems to be little room for his own personal authority and options. The social cues he so energetically seeks are treated as if they were unambiguous cues to action. On the other hand, Ron's own goals and strategies lead him to just "listen" in a radically constructive way—to interpret and transform the context of the freshman class into a plan for action. In many ways, Ron inhabits his own cognitively constructed context of freshman writing in which he acts with a sense of purpose that is at once assertive, bounded, and problematic. The Reading-to-Write study suggested that we needed a theory and language of interaction to understand Ron. It also illuminated some of the difficulties of conducting such research.

Seeing Interaction in Action

If we agree that a theory of interaction is a worthwhile goal, we have not given ourselves an easy task. *Interaction* or situated cognition (Brown,

Collins, and Duguid) is a conditionalized sort of action, operating in response to specific situations, including a context within the writer's own mind which changes as that writer constructs new meaning. Some of the interaction between cognition and context will be predictable and insignificant to us; some will make all the difference. *To build a theory based on those sites where interaction matters most, we must be willing to investigate real acts of writing.* I do not believe we can leap from armchair research to make assertions about the force or role of this particular dialectic without evidence of real sites where conditions and cognition meet with explosive, unacknowledged, or generative force. Nor would it be enough at this stage of knowledge to build self-referential theories of how such interaction *might work* or what such a dialectic *should lead to.*

To do justice to this partly understood, situated process, we would need to shift focus from a big "C" theoretical Context and from big "C" general theories of Cognition, to the small "c" contexts in which writing is going on and the study of strategic cognition in situ. Even though our implicit big "C" theories *affect and guide* our interpretation of lived-in contexts and records of cognition, the process of interaction is no fragile epiphenomenon; it is a robust fact of experience that can stand up to critical examination.

For me the greatest challenge would be to construct a theory of interaction that could itself support action. As an educator, the action I can foster does not go on within a social abstraction or a collective, but in the minds of individual students. The ultimate reason for my research is intervention. I need a vision that preserves the place of the thinking, acting, self-aware writer. I want a vision that can recognize the reality of that writer's bounded intentionality and socially constructed knowledge—and within the center of that vision illuminate the space for possibility, options, and action by individual writers.

PART TWO: OBSERVATIONAL RESEARCH AND INTERACTIVE THEORY

The project I have outlined calls for a kind of theory-building which is not afraid of research and for a kind of research that is willing to grapple with its own limitations in order to go beyond isolated "results" to theory-building. The goal of an interactive theory, it seems to me, is intimately bound up with the problem of how to build one. In the second half of this article, I would like to examine the role observational research might play in such theory building. There are two good reasons to do this. One is the strong premise outlined above—that we can best understand interaction by dedicated efforts to see it in action. The second and more problematic reason is that some members of the broad community of English see research itself as a threat to the humanities, especially research that uses empirical methods. Let me be concrete. Last year at the summer Rhetoric Seminar at Purdue, I talked to a young woman who was working on a degree in literature at another institution. As we were sitting around one night drinking wine, she told me that she "didn't believe in doing research." I was a little taken aback that an aspiring scholar would reject any method of inquiry out of hand, almost as an article of faith. But in talking it became apparent that her vision of empirical research was itself so reductive that she never saw beyond the methods, the numbers, and the tables she couldn't read, to the common sense on which research and its rules of evidence are built or to goals we both cared about. My remarks here are in a sense addressed to that young woman and to our need for a broader vision of research as a tool for building contextualized and integrated theories of writing.

Research and Observation-Based Theory Building

Any theory, if it is to offer a broadly explanatory account of a significant human action or body of knowledge, will have to meet many criteria including logical consistency, clarity, scope, and parsimony. A rhetorical theory which integrates cognition and context must do more. Like other "grounded theories," it must *fit* the situation being studied (that is, it can be applied without force and its categories are clearly reflected in the data); and must *work* (that is, it must offer an explanation of the process that is meaningful to us as both theorists and educators) (Glaser and Strauss). Second, as a theory of *interaction*, it should be built on a fine-grained, richly specified vision of the process in question.

Grand, speculative theories are well-designed to capture the imagination, but they are also associated with the rhetoric of conflict among competing theories, one position striving to preempt the other in a zero/sum game. Fine-grained, observational theories can encourage the rhetoric of exploration and construction. They direct attention to the process under study and open the door to continued modification of themselves. They also allow (even invite) us to recognize significant variations in the way this theory plays itself out in different settings, from a storefront school in a barrio to a college classroom, from one writer to another.

There are many valued paths that lead to theory. Theory can be based on historical scholarship or on extrapolations from prior theories, in much the way we adapt classical rhetoric to modern problems or adapt Burke's dramatistic analysis of literature to composing. Theory can also grow out of what Lauer and Asher call rhetorical inquiry: a deductive process in which the theory-builder both examines and argues for a set of premises and conclusions, a mode that can combine the strengths of a speculative leap with reasoned support. Theory can also grow out of research: a process in which one's orienting premises enter into dialogue with a set of close, systematic observations of writers at work. Observation-based theory building is carried out in rhetoric with an expanding repertoire of empirical methods, ranging from the controlled methods of experimental research to the descriptive methods of ethnography, case studies, and process-tracing using cued recall and protocol analysis.

Any basis for theory-building (whether it is historical scholarship, systematic observation, or personal experience) is merely a springboard, a means to an end. We must remember that theory-building is ultimately a constructive, rhetorical act: to create a structured, explanatory account of an interactive process like writing will inevitably force us beyond available evidence and into the probabilistic reasoning that is at the heart of rhetoric (Perelman and Olbrechts-Tyteca). The path we take will differ from other paths in the kind of argument and evidence it can generate. Let me quote Lauer and Asher's definition of "rhetorical inquiry" as one approach to theory-building:

> Rhetorical inquiry, then, entails several acts: (1) identifying a motivating concern, (2) posing questions, (3) engaging in heuristic search [based on analogy] (which in composition studies has often occurred by probing other fields), (4) creating a new theory or hypothesis, and (5) justifying the theory. (5)

The approach I am calling observation-based theory building will lead to an argument with its own distinguishing features. First, unlike an empirical study using data primarily to test or confirm a carefully delimited assertion, the goal of this process is theory. In trying to construct a more comprehensive, more explanatory account, observation-based theory building draws on research for its heuristic power as well—going a step beyond the data in an attempt to honor the data. Second, it differs from the process Lauer and Asher describe in that it is driven to a greater degree by the generative power of close or systematic observation. Observation is used not merely to justify or test a theory but to help pose questions, structure the search, and frame hypotheses. We can see observation-based approaches at work in emerging theories across the field: Freedman's vision of response to writing as a form of collaborative problem-solving, Dyson's developmental picture of early writing as a child's orchestration of visual, verbal, and social meanings, Bazerman's cumulative analysis of how rhetorical intentions, available schemata, and necessary conventions interact in the history of scientific discourse, Applebee and Langer's studies of writing contexts as a scaffold for learning (see Applebee, *Contexts*), Bereiter and Scardamalia's models of knowledge telling and knowledge transformation, Witte's investigation of pre-text as the point at which plans, situational prompts, and text structure intersect, Heath's picture of how different literate practices function, fit, and misfit in different social settings, and my own attempt to explore how rhetorical situations are mediated by the goals, strategies, and awareness that make up a writer's strategic knowledge. These, and other bodies of work I might have mentioned, reflect a cumulative attempt to build a theoretical picture grounded in observation.

I want to focus the rest of this paper on this particular route to theory building, not to compare it to others or even to argue for its advantages, which, like any method's, are mixed. I want instead to initiate a dialogue about observation-based research by trying to describe some of its goals and limitations as I see them, as well as some of the problems of research itself. I would like to organize my comments around what I see as three features of this particular process of inquiry.

Intuition and Data in Observation-Based Theory Building

Observation-based theory is built from the union of two sources of evidence: it springs in part from an intuition or an argument and in part from the complementary evidence of close, systematic observation and data.

Let me illustrate this joint process with an example and a theoretical dilemma. The Reading-to-Write study referred to earlier left us with an important question: does the strategic knowledge we observed in this situation play a critical role in students' attempt to enter academic discourse; does it really matter for most students? Or would strategic awareness be just a luxury, useful only *after* one has learned the "basics" and the conventions of a new discourse? I could best frame my own intuitions about this strategic process as an argument from analogy. Far from being a luxury, valuable only to well-educated college students, I would argue, this strategic knowledge is closely related to the critical consciousness that provides the starting point in Paulo Freire's literacy programs. Those adults enter literacy, not by first trudging through and *banking* knowledge of the basics, but by using sounds and letters they already recognize to "make up" words that express their own experience and goals. They become makers and users of literacy from their first evening session. As Freire and others like Ann Berthoff argue, knowing your own knowledge, whatever it is, and discovering your own power to make meaning stand at the heart of these astoundingly successful literacy programs. To that I would add, if such knowledge can catapult an unlettered Brazilian farmer into literacy, what might such self-awareness offer to a college student who stands merely on the threshold of a new form of discourse?

I like the spirit of this argument. It captures my own intuitions; it is based on a premise I know is shared by other educators; and it builds on an analogy to a clearly successful case showing the power of strategic consciousness in learning new ways to use language. And yet this argument alone is not enough. One wonders, does the analogy really *fit?* And even if it does apply at some level of generality, does it *work* as a genuinely useful explanation; will it describe the experiential reality of students learning a particular kind of discourse? An argument alone will not tell us what may in fact be happening with our students. For instance, what is the strategic repertoire your students bring to college? Does context or the background of your particular students lead to important differences in their goals or strategies that we could/should anticipate? Does the theory outlined in the Reading-to-Write study even fit the data of your experience and your students at all?

It is in response to questions like these that observation-based theory building turns to a second source of evidence, which is the data of experience. Close observation is demanding; systematic observation even more so. I think of Shirley Heath's detailed descriptions of children's speech spanning a nine-year period and how, from these patterns, consistent, deep-running disjunctions between the culture of home and the culture of school began to emerge. I think of Anne Dyson's systematic study of children's early writing and drawing, a study which eventually contradicted the assumption that narrative is the first and natural mode for all children, and in doing so, showed that certain children (marked as developmentally delayed by their teachers!) were in fact becoming writers by a different but equally "natural" path. I think of the Reading-to-Write data which tracked the unpredictable twists and turns of writers' minds at work; how this record captured the interplay between reading, writing, and thinking that the students' texts did not register, and in doing so revealed some of the dilemmas and decisions a teacher never sees. In all of these studies and others like them, the goal is a more explanatory theory, but the starting point is the data of close observation.

We must not forget that "data" is itself a selected piece of experience—the speech the observer chose to write down, the classroom exchanges the ethnographer was there to capture, the thoughts which occupied the conscious attention of writers as they thought aloud. But compared to more ad hoc forms of personal observation and the fragile records of unprompted memory, these formal records of experience provide a large, detailed, and independent picture the observer must then account for. In being *collected* according to a broad and systematic sampling plan, the data one must be accountable to is itself less likely to be covertly patterned, pat, or biased in an unacknowledged way. Such data actively resists the observer's desire to "discover" that single example which will "prove" a pre-ordained point. Good data is assertive and intractable. In the dialogue that goes on between intuition or emerging theory on the one hand and the data on the other, these records of experience have the habit of contradicting one's cherished assumptions and pet theories. The data always contains more possibilities than we can grasp. It may even ask us to negotiate multiple representations of meaning, multiple symbol systems as when an ethnographer must translate non-verbal actions into words or when we move from a rich intuitive perception to a coding scheme we can explain to someone else (Flower and Hayes, "Images"). This very richness is the source of a central dilemma for research. And that is my second point.

Data and Meaning

Data is only data; a theory is a construction based on data.

All data can do is provide the foundation for interpretation. And in observation-based theory-building, as in much research in rhetoric, we have to take genuine leaps. We have to go beyond the data to probabilities, because our goal is not merely to describe, but to understand—to infer and to explain something we want to know. Data is the grist for an interpretive act. Moreover, theory making is never disinterested. We do research because, as a part of an educational community, we have constructed the burning questions we want to answer; we have already named the mysteries we want to plumb. We use data both to initiate and to constrain our interpretive leaps.

To say that data is only data, is also a statement about epistemology. In taking an observation-based approach to theory-building one cannot treat data as if it were a source of immutable, objective facts or transparent proofs, even when that data comes from personal experience. When data is used to build an interpretive theory, it cannot be "read" directly without reference to the rules of evidence that constitute the discourse of research. To say that the "data shows us" something can only mean, at bottom, that our interpretation of that data has tried to live up to the evidentiary rules of research.

To understand the role of data in theory-building, we should not ask "what the data means" but ask "how it is used to make meaning" within the researcher's interpretive act. I think it is clear to the readers of this journal that to do so one must reject the positivistic assumptions associated with nineteenth-century science and behaviorism. What may be less clear is that to understand the role of data we must also become more critical of the naive readings of empirical research within our own community. We need to be as sensitive to unsophisticated or reductive readings of the language of research as we are to reductive readings of literature. For instance, some readings treat the findings of a single study as an unconditional, generalizable assertion of the "research has shown . . ." variety. In this case the overextension is in the mind of a reader (who may be eager to appropriate a result). Other readings, where the aim is to critique, attribute such overextensions to the researchers themselves. Researchers are imagined to hold a variety of positivistic assumptions, to see their results as unmediated statements of natural fact. The apparent basis for this inference by readers is that research papers typically do not discuss the issue or actively deny these presumptions. Likewise, readers who are unfamiliar with the discourse conventions of research may assume that the act of mounting "evidence," especially statistical evidence, constitutes a broad claim about the validity or truth of a conclusion in some ultimate sense (cf. Knoblauch's clear statement of this issue). Or they may read a correlational claim as no different from a claim of causality. Within the conventions of research, however, the "results" of a given study, especially those which merely show a correlation, are just one more piece of evidence in cumulative, communally constructed argument. The special virtue of a claim that has earned the name "result" is that it has been subjected to a given research community's more stringent rules of inference (Hayes).

Terms such as "evidence," "results," and "validity" are loaded concepts to a reader entering the discourse. They contribute to misunderstandings in part because their meaning must be grasped in *the context of specific research methods*. Seen in situ, they do not refer to ultimates or absolutes, but to *tools* that help build more persuasive arguments. For instance, one could read statements about "significance" and "validity" (expected in a research paper) as if they were general assertions of value, reflecting the common usage of those terms. Whether the reader accepted this reading or assumed the researcher was intending it, the misreading would be the same. In context, these terms of art refer in fact to methods one can use to test the strength of one's evidence. For example, the notion of "construct validity" does not refer to a construct's approximation to Truth, but to the use of procedures for testing its coherence with existing theory or practice. The meaning of "validity" lies in this operational definition: it refers to a set of procedures designed to measure consensus with the rest of a discourse community (cf. Lauer and Asher) or to preclude certain rival hypotheses which other researchers could be expected to pose (Huck and Sandler). To achieve construct validity means to pass such tests.

759

In trying to understand how data is in fact used in the discourse, we must also look skeptically at the practice of decontextualized or anachronistic readings of research, often conducted in the name of discovering hidden assumptions. As humanists we are well prepared to write eloquent critiques of Locke's theory of knowledge, to construct abstract or theoretical dichotomies, and to tease out the manifold implications of key words (e.g., validity, significance, data). But to understand the discourse of modern research we cannot simply extrapolate from history or the OED. A sophisticated reading of research depends on understanding the context of doing research, on knowing how key terms and concepts function as method within the practice of the discourse. Acontextual readings, which do not see the methods behind the words, often overgeneralize about what researchers mean. Or they lead to the peculiarly ahistorical assumption that someone doing empirical analysis does so from a set of nineteenth-century, unqualified, simplistic, or positivistic premises. These premises are not only unnecessary to doing empirical observation, they have been largely long abandoned in even the hard sciences (O'Keefe). For example, compare the following two ways of talking about research.

> [Experimental, Clinical, and Formal research in composition share] the *positivist tradition's fundamental faith* in the describable *orderliness of the universe:* that is, the belief that things-in-the-world, including in this case people, operate according to determinable or *"lawful"* patterns, general tendencies, *which exist quite apart from our experience of them* [italics added]. (North 137)

One wonders how many practicing researchers would agree with North's monolithic account of their premises. By contrast, when Stephen Jay Gould, who is a scientist, comments on the relation of knowledge and culture, one sees an alternative view of research in which social construction and observation both play a part. The following comments are from an article which traced the contribution of three culturally "determined" theories of vertebrate evolution. Although Gould sees each theory as building on an historically shaped and ultimately flawed interpretive framework, his view of research allows data and interpretation to enter a constructive dialogue.

> Popular misunderstanding of science and its history centers upon the vexatious notion of scientific progress. . . . The enemy of resolution, here as nearly always, is that old devil Dichotomy. We take a subtle and interesting issue, with a real resolution embracing aspects of all basic positions, and we divide ourselves into two holy armies, each with a brightly colored cardboard mythology as its flag of struggle. . . .

760

These extreme positions, of course, are embraced by very few thinkers. . . . Science is, and must be, culturally embedded; what else could the product of human passion be? Science is also progressive because it discovers and masters more and more (yet ever so little in toto) of a complex external reality. . . . Science is not a linear march to truth but a tortuous road with blind alleys and a rubbernecking delay every mile or two. Our road map is not objective reality but the patterns of human thought and theories. . . .

But this history [of three views on the development of vertebrates] is not only a tale of social fashion. . . . Each world view was a cultural product, but evolution is true and separate creation is not. (16-24)

Gould takes a strong stance on the interaction of data and ideology—a stance which I think marks observation-based theory building as well. Although empirical methods grew up in the context of logical positivism and 18th- and 19th-century science, the most rigorous sort of empiricism can be carried out with very different assumptions about what those "results" might mean. Ironically, the process which practicing researchers actually argue about is both more interesting and more problematic than these "cardboard mythologies" are.

In practice, research is a process of case building in which data is a privileged form of evidence. Because the conclusions to which we aspire in the humanities and social sciences are not susceptible to logical demonstration or proof, we depend on argument and justification. We are operating in what Perelman and others have described as the province of rhetoric—the truths we arrive at are judgments about what is probable. And, as Toulmin has argued, our judgment about what is probable is intimately related to our purpose in doing research or in making a deliberation. Imagine two groups of researchers wanting to understand the place of Black English in education. Linguists intent on recognizing/justifying linguistic diversity are likely to draw on different methods of analysis and justifications—and to reach different conclusions about the phenomenon—than would educators focused on the effect Black English has on social and economic equality (Donmoyer).

Given that discoveries are contingent on the goals of investigation, the critical question becomes: what constitutes a good argument (Phillips)? This question comes up repeatedly in the exciting debate over quantitative versus qualitative inquiry that has raged for the past seven years in the pages of *Educational Researcher*, the journal of the large American Educational Research Association. This research community lives in a post-positivistic world which acknowledges both the relative nature of knowledge and the social and cognitive process of interpretation in educational research (Garrison, Howe,

Phillips). The problem is how to evaluate the validity, reliability, and meaningfulness of claims made *within* this world (Fetterman, Firestone, Mathison, Peshkin). In this debate research methods operate as rhetorical methods in Perelman's sense—they are ways to evaluate the evidence for an idea. For example, researchers use the technique of "significance testing," not to certify Truth or Significance, but to build a case for themselves and others about the relative strength of their evidence, about the likelihood (probability) that the pattern they saw could be seen by others, or that it might appear again, or elsewhere. However, an even more important way to build a case within the research community is to make one's own process of interpretation—one's methodology—transparent. Miles and Huberman describe this process with exceptional clarity as they talk about the problem of consensus building in qualitative research:

> It seems that we are in a double bind: The status of conclusions from qualitative studies is uncertain because researchers don't report on their methodology, and researchers don't report on their methodology because there are not established conventions for doing that. Yet the studies are conducted, and researchers do fill up hundreds of pages of field notes, then somehow aggregate, partition, reduce, analyze, and interpret those data. In publishing the results, they must assume theirs is not a solipsistic vision. . . . [They] do have a set of assumptions, criteria, decision rules, and operations for working with data to decide when a given finding is established and meaningful. The problem is that these crucial underpinnings of analysis remain mostly implicit, explained only allusively. . . . We need to make explicit the procedures and thought processes that qualitative researchers actually use in their work. (22)

To say that data is only data, then, is to assert that research is a process of case building and justification to one's self and others. Consider the problem which motivates this article: trying to understand the interaction of cognition and context in writing. The goal of an observation-based theory would be to create a finely-grained explanatory theory, to construct a more fully-specified vision of this process, based on the data of experience. But because we cannot *finally know* if the patterns we see are there, the methods of observational research should be read as *attempts* to test and verify one's claims, as *attempts* to create more precise operational definitions, and/or as *attempts* to rest claims upon multiple, independent observations based on multiple methods (cf. Schriver). In this process, empirical observation plays a central and positive role. However, this method of inquiry is not without unavoidable difficulties of its own. In the rest of this paper I want to concentrate on some of the inherent problems of observation and on the limits of evidence from any source. A theory based on observation, like any argument, is still nothing more than a probabilistic statement. The problem is how to respond to the necessary uncertainty of our own interpretations.

My mind goes back to that young woman working on her literary dissertation, developing her own new reading of a text. It was the *spectre of empirical methods* that made her reject research. Why on earth should Anne Dyson do a detailed, even quantifiable, analysis of her six-year-olds? Why should theorists do more than assert, describe, and present persuasive examples of the evocative patterns they see? One answer is that *as theorists and researchers, we inevitably, constantly, and energetically impose meaning and pattern on the data of experience.* We begin a study, we leap to an argument, and yet all too often, when we return to that larger world of our data—when we analyze it more, asking if it fits our hypothesis—we see we were "wrong." Our interpretive act created a lovely, theoretically appealing, logically consistent pattern. It would have made a great journal article. But as a theory aspiring to explanatory breadth it was wrong. Our theory may, for instance, have described the striking performance of Jeannelle and Jason to a "T," but on closer analysis it violated the experience of every other student in the study.

There is a double bind in this profession. We know as theorists that our interpretive acts cannot be "right" in any final sense. But unfortunately, they can be wrong in some important ways: they can fail to fit or account for the experience at hand; they can fail to do justice to the data, to the process, or to the people we are trying to understand. The process of rhetorical inquiry Lauer and Asher described has always been alive to this problem, insisting on the tests of internal coherence and consistency. And, in fact, many tentative perceptions are discarded by those means long before we turn to other, more elaborate filters. But the complexity and data-rich detail that both cognitive and contextual studies generate can create additional problems.

The Contribution of Empirical Methods

Observation-based theory turns to empirical methods because it is sensitive to its own limitations.

Given enough time, people, including teachers, researchers, and literary critics, will always perceive patterns, of some sort, in anything. In the face of this human tendency, observational research relies on two acts of common sense. The first is to subject these observations and interpretations to the test of reliability. As my colleague John Hayes once said, looking at protocols is a little like looking at clouds—if you look long enough you can always see a pattern. The question is, would anyone else see it too? Does this pattern in the data exist only in the eye of the beholder or the mind of the theorist? A formal test of reliability among different observers is a response to this dilemma.

In practice this simply means that the researcher must articulate the pattern he or she perceives into a coding scheme that tells another observer how to read the data (e.g., how to recognize a goal, an act of resistance, or a commonplace of academic discourse when one of these postulated events appears in the data). By convention, researchers expect at least 80% agreement as a basis for asserting reliability.

Sometimes reliability is simply checked at the end of a study and the agreement score reported as another piece of evidence. However, this process of developing a shareable reading of the data can be even more valuable when it is used in the early stages of analysis to create a more sensitive and fine-grained theory. In this process the researcher asks a co-coder to analyze a sample of the data using the tentative theoretical statement (expressed as a coding scheme) that the researcher has developed from his or her own close analysis. The (inevitable) points of disagreement between coder and co-coder become sparks to insight as they challenge a researcher to articulate intuitions, recognize disconfirming evidence, and see the diversity of meaning his or her own categories may embrace. Reliability comparisons, used as a generative technique, can lead to substantial changes in interpretation as a researcher progressively reshapes his or her claims to better reflect the data. What began as a method of confirmation becomes a step in an epistemic process. The exuberance of our pattern-making powers, fueled by an initial piece of evidence, is only problematic, then, if we disregard conflicting messages from the data itself. The test of reliability is one way these "messages" are spoken.

Observational theory building tries to deal with its own limitations at a second critical point, by turning to another method that systematizes common sense. It sends the theorist to the resistant, uncompressed body of the data as a whole, with the injunction to *listen to that data—to construct meaning—in a systematic way.* The metaphor of "listening" to the data is used in research not because people literally assume data can speak for itself without our constructive effort, but to dramatize the need to avoid selective observation and the willful imposition of one's own assumptions. The art of listening to the whole involves not only an openness to contradictory and disconfirming evidence, but a perverse zest for rival hypotheses, and an active search for unpredicted patterns that might be more fully supported by the data than those predicted.

Imagine, for example, that you are at a critical point in theory-building. You have discovered a meaningful pattern:

◆ You have found some striking examples of students creating—and then dismissing—their own personal elaborations as they read and write,

◆ Or you have just done a brilliant explication of a protocol or a student text, or completed a revealing case study,

◆ Or you have noticed that your advanced writers seem willing/able to establish their personal authority early in a text, in ways your basic writers fail to do.

You have the beginnings of a theoretical statement about some of the cognitive/contextual dynamics of authority. As a meaning maker, you have imposed a new order on the data of experience. And the question you must now answer for yourself is whether this new order is an interesting but isolated pattern. Would this local explanation account for the other texts in the folder, would it fit the other protocols, would it describe what those 40 students actually do and how the two classes really differ? *In essence, does your pattern fit the data at hand?*

No theory will be a complete or perfect fit. Indeed, the object of theory-building as opposed to case studies is to isolate certain critical features from the "noise" that constitutes the rest of the experience. And we must remember that we are constructing meaning based on our own definitions of meaningful. Given those premises, there are still some hard questions we want to ask about the fit of our interpretations.

One of the first common-sense methods of empirical research is to test the fit by asking, is there a rival hypothesis that offers a better explanation? Many theories of discourse will seem true at some level of generality—e.g., advanced students of anything have more authority than beginners. However, rival interpretations that challenge the "authority" hypothesis might include these: does my operational definition of "personal authority" really capture a writer's personal attitude or can I only claim to have seen certain textual conventions (such as the use of "I") that seem "authoritative"? Or perhaps the assignment is really producing this effect: maybe the advanced writers are working on a familiar genre for which they know the conventions for asserting and supporting a claim—regardless of their personal investment or confidence, or perhaps the real variable here is topic knowledge: the advanced writers are doing research papers which immerse them in rich bodies of information and evidence—their authority is logos; the basic writers, however, were assigned an expressive/descriptive paper which leaves them swimming against the current, forced to use the subtle conventions for establishing ethos and personal authority in an artful genre. Experimental research methodology has formalized some of the most common sources of rival hypotheses into a set of standard threats to validity (cf. Huck and Sandler). Before making a claim about causality, researchers should be able to eliminate rival hypotheses, such as the effect of "mortality" in which only the students who liked the class or shared the observer's bias remained in the sample at the time of evaluation. Perhaps the most devastating rival hypothesis to an experimental study is that what appears to be causation is only correlation. For example, imagine that children's writing ability was shown to increase with cultural literacy, with shoe size, or with some other variable. One might claim causality, but in fact all of these supposed causes may simply reflect the critical variable of age.

In experimental research one tries to control for outside influences in order to exclude such rival claims in advance. In the more exploratory enterprise of observation-based theory building, it is difficult to deal with rival hypotheses through control. However, this concern still enters the process as an effort to capture observations that escape the mold—to actively explore alternative interpretations of the data. There is a well-documented tendency in studies of reasoning and inference-making for people to look only for positive instances which confirm a hypothesis and to happily ignore counter evidence (Wason and Johnson-Laird). Data-based observation encourages an expectant stance toward new data that can leave the theorist open to revision. But more than that, by asking the researcher to make a theory operational—explicit enough to be reliably used by another observer—it allows the data to speak back on its own resistant terms and may encourage rival, complementary, or more explanatory patterns to emerge.

At times, research methodology allows us to ask how well a theory *fits* and how well it *works* in yet another way: by asking if the pattern or frequency of our observation is strong enough to be surprising. Have we uncovered a broadly descriptive pattern or only another interesting but idiosyncratic event (Hayes)? For instance, the particular ways of negotiating or avoiding authority that we observed in a few of our basic writers may, on a more careful look at the data as a whole, be phenomena that are in fact normally distributed across all sorts of students, maybe even across all sorts of adult writers. Developing a voice and taking a rhetorical stance may be problems we all share. If that were the case, our theory asserting that the texts of basic writers can be distinguished by the absence of personal authority and/or our educational innovation based on the differences we thought we observed would be resting on a very shaky premise. Although we might be able to build a convincing argument about a general relationship between personal authority and writing, when it comes to grounding our theory in the data of experience and testing its explanatory power, the data in observation-based theory building has a chance to reply and tell us that we have not yet captured the "truth" of this experience. Our theory does not yet *fit* or *work* for the situation we hoped to explain.

Here is one place where an estimate of probability, in the form of elementary statistics, can play a useful role in exploratory research. Assume that we have observed a number of cases in which basic writers fit our imagined pattern and fewer cases of advanced writers who do so; or assume we see in our protocol data a growing number of elaborations made during reading and discarded during writing. Is this pattern a meaningful description of the fate of elaborations? Does our pattern of authority-taking actually distinguish one group of students from another? A simple test for statistical significance lets us compare the frequency or distribution of the events we see, with what might occur by chance, at random in a normal population of students or in a data set the size of ours. If our pattern is much more frequent than chance would dictate, it begins to look surprising and the probability that we have found a meaningful category goes up. The conventions for claiming statistical significance are rigorous: for a pattern to appear surprising it must have the probability of appearing by chance less than 5 times in 100 or in some cases less than 1 time in 100, a result that is expressed as a probability (p) that is equal to or less than a given level of occurrence (e.g., $p = .05$ or $p < .05$). Notice too what "significance" means here; it is a conservative and probabilistic statement which only asserts that the pattern we claim to have seen is unlikely to have occurred by chance. Under some circumstances we might choose a statistical tool that is less rigorous than a "significance test" and more sensitive to partial or weak but interesting patterns (Glaser and Strauss)—i.e., we could choose to be a little more easily impressed.

Testing the Constructed Reality of Theory

The point of all this is not to prove a claim but to understand more about the strength and predictive power of the patterns we have created. Statistics, by their very nature as tests of probability, are not designed to prove that a point is *true* but whether it is *probable*. Once we decide to move beyond a single case study and talk about the pattern of the whole, when multiple and complex patterns are interwoven throughout a text or throughout the performance of readers or writers, it is often impossible to grasp the patterns of frequency or distribution without turning to a test of probability or a statistical test of correlation. Simple counts and even averages are often deceptive. More importantly, statistical tests are often the only way to acknowledge the negative evidence and the counterexamples in our data in a rigorous and systematic way. They allow us to fit our theorized pattern, like an imaginary transparency laid over the data as a whole, and see where the pictures match—and where they don't.

To return to that young woman again, what I hope she came to see in our conversation was that the attempt to *systematically test the fit* between your vision and your data is not an attempt to eliminate recognition of variety but actively to attend to it. Nor is it an attempt to certify validity, to assert you have found truth, or to replace the richness of experience with numbers. In a way it is just the opposite—it is a way to listen to more of that experience. It is also a response to the limitations of our own ways of knowing and to our extraordinary ability to see pattern in anything. It is a response to our theory-guided tendency to seek out what we can currently imagine and to see what we already believe. All methods are ultimately weak methods, just as all our theories are only partial. In observation-based theory building these two attempts to test claims—that is, to test for reliability and for a fit to the data with or without statistics—are often powerful not because they are instruments of proof, but because they are a hedge against our own fallibility. But more than that, these instruments of caution can also be turned into generative tools for building more finely-grained theories that are more likely to work and fit.

Let me conclude with a final issue we face in building observation-based rhetorical theories that can integrate rather than polarize cognition and context. My own work offers an example of the problem. The Reading-to-Write study used a rich body of data to build a tentative theory of strategic knowledge and its role in learning to manage academic discourse. This theory emerged from a value-laden interpretive framework concerned with how individual students can take authority over their own writing by gaining awareness of their own interpretive process. At the same time, I believe this theory is a sensible and careful description of the students we observed. And its focus on goals, strategies, and awareness offers at least one way to describe how cognition and context work together as reader/writers construct meaning. But will my description of how cognition and context interact fit the data of your students? Will my more general argument for the role of strategic consciousness itself hold when we examine other contexts? I can't say. A genuine observation-based theory of strategic knowledge in writing, if we as a field develop one, will not be the product of any one study or any one writer or theorist. Observation-based theory building is a cumulative effort. It is shaped by a community of observers working from different points of view, with different methods, and in different contexts of observation. More importantly such a theory will be shaped by the tension between its own two goals, which are to create, on the one hand, a meaningful interpretation of the world and, on the other, to test that constructed reality in clear and careful ways, against the rich and contrary data of experience.[1]

NOTE

1. I especially want to thank Janice Lauer, David Kaufer, Stuart Greene, John R. Hayes—and that young woman visiting Purdue—for their stimulating and supportive discussions of these issues.

WORKS CITED

Ackerman, John. "Translating Context into Action." *Reading-to-Write: Exploring a Cognitive and Social Process.* Linda Flower et al. New York: Oxford UP, in press.

Applebee, Arthur N. "Problems in Process Approaches: Toward a Reconceptualization of Process Instruction." *The Teaching of Writing.* Ed. David Bartholomae and Anthony Petrosky. Chicago: National Society for the Study of Education, 1985. 95-113.

_____. *Contexts for Learning to Write.* Norwood, NJ: Ablex, 1984.

Bartholomae, David. "Inventing the University." *When a Writer Can't Write: Studies in Writer's Block and Other Composing-Process Problems.* Ed. Mike Rose. New York: Guilford Press, 1985. 134-65.

Bazerman, Charles. "Physicists Reading Physics: Schema-laden Purposes and Purpose-laden Schemas." *Written Communication* 2 (January 1985): 3-23.

Bereiter, Carl, and Marlene Scardamalia. *The Psychology of Written Composition.* Hillsdale, NJ: Erlbaum, 1987.

Berlin, James. "Rhetoric and Ideology in the Writing Class." *College English* 50 (September 1988): 477-94.

Berthoff, Ann. "Reading the World . . . Reading the Word: Paulo Freire's Pedagogy of Knowing." *Only Connect: Uniting Reading and Writing.* Ed. Thomas Newkirk. Upper Montclair: Boynton/Cook, 1986. 119-30.

Bizzell, Patricia. "Cognition, Convention, and Certainty: What We Need to Know about Writing." *Pre/Text* 3 (Fall 1982): 213-44.

_____. "College Composition: Initiation into the Academic Discourse Community." *Curriculum Inquiry* 12.2 (1982): 191-207.

Brown, John Seely, Allan Collins, and Paul Duguid. "Situated Cognition and the Culture of Learning." *Educational Researcher* 18.1 (February 1989): 32-42.

Bruffee, Kenneth A. "Social Construction, Language, and the Authority of Knowledge: A Bibliographical Essay." *College English* 48 (December 1986): 773-90.

Donmoyer, Robert. "The Rescue from Relativism: Two Failed Attempts and an Alternative Strategy." *Educational Researcher* 14.10 (December 1985): 13-20.

Dyson, Anne Haas. "Individual Differences in Beginning Composing: An Orchestral Vision of Learning to Compose." *Written Communication* 9 (October 1987): 411-42.

Emig, Janet. *The Composing Processes of Twelfth Graders.* Urbana, IL: National Council of Teachers of English, 1971.

Enos, Richard Leo. *The Composing Process of the Sophist: New Directions for Composition Research*. Occasional Paper. Berkeley: Center for the Study of Writing at University of California, Berkeley and Carnegie Mellon University, 1989.

Fetterman, David M. "Qualitative Approaches to Evaluating Education." *Educational Researcher* 17.8 (November 1988): 17-23.

Firestone, William A. "Meaning in Method: The Rhetoric of Quantitative and Qualitative Research." *Educational Researcher* 16.7 (October 1987): 16-21.

Flower, Linda. "The Construction of Purpose in Writing and Reading." *College English* 50 (September 1988): 528-50.

———. "The Role of Task Representation in Reading-to-Write." *Reading-to-Write: Exploring a Cognitive and Social Process*. Linda Flower et al. New York: Oxford UP, in press.

Flower, Linda, and John R. Hayes. "Images, Plans and Prose: The Representation of Meaning in Writing." *Written Communication* 1 (January 1984): 120-60.

Flower, Linda, Karen A. Schriver, Linda Carey, Christina Haas, and John R. Hayes. *Planning in Writing: The Cognition of a Constructive Process*. Technical Report No. 34. Berkeley: Center for the Study of Writing at University of California, Berkeley and Carnegie Mellon University, 1989.

Flower, Linda, Victoria Stein, John Ackerman, Margaret J. Kantz, Kathleen McCormick, and Wayne C. Peck. *Reading-to-Write: Exploring a Cognitive and Social Context*. New York: Oxford UP, in press.

Freedman, Sarah, with Cynthia Greenleaf and Melanie Sperling. *Response to Student Writing*. Urbana: National Council of Teachers of English, 1987.

Freire, Paulo. *Pedagogy of the Oppressed*. Trans. Myra Ramos. New York: Continuum, 1986.

Garrison, James W. "Some Principles of Postpositivistic Philosophy of Science." *Educational Researcher* 15.9 (November 1986): 12-18.

Glaser, Barney, and Anselm Strauss. *The Discovery of Grounded Theory: Strategies for Qualitative Research*. Chicago: Aldine Publishing, 1967.

Gould, Stephen Jay. "Pretty Pebbles." *Natural History* 97.4 (April 1988): 14-26.

Hayes, John R. "Empirical Research in Rhetoric." National Council of Teachers of English Research Council Meeting. Chicago, 19 Feb. 1988.

Hayes, John R., and Linda Flower. "Identifying the Organization of Writing Processes." *Cognitive Processes in Writing: An Interdisciplinary Approach*. Ed. Lee Gregg and Erwin Steinberg. Hillsdale: Erlbaum, 1980. 3-30.

Heath, Shirley B. *Ways with Words: Language, Life and Work in Communities*. Cambridge, Eng.: Cambridge UP, 1983.

Herrington, Anne. "Teaching, Writing and Learning: A Naturalistic Study of Writing in an Undergraduate Literature Course." Writing in Academic Disciplines. Vol. II of *Advances in Writing Research*. Ed. David Jolliffe. Norwood, NJ: Ablex, 1988. 133-66.

Howe, Kenneth R. "Against the Quantitative-Qualitative Incompatibility Thesis or Dogmask Die Hard." *Educational Researcher* 17.8 (November 1988): 10-16.

Huck, Schuyler W., and Howard M. Sandler. *Rival Hypotheses: Alternative Interpretations of Data Based Conclusions*. New York: Harper, 1979.

Knoblauch, C. H. "Rhetorical Constructions: Dialogue and Commitment." *College English* 50 (February 1988): 125-40.

Lauer, Janice M., and J. William Asher. *Composition Research: Empirical Designs*. New York: Oxford UP, 1988.

Lunsford, Andrea, and Lisa Ede. "Why Write . . . Together: A Research Update." *Rhetoric Review* 5 (Fall 1986): 71-81.

Mathison, Sandra. "Why Triangulate?" *Educational Researcher* 17.2 (March 1988): 13-17.

Miles, Matthew B., and A. Michael Huberman. "Drawing Valid Meaning from Qualitative Data: Toward a Shared Craft." *Educational Researcher* 13.5 (May 1984): 20-30.

Myers, Greg. "The Social Construction of Two Biologists' Proposals." *Written Communication* 2 (July 1985): 219-45.

McCormick, Kathleen. "The Cultural Imperatives Underlying Cognitive Acts." *Reading-to-Write: Exploring a Cognitive and Social Process*. Linda Flower et al. New York: Oxford UP, in press.

Nelson, Jennie, and John R. Hayes. *How the Writing Context Shapes Students' Strategies for Writing from Sources*. Technical Report No. 12. Berkeley: Center for the Study of Writing at University of California, Berkeley and Carnegie Mellon University, 1988.

North, Stephen M. *The Making of Knowledge in Composition: Portrait of an Emerging Field*. Upper Montclair: Boynton/Cook, 1987.

O'Keefe, Daniel J. "Logical Empiricism and the Study of Human Communication." *Speech Monographs* 42 (August 1975): 169-83.

Perelman, Chaim, and L. Olbrechts-Tyteca. *The New Rhetoric: A Treatise on Argumentation*. Trans. John Wilkinson and Purcell Weaver. Notre Dame: U of Notre Dame, 1969.

Peshkin, Alan. "In Search of Subjectivity—One's Own." *Educational Researcher* 17.7 (October 1988): 17-22.

Phillips, D. "After the Wake: Postpositivistic Educational Thought." *Educational Researcher* 12.5 (May 1983): 4-12.

Rose, Mike. "Complexity, Rigor, Evolving Method, and the Puzzle of Writer's Block: Thoughts on Composing-Process Research." *When a Writer Can't Write: Studies in Writer's Block and Other Composing-Process Problems*. Ed. Mike Rose. New York: Guilford Press, 1985. 227-60.

_____. "Narrowing the Mind and Page: Remedial Writers and Cognitive Reductionism." *College Composition and Communication* 39 (October 1988): 267-302.

Schriver, Karen A. "What Are We Doing as a Research Community? Theory Building in Rhetoric and Composition: The Role of Empirical Scholarship." *Rhetoric Review* 7 (Spring 1989): 272-88.

Shaughnessy, Mina. *Errors and Expectations: A Guide for the Teacher of Basic Writing*. New York: Oxford UP, 1977.

Spradley, James. *Participant Observation*. New York: Holt, 1980.

Stein, Victoria. "Elaboration: Using What You Know." *Reading-to-Write: Exploring a Cognitive and Social Process*. Linda Flower et al. New York: Oxford UP, in press.

Toulmin, Stephen. *Foresight and Understanding*. New York: Harper, 1961.

Wason, Peter C., and Philip N. Johnson-Laird. *Psychology of Reasoning: Structure and Content*. Cambridge: Harvard UP, 1972.

Witte, Stephen. "Pre-Text and Composing." *College Composition and Communications* 38 (December 1987): 397-425.

Composition Studies
and ESL Writing

A Disciplinary Division of Labor

PAUL KEI MATSUDA

Specialization leads to its own problems. The discipline or department can become an end in itself.

> —Joel Colton, "The Role of the Department in the Groves of Academe," 317

Although the number of nonnative speakers of English in U.S. institutions of higher education has been increasing continuously during the last four decades, the development of composition studies does not seem to reflect this trend.[1] Until fairly recently, discussions of English as a Second Language (ESL) issues in composition studies have been few and far between. Few composition theorists include second-language perspectives in their discussions, and only a handful of empirical studies written and read by composition specialists consider second-language writers in their research design, interpretation of data and discussion of implications. It almost seems as though the presence of over 457,000 international students in colleges and universities across the nation (Davis 2) does not concern writing teachers and scholars.[2]

The presence of ESL students should be an important consideration for all teachers and scholars of writing because ESL students can be found in many writing courses across the United States. As Jessica Williams' survey of ESL writing program administration suggests, the vast majority of institutions

Reprinted from *College Composition and Communication* 50.4 (June 1999): 699–721. Used with permission.

continue to require undergraduate ESL students to enroll in first-year composition courses, often in addition to special ESL writing courses. In many cases, they are also required by their departments to take professional writing courses. Thus, it is becoming increasingly likely that writing teachers at one point or another will encounter ESL writers in their classrooms. Although working with these students is "not radically different from teaching writing to native English speakers" (Leki xi), some of the linguistic and cultural differences they bring to the classroom pose a unique set of challenges to writing teachers. In a review of empirical research comparing ESL writers and native speakers of English, Tony Silva states that the former not only produced texts that were characterized by native-English-speaking readers as "distinct from and often simpler and less effective" but also "planned and reread their writing less, wrote with more difficulty because of a lack of lexical resources, and exhibited less ability to revise intuitively by ear" ("Differences" 215).[3] In *Teaching ESL Writing*, Joy Reid also writes that "the needs, backgrounds, learning styles, and writing strategies of most ESL students differ dramatically" (vii) from those of native English speakers. Furthermore, she points out that there is considerable diversity even among ESL students "in terms of language and cultural backgrounds, prior education, gender, age, and ESL language proficiency" (vii), which may make working with ESL students challenging for some writing instructors. While there also are many similarities, these and many other differences continue to "cause anxiety and misunderstandings" (Leki xi), suggesting the need for writing instructors to become more sensitive to the unique needs of ESL writers.

This absence of second-language writing discussions reflects and is reflected in the way composition studies has been constructed in its historical context. The second-language component does not appear in the work of influential historians of composition studies—such as James Berlin, Robert Connors, Susan Miller and David Russell—because ESL writing has not been considered as part of composition studies since it began to move toward the status of a profession during the 1960s. This omission poses a serious problem for the status of second-language issues in composition studies because historical studies provide narratives that shape the practice within the profession. That is, the lack of second-language elements in the history of composition studies, and therefore in our sense of professional identity, continues to reinscribe the view that the sole responsibility of teaching writing to ESL students falls upon professionals in another intellectual formation: second-language studies, or more specifically, Teaching English as a Second Language (TESL).[4] This view of the interdisciplinary relationship, or what I call the "disciplinary division of labor," seems to reflect the values of the two intellectual formations that sought, especially during their formative years, to establish their own unique identities as respectable professions or academic "disciplines." As I will argue, this desire to claim their own areas of expertise led to the division of writing scholarship into first- and second-language components. This division of labor, however, is inadequate as a metaphor for the relationship between composition studies and TESL because ESL students, just like their native-speaker counterparts, continue to be affected by the institutional practices within composition studies because of their continued presence in composition classes. Yet, this metaphor not only keeps writing teachers from applying the insights from the growing body of second-language writing scholarship in working with ESL writers in their classrooms but also creates a tension that further divides teachers and researchers in the two fields.[5]

To construct an interdisciplinary relationship that is more responsive to the needs of ESL students in composition programs, it is necessary to understand the historical context in which the disciplinary division of labor is situated. In this essay, I examine how this division emerged between composition studies and TESL. Specifically, I will show how the professionalization of TESL over the period of 1941 to 1966—just when composition studies was also undergoing a revision of its own disciplinary identity—inadvertently contributed to the creation of the disciplinary division of labor that continues to influence the institutional practices in composition programs across the nation.

THE BIRTH OF A PROFESSION

It is not enough for the foreign language teacher to be able to speak English; to be most effective he should know English—its sound system, its structural system, and its vocabulary—from the point of view of a descriptive analysis in accord with modern linguistic science.

—*Charles C. Fries,* Teaching *(13)*

Prior to the 1940s, the teaching of ESL was not regarded as a profession in the United States, although this is not to say that the teaching of English to nonnative speakers had not taken place. By the 19th century, the teaching of English to Native American children was well under way (Spack, *Americas*), and Americanization programs provided some formal English language instruction to immigrants in urban areas during the late 19th century and the early 20th century.[6] At the college level, ESL instruction began to take place during the early 20th century. Harold B. Allen notes that the first English class for international students was taught in 1911 by J. Raleigh Nelson at the University of Michigan. Harvard University offered a similar course in 1927, followed by George Washington University in 1931 ("English" 307).[7] Other institutions, however, failed to recognize the special needs of international ESL students, although by 1930 there were already almost 10,000 international students, mostly from Asia and Europe (Institute of International Education 232–35). Consequently, many ESL students were forced into the sink-or-swim approach to language learning. The teaching of ESL generally did not receive serious attention in the United States, and there seemed to be little respect for ESL teachers (Allen, "English" 307; "Freshman" 156).

A significant change was brought to the status of the ESL teaching profession with the development of U.S. foreign policy. Following President Franklin D. Roosevelt's announcement of the Good Neighbor policy at the Pan-American Conference in 1933, the teaching of English to nonnative speakers—especially in Latin American countries—became a serious concern of the federal government. The subsequent development prompted the U.S. Department of State to promote the teaching of the English language to nonnative speakers as well as the preparation of English language teachers. In the fall of 1939, the State Department funded, in cooperation with the Rockefeller Foundation, a conference at the University of Michigan to decide on a theoretical basis for the teaching of ESL (Allen, "English" 299; Alatis 382). Two of the most promising proposals were presented, according to Allen, by I. A. Richards and by Charles C. Fries:

> Richards, who had just come to Harvard University from England and his association there with C. K. Ogden in developing Basic English, offered a plan to teach English as a foreign language through a combination of lessons involving word and picture correspondence and vocabulary acquisition through the use of Basic English. In sharp contrast, Fries's proposal not only relied heavily upon the principles of Henry Sweet but also added a significant dimension taken from current linguistic theory. This dimension provided for controlled drills, structural study of English and the native language of the learner. ("English" 299)

Fries's proposal convinced the Rockefeller Foundation to provide him with a grant in 1940 to develop teaching materials for Latin American students. In 1941, with additional grants from the Department of State and the Rockefeller Foundation, the English Language Institute (ELI) at the University of Michigan came into being with Fries as its first director.

The opening of the ELI at Michigan was one of the most significant events in the history of TESL in the United States. At the 1956 meeting of the Conference on College Composition and Communication, Paul R. Sullivan of the University of Minnesota referred to the Institute as the starting point of modern English language teaching methods ("Studies" 163–64). Allen later characterized the ELI as "the nation's most dynamic single force in the teaching of English as a second or foreign language" ("English" 298). Indeed, the creation of the ELI at Michigan had a significant influence on the development of TESL as a profession. One of the primary missions of the ELI was to provide specialized intensive language instruction to ESL students. Influenced by the U.S. foreign policy, the ELI initially provided courses designed primarily for Spanish speaking students from Latin American countries, but later it opened itself up to ESL students from other countries who were brought by the conclusion of the World War II. During its first ten years of operation, 2,100 international ESL students at the University of Michigan were enrolled in the intensive language courses offered by the ELI. The Institute also provided a professional preparation program for ESL teachers, thus promoting a sense of professionalism among ESL teachers. In fact, one of the most important consequences of the creation of the Michigan ELI was the rise of what may be called "Michigan professionalism," the principle on which the Institute was founded.

Before the Michigan ELI was established in 1941, it was commonly believed that anyone whose native language was English was qualified to teach English to nonnative speakers—much as some thought any literate person could teach writing. In fact, one of the most significant contributions that Fries's ELI made to the profession was to dispel this myth. As Fries later wrote:

> The native speaker himself however, unless he has been specially trained to observe and analyze his own language processes, finds great difficulty in describing the special characteristics either of the sounds he makes or of the structural devices he uses. His comments about his own language more often mislead than help a foreigner. ("As We See It" 13)

With the creation of the professional preparation program at the University of Michigan, however, the teaching of ESL began to move toward the status of a respectable profession.

The meaning of "professionalism" that emerged among applied linguists at Michigan during the 1940s was quite different from the sense of professionalism embraced by practitioners of TESL during the 1960s. Allen's characterization of the language teaching profession in the inaugural issue of the *TESOL Quarterly* in 1966, for instance, focused on the sense of belonging to a group of teachers who shared common concerns and problems:

> Nor without an organization can a large number of people with common interests effectively further those interests. Without an organization, teachers having a common discipline and a common subject matter will not eas-

ily come to consider themselves a professional group. ("TESOL and the Journal" 3)

In contrast, professionalism, as defined by Fries and his colleagues at Michigan, privileged the knowledge of structural linguistics. What professionalism in language teaching meant to them was the application of the principles of linguistics, hence the use of the term "applied linguistics" in describing the profession of language teaching. The term, in the words of Robert B. Kaplan, was "initially nearly inextricably tied to language teaching," although it has, at least in the United States, acquired a broader meaning (374).[8] In A *History of English Language Teaching*, A. P. R. Howatt points out that Fries' view of applied linguistics was "a hierarchical one" with the linguist "at the 'top'" producing the "basic, scientific descriptions of the source and target languages" to be applied by language teachers (267). That Fries decried the lack of knowledge about linguistic principles among language teachers was apparent in the preface to his *Teaching and Learning English as a Foreign Language* (1945), a textbook for second-language teachers that continued to be influential until the 1970s. He wrote:

> In spite of the fact that there has been more than a hundred years of vigorous linguistic investigation in accord with sound scientific methods, very little of the results of this investigation has actually got into the schools to affect the materials and methods of teaching language and the actual conditions under which language teaching is attempted. (i)

He went on to quote structural linguist Leonard Bloomfield, who complained in 1925 that teachers at all levels "do not know what language is, and yet must teach it, and in consequence waste years of every child's life and reach a poor result" (Bloomfield 5, qtd. in Fries, *Teaching* i). Influenced by a Bloomfieldian view of linguistics as a body of knowledge with practical applications, Fries saw the development of teaching materials at the Michigan ELI as "an attempt to interpret, in a practical way for teaching, the principles of modern linguistic science and to use the results of scientific linguistic research" (*Teaching* i).

Fries's view of professionalism was not always welcomed by language teachers, however, because his hierarchical notion of applied linguistics struck them as condescending. As William G. Moulton notes, Fries's idea of "instruction being based on 'sound linguistic principles' and being supervised by a 'trained linguist' struck them [language teachers] as professional exaggeration, not to say arrogance, on the part of the linguists" (97). Yet, Michigan professionalism became increasingly pervasive both nationally and internationally due to the enormous success in reproducing the values of Fries's ELI through the graduates of its teacher preparation program. Although the number of programs that offered graduate courses and certificate programs in TESL had increased to 22 by the end of the 1950s (Institute of International Education 123), the creation of many teacher preparation programs at various institutions across the nation did not so much diversify the view of the profession as it perpetuated the already influential Michigan professionalism because many of those programs were developed or staffed by people who were associated with the Michigan ELI in one way or another.[9] As Allen wrote:

> Even in many of these newer programs is felt the pervasive influence of Charles C. Fries, for dominant in the list of those who founded or now direct or teach in principal other programs are the names of persons who were either trained in the English Language Institute or, now a second generation, were trained by former graduates or staff members. ("English" 302)

Another significant event that contributed to the perpetuation of Michigan professionalism was the creation of a journal. Graduate students at the Michigan ELI had established the Research Club in Language Learning and, in 1948, began the publication of *Language Learning: A Quarterly Journal of Applied Linguistics,* the first journal of its kind in the United States.[10] It was also "the first journal in the world to carry the term 'applied linguistics' in its title," although L. W. Lockhart had already used the term in the subtitle of his book in 1931 (Editorial 1). The goal of the journal, according to Howatt, was "to bring the ideas developed at Fries's English Language Institute at the University of Michigan to the attention of a wider public" as well as to promote the understanding of linguistics and applied linguistics in general (265). As Robert Lado also noted in his 1960 editorial for the journal, the stated goal of the Research Club in publishing the journal was clearly in line with Fries's view of the profession: "to publish articles exploring the application and implications of linguistics in foreign language teaching" (v). Lado further wrote:

> *Language Learning* steadily continued to fill the need for the publication and distribution of those articles that more or less deliberately applied linguistics to language teaching. . . . *Language Learning* has dared to publish articles which would be rejected as too linguistic for the non-linguist and not linguistic enough for the pure linguist. (v)

The initial goal of the Research Club was met successfully; the journal became widely accepted—in the first ten years of the publication, the circulation rose from 200 U.S. subscribers to 1,200 subscribers in 76 countries (Lado v).

The journal continued to adhere to Fries's view of the language teaching profession until the late 1960s. As a 1967 editorial stated, the journal had been publishing articles that "dealt with applications of linguistic theory in the teaching and learning of languages." However, it was no longer possible to ignore the broadening definition of applied linguistics, which came to include "studies in first language acquisition, in bilingualism, translation (human and machine), in linguistic statistics, in sociolinguistics, in psycholinguistics, in the development of writing systems for unwritten languages, in the development of 'new' national languages, and so on." For this reason the editor announced that the journal would also consider articles "in these and other branches of applied linguistics" but only "to the extent that they are at least of marginal interest to those applied linguists whose primary concern is with language learning and teaching" (1).

The growth of Michigan professionalism and its view of secondlanguage teaching as the application of linguistic principles had a profound impact on the way ESL writing was positioned in the emerging field of composition. Before discussing how the rise of professionalism in TESL contributed to the division of labor, however, it is necessary to understand the place of ESL issues in composition studies during that time. I now turn to a discussion of how ESL issues became a concern among teachers of composition and how they were handled in composition programs.

ESL CONCERNS AT CCCC

Many colleges and universities in the United States, especially large institutions with a reputation abroad, are constantly faced with the problem of what to do with foreign students who do not have a knowledge of English adequate for keeping up, on an even basis, with native students.

—George Gibian, (157)

Despite the development of the Michigan ELI and other innovative local ESL programs, such as the program developed at Queens College (Schueler), the number of institutions that developed specialized ESL programs for international students during the early 1940s was rather small. As Allen reported, "there was no noticeable increase in the numbers of foreign students" and "no one saw any major problem." As a consequence, few institutions were prepared for the large numbers of international ESL students who came to the United States at the conclusion of the Second World War ("English" 307). The development of the Conference on College Composition and Communication during the first decade after the war reflected rising concerns about ESL students. When CCCC was first established in 1947, ESL was not a major component of the organization. Yet, as the number of ESL students continued to increase during the 1950s, institutions were no longer able to ignore the presence of this population, and ESL became an important issue at the annual meetings of the Conference.

In the late 1950s, the problems associated with international ESL students often became a topic of discussion at the annual spring meetings of CCCC. A number of panels and a series of workshops on issues surrounding international students were presented between 1955 and 1966, and were included in the workshop reports printed annually in *CCC*, a practice that continued until the 1970s. The names of prominent ESL specialists—including Kenneth Croft of Georgetown University, Robert B. Kaplan of the University of Southern California, Robert Lado of the University of Michigan, and Paul R. Sullivan of Georgetown University—appeared regularly in those workshop reports.

Among the scholars and teachers who were active in both TESL and composition studies was linguist Harold B. Allen, who later presided over NCTE in 1961 and became the first president of Teachers of English to Speakers of Other Languages (TESOL) in 1966.[11] Allen was a key player during the formative years of CCCC. In a historical review of *CCC*, Phillips, Greenberg and Gibson count Allen among the most frequently published authors of major articles as well as the most frequently cited authors between 1950 and 1964. Characterizing him as one of the "early shapers of the discipline," they also note that Allen "was active in the national organization" and that "his reprinted speeches about the future of the profession were often referred to in *CCC* articles" (452). Allen was a member of the general committee for the first CCCC meeting in 1949, and he chaired a workshop the following year. At the business meeting on November 24, 1950, he was elected associate chair of the committee. He then chaired the Conference in 1952.

Although the lack of English language proficiency was one of the most important concerns among English teachers, it was obvious to many that the difficulties that ESL students faced were not only linguistic. For this reason, discussions at CCCC meetings included a wide variety of topics. The participants in the workshop called "The Foreign Student in the Freshman Course" at the 1955 meeting "quickly agreed that satisfactory handling of the foreign student's problems with English involved more than materials and methods of classroom instruction" ("Foreign Student" 1955, 138). Indeed, topics of discussion in this and subsequent workshops often included a wide range of issues: the need for and the availability of English language proficiency tests, models of special ESL curriculum, the issue of granting college credits for ESL courses, evaluation standards in English classes, admission criteria for international students, the need for orientation programs, and the role of English teachers in the students' cultural adjustment process.

The presence of a large number of ESL students in the English classroom was a serious concern not only among ESL specialists but among teachers whose professional interest or preparation did not include the teaching of ESL. The issue of increasing linguistic diversity in English classrooms was highlighted in a 1956 panel entitled "Studies in English as a Second Language." The panel chair, Paul R. Sullivan, began the session by noting that "all teachers of English frequently teach English as a second language" in effect because of the presence of students who spoke a differing variety of English, if not another language, outside of school. He also pointed out the need to provide specialized instruction for the increasing number of international ESL students ("Studies" 163–64). In the following year, Sullivan chaired another panel on the application of TESL principles to the regular English classes. In this panel, he once again pointed out that it had become "increasingly evident that many teachers are finding themselves faced with the problem of teaching English as a second language" ("English" 10). For this reason ESL workshops attracted many non-ESL specialists; in 1956, faculty from institutions without ESL programs constituted the majority of the participants in the CCCC workshop. One of the central topics of discussion at this workshop was the question of how to deal with international ESL students in the regular composition course at institutions where neither ESL specialists nor separate ESL courses were available—a question that continues to be relevant today. The report also indicated that participants in this workshop "represented an immense range in the kinds of programs (or lack of them) now existing" ("Foreign Student" 1956, 122).

Despite the increasing recognition throughout the 1950s of the presence of ESL students in English classrooms and the unique problems they brought with them, the vast majority of institutions continued to place ESL students into sections of English courses designed only for native speakers of English without making any adjustments or providing sufficient linguistic support. Others placed international ESL students into basic writing courses, or "remedial subfreshman courses" as they were then called, although the needs of international ESL students tended to be quite different from those of basic writers and immigrant ESL students.[12] These courses were often taught by teachers whose interest and preparation were limited to literary studies. Some institutions even sent ESL students to "speech clinics where speech therapists treated them as suffering from speech defects" (Allen, "English" 307).

At other institutions, where a large number of ESL students were enrolled, the problem of writing instruction for ESL students became "too conspicuous to be brushed under the freshman English rug" (307). One type of solution, deemed most desirable by applied linguists at the time, was the creation of intensive English language programs modeled after the ELI at Michigan. Many of those programs, often located outside the traditional institutional structure of the English department, were staffed by specially trained ESL instructors. However, the "special training" for the teachers meant at the time coursework in structural linguistics. The intensive programs were able to meet the needs of beginning or intermediate ESL students who had limited or no background in the English language, but they did not address the needs of ESL students in composition courses. Fries's approach to language teaching, which he termed the "oral approach," focused on the "mastery" of the sound system of the English language and was not intended for the teaching of writing to ESL students at the college level. In Fries's words,

> The practice which the student contributes must be *oral practice*. No matter if the final result desired is only to *read* the foreign language[,] the mastery of the fundamentals of the language—the structure and the sound system with a limited vocabulary—must be through speech. The speech *is* the language. The written record is but a secondary representation of the language. To "master" a language it is not necessary to read it, but it is extremely doubtful whether one can really *read* the language without first mastering it orally. (*Teaching* 6)

To Fries, a language was nothing more than "a set of habits for oral production and reception," and writing, or "written symbols," was used only to the extent that it assisted in the mastery of the spoken language (6). Partly due to the dominance of Fries's view of applied linguistics, the study of written language or the teaching of writing to ESL students did not attract serious attention from applied linguists until the 1960s, and intensive English programs did not pay much attention to the teaching of writing beyond grammar drills at the sentence level.

At many institutions where ESL enrollment was relatively low, creating a separate program staffed by ESL specialists was not a feasible option. Instead, special remedial writing courses were created for ESL students and were often taught by instructors from foreign language departments or English departments. In "College English for Foreign Students" (1951), George Gibian wrote that a special section of remedial English was developed at Harvard in 1949 to meet the "peculiar needs" of "a small group of European students, all of whom seemed to need extra aid" (157). The goal of this course was to teach students communication skills—including writing and reading as well as oral communication—that were necessary to succeed in college courses. Sumner Ives of Tulane University also reported in 1953 the creation of a special ESL writing course offered only in the fall. Although this course was offered on a non-credit basis by default, it sometimes became credit bearing when a significant number of students demonstrated the ability to succeed in the second-semester writing course. While this course was primarily concerned with writing, the curriculum and materials from Michigan's ELI were adopted to help students who needed extra linguistic support. Similarly, William F. Marquardt of the University of Washington created a three-credit ESL course in which writing was the focus of instruction.

Those who were committed to the teaching of ESL argued for the division of labor on the basis of the need for a specially trained ESL instructor. As Ives wrote: "This course should . . . be taught by someone on the permanent staff, for an essential feature is the continuity of judgment which is involved. Moreover, it should be taught by someone with linguistic training" (143). Although these courses were intended to provide the needed linguistic support for ESL students, they were also motivated by the need to release composition specialists from the extra "burden" of teaching ESL students in their classes. Gibian argued, for instance, that "distributing the burden of extra aid and consideration among all instructors of courses which the foreign student takes, without helping by providing a special course, is an inefficient process, wasteful and lacking in organization" (157). The creation of these programs was one of the factors that contributed to the division between first- and second-language specialists. However, it was the combination of this and other factors, such as the rise of applied linguistics and the professionalization of both TESL and composition studies, that ultimately led to the institutionalization of the disciplinary division of labor.

INSTITUTIONALIZATION OF THE DIVISION OF LABOR

If we are to be a profession, we must have standards that the professional worker meets. If we are to be a profession, some agency must establish those standards. If we are to be a profession, some agency must recognize appropriately those institutions that acceptably prepare teachers to meet those standards.

—Harold B. Allen, "The Pros Have It" (117)

As the number of ESL programs and teacher preparation programs increased, more teachers began to receive specialized training in TESL, and the need for professionalization of TESL was increasingly felt. Yet, many institutions continued to staff their ESL programs with junior faculty and graduate students from English and foreign language departments whose primary interest and training were in literary studies and not in the teaching of ESL. This tendency was deemed unacceptable both by applied linguists, who were increasingly committed to promoting the application of linguistic principles, and by TESL specialists who sought to increase the professional status of ESL teachers. As William Slager wrote:

> For linguistic science has made it clear that to teach English (effectiveness, organization and usage) to native-born Americans, and to teach English as a foreign language (mastery of the sound and structure system), are as widely different as two tasks can be. The first in many ways deals with language as an art. The other deals with language as a science: its subject matter and its classroom techniques require special background and training. That both courses are often taught in the same department is coincidental. (24)

To Slager and others, the teaching of ESL required "enough linguistic training to make phonemic and structural comparisons" across languages ("Foreign Student" 1955, 139), and the division of labor between composition teachers and ESL teachers was often suggested as a desirable, if not the only acceptable, solution to the problem of teaching ESL students. In the report from the 1961 CCCC panel, "The Freshman Whose Native Language is Not English," chair Ernest A. Boulay argued for the creation of special programs as a solution to the increasing concerns about ESL students. Implicit in this argument was the division of labor between writing teachers and ESL teachers. He argued for a "separate preparatory course" taught by "a linguistic expert, or experts, so that the student may be prepared for and oriented to some of the vagaries of the English language before the Freshman English teacher meets him" (156). At the same session, other panelists also addressed the issue of teacher qualification and argued for the division of labor. Clara M. Siggins of Boston College argued that the course for ESL students "should not be given by the beginning English teacher in order to 'pick up' experience, nor should it be given as extracurricular activity" and that "a program such as this calls for careful course organization and a special faculty." Clifford H. Prator of the University of California, Los Angeles was of the same opinion. He argued that ESL teaching "can be well done only by a specialist with an analytical knowledge of English and with deep insights into the way the student's native tongue interferes with his learning of the new language. The usual freshman composition instructor is not equipped to do the work, to say nothing

785

of the person whose only qualification is that he speaks English as his mother tongue" (156). Prator's argument was motivated by the need for professionalization:

> The teaching of English as a second language is a perfectly respectable academic field which offers immense opportunities for serious research. This discipline needs more practitioners who will devote their entire career to it and not regard it as a temporary way of winning one's bread while preparing to teach courses in linguistic[s] or literature. It is definitely not a job which some university departments of English can continue with impunity to wish off on the newest member of the faculty and on its most defenseless member. (156)

The arguments for the division of labor were also motivated by Michigan professionalism, which sought to establish, in the language teaching arena, the place of the structural linguists who had "become increasingly interested in applying the results of linguistic methods of analysis to the solution of language problems" (156). In 1965, members of the CCCC workshop, chaired by Robert B. Kaplan, formalized the attitude of ESL specialists at the Conference by putting forth a recommendation that "[w]here it is feasible, speakers of English as a second language should be taught *in special classes* by teachers who have had training in teaching English as a second language" ("ESL Programs" 203).

Some ESL specialists were wary of the possible implications of the division of labor. When professionalization was realized by the creation of TESOL, Allen cautioned TESL specialists that the argument for professionalization should not become an argument for "the *reductio ad absurdum* that no one should legally be entitled to teach a single English word to non-English speaking persons without having obtained a license to practice" ("Pros" 114). Although the argument for professionalization did not lead to a ban on the teaching of ESL by non-TESL specialists, it did lead to a decline of interest in ESL issues among composition specialists. In effect, composition teachers were being told by applied linguists and TESL specialists that they lacked the needed expertise to teach ESL students. At the same time, however, composition teachers might have welcomed the same argument because it would release them from the "burden" of acquiring new knowledge and skills to teach ESL students and from the extra time that they had to spend in working with the unique problems that ESL students brought to the classroom.

The decline of interest in ESL issues among composition teachers was evident as the number of participants at CCCC workshops on ESL issues decreased; in fact, nobody attended the 1965 workshop. Discouraged by the lack of interest in ESL issues among CCCC members, the ESL workshop in 1966, chaired again by Kaplan, made a decision that would, in effect, remove ESL elements from composition studies almost entirely. The "small but loquacious group" of ESL specialists at the workshop resolved "somewhat sadly . . . that, given the small attendance at this workshop for several years under the aegis of CCCC, the group should meet hereafter only at NCTE meetings" ("Teaching" 198). In the same year, TESOL was started as a professional organization to serve the needs of a growing number of ESL specialists (Alatis 386–87; Allen, "English" 315–16; Hook 218). The creation of a professional organization that devoted itself entirely to ESL issues and the decline of interest in those issues among composition specialists led to the separation of writing issues into first-language and second-language components. The disciplinary division of labor was thus institutionalized.

The immediate effect of the institutionalization of the division of labor can best be illustrated by considering the exchange that took place between Joseph H. Friend of Southern Illinois University and Gordon Wilson of Miami University, Ohio. At the CCCC executive committee meeting on April 1967, Friend asked "whether problems of teaching composition to non-English speakers should not be included in the program." Wilson, who was the executive committee chair at the time, responded to Friend's inquiry by pointing out that the "competition of TESOL might prevent a sufficient number of people from attending a workshop." Although Wilson suggested that "a panel [on ESL issues] might be advisable" (Burke 1967, 205), sessions concerning nonnative speakers of English—either in the form of panels or workshops—remained absent from CCCC conventions at least for the next ten years.

Richard Braddock of the University of Iowa, who was the convention chair in 1967, was more sympathetic to Friend's cause. During the same meeting, he appointed Friend to act as a liaison between CCCC and TESOL (Burke 1967, 206–7). When Braddock chaired the executive committee meeting in November 1967, he responded to Friend's brief report by asking him to "continue submitting such reports to CCCC" and by saying that "CCCC is always willing to cooperate with TESL" (Hettich 262). However, the TESOL reports continued only during Braddock's tenure in the executive committee. Friend made another report in April 1968 (Burke 1968), but his name disappeared from these meetings after the November 1968 meeting, when Friend "had no report on TESOL" (Burke 1969, 267). ESL concerns had perhaps vanished even earlier, since the content of neither of Friend's reports were recorded in the secretary's reports on executive committee meetings.

BEYOND THE DIVISION OF LABOR

*That there is, and will be, a clash of cultures between the two disciplines
is ... beyond doubt, and as long as it remains, the immediate needs of the
students will not be met as constructively as they might be if L1 [composi-
tion] and ESL specialists worked jointly and cooperatively.*

— *Terry Santos (89)*

As I have argued, the division of labor between composition specialists and
ESL specialists was inadvertently created between the 1940s and the 1960s
as a byproduct of the professionalization of TESL as well as of composition
studies. The division of labor has had a lasting impact on the relationship
between the two professions. Guadalupe Valdés observes, for instance, that
"individuals who focus on the teaching of English to native speakers generally belong to organizations such as NCTE . . . and CCCC" while "individuals . . . who focus on the teaching of English to nonnative speakers of
English are generally members of TESOL . . . or NABE (National Association of Bilingual Education)." She continues:

> Even though there are segments within CCCC and NCTE that specialize
> in the writing of nonmainstream students, these two organizations are not
> generally known for their expertise on matters related to the teaching of
> English to students from non-English-speaking backgrounds. (88)

Indeed, one of the consequences of the disciplinary division of labor is the
lack of concern about the needs of ESL writers among composition specialists that continues even today. As Alice Roy suggests, there is a "tendency
among administrators and English Department faculties to look for linguists
and ESL specialists to 'deal with' second language writers" (20; see also
Ransdell). Ann Johns also points out that, while some ESL specialists have
been trying to suggest ways to increase the understanding of ESL issues
among composition specialists, ESL panels at CCCC "seem to attract only
the ESL people who attend this conference" ("Too Much" 86). Composition specialists, Johns further writes, "have shown little interest, so far, in
who we are, who our students are, and what we do" (86). Although ESL issues have become somewhat visible at CCCC meetings—thanks to the
work of people such as Carolyn Chitereer Gilboa, Barbara Kroll, Nancy
Duke S. Lay, Ann Raimes, Alice Roy, Tony Silva and Lynn Quitman
Troyka—most CCCC members seem to remain oblivious to the needs and
characteristics of ESL writers.

As a view of the interdisciplinary relationship between composition studies and second-language studies, the division of labor is far from adequate because it is based on the "myth of transience" (Rose; Russell; Zamel, "Strangers")—the assumption that ESL writing can be broken down neatly into a linguistic component and a writing component and that the linguistic problems will disappear after some additional instruction in remedial language courses. Yet, this is often not the case. Even when ESL students are enrolled in special ESL courses before taking required writing courses, the unique difficulties that ESL writers encounter in English composition are not likely to disappear completely after a semester —or even a few years—of additional language instruction, as Ruth Spack demonstrated in her longitudinal study of a Japanese international student ("Acquisition"). Leki also points out that, "after ten years of studying English in classrooms abroad, ESL students still may have trouble writing effectively in English . . . and students who can recite grammar rules . . . are not always able to use those rules in producing language" (23). Similarly, Williams argues that it is unrealistic to expect that ESL writers "should have put their second language problems behind them and be ready to take on the challenges of the composition classroom without further support" (175). Furthermore, ESL students may not be familiar with the culturally constructed values and expectations that are tacitly understood and shared by the majority of teachers and students in the composition program, as a number of studies have suggested (Atkinson; Atkinson and Ramanathan; Fox; Li; Ramanathan and Kaplan). Since ESL students in most cases are required to enroll in composition courses, and since many ESL writers also take professional writing courses, ESL writing issues should be as much a concern for composition specialists as they are for second-language specialists.

I am not arguing, however, that composition studies and second-language studies should be merged. Although the disciplinary division of labor has created a number of serious and unresolved problems for the two intellectual formations, the solution to these problems does not lie in eliminating the division entirely. Since both composition studies and second-language studies have established their institutional identities and practices over the last three decades, attempting to consolidate the diverse practices in the two distinct professions would be unrealistic and even counterproductive. Rather, second-language writing should be seen as an integral part of both composition studies and second-language studies, and specialists in both professions should try to transform their institutional practices in ways that reflect the needs and characteristics of second-language writers in their own institutional contexts.

How, then, can composition studies integrate second-language ele-ments into its institutional practices? One logical place to start is for compo-sition specialists to begin learning about ESL writing and writers by reading relevant literature and by attending presentations, workshops, and special interest group meetings on ESL-related topics at professional conferences. Research on second-language writing also appears regularly in second-lan-guage journals—such as *College ESL, English for Specific Purposes, Journal of Second Language Writing, Language Learning,* and *TESOL Quarterly.* In addition, a few journals in composition studies—most notably the *Journal of Basic Writing, Teaching English in the Two-Year College* and *Written Com-munication*—have come to include an increasing number of articles con-cerning second-language writing issues. A number of bibliographic sources on ESL writing are also available. Dan Tannacito's *A Guide to Writing in English as a Second or Foreign Language: An Annotated Bibliography* pro-vides a fairly comprehensive bibliography through the end of 1993, and the *Journal of Second Language Writing* also has been publishing annotated bibliographies of recent scholarship on the subject since 1993.

Composition scholars, regardless of their areas of interest or modes of in-quiry, should also try to consider second-language perspectives in their work because theories of composition that exclude second-language writers and writing "can at best be extremely tentative and at worst totally invalid" (Silva et al. 402). In conducting empirical studies, composition researchers should acknowledge the presence of ESL writers in writing classrooms and try to include second-language writers in their research design, analysis, and dis-cussion of implications—rather than excluding them as "outliers" or "excep-tions," as many researchers have done. As Paul Prior points out:

> Although nonnative speakers (NNS) of English, whether resident or inter-national students, are now found in many university classes, only one study of writing in the disciplines (Sternglass, 1988) has even mentioned such students, and that mention was brief. The different language, cultural, and educational backgrounds that NNS bring to their courses raise both theo-retical and practical questions that deserve careful attention. (271)

Valdés also writes, "research on bilingual minority writers must be carried out by mainstream researchers as well as minority researchers and viewed as a legitimate focus of activity" (128).

Graduate programs in composition studies should also try to incorporate second-language writing into their curricula because graduate school is where institutional values are instilled in new members of the profession. At some institutions, graduate students in composition studies can take a second-language writing course offered through a graduate program in TESL, although the number of TESL programs offering a course in second-language writing is still small, and various institutional practices may discourage them from taking the course. An alternative is to create second-language writing courses or components within graduate programs in composition studies. A second-language component can easily be added to courses in composition theory and history as publications concerning second-language writing are becoming more readily available (Kroll, *Second Language*; Severino et al.). In empirical research courses, students can discuss how the consideration of second-language writers may complicate research designs and analyses. Readings from second-language writing research can also be included in courses dealing with almost any topic in composition studies, including writing in the disciplines (Belcher and Braine; Johns, *Text*; Zamel and Spack), literacy (McKay; Rodby), assessment (Hamp-Lyons), reading and writing (Carson and Leki), writing program administration (Braine, "ESL"; Kroll, "Rhetoric/Syntax"; Roy; Silva, "Examination"; Williams), and written discourse analysis (Connor; Connor and Johns; Connor and Kaplan; Purves).

Another important site of institutional practice is writing program administration. Since ESL students continue to enroll in writing courses, writing program administrators should make every effort to provide an ESL-friendly learning environment. This can be accomplished in a number of ways. One approach is to place ESL writers into basic writing or "mainstream" sections of composition that are taught by writing teachers prepared to work with ESL writers. Creating an ESL section of required composition courses is also a common response to the presence of ESL writers. Another approach is to create a special section of composition where native and non-native English speakers are systematically integrated and taught by a teacher who has preparation and experience in working with both types of students (Reichelt and Silva). As Silva suggests, what is important is "to offer ESL students as many of these options (and more) as resources permit" ("Examination" 41). Some institutions, however, may not be able to hire enough writing teachers with ESL preparation because of the lack of financial resources or the shortage of such teachers (Kroll, "Teaching"). In those situations, administrators may need to provide opportunities for writing teachers to learn how to work with ESL writers. This can be accomplished, for example, by offering pre-service and inservice workshops on teaching ESL writing, such as the one described by Braine ("Starting"), or by creating a local e-mail list for the discussion of ESL writing concerns. A number of introductory textbooks are available to facilitate the development of new ESL writing teachers (Campbell; Ferris and Hedgcock; Leki; Reid).

The needs of ESL students differ from individual to individual and from institution to institution, and it is not possible to create one solution that fits all situations. Yet, the solution cannot be found in total isolation from other disciplinary perspectives, either. For more than 30 years, ESL specialists have been working to improve the institutional practices for ESL writers in second-language classrooms by incorporating insights from composition studies; it is time for composition specialists to learn from them in developing institutional practices that can meet the needs of an increasing number of ESL students in writing classrooms—and beyond.

NOTES

1. The primary focus of this essay, which covers the period between 1941 and 1966, is on international ESL students at the undergraduate level rather than immigrant ESL students because, whereas the former began to increase in the 1940s, the latter did not reach a critical mass until the late 1960s. The distinction between international, or "foreign," students and immigrant students, who are permanent residents or citizens (as opposed to "non-immigrant aliens") of the United States, was a salient one during the formative years of composition studies and TESL. (See Slager, for example.) Although this dichotomy tends to oversimplify differences within the two groups of students, it continues to be a significant distinction because immigrant ESL students have needs and advantages that are different than those of international students (Leki 42–43). The presence of immigrant ESL students warrants another historical study, which is beyond my scope here.

2. According to the Institute of International Education, the total number of international students in the 1996–1997 academic year was 457,984, including 227,305 undergraduate students (Davis 130). Although not all international students are ESL students, most of them come from countries where English is not the dominant language.

3. It is important to remember that not all ESL texts are "simple" or "ineffective"—overgeneralization of research findings should be avoided at all cost—and that these are relative characterizations based on the expectations of native-English-speaking readers. Texts written by ESL students are often complex in ways that are different than those written by native speakers of English, and the effectiveness of the text is also context dependent. However, my experience as a secondlanguage writer as well as my interaction with ESL students also suggest that ESL writers, especially in the early stages of language learning, often feel frustrated because they are not able to write with the kind of complexity and effectiveness that they can achieve more easily when writing in their native languages.

4. My use of the term "intellectual formation" is inspired by Michel Foucault, whose notion of formation implies dynamic and complex discursive relations rather than a static and coherent body of knowledge. I thank Patricia Harkin for her insightful comment on this point.

5. I do not mean to imply that there has not been any interaction between the two intellectual formations. Second-language writing researchers have been borrowing theoretical and methodological frameworks from composition studies since the 1960s. (See, for example, Kaplan, "Cultural"; Raimes; Zamel, "Teaching," "Recent"). During the 1970s and the 1980s, Mina Shaughnessy, Alice Horning and others also made efforts to incorporate insights from second-language studies in general, although their goal was to help basic writers rather than ESL writers.

6. Spack, "America's"; Allen, "English" 295; see Brown and Singh for accounts of English language instruction to immigrants before 1920.

7. See Rogers for an account of the program at George Washington University.

8. Kaplan claims to be the first in the United States to bear the title of Professor of Applied Linguistics (Kaplan, "TESOL" 374).

9. There were, of course, some exceptions, including programs created at Georgetown University, American University, and the University of Texas, Austin (Moulton 105).

10. The term "Quarterly" was later dropped from the title because of the initial difficulty in maintaining its regular production schedule.

11. Allen contributed significantly to the creation of TESOL and its journal by conducting a status study of the ESL teaching profession (i.e., Allen, *Survey*) and by organizing conferences on ESL teaching between 1964 and 1966 (Hook 218).

12. Slager was among the first to discuss the differing needs of international ESL students and immigrant ESL students, and the placement issue of ESL students continues to be an important topic of discussion among ESL specialists. See Leki for a succinct review of differences between ESL writers and basic writers (27–38), and Silva ("Examination") for a comprehensive review of available placement options.

WORKS CITED

Alatis, James E., with Carol LeClair. "Building an Association: TESOL's First Quarter Century." *State of the Art TESOL Essays: Celebrating 25 Years of the Discipline.* Ed. Sandra Silberstein. Alexandria: TESOL, 1993. 382–413.

Allen, Harold B. "English as a Second Language." *Current Trends in Linguistics: Linguistics in North America.* Vol. 10. Ed. Thomas A. Sebeok. The Hague: Mouton, 1973. 295–320.

———. "The Pros Have It." *TESOL Quarterly* 2 (1968): 113–20.

———. *A Survey of the Teaching of English to Non-English Speakers in the United States.* Champaign: NCTE, 1966.

———. "TESOL and the Journal." *TESOL Quarterly* 1 (1967): 3–6.

Atkinson, Dwight. "A Critical Approach to Critical Thinking in TESOL." *TESOL Quarterly* 31 (1997): 71–94.

Atkinson, Dwight, and Vai Ramanathan. "Cultures of Writing: An Ethnographic Comparison of L1 and L2 University Writing/Language Programs." *TESOL Quarterly* 29 (1995): 539–68.

Belcher, Diane, and George Braine, eds. *Academic Writing in a Second Language: Essays on Research and Pedagogy.* Norwood: Ablex, 1995.

Bloomfield, Leonard. "Why a Linguistic Society?" *Language* 1 (1925): 1–5.

Braine, George. "ESL Students in First-Year Writing Courses: ESL Versus Mainstream Classes." *Journal of Second Language Writing* 5 (1996): 91–107.

———. "Starting ESL Classes in Freshman Writing Programs." *TESOL Journal* 3.4 (1994): 22–25.

Brown, Steven. "ESL Textbooks and Teaching in the Progressive Era." *The Mid-Atlantic Almanac* 6 (1997): 81–94.

Burke, Virginia M. "Secretary's Report No. 56." *CCC* 18 (1967): 204–7.

———. "Secretary's Report No. 58." *CCC* 19 (1968): 263–65.

———. "Secretary's Report No. 59." *CCC* 20 (1969): 266–68.

Campbell, Cherry. *Teaching Second-Language Writing: Interacting with Text.* Boston: Heinle, 1998.

Carson, Joan G., and Ilona Leki, eds. *Reading in the Composition Classroom: Second Language Perspectives.* Boston: Heinle 1992.

Colton, Joel. "The Role of the Department in the Groves of Academe." *The Academic's Handbook.* 2nd ed. Ed. A. Leigh DeNeef and Craufurd D. Goodwin. Durham: Duke UP, 1995. 315–33.

Connor, Ulla. *Contrastive Rhetoric: Cross-Cultural Aspects of Second Language Writing.* New York: Cambridge UP, 1996.

Connor, Ulla, and Ann M. Johns, eds. *Coherence in Writing: Research and Pedagogical Perspectives.* Alexandria: TESOL, 1990.

Connor, Ulla, and Robert B. Kaplan, eds. *Writing Across Languages: Analysis of L2 Text.* Reading: Addison, 1987.

Davis, Todd M., ed. *Open Doors 1996–97: Report on International Educational Exchange.* New York: Institute of International Education, 1997.

Editorial. *Language Learning* 17.1/2 (1967): 1–2.

"ESL Programs: Composition and Literature." CCC 16 (1965): 203.

Ferris, Dana, and John Hedgcock. *Teaching ESL Composition: Purpose, Process, and Practice.* Mahwah: Erlbaum, 1998.

"The Foreign Student in the Freshman Course." CCC 6 (1955): 138–40.

"The Foreign Student in the Freshman Course." CCC 7 (1956): 122–24.

Fox, Helen. *Listening to the World: Cultural Issues in Academic Writing.* Urbana: NCTE, 1994.

"The Freshman Whose Native Language is Not English." CCC 12 (1961): 155–57.

Fries, Charles C. "As We See It." *Language Learning* 1.1 (1948): 12–16.

_____. *Teaching and Learning English as a Foreign Language.* Ann Arbor: U of Michigan P, 1945.

Gibian, George. "College English for Foreign Students." *College English* 13 (1951): 157–60.

Hamp-Lyons, Liz, ed. *Assessing Second Language Writing in Academic Contexts.* Norwood: Ablex, 1991.

Hettich, David W. "Secretary's Report No. 57." CCC 19 (1968): 261–63.

Hook, J. N. *A Long Way Together: A Personal View of NCTE's First Sixty-Seven Years.* Urbana: NCTE, 1979.

Horning, Alice S. *Teaching Writing as a Second Language.* Carbondale: Southern Illinois UP, 1987.

Howatt, A. P. R. *A History of English Language Teaching.* New York: Oxford UP, 1984.

Institute of International Education. *Handbook on International Study: For Foreign Nationals.* New York: Institute of International Education, 1961.

Ives, Sumner. "Help for the Foreign Student." CCC 4 (1953): 141–44.

Johns, Ann M. *Text, Role, and Context: Developing Academic Literacies.* New York: Cambridge UP, 1997.

_____. "Too Much on Our Plates: A Response to Terry Santos' 'Ideology in Composition: L1 and ESL.'" *Journal of Second Language Writing* 2 (1993): 83–88.

Kaplan, Robert B. "Cultural Thought Patterns in Inter-cultural Education." *Language Learning* 16 (1966): 1–20.

_____. "TESOL and Applied Linguistics in North America." *State of the Art TESOL Essays: Celebrating 25 Years of the Discipline.* Ed. Sandra Silberstein. Alexandria: TESOL, 1993. 373–81.

Kroll, Barbara. "The Rhetoric/Syntax Split: Designing a Curriculum for ESL Students." *Journal of Basic Writing* 9.1 (1990): 40–55.

_____. ed. *Second Language Writing: Research Insights for the Classroom.* New York: Cambridge UP, 1990.

_____. "Teaching Writing IS Teaching Reading: Training the New Teachers of ESL Composition." *Reading in the Composition Classroom: Second Language Perspectives.* Ed. Joan G. Carson and Ilona Leki. Boston: Heinle, 1992. 61–81.

Lado, Robert. "New Perspectives in Language Learning." Editorial. *Language Learning* 10.1/2 (1960): v–viii.

Leki, Ilona. *Understanding ESL Writers: A Guide for Teachers.* Portsmouth: Boynton/ Cook, 1992.

Li, Xiao-Ming. *"Good Writing" in Cross-Cultural Context.* Albany: State U of New York P, 1996.

Marquardt, William F. "Composition and the Course in English for Foreign Students." *CCC* 7 (1956): 29–33.

McKay, Sandra Lee. *Agendas for Second Language Literacy.* New York: Cambridge UP, 1993.

Moulton, William G. "Linguistics and Language Teaching in the United States 1940– 1960." *Trends in European and American Linguistics 1930–1960.* Ed. Christine Mohrmann, Alf Sommerfelt, and Joshua Whatmough. Utrecht: Spectrum, 1961. 82–109.

Phillips, Donna Burns, Ruth Greenberg, and Sharon Gibson. "*College Composition and Communication:* Chronicling a Discipline's Genesis." *CCC* 44 (1993): 443–65.

Prior, Paul. "Contextualizing Writing and Response in a Graduate Seminar." *Written Communication* 8 (1991): 267–310.

Purves, Alan C., ed. *Writing Across Languages and Cultures: Issues in Contrastive Rhetoric.* Thousand Oaks: Sage, 1988.

Raimes, Ann. "What Unskilled ESL Students Do As They Write: A Classroom Study of Composing." *TESOL Quarterly* 19 (1985): 229–58.

Ramanathan, Vai and Robert B. Kaplan. "Some Problematic 'Channels' in the Teaching of Critical Thinking in Current L1 Composition Textbooks: Implications for L2 Student-Writers." *Issues in Applied Linguistics* 7.2 (1996): 225–49.

Ransdell, D. R. "Important Events: Second Language Students in the Composition Classroom." *Teaching English in the Two-Year College* 21 (1994): 217–22.

Reichelt, Melinda, and Tony Silva. "Cross-Cultural Composition." *TESOL Journal* 5.2 (1995–1996): 16–19.

Reid, Joy M. *Teaching ESL Writing.* Englewood Cliffs: Prentice, 1993.

Rodby, Judith. *Appropriating Literacy: Writing and Reading in English as a Second Language.* Portsmouth: Boynton, 1992.

Rogers, Gretchen L. "Freshman English for Foreigners." *School and Society* 61 (1945): 394–96.

Rose, Mike. "The Language of Exclusion: Writing Instruction at the University." *College English* 47 (1985): 341–59.

Roy, Alice M. "ESL Concerns for Writing Program Administrators: Problems and Policies." *Writing Program Administration* 11.3 (1988): 17–28.

Russell, David R. *Writing in the Academic Disciplines, 1870–1990: A Curricular History.* Carbondale: Southern Illinois UP, 1991.

Santos, Terry. "Response to Ann Johns." *Journal of Second Language Writing* 2 (1993): 89–90.

Severino, Carol, Juan C. Guerra, and Johnnella E. Butler, eds. *Writing in Multicultural Settings.* New York: MLA, 1997.

Schueler, Herbert. "English for Foreign Students." *Journal of Higher Education* 20.6 (1949): 309–16.

Shaughnessy, Mina P. *Errors and Expectations: A Guide for the Teacher of Basic Writing.* New York: Oxford UP, 1977.

Silva, Tony. "An Examination of Writing Program Administrator's Options for the Placement of ESL Students in First Year Writing Classes." *Writing Program Administration* 18.1/2 (1994): 37–43.

———. "Differences in ESL and Native-English-Speaker Writing: The Research and Its Implications." *Writing in Multicultural Settings.* Ed. Carol Severino, Juan C. Guerra, and Johnnella E. Butler. New York: MLA, 1997. 209–19.

Silva, Tony, Ilona Leki, and Joan Carson. "Broadening the Perspective of Mainstream Composition Studies: Some Thoughts from the Disciplinary Margins." *Written Communication* 14 (1997): 398–428.

Singh, Frances. "Teaching English to Adult Speakers of Other Languages: 1910– 1920." *College ESL* 2.1 (1992): 44–53.

Slager, William. "The Foreign Student and the Immigrant: Their Different Problems as Students of English." *Language Learning* 6.3/4 (1956): 24–29.

Spack, Ruth. "The Acquisition of Academic Literacy in a Second Language: A Longitudinal Case Study." *Written Communication* 14 (1997): 3–62.

———. *America's "Second Tongue": The Ownership of English and American Indian Education, 1860s-1900.* Diss. Lesley College, 1998.

Sternglass, Marilyn S. *The Presences of Thought: Introspective Accounts of Reading and Writing.* Norwood: Ablex, 1988.

"Studies in English as a Second Language." *CCC* 7 (1956): 163–65.

Sullivan, Paul R. "English as a Second Language: Potential Applications to Teaching the Freshman Course." *CCC* 8 (1957): 10–12.

Tannacito, Dan J. *A Guide to Writing in English as a Second or Foreign Language: An Annotated Bibliography of Research and Pedagogy.* Alexandria: TESOL, 1995.

"Teaching English as a Second Language." *CCC* 17 (1966): 198–99.

Valdés, Guadalupe. "Bilingual Minorities and Language Issues in Writing: Toward Professionwide Response to a New Challenge." *Written Communication* 9 (1992): 85–136.

Williams, Jessica. "ESL Composition Program Administration in the United States. *Journal of Second Language Writing* 4 (1995): 157–79.

Zamel, Vivian. "Strangers in Academia: The Experiences of Faculty and ESL Students Across the Curriculum." *CCC* 46 (1995): 506–21.

———. "Teaching Composition in the ESL Classroom: What We Can Learn from Research in the Teaching of English." *TESOL Quarterly* 10 (1976): 67–76.

———. "Recent Research on Writing Pedagogy." *TESOL Quarterly* 21 (1987): 697–715.

Zamel, Vivian, and Ruth Spack, eds. *Negotiating Academic Literacies: Readings on Teaching and Learning Across Cultures.* Mahwah: Erlbaum, 1998.

Acknowledgments: I am grateful to Tony Silva and Irwin Weiser, whose comments and encouragement helped me in developing this essay. I also thank Robert B. Kaplan for his valuable insights, Ruth Spack for discussing many important points with me, and Dwight Atkinson, Margie Berns, Laurie Cubbison, Ted Gallagher, Vai Ramanathan, Carlos Salinas, Michele Simmons, and John Swales for their thoughtful comments and suggestions.

Distant Voices

Teaching and Writing in a Culture of Technology

CHRIS M. ANSON

With the development of the Internet, and . . . networked computers, we are in the middle of the most transforming technological event since the capture of fire.
    —John Perry Barlow, "Forum: What Are We Doing Online?" (36)

August 3, Les Agettes, Switzerland. I am sitting on a veranda overlooking the town of Sion some three thousand feet below, watching tiny airplanes take off from the airstrip and disappear over the shimmering ridge of alps to the north. Just below us is another chalet, the home of a Swiss family. At this time of day, they gather at the large wooden table on the slate patio behind their home to have a long, meandering lunch in the French Swiss tradition. Madame is setting the table, opening a bottle of Valais wine, which grandpère ritually pours out for the family and any friends who join them. As they sit to eat, the scene becomes for me a vision of all that is most deeply social in human affairs. They could not survive without this interconnectedness, this entwining of selves, the stories passed around, problems discussed, identities shared and nourished. For weeks, away from phones, TVs, computers, and electronic mail, a dot on the rugged landscape of the southern Alps, I have a profound sense of my own familial belonging, of how the four of us are made one by this closeness of being. Just now Bernard, the little boy who lives on the switchback above, has run down with his dog Sucrette to see if the kids can play. He is here, standing before us, his face smudged with dirt, holding out a toy truck to entice the boys. For now, it is his only way to communicate with them, poised here in all his Bernard-ness, his whole being telling his story.

Reprinted from *College English* 61.3 (January 1999): 261–80. Used with permission.

Not long after writing this journal entry and reflecting on how different my life had become during a summer without access to computers, I came across an issue of *Policy Perspectives*, a periodical issued by the Pew Higher Education Roundtable, which was intriguingly titled "To Dance with Change." When the *Policy Perspectives* began in 1988, the roundtable members believed that "the vitality of education would be defined by its ability to control costs, its capacity to promote learning, and its commitment to access and equity" (1). Less than a decade later, they had shifted their attention to forces beyond academia, realizing that they had been thinking of the institution itself without considering its connection to broader social pressures and movements. They conclude that "among the changes most important to higher education are those external to it"—economic, occupational, and technological. In particular, the electronic superhighway

> may turn out to be the most powerful external challenge facing higher education, and the one the academy is least prepared to understand. It is not that higher education institutions or their faculties have ignored technology. The academy, in fact, is one of the most important supporters and consumers of electronic technology. . . . The problem is that faculty—and hence the institutions they serve—have approached technology more as individual consumers than as collective producers. For the most part the new capacities conferred by electronic means have not enhanced the awareness that teaching might be conceived as something other than one teacher before a classroom of students. While academicians appreciate the leverage that technology has provided in the library and laboratory, they have not considered fully how the same technology might apply to the process of teaching and learning—and they have given almost no thought to how the same technologies in someone else's hands might affect their markets for student-customers. The conclusion that has escaped too many faculty is that this set of technologies is altering the market for even the most traditional goods and services, creating not only new products but new markets and, just as importantly, new providers. (3A)

In the context of our beliefs about how students best learn to write, many educators are haunted, like the Pew members, by a sense that bigger things are happening around us as we continue to refine classroom methods and tinker with our teaching styles. Theorists or researchers or just plain teachers, we spend much of our time working within the framework of certain fairly stable educational conditions. These conditions include physical spaces that define the social and interpersonal contexts of teaching: classrooms where we meet large or small groups of students, offices where we can consult with students face-to-face, and tutorial areas such as writing centers. We expect students to come to these places—even penalizing them for not doing so—and also to visit other physical spaces on campus such as libraries, where they carry out work connected with our instruction. The textual landscape of writing instruction also has a long and stable history: students write or type on white paper of a standard size and turn in their work, adhering to various admonitions about the width of their margins and the placement of periphera such as names, dates, and staples. Teachers collect the papers, respond in predictable places (in the margins or in the spaces left at the end) and return the papers at the institutional site. Innovations like portfolios are extensions of the use of this textual space, but the spaces themselves remain the same.

While the Pew Roundtable members may be concerned that faculty are not attentive to the frenzy of innovation in computer technology, it is difficult for them to make the same claim about academic administrations. Searching the horizon for signs of educational and institutional reform, administrators are often the first to introduce new campus-wide initiatives to the professoriate, who react with delight, resistance, apathy, or outrage to various proposals for change. In the climate of burgeoning developments in technology that have far-reaching consequences for teaching and learning, such changes will no doubt challenge existing ideologies of writing instruction, in part because of the assumed stability on which we have based our curricula and pedagogies.

In this essay, I will consider two of the ways in which teaching and responding to student writing are pressured by rapidly developing technologies now being introduced into our institutions. The first—the increasing replacement of face-to-face contact by "virtual" interaction—is the product of multimedia technology, email communication systems, and the recently expanded capabilities of the World Wide Web. The second, somewhat more institutionally complex development is distance education, in which students hundreds or even thousands of miles apart are connected via interactive television systems. While these technologies offer an endless array of new and exciting possibilities for the improvement of education, they also frequently clash with some of our basic beliefs about the nature of classroom instruction, in all its communal richness and face-to-face complexity. Of even greater urgency is the need to understand the motivation for these developments. More specifically, new technologies introduced with the overriding goal of creating economic efficiencies and generating increased revenues may lead to even greater exploitation in the area of writing instruction, the historically maligned and undernourished servant of the academy. The key to sustaining our pedagogical advances in the teaching of writing, even as we are pulled by the magnetic forces of innovation, will be to take control of these technologies, using them in effective ways and not, in the urge for ever-cheaper instruction, substituting them for those contexts and methods that we hold to be essential for learning to write.

THE ALLURE: TECHNOLOGY
AND INSTRUCTIONAL ENHANCEMENT

Until recently, writing instruction has experienced the greatest technological impact from the personal computer, a tool that had an especially powerful effect on the teaching and practice of revision. The integration of the microcomputer into writing curricula seemed a natural outcome of our interests and prevailing ways of teaching: it offered students a screen on which they could manipulate texts, but they could still print out their writing and turn it in on paper.

Throughout the 1980s and 1990s, many writing programs experimented with labs or computerized classrooms where students could write to and with each other on local area networks. (For a historical account of computers in the teaching of writing, see Hawisher, Selfe, Moran, and LeBlanc.) Simultaneously, an array of computer-assisted instructional programs became available, allowing students to work through guided activities (typically alone) on a personal computer. Computer-generated questions could prompt students to invent ideas; style checkers could give them an index of their average sentence length or complexity; and outline programs could help them to map out the structure of their essays as they wrote. But even with all the cut-and-paste functions and floating footnotes that eased the writing process and facilitated revision, the "textuality" of academic essays remained relatively unchanged: students continued to meet in classrooms to work on their assignments, and teachers reacted to and assessed their products in conventional ways, by carrying the papers home and grading them. Personal computers offered students and teachers a new tool to practice the processes of writing, but the outcome still emerged, eventually, on paper.

In the field of composition studies, the development of more reasoned, theoretically informed methods of response to students' writing has been framed by assumptions about the perpetuation of these physical and textual spaces. Recent studies of response analyze marginal comments written on students' papers for various rhetorical or focal patterns (see, e.g., Straub; Straub and Lunsford; Smith). Studies that deliberately attend to the contextual factors that influence teachers' responses continue to do so within the traditional parameters of typed or handwritten papers turned in for (usually handwritten) response or assessment (e.g., Prior). While such work is much needed in the field, it largely ignores the sweep of change in the way that many students now create, store, retrieve, use, and arrange information (including text) in their academic work. Artificial intelligence expert Seymour Papert pictures a scenario in which a mid-nineteenth century surgeon is time-warped into a modern operating theater. Bewildered, the doctor would freeze, surrounded by unrecognizable technology and an utterly transformed profession, unsure of what to do or how to help. But if a mid-nineteenth century schoolteacher were similarly transported into a modern classroom, the teacher would feel quite at home. Recounting Papert's anecdote, Nicholas Negroponte points out that there is "little fundamental difference between the way we teach today and the way we did one hundred and fifty years ago. The use of technology is at almost at the same level. In fact, according to a recent survey by the U.S. Department of Education, 84 percent of America's teachers consider only one type of information technology absolutely 'essential' to their work—a photocopier with an adequate paper supply" (220). Yet most statistics show the use of computers, particularly by students in high school and college, increasing at lightning speed. Today, more than one-third of American homes already have a computer, and it is predicted that by 2005 Americans will spend more time on the Internet than watching TV.

That personal computers have done little to disrupt our decades-old habits of working with and responding to students' writing is partly because the channels of electronic media have been separate and discrete. Video has been kept apart from computer text, audio systems, and still pictures, requiring us to use different equipment for each technology (and allowing us to focus on computer text to the exclusion of other media). Whether teachers focus on text to the exclusion of other media is not really the point; as Pamela McCorduck points out, "knowledge of different kinds is best represented in all its complexity for different purposes by different kinds of knowledge representations. Choosing *la représentation juste* (words, images, or anything else) is not at all an obvious thing: in fact, it's magnificently delicate. But we have not had much choice until now because text, whether the best representation for certain purposes or not, has dominated our intellectual lives" (259).

The introduction of hypertext and multimedia refocused attention on the relationship between text and other forms of representation. Experimenting with new technology, teachers of literature dragged laptops and heavy projection equipment into their classrooms and displayed stored multimedia Web sites to students reading *Emma* or *King Lear*, linking such texts to their social and political contexts, revealing connections to pieces of art of the time, playing segments of music that the characters might have heard, or showing brief video clips of famous stage presentations. Early advocates of multimedia in teaching and learning clearly framed its advantages in terms that emphasized the process of absorbing information, however innovatively that information might be structured, and however freely the user might navigate through multiple, hierarchically arranged connections (see, for example, Landow). Multimedia was something *presented* and perhaps *explored*, but it was not "answerable." In all their activity as creators of their own knowledge, students remained relatively passive, now receiving deposits of knowledge from automatic teller machines that supplemented the more direct, human method.

But that situation, as Negroponte has suggested, is rapidly changing, creating potentially profound implications for the delivery and mediation of instruction in schools and colleges. Within a few years, the disparate channels of video, audio, and computerized text and graphics—channels that come to us via airwaves, TV cable, phone cable, CD-ROM and computer disks—will merge into a single set of bits sent back and forth along one electronic highway at lightning speed. Our equipment will selectively manipulate this information to produce various outputs, a process already visible in the rapidly developing multimedia capabilities of the World Wide Web. In turn, users can assemble information and send it back (or out) along the same highway. The effect on both the production and reception of writing may be quite dramatic. Modern newspapers, for example, which are already produced electronically, may largely disappear in their paper form:

> The stories are often shipped in by reporters as e-mail. The pictures are digitized and frequently transmitted by wire as well. And the page layout . . . is done with computer-aided design systems, which prepare the data for transfer to film or direct engraving onto plates. This is to say that the entire conception and construction of the newspaper is digital, from beginning to end, until the very last step, when ink is squeezed onto dead trees. This step is where bits become atoms. . . . Now imagine that the last step does not happen . . . but that the bits are delivered to you as bits. You may elect to print them at home for all the conveniences of hard copy. . . . Or you may prefer to download them into your laptop, palmtop, or someday into your perfectly flexible, one-hundredth-of-an-inch thick, full-color, massively high resolution, large-format, waterproof display. (Negroponte 56)

In the educational realm, the new capabilities emerging from multimedia technology offer many alternatives for teaching and learning, and for assigning and responding to writing, particularly as "papers" and "written responses" are replaced by electronic data. Imagine, for example, a college student (call her Jennifer) coming into the student union a few years from now. She pulls from her backpack a full-color, multimedia computer "tablet," just half an inch thick, plugs it into a slot on a little vending machine, puts three quarters into the machine, and downloads the current issue of *USA Today*. Over coffee, she reads the paper on the tablet, watching video clips of some events and listening to various sound bites. She finds a story of relevance to a project she is working on and decides to clip and save it in the tablet's memory. Then she deletes the paper.

Jennifer's first class of the day is still remembered as a "lecture course" in history, but the lecture material has been converted into multimedia presentations stored on CD-ROM disks (which the students dutifully buy at the bookstore or download onto massive hard drives from a server, paying with a credit card). Students experience the lectures alone and meet collectively only in recitation sections. Because her recitation begins in an hour and she did not finish the assignment the night before, Jennifer heads for one of the learning labs. There, she navigates through the rest of a multimedia presentation while handwriting some notes on her tablet and saving them into memory. She is impressed with the program, and justifiably: the institution is proud to have an exclusive contract with a world-famous historian (now living overseas) for the multimedia course.

The recitation is held in a room fully equipped for distance learning. Cameras face the students and teacher. Enormous, high-resolution monitors provide a view of two distant classes, each located a hundred miles away on smaller campuses. Jennifer sits at one of seventy-five computer stations. The first half of the class involves a discussion of some of the multimedia course material. The recitation coordinator (a non-tenure-track education specialist) brings the three sites together using artful techniques of questioning and response. After raising a number of issues which appear on a computerized screen from his control computer, the coordinator asks the three classes to discuss the issues. Students pair off electronically, writing to each other; some students at the main site pair with students at the distant sites, selected automatically by the instructor using an electronic seating chart and a program that activates the connections for each pair.

After the recitation, Jennifer remembers that she is supposed to send a revised draft of a paper to her composition instructor. She heads for another lab, where she accesses her electronic student file and finds a multimedia message from her instructor. The instructor's face appears on her screen in a little window, to one side of Jennifer's first draft. As Jennifer clicks on various highlighted passages or words, the instructor's face becomes animated in a video clip describing certain reactions and offering suggestions for revision.

After working through the multimedia commentary and revising her draft, Jennifer then sends the revision back electronically to her instructor. Jennifer has never actually met her teacher, who is one of many part-time instructor/tutors hired by the semester to "telecommute" to the institution from their homes.

Because Jennifer is a privileged, upper-middle-class student who has a paid subscription to an online service, her own high-end computer system and modem, and the money to buy whatever software she needs for her studies, she can continue her schoolwork at home. There, she uses her multimedia computer to study for a psychology course offered by a corporation. On the basis of nationally normed assessments, the corporation has shown that its multimedia course achieves educational outcomes equal to or greater than those provided by many well-ranked colleges and universities. Jennifer will be able to transfer the course into her curriculum because the corporation's educational division has been recently accredited. She also knows that, as multimedia courses go, this one is first-rate: the corporation is proud to have an exclusive contract with its teacher-author, a world-famous psychologist. As she checks the courseline via email, she notices that a midterm is coming up. She decides to schedule it for an "off" day, since she will have to go to one of the corporation's nearby satellite centers to take the test at a special computer terminal that scores her answers automatically and sends the results to her via email.

Later that day, Jennifer decides to spend an hour doing some research for her history project. From her home computer, she uses various Internet search programs to find out more about the Civil War battle of Manassas. On her high-resolution, 30-inch monitor (which also doubles as a TV and video player), she reads text, looks at drawings, opens video and audio files, and locates bibliographic material on her topic. She also finds some sites where Civil War aficionados share information and chat about what they know. She sends and receives some messages through the list, then copies various bits of information and multimedia into her computer, hoping to weave them into her report, which itself may include photos, video clips, and audio recordings. Due in less than three weeks, the report must be added (quite simply) to a privately accessed course Web site so that one of the several teaching assistants can retrieve it, grade and comment briefly on it, and send it back to Jennifer with an assessment. Just before she quits her research to watch some rock videos from the massive archives in a subscription server, Jennifer locates a Web site at another college where the students had researched the Civil War. The site includes all twenty-six projects created by the students; one focuses for several electronic pages on the battle at

Manassas. Intrigued, Jennifer copies the pages into her computer, intending to look at them carefully the next day and perhaps use parts of them in her own multimedia project.

While this scenario may seem futuristic, much of the technology Jennifer experiences is already here or soon to be. The Knight-Ridder Corporation, for example, has recently developed a prototype of Jennifer's multimedia news "tablet" weighing about two pounds (Leyden). The Web now has the capability to send software to the receiver along with the actual information requested, and this software enhances the user's capacities to work with the information. Programs are currently available that allow teachers to open a student's paper onscreen and scroll through it to a point where a comment might be made to the student. At that point, an icon can be deposited that starts up a voice-recording device. The teacher then talks to the student about the paper. Further marginal or intertextual icons encase further voice comments. Opening the paper on disk at home, the student notices the icons and, activating them, listens to the teacher's response and advice. Computers with tiny videocameras are already enabling a picture-in-picture window that shows the teacher's image talking to the student as if face-to-face. The technology that now provides teleconferencing, when merged with Web-like storage and retrieval devices, will easily facilitate "one-way" tutorials that project audio and video images from a teacher, superimposed over typed text on which marks, corrections, and marginal notes can be recorded "live," like the replay analyses during televised football games.

When demonstrated, such advances may dazzle teachers because we see them as a promise to simplify our lives and streamline our work. New technologies often seem to improve our working conditions and provide better ways to help our students (seasoned teachers, as they stand at the computer-controlled reducing/collating/stapling photocopier, have only to reminisce about the old fluid-and-ink ditto machines to feel these advantages quite tangibly). Teaching, too, seems if not eased, affected in ways that enhance students' experiences. Positive accounts already show that email can help students to form study groups, interact with their teachers, or carry on academic discussions with students at other locations all over the world. In one experiment, students in an all-black freshman composition course at Howard University teamed up with a class of predominantly white students in graphic design at Montana State University to create a 32-page publication, *On the Color Line: Networking to End Racism*. Using digital scanners and email, the students and teachers were able to bring together two classes 1,600 miles apart to critique each other's work, discuss race-related views, and collaboratively produce a pamphlet (Blumenstyk). Many other accounts of networked classrooms suggest increased participation among marginalized groups (see, for example, Selfe, "Technology"; Bump).

Curiously, these and other positive accounts almost always describe adaptations of new technologies as ancillary methods within classrooms where students interact with each other and with their teacher. In a typical computerized grade-school class, for example, a student might use email to ask kids around the world to rank their favorite chocolates as part of a project focusing on *Charlie and the Chocolate Factory*; but then the entire class tallies the results and shares the conclusions (Rector). At the college level, Rich Holeton describes his highly networked electronic writing classroom and its advantages, especially in the area of electronic groups and discussions, yet still sees face-to-face interaction as the "main action" of the course and electronic techniques as "supplementary." Similarly, Tom Creed discusses the many ways he integrates computer technology into his classrooms, but finds it essential to create cooperative learning groups and build in time for students to make stand-up presentations to the class. Electronic innovations, in other words, appear to be carefully controlled, integrated into the existing curriculum in principled ways that do not erode the foundations on which the teacher-experimenters already base their instructional principles. Recognizing the importance of this configuration, some educators much prefer the term "technology-enhanced learning" to other terms that imply a radical shift in the actual delivery of education, such as "technologized instruction."

Because of improvements in educational software and hardware, however, our profession will feel increased pressure to offer technologically enhanced "independent study" courses. Some campuses are already experiencing dramatic differences in students' use of communal spaces with the introduction of dorm-room email. Clifford Stoll, a former Harvard University researcher and author of *Silicon Snake Oil: Second Thoughts on the Information Highway,* claims that by turning college into a "cubicle-directed electronic experience," we are "denying the importance of learning to work closely with other students and professors, and developing social adeptness" (qtd. in Gabriel). Students may be psychodynamically separated from one another even while inhabiting the same campus or dorm building; even more profound effects may be felt when students and faculty use advanced technologies to link up with each other in a course without ever meeting in person. Although many studies and testimonials affirm the ways that Internet chat lines, listservs, email, and other "virtual spaces" can actually increase the social nature of communication, there is no doubt that the physical isolation of each individual from the others creates an entirely different order of interaction.

DISTANCE, INDEPENDENCE,
AND THE TRANSFORMATION OF COMMUNITY

The teaching of writing, unlike some other disciplines, is founded on the assumption that students learn well by reading and writing with each other, responding to each other's drafts, negotiating revisions, discussing ideas, sharing perspectives, and finding some level of trust as collaborators in their mutual development. Teaching in such contexts is interpersonal and interactive, necessitating small class size and a positive relationship between the teacher and the students. At the largest universities, such classes taken in the first year are often the only place where students can actually get to know each other, creating and participating in an intimate community of learning. Large lecture courses, driven by the transmission and retrieval of information, place students in a more passive role. In her book on the effect of college entrance examinations on the teaching of English, Mary Trachsel points out that the "factory" model of education, which privileges standardized testing and the "input" of discrete bits of information, is at odds with our profession's instructional ideals, which align more comfortably with those of theorists like Paulo Freire:

> The model for [authentic education] is that of a dialogue in which hierarchical divisions are broken down so that teachers become teacher-learners, and learners become learner-teachers. Educational values are thus determined not by a mandate to perpetuate an established academic tradition but by local conditions and by the emerging purposes and realizations of educators and learners in social interaction with one another. This socially situated version of education stands in opposition to the "banking concept" of traditionally conceived schooling. (12)

For such ideological reasons, the teaching of writing by correspondence or "independent study" has always lived uneasily within programs that also teach students in classrooms. Although such instruction can be found at many institutions, few theorists strongly advocate a pedagogy in which students write alone, a guide of lessons and assignments at their elbows to provide the material of their "course," a remote, faceless grader hired by the hour to read assignments the students send through the mail and mail back responses. Next to classrooms with rich face-to-face social interaction—fueled by active learning, busy with small groups, energized by writers reading each other's work, powered by the forces of revision and response—independent study in writing appears misguided.

But in the context of our convictions about writing and response, new technologies now offer educational institutions the chance to expand on the idea of individualized learning. Online communication with students is an idea that seems stale by now but is by no means fully exploited; only some teachers eagerly invite email from students, and only some students end up using it when invited. Those faculty who value their autonomy and privacy find that email makes them better able to control when and where students enter their lives. Departments at many universities are requiring faculty to use email by giving them computers, hooking them up, offering workshops on how to use them, and then saying that faculty have no excuse for not voting on such and such an issue or not turning in their book orders on time. The results have already been felt on many campuses, as meetings give way to electronic communion, turning some departments into ghost haunts. Very few universities have developed policies that disallow the use of online office hours in place of physical presence on campus. As teachers across the country realize the tutorial potential of electronic media, such media may come to substitute for direct contact with students. For faculty busy with their own work, the gains are obvious: consultation by convenience, day or night; freedom from physical space; copyable texts instead of ephemeral talk.

From a more curricular perspective, the concept of independent study is rapidly changing from its roots in study manuals and the US Postal Service to a technology-rich potential for students to learn at their own pace, in their own style, with fingertip access to an entire world of information. Multimedia computers using text, sound, video, and photos provide opportunities to bring alive old-fashioned text-only materials. But it is not just independent-study programs, usually seen as ancillary to "real" education, that will change: multimedia could transform the very essence of classroom instruction. At many institutions, administrators are realizing that creating a state-of-the-art multimedia course out of, for example, "Introduction to Psychology," which may enroll up to five hundred students, represents a major improvement. The quality of faculty lectures is uneven; they come at a high cost; and they are often delivered in settings not conducive to learning—hot, stuffy lecture halls with poor sound systems and ailing TV monitors hung every few rows. In the converted version, a student can choose when to work through a multimedia presentation in a computer lab, can learn at her own pace, can review fundamental concepts, can download some information for later study, and can even test her developing knowledge as she learns. In such situations, as journalist Peter Leyden writes, "the time-honored role of the teacher almost certainly will change dramatically. No longer will teachers be the fonts of knowledge with all the answers that [students] seek. They can't possibly fill that role in the coming era" (2T).

In itself, multimedia technology has not directly challenged the field of composition. True, many educators are working on integrating into their research-paper units some instruction on citing electronic sources, search-ing the Web, or using online databases. The prospect of a teacherless and "community-less" course, however, creates much debate in the composition community, where many see computers as poor substitutes for old-fashioned forms of human interaction. In areas involving context-bound thinking, Stanley Aronowitz maintains, "knowledge of the terrain must be obtained more by intuition, memory, and specific knowledge of actors or geography than by mastering logical rules. . . . Whatever its psychological and biologi-cal presuppositions, the development of thinking is profoundly shaped and frequently altered by multiple determinations, including choices made by people themselves" (130–31). In the face of the trend to increasing "indi-rectness" of teaching, Charles Moran argues, "we will need to be more artic-ulate than we have yet been in describing the benefits of face-to-face teaching, or what our British colleagues call 'live tuition'" (208).

New technologies are also giving a strong boost to distance learning. Like the concept of independent study, distance learning too may power-fully affect the way in which we teach and respond to students. In distance learning, students actually participate in the classroom—they are just not there, physically. Beamed in by cable or broadcast, their personae are repre-sented on TV monitors, which, as the idea expands, are becoming larger and gaining in resolution. As classrooms become better equipped, students at several sites will work in virtual classrooms, writing to and for each other at terminals. Teachers can pair students, using small cameras and monitors at their desks, and then regroup the classes at the different sites for larger dis-cussions using the bigger screens.

Institutions are attracted to the concept of distance education for rea-sons obvious in times of fiscal constraint. Students register for a single course from two or more sites, generating tuition revenue for the parent in-stitution. A course previously taught by several salaried faculty (each on lo-cation, hundreds of miles apart) now needs only one main teacher, aided by non-tenure-track staff "facilitator-graders" or teaching assistants hired inex-pensively at the different locations. If small satellite sites are created, some-times in available spaces such as public schools, community centers, or libraries, new revenue sources can be exploited in remote areas. Even after the cost of the interactive television equipment and link-up is calculated, distance education can generate profit for the institution at reduced cost, using its existing faculty resources as "lead teachers." Such an arrangement is especially attractive to institutions used to delivering instruction via the traditional "banking" model of lectures and objectively scorable tests.

Distance learning is also allowing some pairs or groups of institutions to consolidate resources by sharing programs with each other. Imagine that

University A realizes that its Swahili language program does not have the resources to compete with the Swahili language program at University B; but it does have a nationally recognized Lakota language program. Unfortunately, the Lakota program is not very cost-effective, in spite of its standing, because its student cohort is so small. Likewise, University B recognizes that its own Lakota language program pales by comparison with University A's, yet it boasts a particularly strong Swahili program similarly suffering from its inability to generate profits for the school. Using sophisticated interactive television and multimedia resources, the two institutions team up to exchange programs, swapping the tuition revenues along with their instructional programs. As technology keeps expanding and becoming refined, collaborations like these will become increasingly popular, even necessary. In part, these ideas save money. In part, they also respond to growing competition from non-academic providers of education, a major threat to our present institutions. By collaborating to deliver the "best" programs possible, the institutions protect themselves against the intrusion of industry, of what the Pew Roundtable calls "high-quality, lower-cost educational programming conjoined with the rising demand for postsecondary credentials that creates the business opportunity for higher education's would-be competitors" (3). But the result is almost certain to be a continued reduction in full-time, tenure-track faculty and an increased reliance on modes of instructional delivery that physically distance students from each other and from their mentors.

Practically speaking, the idea of distance learning seems reasonable in the context of Lakota and Swahili—it saves duplication of effort, it cuts costs, it may lead to increased institutional collaboration, and it offers students at different locations the chance to be taught, in some sense of the word, by high-quality teachers. It is when the prospect of fully interactive, technologically advanced distance learning conflicts with our most principled educational theories that we feel an ideological clash. Long privileged in composition instruction, for example, is the interactive teaching style. Writing teachers arrange and participate in small groups in the classroom, talk with students before and after class, walk with them to other buildings, meet them in offices, and encourage students to respond to each other instead of through the teacher. Distance learning has yet to overcome the virtuality of its space to draw all students into such interpersonal relationships. Teachers often report feeling detached from the students at the distant sites, unable to carry on "extracurricular" conversations with them. The savings promised by distance education come from the elimination of trained professionals who reduce teacher-student ratios and offer meaningful consultation with students, face to face. If distance learning becomes the norm in fields where general education courses are usually delivered in large lectures with little chance for students to learn actively or interact with each other or the teacher, it will not be long before writing programs are encouraged to follow suit.

In exploring the concept of humans in cyberspace, we can find, as Anna Cicognani has found, many of the same conditions as those we experience in physical space: social interaction; logical and formal abstractions; linguistic form; corresponding organizations of time; the possibility for rhetorical action; and so on. But it is, finally, a "hybrid space, a system which is part of another but only refers to itself and its own variables." It belongs to the main system of space, but "claims independence from it at the same time." Cicognani's representation of cyberspace as a hybrid, which still allows communities to form and develop but relies for its existence on the physical space from which is has been created, offers a useful metaphor for the continued exploration of the relationships between education and computer technology, as the latter is carefully put to use in the improvement of the former. Yet to be considered, however, are broader questions about the role of teachers in technology-rich educational settings.

RESPONSE, TECHNOLOGY, AND THE FUTURE OF TEACHING

The quality of faculty interaction with students is a product of our *work*— our training, the material conditions at our institutions, how much support we get for developing our teaching and keeping up on research. While to this point we have been reflecting on the possible effects of new technologies on the quality of students' learning experiences and contexts, we must also consider ways in which colleges and universities, as places of employment, may change.

Teachers of composition continue to argue that writing programs provide an important site for active and interactive learning in higher education. Our national standards have helped to keep classes small; our lobbying continues to call attention to the exploitation of part-time faculty. We argue the need for support services, such as writing centers, tutors, and ESL programs. And, in writing-across-the-curriculum programs, we have helped to integrate the process approach in various disciplines and courses with considerable success. But the current cost-cutting fervor will continue to erode these principles. Massy and Wilger argue, for example, that "most faculty have yet to internalize the full extent of the economic difficulties facing higher education institutions, both public and private. . . . [F]ew faculty take seriously the current fiscal constraints. Most believe that the problems are not as significant as administrators and others warn, or that the conditions are only temporary" (25).

As teachers, our own occupational space is clearly defined. We "belong" to a particular institution, which pays us, and the students get our instruction, consultation, expertise, and time in exchange for their tuition or, in public schooling, the revenues generated by local taxes and other local, state, and federal funds. Yet technology will soon change not only how we work within our institutions but also how "attached" we may be to an institution, particularly if we can work for several institutions at some physical (but not electronic) remove from each other. In an article in the Information Technology Annual Report of *Business Week*, Edward Baig lists by category the percentage of sites that plan additional "telecommuters"—"members of the labor force who have chosen to, or have been told to, work anywhere, anytime—as long as it's not in the office" (59). Higher education is placed at the very top of the heap, with over 90 percent of sites planning to increase telecommuting.

Universities once looked upon computer technology as an expense and a luxury; increasingly it is now seen as an investment that will lead to increased revenues and reduced expenses. The standards of work defined by the Conference on College Composition and Communication have not anticipated a new vision of writing instruction involving low-paid reader-responders, tutorial "assistants" for CD-ROM courses taken "virtually" by independent study, or coordinators at interactive television sites where students from many campuses link to a single site requiring only one "master professor." Robert Heterick, writing for Educom, predicts a major shift in resource allocation across institutions of higher education:

> The infusion of information technology into the teaching and learning domain will create shifts in the skill requirements of faculty from instructional delivery to instructional design . . . with faculty being responsible for course content and information technologists being responsible for applying information technology to the content. These changes will increase the number of students the institutions can service without corresponding increases in the need for student daily-life support facilities. (3)

In the area of composition, part-time telecommuters, supplied with the necessary equipment, could become the primary providers of instruction to many students. At some locations, private industry is already exploring the possibility of supplying writing instruction, using technology, to institutions interested in "outsourcing" this part of their curriculum. In the *Adjunct Advocate*, a newsletter for part-time and temporary writing teachers, instructors have expressed considerable concern about administrators' requests that they teach sections of introductory composition via the Internet (see Lesko; Wertner). The "profound change in work" represented by advanced technology may also further isolate women. Although the computer once promised to level gender discrimination by removing direct identity from online forums, some social critics are now seeing the potential for new inequities in the labor force. In her contribution to Susan Leigh Star's *The Cultures of Computing*, for example, Randi Markussen takes up the question of "why gender relations seem to change so little through successive waves of technological innovation" (177). Technology promises the "empowerment" of workers, but it also reinforces and more strongly imposes the measurement of work in discrete units. In her analysis of the effects of technology on practicing nurses, Markussen notes that instead of "empowering" employees by making their work more visible or supporting their demands for better staffing and pay, new computer technology actually places greater demands on nurses to account for their work in "categories of work time," decreasing the need for "interpersonal task synchronization" and cooperation with other people. "The transformation of work," Markussen writes, "puts new demands on nurses in terms of relating the formalized electronic depiction of work to caregiving activities, which may still be considered residual and subordinate" (172).

Like nursing, composition has been positively constructed through its preoccupation with the development of the individual and the creation of an engaging, student-focused classroom. Yet composition likewise suffers from higher education's continued attitude that it serves a "residual and subordinate" role, necessary for "remediation." This gross misconception of the value of writing instruction is directly linked to employment practices at hundreds of colleges and universities, where large numbers of "service professionals," a majority of them women, are hired into low-paid, nontenurable positions with poor (or no) benefits. With the potential for the further automation of writing instruction through the use of telecommuting and other technology-supported shifts in instructional delivery, composition may be further subordinated to the interests of powerful subject-oriented disciplines where the conception of expertise creates rather different patterns of hiring and material support.

Our key roles—as those who create opportunities and contexts for students to write and who provide expert, principled response to that writing—must change in the present communications and information revolution. But we cannot let the revolution sweep over us. We need to guide it, resisting its economic allure in cases where it weakens the principles of our teaching. The processes of technology, even when they are introduced to us by administrations more mindful of balancing budgets than enhancing lives, will not threaten us as long as we, as educators, make decisions about the worth of each innovation, about ways to put it to good use, or about reasons why it should be rejected out of hand. More sustained, face-to-face discussions—at conferences and seminars, at faculty development workshops, and in routine departmental and curricular meetings—can give us hope that we can resist changes that undermine what we know about good teaching and sound ways of working. Such discussions are often difficult. They are highly political, painfully economic, and always value-laden and ideological. But as teachers of writing and communication, we have an obvious investment in considering the implications of technology for working, teaching, and learning, even as that technology is emerging.

Because technology is advancing at an unprecedented rate, we must learn to assess the impact of each new medium, method, or piece of software on our students' learning. Most of the time, such assessments will take place locally (for example, as a genetics program decides whether it is more effective for students to work with real drosophila flies or manipulate a virtual drosophila world using an interactive computer program). But we also urgently need broader, institution-wide dialogues about the effect of technology on teaching, particularly between students, faculty, and administrators. Deborah Holdstein has pointed out that as early as 1984 some compositionists were already critiquing the role of computers in writing instruction; "caveats regarding technology . . . have always been an important sub-text in computers and composition studies, the sophistication of self-analysis, one hopes, maturing with the field" (283). Among the issues she proposes for further discussion are those of access, class, race, power, and gender; she questions, for example,

> those who would assert without hesitation that email, the Net, and the Web offer us, finally, a nirvana of ultimate democracy and freedom, suggesting that even visionaries such as Tuman and Lanham beg the question of access, of the types of literacies necessary to even gain access to email, much less to the technology itself. What *other* inevitable hierarchies—in addition to the ones we know and understand . . . —will be formed to order us as we "slouch toward cyberspace"? (283)

While it is impossible to overlook not only that advanced learning technologies are here to stay but that they are in a state of frenzied innovation, Holdstein's admonishments remind us of the power of thoughtful critique and interest punctuated by caution. In addition to the issues she raises, we can profit by engaging in more discussions about the following questions:

1. What will multimedia do to alter the personae of teachers and students as they respond to each other virtually? How do new communication technologies change the relationships between teachers and students? Recent research on small-group interaction in writing classes, for example, shows labyrinthine complexity, as demonstrated in Thomas Newkirk's study of students' conversational roles. What do we really know about the linguistic, psychosocial, and pedagogical effects of online communication when it replaces traditional classroom-based interaction? (See Eldred and Hawisher's fascinating synthesis of research on how electronic networking affects various dimensions of writing practice and instruction.)

2. How might the concept of a classroom community change with the advent of new technologies? What is the future of collaborative learning in a world in which "courseware" may increasingly replace "courses"?

3. What are the consequences of increasing the distance between students and teachers? Is the motivation for distance education financial or pedagogical? Will the benefits of drawing in isolated clients outweigh the disadvantages of electronically "isolating" even those who are nearby?

4. What will be the relationship between "human" forms of response to writing and increasingly sophisticated computerized responses being developed in industry?

5. How will the conditions of our work change as a result of increasing access to students via telecommunications? Who will hire us to read students' writing? Will we work at home? Will educational institutions as physical entities disappear, as Alvin Toffler is predicting, to be replaced by a core of faculty who can be commissioned from all over the world to deliver instruction and response via the electronic highway? What new roles will teachers, as expert responders, play in an increasingly electronic world?

6. What are the implications of telecommuting for the hiring and support of teachers? Could technology reduce the need for the physical presence of instructors, opening the door to more part-time teachers hired at low wages and few benefits?

7. How will writing instruction compete with new, aggressive educational offerings from business and industry? What will be the effects of competing with such offerings for scarce student resources?

If we can engage in thoughtful discussions based on questions such as these, we will be better prepared to make principled decisions about the effect of new technologies on our students' learning and the conditions of our teaching. And we will be more likely, amid the dazzle of innovation, to reject those uses of technology that will lead to bad teaching, poor learning, unfair curricular practices, and unjust employment.

August 21, Les Agettes, Switzerland. I have met the family below. They tell me grandpère has lost some of his memory. He often spends part of the day breaking up stones, clack, clack, clack, behind the chalet. It's not disturbing, they hope. We haven't noticed, I say. We talk almost aimlessly, wandering around topics. Have we met the priest who rents an apartment below the chalet? Can they tell me what the local school is like? We talk about learning, about computers. As if scripted by the ad agency for IBM, they tell me they are interested in the Internet; their friends have computers, and they may get one too, soon. Later, gazing down toward the bustling town of Sion, I wonder how their lives will change. I imagine them ordering a part for their car over the computer without ever catching up on news with Karl, the guy at the garage near the river. Yet I'm also optimistic. They will use email someday soon, and I can get their address from my brother and write them messages in bad French, and they can share them during their long lunches on the patio, where they still gather to eat and laugh, turning my text back into talk.

WORKS CITED

Aronowitz, Stanley. "Looking Out: The Impact of Computers on the Lives of Professionals." Tuman 119–38.

Baig, Edward C. "Welcome to the Officeless Office." *Business Week* (Information Technology Annual Report, International Edition) 26 June 1995: 59–60.

Barlow, John Perry, Sven Birkerts, Kevin Kelly, and Mark Slouka. "Forum: What Are We Doing Online?" *Harper's Magazine* Aug. 1995: 35–46.

Blumenstyk, Goldie. "Networking to End Racism." *Chronicle of Higher Education* 22 Sept. 1995: A35–A39.

Bump, Jerome. "Radical Changes in Class Discussion Using Networked Computers." *Computers and the Humanities* 24 (1990): 49–65.

Cicognani, Anna. "On the Linguistic Nature of Cyberspace and Virtual Communities." <http://www.arch.usyd.edu.au/~anna/papers/even96.htm>

Creed, Tom. "Extending the Classroom Walls Electronically." *New Paradigms for College Teaching.* Ed. William E. Campbell and Karl A. Smith. Edina, MN: Interaction, 1997. 149–84.

Eldred, Janet Carey, and Gail E. Hawisher. "Researching Electronic Networks." *Written Communication* 12.3 (1995): 330–59.

Gabriel, Trip. "As Computers Unite Campuses, Are They Separating Students?" *Minneapolis Star Tribune* 12 Nov. 1996: A5.

Hawisher, Gail E., Cynthia L. Selfe, Charles Moran, and Paul LeBlanc. *Computers and the Teaching of Writing in American Higher Education, 1979–1994: A History.* Norwood, NJ: Ablex, 1996.

Heterick, Robert. "Operating in the 90's." <http://ivory.educom.edu:70/00/educom. info/html>

Holdstein, Deborah. "Power, Genre, and Technology." *College Composition and Communication* 47.2 (1996): 279–84.

Holeton, Rich. "The Semi-Virtual Composition Classroom: A Model for Techn-Amphibians." *Notes in the Margins* Spring 1996: 1, 14–17, 19.

Landow, George. "Hypertext, Metatext, and the Electronic Canon." Tuman 67–94.

Lesko, P. D. "Adjunct Issues in the Media." *The Adjunct Advocate* March/April 1996: 22–27.

Leyden, Peter. "The Changing Workscape." Special Report, Part III. *Minneapolis Star Tribune* 18 June 1995: 2T–6T.

Markussen, Randi. "Constructing Easiness: Historical Perspectives on Work, Computerization, and Women." *The Cultures of Computing.* Ed. Susan Leigh Star. Oxford: Blackwell, 1995. 158–80.

Massy, William F., and Andrea K. Wilger. "Hollowed Collegiality: Implications for Teaching Quality." Paper presented at the Second AAHE Annual Conference on Faculty Roles and Rewards, New Orleans, 29 Jan. 1994.

McCorduck, Pamela. "How We Knew, How We Know, How We Will Know." Tuman 245–59.

Moran, Charles. "Review: English and Emerging Technologies." *College English* 60.2 (1998): 202–9.

Negroponte, Nicholas. *Being Digital.* New York: Knopf, 1995.

Newkirk, Thomas. "The Writing Conference as Performance." *Research in the Teaching of English* 29.2 (1996): 193–215.

Pew Higher Education Roundtable. "To Dance with Change." *Policy Perspectives* 5.3 (1994): 1A–12A.

Prior, Paul. "Contextualizing Writing and Response in a Graduate Seminar." *Written Communication* 8 (1991): 267–310.

———. "Tracing Authoritative and Internally Persuasive Discourses: A Case Study of Response, Revision, and Disciplinary Enculturation." *Research in the Teaching of English* 29 (1995): 288–325.

Rector, Lucinda. "Where Excellence Is Electronic." *Teaching and Technology* Summer 1996: 10–14. <http://www.time.com/teach>

Selfe, Cynthia. "Literacy, Technology, and the Politics of Education in America." Chair's Address, Conference on College Composition and Communication, Chicago 2 April 1998.

———. "Technology in the English Classroom: Computers Through the Lens of Feminist Theory." *Computers and Community: Teaching Composition in the Twenty-First Century.* Ed. Carolyn Handa. Portsmouth, NH: Boynton/Cook, 1990. 118–39.

Smith, Summer. "The Genre of the End Comment: Conventions in Teacher Responses to Student Writing." *College Composition and Communication* 48.2 (1997): 249–68.

Stoll, Clifford. *Silicon Snake Oil: Second Thoughts on the Information Highway.* New York: Doubleday, 1995.

Straub, Richard. "The Concept of Control in Teacher Response: Defining the Varieties of 'Directive' and 'Facilitative' Commentary." *College Composition and Communication* 47.2 (1996): 223–51.

Straub, Richard, and Ronald F. Lunsford. *Twelve Readers Reading: Responding to College Student Writing.* Cresskill: Hampton, 1995.

Trachsel, Mary. *Institutionalizing Literacy.* Carbondale, IL: Southern Illinois UP, 1992.

Tuman, Myron C., ed. *Literacy Online: The Promise (and Peril) of Reading and Writing with Computers.* Pittsburg: U of Pittsburgh P, 1992.

Wertner, B. "The Virtual Classroom" (letter to the editor). *The Adjunct Advocate* May/June 1996: 6.

The Public Intellectual, Service Learning, and Activist Research

Ellen Cushman

While I support the good intentions of those who have recently proposed definitions of the public intellectual, I find these definitions problematic in their narrow delineation of the word "public"—they focus on a "public" consisting of middle and upper class policy makers, administrators, and professionals, and, in doing so, omit an important site for uniting knowledge-making and political action: the local community. Canvassing the letters submitted to the October 1997 *PMLA* forum on intellectual work in the twenty-first century, one notices numerous tensions regarding the larger public role of the intellectual:

> New and old intellectuals in the twenty-first century need to try to answer such questions as: "What do people(s) want?" and "What is the meaning of the political?" (Alina Clej; Forum 1123)

> In the next century, the intellectual must be willing to take more risks by choosing exile from confining institutional, theoretical, and discursive formations. (Lawrence Kritzman 1124)

> American intellectuals appear to have entered a period of non-engagement, cherishing their autonomy over engagement and retreating into the ivory tower. (Patrick Saveau 1127)

> If there is a task ahead for the kind of intellectual I have in mind, it lies in the attempt to forge a more secure link between the love of art and human decency. (Steven Greenblatt 1131)

Reprinted from *College English* 61.3 (January 1999): 328–36. Used with permission.

[The modern intellectual's] goal would be to enact in one's research an informed concern with specific questions of public value and policy. (Dominick Lacapra 1134)

A postoccidental intellectual [is] able to think at the intersection of the colonial languages of scholarship and the myriad languages subalternized and banned from cultures of scholarship through five hundred years of colonialism. (Walter Mignolo 1140)

Taken together, these statements indicate a growing pressure for intellectuals to make knowledge that speaks directly to political issues outside of academe's safety zones. This urgency comes in part from administrators and legislators who demand accountability, but it also comes from academics who have grown weary of isolation and specialization and who hope their work might have import for audiences beyond the initiated few. They wonder if knowledge-making can take risks while both cultivating aesthetics and leading to political action. Above all, these quotations reveal the nagging suspicion that academics have yet to realize their full potential in contributing to a more just social order. I believe public intellectuals can indeed contribute to a more just social order, but to do so they have to understand "public" in the broadest sense of the word.

The kind of public intellectuals I have in mind combine their research, teaching, and service efforts in order to address social issues important to community members in under-served neighborhoods. You know these neighborhoods: they're the ones often located close by universities, just beyond the walls and gates, or down the hill, or over the bridge, or past the tracks. The public in these communities isn't usually the one scholars have in mind when they try to define the roles of "public" intellectuals. For example, Pierre Bourdieu recognizes that the intellectual has dual and dueling agendas: "on the one hand, he [sic] must belong to an autonomous intellectual world; . . . on the other hand, he must invest the competence and authority he has acquired in the intellectual field in a political action" ("Fourth Lecture" 656). Yet Bourdieu advocates only one kind of political action: "the first objective of intellectuals should be to work collectively in defense of their specific interests and of the means necessary for protecting their own autonomy" (660). Granted, academics must have the secure position that autonomy (typically gained through tenure) provides if the knowledge they make is to be protected from censorship. Yes, academics need to defend their positions, particularly in this socio-economic climate where big business ethics of accountability, total quality management, downsizing, and overuse of part-time labor conspire to erode academics' security within the university. However, the fight for our own autonomy is a limited and self-serving form of political action addressed only to an elite "public" of decision-makers.

Another type of public intellectual, in the limited sense of the word *public*, believes in protecting scholarly autonomy through popularizing intellectual work. Here's Michael Bérubé on this kind of public intellectual: "the future of our ability to produce new knowledges for and about ordinary people—and the availability of education *to* ordinary people—may well depend on how effectively we can . . . make our work intelligible to nonacademics—who then, we hope, will be able to recognize far-right rant about academe for what it is" (176). Going public, turning to mass media, dressing our work in plain garb may help preserve autonomy, may even get intellectuals a moment or two in the media spotlight, but how will this help individuals who have no home, not enough food, or no access to good education? Popularizing scholarship may help solve problems on academe's front lines, but such action does not seem to do democracy any great favors. Popularizing suggests that public intellectuals simply translate their thinking into less specialized terms, then publish in the *New Yorker* or *Academe*. Yet publishing to a greater number of elite audiences works more to bolster our own positions in academe than it does to widen the scope of our civic duties as intellectuals.

Bourdieu and Bérubé belong to the modern ranks of public intellectuals, among whom I might include such currently prominent figures as Henry Louis Gates, Jr., and Stanley Fish. They all share an implied goal of affecting policy and decision-making, and they reach this goal by using their positions of prestige as well as multiple forms of media (newspapers, radio, and television) in order to influence a public beyond the academy, though this public will usually be limited to the educated upper echelons of society. In their dealings with this public, moreover, they typically remain scholars and teachers, offering their superior knowledge to the unenlightened.

When public intellectuals not only reach outside the university, but actually *interact* with the public beyond its walls, they overcome the ivory tower isolation that marks so much current intellectual work. They create knowledge with those whom the knowledge serves. Dovetailing the traditionally separate duties of research, teaching, and service, public intellectuals can use the privilege of their positions to forward the goals of both students and local community members. In doing so, they extend access to the university to a wider community. Academics can reach these goals in two ways: service learning and activist research.

SERVICE LEARNING

To enact citizenship in the larger sense, and to unify the locations of research, teaching, and service, the public intellectual can begin by developing service learning or outreach courses. Service learning asks students (both graduate and undergraduate) to test the merit of what they learn in the university classroom against their experiences as volunteers at local sites such as philanthropic agencies, primary and secondary schools, churches, old-age homes, half-way houses, and shelters. When students enter communities as participant observers, they "begin not as teachers, but as learners in a community setting where the goals and purposes of a 'service' effort are not established beforehand" (Schutz and Gere 145). Students enter the community in a sincere effort to both engage in and observe language use that helps address the topics that are important to community members. When activist fieldwork is a cornerstone of the course, students and community residents can develop reciprocal and dialogic relations with each other; their relationship is a mutually beneficial give-and-take one.

As participant observers, students take fieldnotes that reflect on their experiences with community members and how these experiences relate to the set of readings chosen by the professor. These fieldnotes serve a twofold purpose. First, they offer students a ready supply of examples to analyze in their essays, and second, they become potential source material for the professor. The professors' own notes, video and audio tape recordings, evaluations from the public service organization or area residents, and other literacy artifacts constitute a rich set of materials for knowledge-making. Since the professors also volunteer, teach, and administer the service learning course, they have first-hand familiarity with the important social issues and programmatic needs at the local level, and they tailor the curriculum to fit these. Thus, when activist methods are employed, knowledge-making in outreach courses happens *with* the individuals served. The course must respond to the immediate concerns and longstanding problems of the area in order to remain viable.

In their most limited sense, service learning courses unite in a single mission the traditionally separate duties of research, teaching, and service.

The research contributes

- ◆ to teaching by informing a curriculum that responds to both students' and community members' needs, and

- ◆ to service by indicating emerging problems in the community which the students and curriculum address.

The teaching contributes

- to research by generating fieldnotes, papers, taped interactions and other materials, and
- to service by facilitating the community organization's programmatic goals with the volunteer work.

The service contributes

- to research by addressing political and social issues salient in everyday lived struggles, and
- to teaching by offering students and professors avenues for testing the utility of previous scholarship in light of community members' daily lives and cultural values.

Because service learning includes an outreach component, the knowledge generated together by the area residents, students, and the professor is exoteric (as opposed to esoteric) and is made in interaction (as opposed to isolation).

Among composition and rhetoric scholars, Bruce Herzberg, Linda Flower, and Aaron Schutz and Anne Ruggles Gere, to name a few, have created community literacy projects which include service learning. Joan Schine has recently discussed elementary and secondary programs in service learning, and Barbara Jacoby addresses the practical and political aspects of developing outreach courses at the university level. Although scholars have begun to develop these outreach initiatives, few have offered a methodology that integrates the civic-minded mission of service learning with the politics of research in local settings.

ACTIVIST RESEARCH

One limitation of service learning courses can be students' perception of themselves as imparting to the poor and undereducated their greater knowledge and skills. Instructors in the service learning course that Anne Ruggles Gere and her colleagues developed noted that "their students often entered seeing themselves as 'liberal saviors,' and that the structure of tutoring had the potential to enhance the students' vision of this 'savior' role" (Schutz and Gere 133). Indeed, if the university representatives understand themselves as coming to the rescue of community residents, students will enact this missionary ideology in their tutoring. Service learning courses can avoid this liberal do-gooder stance when they employ activist research methodologies.

Activist research combines postmodern ethnographic techniques with notions of reciprocity and dialogue to insure reciprocal and mutually beneficial relations among scholars and those with whom knowledge is made. Since a central goal of outreach courses is to make knowledge *with* individuals, scholars need a methodology that avoids the traditional top-down approaches to ethnographic research: "The Bororos of Brazil sink slowly into their collective death, and Lévi-Strauss takes his seat in the French Academy. Even if this injustice disturbs him, the facts remain unchanged. This story is ours as much as his. In this one respect, . . . the intellectuals are still borne on the backs of the common people" (de Certeau 25). Traditional forms of ethnographic fieldwork yield more gains for the intellectual than the community residents. On the other hand, activist ethnographic research insures that, at every level of the ethnographic enterprise—from data collection through interpretation to write-up—the researcher and participants engage in openly negotiated, reciprocal, mutually beneficial relations.

Theories of praxis can be united with notions of emancipatory pedagogy in an effort to create a theoretical framework for activist methodology. Scholars who advocate praxis research find the traditional anthropological method of participant observation unsatisfactory because it has the potential to reproduce an oppressive relationship between the researcher and those studied (Oakley; Lather; Bleich; Porter and Sullivan). Instead of emphasizing observation, research as praxis demands that we actively participate in the community under study (Johannsen; for a thoughtful exploration of the connections between critical ethnography and critical pedagogy, see Lu and Horner). Applied anthropology provides theoretical models for how praxis—loosely definable as ethical action to facilitate social change—enters into the research paradigm, but many scholars still need to do the work of intervention, particularly at the community level.

Praxis research can take emancipatory pedagogy as its model for methods of intervention, since notions of emancipatory pedagogy work with the same types of theoretical underpinnings. Paulo Freire's *Pedagogy of the Oppressed* exemplifies the pragmatic concerns of politically involved teaching aimed at emancipating students. His work teaching illiterate peasants in Latin America has been adapted to American educational needs in schooling institutions (Apple and Weis; Giroux; Luke and Gore; Lankshear and McLaren). Emancipatory teaching can only go so far in instantiating activist research, though, because teachers often apply liberating teaching only in the classroom, and they are hard pressed to create solidarity and dialogue within the institutionalized social structure of American schools. In order to adapt Freire's pedagogy to the United States, we must also practice it outside the academy, where we can often more easily create solidarity. In a conversation with Donaldo Macedo, Freire says: "it is impossible to export pedagogical practices without re-inventing them. Please, tell your fellow American educators not to import me. Ask them to recreate and rewrite my ideas" (Macedo xiv). Our revisions of his pedagogy can be more fully expanded if we move out of the institutionalized setting of classrooms and into our communities. In this way, liberatory teaching can be brought together with praxis research to create the activist research useful to service learning.

Although I have conducted a three-and-a-half year long ethnography of literacy in an inner city (Cushman), Spring 1998 offered me the first opportunity to bridge activist research and service learning through a course called "Social Issues of Literacy." The course links Berkeley undergraduates with the Coronado YMCA in Richmond, a place residents of the East Bay call "the forgotten inner city." Undergraduates read scholarship on literacy, volunteer at the YMCA, write fieldnotes, and then integrate theory and data in case studies. The course has met with initial success in three ways.

First, students immediately saw the tight integration of literacy theory and practice. Their essays revealed careful attention to the scholarship and some rigor in challenging the limitations of these readings against their own observations. One student's paper noted that Scribner and Cole's famous work on Vai literacy showed their limited access to Vai females' literacy practices. Her paper then illustrated two interactions where she noticed how girls were excluded by the boys during storytelling, playing, and writing. She considered methods of participant observation that might invite more of the girls to engage in these activities. At the same time, she conducted informal interviews with the YMCA members in order to understand better how their values for oral and literate language shifted along gender lines. She did this with an eye toward filling gaps in knowledge that she saw in the scholarship on literacy that we read in class.

Second, the outreach course has filled a very real need for the YMCA staff. While this particular YMCA had numerous programs, including African dance, sports, teen pregnancy prevention, and scouting, they needed adults to engage youths in language use that would promote their reading and writing—without reproducing a school atmosphere. As one supervisor told me, "if the undergraduates come in here with too much school-like structure, they could turn the kids off to the reading and writing that they'll need to get ahead in school. So let's create a flexible structure for activities." Her point was subtle; area children hold schoolwork in low esteem, but the adults value the reading and writing needed to succeed in education.

With the supervisor's goals in mind, the undergraduates and I ask the YMCA members what kinds of activities they would like to do and offer a broad range of reading, writing, and artistic events in which they can engage. One ongoing literacy event centers around the creation of personal journals. Shawn, a nine-year-old, told me he wanted his "own journal here [at the YMCA] where I can keep all my stories and things." Together with the undergraduates, the children have produced journals with decorated covers bound with staples or yarn. Inside the journals, they keep their stories, math homework, spelling words, drawings, and letters to the undergraduates and myself. Leafing through a set of completed journals, the YMCA supervisor noted that the children "don't even realize that all the art, math, and writing they're doing in these journals will help them with their schoolwork." At the intersection where university representatives and community members meet, these journals offer a brief illustration of the way in which public intellectuals and community members can work together to identify and ameliorate local-level social issues. In this case, we together found ways to engage in reading and writing that would bridge a problematic split in generational values attached to literacy.

Finally, "Social Issues of Literacy" has met with some success in terms of research: the course has generated numerous literacy artifacts and events which could potentially serve as data for an extended study of community literacy. In exchange for the hours I have invested in curriculum development, site coordination, grant writing, and local research, I have the immediate reward of writing this paper. Thus, at least the initial results indicate that everyone seems to benefit from the service learning and activist research in this project.

However, even with examples of outreach and activist research like this, literary scholars may be hard pressed to see their intellectual work as amenable to service learning courses. To put a finer point on it, can outreach courses help forge a more secure link "between the love of art and human decency" (as Greenblatt put it in the *PMLA* forum), between intellectual work which cultivates aesthetics and work which speaks to common, lived conditions of struggle in the face of vast and deepening social inequalities? If public intellectuals hope to find and generate overlaps between aesthetics and politics, they need to first understand that what they count as art or political choices does not necessarily match what community members count as art or political choices. Because university representatives tend to esteem their own brand of knowledge more than popular forms of knowledge, they deepen the schism between universities and communities. Bourdieu described well the production of legitimate (read specialized, publishable, esoteric, academic) language, which gains material, cultural and symbolic capital by implicitly devaluing nonstandard (read colloquial, vernacular, common, vulgar) language. The educational system, particularly higher education, "contributes significantly to constituting the dominated uses of language as such by consecrating the dominant use as the only legitimate one" through "the devaluation of the common language which results from the very existence of a literary language" (*Language* 60–61). How can public intellectuals link the love of art and human decency if we continue to value university-based knowledge and language more than community-based knowledge and language? Unless the love of art and human decency, as they manifest themselves in university culture, justify themselves against local cultural value systems, academic knowledge-making will remain esoteric, seemingly inapplicable, remote, and elitist.

Public intellectuals challenge the value system of academe by starting with the assumption that all language use and ways of knowing are valuable and worthy of respect. To enact this principle, service learning offers meeting places for community and university values, language, and knowledge to become mutually informative and sustaining, places where greater numbers of people have a say in how knowledge is made, places where area residents, students, and faculty explore works of art, literature, and film to find ways in which these works still resonate with meaning and inform everyday lived struggles. Service learning "mak[es] rhetoric into a social praxis . . . assigning students to effective agency in the ongoing struggle of history" (France 608). Public intellectuals can use service learning as a means to collapse harmful dichotomies that traditional university knowledge espouses: literary/vernacular; high culture/low culture; literature/literacy; objective/subjective; expert/novice. Because these dualities place faculty members in a presumably higher social position, they distance academics from those they hope their knowledge serves—from those their knowledge must serve.

Public intellectuals can use their service, teaching, and research for the benefit of those inside and outside the university. Their knowledge, created with students and community members, can have political implications in contexts beyond the university. Their positions as faculty members can have readily apparent accountability, and their intellectual work can have highly visible impact. In the end, public intellectuals can enact the kind of civic-minded knowledge-making that engages broad audiences in pressing social issues.

WORKS CITED

Apple, Michael, and Lois Weis, eds. *Ideology and Practice in Schooling.* Philadelphia: Temple UP, 1983.

Bérubé, Michael. *Public Access: Literary Theory and American Cultural Politics.* London: Verso, 1994.

Bleich, David. "Ethnography and the Study of Literacy: Prospects for Socially Generous Research." *Into the Field: Sites of Composition Studies*. Ed. Anne Ruggles Gere. New York: MLA, 1993. 176–92.

Bourdieu, Pierre. "Fourth Lecture. Universal Corporatism: The Role of Intellectuals in the Modern World." *Poetics Today* 12.4 (1991): 655–69.

———. *Language and Symbolic Power*. Cambridge: Harvard UP, 1991.

Cushman, Ellen. *The Struggle and the Tools: Oral and Literate Strategies in an Inner City Community*. Albany: SUNY P, 1998.

de Certeau, Michel. *The Practice of Everyday Life*. Berkeley: U of California P, 1984.

Flower, Linda. *The Construction of Negotiated Meaning*. Carbondale: Southern Illinois UP, 1994.

Forum. *PMLA* 112.5 (October 1997): 1121–41.

France, Alan. "Assigning Places: The Function of Introductory Composition as a Cultural Discourse." *College English* 55.6 (1993): 593–609.

Giroux, Henry. *Ideology, Culture, and the Process of Schooling*. Philadelphia: Temple UP, 1981.

Herzberg, Bruce. "Community Service and Critical Teaching." *College Composition and Communication* 45.3 (Oct. 1994): 307–19.

Jacoby, Barbara. *Service-Learning in Higher Education*. San Francisco: Jossey-Bass, 1996.

Johannsen, Agneta. "Applied Anthropology and Post Modernist Ethnography." *Human Organization*. 50.1 (1992): 71–81.

Lankshear, Colin, and Peter McLaren, eds. *Critical Literacy: Politics, Praxis, and the Postmodern*. Albany: SUNY P, 1993.

Lather, Patti. "Research as Praxis." *Harvard Education Review*. 56 (1992): 257–77.

Lu, Min-Zhan, and Bruce Horner. "The Problematic of Experience: Redefining Critical Work in Ethnography and Pedagogy." *College English* 60.3 (March 1998): 257–77.

Luke, Carmen, and Jennifer Gore. *Feminism and Critical Pedagogy*. New York: Routledge, 1992.

Macedo, Donaldo. *Literacies of Power: What Americans Are Not Allowed to Know*. Boulder: Westview P, 1994.

Oakley, Anne. "Interviewing Women: A Contradiction in Terms." *Doing Feminist Research*. London: Routledge, 1981. 30–62.

Schine, Joan. *Service Learning*. Chicago: NSSE/U of Chicago P, 1997.

Schutz, Aaron, and Anne Ruggles Gere. "Service Learning and English Studies: Rethinking 'Public' Service." *College English* 60.2 (1998): 129–49.

Sullivan, Pat, and James Porter. *Opening Spaces: Writing Technologies and Critical Research Practices*. Greenwich, CT: Ablex, 1997.

On the Rhetoric and Precedents of Racism

Victor Villanueva

UNA HISTORIA

The scene is Peru. It's the end of the 15th century. Father Valverde, a Franciscan, is speaking to the Incan philosopher-rhetorician about the ways of the world. The Franciscan intends to be instructive, to attempt to raise the indigenous from its ignorance. But the Incan doesn't recognize the developmental mindset and enters into dialectical interplay. Having heard of how things work according to Father Valverde, the Incan responds:

> You listed five preeminent men whom I ought to know. The first is God, three and one, which are four, whom you call the creator of the universe. Is he perhaps our Pachacámac and Viracocha? The second claims to be the father of all men, on whom they piled their sins. The third you call Jesus Christ, the only one not to cast sins on that first man, but he was killed. The fourth you call pope. The fifth, Carlos, according to you, is the most powerful monarch of the universe and supreme over all. However, you affirm this without taking account of other monarchs. But if this Carlos is prince and lord of all the world, why does he need the pope to grant him concessions and donations to make war on us and usurp our kingdoms? And if he needs the pope, then is not the pope the greater lord and most powerful prince of all the world, instead of Carlos? Also you say that I am obliged to pay tribute to Carlos and not to others, but since you give no reason for this tribute, I feel no obligation to pay it. If it is right to give tribute and service at all, it ought to be given to God, the man who was Father of all, then to Jesus

Reprinted from *College Composition and Communication* 50.4 (June 1999): 645–61. Used with permission.

Christ who never piled on his sins, and finally to the pope. . . . But if I ought not give tribute to this man, even less ought I give it to Carlos, who was never lord of these regions and whom I have never seen.

The record of this meeting at Atahualpa notes that,

> The Spaniards, unable to endure this *prolixity of argumentation*, jumped from their seats and attacked the Indians and grabbed hold of their gold and silver jewels and precious stones. (Dussel 53)

A little later, 1524, a little further north, Mexico. Twelve recently arrived Spanish Franciscan missionaries have agreed to a dialogue with the indigenous people of the region. The Aztecan delegation consists of a group of *tlamatinime*, or philosophers. Somewhere between the ages of six and nine, young Aztecs (which might have included women) left their families to join the *Calmécac* community. There, they received a rigorous education based on discussions with teachers, or wise ones *(Huehuetlatoli)*. The discussions will allow the young Aztecs to acquire the wisdom already known *(momachtique)*, a wisdom which is to be rendered in the adequate word *(in quali tlatolli)*. This, then, was the Aztecan trivium, displayed in the rhetoric called the flower-and-song *(in xochitl in cuícatl)* (Dussel 95–97).

The *tlamatinime* address the missionaries in the manner of the flower-and-song, in what could be read as a five-part rhetorical rendition. First, there is a salutation and introduction:

> Our much esteemed lords: What travail have you passed through to arrive here. Here, before you, we ignorant people contemplate you.
>
> What shall we say? What *should we direct to your ears?* Are we anything by chance? We are only a vulgar people.

The *proemium*-like intro done, the *tlamatinime* turn to the matter at hand, an attempt to enter into a dialogue concerning the doctrine that the missionaries had brought. The Aztecan flower-and-song enters into a context-setting that is like the classical Roman *narratio*:

> Through the interpreter we will respond by returning the-nourishment-and-the-word to the lord-of-the-intimate-which-surrounds-us. For his sake, we place ourselves in danger. . . . Perhaps our actions will result in our perdition or destruction, but where are we to go? We are common mortals. *Let us now then die; let us now perish* since *our gods have already died.* But calm your heart-of-flesh, lords, for we will break with the customary for a moment and open for you a little bit the *secret*, the ark of the lord, our God.

Next, *dispositio:*

> You have said the *we do not know* the lord-of-the-intimate-which-surrounds-us, the one from whom the-heavens-and-the-earth come. You have said that our gods were not *true* gods.

> We respond that we are perturbed and hurt by what you say, because our progenitors never spoke this way.

Refutatio takes the form of three topics not unlike Aristotle's: authority, ideology as worldview, and antiquity. The first is authority:

> Our progenitors passed on the *norm of life* they held as *true* and the doctrine that we should worship and honor the gods.

Such doctrine is consistent with the Aztecan worldview:

> They taught . . . that these gods give us life and have gained us for themselves . . . in the beginning. These gods provide us with sustenance, drink and food including corn, beans, goose feet (*bledos*), and *chia*, all of which conserve life. We pray to these gods for the water and rain needed for crops. These gods are happy . . . *where they exist*, in the place of *Tlalocan*, where there is neither hunger, nor sickness, nor poverty.

Then the appeal to antiquity:

> And in what form, when, where were these gods first invoked? . . . This occurred a very long time ago in Tula, Huapalcalco, Xuchatlapan, Tlamohuanchan, Yohuallican, and Teotihuacan. These gods have established their dominion over the entire universe (*cemanauac*).

Conclusio

> Are we now to destroy the ancient *norm of our life?*—the *norm of life* for the Chichimecas, the Toltexs, the Acolhuas, and the Tecpanecas? We *know* to whom we owe our birth and our lives.

> We refuse to be tranquil or to believe as truth what you say, even if this offends you.

> We lay out our reasons to you, lords, who govern and sustain the whole world (*cemanáhualt*). Since we have handed over all our power to you, *if we abide here, we will remain only prisoners.* Our final response is do with us as you please. (Dussel 112–14)

831

No multiculturalism there, no cultural hybrid possible, though some try hard now to reclaim the Incan or Aztecan, try hard to be more than the Eurocentric *criollo* of Latin America.

ALGUNAS IDEAS

As academics and teachers we become accustomed to juggling dozens of constraints at a time. We adjust to the multidimensional nature of our jobs. But just for a little while we'd like to focus on one aspect of our careers, work one thing through. Except for the occasional sabbatical leave some of us are granted in our jobs, however, the best we can usually do is set priorities. It's something of the too-much-to juggle mindset, I would say, that gives rise to multiculturalism. So many inequities, so much rampant bigotry leveled at so many things. None of it should be ignored. But if we're to set priorities, I would ask that we return to the question of racism, the "absent presence" in our discourse (Prendergast). Although gays and lesbians are subject to more acts of hate in this country right now than any other group, the attacks are most often leveled at gays and lesbians of color (Martínez 134). Women of color carry a double yoke, to use Buchi Emecheta's words, being women and being of color. And it's a secret to no one that the greatest number of poor are people of color. This is not to say that the eradication of racism — even if possible — would mean the eradication of bigotry and inequity. It is to say that as priorities go, racism seems to have the greatest depth of trouble, cuts across most other bigotries, is imbricated with most other bigotries, and also stands alone, has the greatest number of layers. According to Mike Davis:

> No matter how important feminist consciousness must be. . . , racism remains the divisive issue within class and gender [and sexual orientation]. . . . The real weak link in the domestic base of American imperialism is a Black and Hispanic working class, fifty million strong. This is the nation within a nation, society within a society, that alone possesses the numerical and positional strength to undermine the American empire from within. (299, 313–14)

The numbers have risen since Davis wrote this in 1984. And he failed to mention the Asian Americans and Pacific Islanders, the amazing percentages that don't succeed and the others who are "model minorities" rather than simply assimilated. Or the American Indians. Racism continues to be among the most compelling problems we face. Part of the reason why this is so is because we're still unclear about what we're dealing with, so we must thereby be unclear about how to deal with it.

Part of that insecurity about what it is we face when we talk or write about racism can be seen in our references to "race and ethnicity." I've used the term myself, to distinguish what we are biologically from how we're treated or regarded, to point to the ways in which racism doesn't always effect those who are visibly different from the majority. But referring to ethnicity is tricky, carries connotations that don't necessarily apply to people of color in the U.S.

Ethnicity grows out of a consciousness of an older, less sustainable racism. The concept of ethnicity first evolved in response to Social Darwinism, traveling through the 1920s to the 1960s, at which time class and colonialist concerns came to the fore (Omi and Winant, Grosfoguel, Negrón-Muntaner, Georas). Since the 1960s, the talk of colonialism has taken a new turn, and the realization that racism remains even when there is class ascension has made for something of a separation between discussions of class and of color. So ethnicity is back, now decidedly associated with race. And with ethnicity comes the concept that was historically a subset of ethnicity, *cultural pluralism* (Omi and Winant 12).

Ethnicity received its most complete treatment in Nathan Glazer and Daniel P. Moynihan's *Beyond the Melting Pot: The Negroes, Puerto Ricans, Jews, Italians, and Irish of New York City*, first published in 1963, with a second edition in 1970. Glazer and Moynihan describe a process that sounds much like hybridity, a postcolonial term enjoying currency. Ethnic groups do not necessarily assimilate, say Glazer and Moynihan:

> Ethnic groups . . . even after distinctive language, customs, and culture are lost . . . are continually recreated by new experiences in America. The mere existence of a name itself is perhaps sufficient to form group character in new situations, for the name associates an individual, who actually can be anything, with a certain past, country, or race.

So something new emerges in the acculturation process—neither fish nor fowl, a new language and culture with ties to something older. And this new thing is an *interest group*. Glazer and Moynihan continue:

> But as a matter of fact, someone who is Irish or Jewish or Italian generally has other traits than the mere existence of the name that associates him with other people attached to the group. A man is connected to his group by ties of family and friendship. But he is also connected by ties of *interests*. The ethnic groups in New York are also *interest groups*. (qtd. in Omi and Winant 18)

From this it wasn't much of a leap to the bootstraps mentality, with Glazer and Moynihan writing in 1975 that "ethnic groups bring different norms to bear on common circumstances with consequent different levels of success—hence *group* differences in status," so that any group that fails does so by virtue of flaws in the group's "norms," as in the stereotypical contention that the dropout rates among Chicanos and Latinos are so high because Latino culture does not prize education like other groups do (qtd. in Omi and Winant 21).

Because this country has always consisted of many groupings (even before the first Europeans), the notion of ethnicity rings true. And because so many ethnicities still feel attachments to their ancestry, even if only as nostalgia, the concept of a cultural plurality sounds right. Ethnicity and the cultural plurality suggested by multiculturalism appeal to common sense in ways that can address racism—and sometimes they do, maybe often—but without tugging at its hegemony with the kind force so many of us would wish.

Racism runs deep. Consider some of the litany of the 1980s with which E. San Juan opens his book on *Racial Formations/Critical Transformations*:

> Vigilante gunman Bernard Goetz catapulted into a folk hero for shooting down four black youths in a New York subway. Fear of Willy Horton, a black inmate helped elect a president. . . . Antibusing attacks in the early eighties in most big cities. The 1982 murder of Chinese American Vincent Chin mistaken by unemployed Detroit autoworkers for a Japanese. . . . The election to the Louisiana legislature of Republican David Duke, former head of the Ku Klux Klan. (1)

And also:

- We watched the 1992 beating of Rodney King, watched Alicia Soltero Vásquez being beaten by Border Patrolmen.

- San Francisco, 1997. Two young Latino children are found completely covered in flour. They wanted their skin to be white enough to go to school, they say.

- Oxnard, 1995, Mexican and Chicana women working at a Nabisco plant are denied toilet breaks. They are told to wear diapers during their shift.

- Rohnert Park, 1997. Police kill a Chinese engineer, father of three, who had come home drunk and angry after having put up with racist insults at a bar. He's loud. A neighbor calls the police. Still drunk, he grabs a one-eighth inch thick stick, brandishes it. He's shot. His wife, a nurse, is disallowed to administer care. He's handcuffed. Dies while awaiting an ambulance. The reason for shooting him? The police were afraid he would use martial arts with that one-eighth inch stick (Martínez 10–11).

We know that incidents like these are ubiquitous. And we know they're on our campuses—at the University of Nevada, at Miami University of Ohio, at my own campus. Everywhere.

Multiculturalism hasn't improved things much, not even at the sites where students are exposed to such things. Maybe the relatively low numbers of people of color on our campuses or in our journals—or the high numbers at community colleges with disproportionately few of color among the faculty—reinforce racist conceptions. The disproportionately few people of color in front of the classrooms or in our publications, given the ubiquity of the bootstrap mentality, reifies the conception that people of color don't do better because they don't try harder, that most are content to feed off the State. The only apparent generalized acknowledgement of racism as structural comes by way of the perception of a reverse discrimination.

Yet the numbers underscore that there is no reversal. Latinos have the highest poverty rates of all Americans—24%, with Navajo close behind, followed by African Americans (Martínez 7). And there's no use blaming insufficiency in English, as Latinos and Navajo lose their native tongues, the Navajo struggling to hold on to their Dine' language (Veltman, DeGroat).

Among Latinos, 64% are native to the U.S. Half of all Latinos never complete high school, the highest percentage for all groups (Dept. of Health). Although segregation by race is no longer legal, there is an economic segregation, a white and middle-class flight from inner cities that relegates African American and Latino students to schools that lack a strong tax base and are thereby poorly funded (Martínez 7). While Latinos make up over 12% of the public school population, less than 4% of faculty or administration are Latina or Latino, and less than 1% of those who sit on school boards as voting members are Latina or Latino.

Of course, some do make it to higher education. Twenty percent of those who receive Associate Degrees are of color. Of that 20%, Latinas and Latinos account for 6%. Those rates are relatively the same through Bachelors and Masters degrees. At the doctoral level, Asian Americans earn about 4.5% of all PhDs, African Americans 3%, Latinos 2%, American Indians, about .3%, and white folks who are not Latina or Latino 61% (the remaining 27% going to foreign nationals) (37, 39). In English Language and Literature for 1995, Latinos and Latinas received 26 PhDs—not 26% but 26: 8 for Latinos and 18 for Latinas—African Americans 37, Asian Americans 35, American Indians 7. White folks who were not Latino received 1,268—of which 743 were awarded to women (U.S. Dept. of Education). That's 1,268 white to 26 Latino or Latina PhDs in English. I have so little patience with reverse discrimination.

These numbers could still be broken down by field within English, but there are no clear numbers that include race breakdowns. If CCCC membership demographics can tell us much, though, the numbers aren't encouraging, with a 92% white membership, 5% African American, 1.4% Chicanos or Latino, 1% Asian American, and 0.5% Native American/American Indian. And there is only the most infinitesimal amount of representation in our journals, with *TETYC* giving the most attention to race issues of the three journals searched (*TETYC*, *CCC*, and *College English*), with none in a search by article titles looking at issues concerning Latinas or Latinos—not even to address the English-Only movement.

Even though members of CCCC and NCTE have tended to treat its members of color with respect and have advanced our numbers into positions of leadership regularly, and even though both NCTE and CCCC will soon be entering into a membership campaign that should increase the pool of people of color, I believe that our best recruiting tool for those graduate students of color, the undergraduates of color, the students who have vaulted the fault line and are in college at all will not be the pictures of people of color in the *Council Chronicle* or in the convention program books or even at our wonderful conventions—since all of those media mainly reach the already-subscribed; rather, it will be through our journals, the journals on library shelves or online, with people of color writing frankly, sympathetically about matters concerning racism, and all of us writing about what matters to those students of color. That's what will attract people of color in sufficient numbers to begin to affect racism. We can do better than 7% among our teachers and scholars of color, better than a representation that is statistically insignificant in our journals.

CUENTOS

A number of graduate students of color in English at my campus write an article for the school newspaper which gains a full-page spread. Its title, "Black Masks, White Masks," parodies a famous book on colonialism and race by Frantz Fanon. The grad students write that they no longer wish to be reduced to wearing white masks if they are to succeed in the university, that the denial of their being of color affords them nothing but their silencing. Among their examples of the racism they feel, they write of a Halloween party in which one of their fellows appeared in blackface (Dunn et al. 6).

A meeting of grad students and department faculty. Tempers run hot. Blackface says he never meant to offend. He was paying homage to the great jazz and blues musicians of the past, playing Muddy Waters tunes. He would have been born in the 1970s, maybe unaware of a dark history of such homages.

> *Holiday Inn:* Bing Crosby in blackface, singing "Who was it set the darkies free? Abraham. Abraham." Mr. Crosby surely didn't mean to offend. But that was then, you might have said before this little *cuentito.*

Stunned silence. A student of color leaves.

A large-seeming fellow, red hair, small, blue eyes, always earnest, always speaking with broad gestures from large, thick hands, all befreckled, always the one to find contradictions. He stands. Says that as he sees it, this thing about silencing doesn't wash, that those complaining about it are the very ones who are always speaking up in classes, and that (without a breath) he can't think of a one from among the faculty present who doesn't speak of multiculturalism, that the damned text used in the first-year composition program is really an Ethnic Studies book, for gosh sake (or words to that effect). (The book is Ronald Takaki's *A Different Mirror,* "a history of multicultural America," according to the subtitle, its author, "a professor in the Ethnic Studies Department" at his university.) All are effectively silenced for a dramatically long moment.

Then, from behind the semi-circle of chairs, a South Asian woman stands. She self-identifies as a person of color, as one of those colonized by another's empire, British accent to her speech, dark brown skin, large black eyes that seem to well with tears, thick black mane framing her small face. She's clearly agitated. Breaks the silence. She speaks about the difference between speaking and being heard, that if one is constantly speaking but is never heard, never truly heard, there is, in effect, silence, a silencing. She says that speaking of ethnic studies or multiculturalism is less the issue than how racism seems always to be an appendage to a classroom curriculum, something loosely attached to a course but not quite integral, even when race is the issue.

She, two Latinas, and one African American woman had attended, then boycotted a graduate seminar on Feminist Theory a few semesters before. Expecting that the most common and longest form of oppression in human history, gender discrimination, would serve as a bond that would tie them to the other class members and the professor, these four women were surprised, then hurt, then angered, at their silencing by their sisters. One of the Latinas does her presentation in Spanish, says "Nobody listens anyway." No one commented, or even acknowledged not knowing what she had said. The African American woman posted a message on an African American listserv warning others not to apply to the school, that it was too deeply racist.

A poem by Puerto Rican poet Victor Hernández Cruz:

Anonymous

And if I lived in those olden times
With a funny name like Choicer or
Henry Howard, Earl of Surrey, what chimes!
I would spend my time in search of rhymes
Make sure the measurement termination surprise
In the court of kings snapping till woo sunrise
Plus always be using the words *alas* and *hath*
And not even knowing that that was my path
Just think on the Lower East Side of Manhattan
I would have been like living in satin
Alas! The projects hath not covered the river
Thou see-est vision to make thee quiver
Hath I been delivered to that "wildernesse"
So past
I would have been the last one in the
Dance to go
Taking note the minuet so slow
All admire my taste
Within thou *mambo* of much more haste.

One of my daughters had had enough with the teacher who singled her and her girlfriends out, except the Latina girlfriend from Venezuela, who bore European features and a French and German name, never called out even though she did in fact cut up with the others when they were cuttin' up. My daughter had shaken her booty at the teacher after a disciplining of one sort or another. The teacher: "That might be okay in your culture, but not in mine." I don't think multiculturalism took.

A meeting with that teacher and the principal. After explanations, I break into a lecture about racism. I do that. Often. From the Principal: "We had some problems with that at the beginning of the year, but we took care of them." And I want to know how he solved the problem of our nation "at the beginning of the year."

A joke to some and not to others tells about an immigration official who detains the Puerto Rican at the border. "But I'm Puerto Rican," says the detained citizen. "I don't care what kind of Mexican you are," says the official.

A poem by Sandra María Esteves:

From Fanon

We are a multitude of contradictions
reflecting our history
oppressed
controlled
once free folk
remnants of that time interacting in our souls

Our kindred was the earth
polarity with the land
respected it
called it mother
were sustained and strengthened by it

The european thru power and fear became our master
his greed welcomed by our ignorance
tyranny persisting
our screams passing unfulfilled

As slaves we lost identity
assimilating our master's values
overwhelming us to become integrated shadows
unrefined and dependent

We flee escaping, becoming clowns in an alien circus
performing predictably
mimicking strange values
reflecting what was inflicted

Now the oppressor has an international program
and we sit precariously within the monster's mechanism
internalizing anguish from comrades
planning and preparing a course of action.

ON BREAKING PRECEDENTS

I have failed some tests, have had a fellow worker bleed in green and red over a paper I had wished to submit for publication, have gotten the maybe-you-could-consider-submitting-this-essay-somewhere-else letter from journal editors. That's just part of the job. But I have only once felt insulted. Some years have passed, and I have forgotten the editor who had written my rejection letter; I've even forgotten the journal, I realize as I write this. But I still bear a grudge. The essay challenged the idea of a postcolonialism, invoking Frantz Fanon. The Rejecter said he saw no reason to resurrect Fanon. The essay also cited Aristotle and Cicero. Their resurrection went unquestioned. Rejecter also said that he feared that in bringing in Fanon, I risked essentializing. *Essentialism*, as I understand the term, is the "belief in real, true human essences, existing outside of or impervious to social and historical context" (Omi and Winant 187). But I had argued in that piece, as I have always argued, that race in America is a result of colonialism, that "racial discrimination and racial prejudice are phenomena of colonialism," to use John Rex's words (75). This is historical, not merely a matter of physiognomy. How was I essentializing?

In the years that have followed that infuriating letter, I have seen my concern of that essay echoed, seen a rekindled interest in Fanon grow and grow, and have heard how others of color have been insulted by a particular use of the word *essentializing*. Henry Louis Gates in an essay titled "On the Rhetoric of Racism in the Profession," for example, writes that

> Long after white literature has been canonized, and recanonized, our attempts to define a black American canon—foregrounded on its own against a white backdrop—are often decried as racist, separatist, nationalist, or "essentialist" (my favorite term of all). (25)

And so maybe that was the problem, that I had been read as taking on an old, 1960s type of argument for nationalism among people of color in bringing up Fanon's rendering of internal colonialism.

Now as I try to think of how this profession can improve on its multiculturalism, do more than assuring that people of color are represented in our materials, more than assuring that people of color are read and heard in numbers more in keeping with the emerging demographics of the nation and the world, I remain tied to the belief that we must break from the colonial discourse that binds us all. What I mean is that there are attitudes from those we have revered over the centuries which we inherit, that are woven into the discourse that we inherit. I believe this happens. But even if not, consider the legacy.

Among all that is worthwhile in the intellectual discourse we inherit from the colonizers of the United States, there is also a developmental and racist discourse. Here is how Kant, in 1784, answers the question as to "What is Enlightenment?"

> Enlightenment (*Aufklärung*) is the exit of humanity by itself from a state of culpable immaturity (*verschuldeten Unmündigkeit*). . . . Laziness and cow-

ardliness are the causes which bind the great part of humanity in this frivolous state of immaturity. (qtd. in Dussel 20)

For Hegel,

> Universal history goes from East to West. Europe is absolutely the *end of universal history*. Asia is the beginning.

> Africa is in general a closed land, and it maintains this fundamental character. It is characteristic of the blacks that their consciousness has not yet even arrived at the intuition of any objectivity . . . He is a human being in the rough.

> This mode of being of the Africans explains the fact that it is extraordinarily easy to make them fanatics. The Reign of the Spirit is among them so poor and the Spirit in itself so intense . . . that a representation that is inculcated in them suffices them not to respect anything and to destroy everything.

And as for Spain, Hegel continues:

> Here one meets the lands of Morocco, Fas (not Fez), Algeria, Tunis, Tripoli. One can say that this part does not properly belong to Africa, but more to Spain, with which it forms a common basin. De Pradt says for this reason that when one is in Spain one is already in Africa. This part of the world . . . forms a niche which is limited to sharing the destiny of the great ones, a destiny which is decided in other parts. It is not called upon to acquire its own proper figure. (qtd. in Dussel 21–24)

This is the legacy of racism. And how is it passed on? The Naturalization Act of 1790—1790!—denying rights of full citizenship to nonwhites (Takaki, "Reflections"). The Chinese Exclusion Act of 1882. The 1928 Congressional Hearings on Western Hemisphere Immigration:

> Their minds run to nothing higher than animal functions—eat, sleep, and sexual debauchery. In every huddle of Mexican shacks one meets the same idleness, hordes of hungry dogs, and filthy children with faces plastered with flies, disease, lice, human filth, stench, promiscuous fornication, bastardly, lounging, apathetic peons and lazy squaws, beans and dried fruit, liquor, general squalor, and envy and hatred of the gringo. These people sleep by day and prowl by night like coyotes, stealing anything they can get their hands on, no matter how useless to them it may be. Nothing left outside is safe unless padlocked or chained down. Yet there are Americans clamoring for more of these human swine to be brought over from Mexico. (Estrada et al. 116)

And after the slurs run through the mind, there comes the question as to how this is an issue of immigration to the Western Hemisphere as a whole, rather than simply to one country of the Western Hemisphere. To understand that, we would need to recognize the discourse of diplomacy toward our neighbors to the South since the time of John Quincy Adams, summed up in a 1920s lecture to new envoys to Central and South America:

> If the United States has received but little gratitude, this is only to be expected in a world where gratitude is rarely accorded to the teacher, the doctor, or the policeman, and we have been all three. But it may be that in time they will come to see the United States with different eyes, and have for her something of the respect and affections with which a man regards the instructor of his youth and a child looks upon the parent who has molded his character. (Schoultz 386)

Or George Bush referring to Daniel Ortega's presence at a meeting as like an unwelcome dog at a garden party (Schoultz vii, 386). And after the summer hurricanes hit Central America during the summer of '98, we all heard Bush's pleas for aid for Honduras, since if such were not granted, those people might come here.

From Kant to our current politicians, from the exclusion of somehow "essentialized" notions of race to ongoing English-Only laws and the end of Affirmative Action, we are steeped in racism. And we are steeped in a colonial discourse, one which continues to operate from a developmental rather than dialectical model—despite our best efforts.

If Latin America is like a child to the U.S., the U.S. continues to act as the colonial offspring of Europe. Here's an analogy from diplomacy. Historian Lars Schoultz writes:

> When a State Department official begins a meeting with the comment "we have a problem with the government of Peru," in less than a second the other participants instinctively turn to a mental picture of a foreign state that is quite different from the one that would have been evoked if the convening official had said, in contrast "we have a problem with the government of France."
>
> What exactly is the difference? To begin, Peru is in Latin America, the "other" America; France is in northwestern Europe, the cradle of the dominant North American culture. Peru is poor; France is rich. Peru is weak; France has nuclear weapons. Peru has Incan ruins . . . ; France has ancient ruins too, but it also has the Louvre. Peru makes pisco; France makes claret. Peru is not so firmly democratic; France is. Peru is a Rio Treaty ally, which, as alliances go, is something of a charade; France is a NATO ally,

which is a very serious alliance. In most of our history, Peru has not mattered much in international relations; France has mattered a lot. . . . U.S. policy toward Peru is *fundamentally* unlike U.S. policy toward France, despite the fact that both policies are driven by self-interest. (xvi–xvii)

Now, imagine the phrase "there is a Mexican philosopher" and compare it to "there is a French philosopher." Which carries the greater weight? The analogy holds.

I began this essay with a reference to the logic of the Incas and the rhetorical training and rhetoric of the Aztecs prior to the European conquest. The source was a series of lectures delivered in Europe by an Argentine philosopher who resides in Mexico City, Enrique Dussel. Apart from a couple of dozen students in one seminar I've taught, I don't believe there are many in this country who know him or his work or the ways he might inform our concern with rhetoric or with liberatory pedagogy. His work mainly concerns the Philosophy of Liberation, and a good deal of it is in translation. We don't look to the South. Freire came to our attention only after he became a member of the faculty at Harvard. We tend to get our Great Thinkers from Europe, and too often only after our literary brothers and sisters, themselves too many and too often still quite literally an English colony, have discovered them. I'm not saying we shouldn't. I am grateful for *habitus* and hegemony as concepts that came from Europe. I have a great affection for the rhetoricians of Greece and Rome. But we must break from the colonial mindset and learn from the thinkers from our own hemisphere as well. There is, for example, a community college with a long record of trying to break through structural racism (now facing bureaucratic problems), Hostos Community College. Do we know who the school is named after? Do we know about his educational philosophy? He was a Puerto Rican philosopher, Eugenio María Hostos. Freire refers to many of the European thinkers, but he also refers to others. Do we know them? Might not knowing them be of some worth?

Break precedent! We are so locked into the colonial mindset that we are now turning to the excolonials of Europe to learn something about our own people of color. There again, I'm grateful for the insights. But what are the ex-colonials of the U.S. saying, the ex-colonials of our hemisphere, now caught in neocolonial dependency? In this essay, for example, I have called on the research of a number of Puerto Ricans, a Filipino, a number of Chicanas and Chicanos, an American Indian, African Americans, as well as an Argentine from Mexico—ex-colonials and contemporary colonials of the United States, writing and researching on their colonial relations to the United States. What we know are the writers. And they have a great deal to say that we should hear. But the Grand Theorists, to our mind, must be of "the continent" (as if the Americas weren't). At Hunter College in New York there is a Center for Puerto Rican Studies. What is being said there, not by postcolonials but by still-colonials? Some Puerto Ricans, for instance, are arguing for *jaiba* politics, a strategy of mimicry and parody that might have application in the classroom, a way to think our ways through the contradiction of a political sensibility in the composition classroom and instruction in academic discourse (Grosfoguel, Negrón-Muntaner, Georas 26–33). I haven't studied the concept of *jaiba* further or its possible application in composition studies yet. But I am hoping more of us will.

We shouldn't ignore the concepts that come of the ex-colonies of Europe, nor should we ignore European attempts to think its ways through bigotries of all sorts, since the problems of racism and hatred are Europe's also—but we also should not ignore the concepts that come of members of the interior colonies like Puerto Rico and the American Indian nations, the internal colonies of the formerly colonized as in America's people of color, the neocolonies of Latin America.

From Sandra María Esteves:

Here

I am two parts/a person
boricua/spic
past and present
alive and oppressed
given a cultural beauty
. . . and robbed of a cultural identity

I speak the alien tongue
in sweet boriqueño thoughts
know love mixed with pain
have tasted spit on ghetto stairways
. . . here, it must be changed
we must change it.

WORKS CITED

Cruz, Victor Hernández, "Anonymous." *Puerto Rican Writers At Home in the USA: An Anthology.* Faythe Turner, Ed., Seattle: Open Hand P, 1991. 119.

Davis, Mike. "The Political Economy of Late Imperial America." *New Left Review* 143 (1984): 6–38.

De Groat, Jennie. Personal Communication, 21 Nov. 1998.

Department of Health and Human Services. Hispanic Customer Service Demographics, *http://www./hhs/gov/heo/hisp.html*, 4 October 98.

Dunn, Cataya, Azfar Hussan, Abraham Tarango, Sumatay Sivamohan. "Black Masks, White Masks" *The Daily Evergreen*, 23 April 1998, 6.

Dussel, Enrique. *The Invention of the Americas: Eclipse of "the Other" and the Myth of Modernity*. Trans. Michael D. Barber. New York: Continuum, 1995.

Emecheta, Buchi. *Double Yoke*. New York: Braziller, 1982.

Esteves, Sandra María. "From Fanon." Turner 186–87.

———. "Here." Turner 181.

Estrada, Leonardo F., F. Chris Garcia, Reynaldo Flores Macias, and Lionel Maldonado. "Chicanos in the United States: A History of Exploitation and Resistance." *Daedalus* 2 (1981): 103–31.

Fanon, Frantz. *Black Skin, White Masks*. Trans. by Charles Lam Markmann. New York: Grove, 1967.

Gates, Henry Louis, Jr. "On the Rhetoric of Racism in the Profession." *Literature, Language, and Politics*. Ed. Betty Jean Craige. Athens: U of Georgia P, 1988. 20–26.

Glazer, Nathaniel and Daniel P. Moynihan. *Beyond the Melting Pot: The Negroes, Puerto Ricans, Jews, Italians, and Irish of New York City*. Cambridge: MIT P, 1970.

Grosfoguel, Ramón, Frances Negrón- Muntaner, and Chloé S. Georas. "Beyond Nationalist and Colonialist Discourses: The *Jaiba* Politics of the Puerto-Rican Ethno- Nation," *Puerto Rican Jam: Rethinking Colonialism and Nationalism*. Grosfoguel et al., eds. Minneapolis: U of Minnesota P, 1997. 1–36.

Martínez, Elizabeth. *De Colores Means All of Us: Latina Views for a Multi-Colored Century*. Cambridge: South End, 1998.

Omi, Michael and Howard Winant. *Racial Formation in the United States: From the 1960s to the 1990s*. New York: Routledge, 1994.

Prendergast, Catherine. "Race: The Absent Presence in Composition Studies." *CCC* 50 (1998): 35–53.

President's Advisory Commission on Educational Excellence for Hispanic Americans. *Our Nation on the Fault Line: Hispanic American Education*. Washington, DC: USIA, September 1996.

Rex, John. *Race, Colonialism and the City*. London: Routledge, 1973.

San Juan, E. *Racial Formations/Critical Transformations: Articulations of Power in Ethnic and Racial Studies in the United States*. Atlantic Highlands: Humanities P, 1992.

Schoultz, Lars. *Beneath the United States: A History of U.S. Policy Toward Latin America*. Cambridge: Harvard UP, 1998.

Takaki, Ronald. *A Different Mirror: A History of Multicultural America*. Boston: Little, 1993.

———. "Reflections on Racial Patterns in America." *From Different Shores*. Ed. Ronald Takaki. New York: Oxford UP, 1987.

Turner, Faythe, ed. *Puerto Rican Writers At Home in the USA: An Anthology*. Seattle: Open Hand P, 1991.

U.S. Department of Education, National Center for Educational Statistics, Integrated Postsecondary Education Data System. "Completions Survey." Washington: US. Department of Education. April 1997.

Veltman, Calvin. "Anglicization in the United States: Language Environment and Language Practice of American Adolescents." *International Journal of Social Languages* 44 (1983): 99–114.

A List of Resources

Anzaldúa, Gloria. *Borderlands/La Frontera*. San Francisco: Aunt Lute Books, 1999.

Applebee, Arthur N. *Tradition and Reform in the Teaching of English: A History*. Urbana, IL: NCTE, 1974.

Aristotle. *The Rhetoric and the Poetics of Aristotle*. Trans. W. Rhys Roberts and Ingram Bywater. Ed. Edward P. J. Corbett. New York: Random House, 1984.

Bain, Alexander. *English Composition and Rhetoric: A Manual*. London: Longman, 1866.

Bartholomae, David, and Anthony Petrosky, eds. *Facts, Artifacts, and Counterfacts: Theory and Method for a Reading and Writing Course*. Upper Montclair, NJ: Boynton/Cook, 1986.

———, eds. *Ways of Reading: An Anthology for Writers*. 4th ed. Boston: St. Martin's, 1996.

Belanoff, Pat, and Marcia Dickson, eds. *Portfolios: Process and Product*. Portsmouth, NH: Boynton/Cook, 1991.

Benson, Thomas W., and Michael H. Prosser, eds. *Readings in Classical Rhetoric*. Boston: Allyn and Bacon, 1969.

Berlin, James A. *Rhetoric and Reality: Writing Instruction in American Colleges, 1900–1985*. Carbondale: Southern Illinois UP, 1987.

———. *Rhetorics, Poetics, and Cultures: Refiguring College English Studies*. Urbana: NCTE, 1996.

———. *Writing Instruction in Nineteenth-Century American Colleges*. Carbondale: Southern Illinois UP, 1984.

Bizzell, Patricia. *Academic Discourse and Critical Consciousness*. Pittsburgh: U Pittsburgh P, 1992.

Britton, James, et al. *The Development of Writing Abilities, 11–18*. Schools Council Research Studies series. London: Macmillan, 1975.

Brody, Miriam. *Manly Writing: Gender, Rhetoric, and the Rise of Composition*. Carbondale: Southern Illinois UP, 1993.

Cooper, Charles R., and Lee Odell, eds. *Evaluating Writing: Describing, Measuring, Judging*. Urbana, IL: NCTE, 1977.

Corbett, Edward P. J. *Classical Rhetoric for the Modern Student*. 3rd ed. New York: Oxford UP, 1990.

Crowley, Sharon. *The Methodical Memory: Invention in Current-Traditional Rhetoric*. Carbondale: Southern Illinois UP, 1990.

———. *Ancient Rhetorics for Contemporary Students*. New York: Macmillan, 1994.

Daiker, Donald A., Andrew Kerek, and Max Morenberg. *The Writer's Options: College Sentence Combining*. New York: Harper and Row, 1979.

Elbow, Peter. *What Is English?* New York: Modern Language Association; and Urbana, IL: National Council of Teachers of English, 1990.

———. *Writing without Teachers*. New York: Oxford UP, 1973.

———. *Writing with Power: Techniques for Mastering the Writing Process*. New York: Oxford UP, 1981.

Emig, Janet. *The Composing Processes of Twelfth Graders*. NCTE Research Report No. 13. Urbana, IL: NCTE, 1971.

Flower, Linda. *The Construction of Negotiated Meaning: A Social Cognitive Theory of Writing*. Carbondale: Southern Illinois UP, 1994.

Fowler, Shelli B., and Victor Villanueva, eds. *Included in English Studies: Learning Climates That Cultivate Racial and Ethnic Diversity*. Washington, DC: American Association for Higher Education, 2002.

Enos, Theresa, ed. *A Sourcebook for Basic Writing Teachers*. New York: Random House, 1987.

Faigley, Lester. *Fragments of Rationality: Postmodernity and the Subject of Composition*. Pittsburgh: U of Pittsburgh P, 1992.

Freire, Paulo. *Cultural Action for Freedom*. Cambridge, MA: *Harvard Educational Review*, 1970.

———. *Pedagogy of the Oppressed*. Trans. Myra Bergman Ramos. New York: Herder and Herder, 1970.

Freire, Paulo, and Donaldo Macedo. *Literacy: Reading the Word and the World*. South Hadley, MA: Bergin & Garvey, 1987.

Gere, Anne Ruggles. *Writing Groups: History, Theory, and Implications*. Carbondale: Southern Illinois UP, 1987.

Gibson, W. Walker. *Tough, Sweet & Stuffy: An Essay on Modern American Prose Styles.* Bloomington, IN: Indiana UP, 1966.

Gilyard, Keith, ed. *Race, Rhetoric, and Composition.* Portsmouth, NH: Boynton/Cook, 1999.

———. *Voices of the Self : A Study of Language Competence.* Detroit: Wayne State UP, 1991.

Golden, James L., and Edward P. J. Corbett. *The Rhetoric of Blair, Campbell, and Whately.* New York: Holt, Rinehart and Winston, 1968.

Gramsci, Antonio. *Selections from the Prison Notebooks of Antonio Gramsci.* Ed. and Trans. Quintin Hoare and Geoffrey Nowell Smith. New York: International, 1971.

———. *Selections from Cultural Writings.* Ed. David Forgacs and Geoffrey Nowell-Smith. Trans. William Boelhower. Cambridge: Harvard UP, 1985.

Graves, Richard L., ed. *Rhetoric and Composition: A Sourcebook for Teachers and Writers.* 2nd ed. Upper Montclair, NJ: Boynton/Cook, 1984.

Havelock, Eric A. *Preface to Plato.* Cambridge, MA: Harvard UP, 1963.

Hawisher, Gail E., and Cynthia L. Selfe, eds. *Global Literacies and the World-Wide Web.* New York: Routledge, 2000.

Heath, Shirley Brice. *Ways with Words: Language, Life, and Work in Communities and Classrooms.* New York: Cambridge UP, 1983.

hooks, bell. *Teaching to Transgress: Education as the Practice of Freedom.* New York: Routledge, 1994.

Horner, Bruce, and Min-Zhan Lu. *Representing the "Other": Basic Writers and the Teaching of Basic Writing.* Urbana, IL: NCTE, 1999.

Irmscher, William. *Teaching Expository Writing.* New York: Holt, Rinehart and Winston, 1979.

Jarratt, Susan C. *Rereading the Sophists: Classical Rhetoric Refigured.* Carbondale: Southern Illinois UP, 1991.

Kells, Michelle Hall, and Valerie Balester, eds. *Attending to the Margins: Writing, Researching, and Teaching on the Front Lines.* Portsmouth, NH: Boynton/Cook, 1999.

Kennedy, George. *Classical Rhetoric and Its Christian and Secular Tradition from Ancient to Modern Times.* 2nd ed. Chapel Hill: U of North Carolina P, 1999.

Kent, Thomas, ed. *Post-Process Theory: Beyond the Writing-Process Paradigm.* Carbondale: Southern Illinois UP, 1999.

Lindemann, Erika. *A Rhetoric for Writing Teachers.* 4th ed. New York: Oxford UP, 2001.

Locke, John. *An Essay Concerning Human Understanding.* Ed. Peter H. Nidditch. Oxford: Clarendon, 1975.

Macrorie, Ken. *The I-Search Paper.* Portsmouth, NH: Boynton/Cook, 1988.

_____. *Uptaught.* New York, Hayden, 1970.

Marrou, H. I. *A History of Education in Antiquity.* New York: Sheed and Ward, 1956.

Matsen, Patricia P., Philip Rollinson, and Marion Sousa. *Readings from Classical Rhetoric.* Carbondale: Southern Illinois UP, 1990.

Mellon, John C. *Transformational Sentence-Combining: A Method for Enhancing the Development of Syntactic Fluency in English Composition.* NCTE Research Report No. 10. Urbana, IL: NCTE, 1969.

Moffett, James. *Teaching the Universe of Discourse.* Boston: Houghton Mifflin, 1983.

Murphy, James J., ed. *A Short History of Writing Instruction: From Ancient Greece to Twentieth-Century America.* Davis, CA: Hermagoras, 1990.

_____. *Rhetoric in the Middle Ages: A History of Rhetorical Theory from St. Augustine to the Renaissance.* Berkeley: U of California P, 1974.

_____, ed. *The Rhetorical Tradition and Modern Writing.* New York: MLA, 1982.

Murray, Donald. *A Writer Teaches Writing.* Boston: Houghton Mifflin, 1968.

Nelson, Cary, and Lawrence Grossberg, eds. *Marxism and the Interpretation of Culture.* Urbana: U of Illinois P, 1988.

Ohmann, Richard M. *English in America: A Radical View of the Profession.* New York: Oxford UP, 1976.

Ong, Walter J. *Orality and Literacy: The Technologizing of the Word.* London: Methuen, 1982.

Piaget, Jean. *The Language and Thought of the Child.* Trans. Marjorie Gabain. New York: World, 1973.

Plato. *Phaedrus.* Trans. R. Hackforth. Cambridge: Cambridge UP, 1952.

Quintilian. *On the Teaching of Speaking and Writing.* Ed. James J. Murphy. Carbondale: Southern Illinois UP, 1987.

Rose, Mike. *Lives on the Boundary: A Moving Account of the Struggles and Achievements of America's Educational Underclass.* New York: Penguin, 1989.

Scribner, Silvia, and Michael Cole. *The Psychology of Literacy.* Cambridge, MA: Harvard UP. 1981.

Shaughnessy, Mina. *Errors and Expectations: A Guide for the Teacher of Basic Writing.* New York: Oxford UP, 1977.

Shor, Ira, and Paulo Freire. *A Pedagogy for Liberation: Dialogues on Transforming Education.* South Hadley, MA: Bergin & Harvey, 1987.

Swearingen, C. Jan. *Rhetoric and Irony: Western Literacy and Western Lies.* New York: Oxford UP, 1991.

Tate, Gary, ed. *Teaching Composition: Twelve Bibliographical Essays.* Rev. ed. Ft. Worth: Texas Christian UP, 1987.

Tate, Gary, and Edward P. J. Corbett, eds. *The Writing Teacher's Sourcebook.* 2nd ed. New York: Oxford UP, 1988.

Villanueva, Victor, Jr. *Bootstraps: From an American Academic of Color.* Urbana, IL: NCTE, 1993.

Vygotsky, Lev. *Thought and Language.* Cambridge, MA: MIT P, 1962.

Yagelski, Robert P. *Literacy Matters: Writing and Reading the Social Self.* New York: Teachers College P, 2000.

Young, Richard E., Alton L. Becker, and Kenneth L. Pike. *Rhetoric: Discovery and Change.* New York: Harcourt, Brace and World, 1970.

Index

853

877

Editor

Victor Villanueva is professor and chair of the English department at Washington State University. A popular writer and speaker, he has won a number of awards for his scholarship, his teaching, and his speaking. He is often anthologized and is often asked to deliver keynote and other addresses. He is the former chair of the Conference on College Composition and Communication and the former co-chair of the organization's Winter Workshop — twice. After family, his central preoccupations are racism, the political more generally, and their embodiment in rhetoric and literacy.

This book was typeset in 11/13 Electra by Precision Graphics.
Typefaces used on the cover and spine were Electra and Gill Sans.
The book was printed on 50-lb. Husky Offset
by IPC Communication Services.